WITHDRAWN

WITH

IDRAWN

WITHDRAWN

This is the first full-scale history of early modern English literature in nearly a century. It offers new perspectives on English literature produced in Britain between the Reformation and the Restoration. While providing the general coverage and specific information expected of a major history, its twenty-six chapters address recent methodological and interpretive developments in English literary studies. The book has five sections: 'Modes and Means of Literary Production, Circulation and Reception', 'The Tudor Era from the Reformation to Elizabeth I', 'The Era of Elizabeth and James VI', 'The Earlier Stuart Era' and 'The Civil War and Commonwealth Era'. While England is the principal focus, literary production in Scotland, Ireland and Wales is treated, as are other subjects less frequently examined in previous histories, including women's writings and the literature of the English Reformation and Revolution. This innovatively designed history is an essential resource for specialists and students.

DAVID LOEWENSTEIN is Marjorie and Lorin Tiefenthaler Professor of English at the University of Wisconsin, Madison. He is the author of *Representing Revolution in Milton and his Contemporaries: Religion, Politics, and Polemics in Radical Puritanism* (Cambridge, 2001), *Milton: Paradise Lost* (Cambridge, 1993) and *Milton and the Drama of History: Historical Vision, Iconoclasm, and the Literary Imagination* (Cambridge, 1990). He has also co-edited *Politics, Poetics, and Hermeneutics in Milton's Prose* (Cambridge, 1990).

JANEL MUELLER is William Rainey Harper Professor, Department of English and the College, at the University of Chicago, where she is currently Dean of the Division of the Humanities. She is the author of *Donne's Prebend Sermons* (1971) and *The Native Tongue and the Word: Developments in English Prose Style, 1380–1580* (1984). More recently she has published on topics in religion and literature and on earlier English women authors.

THE NEW CAMBRIDGE HISTORY OF
ENGLISH LITERATURE

The New Cambridge History of English Literature is a programme of reference works designed to offer a broad synthesis and contextual survey of the history of English literature through the major periods of its development. The organisation of each volume reflects the particular characteristics of the period covered, within a general commitment to providing an accessible narrative history through a linked sequence of essays by internationally renowned scholars. The History is designed to accommodate the range of insights and fresh perspectives brought by new approaches to the subject, without losing sight of the need for essential exposition and information. The volumes include valuable reference features, in the form of a chronology of literary and political events, extensive primary and secondary bibliographies and a full index.

The Cambridge History of Medieval English Literature
EDITED BY DAVID WALLACE

The Cambridge History of Early Modern English Literature
EDITED BY DAVID LOEWENSTEIN
AND JANEL MUELLER

Also in preparation

The Cambridge History of English Literature 1660–1780
EDITED BY JOHN RICHETTI

The Cambridge History of English Romantic Literature
EDITED BY JAMES CHANDLER

The Cambridge History of Twentieth-Century English Literature
EDITED BY LAURA MARCUS AND PETER NICHOLLS

THE CAMBRIDGE
HISTORY OF
EARLY MODERN
ENGLISH LITERATURE

—

EDITED BY
DAVID LOEWENSTEIN AND
JANEL MUELLER

CAMBRIDGE
UNIVERSITY PRESS

PUBLISHED BY THE PRESS SYNDICATE OF THE UNIVERSITY OF CAMBRIDGE
The Pitt Building, Trumpington Street, Cambridge, United Kingdom

CAMBRIDGE UNIVERSITY PRESS
The Edinburgh Building, Cambridge CB2 2RU, UK
40 West 20th Street, New York, NY 10011-4211, USA
477 Williamstown Road, Port Melbourne, VIC 3207, Australia
Ruiz de Alarcón 13, 28014 Madrid, Spain
Dock House, The Waterfront, Cape Town 8001, South Africa

http://www.cambridge.org

© Cambridge University Press 2002

This book is in copyright. Subject to statutory exception
and to the provisions of relevant collective licensing agreements,
no reproduction of any part may take place without
the written permission of Cambridge University Press.

First published 2002

Printed in the United Kingdom at the University Press, Cambridge

Typeface Renard 2 9.5/12.75 pt   *System* LaTeX 2$_\varepsilon$ [TB]

A catalogue record for this book is available from the British Library

Library of Congress Cataloguing in Publication data

The Cambridge history of early modern English literature / edited by David Loewenstein
and Janel Mueller.
p.   cm. – (The new Cambridge history of English literature)
Includes bibliographical references and index.
ISBN 0 521 63156 4
1. English literature – Early modern, 1500–1700 – History and criticism.   1. Loewenstein, David, 1955–
11. Mueller, Janel M., 1938–   111. Series.
PR421 .C26   2002
820.9′003 – dc21   2002023792

ISBN 0 521 63156 4 hardback

Contents

2
THE TUDOR ERA FROM THE REFORMATION TO ELIZABETH I

3
THE ERA OF ELIZABETH AND JAMES VI

4
THE EARLIER STUART ERA

Contributors

CATHERINE BATES · *University of Warwick*
DAVID BEVINGTON · *University of Chicago*
PAULA BLANK · *College of William and Mary,*
Williamsburg, VA
MARTIN BUTLER · *University of Leeds*
KENNETH CHARLTON · *King's College, University of London*
PATRICK COLLINSON · *University of Cambridge*
THOMAS N. CORNS · *University of Wales, Bangor*
DEREK HIRST · *Washington University*
DAVID SCOTT KASTAN · *Columbia University*
REBECCA LEMON · *University of Southern California*
BARBARA K. LEWALSKI · *Harvard University*
DAVID LOADES · *University of Wales, Bangor*
DAVID LOEWENSTEIN · *University of Wisconsin, Madison*
HAROLD LOVE · *Monash University*
LAWRENCE MANLEY · *Yale University*
LEAH S. MARCUS · *Vanderbilt University*
ARTHUR F. MAROTTI · *Wayne State University*
CLAIRE MCEACHERN · *University of California, Los Angeles*
JOHN MORRILL · *University of Cambridge*
JANEL MUELLER · *University of Chicago*
GRAHAM PARRY · *University of York*
JOSHUA SCODEL · *University of Chicago*
WILLIAM A. SESSIONS · *Georgia State University*
DEBORA SHUGER · *University of California, Los Angeles*
NIGEL SMITH · *Princeton University*
JOHANN P. SOMMERVILLE · *University of Wisconsin, Madison*
MARGARET SPUFFORD · *Roehampton Institute, London*
JAMES GRANTHAM TURNER · *University of California, Berkeley*
HELEN WILCOX · *University of Groningen*
STEVEN N. ZWICKER · *Washington University*

Acknowledgements

We have been fortunate to work on this project with several outstanding editors at Cambridge University Press: with energy and imagination, Josie Dixon helped to shape this new history from the outset; once the volume was well along, Ray Ryan continued to offer excellent advice and encouragement. Kevin Taylor offered valuable guidance at the earliest stages. The editors and all the contributors have benefited inestimably from the prompt, acute, felicitous copy-editing performed by Leigh Mueller. She has our deep gratitude. In addition, we would like to thank Barbara Hird for her meticulous and intelligent compilation of the book's index. Numerous colleagues have also given us helpful advice. David Wallace provided excellent counsel based on his experience as the editor of the preceding volume in this new Cambridge series. Steven May, Arthur Marotti and Harold Love helped us with questions regarding manuscripts. Anthony Milton was especially generous when we needed the advice of a first-rate historian. For their thoughtful suggestions, we are grateful to the participants in the Renaissance Workshop at The University of Chicago (April 1998) and the Renaissance conference at the University of Michigan-Dearborn (October 1999). In particular we thank Richard Strier, Katherine Narveson, William Shullenberger and Katherine Eisaman Maus. Taryn Okuma and Jay Gates assisted with the bibliography. Research support has been provided by the Graduate School of the University of Wisconsin-Madison, by the Marjorie and Lorin Tiefenthaler Professorship of English (University of Wisconsin) and by the Division of the Humanities, The University of Chicago.

The publisher has used its best endeavours to ensure that the URLs for external websites referred to in this book are correct and active at the time of going to press. However, the publisher has no responsibility for the websites and can make no guarantee that a site will remain live or that the content is or will remain appropriate.

INTRODUCTION

DAVID LOEWENSTEIN AND JANEL MUELLER

Following *The Cambridge History of Medieval English Literature* edited by David Wallace (1999), this collaborative volume of twenty-six chapters in five Parts narrates the history of English literature written in Britain between the Reformation and the Restoration. *The Cambridge History of Early Modern English Literature* takes account of significant recent discoveries and methodological developments in English literary studies, while providing the general coverage expected of a major critical reference work. We believe that there is a need for an innovatively conceived literary history that examines the interactions between sites of production, reception and circulation, on the one hand, and the aesthetic and generic features of early modern texts, on the other. Our volume provides basic information about and essential exposition of writing in early modern Britain, while exemplifying fresh approaches to the field and the writing of literary history. We hope that this volume, like the one devoted to medieval literature, will prove a valuable resource for scholarly, graduate and undergraduate readers, and that it will influence teaching and research in early modern English literature. We also believe that this *Cambridge History* differs from earlier literary histories in several notable ways.

Our volume is designed to implement what is, at present, a frequently shared working assumption of Anglo-American literary studies, but one that until now has not given shape to the compilation of a literary history. This assumption holds that literature is at once an agent and a product of its culture, simultaneously giving expression to and taking expression from the political, religious and social forces in which its own workings are imbricated. Conceived in this manner, literature can be seen to operate with peculiar power and saliency not just to create culture but also to enliven and enrich it through multiple voices and utterances. In the textual representation, expression and record that is literature, culture finds itself made readable, transmissible, revisable and preservable, while the restrictive and often artificial distinction between 'text' and 'context' dissolves. The design of *The Cambridge History* aims to develop this view of early modern English literature. Designed in this fashion, our history yields multiple accounts based on various institutional sites and therefore does not assume the dimensions of a *grand récit*.

In several fundamental respects our predecessor, the first *Cambridge History of English Literature*, remains a prototype for the current project of a new, multi-volume account of English literary history from Cambridge University Press. That pioneering literary history was published in fourteen volumes between 1907 and 1917 under the general editorship of A. W. Ward and A. R. Waller (the General Index, volume 15, was issued in 1927), and it remained in print until the 1970s. Then and now, the narratives of each literary history are multi-voiced, not single: each chapter has a different author (or, in a few cases, co-authors). Then and now, the structure of each history is poly-faceted, not monolithic: chapters the length of scholarly articles are clustered in chronological or generic subdivisions. Ward and Waller resonantly envisaged themselves and Cambridge University Press as coordinating a grand Baconian and Arnoldian project for collaboratively advancing literary knowledge and understanding among the widest possible English-language readership. In their words, they were aiming 'to provide a history for both the general reader and the student by the combination of a text abstaining as much as possible from technicalities, with bibliographies as full as possible of matter... We are convinced that it is the duty of a university press to endeavour both to meet the highest demands that can be made upon its productions by men of learning and letters, and to enable the many to share in the knowledge acquired by the few.'[1] The premiums that Ward and Waller placed on aids to access and further study, by way of bibliographies and other reference tools, on synoptic perspectives and inclusive treatments of subjects in the framing of chapters, and on information and stimulation for a diversity of readers still carry their weight in this new *Cambridge History*.

The first *Cambridge History* remains particularly commendable for its broad and inclusive conception of literature. This encompasses, for the period covered by the present volume, discussions of chronicle- and history-writing, philosophical and scientific writing, early political and economic writings, and writings on navigation and agriculture, as well as the expected accounts of sonnet sequences, song-books and miscellanies, prose genres from sermons to romances to jest-books and broadsides, and compendious coverage of English drama in the age of Shakespeare – which occupies volumes 5 and 6 – in addition

---

1 A. W. Ward and A. R. Waller (eds.), *The Cambridge History of English Literature*, 15 vols. (Cambridge University Press, 1907–27), 3:iv.

to numerous chapters on single authors. The passage of a century, however, has inevitably dated certain aspects of the earlier *Cambridge History* and provided incentives and opportunities for fresh approaches to writing literary history. Ward and Waller's volumes lack an integrative structural design; the variety of the chapters, initially appealing, registers as a miscellany of works and topics. There are, however, recurrent lines of connection, but these too no longer command the acceptance that these volumes assume. One such line of connection implies that the English Renaissance and Reformation and its immediate aftermath in the seventeenth century (*c.* 1509–1660, though including the later works of Milton, Bunyan and Marvell) was an era of unsurpassed and unmatchable literary greatness, uniquely requiring five volumes for its treatment, while English literature from 'the Age of Dryden' to the nineteenth century receives a total of seven. Another line of connection assumes that the way to understand an individual author lies through his – and it is always his – biography and the evaluation of his character: thus, for example, Bacon's philosophical method is found to be flawed, just as his political career was, and Donne's literary audacity, independence and restless intellect are viewed in reference to his extravagances of behaviour. Perhaps the most encompassing line of connection is the untroubled sense, conveyed by the dozens of contributors to these volumes, that what the major and what the minor literary genres are, what the major and what the minor achievements are within these genres, and who the major and the minor authors and schools of practice are is a matter of established knowledge and consensual judgement. The outlines, volumes and values of the Big Picture are objectively out there, only the specifics need filling in – so runs the implicit message of the first *Cambridge History*. Today's readers inhabit a considerably more contestatory and sceptical moment in the study of literature and literary history, while continuing to credit acquisition of knowledge and exercise of critical judgement. The present volume is designed to honour, extend and reconsider the polyvocal, multifaceted dimensions that are the most enduring and productive legacy of Ward and Waller's collaboratively authored volumes.

Other previous histories differ from the present volume of the *Cambridge History* in tending to relegate certain kinds of political and religious texts to background material; or discussing them (if at all) under such categories as political and religious thought. In Douglas Bush's influential *English Literature in the Earlier Seventeenth Century, 1600–1660* (2nd edn, 1962), there is a long opening chapter on 'The Background of the Age', with subsequent chapters devoted to political thought, science and scientific thought, and religion and religious thought.[2] The present *Cambridge History* not only breaks down the background/foreground dichotomy; it also refuses to treat writers simply in terms of political or religious thought. Instead, our contributors place more emphasis on rhetorical and literary achievements in relation to religious beliefs and political ideologies. Thus, for example, Bush's volume treats the Levellers John Lilburne and William Walwyn in chapters on political and religious thought, while our history takes account of the texture of their polemical writings in a range of chapters concerned with literature and national identity, religion, and the City of London in the Civil War and Interregnum. Similarly, the significant seventeenth-century writer Gerrard Winstanley attracts only passing mention from Bush – mainly in the context of political ideas, where seventeenth-century historians usually place him. But in our literary history the language and texture of Winstanley's idiosyncratic Biblical and apocalyptic mythmaking are interconnected with his heretical religious beliefs and communist agrarian ideology (Chapters 21–3). Our treatment of literature in relation to various institutions or sites of production dispenses with the more traditional series of 'background' chapters, providing an alternative framework in six comprehensive chapters that address the material conditions, production, circulation, patronage and reception of writing in early modern Britain. We restrict our English-language purview to Britain not because we ignore or deny the vitality and interest of the trans-Atlantic dimension of literature in our period, but because this multifaceted subject has been admirably treated in another *Cambridge History*.[3]

We have also chosen to call this a history of 'early modern English literature', while remaining cognisant of the generality and even the ambiguity of the phrase 'early modern'. Although it can be used too facilely to associate literature in our period with the origins of modernity and individualism, or, more generally, to strike a Whiggish, progressivist note, this formulation is serviceable to us as a means of addressing the vexed problem of periodisation. For one thing, it allows us wider scope at both ends of our chronological spectrum. The term 'English Renaissance' – by no means a term we wish to

2 Douglas Bush, *English Literature in the Earlier Seventeenth Century, 1600–1660*, 2nd edn (Oxford and New York: Oxford University Press, 1962), chs. 1, 8, 9, 10. Bruce King's one-volume *Seventeenth-Century English Literature* (New York: Schocken Books, 1982) likewise contains a series of 'background' chapters for the years 1600–25, 1625–60 and 1660–1700, and covering such topics as 'causes of political instability', 'literature and society' and 'art, music and science'.

3 See discussions by Myra Jehlen, 'The Literature of Colonization', and by Emory Elliott, 'The New England Puritan Literature', in *The Cambridge History of American Literature: Volume I (1590–1820)*, ed. Sacvan Bercovitch and Cyrus R. K. Patell (Cambridge University Press, 1994), pp. 13–108, 171–278.

discard – would not have allowed us to configure Part 2 of our volume as we have, with three chapters devoted to literary activity having formative implications for the consolidating culture of the Tudor court, the nascent institution of the Church of England, and the literary expression of national identity. This very era – the middle decades of the sixteenth century – has standardly been regarded as a prologue rather than a notable period of literary culture in its own right. Not so long ago, the 'Golden Age' of the English Renaissance was confidently hailed as arriving with the publication of Lyly's *Euphues: The Anatomy of Wit* (1578) and Spenser's *Shepheardes Calender* (1579).[4]

At the other end of our chronological spectrum, the term 'English Renaissance' would have precluded attention to the vast and varied amount of writing produced during the period of the English Civil War and Interregnum and its immediate aftermath, much of which is typically not taught or read under the rubric 'Renaissance'. Indeed, recent historians have argued that Renaissance culture ends about 1640 if not earlier, though a major anthology of English poetry uses the term 'Renaissance' flexibly enough to include verse up to the crisis of the English republic in 1659.[5] The greatest literary figure of seventeenth-century England, John Milton, lived and wrote during the late Renaissance, the English Revolution and the Restoration. His writings can and should be read in terms of all three chronological perspectives, but cannot be fully understood or defined by any one of them. The phrase 'early modern' allows us to address the crucial decades between the Renaissance and the Restoration, and to explore continuities (as well as differences) between the literature of the 1640s and 1650s and the literature preceding and immediately following it. The result is to challenge and complicate traditional chronological boundaries – such as that between the Interregnum and Restoration (see Chapter 26) – without imposing sharp or simplistic divisions as Jacob

4 See C. S. Lewis, *English Literature in the Sixteenth Century Excluding Drama* (Oxford: Clarendon Press, 1954), p. 64: 'Though "periods" are a mischievous conception they are a methodological necessity ... I have accordingly divided [the mass of literature which I attempt to study in this book] ... into what I call the Late Medieval, the Drab Age, and the "Golden" Age. They ... cannot be precisely dated, and the divisions between them do not apply to prose nearly so well as to verse. The Late Medieval extends very roughly to the end of Edward VI's reign ... The Drab Age begins before the Late Medieval has ended, towards the end of Henry VIII's reign, and lasts into the late seventies ... The Golden Age is what we usually think of first when "the great Elizabethans" are mentioned: it is largely responsible, in England, for the emotional overtones of the word *Renaissance*.'

5 See William J. Bouwsma, *The Waning of the Renaissance, 1550–1640* (New Haven: Yale University Press, 2000). Peter Burke sees the late Renaissance in Europe and England as extending to around 1630: *The European Renaissance: Centres and Peripheries* (Oxford: Blackwell, 1998). See, however, *The Penguin Book of Renaissance Verse, 1509–1659*, ed. H. R. Woudhuysen with an introduction by David Norbrook (Penguin: Harmondsworth, 1993).

Burckhardt famously did between the Middle Ages and the Renaissance in Italy, in order to argue for the emergence of a new self-conscious individualism.[6] Finally, the phrase 'early modern English literature' allows us to develop a more broadly inclusive perspective on literary history, where the word 'Renaissance', meaning rebirth, evokes a world of high or urbane literary culture, often associated with the court, humanism and the great revival of antiquity leading to an emulation of classical models for composition. Because our history also addresses much popular writing and 'cheap print' in English, some of it (including ballads, chapbooks and popular romances) intended for the middling or even lower ranks of society (see Chapter 1), the more general term 'early modern English literature' seems advantageous and appropriate to us.

For the largest purposes of this volume, moreover, we want to construe 'literature' in the sense that it had in sixteenth- and seventeenth-century English, as helpfully detailed by Raymond Williams in *Keywords: A Vocabulary of Culture and Society*.[7] For Sir Francis Bacon in *The Advancement of Learning* (1605), the goal was to become 'learned in all literature & erudition, divine & humane'.[8] Here, clearly, literature is synonymous with the domain of all knowledge that has been preserved and transmitted in written form. The term came into English through the late medieval and early modern valuation of the skills of reading and the qualities of the book, a valuation intensified by the development of printing. There is a close period association between literature and literacy, and our volume aims to honour that inclusiveness by recognising as 'early modern English literature' a broad spectrum of what later would be classified as history, household advice, religious and political tracts, and much else. Not until the cult of authorship in the eighteenth century, compounded with the Romantic premium on the imagination, did the domain of literature become circumscribed to mean, primarily, poetry, fiction, drama and essays. Any treatment of the literary production during either the English Reformation or English Revolution reveals how inclusive we need to be in addressing the full range of writings produced then, yet (until recently) rarely analysed in detail by literary scholars (e.g. in the first instance political treatises, religious tracts

---

6 Jacob Burckhardt, *The Civilization of the Renaissance in Italy*, trans. S. G. C. Middlemore (Harmondsworth: Penguin, 1990); this classic account of the Renaissance was first published in German in 1860. The Burckhardtian spirit remains vital in William Kerrigan and Gordon Braden, *The Idea of the Renaissance* (Baltimore and London: The Johns Hopkins University Press, 1989).

7 Raymond Williams, *Keywords: A Vocabulary of Culture and Society*, rev. edn (New York: Oxford University Press, 1985), s.v. 'literature'.

8 Francis Bacon, *The Advancement of Learning*, ed. Michael Kiernan, The Oxford Francis Bacon, 4 (Oxford: Clarendon Press, 2000), p. 4.

and broadsides; in the latter period also serial newsbooks, heresiographies and so on). Nonetheless, while the new *Cambridge History* emphasises breadth in terms of what constitutes 'literature', its contributors variously attend to considerations of language, form, style, conventions and literary genres in order to address the poetic and rhetorical achievements of the writers and works of early modern English literature. Ultimately, we seek to integrate our premium on the literary more broadly defined with a better informed sense of the roles played, the cultural work done, and the regard achieved (or not achieved) by English literature in the sixteenth and seventeenth centuries.

The new *Cambridge History of Early Modern English Literature* is also unusual in providing no chapters on single authors. Single-author accounts, usually focused on the careers of such consequential writers as Sidney, Spenser, Shakespeare, Donne, Jonson and Milton, have been rendered masterfully in other literary histories of the period, where they are staples of presentation. Our aim here is to achieve freshness by allowing individual authors to be evaluated from multiple perspectives and located in relation to a range of institutional sites. This kind of placement may complicate our sense of an individual author's agency; it does not, however, diminish it. What is more, the detailed Index to this *Cambridge History* will enable our readers to find with ease and precision the discussions of specific authors and their works.

Like the one devoted to medieval literature, this volume examines the relation of literary history to other aspects of history, stressing, in particular, the dynamic interactions between texts and institutional contexts in early modern Britain.[9] In our sequence of chapters, aesthetic issues and questions are not divorced from historical conditions or social functions; rather, verses, plays, masques, prose writings and so on are frequently, though not exclusively, read as participating in, as helping to shape and question social and religious processes and philosophical assumptions. Too often, regrettably, new historical accounts have neglected religious developments and conflicts (e.g. the polemical agenda of Reformation literature in the 1530s, 1540s and 1550s; the polemical agenda of Catholic devotional literature in the 1580s; burgeoning anti-popery and ongoing fears of domestic Catholic conspiracies; the Puritan print campaign against the bishops in the 1580s and 1590s; the divisive repercussions of Laudian ceremonial innovations) in relation to the writing of early modern England. This volume therefore aims to redress the balance and give due weight to the intersection of politics and religion from the later years of Henry VIII

---

9 For acute reflections on the interactions between contexts and texts, see Dominick LaCapra, *Rethinking Intellectual History: Texts, Contexts, Language* (Ithaca, NY: Cornell University Press, 1983), ch. 1.

onward. Indeed, by emphasising the crucial roles of religious discourses, beliefs and institutions in the evolution of early modern literary culture, this literary history underscores their centrality without reductively viewing them as fronts for issues of power. In addition, where our volume explores the intersections between literature and history, it aims to complicate and challenge monolithic views of power and representation in early modern England.

Besides an inclusive chronological scope and the institutional location of various aspects of literary activity, periodisation is a crucial concern in the organisation of this history. The divisions into five Parts set out a sequence of distinct but contiguous phases of national and cultural identity, in which England proportionally produces and circulates more literature in more varied sites than do Scotland and Ireland at this period. Each Part of this volume contributes cumulatively to evoke the historically specific multiple constructions of 'England' as that state, church and language community whose metropolis and matrix was London, site of a quarter of England's population by 1600, and the centre of much literary production, reception and circulation in the sixteenth and seventeenth centuries. Besides the great centripetal pull of London's prodigious vitality in the early modern period, another major source of cultural magnetism was the court and the incentives it offered to literary activity and achievement. Hence, while regnal divisions can sometimes be mechanical devices for organising a historical narrative, here they justify their use as vectors pointing to key directions being taken by literary activity. Parts 2, 3 and 4 of this literary history correspond to groupings of reigns or to a long single reign, in the case of Elizabeth I, signifying the centrality of the figure of the monarch to the culturally authoritative institutions of this early modern era. Yet even Part 3 takes account of the non-synchronous phases of Mary Stuart's and James's reigns as monarchs of Scotland.

This new history of early modern English literature has an important multinational dimension to its design as well, especially with regard to the chapters on literature and national identity (Chapters 7, 10, 15, 21). These chapters demonstrate the productivity of recent scholarship on historically specific senses of national identity and 'the British problem' (as well as the cultural tensions conveyed by this term) in the early modern period.[10] While England

---

10 See, for example, Richard Helgerson, *Forms of Nationhood: The Elizabethan Writing of England* (University of Chicago Press, 1992); Claire McEachern, *The Poetics of English Nationhood, 1590–1612* (Cambridge University Press, 1996); Brendan Bradshaw and John Morrill (eds.) *The British Problem, c. 1535–1707* (Basingstoke: Macmillan, 1996); David J. Baker, *Between Nations: Shakespeare, Spenser, Marvell and the Question of Britain* (Stanford University Press, 1997); Colin Kidd, *British Identities before Nationalism: Ethnicity and Nationhood in the Atlantic World, 1600–1800* (Cambridge University Press, 1999); David J. Baker

is a principal focus, attention is simultaneously devoted to literary production in Scotland and Ireland, with occasional notice of Wales and Ireland in literary representations written in English. For example, Chapter 10 ('Literature and national identity') examines competing conceptions of nationhood: the emerging, multiple visions of Scottish national and independent identity (sometimes in tension with the institution of monarchy) in Scottish Reformation histories (e.g. by John Knox, John Leslie, George Buchanan); the multiple representations of English nationhood in John Foxe, Elizabeth I's writings, Shakespeare's history plays, Samuel Daniel's *Civil Wars* (1595), among other works; images of Ireland (by Richard Stanyhurst, John Derricke, Spenser and others) as negative counter-images of England itself (since there is no discourse of Irish nationhood in the English language at this moment). The subsequent chapter on literature and national identity (Chapter 15) likewise concludes with sections on Scotland and Ireland – a section on Scottish liberties and nationhood (which examines conflicting responses to Buchanan's writings), and a section treating Irish Catholic perspectives on Irish history (e.g. by Philip O'Sullivan Beare and Geoffrey Keating), as well as some of the more hostile literature about the explosive Irish Rebellion. These are just some of the ways, then, that this new *Cambridge History*, provides multi-national perspectives on English literature in Britain.

Within each of the five Parts of this *Cambridge History*, separate chapters are assigned to institutions as they come to the fore and demonstrate their saliency as actively contributing sites of literary production, reception and circulation. So, for example, while the City of London and the household have a long preexistence as institutions, London here first becomes literarily salient in the reign of Elizabeth (Chapter 13), while the household – itself distributed between the godly household and the landed estate – first demands attention as an active literary category under the earlier Stuarts (Chapter 20). Indeed, two of the more novel features of this new literary history are its chapters on literature and the City of London and on literature and the household. Since they locate sites of important cultural activity, chapter headings themselves serve as dynamic elements in the larger narrative of this literary history. They signal a new coincidence of institutional life and cultural vitality, as does the chapter on literature and the theatre under Elizabeth. Or they may modify already operative categories, as do those treating the Civil War and Commonwealth era where the chapter on 'Literature and the court' is omitted but 'Alternative

and Willy Maley (eds.), *British Identities and English Renaissance Literature* (Cambridge University Press, 2002). See also Linda Colley, *Britons: Forging the Nation, 1707–1837* (New Haven: Yale University Press, 1992).

sites for literature' are located and discussed, and a chapter on 'Literature and religion' substitutes for one on 'Literature and the church', signifying the then-prevailing institutional turbulence and religious ferment.

The Cambridge History of Early Modern English Literature also addresses areas of literary history that have received less attention until recently – for example, English and Scottish Reformation literature and the literature of the English Revolution. Since the recently published *Cambridge History of Medieval English Literature* extends its scope to the dissolution of the monasteries and the death of Henry VIII (1547), this subsequent volume retraces some of the early chronology – specifically the final two decades of Henry VIII's reign – from different perspectives, emphasising the literary achievements of the mid sixteenth century and the genres that flourished then (the popular interlude, allegory and satire, millennial prophecy and Biblical translation), as well as certain writers who promoted Reformation concerns. At the other end of our timespan, the unusually large volume of writing produced between 1640 and 1660 (over 22,000 books, polemical pamphlets, newsbooks, broadsides and manuscripts in the George Thomason collection alone) has been evaluated freshly in recent years by a new generation of literary historians. Prominent in this evaluation have been considerations of licensing and censorship: its nature, extent, effectiveness and impact on literary activity. Our history therefore includes several chapters that consider the role of literature and newly emergent forms of writing in the Civil War and Interregnum – a period of crisis when England's view of itself as God's chosen nation and a modern Protestant Israel was severely challenged. This part of the volume also highlights the literary and rhetorical achievements of important writers of political theory (Hobbes and James Harrington besides others mentioned above). It gives some attention to the flourishing of radical religious writing in the mid seventeenth century and to the role of literary republicanism in the 1640s and 1650s. It contests the notion that not much happens in literary history (outside, say, the major contributions of Milton, Marvell and Hobbes) between 1640 and 1660 and examines interconnections between the literary culture of the Interregnum and the Restoration (Chapters 21–6).[11]

Last but far from least, since we have been steadily increasing our awareness and knowledge of women writers and readers, as well as female patronage

---

11 Compare the claim by Robert M. Adams that 'periods of social strife and radical experiment don't generally produce much literature, and the two decades from 1640 to 1660 bear out that rule': *The Land and Literature of England: A Historical Account* (New York: Norton 1983), p. 238. More recently, *The Routledge History of Literature in English: Britain and Ireland*, by Ronald Carter and John McRae (London and New York: Routledge, 1997) hardly mentions any writing between 1640 and 1660.

and friendship in early modern England, the volume prominently incorporates these important areas of literary activity. Historically oriented feminist scholarship has helped to discover many of these authors and has taught us how to read and teach them. There are appreciable numbers of Renaissance and seventeenth-century women writers whose literary achievements and careers have recently received scholarly attention and whose writings figure in the new *Cambridge History*: Katherine Parr, Anne Askew, Queen Elizabeth, Mary Sidney, Isabella Whitney, Anne Clifford, Rachel Speght, Elizabeth Cary, Lady Mary Wroth, Aemilia Lanyer, Lady Eleanor Davies, An Collins, Lucy Hutchinson, Dorothy Osborne, Margaret Cavendish and Katherine Philips (one could easily expand this list). Indeed, only since 1985 has there been any scholarship on Aemilia Lanyer's published volume of Protestant and feminist poetry (*Salve Deus Rex Judaeorum*, 1611), self-consciously addressed to an aristocratic circle of female readers and potential patrons; this first volume of poetry in English by a woman (unmentioned in Douglas Bush's literary history as well as in the earlier *Cambridge History*) may give us the first country-house poem. Moreover, because the new *Cambridge History* dissolves chronological divisions between the late Renaissance and the English Civil War and Interregnum, it responds to the scholarly attention recently devoted to the role of women writers and prophets in the revolutionary decades of the 1640s and 1650s. Our contributors consider such figures as Lucy Hutchinson and Eleanor Davies, listed above, as well as others (e.g. the Fifth Monarchist Anna Trapnel, Margaret Fell the Quaker, and additional Quaker women) who wrote outside the political world of court culture and patronage and were associated with the flourishing religious sects and radical movements. Our literary history addresses interconnections between gender and writing in sixteenth- and seventeenth-century England, while exploring and placing them in the broader framework of early modern literary culture, history and institutions.

These women writers, moreover, receive treatment for the first time in a comprehensive literary history as opposed to one devoted exclusively to early modern women writers. They are not treated in separate chapters but integrated into broader discussions. For example, the chapter on literature and the household in the earlier Stuart period (Chapter 20) shows that households of various kinds (from noble estates headed by literary patrons to private dwellings of the 'middling sort' to the godly household) were prominent sites of literary production for male as well as female authors and offered an alternative to the court or the church. A discussion of Jonson's 'To Penshurst' opens the chapter, followed by an account of the Sidney–Pembroke coterie and of Mary Wroth and her writings; a discussion of Margaret Clifford, Countess of Cumberland,

and her daughter Anne Clifford's writings; an account of Daniel (who lived in the Clifford household) and his verse epistles to Margaret and Anne Clifford; a concise treatment of Aemilia Lanyer; as well as a discussion of Donne at Twickenham. Books of domestic advice as well as Puritan diaries get treated in this chapter, as do some of Milton's early poems – *Arcades* written to celebrate the household of the Protestant Countess of Derby and *A Maske Presented at Ludlow Castle* with its focus on another prominent Protestant household, that of Sir John Egerton, Earl of Bridgewater.

As signalled earlier, *The Cambridge History of Early Modern English Literature* opens with a section of six chapters addressing the material conditions, production, circulation, patronage and reception of writing in early modern Britain. Less focused on chronological periods (like the following demarcated Parts of the volume), these chapters range across the large timespan encompassed by the whole of our volume. They address, among other topics, the conditions of literacy, education and reading practices; the social contexts of manuscript transmission and circulation; print culture as a medium for the shaping of various forms of early modern subjectivity, including the phenomenon of newly self-conscious authorial presentation; the social conditions and dynamics of literary patronage; and the choice of linguistic medium for the production, circulation and reception of literature. We hope that this new history, through its combination of long-range chapters and chapters setting early modern English literature in its various institutional sites, will stimulate readers to rediscover or investigate anew the great diversity of literary texts in our period, encourage fresh debate and criticism, and suggest new lines of research in neglected areas.

1

MODES AND MEANS OF LITERARY
PRODUCTION, CIRCULATION
AND RECEPTION

Chapter 1

LITERACY, SOCIETY AND
EDUCATION

KENNETH CHARLTON AND MARGARET SPUFFORD

The rudiments

In 1607, Christopher Meade, gentleman, and steward of the manor court of Little Gransden in Cambridgeshire, appeared in the Court of Exchequer to give evidence in a suit concerning the size and whereabouts of the demesne and the yardland in Gransden. The purchasers of this former episcopal manor could not, in a fashion not unknown elsewhere amongst this batch of episcopal sales, find their purchase, which had been farmed by the tenants since the fourteenth century. Christopher Meade was an antiquarian of considerable skill and resourcefulness, for he had searched the thirteenth-century episcopal surveys of Gransden, and the medieval reeves' accounts, and then tied the documents to surviving earthworks to reconstruct the layout of the demesne. It is the first record known to us of a local historian 'getting mud on his boots' and doing some fieldwork. Meade, however, had a considerable advantage: he had been to school in the 1570s or 1580s in the chancel of Little Gransden church with a very mixed group of the other witnesses, who, as children, had been schoolfellows. These children had talked about the rumour that houses had once stood in the Bury Close, and played over the surviving tell-tale earthworks.[1] So Meade's gentry status did not prevent his learning the 'rudiments' along with other village children in the church chancel.

Fifty years or so later, in 1624, John Evelyn, son of a Justice of the Peace and later High Sheriff, was nearly four when he was 'initiated' into these same rudiments in the church porch at Wotton, where his father's mansion stood.[2] So Evelyn too, as a small boy, mixed freely with village children. Girls were included in these groups in church porches. School had started early for Evelyn:

---

1 PRO, E.134, 5 Jas. I/Hil.26. Margaret Spufford, *Contrasting Communities* (Cambridge University Press, 1974), p. 35 n. 105 and pp. 188–9.
2 John Evelyn, *Diary*, ed. E. S. de Beer, vol. 1 (London and New York: Oxford University Press, 1959), p. 5.

it was more normal to start at six, like Oliver Sansom, the son of a yeoman, who was born at Beedon in Berkshire in 1636: 'When I was about Six years of Age, I was put to school to a Woman to Read, who finding me not unapt to learn, forwarded me so well, that in about four months' time, I could read a chapter in the Bible pretty readily.'[3] It is well to be clear what these rudiments were: reading and writing were two very distinct and separate skills, taught about two years apart. Sometimes the children had been taught reading by their mothers before even starting school.

The Christian church had always placed great responsibilities on parents in the education of their children. If anything, the Protestant Reformation increased those responsibilities, by insisting, with William Perkins, that the family should be 'the seminarie of all other societies ... the schoole wherein are taught and learned the principles of authoritie and subjection'.[4] Parents were, therefore, constantly urged to see that their offspring learned by heart the elements of their religion – the Lord's Prayer, the Ten Commandments and the Creed – and then to read their Bible, catechism and other godly books.[5] Above all, great stress was laid on the importance of example – by telling the stories of Biblical personages, and more importantly by setting a good example in their own lives and behaviour.[6] Among the clerics Henry Bullinger was not alone in reminding parents that their 'godly and honest conversation in the presence of their children [will] teach them more virtues and good ways than their words, for words although they may do much, yet shall good examples of living do more'. For Robert Cleaver 'verbal instruction without example of good deeds is dead doctrine'. William Gouge likewise insisted that 'example is a real instruction and addeth a sharp edge to admonition'. John Donne had no doubt but that 'as your sons write by copies and your daughters by samplers, be every father a copy to his son and every mother a sampler to her daughter and every house will be a university'.[7] He had in mind the children of the gentry, of course.

Other children, however, also had their intellectual development attended to at home. There is so little statistical evidence bearing on reading ability

3 Oliver Sansom, *An Account of the Many Remarkable Passages of the Life of Oliver Sansom* ... (London, 1710), p. 2.

4 William Perkins, *Christian Oeconomie*, trans. T. Pickering (London, 1609), Epistle Dedicatorie, sig. 3r–v.

5 W. H. Frere and W. P. M. Kennedy (eds.), *Visitation Articles and Injunctions of the Period of the Reformation*, 3 vols. (London: Longmans, Green, 1910), 2:6–7, 21, 48–9 and subsequent diocesan injunctions.

6 Kenneth Charlton, *Women, Religion and Education in Early Modern England* (London: Routledge, 1999), pp. 92–7.

7 H. Bullinger, *The Christian State of Matrimonie*, trans. M. Coverdale (London, 1541), fol. lix v. R. C[leaver], *A Godlie Forme of Householde Gouvernement* (London, 1598), p. 260. W. Gouge, *Of Domesticall Duties* (London, 1622), p. 542. *Sermons of John Donne*, ed. G. R. Potter and E. M. Simpson, 10 vols. (Berkeley: University of California Press, 1953–62), 4:100.

in the seventeenth century that we are forced to use an example from beyond the end of our period.[8] Right at the end of the century, the reading ability of the children entering the school at Aldenham in Hertfordshire was noted. In the 1690s nearly a third of the five-year-olds, and over half the six-year-olds could already read at entry, and had therefore learnt at home or at a dame school. These records cumulatively covered the reading ability of 127 boys, from all social groups, who entered in 1689, 1695 and 1708, aged 3–12 at entry. Of the 127, 60% could already read, and 68% came in at five, six and seven. Only 10% of the three- and four-year-olds could read.

Vernacular elementary schools, or rather their masters, were erratically licensed by the bishops to teach boys 'reading, writing and to caste accomptes'. The boys and girls were therefore taught to read, from their hornbooks, on entry, and usually taught only to read at this stage. Girls were to be taught 'to read, knit and spin', though it becomes apparent that many of them were not at all unfamiliar with casting accounts later in their lives.[9] Learning to read from a hornbook, with its alphabet, Lord's Prayer and perhaps a psalm, also began, of course, the religious teaching of the child, which was then reinforced by the Primer,[10] followed up by the New or Old Testaments. We do not know how widely the flood of schoolbooks and manuals for schoolmasters teaching reading were actually used: the very fact that there was a flood indicates a market.[11] But the references commonly found after the hornbook itself are to the Primer, and then to the New and Old Testaments. The Bible seems to have been the commonest of all the textbooks, and indeed, the one to which the manuals for teachers pointed. Bible stories were gripping, as the seven-year-old Thomas Boston found. He 'had delight' in reading the Bible by that age, and took it to bed at night, observing 'nothing induced me to it, but curiosity, ... as about the history of Balaam's ass'.[12]

The second stage, learning to write, and possibly the third, 'casting accomptes', began later and continued in elementary schools at the point when

---

8 From the unpublished papers of Mr Newman Brown, held by the Cambridge Group for the History of Population and Social Structure. We are deeply grateful to Dr Roger Schofield for drawing them to our attention. There is another set of late statistics, reflecting lower reading ability, from the Great Yarmouth Children's Hospital, 1698–1715; David Cressy, *Literacy and the Social Order: Reading and Writing in Tudor and Stuart England* (Cambridge University Press, 1980), pp. 30–5.

9 Charlton, *Women, Religion and Education*, pp. 44–8, and Amy Louise Erickson, *Women and Property in Early Modern England* (London and New York: Routledge, 1993). See also p. 22 below, on Grace Sherrington.

10 Margaret Aston, *Lollards and Reformers: Images and Literacy in Late Medieval Religion* (London: Hambledon Press, 1984), pp. 124–5 and nn. 71–7.

11 Charlton, *Women, Religion and Education*, pp. 78–84; Cressy, *Literacy and the Social Order*, pp. 19–21.

12 G. D. Lowe (ed.), *A General Account of my Life by Thomas Boston, AM, Minister at Simprin, 1699–1707 and at Ettrick, 1707–32* (London: Hodder & Stoughton, 1908), p. 3.

boys of superior social status left for grammar school, as John Evelyn did. John was eight, despite his early start, when he was 'put to learne my Latine Rudiments and to write', in 1628.[13] His father later complained of his writing when he was fifteen, and he had an intensive 'moneth or two' at a writing-school. Despite that, and the criticisms of his modern editor that his writing in almanacs, while he was up at Oxford, was 'almost illegible', he began 'to observe matters ... which I did set down in a blanke Almanac' when he was eleven, in direct imitation of his father, who also used almanacs for this purpose. Written texts of custumals, for instance, were increasingly thought more credible.[14] A perfect illustration of a boy's new skill of writing survives in the diary of an alderman of Cambridge. Mr Samuel Newton wrote in an evil scrawl, and mostly recorded the consumption of large quantities of sugar-cakes and sack and gratifying corporation occasions. There is little record of his family. Yet on 12 February 1667, he wrote, 'on Tewsday was the first time my sonne John Newton went to the Grammar Free Schoole in Cambridge'. In October of the same year, right in the middle of a page of the paternal scrawl, but with no paternal comment, appear neatly ruled lines, inscribed upon them in the most painstaking child's hand

> I John Newton being in Coates this nineteenth day of October Anno Domini
> 1667 and not then full eight yeares old wrote this by me   John Newton

This newly breeched boy was proud of his accomplishment, and so was his father.[15]

We know less about the teaching of the third of the rudiments, casting accounts, than the other two. Like reading, mathematical skills left no quantifiable data behind. But there are even some hints that reckoning, by whatever method, might have been more valued than writing. John Awdeley, composing a textbook in 1574, wrote 'there be many persons that be unlearned, and can not wryte, nevertheless the craft or science of Awgrym [algorithm] & reckoning

---

13 Evelyn, *Diary*, ed. de Beer, 1:6 and p. 7 n. 1, and Guy de la Bédoyère (selected and ed.), *The Diary of John Evelyn* (Woodbridge: Boydell Press, 1995), Introduction.

14 Adam Fox, 'Custom, Memory and the Authority of Writing', in *The Experience of Authority in Early Modern England*, ed. Paul Griffiths, Adam Fox and Steve Hindle (Basingstoke: Macmillan, 1996), pp. 89–116. Unfortunately, Adam Fox, *Oral and Literate Culture in England, 1500–1700* (Oxford: Clarendon Press, 2000), came out after this text was finished. It would have been very influential. See aso David D. Hall, 'The Chesapeake in the Seventeenth Century', in *Cultures of Print. Essays in the History of the Book* (Amherst: University of Massachusetts Press, 1996), pp. 101–15.

15 J. E. Foster (ed.), 'The Diary of Samuel Newton, Alderman of Cambridge (1662–1717)', *Cambridge Antiquarian Society*, Octavo Publication 23 (1890), 17 and 23. The original is in Downing College Library, and the entry by John Newton appears on fo. 74 of the MS.

is nedfull for them to know'.[16] Recent work has made us much more aware of the need for commercial skills in sixteenth- and seventeenth-century England, and, indeed, has challenged the old assumption that Protestantism as the 'religion of the Book' was the main motor for improved literacy in northern Europe, rather than commerce. 'Traditionally, historians have emphasized the thirst for the printed Word as the prime cause of the thrust towards literacy in protestant countries',[17] but this judgement can no longer stand. In all the main commercial centres of Europe, from medieval Italy to south Germany, through the southern Low Countries to the United Provinces of the seventeenth century, commercial needs for education overrode all others, both before and after the Protestant Reformation, and before and after the Council of Trent. Both Catholics and Protestants were deeply interested in literacy. The post-Tridentine Schools of Christian Doctrine taught enormous numbers of children basic reading, writing and the newly adapted catechism in northern Italy. Religious training and vocational training for earning a living, including literacy, were important to Catholics, since lack of either indicated a deprived condition. The Protestant burghers of a town in Würtemberg did not care for Luther's new Latin schools for the elite:[18] their 'greatest complaint [was] that their sons [had] been deprived of the opportunity to learn reading, writing and reckoning before they [were] apprenticed to the trades'. As England, a century after the Dutch, took off commercially, so also did the records demonstrate the increasing extent of borrowing and lending, and the increasing need for numeracy. The incentive to understand the bond which one had signed or marked with one's name, and which might involve the mortgage of property or the sale of one's goods, must have been a very powerful motive to acquire both skills.

Arithmetic, then, was increasingly needed. Numeracy has been too little studied.[19] We can proceed by the same methods as with reading, which likewise

16 *An Introduction of Algorisme: to learn to reckon wyth the Pen or wyth the Counters*, printed by John Awdeley (London, 1574).

17 John Morgan, *Godly Learning: Puritan Attitudes towards Reason, Learning and Education, 1560–1640* (Cambridge University Press, 1986), p. 160.

18 Margaret Spufford, 'Literacy, Trade and Religion in the Commercial Centres of Europe', in *A Miracle Mirrored: The Dutch Republic in European Perspective*, ed. Karel Davids and Jan Lucassen (Cambridge University Press, 1995), pp. 229–83. For Italy, see p. 242; for German opposition to Luther's Latin schools, see pp. 245–6.

19 The only exceptions are Kenneth Charlton, *Education in Renaissance England* (London: Routledge and Kegan Paul, 1965), pp. 258–69, and Keith Thomas, 'Numeracy in Early Modern England', *Transactions of the Royal Historical Society* 5th ser. 37 (1987), 103–32. They both draw attention to the increasingly frequent publication of textbooks on arithmetic in the seventeenth century.

leaves no quantifiable record. We can show that elementary schoolmasters were licensed to teach this third rudiment as well as the other two,[20] and the seventeenth-century 'spiritual autobiographers' also provide us with enough examples to demonstrate the effects of some of this teaching.

Thomas Chubb was the son of a maltster who died when Thomas was nine. Thomas wrote of himself in the introduction to a lengthy work on the Scriptures:

> The Author was taught to read English, to write an ordinary hand, and was further instructed in the common rules of arithmetick; this education being suitable to the circumstances of his family and to the time he had to be instructed in. For as the Author's mother laboured hard, in order to get a maintenance for herself and family, so she obliged her children to perform their parts towards it.[21]

Thomas ended up as the leader of a group of young journeymen in Salisbury, who were 'persons of reading' and who had 'paper-controversies' or written debates between themselves.

A grammar school education did not necessarily supply either fluent writing or any introduction to the 'common rules of arithmetic'. It is possible that these may have been more familiar to a boy from a vernacular elementary school than to one from a grammar school. On the other hand, Oliver Sansom, whom we know, was taken from his grammar school soon after he was ten: '[I] ... stayed not long there, my father having occasion to take me home *to keep his book* [our italics] and look after what I was capable of in his business, which was dealing in timber and wood'. So Oliver was already capable of giving practical assistance, coming out of a grammar school. John Newton did not stay at grammar school either: his proud father apprenticed him to a dry-salter at fourteen. We become aware of a whole group of yeomen and tradesmen who interrupted their sons' grammar school education at an appropriate point when they were old enough to be of use. We also become aware of increasing references to both 'writing schools', like the one John Evelyn attended, and accounting, or 'reckoning' schools,[22] to which these fathers often sent their sons briefly after grammar school, to prepare them for business. This was the more necessary as the whole system of accounting was changing from the old use of a 'reckoning' board or cloth, marked out in squares, on which a sum was done using counters and roman numerals, to 'cyphering' using arabic numerals. It seems that the

---

20 See below, pp. 20–1, 23, 26.
21 T. Chubb, *The Posthumous Works of Mr Thomas Chubb ... To the whole is prefixed, some account of the author, written by himself* ... (London, 1748), pp. ii–iii.
22 Charlton, *Education*, pp. 259ff.

transition took place during the seventeenth century, when counters stopped being produced in Nuremberg, which had supplied Europe, but that the two systems ran on side by side for some time.[23] The earliest textbook in English already referred to the new system. It was entitled *An Introduction for to Lerne to Recken with the Penne or Counters* (1537). In Bristol, the change can be deduced from the probate inventories, drawn up by men who had been at school some twenty or thirty years before. Around 1610, 90% of inventories still used roman numerals which needed counters, but by 1650 90% were using arabic figures.[24]

The fullest example we have of the ability 'to write and cast accounts', which once again are mentioned together, is that of Gregory King. Here it is necessary to proceed with caution, for not only was Gregory King certainly a prodigy, but he was the son of another Gregory King, who 'being a good grammar scholar had applied himself much to the mathematicks, particularly navigation, gunnery, surveying of land and dyalling . . . at other times teaching to write and cast accounts, and being sometimes employed in designing of the more curious gardens'.

Gregory King senior was probably born in the 1620s, and his son was definitely born in 1648. Unfortunately for our purposes, the elder Gregory helped with his son's education. It was he who taught young Gregory to write when illness kept him at home when he was seven. He had been reading at three. When King wrote his autobiography, he emphasised his expertise in Latin, Hebrew and Greek, and only casually mentioned that he was so far forward by his eleventh and twelfth year that his master gave him permission to leave school early 'that he might have the liberty of attending some scholars of his own, which he then taught to write and cast accounts'. So, with the background of a grammar education, Gregory King could teach writing and casting accounts by the time he was ten and eleven, respectively. At thirteen he was both writing Greek verse of his own and surveying land by himself. But he added that his father taught him much at home until he was ten or eleven, as well as taking him out of school to help with surveying from twelve to fourteen. 'However, the knowledge he had gained in the mathematics did very well recompense' this loss. So we do not know to what extent Gregory King learnt

23 The brass casting-counters used in England were largely made in Nuremberg by two firms, Schultes and Krauwinckel, who manufactured counters specifically for school use. The last dated casting-counters by Krauwinckel were struck in 1610, and the Schultes firm closed in 1612.
24 N. E. and S. George, *Guide to the Probate Inventories of the Bristol Deanery of the Diocese of Bristol (1542–1804)* (Bristol Record Society, 1988), p. xxii.

his mathematics from his father, or whether he also learnt them at school.[25] Nor do we know where Gregory King senior acquired his expertise.

Yet another mystery about this rudiment of numeracy concerns the teaching of women. We know that in elementary schools, girls were to be taught only to read. Yet we also know that educated women and gentlewomen ran their husbands' estates, and 'ordinary women', the widows of the inventoried classes, were financially capable of solving the often tangled business of their husbands' holdings. We know of the distress of the baker's widow in Canterbury who had her chalked-up figures for debts for bread disallowed. But we still do not have the faintest idea how this woman had learned to add.

Very rare references survive to illuminate the position of gentlefolk whose daughters were taught at home. In 1550, George Medley of Wollaton Hall, Nottingham, bought from an itinerant pedlar 'halfe a pounde of counters for my nece to learne to caste with all'. The boarding schools established by the Augustinian canonesses for gentry daughters in Bruges in 1629, and in the later seventeenth century in Paris, included 'casting of accounts' after learning to write well in both syllabuses.[26] Grace Sherrington, of Lacock Abbey, was taught by her aunt at home. A page from her journal relates Grace's everyday activities in detail. It begins: 'When she did see me idly disposed, she would set me to cypher with the pen and to cast up and to prove great sums and accounts'.[27] Grace continues at much greater length about her needlework, music and reading. We are left to wonder whether this basic piece of preparation for a gentleman's wife was not discussed because it was so necessary and obvious that it was assumed. Five-part songs set to the lute were not.

At the point – around seven or eight years old in an elementary school – when writing and arithmetic were to be learnt, the gentlemen's and tradesmen's sons, and the sons of aspiring yeomen, parted social company; those who were to be fully literate in Latin as well as English went on to their grammar schools and different futures. The latter also went on, one may suppose, to their enjoyment of literature, the main subject of the present volume, which may be differentiated from 'cheap print' – ballads, chapbooks and jest-books.

25 'Some miscellaneous notes of the birth, education, and advancement of GREGORY KING, Rouge Dragon Pursuivant, afterward Lancaster Herald', in J. Dallaway, *Inquiries into the Origins and Progress of the Science of Heraldry* (Gloucester, 1793), pp. xxv–xxvii.

26 Caroline Bowden, 'The Education of English Catholic Women in Convents in Flanders and France', *Paedagogica Historica*, Supplementary Series 5 (University of Ghent: Centre for the Study of Historical Pedagogy, 1999), 181–2.

27 Charlton, *Education*, p. 210, and *Women, Religion and Education*, pp. 44–6. J. Collinges, *Par Nobile. Two Treatises at the Funeralls of Lady Frances Hobart and . . . Lady Katherine Courten* (London, 1669), pp. 3–5.

In a sense, this discussion of literate skills might be expected to stop here, or rather to go straight on to the grammar school and university education of these gentlemen and professionals, who must have made up a very large proportion of the readers of the works treated in this volume. But Latined literati were not the only readers of important works; nor were they ignorant of the whole of the contents of the cheap print being produced for those children who had only been to elementary school.

Vernacular elementary schools

A pioneering article in 1954[28] first drew attention to the availability of elementary education between 1625 and 1640 in Leicestershire. In 1555 Queen Mary enacted that all schoolmasters were to be examined and licensed by bishops or other senior church officials,[29] although the records survive patchily. It is very difficult to say much about individual schoolmasters before 1550, although the chantry certificates refer to the practice of some chantry priests additionally teaching the rudiments. It is important to know what type of education was available in these schools for the village, but it is also difficult to establish this. The licences issued for schoolmasters which survive between 1574 and 1604 in the diocese of Ely sometimes simply gave permission to teach and instruct, but frequently the licence was issued for a specific function. It might be 'to teach grammar', 'to teach the rudiments of grammar', 'to teach boys and adolescents to write, read and caste an accompte', 'to write and read the vulgar tongue' or 'to teach young children'.[30] It looks, on the face of it, as though there were both grammar and English schools, and that the latter were divided into the two types described by Professor Stone:[31] petty schools teaching children to write and read, and those teaching English grammar, writing and arithmetic up to the age of sixteen. All these masters were teaching alone, so the modern image of a 'village school' does not fit. Unfortunately, there is a great deal of inconsistency in the type of licence issued for the same village within relatively

28 Brian Simon, 'Leicestershire Schools, 1625-40', *British Journal of Educational Studies* 3 (1954), 42-58.
29 Helen M. Jewell, *Education in Early Modern England* (Basingstoke: Macmillan, 1998), p. 25.
30 Elizabeth Key, 'Register of Schools and Schoolmasters in the Diocese of Ely, 1560-1700', *Proceedings of the Cambridge Antiquarian Society* 70 (1980), 127-89. Of 97 villages in the old county of Cambridgeshire in which Mrs Key found records of education, only 14 had an endowment before 1700: p. 130.
31 Lawrence Stone, 'The Educational Revolution in England, 1560-1640', *Past and Present* 28 (1964), 41-80.

short spaces of time. Licences not uncommonly specified the teaching of the 'vulgar tongue' or 'young children' at one visitation, and grammar at the next, or vice versa. Moreover, the college admissions registers gave evidence that boys were prepared for entrance in some villages where, according to the episcopal records, there had never been a schoolmaster, or there was not a schoolmaster at the right time, or there was only a schoolmaster who taught the 'vulgar tongue'. So licences indicate the minimum number of schoolmasters.

These suspicious contradictions render futile any attempt to establish a typology of local schools. For one thing, the definitions given in the episcopal records may not be reliable; for another, these small village schools probably changed character remarkably quickly. Many existed over a brief period only, or for the working life of an individual teacher. Others, which apparently had no continuous history, may well have had one that escaped episcopal notice. The women who taught reading, like Oliver Sansom's instructor, were hardly ever licensed at all, although, according to ecclesiastical law, they should have been, like the midwives. Yet we know such women were very common.[32] It is obvious that the records are impressionistic, and the impression that they give is of flexibility and change. The school held in Little Gransden should serve as a salutary reminder against too rigid definition. Little Gransden was one of the few villages with no record of any teaching. Yet we know very well from the testimony of Christopher Meade that a school did flourish there in the 1570s and 1580s, and served to teach the local gentry, and others, their 'rudiments'.

Although these Ely schools may have changed rapidly in character between 1574 and 1604, the general quality of the masters teaching in them was extraordinarily high. Nearly two-thirds of the men licensed specifically to teach grammar are known to have been graduates. A number of the remainder may, of course, have graduated as well. Much more surprisingly, a third of the masters licensed merely 'to teach younge children to read write and caste accompte' were also graduates. After 1604, however, when the licences stopped specifying the kind of teaching to be done in the diocese of Ely, no generalisations can be made about the qualifications of teachers in different schools.

In villages with few or no licences it seems probable that individual masters rather than established schools were concerned. The high academic quality of many of these men makes it very likely that they were the products of the bulge in university entrants in the period between the 1560s and the 1580s,

---

32 Margaret Spufford, 'Women Teaching Reading to Poor Children in the Sixteenth and Seventeenth Centuries', in *Opening the Nursery Door: Reading, Writing and Childhood, 1600–1900*, ed. Mary Hilton, Morag Styles and Victor Watson (London: Routledge, 1997), p. 48.

and were reduced to searching for jobs wherever they could find them. They have been found working in every county where schoolmasters' licences have already been examined. The number of college entrants taught by men in villages gives the same impression that isolated individuals were often teachers in villages.[33] Detailed work on the careers of schoolmasters shows that many of them were very young men doing a short spell of teaching between graduation and getting a benefice elsewhere; there was little or no permanence. It is no wonder that endowment, even of a very humble kind, had the immediate effect of establishing a school, when there were so many graduates obviously seeking work which offered an income, however small.[34]

David Cressy's work on the dioceses of London, Norwich, Exeter and Durham covered the counties of Hertfordshire, Essex, Norfolk, Suffolk, Cornwall, Devon, Middlesex and the City of London, Durham and Northumberland. Only the last two were markedly different.[35] He showed a sharp rise in the number of schoolmasters found at visitations in rural Essex and Hertfordshire from 1580 to 1592, followed by a decline in the 1620s, and a 'virtual disappearance' after the Restoration, which might of course only reflect the weakness of the church in enforcing its licensing procedure. The picture in Norfolk and Suffolk was not dissimilar: there was a boom in the number of the schoolmasters teaching in the 1590s, followed by a slump in the early seventeenth century, some recovery by the 1630s, but a severe decline after the Restoration.

In Cambridgeshire, approximately one-fifth of the villages, mainly the larger ones and the minor market towns, had a schoolmaster licensed continuously from 1570 to 1620. Maps of teacher distribution show that except in the poor western boulder clay area and the chalk down areas of the county, some sort of teacher was almost always within walking distance for a determined child in the late sixteenth and early seventeenth centuries.[36] In one village, Willingham, parents set up and endowed their own school. This had a noticeable effect, since it produced a group of farmers who were capable of writing wills for the whole community, as well as a college entrant. Again, there was a diminution in the number of masters recorded in the episcopal records after the Restoration. Cambridgeshire, where one-third of the masters in unendowed schools

---

33 This confirms Stone's impressions in 'Educational Revolution in England, 1560–1640', p. 46, that college entrants were often privately prepared in small hamlets. It is wrong to assume, as W. A. L. Vincent did in *The State and School Education, 1640–60, in England and Wales* (London: SPCK, 1950), that any village in which a college entrant was prepared automatically had a grammar school. His county lists are suspect for this reason.
34 Charlton, *Women, Religion and Education*, pp. 145–53.
35 Cressy, *Literacy and the Social Order*, pp. 112–24.
36 Spufford, *Contrasting Communities*, p. 185.

licensed only to 'teach younge children to read, write and caste accompte' were graduates, did not owe its supply of teachers simply to the work of the university town at the centre of the county. Maps of the schools functioning in Kent show that, again with the exception of the poorest areas in Romney Marsh and on the downs of Canterbury, that county was also reasonably well provided.[37] Between 1601 and 1640, half the settlements had a teacher at some time or another, and one-eighth of them had a school functioning continuously, as opposed to only one-sixteenth of them from 1561 to 1600.

Work on the availability of teachers in north-western England shows a very different chronological picture. In the diocese of Coventry and Lichfield, covering Staffordshire and Derbyshire, north Shropshire and north-eastern Warwickshire, schools had already been established in all the main centres of population by 1640. A large number of new endowments were made between 1660 and 1699. The majority of these were intended for the teaching of reading and writing, and specifically mentioned the poor. Even more interestingly, there was general development of educational facilities between 1660 and 1700, when masters appeared in no fewer than 119 places where there had been no reference to one between 1600 and 1640.[38] In the north-east, likewise, literacy rates improved later in the century, especially among men in cities.[39]

In Cheshire, 132 places had masters teaching at some point between 1547 and 1700. There again, there was an increase in the number of teachers appearing after 1651. Analysis of the number of places for which schoolmasters were licensed in Cheshire in fifty-year periods showed a continuous increase, from 53 before 1600, to 79 in 1601–50, to as many as 105 between 1651 and 1700. Again, a map shows that schools, or rather schoolmasters, were scattered at reasonable distances all over the county, with the exception of noticeably poor areas. The child who lived in Delamere Forest or on the heath area south-west of Nantwich would not find it easy to learn to read or write.[40] This widespread network of elementary schools produced general reading ability except in the poorest areas.

37 Peter Clark, *English Provincial Society from the Reformation to the Revolution* (Hassocks: Harvester Press, 1977), pp. 202–3.
38 A. Smith, 'Endowed Schools in the Diocese of Lichfield and Coventry, 1660–1699', *History of Education* 4.2 (1975), 5–8, and 'Private Schools and Schoolmasters in the Diocese of Lichfield and Coventry', *History of Education* 5.2 (1976), 117–26.
39 R. A. Houston, 'The Development of Literacy: Northern England, 1640–1750', *Economic History Review* 35.2 (1982), 199–216, and *Scottish Literacy and the Scottish Identity: Illiteracy and Society in Scotland and Northern England, 1600–1800* (Cambridge University Press, 1985).
40 C. Rogers, 'Development of the Teaching Profession in England, 1547–1700', unpublished Ph.D. diss., University of Manchester (1975), pp. 245ff.

Literacy levels

Because there was approximately a two-year gap between the teaching of reading and of writing, the discussion of 'literacy' since the 1980s has been bedevilled by misunderstanding. It is the first skill, reading, which brings about cultural change and openness to the spread of ideas. Yet the ability to read leaves no trace on the printed page or in the records. It is unquantifiable. There is only one standard literary skill capable of measurement that can be used as an index for the whole population, and that is the less important ability to sign one's name. Therefore a mass of important work uses this index of 'literacy' which quantifies signatures and establishes their relationship to economic and social status.[41] 'Illiterate' is normally taken by early modernists to mean 'unable to sign one's name'. This skill has been conclusively shown to be tied to one's social status in Tudor and Stuart East Anglia, for the simple reason that some degree of prosperity was necessary to spare a child from the labour force for education once it was capable of work. The gap between learning to read and learning to write is unfortunately crucial. Six or seven, before writing was normally taught, was the age at which a child was thought capable of joining the workforce and starting to bring wages in.[42] This meant that he or she was likely to be removed from school as soon as he or she could contribute: the poorer the family, the earlier the entry into the workforce. Thus the social pyramid of literacy is precisely explained, for it was economically determined by the need for wages as well as the need not to pay the schooldame or master 1d or 2d.

Thomas Tryon, amongst the autobiographers who identified their backgrounds, came from the poorest home, and he certainly had the most prolonged struggle to get himself an education. He was born in 1634 at Bibury in Oxfordshire, the son of a village tiler and plasterer, 'an . . . honest sober Man of good Reputation; but having many Children, was forced to bring them all to work betimes'.[43] The size of the family did much to dictate educational opportunity, for obvious reasons. Again and again amongst the autobiographers,

---

41 See the pioneering work by Dr Roger Schofield, 'The Measurement of Literacy in Pre-Industrial England', in J. R. Goody (ed.), *Literacy in Traditional Societies*, ed. Jack Goody (Cambridge University Press, 1968), pp. 318–25, and 'Some Discussion of Illiteracy in England', 1600–1800' (unpublished). A part of the latter has appeared as 'Dimensions of Illiteracy, 1750–1850', *Explorations in Economic History* 10.4 (1973), 437–54.

42 Margaret Spufford, 'First Steps in Literacy: The Reading and Writing Experiences of the Humblest Seventeenth-Century Spiritual Autobiographers', *Social History* 4 (1979), 407–35, expands the summary given here.

43 Thomas Tryon, *Some Memoirs of the Life of Mr Tho: Tryon, late of London, merchant: written by himself*. . . (London, 1705), pp. 7–9.

only children, or those from small families, appear at an advantage. Despite his numerous siblings, young Thomas was briefly sent to school: 'About Five Year old, I was put to School, but being addicted to play, after the Example of my young School-fellows, I scarcely learnt to distinguish my Letters, before I was taken away to Work for my Living.' This seems to have been before he was six, although his account is ambiguous. At six young Thomas Tryon was either not strongly motivated, as he obviously thought himself from his mention of the importance of play, or not well taught. Yet it is worth remembering that he was removed from school to work at about the age Oliver Sansom began to learn. His early failure to learn to read would take great effort of will to redress.[44]

His contribution to the family economy began immediately and he obviously took tremendous pride in his ability to contribute. He became a spinner. Henry Best described the occupations of children in Yorkshire. His children helped dip sheep, carried mortar, cared for cattle and spread muck and molehills. The 'bigger and abler sort' were paid 3d a day and the 'lesser sort' 2d a day.[45] The physical ability of the child to earn 'wages' at six, or at least seven, dictated that child's removal from school, just as he was about to learn to write. Only the more unusual children overcame this handicap. Yet he, or even she, could almost certainly read. A note of caution needs to be sounded, however. The ability to 'read' at this age inevitably varied widely. One might place under the heading 'reading ability' a group of Gloucestershire shepherds who could sound out words to teach an eager boy to read, and a Wiltshire labourer who could read *Paradise Lost* with the aid of a dictionary. What all these probably had in common was the ability to read or recite the New Testament.

The social pyramid meant in practice that 'literacy could be taken for granted among the gentlemen [and professionals] of England, and although their educational experience may have altered along with fluctuations in their taste in books there was no variation from their virtually universal ability to sign'. The only exceptions were 'gentlemen' in the diocese of Durham: the north-east was more backward, and illiteracy rates amongst the gentry did not start to drop until the 1590s. However, there were no illiterate 'gentlemen' by the 1620s.[46] Nor understandably, were there any illiterate professionals. Those who made

44 See below, pp. 30–1.

45 Donald Woodward (ed.), *The Farming and Memorandum Books of Henry Best of Elmswell, 1642,* Records of Social and Economic History, new ser., 8 (London: Oxford University Press for the British Academy, 1984), pp. 21, 24, 126, 146, 152.

46 Cressy, *Literacy and the Social Order*, pp. 142–3, Graph 7.1 showing disappearance of gentry illiteracy measured in terms of ability to sign in the diocese of Durham, 1560–1630.

their living by reading and writing might be expected to be, as they were, totally literate.[47] Between 1580 and 1700, 11% of women, 15% of labourers and 21% of husbandmen could sign their names, against 56% of tradesmen and crafts-men, and 65% of yeomen in East Anglia.[48] Grammar school and, even more, university education were heavily restricted socially. From amongst the peas-antry, only sons of yeomen had much chance of appearing in grammar school or college registers. There was, however, 'general and substantial progress in reducing illiteracy' amongst all social groups except labourers in the late six-teenth century, followed by some stagnation or decline both in the 1630s and the 1640s, and in the late seventeenth century. It is possible, though, that the improvements and decreases in literacy levels in East Anglia may have been quite differently timed in other parts of the country, since increasing num-bers of teachers were found at periods after the Restoration in the dioceses of Coventry, Lichfield and Chester. Examination of literacy rates elsewhere might, therefore, give a substantially different picture.

The Protestation returns of 1642, which should have been signed or marked by all adult males, give, where they survive, the only seventeenth-century evi-dence providing a comprehensive cross-section of the results achieved by those teachers who appear in the episcopal records, and also comparisons between dif-ferent parts of the country of the percentages of those unable to sign. They have been extensively quarried by historians, and are fully discussed by Schofield, Cressy and Houston. Briefly, they reveal that, from parish to parish in the coun-tryside, a proportion of men varying between 53% and 79% were unable to sign their names.[49] The average was around 70%. In accordance with international convention, these figures are always expressed in negative terms, and 'illiteracy' rates rather than 'literacy' rates are cited. Despite the somewhat gloomy inter-pretation Schofield and Cressy have put on their analyses of the 1642 returns, it appears equally possible to reverse the image. One can point out that, where the negative statement can be made that the least advanced parishes in England had not less than 79% of illiterate adult males, so equally can the positive statement that, even in the most backward parishes in England, one-fifth of men could write their names. There was therefore an absolute minimum reading public of 20% of men in the least literate areas in 1642. Nineteenth-century evidence

---

47 Below, pp. 46–7, and Spufford, 'First Steps', 424–7. Houston, *Scottish Literacy*, pp. 30, 31 and 33.

48 The dates are Cressy's, *Literacy and the Social Order*, Table 6.1, p. 119. He then examines illiteracy in the dioceses of Exeter, Durham and London in Tables 6.2–6.5. See his p. 112 for discussion of the dates of his sources which 'are usually lacking before the Elizabethan period'.

49 Mapped by David Cressy as 'Illiteracy in England, 1641–4', *ibid.*, Map 1, p. 74.

suggests that those who could sign their names could also read fluently. It also shows that as many as three-quarters of the women making marks could read, since writing was normally omitted from the elementary school curricula for girls from the sixteenth to the nineteenth centuries.

The passionate reader

Two years after it was ordained that the Great Bible of 1539 should be bought and placed in every parish church 'where your parishioners may most commodiously resort unto the same and read it', Thomas Becon was enquiring 'But how many read it? Verily a man may come into some churches and see the Bible so enclosed and wrapped with dust... that with his finger he may write upon the Bible this epitaph: ecce nunc in pulvere dormio, that is to say "behold I sleep now in the dust".'[50] If Becon is to be believed, in 'some churches' even the Prayer Book's ordering of the reading of the Lessons was not proving effective. However, there were certainly those who were longing to read the Scriptures for themselves. William Maldon, a twenty-year-old apprentice of Chelmsford in Essex, reported that soon after the orders for the Great Bible were given, various poor men of Chelmsford bought the New Testament for themselves, and sat reading at the lower end of the church on Sundays, 'and many would flock about them to hear their reading'. Maldon was enthused by hearing 'their reading of that glad and sweet tidings of the Gospel... Then thought I, I will learn to read English, and then will I have the New Testament and read thereon myself.' So he obtained an English primer and learnt to read from it, then clubbed together with another apprentice to buy an English New Testament, which they hid in their bed straw.[51] Basic literacy could be acquired even when the acquisitor had not been able to attend a vernacular school.

Over a century later, another boy out of reach of schooling also 'bought him a primer'.[52] At last the desire for literacy gripped Thomas Tryon about 1647:

> now about Thirteen Years Old, I could not Read; then thinking of the vast usefulness of Reading, I bought me a Primer, and got now one, then another, to teach me to Spell, and so learn'd to Read imperfectly, my Teachers themselves not being ready Readers: But... having learn't to Read competently well, I was desirous to learn to Write, but was at a great loss for a Master, none of my Fellow-Shepherds being able to teach me. At last, I bethought myself of a... Man who

50 Thomas Becon, *The Early Works of Thomas Becon*, ed. J. Ayre, Parker Society, 2 (Cambridge University Press, 1843), p. 38.
51 Aston, *Lollards and Reformers*, p. 214.   52 See above, pp. 27–8.

taught some poor People's Children to Read and Write; and having by this time got two Sheep of my own, I applied myself to him, and agreed with him to give him one of my Sheep to teach me to make the Letters, and Joyn them together.

The difficulty Thomas found in learning to write, as opposed to learning to read, seems very important. Although his fellow shepherds, as a group, were not 'ready readers' they did, again as a group, possess the capacity to help him to learn to spell out words. He was not dependent on only one of them to help him. But these Gloucestershire shepherds could not write at all. A semi-qualified teacher was called for, and it took some effort to find him.

Thomas Tryon eventually went to London as an apprentice. His addiction to print continued. He made time to read by sitting up at night for two or three hours after his day's work was finished. His wages went on education. 'Therewith I furnished myself with Books, paid my Tutors and served all my occasion.' By the end of his life, his own written works reflecting his range of interests included *The Country Man's Companion, The Good Housewife Made a Doctor, Dreams and Visions, Book of Trade, Friendly Advice to the People of the West Indies, A New Method of Education* and, most surprisingly of all, *Averroes Letter to Pythagoras*. It is a remarkable publication list for a boy who left school at six before he could read.

Tryon was the most dedicated self-improver we know of, but other examples of people thirsting for print exist. The unfortunate Rhys (or Arise) Evans, who initially could read but not write, made his way from the Welsh borders to London on foot after emerging from his apprenticeship. A book to read could delay him, however. He tells us:

> And at Coventre I wrought and stayed a quarter of a year, by reason of an old Chronicle that was in my Master's house that showed all the passage in Brittain and Ireland from Noahs Floud to William the Conquerour, it was of a great volume, and by day I bestowed what time I could spare to read, and bought Candles for the night, *so that I got by heart the most material part of it.*[53]

This desire for information, together with the problems of even finding time to absorb it during the working day, or a source of light to read it by at night, seems to have been common to all largely self-educated working men. The physical difficulties the autobiographers encountered in the seventeenth century were fundamentally the same as those of their nineteenth-century heirs.[54]

---

53 Rhys (or Arise) Evans, *An Eccho to The voice from heaven*... (London, 1652), p. 13.
54 David Vincent, *Bread, Knowledge and Freedom: A Study of Nineteenth-century Working-class Autobiography* (London: Europa, 1981), ch. 5.

Print: availability and use

If a large number of people could read in the seventeenth century, what was there available to read? The early modern period saw a massive increase in the production of printed books, and it is not difficult to show the increased availability of books of all sorts, from multi-volumed works to broadsheets and chapbooks, from fictive literature to doctrinal treatises.[55] The more difficult question remains: What evidence is there that they were read and by whom? Some does exist. John Foxe's originally Latin, folio volumes of 'The Book of Martyrs' were first of all Englished, then enlarged, and later abridged and imitated to widen their readership. Thomas à Kempis's *Imitatio Christi* was translated and protestantised to the same end.[56] Margaret Hoby's diary frequently refers not only to her daily reading of the Bible and other godly books but also to her reading to other members of her household. That of the literate Anne Clifford mentions what was obviously a regular practice of having various members of her household read to her from, amongst others, Ovid's *Metamorphoses* (presumably in Arthur Golding's translation of 1565–7), Sidney's *Arcadia*, Spenser's *Faerie Queene*, Montaigne's *Essays* (in John Florio's 1603 translation), as well as readings from the Bible, Thomas Sorocold's *Supplication of the Saints* (1612) and Robert Parsons's *Resolutions of Religion* (1630).[57] Though the accounts of Samuel Blithe, Fellow of Clare Hall, Cambridge, from 1658 to 1693, show that he bought and sold to his students the usual logic and rhetoric texts of the period, he nevertheless included Donne's *Poems* (1633), George Herbert's *The Temple* (1633), Richard Crashaw's *Steps to the Temple* (1646) and the works of Abraham Cowley, as well as Richard Allestree's *Whole Duty of Man* (1658), Thomas à Kempis's *The Following of Christ* (1673 edn) and, most unusually in the context, the *Poems* of Katherine Philips, 'The Matchless Orinda'.[58]

---

55 On the production of printed books, see also Chapter 3 in this volume.
56 D. M. Loades (ed.), *John Foxe and the English Reformation* (Aldershot: Scolar Press, 1997); W. Haller, *Foxe's Book of Martyrs and the Elect Nation* (London: Jonathan Cape, 1963); D. Crane, 'English Translations of the *Imitatio Christi* in the Sixteenth and Seventeenth Centuries', *Recusant History* 13 (1975), 79–100; E. K. Hudson, 'English Protestants and the *Imitatio Christi* 1580–1620', *Sixteenth Century Journal* 19 (1988), 541–58.
57 Margaret Hoby, *The Private Life of an Elizabethan Lady: The Diary of Lady Margaret Hoby, 1599–1605*, ed. Joanna Moody (Stroud: Sutton, 1998), pp. xxxvi–xlii; Anne Clifford, *The Diary of Anne Clifford, 1616–1619. A Critical Edition*, ed. Katherine O. Acheson (New York: Garland, 1995), pp. 45, 51, 59, 65, 73, 76, 79, 81, 90, 102, 103, 113.
58 J. Gascoigne, 'The Cambridge Curriculum in the Age of Newton as Revealed in the Accounts of Samuel Blithe', in his *Science, Politics and Universities in Europe, 1600–1800* (Aldershot: Ashgate, 1998), ch. 3. In 1675 Brasenose College bought copies of the verse of Spenser, Cowley and Katherine Philips: I. G. Philips and P. Morgan, 'Libraries, Books and Printing', in *The History of the University of Oxford*, gen. ed. T. H. Aston, 8 vols. (Oxford: Clarendon Press, 1984–94), 4:676. See also P. Clarke, 'The Ownership of Books in England 1540–1640'.

Contemporary poetry, aiming always 'to profit men and also to delight', as Arthur Golding reminded his readers in 1565,[59] was usually 'distributed' by means of circulation in manuscript from among the families of the upper class, but by the mid sixteenth century the printed press was beginning to provide for a wider readership. *The Songes and Sonnettes* of Thomas Wyatt, Henry Howard, Earl of Surrey, and other versifiers, gathered and printed by Richard Tottel in 1557, was for thirty years one of the most popular collections of lyric poetry, commonly known as *Tottel's Miscellany*. At the end of the century Robert Allott's collection *England's Parnassus*, Anthony Munday's *Belvedere or the Garden of Muses* and Nicholas Ling's *England's Helicon*, all published in 1600, provided the reading public with an introduction to 'the choycest floures of our moderne poets', *England's Helicon* figuring in a seventeenth-century collection of books with the inscription 'Frances Wolfreston hor bouk'.[60] Translation, too, was making available both classical and continental literature, and by 1600 'with the exception of Greek lyric poetry and drama the whole of the classical heritage was within the grasp of a travelled man though he possessed little Latin and less Greek'.[61] Moreover, there were available for the busy or impatient the early modern equivalents of the medieval *florilegia*, of which William Caxton's *Dictes and Sayinges of the Philosophers* (1477, etc.) was an early progenitor. The most popular was William Baldwin's *A Treatise of Morall Philosophie Contayning the Sayings of the Wise*, first published in 1547, reprinted in 1550, 'augmented' by Thomas Palfreyman in 1555 and 1557, reissued by Richard Tottel, and 'now once again enlarged by the first author' in 1564. Altogether twenty-four different editions were printed between 1547 and 1651.

Below these levels were the layers of romances, broadsheets and ballads frequently complained of by the moralists. In the 1980s we learnt an enormous amount about this cheap print.[62] Bunyan himself described his favourite

The Example of Some Kentish Townsfolk', in L. Stone (ed.), *Schooling and Society. Studies in the History of Education* (Baltimore: Johns Hopkins University Press, 1976), pp. 95–111, and Charlton, *Women, Religion and Education*, pp. 177–87.

59 Arthur Golding's metrical preface to his translation of Ovid's *Metamorphoses, The fyrst fower bookes of P. Ovidius Nasos worke intitled Metamorphosis* (1565), sig. Biii v, and more famously in Sidney's *Apologie for Poetrie* (London, 1595), sig. C3 v.

60 P. Morgan, 'Frances Wolfreston and "Hor Bouks", A Seventeenth-Century Woman Book-Collector', *The Library* 6th ser., 11 (1989), 197–219.

61 R. R. Bolgar, *The Classical Heritage and Its Beneficiaries* (Cambridge University Press, 1954), p. 328. See also H. R. Palmer, *List of English Editions and Translations of Greek and Latin Classics Printed Before 1641* (London: Blades, East & Blades, 1911); H. B. Lathrop, *Translations From the Classics into English from Caxton to Chapman, 1477–1620*, Studies in Language and Literature, 35 (Madison: University of Wisconsin Press, 1933).

62 The change in emphasis that this has led to amongst historians as the new area has been explored is well illustrated by comparing passages written by Patrick Collinson in 1981 (*The*

reading as a youth, probably in the 1640s, in terms fuller than those of any other 'spiritual autobiographer'. It was chapman's ware. He wrote 'give me a Ballad, a News-book, *George on Horseback* or *Bevis of Southampton*, give me some book that teaches curious Arts, that tells of old Fables; but for the Holy Scriptures, I cared not. And as it was with me then, so it is with my brethren now.'[63] Plainly either Bunyan's relations or his peer group were, at the time Bunyan was writing in the 1660s, avid readers of the ballads and chapbooks which Bunyan himself avoided after his conversion.

Bunyan's reading seems to have left a mark on him. *Bevis of Southampton* was a typical, breathless, sub-chivalric romance in which adventure follows adventure in quick succession. The hero's mother betrays his father to death and marries his murderer. Her son first escapes and keeps his uncle's sheep on a hill near his father's castle, then is sold into slavery to the 'paynims'. There he refuses to serve 'Apoline' their god, kills a gigantic wild boar, is made a general over 20,000 men, and wins the love of the princess. Alas, he is betrayed, and thrown into a dungeon with two dragons who quickly get the worse of it. After seven years on bread and water, he is still able to kill his jailer, and runs off with the princess and a great store of money and jewels. He is next attacked by two lions in a cave, meets 'an ugly Gyant thirty foot in length and a foot between his eyebrows', defeats him and makes him his page, and kills a dragon forty feet long. He then has the heathen princess baptised, and after numerous further adventures invades England, avenges his father's death, marries his paynim lady, and is made Lord Marshal. There is no attempt at characterisation and the whole piece of blood-and-thunder writing seems aimed at pre-adolescent or adolescent males – very successfully, if Bunyan's testimony is to be believed. Although his own writing was very far removed from this, some of his imagery does seem to have come from his early reading. The lions Christian meets by the way, the description of the monster Apollyon and the cave where the giants

---

Religion of Protestants (Oxford University Press, 1982), pp. 233–4) and 1988 (*The Birthpangs of Protestant England: Religious and Cultural Change in the Sixteenth and Seventeenth Centuries* (Basingstoke: Macmillan), p. 124). Both opinions were amply justified by the state of knowledge at the time.

63 John Bunyan, *A Few Sighs from Hell, or, The Groans of A Damned Soul* (London, 1658), pp. 147–8. The italics are his. In 1631, Richard Brathwait in *Whimzies: or, A New Cast of Characters* had not been complimentary about the 'Corranto-Coiner' who was presumably the source of the news-books Bunyan enjoyed. 'His mint goes weekly, and he coins monie by it...', Brathwait wrote. 'The vulgar doe admire him, holding his novels oracular; and these are usually sent for tokens... betwixt city and countrey...' A copy of *Bevis of Southampton* survives in Samuel Pepys's collection of 'Vulgaria', 3, item 10, Pepys Library, Magdalene College, Cambridge. 'George on Horseback' is probably the chapbook *St George*. There is a copy in Pepys's 'Penny Merriments', 2, pp. 105–28, of the edition printed in the 1680s.

Pope and Pagan dwell all owe something to it, as, perhaps, does Giant Despair himself. It is worth remembering also that Bunyan's own voluminous output was surely aimed at the rural readership he knew in the villages around Bedford amongst which he had his ministry. He knew his readership was familiar with the giants, lions, dragons and battles of the chapbooks, just as it was with the cadences of the Authorised Version. We now know that the congregation of Open Baptists for whom Bunyan primarily wrote was the poorest dissenting congregation for which we yet have information in England,[64] yet this was the 'reading public' of whom many could not write the letters of their names. This was the stock of metaphor and simile available to them and these were the stories they knew.

The whole process had, of course, started much earlier. In 1520, the Oxford bookseller John Dorne sold 170 ballads at a halfpenny each, with concessions for batches.[65] These concessions show the ballad trade was already a hawking trade. That it was a successful hawking trade is demonstrated by the offer of a Cambridgeshire man in an alehouse in the village of Orwell in 1555 to display a derogatory ballad called 'maistres mass'.[66] In all, there were probably some 3,000 different ballads in circulation in the second half of the sixteenth century, according to the Stationers' Company Register. Depending on the size of the print-runs, a minimum of 600,000 ballads were circulating at that time. The broadside ballads were much criticised as a vehicle for mass bawdiness and titillation. Miles Coverdale grumbled in the 1530s that 'women at the rockes and spynnynge at the wheles' should be better occupied than with 'hey nonny nonny-hey trolly lolly', and 'such like fantasies' and himself produced a volume of *Goostly Psalmes* (before 1539) to replace the 'ballads of filthiness (and) naughty songes of fleshly love and wantonness'.[67] It was the first of a flood of such ballads, which make up as much as a third of the whole output. But in the 1570s and 1580s the effort was largely abandoned in favour of the psalms as definitive godly songs.[68] Even so, the stock of the newly formed

64 W. Stevenson, 'The Social and Economic Status of Post-Restoration Dissenters', in Margaret Spufford (ed.), *The World of Rural Dissenters, 1520–1725* (Cambridge University Press, 1995), pp. 334–8. Over half of the Open Baptists lived in a house with a single hearth, and 17% of them were exempt from the hearth tax on grounds of poverty.

65 F. Madan (ed.), 'The day-book of John Dorne, bookseller in Oxford 1520', *Collectanea*, Proceedings of the Oxford Historical Society, 1st series (1885), 17–178.

66 Spufford, *Contrasting Communities*, p. 245.

67 For a consideration of their varied nature and influence, see K. Charlton, ' "False Fonde Bookes, Ballades and Rimes": An Aspect of Informal Education in Early Modern England', *History of Education Quarterly*, 27 (1987), 449–71.

68 Tessa Watt, *Cheap Print and Popular Piety, 1550–1640* (Cambridge University Press, 1991), pp. 47, 55–7, 82, 107, 117.

Ballad Partners of the 1620s contained a group of religious ballads which were proven favourites, and reprinted over and over again, some even for a whole century. They ranged in content from the death-bed scene of the pious 'Clarke of Bodnam' as his 'passing-bell is towling, sweetly' and his justification by his faith, to the attractions of David's Bathsheba whose

> body like a Lilly Flowere
> was covered with her golden haire.

Ballads were the cheapest of the cheap print, with the exception of single-sheet pictures alone. The seventeenth-century ballads were increasingly illustrated,[69] as Cokes remarks to Mistress Overdo in Ben Jonson's *Bartholomew Fair* (1614), 'O sister, doe you remember the ballads over the nursery chimney at home of my own pasting up? These be brave pictures.' After a good day's fishing Izaak Walton's Piscator in 1653 proposed to lead the highly respectable Viator 'to an honest alehouse where we shall find a cleanly room, lavender in the windowes and twenty ballads stuck about the wall', a collection which might even have included 'A Looking Glasse for the Soule Worth to be Hung Up in Every Householde in the Kingdom and to be Looked at Daily', or 'A Right Godly and Christian ABC Shewing the Duty of Every Degree',[70] or 'A Christian Belief Concerning Bishops' or 'A Table Pointing Out Such Places of Scripture . . . Condemning the Principal Points of Popery'.[71] These illustrated ballads might well carry little pictures of the holy family or Christ in glory, which was the commonest 'godly' woodcut,[72] but the single-sheet woodcut to stick on the wall remained popular and became more cautious in its imagery. There is some evidence that the trade in cheap woodcut pictures grew in scale in the second decade of the seventeenth century.[73] In 1664, one of the chief publishers in the trade had at least 1,000 pictures in stock, worth a halfpenny each.[74]

The 1620s begin to appear as a decade not only of increased ballad production, but of an explosion of cheap print. In general, the monopoly on printing almanacs had gone to the Stationers' Company in 1603. We do not, unfortunately, have figures of their output, but only the increasing number of titles and the

69 *Ibid.*, p. 78 and n. 28.   70 Illustrated in *Ibid.*, p. 236.

71 Tessa Watt closes *Cheap Print* with just such an 'art of memory' scene, projecting the early seventeenth century with its very various secular and sacred, Reformed and pre-Reformation imagery onto the walls of a respectable alehouse: *ibid.*, pp. 331–2.

72 *Ibid.*, pp. 167, 172, 177.   73 *Ibid.*, pp. 143, 147.

74 *Ibid.*, p. 140; Margaret Spufford, *Small Books and Pleasant Histories: Popular Fiction and its Readership in Seventeenth-Century England* (London: Methuen, 1981), pp. 91–101, from the PRO, Kew, Prerogative Court of Canterbury, Prob. 4 8224.

information that, by the 1660s, sales averaged about 400,000 copies annually, or one for every three families in the kingdom.[75] We have seen how the eleven-year-old John Evelyn imitated his own father by setting down events 'in a blanke Almanac'. Such examples can be multiplied.

The newsbooks, or corantos, first appeared in folio in the Low Countries in December 1620, and then in London. From October 1621, quarto corantos were printed by partnerships of London stationers,[76] and their publishing history continued, with interruptions, until 1641. Government officials were appointed to license corantos. This was especially important in the early 1620s while King James negotiated with Spain for the marriage of Prince Charles with the Infanta, and for the peaceful restoration of his son-in-law, Frederick V, to the throne of the Palatinate – all of these against the wishes of 'Puritan' pamphleteers. Oblique criticism of James's pacific foreign policy was voiced by the corantos, which seemed to represent Protestant opinion. There may have been up to 50,000 copies in each series.

In 1624 the Ballad Partners, who had a well-organised distribution network into the countryside, were responsible for the appearance of a new genre, the chapbooks, which sold at 2d by the time Samuel Pepys collected them in the 1680s. There had been small octavos before: indeed, John Dorne had had some in 1520. His peak sale was four in a year, however, against, for instance, *The Plain Man's plain path-way to heaven*, John Hart's abridgement of Arthur Dent's classic (1601), which was published by John Andrews at Pye Corner in 1656, and reached its 'seventeenth edition' in three years.[77] These chapbooks were known in the trade as 'small godlies, small merries, and pleasant histories', 24-page octavos or duodecimos selling at 2d, which Samuel Pepys later had bound together as 'Penny Merriments', 'Penny Godlinesses' and 'Vulgaria'. Some of the latter were 24-page quartos known as 'double-books', which sold at 3d or 4d. We have to depend on his post-Restoration collection, since the only earlier one, that of Frances Wolfreston, was sold in the nineteenth century.[78] This is not as much of a handicap as it may seem, for very many of the stories

75 Bernard Capp, *English Almanacs, 1500–1800. Astrology and the Popular Press* (London: Faber, 1979), pp. 23, 29, 33.
76 Michael Frearson, 'The English Corantos of the 1620s', unpublished Ph.D. thesis, University of Cambridge (1993), pp. 84 *et seq.*, 116–17 and ch. 5. We are much indebted to Dr Frearson for permission to quote his thesis.
77 Watt, *Cheap Print*, pp. 269, 272.
78 *Ibid.*, pp. 315–17. For a full analysis of the Pepys collection, see Spufford, *Small Books*. There are separate chapters on the contents of 'godlies', 'merries' and 'pleasant histories', and possible readership is deduced from these contents.

were retold, and told again, from a much more distant past. In 1664, Charles Tias, just one of the specialist publishers, had around 90,000 octavo and quarto chapbooks in his shop on London Bridge, house and warehouse. There is no means of estimating his turnover, but this is at least one-fifth or a quarter of the Stationers' Company production of almanacs, and possibly more. Tias alone had in stock around one chapbook for every fifteen families in the kingdom.[79]

The trade origins of this newly produced genre remained a mystery until Tessa Watt engaged in a truly heroic act of analysing all of the non-ballad output of a selection of ballad publishers of the sixteenth century and seventeenth century, on the reasonable supposition that these men (or their active widows) were likely to be the pioneers.[80] This supposition was right. Moreover, Dr Watt was able to date the appearance of the chapbooks with some precision. Some late sixteenth-century 'penny miscellanies' came into the hands of the ballad publishers about 1614, and new 'penny merriments' were created in the late 1620s and 1630s. The 'godlinesses' began to be written in 'penny' format about 1616 and were acquired by the ballad publishers from the later 1620s. The 'merry' quartos later known as 'double-books' and 'histories' were acquired at the same time. So in the 1620s a deliberate publishing venture enormously expanded the range of cheap print available to humble readers. We have already considered the expanding range of elementary vernacular schooling and the basic literacy rates. Although caution is needed, we are surely entitled to think these businessmen, as they were, were responding to an expanded and expanding market.

By the time Pepys was collecting, 28% of the chapbooks on the specialist publishers' trade lists[81] were 'small godly' books and 72% were 'merry books'. Of this 72%, 23% were the quarto 'pleasant histories', which cost 3d or 4d rather than 2d. The English godly books laid immense stress on bringing the reader to repentance, and so to a fit state for conversion, and on his, or her, desperate need of the justifying grace of God, to be apprehended through faith.[82] The most striking thing about the religious chapbooks is the domination, both in words and woodcuts, of the skeletal figure of Death. In the

---

79 Using Gregory King's estimate of 1688.
80 Watt, *Cheap Print*, pp. 274–8; also the whole of chs. 7 and 8.
81 Spufford, *Small Books*, Table 2, p. 134. The percentages given here are not the percentages on the table, which were those collected by Pepys out of the works on the market, but the proportions of the 278 books on seven publishers' trade lists made up by each type of 'small books'. For further details, see ch. 6 of *Small Books*; and for the publishers themselves, ch. 4.
82 Eamon Duffy has given a more subtle interpretation in 'The godly and the multitude in Stuart England', *Seventeenth Century* 1 (1986), 31–55.

English chapbooks, Death has been removed from its place as a separate topic in popular culture, stemming from the medieval Dance of Death, and has now become a pedagogue of the small godlies, pointing a bony finger at the way to conversion. It is striking that over a quarter of this 'new' cheap print was religious. It suggests that popular interest in religion spread widely amongst conformists, as well as the 4% of nonconformists[83] in society who might justifiably have been expected to take a special interest. The 48% of 'small merriments' on the trade lists fell into many different groups. The reprinted jest-books of John Scoggin and George Peele, which had been very popular in the sixteenth century, and still were, if their appearance in the Pepys collection is evidence, had no continuous narrative line at all. They were a series of disconnected anecdotes about the 'merry' doings of central figures, who acted as link devices. Both Scogin and Peel were Oxford students, and therefore moved at least on the fringes of educated society. The 'heroes' of the burlesques which replaced them did nothing of the kind. *Tom Stitch the Tailor, Robin the Merry Saddler of Walden, The Unfortunate Son* and *The Unfortunate Welshman* moved from one drunken and very frequently scatological amorous adventure into another. There was no concept of marriage in the burlesques or in the group of anti-female satires; the chapbook version of that supposedly honourable estate equated it with cuckoldry.

The art-of-compliment chapbooks and the courtship dialogues giving instructions that were very frequently satirical, on how to woo both virgins and widows, tell a somewhat different story. The importance of courtship, whether in deadly earnest or in mockery, was obviously an extremely important, almost obsessive topic amongst the humble in Restoration England. It was therefore a best-selling line for the publishers who catered for the humble. The god of the merry books was Cupid, whose pretty, lethal figure, armed with bow and arrow, appeared in many woodcuts dominating stockyard and city alike, slaying Somerset labourers and court fops with equal zest. His representations in the woodcuts seem frequently to have a conscious iconographic reference to his brother Death of the godly books, who was also armed with arrows. The implication was that Cupid's reign, also, was universal.

The past of the chapbooks was a pre-Reformation past, replete with lascivious friars and kings in disguise who brought good fortune. The stories of royal mistresses were excuses for juicy accounts of adultery, high life, rich living

83 Figure from Anne Whiteman (ed.), *The Compton Census of 1676: A Critical Edition*, Records of Social and Economic History, new ser. 10 (London and New York: Oxford University Press for the British Academy, 1986).

and repentance, with a moral at the end. Among the quarto double-books and the 'histories' there are genuine chivalric romances. Bunyan's beloved *Bevis of Southampton*[84] drew on a thirteenth-century Anglo-Norman romance which in turn probably drew on much earlier popular themes.[85] These descendants from knightly high society were so popular that they were joined, at the end of the sixteenth century, by a whole wave of neo-chivalric imitations, some of which were almost unbelievably threadbare.[86] These are the romances 'of the type that drove the good knight of La Mancha mad'.[87] The 24-page duodecimo translation of *Don Quixote* in Pepys's collection has never seemed so funny as after reading the fake chivalrics, and, indeed, reads as if it had been written expressly for a rustic audience that was familiar with the giants, dragons and heroes of the romances, but which also lapped up both slapstick and satire.

In many ways, the most interesting 'historical' works were the beginnings of the 'realistic' novel in Deloney's works with clothier heroes. Their cut-down versions were especially adapted to appeal to the poor, and the poor were especially encouraged to see their way to success in a trade, however low their birth. Alongside these, again, another little group of chapbooks appeared with heroes or heroines drawn from somewhere near the bottom of society: vagrants, servants and day-labourers, who had all, at some time in a past which was often mythical, made their fortunes.

The English chapbooks, however unrealistic they were, made some attempt to adjust to social reality and to please their readers. The English reader might imagine himself a hero against the Turks; but he could also imagine himself a wealthy clothier, a Lord Mayor of London or even making good as a minor country gentleman. These chapbooks attempting to gratify the dreams of their readers, did not, it seems, prove most pleasing to the grammar school boys who were either gentry or intended for the professions. The different fantasy of the 'chivalrics' suited them better.

Francis Kirkman, who was so enraptured by his boyhood reading that he not only frustrated his father's plans for him to become a bookseller but also wrote additional parts for the Palmerin cycle in the late seventeenth century, recorded his taste in fiction in 1673, when he had been at St Paul's School:

84 Spufford, *Small Books*, pp. 219–24.
85 L. A. Hibbard, *Medieval Romance in England* (New York: Oxford University Press, 1924), pp. 115–26.
86 Spufford, *Small Books*, pp. 232–7.
87 Margaret Schlauch, *Antecedents of the English Novel, 1400–1600* (Warsaw: PWN-Polish Scientific Publishers, 1963), pp. 164–74.

Once I happened upon a Six Pence, and having lately read that famous Book, of the *Fryar and the Boy*, and being hugely pleased with that, as also the excellent History of the *Seven wise Masters of Rome*, and having heard great Commendation of *Fortunatus*, I laid out all my mony for that, and thought I had a great bargain ... I proceeded on to *Palmer of England*, and *Amadis de Gaul*; and borrowing one Book of one person, when I read it my self, I lent it to another, who lent me one of their Books; and thus robbing Peter to pay Paul, borrowing and lending from one to another, I in time had read most of these Histories. All the time I had from School, as Thursdays in the afternoon, and Saturdays, I spent in reading these Books; so that I being wholy affected to them, and reading how that *Amadis* and other Knights not knowing their Parents, did in time prove to be Sons of Kings and great Personages; I had such a fond and idle Opinion, that I might in time prove to be some great Person, or at leastwise be Squire to some Knight.

He thus indicated not only that he, a London merchant's son, read a corpus of popular tales that was collected in its entirety by Pepys in the 'Vulgaria' in the next decade, but also that a lively system of exchange and barter of sixpenny quartos existed among his schoolfellows. It sounds as if a very high proportion of the boys would have read the stories in the 'Vulgaria'. Many well-educated people confessed in later life that they had 'wasted' their time in reading such stories in their youth. John Milton, Richard Baxter and John Bunyan ranked among them, as well as Margaret Cavendish, Mary Rich and Elizabeth Delaval,[88] the last reporting 'I was but a few months past ten years old before I had read several great volumes of them: all Cassandras, the Grand Cyrus, Cleopatra and Astrea'.[89] Nor was such reading confined to the 'better sort'. Sir Thomas Overbury's 'chambermaid' would read romances rather than godly books: 'she reads Green's works over and over, but is so carried away with The Myrrour of Knighthood that she is many times resolved to run out

88 J. Milton, *An Apology for Smectymnuus* (London, 1642), pp. 16–17. Richard Baxter, (ed.), *The Autobiography of Richard Baxter*, ed. N.H. Keeble (London: Dent, 1974), p. 517. Bunyan, *A Few Sighs from Hell*, pp. 156–7. M. Cavendish, *Sociable Letters* (London, 1664), p. 39. *The Autobiography of Mary, Countess of Warwick*, ed. T. C. Croker (London, 1848), p. 21. *The Meditations of Lady Elizabeth Delaval Written Between 1662 and 1671*, ed. D. G. Greene Publications of the Surtees Society, 190 (Gateshead: Northumberland Press, 1978), p. 32.

89 Sir Charles Cotterell (trans.), [Gualtier de Coste, Seigneur de La Calprenède,] *Cassandra. A Romance* (London, 1652), and Robert Loveday (trans.), [Gualtier de Coste,] *Hymens praeludia or Loves Masterpiece, Being the first part of Cleopatra* (London, 1652). Madeleine de Scudéry, *Artemenes, or the Grand Cyrus*, trans. F. G. (London, 1653). Honoré d'Urfé, *Astrea. A Romance*, trans. J. Davies (London, 1657). Dorothy Osborne offered to lend her copy of *Cleopatra* to William Temple: Osborne, *Letters to Sir William Temple*, ed. Kenneth Parker (London and New York: Penguin Books, 1987), pp. 57, 59–60.

of herself and become Lady Errant'.[90] So the cheap print had a wide impact among the reading population.

Alongside the undoubtedly undesirable there was plenty of romantic and dramatic literature which could widen the imaginative compass of those who could read (to say nothing of those who were read to), and even remind them of courage, justice and compassion in a society (at least their part of it) that might seem singularly short of these qualities. In addition to what Andrew Boorde in the 1520s categorised as 'laudable myrth',[91] the cathartic effect of vicarious violence and bawdry gave large numbers of participants – such as those comprising the theatre audience so vividly described by Thomas Dekker in his *Gull's Hornbook* (1609) – a sense of sharing a range of basic emotions not only with their peers but also with their 'betters'. As Philip Sidney acknowledged at the time, 'Truely I have known men that even with reading *Amadis de Gaule* (which God knoweth wanteth much of a perfect poesie) have found their hearts moved to the exercise of courtesie, liberalitie and especially courage.'[92] Samuel Pepys noted with ill-concealed disapproval his wife's reading of the verbatim love-letters which were a feature of such romances, though, by contrast, Dr Arnold Boate, recalling his pious wife's reading of them, noted that she was 'wonderfully pleased as with the beauty of their language and conceptions, so with the characters of all kinds of heroic virtues which therein are held forth, most lively in the persons of both sexes'. Hannah Woolley similarly listed with approval 'such romances which treat of generosity, gallantry and virtue'.[93]

The depth of the transformation brought about by cheap print and increased opportunities for basic literacy in the sixteenth and seventeenth centuries can most vividly be demonstrated by the effect of the ballad trade. Of the folksongs

90 T. Overbury, *Characters* (London, 1614), many times enlarged and reprinted; W. J. Paylor (ed.), *The Overburian Characters* (Oxford: Blackwell, 1936), p. 43; R. Greene, *A Quip for an Upstart Courtier* (London, 1592); Margaret Tyler (trans.), [Diego Ortuñez de Calahorra,] *The Myrrour of Princely Deedes and Knighthood* (London, 1578). As an example, Henry Gostling had copies of d'Urfé's *Astrea* and de Coste's *Cassandra* amongst his books: B. Dickins, 'Henry Gostling's Library: A Young Don's Books in 1674', *Transactions of the Cambridge Bibliographical Society* 3 (1961), 216–24.

91 A. Borde, *The Breuiary of Helthe* (London, 1547), fols. lxix v–lxxiii v. See also N. Grimald's song 'Of Mirth' in Richard Tottel, *Tottel's Miscellany* (London, 1557), ed. Hyder E. Rollins, 2 vols. (Cambridge, MA: Harvard University Press, 1928–9), 1:99, and Prologue to N. Udall, *Ralph Roister Doister* (London, 1566, but written before 1553).

92 T. Dekker, *Gull's Hornbook* (London, 1609), ch. 6. P. Sidney, *An Apologie for Poetrie* (London, 1595), sigs. E4v–F1r.

93 A. Boate, *The Character of a Trulie Vertuous Woman . . . Mistris Margaret Dungan, Wife to Dr Arnold Boate* (Paris, 1651). Samuel Pepys, *Diary: A New and Complete Transcription*, ed. Robert Latham and William Matthews, 11 vols. (Berkeley and Los Angeles: University of California Press, 1970–83), 8:312 (7 December 1660); H. Woolley, *The Gentlewomans Companion* 2nd edn (London, 1675), p. 9.

gathered in the major twentieth-century collections, 80% were derived from printed broadsides. Ninety songs gathered by collectors can only derive from broadsides printed before 1700. Likewise the *Dictionary of English Folk Tales*[94] contains 6% of titles which overlap with those of chapbooks or ballads printed before 1700.[95] The most telling evidence of all demonstrates that groups of people who were annoyed by the behaviour of their social superiors gathered in alehouses and were so familiar with ballad forms that they were able to adapt them to make abusive rhymes about these same superiors. With a quart or two of wine they then 'paid' someone who could write, to copy out their lampoons. The copies were pinned up in conspicuous places like church doors and market crosses to attract the derision of the local community. Cheap print was substantially modifying culture, even at the lowest social levels, in the alehouses. The situation has been summarised thus: 'The striking feature that nearly all verses were ... also written down is indicative of the fact that early seventeenth-century England was a "partially-literate" society ... The value of the written word was appreciated quite clearly even at the lowest social levels.'[96]

Before 1550, provincial England was a late medieval peasant society, in which people were well aware of the value of the written instrument, but in which reading and writing were still special skills exercised by experts on behalf of the community. Between 1500 and 1700, however, it was transformed into a society in which writing, and particularly reading, were widely used in many areas of human activity, including pleasure and self-education, by many more members of the community, including some of the labouring poor.

Grammar schools

From the second half of the sixteenth century, more and more grammar school foundations included the teaching of English language skills as part of their provision, though always as a necessary preliminary to the study of Latin.[97] In a small school the master would make a start in the matter. In a larger,

---

94 Katherine Briggs, *A Dictionary of English Folk Tales*, 2 vols. (London: Routledge, 1970–1).
95 For the flexible overlap between orality and reading literacy, see the survey by Barry Reay, 'Orality, Literacy and Print', in his *Popular Cultures in England, 1550–1750* (London: Longman, 1998), pp. 36–70.
96 Adam Fox, 'Ballads, Libels and Popular Ridicule in Jacobean England', *Past and Present* 145 (1994), 64. This is much expanded in Fox, *Oral and Literate Culture*, ch. 6.
97 A. A. Mumford, *Manchester Grammar School 1515–1915* (London: Longmans, 1919), p. 479. J. Whitaker, *The Statutes and Charter of Rivington School* (London: Whittaker, 1837), pp. 165–6.

better endowed school it would be the responsibility of the master's assistant, the usher, and even if the founder had included in his statutes a stipulation that a boy should be able to read before being admitted,[98] the economics of schoolmastering might well have pushed the master to ignore this and recruit boys who needed to be taught their English 'letters'.

The Chantries Act of 1547 had abolished the chantries and their prime religious purpose of saying prayers for the souls of the donor and his dead relations. Where the founder had made an additional educational provision the 'school' was in most cases 'continued', either at the insistence of the commissioners or after a supplication by the local community.[99] Thereafter, the medieval practice of lay men and women and clerics providing funds to endow a grammar school continued apace, without, however, there being any sign of a systematic provision for grammar schools.[100]

Once in the grammar school, the prime purpose was to acquire a knowledge of the Latin language, its vocabulary, accidence and syntax, in order to enter into a study of select Latin authors. A start on the study of Greek would be undertaken only by those few boys in the upper forms of the larger schools. At the same time some pupils would have been withdrawn by their parents once they had become literate in the English language, with a view to their starting on some kind of vocational training. Significantly, one of the earliest printed grammar texts of the period was the *Lac Puerorum or Mylke for Chyldren* (1497), written in English by John Holt, usher of Magdalen College School, Oxford, under John Stanbridge, who with his pupil Robert Whittinton produced a revised grammar in 1520. These were in turn replaced by the composite grammar which came to be known as Lily's Latin Grammar, or the Royal Grammar since it came to be prescribed in the Royal Injunctions of Edward VI (1547) and Elizabeth (1559), as well as in the Ecclesiastical Canons of 1571 and 1604.[101] It remained the standard though by no means the only grammar until

---

98 For example at St Paul's, J. H. Lupton, *A Life of Dean Colet DD* (London: Bell, 1887), p. 277; at Merchant Taylors', H. B. Wilson, *A History of Merchant Taylors' School*, 2 vols. (London, privately printed, 1812–14), 1:16; at Eton, H. C. Maxwell-Lyte, *A History of Eton College* (London: Macmillan, 1889), pp. 581–3; at St Albans, N. Carlisle, *A Concise Description of the Endowed Schools of England and Wales*, 2 vols. (London: Baldwin, Craddock and Joy, 1810), 1:517.

99 J. Simon, *Education and Society in Tudor England* (Cambridge University Press, 1966), pp. 179–96, 223–44.

100 Charlton, *Education*, pp. 92–3.

101 For the Magdalen grammar school, N. Orme, *Education in Early Tudor England. Magdalen College and Its School, 1480–1540*, Magdalen College Occasional Papers, 4 (Oxford: Magdalen College, 1998); V. J. Flynn, 'The Grammatical Writings of William Lily 1468–?1523', *Papers of the Bibliographical Society of America* 37 (1943), 85–113; C. G. Allen, 'The Sources of Lily's Grammar: A Review of the Facts and Some

it, too, was replaced by the introduction of the Eton Grammar in 1758. The attempt to systematise the teaching of English had to wait until 1570 when the spelling-reformer John Hart produced his *Methode or Comfortable Beginning for all Unlearned Whereby they may be Taught to Reade English in a very Short Time with Pleasure*, which included a pictorial alphabet and 'in a great letter the Christian Belief, the Ten Commandments of God and the Lord's Prayer, where the syllables are sundered for the ease of all learners old and young'.[102] Hart's book was soon followed by Francis Clements's *Petie Schole with an English Orthographie wherein is taught by rules lately prescribed a method to enable both a childe to read perfectly within one moneth and also the imperfect to write English aright* (1578), William Kempe's *Education of Children in Learning* (1588) and Edmund Coote's *The English Scholemaister* (1596), the latter so popular that it reached a 25th edition by 1635 and a 54th in 1737. In addition to the introductory sections and the more advanced reading exercises, it included a short catechism, a prayer, several graces to be said before meals and extracts from the Bible. In other words, in a more detailed and systematic fashion, it followed the pattern of the horn book.[103]

Significantly, Kempe and Coote were grammar school masters, Kempe at Plymouth and Coote at Bury St Edmunds, both well aware of the difficulties of preparing a boy to become literate in his own language before going on to his Latin studies, which themselves required some skill in English as the boy moved on from the accidence to the practice of double translation – English into Latin and back into English – as part of his rhetorical training.[104] What is more, the duties of a grammar school master included leading his pupils in prayers at the beginning and ending of every school day, as well as catechising them and taking them to church on Sundays, when the older boys would be charged with

---

Further Suggestions', *The Library* 5th ser. 9 (1954), 85–100. The grammar is reproduced in facsimile in V. J. Flynn (ed.), *A Shorte Introduction to Grammar* (Gainesville, FL: Scholars' Facsimiles and Reprints, 1945). For its printing history, see F. Watson, *The English Grammar Schools to 1660* (Cambridge University Press, 1908), pp. 241–75.

102 Reprinted in B. Daniellson, *John Hart's Works on English Orthography and Pronunciation*, Stockholm Studies in English, 5 (Stockholm: Almqvist, 1955).

103 I. Michael, *The Teaching of English from the Sixteenth Century to 1870* (Cambridge University Press, 1987), chs. 2 and 3.

104 As in R. Ascham, *The Scholemaster* (London, 1570), fols. 1v and 34v, and at Chipping Barnet in F. C. Cass, 'Queen Elizabeth School at Chipping Barnet 1570–1665', *Transactions of London and Middlesex Archaeological Society* 5 (1876), 30; Steyning grammar school in W. B. Breach, 'William Holland, Alderman of Chichester and Steyning Grammar School', *Sussex Archaeological Collections* 43 (1990), 79; Durham Grammar School, in *Victoria County History: Durham*, 1 (1903), 377. The practice was also recommended by J. Brinsley, *Ludus Literarius* (London, 1612), p. 255, and C. Hoole, *A New Discovery of the Olde Arte of Teaching School* (London, 1660), pp. 270–1.

the task of taking notes on the sermon, to be repeated to the other pupils on Monday morning.[105] John Milton, like others before him, had no doubts that 'the end then of learning is to repair the ruins of our first parents by regaining to know God aright, and out of that knowledge to love Him, to imitate Him, to be like Him'.[106] It must be remembered, too, that these schools existed in a recently Protestantised nation, in which the state, with the church as its agent, attempted to keep some sort of control over what went on in them. Hence a royal Grammar was accompanied by the approved catechism of Laurence Nowell, and an approved Bible, whether the Great Bible of 1539, the Bishops' Bible of 1569 or the Authorised Version of 1611. It was, of course, one thing to assert by legislation and injunction the nature of 'God's true religion now set forth by public authority'.[107] It was quite another to maintain such uniformity in the face of the doctrinal and ecclesiastical debates which characterised Tudor and Stuart England, as the popularity of the Geneva Bible (1560) and the host of alternative catechisms made plain.

Traditionally the grammar school was the milieu of the 'poor and needy scholar', with the prime purpose of producing future clerics, the sons of the upper classes being educated at home by a tutor-chaplain or in the household of another family. The early modern grammar schools continued to provide education for future clerics: Lancelot Andrewes at Merchant Taylors' in London, William Laud at Reading, William Sancroft at Bury St Edmunds, for example, amongst many others. But increasingly the aristocracy, recognising that the chivalric education deemed appropriate for their ancestors was no longer appropriate to sustain their claim to a role as governors in the Tudor state – a view expressed in Sir Thomas Elyot's much reprinted *Boke named the Governour* (1531) – began to send their sons to grammar schools, especially those that took boarders, thus enabling them to continue the practice of sending their sons away from home for their education. The professional classes and the gentry equally saw that a 'liberal' education would not only equip them for state service, whether in London or the localities, but also increase their status in society. Grammar school registers (where they have survived) thus began to show

---

105 See, for example, Bishop Pilkington's 1566 requirements of his master and scholars in his Rivington and Blackrod school, in M. M. Kay, *The History of Rivington and Blackrod Grammar School* (Manchester University Press, 1931), pp. 170–4, and the Royal Injunctions for Winchester College 1547, Frere and Kennedy (eds.), *Visitation Articles*, 2: 150–1.

106 J. Milton, *Of Education* (London, 1644), p. 2.

107 Frere and Kennedy (eds.), *Visitation Articles*, 3:21. P. H. Hughes and J. F. Larkin (eds.), *Tudor Royal Proclamations*, 3 vols. (New Haven: Yale University Press, 1964–9), 2:27. See also the Preface to the 1545 Primer, 'one uniform manner or course of prayer throughout our dominions': J. E. Cox (ed.), *Miscellaneous Writings and Letters of Thomas Cranmer*, Parker Society, vol. 16 (Cambridge University Press, 1846), p. 497.

the admission of the sons of each of these social groups. Even so, we do well to beware the optimism of W. K. Jordan, who saw in these developments the beginnings of equal opportunity for all, and heed the cautions of David Cressy that there were expenses to be incurred in attending grammar schools, which precluded the admission of boys lacking the family resources of the relatively prosperous sections of society.[108]

Universities

Once prepared in an elementary study of Latin grammar and composition, some few boys would then be sent to university, or rather to a college of one of the two universities. On admission, their mastery of the elements of the Latin language would be taken for granted, as they prepared to engage in a four-year study of the Arts course for the degree of BA. Though the early part of the sixteenth century had seen the importation of Italian humanist ideas into England, by continental scholars or by Englishmen who had studied in Italy, the impact was confined for the most part to a few colleges with innovative founders, Masters or fellows, for example Christ's and St John's, Cambridge, or Corpus Christi, Oxford.[109] By the middle of the century, however, the Arts course, originally intended to cover the whole of the seven liberal arts, had become for all practical purposes an increasingly detailed study of dialectic and rhetoric, reinforced at both university and college level by regular participation in disputation.[110] By then, too, the medieval practice of newly graduated masters being required to lecture, for two years, to the undergraduate body 'publicly in the Schools', the university lecture halls, had for a variety of reasons lapsed.[111] More and more, the colleges undertook that duty, assigning it either to the fellows or to the increasing numbers of newly appointed stipendiary

108 W. K. Jordan, *Philanthropy in England 1480–1660* (London: Allen and Unwin, 1959), pp. 279ff. D. Cressy, 'Educational Opportunity in Tudor and Stuart England', *History of Education Quarterly* 16 (1976), 301–20, and M. Feingold, 'Jordan Revisited: Patterns of Charitable Giving in Sixteenth- and Seventeenth-Century England', *History of Education* 8 (1979), 257–73.
109 Charlton, *Education*, ch. 3.
110 L. Jardine, 'The Place of Dialectic Teaching in Sixteenth-Century Cambridge', *Studies in the Renaissance* 21 (1974), 31–62, and 'Humanism and Dialectic in Sixteenth-Century Cambridge', in R. R. Bolgar (ed.), *Classical Influences on European Culture AD 1500–1700* (Cambridge University Press, 1976), pp. 141–54; A. Grafton and L. Jardine, *From Humanism to the Humanities* (Cambridge, MA: Harvard University Press, 1986), chs. 3, 4 and 5.
111 For college tutoring, see R. O'Day, *Education and Society 1500–1800* (London: Longman, 1982), pp. 115–16; M. Feingold, *The Mathematician's Apprenticeship* (Cambridge University Press, 1984), pp. 35–41; J. Looney, 'Undergraduate Education in Early Stuart Cambridge', *History of Education* 10 (1981), 9–19.

lectors as part of their statutory duty. In the later sixteenth and early seven-teenth centuries, the students were helped by the production of large numbers of compendia written by college fellows that covered the two arts of common language discourse at an elementary level,[112] following the example of the revi-sionist dialectics of Rudolph Agricola and Philip Melanchthon. Those of John Seton and Bartholomew Keckermann were perhaps most popular, outlasting the comet-like appearance and influence of Ramist texts in the 1570s and 1580s. A study of contemporary drama, poetry and prose fiction did not figure at all in the statutory prescriptions of university or college, though plainly fellows and students alike were well aware of such literature. The newly founded Lady Margaret Professorships of Divinity, one at each university, and the Regius Professorships of Theology, Greek, Hebrew, Civil Law and Medicine were de-signed chiefly for those studying in the higher faculties, particularly for those in their theological studies who would require a knowledge of the original bib-lical languages as well as an awareness of the Erasmian approach to the study of the Bible and to the practice of exegesis which the Protestant reformers found congenial.[113] The undergraduates were required to attend sermons in the college chapel as well as the lectures given by the college catechist, as part of their general education.

By the end of the fifteenth century the medieval idea of a college being a centre in which graduate students and fellows prepared for study in the higher faculties of theology and law (canon and civil) had in some degree been eroded by the foundation of colleges such as New and Magdalen at Oxford and the King's Hall (later to be transformed into Trinity) at Cambridge, whose statutes provided for the admission of fee-paying undergraduate 'commoners'. The practice was continued on a grand scale by Bishop Richard Fox when he founded Corpus Christi College, Oxford, in 1517, and his example was followed not only by the new foundations of the sixteenth century but also by the revision of the statutes of the older colleges.[114] What had started as a trickle in the late medieval period had thus by the mid sixteenth century become a decided 'influx'. The advent of the gentleman-commoners certainly changed the social mix of the

---

112 For compendia, M. Feingold, 'The Humanities', in *The History of the University of Oxford*, gen. ed. T. H. Aston, vol. 4 (Oxford: Clarendon Press, 1986), pp. 296–9.
113 F. D. Logan, 'The Origin of the So-Called Regius Professorships', in *Renaissance and Re-newal, Studies in Church History* 14 (1977), 271–8. G. D. Duncan, 'Public Lectures and Professorial Chairs', in *The History of the University of Oxford*, gen. ed. Aston, vol. 3, *The Collegiate University*, pp. 335–61. For a useful summary of the limited library facilities available, see O'Day, *Education and Society*, pp. 118–24.
114 J. K. McConica, 'The Rise of the Undergraduate College', *The History of the University of Oxford*, 3:1–68.

university undergraduate population, but their proportion was nevertheless outweighed by the number of students who attended in order to prepare for the professions of church, school-teaching and state administration.[115] Whether the change from the much-criticised late medieval trends in scholastic logic and theology to a course of study which emphasised the skills of common language use resulted from recognising the needs of those students who would come to play their part in both local and central government is a very moot point indeed. To emphasise their needs would ignore the fact that the universities continued to see their main role as producers of the country's professional classes, especially its clergy, as the new foundations of Emmanuel (1584) and Sidney Sussex (1596) were clearly intended to show.

In one important particular, however, all types of students were affected by the result of another change which characterised life in the universities of the sixteenth and seventeenth centuries: the matter of control. The Henrician Reformation and its subsequent development insisted not only that the new state religion be enforced in the universities as elsewhere, but also that their students and teachers alike should make formal acceptance of the articles of religion and formal recognition of the monarch as head of the church.[116] For a variety of reasons the relationship between state and university remained one of (not always benevolent) patronage and (usually willing) acceptance. If there was an 'educational revolution' in the early modern universities – and that is highly doubtful[117] – it was only in a very restricted sense of the term. Lawrence Stone's conclusion is nearer the mark: 'The university, like the family and the church, is one of the most poorly integrated of institutions, and again and again it has been obstinately resistant to changes which were clearly demanded by changing conditions around it.'[118] Changes there were, though they were not always in one direction or consistent throughout the collegiate universities.

115 For the Inns of Court, described by Sir George Buck as *The Third Universitie of England* (London, 1612), see W. R. Prest, 'Legal Education and the Gentry at the Inns of Court', *Past and Present*, 38 (1967), 20–39, and *The Rise of the Barristers. A Social History of the English Bar 1590–1640* (Oxford: Clarendon Press, 1991); D. Lemmings, *Gentlemen and Barristers. The Inns of Court and the English Bar 1680–1730* (Oxford: Clarendon Press, 1990); L. A. Knafla, 'The Matriculation Revolution and Education at the Inns of Court in Renaissance England', in A. J. Slavin (ed.), *Tudor Men and Institutions. Studies in English Law and Government* (Baton Rouge: Louisiana State University Press, 1972), pp. 232–64.

116 L. L. Shadwell (ed.), *Enactments in Parliament Especially Concerning the Universities of Oxford and Cambridge*, 4 vols., Oxford Historical Society, Nos. 58–61 (Oxford: Clarendon Press for Oxford Historical Society, 1911–12), 1:119. S. Gibson (ed.), *Statuta Antiqua Universitatis Oxoniensis* (Oxford: Clarendon Press, 1931), pp. 403ff., 421.

117 Kenneth Charlton, 'A Tudor Educational Revolution? An Inaugural Lecture at King's College, University of London, 18 February 1974' (London, King's College, 1974).

118 Lawrence Stone (ed.), *The University in Society*, 2 vols. (Princeton University Press, 1974) 1:v.

What did not change, however, was the overriding insistence of the state in maintaining its control over the institutions of higher learning in the cause of 'true religion' (of whatever hue).

Women

In church, in the grammar schools, and in the universities the agents of the educative process were invariably male. The question remains, therefore: Were women never agents in their own education or in the education of others? Any enquiry which goes beyond the stereotypic male-dominated world of early modern England will quickly reveal a relatively important contribution. Though women were denied a place in the pulpits of parish churches, the pages of Foxe's 'Book of Martyrs' provide plenty of evidence of women maintaining a heterodox doctrinal position, especially concerning the nature of the Eucharist. They also contributed to the religious education of members of their families, neighbours and friends, as the records of ecclesiastical and common law courts show them engaging in and being punished for 'preaching the Word'. There are, in addition, examples of women who could not themselves write, who deliberately fostered reading skills. Oliver Heywood's mother, wife of a Lancashire fustian-weaver, seems only to have been able to read. As a young girl after her conversion in 1614 she 'took her bible with her and spent the whole day in reading and praying'. Later her son went with her to Puritan exercises and sermons. Afterwards he wrote, he 'was in some measure helpful to her memory by the notes of sermons I took'. He regularly sent her notes of sermons when he went up to Cambridge, and as an old woman she meditated on these: 'it was her constant course in the night when she lay waking to roll them in her mind, and rivet them there'. She took great pains over her children's education – 'She was continually putting us upon the scriptures and good bookes and instructing us how to pray' – and this work extended outside her own family: 'It was her usual practice to help many poore children to learning by buying them bookes, setting them to schoole, and paying their master for teaching, whereby many a poore parent blessed god for help *by their childrens reading*' [our italics].[119]

The General Baptist, Sister Sneesby, was in a state of great spiritual torment in 1654, when she was visited by the Baptist messengers. They reported:

119 J. Horsfall Turner (ed.), *The Rev. Oliver Heywood, BA, 1630–1702: His Autobiographies, Diaries, Anecdote and Event Books* (Brighouse: A. B. Bayes, 1882), 1:42, 48, 51 and 234.

we found [her] in a very sad and deplorable condition . . . We told her, that we heard one of those commonly called Quakers was at her house and preached there: and we were afraid his preaching had brought her into that condition. She answered that she could hear very little that he said [she seems to have been deaf] but she said she had read many of his books. Then we asked her whether the reading of them were not the cause of her trouble?

When she confessed this might be so, she was advised 'to continue reading' the Scriptures. Nevertheless, she was converted to Quakerism by her reading, despite the fact that she was a poor woman who earned her living by day-labour in her widowhood.[120] Women from the upper and more prosperous middle classes are also to be found acting as founders and benefactors to the universities, contributing both to the founding of colleges and to the support of individual students. They acted as governesses in the houses of the wealthy and they figured as founders or as schoolmistresses of seventeenth-century elementary schools. Above all in their roles as mothers they were prime movers, with divine sanction and the support of classical and biblical exemplars, in the education of their children. Men and women who wrote of their early years, whether in autobiography or familial letter, frequently took the opportunity to express their gratitude to their mothers for teaching them to read, for catechising them, for rehearsing sermons with them, for reading the Bible with them, and above all, echoing the injunctions of the bulk of prescriptive literature, for stressing the importance of example in their upbringing.[121]

Among the many brief accounts of mothers as educators there is one very full record, that relating to Elizabeth Walker (1623–90), the wife of Anthony Walker, Rector of Fyfield in Essex. He wrote a 'Holy Life' very shortly after her death whilst the memory was fresh, based on documents (no longer extant) she herself had written during her life.[122] It is characterised by a wealth of detail which he gathered under such headings as 'How she did spend her day' and 'Her care in the education of her children', drawn from a collection of her letters and an autobiographical manuscript 'left under her own hand . . . [in] . . . a large book in octavo of the best paper she could buy, neatly bound, gilded and ruled with red', together with a commonplace book of scriptural passages

120 E. B. Underhill (ed.), *Records of the Churches of Christ gathered at Fenstanton, Warboys and Hexham, 1644–1720* (London: Hanserd Knollys Society, 1854), 120; Spufford, *Contrasting Communities*, pp. 216–17.

121 Charlton, *Women, Religion and Education*, pp. 216–19.

122 A. Walker, *The holy life of Elizabeth Walker . . . with some useful papers and letters written by her on several occasions* (London, 1690).

arranged under headings such as 'Prayer', 'Fear of God', Promises of Pardon of Sin', 'An Abbreviation of Faith and Christian Principles', each provided with appropriate chapter and verse. Elizabeth married in 1650; her first child was born in the following year, and in the next fourteen years she had 11 full-term births, of which 3, including her last, were stillborn. As mistress of a country parsonage she involved herself in needlework, cooking, brewing, baking and dairy management, together with 'the making of all kinds of English wines, gooseberry, currant, cowslip, quince etc.'. But as her husband recalled, 'all this was by-business comparatively ... she considered her children as the nursery of families, the church and the nation ... her business was to cultivate their minds, improve their intellectuals, to season their tender hearts with a due sense of religion', which she did in a highly systematic fashion, paralleled only, in the records at least, by the activities of three generations of Ferrar women at Little Gidding during the 1630s to 1650s, and later of Susanna Wesley.

To conclude that the role of women was merely as agents in the education of others, however, would be to ignore what Peter Lake has called their 'urgent autodidactism'.[123] This was expressed in their reading of the mass of printed material which they considered would improve not only their own lives but the lives of those around them, as well as in their engagement in prayer and meditation, whether in the privacy of their own closet or, again following biblical example, in the quiet of a garden, open field or wood. Their ownership, reading or recommendation of the poetry of George Herbert, for example, is a case in point. Of Susanna, Countess of Suffolk, it was reported: 'Begin a religious ode of Mr Herbert's which she had read and she would ordinarily repeat the rest without sticking or missing.' Anne and Mary Collett, nieces of Herbert's close friend, Nicholas Ferrar, copied out his poems at Little Gidding. In her autobiographical meditations Elizabeth Delaval noted 'the beauty I am speaking of be like what Mr Herbert describes in his poems' and goes on to quote lines from the poem 'Vertue'.[124]

It was not until the seventeenth century that a new kind of educational provision for girls of the upper and middle classes appeared. This took the form of boarding schools, 'academies for the daughters of gentlemen', phrasing that indicates a widening of the social spread of the clientele and a different institutional form that largely replaced the earlier practice of sending girls away

---

123 P. Lake, 'Feminine Piety and Personal Potency: The Emancipation of Mrs Jane Ratcliffe', *Seventeenth Century* 2 (1987), 143–65.

124 S. Clarke, *The Lives of Sundry Eminent Persons* (1683), p. 210; J. E. B. Mayor (ed.), *Nicholas Ferrar. Two Lives by his Brother John and Dr Jebb* (Cambridge: Macmillan, 1855), Appendix; Delaval, *The Meditations*, p. 56 and n. 42.

from home to be brought up in the household of another family.[125] When John Batchiler wrote his *The Virgins Pattern* (1661) to memorialise 'the life and death of Mistress Susanna Perwich...who died July 3 1661' when she was twenty-five years old, he dedicated it 'To all the young ladies and gentlewomen of the several schools in and about the city of London and elsewhere'. His reason for doing this arose from the fact that Susanna was the daughter of Robert Perwich, who had such a school in Hackney where she had finished her own schooling and had then become a teacher. Hackney was at the time a salubrious village to the north of the City of London, where many prosperous middle- and upper-class people had taken up residence, and where several other schools of a similar kind were to be found. It was in 1636 that the eight-year-old Katherine Fowler arrived in Hackney to join the school run by a Mrs Salmon. Fowler would later marry and, as Katherine Philips, make her name as a poet, 'the Matchless Orinda'. The two eldest daughters of Sir John Bramston were also sent to Mrs Salmon's school after the death of their mother in 1648. Samuel Sainthill of Bradninch north of Exeter sent his sister there during 1652–3. Mary Aubrey, a cousin of the antiquary, also attended the school; and in 1675 Ralph Josselin's two daughters, Mary and Elizabeth, arrived there with their mother from Earls Colne in Essex. Samuel Pepys, in typical fashion, recorded in his diary his visit on Sunday 21 April 1667 to Hackney parish church, St Augustine's, undertaken chiefly in order to run his eye over the 'young ladies' of the schools.[126] Schools of a similar kind circled London, in Tottenham, where Bathsua Makin ran a school, in Islington, Stepney, Chelsea, Deptford and upstream at Putney, which John Evelyn visited in 1649. The evidence for such schools beyond London is much more scattered, though their emphasis on dancing, music, needlework and 'behaviour' was criticised by, amongst others, John Dury in his *Reformed School* (1649?, 1651). The criticism led Edward Chamberlayne to propose *An Academy or College Wherein Young Ladies and Gentlewomen may at very small expense be duly instructed in the true Protestant religion* (1671). Mary Astell in her *Serious Proposal to the Ladies for the Advancement of Their True and Great Interest*, published in two parts in 1694 and 1697, expresses the hope for an education that would produce a woman 'who is a Christian out of choice not in conformity to those about her...[and who] acquires a clear understanding as well as a regular affection' – the kind of Christian life which Damaris Masham, daughter of the Cambridge Platonist Ralph Cudworth, achieved in her life and writings.

125 Charlton, *Women, Religion and Education*, pp. 131–41.   126 Pepys, *Diary*, 8:174.

Conclusion

Our discussion of education in early modern England has required an inclusive rather than an exclusive use of the term 'education', and, more particularly, has avoided equating 'education' with 'schooling', if by that is meant what was transacted in the formal institution called 'school'. We have also acknowledged that both religious and commercial incentives were a prime and necessary part of the story, especially when justificatory arguments relied on the Scriptures to provide proof-texts for just about every level and kind of claim in the matter. Shakespeare was merely reflecting a common awareness when he had Antonio warn Bassanio that 'The Devil can cite scripture for his purpose'.[127] Moreover, we have noted that the oral mode of education applied as much to the literate as the illiterate section of the population, a point well recognised by John Milton (who may have the last word) as he reminds us that 'whatever thing we hear or see, sitting, walking, travelling or conversing, may fitly be called our book, and is of the same effect as writings are'.[128]

127 W. Shakespeare, *The Merchant of Venice*, 1.3.93.
128 J. Milton, *Areopagitica* (London, 1644), p. 18.

Chapter 2

MANUSCRIPT TRANSMISSION
AND CIRCULATION

HAROLD LOVE AND ARTHUR F. MAROTTI

By 1476 when William Caxton issued the first book from his press at Westminster, England had already experienced considerable exposure to imported print. Caxton himself had printed some Latin during his time at Bruges, as well as a pioneering English text, the *Recuyell of the Historyes of Troye*. Already, we may surmise, printed copies had replaced manuscripts of the same work in progressive libraries. But on the whole, as would remain the case for many decades, most 'publication' of texts was still carried out through writing and voice. The pen of the scribe scratched on regardless of the first creakings of the wooden press. Increasing literacy, the outcome of a modernising business and administrative order, fuelled an expansion of both systems of production: it was not a matter of the new one expanding at the expense of the old. Instead, each came to meet particular needs. While the press dealt best with longer texts and those required in large numbers, shorter ones directed at specialised readerships remained the preserve of the pen. The loss in the late 1530s of the scriptoria in which monks had toiled as an act of communal devotion was compensated for by the Protestant recognition of writing as an exercise of personal virtue and by an expansion of both private and public record-keeping.

It is salutary to remember how, even as late as the early seventeenth century, the activities of the law and Parliament were conducted with hardly any recourse to the printed word. Juridical proceedings were preserved only in tenacious memories and handwritten précis: even law textbooks were as likely to be manuscript copies as printed.[1] Parliament had no Hansard: the only permanent records of debates were in private notes made by members and the barest summaries of decisions in the clerk's book. It is true that by the early seventeenth century a market was developing in unofficially compiled 'Diurnalls', but these,

---

1 See D. F. McKenzie, 'Speech–manuscript–print', in *New Directions in Textual Studies*, ed. Dave Oliphant and Robin Bradford (Austin: Harry Ransom Humanities Research Center, University of Texas, 1990), pp. 97–9.

until the eve of the Civil War, were exclusively in manuscript.[2] In scriveners'
and attorneys' offices, in diocesan chanceries, in counting houses and colleges,
and in the 'closets' of the gentry, the quill maintained its primacy. Even the
theatres relied almost wholly on handwritten copies and frowned upon the
printing of plays for private reading.[3] There was always a huge preponderance
of professional scribes and amanuenses over printing operatives.

In particular, a great many shorter literary works, and even a few longer
ones, continued throughout to be circulated primarily in handwritten copies.
Poets as influential as Sidney, Ralegh, Donne and Carew circulated their verse
almost exclusively through the scribal medium.[4] Lengthy prose romances such
as Sidney's two *Arcadias* and the second part of Mary Wroth's *Urania* (after
the printing of the first part had led to scandal and suppression) and political
tracts such as *A View of the present state of Ireland* (long ascribed to Spenser) and
Ralegh's *A Dialogue between a Counsellor of State and a Justice of the Peace* were
intended by their writers for scribal transmission and only deviated into print
years or decades after composition, often in unauthorised editions. Much lyric
verse and nearly all topical satire did likewise: the more popular examples of
these kinds still survive in dozens of copies. To complement the impressive
record of press productivity offered by the two *Short-Title Catalogues*,[5] we need
to recognise that the major libraries of Britain and North America preserve a
huge heritage of manuscripts written during the first two centuries of print's
supposed dominance which were not copies from printed originals, and that
these are only a small fraction of what once existed.[6]

Many writers from the gentry and aristocracy shunned print publication
as conferring a mechanic, stipendiary status,[7] but for others the decision to
promulgate a text in one medium or the other meant no more than an efficient
matching of ends to means. Even the professed, print-publishing writer might
turn to script for a work whose presentation to a patron would yield a higher

2 Harold Love, *Scribal Publication in Seventeenth-Century England* (Oxford: Clarendon Press,
  1993), pp. 87–109.
3 Discussed in Harold Love, 'Thomas Middleton: Oral Culture and the Manuscript Economy',
  in *Thomas Middleton and Early Modern Textual Culture*, ed. Gary Taylor (Oxford University
  Press, forthcoming).
4 Ernest W. Sullivan, II, has pointed out in *The Influence of John Donne: His Uncollected
  Seventeenth-Century Printed Verse* (Columbia: University of Missouri Press, 1993) that more
  of Donne's verse appeared in print than has previously been suspected, but the proportion
  is still a very small one of the whole circulating in manuscript.
5 Bibliographical information is given in full in the headnote to this volume's select Bibliography (p. 879).
6 Those by canonical authors are exhaustively listed in Peter Beal's invaluable *Index of English
  Literary Manuscripts*, vol. 1, *1450–1625*, and vol. 2, *1625–1700* (London: Mansell,1980–93).
7 See J. W. Saunders, 'The Stigma of Print: A Note on the Social Bases of Tudor Poetry', *Essays
  in Criticism* 1 (1951), 139–64.

return than could be extracted from the booksellers. Scribal circulation might also be chosen for the speed with which texts could be put into circulation. Ten, twenty or more copies of a new 'libel' or parliamentary speech could be produced by a single scribe in the time it would take for it to pass through the more cumbersome processes of print production, and several times that number could be produced by a scriptorium. Once sent on their way, texts would frequently pass from copyist to copyist along chains linked by personal acquaintance and common interest, which were perfectly adapted to bring them to their desired audience. Communities of the like-minded in every field of cultural and intellectual endeavour were created or confirmed through the regular exchange of manuscripts.[8]

A version of the same work from the press (assuming it was allowed to be printed in the first place) would as a rule be censored or supervised – if not directly by a state-appointed licenser, then as a result of self-policing by the Stationers' Company. If, as was often the case, this version came from a copy casually encountered in scribal transmission, it might well be textually inferior to the better manuscripts. By being available promiscuously from booksellers, stallholders and hawkers, it would have lost the 'reserved' character which made it a prized object for collectors of texts circulating only in manuscript. The scribal text carried with it an intimacy arising from script's greater power of projecting the individuality of the inscriber, especially in the days of exuberant secretary and idiosyncratic 'mixed' hands. Having made a copy (often into a substantial personal miscellany or commonplace book), the reader would have made a personal appropriation of the text concerned.[9] Print replaced manuscript with an objectivity that was both a remoteness and a fixity. Even to annotate a printed book was not a simple matter because printing paper contained less sizing than writing paper, and it was usually necessary to rub the surface first with resin.[10]

8 H. R. Woudhuysen, *Sir Philip Sidney and the Circulation of Manuscripts 1558–1640* (Oxford: Clarendon Press, 1996), p. 297, for example, discusses the exchange of poetry in the Sidney–Greville–Dyer–Spenser circle. Later, John Donne exchanged some work with Sir Edward Herbert (Arthur F. Marotti, *John Donne: Coterie Poet* (Madison and London: University of Wisconsin Press, 1986), pp. 195–202).

9 On the practice of keeping commonplace books, see Mary Thomas Crane, *Framing Authority: Sayings, Self, and Society in Sixteenth-Century England* (Princeton University Press, 1993), and Peter Beal, 'Notions in Garrison: The Seventeenth-Century Commonplace Book', in *New Ways of Looking at Old Texts: Papers of the Renaissance English Text Society, 1985–1991*, ed. W. Speed Hill (Binghamton, NY: Medieval and Renaissance Texts and Studies, 1993), pp. 131–47.

10 Nevertheless, as the marginalia of such book owners as Gabriel Harvey and Ben Jonson attest, readers of printed books continued older practices that assumed an interactive relationship with texts. On the connections of marginalia, including Harvey's, both to print culture and to manuscript culture, see Love, *Scribal Publication*, 224.

Evidently then, to be an author or a reader in one medium or the other was a significantly different activity. Authorship for the press was public, supervised and divorced from any sense of personal contact with the reader, except insofar as this could be simulated through the tone of the actual writing. Its end product was not the individuality and expressive irregularity of script, but arrays of type impressions which, apart from the deformations of wear, were each indistinguishable products of the originating punches. Arranged in regular, parallel lines with an exactness impossible to achieve in script, they emblematised what Walter Ong has called a 'technologising' of the word, fostering also a spatialisation of thought whose cultural consequences were many.[11] Print required that personal reponsibility be taken for what was uttered: the law insisted that a printed text should bear the name of the agents responsible for its physical production. Hideous punishments were prescribed for those who evaded these requirements and, as the case of the Marprelate tracts proves, the government was willing to go to great lengths to track down the authors and printers of illicit texts.[12] Given all these considerations, readers of a printed text could not expect it to address them intimately as individuals; nor did they have any way of altering the condition in which the text was to reach readers of other copies. Thus, they would only have enjoyed a diminished sense of ownership: while they may have acquired a copy, the work itself remained the publicly protected property of the publisher who had entered it in the Stationers' Register.

Authorship in the scribal medium was in every sense more intimate. Writers would have written to be read in their own hands or in those of close friends and associates:[13] as the example of Sidney's 'Old' *Arcadia* demonstrates, their readers would have been present to their imagination as they wrote in a way that was difficult if not impossible for the print-publishing author. That many texts transcended these bounds to the extent of becoming generally available can only seldom have been a consideration at the time of writing. Paradoxically the medium also encouraged anonymity: the scribal author, so powerful as a presence, is very frequently without a name. In the manuscript system, the

---

11 Walter J. Ong, *Orality and Literacy: the Technologizing of the Word* (London and New York: Routledge, 1982).

12 See H. S. Bennett, *English Books and Readers, 1558–1603* (Cambridge University Press, 1965), pp. 81–6.

13 In some cases, however, he or she had an amanuensis or professional scribe produce a fair copy for presentation to a particular person, as John Harington of Kelston did with his epigrams. For a discussion of Wyatt's, Greville's and Harington's uses of scribes to make fair copies of their work, see Woudhuysen, *Sidney and the Circulation of Manuscripts*, pp. 103–9.

ascription of particular works to particular writers was less important than it was in print (where an author's name might have had market value). This unascribed presentation resulted from two factors: (1) texts were more social and appropriable in the manuscript system; and (2) in many cases ascription was unnecessary, since those receiving manuscript texts knew who wrote them. Even if a text did carry the initials or the full name of a writer, the contemporary reader had no way of knowing whether the identification was correct.

Scribal transmission encouraged a fusing of the three roles – author, producer and reader – which print kept separate. While it needs to be recognised that professional scribes were at work in the field from its beginnings, most sources were copied for record or further transmission by, or under the supervision of, their readers. Those compilers of personal miscellanies who were not already authors were encouraged by the medium to become so. The beginning might be humble enough, since it was rare for a scribally transmitted text not to require some editorial repair work. Many transcribers went beyond this to reshape the work itself to accord with their own tastes and interests: there was no sense of its being the unchangeable possession of its author or of some intervening capitalist. The manuscript histories of some poems, such as Dyer's 'Phancy' and Ralegh's 'The Lie' testify to the active involvement of compilers in modifying and supplementing the texts they received.[14] In some collections we can observe correction and revision spurring the desire to create fresh works in the same genre. The sense of belonging to a privileged community would inspire the individual to take an active part in its debates. Compilers composed their own alterations, supplements and responses to the texts they received. Competitive versifying was encouraged by the manuscript medium, especially when commonplace-book anthologies issued from a group effort, as they sometimes did in the universities, aristocratic households or the court. Academic exercises in translation and imitation, together with composition in response to the setting of a theme, carried over from the grammar school to the university to aristocratic, courtly and Inns of Court social worlds, producing competitive versifying of various sorts, including the writing of 'answer-poems' and of rival poems on a particular topic.[15]

14 On the first, see Ruth Hughey (ed.), *The Arundel Harington Manuscript of Tudor Poetry*, 2 vols. (Columbus: Ohio State University Press, 1960), 2:206; on the second, see Michael Rudick (ed.), *The Poems of Sir Walter Ralegh: An Historical Edition* (Tempe, AZ: Renaissance English Text Society in conjunction with Arizona Center for Medieval and Renaissance Studies,1999), pp. xlii–xlvii.
15 See E. F. Hart, 'The Answer-Poem of the Early Seventeenth Century', *RES* n.s. 7 (1956), 19–29, and Arthur F. Marotti, *Manuscript, Print and the English Renaissance Lyric* (Ithaca: Cornell University Press, 1995), pp. 159–71.

Of course, few readers were exclusively wedded to one or the other medium, a fundamental fact obscured by attempts to make hard-and-fast distinctions between print consciousness and script consciousness, although the 'stigma of print' may have tipped the balance markedly in favour of the older medium for those high on the social scale or most of those who sought their patronage. Our model should rather be one of different experiences of readership and authorship undergone by the same individuals at different times and under different circumstances. We can still appreciate that difference today when we turn from a scribal 'separate' in a library to an early printed version of the same text. For a text of our period this will be a very different experience from that of, say, turning from a nineteenth-century author's manuscript to its printed outcome, for that kind of manuscript was never intended to be read except by the author, the publisher and the compositor. The scribal separate, on the other hand, was a communication in its own right which might well pass through dozens of hands and give rise to dozens of copies, and would generally, because of its rarity and the sense of privilege attached to its possession, be read with greater attention and personal involvement than the products of the press.

Preservation and circulation of lyric, dramatic and prose texts

Although literary works in a variety of genres were circulated and collected in manuscript in the early modern period, lyrics constitute a high percentage of the total. The manuscript transmission of poetry communicates two contradictory messages: first, that such work was socially occasional and ephemeral, and second, that it was worth preserving. The first indicates a very different attitude towards texts than that found in established print culture. Poems were associated with such social occasions as the paying of compliments, epistolary communication, witty extemporaneous performance, the sending of New Year's greetings, and congratulations on births or condolences on deaths. The connection to social compliment, for example, is evident in personal manuscript-collecting and compiling as well as in the professional copying of individual works or collections used for presentation to patrons. There was, of course, a continuum from manuscript to print, where the collecting efforts of individuals like John Harington of Stepney and Francis Davison often resulted in print publications.[16]

---

16 Hughey (ed.), *Arundel-Harington Manuscript*, 1:43–62, points to connections between the Harington manuscripts and the collection that was the main source for *Tottel's*

Since most lyrics were social communications, their initial circulation as individual poems or sets of poems made sense. Their entry into personal commonplace books followed. Group efforts of composition and collection, associated, for example, with the universities and Inns of Court, resulted in the circulation of verse in larger units. So, too, literarily self-conscious poets who released a body of verse into more or less restricted circulation made it possible for individual collectors to transcribe substantial collections that, in many cases, included the work of other writers. Thus copyists down the line of manuscript transmission might have had access not only to individual pieces and collections, but also to collections of collections.

The surviving manuscript documents containing lyric poetry represent a range of circulation and compilation practices: these include the passing-on of a poem or small group of poems on a single sheet or as an enclosure in a letter, the use of a quaternion or quire to hold a group of poems, and the gathering of poems into a booklet.[17] Larger collections were formed either by binding loose manuscript 'separates' or by transcribing single poems and collections of poems into already-bound volumes ranging in size from pocket-sized notebooks to impressive folios. Such collections of verse either constitute manuscript poetical anthologies or become parts of commonplace-book gatherings of various kinds of writing. In the latter case, poetry is found along with personal letters, diaries and journals, household accounts, medical receipts, recipes and other useful forms of information – a sign that literary texts were part of a fabric of social life, not artificially segregrated from the everyday world as they came to be in a developed print culture.

The manuscripts containing poetry were mainly associated with the university, the Inns of Court, the court, the aristocratic or middle-class household, and familial or social networks or scribal communities. Some collections belonged to more than one of these milieux, especially in the case of those manuscripts whose owners moved from the university to London, where (perhaps either at court or in the Inns of Court) they continued their transcription of texts. Some social environments, such as the universities, the Inns of Court and the royal court, were especially conducive to transcription and transmission of manuscript separates and collections. Individual networks of

---

Miscellany (1557). Davison, who collected a large body of verse from the late Elizabethan period, produced in *A Poetical Rhapsody* (1602) perhaps the richest of the Elizabethan printed miscellanies.

17 See J. W. Saunders, 'From Manuscript to Print: A Note on the Circulation of Poetic MSS in the Sixteenth Century', *Proceedings of the Leeds Philosophical and Literary Society* 6.8 (1951), 502–28.

transmission associated with particular families (and, sometimes, with their clients), with political factions and with a dispersed religious minority such as English Catholics also account for the production and dissemination of a large body of manuscript texts.

Contrary to what we might expect, at least as far as 'literary' manuscripts are concerned, there are more surviving manuscripts from the seventeenth century than from the sixteenth: of the approximately 230 pre-1640 surviving manuscript collections of poetry that were not single-author collections only 27 belong to the sixteenth century.[18] This may be due to a number of factors, including the increase in manuscript circulation of texts at the university and the Inns of Court, perhaps the two most important centres of manuscript literary transmission and collection; widespread dissemination of materials through professional scribes and scriptoria; and the reliance on manuscript communication by factions and minorities in a period of censorship and political turmoil. Nevertheless, the traces of the social circulation and collecting of texts – including some written by such canonical authors as Wyatt, Sidney and Donne – are numerous enough for us to perceive the workings of this system of literary transmission.

The manuscript poetry collections that survive from the early Tudor period include books of songs and lyrics.[19] The most important manuscripts, however, are those associated with the poetry of Sir Thomas Wyatt. Because of their connection with the publication of the most influential sixteenth-century printed anthology of poetry, *Tottel's Miscellany* (1557), the manuscripts in which we find Wyatt's poetry have received the most scholarly attention. We have not only the Egerton Manuscript of Wyatt's verse (BL, MS Egerton 2711) with its holograph authorial corrections and the 'Blage' Manuscript (Trinity College, Dublin MS 160, pts 2 and 3), which includes a large selection of Wyatt's verse, but also the Devonshire Manuscript (BL, MS Additional 17492), which was a product of a courtly coterie circulation of texts, both Wyatt's and those of other authors, including some of the transcribers.[20]

18 Woudhuysen, *Sidney and the Circulation of Manuscripts*, p. 157.
19 For example, these manuscripts in the British Library, hereafter 'BL': the Fayrfax Manuscript (BL, MS Additional 5465), Ritson's Manuscript (BL, MS Additional 5665), Henry VIII's Manuscript (BL, MS Additional 31922) and BL, MS Cotton Vespasian A-25. For the first three, see John Stevens, *Music and Poetry in the Early Tudor Court* (Lincoln: University of Nebraska Press, 1961), pp. 338–425. For the last, see *Tudor Songs and Ballads From MS Cotton Vespasian A-25*, ed. Peter Seng (Cambridge, MA, and London: Harvard University Press, 1978).
20 See Richard Harrier, *The Canon of Sir Thomas Wyatt's Poetry* (Cambridge, MA: Harvard University Press, 1975), pp. 23–54; Elizabeth Heale, 'Women and the Courtly Love Lyric: The Devonshire MS (BL Additional 17492)', *Modern Language Review* 90 (1995), 296–313;

The Devonshire Manuscript is, perhaps, the best surviving sixteenth-century example of a blank book that was used as a medium of social intercourse. It circulated within a group of male and female courtiers connected with the Howard family, accruing texts in that late Henrician courtly circle before moving, with one of its principals, Margaret Douglas, to Scotland, where Lord Darnley (James I's father) added a poem of his own. Apart from a (textually unreliable) selection of Wyatt poems, this manuscript includes pieces by Thomas Clere (to his love Mary Shelton), Richard Hattfield, John Harington, Sir Edmund Knivet and other courtly amateurs. It has a section preserving a run of love poems by Margaret Douglas (Henry VIII's niece) and Thomas Howard associated with their unauthorised, ill-fated marriage.

Margaret Douglas is one of five women of the Howard family who were connected to the manuscript as collectors, transcribers or subjects of the verse. The mixed society of the court and the aristocratic household made it possible for women to be involved in the composition, circulation and compilation of manuscript verse. Given the limited opportunities for women to have their writings printed, it is not surprising that they should have relied strongly on manuscript transmission.[21] Later in the century Ann Cornwallis was associated with a small poetry collection (Folger Shakespeare Library MS V.a. 89) and Lady Ann Southwell kept a manuscript commonplace book in which she inserted her own and others' poems (Folger Shakespeare Library MS V.b. 198).[22] In the mid-to-late seventeenth century the women of the Catholic Aston family composed, circulated and collected texts from their familial and social networks.[23] Given women's involvement in the manuscript circulation and preservation of texts, it is not surprising to read the professional writer Thomas Nashe's complaint about the exclusiveness and relative inaccessibility of manuscript verse 'oftentimes imprisoned in Ladyes casks'.[24]

and Seth Lehrer, *Courtly Letters in the Age of Henry VIII* (Cambridge University Press, 1997), pp. 143–60.

21 See Margaret J. M. Ezell, *The Patriarch's Wife: Literary Evidence and the History of the Family* (Chapel Hill and London: University of North Carolina Press, 1987), pp. 62–100.

22 See Arthur F. Marotti, 'The Cultural and Textual Importance of Folger MS V.a. 89', *English Manuscript Studies 1100–1700* 11 (2002), 70–92; *The Southwell–Sibthorpe Commonplace Book, Folger MS. V.b. 198*, ed. Jean Klene, CSC (Tempe, AZ: Renaissance English Text Society in conjunction with Arizona Center for Medieval and Renaissance Studies, 1997).

23 Texts from this circle were published in *Tixall Poetry*, ed. Arthur Clifford (Edinburgh: James Ballantyne, 1813). See *The Verse Miscellany of Constance Aston Fowler: A Diplomatic Edition*, ed. Deborah Larson (Tempe, AZ: Renaissance English Text Society in conjunction with Arizona Center for Medieval and Renaissance Studies, 2000), which is based on Huntington Library MS HM 904.

24 In his Preface to Newman's 1591 edition of *Astrophil and Stella*, in *Elizabethan Critical Essays*, ed. G. Gregory Smith, 2 vols. (London: Oxford University Press, 1904), 2:224.

One of the most interesting family manuscripts from the Tudor period is
the Arundel-Harington Manuscript, the album used by Sir John Harington of
Stepney and his son Sir John Harington of Kelston – a rich collection of over
300 poems from a six-decade period (1540–1600) comprising, on the one hand,
the work of the elder Harington (who died in 1582), Wyatt, Surrey, Lord Vaux,
Churchyard, Richard Edwards and others and, on the other, that of such poets as the younger Harington, Sidney, Oxford, Daniel, Ralegh, Greville, Dyer,
Constable and Spenser. John Harington of Kelston continued his father's poetical anthology by adding pieces from the later Elizabethan era: even in its
surviving mangled form (the result of an eighteenth-century editor's removing
pages while editing *Nugae Antiquae*, an anthology of Harington family writing), the Arundel-Harington Manuscript includes many poetical texts that were
prized in Tudor courtly society.[25] Besides transcribing poems to which other
collectors had ready access, the younger Harington also, through his connection to the Sidney–Pembroke circle, was able to copy some of the texts of Sir
Philip Sidney that were initially quite restricted: these include manuscripts
of the *Arcadia, Astrophil and Stella*, some of the *Certaine Sonnets*, and the
Sidney / Countess of Pembroke translations of the Psalms.[26] Harington translated a salacious section of Ariosto's *Orlando Furioso*, circulating it in manuscript
to a courtly readership that included Queen Elizabeth's maids of honour, an
act for which he was banished from court until he did penance by translating
the whole work – which he put into print in an expensively illustrated, but
comically annotated edition. He wrote epigrams for manuscript circulation,
which then posthumously found their way into print.[27] Despite his personal
eccentricity, the younger Harington is a good example of the gentleman au-
thor/collector in late manuscript culture, one who, nevertheless, felt free, as
his Ariosto translation and his Menippean *Metamorphosis of Ajax* demonstrate,
to move his work into print without fear of social stigma.

Like the collection begun by the elder Harington, George Bannatyne's 1568
compilation contains a large variety of Scottish texts, preserving many pieces
that otherwise would have been lost.[28] Although Bannatyne originally planned

25 See Hughey's description of this manuscript, *Arundel-Harington Manuscript*, 1:3–75.
26 See Peter Beal, *In Praise of Scribes: Manuscripts and Their Makers in Seventeenth-Century England* (Oxford: Clarendon Press, 1998), p. 122n.
27 BL, MS Additional 12049 is a copy made for Prince Henry; Beal, *Index*, 1.2.122, notes Harington sent an autographed copy of his epigrams to King James; Harington died in 1612 and the two editions of the poems appeared in 1615 and 1618.
28 See *The Bannatyne Manuscript: National Library of Scotland Advocates' MS 1.1.6* (facsimile edn.), ed. Denton Fox and William A. Ringler (London: Scolar Press, 1980). Fox and Ringler point out, for example, that this manuscript is 'the most important single witness for

to include only religious and moral poetry, he revised his plan and grouped the poems in four sections: 'ballatis of theoligie', 'ballatis full of wisdome and moralitie', 'ballatis mirry' and 'ballatis of luve'.[29] Linking late medieval and sixteenth-century Scottish culture, this anthology numbers more than 400 items and stands as the most important Scottish literary manuscript from the sixteenth century, including (in addition to Dunbar, Henryson and Scott) such writers as Sir William Alexander, Chaucer, Gavin Douglas, John Heywood, Walter Kennedy, John Lydgate, Alexander Montgomerie and William Stewart.

Four especially interesting Elizabethan manuscript collections shed light on the texts that circulated in both courtly culture and the related university Inns of Court and aristocratic environments: those of John Finet (Bodleian (hereafter 'Bod.') MS Rawlinson Poetical 85), Humphrey Coningsby (BL, MS Harley 7392), Henry Stanford (Cambridge MS Dd.5.75) and John Lilliat (Bod. MS Rawlinson Poetical 148).[30] The first two share a large group of poems by such courtly authors as Sidney, Dyer and Oxford. Finet collected and transcribed verse both at court and at the university, producing both a personal and a culturally symptomatic anthology of poetry from the latter part of Elizabeth's reign, including work by Oxford, Ralegh, Breton, Dyer, Sidney, Gorges, Spenser and Queen Elizabeth as well as student poetry from Cambridge.[31] Coningsby, whose family was related by marriage to the Sidneys, was associated both with Christ Church, Oxford, and with the Inns of Court. His collection, which overlaps considerably with Finet's, in addition to pieces by a number of individuals identified only by their initials, has at its core a substantial anthology of Elizabethan courtly verse by such poets as Oxford, Ralegh, Gorges, Sidney, Breton and Queen Elizabeth.[32] Stanford, who was educated at Trinity College, Oxford, and served as a chaplain or tutor in three aristocratic households, not only collected courtly verse by such accomplished

---

[William] Dunbar' (p. xli); for six of Henryson's fables, Bannatyne has the only text (p. xli); most of the poems of Alexander Scott it contains are unique texts (p. xlii).

29 *Ibid.*, p. xiv.

30 The first has been edited by Laurence Cummings: 'John Finet's Miscellany' (unpublished Ph.D. thesis, Washington University, 1960); the third by Steven W. May: *Henry Stanford's Anthology: An Edition of Cambridge University Library Manuscript Dd.5.75* (New York: Garland Press, 1988); and the fourth by Edward Doughtie: *Liber Lilliati: Elizabethan Verse and Song (Bodleian MS Rawlinson Poetry 148)* (Newark: University of Delaware Press, 1985). Fols. 23–63v of Stanford's collection resemble Rawlinson Poetical 85 and Harley 7392, with some riddles and epigrams included.

31 See Cummings (ed.), 'John Finet's Miscellany', pp. 9–14.

32 On this manuscript and its compiler, see Woudhuysen, *Sidney and the Circulation of Manuscripts*, pp. 278–86.

poets as Sidney, Dyer, Breton and Gorges, but also transcribed the juvenile efforts of his pupils.[33] John Lilliat, a cathedral musician, compiled a lyrical and musical collection on sheets bound to Thomas Watson's *Hekatompathia* (1582). His compilation includes pieces by such well-known writers as Dyer, Sidney, Essex, Marlowe, Thomas Campion, Ralegh and Sir John Davies, as well as the work of minor or unknown secular and clerical versifiers, including the compiler himself.

Sir Philip Sidney is clearly the most important manuscript author of the Elizabethan period. He severely restricted the circulation of the texts of the (unrevised 'Old' and revised 'New') *Arcadia, Certaine Sonnets* and *Astrophil and Stella*: ironically the Sidney text that was circulated most broadly in manuscript was his politically hazardous 'Letter to the Queen', whose publicity damaged his career.[34] If we look at the manuscript remains of Sidney's writings, we can detect the network of family, neighbours and friends to whom they were passed. After his death, however, under the joint literary executorship of his sister, the Countess of Pembroke, and Fulke Greville (whose poetry was printed only posthumously in 1633), Sidney's partially revised prose romance came into print in 1590 – republished in 1593, 1598 and 1617 in a fuller version created by adding the unrevised parts of the 'Old' *Arcadia* needed to complete the story. The older version of the work, which Sidney supposedly had sent in a series of manuscript instalments to his sister and her friends in the early 1580s and whose projected publication was thwarted by Greville and Sir Francis Walsingham,[35] had to wait until the twentieth century for rediscovery and print publication. The printing of the more private *Astrophil and Stella* in 1591 was an unauthorised though fortunate one, since it initiated the Elizabethan vogue for sonnet sequences. Once the *Arcadia* and the sonnet sequence were published, print publication of all of this author's works by one means or another was inevitable.

One change that marks the late Elizabethan era is the elevation of the socio-cultural status of lyric poetry, especially of amorous verse. Before the 1580s and 1590s poets writing secular lyrics had to be especially apologetic about publishing their 'poetical toys' in an age that condemned such work as immature and frivolous: George Gascoigne, for example, had to fight this prejudice. In the last two decades of the century, partly through the cumulative effect of the published poetical miscellanies and partly through the posthumous influence

---

33 May (ed.), *Henry Stanford's Anthology*, pp. vii–lxiv.
34 See Beal, *In Praise of Scribes*, pp. 109–46.
35 Woudhuysen, *Sidney and the Circulation of Manuscripts*, pp. 224–5.

of Sidney, gentlemen and professional authors had less fear of print publication. Samuel Daniel, for example, felt free to have his poetry printed once the precedent was set by the appearance of Sidney's verse: his sonnet sequence *Delia* appeared in 1592, the initial version of *The Civil Wars* in 1595, and his collected works in 1601 and 1623. Since manuscript circulation and print were both available, some writers chose to exploit both forms of publication. Some late sixteenth- and early seventeenth-century authors who aspired to 'laureate' status,[36] most especially Edmund Spenser and Ben Jonson, took care to bring their work into print in impressive forms, while actively participating in the system of manuscript transmission as well – at least by circulating texts to friends and (actual or potential) patrons. Spenser gave manuscript texts of his work to members of the Sidney circle (including Fulke Greville and Sir Edward Dyer), and to friends such as Gabriel Harvey, Lodowick Bryskett and Sir Walter Ralegh; Jonson sent individual pieces to such individuals as the Countess of Bedford, the Earl of Pembroke, John Donne and Sir Robert Cecil – both before and after the production of his self-advertising 1616 folio *Workes*. The ready availability of some of Jonson's lyrics in the manuscript system in the 1630s and 1640s, before their posthumous publication in *Under-Wood* (1640/41), testifies to his continuing involvement in this older system of publication.

Though print was the primary means for their preservation for future eras, some dramatic texts were transmitted in manuscript. We have evidence, for example, of the manuscript circulation of civic and academic drama in the sixteenth century, both Latin and English.[37] Although, for professional drama, the most solid evidence exists for seventeenth-century (post-Shakespearean) examples of the practice, Richard Dutton has made an interesting circumstantial case for Shakespeare's circulation of some of his plays in manuscript and he argues that between 1590 and 1642 this was a common practice.[38] Dutton infers from the circulation of manuscript texts of plays, which usually were

---

36 See Richard Helgerson, *Self-Crowned Laureates: Spenser, Jonson, Milton and the Literary System* (Berkeley and Los Angeles: University of California Press, 1983).

37 See Woudhuysen, *Sidney and the Circulation of Manuscripts*, pp. 134–45. See the list of manuscript plays in E. K. Chambers, *The Elizabethan Stage*, 4 vols. (Oxford: Clarendon Press, 1923, 1951), 4:404–6. G. E. Bentley indexes manuscript copies of early Stuart plays in *The Jacobean and Caroline Stage*, 7 vols. (Oxford: Clarendon Press, 1941–68).

38 Richard Dutton, 'The Birth of the Author', in *Texts and Cultural Change in Early Modern England*, ed. Cedric C. Brown and Arthur F. Marotti (Basingstoke and London: Macmillan; New York: St Martin's Press, 1997), pp. 153–78. On the authorial publication of play-texts in manuscript, see Love, *Scribal Publication*, pp. 65–70.

well over the average length designed for performance (2,500 lines), that authors deliberately produced longer versions of their dramas for private reading.
Harold Love observes: 'The six surviving manuscripts of Middleton's *A Game
at Chess* ... are not just the product of unusual political topicality, but rather a
sign of an alternate means of publicising dramatic writing – in which Beaumont
and Fletcher, for example, certainly participated.'[39] In addition, as the Dering Manuscript's conflated and altered text of Shakespeare's *Henry IV*, parts
I and II, indicates, dramatic texts, like lyric poetry, could be altered within
the manuscript system of transmission.[40] Edward Pudsey's commonplace-
book collection of citations from the drama (Bod. MS English Poetry d.3)
demonstrates how printed dramatic texts could be excerpted and compiled in
manuscript form.

The numerous fictional and non-fictional prose texts circulated in multiple manuscript copies include, in addition to Sidney's *Arcadia* and his 'Letter
to Elizabeth', prose lives of Cardinal Wolsey and Sir Thomas More; political
libels such as *Leicester's Commonwealth*; Robert Persons's 'A Memorial for the
Reformation of England'; the letter from the Catholic Philip Howard, Earl
of Arundel, to Queen Elizabeth; Robert Southwell's apologetic letter to his
father; Edmund Campion's *Historie of Ireland*; and papers associated with
Robert Cotton and the Society of Antiquaries.[41] Apart from his *Discoverie
of ... Guiana* (1595) and his monumental, but abortive, *History of the World*
(1614), all of Sir Walter Ralegh's prose works circulated in manuscript during
his lifetime and for some time after his death, reaching print only in altered political circumstances and, therefore, bearing new topical meanings.[42] Letters by
important individuals and excerpts from trials of prominent figures like Ralegh
and the Earl of Essex were sometimes included in manuscript miscellanies.
Of course, newsletters and reports of proceedings in Parliament proliferated,
especially in the first four decades of the seventeenth century.[43]

39 'Thomas Middleton: Oral Culture and the Manuscript Economy'. Woudhuysen, *Sidney and
the Circulation of Manuscripts*, p. 142, notes that 'Jonson exchanged plays in manuscript with
Beaumont and Fletcher'.
40 Barbara Mowat, 'The Problem of Shakespeare's Text(s)', in *Textual Formations and Reformations*, ed. Laurie E. Maguire and Thomas L. Berger (Newark: University of Delaware Press,
1998), pp. 131–48, 145n.
41 See Love, *Scribal Publication*, pp. 83–9.
42 See Anna R. Beer, *Sir Walter Ralegh and His Readers in the Seventeenth Century* (Basingstoke
and London: Macmillan; New York: St Martin's Press,1997).
43 See Love, *Scribal Publication*, esp. pp. 9–22, 124–6, 134–7; Richard Cust, 'News and Politics
in Early Seventeenth-Century England', *Past and Present* 112 (August 1986), 60–90; and
F. J. Levy, 'How Information Spread Among the Gentry, 1550–1640', *Journal of British
Studies* 21(1982), 11–34. For a general discussion of prose texts in manuscript circulation,
see Woudhuysen, *Sidney and the Circulation of Manuscripts*, pp. 145–53.

Manuscript circulation – authors' choices, collectors' connoisseurship

From the end of the sixteenth and through most of the seventeenth century manuscript circulation of their literary texts remained a preferred medium for most gentleman authors. Among those who deliberately chose to restrict their texts to this medium, John Donne is the most prominent case. Except for the carefully staged performances represented by his published polemical and devotional prose – *Pseudo-Martyr* (1610), *Ignatius His Conclave* (1611) and *Devotions upon Emergent Occasions* (1624) – and his public sermons (some of which were printed in his lifetime), Donne was basically a coterie author. Throughout his erratic career – from his Inns of Court days,[44] to those of his courtly employment as secretary to the Lord Keeper, Sir Thomas Egerton,[45] to his three-year social exile in the country following his elopement and its disastrous consequences, to the period of his renewed search for patronage and courtly employment, to, finally, his life as a minister, then Dean of St Paul's – Donne addressed his poetry and much of his prose to various special and restricted audiences of friends, patrons and patronesses, keeping some pieces (such as 'A Nocturnal upon S. Lucies Day' and the prose treatise on suicide, *Biathanatos*) quite close. As the manuscript evidence indicates, they reached a wider audience only some years after their original limited circulation. Among Donne's poems, the striking exceptions are the two *Anniversaries*, whose publication the author deeply regretted. The story of how Donne's poetry finally (after 1615) began to be circulated widely in university, courtly and aristocratic circles is a complex one, demanding both textual and social-historical analysis, but the important thing to note is that, as Peter Beal has indicated, with some 250 surviving manuscripts containing his verse, Donne is the poet who was most widely disseminated in manuscript in the seventeenth century.[46]

Although Donne severely restricted the circulation of some individual pieces – particularly the lyrics grouped under the heading *Songs and Sonets* in the 1635 edition – he released some of his work more freely: for example, the set of his *Satires*, which his friend Ben Jonson transmitted with a cover poem to the

44 Other writers, including Sir John Davies at the Middle Temple and Thomas Campion at Gray's Inn, also circulated their work in manuscript in the Inns environment before allowing it to reach print.

45 Woudhuysen, *Sidney and the Circulation of Manuscripts*, pp. 67, 79, notes that other secretaries who produced writing of their own include Edward Dyer, Edmund Campion, Edmund Spenser, John Lyly, George Turbervile, Thomas Lake, John Finet, Robert Naunton, Sir Thomas Smith, Roger Ascham, James Howell, Frances Quarles and John Milton.

46 Beal, *Index*, 1.1.245.

Countess of Bedford. Some or all of Donne's *Elegies* probably circulated as a group. The *La Corona* sonnets and some of the *Holy Sonnets* were presented to friends and social superiors. Donne's close friend Rowland Woodward compiled (probably for his patron the Earl of Westmorland) a manuscript collection that includes the five satires, thirteen elegies, the Lincoln's Inn epithalamion, a selection of the verse letters, nineteen Holy Sonnets, *La Corona*, prose paradoxes, epigrams and one lyric, 'A Jeat Ring Sent' (New York Public Library, Westmorland MS, Berg Collection). Examining the manuscript remains of both Donne and Henry King, Margaret Crum has convincingly argued that both poets probably originally circulated their work in loose sheets and quires or booklets, rather than in large collections – though, of course, eventually their work was gathered by compilers.[47]

Most of the surviving manuscript remains of the broad circulation of Donne's poems date from about 1620, so that the full impact of work he wrote much earlier was considerably delayed, reaching its widest audience only with the 1633 and subsequent printed editions. We know that at least twice in his life, Donne deliberately collected his poetry: in 1614, with a thought of producing only a few printed copies for presentation to patrons; in 1619, to entrust his verse to his friend Sir Robert Ker on the occasion of going abroad on a diplomatic mission. The surprising thing is that, in the first case, the poet had to ask his good friend Sir Henry Goodyer to return to him a manuscript book of his poems since he did not have a collection in his possession. Donne risked the loss of all or much of his poetry by letting such a manuscript out of his hands; apparently a unique collection of the poems of John Hoskyns, larger than Donne's collected poems, was lost by such means.[48] The manuscript system, evidently, could either imperil or preserve texts.

In the proliferating seventeenth-century manuscript collections, Donne's poetical texts and, to some degree, Jonson's and Ralegh's connect the Elizabethan and early Jacobean literary world with that of the late Jacobean, Caroline and Interregnum periods. Many university, Inns of Court, aristocratic and courtly anthologies from the 1620s through the 1650s contain substantial numbers of lyrics by these older poets alongside the work of a younger generation of writers strongly influenced by Donne and Jonson. One of the motives for preserving older verse was political. Texts such as the collaboratively written 'Parliament Fart' and Wotton's 'Dazel'd thus, with height of place' could be

---

47 'Notes on the Physical Characteristics of Some Manuscripts of the Poems of Donne and of Henry King', *The Library* 16 (1961), 121–32.
48 Mary Hobbs, *Early Seventeenth-Century Verse Miscellany Manuscripts* (Aldershot: Scolar Press, 1992), pp. 9–10, citing John Aubrey as source.

retranscribed (and, in the case of the former, expanded) at times removed from their immediate contexts to convey new political meaning.[49] Especially during the period before, during and just after the Civil War, manuscript collections registered the political tensions and alienation of the compilers and their contacts.[50] Royalists in the Interregnum, like Catholics[51] from the Elizabethan period through to the later Stuart era, and Jacobites after the Glorious Revolution (1688), used manuscript communication to foster group solidarity.

Some of the manuscript collections of the seventeenth century, especially in the period between 1620 and 1660, are impressively large and varied: the practice of anthologising represented by a late Elizabethan printed anthology such as Francis Davison's *A Poetical Rhapsody* (1602) was redirected back into the manuscript system, for, after Davison's collection, few new, respectable poetry anthologies were printed before the Restoration. Some of these large manuscript compilations were made for aristocrats, some (for themselves) by individual connoisseurs. Characteristically, they recovered texts from as far back as the late Elizabethan era, but also included major and minor verse from their own times. Often these anthologies were compiled by combining separate smaller collections of poems: the Skipwith MS (BL MS Additional 25707), for example, conflates five separate collections and some loose papers.[52]

Many of these documents trace their origin to a circle of poets and friends formed in the 1620s at Christ Church, Oxford. In her study of the literary culture of the university, especially the poets and collectors at Christ Church, Mary Hobbs traces the collecting efforts that were continued beyond the university when some individuals moved into other environments, such as that of the Inns of Court, and either personally, or through professional scribes or amanuenses, compiled large anthologies of manuscript verse. Christ Church poets such as William Strode, Richard Corbet and Henry King (the last named by Donne as his literary executor) wrote and exchanged verse as well as passed around

49 On the first, see Baird W. Whitlock, *John Hoskyns, Serjeant-at-Law* (Washington, DC: University Press of America, 1982), 283–93; on the second, see Ted-Larry Pebworth, 'Sir Henry Wotton's "Dazel'd Thus, with Height of Place" and the Appropriation of Political Poetry in the Earlier Seventeenth Century', *Papers of the Bibliographical Society of America* 71 (1977), 151–69.

50 See, for example, Bod. MS Malone 23, which is almost entirely a political collection from the 1620s and 1630s. Bod. MS Rawlinson Poetical 26 is a large collection of political verse assembled over a long period of time, from about 1615 to 1660 (Beal, *Index*, 1.2.379). See the discussion of manuscript poetry and the political world in Marotti, *Manuscript*, pp. 82–133.

51 Catholic manuscripts include the Wellys anthology (Bod. MS Rawlinson C.183), BL, MS Additional 15225, Bod. MS Ashmole 48, Edward Bannister's manuscript (BL, MS Additional 28253) and the yeoman Thomas Fairfax's manuscript (Bod. MS English Poetry b.5).

52 See Hobbs, *Miscellany Manuscripts*, pp. 62–7.

growing collections of miscellaneous verse. Despite the (inadequate) editions of Corbett of 1647 and 1648 and the eventual printing of Henry King's lyrics in 1657 with their author's consent, Strode, Corbet and King should be regarded as fundamentally manuscript authors, whose work circulated first among fellow academics, then in a somewhat wider social sphere as former students and colleagues moved into environments outside the university.[53] In Caroline England, writers like Thomas Carew and Robert Herrick also functioned as manuscript poets. Carew wrote an elegy on Donne that is a sympathetic response of one manuscript poet to another.[54] Before and after their printing in *Hesperides* (1648), many of Herrick's poems found their way into manuscript compilations. Richard Crashaw circulated scribal copies of his poems at Cambridge in the 1630s.[55]

Though dozens of manuscript collections of poetry survive from the late Jacobean period to the Restoration (and beyond), several are especially rich in their contents. One of them, the first part of the large Haselwood-Kingsborough Manuscript (Huntington Library MS HM 198, pt 1), was transcribed for Edward Denny, Earl of Norwich, before his death in 1630. In addition to sixty-five poems by Donne, this 205-page folio anthology contains verse by Jonson, Beaumont, Carew, Herrick, Corbet, Strode and Randolph – that is, the work of both Jacobean and early Caroline poets – as well as numerous political poems from the Jacobean period. Many of the pieces are answer-poems, including eight lyrics by William Herbert, Earl of Pembroke, and Sir Benjamin Rudyerd – one of the largest groups of their poems to be found in manuscript before the 1660 printed edition of their work. Like so many other manuscript collections, this anthology documents its interest in socioliterary relationships and political topicality.[56]

In the 1640s and 1650s, Peter Calfe and his son of the same name assembled, in turn, two large quarto collections of verse (BL, MSS Harley 6917 and 6918).[57] The first, with over 213 poems on some 106 leaves, was compiled in

---

53 *Ibid*, pp. 116–29.
54 Printed in the second edition of Donne's poetry (1635). See John Kerrigan, 'Thomas Carew', *Proceedings of the British Academy* 74 (1988), 311–50, for a discussion of Carew's functioning as an early Stuart manuscript poet.
55 Love, *Scribal Publication*, p. 52.
56 See C. M. Armitage, 'Donne's Poems in Huntington Manuscript 198: New Light on "The Funeral"', *Studies in Philology* 63 (1966), 697–707, and Herbert Berry, *Sir John Suckling's Poems and Letters from Manuscript* (London, ONT: University of Western Ontario Press, 1960), pp. 33–8.
57 See Hobbs, *Miscellany Manuscripts*, pp. 67–71, for a discussion of these manuscripts and of the relationship of Peter Calfe Sr to a London literary circle that included Thomas Manne, Henry King's amanuensis, who would have had a large body of poetry from Christ Church, Oxford.

the 1640s, ending with a poem mourning the executed Charles I; the second, made in the next decade, has a comparable number of poems on 200 pages. The first collection, which numbers its items and, where possible, notes authorship, is prefaced with a first-line index of 198 of the poems: it represents a deliberate act of poetical anthologising that might, in the late Elizabethan period, have resulted in a printed poetical miscellany. Among the forty or so identifiable authors, Carew, Henry King and other members of the King family are most strongly represented. The second collection is a typical Cavalier anthology that emphasises anti-Puritan and anti-Parliament pieces as well as Royalist exhortations. Here Cleveland's work looms large (15 poems), but there is also verse by Donne, Cowley, Randolph, Herrick, King, Felltham, Strode, Fanshawe, Carew and Lovelace, as well as poems by the compiler himself (fols. 96–102). Because Calfe Sr, according to Hobbs, 'evidently copied wholesale other people's collections' and, through a neighbour, Thomas Manne, had access both to poetry from Christ Church, Oxford, and to King family texts, these anthologies represent an extended process of manuscript anthologising that began at Oxford and continued in London in new socioliterary and historical circumstances.

From the 1630s to around 1660, Nicholas Burghe, a Royalist captain in the Civil War, amassed a huge folio anthology of verse and some prose (Bod. MS Ashmole 38).[58] On some 243 leaves he recorded hundreds of poems by dozens of poets, both the well-known and the obscure or unknown, some from printed editions.[59] Burghe, who included a number of his own poems in the volume, seems to have avoided copying many poems by any one writer, the poets most strongly represented being Constable, Jonson, Carew and Herrick. This collection reflects a strong interest in political poetry – including pieces on the scandalous Somerset–Howard marriage and the couple's trial for Sir Thomas Overbury's murder, on Francis Bacon's fall, on the Duke of Buckingham and on Puritans. But the most remarkable feature of the collection is the group of over 200 epitaphs and funeral elegies, a feature that highlights the importance of elegiac and funerary poetry in the social life of the time.

By the time that the two Calfes and Burghe assembled their poetry collections, manuscript anthologising had developed widely as a connoisseur activity among literary amateurs. Manuscript circulation was still valued for its social cachet, but printed books were drawn on for some of the contents of manuscript collections – as they had served earlier as sources of quotes for personal commonplace books. Especially after the publication of Donne's poems in 1633 and

---

58 See Beal, *Index*, 1.2.10, and Marotti, *Manuscript*, pp. 72–3.
59 Earlier manuscripts copied largely from printed editions include BL MSS Harl. 6910 and Additional 34064.

of a series of (mostly posthumous) volumes by Cavalier poets in the 1640s and 1650s, the social boundary between the two systems of literary transmission was blurred. The next change, in the Restoration period, was for booksellers to set up modern scriptoria to produce, on demand, collections of verse for socially elite customers who preferred restricted-circulation handwritten documents to the products of the press.

The political underground of manuscript circulation

At a certain point which can conveniently be identified with the closing years of Elizabeth I, the manuscript text acquired a new function which many found liberating but others deeply threatening. In September 1599 Lord Treasurer Buckhurst fulminated that 'viperous and secrete Libellore[s] doe much more in my opinion deserue death, then those wch Committ open rebellion agaynst the state ... I protest yf there weare a Parliament, I should more willingly give my voyce to establish a lawe of death agaynst them than agaynst the Theife or Murderer.'[60] The medium had become a vehicle for the free circulation of 'libels', 'satyrs' and what were later to be called 'state poems'. In the same year Archbishop Whitgift banned the publication of printed satires and epigrams, but there was no effective way of preventing the transmission of similar pieces by means of manuscript and voice. Indeed, as Whitgift's body lay in state in 1604, a Puritan satire was surreptitiously pinned to his hearse.[61] Moreover, while the printed satire, priding itself on its classical lineage and moral intention, had observed the precedent of the older tradition of verse 'complaint' by attacking the sin rather than the individual sinner, the scribal satire was normally an invective against a named living individual or group of individuals.[62] An important study of the political impact of this underground verse identifies the increase in the number and readership of these pieces (many containing uninhibited commentary on court scandals and unpopular ministers) as variously 'a crude adult education' and even 'as close to a mass media as early Stuart England ever achieved'.[63]

---

60 PRO, Kew, SP 12/273, 64; discussed in M. Lindsay Kaplan, *The Culture of Slander in Early Modern England* (Cambridge University Press, 1997), p. 24.
61 Alastair Bellany, 'A Poem on the Archbishop's Hearse: Puritanism, Libel and Sedition after the Hampton Court Conference', *Journal of British Studies* 34 (1995), 137–64.
62 For 'complaint' see John Peter, *Complaint and Satire in Early English Literature* (Oxford: Clarendon Press, 1956).
63 Thomas Cogswell, 'Underground Verse and the Transformation of Early Stuart Political Culture', in *Political Culture and Cultural Politics in Early Modern England: Essays Presented to*

There is much evidence to support this claim. So far there has been no attempt at a comprehensive study of this material or to enumerate the corpus of surviving topical satire from the period 1600–60.[64] Historians still routinely quote from Frederick W. Fairholt's *Poems and Songs relating to George Villiers, Duke of Buckingham; and his Assassination by John Felton* which appeared as long ago as 1850. But much can be learned from its more closely studied successors of the succeeding half-century. The seven-volume Yale *Poems on Affairs of State 1660–1714* presents a selection of political poems from both manuscript and printed sources, annotated and carefully placed in their historical contexts. The earlier part of the seventeenth century could easily support at least as impressive a collection. That the sources for this body of verse have been less studied for the earlier than for the later period may be the consequence of a relative absence of contributions from the major poets of the age, whereas Rochester, after 1660, was the very model of a scribally publishing 'Libellor'.[65] Thus Peter Beal's listings for Restoration poets in his *Index of English Literary Manuscripts* include many more collections devoted to topical satire than do his entries for Donne and his contemporaries.[66]

The poetic forms employed in the libel (as we will call it for convenience) were generally straightforward, requiring no great literary sophistication. The most common kind is written in stanzas to some well-known broadside ballad tune. (The shape of the stanza will often reveal the intended melody even when this is not declared in the title.) This form was frequently used to pick off a different victim in each stanza, a subgenre sometimes described as the 'shotgun' libel, though its method is closer to that of a sniper despatching target after target in succession. Alternatively, different aspects of a single target might be explored in successive stanzas or a narrative pursued. In all these respects the stanzaic libel reveals its affinities with abusive folk libels, which mostly take the form of a string of crude verses directed at an unpopular authority figure or figures

---

David Underdown, ed. Susan D. Amussen and Mark A. Kishlansky (Manchester University Press, 1995), pp. 278, 287.

64 However, Andrew McRae has commenced such a study. See his 'Renaissance Satire and the Popular Voice', in *Imperfect Apprehensions: Essays in English Literature in Honour of G. A. Wilkes*, ed. Geoffrey Little (Sydney University Press, 1996), pp. 5–17; also the valuable specialised studies by Alastair Bellany, Thomas Cogswell ('Underground Verse'), Pauline Croft, Adam Fox (n. 67 below) and Timothy Raylor listed in the Bibliography.

65 See in particular his verse duels with Mulgrave and Scroope in *The Works of John Wilmot, Earl of Rochester*, ed. Harold Love (Oxford: Clarendon Press, 1999), pp. 92–108.

66 It must also be acknowledged that there has been no single enthusiast corresponding to James M. Osborn, who assembled the enormous collection of manuscripts of post-1660 state satire and libertine verse now at the Beinecke Library, Yale, and was the initiator of the Yale University Press series.

in a village or small town. We know about the circumstances of composition of several of these pieces because they were narrated in the records of court cases for slander, which sometimes also contain texts.[67] The same form in the hands of a Suckling or some competent Inns of Court versifier was obviously going to be a much more polished production, but as long as it was written to a broadside ballad tune it still acknowledged its popular roots.

Another predominant form of satire was written in pentameter or tetrameter couplets and divided irregularly into paragraphs. While methods of development vary, such a piece will often follow a perfunctory introduction with a series of epigram-like attacks. Here folk influences are supplemented by those of the classical satire and epigram, in some cases as mediated through the experiments of Donne, Hall and Marston. The classicising satirists of the 1590s had also established a concept of satire as abstruse in its vocabulary and harsh in its rhythms. This was not on the whole to prove a lasting influence on the libel, though elements of it survive in Cleveland. It is often difficult to tell whether roughness of rhythm and oddities of language in a scribally circulated libel arise from the demotic, colloquial roots of the genre or are a conscious tribute to the 'satyr-satirist' of the 1590s. Some such features must also result from the compromised textual condition of the surviving sources of these much-copied texts.

Libels also appear in the form of acrostics, characters, emblems, mock epitaphs, railings, epistles, dialogues and parodies of all kinds. The sung stanzaic genre is particularly fruitful in parodies since it was already the practice for the standard broadside melodies to be supplied over and over again with new words.[68] As with the lyric, a pattern of poem and answer-poem is frequent, the two (or more in longer series) often circulating as a single work. In the tradition of Dunbar and Skelton, a poem of pure personal invective may be directed in the second person as though its victim were actually present. One subgenre allowed a text to be read with two opposed meanings, either by ambiguous punctuation or by lining up the stanzas in two parallel columns which could be read either horizontally or vertically. An immediately apparent aspect of the libel is its sexual grossness. In libels directed at Buckingham in the period of the proposed Spanish marriage for the future Charles I, innocent friendships become torrid love affairs and political opponents are graphically characterised as

---

67 See Adam Fox, 'Ballads, Libels and Popular Ridicule in Jacobean England', *Past and Present* 145 (1994), 47–83, and Love, *Scribal Publication*, pp. 232–4.
68 Here Claude M. Simpson's *The British Broadside Ballad and its Music* (New Brunswick, NJ: Rutgers University Press, 1966) is an indispensable resource.

adulterers, cuckolds and sodomites.[69] These squibs undoubtedly struck home, and late in 1622 Buckingham offered a £1,000 reward for the identity of the author of one song.

Much satire was addressed to specialised audiences or communities, though it would frequently migrate beyond these. Erudite libels (often in Latin) were written for dons; anti-Popish and anti-prelatical libels for Puritans; and anti-Protestant libels for Catholics. Inns of Court satire numbered the court among its targets, as the (non-topical) work of Donne and Sir John Davies shows: it is also likely that much satire on state themes originated at the Inns. At court we may assume that much transmission took the form of the passing of separates from hand to hand during tedious periods of 'waiting'. Since much court satire was factional in origin, a new libel would often be dropped in places of assembly or posted up in some prominent place. In iv. i of *Valentinian*, Fletcher introduces a letter 'Scatter'd belike i'th Court' into his ancient Roman setting where it is an obvious anachronism. Archbishop Laud noted in 1641 that libels were 'continually set up in all places in the city'.[70] Among the wider circle of educated metropolitan readers, we have references to the reading of verse over or after dinner: John Hoskyns composed one famous example for a meeting of the wits at the Mermaid, while Ben Jonson mentions the practice in poems to Camden and Lady Digby. On one occasion when Jonson was the guest of Sir Robert Cotton, the poem read was a libel praising Felton, Buckingham's assassin.[71] This episode links the transmission of contemporary libels to that of antiquarian manuscripts, of which Cotton was a famous accumulator. Antiquarian historical scholarship as practised by Cotton was highly politicised, since his collections were regularly quarried for legal and parliamentary precedents which could be used to embarrass the crown or a rival officeholder. This activity became so provocative that in 1629 Charles I seized the collection. Cotton's own historico-political essays, later printed in *Cottoni posthuma* (1651), had already by that date been widely distributed in manuscript.

Libels (usually town productions) travelled regularly to the shires, sometimes by the still primitive mail services or the carrier's cart but probably more often in the pockets of masters or their trusted servants moving between a family's London and country houses. From the latter they would move into

---

69 Thomas Cogswell, 'England and the Spanish Match', in *Conflict in Early Stuart England: Studies in Religion and Politics, 1603–1642*, ed. Richard Cust and Ann Hughes (London and New York: Longman, 1989), pp. 124–5.

70 Cogswell, 'Underground Verse', p. 288.

71 Kevin Sharpe, *Sir Robert Cotton 1586–1631: History and Politics in Early Modern England* (Oxford University Press, 1979), p. 212.

transmission through local networks already established for the exchange of other kinds of manuscripts and of correspondence.[72] Much still remains to be discovered about the geography of such transmissions. The simultaneous existence of regional, familial and wider-ranging interest-based networks of exchange, all frequently overlapping with one another, meant that texts could travel with astonishing speed throughout the country. A libel might travel from one antiquarian to another with the transcript of a charter, or from one collector of viol music to another with a new fantasy by Coprario or Jenkins. Writers of newsletters were particularly important for the circulation of libels. We have no clear evidence as yet for the commercial copying and sale of libels which is such a feature of textual circulation in general between the late 1670s and 1700. However, the scriptoria which later produced so many copies of parliamentary proceedings or which dealt in forbidden prose texts such as Thomas Scott's *Vox populi* (1620) were so well adapted to turn to libels in slack times that it seems unlikely that there was not an unofficial trade in such highly sought-after documents.

The material vehicles of these texts were the same as those of other forms of scribally transmitted verse. After circulating orally, as separates or as posted notices, they would be transcribed either in 'linked groups' of verse on a common theme, or into larger collections: the personal miscellany or the scribal anthology. In the miscellany they would take their place in the manner previously described, alongside whatever other materials interested their owners. The Burghe Manuscript, mentioned earlier, is an example which mingled satirical material with lyrics and occasional verse of various kinds. The scribal anthology might devote itself entirely to a single genre. When that genre was satire, these were dangerous books to possess, and it is likely that many were deliberately destroyed during the Civil Wars, and others after the deaths of their original compilers.

The oral transmission of verse libels has been documented in connection with the folk libel, which was generally sung. Other sung libels are also likely to have been transmitted memorially. In 1655 Robert Overton, the radical military leader, was caught in possession of a libel against Cromwell. Overton's servant revealed that his master had copied the verses down after 'hearinge a fidler's boy singe them'. Timothy Raylor notes that 'Differences between it and the version later published in *Cleaveland Revived* suggest the possibility that distinct versions of the poem were in circulation, one for singing and one for

---

72 Love, *Scribal Publication*, pp. 177–230; Woudhuysen, *Sidney and the Circulation of Manuscripts*, passim; and the articles by Cust and Levy, cited in n. 43, above.

reading . . . While the former is written in a rollicking ballad meter, suitable for singing, the latter adopts a more stately iambic form.'[73]

The sense of a change in the very nature of political culture brought about by the explosive growth in the writing and discussion of such material was widespread. The Elizabethans had been familiar with satire as a genre, at least in its classical or neo-classical form and in the demotic insult poetry of their own day. The licensed fool kept in many households as late as 1600 enjoyed a fairly complete liberty of jeering. The medieval flyting in which two partici-pants competed in invective still had occasional successors, while academic and Inns of Court life sustained a culture of disputation and declamation which was also hospitable to outrageous travesties, such as the Latin speeches of the Oxford *terrae filii*.[74] But personal invectives of this kind, often associated with seasonal festivities, did not give rise to social anxiety because they were seen as communally contained. Only the dissident productions of militant Catholics on one side and the more extreme Puritans on the other gave any real cause for concern. Since it was hard to disguise one's membership of these communities and even possession of such a text might be judged treasonous, fear inhibited their free circulation. Exceptional public outbreaks of abuse in print such as the Nashe–Harvey controversy and the satires of Hall and Marston could easily be dealt with through the recognised disciplines of church and state: we have no evidence of any surreptitious reprintings of these books or of manuscript trans-mission after they ceased to be available. Yet, from the 1590s onward, with the appearance and wide circulation of manuscript libels directed at leading figures in the state, we become aware of a generational gap: texts that delighted many of the young were resented and deeply distrusted by most of their elders.

An early example, which may well be the crucial one, was the body of libels that appeared following the death of Robert Cecil, Earl of Salisbury, in 1612. Pauline Croft's study of the attacks (chiefly in manuscript) and the defences (chiefly in print) to which Cecil's reputation was subject points to the aston-ishing power of the verse libel to influence public opinion. Cecil had been a loyal servant to Elizabeth and James; he had done much good work in reform-ing the royal finances; and, apart from being an enthusiastic encloser, he was not excessive, for his time, in his rapacity. Many of the policies for which he was blamed were the King's, not his own. Some had been adopted against his

---

73 Timothy Raylor, *Cavaliers, Clubs, and Literary Culture: Sir John Mennes, James Smith, and the Order of the Fancy* (Cranbury, NJ, and London: Associated University Presses, 1994), pp. 205, 290.

74 For flytings see Douglas Gray, 'Rough Music: Some Early Invectives and Flytings', *Yearbook of English Studies* 14 (1984), 21–43.

advice, though, once they were adopted, like a good civil servant, he considered himself obliged to implement them as effectively as possible. That he had assisted in bringing down the popular Earl of Essex made him many enemies; but even these, if pressed, would have conceded that the abortive rebellion of 1601 was an act of sublime political folly. Little of this was of interest to the anonymous libellers, however. To them Cecil was simply an embodiment of every aspect of royal policy which they disliked. From this they created an image of the archetypal disloyal statesman, diminutive and misshapen (he had a spinal deformity), ruthless in sacrificing others, insatiate in his greed, a betrayer of his country and, needless to say, consumed by the pox (his actual ailments seem to have been scurvy and cancer). His friendships with the Countess of Suffolk and Lady Walsingham were represented as lustful depravity. This image, which is illustrated by Croft with extensive quotations from the libellers, took such a powerful hold that it could be dusted off and revived almost without alteration for representations of the first Earl of Shaftesbury in the 1670s. Those who knew and admired Cecil were shocked by the attacks of the libellers but could do little to soften them, any more than they could with numerous libels later directed at Northampton, Somerset, Buckingham, Strafford and Laud. There was a disturbing awareness that the terms of public discourse had changed in a way that pointed towards wider kinds of disruption. These were not to be long coming. The Civil Wars were being fought through the quill long before the first cannons barked at Edgehill.

Chapter 3

PRINT, LITERARY CULTURE AND
THE BOOK TRADE

DAVID SCOTT KASTAN

The advent of printing in England

In Shakespeare's 2 *Henry VI*, the rebel Jack Cade orders Lord Saye to be beheaded on the anachronistic grounds that he had 'caused printing to be used' and had 'built a paper mill' (4.7.30–3). William Caxton would not in fact set up the first printing press in England until 1476, some twenty-six years after the encounter the play represents, and still another twenty years would pass before John Tate would establish the first paper mill on English soil. Yet if Cade is an unreliable historian as he seeks a justification for his reflexive opposition to authority and order, he correctly intuits that print would have a profound effect upon the social life of England.

Certainly it could be claimed that print was one of those inventions that, in Bacon's famous phrase, 'changed the fate and the state of things in all the world',[1] although it did not work quite as bluntly as Jack Cade feared to secure aristocratic power and privilege. Its effects were unpredictable and slow to be felt at first, and few in the first decades of printing could have sensed its eventual impact. Initially it was little more than an improved means of textual reproduction, a technique of 'artificial writing' that served as a faster, cheaper way of producing multiple copies of the texts that had previously circulated in manuscript. Indeed early printed books tried very hard to reproduce the form and feel of manuscripts (typefaces, for example, mimicking the popular forms of script), though, of course, their ability to do so did not bring the age of manuscript production to an end. Well into the seventeenth century and beyond, professionally handwritten texts continued to be produced and desired; print and manuscript circulated alongside one another, sometimes in the very

---

1 Francis Bacon, *Novum Organum*, Aphorism 129, trans. G. W. Kitchin (Oxford University Press, 1855), p. 110.

same book.[2] By the middle of the sixteenth century, however, printed books had established themselves as the primary form in which readers encountered the written word, and the very scale of textual production that printing thereby enabled made it clear that print marked a revolution in information technology and not a mere refinement of the existing one.

It is in that sense that it is perhaps fair to consider print as 'an agent of change', in Elizabeth Eisenstein's now famous phrase.[3] The extraordinary productivity of print – by 1500, already about 20 million individual books had been produced in the almost 300 European cities and towns that had presses[4] – meant that written material was now available in hitherto unimaginable quantities and circulating into hitherto unreachable segments of the social world. Where, previously, desiring readers had to find books, books, it could be said, now found (and even made) readers, and their widespread availability did have significant social as well as psychological consequences.

Yet we must be careful not to embrace an unconsidered technological determinism as we consider the impact of print. Too easily the new technology has been accorded a power of its own to produce powerful social effects, as though the agency rested mainly in the technology rather than its products and its users. If print could function, as Cade apprehended, to reinforce pre-existent forms of power, it also allowed, as Henry VIII would fear (especially as he resisted the spread of an English Bible), those forms to be subjected to a previously unknown public scrutiny. Even as print came to serve the interests of authority, it equally came to serve the interests of those who would resist that authority, allowing dissident ideas to circulate and coalesce, in many cases allowing new communities to form through the lineaments of a book trade. And of course print functioned in more immediate and obvious ways to circulate news and information, rumours and lies, history and fiction, works of controversy and the Scriptures themselves. Thus it brought about various, unpredictable and often

---

2 On the continuity of manuscript circulation, see Harold Love, *Scribal Publication in Seventeenth-Century England* (Oxford: Clarendon Press, 1993). See also Love and Arthur F. Marotti, 'Manuscript Transmission and Circulation' in this volume, pp. 55–80.

3 Elizabeth L. Eisenstein, *The Printing Press as an Agent of Change*, 2 vols. (Cambridge University Press, 1979). It is, however, important to register Eisenstein's own insistence that she regards 'printing as an agent, not the agent, let alone the only agent, of change in Western Europe'; see her redaction of the earlier book, *The Printing Revolution in Early Modern Europe* (Cambridge University Press, 1983), p. xiii. For a powerful critique of Eisenstein, though one focused mainly on the second half of the seventeenth century, see Adrian Johns, *The Nature of the Book: Print and Knowledge in the Making* (University of Chicago Press, 1998); see also Anthony Grafton's review of Eisenstein, 'The Importance of Being Printed', *Journal of Interdisciplinary History* 11 (1980), 265–86.

4 Antonia McLean, *Humanism and the Rise of Science in Tudor England* (London: Heinemann, 1972), p. 14.

contradictory effects – consequences, surely, more of the uses to which it was put than of the techniques of its production.

It is, however, worth pausing to consider exactly what those techniques were. Johann Gutenberg's invention of the printing press is usually recognised as the motor of the last major revolution in information technology before the computer age, although it was not the press itself that brought about the changes that print would encourage. The press, in truth, merely adapted a pre-existent tool to a new form of manufacture. Wine and olive screw-presses, like the linen press, had made use of the same essential mechanism and had been in use for hundreds of years. What Gutenberg may have invented, however, was a means of enabling the mass production of reusable, movable type (letter forms produced from an individual cast, each piece standing on a shank of identical length).[5] Before the availability of movable type, books could be printed but would have to be set page by page from engraved blocks cut from wood or metal. Such blocks, of course, would be reusable only for the particular page of the particular book to be printed; but movable type allowed printers to set any text, combining the letter forms into whatever composition was required.

Nonetheless, even this innovation would have had little effect upon the reproduction and circulation of texts without the availability of a large paper supply on which to print them.[6] Vellum or parchment, the scraped and softened animal skins on which most writing had previously been preserved, was both slow to prepare and expensive. A large book on vellum might require the skins of over 300 sheep; but paper could be produced relatively cheaply from pulped rags, and its availability in virtually unlimited quantity was critical to the spread of commercial printing. The need for a substitute for parchment intensified with print, since on average about 1,000 sheets per day could be printed on a single press.[7] Inks, too, needed to be developed for the new technology. Inks, of course, existed before printing, but new ones were now needed to adhere to

5 For a concise account of the techniques involved, see Philip Gaskell, *A New Introduction to Bibliography*, rev. edn (Oxford University Press, 1974), pp. 9–12. Recent discoveries by Paul Needham and Blaise Aguera y Arcas, however, suggest that Gutenberg may not have invented interchangeable, movable type. See Dinitia Smith, 'Has History Been Too Generous to Gutenberg?', *New York Times*, 27 January 2001:B9.

6 Mark Bland estimates that by 1600 'printing-house activity in England probably used six million sheets of paper a year'. See his 'The London Book-Trade in 1600', in *A Companion to Shakespeare*, ed. David Scott Kastan (Oxford: Blackwell, 1999), p. 460. See also Graham Pollard, 'Notes on the Size of the Sheet', *The Library* 4th ser. 22 (1941), 105–37.

7 For an example of the variability and scale of press-work at Cambridge, see D. F. McKenzie, 'Printers of the Mind: Some Notes on Bibliographical Theories and Printing-House Practices', *Studies in Bibliography* 22 (1969), 1–75.

the metal types and stand up to the process of producing thousands of printed copies.

The 'invention' of printing, then, was in reality an adaptation and synthesis of a variety of different tools, techniques and materials that made possible a previously unimaginable level of efficiency in the mechanical reproduction of texts. What would have taken scribes years to produce could be accomplished in a matter of weeks. Printing allowed books to become a means of mass communication, and within a few decades of Gutenberg's establishment of a printing house in Mainz in the early 1450s presses were in operation in almost every country in Europe.

The English book trade, it must be said, was not in the vanguard in embracing the new technology. Over twenty years would pass before William Caxton established his printing house in 1476 in the abbey precincts at Westminster. Printed books, however, had already reached English shores, the first apparently arriving when James Goldwell, Dean of Salisbury, returned with a copy of Durandus's *Rationale divinorum officiarum* from a diplomatic mission to Hamburg in 1465; and a second two years later, when John Russell, Archdeacon of Berkshire, brought home an edition of Cicero's *De Officiis* and *Paradoxa* from Bruges, where he had travelled as one of a group representing Edward IV to the Duke of Burgundy. Printed books also were sent from the continent to English readers: for example, the two Latin Bibles that the Earl of Worcester, John Tiptoft, received from Cologne in 1468, or the printed copy of Cardinal Bessarion's *Orationes* that Edward IV received in 1472.[8]

But it was Caxton himself who first targeted in England an audience for printed books that was broader than a few isolated, aristocratic readers. While still at work in the Netherlands, Caxton published Raoul Le Fèvre's *The Recuyell of the Histories of Troy* (1475?), the first printed book in the English language. As Caxton said in the prologue, copies were in demand by many readers and the book was, therefore, 'not wreton with penne and ynke as bokes ben', but printed 'to thende that euery man may haue them attones'.[9] The book, Caxton's own translation from the French, was intended primarily for sale to the English Burgundian colony but also, no doubt, for import across the Channel; and an

---

8 See Margaret Lane Ford, 'Importation of Printed Books into England and Scotland', in *The Cambridge History of the Book in Britain: Volume 3, 1400–1557*, ed. Lotte Hellinga and J. B. Trapp (Cambridge University Press, 1999), pp. 179–201; and Elizabeth Armstrong, 'English Purchases of Printed Books from the Continent 1465–1526', *English Historical Review* 94 (1979), 268–90. See also Nelly J. M. Kerling, 'Caxton and the Trade in Printed Books', *Book Collector* 4 (1955), 190–9.

9 *The Prologues and Epilogues of William Caxton*, ed. W. J. B. Crotch, Early English Text Society, orig. ser., 176 (London: H. Milford/Oxford University Press for EETS, 1928), p. 7.

active import business remained part of Caxton's activity in the book trade even after he moved his printing house to English soil.[10] As the demand for printed books gradually increased, printers other than Caxton recognised the commercial opportunities that existed in England. Caxton's arrival in London was soon followed by Theodoric Rood's in Oxford, where he operated a press between 1478 and 1485 (Rood's edition of Rufinus's *Exposicio Sancti Hieronomi Apostolurum* misprinted the 1478 date as MCCCCLXVIII, giving rise to a tenacious story of English printing's introduction in Oxford rather than at Westminster); and a press was established about the same time at the Abbey of St Albans in Hertfordshire. Johannes Lettau (probably, as his name suggests, a Lithuanian) printed several books and a number of indulgences in London in 1480; and he soon was joined by William de Machlinia (i.e., of Malines in Flanders), the two men printing law books until Lettau's retirement probably sometime in 1483. Machlinia continued to print in various London locations until about 1490, when his business apparently passed to Richard Pynson, who had come to London from Normandy. Pynson established a successful business mainly printing legal documents and religious texts, first in a shop in the parish of St Clement Danes and later at the corner of Fleet Street and Chancery Lane, at the very centre of legal and governmental activity. In 1508, he was appointed printer to the King.

It would be some time, however, before the various printers working in England were themselves capable of meeting the growing requirements of English readers. In 1500 there were still only five printers working in England. The great majority of printed books, therefore, necessarily came from continental printing houses, and the trade in imported books was specifically protected by the government. In 1484, an act otherwise designed to limit the activities of foreign craftsmen and merchants, specifically exempted 'any Artificer or merchaunt straungier of what Nacion or Contrey he be or shalbe of' from any restriction on 'bryngyng into this Realme, or sellying by retaill or otherwise ... such bokes, as he hath or shall have to sell by wey of merchaundise'.[11] The following year, Peter Actors, born in Savoy and hence an 'alien' as the custom rolls term him, was appointed stationer to the King, with a 'licence to import, so often as he likes, from parts beyond the sea, books printed and not printed ... and to dispose of the same by sale or otherwise without

10 G. D. Painter, *William Caxton: a Quincentenary Biography of England's First Printer* (London: Chatto & Windus, 1976), pp. 59–64. On Caxton's imports, see Kerling, 'Caxton and Printed Books', esp. p. 197.

11 'An Act touching the Marchauntes of Italy' (1484), 1 Richard 111, c. 9; *Statutes of the Realm*, ed. A. Luders *et al.*, 10 vols. (London: G. Eyre and A. Strahan, 1810–28), 2:493.

paying customs etc. thereon and without rendering any accompt thereof' (and with the unfortunate result for later scholarship that most of his activities, therefore, have disappeared from the records).[12] From 1492, the likely year of Caxton's death, to 1534, the names of almost 100 agents appear in customs rolls, importers paying duty on books brought in from the continent. Most of these merchants were foreigners, like Henry Frankenbergh, a Dutchman, or the Parisian bookseller, Michael Morin; but native-born Londoners were also involved in the emerging trade in printed books. Richard Brent, Thomas Marbury and John Collins were among the Englishmen importing books, which almost always arrived from continental printing houses in barrels of unbound sheets that individual purchasers would then have bound according to their own requirements.[13]

Gradually, however, native printing houses (though not native printers: Caxton and Thomas Hood, who worked with Rood in Oxford, were the only early printers of English birth) would come to satisfy the bulk of the English market. Caxton printed about 100 editions of various books in his shop in Westminster, located there to capitalise upon both its proximity to the learned monks of the Abbey and his contacts at court. Most of his books were large folios: translations of Latin and European vernacular essays, histories, heraldic works and romances, as well as English texts, including the first printed edition of *The Canterbury Tales* (1477); though he also printed some 'small storyes and pamfletes' – as Robert Copland says in his preface to *Kynge Appolyn of Thyre* (1510) – and hand-sized, octavo devotionals. While Caxton no doubt hoped these smaller-formatted books would find a broad audience, the majority of his publications were targeted more selectively, like his edition of Cicero's *Of Olde Age* (1481), which he admits 'is not requysyte ne eke conuenyent for euery rude and symple man . . . but for noble, wyse, & grete lordes[,] gentilmen and marchau[n]tes that haue seen & dayly ben occupyed in maters towchyng the publyque weal'.[14]

In general, Caxton's books reflected his own sophisticated intellectual interests and the tastes and means of his noble patrons, but with his death and the passing of his business to his assistant, Wynken de Worde, a native of Alsace but a longtime resident of England, the English book trade began successfully

12 Quoted in E. Gordon Duff, *A Century of the English Book Trade* (London: The Bibliographical Society, 1905), p. xiii.
13 See C. Paul Christianson, 'The Rise of London's Book-trade', in *The Cambridge History of the Book in Britain: Volume III, 1400–1557*, ed. Hellinga and Trapp, pp. 141–3.
14 Caxton, *Prologues and Epilogues*, pp. 42–3. See also Seth Lerer's chapter, 'William Caxton', in *The Cambridge History of Medieval English Literature*, ed. David Wallace (Cambridge University Press, 1999), pp. 720–38.

to solicit a wider audience for its offerings. De Worde quickly recognised the commercial potential of less expensive books, and, most likely in response to his sense of who (and where) his customers were, in 1500 he moved his business from Caxton's shop in Westminster to London, establishing a shop in Fleet Street near St Bride's Church, and later adding a book stall in St Paul's churchyard. During his forty-year career, de Worde printed over 800 editions of more than 400 different titles, some numerous times, like the Latin grammar by Robert Whittinton, which itself went through 155 editions.[15] The few large folio volumes he printed were, for the most part, reprints of Caxton's books, but the majority of his printing was small, affordable editions of school books and liturgical texts (including a primer in 1523 that contained the first appearance in print of 'the Pater noster in englysshe'[16]).

If Caxton has been justly celebrated for bringing printing to England, de Worde should be better recognised for insuring its success. Caxton's business depended upon his contacts with an elite coterie of readers and the support of aristocratic patrons, and he alone, of the first generation of printers in England, thrived. De Worde, however, recognised the possibility of appealing to a broad reading public, and he provided easy access to books that both satisfied and expanded it. Grammar books, popular religious writing and contemporary literature (e.g., the poetry of John Skelton and Stephen Hawes, and even what may be the first printed play, the anonymous *Hyckescorner* published about 1515) were part of the new materials he made available in print.[17]

Just as important as his enlargement of the range of available texts, however, was his recognition of the need to change production practices. Some of these changes were motivated by financial considerations. De Worde, for example, was the first printer to use English-made paper, produced at John Tate's mill in Hertfordshire, no doubt allowing the publisher to save money by reducing the transportation costs. Caxton had imported his paper from the Low Countries. But Tate was the only English paper maker for the next half-century, and de Worde and later publishers would continue to purchase paper from the continent, usually from mills in Normandy. Indeed not until the 1670s

15 See H. S. Bennett, Appendix I, 'Handlist of the Publications of Wynken de Worde, 1492–1535', in *English Books and Readers 1475–1557*, 2nd edn (Cambridge University Press, 1969), pp. 239–76.

16 *Hore beatissime virginis Marie ad co[n]suetudinem insignis ecclesie Sar. Nuper emaculatissimi multis orationibus pulcherrimis* (London, 1523).

17 Three early printed playbooks exist, all published about the same time (1512–19): *Hykescorner*, published by de Worde; *Everyman*, published by Pynson; and *Fulgens and Lucrece*, published by John Rastell. See Greg Walker, *The Politics of Performance in Early Renaissance Drama* (Cambridge University Press, 1998), pp. 9–11.

would a native paper industry be able to supply the majority of English paper needs.[18]

De Worde, moreover, introduced technical innovations that affected the physical appearance of the book. Though sometime around 1482 de Machlinia printed the first book with a title page, de Worde was the first English-based printer to develop the title page as a marketing tool, elaborating the page to identify and promote the book.[19] He was the first to include a short description of the text (in 1493 for *The Chastysing of Goddes Chyldern*) and the first to make full use of illustrative material to identify the book's contents or author (for example the cut of Richard Rolle that appears in 1506 for an edition of *The Contemplations*). About 20 of Caxton's books had made use of woodcuts, but de Worde far more extensively included pictures or decorations on the pages he printed (some 500 of the books he printed are in some way illustrated), even if the quality of book decoration in England still lagged well behind continental standards.[20] De Worde was also the first to print musical notes (in 1495 in his edition of the *Polychronicon*), as well as the first to use an italic font (in 1528 in Lucian's *Complures Dialogi*). It is perhaps noteworthy as well that de Worde was also the first publisher to bring a claim of piracy against another publisher (against Peter Treveris for violating the privilege to print Whittinton's *Syntaxis*). Caxton was, of course, the originary figure in English printing history, and therefore his reputation has understandably eclipsed that of any of the other individuals active in the early days of printing in England. But de Worde's innovations, not least among them his acute measure of the variegated marketplace for print that existed, determined the direction of what would become a vibrant English book trade.

The triumph of the book

Nonetheless, it could not have been obvious in the early days of English printing that the book trade would develop as it did. As the new technology reached England, the universities, monasteries and cathedrals quickly set up presses to

---

18 See Richard Hills, *Papermaking in Britain, 1488–1988* (London: Athlone, 1988), esp. pp. 5–9 and 50–3. See, also, D. C. Coleman, *The British Paper Industry, 1495–1860: A Study in Industrial Growth* (Oxford University Press, 1958), esp. pp. 40–52.
19 Margaret M. Smith, *The Title-Page: Its Early Development, 1460–1510* (London: British Library, 2000).
20 See Henry Plomer, *Wynken de Worde and his Contemporaries from the Death of Caxton to 1535* (London: Grafton, 1925); and two essays by N. F. Blake: 'Wynken de Worde: the Early Years', *Gutenberg Jahrbuch* 46 (1971), 62–6, and 'Wynken de Worde: the Later Years', *Gutenberg Jahrbuch* 47 (1972), 128–38.

meet their own specialised needs, and the early domination of the literate segments of society by those institutions allowed these operations some initial success. But each lacked the concentration of skilled labour, capital and, arguably most importantly, access to the rapidly expanding literate markets necessary to become more than a small, specialised business; and the book trade ultimately consolidated in London, independent of any secular or clerical institution.

Although Oxford and Cambridge would always play a role in the production of English books (especially once the two University presses were established in the 1580s),[21] London became the vital centre of the English book trade. There it thrived in the hands of individual entrepreneurs, and the patterns of their activity in the early years established the direction it would in general follow for the future. From the first, its dominant characteristic was what John Feather has called 'the Englishness of English publishing', clearly not referring to the nationality of those active in the trade, but to its almost exclusive focus on English consumption rather than on international markets, with the result that most printing was of English books rather than of Latin texts that might have found a continental audience.[22]

While foreign artisans dominated the early years of the book trade, as the industry developed, the government increasingly worked to defend the interests of English tradesmen. In a series of regulatory statutes (in 1515, 1523 and 1529), it successively limited the number of foreigners that could be employed, prevented the ones already at work from opening new shops, and ordered them to take on only English apprentices.[23] In 1534, the government consolidated these various measures, formally repealing the permissive Act of 1484 that had exempted foreigners in the book trade from restrictions on their activities. The unusual privileges, once understood as necessary when 'there were but fewe bokes and fewe prynters within this Realme', were confidently rendered 'voyd and of none effect' by the new Act, as now 'there be within this Realme a great nombre connyng and expert in the seid science or craft of prynting'. Two new conditions were added: one, that no bound books could be imported or sold, and another, that no undenizened foreigner could sell printed books.[24] The

---

21 For the early history of printing at Oxford and Cambridge, see Harry Graham Carter, *A History of the Oxford University Press* (Oxford University Press, 1975); and David McKitterick, *A History of Cambridge University Press: Volume 1, Printing and the Book Trade in Cambridge, 1534–1698* (Cambridge University Press, 1992).
22 John Feather, *A History of British Publishing* (London and New York: Routledge, 1988), p. 12.
23 The statutes were 7 Henry VIII c. 5; 14 and 15 Henry VIII c. 2; and 21 Henry VIII c. 16. See the accounts in E. Gordon Duff, *The Printers, Stationers and Booksellers of Westminster and London from 1476 to 1535* (Cambridge University Press, 1906), pp. 236–7; and in Graham Pollard, 'The Company of Stationers before 1557', *The Library* 4th ser. 18 (1937), 23–4.
24 25 Henry VIII c. 15.

result was that the book trade passed firmly into the hands of English-born tradesmen or legally resident aliens.

Although to some degree the legislative involvement must be seen as of a piece with governmental economic policies designed to protect other forms of domestic manufacture, the Crown clearly had an unusual interest in the book trade, recognising in the unregulated circulation of printed materials a particular threat to its security. The government's actions, therefore, were not solely conceived as protection for native artisans and merchants, but were also designed to allow it to exert some control over the industry that was forming. As early as 1524, booksellers in London were forbidden by Cardinal Wolsey from trading in books that promoted Lutheranism, and ordered to obtain ecclesiastical approval for all imported books offered for sale. A year later the restrictions were extended to include a provision that no new book could be printed without prior approval.[25]

As the religio-political conflicts of Henry's reign intensified, government concern over the role of the press deepened. In 1529, a new proclamation was issued prohibiting the import, sale or possession of 'any book or work printed or written, which is made or hereafter shall be made against the faith Catholic, or against the holy decrees, laws, and ordinances of Holy Church, or in reproach, rebuke, or slander of the King, his honourable council, or his lords spiritual or temporal', and listing fifteen books that were specifically prohibited from being sold, received or kept, including several volumes of Tyndale's translations of the Bible into English.[26] In 1530, further efforts were made to prevent the dissemination of 'blasphemous and pestiferous English books, printed in other regions and sent into this realm', decreeing that subjects were not to 'buy, receive, or have' any 'erroneous books' and ordering that no book in English 'concerning Holy Scripture' be printed 'until such time as the same book or books be examined and approved by the ordinary of the diocese where the said books shall be printed'.[27]

From the government's perspective, undoubtedly the most 'pestiferous' of the English books were the copies of William Tyndale's translation of the New Testament, which had begun circulating in England shortly after the first edition was printed in Germany in 1526. Within ten years, over 60,000 copies of

---

25 Arthur W. Reed, 'The Regulation of the Book Trade Before the Proclamation of 1538', *Transactions of the Bibliographical Society* 15 (1919), 162–3.

26 *Tudor Royal Proclamations*, ed. Paul L. Hughes and James F. Larkin, 2 vols. (New Haven, CT, and London: Yale University Press, 1964–9), 1:185–6.

27 *Ibid.*, 1:194–5.

Tyndale's translation had been printed and secretly imported.[28] Although an English Bible seemingly was an inevitable response to the *sola scriptura* theme of early Protestantism, Tyndale's New Testament was aggressively condemned by the government that had not yet broken with the Church of Rome. King Henry himself criticised the translation and 'determyned the sayde corrupte and vntrue translatyons to be brenned, with further sharpe correction & punysshment against the kepars and reders of ye same'.[29] Bishop Cuthbert Tunstall ordered the dioceses of London, Middlesex, Essex and Colchester to 'bring in and [readily] deliver unto our vicar-general, all and singular such books as contain the translation of the new testament in the English tongue'.[30] Hundreds of people were interrogated, many were tried for heresy for possessing the translated Testament, some indeed burned (as was Richard Bayfield in 1532); and the prohibited books were sought out, confiscated and many destroyed.

Only three copies of the 1526 edition have survived,[31] though it is unclear whether the disappearance of the edition testifies more to the success of the censorship or to the enthusiasm with which the book was read. The government tried to prevent the circulation of the translated Bible, but the unauthorised Scripture was readily available, provoking Bishop Richard Nix of Norwich to conclude anxiously: 'It passeth my power, or that of any spiritual man, to hinder it now, and if this continue much longer, it will undo us all.'[32] Whether or not the political nation was in any sense undone by the spread of vernacular Scripture, certainly the English Bible promoted the spread of literacy, creating a nation of readers and interpreters that did successfully resist the monopoly on scriptural interpretation claimed by church and state.

28 See J. F. Davis, 'Lollardy and the Reformation in England', *Archiv für Reformationsgeschichte* 73 (1982), 230. It was, however, in 'pirated' editions that it usually reached England, mainly published in Antwerp by Christopher and, later, Catharine van Endoven. See David Scott Kastan, '"The Noise of the New Bible": Reform and Reaction in Henrician England', in *Religion and Culture in Renaissance England*, ed. Claire McEachern and Debora Shuger (Cambridge University Press, 1997), pp. 46–68; and for a collection of essays exploring the early printing of the Bible, see Paul Saenger and Kimberley Van Kampen (eds.), *The Bible as Book: the First Printed Editions* (London: The British Library, 1999).

29 *A copy of the letters, wherin the most redouted & mighty prince our souerayne lorde kyng Henry the eight . . . made answere vnto a certayne letter of Martyn Luther* (London, 1527), sigs. A6r–v.

30 John Foxe, *Acts and Monuments of John Foxe*, ed. Stephen Reed Cattley, 8 vols. (London: R. B. Seeley and W. Burnside, 1837–41), 4:667. 'Readily' reads in this edition 'really'.

31 One of the surviving copies, lacking only its title page, was owned by Bristol Baptist College and was purchased in 1994 by the British Library; another, missing seventy-one leaves, is in the library of St Paul's Cathedral; the third, complete with title page, was found in 1998 in the Würtembergische Landesbibliothek in Stuttgart, Germany.

32 Quoted in H. S. Bennett, *English Books and Readers 1475–1557*, p. 34.

The incontrovertible evidence of the popularity of the heretical publications finally led some in authority to suggest another tack. If unauthorised translation could not be prevented from reaching England, England could authorise a translation. Thomas Cranmer energetically urged an English Bible, succeeding in December 1534 in getting the synod of Canterbury to petition the King for such a translation. Sections of the Bible were then assigned 'vnto the best lernyd Bisshops, and other lernyd men', but the project foundered, as many refused to participate. The Bishop of London, John Stokesley, protested: 'I maruaile what my Lord of Canterbury meaneth, that thus abusethe the people gyving them libertie to reade the scriptures, which doith nothing els but infect them with herysis, I haue bestowed neuer an howre apon my portion nor neuer will.'[33] Others resisted less confrontationally, claiming to be too busy to complete their assigned portion or arguing over insignificant details. Eventually Cranmer realised his project would fail, and he urged the licensing of John Rogers's so-called Matthew Bible, 'until such time as we Bishops shall set forth a better translation, which I think will not be till a day after doomsday'.[34]

The Matthew Bible appeared in 1537, but even before the large folio reached print, another English Bible was published. In 1535, Miles Coverdale's version appeared, the first complete Bible in English and tactfully dedicated to the King. The authorities allowed this Bible to 'go forth under the King's privilege', as indeed they permitted the Matthew Bible to be published by Richard Grafton and Edward Whitchurch with the King's 'most gracyous lyce[n]ce'.[35] Certainly the two licences owed as much to Cromwell's committed evangelism as to any real enthusiasm on the part of the King; though, after his break with Rome in 1533, Henry may well have recognised that an English Bible would help establish the newly asserted royal supremacy. Although the King was willing to have the Bible published, neither edition was printed in England; Coverdale's was most likely printed in Germany, probably in Cologne or Marburg, and Rogers's in the Netherlands, probably in Antwerp at the press of Matthew Crom.

The English editions were printed abroad rather than at home, in part because orders drawn up by the clergy at Oxford in 1408–9 and at Canterbury in 1409

---

33 Quoted in Alfred W. Pollard (ed.), *Records of the English Bible* (London: Oxford University Press, 1911), pp. 196, 197.
34 J. E. Cox (ed.), *Miscellaneous Writings and Letters of Thomas Cranmer*, Parker Society, vol. 16 (Cambridge University Press, 1846), p. 344.
35 The Coverdale privilege is mentioned by a Southwark printer, James Nicholson, in a letter to Cromwell; see *Letters and Papers, Foreign and Domestic, of the Reign of Henry VIII*, comp. and arr. James Gairdner, vol. 9 (London: Her Majesty's Stationers' Office, 1886), p. 75; Cranmer, *Miscellaneous Writings*, p. 346.

(and confirmed by Parliament in 1414), banning scriptural translation into English, remained in force, but perhaps more because English printing, not least because of the exclusion of foreign tradesmen, was not yet as refined as was continental practice.[36] Thus in 1538 when Richard Grafton and Edward Whitchurch were arranging for the printing of the Great Bible (so-called because of its size), this edition fully authorised by governmental authorities and ordered to be 'set up in some convenient place' in the parish churches, they again looked abroad, this time to Paris and the presses of François Regnault.[37] Printing of this Bible began early in 1538, with Grafton and Whitchurch in attendance, but Regnault was interrupted by 'the inquisitors of the faith', who confiscated the printed sheets, as Foxe reports. Grafton and Whitchurch fled back to England. Later, with Cromwell's help, they returned to France and 'got the presses, letters, and servants of the aforesaid printer, and brought them to London', where in the precinct of the Grey Friars, they 'became printers themselves (which before they never intended) and printed out the said Bible'.[38]

The vicissitudes of the Great Bible were only a more extreme example of the hazards in undertaking any large publishing project. While working on the Matthew Bible, Grafton had successfully argued for an exclusive privilege of publication to insure he could recover the considerable production costs, and he and Whitchurch also held a monopoly on the publication of the Great Bible, which, as it was reissued nine times within three years, proved an extremely lucrative project. This practice of short-term privileges granted by the crown served in lieu of a system of copyright to protect the investment of publishers.[39] The oldest surviving privileges from England are from Henry VIII to Richard Pynson, for two Latin sermons – one by Cuthbert Tunstall, Prebendary of York, and the other by Richard Pace, Dean of St Paul's – both of which Pynson printed

36 David Wilkins (ed.), *Concilia Magnae Brittaniae et Hiberniae* (London, 1737), 3:317; 2 Henry V I c. 7. In 1529, Thomas More sanctioned the suppression of the Tyndale Bible on the grounds 'that the clergy of this realm hath before this time by a construction provincial prohibited any book of scripture to be translated into the English tongue'. See *A Dialogue Concerning Heresies*, in *The Complete Works of St Thomas More*, vol. 6, part 1, ed. Thomas M. C. Lawler, Germain Marc'hadour and Richard C. Marius (New Haven, CT, and London: Yale University Press, 1981), p. 28.
37 For the order to place the Great Bible in parish churches, see Walter Howard Frere and W. M. Kennedy (eds.), *Visitation Articles and Injunctions of the Period of the Reformation* (London: Longmans, Green, 1910), 2:35–6. Foxe, *Acts and Monuments*, 5:411, says that the Great Bible was initially taken to France for printing because of the availability there of cheaper paper and better workmen.
38 Foxe, *Acts and Monuments*, 5:411.
39 For a full consideration of this practice, although in France, see Elizabeth Armstrong, *Before Copyright: The French Book-Privilege System, 1498–1526* (Cambridge University Press, 1990).

in November of 1518. The privileges themselves appear in the colophon: *Cum privilegio a rege indulto ne quis hanc orationem infra biennium in regno Angliae imprimat aut alibi impressam et importatam in eodem regno Angliae vendat* (With privilege granted by the King so no one may print this sermon within two years within the kingdom of England or sell it if printed elsewhere and imported). Others soon sought similar exclusive rights for their projects, and either petitioned for or purchased a monopoly for varying lengths of time. When, for example, Thomas Berthelet published Thomas Elyot's English–Latin dictionary in 1538, he was granted a six-year exclusive patent on the book, and it was printed, as its title-page announced, *Cum privilegio ad imprimendum solum*, the privileges defined, as would become common, for printing only and with no implication of any official approval of the text.[40] The most enterprising publishers sought privileges not merely for single titles but for whole classes of books. Richard Tottel, for example, in 1552 was granted a monopoly on the publication of common law books for seven years, as Grafton and Whitchurch in 1543 had been granted an exclusive patent on the liturgical books of the Sarum use and four years later would receive a seven-year privilege for the reformed service books which replaced the Sarum liturgy.

Most books, however, were not covered by any privilege or other forms of commercial protection. Publishers acquired copy and arranged for its printing. In the absence of a privilege, nothing prevented another publisher from reprinting a popular book, which could in fact be done more cheaply and with less risk than it was originally. Such poaching was common enough. In 1490 Pynson published an edition of Chaucer's *Canterbury Tales*, though it had twice been published by Caxton; and Pynson himself, after printing seven editions of Thomas Littleton's *Tenures*, objected to the intrusion into his domain by another publisher, Robert Redman, or, as Pynson disdainfully puns, 'more properly Rudeman, because among a thousand men you will not easily find one more unskillful'.[41] But Pynson's irritation reveals how little remedy was in fact available. Redman's editions of Littleton's *Tenures* were not in any sense illegal, and Pynson could do no more than re-issue his own edition and proclaim Redman's lesser competence.

Though Robert Copland complained in his preface to the second edition of William Neville's *Castell of Pleasure* (1530?) that in these times 'bokes be not

---

40 Scholars have argued about the precise meaning of the phrase, whether it means 'for printing only' or 'the exclusive right of printing'; see W. W. Greg's account of the problem: 'Ad Imprimendum Solum', in *Collected Papers*, ed. J. C. Maxwell (Oxford University Press, 1966), pp. 406–12.
41 *Lytlytons Tenures Newly and Most Truly Correctyd and Amendyd* (London, 1525), sig. A1v.

set by',[42] in truth the demand for books was rapidly growing, and publishers energetically sought to satisfy it. Literacy was clearly on the rise, encouraged not least by the increasing availability of things to read. If Rastell's enthusiastic claim that 'the vnyuersall people of this realm had greate pleasure and gaue themself greatly to the redyng of the vulgare englysshe tonge' is certainly overstated,[43] Stephen Gardiner's assertion that the literate comprised 'not the hundredth part of the realme' is no less an exaggeration.[44] More than four times as many titles were printed in 1550 as in 1500, and the number of printers at work in London had grown proportionally, from five to more than twenty. In 1548, Philip Nicolls remarked on the 'nu[m]bre of bookes ther be abrode in euery ma[n]s hand of dyuers & sundry maters which are very gredely deuoured of a greate sort'.[45] Although it is impossible to calculate exactly how 'greate' was that sort, the evidence for a considerable reading public is unmistakable.[46]

Religious, homiletic, educational, legal, historical, scientific and even literary texts were published and were 'gredely deuoured' by eager readers. The market for books became both larger and more diverse, and popular texts went through multiple editions. Religious works made up about half of the output of printed books. Not merely Bibles, but liturgical, devotional, instructional and increasingly controversial books, were part of what was available for 'the gostly edifycacyon of all them that be, or entend to be, the spouses of our Redemour'.[47] But secular books, too, found a substantial audience. In many cases the interest was professional; books of statutes, abridgements of the laws, and the annual yearbooks of cases were in great demand by the growing numbers of lawyers, some 260 volumes of legal yearbooks, for example, having been published by 1557. Grammars were published for schoolboys, those by John Stanbridge and Robert Whittinton among the age's early best-sellers, until they were superseded by William Lily's in 1540, which itself went through more than fifty editions in the next hundred years. Dictionaries and collections of proverbs, adages and similes also found buyers among students and others who recognised the opportunities that now existed for those who could write with precision and grace. Additional kinds of self-help books were published:

---

42 Neville, *Castell of Pleasure*, 2nd edn (London, 1530?), sig. A2r.
43 *The Statutes Prohemium Johannis Rastell* (London, 1527), sig. A2r.
44 *The Letters of Stephen Gardiner*, ed. J. A. Muller (Cambridge University Press, 1933), p. 274.
45 Nicolls, *Here Begynneth a Godly Newe Story of .xii. Men That Moses Sent to spye Owt the Land of Cannan* (London, 1548), sig. A3v.
46 See Kenneth Charlton and Margaret Spufford, 'Literacy, Society and Education' in this volume, pp. 15–54.
47 William Bonde, *The Directory of Conscience* (London, 1527), sig. A2v.

books of natural history, like *The Grete Herball* (1525 and twice reprinted), not only described the various plants but indicated their medicinal properties; and other books offering compilations of practical information, like *The Treasure of Pore Men* (1526 and reprinted nine times by 1560) which gave the symptoms of various illnesses and prescribed appropriate remedies. History writing also found a substantial audience. Among the first books printed by Caxton were *The Chronicles of England* (1480), a translation of the *Brut*, an Anglo-French chronicle of Britain, beginning, as its name suggests, with its mythical founding by Brutus, a descendant of Aeneas, and carrying the history forward to the battle of Halidon Hill in 1333; and a translation of Ranulph Higden's *Polychronicon* (1482), a universal history in seven books starting with Adam and Eve and continuing to 1358, with Caxton himself adding an eighth book in his printed edition extending the history to 1460. Both Caxton publications went through multiple editions; by 1530, *The Chronicles* had been published thirteen times; the *Polychronicon* six. Works of history continued to be popular, as antiquarian, moral, theological and political interests motivated both their enthusiastic writing and their reading. Fabyan's *Chronicle*, first published posthumously in 1516, went through six more editions in the next fifty years and gave rise to the great chronicle tradition of Hall and Holinshed. Most readers, however, with neither the time nor the money for these massive folio volumes, would have encountered this history in the increasingly popular abridgements, of which Thomas Cooper's *Epitome of the Chronicles* (1549) was the first of many.

Most of what sold well was self-consciously devotional or instructional, but literary works began to appear, even as the category of literature began to consolidate itself. Chaucer and Lydgate were arguably the most popular of the published poets, and of the two, perhaps surprisingly, Lydgate the more. In the first half of the sixteenth century, over thirty editions of his works were printed as against some eighteen of Chaucer's. These two poets, in their remarkable visibility, came to represent the English literary past. Interestingly, where Gower and Hoccleve were seemingly their equals in popularity in the fifteenth century (some fifty manuscripts of Gower's work survive and almost the same number of Hoccleve's), only two printed editions of Gower appeared in the sixteenth century and none of Hoccleve. Lydgate and Chaucer, however, successfully made the transition into print, and not least because they were identifiable, or were at least identified, as the well from which English letters flowed. Chaucer, for example, was hailed by Caxton as the 'fader and founder' of the 'laureate scyence', and Lydgate is praised by Hawes as the 'most dulcet sprynge / Of famous rethoryke'.[48] Of contemporary poets, Skelton was the most popular in the early Tudor period, some fifteen editions of his poetry appearing by 1557; and to him goes the honour of being the first literary figure to write for the press, when de Worde published Skelton's *Bowge of Court* in 1499. De Worde's publishing was always with an eye to the developing market, and, while indeed publishing works clearly designed to appeal to sophisticated literary tastes, he also published works like *A Lytell Geste of Robin Hood* (first published by Pynson), knowing the popular ballad would please a less refined audience.

Publishers saw that the ever-expanding reading public was hardly monolithic. It had varying tastes and varying levels of cultural sophistication, and publishers provided books to satisfy the interests of all. Though hand illumination and fine binding still allowed a printed book to achieve an aura of preciousness not unlike a beautifully illuminated manuscript, books, by mid-century, had become familiar, mass-produced commodities, and publishing itself had largely become a commercial activity driven by the same risk-aversions and profit-motives as any other form of manufacture and merchandising.[49]

The consolidation of the book trade

The very success of the book trade demanded some effort to regulate its increasingly lucrative practices. With considerable income to be made from some titles, publishers understandably sought to defend their property. The system of privileges protected some publishers, of course, from opportunistic raiders who might otherwise profitably take over titles already in print (thus avoiding some of the financial risks of the first printing by choosing books whose audience was already proven and easing the complexities and expenses of production by setting them from printed copy for which no payment for rights had been made). Yet such monopolies produced resentment from others in the trade who claimed that privileges drove up the prices of the protected books and, no doubt more to the point, thought themselves unfairly excluded from access to valuable material and from the work it would provide. In order for

---

48 *The Book of Courtesye*, ed. F. J. Furnivall, Early English Text Society, orig. ser., 32 (London: M. Trübner for Early English Text Society, 1868), lines 330, 332; and Stephen Hawes, *The Pastyme of Pleasure*, ed. William Edward Mead, Early English Text Society, orig. ser., 173 (London: H. Milford for EETS, 1928), p. 5.

49 For a compelling account of the book as commodity in early modern Europe, see Lisa Jardine, *Worldly Goods: A New History of the Renaissance* (London: Macmillan, 1996), pp. 133–80.

the industry to expand in an orderly and efficient manner, some other form of regulation was necessary.

A craft guild of scriveners and illuminators had been in existence since the mid fourteenth century, and in the early fifteenth century they had re-formed to include both booksellers and bookbinders.[50] This informal guild regulated the production and sale of books in the City of London, but, even after print began to transform the book trade, the printers seem not to have been immediately included. Most were aliens and so technically ineligible; and those few English-born printers, like Caxton, were working outside of London and were thus free of the restrictions of the City. Gradually, however, it became obvious that printers must be allowed to join the guild, and by 1557 they were at the forefront of the organisation when Queen Mary and King Philip formalised its existence, granting a charter to ninety-seven men (thirty-three of whom were printers) who made up the 'Community of the mistery or art of Stationery of the City of London'.[51] A 'stationer', a term derived from the relatively permanent, or stationary, stall from which many early tradesmen, including booksellers, sold their wares, came to define all those involved in the book trade: publishers, printers, booksellers, binders, even clasp-makers. Some members of the guild fulfilled multiple roles in the trade, functioning, for example, as both publisher (the person who owns the copy and arranges for the printing) and printer (the person who owns the press and type and produces the printed pages), and sometimes even as the primary bookseller of a particular title. It was only in the late seventeenth century that 'stationer' assumed its modern meaning of a seller of writing materials.

The Company's rules brought some needed order to the book trade. It granted its members the authority to publish and regulated their activities. With a 'licence' from one or more of the Company's officers, a member established his right to publish a specific text. Before 1582, the fee for a licence was one penny for every three sheets; on 26 March 1582, the fee was set at fourpence for a ballad or pamphlet and sixpence for a book. After 1587, all publications were licensed at the higher fee. Having established rights to the copy and permission to print, a member might also pay, usually fourpence, to have his title entered in the Register in order to record his ownership. While

---

50 See Pollard, 'Company of Stationers', 5–9.
51 Edward Arber (ed.), *A Transcript of the Registers of the Company of Stationers of London 1554–1640*, 5 vols. (London and Birmingham: privately printed, 1875–94), 1: xxix. All subsequent references to the Registers will be cited parenthetically in the text. For the standard history of the Company, see Cyprian Blagden, *The Stationers' Company: A History 1403–1959* (London: Allen & Unwin, 1960).

such 'entrance' seems a wise policy, in practice many books – perhaps over a third of all that were published – were never formally registered, no doubt to save the expense of doing so. Registration offered a stationer extra protection for his copy but was not required by the Company; and unregistered books were not in themselves surreptitious or illegal publications.[52]

Before a book could be published, however, it had to be approved by some designated ecclesiastical or governmental authority. The policy dated back at least to 11 August 1549 when the Privy Council decreed that 'no prenter sholde prente or putt to vente any Englisshe booke butte suche as sholde first be examined by Mr Secretary Peter, Mr Secretary Smith, and Mr Cicill, or the one of them, and allowed by the same', but this order itself found precedent in Henry VIII's designation of responsibility for approving books for publication in England to 'some of his grace's Privy Council, or such as his highness shall appoint'.[53] This official 'allowance' was obviously different from the Company's 'licence', although, as the Company wardens might refuse a licence in the absence of proper allowance and issue a licence in the absence of an allowance if the book seemed sufficiently innocuous, the two at times served similar functions.[54] The Company's system of registration, however, mainly existed to protect individual stationers from infringements of their rights to particular titles, and, although it could be used to re-enforce the government's desires to control subversive printing, its primary purpose was to insure an orderly marketplace in the interest of its members.

The charter of the Stationers' Company granted its members a virtual monopoly over the printing and retailing of books within England. No one was permitted to print anything for sale unless 'the same person at the time of his foresaid printing is or shall be one of the community of the foresaid mistery or art of Stationery of the foresaid city, or has therefore licence of us, or the heirs and successors of us the foresaid Queen by letters patent of us, or the heirs and successors of us the foresaid Queen'. To defend their monopoly over all printing except that which was otherwise reserved by privilege, the Company was allowed 'to make search whenever it shall please them in any place, shop,

52 Peter W. M. Blayney, 'The Publication of Playbooks', in *A New History of Early English Drama*, ed. John F. Cox and David Scott Kastan (New York: Columbia University Press, 1997), pp. 400–4.

53 *Acts of the Privy Council of England*, ed. John Roche Dasent, new series (London: Eyre and Spottiswoode for HMSO, 1890–1907), 2:312; *Tudor Royal Proclamations*, ed. Hughes and Larkin, 1:271–2.

54 The standard account of the relevant regulations is in W. W. Greg, *Some Aspects and Problems of London Publishing between 1550 and 1650* (Oxford University Press, 1955); but see Blayney, 'The Publication of Playbooks', pp. 396–405.

house, chamber or building of any printer, binder or bookseller' for irregularly printed books and 'to seize, take, hold, burn, or turn to the proper use' all that had been printed 'contrary to the form of any statute, act, or proclamation made or to be made' (Arber, 1:xxxi).

No doubt the Crown's motive in allowing the incorporation of the Stationers was not merely to establish a well-regulated industry but also to shore up its own efforts to control sedition and heresy. For Queen Mary, the monopoly of the Stationers provided a 'suitable remedy' against the 'detestable heresies against the faith and sound Catholic doctrine of Holy Mother Church', which were circulating in print (Arber, 1:xxvii). In exchange for their right to restrict competition, reserving the economic benefits of the book trade for its members, the Stationers themselves would limit the spread of subversive materials. If this was not quite the same as turning the Stationers into an agent of government policy, it was a shrewd recognition of how their commercial interests might serve the political interests of the monarch.

The charter conferred upon the Stationers rights to regulate their business that were not in fact very different from those permitted other companies. Only the reservation of printing for its own members, instead of being a trade available to the freemen of any company, was unusual, and that no doubt reflects the overlap of interests of company and crown in restricting the flow of print. The Stationers' charter was reconfirmed by Elizabeth in November 1559, even if the new Queen must have felt differently than did her half-sister about the 'sound Catholic doctrine of Holy Mother Church'. That same year, therefore, Elizabeth issued an injunction ordering that no book was to be published unless it had been already licensed by the Queen herself, or six members of the Privy Council, or two ecclesiastical officials (one of whom had to be the ranking authority in the jurisdiction the book was printed) or the chancellor of one of the Universities. A further provision required that the name of the licensers should 'be added in the end of every such work for a testimony of the allowance thereof'. Standard classical works were exempted.[55]

Although the regulations seem not to have been universally obeyed, they were not lightly disregarded either. No prosecution of any printer or publisher is recorded in surviving governmental records, but the Stationers' Register indicates that thirteen printers were fined by the Company in 1559 and one imprisoned 'for pryntinge withoute lycense'. The more severe penalty was meted out to Richard Lant for the tactless publication of *An Epitaph of Queen Mary* (Arber, 1:100–1). In June 1566, the government strengthened the licensing

55 *Tudor Royal Proclamations*, ed. Hughes and Larkin, 2:128–9.

system by increasing the penalties for violation: any person who printed, published or imported an unlicensed book or one held in privilege was subject to the forfeiture of all copies, permanent revocation of the right to print, and three months' imprisonment. Binders of unlicensed or otherwise illegal books were liable to a penalty of twenty shillings per copy. A further provision required all stationers to pledge 'reasonable summes of monie' that they would observe the Company's regulations and aid its Wardens in their enforcement (Arber, 1:322).

In the wake of the 1566 order, Thomas Purfoot and Hugh Singleton 'rode abrode' to conduct a search with the written authority of the Stationers' Company. In May 1567, they presented the ecclesiastical authorities at York with a list of unlawful books they had discovered. Some, unsurprisingly, were Catholic books, but most were books printed in violation of existing privileges. Certainly the result of the search served as much to enforce the Company's regulations as to protect the established church. Fines were levied by the Company against seven stationers, and Purfoot himself was fined for illegally selling primers when some of the men he had exposed seemingly brought charges against him (Arber, 1:346–8). This was the first search authorised by the Company, and it would be a decade before another was undertaken. When, in 1576, twenty-four stationers were paired up and authorised to undertake weekly searches of the printing houses, the charge was to make note of the number of presses, the number of journeymen and apprentices, and the titles and quantities of every book printed. These new searches were seemingly motivated by a decree in March 1576 against the printing and distribution of 'Libells full of malice and falshood . . . tending to sedition, and dishonourable interpretations of her Maiesties godly Actions and purposes' (Arber, 1:474), and, if the results were meagre (merely four small fines in the next year), the fact alone of such authorised surveillance must have served as a strong deterrent to seditious publishing.

The searches indicate the Company's sensitivity to the Crown's displeasure. The government was eager to exert controls over the circulation of printed matter, and the Company was willing to help, though at least as much out of self-interest as on political grounds. Direct government interference in the book trade could undermine the trade's independence, and a well-regulated industry would theoretically provide work and profits for all. The Stationers, therefore, while never a systematic agency of government censorship, were willing to be used on occasion to that end. For them, however, the central goal was less to inhibit the distribution of controversial texts than to protect the increasingly valuable property rights that certain titles represented.

Over the next decades, the fight over property became the main concern of the Company. Privileges came under renewed attack, with the Company usually in the position of defending them on behalf of the holders who were among the Company's most powerful members. Nonetheless, in February 1576, the Company itself petitioned Lord Burghley against a privilege 'for the sole imprintinge of all balades Damaske paper and bokes in prose or metre from the quantitie of one sheete of paper to xxiiij tie' on the grounds that these were the primary means by which members of the Company were maintained and 'if the same be taken away from them by way of previledge they shalbe vtterlie undone'.[56] This petition succeeded, but the privilege system remained in place and continued to produce resentment. In 1577, journeymen printers, along with glass-sellers and cutlers, filed a complaint against 'priuiliges graunted to privatt persons', with nine book privilege holders named as contributing to the decline in opportunities for printers and the resultant rise in the price of books. In 1582, the printers twice more complained to the Privy Council. John Wolfe was the most aggressive of those attacking the monopolistic practices, blatantly infringing a number of valuable privileges and identifying himself as an idealistic reformer: 'Luther was but one man, and reformed all [th]e world for religion, and I am that one man, [th]at must and will reforme the gouernment in this trade, meaning printing and bookeselling' (Arber, 2:781).

Wolfe's challenge was met head on. In December 1582, Christopher Barker wrote an extensive report on privileges, attacking Wolfe and several other privilege-violaters as 'idle, vndescrete, and vnthriftie persons' that have forgotten 'their owne Dutie toward God, toward their prince and their neighbour', but also insisting that, in any case, few privileges were worth anything to their holders. Unsurprisingly, however, Barker, as the holder of valuable privileges for the Bible and the Book of Common Prayer, went on to defend the system, claiming that it worked in the interest both of the nation and of the industry's labourers, who 'both knowe and confesse that if priviledges were Dissolved they were vtterlie undone'.[57] The benefits of privileges were certainly obvious to their holders, and Wolfe himself reversed course when he was given a share of Richard Day's privileges, becoming an orderly member of the Stationers' Company and eventually Printer to the City of London (and, ironically, himself bringing suit for a violation of one of his own privileges by John Legatt in 1591).[58]

56 Quoted in Marjorie Plant, *The English Book Trade: An Economic History of the Making and Sale of Books*, 2nd edn (London: Allen and Unwin, 1965), p. 104.
57 *Ibid.*, pp. 105–8.
58 For an account of Wolfe's suit, see McKitterick, *Cambridge University Press*, 1:63–6.

With the fiery Wolfe's co-optation, pressure against the system eased, but additional steps were undertaken to restore confidence in the Company's procedures. Some privileges were given up by wealthy stationers to be used for aid to the poor of the Company, and an earlier order promising support for the request of any poor member 'to haue allowance to him of anie lawfull copie wherevnto noe other man hath righte or whereof there is noe number remaynynge by the fourmer printer vnsold'[59] was confirmed by grants like that to Timothy Rider, for an abandoned title to a book of home remedies (Arber, 2:430). In granting Rider's title, the Court also ordered that the printing was to be offered to Robert Waldegrave, and such specifications seem part of a policy carefully designed to placate the dissidents, allowing the Company at once to protect existing title claims and address the wider well-being of its membership by imposing conditions that would spread the work.[60] In 1583, for example, Henry Bynneman's titles to a number of potentially profitable classical texts were allowed by the Court of Assistants but only on the condition that the printing be shared with five other stationers (Arber, 2:422).

Clearly the Company was trying to respond both to the dissatisfaction produced by the system of privileges and to other circumstances that adversely affected the working conditions of its members, but the discontent was severe enough to cause the Privy Council to appoint a Commission to investigate the situation. Its report was issued in 1583 and served as the basis for the 1586 Decrees for Orders in Printing. These sought to impose order on the profession by limiting the number of master printers, restricting the number of apprentices (three for the Company's high-ranking officials, two for other liverymen, and one for all other members other than journeymen) and ordering that no new presses be established. Soon after, the Stationers themselves issued some orders that limited the number of copies that could be printed of most books to '1250 or 1500 at one ympression' and decreed that no books were to be reprinted from standing type, two provisions that also worked to ease the problems of too many Stationers competing for too little work (Arber, 2:43).

The 1586 Decrees also reiterated the requirement that no books be printed without the allowance of the Archbishop of Canterbury or the Bishop of London, or contrary to any rule of the Stationers' Company itself, or in violation of any existing privilege. In addition, they confirmed the Company's right to search for and seize unlawful publications and provided further for

59 W. W. Greg and E. Boswell (eds.), *Records of the Court of the Stationers' Company, 1576–1602* (London: The Bibliographical Society, 1930), pp. 3–5.
60 Blagden, *The Stationers' Company*, pp. 68–9.

offenders to be barred from printing, to have their printing materials defaced and to be imprisoned for six months (Arber, 2:807–12). These provisions were no doubt occasioned by the government's desire to control oppositional publication. The preamble notes the 'sondrye intollerable offences and troubles and disturbances' in both the church and government caused by the unrestrained abuses in the book trade. The Decrees themselves, however, were more directly motivated by the wish to resolve the often contentious disputes within the industry, and indeed the legislation was actively promoted by the Stationers. Leading members of the Company made sizeable contributions to the Commission's expenses (Arber, 1:518, 524), a lobbying tactic used by other companies that sought government-imposed order for their trade practices, and it was here, as in the efforts of several other companies, successful. The Decrees were quite conservative in nature and in essence confirmed the rights and prerogatives granted by the terms of the Company's charter.

The new licensing provisions, however, did mark at least one major change, now putting responsibility for allowing books firmly in the hands of the ecclesiastical authorities, though it was never intended that the Archbishop and the Bishop would themselves oversee every book that would be published. Initially it was assumed that their secretaries and chaplains would make recommendations, but by 1588 a panel of 'certan prechers [and others] whome the Archbishop of Canterbury hathe made Choyse of' was established 'to haue the perusinge and alowinge of Copies'.[61] The new system resulted in a markedly higher percentage of books being formally allowed; in 1580, for example, fewer than 20 per cent of the books were authorised, while in 1590 only about 15 per cent were not. Much of the authorisation, however, was inevitably perfunctory, and the effects of the Decrees were, finally, less to ensure orthodoxy in politics and religion than to regulate labour practices and reinforce the monopoly of the Stationers over the book trade.[62]

Although the 1586 Decrees were not completely successful in bringing order to the profession, they did provide a mechanism for the Stationers to assert control over their own unruly members and the book trade in general. Throughout the last decades of the sixteenth century, a number of drapers were profitably participating in the book trade, invoking the traditional custom of the City to allow freemen of any company to engage in any of the City's commercial activities. The Stationers brought suit, appealing to the provisions of the 1586

61 Greg and Boswell, *Records*, pp. 28–9.
62 See Cyndia Susan Clegg, *Press Censorship in Elizabethan England* (Cambridge University Press, 1997), pp. 30–65. See also Fredrick Seaton Siebert, *Freedom of the Press in England, 1476–1776* (Urbana: University of Illinois Press, 1952).

Decrees, and won a judgement that confirmed the Stationers' sole right to 'exercise . . . the Arte or mystery of printynge'. In 1600, those drapers who continued to want to print and publish were received into the Stationers' Company, requiring only that they pay the normal fee, three shillings and four pence, for their admission, and indeed several of the translated drapers would eventually become office holders in their new company.[63]

But if the victory over the Drapers in the courts confirmed the power of the 1586 Decrees to assert the Stationers' monopoly over the custom of the City, what finally consolidated the Company's authority was what became known as the English Stock. In the wake of King James's proclamation of 7 May 1603 against individuals holding monopolies, the Company itself obtained a privilege late in 1603 for 'Prymers Psalters and Psalmes in meter or prose with musycall notes or withoute notes both in greate volumes and small in the Englishe tongue', though this did not extend to the rights to the Book of Common Prayer and its accompanying psalter. The Stock also included 'all manner of Almnackes and prognosticac[i]ons whatsoever in the Englishe tongue'.[64] Soon after these grants, a privilege for common law books was purchased and added to the Stock, and later a privilege for schoolbooks. There were 105 partners drawn from the three grades of the Company membership – 15 assistants, 30 liverymen and 60 yeomen, their shares weighted by rank – who comprised the stockholders. Dividends were paid, usually quarterly, on the considerable profits the Stock made, perhaps as much as £3,000 to be shared in some years. The privileges which had earlier disrupted the orderly operation of the Company became, once they were corporate rather than individual, a means of promoting good order, giving most members a vested interest in the Company's success, contributing significant profits to the shareholders, providing needed work for many of the others, and allowing £200 a year to be paid from the profits to the Company's poor. While the development of the English Stock did not completely end the struggle over privileges, it did provide the Stationers' Company itself a means to resist the centrifugal force of its entrepreneurial members, encouraging, if not quite ensuring, the well-regulated markets and labour practices that would allow the book trade as a whole to thrive. Nonetheless, privileges continued to cause problems, some seventy still being in effect through the seventeenth century, and journeymen printers continued to be at best marginally employed.

---

63 Gerald D. Johnson, 'The Stationers Versus the Drapers: Control of the Press in the Late Sixteenth Century', *The Library* 6th ser. 10 (1980), 12–16.
64 William A. Jackson, *Records of the Court of the Stationers, 1602–1640* (London: The Bibliographical Society, 1957), pp. viii–x.

In 1637, a new decree 'Concerning Printing' was issued by the Star Chamber, attempting once again to establish order in the trade. No doubt this was, like the 1586 Decrees, actively promoted by the Stationers themselves, and tellingly soon after its issue they authorised a gift of £20 to Attorney-General John Bankes, who had drawn up the document, 'for his Loue & Kindnes to the Company'. The provisions of the 1637 order largely restated or reinforced existing ones (including for the first time making entrance to the Company mandatory), clarifying or slightly modifying allowance procedures (but adding a new provision that all reprints were to be re-allowed, aware that changing times might make a once innocent text contentious), insisting on some new controls on bookselling (including regulations that no English books were to be printed abroad for import and that all imported books were to enter at the Port of London) and further regulating the shape of the trade itself (by maintaining the number of master printers at twenty, limiting the number of presses each might have to two, or three in the case of those who had served as a company official, and restating the 1586 rules on the number of workers any shop might employ, though requiring that each house provide work for at least one journeyman). One new feature of the decree was the provision that a copy of every new book was to be provided free to the University Library at Oxford (confirming an agreement of 1611 between Thomas Bodley and the Company that many stationers had simply chosen to ignore).

Though the Company again received support from the government for its practices, and again because the political interests of the government and the financial interests of the Company aligned, this new decree, like its predecessors, was never completely successful in regulating the trade. In part the problem was simply too little work for too many workers. From 1580 to 1589, 186 men were made free of the Company; between 1630 and 1639, the number almost tripled to 415.[65] The alliance between the Company oligarchy and the Crown was increasingly destabilised by tensions in the Company itself between its officials, who in the main represented the prosperous publishers and booksellers, and its increasingly unhappy journeymen printers. But other circumstances worked to undermine the Company's confidence and authority. A powerful monopoly in the hands of Robert Young, Miles Flesher and John Haviland threatened, as one stationer worried, to 'ingrosse all worke here in London, that the poorer sort can get little work'.[66] Similarly, Michael Sparke's

65 Blagden, *The Stationers' Company*, pp. 284–6.
66 Donald W. Rude and Lloyd E. Berry, 'Tanner Manuscript No. 33: New Light on the Stationers' Company in the Early Seventeenth Century', *Papers of the Bibliographical Society of America* 66 (1972), 108.

pamphlet *Scintilla* (1641), proudly 'Printed, not for *profit*, but for the Common Weles good; and no where to be *sold*, but some where to be given', attacked the monopolists, claiming again that their practices limited work for tradesmen and artificially inflated the prices of books, thus picking the 'pockets' of common men 'that eat brown bread to fill the *sleeping Stationers* belly with venison and sacke'.[67]

Within a few years, the collapse of royal authority would leave the trade with no secure means of regulation, and the ensuing Civil War was fought as fiercely with printed words as with muskets and cannon. Though Parliament itself attempted to restore order to the book trade, its efforts were largely unsuccessful, and an unregulatable book trade produced propagandistic newsbooks and pamphlets at a remarkable rate. The London bookseller George Thomason collected over 22,000 items in the 1640s and 1650s, a number that probably represents only about two-thirds of what was actually printed. More items were published in the twenty years after 1640 than in the entire previous history of English printing, the sheer volume evincing how dramatically the nature and function of the book trade was being reshaped in the new world of general literacy and mass production. In the short run, it allowed printers to flourish at the expense of booksellers, earning a great deal of money by serving the needs of the political antagonists in printing pamphlets that were hawked in the streets rather than sold in the bookstalls. The numbers of printers increased, as they ignored the existing regulations concerning their hiring practices. By 1663, the twenty allowed master printers had grown to fifty-nine.

In 1662, a new printing act attempted to restore order to the trade. In many ways the new measures served to reinstitute much of the organisational structure that existed before 1640; indeed they included almost verbatim much of the 1637 Decree. Understandably many printers were unhappy with the mandated return to old practices. For them it only meant the restoration of an institutional structure that made them dependent for their livelihoods upon the wealthy publishers and booksellers who had been 'much enriched by Printers impoverishment' and had their power 'chiefly built upon their ruins'. There is 'hardly one Printer to ten others that have a share in the Government of the Company'.[68] Such concerns drove eleven printers in 1663 to seek independence from the Stationers, as some others had previously done to no avail twelve years earlier, but this new effort also failed. Conservative forces in the government and within the Company itself succeeded in reconfirming a structure

---

67 Sparke, *Scintilla: or, a light broken into darke warehouses* (London, 1641), sig. A4r.
68 *A Brief Discourse Concerning Printing and Printers* (London, 1663), sig. B2v.

that established the oligarchy that had existed before the Civil War, returning power to those who controlled copy.

Some things, of course, did change. At the Restoration a new position had been established, Surveyor of the Press, a government official charged with press supervision, and this fundamentally altered the process of licensing. The 1662 Act, with its recognition of this new office and the proviso that every book print its licence at the beginning of the book, became widely known as the Licensing Act. Marking an even greater difference from what came before, however, authority for the Act now rested in parliamentary legislation rather than in the royal prerogative – a telling measure of how much indeed had changed after the Civil War, even with the restored monarchy. Before the century's end still another telling change would register. Though the Licensing Act was renewed in 1685 and again in 1693, it was allowed to lapse two years later as the Commons found its provisions for scrutiny an undesirable restraint of trade.

The emergence of the author

For the senior officials of the Stationers' Company, the most important thing about the 1662 Act was its confirmation of the traditional rights of a publisher or the Company itself to claim property in a title. Throughout the history of the various efforts to regulate the book trade in England, the central issue, from a commercial point of view, was inevitably the right to publish a particular text. Though there were competing authorisations of such right – one from the crown in the form of a privilege, one from the Stationers themselves by virtue of a licence – a principle of an existing right in copy as a form of property was clearly in place from the mid sixteenth century, and what insured the success of the Company was that the practice of such rights conferred them only on its members. Rights belonged to Stationers, not to authors, and the record is filled with examples of publishers confidently asserting these, not only in the Stationers' Court but in the pages of their books. Valentine Simmes, for example, in his preface to Robert Tofte's sonnet sequence *Laura* (1597), unselfconsciously admits 'What the Gentleman was that wrote these Verses I know not... but thus much I can say, that as they came into the hands of a friend of mine by mere fortune; so happ[e]ned I vpon them by as great a chaunce'. As the unnamed friend says at the end of the volume: 'Without the Authors knowledge, as is before said by the Printer, this Poem is made thus publiquely knowen'.[69]

---

69 Tofte, *Laura* (London, 1597), sigs. A3v, E7r.

But publishing a book 'without the Authors knowledge' was in no way illegal – or even particularly unusual – although it often occasioned the author's anger. Samuel Daniel claimed that he was 'forced to publish' what he termed 'the priuate passions of my youth', since 'the indiscretion of a greedie Printer' had sent some of his 'secrets bewraide to the world, vncorrected'.[70] Some of Daniel's irritation is conventional, a somewhat disingenuous protest to escape the 'stigma of print'[71] attaching to gentlemen who became published authors; but books indeed were regularly printed with neither the approval nor even the knowledge of their authors. The publisher's preface to *The Second Parte of the Mirrour for Magistrates* (1578) admits that the author 'is now beyond the Seas, and wyl marueile at his returne, to find thys imprinted. For his intent was but to profite and pleasure one priuate man, as by his Epistle may appear'.[72] The author's 'intent', however, was of little significance to the publisher, who, coming into possession of a manuscript that he deemed marketable, could legally establish title to it by having it licensed by the Company and then publish it for his profit. The publisher and bookseller John Marriot disarmingly admits in his preface to Robert Gomersall's *Poems* (1633) that 'To praise the worke were to set my selfe to sale, since the greater its worth is, the more is my benefit, & not the Authors'.[73]

In most cases, however, authors were at least paid for their work, even if the rights to it as copy belonged to the publisher. The going rate for a pamphlet was seemingly £2. George Wither, for example, notes in his *Schollers Purgatory* (1624) that publishers 'cann hyre for a matter of 40 shillings, some needy Ignoramus'.[74] Many times, however, authors must have received less, perhaps no fee at all but merely a number of copies of the printed book, as Richard Robinson did for various of his translations, usually receiving twenty-six copies, one of which he presented to a patron and the other twenty-five of which he sold.[75] Occasionally an author might get a bit more: John Stow received £3 for his

70 Daniel, *Delia. Contayning certayne sonnets: with, The complaint of Rosamond* (London, 1592), sig. A2r.

71 J. W. Saunders, 'The Stigma of Print: A Note on the Social Bases of Tudor Poetry', *Essays in Criticism* 1 (1951), 139–64; Steven W. May, 'Tudor Aristocrats and the Mythical "Stigma of Print"', *Renaissance Papers* (1980), 11–18.

72 *The Second Parte of the Mirrour for Magistrates, conteining the falles of the infortunate Princes of this Lande* (London, 1578), sig. *2r.

73 Robert Gomersall, *Poems* (London, 1633), sig. A3r.

74 George Wither, *The Schollers Purgatory, discovered in the Stationers common-wealth* (London: G. Wood for the Honest Stationers, 1624), sig. I1r.

75 George McGill Vogt, 'Richard Robinson's *Eupolemia*', *Studies in Philology* 21 (1924), 629–48. See also M. B. Bland, 'Jonson, Stansby and English Typography 1579–1623', D.Phil. diss., Oxford University (1995), 1:19–21.

Survey of London and forty copies of the book, which, like Robinson's, would then be sold or offered as gifts to potential patrons. Hooker received £10 for the first four books of his *Lawes of Ecclesiastical Politie* and £20 for Book 5.[76] Milton, famously (or infamously) received £10 in two instalments for *Paradise Lost*, and was eligible for an additional £10 when the next two editions sold out.[77]

Milton's contract with Samuel Simmons gave the publisher 'all that Booke Copy or Manuscript' of the poem, 'togeather with the full benefitt profitt & advantage thereof or which shall or may arise thereby'. Though Milton's early biographers were often scandalised by the apparent exploitation of the poet, the terms are unusual only in that they are in fact relatively generous (not only by virtue of the size of the royalty but also in the recognition of some obligation to pay for subsequent editions) and also in that they are explicit, the contract being the first that survives between a writer and a publisher. They reflect the reality of early modern copyright in their recognition of the publisher's ownership of the copy.

Still, the modern notion of copyright as the legal expression of the rights of an author to be recognised as the creator and owner of a literary property, which dates formally only from 1814, had some important anticipations.[78] In rare cases, privileges had been granted to authors from the Crown. As early as 1563, Thomas Cooper was granted a privilege for his Latin–English dictionary for a period of twelve years. A decade later, Lodowick Lloyd was given an eight-year privilege for a translation of Plutarch's *Lives*. The Stationers willingly acknowledged these authorial privileges, for example, in March 1618 when the Company formally recognised Reynold Smith's right 'to ymprint his table and Computac[i]on that he hath made and to sell them w[i]thout interruption of the Company' (Arber, 3:107), knowing that the printing job would inevitably go to

---

76 W. Speed Hill, *Richard Hooker: A Descriptive Bibliography of the Early Editions: 1593–1724* (Cleveland: Case Western Reserve Press, 1970), pp. 10–17.

77 On Simmons's contract with Milton, see Peter Lindenbaum, 'Milton's Contract', in *The Construction of Authorship: Textual Appropriation in Law and Literature*, ed. Martha Woodmansee and Peter Jaszi (Durham, NC: Duke University Press, 1994), pp. 175–90; see also Stephen B. Dobranski, *Milton, Authorship, and the Book Trade* (Cambridge University Press, 1999), esp. pp. 35–6.

78 A copyright law enacted formally in 1710 (8 Anne c. 19) did permit authors to acquire the copyright of their works, a prerogative previously limited to Stationers, but the modern idea of copyright being vested in the author is not fully established in law until 1814, and even then, as Wordsworth and others objected, only for a period of twenty-eight years after publication or the author's lifetime, whichever was longer. On the emergence of copyright law, see Lyman Ray Patterson, *Copyright in Historical Perspective* (Nashville, TN: Vanderbilt University Press, 1968); and Mark Rose, *Authors and Owners: The Invention of Copyright* (Cambridge, MA: Harvard University Press, 1993).

a Company member and that most of the books would be sold at a stationer's stall.

Authors' rights to their own copy were, thus, rare but not unknown, and no doubt some individual arrangements between authors and publishers existed that have not survived. One that has is Robert Burton's will, which makes clear that somehow the rights to *The Anatomy of Melancholy* had been divided between the author and its publisher, and Burton is able to leave 'halfe [his] melancholy Copy' to his wife, acknowledging that 'Crips [i.e., Henry Crips, an Oxford publisher] hath the other halfe'.[79] In general, however, the author's composition, once it reached a publisher's hand, was not his own possession, but this did not prevent a notion of intellectual property from gradually developing. We can see this clearly even in the mid sixteenth century. William Baldwin, for example, compiled what is in essence a commonplace book called *A Treatise of Morall Philosophy*. The book, first published by Edward Whitchurch in 1547, became a best-seller, four editions appeared within six years, and eventually more than twenty were published by 1620. In 1555, however, Thomas Palfryman undertook an unauthorised enlargement of Baldwin's *Treatise*, which was published by Richard Tottel. In 1556, Baldwin reissued his *Treatise*, now published by John Wayland, expressing irritation that some other would dare 'plow with my oxen', though clearly with no sense that there was any legal remedy for the unauthorised appropriation.[80] Similarly, Richard Grafton and John Stow engaged in a caustic feud over their respective abridgements of the chronicles. Grafton maintained, even as he acknowledged the difficulty of a writer of history in making any claim to originality, that 'he that gathereth flowers, & maketh a nosegaie, is worthy of some commendacion for his paines', and Stow accused his competitor of 'setting as it were his marke on another mans vessel'.[81] But again the rivals, however acrimoniously, issued their competing editions and lodged their charges and counter-charges of plagiarism without any sense that a legal right had been violated.

Baldwin, Grafton and Stow, however, all felt strongly that some moral right had been transgressed in the unauthorised and unacknowledged appropriation of their intellectual labour. That right would in time underpin the modern

---

79 Quoted in Robert Burton, *The Anatomy of Melancholy*, vol. 1, ed. Thomas C. Faulkner, Nicolas K. Kiessling and Rhonda L. Blair, corr. edn (Oxford University Press, 1997), p. xli.
80 Baldwin, *The tretise of morall phylosophy* (London, 1556), sig. A2r.
81 Grafton, *A Manuell of the Chronicles of England* (London, 1565), sig. A3r; Stow, *The Summarye of the Chronicles of Englande* (London, 1573), sig. A7v; see also David Scott Kastan, 'Opening Gates and Stopping Hedges: Grafton, Stow, and the Politics of Elizabethan History Writing', in *The Project of Prose in Early Modern Europe and the New World*, ed. Elizabeth Fowler and Roland Greene (Cambridge University Press, 1997), pp. 66–79.

conception of copyright. In his *Schollers Purgatory*, George Wither attacked the Stationers for having 'vsurped vpon the labours of all writers', insisting that 'according to the lawes of nature' he should be able to 'enjoy the benefit of some part of myne owne labours'.[82] In 1643, even a member of the Stationers' Company could claim that 'there is no reason apparent why the production of the Brain should not be as assignable, and their interest and possession (being of more rare, sublime, and publike use, demeriting the highest encouragement), held as tender in the Law, as the right of any Goods or Chattells whatsoever'.[83] But some 170 years would pass before such 'reason' would find full legitimation in law.

In the interim, authors took what payments they could get. Professional writers regularly protested the small compensation that was available, and many must have survived by peddling the copies of their books that they were given by their publishers, like Ingenioso in the first part of *The Return from Parnassus*, who is mocked for 'fidlinge thy pamphletes from doore to dore like a blinde harper, for breade & cheese'.[84] Writers, however, had little leverage to challenge the system, being dependent for publication upon the very Stationers against whom they complained.

Authorship was in most cases poorly paid piecework, but, nonetheless, the English author in a recognisable modern form came into being with print and at least as much as a function of the ambitions of the book trade as of the ambitions of English writers. The oft-remarked prejudice against print publication worked to prevent aristocrats (or those pretending to gentility) from seeking more than manuscript circulation for their verses. ''Tis ridiculous for a lord to print Verses', John Selden wrote in an extreme expression of the social prejudice; ''tis well enough to make 'em to please himself, but to make them public is foolish'.[85] Though a coterie manuscript system thrived well into the seventeenth century, print increasingly became the primary means of poetry's distribution, making possible lyric's eventual absorption into the literary culture. John Harington observed somewhat ruefully that 'Verses are grown such merchantable ware, / That now for Sonnets, sellers are, and buyers'.[86]

82 Wither, *The Schollers Purgatory*, sig. A3r.
83 Plant, *The English Book Trade*, pp. 113–14.
84 *The Return from Parnassus*, lines 396–7, in *The Three Parnassus Plays (1598–1601)*, ed. J. B. Leishman (London: Nicholson and Watson, 1949), p. 155.
85 *The Table-Talk of John Selden*, ed. Samuel Harvey Reynolds (Oxford University Press, 1892), p. 135.
86 Sir John Harington, *Letters and Epigrams of John Harington*, ed. Norman Egbert McClure (Philadelphia: University of Pennsylvania Press, 1930), p. 164.

Verses did become 'merchantable ware', although it was arguably only with the publication of Sidney's *Astrophil and Stella* that the prejudice against printed verse largely disappeared, as Sidney's massive cultural presence lent the lyric some of his own prestige. The first edition in 1591 was published by Thomas Newman as *Syr P. S. His Astrophel and Stella*, but although it indeed was Sidney's composition – 'His', as the title-page emphasises, regarding that part of the text appearing before the twenty-eight poems 'of sundrie other Noble men and Gentlemen' that conclude the volume – the edition belonged to Newman. He had come into possession of the manuscript and dedicated *his* edition to Francis Flower, as 'the first fruits of my affection'. If Newman claims to 'haue been very carefull in the Printing of it', scrupulously 'correcting and restoring it' from the corruption of its 'written Coppies',[87] he does so with no help from or obligation to the poet (and in point of fact his professed care was little more than notional). Sidney himself had been dead for some five years, and the manuscript of the sequence had come into Newman's possession from some unauthorised source.[88] Normally an author, or his agent, would have no recourse to oppose publication, but something happened to enforce 'the takinge in' of the unlicensed quarto (Arber, 1:555). The Stationers' Register does say that the Company thought to consult with Burghley on the matter, and perhaps members of the powerful Sidney family had objected to the publication either because of its subject matter or perhaps because Sidney's sister, the Countess of Pembroke, had her own plans for its publication. Nonetheless, a second edition was published by Newman the same year and another by Matthew Lownes some seven years later.

Samuel Daniel, in protesting the unauthorised publication of his own poetry in Newman's edition of Sidney, notes that Sidney's poems themselves 'haue indured the like misfortune' in Newman's book.[89] Sidney had consistently insisted upon his reluctance to appear 'in the company of the Paper-blurrers', never admitting any desire to appear in print or that 'there should be / Graved in mine Epitaph a Poet's name'.[90] But print insured it so. Once printed, occasional verse became literary, and Sidney achieved his unsought-after 'Poet's name'. To the familiar epithets surrounding the Protestant hero–martyr now had to

---

87 [Philip Sidney], *Syr P. S. His Astrophel and Stella* (London, 1591), sigs. A2r–v.
88 See Henry Woudhuysen, *Sir Philip Sidney and the Circulation of Manuscripts 1558–1640* (Oxford: Clarendon Press, 1996), pp. 365–84.
89 Daniel, *Delia*, sig. A2r.
90 *An Apology for Poetry*, ed. Geoffrey Shepherd (Manchester University Press, 1973), p. 132; *Astrophil and Stella*, sonnet 90, *The Poems of Sir Philip Sidney*, ed. William A. Ringler, Jr (Oxford: Clarendon Press, 1962), p. 224.

be added, in Gabriel Harvey's phrase, 'the Paragon of Excellency in Print',[91] in spite of the fact that 'Print' served Newman's interests far more than Sidney's own and that the 'Excellency' the poet achieved was in many places betrayed by Newman's unauthorised and often careless publication.

The most obvious example, however, of a writer whose printed work reflects less his own ambitions than those of his publishers is Shakespeare.[92] Ironically the playwright who has become the iconic figure of authorship itself showed remarkably little interest in the assertions of authorship conferred by publication. Although he did contribute elaborate and signed dedications to both *Venus and Adonis* and *Rape of Lucrece*, the two narrative poems printed by his fellow Stratfordian Richard Field and published during an enforced closure of the theatres in 1593 and 1594, neither appeared with the author's name on the title-page; and the edition of *Shake-speares Sonnets* published by Thomas Thorpe in 1609 seems likely to have been issued without the poet's cooperation, as the absence of a dedication might suggest.[93] Even less ambiguous and far more important is the fact that none of the plays, unquestionably the achievement on which Shakespeare's massive cultural authority rests, shows any sign of his involvement in its publication.

Eighteen of the plays did reach print before his death in 1616, but their publishers show as little interest in their author as their author did in their publication. Seven plays were published before one was issued with Shakespeare's name on the title-page. Not until 1598, with Cuthbert Burby's edition of *Love's Labour's Lost*, did Shakespeare's name appear; and Burby's title-page acknowledgement is muted, modestly printing the dramatist's name in small italic type, identifying the play as 'Newly corrected and augmented *By W. Shakespere*'. Scholars have often remarked the growth of Shakespeare's reputation, as well as of the cultural status of the drama, measured by the change between this early history and the appearance in 1608 of Nathaniel Butter's edition of *King Lear*, which emblazons Shakespeare's name across the top of the title in the largest font on the page: 'M. William Shak-speare: / *HIS* / True Chronicle Historie of the life and / death of King LEAR and his three / Daughters'. Here the play is enthusiastically celebrated as Shakespeare's own, though it, of course, no more belongs to him in any legal sense than any of

91 *Elizabethan Critical Essays*, ed. G. Gregory Smith (Oxford University Press, 1904), 2:265.
92 For an extended account of Shakespeare's relationship to the book trade, see David Scott Kastan, *Shakespeare and the Book* (Cambridge University Press, 2001).
93 For a contrary view, see the claim that 'in 1609 Shakespeare had assumed control of his own text of his Sonnets': *Shakespeare's Sonnets*, ed. Katherine Duncan-Jones (Walton-on-Thames: Thomas Nelson, 1997), p. 3.

his other plays that had been published and whose copy belonged to their publishers.

The play, at least as copy, belongs to Butter, who asserts Shakespeare's authorship to market his publication, trying either to capitalise on his growing reputation (Thomas Walkely would say in 1622 in his edition of *Othello* that 'the Authors name is sufficient to vent his work') or, more likely at this date, to differentiate the play from an anonymous play, *The True Chronicle Historie of King Leir*, published by John Wright in 1605. Shakespeare's name clearly identifies an author on the 1608 *Lear* quarto but functions less to designate the play*wright* than the play*book*. The 'Shak-speare' of Butter's title-page is the publisher's Shakespeare, a simulacrum devised to individualise and protect the publisher's property. The playwright apparently received nothing for the text, and seems to have been untroubled by its sloppy printing. The 'author', however, at least enabled the publisher to sell some books.

Neither Sidney nor Shakespeare can, of course, be thought normative examples of early modern writers, for in fact every writer provides a singular case. Certainly to observe their lack of interest in the forms of individuation that print allowed or their uninvolvement in the publishing procedures that insured their fame is not to suggest that writers generally lacked literary ambitions. The case of the drama is perhaps anomalous, in that it is essentially a collaborative activity, and professional performed plays, in any case, were still largely considered sub-literary. But even in the professional theatre, literary ambitions emerged. Ben Jonson provides, of course, the obvious example, aggressively using print to establish the authority of his dramatic texts and his authority over them. Jonson became an 'author', as he was the first to claim on a play title page, as he turned his plays into 'works' through the medium of print. Some contemporaries thought his claim an unmerited pretension; others, a proper measure of his artistry.[94] What provoked scorn was not Jonson's literary ambitions themselves but his ambitions for commercial play scripts. Jonson was unusual only in classing plays written for the theatre within the category of literature – and in helping to make them so by his act of classification.

Jonson, however, was not alone in his ambitions. Many writers actively pursued a literary reputation, if rarely with the determination and sophistication

---

94 One anonymous poet mockingly wrote of Jonson's 1616 *Works*, 'Pray tell me Ben, where doth the mystery lurke / What others call a play you call a worke', in *Wits Recreations* (London, 1640), sig. G3v. Conversely, a verse in a copy of the 1616 Jonson folio once owned by Mildmay Fane admires the 'deep Conceptions' of Jonson's drama that permit us to 'turne his Playes into a Worke'. See Joseph T. Roy, Jr, and Robert C. Evans, 'Fane on Jonson and Shakespeare', *Notes and Queries* 239 (1994), 156–8.

of Jonson. The stigma of print was largely an aristocratic affectation, and, even as early as 1589, would-be authors of poetry were urged not to 'be any whit squeimish to let it to be publisht under theire names'.[95] Increasingly they were not at all 'squeimish' about seeking publication. Indeed in 'this scribbling age', as Robert Burton quipped, '*Presses be oppressed*, and out of an itching humour, that every man hath to shewe himselfe, desirous of fame and honour'.[96]

However much that 'itching humour' demanded to be acknowledged, the literary ambitions of early modern writers inevitably had to express themselves in the material forms that print made available and function within the limits imposed by the institution of the book trade. The book trade unified and stabilised their texts, allowed their work to circulate and indeed was what made possible the consolidation of the very category of literature. From Caxton's endowing Chaucer with 'the name of a laureate poete' in the proem to his second edition of *The Canterbury Tales*[97] to Humphrey Moseley's publications in the mid seventeenth century of a group of contemporary writers, including Milton, Suckling, Waller, Carew, Shirley, and Beaumont and Fletcher, in formats and layouts that declared them the worthy inheritors of the English literary tradition that Chaucer began, a notion of literature steadily emerged and its canon was gradually defined. But it was so defined, it must be said, every bit as much by the interests and activities of the early modern book trade as by those of the writers whom it at once exploited and served.

95 Puttenham, *Arte of English Poesie*, in *Elizabethan Critical Essays*, ed. Gregory Smith, 2:23–4.
96 *Anatomy of Melancholy*, 1:8.
97 Geoffrey Chaucer, [*The Canterbury Tales*] (London, 1483), sig. a2r.

Chapter 4

LITERARY PATRONAGE

GRAHAM PARRY

Following the suppression of the monasteries and the turmoil in the church in the 1530s, the patronage of writers became almost exclusively secular, with the monarch and the nobility broadly accepting that the encouragement of learning was one of the functions of power and authority. In a complementary way, authors and printers knew that a book could not come abroad without the name of a patron affixed in order to signal that a powerful figure stood behind the exposed and vulnerable author. Patronage in the early Tudor period was neither systematic nor sustained, and its recipients had limited expectations. In general, a writer would be satisfied with the presence of a protective name at the head of his work; reward was not a significant factor in dedications, for most authors (themselves not a numerous group) already had a post in life, and an affiliation with some great household. Their dedications were mostly expressions of loyalty or gratitude rather than anglings for future favours. Hope of reward in the form of office, advancement or money is a feature of later Elizabethan times, when writers proliferated and aspired to earn a living or advance their careers by publication. In the earlier Tudor period, however, when the number of printed books was relatively modest, and readership limited to the educated, a book needed a guarantee of its worth. The importance of a titled dedicatee has to be recognised: in an aristocratic age a noble name offered assurance that the contents had merit, and reassurance that there was no harm, political or religious, in the work. It seems as if, in the sixteenth century, and well into Elizabeth's reign, the purchase and possession of a book was considered in some subliminal way to be a risky business, and the reader needed some means of allaying fears. Whether this attitude reflected vestigial feelings about the magical potency of books is an open question; there may have been also the pragmatic consideration that the possession of certain books could be compromising in the frequently changing and unpredictably threatening world of post-Reformation England, when suspicion of disloyalty or of one's religious affiliations was a constant background and anxiety.

A curious feature of publication is the commonly expressed belief that the patron will be a preservative against 'malicious tongues', 'backbiting', 'detraction', 'serpents' and the like. This is so general a sentiment, often expressed in forceful language, that there must have been genuine grounds for concern throughout the century. It would be understandable if this fear were expressed mainly in connection with religious books, which might easily be contentious, but it accompanies the publication of books of medicine, law, history, philosophy and poetry as well. One has therefore to assume that publication exposed an author to a good deal of bitter griping and condemnation in the social circles of the time. Though authors were few, critics were evidently many. There seems to have been widespread resentment against writers, arising from any number of sources – envy, factionalism, small-mindedness, anti-intellectualism, cultural hostility – so that a decision to publish was, in effect, to put one's head above the parapet and be a target for all manner of abuse. The modern writer is accustomed to negative criticism in reviews, but the Tudor writer apparently had to endure a great deal of social malevolence. Publication aroused the attention of 'the cruel carper and malicious quarreller [who] leaveth no mans worke unreproved', 'the Criticall censores whyche do nothynge them selfes that good is, but carpe and reprehende other mens doings', and provoked 'the causeless censures of the ignorant, and the biting teeth of the Carper'.[1] A translator of Thucydides feared that his work would incite 'curyous, fantasticall persons. Pryvey diffamours of dylygent and virtuous laboure... grievously pynched with envye'.[2] The writer of a conduct book published in 1547 expected it to be devoured by 'cankerde and envyous stomakes' and scorned by 'malencoly minds replered with venym of intoxicate malyce'.[3] A seriously unpleasant social scene is revealed by many dedications of the sixteenth century, and one can understand why a patron's name might make wanton censurers hold their tongues for fear of retaliation from a powerful hand. Even the distinguished Sir Thomas Elyot, when he published his *Book Named the Governour*, on the education of men who would conduct the affairs of state, explained in his dedication to Henry VIII that 'I am nowe dryven throughe the malignity of this present tyme, all disposed to malicious detraction' to ask the King's protection 'agayne the assaultes of

---

1 The quotations are from the dedications to John Bale's *The Image of Both Churches* (1545), William Hughe's *The Troubled Mans Medicine* (1546) and Miles Mosse's *The Arraignment and Conviction of Usurie* (1595). These examples are cited in H. S. Bennett, *English Books and Readers 1475–1557* (Cambridge University Press, 1969), 1:50; 2:32.

2 Thomas Nicolls, *The Hystory writtone by Thucidides* ([London], 1550).

3 Robert Whittinton, *The Myrrour or Glasse of Maners* (1547), cited in H. S. Bennett, *English Books, 1475–1557*, 1:51n.

maligne interpretours'.[4] Given this prevailing mood of hostility, the fulsome flattery of patrons in dedications also becomes more comprehensible.

One group of writers clearly needed patronage and protection more than most: the Protestant reformers, who were often exposed to 'detraction'. In the dangerous last years of Henry's reign and in the precarious reign of Edward VI, some of the most powerful women in the land proved to be invaluable patronesses. Catherine Brandon, Duchess of Suffolk; Mary Fitzroy, Duchess of Richmond; and Anne Seymour, Duchess of Somerset – all supported the cause of Reformation and used their authority to protect both Protestant controversialists such as John Bale and Robert Crowley, and the key publishers John Day and William Seres. All these women had been associated with Katherine Parr, who sympathised with the process of reform, and who helped to nurture Princess Elizabeth's Protestant sympathies. Catherine Brandon retained the reformer Thomas Wilson as tutor to her sons, and employed Hugh Latimer as her chaplain at her great house at Grimsthorpe in Lincolnshire. Latimer's sermons were, predictably, dedicated to her. In the year 1548–9 she was highly visible as a champion of the reformed religion, with her coat of arms appearing on translations of the New Testament, the Apocrypha, on Latimer's 'Sermon on the Plowers' and on a reprint of William Tyndale's 'Exposicion uppon Matthew'. Mary Fitzroy maintained John Bale and John Foxe at her London residence, Mountjoy House, and Foxe wrote his early works whilst living in her household. Anne Seymour reinforced the patronage of her husband, the first Protector of the realm in the minority of Edward VI, encouraging Protestant activists, including Richard Grafton, Edward Whitchurch and Miles Coverdale.[5]

The patronage commitments of these noblewomen complemented those of the leading Protestant lords: Lord Wentworth, who had been responsible for the conversion of John Bale, and who promoted the career of the prolific divine Thomas Becon, and Edward Seymour, Duke of Somerset, the mainstay of the new Protestant writers. Latimer, Hooper, Becon, Coverdale, Grafton, Whitchurch were all recipients of his favour, and he extended his protection to continental reformers who came to England, including Martin Bucer, Peter Martyr and the mercurial Bernardino Ochino. But Seymour was also responsive to the appeal of humanist scholarship, supporting John Cheke, the preeminent Greek scholar of the mid-century, as well as Thomas Smith the Grecianist, legal scholar and diplomat who wrote the important work on the Tudor constitution

---

4 Thomas Elyot, *The Boke named the Governour* (London, 1531), sig. iii v.
5 Details of the Protestant patronesses are taken from John N. King, *English Reformation Literature* (Princeton University Press, 1982), pp. 104–11.

De Republica Anglorum (written in English in spite of its Latin title, and published posthumously in 1583). One of Seymour's secretaries was William Cecil, who effectively managed his master's patronage relations with clients, and whose own later culture of patronage was formed by his experience in the service of the Protector, fostering both religious writers and humanist scholars. Even at this early stage, however, Cecil was able to offer support to the Italian historiographer Polydore Vergil and to the Hebrew scholar Immanuel Tremellius, who was also of Italian origin. An indication of Cecil's early reputation as a friend to learning was Ralph Robinson's dedication to him of his English translation of More's *Utopia* in 1551; even though Cecil had not commissioned this work, he accepted the dedication and then employed Robinson in his household.

Queen Mary's reign was entirely unpropitious to the production of literary works, or any work of intellectual eminence. With her attempt to restore the Catholic religion, most of the active advocates of Protestantism fled abroad, and such was the climate of fearful anxiety in her short reign that few writers were willing to risk calling attention to themselves by publication. It has been noted that in these years publishers turned to authors who were safely dead, reprinting works by Gower, Malory and More, and giving readers a first sight of poems by Thomas Wyatt and the Earl of Surrey.[6] Wyatt and Surrey appeared in *Tottel's Miscellany* (1557), an anthology of verse from the 1530s onwards that went through numerous editions up to 1587. Of equally durable appeal was *A Mirror for Magistrates* (1559), an assemblage of verse 'tragedies' in seven-line stanzas written by various hands, almost all illustrating the theme of the 'fall of princes' by examples from English history of the previous century. The nominal aim of the collections was to warn the governors of the country to act prudently and responsibly in the exercise of their authority. Put together by four editors, of whom William Baldwin and George Ferrers were the principal ones, the work was reprinted with additions in 1563, 1578 and 1587.[7] Dedicated 'To the nobilitye and all other in office' – the ostensible readership of the book – the work in fact proved broadly popular and secured an independent position in the marketplace. The success of the *Mirror* demonstrated that a literary work might forgo traditional patronage if supported by purchasers and made profitable to its printer and bookseller. *Tottel's Miscellany* likewise

6 A helpful sketch of publishing activity in the reign of Mary can be found in James K. McConica, *English Humanists and Reformation Politics under Henry VIII and Edward VI* (Oxford University Press 1965), pp. 412–16.

7 The publishing history of this book is amply described in *A Mirror for Magistrates*, ed. Lily B. Campbell (Cambridge University Press, 1938; rpt, New York: Barnes & Noble, 1960).

flourished in the open market without a patron, by directly staking its appeal to the reader in a forward-looking way.

The literary scene changed markedly in the time of Elizabeth. As political stability increased, the primary concern of the Queen and her ministers was the successful settlement of the Church of England. The new Protestant society began to express itself in a distinctive literature that reflected a new set of values. Its confident side consisted of religious polemic and Biblical interpretation, pursued with all the zeal and passion that attended a cause of national urgency, and with a freshness that free access to the Bible encouraged. More insecure and hesitant was the secular enterprise – the English attempt to engage with the revival of classical learning – a process begun in early Tudor times but delayed and marginalised by the Reformation. For the most part, translation was needed to put the significant works of ancient Rome and modern Europe before an English audience; but the underdeveloped lexical resources in English in relation to other languages made this seem a daunting task. The religious and humanist missions needed purposeful patrons because the advancement of learning is slow and laborious and, in most ages, poorly rewarded. Learning also needed its champions and standard-bearers, to show that there were great men and women who valued a high literary culture and who would take the lead and encourage it for the honour of the nation and for their own reputation. The leading Elizabethan patrons took a much more sustained and focused view of their role than their predecessors in early Tudor times.

In tandem with leading noblemen, the colleges of Oxford and Cambridge might have been expected to promote new learning. Indeed, the colleges produced a good deal of religious polemic written by men with secure fellowships who might be further rewarded with college livings – positions in the church controlled by the universities. But because Oxford and Cambridge existed primarily to educate men for the church, they did not produce secular writing to any great extent. Henry Savile's translation of Tacitus (1591) was one of few valuable humanist works to come out of Elizabethan Oxford. The effective patrons of both humanist scholarship and Protestant writing were those aristocratic figures whose lives were devoted to the service of the English nation in political, military, diplomatic and cultural ways: Lord Burghley, the Earl of Leicester, Sir Philip Sidney and the members of the interrelated Sidney and Herbert families.

William Cecil, Lord Burghley (1520–98), Secretary of State and chief minister to Elizabeth for most of her reign, took a responsible view of his role as the leading statesman of England. Highly educated himself, and Chancellor of Cambridge University from 1559, he undertook to encourage scholarship, religion and good letters. His early experience as secretary to Edward Seymour, Duke of Somerset, had given him a model of good practice, which he improved on in the more favourable conditions of the Elizabethan state. He offered hospitality to scholars and writers at Cecil House on the Strand in London or at Burghley House near Stamford, rewarded dedications and found posts and pensions for several of his protégés. He was friendly with the educators John Cheke and Roger Ascham, and he assisted the translator Arthur Golding, who dedicated his versions of Caesar and Pomponius Mela to Cecil; he showed favour also to Gabriel Harvey, the Cambridge humanist. Though Cecil did not show any unusual favour to poets, George Puttenham dedicated the *Arte of English Poesie* to him in 1589, perhaps to increase his awareness of the remarkable literary developments currently taking place. Altogether Cecil was the dedicatee of some ninety books. Their dedicatory epistles cumulatively reveal an openminded man who admired learning and learned men, and who sincerely wanted to improve the state of education in England because he believed that nations were judged by their achievements in learning and literature. The preface to Ascham's *The Scholemaster* (1570) recalls Cecil's attentive consideration to scholars: 'at dinner time . . . he ever findeth fitte occasion to talk plesantlie of other matters [than statecraft], but most gladlie of some matter of learning: wherein he will curteslie hear the mind of the meanest at his table'. Here is a writer's dream fulfilled: access to a great man's household, hospitality and respect.

If one had to specify the most appropriate volume dedicated to Cecil, it would be William Camden's *Britannia* (1586), the work that effectively established the identity of the nation, historically and topographically, and formed one of the supreme productions of humanist scholarship in the Elizabethan era. Celebrating the excellence and antiquity of Britain, and written in Latin, *Britannia* was aimed as much at a European audience as at an English one. Sir Philip Sidney and Sir Fulke Greville had been the first to encourage Camden's grand scheme, but Burghley had taken over; Camden's dedication gratefully acknowledges his patron's enthusiasm for the project and his willingness to make his library available to the author. Burghley also helped Camden to a post at Westminster School, of which Burghley was a patron, and where Camden spent the rest of his days. Topographic scholarship further benefited from Burghley's interest, for he supported John Norden's county survey *Speculum Britanniae* (1593) and sponsored Christopher Saxton's scheme to map the country.[8] Characteristically for his time as well, Burghley used his authority to support the reformed religion, patronising translations of Calvin's sermons and Biblical commentaries,

8 See Richard Helgerson, *Forms of Nationhood: The Elizabethan Writing of England* (University of Chicago Press, 1992), pp. 107–47.

accepting the dedications of numerous English sermons, including those of Bishop John Jewel, and backing anti-Jesuit writings by men such as Meredith Hamner and Anthony Munday.

Burghley's patronage closely resembled that of his political rival, Robert Dudley, Earl of Leicester, who was Elizabeth's favourite in the early decades of her reign. His generous career has been surveyed by Eleanor Rosenberg in a study that traces his policy of encouraging writers across a broad spectrum of scholarship, as befitted a man who became Chancellor of Oxford University in 1564.[9] Leicester understood the value of translation to a country with a meagre intellectual heritage, so he became the dedicatee of works on medicine, cosmography, military tactics and theology. Like Burghley, he patronised Golding, who began his translations of Ovid's *Metamorphoses* for Leicester in 1575. History held particular importance in Leicester's mind, both for arousing national pride and for inculcating a knowledge of statecraft. He patronised the chroniclers Richard Grafton, John Stow and Ralph Holinshed, and accepted the dedications of the translations of Philippe de Commines's modern French history and a history of the wars in the Low Countries, in which he himself had participated. In matters of religion, he reinforced Calvinist theology by encouraging translations of works by Calvin, Peter Martyr and Theodore Beza, by contributing towards the printing of plain Protestant sermons and supporting writers of anti-Catholic polemics.

This combination of humanism and vigorous Protestantism was sustained by Leicester's nephew, Sir Philip Sidney, who, though lacking the spacious means of his uncle, showed an unusual responsiveness to his protégés that established his reputation as an ideal patron. The recipient of some twenty-five dedications, he stands out for his early patronage of Spenser, an aspect of his desire to foster the 'New Poetry' of which he was both advocate and practitioner. His generosity towards Spenser ensured the publication of *The Shepheardes Calender* in 1579. Spenser's various elegies on Sidney after his death from wounds in 1586 movingly evoke the sorrow felt by aspiring English poets at his loss. Sidney's relations with Spenser exhibit the effectiveness of serious patronage. Sidney was able to advance a cause he believed in – the development of a new style of poetic expression, involving finer craftsmanship, more learning, allusiveness and musicality than was currently the case – and his advocacy of this cause added to his cultural credit at the English court and in the community of continental scholars whom he personally knew. But Sidney was also able to further the career of his favoured poet, for he recommended Spenser as secretary to Lord Grey de Wilton, who went to Ireland as Lord Deputy in 1580.

9 Eleanor Rosenberg, *Leicester, Patron of Letters* (New York: Columbia University Press, 1955).

So Spenser was settled in a profitable post, although at the expense of exile from England.

Sidney showed signs of being a more adventurous patron than Leicester, for he was willing to offer protection to the erratic metaphysician Giordano Bruno when Bruno moved to England in 1583–5. The winds of persecution had unexpectedly driven into England one of the most complex figures of the late Italian Renaissance: a profoundly learned Neoplatonist, a hermeticist, a passionate poet of love and of the soul's quest for union with the divine mind. He was a Copernican able to elicit a vision of an infinite universe with a plurality of worlds from the philosophical implications of astronomical discoveries. Sidney accepted the challenge of responding, and through his hospitality, support and sympathetic questioning of Bruno's ideas, Sidney gained access to an esoteric world scarcely known to English minds. Bruno's admiration for Sidney and gratitude for favours received are expressed in the philosophical dialogues of *La Cena de le Ceneri* (1584), the Ash Wednesday discussions about an infinity of worlds and the motions of the planets. Bruno also dedicated two substantial works to Sidney: *Lo Spaccio della Bestia Trionfante* (1584), a moral-mythological fantasy, and *Degli Eroici Furori* (1585), the enraptured Neoplatonic love poems with prose commentaries that must have astonished Sidney with their daring flights. The publication of these works realised for Sidney his internationalist ambitions that English writers should share the same intellectual fare as their continental counterparts.

Sidney's European outreach is also evident in his promotion of the educational and dialectical systems of Peter Ramus in England. Sidney had met Ramus in Paris in 1572, shortly before his death in the St Bartholomew's Day massacre, and Sidney came to act as a sponsor for Ramist works in England; a life of Ramus by a French disciple, Théophile de Banos, was dedicated to him, as was a volume of dialectics by William Temple in 1584. (Sidney also paid for the Cambridge education of Abraham Fraunce, who became a well-known Ramist scholar.) In the years before his death, Sidney was beginning to develop interests beyond Europe. As a friend of Drake and Ralegh, he shared their desire for English overseas expansion; his patronage of Richard Hakluyt, who dedicated to Sidney his *Divers Voyages touching the Discoverie of America* in 1582, may have signalled a disposition towards involvement in the colonial venture.[10]

For figures such as Burghley, Leicester and Sidney, literary patronage was an important part of their public lives. It enabled them to influence their society in

10 For Sidney's patronage, see John Buxton, *Sir Philip Sidney and the English Renaissance* (London: Macmillan, 1954), especially pp. 133–72.

ways they desired: to express support for moderate Puritanism and the cause of international Protestantism, to develop the educational system of Elizabethan England and assist the growth of a literary culture. Patronage gave noblemen additional status in a society that was becoming conscious of the desirability of a literary dimension to aristocratic life, as Italian notions of courtly behaviour proposed. In the scholarly and religious worlds, patronage also helped to build up a network of clients with a favourable view of the patron. Classical models of great men with their entourage of poets, scholars and artists were there in the background, and the name of Maecenas was often invoked. The benefits of patronage were reciprocal, for the successful writer might receive any of a great range of rewards: a gift of £2 or £3 for an acceptable dedication, hospitality, a post as tutor or even secretary in the household. For the truly successful, a modest pension, a church living, a fellowship or a minor office at court might be forthcoming. The support of authors in this period was primarily an aspect of aristocratic life, for the church's impoverishment had reduced its influence, although the archbishops practised their traditional clientage.

The anomaly of the Elizabethan system of patronage was the monarch's non-participation. The Queen left such matters to her courtiers. She did not extend patronage to writers, artists or architects. Elizabeth would accept dedications, but she gave nothing in return. An author might as well dedicate a book to the moon for all the benefit it brought. John Foxe dedicated his *Actes and Monuments* (the 'Book of Martyrs') to Elizabeth in 1563, but took care to offer the dedication to Jesus Christ as well, since any spiritual benefits would undoubtedly outweigh the temporal. Spenser dedicated his *Faerie Queene* to Elizabeth, but added dedications to sixteen courtiers from whom he might expect more than a nod of approbation. The geographer John Norden, who had benefited from Burghley's patronage, presented the second part of his *Speculum Britanniae* to Elizabeth in 1598 with an appeal written on the flyleaf: 'In this business I have spent above a thousand marks and five years' time... Only your majesty's princely favour is my hope, without which I myself most miserably perish, my family in penury and the work unperformed, which, being effected, shall be profitable and a glory to this your most admired empire'.[11] All was to no avail. Norden was left to perish. John Lyly, who had written several plays for the court, petitioned Elizabeth for some recompense beyond the elusive promise of a post at court: 'Thirteene yeeres your Highness servant: but yet nothing... my last Will is shorter then my Inventorie: But three Legacyes, Patience to my Creditors, Melancholly without measure to my

---

11 Quoted in Helgerson, *Forms of Nationhood*, p. 125.

frendes, and Beggary without shame to my posterity'.[12] Elizabeth remained unmoved.

The Leicester–Sidney line of patronage continued into the seventeenth century with Sidney's sister, Mary, who became Countess of Pembroke, and her sons William and Philip Herbert, who became the third and fourth Earls of Pembroke respectively. Mary was herself an author of some range and repute, and her son William a competent poet. In consequence, perhaps, they gave particular attention to writers of imaginative literature, and their house at Wilton became known as a kind of arcadian academy. Samuel Daniel, Michael Drayton, William Browne, Ben Jonson, William Shakespeare, Philip Massinger, John Ford and lesser figures such as Thomas Churchyard, Abraham Fraunce and Nicholas Breton were all associated with the family and experienced Pembroke hospitality.[13]

The presence of playwrights in this roll call is a reminder that the theatre needed patronage and protection in Elizabethan times. Although the theatres paid their own way, the companies needed lords to keep the local authorities from clamping down on them and to stop puritanically inclined officials from interfering with actors or performances. Noblemen needed actors to present plays for their entertainment, and recognised the value of the goodwill attracted by support for a popular medium. A number of companies bore a lord's name: Leicester, Worcester, Oxford, Sussex, Essex, Derby, Shrewsbury, while Nottingham stood behind the Admiral's Men and Lord Hunsdon behind the Chamberlain's Men. A theatre company was a distinctive Elizabethan status symbol.

Although an appreciable group of public-spirited noblemen were prepared to assist the writers of literary, scholarly and religious works, by the 1590s the number of writers far outstripped the capacity of patrons to provide support. The proliferation of printing presses, the expansion of the book trade, the rapidly increasing number of university graduates who tried to live by writing – all contributed to that familiar phenomenon, the struggling, near-destitute author, lacking a patron and unable to persuade a publisher to pay him adequately for his work. Publishers in the sixteenth and seventeenth centuries made a simple payment for the manuscript, often a very small payment, at the time of delivery. Books were not sold for the benefit of the author, but for the stationer who bore all the expenses of publication. Elizabethan and Jacobean literary works resound with the distress calls of authors.

12 Second petition to the Queen, in A. Feuillerat, *John Lyly* (Cambridge University Press, 1910), pp. 561–2.
13 Pembroke patronage is exhaustively discussed by Michael Brennan in *Literary Patronage in the English Renaissance: The Pembroke Family* (London: Routledge, 1988).

Thomas Nashe was among the most vocal. Although Nashe habitually exaggerated his response to circumstances, he seems to have been on the receiving end of many a rebuff in his search for patrons. His recollections of a literary life in *Pierce Penilesse* (1592) are particularly distressing:

> All in vaine, I sate up late, and rose earely, contended with the colde, and conversed with scarcitie: for all my labours turned to losse, my vulgar Muse was despised and neglected, my paines not regarded, or slightly rewarded, and I my selfe (in prime of my best wit) laid open to povertie. Whereupon, I accused my fortune, raild on my patrones.[14]

Next comes a vivid glimpse of the hapless writer waiting on a gentleman he has targeted with his dedication or his presentation copy: 'Alas, it is easie for a goodlie tall fellow that shineth in his silkes, to come and outface a poore simple Pedant in a thred bare cloake, and tell him his booke is pretty, but at this time he is not provided for him'.[15] Nashe was one of the most vigorous writers of the time, but this did not seem to impress his patrons. Although he caught the attention of the Earl of Southampton and the Carey family, he did not manage to hold their favour on a literary scene where there were so many rivals. Perhaps his restless personality did not please, or the tenor of his writings was too acrimonious.

Even the great Spenser wandered in the wilderness of neglect for a while, as the complaints in 'Mother Hubberds Tale' (1591) indicate. At the other end of the literary scale, however, a hack writer's life was almost unbearably miserable. Richard Robinson, a translator and aspiring man of letters, gave a sad account of various rejections. He offered Queen Elizabeth his translation of a Protestant devotional work by Strigelius, *The Harmony of King David's Harp*, as she progressed to chapel at Richmond on All Saints' Day, 1595 (the presentation of books to the monarch during her formal progress to chapel was a routine event, as were petitioning and the making of requests). 'It pleased your excellent majesty to receive this my pore labour gracyusly. I pore man expected Comfort for the same deservingly.' The Master of Requests told Robinson that 'your Majesty thanked me for my good will, your Highness was glad yow had a subject could do so well, and that I deserved commendacions. But for any gratification for any suche laboures youre Majesty was not in mynde as then to bestow any suche relief oppon me.' Robinson then tried to present a dedicated copy to Sir Thomas Egerton. 'In the presence of six clerks in the Chancery; his Lordship grutching to recyve my Booke, or to render mee any rewards, his eloquent

---

14 *Pierce Penilesse his supplication to the divell*, in *Works of Thomas Nashe*, ed. R. S. McKerrow, 5 vols. (London: A. H. Bullen *et al.*, 1904–10), 1:157.
15 *Ibid.*, 1:241–2.

tongue tripped mee in my suite saying "What have we here? Literae petaces
[literary farts]?"' and so brushed him off.[16] On a slightly better day, Robinson
was able to get 2 shillings from the Bishop of Chichester for the dedication of
a work. He applied relentlessly to eminent men, and occasionally struck gold:
he once got £2 from the Earl of Rutland, and £2 from Sir Christopher Hatton,
and he lists the names of ten people from whom he received small sums. But
over the years these were slender returns for Robinson's literary labours, and
he lived a most penurious life.

The general situation improved somewhat under James I, for a new reign
gave rise to new hopes, and the King and Queen were much more responsive
and generous to authors than Elizabeth had been. The optimistic and acclam-
atory character of much early Jacobean writing was partly occasioned by the
successful transfer of the crown and the union of England and Scotland, but
it was also caused by the knowledge that James was a bookish king who enjoyed the company of literary men. The King was an author himself, as he
liked to observe – a poet, a theological writer and a composer of treaties on
statecraft. He believed that good letters were an ornament of the kingdom,
and he set an example. Court life flourished under James, was more open than
under Elizabeth, and writers were more welcome: poets, playwrights, philosophical and religious writers all had an entrée to Whitehall. Noblemen and
noblewomen usually liked to have a few authors orbiting around them. The
King directly patronised a theatre company, the King's Men, with Shakespeare
as its leading playwright, and the Queen also had her own company. Queen
Anne's patronage was responsible for the appearance of a new art form, the
court masque, from 1604 onwards, and King James developed a working relationship, perhaps even a friendship, with Ben Jonson, the principal deviser of
masques in the reign.

The most significant act of patronage by King James, however, was the translation of the Bible that he initiated and oversaw. This was a disinterested kind
of patronage, serving in principle the cause of religious harmony and also exploiting the resources of Biblical and linguistic scholarship that had developed
in England in the decades since the Reformation. The proposal for a new translation had come from the Puritan side at the Hampton Court Conference that
James had convened, just after his accession, to settle the differences in the
church. The King rejected most of the Puritan suggestions concerning doctrine
and discipline, but he did respond to the idea that a new translation of the Bible,
scholarly and authoritative, should replace the two competing versions then

16 Quoted in H. S. Bennett, *English Books 1558–1603*, p. 50.

in use: the Bishops' Bible adopted by the Church of England, and the Geneva Bible preferred by the laity. Some fifty translators worked in six groups and consulted frequently. They included such scholars as Lancelot Andrewes, then Dean of Westminster; William Bedwell the orientalist; Laurence Chaderton, Master of Emmanuel College, Cambridge; John Overall, Dean of St Paul's; Sir Henry Savile, Warden of Merton College, Oxford; and George Abbot, Master of University College, Oxford, and future Archbishop of Canterbury.[17]

The King took a serious interest in the progress of the work, and set certain guiding principles: the Bishops' Bible was to be the model, the established ecclesiastical and theological terms kept, and the proper names of Biblical figures, familiar to the people, should be retained. It may seem astonishing that committees could produce such uniform excellence of style, rendering the text with dignity, terseness and clarity in language that achieves gravity but does not lose touch with the popular idiom, all harmonised by noble and moving cadences, wonderfully suited to public utterance. James's active concern for the new translation was indeed enlightened patronage, and he entirely deserved the dedication of the Bible when it was published in 1611.

Although the King was the ultimate fount of patronage, he was less bountiful towards writers than might have been expected of a literary monarch. A few did benefit, however; Jonson managed to derive a fairly regular income from the King for court masques throughout the reign, for these almost-annual commissions could bring in almost £40 a time. In general, however, neither money nor offices nor sinecures were much in evidence as royal rewards for writers in this reign. James's most valuable service to literature was to encourage John Donne to take holy orders, promising him advancement in the church. The King was responding to Donne's prose writings that dealt with the position of the Catholics: the learnedly witty satire against the Jesuits, *Ignatius his Conclave*, and more particularly, *Pseudo-Martyr*, written to justify the taking of an Oath of Allegiance that would ensure the primary loyalty of the English Catholics to the King of England rather than to the Pope of Rome. Donne had hoped for secular advancement, but the King made clear his own conviction that Donne's talents would be best employed in the church. Lacking an alternative, Donne somewhat reluctantly took orders early in 1615, and promptly became a royal chaplain, attending regularly upon the King; he consequently received a Doctorate of Divinity from Cambridge by royal mandate, and soon

---

17 Informative accounts of the production of the Authorised Version are given by C. C. Butterworth in *The Literary Lineage of the King James Bible, 1340–1611* (Philadelphia: University of Pennsylvania Press, 1941), and by A. C. Partridge in his *English Biblical Translation* (London: Deutsch, 1973), pp. 105–58.

acquired two church livings. In 1616 Donne was appointed Reader in Divinity at Lincoln's Inn, and in 1621 the King named him Dean of St Paul's, ensuring his presence at the centre of London ecclesiastical life and giving him a major auditory for his sermons. Of course, James wanted Donne's talents to fulfil the royal policy of creating a learned ministry for the church; he also wanted Donne's eloquence to preach the Word and reinforce the reformed faith. In longer perspective, however, the King's patronage secured the livelihood of one of the most adventurous literary intelligences of the age, and was incidentally responsible for one of the glories of the religious arts in England – the sermons Donne preached in the last fifteen years of his life.

Until his effectual rescue by the King, Donne's career exemplified the uncertainties and disappointments of a literary life in Elizabethan and Jacobean times. We, today, are inclined to regard Donne as a man of letters, for he comes down to us as a poet of love, devotion and philosophical speculation, as a writer of occasional verse, a deviser of strenuously argued paradoxes and polemics. Donne, however, probably regarded himself as a versatile man of wit whose writings in poetry and prose were a form of intellectual display and self-advertisement. He designed his writings to cut a figure to impress and attract the attention of men or women of authority who might offer him employment, commensurate with his abilities, as an adviser or a functionary at court or in the complex systems of the political and legal establishments. This is not to underrate the literary value of Donne's poetry, but rather to indicate its important social dimension. For almost twenty years he had failed to secure a constant patron, although he had brief successes with Sir Thomas Egerton, Lucy, Countess of Bedford, and Magdalen Herbert. King James was his salvation, finally responding to the accumulated evidence of Donne's mastery of language and ideas.

Patronage at the highest level was not always a matter of simple reward for literary production. Francis Bacon, for example, was not seeking a place or a pension or remuneration when he dedicated to King James his series of works calling for the expansion of knowledge. *The Advancement of Learning*, the *Novum Organum Scientiarum* and the comprehensive description of his ambitious programme of intellectual enquiry, the *Instauratio Magna*, were all offered in the hope that the cogency of Bacon's arguments would induce James to become the patron of the new learning, preferably by founding a college for what we would call scientific research, as envisaged in Bacon's posthumous work *New Atlantis* (1626, dedicated to King Charles by its editor). James accepted Bacon's presentation copy of the *Novum Organum* (1620) with the resonant quip that 'like the peace of God, it passed all understanding'. The King remained indifferent to the opportunity to sponsor the systematic study of natural philosophy. Instead, he chose to found a college of polemical divinity at Chelsea, which he believed would meet the urgent needs of the time: defending and justifying the position of the Church of England.

The record of royal patronage in James's reign brings forward Queen Anne and Henry, Prince of Wales, as more active patrons than the King himself. Both incorporated writers into their households, providing secure bases for continuing creativity. The Queen maintained the Protestant John Florio, the leading interpreter of contemporary Italy to the English, as a tutor to her children, and she retained the poet Samuel Daniel as the controller of her entertainments. She also patronised Inigo Jones, the best approximation of a Renaissance universal man that Britain could show; and the Dutch painter Paul van Somer, a suave and stylish modernist, lived in her household for several years. Court masques at Whitehall developed primarily under Anne's patronage, first through her employment of Samuel Daniel in 1604, and thereafter of Ben Jonson, innovators in the new court genre of the masque: symbolic drama that incorporated poetry, song, music, dance, costume and scenery in baroque spectacles of pleasure, wealth and power. Once the Queen commissioned Inigo Jones to design the staging of these masques from 1605 onwards, often in conjunction with Jonson, the distinctive form of the Stuart court festival began to emerge. Queen Anne's initiative propelled these masques into being, and they remained effectively in her control until *Love Freed from Ignorance and Folly* in 1611. These extravagant spectacles scattered money to a range of creative figures in court circles, from poets to tailors. For the last-mentioned masque, for example, Ben Jonson and Inigo Jones both received £40, but the choreographer topped the list of rewards with £50. Anne's interest in masquing waned after the death of her eldest son, Prince Henry, in 1612, when the King seems to have assumed charge, delegating the invention and production of masques to Jonson and Jones.

The heir to the throne, Prince Henry, took the responsibilities of patronage seriously, building up an entourage of writers and artists who would reflect his chosen self-image as a Renaissance prince in the Italian style: soldier, scholar, collector, connoisseur and Christian. Precocious and short-lived (1594–1612), Prince Henry uniquely among the Stuarts had a fully developed sense of a court as a centre of structured cultured activity, where patronage was an essential means of representing the complex figure of the prince in the public eye. Henry employed George Chapman as a member of his household at St James's Palace. Here Chapman undertook his translations of Homer, which would give an appropriately heroic aura to the Prince's court. Chapman claimed that Henry had promised him £300 on the completion of the work – a lavish sum that gives some indication of how highly the Prince valued the work. Chapman wrote his tragedies of French political affairs while in the Prince's service, reflecting Henry's identification with Henri IV (assassinated in 1610), and projecting the values of the Prince of Wales's court in plays that combined political analysis with philosophical reflection, set in a world of noble strife. *The Revenge of Bussy d'Ambois* and *The Conspiracy of Byron* are characteristic of this phase of Chapman's work. Another poet highly favoured by Prince Henry was Michael Drayton, who received a regular pension of £10 per annum, and whose principal work for the Prince was *Poly-Olbion* (1612), a lengthy topographical poem that surveyed the kingdom by tracing the course of its rivers and narrating the stirring events associated with them. Polonius might have described *Poly-Olbion* as epical-historical-pastoral; its mixture of patriotism, chivalry and antiquity evoked an illustrious heritage that, by implication, would be extended by Prince Henry's achievements.

Henry inspired and apparently welcomed the dedication of books that reflected his ambitions and enhanced the reputation of his court. Henry Peacham's attractive emblem book, *Minerva Britanna, or a Garden of Heroical Devises* (1612), represented the court in a series of naïve woodcuts with suitable verses as a place where men aspired to the highest ideals of chivalric honour, morality and piety. Militant Protestants saw Prince Henry as the figure destined to lead the forces of the reformed religion against the iniquities of Rome, a role Henry himself seems to have entertained. A number of books urging him to take the field against the Catholic powers were dedicated to him, including one by Robert Abbot, brother of the Archbishop of Canterbury, expressing the hope that Henry would enact 'the glorious revenge of the cause of Almighty God' by smiting that 'antichristian and wicked state' ruled by the Pope.[18] Notable among Prince Henry's chaplains was Joseph Hall, the moderate Anglican who would successively become Bishop of Exeter, then of Norwich. Hall composed a number of sermons for Henry's edification, and dedicated to him his *Epistles* (1608) and his *Contemplations* (1612), works of moral precept that the Prince took to heart.

On another front, Henry offered encouragement to Sir Walter Ralegh, whose accomplishments he admired and whose counsel he valued. But since Ralegh was locked up in the Tower after 1603, on suspicion of involvement in a plot to overthrow King James, the Prince was unable to provide any effective protection. Nevertheless, Ralegh wrote several works advising the Prince on statecraft and on the use of naval power, and he posthumously dedicated to Henry the

18 Robert Abbot, *The True Ancient Roman Catholike* (London, 1611), p. 18.

immense, unfinished *History of the World* (1614) that he had been compiling for many years in prison, displaying God's judgements in history and his special care for the English in the latter days. Ralegh's preface declared, 'It was for the service of that inestimable Prince Henry that I undertook this work', aiming to give the Prince an overview of the world scene on which he was expected soon to become an actor. When the Prince contracted his sudden, fatal illness in 1612, Ralegh sent him a cordial, probably quinine, that he had discovered to be effective against fever in his South American expedition, but it was too late. Ralegh's imprisonment and Henry's premature death severed a connection of great potential, based on neither money nor position, but on the felt need of an ambitious young prince for an experienced adviser.

A noteworthy feature of patronage in Jacobean times was the prominence of females. A group of bright, educated women, mostly friends of the Queen, regarded the encouragement of writers as a natural part of their aristocratic lifestyle. Several of these women were writers themselves, who understood something of the trials of literary composition; they also appreciated the lustre that dedications and complimentary poems could add to their names in a society where literary awareness was high. The leading light of this group was Lucy, Countess of Bedford, a member of the Harington family, niece of the poet and translator Sir John Harington. Her husband had been politically reduced by his involvement in the Earl of Essex's rebellion of 1601, and ill health later restricted his presence at court. The wealth and honour of the Bedfords were largely in Lucy's control. Her houses at Twickenham and Moor Park were centres of social activity where writers seem to have been most welcome. Poems by Jonson and Donne testify that hospitality was offered and gratuities given, but the real attraction was the access to a setting where wit was valued and writers could display their talents and exchange opinions with the more cultivated members of the Jacobean court. Drayton, Chapman and John Davies of Hereford had entrée to the Countess's circle at various times. Lucy Bedford herself wrote poetry, now unfortunately lost, some in the form of verse correspondence with her familiar poets – an exercise which must have given the poets a pleasing though temporary sense of equality with their aristocratic patron. According to Jonson, Lady Mary Wroth, Sir Philip Sidney's niece, was also a generous patron in her Jacobean heyday; Jonson dedicated epigrams and his play *The Alchemist* to her. Wroth's elaborate romance *Urania* (Part I, 1621) was dedicated to Lady Susan Vere, another of Queen Anne's bright ladies, who showed favour to Jonson and Chapman. Elizabeth, Countess of Rutland, Sir Philip Sidney's daughter, offered friendship to poets in a way almost instinctive among members of the Sidney clan. 'With you, I know, my offering will find grace', remarked Jonson in his epistle to her printed in *The Forest*. She too wrote poetry, for which Jonson expressed admiration in his conversations with William Drummond. Penelope Rich, sister to the second Earl of Essex, dispensed her patronage broadly to musicians such as William Byrd and John Dowland, to the miniaturist Nicholas Hilliard, and to the poet and dramatist John Ford. She was the dedicatee of the English translation of the popular Spanish romance, *Diana*, by Jorge de Montemayor. The two successive Countesses of Derby complete this list of aristocratic patronesses who did so much to sustain poetry and poets in this period. The elder, Alice Spencer, has the unrivalled record of patronising Spenser, Shakespeare and Milton, as well as Donne, Jonson, Marston and John Davies of Hereford, while her successor Elizabeth de Vere (for whose wedding Shakespeare may have written *A Midsummer Night's Dream*) was acknowledged for her generous hospitality to poets and theatre men.[19]

For showing how a poet might succeed through patronage, the career of Samuel Daniel (*c.* 1562–1619) is instructive; he was characteristic of many writers in being well educated but poorly endowed financially, and determined to live by letters. After his education at Oxford, he was taken up by Sir Edward Dymoke, the Queen's Champion, a man naturally interested in war, tournaments and chivalry. He encouraged Daniel to translate Paolo Giovio's book on impresas or military emblems from the Italian, a language Daniel had managed to learn in England. His connection with Dymoke led to employment by Sir Edward Stafford, the English ambassador in Paris in the 1580s, and Daniel hoped to study there, but instead went as Dymoke's servant on a tour of Italy, where he met the great Ferrarese pastoralist Guarini. On his return, eager to write poetry, Daniel soon came to the attention of Mary, Countess of Pembroke. She was enthusiastic about his European experiences and encouraged him to write for the honour of English poetry, offering him financial support and a place in her household at Wilton. There in the first half of the 1590s, Daniel composed his best poetry. He dedicated his sonnet sequence, *Delia*, and his long *Complaint of Rosamond* to the Countess in 1592. Influenced by the Countess's translation of the French drama *Marc-Antoine*, by Robert Garnier, Daniel wrote his philosophical tragedy *Cleopatra* (registered in 1593) and then began work on his long sequence of poems on the Wars of the Roses. Some unknown incident in 1595 caused him to leave Wilton, but he was promptly taken up by those friends of poetry Fulke Greville and Charles Blount, Lord Mountjoy, who found him accommodation and presumably provided financial support. In this era many aristocratic men and women felt strongly about the condition of English letters and were prepared to patronise promising poets who might add distinction to the national name. Ever since Sidney had drawn attention to the relative backwardness of English imaginative writing in his *Apologie for Poetrie* (*c.* 1581), calling for a national literature that could equal that of France and Italy, educated Englishmen and women of eminent families had recognised that talented men of letters should be supported and encouraged as a matter of patriotic pride.

About 1600 Daniel made an advantageous move into the household of Lady Margaret Clifford, Countess of Cumberland, where he became tutor to her independent-minded daughter, Lady Anne Clifford. He taught her languages, history, philosophy and made her a lifelong lover of poetry. For several years this pleasant state of affairs continued, enhanced by recommendations to Lucy, Countess of Bedford, Margaret Clifford's close relative, and then to the Queen. Daniel's commission for the masque *The Vision of the Twelve Goddesses* came out of these new relationships at court. He still enjoyed Lord Mountjoy's favours and about 1604/5 added the patronage of the rich Earl of Hertford to his portfolio. By this time literate aristocrats were competing for a share in the work of Samuel Daniel. He acquired a house in the City of London, became a Groom of the Queen's Privy Chamber sometime in 1607, advancing to Gentleman Extraordinary in 1613 with a salary of £60, and remaining in her household until the Queen's death in 1619. His principal literary service to her was the masque *Tethys Festival*, composed for the installation of Prince Henry as Prince of Wales in 1610. Daniel kept lines of communication open to old patrons, dedicating *Musophilus* to Sir Fulke Greville in 1611, for example. When he died in 1619, and was buried in his native village of Beckington in Somerset, Daniel's attentive patrons continued to care for him even after death, for Lady Anne Clifford composed a memorial inscription for him and paid for his modest monument in the parish church.[20]

If Daniel's career shows the successful manipulation of patronage, its complete failure is exemplified by the case of Aemilia Lanyer, the wife of a court musician, who published her devotional volume, *Salve Deus Rex Judaeorum*, in 1611. Here was a rare instance of a woman appearing in print, and aspiring to divine poetry too. Half as long as the main poem was a prefatory series of

---

20 Daniel's career can be followed in detail in Joan Rees, *Samuel Daniel* (Liverpool University Press, 1964).

ten dedicatory poems addressed to the powerful women of the Jacobean court, starting with the Queen. Some of these women Lanyer had known slightly, others are figures she admires from a distance, and she appeals for their patronage in the name of religion and feminine solidarity to support her work. Lanyer evidently had not sought permission to offer these dedications, so they belong to that familiar class of hopeful supplications that came unsolicited and went unacknowledged. Although her dedicatory poems to Princess Elizabeth, Arbella Stuart, Lucy Bedford, Margaret Cumberland, Anne Dorset and other peeresses evoked a spirit of enlightened feminine co-operation, Lanyer appears to have been totally neglected. Why, one wonders? Possibly because she had no history as a writer, or because her unbidden dedications were regarded as impertinent, or because a woman's verses were not thought to add lustre to a patron's name or to the reputation of English letters. Lanyer vanished from the literary scene after her one brief appearance.

The reign of Charles I saw an overall tendency for serious literary patronage to decline. There were few outstanding patrons, and probably less need for financial support or provision of places because many of the writers of the time were either gentlemen of private means or had some form of settled employment, often in the church. A dedication to a friend – often one of higher social status than the author – became a normative pattern, and commonly the dedication dwelt on the shared values of author and dedicatee. For example, William Davenant dedicated his volume of poems *Madagascar* (1638) to Endymion Porter and Henry Jermyn. However, many volumes of verse now appeared without any dedication at all: the posthumous volumes of Donne's *Poems* (1633) and Herbert's *The Temple* (1633) had no dedicatees, nor did Thomas Randolph's volume of poems published in 1638 or Thomas Carew's in 1640. The number of books dedicated to the most important men in the state noticeably declined. Fewer books were offered to Charles I than had been dedicated to James, by a ratio of about ten to fifteen a year over a decade. Archbishop Laud received remarkably few dedications, only four or five a year throughout his period in office, and only a dozen books were dedicated to Sir Thomas Wentworth during the 1630s.[21] Even Philip Herbert, Earl of Pembroke, the head of the family with the greatest tradition of literary patronage in the country, received fewer dedications after he inherited the title in 1630 than he had as the heir apparent in Jacobean times. The fashion for cultivating writers, which had conferred social distinction in James's time, lapsed under Charles. This may

---

21 Details from Franklin B. Williams, *Index of Dedications and Commendatory Verses* (London: Bibliographical Society, 1962).

have been because Charles was much more interested in the visual arts than in books. The theatre companies and dramatists had less need for patrons in the later reign, and could survive more or less independently in the open market.

Even in these relatively palmy days, a professional writer might experience great difficulty in scraping together a living, especially if he had a restless temperament and a prickly personality. James Shirley is a case in point. A play-wright, poet, masquemaker, Shirley appealed for patronage to many different people – some of the highest eminence – during the 1630s and 1640s. Yet no relationship endured. Shirley became a servant of Queen Henrietta Maria for a short time, then became the resident playwright at Wentworth's viceregal court in Dublin in 1636. After Wentworth's demise, he was taken up by the Earl of Newcastle, who did more to help Shirley's career in the Royalist army than in the Caroline literary world. Patron gave way to patron, and virtually every one of Shirley's many publications was dedicated to a different person. His *Poems* (1646), his most personal creation, was dedicated to a man he did not even know, a prosperous London merchant, Bernard Hyde, in vain hope of reward. Shirley's restlessness and instability emerge too in his constant change of publishers: he used at least twenty-five publishers and booksellers in the course of his long career. He kept writing to the end, buoyed up by the tem-porary literary patronage from many quarters, but a huge expense of time and effort must have been required to keep afloat.[22]

With the outbreak of the Civil War in 1642, conventional patronage patterns broke down. The court dissolved, and gentlemen had other things to think about than encouraging literature. Censorship broke down too, and publish-ing faced free market forces for the first time. The vast number of pamphlets that now poured out from the press did not need patrons, for they addressed contemporary issues, and they sold cheaply on their merits. A distinctive fea-ture of literary publication in the 1640s was the number of volumes of poetry and plays by Royalists such as Carew, Waller, Crashaw, Vaughan, Suckling, Shirley, Herrick, Cowley and Fanshawe, together with the posthumous folio collections of Jonson and Beaumont and Fletcher. It seems that poems were published because their real audience amongst courtiers and churchmen and country gentlemen had been dispersed by war, and publication allowed them to find what audience they could in the country at large. The volumes also served, however, to rally Royalist sentiment and to uphold the cause of church and King in times of opposition and defeat. Patrons were not required, although

22 See Sandra A. Burner, *James Shirley: a Study of Literary Coteries in Seventeenth-Century England* (Lanham, MD: University Press of America, 1988).

several dedications went to the King and Prince of Wales as gestures of faith in the eclipsed monarchy. After the execution of Charles in 1649, in the new ethos of republican Britain, old-style patronage that encouraged and protected the recipient almost disappeared. Most books were dedicated to friends or to well-wishers, or to appropriate bodies such as colleges or the Inns of Court, gentlemen of a shire or to Members of Parliament. The most dangerous book of the age, Hobbes's *Leviathan*, with its secular, amoral analysis of political power, was dedicated to Francis Godolphin, brother of Hobbes's friend Sidney Godolphin, who had been killed in the Civil Wars. Hobbes was not persecuted for his sceptical – some would say atheistical – views, nor was the book banned. Hobbes had no need of a patron or protector in the relatively tolerant climate of the 1650s. Yet he was a product of the old patronage system, having been maintained for many years before the war by the Cavendish family, who gave him the time and the means to develop his thought in an agreeably sheltered setting.

One special category of book enjoyed a particular prominence in the 1650s: the major scholarly work, usually in folio, immensely expensive to produce yet appealing to only a small readership. An early example would be Sir Henry Savile's edition of St John Chrysostom's works in eight volumes, published in 1619–22. This particular enterprise was supported by Eton College, and dedicated to King James, who, one assumes, contributed generously towards a work that tended to the honour of a scholarly Church of England. The 1650s saw a number of major projects come to press, notably books by William Dugdale: the *Monasticon Anglicanum* (1655) *and The Antiquities of Warwickshire* (1656). The *Monasticon*, the first book on the foundation and history of monasteries in England, was filled with details of charters and land grants, and illustrated with numerous plates of monastic sites. Although Dugdale invested much of his own money in this work, its publication was facilitated by the subscription system; supporters of the project each sponsored a plate for £5, for which they had their name, coat of arms and a Latin phrase engraved in a cartouche. Others engaged to buy a copy of the published book. This method of subscription was in effect an inexpensive form of patronage that allowed many individuals to associate themselves with the book, and allowed the book to represent a constituency of readers when it was published. Dugdale's other works were brought out under the same system.[23] The pioneering *Dictionarium Saxonico-Latino-Anglicum* compiled over many years by William Somner, which made the

---

23 For publication of Dugdale's books, see Graham Parry, *The Trophies of Time: English Antiquarians of the Seventeenth Century* (Oxford University Press, 1995), ch. 8.

Anglo-Saxon language broadly accessible for the first time, was published in 1659 by means of the subscription method.

Of all these Commonwealth scholarly projects, the largest was the Polyglot Bible, printed during the years 1654 to 1657 under the general editorship of Brian Walton, who later became Bishop of Chester. In six volumes, with texts in nine languages, and drawing on many ancient renderings of the Scriptures, this work was the supreme achievement of Biblical scholarship in seventeenth-century England. It was supported by subscription, at least £10 for a set, and by free gifts from well-wishers. By these means the impressive sum of £8,000 was raised. The Council of State approved the project, and promised £1,500, but the sum was never paid. Oliver Cromwell desired to have the dedication of the work, but its editor Walton resented the non-payment of the subsidy, and he was, besides, an Anglican and a royalist. He wanted to dedicate the Bible to the exiled Prince Charles as Charles II of England, but he was dissuaded by the other movers of the work from this provocative gesture. The Bible finally appeared without a dedication, but with two prefaces, variously present in different copies, one acknowledging the Protector Cromwell and the Council of State, the other mentioning neither of these parties nor Prince Charles. The confused preliminaries of the Polyglot Bible reveal the tensions and divided loyalties of the time, but the successful publication of the Bible was a convincing demonstration of the viability of the subscription system, which became a normal form of publication for learned works after the Restoration.[24]

This account cannot close without some mention of John Milton. As a young man in the 1630s he willingly accepted commissions from the Countess of Derby and the Egerton family, and aspired to gain the support of Sir Henry Wotton at the beginning of his Italian journey in 1637. But as Milton grew more radical after the assembling of the Long Parliament, he had no use for patrons: free-born Englishmen should speak their minds openly, and be indebted to no man. Hence Milton did not dedicate his writings, but he did address some that proposed reform, such as *Areopagitica* or the divorce tracts, to 'the Parliament of England' as the main engine of reform in the country. His *Poems* of 1645 carried no dedication, nor did *Paradise Lost* in 1667. However, the writing of *Paradise Lost* gave rise to a new concept of patronage. While Milton felt entirely independent of all earthly obligation, his experience of divine inspiration during the process of composition led him to discover the perfect patron in the Muse of Divine Poetry. This inspirational power, on occasion called Urania,

---

24 The progress of the Polyglot Bible can be traced in Henry John Todd, *Memoirs of the Life and Writings of the Rt Rev. Brian Walton*, 2 vols. (London: F. C. and J. Rivington, 1821).

is sometimes indistinguishable from the Holy Ghost in the blending of classical and Christian ideas in Milton's mind. It is entirely characteristic of Milton at the height of his career that he should recognise the only true patron for his soaring imagination as a spiritual, indeed a divine being. Accordingly he invokes, at the beginning of Book IX:

> My Celestial Patroness, who deignes
> Her nightly visitation unimplor'd,
> And dictates to me slumbring, or inspires
> Easie my unpremediated Verse.

The conflation of muse and patron was a satisfying synthesis for the most independent of poets, one that transposes the whole concept of patronage onto a higher plane. For all other writers who published in the years after the Restoration, conventional patronage, often signalled by a dedication to a member of the restored aristocracy, became once more the norm.

Chapter 5

LANGUAGES OF EARLY MODERN
LITERATURE IN BRITAIN

PAULA BLANK

The *questione della lingua*: *that* is the question or, at least, the one that was posed by early modern Italians regarding the status of the vernacular in the sixteenth century. Renaissance Italian writers involved in the debate widely known as the 'question of the language' considered their options: they had to choose, first, between the native tongue and Latin, still the lingua franca of European culture; and second (if they chose Italian), they had to discriminate further among the several dialects of Italian then current. Early modern British authors, too, often faced such choices – whether to write in Latin or in the mother tongue and, if in the latter, what form of the vernacular to choose. Although the question of selecting among regional dialects had been more or less settled with regard to the written language, the British vernaculars were not yet standard languages; that is, they were neither uniform nor fixed by rule.[1] The Renaissance in Britain has long been identified with a prodigious variety and plasticity in the forms and uses of native languages, a 'linguistic exuberance' characteristic of its greatest poets, including Edmund Spenser, William Shakespeare and John Milton. The Renaissance was no linguistic free-for-all, however: sixteenth- and early seventeenth-century writers, across a range of disciplines, address the question of the language by discriminating among available forms and experimenting with new ones. The linguistic choices made by Renaissance British writers, and what was at stake in the choosing, will be the subject of this chapter.

In the almost six centuries from 1100 to 1660 – roughly, from the Norman Conquest to the Restoration – Latin was the dominant language of a transnational, European, lettered culture. The latter days of the long reign of Latin over European literature – the early modern period, from 1500 to 1660 – are distinctive, however, in one important and apparently contradictory way:

---

1 Classical Gaelic, the language of bardic poetry in Gaelic Scotland and Ireland, is an exception. See observations below, p. 162.

Renaissance writers subscribed anew to the preeminence of Latin, yet at the same time presided over Latin's decline. As a period term the 'Renaissance' refers in large part to the humanist recovery and imitation of Greek and Latin classics; the period thus defined itself by its endorsement of writing in those languages. The Renaissance also saw the proliferation of *neo*-Latin literature, a conscious effort to compose new works in the classical language across the range of early modern arts and sciences. Until the middle of the seventeenth century, there is a clear humanist consensus that Latin is superior to the vernaculars, aesthetically, spiritually and socially; Latin is widely revered as a model of eloquence and grammatical rule, the way to sacred truths, a mark of literacy, education and social ascendancy. Classical Latin was regularly deemed a 'perfect' language, all the more for being a dead language, no longer subject to degenerative change. It was, and continued to be, the model for what might be achieved through the written word.

Thus when the sixteenth-century Scottish poet Gawin Douglas said that 'Besyde Latyn our langage is imperfite',[2] he was only reiterating a commonplace of Renaissance comparative linguistics. The six vernacular languages in use in Renaissance Britain included two modern descendants of Anglo-Saxon – English and Scots – and four Celtic languages: Cornish, Welsh, Irish Gaelic and Scottish Gaelic. By 1603, England's closest neighbours, Wales, Scotland and Ireland, had all been the object of English efforts towards annexation or union, with coextensive efforts towards linguistic union, or 'anglicisation'. The anglicisation of British writing is testimony to what has been called the 'triumph of English' in this period.[3] But it is essential to note that Latin, the language of imperial Rome, provided the model for a 'universal' English in Britain. As Spenser observed, '[I]t hath ever been the use of the conqueror to despise the language of the conquered, and to force him by all means to learn his. So did the Romans...', and many concurred that in Rome as elsewhere 'this communion...of language hath always been observed a special motive to unite...the minds of all nations'.[4] Uniting minds by uniting language, as we will see, was one of the declared motives behind language policy throughout the period. Despite, and sometimes because of, the long-standing catholicity

---

2 Gawin Douglas, *Virgil's Aeneid Translated into Scottish Verse* (1553), ed. David F. C. Coldwell (Edinburgh: William Blackwood,1957), Proloug, line 359.
3 Richard Foster Jones, *The Triumph of the English Language* (Stanford University Press, 1953).
4 Edmund Spenser, *A View of the Present State of Ireland* (1596), in *Elizabethan Ireland: A Selection of Writings by Elizabethan Writers on Ireland*, ed. James P. Myers, Jr (Hamden, CT: Archon Books, 1983), pp. 96–7; Fynes Moryson, *An Itinerary* (1617 – c. 1626), in *Elizabethan Ireland*, p. 207.

of Latin, the British vernaculars were increasingly pronounced the *new* voices of consensus, conformity or cultural identity.

I will begin with a brief overview of the status of the vernacular languages in Renaissance Britain before proceeding to a closer investigation of language choices in selected fields of Renaissance writing. First, the fate of both spoken and written Cornish, the Celtic language native to southwestern England, can be dealt with summarily here. Although in 1547 Andrew Borde reported that many men and women in Cornwall spoke no English but only Cornish, by 1602 a *Survey of Cornwall* sees the situation reversed: '[M]ost of the inhabitants can speak no word of Cornish, but very few are ignorant of the English'.[5] The only extant Cornish writings of the period are two plays on Biblical themes, from 1504 and 1611, respectively, and about a dozen homilies translated from English. This in itself is not incidental, since the transmission of the Celtic languages, in general, would occur largely through literary and theological writing.

The anglicisation of Wales, Ireland and Scotland, however, called for more deliberate political and legal action. The political border between Wales and England was abolished by the Act of Union of 1536 when, in the words of one early seventeenth-century playwright, 'faire *Wales* her happy Vnion had, / Blest Vnion, that such happinesse did bring'.[6] In addition to imposing English religion and English law, the Union made specific provisions for the Welsh language, banning Welsh speakers from pursuing justice in their native tongue or from holding municipal office of any kind, unless 'they use[d] and exercise[d] the speche or langage of Englisshe'.[7] The anglicisation of Wales proceeded apace with the help of the Welsh gentry, many of whom sent their sons to be educated at English schools. As contemporary chorographies of the region report, however, Welsh remained the dominant form of speech in the region (except in Pembrokeshire, sometimes called 'Little England beyond Wales'), despite the steady progress of anglicisation in writing.[8]

The English did not have to resort to violence in their efforts to unite with the Welsh, although they did demand certain cultural sacrifices of them. With the Irish, it was another story. After centuries of native resistance, Ireland was

5 Andrew Borde, *The fyrst boke of the Introduction of knowledge* [1542]; Richard Carew, *Survey of Cornwall* (1602), qtd in Glanville Price, 'Cornish Language and Literature', in *The Celtic Connection*, ed. Glanville Price (Gerard's Cross: Colin Smythe, 1992), p. 302.

6 R. A., Gent., *The Valiant Welshman* (1615) (New York: AMS Press, 1970), i. 56–7.

7 Qtd in R. Brinley Jones, *The Old British Tongue: The Vernacular in Wales, 1540–1640* (Cardiff: Avalon Books, 1970), p. 33.

8 See, for example, George Owen, *The description of Pembrokeshire, by George Owen of Henllys*, ed. with introduction and notes by Dillwyn Miles (Llandysul, Wales: Gomer Press, 1994).

explicitly an object of conquest and subjugation rather than 'assimilation'. The official effort to suppress native Irish culture, including the Irish Gaelic language, is generally dated to the fourteenth-century Statutes of Kilkenny. Although they had never actually been repealed, these Statutes were newly enforced in the early part of the sixteenth century. In 1537 Henry VIII issued 'an act for the English order, habite, and language' which promised to use education and religion to propagate the English language in Ireland.[9] The Tudors took the initiative in renewing the lapsed campaign to extirpate Irish culture, but James I was more successful than his predecessors in planting the English language in Ireland, especially through colonisation. Like Irish Gaelic, Scottish Gaelic was repressed by English legislation, as promulgated, again, by the Scottish James I. In 1609 James decreed that the highland clans must send their eldest sons to school in the lowlands to learn English. In 1616, he went further: an Act of the Scottish Privy Council required that 'the vulgar Inglishe toung be universallie plantit, and the Irishe language, whilk is one of the cheif and principall causis of the continewance of barbaritie and incivilitie amongis the inhabitantis of the Ilis and Heylandis...be abolisheit and removit'.[10] Branded as 'Irish', Scottish Gaelic and its speakers were designated as aliens within their own nation.[11]

Scots, not Gaelic, was the national language of Scotland at the start of our period; the Acts of Scottish Parliaments, for example, had been recorded in Scots since 1424. Linguistically, Scots closely resembled the dialect of English spoken just on the other side of the national border; both were descended from the Northumbrian dialect of Anglo-Saxon. Many Renaissance Scotsmen considered Scots and English to be of 'ane langage'. Before 1500, the Scottish referred to their own vernacular as 'Inglis' and the term 'Scots', first used by a Scottish writer in 1494, is used almost interchangeably with 'Inglis' throughout the sixteenth century. When James I, at the opening of the English Parliament in 1603, made the case for the union of his kingdoms, he called language to witness: 'Hath not God first vnited these two Kingdomes both in Language, Religion, and similitude of maners?'[12]

9 Brian O'Cuiv, 'The Irish Language in the Early Modern Period', in *A New History of Ireland*, vol. 3, eds. T. W. Moody, F. X. Martin and F. J. Byrne (Oxford: Clarendon Press, 1976), p. 509.
10 Qtd in Richard W. Bailey, 'The Conquests of English', in *The English Language Today*, ed. Sidney Greenbaum (New York: Pergamon, 1985), p. 16.
11 Nancy C. Dorian, *Language Death: The Life Cycle of a Scottish Gaelic Dialect* (Philadelphia: University of Pennsylvania Press, 1984), p. 20.
12 James I, *A Speach, As It Was Delivered...March 1603. Being the First Day of the First Parliament*, in *Political Writings: James VI and I*, ed. Johann P. Sommerville (Cambridge University Press, 1994), p. 135.

The nature of the British vernaculars, and their relationship to British national identities, were questions implicit in linguistic debate throughout the period. This was especially true with regard to the native English word-stock. Compared with the major syntactic revolutions of the medieval period, early modern English witnessed modest grammatical changes; English phonology, by contrast, underwent a 'Great Vowel Shift', to which we owe many of the complexities and inconsistencies of modern English orthography. But the most revolutionary change from middle to early modern English occurred in the lexicon. It has been estimated that between 10,000 and 25,000 new words were introduced into the native vocabulary, with the period of greatest growth from the 1580s to the 1630s. The veritable explosion of new words in early modern English was partly the result of cultural expansion, fostering a new trade in foreign words and borrowings. Thousands of new words were also deliberately introduced by writers seeking to enrich a language that they believed inadequate to express ideas, especially in fields previously dominated by Latin or Greek. What may be most significant about the expansion of the English lexicon in the Renaissance, for the purposes of this chapter, is the way it relocated the contests between the vernacular and Latin within the English language itself. Newly invented words – generally employing Latin roots and affixes, but sometimes other imported ones – were often referred to as 'inkhorn' terms. For its detractors, inkhorn language was 'outlandishe English' – strange or alien English, perhaps not even English at all. The 'triumph of English' in the early modern period was a function not only of the ascendancy of English over Latin, or Welsh, or Scots, but of the successful assimilation of foreign elements within English itself.

A new awareness of the 'multicultural' nature of Renaissance English opened the way for vernacular lexicography, one of the most important developments in language study of the period. Early modern dictionaries emerged in response to the perception that the country was, as one of them put it, 'a self-stranger Nation'.[13] Sometimes known as 'hard words' dictionaries, these works were not comprehensive guides to English lexical usage, as dictionaries are today. They didn't differ much, in fact, from the foreign-language dictionaries that preceded them: both listed and defined strange or foreign terms and translated them into 'common' English. The first English dictionary, Robert Cawdrey's *Table Alphabeticall* (1604), advertises itself on its title-page as a collection of hard words 'borrowed from the Hebrew, Greeke, Latine, or French, & c. With

13 Thomas Blount, *Glossographia* (London: Thomas Newcomb, for Humphrey Moseley and George Sawbridge, 1656), 'To His Honored Friend Mr. T. B.'

the interpretation thereof by plaine English words'. Cawdrey offers his work for the benefit of women 'or any other unskilfull persons' who lack knowledge of foreign tongues. Everyone should have access to the meanings of hard words because, as he asks, 'Do we not speak, because we would haue other[s] to vnderstand vs?' By making strange words common Cawdrey claimed to be promoting 'one manner of language' for all. But it seems that the early English lexicographers sensed some opposition to their project of levelling what Cawdrey called the 'difference of English'.[14] John Bullokar prefaces his own dictionary of hard words (*An English Expositor*, 1616) with an apology 'To the Courteous Reader': 'I hope such learned will deeme no wrong offered to themselues or dishonour to Learning, in that I open the signification of such words, to the capacitie of the ignorant... for considering it is familiar among best writers to usurpe strange words... I suppose withall their desire is that they should also be understood.'[15] Henry Cockeram, who followed with his own *English Dictionary* in 1623, was less deferential than reproachful towards those 'who study rather to bee heard speake, than to vnderstande themselues'.[16] The first English lexicographers make it clear that the language recorded in their dictionaries was created by and for the use of a certain social class, one educated in foreign languages. The simultaneous rise of glossaries of 'cant' or 'pedlar's French' – the invented language allegedly used by a criminal underworld – is further evidence that English lexicography began as a response to social as well as formal stratification within the vernacular.

Although dictionaries of Scots and Gaelic were products of a later time, Wales also saw the rise of vernacular lexicography in this period. The humanist William Salesbury compiled the earliest English–Welsh dictionary (1547) as an aid to the progress of anglicisation within Wales. Salesbury applauds the language policy of Henry VIII and celebrates the union of language and law as an expression of a unity of hearts: 'What a bonde and knotte of love and friendship the comunion of one tonge is... [T]hey that be under dominion of one most gracious hedde and kynge shall use also one language'. In his later works, however, Salesbury made a place for his native language in Henry's regime. Exploiting the popularity of the 'matter of Britain' and the Tudors' own Welsh origins, he advanced what he now preferred to call the 'British' language: By 'Brytyshe', he explained, 'I meane the language that by

---

14 Robert Cawdrey, *A Table Alphabeticall* (London: J. Roberts, for E. Weaver, 1604), 'To the Reader'.
15 John Bullokar, *An English Expositor* (London: J. Legatt, 1616), 'To the Courteous Reader'.
16 Henry Cockeram, *The English Dictionarie* (London: Eliot's Court Press, for N. Butter, 1623), 'Premonition to the Reader'.

continuall misnomer... is called Walshe'.[17] Salesbury laid the foundation for further study of the language, including the important linguistic works of John Davies of Mallwyd (especially his *Antiquae linguae Britannicae* of 1621), devoted to preserving Welsh for its own sake. Although Welsh lexicography began by paying tribute to the King and his English, it evolved into a site of emergent Welsh nationalism.

The rise of vernacular lexicography is closely linked to the ideologies of translation in Renaissance Britain – the project of rendering Latin, Greek and other foreign works into native form. To some extent, Renaissance English translators were motivated by the spirit of nationalism as (it was believed to be) embodied in language; Thomas Phaer, for example, claims his motive for translating Virgil to be 'defence of my country's language'.[18] As a centrepiece of the larger humanist programme, however, the primary purpose of translation was the dissemination of knowledge. As a social movement, translation was thus closely tied to the print revolution, both bringing more and more previously unavailable texts – literary, historical, philosophical, scientific – to more and more readers. 'Englishing' these works, however, was not such a simple matter. Given the dearth of English terms as compared with Latin and Greek, especially the terms of specialised arts and sciences where the classics had long dominated, how could English serve?

Many translators took the opportunity to enrich English by incorporating Latin or other foreign elements to create new words, the inkhorn language of the new vernacular dictionaries. The trouble was that such language was, for many readers, still too 'hard'. Whatever their usefulness, inkhorn words and foreign borrowings in many ways reproduced the older social distinctions between those who could read foreign languages and those who could not. For Renaissance writers on both sides of the issue, the debate over translation was fundamentally a debate over access to what had been, both linguistically and culturally, privileged information.

John Bullokar stated that his dictionary would include not only words derived from foreign languages but also 'diuers termes of art, proper to the learned in Logicke, Philosophy, Law, Physicke, Astronomie, etc., yea, and Diuinitie it selfe, best knowen to the seuerall professors thereof'. The second part of this

17 William Salesbury, *A Dictionary in Englyshe and Welshe* (London: [N. Hill for] J. Waley, 1547), 'To the... Redoubtede Prince Henry'; *A Briefe and A Playne Introduction, Teachynge How to Pronounce the Letters in The British Tong* (London: [R. Grafton for] R. Crowley, 1550), p. 37.
18 Thomas Phaer, *Master Phaer's Conclusion to his Interpretation of the Aeneidos of Virgil* (1573), qtd in Flora Ross Amos, *Early Theories of Translation* (New York: Columbia University Press, 1920), p. 98.

chapter will focus on three representative disciplines, from the spectrum of the Renaissance arts and sciences, in which the issues of translation and language choice were particularly and tellingly contested: 'diuinitie', 'physicke' (or medicine) and poetry. Of special concern will be the ways that writers choose among the 'termes of art' appropriate to each. For all of the contemporary claims regarding the aesthetic and social preeminence of Latin, nine out of ten works printed in early modern England are in English. Although the triumph of the English language throughout the British Isles is no doubt the major linguistic phenomenon in each of the fields surveyed here, the rise of vernacular writing in the Renaissance is not just a story about English. Just as English authors were inspired by a new national consciousness, so too Welsh, Scottish and Irish authors began to promote a need for works in their own, native vernaculars. Throughout Britain, early modern writers started redrawing the bounds of what Edmund Spenser referred to as 'a kingdom of our own language',[19] discipline by discipline.

The Protestant Reformation and the 'reformations' of language

Is the kingdome of God become words or syllables?
– King James Authorised Version of the Bible (1611)

The impact of the Protestant Reformation on language choice was complex, even contradictory. On the one hand, it was the period's greatest spur to the anglicisation of Britain, since the dissemination of the new faith proceeded by way of new, vernacular writings. But Protestantism, and resistance to it, also inspired a resurgence of neo-Latin and original Celtic works. Whether or not to translate the Scriptures and accompanying religious texts into the vernaculars, and how to translate them faithfully, proved the most contested questions about language of the period. At stake here for Renaissance writers were not merely words but the Word of God. This section will trace how and why the Reformation in Britain led to acts of linguistic supremacy, linguistic uniformity, and counter-reform movements within the written language.

From a linguistic standpoint, the way for sixteenth-century Bible translation in England had been prepared by the 1488 printing of the Hebrew Old Testament, and by Erasmus's 1516 Greek New Testament (to which he appended his own Latin translation). These works quickly superseded the

---

19 Quoted and discussed in Richard Helgerson, *Forms of Nationhood: The Elizabethan Writing of England* (University of Chicago Press, 1992), pp.1–18.

imperfect Latin Vulgate as source texts for translators. The first sixteenth-century English translations of the Scriptures were produced by William Tyndale, who published his version of the New Testament in Germany in 1525. Although Henry VIII had originally sustained the force of earlier legislation against the Lollards (the Oxford Constitutions of 1408-9) by prohibiting the printing or importing of vernacular Bibles, Tyndale's version (albeit not identified as such) received official sanction. Miles Coverdale's English Bible, probably printed in Germany, followed in 1535. Edward Whitchurch and Richard Grafton were granted permission soon after for incorporating Tyndale and Coverdale (1537), once again with the King's 'gracious license'. By the following year, however, the royal patent secured by Thomas Cromwell for the printing of the Bible was stressing the need for a single, official translation, since 'the frailty of men is such that the diversity thereof may breed and bring forth manyfold inconveniences'.[20] The result was the Great Bible (1539), complete with a frontispiece showing Henry VIII handing down the Word of God to his bishops, and they in turn to his people. Nevertheless, the proliferation of variant translations continued. During Mary's reign Coverdale and William Whittingham published a New Testament, with a preface by Calvin himself (Geneva, 1557), yet it is only the later Geneva Bible, produced by Whittingham, Anthony Gilby and Thomas Sampson, that took firm hold in England, with more than 150 editions printed between 1560 and 1644. The Bishops' Bible, made for official ecclesiastical use, was published in 1568; soon thereafter, Catholic refugees in the Low Countries arranged for the publication of their own New Testament in France (Rheims, 1582). The triumph of the English Bible, however, is no doubt the Authorised Version (1611) commissioned by King James, a milestone achievement not only in the history of ecclesiastical literature but in the history of the English language as well.

This brief summary is enough to reveal a certain irony about the first English Bibles: from Tyndale forwards, the englishing of Scripture was largely a continental enterprise. Worms, Antwerp and Geneva saw the first printing of most of the early English versions of the Bible, while the Great Bible was set up in Paris. Richard Grafton remarked to Cromwell how 'Dutchmen dwelling within this realm go about the printing of it, which can neither speak good English, nor yet write none', while Coverdale and Grafton asked Cromwell to ensure that François Regnault, the French printer, 'henceforth ... print no more in the English tongue, unless he have an Englishman that is learned to be his corrector'.[21]

---

20 Qtd in Amos, *Early Theories of Translation*, p. 51.   21 *Ibid.*, p. 52.

But the disadvantage of relying on foreign printers was perhaps the least of the problems raised by and about the language of early Bible translation. While those who favoured translation cited the humanist aim of bringing truth and knowledge to all through the medium of writing, those who opposed it saw translation as a form of blasphemy, and charged translators with manipulating forms to propagate Protestant meanings. Against Thomas More, Tyndale defended his use of English on the grounds that the gospel was, after all, originally preached in the apostles' mother tongues. The effort to suppress English Bibles, he claimed, was an attempt by the old religious hegemony to 'kepe the world still in darkenesse'.[22] Nor was his charge ungrounded. The Catholic translators of the Rheims Bible, explaining that their own version was produced in an effort to emend all the errors perpetrated in the Protestant Bibles, insisted that the Scriptures were not written 'to be read indifferently of all, or... [to be] easily vnderstood of euery one that readeth or heareth them'. In the old days of western Christendom, they write, the Bible was not available for the understanding of 'euery prophane person' who 'could neither reade nor know the sense, meaning, and mysteries of the same'.[23] Those who objected to Protestant translations of the Bible regarded Hebrew, Greek and Latin as lending a veil to the 'mysteries' of Scripture, a needful interposition for those too ignorant or too unworthy to receive the Word directly.

But the steady proliferation of English Bibles in the sixteenth century made clear that the case against translation itself was futile (even the compilers of the Rheims edition acknowledge this), and the debate soon shifted to the relative merits of competing versions as renderings of sacred writ. Some considered whether it was necessary to use the same number of words as appeared in the original texts. The heart of the debate soon centred on vocabulary – the question of how to translate traditional Greek and Latin ecclesiastical terminology. Catholics tended to emphasise the difficulties of finding English equivalents and argued for the 'faithful' preservation of original words; the Rheims New Testament, for example, retains *pontifex, ancilla, lites, egenus, zizania, corbana, parasceve, pasche, azymes* and a host of other more or less direct transpositions. William Fulke wrote a treatise in support of Protestant Bible translations (1589), arguing that such terms as *azymes, pasche* and the

---

22 *The Preface of master William Tyndall, that he made before the fiue bookes of Moses* (1530), in *The whole works of W. Tyndall, John Frith, and Doct. Barnes*, [ed. J. Foxe], (London: J. Daye, 1573), p. 1.
23 *The New Testament of our Lord and Saviour Jesus Christ... translated out of the Latin vulgate*, Preface (Rheims: J. Fogny, 1582).

like were 'not understood of mere English ears'.[24] The Geneva Bible, mean-while, had promised to observe 'the sense' and to keep 'the propriety of the words' while allowing for the 'interpretation' of Hebrew and Greek phrases by more common English ones.[25] At the other extreme, the Protestant humanist Sir John Cheke had attempted a translation of Matthew and Mark using only words of English derivation. For the Catholic translators, however, even the most conservative Protestant translations were heretical efforts to twist 'all the authentical and Ecclesiastical wordes vsed sithence our Christianite into new prophane nouelties of speaches agreable to their doctrine'.[26]

The Authorised Version of 1611 was in many ways the culmination of the linguistic debates on the Bible. Representing the combined efforts of conserva-tive and more reform-minded scholars, the Authorised Version took a middle way:

> We haue on the one side avoided the scrupulositie of the Puritanes, who leaue the olde Ecclesiasticall words, and betake them to other, as when they put washing for Baptisme, and Congregation in stead of Church, as also on the other side we haue shunned the obscurities of the Papists, in the Azimes, Tunike, Rational, Holocausts, Praepuce, Pasche whereof their late Translation is full, and that of purpose to darken the sence, that since they must needs translate the Bible, yet by the language thereof, it may bee kept from being understood. But we desire that the Scripture may speake like it selfe that it may bee vnderstood euen of the very vulgar.[27]

In part under the influence of Fulke, the King James Bible dissociated the meanings of religion from specific linguistic forms, as its compilers ask, 'Is the kingdome of God become words or syllables?' With hindsight, the year 1611 – given the eventual success of the Authorised Version – marks the end of the debate over specialised ecclesiastical terms. Yet a year later the clergyman Thomas Wilson published *A Christian Dictionarie*, 'Opening the signification of the chiefe wordes dispersed generally through Holie Scriptures'. Religion too, it seems, had become a discourse of 'hard words'.

It would be misleading, however, to suggest that all translations of the Bible produced in this period were English ones. Following Erasmus's lead, many new Latin translations of the Bible and of Greek theological treatises were produced for international use. English works, too, were sometimes latined for

---

24 Qtd in Amos, *Early Theories of Translation*, p. 74.   25 *Ibid.*, p. 61.
26 Preface to the Rheims New Testament.
27 The Holy Bible, facsimile edition of Authorised Version of 1611 (Oxford University Press, 1911), 'The Translators to the Reader'.

a wider European audience; the Book of Common Prayer (1549), first compiled in English to make uniform the current 'diuersitie in saying and synging', also appeared in Latin versions, both in England and abroad.[28]

Not surprisingly, perhaps, the contests between Latin and the vernacular as the medium of religious discourse intensified during the Civil War and Commonwealth periods. After 1640, the Puritans became the most important and vocal advocates of the vernacular, in all fields, but most vehemently in religion, science and education. For some of the most fanatical Puritans, Latin, by association with the Vulgate, the Catholic church and a professionally trained clergy, was the 'Language of the Beast'. Cynics scorned the Puritan bias against classical languages: '[S]uch *witlesse lack-latin Zelots* ... tell their *silly disciples* ... That *Latin* and *Greek* are the languages of the Beast; that all books but the Bible ... are *Antichristian* and to be *destroyed*'.[29] But the alliance between the new science of the seventeenth century and Puritan theology, alone, gives the lie to the idea that their intolerance towards Latin was based, narrowly, in anti-intellectualism or ignorance.

In Wales, Scotland and Ireland, the revolutions transforming the relationship between church and state also shook the domain of language. While state laws were enforced against the Celtic languages in Britain, the 'Thirty-Nine Articles of Religion' (1562) insisted that 'Publicke Prayer, and the Sacraments, must be ministred in a Tongue understood of the common People'.[30] In Renaissance Britain, it seems, acts of religious uniformity ultimately took precedence over acts of linguistic uniformity. Just as Wales was the first region of Celtic Britain to advance the study of the native language, it also saw the first sustained and successful efforts to translate the Bible and Prayer Book. In an Act for the Translation of the Bible and the Divine Service into the Welsh Tongue (1563), Queen Elizabeth permitted the Bible and the Prayer Book to be published in Welsh, with the stipulation that they be accompanied by English versions in churches. The Welshman John Penry even suggested that translating English religion into Welsh terms might advance the cause of anglicisation in the long run: '[A]l should be brought to speak English ... [but] shal we be in ignorance vntil wee all learne English? This is not hir Maiesties will wee are assured. Raise vp preaching euen in welsh, & the vniformity of the language wil bee

---

28 *Booke of the common prayer and administration of the Sacramentes* (London: E. Whitchurche, 1549), Preface. Latin versions were published in England in 1560, 1574, 1594 and 1604, and abroad in 1551(Leipzig) and 1577 (Basle).
29 Qtd in R. F. Jones, *Triumph of the English Language*, p. 314.
30 *The Faith, Doctrine and Religion, Professed, and Protected in the Realm of England* ... *Expressed in Thirty-Nine Articles, 1562 and 1604* (London: J. Field, 1661), Article 24, p. 141.

sooner attained.'[31] By 1567 William Salesbury himself had translated the Book of Common Prayer and much of the New Testament. His work was revised by William Morgan, whose complete Welsh Bible appeared in 1588; one year later, Morgan revised Salesbury's Book of Common Prayer as well. In the dedication of his Bible to Queen Elizabeth, Morgan hoped to reconcile the contradictions in the English language policy towards Wales by proposing a hierarchy of objectives:

> If there are any who maintain that in order to retain agreement our country-men had better learn the English tongue than that the Scriptures should be translated into our own, I would wish that while they study unity, they would be more cautious not to hinder the truth . . . [t]here can be no doubt that sim-ilarity and agreement in religion rather than in speech much more promotes unity.[32]

The English Crown evidently agreed that religious uniformity was more polit-ically expedient than other forms of cultural union. Authorised Welsh versions of the Bible and Prayer Book, perhaps inspired by their English counterparts, were available by the 1620s. As in England, however, Counter-Reformationists responded with their own, Welsh Catholic version of the Scriptures.

In Ireland, the project of promoting a reformed religion led the Crown to speak at cross-purposes on the question of anglicisation. Queen Elizabeth herself encouraged the use of Irish as a means of disseminating the doctrines of the national church, even within the English Pale. After providing funds for a type and a press to print an Irish Bible, the Queen threatened to with-draw these funds as a ploy for quickening the pace of translation. Yet while Sir William Herbert in Munster was celebrating the translation of the Lord's Prayer and other religious materials into Irish in 1587, the Lord Deputy in Dublin was demanding that the Statutes of Kilkenny, including the provisions about language, be put into effect 'with all severity in due execution'.[33] The New Testament was translated into classical Irish Gaelic by William O'Donnell and published in 1603. Yet even as the use of Irish Gaelic was an arm of the English colonisation of Ireland, Gaelic became the chief medium of the Counter-Reformation in Ireland for the several Catholic nationalists who chose to write, polemically, in their native tongue.

---

31 Qtd in R. Brinley Jones, *The Old British Tongue*, p. 39.
32 William Morgan, 'Dedication' to the Welsh Bible of 1588, in Albert Owen Evans, *A Mem-orandum on the Legality of the Welsh Bible and the Welsh Version of the Book of Common Prayer* (Cardiff: William Lewis, 1925), Appendix IV, p. 134.
33 Qtd in O'Cuiv, 'Irish Language', p. 513.

The situation in Gaelic Scotland was not unlike that of Ireland. The first printed book in any Celtic language was in fact a translation of the Book of Common Order, done by John Carswell into classical Gaelic for the use of Scottish Gaels (1567). Robert Kirk's Scottish Gaelic New Testament (1603) was a slightly modified version of O'Donnell's Irish Bible. The Reformation in the lowlands, on the other hand, was transmitted largely through English materials, in part because, as discussed earlier, many were prepared to accept English and Scots as the same 'Word'. Only a single attempt was made to translate the Bible into Scots, in 1513–22, but this text was never printed. Yet Scottish Counter-Reformationists, like their co-religionists in Celtic Britain, sometimes chose their native vernacular as a vehicle of reaction and resistance to the Reformed Church: 'Gif King James the fyft war alyue, quha hering ane of his subjectis knap suddrone [southern; i.e. English], declarit him ane trateur: quhidder wald he declaire you triple traitours, quha not only knappis suddrone in your negative confession, but also hes causit it be imprentit at London in contempt of our native langage?'[34] It would be more than a century, however, before writing in Scots or Gaelic would be recognised as an overt and unmistakable political act. In the early modern discourses of religion, the question of which language best represented national and regional identities of Britain had yet to be resolved.

Language and Renaissance medical writing

Nothing here sours our looks, no such strong phrase,
That might perplex us worse than a Disease.
  R. W., Dedicatory Poem to Nicholas Culpepper's *School of Physick* (1659)

Medical practitioners and clerics had much in common in the Renaissance. Although doctors were popularly suspected of atheism – 'the general scandal of my profession', according to Thomas Browne in *Religio Medici*[35] – the care of the soul and the care of the body were allied concerns in this period. Their linguistic concerns, at the very least, are markedly similar. In the case of the medical professions, Greek, Latin and Arabic are the 'hard' languages of origin

---

34 Qtd in J. Derrick McClure, *Scots and Its Literature* (Amsterdam and Philadelphia: John Benjamins, 1995), p. 53. 'If King James V were alive – who, hearing one of his subjects talk Southern, declared him a traitor – would he declare you triple traitors, who not only talk Southern in your negative confession, but also has caused it to be inprinted at London, in contempt of our native language?'
35 Sir Thomas Browne, *Religio Medici*, in *The Works of Sir Thomas Browne*, ed. Geoffrey Keynes, 4 vols. (London: Faber, & Faber, 1964), 1:5.

for the canonical works of the discipline, with many reforms, once again, originating on the continent. Physicians and (to a lesser extent) surgeons depended
on a knowledge of Latin, if not Greek and Arabic, and they present themselves as possessors of knowledge privileged not only in its learned matter
but in its difficult forms. Like Protestant polemicists writing in the vernacular, medical practitioners who chose to write in English professed to do so
as a means of disseminating that knowledge in a language that all could understand. As in the debates among translators of the Bible, however, doctors,
herbalists, apothecaries and midwives quarrelled over the question of incorporating or adapting Greek and Latin medical vocabulary into English; that
is to say they quarrelled, as 'R. W.' would have it, over the 'disease' of hard
words. Yet science proves a more conservative discipline than religion in this
period, with regard to language. While the Protestant Reformation inadvertently promoted the nationalisation of religion, and, with it, English writing,
the scientific revolutions of the Renaissance remained broadly European in
context.

Of the roughly 200 medical, surgical and anatomical treatises published in
England from 1500 to 1660 (many of these in multiple editions), about 50 are
in Latin. The fact that Latin medical works represent only a quarter of those
printed is misleading, however, since several of them are disproportionately
influential in this period. Latin translations of the works of Galen, above all,
served as essential medical texts of the Renaissance, providing the basis for the
training, examination and licensing of physicians. To be sure, many of the English medical works published in these years are also translations or adaptations
of Galen. The most important contemporary medical breakthroughs, including
that of Vesalius on anatomy (1543), and William Harvey on the circulation of
the blood (1628), first appeared as Latin works. Several English physicians and
surgeons wrote in both Latin and English, including Thomas Paynell (1530s),
John Caius (1540s) and Timothy Bright (1580s). Although English physicians
are often considered the elite among Renaissance medical practitioners (or so,
at least, they considered themselves), it is worth noting that after 1557 members of the guild of Barber-Surgeons were likewise required to be familiar with
Latin as a precondition for apprenticeship.[36]

Sir Thomas Hoby, in the mid sixteenth century, cites a consensus regarding
the translation of scientific treatises: '[O]ur learned menne for the most part

---

36 Margaret Pelling and Charles Webster, 'Medical Practitioners', in *Health, Medicine, and
Mortality in the Sixteenth Century* ed. Charles Webster (Cambridge University Press, 1979),
p. 175.

holde opinion, to haue the sciences in the mother tunge, hurteth memorie and hindreth lerning'.[37] But by the 1540s England had already witnessed the rise of a healthy vernacular medical literature. Many translators and authors of original vernacular works of 'physick' defend their choice of English, just as Tyndale and other reformers did, by reminding their readers that the original medical writers used their native tongues, and did so precisely in order to be understood. If their intention had been to be obscure, Sir Thomas Elyot writes in his *Castel of Helth* (1541), they would have found a way: '[I]f they had bene as moche attached with enuy and couaytise, as some nowe seeme to be, they wolde have deuysed somme particuler language, with a strange syphre or fourme of lettres, wherin they wold haue writen their science'.[38] But the physician George Baker confesses that many of his contemporaries value medical science to the extent that only a few understand it, and in general 'esteeme of nothing but that which is most rare, or in harde and vnknowne languages'.[39]

   In fact, the operative word among medical writers, on both sides of the question of scientific language, was 'secret'. Just as reformers and their opponents debated the spiritual consequences of opening the 'mysteries' of God's Word through English writing, medical writers considered the advantages and disadvantages of exposing knowledge of the human body. Nearly every English medical treatise composed between 1550 and 1660 advertises itself as revealing the secrets of a once private trade.[40] Despite the hundreds of medical works in English circulating by the middle of the seventeenth century, it was still deemed necessary or perhaps desirable to call attention to the idea of forbidden disclosure: 'It is not unknown with how great an applause this book was attended when it was first made publique. For it overcame the general envy... in disclosing even to mean capacities the rarest and deepest mysteries of Physicke, which till now were concealed and lockt up in unknown Languages'.[41]

   The source of that 'general envy', according to advocates of vernacular medicine, was largely economic: doctors were attempting to retain their

37 Sir Thomas Hoby (trans.), *The courtyer of count Baldessar Castilio* (London: [S. Mierdman for R. Jugge], 1561), Epistle.
38 Sir Thomas Elyot, *The Castel of Helthe* (London, 1541),'Proheme'.
39 George Baker (trans.), *The newe jewell of health* (London: H. Denham, 1576), 'George Baker to the Reader'.
40 Many Renaissance medical treatises highlight such 'secrets' in their titles, e.g., Robert Copland, *Secreta secretorum: the secrete of secretes of Aristotle* (London: R. Copland, 1528); William Ward, *The secretes of the reverende Maister Alexis of Piedmont* (London: J. Kingston for N. Inglande, 1558); John Hester, *A compendium of the rationall secretes of L. Phioravante* (London: J. Kingston for D. Pen and J. Hester, 1582); John Partridge, *The treasurie of commodius conceits and hidden secrets* (London: R. Jones, 1573).
41 Nicholas Culpeper, *Culpeper's Astrologicall judgment of diseases from the decumbiture of the sick* (London: for N. Brooke, 1655), 'To the Reader'.

monopoly on medical care. While Tyndale argued that Catholics were hiding true doctrine 'to satisfy their filthy lustes, their proude ambition, and unsatiable couetnousnes',[42] Thomas Phaer complained that knowledge of the human body 'ought not to be secrete for Lucre of a few... or what make they themselves? Marchauntes of our lyues and deathes, that we shulde bye our health only of them, and at theyr pryce?'[43] Many vernacular works offer their remedies for the disadvantaged; for example, Thomas Moulton, author of the most popular medical treatise of the sixteenth century, *The myrour or glasse of helthe* (appearing in at least seventeen editions between 1530 and 1580), claims to write out of the 'compassion that I haue of the poore people'.[44] Nicholas Culpeper turns compassion to social outrage, arguing that the poor have been 'hoodwinkt, and muffled in such darkness, sacrificed to the ambitions and covetousness of such uncharitable persons... I appeal to all men in their Wits, whether there are such unnatural Monopolizers in the world?'[45]

But opponents of dispensing medical information to the 'vulgar people' were many – even, surprisingly, among those who wrote in English. No one, it seems, wanted to see ploughmen and cobblers turn surgeons, or 'euery old wyfe presume not without the mordre of many, to practyse Phisick'.[46] Women counted among the many unlicensed doctors practising in England (between 1581 and 1600 the College of Physicians prosecuted twenty-one of them), but midwives, many licensed by ecclesiastical authority, made up the majority of women practising physic in the period. Although the first book of midwifery by a woman did not appear until 1671, its author, Jane Sharp, insisted on dissociating Nature's truths about the human body from the mysteries of language: 'It is not hard words that perform the work, as if none understood the Art that cannot understand Greek. Words are but the shell, that we ofttimes break our Teeth with them to come at the kernal.'[47]

The idea that 'truth' must be distinguished from mere words was a basic premise of the scientific investigation of language inaugurated by men like Francis Bacon and pursued by writers, many of them Puritans, throughout the seventeenth century. For some Puritans, especially, Latin had associations not only with the errors of the Catholic Church but with the benighted science of the medieval past; the new science, following Bacon, was to emphasise

---

42 Tyndale, *Whole Works*, p. 1.
43 Thomas Phaer, *A new booke entyteled the regiment of lyfe*, 2nd edn (London: E. Whitchurch, 1544), sig. Aiii r.
44 Thomas Moulton, *The myrour or glasse of helthe* (London: R. Redman, 1540), sig. Avii r.
45 Nicholas Culpeper, *Culpeper's school of physick*, 2nd edn (London: for O. B. and R. H., to be sold by Robert Clavel, 1678), Preface.
46 William Turner, *A new herball* (London: S. Mierdman, 1551), 'Prologe'.
47 Jane Sharp, *The Midwives' Book* (1671) (New York: Garland Publishing, 1985), pp. 3-4.

direct observation of the natural world and experimentation.[48] The physician John Webster, a Puritan and a Baconian, declares skills in classical languages irrelevant to the pursuit of the new science, good only for those who wish 'like Parrots to babble and prattle'.[49] Nicholas Culpeper repeatedly invites his readers to 'see the truth and themselves' in his works, drawing a direct analogy between physicians and Catholics: 'The truth is, throughout the whole World there are not such slaves to the Doctors, as the poor English are; most of them profes themselves Protestants, but their practises have been like those of the Papists, to hide the grounds of Physick from the vulgar.'[50]

As in the case of ecclesiastical writing, however, the aim of presenting the plain, unadulterated, unmediated truth in English, this time about the body rather than the spirit, was easier said than done. The medical lexicon, including the names of body parts, diseases and remedies, traditionally consisted of Greek, Arabic and Latin terms, and there were no equivalent terms available in early modern English. Among English medical writers, however, relatively few attempted to remedy the situation with inkhorn language. Andrew Borde is the notable exception. In the Preface to his *Breuiary of helthe* (1547), he claims to 'haue translated all such obscure wordes and names in to englyshe, that euery man openly and apartly may understande them'.[51] His practice, in general, was to give the Greek, Latin and Arabic names and then one or more English equivalents, some of them of his own coining: 'Abstinencia is the latyn word. In greke it is named Apochi. In englyshe it is named Astynence or fastynge, or forbearynge of meates and drynkes.'[52] Some apparently found his linguistic innovations alarming: 'Was there euer seene from a learned man a more preposterous and confused kind of writing; forced with so many and such odde coyned tearmes?'[53] But Borde's practice may be most interesting for the way it reflects contemporary ambivalence towards opening up the 'secrets' of medicine through language. While he claims to be aiming for transparency, so that all might understand, Borde is sometimes reluctant to tell all: 'Where that I am very briefe in shewyng brefe medicines for one sickness . . . the first cause is that the archane science of physicke shulde nat be to[o] manifest

48 Richard Foster Jones, 'Science and Language in England in the Mid-Seventeenth Century', *Journal of English and Germanic Philology* 31(1932), 315–31.
49 Qtd in R. F. Jones, 'Science and Language', 319.
50 Culpeper, *School of Physick*, Preface.
51 Andrew Borde, *The breuiary of helthe* (London: W. Myddelton, 1547), 'The Preface to reders of this boke'.
52 *Ibid.*, sig. Biv r.
53 Angel Day, *The English secretorie* (London: R. Waldegrave,1586), p. 39.

and open . . . [or] doctours the which hath studied the faculties shulde nat be regarded so well as it is'.[54]

In fact, the majority of Renaissance English physicians and surgeons tend to retain Greek and Latin terms in their English works, with anglicised spellings, even when they complain about the lack of English words for their purposes. Some clearly prefer a bit of mystery. The surgeon John Banister notes with satisfaction the way that Latin and Greek terms make for a 'harder shell then you shalbe able to cracke', while the physician George Baker's refusal to 'English' certain terms is put rather more bluntly: 'I would not haue euery ignorant ass to be made a Chirurgian by my Book'.[55] Those that address women readers, in particular, seem vexed about a full translation, especially when it comes to the terms for the 'privy parts'. While male physicians assert their intention to 'stoop to [women's] capacities in avoiding hard words',[56] even Culpeper, despite his characteristic polemic against 'former Ages [which] have used to muffle up our Eys, least we should see the Truth', leaves the terms for the genitals untranslated in his text, preferring to explain them in a glossary at the end of his work.[57]

The Renaissance is the source of our modern practice of deriving scientific and technical terms from Latin and Greek. Apparently, we still expect a certain degree of mystification when it comes to the sciences, to remind ourselves that we are in the presence of an art that requires, now more than ever perhaps, interpretation by a specialist.

Poetry and the terms of imaginative art

[W]e always bewray our selues to be both vnkinde and vnnaturall to our owne natiue language, in disguising or forging strange or vnusuall wordes, as if it were to make our verse seeme another kind of speach out of the course of our usuall practise.   – Samuel Daniel, A Defence of Ryme (1603)[58]

It should be clear by now that one question about English cuts across the disciplines of Renaissance writing: which words, within the expanding lexicon, are

54 Borde, Breuiary, Preface.
55 John Banister, The Historie of Man, sucked from the sappe of the most approved Anathomistes (London: J. Daye, sold by R. Daye, 1578), 'Epistle to the Chirurgians'; George Baker, The Composition or making of the oil called oleum magistrale (London: J. Alde 1574), sig. Qii r.
56 John Sadler, The sicke womans private looking-glasse (London: A. Griffin for P. Stephens and C. Meridith, 1636), 'The Epistle Dedicatory'.
57 Culpeper, A directory for Midwives, 2nd edn (London: Peter Cole, 1656), sig. B3 r.
58 Samuel Daniel, A Defence of Ryme (1603), in Elizabethan Critical Essays, ed. G. Gregory Smith (Oxford: Clarendon Press, 1904), 2:384.

to be considered natural, native, undisguised, genuine, familiar, usual – that is, really and truly English? In terms of the sheer variety and ingenuity of answers to this question, imaginative literature is surely the most prodigious among cultural discourses of the period. Although the range of linguistic variation among the numerous and diverse literary authors of the period makes this a subject too broad to cover here, I will survey the issues involved in determining the language appropriate to British poetry and to British poetics, before focusing on the choices made by three major poets of the period: Spenser, Shakespeare and Milton. Moving from the soul to the body to the 'wit' or imagination, the last section of this chapter will suggest the extent to which Renaissance poets responded creatively to the question of the national language.

Greek and Latin poetry ranks, of course, among the most important of the classical writings recovered by British humanists. But besides the increased circulation of Greek and Latin literary works, the period also sees the proliferation of neo-Latin poetry, especially from the mid sixteenth century onward. Among the Renaissance poets writing original works in Latin are Thomas More, John Foxe, Thomas Campion, Queen Elizabeth, George Buchanan, John Donne, George Herbert, Abraham Cowley and, preeminently, John Milton. This abbreviated list is perhaps misleading, because the new humanist curriculum, at the grammar school and university levels alike, demanded that everyone who passed through the system write poetry, among other things, in Latin. Latin verse was often composed for university and occasional collections, especially those compiled to mark an official event – the birth, marriage or death of royal and aristocratic personages, the triumphal entry of a monarch into a city, the visits of monarchs to universities, and so on. Indeed, most neo-Latin writing of the Renaissance is public and formal.[59] Scotland, with England, experienced its own Renaissance in Latinity after 1500; the greatest of the British latinists is no doubt the Scottish humanist George Buchanan. The Renaissance in Scotland included a few attempts to produce a national epic, notably Andrew Ramsay's *Creationis rerum descriptio poetica* (1633), an analogue, possibly even a source, for Milton's epic undertakings. The culminating moment of the Scottish Renaissance, the 1637 publication of the *Delitiae poetarum Scotorum huius aevi illustrium*, included the Latin works of thirty-seven poets.

Along with Latin and Greek poetry, the Renaissance saw the printing of many Greek and Latin works on poetics – especially, on the rules of rhetoric. The works of Aristotle, Cicero, Quintilian and others, like Greek and Latin

59 J. W. Binns, *Intellectual Culture in Elizabethan and Jacobean England: The Latin Writings of the Age* (Leeds: Francis Cairns, 1990), p. 34.

medical writings, had a disproportionate influence on the art of writing English poetry; among continental works circulating in England, Julius Caesar Scaliger's *Poetices libri septem* (Lyons, 1561) dominates, especially in the field of genre theory. Sixteenth- and early seventeenth-century England produced a number of vernacular works on poetics, including Thomas Wilson's *Arte of Rhetorique* (1553); Henry Peacham's *Garden of Eloquence* (1577); Abraham Fraunce's *Arcadian Rhetoricke* (1588); George Puttenham's *Arte of English Poesie* (1589); Philip Sidney's *Apologie for Poetrie*, also called *The Defence of Poesie* (publ. 1595); and Daniel's *Defence of Ryme* (1603). Although many of these make reference to the status of vernacular poetry, there is little that is distinctively 'English' about the poetic theories promulgated in these works. What is most interesting about Renaissance vernacular poetics, from the standpoint of linguistic choice, is the tendency to leave the terms of literary art – especially, the names for rhetorical figures – in Latin or Greek (often with anglicised spellings). A notable exception is Puttenham's treatise, which attempts to introduce 'Englished' terms for the tropes, such as 'ringleader' for *prozeugma*, 'trespasser' for *hyperbaton*, and 'misnamer' for *metonymia*.[60] His innovations failed to catch on, however, and – as any modern handbook of rhetoric will show – we are still using the old, 'hard' terms of literary art today. The democratisation of Renaissance English literature did not extend, it seems, to the domain of rhetorical art.

Scots poetics fell under the dual influence of native English and classical works in this period. English poetry had circulated widely in Scotland from the fourteenth century or earlier, and Chaucer's influence on native Scots poets is well known. Scottish 'makars' of the fifteenth and sixteenth centuries not only imitated Chaucer's style, but tried out English spellings and English locutions as well. By 1560, Scots poetry was already using a mixed dialect, with pairs of spellings like *ony* and *any*, *gude* and *good*, *quha* and *who*, occurring side by side, sometimes in the same work.[61] Many sixteenth- and seventeenth-century Scottish poets, such as George Buchanan, alternately wrote in Scots and in 'sudron'; others, with Sir William Alexander (born 'MacAlastair'), gradually eliminated Scoticisms from their writings over the course of their careers. After the Union of the Crowns in 1603, authors such as Alexander quickly stepped up their efforts to conform their language to that of the English court.

Although King James I claimed that the Scottish and the English were already united by language, his own self-conscious efforts to anglicise his political works reveal that he must have considered their languages different enough.

60 George Puttenham, *The Arte of English Poesie (1589)*, ed. Gladys Doidge Willcock and Alice Walker (Cambridge University Press, 1936; repr. 1970), pp. 163–260.
61 *The Concise Scots Dictionary* (Aberdeen University Press, 1985), p. x.

James was also the author of Scots poetry and, more remarkably, a treatise on Scots poetics, his *Reulis and Cautelis to be observit and eschewit in Scottis Poesie.* The language of this treatise appears nearly to have bypassed anglicisation altogether, in contrast to everything else printed in his *Essayes* of 1584. James explained to his readers that he wrote the work because nothing of the kind had ever been 'written in our language': 'For albeit sindrie hes written of it in English, quhilk is lykest to our language, 3it we differ from thame in sindrie reulis of Poesie, as 3e will find be experience.'[62] Significantly, James was willing to set Scots apart as 'our language' when it came to questions of poetry. Indeed poetry or, at least, popular verse emerged as the chief medium for the transmission of Scots into the seventeenth century, especially Scots ballads. The great 'ballad zone' incorporating northern England, Lowland Scotland and English-speaking Ireland remained indifferent to the political and religious boundaries within the British Isles in the early modern period.

Celtic Scotland and Ireland represented another common literary culture. Though Scottish and Irish Gaelic, as spoken languages, became distinct during the Renaissance, classical Gaelic remained a single, even standardised written dialect, preserved through a shared bardic culture. Both Henry VIII and Elizabeth, however, identified the bardic schools as sites of political resistance, and legislation was passed for their suppression. In 1609 the Scots Parliament furthered this endeavour with the Statutes of Icolmkill; during the Cromwellian campaigns of 1649–52, finally, bardic culture was systematically wiped out, although the source of its patronage, a Gaelic-speaking aristocracy, had long been in decline.[63] The *Book of the Dean of Lismore*, a manuscript of verse from the first half of the sixteenth century, contains much of what is known about the work of the professional Scottish and Irish bards.

The fate of Welsh bardic poetry was somewhat different, largely because of efforts by Welsh humanists such as William Salesbury to reconcile the native tradition with the new humanist poetics. While many Welsh bards resisted this, even passing legislation to keep their art a secret, Welsh humanists published treatises on native poetics and translated works of classical poetics into Welsh for the benefit of native poets. Yet despite their efforts, few of the characteristic Renaissance poetic genres took root in Welsh.[64] Meanwhile, nobody in Britain thought to suggest that the great contemporary writers of Welsh origin – Philip

---

62 *The Poems of James VI of Scotland,* vol. 1, ed. James Craigie (Edinburgh: William Blackwood, 1955), p. 67.

63 John Macinnes, 'The Scottish Gaelic Language', in *The Celtic Connection,* ed. Price, p. 115.

64 R. Geraint Gruffydd, 'The Renaissance and Welsh Literature', in *The Celts and the Renaissance: Tradition and Innovation,* ed. Glanmor Williams and Robert Owen Jones (Cardiff: University of Wales Press, 1990), pp. 28–30.

Sidney, John Donne, George Herbert and Henry Vaughan among them – were anything but English poets.

As compared with contemporary debates over translating works in religion and medicine, relatively few objections were raised to translating foreign poetry into English; a greater licence with language generally ruled in this domain. But the problem of finding (or inventing) appropriate English words, for translations as well as for original English works, was just as pronounced. In the case of Renaissance literary writing, the problem of 'hard' or 'obscure' terms may be identified with the emergent notion of 'poetic diction' – a distinctive language of poetry. In a well-known passage, Puttenham advised poets to avoid unusual language, including inkhorn terms, archaisms and dialect words, and rather 'take the usuall speach of the Court, and that of London and the shires lying about London'.[65] Yet 'un-usuall' words, including those Puttenham explicitly proscribed, are frequently associated in this period with literary writing. The three major poets of the period in England – Spenser, Shakespeare and Milton – have all been judged, in our own time as in theirs, by their poetic language, and the question of how 'English' their diction really is. I will now turn to an examination of the lexical choices of these poets. The distinctiveness of each, in itself, argues the flexibility and liberality of Renaissance literary writing in comparison with other contemporary discourses. But the greater licence exercised by Renaissance poets does not mean that there was anything less at stake in the answers they offered, respectively, to the question of the language.

The language of Edmund Spenser's poetry was notorious in its own time, as apparently Spenser anticipated it would be. His early collection of eclogues, *The Shepheardes Calender* (1579), appeared with a letter from one 'E. K.' to Gabriel Harvey, an extended explanatory gloss centred on defending the language of the poem. E. K. admits to Harvey that much about the eclogues will seem unfamiliar to readers, but 'of many thinges which in him be straunge, I know [the language] will seeme the straungest'. He attributes the strangeness of Spenser's language to his profuse borrowings from Chaucer, words that have since become 'something hard, and of most men unused'.[66] Archaism was indeed the most conspicuous feature of the language of this poem as well as that of Spenser's major work, *The Faerie Queene* (1590, 1596). The early reception of the *Calender* reveals the immediate controversy generated by Spenser's language:

---

65 Puttenham, *Arte of English Poesie*, p. 145.
66 E. K., 'Epistle to Gabriel Harvey', *The Shepheardes Calender* (1579), in *The Works of Edmund Spenser*, 11 vols., ed. Edwin Greenlaw *et al.* (Baltimore, MD: Johns Hopkins University Press, 1932–57), 7:7–11.

> Some blame deep *Spencer* for his grandam words
> Others protest that, in them he records
> His maister-peece of cunning giuing praise,
> And grauity to his profound-prickt layes.[67]

Samuel Daniel deemed Spenser's archaisms 'vntimely', and Sidney famously censured Spenser's choice of words: 'That same framing of his style to an olde rusticke language, I dare not allow.' Ben Jonson fulfilled E. K.'s prediction that many would find Spenser's English 'gibbrish', denying that his diction was English at all: 'Spencer, in affecting the Ancients, writ no Language.'[68] Long after their publication, Spenser's eclogues remained a repository of 'hard words': Bathurst's edition of the *Calender* (1653) included a glossary; and John Ray included words from Spenser in his dialect dictionary, *A Collection of Words Not Generally Used* (1674). Although many modern critics have worked to demystify Spenser's language and assimilate it to sixteenth-century poetic practice,[69] it seems clear that in his own time it was considered 'strange' enough.

E. K. defends archaising as an effort to recover a purer English; the poet, he says, 'hath laboured to restore, as to theyr rightfull heritage such good and naturall English words, as haue ben long time out of vse and almost cleane disherited'. This 'disinheritance', he notes, has caused writers to eke their verses out with 'peces and rags of other languages, borrowing here of the French, there of the Italian, every where of the Latine', making contemporary English 'a gallimaufray or hodgepodge of al other speches'. Spenser's language, by contrast, is true English, however unrecognisable it might be to his readers. E. K. tries to forestall the criticism of his countrymen who 'if them happen to here an olde word, albeit very naturall and significant, crye out streight way, that we speak no English, but gibbrish' by practising some patriotic one-upmanship: '[Their] first shame is, that they are not ashamed, in their own mother tonge straungers to be counted and alienes'. E. K. thus represents what seems most foreign in Spenser's diction as what is, if rightly understood, most native to the English language.

---

67 Qtd in R. M. Cummings, *Spenser: The Critical Heritage* (New York: Barnes & Noble, 1971), p. 288.

68 Samuel Daniel, *Delia* (1592), in *The Complete Works of Samuel Daniel in Verse and Prose*, 5 vols., ed. Alexander B. Grosart (London: Russell & Russell, 1885), vol. 1, Sonnet 55, line 2; Philip Sidney, *Defence of Poesie* (1595), in *Prose Works*, 4 vols., ed. Albert Feuillerat (Cambridge University Press, 1962), 3:37; Ben Jonson, *Discoveries* (1640), in *The Works of Ben Jonson*, vol. 8, ed. C.H. Herford, Percy Simpson and Evelyn Simpson (Oxford: Clarendon Press, 1947), p. 618.

69 See, for example, Bruce Robert McElderry, Jr, 'Archaism and Innovation in Spenser's Poetic Diction', *PMLA* 47.1 (1932), 144–70.

Although archaism is the most marked aspect of his poetic diction, Spenser tapped other sources for unusual words as well. He sometimes employs latinate words; for example, when 'two naked Damzelles' confronted by Guyon in *The Faerie Queene* 'th'amarous sweet spoiles to greedy eyes revele'. Spenser's spelling 'amarous' was a variant of 'amorous' in the 1590s, but is also no doubt meant to evoke the Latin *amarus*, meaning bitter.[70] Spenser also made use of continental loanwords (such as *faytours*, *peregall* and numerous words ending in the French suffix-*ance*, such as *jouyssance* and *miscreaunce*) along with northern dialect words, and neologisms, the most famous of which is *derring-doe*.[71] He may well have been influenced in the range of his lexical choices by the poetic theories of the Pléiade, a circle of sixteenth-century French poets including Joachim du Bellay and Pierre Ronsard, who encouraged poets to search out new sources of diction in order to promote an expanded vernacular. The best way to understand Spenser's poetic diction, however, is as an attempt at linguistic 'originality' – a language at once old and new, native and strange – an experiment in cultural restoration and revitalisation through language.

Despite E. K.'s rhetoric of linguistic recovery and inheritance, Spenser's poetic diction had no material effect on the development of a national language in sixteenth-century England. Instead, the language of *The Shepheardes Calender* and *The Faerie Queene* became a model for *literary* diction. George Peele was among the first of many poets who would borrow directly from Spenser's idiom, especially for pastoral verses: 'Herdgroom, what gars thy pipe to go so loud? / Why bin thy looks so smicker and so proud?'[72] Later Spenserians, including the young Keats, would try to imitate it as well. Yet for all E. K.'s insistence that Spenser's diction was natural English, literary history would have the last word, for most readers would judge it as an example of the strangeness and artificiality of pastoral language.

If Spenser is generally known today as the inventor of a rather affected 'poetic diction', Shakespeare (along with the King James Bible) has been treated as one of the very makers of our language. What did Shakespeare do with words that has made him seem an integral, inalienable part of a collective cultural identity? First of all, Shakespeare has perhaps the largest vocabulary of any English writer; the sheer size of his lexicon seems to reflect a sense of comprehensiveness and universality. Some 600 inkhorn terms, many still in use today,

---

70 This example and others are discussed by John K. Hale, *Milton's Language: The Impact of Multilingualism on Style* (Cambridge University Press, 1997), pp. 107–8.

71 See McElderry, 'Archaism and Innovation', for a full account of Spenser's poetic lexicon.

72 George Peele, 'An Eclogue Gratulatory' (1589), in *The Workes of George Peele* (1589), vol. 2, ed. A. H. Bullen (London: John C. Nimmo, 1888; Port Washington, NY: Kennikat Press, 1966), lines 1–2.

have been attributed to him, including 'accommodation', 'assassination', 'dexterously', 'frugal', 'indistinguishable', 'misanthrope', 'obscene', 'pedant', 'premeditated' and 'submerged'. Shakespeare's use of new words, however, is itself often new; they are employed to numerous ends and effects:

> Will all great Neptune's ocean wash this blood
> Clean from my hand? No; this my hand will rather
> The *multitudinous* seas *incarnadine*,
> Making the green one red.[73]

'Multitudinous' is Shakespeare's coining, while 'incarnadine' is a neologism first recorded in 1591 as a colour adjective. But Shakespeare innovates further by using 'incarnadine' as a verb, and by possibly evoking in this context the idea of human flesh (from Latin *caro*). Next, Shakespeare crash-lands Macbeth's lofty flight of words onto the plain, hard surface of the final line, 'Making the green one red'. In this sequence of clear, monosyllabic, Anglo-Saxon words – ending, significantly, on 'red' – we get a straight, vivid, even violent answer to the question that opens the passage.

Yet if Shakespeare proves himself a partisan of the project of linguistic enrichment by the number of words and idioms he added to the native word-stock, he also calls attention to what he saw as a contemporary embarrassment of linguistic riches. In *Love's Labour's Lost*, he creates what has been described as 'a comedy on the English *état de langue*'.[74] The focus of his satire is the comic trio, the pedant Holofernes, the curate Nathaniel and the pretentious Spaniard, Armado. Armado is described by the others as a man who 'hath a mint of phrases in his brain', 'a man of fire-new [newly coined] words'.[75] Armado deigns to translate his 'hard words' to the clown, Costard: speaking of Costard's 'enfranchisement', Armado explains, 'I mean setting thee at liberty, enfreedoming thy person: thou wert immured, restrained, captivated, bound' (3.1.123–35). Although Holofernes and Nathaniel deride Armado's speech, their own conversations are strewn with Latin words and latinate coinings such as 'thrasonical', 'peregrinate' and 'verbosity'. For all their condescension towards the language of others, they use it themselves as a means to thrive, to assert their social ascendancy, as Costard knows: 'O, they have liv'd long on the alms-basket of words' (5.1.38–9).

---

73 William Shakespeare, *Macbeth*, in *The Riverside Shakespeare*, ed. G. Blakemore Evans, 2nd edn (Boston: Houghton Mifflin,1997), 2.2.57–60, emphasis added. This example is also discussed by Gert Ronberg in *A Way With Words: The Language of Renaissance English Literature* (London: Edward Arnold, 1992), pp. 19–20.
74 William Mathews, 'Language in *Love's Labour's Lost*', *Essays and Studies*, new ser., 7 (1964), 1.
75 *Love's Labour's Lost*, 1.1.165, 178.

In *Love's Labour's Lost*, Shakespeare satirises some of the new 'authors' of English – but how, exactly, are we to distinguish them from the playwright himself? Although Shakespeare may have deemed some of the 'fire-new words' used by Armado or Holofernes pretentious, he uses many of them elsewhere; while 'perambulate', 'peregrinate' and 'verbosity' only occur in this play, 'peremptory', 'thrasonical', 'audacious', 'impudency', 'excrement' and 'eruption', for example, all occur in other plays as well as this one, and in passages where no satire is intended. Shakespeare's parody is not really directed at particular words, but at particular people – not just Armado and Holofernes, but the countless comic characters in his plays (Dogberry, Bottom and Mistress Quickly among them) who are either too affected or too ignorant to use such words wisely. If the popular claim that Shakespeare is a universal poet, speaking for and about all people everywhere, is exaggerated, so too, perhaps, is the idea that he speaks a universal language, intended for all to share. But that should in no way diminish our admiration for the wealth of words in his plays and his bounteousness in their use.

John Milton is no doubt the greatest English poet to write Latin poetry, so perhaps it is not surprising that the spectre of latinity has seemed, to many readers, to haunt his English works. At the same time, Milton is famous for his self-conscious determination to leave Latin behind in favour of English verse, a decision prefigured in the 'part Latin, part English' lines 'At a Vacation Exercise' (1628), written while still at Cambridge. This poem shifts from one language to the other ('the Latin speeches ended, the English thus began') with a salute to the vernacular, 'Hail native Language'.[76] Milton's 'Epitaphium Damonis' (1639) discusses his decision in a long passage (one scholar has suggested that Milton lays Latin in a grave alongside 'Damon').[77] Three years later, in *The Reason of Church Government*, Milton restated his commitment 'to the adorning of my native tongue', citing contemporary Italian authors as his model.[78] In fact, Milton never abandoned Latin altogether, although it became only rarely the medium of his verse; almost half of his copious prose, composed throughout his career, is in Latin.[79]

Yet despite his dedication to the native tongue, readers from Samuel Johnson onwards have continually found Milton's poetic language somehow

---

76 John Milton, 'At a Vacation Exercise', in *John Milton: Complete Poems and Major Prose*, ed. Merritt Y. Hughes (Indianapolis: Bobbs-Merrill, 1957), line 1.

77 Hale, *Milton's Language*, p. 58.   78 *Ibid.*, p. 61.

79 Milton's one substantial Latin poem after this time is his 'Ad Ioannem Rousium' (1647). For a recent account of Milton's neo-Latin works, see Stella P. Revard, *Milton and the Tangles of Neaera's Hair: The Making of the 1645 Poems* (University of Missouri Press, 1997).

'unEnglish'. Johnson criticised the 'second Babel' in his verse, even invoking Jonson's quip that Spenser 'wrote no language'.[80] In the 1930s T. S. Eliot charged Milton with doing 'damage to the English language' because of the foreign character of his idiom. Milton's early poetry contains numerous archaisms culled from Spenser ('Beldame' Nature; 'dew besprent'; 'cedarn'; 'yclept'). But the 'foreign' quality of his later verse, including *Paradise Lost* (1667), *Paradise Regain'd* and *Samson Agonistes* (both 1671), owes very little to archaism. Although the latest critical consensus is that Milton's diction largely conforms to English usage of his own day, most scholars agree that he often evokes foreign meanings – Latin, Greek, Hebrew and Italian – as a secondary sense. For example, 'Hebrew meets Greek' in his play, *Samson Agonistes* – even in its very title. He adapts words from Dante, including 'adorn', 'fugue', 'outrageous' and 'imparadis't'. The latinate character of his major poetry owes much to his syntax, for he adapts characteristic Latin constructions such as the ablative absolute (as in his phrase 'Satan except'). Milton also evokes the original Latin meanings of words, though he rarely invents latinate words outright ('omnific', 'displode' and 'gurge' are some exceptions). Milton especially liked multilingual puns: for example, Sin and Death's bridge from earth to hell in *Paradise Lost* is described as 'Wondrous art / Pontifical', where 'pontifical' evokes the Latin *pons, pontis* ('bridge') as well as a folk etymology of *pontifex* ('pope'); in a word, Milton allies their devilish craft with Papism. When Satan 'springs upward like a pyramid of fire', the Greek *pyr* or 'fire' lends greater intensity to the phrase.[81] If Milton's diction is not as 'foreign' as it is sometimes judged to be, there is no question that his poetry is as allusive linguistically as it is culturally and intellectually. Arguably, it is not the mercurial Shakespeare but the densely allusive Milton who, in his fluency with a range of languages and cultural traditions, ought by rights to have a better claim to being a 'universal' poet. But attentive readers of his work have also perceived, not without reason, that Milton's 'universality' is not unlike that of Latin itself in the early modern period – 'common' to a *lettered* culture.

English a universal language?

The end of this story of English and other languages of Renaissance British writing returns, in some ways, to its beginning: if the period begins with the

---

80 See Samuel Johnson, 'Milton', in *Lives of the English Poets*, vol. 1, ed. George Birkbeck Hill (Oxford: Clarendon Press, 1905), pp. 189–91.

81 For these and further examples of Milton's poetic language, see Thomas N. Corns, *Milton's Language* (Oxford and Cambridge, MA: Basil Blackwell, 1990); and Hale, *Milton's Language*.

predominance of Latin across the disciplines of writing, it ends on the eve of the earliest efforts to create or recover a 'common' language. But fifty years before members of the Royal Society of London (founded in 1662) set about the task of devising a universal language – this time to be based on 'universal' properties of the human mind – the English grammarian Alexander Gill proposed his own solution to the 'Babel' of the early modern world: 'Since in the beginning all men's lips were identical, and there existed but one language, it would indeed be desirable to unify the speech of all peoples in one universal vocabulary; and were human ingenuity to attempt this, certainly no more suitable language than English could be found.'[82] Several years later the Puritan James Hunt, penner of 'spiritual verses', had a similar thought:

> For God will gather all Nations into Religion one
> So by degrees all shall be taught the English tongue.[83]

The idea that English might one day serve all nations as a universal language was an elaboration of the dream of anglicisation, like that of Sir John Davies for Ireland: '[W]e may conceive an hope that the next generation will in tongue and heart and every way else become English, so as there will be no difference or distinction but the Irish sea betwixt us'.[84] The idea of English as a 'common' language – reflecting a common mind, a common spirit or a common purpose – would find its advocates in future centuries, including our own. For the time being, an unprecedented heterogeneity of forms held sway in Renaissance writing, at least in English. Scots and Gaelic were once and future literary kingdoms. Throughout Renaissance Britain, however, the question of the language was fundamentally a question about access to knowledge; the linguistic choices surveyed here all served (or resisted) the transmission of culture. Although relationships between language and other social forms were not yet fixed, the die was cast: soon enough, the British languages would answer, more directly, to questions of social, regional and national identity.

---

82 Alexander Gill, *Logonomia Anglica (1619)*, trans. Robin C. Alston, ed. Bror Danielsson and Arvid Gabrielson, *Stockholm Studies in English*, 26–7 (Stockholm: Almqvist & Wiksell, 1972), p. 86.
83 Qtd in R. F. Jones, *Triumph of the English Language*, p. 321.
84 Sir John Davies, *A Discoverie of the true causes why Ireland was never entirely subdued* (1612), in *Elizabethan Ireland*, ed. Myers, Jr, p. 174.

Chapter 6

HABITS OF READING AND EARLY
MODERN LITERARY CULTURE

STEVEN N. ZWICKER

My subject is the consumption and production of vernacular literature in early modern England – of epic and romance, of history and pamphlet, of song and sonnet, ode and epistle, satire and epigram – and more especially the ways in which habits of reading created a field of expectations in which literature was imagined and into which texts were issued. I want to begin, however, with a personal letter, and not a canonical literary text, because the letter touches on both the production and consumption of literature, and at a number of points. In December of 1614, shortly before he took orders, John Donne wrote to Sir Henry Goodyer for help in retrieving his scattered verse, not exactly, it turns out, because Donne was ashamed of his literary vocation – though there is a sense of valediction in the letter that covers Donne's secular writing – but rather to secure scattered manuscript copy with a view to print publication. Donne had been contemptuous of print and was aware that others knew of that contempt,[1] but necessity pressed him, and the appeal to Goodyer points not only to the dilemmas and desires of a poet, c. 1600, but also to the merits of script and print, the status and uses of verse, and the ways in which poems and letters might be read and remembered:

> One thing more I must tell you; but so softly, that I am loath to hear myself: and so softly, that if that good Lady [the Countess of Bedford] were in the room, with you and this Letter, she might not hear. It is, that I am brought to a necessity of printing my Poems, and addressing them to my L. Chamberlain. This I mean to do forthwith; not for much publique view, but at mine own cost, a few Copies. I apprehend some incongruities in the resolution; and I know

1 See, for example, Donne's letter to George Gerrard (Paris, 14 April 1612): 'Of my *Anniversaries*, the fault that I acknowledge in myself is to have descended to print anything in verse, which, though it have excuse, even in our times, by example of men which one would think should as little have done it as I; yet I confess I wonder how I declined to it, and do not pardon myself'; or, Donne's letter to Sir Henry Goodyer (Paris, April? 1612). Texts cited from *John Donne*, ed. John Carey (Oxford University Press, 1990), pp. 233–4.

what I shall suffer from many interpretations: but I am at an end, of much considering that... By this occasion I am made a Rhapsoder of mine own rags, and that cost me more diligence, to seek them, than it did to make them. This made me aske to borrow that old book of you, which it will be too late to see, for that use, when I see you: for I must do this, as a valediction to the world, before I take Orders. But this is it, I am to aske you; whether you ever made any such use of the letter in verse, *A nostre Countesse chez vous*, as that I may not put it in, amongst the rest to persons of that rank; for I desire very very much, that something should bear her name in the book... I pray tell me as soon as you can, if I be at liberty to insert that: for if you have by any occasion applied any pieces of it, I see not, that it will be discerned, when it appears in the whole piece. Though this be a little matter, I would be sorry not to have an account of it, within as little after New years tide, as you could.[2]

Like his poetry, Donne's letter suggests privileged exchange, even whispered intimacy. But its language also points to a more public sociability, to the qualities of Donne's writing as colloquy and conversation. The letter reminds us of poetry's audience, in the English Renaissance, among men and women of courtly and aristocratic rank, and of the private circulation of verse in manuscript as well as of the gradations of public space that manuscript and print might occupy.[3] It points to the importance too of patronage and publication to the business of advancement – sacred, social, literary and economic – and it underscores the role of writing and reading, and of the cultivation of literary distinction, in achieving it. Donne's letter also allows us to see how, and under what constraints, a book might be put together by recalling scattered leaves of verse, and the ways in which poetry circulates from one writer's page to another's lips or hand and back again.

Donne seeks the manuscript compilation from Goodyer because he has not, apparently, retained his own copy,[4] though that request may partly cover a more delicate inquiry: not if Goodyer has kept Donne's copy, but if he has borrowed Donne's language. Would the Countess of Bedford remember, and from another's voice or hand, Donne's words? He wants a place for her name in his book, but Donne cannot include the verse epistle if the Countess of Bedford already knows 'pieces of it'. We are aware from work on Renaissance protocols

---

2 The text is cited from *John Donne, Selected Prose*, ed. Helen Gardner and Timothy Healy (Oxford University Press, 1967), pp. 144–5; and see the discussion of the letter and the project of print publication and other examples of Goodyer's 'borrowings' from Donne in R. C. Bald, *John Donne: A Life* (Oxford University Press, 1970), pp. 166–8, 295–6.

3 See Harold Love and Arthur Marotti, 'Manuscript transmission and circulation' in this volume (Chapter 2).

4 In *John Donne: Coterie Poet* (Madison: University of Wisconsin Press, 1986), p. 291, n. 2, Arthur Marotti cites the example of Sir John Davies making a similar request.

of imitation and adaptation that standards of plagiary and originality quite different from our own were supposed to cover the subject that Donne raises – and Donne's casual assumption that Goodyer may indeed have appropriated his language is not itself at issue.[5] Authorship and originality, however, surely do animate Donne's nervous query: 'But this is it, I am to aske you; whether you ever made any such use of the letter in verse, *A nostre Countesse chez vous*, as that I may not put it in'. Donne's language expresses, if not exactly a claim to literary property, certainly an awareness that reading situates Donne's verse in a competitive system; that friends and patrons constitute a knowing audience; that not only manuscripts but words and phrases, perhaps lines and whole stanzas, circulate among these readers, and under various names; that authorship and originality are qualities for which the Countess of Bedford reads; and that she has a discerning eye and a quick memory.

The letter is rich in implications for our understanding of literary culture, *c.* 1600, and it would be easy enough to deploy its sentences in describing this culture according to a familiar and fruitful model of literary study, one imagined from the point of view of authors and their work: Donne's needs, his expressiveness, his awareness of the idioms of compliment and their modes of currency. These are traditional materials of literary scholarship, and the insertion of Donne's remarks on patronage into such an account of literary production brings this model closely up to date.[6] Moreover, registering the porous relations between manuscript and print here documented deepens our appreciation of the varied textures of early modern writing, circulation and publication.[7]

But Donne's letter also invites us to imagine literary history from a different perspective, one conceived, at least in part, from the point of view of

5 See Stephen Orgel, 'The Renaissance Artist as Plagiarist', *ELH* 48 (1981), 476–95; and on ownership, circulation and appropriation in the Restoration, see Harold Love, 'Rochester's "I" th' isle of Britain": Decoding a Textual Tradition', *Manuscript Studies, 1100–1700* 6 (London: The British Library, 1997), 175–223.

6 On early modern literary patronage, see Dustin Griffin, *Literary Patronage in England 1650–1800* (Cambridge University Press, 1996); Cedric Brown (ed.), *Patronage, Politics, and Literary Traditions in England, 1558–1658* (Detroit: Wayne State University Press, 1993); and Margaret Hannay, *Philip's Phoenix: Mary Sidney, Countess of Pembroke* (Oxford University Press, 1990). See also Chapter 4 in this volume.

7 On scribal and print publication in early modern England, see Peter Beal, *In Praise of Scribes: Manuscripts and their Makers in Seventeenth-Century England* (Oxford: Clarendon Press, 1998); H. R. Woudhuysen, *Sir Philip Sidney and the Circulation of Manuscripts 1558–1640* (Oxford: Clarendon Press, 1996); Arthur Marotti, *Manuscript, Print, and the English Renaissance Lyric* (Ithaca: Cornell University Press, 1995); Mary Hobbs, *Early Seventeenth-Century Verse Miscellany Manuscripts* (Aldershot: Scolar Press, 1992); and Harold Love, *Scribal Publication in Seventeenth-Century England* (Oxford: Clarendon Press, 1993).

consumption rather than production: a history that allows us to see how verse letters, for example, are composed not only within and against the norms of demonstrative rhetoric and traditions of epideictic poetry, but also with an individual reader and with a class of sophisticated, courtly consumers in mind. Indeed, the study of literary consumption invites us to contemplate a broad range of negotiations between reading and writing, to imagine writing not only as a complex formal and social practice, but also as a field of gestures within and through which authors might anticipate the reception, circulation and reproduction of their words and work.

Donne's verse letters to the Countess of Bedford display all the compression and angularity of his lyrics, and their hyperbolic figures are the practised idiom of his language of compliment; but the theological boldness of Donne's address to Bedford – she appears variously in these letters as 'God's masterpiece', 'His factor for our loves', indeed 'divinity' itself – and especially the touches of intimacy, anxiety and need that Donne betrays, bespeak ways of writing that spring not only from convention but also from a particular and self-conscious knowledge of the character and the habits of a specific reader and more broadly of a circle of readers for whom and to whom Donne wrote his poetry. Like the court masque, Donne's verse epistles are situated within a geography of graduated privilege: one reader is entitled to the perspective of full comprehension and compliment; others read at angles more oblique to its spectacle.[8] The emblems, half-secrets and knowing glances of the verse epistles – Donne's sly allusion, for example, to the daring 'see-through' costume that the Countess wore in Jonson's *Masque of Queenes*[9] – are staged for the complete but not completely private experience of an aristocratic patron reading from Donne's autograph, as well as for the pleasure of those privileged to witness (in this instance by reading manuscript copy, though not likely Donne's autograph) his bold display.[10]

Such graduated scales of privacy and publicity and such legible traces of a writer's address to a reader's social standing and taste are to be discovered not only in Donne's brilliant verse epistles but also in a broad range of early

8 On the court masque and privileged perspective, see Stephen Orgel, *The Illusion of Power: Political Theater in the English Renaissance* (Berkeley: University of California Press, 1975).

9 See Barbara K. Lewalski, 'Lucy, Countess of Bedford: Images of a Jacobean Courtier and Patroness', in *Politics of Discourse: The Literature and History of Seventeenth-Century England*, ed. Kevin Sharpe and Steven N. Zwicker (Berkeley: University of California Press, 1987), pp. 58–9.

10 For a discussion of autograph and manuscript copies of Donne's verse, see the *Index of English Literary Manuscripts, Vol. 1: 1450–1625*, compiled by Peter Beal, Part I *Andrews-Donne* (London: Mansell; New York: Bowker, 1980), pp. 244–50.

modern writing: in poetry of compliment and complaint as early as Wyatt's satirical verse epistles, in acts of devotion and contemplation, and in the literature of patronage and place that stretches from Jonson's epigrams and panegyrics or Lanyer's 'Description of Cooke-ham' across the succeeding decades to include Herrick's odes and carols, and the poetry that he wrote to the Earl of Westmorland; the poems that Westmorland, in turn, addressed to Herrick; Carew's verse letters, epitaphs and addresses; Denham's *Coopers Hill*; Waller's Penshurst poetry and his verse 'On St. James' Park'; Dryden's hopeful addresses to the good and the great; even Lord Rochester's casual and scandalous verse – poetry that could only have been written with an intimate knowledge of the social, sexual and readerly tastes and discriminations of its readers who passed copies of the verse among themselves and who all, no doubt, were known by the Earl.

If we would examine the most brilliant and complex and telling instance of poetry written into the privacy of a reader's pleasures, exigencies and vanities, we can do no better than read across the stanzas of Andrew Marvell's 'Upon Appleton House', a text both personal and polemical, verse that caresses and corrects, poetry written to and for and beyond Marvell's patron, Thomas, Lord Fairfax, his family, and his circle of Yorkshire antiquaries and friends.[11] In Marvell's careful and witty compliments to his patron's interests and passions (Fairfax's antiquarianism, his interest in family genealogy and church history, his ethical scrupulousness), in the poet's indulgent account of Fairfaxian morals and martial history, and in the ways that Mary Fairfax is imagined as both virtuous tutee and the sacred vessel of Fairfaxian destiny, we might sense Marvell's cultivation of the taste and concerns of particular readers within a Puritan aristocratic household. But more fully to address the ways in which Lord Fairfax might have read Marvell's little country-house epic, or more exactly to engage Donne's verse epistles as reading copy, or to imagine Herrick's carols as social and patronage performance, and more broadly to write of early modern English literature from the point of view of its consumption raises problems not simply of re-imagining the past but of evidence of that past.[12] It would be nice to know how, and with what degree of pleasure, the Countess of Bedford encountered Donne's epistles, or to glance over her shoulder as she read his

---

11 On *Upon Appleton House* and its engagement with Lord Fairfax, see Derek Hirst and Steven Zwicker, 'High Summer at Nun Appleton, 1651: Andrew Marvell and Lord Fairfax's Occasions', *Historical Journal* 36 (1993), 247–69.

12 On reading and the problem of evidence, see the 1992 reprint of Carlo Ginzburg's *The Cheese and the Worms*, trans. John Tedeschi and Anne Tedeschi (Baltimore: Johns Hopkins University Press, 1992), which contains Ginzburg's response to his critics.

verse, perhaps recognising the odd phrase from a letter or conversation with another friend or client; failing that, we would do well to have her marked copy of Donne's verse. No such records of her reading or marking, however, have come to light. And though we have copies of Fairfax's translations of St Amant,[13] a poet whose verse Marvell wove into the fabric of 'Upon Appleton House' as he laced the poem with Fairfaxian markers,[14] we do not know with what sense of recognition Fairfax read 'Upon Appleton House', or indeed if Fairfax read, or even saw, the tutor's poem.

Reading and the problem of evidence

Writers leave their traces everywhere: we have their drafts and revisions, their letters, notes and diaries, we have their literary theorising, perhaps even their formal literary criticism as well as the internal evidence of borrowing and allusion. Reading seems quite another matter. Like other modes of consumption – like eating, or listening, or looking – reading seems to deny its material premise. Reading is silent, private, often immobile; we read in bed or in the bath, we read by ourselves, we read in studies, offices or libraries; but once we have finished, we remove our body from the act – the event often vanishes without a trace.[15] To reconstruct, rather than simply to reimagine, the history of literature from the point of view of its consumption might seem a very difficult task.

Reading in the Renaissance, however, was not always private, silent and immobile, nor did early modern reading vanish quite without a trace. Not only did the act of reading provide repeated subject matter for painted and engraved portraits with their familiar icons of early modern reading (fingers holding and marking different places in the book, pen and ink ready to hand,

---

13 See Hilton Kelliher, *Andrew Marvell, Poet & Politician: An exhibition to commemorate the ter-centenary of his death* (London: The British Library, 1978), pp. 45–8; Fairfax's translations can be consulted in *The Poems of Thomas, Third Lord Fairfax*, ed. Edward Bliss Read, Transactions of the Connecticut Academy of Arts and Sciences, 14 (New Haven, CT: Auspices of Yale University, 1909).

14 See the commentary to *Upon Appleton House* in *The Poems and Letters of Andrew Marvell*, ed. H. M. Margoliouth, 3rd edn revised by Pierre Legouis with the collaboration of E. E. Duncan-Jones (Oxford: Clarendon Press, 1971), 1:279–93.

15 Most contemporary references to and representations of reading in the early modern period underscore its formal settings, but there are occasional references to reading in bed; see, for example, Sir Kenelm Digby's remarks on reading *Religio Medici*, in *Observations Upon Religio Medici* (London, 1643); or *Familiar Forms of Speaking Compos'd for the Use of Schools, formerly fitted for the Exercise of a Private School only, now published for Common Use*, 3rd edn (London, 1680), p. 108: 'I make Verses best in Bed. My Bed-chamber is my best Study'; this text is an adaptation of Erasmus's *Familiarum Colloquiorum Formulae*, which was first published in 1519.

the contemplative gaze, the open texts on the studio table)[16] and appear frequently and emblematically on the early modern stage ('*Enter Hamlet reading on a Booke*'; 'Read on this book, / That show of such an exercise may colour / Your loneliness'),[17] but the intimacy of reading with writing throughout the early modern period provides important materials for an archaeology of literary consumption.

Indeed, writing was among the most widespread habits of early modern reading.[18] To read with pen in hand underscoring or otherwise marking memorable passages; to correct errors or emend the text and cite variant readings; to gloss or interline with technical or rhetorical terms or with translations and citations; to summarise and cross-refer; to outline and paraphrase; to make synopses and provide interpretations; to extract maxims from Scripture and sermons, from plays and poems, from prayers and devotions; to move themes, arguments and topics, indeed whole poems, elegies and epitaphs, recipes and remedies, speeches and letters from one transcript to another, from printed book or manuscript text to commonplace compilation, notebook or miscellany – these indeed were the commonplaces of Renaissance reading.

Such signs of reading are to be found repeatedly in the printed and manuscript records of early modern England. At times they are made by owners dating and otherwise marking their books; sometimes by multiple owners who occasionally respond to earlier marking. One owner of Clement Walker's *Compleat History of Independency* (1661) remarks that his copy of the book once belonged to 'some spitefull ffanatick', 'as appears by the malevolent marginall notes'.[19] Sometimes marks are made by aristocratic and royal readers: Charles I's copy of Xenophon's *Treatise of Housholde* (1534) inscribed to him in 1615, with its proverbial matter underscored in manuscript, or the King's copy of

---

16　See Peter Stallybrass, 'How Many Hands Does It Take to Read or Write a Book', University of Virginia Lecture, Rare Book School, 16 July 1997.

17　For a discussion of this scene, see Eve Sanders, *Gender and Literacy on Stage in Early Modern England* (Cambridge University Press, 1998), pp. 69–71.

18　For illustrations of the Renaissance systems of interlinear gloss and marginal commentary, see Roger E. Stoddard, *Marks in Books, Illustrated, and Explained* (Cambridge, MA: Harvard University Press, 1985); and Bernard M. Rosenthal, *The Rosenthal Collection of Printed Books with Manuscript Annotations: A Catalogue of 242 Editions Mostly Before 1600 Annotated by Contemporary or Near-Contemporary Readers* (New Haven, CT: Yale University Press, 1997).

19　See the Folger copy of Clement Walker's *Compleat History of Independency* (London, 1661) where, at the close of the prefatory epistle the owner writes, 'this booke was bought by me...AD 1671, in Westminster Hall of Mr Henry Mortlock Stationer, at the sign of the White Hart: which book (as appears by the malevolent marginall notes, in the other page) did formerly belong to some spitefull ffanatick.'

Shakespeare.[20] We have books that were shared within families, passed from husband to wife, and from one generation to the next, and such copies reveal the ways in which individual readers and communities of readers used, marked and understood their texts. The case of writers consuming the works of their peers and predecessors affords an especially heightened and attentive model of reading, understanding and applying. Jonson's copy of Martial, for example, provides a fascinating glimpse of consuming and producing. Jonson's predominant habits as a reader were to underscore and to mark with various signs in the text: with daisies, with pointing hands, with occasional remarks that indicate intertextual moments within Martial's work or lines of special interest. He underscores every single line of Martial's Epigram, 'In Bassum', and at line 4 intrudes a pointing finger, writing in the margin 'vide Lib. VI. Epig. CXCIII'.[21] If we attend to Jonson's marking of Martial we can map, in this highly articulate instance, some of the traffic between consuming and producing, between Jonson noting a particular turn of phrase or figure in Martial – a slighting, offensive or defamatory move – and the abstraction, the appropriation often by literal translation, or the application of that idiom. From marks and underscoring, from the highlighted or cross-hatched and even, at times, wholly obliterated pages, from pointing fingers and marked commonplaces, and especially from annotations in the margins of books we might, then, achieve at least a partial recovery of early modern reading, that often silent, seemingly ephemeral, and most intimate form of intellection and engagement.

Annotation is not of course an invention of the early modern reader. Medieval manuscripts are covered by a repertoire of signs – punctuation, foliation, rubrics, reading accents, cross-referencing and annotation – and by scribal illustrations that allow us to construe a field of 'visual politics' in these texts.[22] Yet the powerful and regulated impulses of humanist education spread annotation far beyond the professional class of readers. Marginalia in the Renaissance

20 See Folger STC 18345; for Charles's Shakespeare see T. A. Birrell, *English Monarchs and Their Books: From Henry II to Charles II*, The Panizzi Lectures, 1986 (London: The British Library, 1987), pp. 44–5.
21 See Folger STC 17492, copy 1, and also the Folger copy of Speth's *Chaucer* (1602; STC 35489) with Jonson's annotations. On Jonson's marginalia, see Robert C. Evans, *Habits of Mind: Evidence and Effects of Ben Jonson's Reading* (Lewisburg, PA: Bucknell University Press, 1995), and on Jonson as reader of Spenser, see James A. Riddell and Stanley Stewart, *Jonson's Spenser: Evidence and Historical Criticism* (Pittsburgh: Duquesne University Press, 1995).
22 See Kathryn Kerby-Fulton and Denise L. Despres's *Iconography and the Professional Reader: The Politics of Book Production in the Douce 'Piers Plowman'* (Minneapolis: University of Minnesota Press, 1999); and, more generally, Michael Camille, *Image on the Edge: The Margins of Medieval Art* (Cambridge, MA: Harvard University Press, 1992).

were the property not only of cleric and scribe, but of aristocrats and their secretaries, of scholars and schoolboys, and, eventually, of a wider, more socially diverse and, by the middle of the seventeenth century, more contentious and combative field of readers.[23] What bound such early humanists as More and Erasmus together was not only a shared rhetorical tradition and the impulse to mark but the importance of exemplarity to their habits of reading, and admiration to their modes of consumption. The Marquis of Winchester published a collection of precepts in 1586, underscoring, in the very title of his book – *The lord marques idlenes; conteining manifold matters of acceptable devise; as sage sentences, prudent precepts, morall examples, sweete similitudes, proper comparisons, and other remembrances of speciall choise. No lesse pleasant to peruse* – the relationship between exemplarity and application, between morality and memory.[24] And when Edward Lumsden annotated Montaigne's *Essays* (1603), he turned the title-page of his copy into an index of the book's themes and 'sentences'.[25]

What distinguished the heirs of these humanists in the growing turbulence of the 1630s and 1640s, and in the nervous and disillusioned decades that followed, was the willingness to abandon sweet similitude and sage sentence,[26] to press controverting habits well beyond the tracks of religious controversy where they had been so deeply laid by the Reformation, to cover with increasingly hostile response a broad field of texts, to arm and intensify annotation, indeed, at points, almost to flood with suspicion and hostility an entire marketplace of texts from news-sheet to epic poem, from broadside and pamphlet (where we might well expect the mark of controversy) to song and strophic ode.

We can trace a strong tradition of religious animadversion from the earliest years of the Reformation to the Restoration and beyond. There is no question

---

23 For commentary on the general lack of marginalia in books owned by women in the early modern period, see Heidi Brayman Hackel, '"Boasting of Silence": Women Readers and the Patriarchal State', in *Renaissance Reading*, ed. Kevin Sharpe and Steven N. Zwicker (Cambridge University Press, 2002). Lady Eleanor Davies Douglas provides an interesting exception to the general silence of women in the margin; she dated and annotated her own pamphlets including *The Crying Charge* (n.p., 1649); *Elijah the Tishbite's Supplication* (n.p., 1650); *The Excommunication out of Paradice* (n.p., 1647); see the Folger Library collection of Douglas's pamphlets, D2010.

24 *The Lord Marques Idlenes: Conteining manifold matters . . . compiled by the right Honorable L. William Marques of Winchester that now is* (London, 1586). Folger STC 19485, copy 3, is annotated by hand.

25 Folger V. b. 327, *The Essays or Moral Politike and Millitarie Discourses* (London, 1603).

26 See R. A. Beddard, 'A Traitor's Gift: Hugh Peter's Donation to the Bodleian Library', *Bodleian Library Record* 16 (April 1999), 374–91, which documents the disillusionment with humanist education in the 1650s: 'As a senior member of Merton College, Anthony Wood had closely followed the menacing dispute. He bound in one volume many of the pamphlets in the controversy, and labelled it, "For and against, humane learning".'

of the savagery of such contest, of the obsessive and often violent temper of its invective, or of its tenacity.²⁷ Nor should we be surprised to find that the consumption of religious polemic or, even, of devotional texts, was animated by this spirit, that copies of religious books reveal woodcut portraits of Catholic martyrs that have been struck through, or the offending language of sanctification obliterated,²⁸ or on the other side of the divide to find religious texts sharply marked by Catholic sympathies. In one French history of the English 'heresy', an English Catholic has deeply marked the passages on English religion and written the word 'abominable' next to an account of the martyrdom of John Nelson, an English Catholic.²⁹ Moreover, religious tracts often appropriate in the form of printed marginal commentary the well-worn pattern of readerly objection and repudiation, and pamphlets often deploy the voices of dialogue and disputation in the texture of their writing, even in their print styles and typeface.³⁰

Of course, suspicion and hostility, even in the sixteenth century – well before the Civil Wars had so broadly spread the arts of contentious reading – are not confined to the domain of religious controversy. No doubt literary envy is as old as composition itself, and certainly the fear of caviling and competition is recorded in a variety of literary prefaces, dedications and satiric texts. Jonson's epigrams, for example, scatter a bright if irregular light on a broad spectrum of writerly apprehensions and readerly suspicion; he repeatedly anticipates, and hedges against, misreading and misprision. In the very first poem of *Epigrams* Jonson posts danger signs, 'Pray thee, take care, that tak'st my book in hand, / To read it well: that is, to understand', and throughout his book he scatters gestures that both warn and caress. Perhaps Jonson's defensiveness and aggression seem rather more pathology or bravado than part of a common literary culture, but

---

27 See G. R. Elton on Sir Thomas More, *Studies in Tudor and Stuart Politics: Papers and Reviews, 1946–1972*, 3 vols. (Cambridge University Press, 1974), vol. 3.

28 See, for example, the University of Aberdeen copy of Jacobus de Voragine, *The golden Legend* (1483) [Boyndlie Inc 225a] where the saints' images are mutilated, a number of woodcuts removed and words like 'seynt' are struck through.

29 See the Folger Library copy of *L'Histoire de la Naissance, progrez et decadence de l'heresie de ce siecle* (Paris, 1610), 'Chapitre XI, Livre Sixieme. La difference de la Religion des Anglois, & de autres sects', p. 745.

30 See, for example, *An Oration or Funerall Service uttered at Rome at the buriall of the holy Father Gregory the 13 . . . Faithfully translated out of the French Copie, printed at Paris for Peter Jobert, dwelling in Harpe streate. 1585*. On p. 8, the printed text reads, 'wherein although I can not (as in truth I am not able) atteyne to the least parcell of thy desertes; which are not well to be expressed, yet at all adventures I assure my selfe, O happy soule, that as in thy lyfe time thou didest pardon mee a number of other imperfections, so now thou wilt likewise forgive mee this'. The printed marginal comment is 'Beastly and blasphemous devinitie fit for so leaud a Bishop and so unlearned a Chaplaine.'

Jonson was not alone in these moods.[31] George Chapman protested, perhaps with a touch of the same paranoia, the innocence of his *Andromeda Liberata* (1614):

> a malicious reader by straining the Allegorie past his intentionall limits, may make it give blood, where it yeeldes naturally milke, and overcurious wits may discover a sting in a lie: But as a guiltless prisoner at the barre sayd to a Lawyere thundring against his life, Num quia tu disertus es, ego peribo? Because malice is witty, must Innocence be condemned?... Doth any rule of reason make it good, that let the writer meane what he list, his writing notwithstanding must be construed in mentem Legentis? To the intendment of the Reader?[32]

Chapman's delicate negotiation between intention and understanding, between a writer's innocence and a reader's malice, suggests a well-developed understanding of the dangers of writing in an unpredictable interpretive community.

Jonson's epigrams, however, tell more than suspicion's story; their title may carry 'danger in the sound', but Jonson also celebrates the epigrams as a theatre of virtue.[33] Like his models Martial and Horace, Jonson both caresses and corrects; he names virtuous names, but he also anticipates the wicked and the guilty reading themselves into and out of his poetry. Keys and ciphers mark Restoration literature at every turn, but Jonson renders for us an atmosphere of secrecy and suspicion and spying that characterise Jacobean politics and Jacobean hermeneutics:

> When I made them [epigrams], I had nothing in my conscience, to expressing of which I did need a cipher. But, if I be fallen into those times, wherein, for the likeness of vice, and facts, everyone thinks another's ill deeds objected to him; and that in their ignorant and guilty mouths, the common voice is (for their security) 'Beware the poet', confessing, therein, so much love to their diseases, as they would rather make a party for them than be rid, or told of them . . . I have avoided all particulars, as I have done names . . . [but] some will be so ready to discredit me, as they will have the impudence to belie themselves . . . For such, I would rather know them by their vizards, still, than they should publish their faces, at their peril, in my theatre, where Cato, if he lived, might enter without scandal.[34]

31 See, for example, Joseph Hall's epigrams, *Virgidemiarum. The three last Bookes* (London, 1598).
32 Chapman, *The Poems*, ed. Phyllis Brooks Bartlett (Oxford University Press, 1941), pp. 329–30.
33 See Jonson's dedication of *Epigrams*, 'To the great example of honour and virtue, the most noble William, Earl of Pembroke', in Ben Jonson, *The Complete Poems*, ed. George Parfitt (New Haven; CT: Yale University Press, 1975), pp. 33–4.
34 Text cited from the Parfitt edition; and cf. Jonson's proclamations of authorial innocence in the 'Apologetical Dialogue' to *Poetaster*, 'My books have still been taught / To spare the

Though Jonson protests the innocence of his motives and the purity of his poetry – he has published no names and particulars, the texture of his verse is free of cipher and indirection – by projecting the guilt of application and innuendo onto the mind of his readers and the manner of his times, he allows his verse at once to stand free of innuendo and to dwell within the excited atmosphere of injury and application.

The course of the century that was to unfold after the publication of Jonson's *Workes* (1616) witnesses an intensification, indeed at points a transformation, of relations between consumption and production that makes Jonson's anxiety and abrasion seem the very model of the coming age. His language of ciphers and disguise, his exposing of vice and publication of scandal, his sense of cabinets opened and secrets revealed seem as much to predict the circumstances of rebellion, revolution and Restoration as to name Jacobean practices. Certainly by the time of the Civil Wars, and for decades thereafter, competition and antagonism, and not simply scepticism, became a dominant force in the relations between readers and their texts. Indeed, when Charles I's cabinet of private letters was forced open, those who published the letters assumed that the mere act of reading them would convict the King of secret hostility and treasonous enmity, and that only malignants could read them otherwise.[35]

Until the Civil Wars ceased to be living memory, suspicion and contempt were the shadow under which many transactions between consumption and production took place. The consequences were difficult to avoid in a world riven by civil and religious dissent, fractured by rebellion and revolution, and then marked by a broad political ethos of irony, duplicity and mistrust.[36] They were in fact the very conditions that produced the brilliant and complex culture of royalism in retreat, of ardency and republicanism, and of those incomparable ironies and culpable morals of the Stuart Restoration.

Perhaps, however, we thrust Jonson's fears and apprehensions too quickly forward into the political and social ethos of rebellion and restoration. The literary culture of the late sixteenth century was itself spiked by controversy

---

persons and to speak the vices': *Poetaster*, ed. Tom Cain (Manchester University Press, 1995), 266, lines 71–2.

35 *The Kings Cabinet opened: Or, Certain Packets Of Secret Letters & Papers, Written with the Kings own Hand, and taken in his Cabinet at Nasby-Field, June 14. 1645* (London, 1645), sig. A4 r: 'if thou art a perfect malignant, and dost not stick to deny, that there is anything in these letters unbeseeming a Prince... Then know, that thou art scarce worthy of any reply, or satisfaction in this point.'

36 See Steven N. Zwicker, 'Irony, Modernity, and Miscellany: Politics and Aesthetics in the Stuart Restoration', in *Politics and the Political Imagination in Later Stuart Britain: Essays Presented to Lois Green Schwoerer*, ed. Howard Nenner (University of Rochester Press, 1997), pp. 181–95.

and competition. The 'War of the Theaters' and the Nashe-Harvey debates, the ballad literature and the Marprelate tracts all give ample and varied evidence of the controversial strands of Elizabethan print culture.[37] Such texts stimulated political, literary and religious dissent and they contributed to the practices of controversial and dissonant reading so vividly illustrated in an annotated copy of Rachel Speght's *A Mouzell for Melastomus* (1617) where the reader explodes with hostility in a set of contemptuous, witty and occasionally indecent polemics against Speght's text.[38] Speght inveighs against malice and misogyny, 'Good it had beene for you to have put on that Muzzel, which Saint James would have all Christians to weare; Speak not evill one of another', and in the margin of his copy, Speght's antagonist wrote, 'Likewise it is sayd, revile not those that revile: which muzzell would verie well have fitted your mouth in manie places of this booke'.[39]

Exemplarity and admiration

The more important, and, by far, the more dominant models of Renaissance literary consumption, as well as the more prominent intellectual features within a broad field of readerly expectations, were, however, imitation, exemplarity and admiration.[40] The detailed portraits we possess of figures like Gabriel Harvey, John Dee and, now, of Sir William Drake, and of their work as lay and professional readers,[41] argue not simply the applied agency of the humanist intellect but the overarching model of exemplarity which guided and informed the reading of courtiers, aristocrats and connoisseurs, and of their professional servants and protégés. Exemplary reading – the careful study of texts for patterns of virtue, the imbibing of classical wisdom, and the exportation of models of conduct and expression – was reinforced by a culture of imitation which spread far

---

37 On Elizabethan pamphlet culture, see Alexandra Halasz, *The Marketplace of Print: Pamphlets and the Public Sphere in Early Modern England* (Cambridge University Press, 1997); Herbert Grabes, *Das englische Pamphlet: Politische und religiose Polemik am Beginn der Neuzeit* (1521–1640) 2 vols. (Tubingen: Max Niemeyer Verlag, 1990); and, more broadly, M. Lindsay Kaplan, *The Culture of Slander in Early Modern England* (Cambridge University Press, 1997).
38 The Speght volume is in the Beinecke Library at Yale University and the text and marginalia have been edited by Barbara K. Lewalski, *The Polemics and Poems of Rachel Speght* (Oxford University Press, 1996).
39 *Ibid.*, p. 95.
40 See, however, the essays collected in the *Journal of the History of Ideas* 59.4 (October 1998) under the title, 'The Renaissance Crisis of Exemplarity'.
41 See Anthony Grafton and Lisa Jardine, ' "Studied for Action": How Gabriel Harvey Read his Livy', *Past and Present* 129 (1990), 3–50; for John Dee as Renaissance reader, secretary, intellectual facilitator and magus see William H. Sherman, *John Dee: The Politics of Reading and Writing in the English Renaissance* (Amherst: University of Massachusetts Press, 1995); and on Sir William Drake and early modern reading, see Kevin Sharpe, *Reading Revolutions: The Politics of Reading in Early Modern England* (New Haven: Yale University Press, 2000).

beyond the study or the diplomatic and courtly conference.[42] Imitation and admiration inhabit the schoolroom and the rhetorical handbook, they inform the literary experimentation of euphuism and quantitative metres,[43] and they animate the creation of a rhetorical culture of extravagance and amplification – Spenser's *Hymns* and *The Faerie Queene*, the Elizabethan sonnet sequences, and the burgeoning miscellanies, songbooks and madrigals.[44] These texts evidence a particular convergence of cultural style and literary habit, a kind of complicity between consuming and producing, of reading for wonder, for admiration and imitation, and of writing into that very market. But modes of reading and writing inform one another not only in and through the economy of demand and supply – though that is surely an important economy – they also create a nexus of social and psychological circumstances shared by all those who read and write.

The most familiar case study of humanist reading and marking is that provided by Anthony Grafton and Lisa Jardine's work on Gabriel Harvey. Though Grafton and Jardine emphasise the plurality of Renaissance reading and its critical, even sceptical, dimensions,[45] the very premise of Harvey's study and application is a belief in the authority and wisdom of the text. As secretary to the Earl of Leicester, he studied the historians and political theorists of Renaissance Italy and classical antiquity with the aim of extracting their wisdom and reflecting the lessons that history taught on present circumstances, making such wisdom an act of counsel and service. Nor is Gabriel Harvey our only exemplar of Renaissance reading, nor is the case study our only form of evidence. Commonplacing itself provides a model of exemplarity, and it is practised across the social spectrum and over the whole of the early modern period: readers marking and copying – revolving, reducing and digesting to practice – the text that lay before them.[46] A number of the most striking images and accounts of

---

42 On reading for scholarly and diplomatic purposes, see Lisa Jardine and William Sherman, 'Pragmatic Readers: Knowledge Transactions and Scholarly Services in Late Elizabethan England', in *Religion, Culture, and Society in Early Modern Britain*, ed. Anthony Fletcher and Peter Roberts (Cambridge University Press, 1994), pp. 102–24.

43 See Derek Attridge, *Well-weighed Syllables: Elizabethan Verse in Classical Metres* (Cambridge University Press, 1974), pp. 119–20: 'The concept of "imitation" was, of course, central to the whole quantitative movement.'

44 Terence Cave provides the best introduction to the rhetoric and arts of Renaissance copia: *The Cornucopian Text: Problems of Writing in the French Renaissance* (Oxford: Clarendon Press, 1979).

45 On Jonson and Selden as sceptical readers, see Jason P. Rosenblatt and Winfried Schleiner, 'John Selden's Letter to Ben Jonson on Cross-Dressing and Bisexual Gods', *English Literary Renaissance* 29 (Winter 1999), 48–9.

46 See Archibald Campbell, Marquis and eighth Earl of Argyll, *Instructions to a Son* (Edinburgh and London, 1661), pp. 102–4: 'Think not cost too much in purchasing rare Books; next to that of acquiring good Friends I look upon this purchase; but buy them not to lay by,

early modern readers – Holbein's portraits of Erasmus and Sir Thomas More, Quentin Metsys's portrait of Peter Gilles, the portrait of Lady Anne Clifford among her books[47] – reinforce this sense of reading's exemplary modes and practices: reading as the veneration and imitation of antiquity, reading as conformity to Scripture, reading as the comparing and conflating of texts, reading as the appropriation of wisdom.[48] Perhaps commonplacing put anachronistic pressure on some classical texts, but it was certainly no anachronism for contemporary texts which often seem written to order for such work: proverbs, sentences, adages, axioms and examples all marked for extraction and when not literally marked easy to discover and appropriate.[49]

When Harvey annotated his Tacitus,[50] or Jonson marked his Martial,[51] when Lady Mary Sidney annotated Hall's *Chronicles*,[52] or Charles I marked his Shakespeare,[53] and when lawyers marked their collections of statutes or

or to grace your library, with the name of such a Manuscript, or such a singular piece, but read, revolve him, and lay him up in your memory where he will be far the better Ornament. Read seriously whatever is before you, and reduce and digest it to practice and observation, otherwise it will be Sysyphus his Labour to be always revolving Sheets and Books at every new Occurence which may require the Oracle of your reading. Trust not to your Memory, but put all remarkable, notable things you shall meet with in your Books *sub salva custodia* of Pen and Ink, but so alter the property by your own Scholia and Annotations on it, that your memory may speedily recur to the place it was committed to.'

47 See Graham Parry, 'The Great Picture of Lady Anne Clifford', in *Art and Patronage in the Caroline Courts*, ed. David Howarth (Cambridge University Press, 1993), pp. 202–19.

48 For contemporary Dutch images of reading, see *Leselust: Niederlandische Malerei von Rembrandt bis Vermeer*, ed. Sabine Schulze (Stuttgart: Gerd Hatje, 1993).

49 See, for example, the Speght Chaucer, *The Works of our Ancient and Learned English Poet...newly printed...*(London, 1602), with its printed hands pointing to sententious materials (and the Folger Library copy, STC 5080, copy 3, with Jonson's underscorings); or the beautifully marked Folger copy of Sidney's *Countesse of Pembroke's Arcadia* (STC 22540, copy 1) with its printed marginal commentary and elaborate series of manuscript citations to Sidney's literary sources and its carefully marked maxims and sentences; or the annotated copy of More's *Utopia* (London, 1551), Folger STC 18094, copy 2, with its sententiae picked out and noted with carefully inked points, quotation marks and 'notas'. Even so late as the 1670s Marvell mocks such a preparation of texts; see *The Rehearsal Transpros'd*, ed. D. I. B. Smith (Oxford: Clarendon Press, 1971), p. 84: 'Our Booksellers have many Arts to make us yield to their importunity: and among the rest, they promise us, that it shall be printed in fine paper, and in a very large and fair letter...that wheresoever there is a pretty Conceit, it shall be marked out in another Character, that the Sentences shall be boxed up in several paragraphs, and more Drawers than in any Cabinet.'

50 These can be consulted in *Gabriel Harvey's Marginalia* collected and edited by George Charles Moore-Smith (Stratford-upon-Avon: Shakespeare Head Press, 1913).

51 Jonson's marked copies of Martial are in the Folger Library: *Epigrammaton libri* (London, 1615), STC 17492, copy 1, and *M. Val. Martialis nova editio* (London, 1619), PA 6501, A2, 1619 Cage. See, as well, the marked Folger copy of Sidney's *Countesse of Pembroke's Arcadia* (STC 22540, copy 1); and the Folger copy, STC 26071, of Xenophon's *Treatise of Housholde* (London, 1537), inscribed to Prince Charles in 1615 with its proverbial matter underscored.

52 Folger STC 1272, copy 2.   53 See Birrell, *English Monarchs and their Books*, pp. 44–5.

Members of Parliament annotated political pamphlets, they all participated in a common cultural literacy. These are but the most obvious exemplars; the archive of marginal annotation in any of the great repositories of early modern books provides a wealth of texts so marked and used, and from such markings we might well begin the recovery of early modern habits of reading. But evidence of the margin is not our only archive for this history, nor does the margin itself always provide evidence that is easy to sift and evaluate or indeed, at times, even to decipher.[54] The arts of reading can be inferred from other sources and other forms of evidence: from the kinds of training readers received; from the dominant texts of the culture and the ways they were presented, distributed and used; and from all the paratexts of early modern books – frontispieces, tables, commendatory verse, indexes, plates and, most intriguingly, those dedications and addresses in which writers, publishers and printers at once imagined and conjured the early modern patron, reader and marketplace for books.

The majority of early modern readers and writers of classical and vernacular literature were socially and economically privileged males trained in the reading and translating of Virgil and Horace, Martial and Catullus, Juvenal and Persius.[55] They learned to read from private tutors and in schoolrooms, and their personal and institutional experience constitutes an important source of information for reconstructing the experience of individual readers and of a significant class of consumers.[56] They were saturated with editions of classical

54 The relations between book collecting and marginalia might themselves form a significant chapter in the history of books; the appeal of marked copies has varied widely over the course of the nineteenth and twentieth centuries, and the interest of collectors in clean copies has often determined which copies of early modern books were saved, which washed or cropped, and which discarded.

55 On Renaissance literacy, see David Cressy, *Literacy and the Social Order: Reading and Writing in Tudor and Stuart England* (Cambridge University Press, 1980); Cressy's statistics have been questioned by Margaret Spufford, *Small Books and Pleasant Histories* (Athens: University of Georgia Press, 1981); by Keith Thomas in 'The Meaning of Literacy in Early Modern England', in *The Written Word: Literacy in Transition*, ed. Gerd Baumann (Oxford University Press, 1986); and by Tessa Watt, *Cheap Print and Popular Piety, 1550–1640* (Cambridge University Press, 1991), pp. 7–8. For an account of the reading of a young dissenter, see *An Astrological Diary of the Seventeenth Century: Samuel Jeake of Rye, 1652–1699*, ed. and with an introduction by Michael Hunter and Annabel Gregory (Oxford University Press, 1988), which includes a list of all the books Jeake had read by the age of fifteen. There were of course notable exceptions among aristocratic girls and women throughout this period; Lady Jane Lumley made a translation of *Iphigenia at Aulis* in her commonplace book, BL Royal MS 15.A.ii, printed for the Malone Society (London: C. Whittingham, 1909), and Anne Cornwallis Campbell, Countess of Argyll (d. 1635) made a commonplace book (Folger V.a. 89) which shows her wide contemporary reading.

56 On the schoolroom and its training, see M. L. Clarke, *Classical Education in Great Britain 1500–1900* (Cambridge University Press, 1959); Anthony Grafton and Lisa Jardine, 'Teacher, Text, and Pupil in the Renaissance Classroom', *History of Universities* 1 (1981), 37–70; and, more recently, Alan Stewart, *Reading and Homosociality* (Princeton University Press, 1998).

authors whose printed texts were surrounded by a sea of commentary.[57] Readers and writers shared these editions as the common property of an education in humane letters, and in their modelling of text and commentary they shaped the creation and presentation of early modern literary texts from Spenser's *Shepheardes Calender* (1579) to Cowley's *Davideis* (1656) and from Harington's *Orlando Furioso* (1591) to Hobbes's Thucydides (1629) and beyond. Printed commentary bolstered the authority of the text and guided its interpretation by situating the contemporary text and the contemporary reader in a community of learning and within a set of interpretive protocols.

Of course reading was inflected by other models, none more important than Scripture. The English Bible was the great vernacular text whose histories, verses, epistles and prayers supplied the steady continuo against which so many early modern literary texts were written and read.[58] Scripture was read in the home and from the pulpit; and sermons and homilies, paraphrases and commentaries, psalters, hymns and prayers flowed from divines and scholars through printing presses and booksellers to readers throughout this period. Nor should we think that the parsing or paraphrasing of Latin poetry and the explication of Scripture were contradictory modes of thought or feeling. One of the great interpretive projects of the European learned community was the harmonising of sacred and secular histories and mythologies.[59] Indeed, the texts of Hebrew and classical antiquity were the twin foundations on which the structure of exemplary reading was based.

Habits of imitation and admiration, of application and attentiveness, were formed by parsing, translating, memorising and replicating both the Scriptures and the classics. These habits focused the mind on the exemplary force of the text, on what was translatable and transportable, on the 'commonplace' and the proverbial, on the didactic and moralising, and on ethical and spiritual thematics. When Sidney defended poesy, it was for literature's moving

---

57 Anthony Grafton cites the superb example of Niccolo Perotti's *Cornucopiae* with its 1,000 folio columns devoted to commentary on one book of Martial's epigrams; see Grafton's *Joseph Scaliger: A Study in the History of Classical Scholarship* (Oxford University Press, 1983), 1:17; and, more generally, L. D. Reynolds and N. G. Wilson's *Scribes and Scholars: A Guide to the Transmission of Greek and Latin Literature*, 3rd edn (Oxford University Press, 1991).

58 On the ways in which Scripture shaped the creation of early modern devotional poetry, see Barbara K. Lewalski, *Protestant Poetics and the Seventeenth-Century Religious Lyric* (Princeton University Press, 1979), and Rivkah Zim, *English Metrical Psalms: Poetry as Praise and Prayer 1535–1601* (Cambridge University Press, 1987); for the importance of Scripture to early modern English prose, see Janel M. Mueller, *The Native Tongue and the Word: Developments in English Prose Style, 1380–1580* (University of Chicago Press, 1984).

59 See R. R. Bolgar, *The Classical Heritage and its Beneficiaries* (Cambridge University Press, 1954), and Bolgar (ed.), *Classical Influences on European Culture AD 1500–1700* (Cambridge University Press, 1976).

and imaginative moral life; when Lady Anne Clifford consoled herself with Chaucer, it was for 'his devine sperett';[60] and when Henry More recalled his father reading Spenser, he remembered a poem 'richly fraught with divine morality'.[61] Such modes of reverence and methods of understanding and application were echoed and reinforced by the literary, even the typographical, texture of vernacular literature: the adages and axioms marked for extraction, the exemplary materials set in italic type,[62] the commonplaces marked by inverted commas,[63] and when not literally marked, easy to discover and export.[64] We might even think that reading was programmed by physical markers that became internalised, habitual to the act of reading, indeed to the ways in which both those who read and those who wrote imagined the work of the text. In the flourishing literature of 'sentences', in the training to commonplace, in Biblical hermeneutics and particularly in the methods of personal and national application so important to reformed traditions of reading Scripture, we find a powerful set of models for the consumption of a broad variety of texts. Manuscript commonplace books into which early modern readers transcribed miscellaneous materials – prose passages, verse extracts, poems, prayers, moral proverbs, observations – from a broad variety of their reading according to a set of abstracted categories not only provided these readers with materials for their own literary, political and intellectual labour, but they provide us with ways of looking at the experience of reading for extract and exemplarity and of gauging the pressure that reading for exemplarity placed on the experience of reading itself.

60 *The Diary of Anne Clifford, 1616–1619*, ed. Katherine O. Acheson (New York: Garland, 1995), pp. 164–5: 'If I had nott exelent Chacor's booke heere to comfortt mee I wer in a pitifull case, having so many trubles as I have, but when I rede in thatt I scorne and make litte of tham alle, and a little partt of his devine sperett infusses itt selfe in mee.'

61 Henry More, *Philosophicall Poems* (Cambridge, 1647), sig. A2r.

62 In Hobbes's translation of *Eight bookes of the Peloponnesian Warre written by Thucydides* (London, 1629) italic type is used for exemplary material throughout the text; in the Folger copy, STC 24058, the italic materials are underscored by pen.

63 See Robert Garnier, *Two Tragedies: Hippolyte and Marc Antoine*, ed. Christine M. Hill and Mary G. Morrison (London: Athlone Press, 1975), pp. 24–5, where the editors discuss this marking of sentences.

64 See, for example, the Folger Library manuscript commonplace book, V.b. 93, in which a very large number of printed literary texts – indexed alphabetically at the back of the volume by title and author – are excerpted in order to illustrate and provide quotations for a large number of alphabetically organised topics, e.g., *acquaintance, actions, adultery, adventure, adversity*. The heavily used book is marked by a complex system of signs. Among the authors commonplaced are Beaumont, Burton, Cartwright, Chapman, Crashaw, Digby, Fuller, Heywood, Jonson, Milton, Ogilby, Quarles, Randolph, Sandys, Shakespeare, Shirley, Sidney, Stanley, Suckling and Sylvester. On commonplacing and the Renaissance reader, see Terence Cave, 'Problems of Reading in the *Essais*', in *Montaigne: Essays in Memory of Richard Sayce*, ed. I. D. McFarlane and Ian Maclean (Oxford University Press, 1982), 136–7.

Yet to note the dominant modes of early modern textual production and consumption is not to predict every event that took place within this frame, nor is it to calculate the angles of complicity, resistance or irony from which those modes were practised or at which they were mingled, applied and experienced, even within a culture of humane letters. To return for a moment to the relationship between Donne and the Countess of Bedford with which we began, what we might hear in the complex address of Donne's verse epistles to the Countess – 'Madam, / Reason is our soul's left hand, Faith her right, / By these we reach divinity, that's you' or 'Honor is so sublime perfection' – are both the continuous presence of courtly and theological commonplaces and the frequent risking of those honours and refinements. The idioms of admiration and exemplarity brighten the texture of this verse, but they are also compromised, at points almost exploded, by the pressure of inflated rhetoric. And further to complicate our assessment of dominant models of consumption, we must allow that attitudes and protocols were not shared evenly across the culture: in some of its modes like the verse epistle they lingered uneasily, in others like satire they were often not present at all. Under repeated political, social and ideological stress, all the counters of intellectual life, of reading and its arts, suffered change.

The culture of exemplarity, however, did not simply or quickly disappear. We are right to sense a mood of admiration and extravagance well beyond the turn of the sixteenth century, in the thickets of commendatory verse that prefaced the folios that Humphrey Moseley published of Beaumont and Fletcher (1647) and William Cartwright (1651) – though in the very density of commendation we might detect a defensive posture – even in the recessive, self-conscious pastoralism and pastiche of Walton's *Compleat Angler* (1655).[65] These writers shared a trust in the community of reading, and Walton's anthologising of Elizabethan and Jacobean ballads and sonnets, like his patchwork quotation of stanzas of Du Bartas and Donne, seems an effort at once to assert and to create such commonality and community of literary culture. Or perhaps we ought to say that these signs suggest a fantasy of that commonweal, a fiction that the Civil Wars put under stress and at points exploded. Nor are we wrong to feel more than a shadow of that combustion passing over Cavalier poetry, over even Herrick's bright and innocent lyric turn. His sense of public and literary

---

65 In the prefatory address to Richard Brome's *Five New Playes* (London, 1653), Alexander Brome acknowledges both the variety of readers of a volume of plays published after the closing of the theatre and their essential solidarity: 'Beloved, Being to write to a multitude of you, (for I know you will be many) I forbear Epithets, because the same will not fit all; and I hate to make difference among Friends.'

ruin – of poetry written into and against the envy, suspicion and the indignation of the times – is eloquent testimony to the ghosts that haunted his verse, even that poetry's easy congress with antiquity. Marvell warned against 'Word-peckers, Paper-rats, Book-scorpions';[66] Herrick imagined his own volume so damaged and torn.[67] *Hesperides* is a book designed for browsing and borrowing, for copying and commonplacing,[68] but among those happy continuities with the past we can also hear the poet's loss of faith in the very culture that was meant to support the reading, circulation and reproduction of *Hesperides*. Herrick maps both his poetry's use and its destruction – even as he wrote, Herrick imagined his poetry as 'orphaned verse'.[69]

Reading and rebellion

The transformation of reading practices is, however, evidenced by more than reading's representation: the simple numbers of print publication tell a powerful story in the years preceding and following the Civil Wars. If we track London imprints through the 1620s, the approximate number of individual titles for any given year stays well below 500; 1630 itself is marked by over 500 imprints, and through the 1630s these numbers remain above 400. Then in 1640 the number reaches 800; in 1641 there are over 2,500 imprints, and in 1642 the number reaches 4,000. From that high, the numbers begin to drop: 2,000 in 1643, 1,300 in 1644, down to a low for the decade of 900 in 1645 and then above 1,000 for each year through the rest of the decade.[70] We know that the mechanisms for enforcing the licensing laws collapsed in 1641, and that the general confusion over licensing had the effect of stimulating print publication (various efforts at re-imposition over the following decades may help to account for some of the fluctuating numbers of print publication), but lapses in the enforcement of regulations do not create a market. The numbers evidence both a remarkable history of printing and licensing at mid-century and a tremendous appetite for print products of all kinds in

---

66 *The Poems and Letters of Andrew Marvell*, 1:3.
67 See Herrick's repeated address to his book, *The Poetical Works of Robert Herrick*, ed. L. C. Martin (Oxford: Clarendon Press, 1956), pp. 6, 155, 212, 275, 300.
68 On the qualities of *Hesperides* as miscellany, see Randall Ingram, 'Robert Herrick and the Making of *Hesperides*', *Studies in English Literature* 38.1 (Winter, 1998), 127–49.
69 *The Poetical Works*, 'To his Verses', p. 218.
70 These estimates are derived from WorldCat, an OCLC database that is searchable by year and place of publication; the WorldCat data may give a high estimate. On these estimates, see M. Bell and J. Barnard, 'Provisional Count of STC Titles 1475–1640', *Publishing History* 31 (1992), 48–64, and Bell and Barnard, 'Provisional Count of Wing Titles 1641–1700', *Publishing History* 55 (1998), 89–97.

London. Print publication in the provinces tells a similar story, and of course London products are not limited to London circulation. Moreover, if we examine titles and keywords the story comes into sharper focus. To follow, for example, the fortunes of such words as 'opinion' and 'rebellion' or 'schism' and 'remonstrance' is to discover the rapid expansion of print publication inflected by particular themes and concerns, by the outburst of political anger and accusation, and by the suspicion of religious motives and practices. And print publication itself is only one part of the story of production and consumption. Throughout the early modern period all sorts of materials – letters and news reports; satires, squibs and scandals; prayers, meditations and animadversions – circulated in manuscript, at times only among intimates or between friends; but also more widely among social and literary peers; within religious communities; between political allies and sometimes, like printed pamphlets, scattered anonymously. Books that were too dangerous to print in London were produced, or carried false imprints of production, in Amsterdam, Brussels and Leiden, and books that were too dangerous to be sold were simply given away, dropped in the streets, left at the door, hung on hedges in the highway.[71]

Numbers of production and modes of distribution indicate part of the story of consumption. Dedications tell us more exactly of the ways that writers anticipated reading and hoped to shape response: to persuade and to caution, to move and to inflame. Often dedications were accompanied by yet more explicit addresses to the reader, indeed to specific kinds and communities of readers: to the courteous reader, the serious reader, the candid reader, the discerning reader, the ingenuous reader, the Christian reader, the impartial reader, the unprejudiced reader, the vulgar reader, the inquisitive reader – individuals and collectives brought ever more sharply and determinedly into focus by civil and religious conflict. What publication numbers and the language of dedication and preface, however, cannot tell us is exactly how courteous and candid readers consumed their letters, pamphlets and books.

Of course, not all reading was courteous and compliant. Indeed we have mounting evidence over the 1630s, 1640s and 1650s, both occasional and programmatic, of some spectacularly discourteous acts of reading, and I want to pause over one such example because it provides us with the very model of readerly suspicion and deconstruction. 'In words which admitt of various sense, the libertie is ours to choose that interpretation which may best minde us of

71 Keith Sprunger, *Trumpets from the Tower* (Leiden: E. J. Brill, 1994), p. 163.

what our restless enemies endeavor, and what wee are timely to prevent.'[72] So Milton glossed Charles I's Latin epithet in the *Eikon Basilike* (1649), '*Vota dabunt, quae bella negarunt*', and so this humanist reader, trained in the modes of admiration and exemplarity, went about sniffing behind enemy lines for restless endeavour. In one way, reading for action is exactly what John Milton, Renaissance humanist, did with the text of Charles I. But the powerful assertion of individual will, the haunting suspicion, the determination to penetrate and decode – though they may have been latent in commonplacing or reading for action – had all been intensified and transformed through the poet's, and the nation's, experiences of civil war and regicide.

The *Eikon Basilike* boasts one of the most astonishing print histories in early modern Europe. It was issued and sold in the streets on the day of its author's execution, and within the first year of publication it had gone through thirty-five separate London editions.[73] It was published in large quartos but also in pocket editions, rubricated, bound in leather, and intended for wearing near the heart. It was imitated, adored and adapted; it was both memorial and talisman. With its interleaving of personal narrative and prayer, the book wrote its own modes of reading, but not every reader would be mesmerised by its idioms. Milton became official respondent to the *Eikon Basilike* by parliamentary appointment, but it was not Parliament alone that had made him into textual editor, literary critic and sociologist of reading. What Milton proposed in *Eikonoklastes* was to contest every aspect and endeavour of the King's book, to practise reading as preemptive military strike. His was a programme of political and intellectual liberation from the bonds of admiration and exemplarity. And in that endeavour *Eikonoklastes* is armed to the teeth. Milton conceives of reading as intellectual combat, and the language of armed engagement – of gauntlets and fields of contest, of 'force and equipage of arms', of liberty, tyranny and glorious warfare – pervades *Eikonoklastes*; he understands reading as an anatomising force that would contest history, disparage eloquence and destroy images. By emphasising the connections between the King's book and the masque, by aligning its effects with spectacle, romance and theatre, Milton aimed to discredit the King's aesthetics and politics and at the same time to humiliate and re-educate those who read by adoring its images and affect. Milton would shake the 'Common sort' from intellectual torpor, from their habits

72 Citations of *Eikonoklastes* are from the *Complete Prose Works of John Milton*, ed. Don M. Wolfe *et al.*, 8 vols. (New Haven, CT: Yale University Press, 1953–82), 3:342.

73 The standard bibliography is Francis F. Madan, *A New Bibliography of the Eikon Basilike of King Charles I* (Oxford University Press, 1950).

of reading 'without industry or the paines of well judging, by faction and the easy literature of custom and opinion'.[74]

Nor was Milton alone in such practices. We can find a multitude of examples of reading as anatomy and destruction; the King's book excited other answers and animadversions, each one of which is in the first instance an act of hostile and suspicious reading. Evidence of reading as hostility and suspicion is superbly demonstrated by the publication of *The Kings Cabinet Opened* (1645). After the king's defeat at Naseby, the parliamentary forces captured Charles's letters to his wife and arranged their print publication with editorial annotations which acted as hostile and suspicious readings of the King's correspondence and more largely of the King's character, domestic relations and politics. Combat and contest also mark the work of less articulate expressions of reading – acts that took place in the margins of books and between lines of print, indeed at times over the printed line itself, and at times over other marginalia in the form of deeply incised cross-hatching.[75] Moreover, when such reading intended more than obliteration, it contested and engaged through correction, denial and repudiation. Throughout the 1640s and 1650s marginal annotation – itself, as we have seen, a venerable humanist practice – turned partisan and harshly polemical. Insults were scrawled across title-pages, scandals were cast on 'schismatics' and 'delinquents', aspersions were written on flyleaves and up and down the sides of pages.[76] Politics drove the consumption of texts just as writing was absorbed to 'Partie Projects'.[77] Books from this period are covered with signs of active reading, but these no longer gave evidence of a commonwealth of meanings; they exemplified rather a world of politics, partisanship and passions.

It may not be surprising that books of such notoriety as *Eikon Basilike* drew the attention of readers armed for combat, and my citation of the *Eikon Basilike* and Milton's reading of that book is intended to suggest the power and thoroughness of consumption as combat and contest. But if the practice of contestatory

74 *Complete Prose Works*, 3:338.
75 See, for example, the Folger Library copy, P4109, of William Prynne, *The Treachery and Disloyalty of Papists to their Soveraignes* (London,1643) which is marked by a score of marginal comments, each one defaced and rendered illegible.
76 See the Folger Library copies of Prynne's *New Discovery of the Prelates Tyranny* (London, 1641), Folger Library copy, P4018; *Cabala, Mysteries of State* (London, 1654), Folger Library copy, C7175; John Vicars, *Former ages never heard of, and after ages will admire. Or a brief review of the most material Parliamentary transactions*, 2nd edn (London, 1656), a collection of eight pamphlets, Folger Library copy, V306.2
77 See William Ashhurst, *Reasons Against Agreement with a late Printed Paper, intituled, Foundations of Freedome* ([London], 1648), p. 14: 'But let us lay aside this Paper, and all dividing and Partie Projects'.

reading were exclusive to such programmatic texts, we would extend our understanding of only one aspect of civic culture. Rather, my aim is to suggest a broad transformation of intellectual practices, of reading as suspicion and combat applied to a wide range of texts and textual practices. Once the field of reading had been transformed so thoroughly into a territory of combat, it was difficult to imagine and experience it otherwise. What Milton had done to *Eikon Basilike* might foreshadow, though perhaps in cooler and more oblique ways, the reading of a broad range of texts and forms.

Consider, for example, the reading that Marvell may have anticipated, and that may – I would argue – have shaped and inflected his *Horatian Ode*. The poem has long been studied as the quintessence of intellectual integrity and independence of spirit; and, without denying its poise or refinement, I would challenge integrity and independence as the mainspring of its strategies and modes of ambivalence. By situating the poem within a historical field of reading, it becomes possible to see the text not as an act of delicate intellection but as a set of postures and negotiations, a repertoire of gestures and imaginative constructs whose aim is to baffle partisanship. The poem offers its readers a structure in which to contemplate their circumstances amidst powerfully conflicting loyalties and ambitions. The verse carries signs of the royalist past and auguries of the republican future, but it remains scrupulously free of commitment to either position.[78] The ode would baffle partisan reading by draping royalist forms over republican facts; hence it might seem either to regret or to celebrate, a self-service poem offering its wares without recommendation.

Marvell designed the poem to withhold opinion. The ode is supremely sensitive to the conditions of reading in a polemical culture, but it does not so much resist or rewrite those conditions as acquiesce in and use them. In a zone of combat and contest, the work of the *Horatian Ode* is to anticipate and neutralise the suspicions and destructive impulses of its readers, to offer a dialectic in which the consequences of choice are aestheticised, or, indeed, anaesthetised. Milton had written of the liberty to choose an interpretation 'in words which admit of various sense'; Marvell's ode seems designed to generate exactly such a variety of sense, but also to take the sting out of the consequences of that variety. One might read the poem and experience simultaneously a nostalgia for old forms – the very title of the poem conjures a world of aristocratic literary culture – and a commitment to new engagements, and feel those contradictions resolved or melted away by the rhythms and idioms of a poem which allows the reader to

---

78 But see David Norbrook's *Writing the English Republic* (Cambridge University Press, 1999), for the classic republican reading of Marvell's verse.

contemplate the destruction of an aristocratic political model within an aristocratic literary form whose intricate stanzas and exacting diction both preserve the culture and allow the contemplation of its destruction. The poem services a readership that could take comfort in its baffling moves, its dialectical way of holding at bay the pressures of partisan feeling that had erupted in the wake of the Civil War, the regicide and the creation of a republic. The *Horatian Ode* takes on a very different sense when it is inserted into the centre of the world of readerly violence Milton epitomises in *Eikonoklastes*, for it is exactly that penetration, that anatomising force the poem would resist.

Ironies and subversions

Though the pressures of partisanship would change, they would not get any simpler when the strenuous republicanism of the 1650s gave way to that force field of ironies that constituted Restoration culture. It is possible to see the rise of party politics over the course of the Restoration as a civilising innovation, a gradual reduction of the stakes of political combat from armed conflict to paper skirmish, but I would not want to exaggerate the rapidity with which civic violence was translated into mere partisanship, or a consequent sense of diminished dangers or diminished stakes for the invention, publication and distribution of texts. If anything, print culture in the Restoration is ever more closely and overtly implicated in politics, and the field of reading more hazardous and volatile. The dense topicality of civic texts is one sign of that implication; more broadly, the entire culture of hints and allusions, of masking, allegory and innuendo, suggests not simply intimate but something like claustrophobic relations between consumption and production. The Advice-to-Painter poems superbly illustrate these complicities, and none more so than Marvell's *Last Instructions to a Painter*. Its gossipy retailing of parliamentary debate, its portraits of aristocratic corruption and astonishing imagery of the King in sexual heat argue at once a deeply polemicised market and a taste for scandal, together with a set of highly developed skills and, we might think, partisan self-consciousness for its deciphering and decoding.[79] Marvell's own reading and application of Milton's allegory of Sin and Death to the creation of Excise also suggest a broader scheme

---

79 *The Last Instructions* is one of the first texts in which we discover the language of court and country applied to factional politics; see lines 105ff.: 'Draw next a Pair of Tables op'ning, then / The House of Commons clatt'ring like the Men.' The *OED* cites Bolingbroke's *On Parties* (1735–8) as the initial entry for 'country party'. On deciphering and decoding, we might think of the ways in which, both in manuscript and when poems reach print, the names of courtiers, politicians and other public figures are concealed, but sometimes barely so, behind initial letters.

of reading practices in the Restoration. For what Marvell has done is to situate the drama of parliamentary politics within the spaces of Milton's allegory, to read Milton's powerful and intricate drama of the incestuous creation – itself a parody of divine creation – as a gloss on and a parody of parliamentary creation. Marvell borrows the moral grandeur and the sexual resonance of Milton's verse at once to stain and to explicate the sordid manoeuvring of parliamentary politics:

> ... a Monster worse than e're before
> Frighted the Midwife, and the Mother tore
>
> * * *
>
> She stalks all day in Streets conceal'd from sight,
> And flies like Batts with leathern Wings by Night.
> She wastes the Country and on Cities preys.
> Her, of a female Harpy, in Dog Days:
> Black Birch, of all the Earth-born race most hot,
> And most rapacious, like himself, begot.
> And, of his brat enamoured, as't increast,
> Bugger'd in Incest with the mungrel Beast.[80]

Marvell was putting the finishing touches on *The Last Instructions* in late summer of 1667, perhaps a month or two before *Paradise Lost* was published,[81] but not before it was circulated and read. What the passage so powerfully conveys is the availability of *Paradise Lost* to the sharpest sort of partisan reading and rewriting – a sense that Marvell understood the ways in which Milton's poem was implicated in Restoration politics, tied to the rankness and indecencies so amply illustrated in the rest of Marvell's brilliant essay on court corruption. Nor was Marvell alone in appreciating that proximity; the first edition of *Poems on Affairs of State* figures Milton prominently among its 'wits', claiming his authority for *The Second Advice* 'said to be written by Sir John Denham, but believed to be writ by Mr Milton'.[82]

It was Toland's spiritualised life, the print annotations of the 1690s, and the late seventeenth- and eighteenth-century practices of editing and presenting

---

80 Text cited from *The Poems and Letters of Andrew Marvell*, 1:141, lines 131-2, 141-6.
81 On the dating, see ibid., 1: 346; Margoliouth conjectures its completion 'some time after 30 August 1667, when Clarendon resigned the seals, and before 29 November 1667, when he fled to France (it contains no reference to his flight)'. Nicholas von Maltzahn speculates on a publication date in October or early November, 1667, for *Paradise Lost*; see Von Maltzahn, 'The First Reception of *Paradise Lost* (1667)', *Review of English Studies* 47 (November 1996), 481.
82 *Poems on Affairs of State... Written by the greatest Wits of the Age. Viz. Duke of Buckingham, Earl of Rochester, Lord Bu ----- st, Sir John Denham, Andrew Marvell, Esq; Mr Milton, Mr Dryden, Mr Sprat, Mr Waller. Mr Ayloffe, &c.* (n.p., 1697), sig. A6r, 'Directions to a Painter, said to be written by Sir John Denham, but believed to be writ by Mr. Milton.'

Milton's poetry separate from his prose – and of course the gradual loss of a readerly intimacy with the forces and circumstances under which the poem was meditated, produced and initially read – that distanced *Paradise Lost* from the habits and capacities of polemical reading and rewriting.[83] Even when Francis Atterbury made marginal annotations in his copy of *Paradise Lost*, perhaps in the 1680s, and certainly at some remove from its initial publication, he understood and replicated the ways in which Restoration politics were read into and read out of Milton's poetry. Next to the portrait of Moloch in Book 2 (ll. 106–8) Atterbury wrote, 'This probably ye picture of some great man in Milton's time.'[84] Was the episcopal licenser Thomas Tomkins wrong in 1667 to read *Paradise Lost* and suspect treason where Milton suggested that the 'dim Eclipse disastrous Twilight sheds / On half the Nations, and with fear of change / Perplexes Monarchs' (1, 597–9)? In the 1690s Toland mockingly retailed this story, but Tomkins's responsiveness not simply to Milton's reputation but to the conditions of reading in the first years of the Restoration seems in fact less anachronistic than Toland's scorn for what he calls Tomkins's 'frivolity and superstition'.[85]

Nor was Dryden's superb rendering, or rather reduction and defanging, of *Paradise Lost* in *The State of Innocence* (published 1677), and his laying it at the feet of the sixteen-year-old Roman Catholic bride of the now publicly Roman Catholic Duke of York, any less a political act and a politicised reading of *Paradise Lost* than was Marvell's *Last Instructions*. *The State of Innocence* has been understood as a trimming of Milton's epic to the theatrical tastes and aesthetic standards of the 1670s, but this is too simple, too innocent a reading of Dryden's motives. He was quite sensitive to the politics as well as the grandeur, the sublimity, the learning of Milton's poem; he was a superlative reader of Milton's verse, but he had motives other than appreciation in his management of *Paradise Lost*. Dryden had a sense of the design of the poem on its audience, and he aimed to make *Paradise Lost* safe for the Restoration reader. *The State of Innocence* is like an infra-red map of *Paradise Lost*; where Dryden sensed danger, there he excised and simplified.

Of course we have other evidence, not quite so brilliant or peculiar or partisan, of the contemporary reading of *Paradise Lost*. One marked copy gives evidence

83 See Sharon Achinstein, *Milton and the Revolutionary Reader* (Princeton University Press, 1994), pp. 173–6, and ch. 4, 'Milton and the Fit Reader'.

84 John Milton, *Paradise Lost. A Poem in Twelve Books* (London, 1678), Beinecke Library, Yale University, Osborn Collection, pb 9.

85 *A Complete Collection of the Historical, Political, and Miscellaneous Works in English and Latin of John Milton*, ed. John Toland 2 vols. (Amsterdam, 1698), 1:40–1; and see von Maltzahn, 'The First Reception of *Paradise Lost* (1667)', 482–7.

of a serious struggle to make sense of the poem, especially its chronologies; in this book the flyleaf is used to map the timeline of *Paradise Lost* in a way that identifies which of the poem's events occurred before and which after the work of Creation.[86] Other copies suggest a profound absorption in the poem's piety and scripturalism; one reader turned *Paradise Lost* into a virtual concordance of Scripture.[87] Nor should we expect less from a poem put to market in the shops of Peter Parker, Mathias Walker and Robert Boulter, booksellers busy with the publishing and vending not of epic poetry but of religious nonconformity – the writings of Calvinists, Presbyterians and ejected ministers.[88] Neither the strenuously politicised nor the intensely spiritualised readings of *Paradise Lost* will much remind us of poetry so long regarded as a glacial monument of Renaissance humanism. But we should not think that Milton, who had gone to school in the furious polemical skirmishing of the 1640s and 1650s, had forgotten earlier modes of contemplation and other ways of thinking and feeling. Perhaps *Paradise Lost* is best understood as a palimpsest from which we might glean a long history of reading. Here is a text capable of supporting the widest variety of readerly practices and protocols; Milton scholarship has done justice to the learning and elevation and to certain forms of the poem's expressive complexity, to ways in which it spoke to and was read by eighteenth-century editors, Romantic poets and twentieth-century scholars. But the poem also spoke, if with less elevation then certainly with no less urgency, to those who read the text in November of 1667 and in the months and years following.[89] Those readers may not have appreciated all of the poem's challenging erudition, but I suspect, whatever their allegiances, they felt its politics – the powerful resonance of its lines on the eclipsing of monarchy, or its lurid catalogues of pagan monarchs and deities – with a quickness now difficult fully to imagine.

To address the ways in which books were read in the past – in the context of humanist practices, under the shadow of Scripture, in the turmoil of civil war and revolution and, when the winds had shifted and loyalties turned, under pacts of oblivion and in the midst of new political and aesthetic formations – is

---

86 See the Case Western Reserve University copy, PR 3560, 1674, 800722, in which the verso of the title-page is used to make a topical index to *Paradise Lost* for such themes as 'hell', 'tower of babel' and the 'devil his world'; further, there is a manuscript chronology within the index that seems to have been used to clarify and organise the poem through two categories: 'world not made' and 'world made'.

87 British Library copy, C.14.A.9.

88 Their publications records may be consulted through Paul G. Morrison's *Index of Printers, Publishers and Booksellers in Donald Wing's Short Title Catalogue* (Charlottesville: University Press of Virginia, 1955).

89 See Nicholas von Maltzahn, 'Laureate, Republican, Calvinist: An Early Response to Milton and *Paradise Lost* (1667)', *Manuscript Studies* 29 (1992), 181–98.

to acknowledge, perhaps even to overcome, that difficulty of imagination. And so to contemplate this poem, and so to contemplate early modern writing, is for us to read with an understanding of the complex, even (we might admit) imponderable ways in which production anticipated consumption, in which early modern texts were written into an imagination of their contemporary reading.

2

THE TUDOR ERA FROM THE REFORMATION TO ELIZABETH I

Chapter 7

LITERATURE AND NATIONAL IDENTITY

DAVID LOADES

England

At one level national identity is little more than xenophobia: that gut reaction which provokes verbal and physical violence against strangers and outsiders. It had appeared in fifteenth-century riots against Flemings and Italians; and it appeared in the 'Evil May Day' riot of 1517 against foreigners. An anonymous Italian observer, writing of the English about 1500, declared 'They have an antipathy to foreigners, and imagine that they never come into their island but to make themselves masters of it, and to usurp their goods.' There was a positive side to such feelings, but it was equally unattractive. The same observer continued: 'The English are great lovers of themselves, and of everything belonging to them; they think there are no other men than themselves, and no other world but England. And whenever they see a handsome foreigner, they say that "he looks like an Englishman".'[1] Such sentiments do not appear in English writings of the period, which were seldom aimed at a popular readership, but they were widespread at all social levels. English nobles attending Henry VIII in the highly competitive atmosphere of the Field of the Cloth of Gold (1520) declared that if any French blood ran in their veins, they would cut it out with a knife.[2] Popular and semi-popular writing on patriotic themes focused either on the power and splendour of the King, or on God's special favour to the realm;

> Regnum Anglorum regnum Dei est,
> As the Aungelle to seynt Edwarde dede wyttenesse

---

1 Charlotte A. Sneyd (ed.), *A Relation ... of the Island of England ... about the year 1500*, Camden Society, old ser., 37 (London: The Camden Society, 1847), pp. 53–4. The best-known account of England by a Renaissance scholar also reflected an Italian point of view: Polydore Vergil, *Historiae Anglicae libri viginti septem* (Basle, 1534). The best modern edition is *The Anglica Historia, AD 1485–1537*, ed. and trans. Denys Hay, Camden Society, 3rd ser., 74 (London: Royal Historical Society, 1950).
2 J. G. Russell, *The Field of Cloth of Gold* (London: Routledge, 1969), p. 188.

an anonymous Yorkist poet had written in 1460.[3] In the words of John McKenna, God had become an Englishman in the context of the Hundred Years' War, and that sense of identity, framed in a confrontational spirit, not only against the French but also against their allies the Scots, forms the background to the period with which we are concerned.[4]

Writings aimed at the basically literate, designed to arouse feelings of loyalty and affection towards King and country, and of corresponding antipathy to those seen as a threat, form one category of work to be noticed. A second category consists of treatises on the laws and government of England. These vary from technical case books to political commentary which is highly engaged with current affairs. The identity of every community was expressed in its law, and it was of the greatest importance to England that it had a common law, which was uniformly administered by royal writ. Thirdly, it is necessary to examine briefly the enormous literature generated by Henry VIII's Great Matter – the annulment of his marriage to Catherine of Aragon. The King's repudiation, not only of papal suzerainty but also of the spiritual jurisdiction of Rome, caused a flurry of controversy over the proper limitations of royal power, and consequently over the extent of what would later be called 'national sovereignty'. This controversy was subsequently extended in two directions: by those Protestants who sought to emulate the claims of the papacy by denying the legitimacy of regimes with which they were in dispute; and by those who claimed that a woman's right to rule was circumscribed by her gender and by the customs of Christian marriage. Finally, it is necessary to notice the various ways in which the identity of England was located: in the law, in the monarchy, in the land, in the will of God, in the people and even in the Parliament. Scotland was following a similar track, but with less emphasis upon positive constitutional features and more upon loyalty and popular sentiment. In Wales, where there was no institutional focus, the main emphasis was upon language, custom and kinship.

English-language chronicles, of which many were published in the early sixteenth century, were a fairly humble form of literary life, but undoubtedly intended to engender a sense of identity.[5] A typical specimen was *This is the Cronycle of all the kynges names that have ben in England* (1518), starting with Brute and remaining highly mythological until about the tenth century.[6] This

---

3 R. H. Robbins (ed.), *Historical Poems of the XIVth and XVth Centuries* (New York: Columbia University Press, 1959), pp. 207–10.

4 J. W. McKenna, 'How God became an Englishman', in *Tudor Rule and Revolution: Essays for G. R. Elton from his American Friends* (Cambridge University Press, 1982), pp. 25–43.

5 For a discussion of this type of antiquarian interest and its development, see May Mackisack, *Medieval History in the Tudor Age* (Oxford: Clarendon Press, 1971).

6 *Short-Title Catalogue of Books Printed in England, Scotland and Ireland, and of English Books Printed Abroad, 1475–1640*, ed. A. W. Pollard and G. R. Redgrave (London: Bibliographical Society,

anonymous list contained the names of two women, 'Gwentolyn, wife of Bladud' and 'Credel, daughter of Lyne', both equally mythological, but interesting in view of the fact that there had been, at that point, no historically authentic female ruler. The only serious claimant, Matilda, had failed to obtain possession of the Crown in 1141. To emphasise its main point this doggerel recital also referred to 'Newe Troy (that now is callyd London)'. In spite of its title, it was the antiquity and integrity of the realm which was in question in this work, rather than the genealogy of its rulers. Edward Hall's *Union of the two noble and illustre famelies of York and Lancaster* (1548) was an altogether more sophisticated piece of work, but its basic aim was the same, topping off its narrative with a highly positive assessment of the Tudor achievement.[7] Accounts of victories in battle, although much narrower in focus, belong to the same category, for example *Hereafter ensueth the trew encounter between England and Scotland* (1513), which celebrated the battle of Flodden; *The late expedicion in Scotlande* (1544) (Solway Moss) and William Patten's similar account of Pinkie Cleugh in 1548.[8] Tales of heroic exploits at sea, not only victories but voyages of discovery, served a similar emotional purpose, but belong to a later period.[9]

An early sixteenth-century Englishman certainly saw himself as a loyal subject of the King, but the King had other subjects who were not English, and certainly not English-speaking. *The fyrst boke of the Introduction of knowledge*, by Andrew Borde (1542), explored the whole question of identity rather interestingly: 'In England, and under the dominium of the dominum of England be many sondry speeches besides English; there is French used in England, specialy at Calys, Garnsey and Jersey. The Walshe tongue is in Wales. The Cornyshe tongue in Cornwall and Iryshe in Irelande . . . There is also the Northern tongue, the whych is true Scottyshe.'[10] Borde then proceeded to describe the 'natural dispositions' of a variety of nationalities, distinguishing not only Scots, Flemings, French and many others from the English, but also Irish, Welsh and Cornish. Consequently for Borde identity was not focused upon allegiance, but rather upon language and 'characteristics'. He was not unduly flattering in

1926); revised by W. A. Jackson, F. S. Ferguson and K. Pantzer (London: Bibliographical Society, 1976, 1986). (*STC: Short-Title Catalogue*), 9983.3.

7 *STC* 12721. The publishing history of this work is exceedingly complex. It was later continued by Hall's printer, Richard Grafton. The standard edition is by Henry Ellis, London, 1809.

8 *STC* 11088.5; 22270; 19476.5. Patten's account was edited by A. F. Pollard in *Tudor Tracts* (Westminster: Constable, 1903), pp. 53–158.

9 For example, Thomas Greepe, *The True and perfecte newes of the exploytes performed by Syr Francis Drake* (London, 1587); *Newes out of the coast of Spaine* (London, 1587); and above all Richard Hakluyt, *The Principall Navigations, Voiages, Traffiques and Discoveries of the English Nation* (London, 1589).

10 *STC* 3383, sig. Bi.

his description of any nationality, including the English, but his comment on the country itself was more enthusiastic.

> For as much as the most royall realme of Englande is cituated in an angle of the world; having no region in christendom nor out of Christendom equivalent to it. The commodities, the qualitie and the quantitie with other and many thinges considered within & aboute the sayd noble realme, whereof if I were a Iewe, a Turke or a Sarasin, or any other infidel, I yet must prayse and laud it.[11]

Shakespeare's John of Gaunt was to say much the same thing more eloquently half a century later. England, therefore, was a 'noble realm', owing allegiance to one king and one law, but occupied by several different peoples, of whom the English proper were only the most numerous. Borde's popular, but not entirely consistent, cocktail of emotions remained an important factor throughout the century, but those who sought to construct a more effective and distinctive identity inevitably looked elsewhere.

Personal loyalty to the monarch, as something which transcended 'nationality', was often evoked, as much in the 'mab darogan' (son of prophecy) literature of Wales as in the popular ballads which circulated on the streets of London. *The maner of the tryumphe at Caleys and Bulleyn* (1533) and *A newe ballade of the marigolde* (1554) provide examples of the latter,[12] both linked to popular discontent with aspects of royal policy which it was considered necessary to overcome. Henry VIII's Great Matter and Mary's marriage to Philip of Spain both pitted loyalty to the monarch against other claims on the subjects' allegiance. Those who defended the integrity of Henry's first marriage against the King's wishes were invoking not only emotions about a 'wronged woman', but urging the prior claims of canon law and the Pope over the royal will and the positive law of England. They claimed that both the Crown and the law of England were constrained by the prior claims of divine law as expressed in the jurisdiction of the church. Against them, the King's supporters argued that the divine law was enshrined in the Scriptures, not in the decrees of the church, and that the King's interpretation of Scripture was correct. The so-called *plenitudo potestatis* was a human invention, designed to further the interests of greedy clergy, and consequently the King had a perfect right, under God, to exercise control over the church within his realm. Deny that claim and the clergy became 'but half his subjects, yea and scarce his subjects', impairing the integrity of the state. A barrage of publications defended Henry's actions:

---

11 *STC* 3383, sig. Ei.
12 *STC* 4350; 11186. The first of these was royal propaganda in favour of the unpopular Boleyn marriage; the second 'by William Forrest, priest', was intended to drum up enthusiasm for Mary's marriage to Philip.

The glasse of the truth (1530), the *Determinations of the moste famous ... universities*, both in English and Latin (1530/1), and William Marshall's 'translation' of Marsilius of Padua's *Defensor Pacis* (1535).[13] The learned case for the other side was expressed by John Fisher in *De causa matrimonii serenissime Regis Angliae* (1530), prudently published in Alcala, and the popular case, a generation later, by William Forrest in his 'History of Grisild the second' (1558), which was not published until the nineteenth century.[14]

Once Henry had imposed his own solution, between 1533 and 1535, the stakes were raised still higher. It became high treason to deny that 'this realm of England is an Empire'; that the King was, and always had been, Supreme Head of the church; and that the King, with the consent of Parliament, could arrange the succession to suit himself. The relevant statutes, and the proclamations implementing them, were printed by Thomas Berthelet, the King's printer, and circulated widely.[15] Further polemical publications defended this position, notably *De vera obedientia oratio* by Stephen Gardiner (1535), *Oratio qua docet ... hortatur* by Richard Sampson (1533), *A Lamentation in which is showed what ruin and destruction cometh of seditious rebellion* by Richard Morison (1536) and *An exhortation to the people instructynge them to unitie and obedience* by Thomas Starkey (?1540).[16] The first two of these were addressed to a learned audience, both in England and beyond, and how far they contributed to a sense of identity is difficult to say. It was too dangerous to publish rebuttals of these arguments in England, so Reginald Pole's defence of the unity of the church was printed in Rome, to Henry's bitter annoyance.[17] In the same way, that powerful popular sentiment which held that the King had endangered himself and his realm by offending God, frequently articulated by preachers and ale-house gossips, did not find its way into print.[18] In fact, Henry had disrupted a great deal more than the unity of the church. As the leaders of the Pilgrimage of Grace argued

13 For a discussion of these works and their impact, see Edward Surtz, SJ, and Virginia Murphy (eds.), *The Divorce Tracts of Henry VIII* (Angers: Moreana, 1988); and Guy Bedouelle and Patrick Le Gal (eds.), *Le 'Divorce' du Roi Henry VIII: Etudes et documents*, Travaux d'Humanisme et Renaissance, 221 (Geneva: Droz, 1987). On Marshall see S. Lockwood, 'Marsilius of Padua and the Case for the Royal Ecclesiastical Supremacy', *Transactions of the Royal Historical Society*, 6th ser. 1 (1991), pp. 88–119.

14 *The History of Grisild the second: a narrative, in verse, of the divorce of Queen Katharine of Aragon*, ed. W. D. Macray, Roxburghe Club (London: Whittingham and Wilkins, 1875).

15 The printing of individual statutes and proclamations is listed in *STC*, under 'England'.

16 *STC* 11584, 21681, 15185, 23236. A modern edition of Gardiner is printed in Pierre Janelle, *Obedience in Church and State* (Cambridge University Press, 1930).

17 *Pro ecclesiasticae unitatis defensione* (1536). For an examination of the response to this attack in England, see G. R. Elton, *Policy and Police* (Cambridge University Press, 1972), pp. 202–5.

18 Eamon Duffy, *The Stripping of the Altars: Traditional Religion in England, 1400–1580* (New Haven, CT: Yale University Press, 1992), pp. 377–447, gives the best recent account of this reaction; see also Elton, *Policy and Police*.

in 1536, by following base and unworthy counsel, the King had broken his coronation oath, and with it the bond of mutual respect and obedience which bound him to his nobility. Lord Darcy declared himself to be dishonoured by an allegiance which he considered that Henry had annulled.[19]

At the end of the day, these outraged sensibilities counted for little, and the changes which the King had wrought were pragmatic rather than theoretical. By defeating or outfacing opposition, no less than by declaring his new position, Henry changed the political landscape. After 1535 both the clergy and the nobility were his subjects in a new sense. In the case of the latter, the change was subtle, but profound. The pride of ancestry, and codes of honour, which had been so powerful in the early years of the century, now counted for little. Nobles were primarily the King's servants, and their political vehicle was the House of Lords. New noble families, Boleyn, Seymour, Dudley, took the place of the Percys, the Poles and the Courtenays. Within a decade the Parliament, to which Henry had been forced to resort to give his intentions the force of law, had changed from being a well-established but essentially limited institution, into a legislative body of unknown potential and an essential instrument of government.[20] In so far as England had a coherent political philosophy in the early sixteenth century, it was still that articulated by Sir John Fortescue in *De laudibus legum Angliae*, and *The governance of England*, written in the 1470s.[21] Fortescue is remembered for describing England as 'dominium politicum et regale', which means roughly that the King's power to govern is circumscribed by the laws and customs of the land. The limitations also imposed by the church were taken for granted. That doctrine was not abrogated by the new developments, but given a new and altogether more precise meaning. Law and custom became institutionally embodied in the Parliament. In order to free himself from the constraints of ecclesiastical control, the King had been forced to accept the far more tangible limitations imposed by the assembled Lords and Commons. This transformation was not immediately clear to anyone – least of all Henry VIII. He had always regarded the Parliament as an instrument in his hand, and during his lifetime it did very little to disabuse him of that illusion.

---

19 M. E. James, *English Politics and the Concept of Honour, 1485–1640, Past and Present* Supplement, 3 (1978).

20 G. R. Elton, *The Tudor Constitution*, 2nd edn (Cambridge University Press, 1982); S. E. Lehmberg, *The Reformation Parliament, 1529–1536* (Cambridge University Press, 1970); Lehmberg, *The Later Parliaments of Henry VIII, 1536–1547* (Cambridge University Press, 1977).

21 Although these works were very influential, neither of them was published in its original form during this period. The *Governance* appeared as *De politica administratione et legibus civilibus Angliae commentarius* in 1543; *De Laudibus* was not published until 1616 (*STC* 11197). There is a modern edition of the *Governance* by C. Plummer (Oxford: Clarendon Press, 1885).

However, by the time that Sir Thomas Smith wrote *De republica Anglorum* (in English in spite of its title) (1565), perceptions had radically changed:

> The most high and absolute power of the realme of England is in the Parliament... That which is done by this consent is called firme, stable and *sanctum* and is taken for lawe. The Parliament abrogateth olde lawes, maketh newe, giveth orders for thinges past, and for thinges hereafter to be followed, changeth rights and possessions of private men, legittimateth bastards, establisheth forms of religion, altereth weights and measures, giveth formes of succession to the crowne... For everie Englishmen is entended to bee there present, either in person or by procuration and attornies, of what prehemi-nence, state, dignitie or qualitie soever he be, from the Prince (be he King or Queene) to the lowest person of Englande. And the consent of the Parliament is taken to be everie mans consent.[22]

Henry had not only conferred this kind of omnicompetence upon the Estates, he had also made its representative character more convincing by enfranchising Wales and Calais in the process of unifying (by statute) the administration of the realm.[23] Although the person of the monarch remained the emotional focus of English identity, the composite institution of monarch, Lords and Commons had become the constitutional and political focus. This essentially new development, which converted the Parliament from an instrument of occasional resort into a regular institution of government, was firmly in place by the beginning of Elizabeth's reign. Significantly, the parallel ecclesiastical institutions, the convocations of the two provinces of Canterbury and York, not only remained divided, but were completely overshadowed by Parliament, both in power and representative function. Henceforth all major questions of religion would be resolved by the secular legislature.

The increased willingness of Parliament to legislate also had the effect of reinvigorating the common law, which, as we have seen, was another focus of identity. Law textbooks of one kind and another had come from the London presses since such things first existed in the 1470s, and many of the mid sixteenth-century products were of the same nature, such as John Perkins, *A verie profitable booke... treating the lawes of this Realme* (1555), or William Stanford, *Les plees del coron* (1557).[24] However, there were also others which showed a greater

---

22 *De Republica Anglorum*, ed. Mary Dewar (Cambridge University Press, 1982), p. 78. The original work survives in three complete and numerous incomplete manuscripts. It was first published in 1583. *STC* 22857. Also see Chapter 10 below, p. 326.

23 27 Henry VIII c. 24; 34 & 35 Henry VIII c. 26; *Statutes of the Realm*, 10 vols. (London: G. Eyre and A. Strachan, 1810–28), 3:555–8, 926.

24 *STC* 19633; 23219.

sensitivity to the changing situation, most notably the works of Christopher St German: *A dyalogue in Englyshe betwyxt a doctoure of dyvynyte and a student in the lawes* (1531), *A treatise concernynge the division betwene the spiritualitie and temporalitie* (1532) and *An answere to a letter* (1535).[25] St German wrote as much in defence of the King's proceedings as in explanation of the law, but became increasingly fearful that the undermining of the canon law might leave the common law vulnerable to similar subversion. Consequently he emerged eventually as a strong advocate of the Parliament as the safeguard of the law, which was basically the position taken later (and more famously) by Sir Edward Coke.[26] Nor was Smith the only writer to be interested in the legal aspects of the royal prerogative as that emerged from the creative political and ecclesiastical changes of Henry VIII. William Stanford, a Member of Parliament and later a judge of Common Pleas, published in 1567 *An exposition of the kinges prerogative*, which, although it drew largely on Fitzherbert and earlier authors, was nevertheless a standard work of reference until beyond the turn of the century.[27] Given the nature of Tudor government, it is often hard to distinguish between legal treatises and works of political theory. However, in spite of being known as the 'King's law', because he had the responsibility for enforcing it, the common law of England continued to be regarded as the property of the community (and conseqently a defining element in determining the nature of that community), an ownership which the developments of the mid-century vested eventually in the Parliament.

Although it is seldom noticed in the same way, Mary's marriage in 1554 raised questions which were just as fundamental as those addressed at the time of her father's declaration of independence. One of the main reasons why Henry had moved heaven and earth to free himself from his first wife was that their only child was a daughter. There was no Salic law in England, and consequently a woman was entitled to inherit the crown. However, there was no historical precedent for a female ruler, and therefore complete uncertainty as to what the nature of her authority might be. The common law was reasonably generous to the 'femme seul', whether spinster or widow, recognising her right to hold and control her own property, but the 'feme covert', or married woman, was

---

25 *STC* 21561; 21586; 21558.5. St German wrote a number of other treatises, which are fully discussed in J. A. Guy, *Christopher St German on Chancery and Statute* (London: Selden Society, 1985).

26 For a full description of Coke's position, see Stephen D. White, *Sir Edward Coke and 'the grievances of the commonwealth', 1621–1628* (Chapel Hill: University of North Carolina Press, 1979).

27 *STC* 23213.

in a different position entirely.[28] Her identity was absorbed in her husband's, and he had full control over her property (except that he could not dispose of it without her consent). That a female ruler might resolve this problem by remaining unmarried was scarcely considered; after all the succession had to be provided for. It was therefore extremely likely that whoever the Princess Mary married would become King of England and, although a joint ruler in theory, would in practice exercise full control over the realm. Not only was this an unacceptable prospect to Henry, it was abhorrent to most of his subjects as well, and although both Catherine and Mary remained popular, the action which the King took to forestall it was generally approved.[29] Once Edward was born, in 1537, Henry became more relaxed about his daughters, and ended by including them in the succession should Edward have no heir of his own body.[30] The king had done his duty to God and the realm by begetting a son, and thereafter the situation was in the hand of Providence.

When Edward died unmarried in 1553, Mary therefore succeeded, her task made easier by the fact that the rival put up against her was also female. At that point nobody tried to argue that female succession was unlawful, or even undesirable. The case against her rested (paradoxically) on the fact that she was unmarried, whereas her rival, Jane Grey, was safely espoused to a younger son of England's most powerful nobleman, the Duke of Northumberland. Mary, her opponents claimed, would almost certainly marry a foreign prince and bring the realm into 'beastly servitude'.[31] At the time, such arguments carried little weight, but the new Queen had been on the throne less than six months when the prophecy began to be fulfilled. At first Mary had no problem with the 'gender trap'. Parliament sensibly and conveniently declared that her authority was identical with that of any of her progenitors 'kings of this realm'.[32] Marriage, however, raised the problem unavoidably, especially as her chosen mate was Philip, Prince of Spain, the only legitimate son of the Holy Roman Emperor. The success which the Tudors had so far enjoyed in symbolising the

28 T. E., *The Lawes Resolutions of Women's Rights or the Lawes Provision for Woemen* (London, 1632).
29 Attitudes towards Henry's 'Great Matter' have been endlessly discussed in articles and monographs. The standard treatment is still J. J. Scarisbrick, *Henry VIII* (London: Methuen, 1968; New Haven, CT: Yale University Press, 1997); the most recent discussion is in A. Chibi, *John Stokesley: Henry VIII's Conservative Bishop* (Bern: Peter Lang, 1998).
30 35 Henry VIII c. 1; *Statutes of the Realm*, 3:995.
31 Robert Wingfield of Brantham, 'Vita Mariae Reginae', ed. D. MacCulloch, *Camden Miscellany* 28 (1984), pp. 181–301. One of the principal offenders was Bishop Nicholas Ridley of London, who preached to this effect on 9 July.
32 1 Mary, session 3, c. 1; for a discussion of this act and its significance, see J. Loach, *Parliament and the Crown in the Reign of Mary Tudor* (Oxford University Press, 1986), pp. 96–7.

realm in their own persons now became a liability to Mary. She was popular, and no one seriously denied her right to choose her own husband, but the image of England as the bride of Spain, absorbed by the imperial ambitions of that country, was one which no Englishman could contemplate with equanimity. There were two possible reactions: one was to frustrate the marriage by political opposition and even rebellion; the other was to make the best of it by negotiating a favourable marriage treaty. The former was tried early in 1554, rebel propaganda claiming (plausibly but mendaciously) that the Queen should forfeit the throne because she was proposing to marry without the consent of her council, as had been stipulated in her father's will.[33] The Wyatt rebellion (as it was known) was defeated, although the arguments which had supported it did not disappear; and the alternative plan was successfully implemented.

The marriage treaty, which was proclaimed in January 1554 and confirmed by Parliament in April, in theory provided England with almost complete protection against Spanish (or Imperial) domination. Philip was given very little authority in his own right, and his interest in the realm was to cease if Mary predeceased him without heirs.[34] The Prince of Spain duly arrived in July 1554, and the marriage took place without any further disruption. The problems, however, did not go away. Philip behaved with discretion, but could scarcely conceal his disappointment with the treaty, and many commentators, both English and Spanish, believed that it would become a dead letter once the new King had established himself, particularly if the Queen had a child. Hatred between the two nations festered, erupting in periodic violence, and works began to appear in print denouncing Philip and his supposed ambitions. John Bradford's *The copye of a letter...*, clandestinely published in 1556, was partly crude sexual abuse, accusing the King of betraying his wife with numerous 'bakers daughters and such like poore whores' while he was safely out of her sight in the Netherlands.[35] More seriously, it accused her of conspiring to hand the realm over to him, in defiance of her own treaty: 'There is no law confirmed and past by whiche the Queene may lawfully disinherit the realme of the crowne'.[36] The crown, he pointed out, was not her personal property but a trust held on behalf of the realm, which must by law be passed to the rightful

33 J. Proctor, *The historie of Wyates rebellion* (London, 1554), (*STC* 20407), p. 73. Reprinted in Pollard's *Tudor Tracts*, pp. 199–258.

34 J. L. Hughes and P. F. Larkin, *Tudor Royal Proclamations* (New Haven, CT: Yale University Press, 1969), 2:21–6.

35 *STC* 3504.5. For a discussion of this work, see D. Loades, 'The Authorship and Publication of *The copye of a letter...*' in *Politics, Censorship and the English Reformation* (London: Pinter, 1991), pp. 91–6.

36 *Ibid.*, pp. 91–6.

heir – in this case Elizabeth. By 1556 there was an edge to this argument, because Mary's 'pregnancy' in the previous spring had turned out to be false, and thereafter there was little chance of a healthy child. Bradford was not the only writer to make the point; it appeared also in *A warninge for Englande* (1555) and *A supplycacyon to the Queenes Maiestie* (1555).[37] These were all popular works of anti-Spanish polemic, claiming loyalty to Mary, whom they represent as being deceived and abused by sinister foreign conspiracies. However, the most articulate and coherent presentation of this theory of responsibility did not trouble with any such disguise. The Protestant exile John Ponet, whose *Shorte Treatise of Politike Power* appeared in Strasbourg in 1556, blamed Mary directly for subverting the integrity of her own realm, and claimed that she had thereby forfeited any right to the throne: 'But thou wilt saie, it is the Queenes owne and she maie lawfully do with her own what she lusteth ... But I answere that albeit she have it by inheritaunce, yet she hath it with an oathe, lawe and condicion to kepe and mayntene it, not to departe with it nor diminishe it.'[38] In the event no crisis developed. Frustrated in his hope of an heir, and disillusioned with England, Philip busied himself with other concerns after 1555. Mary, left perforce very much to her own devices, exercised her authority without further challenge or ambiguity. Although her subjects did not like it, they did not dispute her right to involve them in Philip's war with France in 1557, and by the following year her health was visibly deteriorating. In spite of her extreme distaste for her half-sister, she eventually recognised Elizabeth's right to succeed, and a repetition of 1553 was avoided. Partly because of her childlessness, and partly because of Philip's other priorities, Mary did not force a showdown on the issue of responsibility. However, like her father's actions twenty years before, Mary's policies put the issue of lawful limitation firmly on the agenda again, thereby raising once more the whole question of where the identity of the realm should be located.

The English had always thought of themselves as a very pious nation, and the Italian observer quoted at the beginning of this chapter (no very great admirer) confirmed as much. By striking at the papacy, Henry VIII had struck the traditional church at its weakest point, its reliance on 'foreign' authority. As the Reformation issues began to clarify after 1535, and in response to the King's own idiosyncratic vision, the English church acquired a new identity. The papacy, it soon transpired, had mattered little; and the religious orders were

---

37 *STC* 10023.7; 17562.
38 *STC* 20178, sig. Eii v. Reprinted in facsimile in W. S. Hudson, *John Ponet: Advocate of Limited Monarchy* (University of Chicago Press, 1940).

equally dispensable; but traditional rites, and particularly the mass, mattered a great deal.[39] The new Protestant ideas (although in some respects they resembled indigenous Lollardy) were 'foreign' – mainly German or Swiss. The papacy was also foreign; but Henry's church, with its traditional rites, English Bible and national Headship – that belonged to the realm. There was little ecclesiastical coherence about this, and both Protestants and Catholics rejected it, but 'religion as King Henry left it' acquired a firm grasp on the popular imagination. When Edward VI and his advisers converted the national church to a form of Swiss Protestantism between 1547 and 1553, the changes were deeply resented, but they were accepted because the King's authority was accepted. In the last analysis the spiritual state of the realm was the King's responsibility. Englishmen had accepted that lesson from Henry VIII, and therefore their obedience to his son absolved them from responsibility. If the King had got it wrong with God, that was his fault, not theirs. In accepting Protestant forms, Englishmen saw no reason to accept Protestant visions of godliness as well, and at the height of their power, the evangelical preachers despaired.[40] Consequently, although the Protestant establishment was properly owned by the realm, and to that extent a part of its identity, it attracted little emotional allegiance outside its main strongholds in the southeast of England.

Unfortunately, Mary in this respect completely failed to understand her own subjects. Living in a simplified world of error and truth, she did not realise the qualifications with which most people surrounded their allegiance to the old ways. Had she been content (as most people expected) to restore her father's settlement, religion would hardly have been an issue, except to that small minority which had genuinely embraced Protestantism during the previous reign. By deciding to restore the papal jurisdiction, however, she fatally muddied the waters. Ironically, her own personal religion was extremely insular, owing much to the Erasmianism of the 1520s and virtually nothing to the spirituality of the Counter-Reformation.[41] However, once Parliament had dutifully repealed the Acts of Supremacy and a papal legate started sending heretics to the fire, the old demons of 'foreign power' were quickly resurrected. The fact that Philip played a significant part in bringing this about was (as both Reginald Pole and Stephen Gardiner realised at the time) singularly unfortunate. The King and the Pope became united in a foreign conspiracy to subvert the liberties

39 Duffy, *Stripping of the Altars*, pp. 424–77; C. Haigh, *English Reformations: Religion, Politics, and Society under the Tudors* (Oxford University Press, 1993).

40 For a full discussion of these evangelical frustrations, see D. MacCulloch, *Thomas Cranmer* (New Haven, CT: Yale University Press, 1996), pp. 454–513.

41 D. Loades, *Mary Tudor: A Life* (Oxford: Basil Blackwell, 1989), pp. 118–19.

of England. The fact that Philip and Paul IV were soon at war, and that Parliament had sanctioned the new situation, made little difference to popular attitudes. Although pro-government writers such as John Proctor, John Christopherson and Miles Hogarde made much of 'the Queens Godly proceedings', and hardly mentioned the pope, they did not succeed in recovering the initiative.[42] Thanks partly to the effectiveness of Protestant propaganda, and partly to a persecution of unprecedented severity, which inflicted nearly 300 deaths in three and a half years, the conservative majority in the English church was weakened and confused by 1558. Was the old faith English, or was it Spanish and Italian?

National 'ownership' of the church could only be secured by the royal supremacy, and when explicitly Protestant polemicists like Christopher Goodman in *How superior powers oght to be obeyd* (1558) argued that only the Reformed faith could guarantee legitimate royal government, they found an attentive audience.[43] By returning to her brother's settlement early in 1559, Elizabeth forced this issue. As long as she survived, she would control a Protestant church which, like herself, was 'mere English'.[44] It would be an exaggeration to claim that England's national identity had become bound up with the Reformed faith by 1565, but by that date the country had a distinctive church, with a vernacular liturgy and Scriptures, and a cross-bred theology which came out of no one stable. At the same time 'religion as King Henry left it' had ceased to be a viable option, having been eroded from both sides, whilst Catholicism proper was becoming increasingly 'un-English'. As this delicate work of definition was going on, and the country braced itself for what the next royal marriage would bring, John Knox lobbed in his firecracker *The First Blast of the trumpet against the monstruous regiment of women* (1558) declaring that all female rule was contrary to the law of God.[45] His timing could hardly have been worse. Aimed at Mary Tudor, Mary of Guise and Catherine de Medicis, it seemed to threaten Elizabeth from within the very confession which she had

---

42 Proctor, *The historie of Wyates rebellion*, already cited in n. 33; Christopherson, *An exhortation to all menne to take hede and beware of rebellion* (STC 5207); Hogarde, *The displaying of the protestantes* (STC 13557), *A treatise declaring how Christ by perverse preachyng was banished out of this realme* (STC 13560.5).

43 STC 12020. D. Loades, *The Reign of Mary Tudor* (London: Longmans, 1991), p. 376. J. E. A. Dawson, 'The Early Career of Christopher Goodman and his Place in the Development of English Protestant Thought' (University of Durham Ph. D. thesis, 1978). A modern facsimile of Goodman's treatise was printed in New York in 1931.

44 Wallace MacCaffrey, *Elizabeth I* (London: Arnold, 1993), pp. 48–60. Haigh, *English Reformations*.

45 STC 15070. Reprinted in *The Works of John Knox*, ed. D. Laing, 6 vols. (Edinburgh: Bannatyne Society, 1846–64), 3:349–422.

embraced. Had Knox been taken seriously, English Protestants could quickly have found themselves trapped between the law of the land and the law of God. That did not happen, partly because English opinion was never logical and partly because John Aylmer's *An Harborowe for faithfull and trewe subjectes* (1559), written as a direct refutation of Knox, quickly offered an acceptable escape by declaring that God, being omnipotent, could work through righteous women as well as men.[46] Soon after, the immensely influential *Actes and monuments of these latter and perilous dayes* (1563) by John Foxe clinched the matter by hailing Elizabeth as the New Constantine.[47] Whatever gender problems the Queen might have thereafter, the law of God did not enter into them.

The partnership between the realm and the monarch was a little like that between a horse and rider. No Tudor could (or would) have said with Louis XIV, 'L'état, c'est moi.' Because of the limitations, both tangible and intangible, which restricted the authority of the English Crown, obedience was the central theme of royal propaganda. This was particularly the case when controversial or unpopular policies were embraced, or when a foreign war was looming. In this respect the royal supremacy was an asset, helping to mobilise religious duty in the service of the Crown, so that obedience became an issue of conscience, unchallenged by rival claims to spiritual allegiance.

There were many tracts urging this duty, but typical examples were Richard Morison's *Remedy for sedition* (1536), John Cheke's *Hurte of sedition* (1549), and John Christopherson's *Exhortation to all menne to take hede and beware of rebellion* (1554).[48] There was also an 'Exhortation concerning good order and obedience' among the *Homilies appoynted by the kynges maiestie to be read in churches* (1547).[49] Support for the King's wars was also occasionally invited, providing further occasions to instil a sense of duty. In 1539, when widespread religious disaffection may have been feared, Morison also wrote an *Exhortation to styrre all Englyshe men to the defence of theyr contreye*, and in 1545, when England had been abandoned by her allies, Edward Walshe published *The office and duety in fightyng for our countrey*.[50] The frequency with which the Tudors felt it necessary to persuade their subjects of the rightness of the courses which they

---

46 *STC* 1005. Reprinted in J. Ayre, *The Works of John Aylmer*, 4 vols. (Parker Society, 1845–50).
47 *STC* 11222. For discussions of this work and its impact on the early Elizabethan church, see: J. F. Mozley, *John Foxe and his Book* (1940; rpt, New York: Octagon, 1970); V. Norskov Olsen, *John Foxe and the Elizabethan Church* (Berkeley: University of California Press, 1973); D. Loades (ed.), *John Foxe and the English Reformation* (Aldershot: Scolar Press, 1997). Also see Chapter 10 below, p. 330.
48 *STC* 18113.5; 5109; 5207.
49 *STC* 13638.5. Reprinted in *The Two Books of Homilies Appointed to be Read in Churches*, ed. J. Griffiths (Oxford, 1859).
50 *STC* 18110.

were taking is significant. When the Duke of Somerset decided to resurrect the Treaty of Greenwich (1543) for a marriage between Mary of Scotland and Edward VI, he issued what was ostensibly an open letter to the Scots, arguing the advantages of such a course. Whether the *Epistle or exhortation... to unitie* (1547) had any influence north of the border may be doubted, but it was widely read in England, and probably influential.[51] Despite the institutional strength of the English Crown, the monarch had to lead his country; he could not drive it, and that reflected the way in which Englishmen perceived their communities. There was at this time no overt talk of Magna Carta, or of the 'liberties of freeborn Englishmen', but Andrew Borde makes his Englishman say of himself:

> I do feare no manne, all menne feareth me
> I overcome my adversaries by land and by see
> I had no peere yf to my selfe I were trew
> Because I am not so, divers times I do rew.[52]

Such sentiments interestingly foreshadow the patriotic rhetoric of the next generation:

> Come the three corners of the world in arms,
> And we shall shock them
> Naught shall make us rue
> If England to herself do rest but true.[53]

The unanswered question, at least in 1542, was exactly where that elusive English integrity rested. England claimed, or at least the Parliament claimed on her behalf, that she was an Empire: 'and so hath been accepted in the world, governed by one supreme head and king having the dignity and royal estate of the Imperial crown of the same, unto whom a body politic... be bounden and owe to bear next to God a natural and humble obedience'.[54]

Scotland

Scotland, by contrast, had no such pretension. Through most of the sixteenth century it defended itself against Tudor claims to feudal overlordship by entering into a dependent relationship with France. The most that it could hope to do was to preserve a precarious independence. A sense of national identity had

---

51 STC 22268. For an assessment of this work and its possible influence, see M. L. Bush, *The Government Policy of Protector Somerset* (London: Edward Arnold, 1975), esp. pp. 10–11.
52 *The fyrst boke*, sig. Ai.
53 William Shakespeare, *King John*, 5.7.116–19 (the last lines of the play).
54 Preamble to the Act in Restraint of Appeals (24 Henry VIII c. 12). *Statutes of the Realm*, 3:427–9.

certainly existed since the fourteenth century, fuelled, as early English sentiment had also been, by the desire to differentiate from a threatening enemy.
Just as the Englishman first knew that he was not French, so the Scotsman first
knew that he was not English. By 1500 the Scots were recognised abroad by
the scholars and soldiers who sought opportunities for employment outside
their own confined country. Pedro de Ayala in 1498 saw them as a handsome
people, vain, ostentatious and courageous;[55] but how they saw themselves is
less clear.

Scotland was far less unified than England, and its government lacked bureaucratic strength. Whereas in England the Welsh and the Cornish were small
minorities, in Scotland the Gaelic-speaking clans constituted half the population, and occupied more than half the land. They were, more or less, subjected
to the Scottish Crown, but shared no identity with the lowlanders, who spoke
an English dialect and regarded themselves primarily as the King's subjects.
Superficially the polity of lowland Scotland resembled that of England; there
was a Parliament, royal courts and a code of law. There were towns, universities
and a flourishing overseas trade. On the other hand the Crown was both poorer
and weaker in relation to its subjects than was the case in the southern kingdom. Scottish domestic politics were turbulent, not just occasionally but all
the time, and the theoretical allegiance which the nobles owed to the King did
not prevent them from running their patrimonies as best pleased themselves.
Hardly any of the characteristics required for the development of an articulate
sense of national identity were present.[56]

There was a modest chronicle literature, including such works as John
Major's *De gestis Scotorum* (1521) and Hector Boece's *Historia gentis Scotorum*
(1527), the latter 'translated into Scotch' by John Bellenden in 1540. However,
the former of these was published in Paris, as was *The complaint of Scotland* (1549),
which was a distinctly negative assessment of the country's unity and strength.
Edinburgh printing remained on a very small scale until later in the century.[57]
There was also a flourishing tradition of courtly poetry, but none of this
provided a focus for patriotism. James V deliberately rejected all suggestions

55 Cited by Mark Nicholls in *A History of the Modern British Isles*, 1529–1603 (Oxford: Blackwell,
    1999), p. 77.
56 H. L. MacQueen, ' "Regiam Maiestatem", Scots Law and National Identity', *Scottish
    Historical Review* 74 (1995); J. Wormald, *Court, Kirk and Community, 1470–1625* (London:
    Edward Arnold, 1981); Wormald, 'Bloodfeud, Kindred and Government in Early Modern
    Scotland', *Past and Present* 87 (1980), 54–97.
57 *STC* 3203; 22009. Bellenden was printed in Edinburgh; Major's book, being in Latin and
    printed in Paris, does not appear in *STC*. A new edition of Bellenden's translation in 2 vols.
    was published in the Scottish Text Society: *The Chronicles of Scotland*, 3rd ser., vols. 10 and
    15 (1938, 1941).

that he should follow Henry's lead against the papacy, and although this earned him a papal sword and cap of maintenance, it also meant that the Scottish church was in no sense owned by the nation, and could not contribute to any image of identity in the way that the English royal supremacy did. Moreover, just at the point where the Crown might have moved ahead as a focal point for unity, James V died and was succeeded by his infant daughter. It was to be over forty years before Scotland again had an adult King who could to some extent impose himself upon the situation. A prolonged and eventually successful war with England from 1542 to 1550 gave the Scots military confidence and self-respect, but did little to create internal coherence. Throughout most of this period there was a pro-English party of varying strength in Scotland, and although their enemies were not necessarily pro-French, they inevitably appeared so, and abetted French control. In 1548 the infant Queen Mary was betrothed to the Dauphin, and shipped off to France.[58] From the factional quarrels which followed, her mother, Mary of Guise, emerged as Regent in 1555, and when Henry II of France was unexpectedly killed in the summer of 1559, the younger Mary became Queen of France by marriage, as well as Queen of Scotland by inheritance.

None of this did anything for Scotland's sense of identity, but a solution was already approaching. James V had remained loyal to the old faith because, as far as he could see, he had nothing to gain by defecting from it. However, by 1550, thanks partly to the activity of Cardinal David Beaton, traditional religion was closely linked to the French ascendancy. For this reason England (which was officially Protestant from 1549 to 1553) encouraged the Scottish reformers to challenge that ascendancy, and the pro-English party became strongly tinged with Protestantism.[59] Once the English war was over, and England had reverted to Catholicism, the Scottish reformers were left to their own devices, and this turned out to be greatly to their advantage. By 1555 they were able to ride with the anti-French factions, unencumbered by any association with the 'auld enemy'. By 1559 the so-called 'Lords of the Congregation of Jesus Christ' were in open rebellion against the French-controlled Regency. Whether they would have succeeded without assistance is an open question, but at that point the English government again became Protestant, and had the same interest as its predecessors in getting the French out of Scotland. Elizabeth's intervention was hesitant, and not directly very effective, but combined with the death

---

58 Bush, *Government Policy*, p. 27; and citing BL, MS Harley 523, f. 28b.
59 James Kirk, 'The Religion of Early Scottish Protestants', in *Humanism and Reform: the Church in Europe, England and Scotland, Essays in Honour of James K. Cameron*, ed. Kirk (Oxford: Blackwell, 1991).

218   DAVID LOADES

of Mary of Guise and the onset of religious war in France, it was sufficient
to give the Lords of the Congregation victory. The Treaty of Edinburgh in
1560 ushered in a new era in Anglo-Scottish relations.[60] Elizabeth had no
interest in reviving the old claims to suzerainty, and no desire to impose a
religious settlement upon the Scots. On the other hand, she had every interest in
maintaining the Protestant ascendancy which, if threatened, would inevitably
look to her for assistance. The advance of the Reformation was patchy, and
extremely slow beyond the highland line, but by 1570 Scotland was well on
the way to having a national faith.[61]

This came about partly because of Elizabeth's abstemious resolution not to
meddle, and partly because of the religious affiliations of such Scottish divines as
John Knox and John Wullocke. Although both had spent time in England during Edward's reign, neither was enthusiastic either about the royal supremacy
or about the episcopal system of government which was retained in the English
church. When Mary came to the throne, the situation in their own country was
unpropitious, so both withdrew to the continent, Wullocke to Emden and
Knox first to Frankfurt and then to Geneva.[62] By the time that the victory
of the Lords of the Congregation drew them back to Scotland in 1559, both
were committed to a full Calvinist discipline and doctrine, and Knox quickly
established himself as the leader of the emerging reformed kirk. There had already been a few works of Protestant devotion published in Scotland, such as
Patrick Cockburn's *In dominicam orationem pia meditatio* (1555), or abroad in
Scots, such as *The richt way to the Kingdome of hevine* (1533), which had appeared
in Malmö.[63] However, the first defining work was *The confessioun of faith profesit
and belevit be the protestantes within the realme of Scotland* (1561), which set out the
agenda for a distinctive Reformed church.[64] The return of the widowed Queen
Mary in 1561 disturbed but did not overturn the control which Knox and his
friends had by then established, and although Scotland's secular politics continued to be turbulent for another twenty years, the kirk steadily advanced,
penetrating the countryside from the towns and gradually commanding the
allegiance of the whole country below the highland line.

60 Wallace MacCaffrey, *The Shaping of the Elizabethan Regime: Elizabethan Politics, 1558–1572*
   (Princeton University Press, 1969); Wormald, *Court, Kirk and Community*.
61 For an examination of this advance, see Michael F. Graham, *The Uses of Reform: 'Godly Discipline' and Popular Behaviour in Scotland and Beyond, 1560–1610* (Leyden: E. J. Brill, 1996).
62 C. H. Garrett, *The Marian Exiles* (Cambridge University Press, 1938).
63 *STC* 5458; *The richt way*, by John Gau (a translation from Danish), was edited by A. F. Mitchell
   (Edinburgh: Scottish Text Society, 1888).
64 *STC* 22016. Incorporated into Knox's *History*, this appears in Laing's edition of *The Works
   of John Knox*; there is also a more recent edition by G. D. Henderson (Edinburgh, 1937).

The kirk thus provided in Scotland what the secular state had failed to provide, a focus of identity which was meaningful, and distinctively Scottish. There was, and had been for some time, an emotional xenophobia which shifted uneasily between the English and the French, but it had had little positive content. Andrew Borde had been in no doubt about what distinguished a Scot in his eyes:

> I am a Scotyshe man, and trew I am to France,
> In every country I do myself avaunce
>
> ...
>
> An Englyshe man I cannot naturally love
> Wherefore I offend them and my lorde above.[65]

However, that was in 1542, and he was biased. Unlike the situation in England, loyalty to the King was not different in nature from loyalty to any other lord, and the weakness of the Crown throughout the mid-century effectively removed it as a contender. Beyond the highland line the Reformation advanced only very slowly, and the clansman's sense of identity remained focused upon his chieftain and his sept until the eighteenth century. A fierce attachment to the clan territory was the nearest equivalent to nationalism that the Highlands produced until very much later. Ironically, most of the symbols of modern Scottishness – the tartan, the bagpipes, the highland dancing – are nineteenth-century adaptations of Gaelic practices. The initial test of that Scottish identity created by the kirk came when first James VI and then Charles I tried to anglicise its worship and government between 1610 and 1640. The result was first the National Covenant, and then civil war.[66]

Wales and Ireland

Wales and Ireland differed fundamentally from Scotland in that neither was an independent state, and therefore did not even have the opportunity to focus a sense of identity upon its machinery. Wales had been a single political entity ('state' would be an anachronism) for just a few years in the thirteenth century. Before that it had been a collection of separate, and often warring, principalities; and soon after it became a dependency of the English Crown. Like the Scot, the Welshman identified himself as being not English, and if anyone doubts the strength of that emotion it was powerfully expressed in Owain Glyndwr's

---

65 *The fyrst boke*, sig. Di.
66 Peter Donald, *An Uncounselled King: Charles I and the Scottish Troubles, 1637–1641* (Cambridge University Press, 1990).

propaganda from the early fifteenth century.[67] After Glyndwr's revolt, for over a hundred years, the Welsh were a subjugated people: second-class citizens in their own land. In the early sixteenth century controls relaxed and resentment waned. The Tudors acknowledged a partially Welsh origin, and both Henry VII and Henry VIII extended their favour to a number of Welsh gentry. The real changes, however, came in 1536 and 1543, when two statutes reorganised the government of Wales, converting it to shire ground on the English model, with parliamentary representation and (most important of all) commissions of the peace staffed by local gentry.[68] The creation of this degree of local autonomy, and the opportunities of service under the English Crown, largely reconciled the natural leaders of Wales to the political status quo, and, as the Reformation developed, the pre-Augustinian origin of the Welsh church commended itself to those who were seeking to prove the ancient independence of the realm from Rome.[69] By the end of the sixteenth century antiquarian curiosity was beginning to add some elements of Welshness to the English national identity, but it would be difficult to argue that for the period with which we are concerned.

In the mid sixteenth century Welsh identity had no political or ecclesiastical focus, and the negative focus of hostility to England was waning. What Wales did have was a distinctive social structure, a number of codes of customary law, and above all a language. Bardic 'praise poetry' was an ancient literary genre. Bards were traditional poets and singers, sometimes itinerant, sometimes attached to an aristocratic household, who sang the praises of their hosts and patrons, and recited the deeds of their ancestors. They saw themselves, and were seen by others, as the guardians of the soul of Wales, who had kept its customs and culture alive when there were few other methods of doing so.[70] It was the bards who had hailed Henry VII as the 'son of prophecy'.[71] The prophecy in question was one attributed to Merlin, in which he had allegedly foretold that one day the true British royal line would be restored, and the *cymru* (Welsh) would recover control of *loegre* (Britain). Henry had no intention of honouring that expectation, but it was useful to him and the bards never entirely lost faith in the Tudors. At the same time the attitude of the English

67 R. R. Davies, *The Revolt of Owain Glyn Dwr* (Oxford University Press, 1995), pp. 153–73.
68 27 Henry VIII c. 24; 34 & 35 Henry VIII c. 26.
69 Mackisack, *Medieval History*, pp. 26–49; Glanmor Williams, 'Bishop Sulien, Bishop Richard Davies and Archbishop Parker', *Journal of the National Library of Wales* 5 (1948).
70 Thomas Parry, *Hanes llenddiaeth Gymraeg hyd 1900* (Cardiff, 1944); W. G. Jones, 'Welsh Nationalism and Henry Tudor', *Transactions of the Cymmrodorion Society* (1917–18), 1–59.
71 David Rees, *The Son of Prophecy: Henry Tudor's Road to Bosworth* (London: Black Raven Press, 1985; 2nd edn. Ruthin: John Jones, 1997); R. A. Griffiths and R. S. Thomas (eds.), *The Making of the Tudor Dynasty* (Gloucester: Alan Sutton, 1985).

government to the Welsh language was ambivalent. The Acts of Union forbade
its use in the courts of law or in government, and required all Welsh Justices of
the Peace to be fluent in English; but the Book of Common Prayer was translated into Welsh in 1549, the New Testament in 1567, and the whole Bible
in 1588 as a means of promoting a 'Godly reformation'.[72] Consequently the
church in Wales never used (nor was required to use) a liturgy or Scriptures in
English. It went straight from Latin to Welsh. On balance, Welsh was probably
strengthened rather than weakened as a literary language by the intervention of
government. The bards, however, suffered, particularly as a result of the Acts
of Union, which involved so many of the more important figures in Welsh
society in the business of administration. Most Welsh gentlemen considered
that learning English was a small price to pay for a recognised (and rewarded)
place in the service of the Crown, and the anglicisation of the Welsh gentry
was already well under way by 1560. The bards became first old-fashioned, and
then irrelevant, as the church took over the role of cultural guardian.

Welsh laws and customs were also heavily eroded as a result of the Acts.
English common law had been in use in the principality for some time, mainly
for criminal pleas, and landholders preferred it for inheritance purposes because it helped to keep estates together. However, in the marcher lordships
the old customs of partible inheritance, and even financial compensation for
criminal offences, were still in use. These customs contributed significantly to
the poor opinion which the English had of the Welsh, because it was believed
that the failure to distinguish between legitimate and illegitimate children for
inheritance purposes meant that marriage was not taken seriously; and the use
of the compensation system meant that bloodshed was not taken seriously either. When the lordships were abolished, the use of Welsh law was abolished
with them, or, more accurately, relegated to minor and private jurisdictions.[73]
There were those who thought that with these ancient customs another part of
the soul of Wales had departed. But on the whole the practical benefits of the
new system, and eventually a significant reduction in lawlessness, convinced
most that the price was well worth paying. In the mid-century period there
is little evidence of a coherent self-consciousness in Wales. The best account
probably comes again from the English-biased Andrew Borde. Although he has
his Welshman declare

72 Although Sir John Price appears to have made his first translation of the Prayer Book as soon
as it was published in English, it did not become generally available until 1567 (*STC* 16435),
the same year in which the New Testament was issued (*STC* 2960). William Salesbury's
Welsh Bible took another twenty years (*STC* 2347).
73 See, for example, J. G. Jones, 'Lewis Owen, Sheriff of Merioneth and the "Gwylliaid cochion"
of Mawddwy in 1554–5', *Merioneth Historical and Record Society Journal* 12 (1996), 221–40.

> I am a Welsheman and do dwell in Wales
> ...
> I love not to labour, nor to delve nor to dyg
> My fyngers be lymed lyke a lyme twygg,

he also adds 'The Welshe men be hardy men, strong men and goodlie men ... they do set much by their kindred and prophecies'.[74] Wales itself, he concludes, is clearly divided into north and south, and south Wales 'is better in many things'. There was also, he noted, 'much povertie'. The bards had their own more positive vision of the *cymru*, but, as Borde realised, it was focused on kindred and prophecy, rather than more tangible qualities. It was not until the works of Thomas Churchyard and Humphrey Llwyd were published in the 1580s that an identity based upon the history and topography of the whole land began to emerge.[75] Welsh identity was also hindered until much later by the absence of any university or printing press in Wales; there was Welsh-language printing, but it was undertaken in London or in Oxford.

Ethnically, Ireland was very similar to Wales, but its whole political history had been very different, and there is little comparison between the two lands in the early Tudor period. Where the whole of Wales was under effective English control, and concessions to the desire for local autonomy were constructive, Ireland was divided into three distinct zones. The Pale, east and south of Dublin, had been an English enclave for centuries. The language and the law were English, and allegiance to the Crown was unquestioned. Beyond that, mainly to the south and southwest, were the so-called 'obedient lands'. These included English towns, such as Wexford, Galway and Cork, but were mostly Anglo-Irish lordships, controlled by families such as the Ormondes, the Fitzgeralds and the Butlers. These were families of Anglo-Norman origin, who held titles derived from the English Crown, but who had long since intermarried with the Irish chieftains, and who used local customs and the Gaelic language indifferently with English and the common law. Their estates were effectively franchises, which owed allegiance to the Crown (hence their name), but effectively controlled their own affairs. Beyond these again, to the north and west, were the 'wild Irish' tribes. Although theoretically occupying part of the Lordship of Ireland, they had never been under English control, and had been little influenced by English customs, law or language.[76]

74 *The fyrst boke*, sig. Biii. E. V. Evans, 'Andrew Borde and the Welsh People', *Y Commrodor* (1919), 44–55.
75 Thomas Churchyard, *The worthines of Wales* (1587) (*STC* 5261); Humphrey Llwyd, *The Breviary of Britayne* (1573) (*STC* 16636). Churchyard was reproduced in facsimile by the Spenser Society in 1876.
76 S. G. Ellis, *Tudor Ireland: Crown, Community and the Conflict of Cultures* (London: Longman, 1985), pp. 33–53.

At the beginning of the Tudor period, even the Pale was mainly run by local Anglo-Irish families, and Henry VII had been content, after his victory over Lambert Simnel (who had much support in Ireland) in 1487, to reimpose the loose obligations of overlordship on the great nobles, and effectively to leave them to run the country in their own way.[77] His son was not satisfied with this degree of devolution, and both Wolsey and Cromwell sought to bring English Ireland under more effective control. There was good reason for this as the powerful Earls of Kildare governed in their own interest, using the office of Lord Deputy to suppress their rivals at least as much as to serve their overlord. Henry became increasingly suspicious, and the ninth Earl survived a number of crises in his relations with the Crown during the 1520s.[78] Irish identity was not a factor in this increasing tension, which developed almost entirely within the Anglo-Irish community. Irish-language chronicles, such as the 'Annala Uladh' (Annals of Ulster), written in this period, were not printed until much later, and are specifically local in their focus. If the Fitzgeralds had sought to identify themselves in the later fashion, they would probably have called themselves 'old English', and would have claimed a natural right to rule in the King's name. The politics of the following decade were extremely complex, but the basic fact is that Thomas Cromwell sought to diminish Kildare's power, and to introduce 'new English' officers who would be more directly answerable to Westminster. The 'old English' thus felt themselves under threat, and made common cause with the conservative opposition in England to the King's 'Great Matter'. The result was a rebellion in 1534–5, led by Lord Ossory, the Earl of Kildare's son, known as 'Silken Thomas'.[79]

At the time it was thought that the main danger of this revolt lay in the possibility that it would attract aid from the Emperor, who was thoroughly alienated by Henry's treatment of his aunt Catherine. However, that did not happen, and with hindsight it appears that Ossory's decision to take refuge among the Irish tribes when his rebellion began to falter was its most lasting consequence. For several months a leading Anglo-Irish nobleman raided the Pale in alliance with the 'wild Irish', and began to identify with the anti-English sentiments of the tribes.[80] In the short term Ossory's defiance led him and a number of his kindred to the scaffold, but the problems created by the destruction of the Kildare ascendancy were eventually to prove intractable. For thirty years after the suppression of 'Silken Thomas's' rebellion successive English

77 *Ibid.*, pp. 85–107.   78 *Ibid.*, pp. 113–120.
79 B. Bradshaw, *The Irish Constitutional Revolution of the Sixteenth Century* (Cambridge University Press, 1979), pp. 163–6; Bradshaw, 'Cromwellian Reform and the Origins of the Kildare Rebellion, 1533–4', *Transactions of the Royal Historical Society* 5th ser. 27 (1977), 69–93.
80 Ellis, *Tudor Ireland*, pp. 125–7.

governments strove to establish a secure basis for direct control. However, the main result was that by the beginning of Elizabeth's reign there were three ethnic groupings in Ireland: the 'new English' – planters, soldiers and settlers, who were Protestant in religion and regarded the Irish with undisguised contempt; 'old English', who were conservative in religion and deeply resentful at losing their traditional role; and native Irish, who were traditional in religion, Gaelic in speech and fiercely independent in temperament.

There are comparatively few writings from the period which reflect this situation, and fewer still which were published. *The copye of the submissyon of Oneyll* (1542) was government propaganda, and John Bale's *Vocacyon . . . to the Bishoprick of Ossorie in Irelande* (1553) a piece of anti-Irish bile from a disappointed Reformer. Rowland White, an old English Protestant, wrote 'A Discors touching Ireland' in about 1569, and 'The dysorders of the Irisshery' two years later. Both were examples of the reform proposals which proliferated from English and Anglo-Irish pens in the mid century. Neither was published, and both reflect an English rather than an Anglo-Irish attitude towards the 'wild Irish'.[81]

There was no such thing as an Irish identity, because the Irish did not even begin to think of themselves as one nation until the Tyrone revolt at the end of the century. There was a flourishing Gaelic culture, which resembled the Welsh in that it was focused on language, prophecy and kindred, but it was only under pressure from the English plantations after 1570 that it began to perceive itself as Celtic and Catholic.[82] The Irish, like the Scots and the Welsh, defined themselves as being not English, and the old English, caught between undesirable alternatives, began to move in the direction of an Irish identity – which is why the example of 'Silken Thomas' was so important. The erection of the Lordship of Ireland into a kingdom in 1541 – a move designed to increase Henry's authority – did nothing for Irish identity. The Protestant Reformation, which quickly became associated with the 'new English' ascendancy, was divisive but scarcely touched the native Irish. There was no Gaelic liturgy or New Testament until the following century, when it was already too late to prevent the old faith from being a hallmark of Irishness. There were Irish chronicles in both Gaelic and Latin, but none of them were published during this period, and most of the numerous English accounts on the general theme of 'what is wrong

---

81 STC 11813 (published by John Gough); STC 1307; on White, see N. Canny, 'Rowland White's "Discors touching Ireland", c. 1569', *Irish Historical Studies* 20 (1976–7), 439–63, and 'Rowland White's "The dysorders of the Irisshrey", 1571', *Studia Hibernica* 19 (1979), 147–60.

82 Ciaran Brady, 'England's Defence and Ireland's Reform: the Dilemma of the Irish Viceroys, 1541–1641', in *The British Problem, c. 1534–1707*, ed. Bradshaw and Morrill (Basingstoke: Macmillan, 1996), pp. 89–117.

with Ireland' were not written until after 1570.[83] Even the ubiquitous Andrew Borde had little to say about Ireland. The people of the Pale were civil, if somewhat tetchy, and the wild Irish were simply idle, caring nothing for wealth and not bothering to till the soil. The fierce and explicitly anti-English nationalism which began to characterise the native Irish from the mid seventeenth century did not exist in this period.

Regional and civic loyalties

There were some local identities within England which also deserve a passing mention. Andrew Borde noticed the separateness of the Cornish, commenting 'In Cornwall is two speeches... the one is naughty englyshe and the other is Cornyshe... there be many men and women whiche cannot speake one word of English', a point also made in 1549 by objectors to the English Prayer Book.[84] The Cornish certainly resented outside interference, but they had to put up with it, and their separateness had no focus apart from the language. The last time that they drew violent attention to that sense of identity was in 1497, their participation in the revolt of 1549 not differing much from that of their Devon neighbours. The 'northern men' similarly resented interference from the south, and drew attention to that grievance in 1536 and 1569, but they had no distinctive language, and there is no literary expression for any positive sense of identity.[85] Such an identity did exist among the kindreds of the Anglo-Scottish border, where the primitive loyalties of the reivers, or cattle thieves, were expressed in the fifteenth-century border ballads. This distinctive society, which was neither English nor Scots, survived until almost the end of the sixteenth century, increasingly under seige as central authority was strengthened both in London and in Edinburgh. As with the highlanders, the central focus of identity was the 'surname'; but unlike the highlanders the borderers were distinguished from their more civilised neighbours by neither speech nor religion, and their predatory lifestyle was more easily contained when the previously endemic Anglo-Scottish hostility petered out after 1560.

At what was virtually the opposite end of the social spectrum, many towns also had a sense of identity, fostering the civic pride which led to so many

---

83 E.g. Edmund Spenser, *A view of the state of Ireland... in 1596*, first printed by James Ware in *Two histories of Ireland* (London, 1633).

84 *The fyrst boke*, sig. Bii. N. Pocock (ed.), *The Troubles Connected with the Prayer Book of 1549*, Camden Society, new ser. 37 (London: Camden Society, 1884).

85 M. L. Bush, 'The Problem of the Far North: a Study in the Crisis of 1537 and its Consequences', *Northern History* 6 (1971), 40–63; Bush, *The Pilgrimage of Grace* (Manchester University Press, 1996).

new incorporations in the mid-Tudor period, and to an outburst of Town Hall building.[86] Naturally London is the most conspicuous example. By the fifteenth century London was virtually a self-contained commonwealth, with which Kings had to bargain on equal terms. In theory it enjoyed nothing like the autonomy of the Imperial Free Cities, or the great commercial centres of the Low Countries, but in practice its wealth and population (about 150,000 by 1550) made it a place apart. A number of town chronicles expressed that sense of distinctness, not to say self-importance, and with the advent of the Reformation, London became the earliest, and by far the most powerful, centre of the new faith.[87] London drew in population from all over the country, and indeed from all over Europe, so its identity was never ethnic or linguistic, but was based rather on residence and function. It could be argued that London saw itself as 'essential England'. As the community which best represented or symbolised the realm as a whole, it did not see itself as distinctive, but the 'London pride' of later centuries can be clearly seen in the dealings of the city with the early Tudors. Although London produced the first chronicles, it was not alone. Another precocious example was Richard Ricart's *Maire of Bristowe is Kalendar* (1484), and a number of other towns followed.[88] Urban identity never challenged national, any more than did the sense of 'belonging' to a major noble affinity. The days when a gentleman might see the Earl of Derby or the Duke of Buckingham as a more meaningful lord than the King were past by 1535, and even the most enthusiastic Londoner did not believe that the Guildhall was more powerful than the court. Such identities were essentially secondary, and were seen in that way at the time. The most meaningful body to which all the King's subjects belonged was the realm of England, and when that also became co-extensive with the Church of England, its significance was greatly increased.

In spite of the comparatively developed nature of the English state, and the defining fires through which it passed in the early sixteenth century, literary expressions of identity are few and indirect. Royal propaganda was naturally strong on allegiance, and upon the unity of realm and monarch; opposition propaganda, whether radical or conservative, emphasised limitation and sought to detach the nation, if not from the Crown at least from a particular monarch. The great histories of Holinshed, Stow and Camden were foreshadowed by

---

86 Robert Tittler, *Architecture and Power: The Town Hall and the English Urban Community, 1500–1640* (Oxford University Press, 1991).

87 S. E. Brigden, *London and the Reformation* (Oxford: Clarendon Press, 1989); C. L. Kingsford (ed.), *Chronicles of London* (Oxford: Clarendon Press, 1905).

88 Alan Dyer, 'English Town Chronicles', *Local Historian* 12.6 (1977), 285–91. Ricart's work was not printed.

Fabyan, Hall and Grafton, but they addressed the issue of identity only indirectly.[89] More important was John Bale's *The Laboryouse journey and serche of Johan Leylande for Englande's antiquities* (1549), which showed a clear appreciation of the importance of the land itself and its heritage in the process of definition.[90] Leland's own work was not published until the eighteenth century, but Bale adequately expressed the nature of his preoccupation, and demonstrated that it was not the eccentric foible of a single man. Sir Thomas Smith wrote what was probably the most complete expression of the realm as a legal and constitutional entity, but although that was composed in 1565, while he was ambassador in France, it was not published until 1584.[91] Apart from Leland/Bale, the most important work of identity published within the period was probably that of John Foxe. The *Acts and monuments* was not 'nationalistic' in the later sense, and did not articulate the notion of England as an Elect Nation. It did, however, evoke a special providence. God expressed his purposes 'first, as is his wont, unto his Englishmen'. It was Aylmer and not Foxe who had earlier declared that God was English, but the martyrologist was quite clear that the realm of England was something distinctive in the sight of God. Henry, Edward and Elizabeth (particularly the latter two) were great servants of His truth, but it was the country rather than the monarch which was favoured. By the end of Elizabeth's reign Protestantism was to be one of the salient characteristics of Englishness.

Finally the social commentaries which appeared in connection with the upheavals of 1548/9 should also be mentioned. They purport to show a traditional order disintegrating under the assaults of greed and irresponsibility. Such writings as 'Certayne causes gathered together wherein is shewed the decaye of Englande only by the great multitude of shepe' (1552) and *A discourse of the Common weal of this realm of England* (1549, but not published until 1581), show an awareness of the realm as community which owes nothing to either the church or the Crown.[92] The King is invoked as the guardian of

---

89 Robert Fabyan's *Cronycle* went through several editions (1516, 1533, 1542, 1559) before being superseded. Grafton was the continuer of Hardynge (1543) and Hall (1547), before beginning in his own right with *An abridgement* (1562).

90 *STC* 15445.

91 *STC* 22857; see, above, n. 22. It may have been originally intended for a French readership, but since it was written in English, rather than in Latin or French (both of which Smith wrote), that may be doubted.

92 The *Discourse* was first printed in a collection by William Stafford, *A compendious or briefe examination of certayne ordinary complaints* (1581). The 'Certayne causes' remained in manuscript until it was printed by F. J. Furnivall and J. Meadows Cooper for the Early English Text Society (EETS) in 1871. There was an extensive 'commonwealth' literature printed at the time, including William Forrest's *The pleasaunt poesye of princlie practise* (1548; EETS, ed.

the social order, but not as its creator. The vision of these writers was nostalgic, and not entirely real, but it should remind us that there were other ways of identifying the realm of England apart from those approved by the Tudors and their Parliaments. Of British identity, as opposed to English or Scottish, there is very little sign in this period. Somerset's somewhat disingenuous propaganda on union was matched by James Harrison, a London-based Scot, who published *An exhortacion to the Scottes, to conforme them selfes to the honorable, expedient and godly union betwene the two realmes of England and Scotlande*, also in 1547,[93] and John Foxe wrote (perhaps inadvertently) of 'this realme of England and Scotland', but such swallows do not make even a spring, let alone a summer. 'Britain' had to await the politicians, and historians, of a later generation.

S. J. Herrtage, 1878); Thomas Lever's *Sermons* (1550; ed. E. Arber, English Reprints, 1871); and Robert Crowley's *Way to Wealth* (1550; EETS, ed. J. M. Cowper, 1872).
93 *STC* 12857.

Chapter 8

LITERATURE AND THE COURT

WILLIAM A. SESSIONS

The dynamics of literature in the early Tudor court

In the summer of 1537 Henry Howard, Earl of Surrey, was imprisoned by order of the King. This was the first of four such occasions (from the last, in the Tower, he would not return). 'The most folish prowde boye that ys in Englande', the 21-year-old heir to the greatest title outside the royal family, was boxed in. If his punishment was mild – confinement in Windsor Castle, silent without the court's activity, where walls without tapestries returned 'a hollow sound of plaint' – Surrey's dilemma was not. In his stanzaic poem beginning 'So crewell prison', the longer of two texts he wrote to dramatise his situation, Surrey's speaker is losing his 'freedom', a pun ambiguously situated between 'liberty' and 'blood-nobility'. In actual fact, Henry VIII had sequestered his cousin, and the personal humiliation for the stylish aristocrat was worse than the public. Accordingly, in conversation, the courtier George Constantyne answers the attack on Surrey as a 'prowde' show-off by responding: 'What then? he ys wise for all that' and 'no mervell though a yonge man so noble a mans sonne and heyre apparante be prowde'.[1] The courtier on the lower rung identifies the very public place Surrey held in the stratified space – physical and cultural – called the court in 1537.

Surrey's problem illustrates the tension of writing in the early Tudor court. The Howard heir responded by inventing two lyrics – original in English both because of their subject, love for another male, and because of their verse innovations: the first sonnet in the English form and the first sequence in heroic quatrains. This response reveals the dynamic of literature in the early Tudor court – how to write it and how to read it. In 1537 Surrey was trapped between the power of an increasingly absolute monarch – the real audience in

---

1 Henry Howard, Earl of Surrey, 'So crewell prison', line 51, in *Poems*, ed. Emrys Jones (Oxford: Clarendon Press, 1964). *Archaeologia: Or Miscellaneous Tracks Relating to Antiquity* (London: Society of Antiquaries, 1831) 28:62.

the early Tudor court – and the desire of a courtier to project the authenticity, even market-value, of his own text and particular self-representation. Standing at the highest peak of a nobility that was slowly being displaced at court, the young Earl needed the King's attention. His texts would remind Henry VIII of Surrey's once high place as the close friend of the Duke of Richmond, Henry VIII's bastard son, and heir to the throne before his sudden death in 1536. The King's patronage could repair the Howard fortunes after the beheading of Anne Boleyn, Surrey's first cousin, and the traumatic events of the Pilgrimage of Grace, also in 1536, that had led to Surrey's imprisonment.

Surrey's situation illustrates that, whatever grief or love he actually felt, his text had to count for more than sincerity or a brilliant variation on Petrarchan extremes of love. The lyrics had to enter 'circulations of social energy' at the Tudor court.[2] In this system that encompassed both the increased text-making and the new audiences for these works, nothing could be assured, as Spenser would show in Philotimé's court in *The Faerie Queene*, where courtiers leap to touch 'the great gold chaine ylincked well' but are destroyed because 'every one did striuve his fellow downe to throw' (II, vii, 46). An enduring literary form or major text might emerge, might even survive, but this was as much accident as intention. Three writers who did achieve lasting texts (ironically, not by their own agency) provide a spectrum for surveying what may be called 'literature' in the period from Henry VIII to Mary I. The trio also illustrate the tensions between the court and the writer of texts in their shared fate of destruction, although socially each represented a different part of the spectrum: Surrey the highest aristocracy, Wyatt the powerful centre of 'new men' at the court, and Anne Askew the margins, although she was supported by a Queen and other persons in the highest circles.

Active in the last decade of Henry VIII's reign, the two male poets established in their texts (and significantly in their lives as well) patterns for later Tudor and Stuart courtiers. Reading them, other courtiers could deal with the interplay at court between would-be absolute monarchs and individual text-makers strong in their desire to create. George Puttenham's revisionist reading of early Tudor poetry in the 1580s recognised Wyatt and Surrey as 'courtly makers',[3] thus indicating their cultural originality as models whose literary achievements survived the courtly tensions Elizabethans knew. Puttenham's formulation only encapsulated, however, what a revolutionary book had established thirty years earlier in the reign of Queen Mary. *Tottel's Miscellany*, with its almost equal

---

2 Stephen Greenblatt, *Shakespearean Negotiations: The Circulation of Social Energy in Renaissance England* (Berkeley: University of California Press, 1988).

3 George Puttenham, *The Arte of English Poesie*, ed. G. D. Willcock and A. Walker (Cambridge University Press, 1936; rpt 1970), p. 60.

measure of erotic and elegiac poetry, had focused on Surrey and Wyatt, with the politically significant title *SONGES AND SONETTES, written by the ryght honorable Lorde Henry Haward late Earle of Surrey, and other.*

Richard Tottel showed almost perfect timing in launching his product. In the Edwardian era, such a collection of poetry could not have been published because of its erotic subject matter, but in the more sophisticated Marian world – especially because the book would honour the Howards and Surrey's son Thomas, the recently ascended 4th Duke of Norfolk – Tottel found his moment. In that summer of 1557 not only did Tottel produce his miscellany of poetry but he took a 1554 published text of Surrey's, the translation of the fourth book of the *Aeneid*, revised it and then added to it his new-found second book translated by Surrey. Finding other manuscripts saved from the Howard dynastic collapse a decade earlier, he achieved a coup for the Marian court. As a result, he brought out the only two books of Virgil's epic that remain of Surrey's translation of Virgil in his new heroic form, later called blank verse. In all his published texts that summer, each associated in some way with the martyred young Earl, Tottel inaugurated a new kind of consumerism within early modern print culture and thereby institutionalised the English lyric[4] and a classic English verse form.

Tottel was too good a merchant not to leave room for further transition. He combined Marian nostalgia and the renewing of an icon with the Edwardian glorification of the printed book. Thus, when Mary I died seventeen months after the *Miscellany* appeared, Tottel had a best-selling text for Elizabeth I, the daughter of Surrey's first cousin, when she ascended the throne. Eventually, this book – by the 1580s called 'the Earl of Surrey's lyrics' – became one of the four English texts that Sir Philip Sidney thought worthy of any literary consideration. Another of Tottel's marketing instincts was less prescient: his audience was not to be his own bourgeois class and certainly not any lower. His audience were courtiers, and the more exalted the bloodline the better – the blessed Queen herself intended as the ultimate reader. With the pointed snobbery that characterised a great deal of English and European humanism, Tottel's preface – a typical early Tudor polemical text – attacks 'the rude skill of common eares', and with a courtly rhetorical flourish, he exhorts 'the vnlearned, by reading to be more skilfull, and to purge that swinelike grossenesse, that maketh the swete maierome [marjoram] not to smell to their delight'.[5] But

---

4 See Arthur Marotti, *Manuscript, Print and the English Renaissance Lyric* (Ithaca, NY, and London: Cornell University Press, 1995), p. 216. Cf. Wendy Wall, *The Imprint of Gender: Authorship and Publication in the Renaissance* (Ithaca, NY, and London: Cornell University Press, 1993).
5 Richard Tottel, preface to *Tottel's Miscellany (1557–1587)*, ed. Hyder Edward Rollins, 2 vols. (Cambridge, MA: Harvard University Press, 1928–9). For the snobbery of early modern

Tottel's texts quickly moved from the intended aristocratic audience to lower classes, as both Shakespeare's Gravedigger and Shallow demonstrate in their enthusiasm for the book and its lyrics.

If Tottel and his imitators marketed the upscale – necessary in the Tudor court – the commodity-value of Anne Askew was evident from the beginning. Only months after she was burned at the stake by Henry VIII in the summer of 1546 for denying the Real Presence, John Bale compiled a text for the new Edwardian court. Not only would this book and its martyrology, together with his other polemical texts, win him an Irish bishopric, but also this new courtier-cleric would inaugurate a new Christian anthropology. With typical brashness, the ex-Carmelite monk textualised the modern hero-saint as a woman burned alive for Christ. This prophetic sign of a woman, descended from Lincolnshire gentry, had the highest patronage at court in Henry VIII's last Queen, Katherine Parr. Her circle of evangelicals included the Hobys (one of whom at the Marian court would make the first English translation of Castiglione); the Seymours, future Duke and Duchess of Somerset; the Princess Elizabeth; and Surrey's sister the Duchess of Richmond, herself one of the keepers of the most famous lyric anthology in early Tudor England, the Devonshire manuscript. It was precisely from this circle that Anne Askew received money and books, and possibly manuscript poems of Surrey.

Bale's marketing notably revised English cultural history. He had 'The Balade whych Anne Askewe made and sange when she was in Newgate' printed in Germany, and he added to it and to Askew's report of her interrogations his commentary that effectually canonised her – the first making of a saint by means of a printed book, in England and probably in Europe. Bale self-consciously notes: 'Thus is she a gyant canonysed in Christes bloude, though she never have other canonysacyon of pope, preest, nor Byshopp.' John Foxe, whom Bale first met in the Duchess of Richmond's household, gives Askew's cult-narrative a crucial placement in his *Actes and Monuments*, which saw a Latin version in Strasbourg during the Marian regime. In this revisionist book of martyrs that would be almost as decisive for a providential sense of nationalism as the new English Bibles and Cranmer's Book of Common Prayer, Foxe borrows heavily from Bale, elaborating the symbolism latent in Bale's woodcut in the first edition. In Bale, a woman steps forward, bearing a palm frond in her right hand, as history's prototype of the ancient maxim (renewed by Erasmus in his *Adagia*) *Veritas filia temporis* ('Truth is the daughter of Time'). The young woman

humanism, see Vernon Hall, *Renaissance Literary Criticism: A Study of its Social Content* (Gloucester, MA: Peter Smith, 1959), and also Fernand Braudel, *The Mediterranean and the Mediterranean World in the Age of Philip II*, trans. Sian Reynolds, 2 vols. (London: Collins, 1972–3), 2:725–33.

represents resurrection in a prophetic era. In her own public-relations coup, Queen Mary would make this powerful humanist Christian maxim one of her coronation texts, and the appropriation was repeated in Richard Mulcaster's account of Elizabeth's coronation procession from the Tower to Westminster.

Askew's ballad announces her fight for the truth she finds in her greater self-consciousness and her right to act as she believed. For her, the Real Presence of Christ is everywhere. In struggling to write a text of the self pitted against the world – i.e., the Tudor court in 1546 – she saw herself as a transformed courtier of the old nobility, a modern woman-knight (adumbrating Spenser's Britomart in fiction and, in actual history, a queen of nine days, Lady Jane Grey). Askew saw herself as a new Christian authenticating the Ephesian imagery of St Paul:

> Lyke as the armed knyght
> Appointed to the fielde
> With thys world wyll I fyght
> And fayth shall be my shield.

In her fashion, Askew follows Luther and possibly her patron Katherine Parr, who may have been composing her autobiographical *Lamentations* during Askew's imprisonment, interrogation and final ordeal. The young woman internalises not only her act of faith but her own act of writing:

> I am not she that lyst
> My anker to lete fall
> For euerye dryslynge myst
> My shyppe substanciall.
>   Not oft use I to wryght
> In prose nor yet in ryme
> Yet wyll I shewe one syght
> That I saw in my time.

This 'syght' that provokes a text is none other than the horror of Henry VIII, whose surrogates are torturing and killing her. This is a new kind of *speculum principis* or 'mirror' for princes. In Askew's lyric definition of the self in tension with the Tudor monarch, a strategic intertextual transfer occurs: she borrows lines from the Earl of Surrey. Earlier, after his disgraceful return from the French wars in 1546, Surrey had continued his free, highly subjective Biblical paraphrases. One, working from Ecclesiastes, ch. 3, identifies Henry VIII in language that Askew appropriates. Surrey's poulter's measure, 'I saw a royal throne whereas that Justice should have sit; / Instead of whom I saw, with fierce and cruel mode', becomes Askew's ballad metre, 'I saw a ryall trone / Where Justyce should haue sytt / But in her sted was one / Of modye cruell wytt.' Characterising the King as 'Sathan in hys excesse' (Askew's phrase)[6], both texts reveal the dangers of writing at the Tudor court. Askew's language expresses the faith not just of the new Christian but of the originating self in the Henrician court.

It was Sir Thomas Wyatt who best understood the dangers of opposing textual and courtly power. He survived execution, but lived only to the age of thirty-nine, exhausted by his labours as a diplomat and by the King's imprisonings of him in the Tower. He was released from the last of these in 1541 through Surrey's intercession with his teenaged first cousin Queen Catherine Howard. As early as his first Tower imprisonment in 1536, any illusion Wyatt might have had regarding the relative freedom of the self at court vanished. Looking out of his cell window and watching Anne Boleyn beheaded, he could only evoke the event in subjective terms surfacing from his deepest humanist training. As the Latin phrase indicates, the scene recapitulates the horrors witnessed by Seneca at the court of Nero:

> These bloody days have broken my heart.
> My lust, my youth did them depart,
> And blind desire of estate.
> Who hastes to climb seeks to revert.
> Of truth, *circa regna tonat*.[7]

Lyric and didactic projections

The cause of Wyatt's 'bloody days' was the political shifts all three poets had lived through. Hans Holbein's (or his school's) frontispiece for the 1539 Great Bible illustrates the new changes at the Tudor court. It portrays graphically the 'circulations' of power descending from the uppermost central image of Henry VIII. As never before, all courtiers, whether the upwardly mobile or the old nobility, were being squeezed into a political antithesis of an increasingly centralised monarchy and less and less powerful secular and spiritual hierarchies, the ancient three estates rapidly becoming one. What Lord Privy Seal and

---

6 Askew's texts can be found in *The First Examination of Anne Askew, Lately Martyred in Smithfelde, by the Romysh Popes Upholders, with the Elucydacyon of Johan Bale* (Marburg, 1546), STC 848: 3, 49, 62–3. For a comprehensive introduction and textual history, see *The Examinations of Anne Askew*, ed. Elaine V. Beilin (New York and Oxford: Oxford University Press, 1996). For Surrey's text, see Henry Howard, Earl of Surrey, *Poems*, ed. Jones. All further references to Surrey will be from this edition and cited, where necessary, in the text. I have modernised the spelling of Surrey's poems.

7 *The Complete Poems of Sir Thomas Wyatt*, ed. R. A. Rebholz (New Haven, CT, and London: Yale University Press, 1975), CXXIII. All further references to Wyatt's poetry will be from this edition and cited in the text.

Vice-gerent for Spirituals, Thomas Cromwell, declares in clear, objective language – the Pope had robbed 'the King's Majesty, being only the Supreme Head of this his realm of England immediately under God, of his honour, his right, and preeminence due unto him by the law of God' – Holbein would further portray in a vast iconic mural on the wall of the Privy Chamber at Whitehall.[8] Through its crucial placement, the gigantic immediacy of this English king with spread legs and upright phallus dominated the vision of all Tudor and Stuart courtiers until Oliver Cromwell and the revolution whitewashed it.

Unintentionally and even unpredictably, the forms of the lyric, epic, theatre and devotional employed by writers at the early Tudor court were called forth by the outward political shifts compressing a cultural revolution in England. The very spaces of this court registered one central fact: from the monarch, whether Henry VIII, Edward VI or Mary I, all blessings flowed. No text, however lyric or subjective, could reach any audience in such spaces unless directly or indirectly it reflected this political reality and its resultant 'circulations' of power. In these spaces, time operated, in Thomas Cromwell's phrase, 'immediately' (the past either transformed or obliterated). Furthermore, since total concentration of power can never be a total success, social controls, including new icons and new murals, had to be introduced by way of new technologies.

At the heart of these technologies in the early Tudor court lay new or newly transformed systems of communication with their special texts and languages. George Orwell provides a more apposite image for this new technology than Spenser and the Tudor court, operating less like the old Virgilian simile of a beehive and more like the scurrying main floor of a modern international network communications centre (say, CNN), where texts are produced and transmitted in and to constantly changing space and time. Literature for such a court entailed not only control of humanist letters as reservoirs of social technology with their dogma of permanent texts (Virgil, Cicero, the Bible). It also entailed more ubiquitous and flexible concepts of writing and communication. Courtiers in the new era understood what Surrey, Wyatt and Askew realised preeminently in their texts and lives. No text-making can proceed unless it addresses what Wyatt calls 'the presse' of court, centred in the monarch, and its pageants, ceremonies, plays, prayers, liturgies, processions, sermons and speeches on the scaffold.[9]

8 *Statutes of the Realm (1509–1547)* (London, 1817) 3:363. See also Helen Miller, *Henry VIII and the English Nobility* (Oxford: Blackwell, 1986), and Roy Strong, *Holbein and Henry VIII* (London: Routledge & Kegan Paul, 1967).
9 See the relevant definitions in Raymond Williams, *Keywords: A Vocabulary of Culture and Society* (New York: Oxford University Press, 1985).

The Henrician court now depended on a new communications-theatre in which the making of texts became essential. Sir Thomas More had noted this shift in introducing an ancient metaphor – the court as theatre – in the English text of his *History of Richard III*. While earlier English courts had performed the same high ceremonies and processions as the Tudors, they had never been quite so directed towards a single spectator who could applaud but also kill. Written at the same time as More's less ideologically transparent *Utopia*, the *History of Richard III* was never finished, possibly because More realised the evil it depicted still continued at the Henrician court. With the new political shifts, other models, updated *specula principis*, began to appear. In 1535, the year More was beheaded, both monarch and courtier could read Lord Berners's translation of *The Golden Book of Marcus Aurelius* from the popular Renaissance text of Antonio de Guevara. Berners, the translator of *Froissart's Chronicles* for the youthful court of Henry VIII, the old aristocrat and uncle of Anne Boleyn and Surrey, retained in his new book the Arthurian ideology of Froissart but made it more fashionably humanist in the guise of a 'mirror' of a Roman emperor. The old ideology would serve as a reminder: Berners defines his Roman court as a relationship of 'divers men and one lord' and defines honour as the bond between the two, not with the King above it.[10]

Even though Wyatt and Surrey welcomed many of Henry VIII's political changes, they had been bred in the ideology of Lord Berners and perceived the stark differences in the new technologies. Wyatt particularly understood the new terms for survival and inventing texts. Without the control of language that his humanist masters had taught him and his applications of this highly developed language, Wyatt knew he would be squeezed in the 'presse' of court. His life as a diplomat taught him the necessity of ready language. In reporting to Henry VIII from Brussels on 3 February 1540, Wyatt describes his exchange with the Holy Roman Emperor, Charles V. The most powerful man in Europe, 'in all the processe, not ons or twise, but offten . . . clypped my tale with imperious and brave wordes ynow, wherby dryven to replie, to retorne to the matter, and to disgresse, other wise then euer with hym I have bene acustomid, skant my memory can containe the particular incidentes, wyche to me were as notable as the principall'.[11] In such a world, Wyatt's 'tongue served', as Surrey noted in his 1542 elegy on his friend, 'in foreign realms his king'.

---

10 Sir Thomas More, *The History of King Richard III*, ed. Richard S. Sylvester (London and New Haven, CT: Yale University Press, 1963), p. 274. Antonio de Guevara, *The Golden Boke of Marcus Aurelius*, trans. John Bourchier, Lord Berners (London, 1535), STC 12436.
11 Kenneth Muir, *Life and Letters of Sir Thomas Wyatt* (University of Liverpool Press, 1963), p. 134.

Earlier still at the Tudor court, Wyatt had perceived the only dynamic by which he could survive. This he articulated in his first printed work, his translation of *Plutarckes boke of the Quyete of mynde*, dedicated to Queen Catherine of Aragon at the onset of her disgrace. Wyatt's luminous syntax shifted Latin rhetorical forms into native English patterns, as it focused on the necessity for a still point in a quickly turning world. Roman stoicism had become a part of his (and Lord Berners's) response to the Tudor court. Wyatt's title, moreover, became a kind of code word ('quiet mind') for courtiers in the late 1530s and 1540s. Sir Ralph Fane, one of the Devonshire Manuscript circle and a courtier executed by Dudley in the last Edwardian years, used this phrase in a letter from the war-front in France in 1543.[12] Lesser courtiers also realised how literary texts and the right language could become referents for understanding their own fates.

In a period of respite from arrests and imprisonments, possibly after 1541, Wyatt wrote another of his Roman satires revealing courtly tensions. His Horatian verse letter is addressed to his fellow courtier, John Poins, who had asked 'to know / The cause why that homeward I me drawe, / and fle the presse of courtes wher soo they goo'. Wyatt no longer wants 'to lyve thrall, vnder the awe / Of lordly lokes, wrappid within [his] cloke'. The first part of the poem attacks the Tudor court, hardly different from courts Wyatt had seen in Madrid, Paris, Bruges and Rome. After this first powerful description in English of what Spenser would later term the Blatant Beast, Wyatt prefers 'inward resort' though tempted by 'glorye' and courtly 'honour'. His sense of self is as adamant as Anne Askew's: 'I cannot, I. No, no, it will not be.' But the dichotomy drawn between active life at court and contemplative life in Kent discloses Wyatt's recognition that he could not escape the court. The lyric beginning 'Stand whoso list upon the Slipper toppe / Of courtes estates, and lett me heare reioyce' contrasts the dangerous life of arguing with emperors to his own private needs: 'use me quiet without lett or stoppe, / Unknowen in courte . . . In hidden place' so that 'I maye dye aged after the common trace'. This is the end he desires, not that of the courtier endlessly caught in 'circulations' and dying without self-knowledge, 'dazed with dreadfull face'.

No such image of an English courtier had been articulated before. Wyatt's startling originality only made it clearer how different the English court had become. Or, if the court had not actually changed from the brutality of the War of the Roses, the sensibilities trained in elaborate humanist technologies

---

12 *Letters and Papers, Foreign and Domestic, of the Reign of Henry VIII* (London: Longman, 1862–1932), vol. 18, pt 2, p. 190.

had. A new kind of literature had sprung up in the wake of Duke Humphrey of Gloucester and mid fifteenth-century contacts with Italy and the continent. By late Henrician times, the texts of Erasmus were everywhere, imbuing Tyndale's Bible translations – culturally and linguistically the most influential texts of the period. Text after text outlined educational programmes offering courtiers opportunities to prosper from the change of intellectual climate that followed Henry VII's introduction of humanists to his court. Tutored by John Skelton, Henry VIII took pride in his facility with languages and his early compositions of music and verse, especially 'Pastime with good company' that resounds with the bluff jollity of a far less anxious court. Court officials with proficiency of language continued in steady demand – from Richard Pace (whose *Benefit of a Liberal Education*, published in Latin in 1519, deciphers linguistic theories of the early court), to Thomas Cromwell (master of Tudor documentary prose and the humanist friend of Wyatt), to the King's Erasmian brother-in-law, Edward Seymour, later Duke of Somerset (who would rule the kingdom as Edward VI's Protector). Henry VIII also named the universally learned John Leland, England's first antiquarian, Court Librarian and thereby instituted the policy of textual conservation – a cause Leland's friend John Bale would advocate at the Edwardian court after Leland went insane.

Henry VIII obviously admired rhetorical displays. So did his son Edward listening to Hugh Latimer preach, and his daughter Mary hearing Cardinal Reginald Pole. Queen Catherine of Aragon had instructed Juan Vives, the Spanish humanist, to write a textbook, *The Instruction of a Christian Woman*, for her daughter, the Princess Mary. It was translated into English by Richard Hyrde, one of many courtiers active at court in the new technology of texts. When Thomas More published his *Utopia* in 1516, his mastery of Latin revealed the success of the educational systems pioneered by John Colet and William Lily. Written as a Renaissance 'courtesy book' before Castiglione's, More's own variation on the *speculum principis* tradition was one more meditation on the nature of power at court. The dialogic method in *Utopia* – open-ended and still hopeful that courtiers might function in a renewed polity – shifted to monologue in More's final *Dialogue of Comfort Against Tribulation* (1534). Now the text-maker in the Tower assesses the transformation of his time: 'the world is here waxen such / & so gret perilles appear here to fall at hand'.[13]

In 1529 Thomas Starkey answered the arguments of *Utopia* in his unpublished *Dialogue between Reginald Pole and Thomas Lupset*, which, in the spirit of

13 *Dialogue of Comfort Against Tribulation*, ed. Louis L. Martz and Frank Manley (New Haven, CT, and London: Yale University Press, 1976), p. 3.

the humanist Machiavelli and in vigorous Tudor phrasing, outlines a theory of service for a controversial polity. Here Reginald Pole figures as the centre of a new, less autocratic and more nobility-based regime. Sir Thomas Elyot's *The boke named the Gouernour* (1531) was dedicated to Henry VIII and also directly undertook to answer More's ambiguous 'courtesy book'. For Elyot, service to the King within the new Tudor distribution of power could be expressed in quite specific ways, from dress to dancing to modes of thought and composition. Elyot carried over the image of the ideal monarch in his different *Image of Governance* (1540) – a work based on another Roman emperor, Septimus Severus, and dedicated to Surrey's father. Extending models of text-making for the court, Elyot wrote treatises on health and proverbial wisdom and compiled a Latin–English *Dictionary*. With Richard Taverner, who englished a selection from Erasmus's *Adagia*, he prepared the way for the more advanced rhetorical handbooks of the Edwardian and Marian reigns. Thomas Wilson's *Art of Rhetoric* (1553), itself influenced in its structure by Leonard Cox's lists and categories in *Art or Craft of Rhetoric* (1529), and Richard Sherry's *Treatise of Schemes and Tropes* (1555) offered technically brilliant catalogues for courtiers to use in the new technology of communication.

By the advent of Queen Mary I, the courtier had become identified, in fact, with the power of language. By then the highest such precedent had been set by royalty itself: by Henry VIII, his Spanish Queen, his first Howard Queen, Anne, and his last, Katherine; by Edward VI, with his precocious Latin style; and by Lady Jane Grey, with her copy of Plato's *Phaedo* in hand, in Ascham's famous description. Now, whatever the ideology, no courtier could survive without skills in the technology of rhetoric, as earlier courtiers could not survive without martial and athletic skills. Roger Ascham is aware in his *Toxophilus* (1545), dedicated to the ageing Henry VIII, that only control of native English can return the nation to the dominance it once held with the longbow, whose demise his text laments. Mixing Latin syntax with native English rhythms (for example, his attack on popular music as 'nice, fine, minikin fingering') here and in his *Scholemaster*, Ascham confirms the educational theories not only of Elyot but of his beloved teacher, Sir John Cheke, a tutor of Edward VI and associated not only with the Earl of Surrey but with his brother-in-law William Cecil (Elizabeth I's Lord Burghley). Ascham's crucial teaching of the superiority of native diction over foreign models shaped the next decades of English compositional theory. The immediate effect of such literary and rhetorical strategies was to prepare the courtier for his encounters at court – new analogues of the old Arthurian battles that Erasmus and Ascham had condemned as fiction. That 'real world' of the Tudors required, however, dealing with literature in a larger context and as a kind of organic structure where the various models could synthesise. To prepare the synthesis, language, from these new resources and technologies, had to create myth.

Well into Elizabeth I's reign, the Tudor court imagined itself through idealising texts like Edward Hall's *The Union of the two noble and illustre famelies of Lancastre and York* (1548), which set the chivalric mythology for the late Elizabethan and Stuart courts (e.g., James VI's idolising of Surrey's flamboyant grandfather, the original Duke of Buckingham). The myth would last until the English Revolution and, in various guises, even longer. Hall's essential myth of chivalry was further disseminated by the more realistic but still glory-focused histories like those of Richard Grafton and Raphael Holinshed. Hall demonstrates, often with rapture, how court literature, drama and symbolic action generally exerted political coercion over foreign ambassadors and merchants and the general populace. Hall appears ready to end his history, for example, with images of a radiant and radiating court. He exalts Henry VIII's final magnificence in the banqueting and receptions for the French Lord Admiral in August 1546. Then, suddenly, he appends three shocking deaths: Anne Askew's burning (the previous month), the Earl of Surrey's sudden arrest and beheading, and Henry VIII's own death in the following January. In this first major text of Tudor historiography in native English, Hall provided an ideal Burgundian model even for Seymour and John Dudley (Sidney's grandfather). The text also gave Queen Mary dynastic hope. Its conclusion, with its sharp contrast of magnificence and death, tells a different story, however, warning implicitly of the court tensions in which death remains the first reality. George Cavendish's *Life and Death of Cardinal Wolsey* carries the same warning. Written during Mary's reign, Cavendish builds on Hall's sense of the rise and fall of a great magnate. This nostalgic text is structured in the *de casibus* tradition; the middle of the narrative is exactly the point of downturn for Wolsey's career. It is as much a *memento mori* – the equivalent of Yorick's skull for Prince Hamlet – as a 'mirror for princes'.

Dramatic representations: England and Scotland

Of all the forms of the 'presse' of court, theatre and drama could most easily become, by their public nature, instruments of the monarch: vehicles of propaganda seemingly impervious to any personal text or even subtext. But the placid surfaces of Henrician interludes, of Edwardian morality plays and of Marian political and educational theatre may be deceptive. Plots of rather wild comedy (in John Heywood, or example) or a five-act Latinate structure (in Nicholas Udall, for example) carry, in one critic's biological metaphor, 'protective coloration'.[14] Under the full threat of censorship exercised by every Tudor monarch, especially during the political shifts in the late Henrician, Edwardian and Marian courts, writers for theatre had no recourse but to submit. For a courtier who would gain access to power or survival, as Surrey learned in 1537, the real test was how to represent a self that perceived itself not just as personal but collective. Virtually all the major dramatic texts of the Tudor court before 1558 reveal themselves, whatever the shifting power alignments, as *specula principis*. If the monarch can be properly advised, however indirectly, the political order, the total community, might be redeemed. In this way subjectivity – the perceptions of the writer's private self – expressed in a public text might define or even regulate the court.

From the beginning, the Tudors had particularly recognised the special force of theatre as a means of public control. They were not concerned with the popular morality plays and the religious mystery cycles for the lower classes – flourishing genres until Edward VI closed them down, Mary tried to revive them, and then Elizabeth I, encouraging the moralities, killed the mystery cycles. The theatre audience that counted was the court and academic elite and little else. From Henry VII on, Tudor monarchs supported troupes of players or performers connected with the Chapel Royal. The Yorkists and earlier aristocrats had also done so, but now professional entertainers could advance the new production of myth. The convergence met Tudor objectives perfectly, as language and performance celebrated the image of the monarch. Extending the courtly traditions of Henry Medwall and John Rastell, More's brother-in-law, John Skelton accepts and then cautions this new power in *Magnyfycence*. The poet–priest transforms a *speculum* focus by fitting direct historical commentary within the allegorical frame of a morality. Here the realism of an actual event – the expulsion of certain 'new men' from court in 1519 – denatures the homiletic abstractions of the Four Virtues and the Four Vices. *Magnyfycence* thus varies the standard abstract pattern of most Tudor morality plays, a fall from prosperity that leads to penance and restitution. Skelton may still offer his audience an idealised king reconciled to Measure and the Virtues, but Magnificence has been tricked earlier by the Vice figures – Courtly Abusion and Cloaked Collusion – and he appears to have listened more to Fancy than to Measure: 'Measure is mete for a marchauntes hall / But largesse becometh a state ryall.' Whatever 'protective coloration' of encomium and allegory

14 David Bevington, *Tudor Drama and Politics* (Cambridge, MA: Harvard University Press, 1968), p. 65.

may figure here, Skelton pointedly signals the dangers of the new Tudor magnificence.

The allegory of the *Enterlude of the Vertuous and Godly Queene Hester* also seems controlled by topical allusion, providing a realistic frame through which to project commentary on the conduct of the court. The Old Testament analogue is obvious in the text: Esther represents an English Queen married to King Assewerus or Henry VIII and threatened by Aman, the King's chief minister. The problem lies in identifying which Queen and which chief minister. Is Esther the beleagured Catherine of Aragon, and Aman, Cardinal Wolsey, who had already begun the dismantling of the monasteries (a clear political subtext here)? Or is Esther the hapless Catherine Howard, and the fall of Cromwell the fall of Aman by which the righteous faction in the state – the Howards and old nobility as the Jews – rises again? Either possibility finds a conservative faction pushing its case as strongly as the Christians influenced by Luther would soon be doing. Yet, if the drama's solution to the political débâcle of the Henrician court is collective, the unknown courtier's perceptive text is his own.

A more developed text on the role of the King in the dangerous currents of his court, John Heywood's *A Play of the Weather*, takes a deceptively comic classical ploy. It purports to advise the King on the 'weather' of religious dispute around 1530. A metatheatrical gesture situates the play in the Great Hall or Presence Chamber of Jupiter, where the true Father of Heaven appoints a courtier-servant, Merry Report, to hear complaints about the weather and report back. Merry Report, an updated Vice, receives complaints across a social spectrum – water-miller, laundress and little boy, none of whom will compromise on a definition of the right weather. Heywood manages to affirm the King's authority (a hope for conservatives in 1530) by having Jupiter decide that each may have his or her desired weather but only through an obligatory system of interdependence and cooperation. The play ends with two stanzas of Chaucerian rhyme royal, in which Jupiter appropriately congratulates himself. The theatricality of *A Play of the Weather* confirms the ingenuity of a master showman who started as 'singer', then 'player of virginals' at the Tudor court, and in 1528 became Steward of the Royal Chamber, a position he held through three reigns until the advent of Elizabeth. The father of two Jesuits (one of them, Jasper, the first translator of a Senecan play into English) and the grandfather of John Donne, Heywood wrote constantly through his time at court and was preparing an Easter play for Edward VI when the young King died.

John Bale defined the other end of the theatricalised political struggle. Cromwell supported a performance of *King Johan* by Bale's players in 1538 because an important source for the text is a passage in Tyndale's 1528 *Obedience of a Christian Man* portraying the medieval King John as a royal martyr to un-bridled papal power. Like Tyndale, Bale presented his historical exemplum without ambiguity or irony. For Bale, the past existed to reveal a triumphant future. The struggle between King and established church in *King Johan* may be as radical in its topical realism as Bale's text canonising Anne Askew, but its dramatic structure turns on streamlined psychomachia – absolute good and absolute evil. Bale's subjectivity as centred in his faith asserted itself, moreover, in the confidence that he was on the winning side. Thus, when the play ends by harmonising Veritas and Imperial Majesty, Bale's text authorises a new history. Anything partial or tendentious in this courtly act of writing and performance translates into an 'uncontested and uncontestable reading' so that England's past and even its prophetic future can be actualised in the present moment of history the providence of God has brought forth.[15]

Such prophetic assurance defines most of the dramatic literature from the reign of Edward VI. Now the old forms could be accommodated for a new purpose. As with Bale and Henry VIII, colouration was still necessary and demanded tact and decorum in handling political representation. Here *Realpolitik* was successively determined by two Dukes, Somerset (Edward Seymour) and Northumberland (John Dudley). Yet, whatever their power, subjective commentary, even critical, found its channels of expression. The tri-partite structure of R. Wever's *Lusty Juventus* – conversion, degeneration and recovery – echoes, in its simplified shape, Skelton's *Magnyfycence*. Here, the Aris-totelian and Scholastic Virtues and Vices of earlier morality plays like *Everyman* and *The Castle of Perseverance* are changed into more topicalised names: Good Counsel, Satan, Hypocrisy, Fellowship, Abominable Living and God's Merciful Promises. Somerset's suspension of censorship energised Protestant courtiers like Wever who had felt repressed in the ambiguous Henrician court, although the refrain of a popular ballad at court resonated with a sense of Catholic ex-clusion: 'I'm little John Nobody, / Little John Nobody that durst not speak.'[16] With this new energy, courtiers looked to the Bible for sources. The Christian parable of the Prodigal Son is the source for *Lusty Juventus* as well as *Nice Wanton* (containing a Prodigal Daughter), performed around 1550. These comic texts not only dramatise individual Bible stories but incorporate Biblical passages in dialogue and action. Thomas Becon's *A New Dialog between thangell of God, & the*

---

15 David Kastan, ' "Holy Wurdes" and "Slypper Wit": John Bale's *King Johan* and the Poetics of Propaganda', in *Rethinking the Henrician Era: Essays on Early Tudor Texts and Contexts*, ed. Peter C. Herman (Urbana: University of Illinois Press, 1994), p. 279.

16 John King, *English Reformation Literature: The Tudor Origins of the Protestant Tradition* (Princeton University Press, 1982), p. 217.

Shepherdes in the Felde (*c.* 1547) and Lewis Wager's *Life and Repentaunce of Marie Magdalene* (*c.* 1550) update the old morality and miracle plays. They exemplify the new Protestant literary method of parody (sacred imitation) and the fine line between theatre and sermonising that a preacher like Hugh Latimer would exploit.

At a remove from the respective party lines of the Edwardian and Marian courts, two comedies of the era offer personal commentary, through structurings of irony that are more sophisticated and intellectual than simply didactic. Both are products of academic theatre. *Gammer Gurton's Needle* was written at Cambridge University by an unknown academic, and *Ralph Roister-Doister* by Nicholas Udall entertained student audiences. Both anticipate the comedies of the next eighty years in England by fusing the old allegorical morality with a sharp realism introduced by new humanist methods of literary analysis and new Protestant forms of psychological reflection. In *Gammer Gurton's Needle*, the characters speak a Somerset dialect, providing extra laughs for Cambridge University wits. In this farcical treatment of Gammer Gurton's lost needle and the communal uproar of the search, Diccon (another updated Vice) misdirects such villagers as Doctor Rat and Dame Chat, but all concludes didactically. Countering the demand by the vengeful Rat that Diccon should die, the genial Chaucerian magistrate Master Bailly suggests an 'open kind of penaunce', namely that Diccon should kiss Hodge's rear end (in which process the needle is discovered to be embedded in Hodge's breeches). Also 'open' are deeper resonances in the scatological farce that reflect on the hunger and poverty resulting from the economic disasters of the Edwardian reign: Could the polity again be compassionate? Could citizens put public duty before personal wealth or maintain, as in the pre-Henrician days, support systems for the poor?

Matthew Merrygreek in Udall's *Ralph Roister Doister* parodies Heywood's Merry Report, and the differences between the two reveal the shape of the new realistic comedy. Udall's play exhibits the formal structure of Latin five-act comedy, and, like *Gammer Gurton's Needle*, adapts the ancient Roman comic devices to a realistic contemporary English scene and the capacities of schoolboy actors. Headmaster at Eton College until his dismissal for sodomy and robbery (neither of which he ever denied), Nicholas Udall performed as an impresario in Edward's and Mary's courts and even wrote a parody of the old miracles, *Jacob and Esau*, for Edward. Such a backward-looking gesture, however, would not appeal to Queen Mary, as Udall soon recognised. In the 1540s, Princess Mary had translated Erasmus's Latin *Paraphrase* of St John's Gospel under Udall's tutelage, showing herself as capable of new readings of the old as her brother Edward, but opting for an alternative mode – more European, stylish and Counter-Reformation. Thus, it is probable that Udall directed his choir boys in the songs and pealing of bells to celebrate the Queen's first Christmas of 1553, staging a deliberate return to the previously outlawed Twelfth Night festivities. Appealing to this sophisticated and humanist court, Udall also adapted Terentian character types. Roister Doister becomes an updated Marian Thraso whose love tokens are refused by Dame Christian Custance, and who is outwitted and ridiculed by Matthew Merrygreek, a modernised English Gnatho. Two burlesques – of the Catholic requiem mass and a chivalric battle – are the kind of parodies the older world of the Queen's mother, Catherine of Aragon, had long recognised. Udall's battle deliberately recalls classical drama when Dame Custance and her household women, Madge Mumblecrust, Tibet Talkapace and Annot Alyface, rout the show-off Ralph, who has a cooking pot for his helmet. The Dame emerges, with her dry humour and clever political alliance with Matthew Merrygreek, as a model of wisdom and proof of the constancy of her name. Indeed, if Queen Mary attended the acting of this play, its principal character would subtly remind Udall's former pupil of the need for humour and political savvy.

Advising the new Tudor monarch is the clear intent of Udall's moral interlude, *Respublica*, perhaps presented in the same Christmas season. Combining praise and hope, produced in 'the first yeare of the moost prosperous Reigne of our most gracious Soveraigne Quene Marye the first', the text provides one further way to read Tudor court literature. Once more, with the irony of a courtly text-maker, Udall's *Respublica* advances a radical suggestion with seemingly conformist counsel. Revising Skelton's *Magnfycence*, the eponymous heroine is not a prince but a nation who has become a 'poor wydowe' in need of good ministers. At first she listens to the Vices, including Avarice disguised as Policy, Insolence as Authority, and Oppression as Reformation – each a comment on the Dukes of Somerset and Northumberland and the nobility to whom the wealth of the Catholic church had been given. An honest rustic, People is even thrown out of the new polity. In this Marian psychomachia, only the arrival of the four daughters of God, Misericordia, Veritas, Justicia and Pax can effectively counter the Vices. Their entire expulsion, however, awaits the *dea ex machina* Nemesis – specifically, as the prologue states, a figure for the new Queen Mary. But, if the late appearance of the overtly identified Queen concludes the play on a note of ideological triumph like that of the Henrician analogues in *Magynificence* and *The Play of the Weather*, Udall's text remains more subtle. The play's other ruling woman appears quite vulnerable in her choices. Respublica falls victim to her own weakness, becoming the thrall of her Vice-ministers. Even in John Heywood's laudatory beast allegory written during this same period,

The Spider and the Fly, the Queen, outwardly the Nemesis-figure of a housemaid who sweeps away all cobwebs, is admonished through the allegory to reconcile all political leaders and form a true republic of Catholics and Protestants. Udall's more sophisticated theatre-text employs the inherent dramatic tension between his two types of women to convey the same message: save the nation through reconciliation of factions.

This is the same message dramatised in the Scottish panoramic satire *Ane Satyre of the Thrie Estaitis* by Sir David Lindsay of the Mount, performed in the palace of Linlithgow in 1540 before James V and then in Edinburgh in 1554 before the Dowager Regent, Marie de Guise, the infant Mary Stuart's mother. For one of the most public occasions the Scottish court could offer, Lindsay, its most courtly figure, crafts an officially panegyric text. But the action of the satire warns both rulers – in differing ways – of the perils confronting Scotland. Lindsay had seen the Scottish court decay from its height under the most chivalric king in northern Europe, James IV, whose intellect, fluency in six languages, and Burgundian courtliness were legendary. James was fatally defeated in 1513 at Flodden Field at the hands of the English. Over half the court died with their King, and Scotland was left with an infant as King: James V.

In the royal household, Lindsay as Lyon King acted as a mentor of the highest order and guardian of Scottish arms and pedigree. Thus, perhaps more than other text-makers at court, Lindsay felt a personal as well as collective responsibility for the health of the nation. His 'enterluyde played in the feaste of the epiphanne of our lorde last paste', 6 January 1540, offered a rather startling 'Declaration of the noughtiness in Religion' and suggested measures for avenues of reform – which James V was getting underway, when he died shortly after the Scottish defeat at Solway Moss in 1542. Scotland now plunged into new chaos under a foreign regent for his infant daughter. In Lindsay's revised text of 1554, the rewritten portion appears more structured, comprising two sections and an interlude between. The plot – the usual fall and rise of a young King surrounded by stock allegorical abstractions of evil and good – varies in the second section. In it, the Scottish Parliament is convened to reform the nation, and attempts to weed out the clerical representatives. However, the central effect is the breakdown of authority, seen not least in the feckless King and his weak advisors Gude Counsall and Correctioun, and even in Verity and Divyne Correctioun. In 1554, royal authority is nowhere, neither in the audience nor on stage, and Foly's scatological jokes and a sermon on fools convey the author's anguished response to the collapse of Scotland.

As Lindsay's text and his court career demonstrate, the monarchy that had achieved an all but total concentration of power in England gradually became chaotic polity in Scotland. The three greatest poets of this half-century demonstrate the decline in Scotland's royal court. On the one hand, William Dunbar represented the old Scottish tradition of allegorical panegryric, writing *The Thrissill and the Rois* to celebrate James IV's marriage to Margaret Tudor in 1503. The vivid imagery in his religious poetry sets a style for later Scottish literature: 'All fishe in flud and foull of flicht / Be myrthfull and mak melody: / All *gloria in excelsis* cry.'[17] Gawain Douglas, from this same period, wrote two works displaying the grandeur of the early Jacobean court: *The Palice of Honour*, an allegorical text steeped in Burgundian chivalry but already demonstrating the power of inventive phrase that would next mark his most famous work, his translation of Virgil's *Aeneid*. Douglas writes almost nothing, however, after 1513 and the death of the King in the Scottish defeat by the English at Flodden, a loss personally devastating to Douglas. The decline after Flodden also marks the lyrics of Sir David Lindsay. From the *Dreme*, with its vision of John Commonwealth 'all raggit, revin, and rent', to 'The Complaynt to the King', with its 'flyting' of the evil counsellors, to his imitation of Skeltonic satire in 'Testament and Complaynt of the Papyngo', to his blending of realistic history with court critique in *A Tragedie of the Cardinall*, his poem on the murder of Cardinal Beaton in 1546, Lindsay sustains a single purpose: to reform the court and prevent further breakdown for a court without a centre.

The impact of the Reformation at court

In this same period, the Tudor court witnessed its centre grow more centripetal, the magnetism of the monarch drawing in on itself more and more. The last years of Henry VIII and the diametrically opposite ideological centres in the courts of Edward VI and Mary allowed little or no political dialectic or ambiguity. Ironically, the writers in this period found their own way to write very individual texts or edit earlier ones of remarkable self-realisation. This freedom to make their own texts of subjectivity came through the increasing use of two European models, Petrarch and Luther. The influence was both ideological and stylistic, and, combined or separately, the two figures influenced the reigns of both the brother and the sister monarchs and lasted well into the reign of their little sister. If, as I shall show in the next section, the Petrarchan influence was vast and enduring, the Lutheran Reformation would transform the English court in less than three decades, Calvin influencing the majority of English courtiers comparatively late.

17 C. S. Lewis, *English Literature in the Sixteenth Century Excluding Drama* (Oxford: Clarendon Press, 1954), p. 96.

The first powerful Lutheran influence came through William Tyndale in his forceful and eloquent formulations of a new Protestant dispensation of power, especially in his ringing exchanges with Sir Thomas More. If Tyndale, following Luther, emphasised the supreme power of a monarch for a potentially chaotic society of souls made equal only by their original and continuing condition of sin, the sinner in the society had also the supreme individual option of justifying faith. In this experience of Jesus Christ, a totally subjective realisation gave renewed strength to each newly born self – including, one might add, the renewed ability to form texts. This dialectic was based on a positive inward encounter, and against the total power of a monarch now existed a self-making freedom open to all. In his last sermon before Edward VI, in Lent of 1550, Hugh Latimer enunciated these implications of Lutheran dichotomy: 'They in Christ are equal with you. Peers of the realm must needs be. The poorest plowman is in Christ equal with the greatest prince there is.'

As the Lutheran dialectic slowly gained power in Tudor England, troubling questions inevitably arose and they turned on this question of the self-discovery of the writer and the necessity of a supreme monarch to keep society from falling into chaos. What happens, for example, to the self and its text-making within the total obedience due the monarch? How can Protestant concepts of purifying the self through reading the text of texts, the Bible, be accommodated to less purifying texts that incorporated elements of art? In his majestic translations of the Bible, Tyndale followed the example of Luther and made his English language a model for the rest of English history. Humanism reaches one of its heights with these translations, for the classicist Tyndale serves both Athens and Jerusalem in language that became the fundament of that matrix of modern English, the King James Bible. If Tyndale answered the questions, others lacked his genius at synthesis, however. Although these ambiguities were hardly new (the early Greek fathers had debated them and Jerome and Augustine among the Latin fathers gave harsh answers), they would haunt Tudor and Stuart literature and culture.[18]

What was clear without question was that the Lutheran dialectic had made its mark on early Tudor society. This mark was seen not least in its generating a special self-consciousness that might begin in religion but move elsewhere in its freedom. Typically, the most powerful of these promulgators of the Lutheran dichotomy were like Tyndale: they could work a transformation, through adaptation, of the classical humanist prose tradition so recently regenerated

18 Patrick Collinson, *The Birthpangs of Protestant England: Religious and Cultural Change in the Sixteenth and Seventeenth Centuries* (New York: St. Martin's Press, 1988), p. 98.

in England and in religion make their own works of art. They reaffirmed the ancient role of language as a means not only of conveying ideology but of offering the best representations of the mysteries of human experience. In the reign of Edward VI Hugh Latimer was the chief instrument and exemplar of this transformation of style.

At once bishop and courtier (his patron the powerful evangelical Duchess of Suffolk) Latimer set for sermons in English a pattern that has endured for over 400 years. His realism, anecdotes, personalising of Scripture and sense of intimacy still animate preaching, whether on world television or in cathedrals of glass as in Los Angeles. The purpose of all preaching is to exhort and arouse the listener. For Latimer, that entailed a precise act of subjectivity. The self examines the sinner-self in order to move from despair to a saving faith in Christ that enables a new life and, where possible, action in a society itself broken by sin. To represent his process of regeneration, Latimer would often use a bold, topical metaphor. 'Faith', he exclaims in the dramatic *peroratio* of his seventh sermon before the young King, 'is a noble duchess, she hath ever her gentleman-usher before her – the confessing of sins; she hath a train after – the fruits of good works, the walking in the commandments of God.'

Fifteen years later John Foxe's myth-making account of this period in *Actes and Monuments* includes a woodcut showing Latimer preaching to a massive crowd in the garden of Westminster Palace, the young King at his window and in the next the Duke of Somerset. In this privileged place, Latimer would rail ('But how long hast thou, England, thou England?') and cajole as well as continue the verbal iconoclasm against Catholic traditions, utilising burlesque and native vernacular devices like alliteration and parison: false prayer 'is but lip-labour and vain babbling and so unworthy to be called prayer, as it was in times past used in England'; and 'the saints have not so sharp eyes to see down from heaven' because 'they be spur-blind, and sand-blind'. A transformative use of anaphora, ploce, zeugma within the balancing act of a Ciceronian syntax subverts perceived paganism with pagan modes of eloquence: 'They saw the intolerable abuses of images. They saw the perils that might ensue of going on pilgrimage... Surely, somewhat they saw.'[19]

By the time of Latimer's death, both Edward VI and Queen Mary had realised the power of text-makers at court. In fact, the young King became one. He had always been gifted in his Latin compositions, especially in his letters to his step-mother Queen Katherine Parr, and in 1546 he spoke to the French ambassador

19 *Selected Sermons of Hugh Latimer*, ed. Allan G. Chester (Charlottesville: University Press of Virginia, 1968), pp. 149, 137, 146, 194, 161, 165 and 24.

(his first public display) in highly praised Latin. His most remarkable texts were his ventures into self-expression, into a new kind of self-consciousness. He wrote a lyric on the Eucharist ('I say that Christ in flesh and bloud / Is there continually: / Unto our soule a speciall food / Taking it spiritually') that defended, against Cranmer and others, the Real Presence as his father had transubstantiation. Remarkably, he also composed a diary-like compilation on events which took place at court, during Privy Council meetings, and in the nation. It was a text he himself called a *Chronicle*.

The young King's *Chronicle* began probably as a writing exercise for his tutors: Sir John Cheke, the first Regius Professor of Greek at Cambridge, or Francis Bacon's grandfather, Sir Anthony Cooke. Cheke's own powerful tract *Hurt of Sedition*, written in Edward's reign (1549) and a model of rhetorical expertise, demonstrated the humanist truth Cheke taught his pupil Ascham and no doubt his royal pupil: control of language means a control of both the moral and spiritual life, both one's own and that of one's greater community. By no accident, then, the listing of events may be spare in the *Chronicle*, as in the boy's record of the deaths of his two Seymour uncles who had watched over him from infancy– 'Also the Lord Sudeley, Admiral of England, was condemned to death and died the March ensuing' and 'The Duke of Somerset had his head cut off upon Tower Hill between eight and nine o'clock in the morning.' They show, however, the twelve-year-old developing into an astute fifteen-year-old with ideas for reforming the government. He also has plans for the nation: 'a privy search made through all Sussex for all vagabonds, gypsies, conspirators, prophets, ill players, and such-like'.[20] No Tudor monarch had quite written texts like those of the serious young King. The distance between the father's early songs and the son's plain-style religious lyric and *Chronicle* further signals the profound change in the Tudor court and the way it viewed literature.

Part of that evolution had come from a revolutionary text by none other than an English Queen. Published only after Henry's death in the reign of her stepson, Katherine Parr's *The Lamentation of a Sinner* attests the direct influence of Luther's doctrine of justification by faith and has the self-consciously abject sub-title *Bewailing the ignorance of her blind life led in superstition*. Aware of the autobiographical texts by the French evangelical Marguerite of Navarre, the sister of Francis I, Henry VIII's last Queen had a conversion experience which she dramatises as the inward struggle each redeemed Christian must undergo.

20 *Literary Remains of King Edward the Sixth*, ed. John Gough Nichols (1857; rpt, New York, 1966), pp. 206–8. *The Chronicle and Political Papers of King Edward VI*, ed. W. K. Jordan (Ithaca, NY: Cornell University Press, 1966), pp. 10–11, 107, 37.

She wrote this text explicitly identifying herself as Henry VIII's wife, the Queen of England. That kind of consciousness – her sinful self speaking to her royal self – was original. The opening of the royal self to make a text of self for one's own court may have set an example of subjectivity for the young King Edward. The textual results were radically different, however.

Nowhere does this teenaged 'Supreme Head of the Church of England and Ireland' reveal, for example, like his stepmother, any sense of his own vulnerability or of himself as sinner. This is not true of the texts by the monarch whom the young Tudor King chose for his successor. Lady Jane Grey may have been Queen for only nine days, but her intensive humanist training became evident in texts that prepared her for a brief life. 'Live still to die', she wrote to the Lieutenant of the Tower in her little book of prayers, 'that by death you may purchase eternal life.' As Foxe records, on the scaffold she cried out 'Good people, I am come hither to die and by a law I am condemned to do the same' and, as she was wringing her hands, continued 'I do wash my hands thereof in innocence, before God and the face of you, good Christian people, this day.' In the hours before her death, she wrote three other texts in her prayer book, one in Latin, one in Greek, and one in English that said: 'If my faults deserve punishment, my youth at least and my imprudence were worthy of excuse. God and posterity will show me favour.'[21] Her assurance of survival and 'favour' appears to lie as much in the languages she was writing as in anything else.

The Edwardian court had concurred with its King. It too sought to represent the ideas, beliefs and passions of the individual self. Here the Lutheran mode of self-consciousness led to new texts, not least personal remakings of established communal texts. Although angry underground Catholics were writing outbursts like Miles Hogarde's *The Assault of the Sacrament of the Altar*, 'Gospelling' poetry flourished at court in the metrical psalms of Thomas Sternhold, Robert Crowley's *Psalter*, Thomas Becon's *Davids Harpe* and William Baldwin's *Canticles or Balades of Salomon* (in which the poet complains about the 'baudy balades of lecherous love' sung by 'idle courtyers in princes and noble mens houses'[22]). Three writers took this militantly evangelical text-making of the Edwardian court in innovative directions. Luke Shepherd parodies Skelton's subject matter and verse form to present a new type of Protestant satire; the Colin Clout figure becomes a Protestant common man as capable of religious insight as any priest or Doctor Double Ale. Robert Crowley's editing of

21 Mary Luke, *The Nine Days' Queen: A Portrait of Lady Jane Grey* (New York: W. Morrow, 1986), pp. 401–2.
22 William Baldwin, *The Canticles or Balades of Salomon Phraselyke Declared in English Metres* (London, 1549), p. 225.

The Vision of Piers Plowman exemplifies the same new method of Protestant parody and, as in his *Voyce of the Laste Trumpet* and *A New Yeres Gyfte*, creates a poet's voice warning of avarice amid the rebellions and political chaos of Edward VI's reign. From these, Crowley turns to his finest representation of the turmoil of the new Protestant court. In that national centre of power, Crowley discovers his personal ideology has been betrayed in a terrible irony – the insatiable materialism of this purported spiritual regime. His anguished personal response is to write a verse satire based on morality plays, *Philargyrie of Greate Britayne* (1551). In the title-page woodcut, a 'great Gigant' whose Greek name means 'lover of silver' is a fur-clad Protestant aristocrat who uses his Bible to rake glittering coins into a sack. Crowley here poses the crucial question from *Utopia* onward, now with special updating and parody: Where can the ideal royal counsellor be found? In a broken world, how can he be recognised by the honest text-maker and courtier? Written as another psychomachia but in the plain style for which Protestant courtiers would become notable, *Philargyrie* builds on suspense until the true King, holding the Bible in one hand and the sword in the other, drives out, urged on by Truth, the Vice-figures of the giant and the false counsellors Hypocrisy and Philaute (Self-Love).

In 1553 William Baldwin, the future editor of *A Mirror for Magistrates*, produced *Beware the Cat*, a text that experiments, like modern fiction, with types of narration and shifting points of view. A Rabelaisian combination of beast fable, satire, parody, and almost every narrative technique and genre available, *Beware the Cat* asks the central question of all such satires, posed now by Baldwin in the new frame of Reformation England. It is a question relayed by a dizzying regress of narrators and the absurdity of the plot (cats talking and stalking men): How can the naïve protagonist Streamer and the *persona* Baldwin, within themselves or as social beings, escape the enveloping irrationality, about which the cats tell Streamer? The Lutheran leap to faith in the final 'Hymn' concludes the text but typically does not solve the naïve protagonist's dilemma (and Streamer is as simple as Swift's later Gulliver): How to survive time and history in a world where cats are always around?

Tottel's moment: Wyatt and Surrey as Marian poets

Finally, the court of Queen Mary I produced little originating literature, although it did bring a new phenomenon to fruition: English Petrarchism. The first English Queen regnant in four centuries wanted her own bold and provocative signs, several of which her sister Elizabeth I took as her own.

Under Mary's cultural impetus of trying to combine the old aristocratic culture with the new Counter-Reformation reality of modern Europe, an ideology more encompassing and European than her brother's was required. She was surprisingly successful in her attempt at synthesis. The Council of Trent, for example, later based its most important decree, the mandated renovation of seminaries, on the model Queen Mary and Cardinal Pole set in the Tudor court of 1553–8.[23] As this granddaughter of Isabella of Spain knew well, Petrarchism had been the common language and style of European courts since Chaucer's visit to Italy in the 1370s. Yet the innovative features of the poetry of the 1530s and 1540s at the Tudor court, which Mary herself heard read and performed, had never found their full audience. With this concern, Mary not only brought the remains of Chaucer to Westminster Abbey but created what became 'Poet's Corner' in that most central church of the nation. Thus Tottel found his moment. He understood how, with the new Queen inheriting her father's and brother's total authority and desiring to remake the monarchy, such a movement towards Petrarchism could serve her own purposes of cultural restoration – and he could make a profit.

If the Earl of Surrey was the reigning star of *Tottel's Miscellany* for the Marian court, the texts of Sir Thomas Wyatt have remained its most enduring achievement. Wyatt had published his first lyrics in the Tudor miscellany of the 1530s, *The Courte of Venus*. These lyrics show Wyatt changing from the convivial English song poetry of the earlier Henrician court to his famous Petrarchan introspective innovations that, with Surrey's, would help to shape lyric writing during the next centuries. Like Petrarch's, Wyatt's emphasis is on the self of the writer, his pain and suffering voiced as living contradiction – 'I fear and hope, I burn and freeze like ice' – or mediated through translations like 'The long love that in my thought doth harbour' (which Surrey in turn adapted). The extravagantly solipsistic ending of 'My galley charged with forgetfulness' characterises Wyatt's legacy of Petrarchan flourish: 'And I remain despairing of the port.' Wyatt's court elegy on Thomas Cromwell (an imitation of Petrarch's on Cardinal Colonna), 'The pillar perished is whereto I leant', characterises his second legacy of Petrarchan introspection. In such lyrics as these, Wyatt naturalises the Petrarchan sonnet in English, as he introduces verse satire into the language and invents poulter's measure – one of the most popular metres in Tudor England – for two poems of introspection: his long soliloquy 'In Spain' and the monologue 'Iopas' Song' from the *Aeneid*. Readers, caught by Wyatt's

---

23 Eamon Duffy, *The Stripping of the Altars: Traditional Religion in England, 1400–1580* (New Haven, CT, and London: Yale University Press, 1992), p. 525.

personal intensity, often overlook just how innovative Wyatt was in his variety of forms and prosody. In his greatest lyrics this intensity of form and subject never slackens. The so-called Anne Boleyn poems – the ballad 'They flee from me that sometime did me seek'; the sonnet 'Whoso list to hunt, I know there is an hind'; and the epigram 'Sometime I fled the fire that me brent' – project a personal ferocity amid the intrigues and 'presse' of a terrifying court. Even Wyatt's lightness in a ballad like 'Blame not my lute for he must sound' and the song 'My lute, awake! Perform the last' must be counterpoised with a prison epigram such as 'Sighs are my food, drink are my tears / Clinking of fetters such music would crave.' Writing at the court of Henry VIII necessitated such double awareness if literature were to be made.

What Wyatt had discovered in Petrarchan texts were ready-made representations of subjectivity as intense as any Luther could want, the suffering of the 'I', the emphasis on the voice speaking, not necessarily on the cause or effect of such suffering. By no accident, Wyatt's most original adaptation of Petrarch occurred in combination with Lutheran subjectivity. This sequence of poems, *Certayne Psalmes... drawen into Englyshe Meter*, was published in 1549 under Edward VI as another kind of devotional and metrical paraphrase of Scripture. But, as Surrey's lyric praising Wyatt's paraphrases shows ('What holy grave, what worthy sepulcher / To Wyatt's Psalms should Christians then purchase?'), the late Henrician court considered Wyatt's *Psalmes* his masterpiece. Such paraphrases and especially metrical Psalms were 'the best secret weapon of the English Reformation'[24] because they synthesised public and private in a single language. Now language for acts of worship, the most explicitly prescribed of court 'circulations', could double as language for private devotions, where the self could freely confront its inward depths. In his last years, even the King who had earlier written light songs let himself be depicted in an illuminated manuscript of Psalms as a singer and reader of them. As Wyatt knew, in the Psalms, the early Tudor lyric found a frame for reaching the monarch and other courtiers through public performances of the soul.

For imitating Petrarch in his Penitential Psalms, Wyatt deliberately chose one of the Italian master's more contemplative forms. Modelled on Dante, the *capitolo* was a meditation in continuous *terza rima*, and to this form, for his actual translations, Wyatt sets up a metric counterpoint of *ottava rima* in his preface (adapted from Aretino) and narrative links. This metrical counterpoint differentiates the public frame from the David-self and his Petrarchan anguish:

24 Diarmaid MacCulloch, *Thomas Cranmer: A Life* (New Haven, CT, and London: Yale University Press, 1996), p. 618.

'I wash my bed with tears continual, / To dull my sight that it be never bolde / To stirr mye hart agayne to suche a fall.' If Wyatt's protagonist is at times 'Surprised with joy' and 'plunged up, as horse out of the mire / With stroke of spur', he is always aware of his essential condition, the self as characterised by Luther: 'For I myself, lo thing most unstable / Formed in offence, conceived in like case, / Am nothing but sin from my nativity.' It is not 'outward deeds that outward men disclose', as at court, but 'The sacrifice that the lord lykyth most', the 'spirit contrite', the 'Inward Sion, the Sion of the Ghost'. This is the perceived pattern of his life: 'thou didst lift me up to throw me down / To teach me how to know my self again'.

If Wyatt hoped that his Penitential Psalm sequence might have an audience even greater than courtiers, Henry Howard's first major lyrics – published twenty years later in *Tottel's Miscellany* – were written to gain the attention not only of the court but of King Henry himself, who could, the young Surrey knew, restore his dignity after his imprisonment at Windsor Castle. In composing these texts, Surrey exerted his greatest skills and transformed the Petrarchan language of his friend Wyatt by inventing the so-called English sonnet for one poem and, for the other, the heroic quatrain that later served him (and Thomas Gray) as elegiac vehicle. He also makes his Petrarchan lament as specific and English as possible, setting both poems at Windsor Castle, the matrix of English systems of honour. In these realistic settings – tapestries, walls, fields and festivities he had known at Windsor with his beloved Richmond – Surrey creates a personal voice. Technically, he revises the Petrarchan lyric outburst and implied narrative by subsuming these into soliloquies of self. The old *ubi sunt* theme of loss and mutability – nowhere is his friend Richmond to be found in the places they both had loved – is now identified with a specific voice lamenting a specific historical person.

Surrey's 1542 elegy on Wyatt proceeds with this same evocation of a real person in a historical setting, the English courtier in the Tudor world. The form of this extended lament is the same heroic quatrains invented to mourn the higher-ranked Richmond. The historical Wyatt becomes, in Surrey's elegy, a model for the entire Tudor court. Surrey's catalogue reads as a blazon for a new kind of hero, a text-maker who knew himself how to master writing and survive at the early Tudor court. If Surrey's elegy on Wyatt is his lyric masterpiece, his constructed subjectivity – his personal utterance voiced within a denoted historical situation – also inscribes the two books of Surrey's translation of the *Aeneid*. Here he attempts to reproduce the heroic line of Virgil in Tudor English – his most famous achievement. To represent epic language, Surrey invents a form of unrhymed iambic pentameter lines whose conversational

rhythms suit the English of a new Tudor courtier. Within such social language
Surrey brought a new and objective representation of intense subjectivity. His
new English line accommodates the painful monologue of Aeneas' retrospective of the night Troy fell (with its echoes not only for the Henrician court
but for the Marian one in which it appeared) and it heightens the anguished
love soliloquies of Dido (the abandonment of whom also fits the abandoned
Mary who read the printed text a year before her own death).

This innovation in verse form, devised for specific Tudor courts, would become the standard not only for the later English epic (especially after Milton
and those who wrote in his wake) but more immediately and pervasively for the
so-called 'blank verse' (as Gascoigne termed Surrey's line) of a drama famous
for the power of its monologues and soliloquies. Surrey's blank verse would
promote dramatic or epic interplay by providing language that registers, on the
one hand, 'the presse' of court in narrative or dramatic social 'circulations' and,
on the other, the most intense and intimate introspection, whether Hamlet's,
or the Miltonic Satan's, or the Wordsworthian hero's, or Robert Frost's farmers', or that of Wallace Stevens's speaker on a Sunday morning. For Surrey and
all the other text-makers, writing at and for the early Tudor court required
incorporating such tensions of self and court, if a text or literature of any kind
were to be made for the audience of monarch and other courtiers. Whatever the
ultimate fate of the individual text-maker, this kind of interplay, this dialectic
of history realised in a text, would give such literature at the Tudor court the
chance and, not infrequently, the power to survive it.

Chapter 9

LITERATURE AND THE CHURCH

JANEL MUELLER

This chapter addresses the advent of the English Reformation from its political inception in the 'Great Matter' of Henry VIII's divorce suit to its formal reinstatement in the first year of Elizabeth's reign. Here the phrase 'English Reformation' will have a dual reference, both institutional and textual – denoting, on the one hand, the emergent entity of an autonomous national church comprehending England, Wales and parts of Ireland, and, on the other, the literature in English that articulated, probed, contested and projected the religious claims and aspirations of this thirty-year period.

Prior to these tumultuous decades of the sixteenth century, the domain of religious adherence, faith and practices had been a Christendom imagined as universal through its obedience to the Pope, but in fact experienced much more locally, in the human associations and the sacred traditions of one's own parish church. It has long been commonplace to observe that the national Church of England began as a top-down imposition by successive Tudor sovereigns, eventually acquiring an identity that a popular majority came to embrace as its own. While accurate enough regarding the beginning and end of a sometimes ruptural, sometimes gradual, always complex process, this commonplace sheds no light on intermediate phases. Across a spectrum of recent historical scholarship, however, the English Reformation has taken interpretive shape as a series of confrontations and negotiations that effected transformations in English culture in the 1530s, 1540s and 1550s as successive political agendas appropriated and forefronted certain religious issues.[1] The force of political agendas originating with the Crown and its chief adherents is a main fact of the period.

---

1 See, for example, Susan Brigden, *London and the Reformation* (Oxford: Clarendon Press, and New York: Oxford University Press, 1989), esp. chs. 5–8, 12–13; Christopher Haigh (ed.), *The English Reformation Revisited* (Cambridge University Press, 1987), and Haigh, *English Reformations: Religion, Politics, and Society under the Tudors* (Oxford University Press, 1993), extending and revising foundational work by G. R. Elton in *Reform and Reformation, England 1509–1558* (Cambridge, MA: Harvard University Press, 1977), and *Policy and Police: The Enforcement of the Reformation in the Age of Thomas Cromwell* (Cambridge University Press,

There can be no disputing the general effectiveness of royal power deployed through new levels of organisation and centralisation in Tudor bureaucracy to enforce laws and injunctions, whether through special commissions or by more ordinary means – for example, Justices of the Peace – and to quell armed resistance when it sporadically arose.[2]

But this is not to grant that the cultural transformations wrought by the English Reformation were forcibly imposed – or could have been forcibly imposed – on the people as a whole. As we shall see, a given religious tenet or disposition acquired significance and saliency when legitimated and enforced by political authority. Yet any such tenet or disposition became culturally transformative only to the degree and in the measure that psychological, ethical and rhetorical suasion operated to make it appealing, energising, even directive in people's thoughts and lives. For the study of a past as distant as the English Reformation, literature affords the richest residue of the expressive and communicative power of language that by turns anticipates, affirms, resists or outgoes royal or parliamentary determinations in matters of religion – thus rendering the literary record significantly more indicative of the course of cultural transformation than the purely political record can be. This chapter traces crucial interrelations between literature and the Church in this cataclysmic era.

From papal supremacy to royal supremacy:
Henrician measures

Though Henry VIII had no prior intention of launching the Reformation in England, Edward Hall's chronicle, a contemporary's narration of the events of the last two decades of the reign, repeatedly depicts the King in what would become a recognisably Protestant attitude. Sorely troubled in conscience about the validity of his marriage to Catherine of Aragon, his brother Arthur's widow, Henry obsessed fearfully over Leviticus 20:21, 'If a man shall take his brother's wife, it is an unclean thing: ... they shall be childless'. Hall's report of the address that the King made to his assembled nobility and counsellors at his palace

---

1972), and by A. G. Dickens, *The English Reformation* (New York: Schocken Books, 1964), chs. 6–11.

2 The principal source is G. R. Elton, *The Tudor Revolution in Government* (Cambridge University Press, 1953); see also C. Coleman and D. R. Starkey (eds.), *Revolution Reassessed: Revisions in the History of Tudor Government and Administration* (Oxford University Press, 1986).

of Bridewell in late 1528 abounds with polarised moral terms that expressively register a divided heart and mind – or, as Henry says, 'conscience':

> Our trustie and welbeloved subjectes..., it is not unknowen to you how that we, both by Goddes provision and true and lawful inheritaunce have reigned over this realme of England almost the terme of xx. yeres... But ... if our true heire be not knowen at the time of our death, se what mischiefe and trouble shal succede to you and your children... And although it hath pleased almighty God to send us a fayre doughter of a noble woman and me begotten to our great comfort and joy, yet it hath ben told us by diverse great clerkes, that neither she is our lawfull doughter nor her mother our lawful wyfe, but that we lyve together abhominably and detestably in open adultry... Thinke you my lordes that these wordes touche not my body and soule, thinke you that these doynges do not daily and hourly trouble my conscience and vexe my spirites, yes we doubt not but that yf it wer your owne cause every man would seke remedy, when the peril of your soule and the losse of your inheritaunce is openly layd to you... These be the sores that vexe my minde, these be the panges that trouble my conscience, and for these greves, I seke a remedy.[3]

Henry wanted a legitimate son to assure the succession in the Tudor line, but his only living child was a daughter, Mary, and Catherine was past childbearing when Henry fell in love with one of her ladies-in-waiting, Anne Boleyn, in 1527. Hall records the equivocal feelings that Henry's dilemma evoked in the people: 'Some syghed and sayd nothynge, other were sory to heare the kyng so troubled in his conscience. Other that favored the quene much sorowed that this matter was now opened, and so every man spake as his hert served him' (Hall, *Triumphant Reigne*, p. 147). In the event, apart from the brief notoriety of Elizabeth Barton, the 'Maid of Kent', and her sensational prophecies of Henry's impending doom, which Hall reports (pp. 244–5), popular affection for Queen Catherine and suspicion of Anne made for slender literary response.

In his *Practice of Prelates* (1530) William Tyndale did take polemical aim against the divorce initiative and in support of Queen Catherine as part of a broadside attack on Cardinal Thomas Wolsey, the King's chief minister. But in casting Wolsey as 'this wylye wolf... and raginge see and shipwracke of all Englond' – that is, as the conniving author of a dangerously misguided

---

3 Edward Hall, *Henry VIII by Edward Hall: The Triumphant Reigne of Kyng Henry the VIII* [written between 1532 and 1548], ed. Charles Whibley (London: T. C. & E. C. Jack, 1904), pp. 145–7: subsequent references are given parenthetically in text. Other mentions of the king's anguished 'conscience' occur on pp. 151, 172, 209–10. John Foxe also transmits Hall's text of this speech in *Acts and Monuments of John Foxe*, ed. Stephen Reed Cattley, 8 vols. (London: Seeley, Burnside, and Seeley, 1843–9; rpt New York: AMS Press, 1965), 5:48–9.

initiative – Tyndale had the facts the wrong way around.[4] Despite Wolsey's best influence-wielding, Henry's attempts to secure a papal annulment of his marriage were doomed, for Pope Clement VII was Queen Catherine's nephew. Wolsey was summarily deprived of his vast powers and died shortly thereafter in disgrace. A less ambiguous issue than Henry's divorce would be required to combine political power and rhetorical suasion in the transformative cultural dynamic of reformation. Thomas Cranmer first came to the King's notice and favour with his suggestion that a divorce from the Queen be sought – necessarily in the church courts. But however many theological faculties of Europe would declare on Henry's behalf – and Hall documents their number at some length (Hall, *Triumphant Reigne*, pp. 185–95) – still a divorce would be of no use if the Queen were to appeal to the Pope as supreme arbiter. The King's 'Great Matter' required that English jurisdictional authority be free and independent of Rome, both to carry out the divorce and to debar any parties to it from seeking redress from any purported higher power beyond the borders of England.

Wolsey's protégé and close associate, Thomas Cromwell, addressed the King's predicament in a proactive plan. He set a trusted group of humanist lawyers and clerics to work scanning ancient sources for precedents and rationales that could vindicate the supreme authority and autonomy of the English crown – and, by extension, of the English church – against any foreign power. For Cromwell's purposes, the apex of these scholarly labours was the *Collectanea satis copiosa* (Sufficiently Plentiful Compilation) prepared by Thomas Cranmer and Edward Foxe and presented to Henry in 1530. Drawing on the Old Testament, the Church Fathers, late medieval jurists, Anglo-Saxon laws, English histories and chronicles and various other authorities, this manuscript compilation radically recast the relation of royal and ecclesiastical power. Ever since the Anglo-Saxons converted to Christianity, so the *Collectanea* argued, the kings of England had possessed secular imperium and spiritual supremacy like their counterparts, the later Roman emperors; what was more, the English church always had been a separate province of Christendom subject only to royal jurisdiction, and the papacy had once recognised it as such.

In late 1529 Henry convened what came to be known as the 'Reformation Parliament', concurrent with Wolsey's arraignment under a charge of *praemunire* – that is, disloyalty to the English crown, committed by acknowledging

---

4 W[illiam] T[yndale], *The practyse of prelates: Whether the Kinges grace maye be separated from hys quene / because she was his brothers wyfe* (Marburg: n.p., 1530), unpaginated; section entitled 'The practyse of oure tyme'.

papal supremacy and punished mainly by forfeiture. In 1531 the King extended the threat of *praemunire* charges to the entire English clergy, triggering their wholesale suit for royal pardon and their payment of a huge fine. As for the Parliament, its epoch-making legislative programme kept it in session, with intermittent recesses, until 1536; the years 1532–6 witnessed its greatest activity. In May 1532 Cromwell exploited parliamentary hostility to the clergy and obtained passage of the following statutes: the clergy would henceforth require the King's permission to assemble in Convocation as well as his assent to enact new canon laws; a royal commission would review all existing canon laws and those found prejudicial to royal prerogative would be annulled. Sir Thomas More, the preeminent Catholic lay traditionalist, instantly resigned his seat in Parliament. The death of the traditionalist Archbishop of Canterbury, William Warham, in the same year, enabled Henry's appointment of Thomas Cranmer to the highest ecclesiastical office of the realm. Late January 1533 saw Cranmer's confirmation as Warham's successor and then the secret marriage of Henry VIII and Anne Boleyn.

As the King's chief minister, Cromwell now moved to make Henry and Anne's marriage unassailable by means of the first legal instrument of England's break with Rome – the Act in Restraint of Appeals, which Parliament ratified in April 1533. Citing the authority of 'sundry old authentic histories and chronicles' – a nod to the *Collectanea* – the act's preamble roundly affirmed that England was 'an empire' governed by 'one supreme head and king'. Henry's imperial mandate rested in his 'whole and entire power' to govern his subjects without interference from 'any foreign princes or potentates'. It further entailed the independence of the English church under the independent English crown, and still further implied that the crown had the power to take back from the church what it had originally granted – for example, the earliest monastic foundations. Without explicit reference to Queen Catherine's case, this act terminated all appeals to papal authority, directing these to be presented thereafter in English church courts, and referring any appeal naming the King to the upper house of the clergy in Convocation. Yet, for all of its sweeping reformulations, the revolutionary logic of the Act in Restraint of Appeals had a paradox at its core. While the act itself asserted that the royal supremacy was God-ordained – was, in effect, a divine right – the passage of the act by parliamentary vote signified that the people had given the supremacy to Henry through their representatives. With time this paradox would have the effect of strengthening the power of Parliament in relation to Crown prerogatives, for both Mary and Elizabeth would have to resort to Parliament's agency: the one, in order to divest herself of the supremacy; the other, in order to reassume it.[5] The immediate implication, however, was to exalt Henry's sole, supreme sovereignty as King of England and his exclusive claims to his subjects' obedience.

While parliament debated and the bishops in Convocation found Henry's and Catherine's marriage invalid, Archbishop Cranmer annulled the marriage, proclaiming the validity of Henry's and Anne Boleyn's union in May 1533. Although popular sentiment lay strongly with the disavowed and disgraced Catherine, Anne – already six months pregnant – was proclaimed and displayed as Queen in a lavish public spectacle on 1 June. In the longest narrative sequence in his account of Henry VIII's last decades, Hall details the 'ryche pageaunt full of melodye and song' that presented Anne with a tripartite golden ball, hailing her as the favourite of Pallas, Juno and Venus in her 'wysdome, ryches and felicitie' and then exalting her far more highly as a living instance of fidelity to Scripture, with a gift of gold and silver tablets engraved with verses from Canticles and the Psalms: *'Veni amica coronaberis'* ('Come, my beloved, thou shalt be crowned'), *'Domine directe gressus meos'* ('Lord, direct my way') and *'confido in domine'* ('I trust in the Lord'). Princess Elizabeth was born in early September.[6]

Parliament further demonstrated its utility as an instrument for advancing royal power at the expense of the Pope and the Church (as well as Anne's claims over Catherine) by passing a series of acts that reinforced the break with Rome. The Succession Act of 1534 turned Cranmer's judgements into statute, legitimating Queen Anne and her issue, making it high treason to dispute Henry's title to the crown or his marriage with Anne. The Act for the Submission of the Clergy and the Dispensations Act, also of 1534, reasserted Henry's royal supremacy and extended lay powers of judgement in ecclesiastical cases, licences and dispensations, in particular placing under royal supervision monasteries that had claimed papal privilege. This same session saw the relaxing of *De haeretico comburendo*, the mandating of death by burning for anyone confirmed as a heretic, by which the Crown and Parliament in 1401–14 had sought to extinguish the menace of Lollardy (Gee and Hardy, *Documents*, pp. 133–7). The immediate implication of this momentous statutory turnaround was to

5 For the text of the act, see Henry Gee and William John Hardy (eds.), *Documents Illustrative of English Church History* (London: Macmillan, 1896), pp. 187–95. The alleged evidence for papal acknowledgement of English royal supremacy was Pope Eleutherius's supposed letter (*c*.187) to the mythical King Lucius I of Britain, addressing him as 'vicar of God' within his realm. The *Collectanea*, preserved as British Library, MS Cotton Cleopatra E. VI, fols. 16–135, is discussed by Alistair Fox and John Guy, *Reassessing the Henrician Age: Humanism, Politics, and Reform, 1500–1550* (Oxford University Press, 1986), pp. 151–78.

6 Hall, *Triumphant Reigne*, pp. 229–47; quotations at p. 235.

permit open speaking in England against the Pope's authority – with rapid consequences for reformist preaching and printing.

A complementary Treason Act made it high treason to rebel against or threaten, even verbally, the royal family or to deny their titles, or to call the King a heretic, schismatic, tyrant, infidel or usurper. Parliament's crowning Act of Supremacy of 1534 ascribed all-encompassing temporal and spiritual powers to the King, enjoining that he 'be taken, accepted and reputed the only supreme head in earth of the Church of England called *Anglicana Ecclesia*, and shall have and enjoy annexed and united to the imperial crown of this realm as well . . . all honours, dignities, preeminences, jurisdictions [and] authorities . . . to the said dignity of supreme head of the same Church belonging and appertaining' (*Documents*, pp. 243–4).[7] For his silence when charged to swear to the Act of Supremacy, More went to prison in the Tower of London. This cumulative judicial and legislative record marks the first high point of the efforts of Cromwell, Cranmer and their supporters to restructure the institution of the English church – thereby to free Henry from his impasse with the Pope as well as to promote the cause of Queen Anne for their own reformist purposes. For their part, the Anglo-Irish members of the Irish Parliament were equally compliant, abolishing papal authority in 1536. Henry assumed the titles of 'King of Ireland' and 'Head of the Church in Ireland' in 1541.[8]

The Act in Restraint of Appeals and the Act of Supremacy laid the foundations of an autonomous national church coextensive with the boundaries and jurisdictions of the sovereign political state. Under Henry VIII, Edward VI, Mary I and Elizabeth I, the successive exercise of royal supremacy inaugurated, recast, dismantled and refounded the institution that became the 'Church of England'. However, Henry's repudiation of papal authority could only eventuate in a national church and an attendant sense of national identity if these radical measures met with popular compliance. And they did. At its inception, the royal supremacy silhouetted the figures of More, Bishop John Fisher and the London Carthusians as a handful of martyred resisters against a backdrop of general acquiescence – or at least, quiescence – in England and in the parts of Ireland under Anglo-Irish control. Beyond this, a uniquely Welsh fervour for Henry VIII as the sovereign who had spent his childhood and youth among them seems to have prompted the premier Welsh poet of the age, Lewis

---

7 On the 1534 parliamentary session and its context see G. R. Elton, *The Tudor Constitution*, 2nd edn (Cambridge University Press, 1982), pp. 364–5; John Guy, *Tudor England* (Oxford University Press, 1988), pp. 133–6.
8 Elton, *Reform and Reformation*, pp. 208–10.

Morgannwg, to address the Supreme Head of the Church and hail his triumph
over the Pope and other enemies in rhapsodic verse:

> Helmsman, defender of the faith,
> Head under Christ, chief in Christendom,
> Head of the church in thy island, the pinnacle hast thou attained,
> Head of the faith, and always its defender.[9]

Stephen Gardiner, Bishop of Winchester, who would become the ranking
exponent of English religious traditionalism and reunion with Rome in Mary's
reign, likewise declared forthright support of the royal supremacy in 1535.
His confident phraseology, however, is freighted with legalistic redundancy
and over-specificity that bespeak some defensiveness about this supposedly
natural concept:

> Surely I see no cause / why any man shoulde be offended / that the kinge is
> called the headde of church of Englande / rather than the headde of the realme
> of Englande ... seinge the churche of Englande consisteth of the same sortes
> of people at this daye / that are comprised in this worde realme / of whom / the
> kinge is called the headde: shall he not / beinge called the headde of the realme
> of Englande / be also the heade of the same / when they are named the churche
> of Englande? ... / the churche of Englande / ... / is iustlie to be called the
> churche / because it is a communion of christen people / and of the place / it
> is to be named / the churche of Englande/[10]

Besides Gardiner, other ranking ecclesiastics who published tracts and sermons
in favour of Henry's royal supremacy included Edward Foxe, Richard Sampson,
Cuthbert Tunstall, John Stokesley and Edmund Bonner.[11] The sole dissenting
pen was that of Reginald Pole, Henry's cousin, who would return to England

---

9   'Llywiawdr, ymddiffyniawdr ffydd, / Penn dan Grist, penna dan Gred, / Penn eglwys d'ynys,
    pinagl ystynnaist, / Penn ffydd a ffaunydd yr amddiffynnaist.' Cited in Glanmor Williams,
    Wales and the Reformation (Cardiff: University of Wales Press, 1997), p. 113.
10 Stephen Gardiner, 'The Oration of True Obedience', in *Obedience in Church and State: Three
    Political Tracts by Stephen Gardiner*, ed. Pierre Janelle (Cambridge University Press, 1930),
    pp. 93, 95. Gardiner published the Latin text of *De vera obedientia in* 1535; the English
    translation, which Janelle agrees is John Bale's work, appeared in 1553.
11 See, variously, [Edward Foxe], *Opus eximium, de vera differentia regiae potestatis et ecclesiasticae*
    (London, 1534), Eng. version entitled *The true dyfferens between the regall power and the
    ecclesiasticall power*, trans. Henry, Lord Stafford (London, [1548]); *Oratio, qua docet, anglos
    regiae dignitati ut obediant* ... (London, [1535?]); *A letter written by Cuthbert Tunstall and J.
    Stokesley somtime byshop of London, sent vnto R. Pole, cardinall* (London, 1560); *The seditious
    and blasphemous oration of cardinal Pole intytuled the defence of the eclesiastical vnitye*, trans. F.
    Wythers (London, [1560]).

after decades of exile and attempt to reverse the course of Reformation as cardinal and papal legate under Queen Mary.[12]

A sizeable output of vernacular literature secured a hold in popular consent for the royal supremacy and its widespread, successive alterations in the Church of England by forefronting a complex of themes and compellingly representing these as beliefs and attitudes necessary to being English. Obedience to the sovereign was the chief theme, grounded in such proof-texts as 1 Peter 2:17, 'Fear God; honour the king', and exemplified by order and hierarchy as the founding principles of social life, stability and well-being. No other theme is so extensively treated in the religious literature of the English Reformation. On the historical evidence, the absence of religious wars like those that ravaged France and the Netherlands in the sixteenth century and of unmanageable local armed rebellion like the Peasants' Revolt (1525) and the later Münster uprising (1534) in Germany suggests an underlying consonance between the behaviour of the people and the ceaseless admonitions to obey one's sovereign, to sustain cosmic order.

It is, however, of particular literary significance that William Tyndale's widely circulated tract, *The Obedience of a Christian Man* (1528), anticipated the Act of Supremacy by nearly a decade. John Foxe reports that Anne Boleyn gave a copy to Henry, who declared this a book for him and all kings to read. To Tyndale, obedience was one half – the indispensable, preparatory half – of the message of the Bible, to be reconfirmed after the experience of saving faith in a life of continuing obedience. The *Obedience* exhorts the clergy to undertake a two-step programme of religious education in England. First they are to

> teach the people Gods lawe, and what obedience God requireth of vs vnto father and mother, mayster, Lord, King, and all superiours, and wyth what frendly loue he commaundeth one to love an other. And teach them to know that naturall vename, and byrth poison, which moueth the very harts of vs to rebell against the ordinaunces and will of God, and proue that no man is righteous in the sight of God, but that we are all damned by the lawe.

Then, when the people have been 'meeked' and 'feared … wyth the lawe', 'teache them the testament, and promises which God hath made vnto vs in Christ, and how much he loueth us in Christ; and teache them the principles, and the ground of the fayth, and what the sacraments signifie, and then shall the spirite worke wyth thy preaching, and make them feele'.[13] Tyndale's phrasal

---

12 See Janelle's Introduction to Gardiner, *Obedience in Church and State*, pp. xiv, xxi.
13 William Tyndale, *Obedience of a Christen man, and how Christen rulers ought to gouerne*, in *The whole workes of W. Tyndall, John Frith, and Doct. Barnes* (London, 1573), p. 107.

catalogues and his repetitions of verb phrases (teach, and prove, teach them, teach them) and key nouns (God, law, Christ) produce an emphatic rhythm that trains attention on the prime subject, 'The obedience of Subiects vnto Kinges, Princes, and rulers'. This Tyndale introduces with the era's ubiquitous proof-text for divine right, Romans 13, which he translates thus:

> Let every soule submit him selfe vnto the auctorite of the hyer powers. For there is no power but of God. The powers that be / are ordeyned of God. Whosoever therefore resysteth the power / resisteth the ordinaunce of God. And they that resist / shall receave to them selfe damnacion. For rulars are not to be feared for good workes / but for evyll.

Stark clausal antitheses present key precepts ('there is no power but of God', 'rulars are not to be feared for good workes / but for evyll') while soundplay on r's and s's compounds with the rhetorical figure of *gradatio* to shape and instil a solemn admonition – that resisting power entails resisting God's ordinance, and resisting God's ordinance entails receiving one's own damnation. Significantly Tyndale completes this topic by disparaging popes and bishops, monks and friars, as so many illusory authorities in comparison with Henry's divine right and royal supremacy:

> No person, neither any degree may be exempt from thys ordinaunce of God. Neither can the profession of Monkes and Fryers, or any thyng that the pope or Byshops can laye for themselues, except them . . . Here is no man except, but all soules must obey . . . The kyng is, in thys worlde, without lawe, & may at his lust doe right or wrong, & shall geue acomptes, but to God onely.
>
> (*Whole Workes*, pp. 109, 111–12)

In the event, among many other sermons and tracts, the authorised *Books of Homilies* published in Edward's reign (July 1547) and Elizabeth's (August 1563), through their many refinements and enlargements, would implement Tyndale's programme for religious education in England, centring around faith and its fruits. In 1547, the only fruit to draw separate, special treatment in 'three Parts' would be 'Good Order and Obedience to Rulers and Magistrates', supplemented by a prolix new homily 'in six Parts . . . against Disobedience and Wilful Rebellion' in 1571, after the suppressing of the Northern Rebellion.[14] As already glimpsed in Tyndale's antitheses and elaborations, a particular dynamic characterises these texts. The earlier Edwardian homily exhorting to

---

14 See the editorial preface, census of editions, and notes on variant readings in John Griffiths (ed.), *The Two Books of Homilies Appointed to be Read in Churches* (Oxford University Press, 1859), pp. vii–xxvi, xlvii–lxxx.

obedience elicits a later Elizabethan homily, more than twice as long, against disobedience. What begins as a positive emphasis – obedience rightly owing to the sovereign – inevitably gradates into negative reflexes and repercussions. By a process now thoroughly familiar from recent studies of national formation, identification with a collective entity – here, the King and Church of England – proceeds by declaring and defining an opposite, or 'other', that must be reviled and rejected.[15] At its narrowest in the English Reformation era, this 'other' is the authority of the papacy, including its alleged vices and stratagems. Quickly, however, the scope of this 'other' enlarges to clerical orders and traditional beliefs and practices undergirded by papal authority – for example, the begging and preaching of friars, the sale of indulgences, belief in purgatory, the cult of the saints and their relics. At its most inclusive and its most destructive, what the English Reformation 'othered' was anything with traditional sacred significance – church altars, stained-glass windows, rood-screens, the clergy's vestments, the sign of the cross in baptism, the wafer consecrated and distributed by the officiating cleric. Yet, as we shall be seeing, this violently disjunctive cultural dynamic does not ultimately engender the most enduring literary legacy of the Church of England in the Reformation era.

Although a negative extreme of the dynamic of reformation is reached in the iconoclasm and polemical violence of Edward VI's reign, there is no steady, systematic pattern of intensification to be traced in preceding rhetorical ambits of force and counter-force. As early as February 1529 Simon Fish circulated his *Supplication for the Beggars*, employing heaps of nouns and verb phrases, intermixed with statistics on taxes, rents and land values, to call upon Henry to exercise his royal authority against 'the rauinous wolues going in herdes clothing, deuouring the flocke, the Bisshoppes, Abbottes, Priours, Deacons, Archedeacons, Suffraganes, Prestes, Monkes, Chanons, Freres, Pardoners and Somners'. Fish implores the King to punish the moral laxity of the clergy and religious orders, to turn the monasteries into hospitals for the lepers, the lame and the famished of the realm, and to expose the 'ypocrasie' of belief in purgatory and prayers for the souls of the dead. He does not name but purports to speak for 'many men of greate litterature and iudgement' in declaring that 'there is no purgatory, but it is a thing inuented by the couitousnesse of the

---

15 See Claire McEachern, *The Poetics of English Nationhood, 1590–1612* (Cambridge University Press, 1996), pp. 5–33, remarking (p. 7) on the 'xenophobic force of English nationhood'; and Linda Colley, *Britons: Forging the Nation, 1707–1837* (New Haven: Yale University Press, 1992), ch. 1, on the insistent eighteenth-century characterisation of Britain as a Protestant nation, which muted recognition of local and regional differences while forefronting differences with the countries of Catholic Europe.

spiritualtie, onely to translate all kingdomes from other princes vnto theim, and there is not one word spoken of hit in al holy scripture'. As in Tyndale's prose, an alert sounded in brief, reiterated antitheses gives way to rhetorically linked, serial clauses that perform a stepwise procedure. In the following passage from Fish, the links are the 'ifs', and the procedure is a *reductio ad absurdum* of papal exactions for pardons (and, it seems, of purgatory as well):

> If there wer a purgatory, And also if that the pope with his pardons for money may deliuer one soule thens; he may deliuer him as wel without money: if he may deliuer one, he may deliuer a thousand: yf he may deliuer a thousand, he may deliuer theim all, and so destroy purgatory. And then is he a cruell tyraunt without all charite, if he kepe theim there in pryson and in paine till men will giue him money.[16]

Fish serves Henry with a frontal challenge: 'where is your swerde, power, crowne, and dignite become that shuld punisshe (. . . euen as other men are punisshed) . . . this sinfull generacion? where is theire obedience become, that shulde be vnder your hyghe power yn this mater? ys not al to-gither translated and exempt from your grace vnto theim? yes, truely' (Fish, *Supplicacyon*, p. 7). The tract ends with an evocatively rhythmed imagining of a reformed England brought into being by the King's just actions that pursues its everyday rounds of life in good order, stability and prosperity. Fish's lavish use of anaphora – identical clausal beginnings, here, with future-tense verbs (Then shall . . . Then shall) – compounds with an expressive sequence of homoioptoton, or similar word and sentence endings (decrease, cease, increased, increase, preached). The result is a nearly incantatory assurance that well-being will ensue here, and here, and there, and there, and everywhere in the realm – if Henry will but assert his due supremacy and energise his people:

> Then shall, aswell the nombre of oure forsaid monstruous sort, as of the baudes, hores, theues, and idell people, decreace. Then shall these great yerely exaccions cease. Then shall not youre swerde, power, crowne, dignite, and obedience of your people, be translated from you. Then shall the idell people be set to werke. Then shall matrimony be moche better kept. Then shal the generation of your people be encreased. Then shall your comons encrease in richesse. Then shall the gospell be preached. Then shall none begge our almesse from vs. Then shal we haue ynough, and more then shall suffice vs; whiche shall be the best hospitall that euer was founded for vs. Then shall we daily pray to god for your most noble estate long to endure.   (Fish, *Supplicacyon*, pp. 14–15)

16 Simon Fish, *A supplicacyon for the beggers, Written about the Year 1529 by Simon Fish*, ed. Frederick J. Furnivall, Early English Text Society, extra series, 13 (London: Trübner, 1871), pp. 1–2, 11–12.

Also in 1529, Thomas More undertook a tactical and literary counter-offensive in a tract entitled *The Supplication of Souls . . . against The Supplication of the Beggars*. Ten times as long as Fish's original, More's tract disputes Fish's statistics, massively alleges the falsity of his accusations of the immorality and venality of the spiritual orders, denies that papal and clerical authority threaten that of the King and Parliament, and charges Fish with wanting to bring the so-called 'gospel' of Luther and Tyndale into England, thus fostering heresy and sedition. Thomas More climactically pits against Fish's vision of a reformed, present-day England the haunting, voluble pleadings of dead English souls in purgatory, who ask to be remembered and relieved in their torments by the prayers that the living can provide for them by alms and by extra payments for the services of the clergy:

> If euer ye lay syk and thought the nyght long / & longed sore for day whyle euery howre semed longer than fyue: bethynk you then what a long nyght we sely soulys endure / that ly slepelesse / restlesse / burnyng / and broylyng in the dark fyre one long nyght of many days / of many wekys / and sum of many yeres to gether . . . Thynk how sone ye shall cum hether to vs: thynk what great grefe and rebuke wolde then your vnkyndnes be to you: what cumfort on the contrary part when all we shall thank you: what help ye shall haue here of your good sent hether . . . Now dere frendys remember how nature & crystendom byndeth you to remember vs . . . so mote god make your ofsprynge after remember you: so god kepe you hens or not long here: but brynge you shortely to that blysse / to whych for our lordys loue help you to brynge vs / and we shall set hand to help you thyther to vs.[17]

As early, then, as the opening of the 'Reformation Parliament', the issue of the royal supremacy becomes the rhetorical and imaginative occasion for Fish's and More's opposed constructions of English community. Fish evokes a godly, sober commonwealth of the here and now, reformed and energised by equity and social action that benefit the living; More conjures an extended kinship that obligates the living to remember and relieve the torments of the dead, binding both in supernatural bonds of sin, mortality and need for salvation. Conceivably the ongoing contests between reformers and traditionalists might have been contained within the thrust and counterthrust of their own copious polemic – as seems to happen in the foregoing exchange between Fish and More.

But a broader framework for such competing visions as these requires to be sought in what, by the 1520s and 1530s, was becoming a combinatory cultural

17 *The supplycacyon of soulys Made by syr Thomas More . . . Agaynst the supplycacyon of beggars*, ed. Frank Manley, Germain Marc'hadour, Richard Marius and Clarence H. Miller, in *Complete Works of St Thomas More*, vol. 7 (New Haven, CT: Yale University Press, 1990), pp. 225, 228.

dynamic of English religious reform. The top-down implications of the Act in Restraint of Appeals and the Act of Supremacy were ruptural and revolutionary, and not merely so in voiding papal authority over the laity as well as the clergy and monastics and their jurisdictions and properties. Also voided was the papal warrant for the comprehensive system of traditional religious practices by which the living might transfer to the dead pardons and alleviations from the so-called 'treasury of merits' – masses for the souls of the deceased, prayers and candles offered to the saints as intercessors, pilgrimages to the shrines of the saints' relics, all of these anchored in the belief in purgatory. Such abrogation of many of the central daily practices of popular Catholic religion was certainly not an effect that Henry VIII had envisaged, much less sought, when he broke with Rome.

Old faith, new learning: Henrician contestations

In the early 1530s Hugh Latimer, a Cambridge graduate, a supporter of the King's divorce, and the man who under Henry and Edward would become the most celebrated preacher of reform in England, began a vigorous sermon campaign against 'pickpurse purgatory', 'this monster purgatory' and its affiliated religious practices. Latimer's racy colloquialisms and fiery zeal brought to a populace selectively acquainted with the Gospels a native analogue of Jesus' chastisement of the hypocrisy of the Pharisees by calling them 'whited sepulchres' or his tongue-lashing and expelling of the money-changers in the Temple at Jerusalem. Latimer's iconoclastic challenge provoked at least as much public outcry as public interest, eliciting the charge that he was spreading 'new learning' – that is, heresy.[18] Nonetheless, he was the Lenten preacher at court in 1534, and was appointed Bishop of Worcester in 1535. At the opening of the Convocation of the English clergy concurrent with the Parliament of 1536, he delivered a provocative Latin sermon calling for the replacement of popular religious practices by frequent preaching and sound reading matter to instruct the laity. Yet this same Parliament witnessed the arraignment and execution of Queen Anne Boleyn, an advocate of the 'new learning', as a faithless wife and betrayer of the King.

18 See two studies by Allan G. Chester, 'The "New Learning": A Semantic Note', *Studies in the Renaissance* 2 (1955), 139–47, and *Hugh Latimer: Apostle to the English* (Philadelphia: University of Pennsylvania Press, 1954); also, N. H. Keeble, '"Take away preaching, and take away salvation": Hugh Latimer, Protestantism, and Prose Style', in *English Renaissance Prose: History, Language, and Politics*, ed. Neil Rhodes (Tempe, AZ: Medieval and Renaissance Texts and Studies, 1997), pp. 57–74.

The mid and later 1530s were a fractious era, with Henry and his chief ministers inciting both sides in the fray over religion. On the one hand, Cranmer and
the leading traditionalists among the bishops, John Longland, John Stokesley
and Stephen Gardiner, concurred in banning contentious preaching for a year
starting at Easter 1534 – an ostensible check to Latimer – and Henry would
issue his own brief against contentious preaching in January 1536. Preachers
were to uphold the royal supremacy and denounce the Pope's power, but were
to preach 'neyther with nor against purgatory, honoring of saynts, that priests
may have wives, that faith only justifieth; to go on pilgrimages, to forge miracles, . . . considering that thereupon no edification can ensue in the people, but
rather occasions of talk and rumour, to their great hurt and damage'.[19] On the
other hand, during the summer of 1535, Henry authorised a royal visitation of
smaller monasteries to investigate the use of relics in promoting pilgrimages
and the cult of the saints; between 1537 and 1540, this initiative became a full-
scale process of dissolving the larger monasteries, dismantling their shrines and
expropriating their properties for the Crown.

In the devotional register, too, there were symptoms of severe conflict. In
1534 William Marshall issued an English primer with a preface sharply critical
of the cult of the saints and the treasury of merits; the text itself made heavy
use of Luther's writings and contained neither prayers for the dead nor the
litany of the saints. While his second edition of 1535 restored the litany and
the '*Dirige*', Marshall's new preface was even more stridently contemptuous of
prayers for the dead. Another reformed primer issued by Robert Redman in
1535, which like Marshall's two primers claimed to print by royal privilege,
omitted all the pardon rubrics stating the exculpatory value of specific prayers
and devoted its preface to hailing 'elect princes, and true pastours' who now
have been inspired by God 'to purge the fylthynes of false doctrine'.[20]

By the mid-1530s the 'othering' dynamic that abounds in the writings of
Tyndale, Latimer and many other reformers had conjoined the issue of pretended papal power with belief in purgatory and the efficacy of alms, masses
and prayers for the souls of the dead frequently enough to prompt More to
counter with two further, voluminous diatribes detailing recent heresies and

19 Gilbert Burnet, *History of the Reformation*, 1850 edn, 2: ccxlvii, cited in Eamon Duffy, *The
Stripping of the Altars: Traditional Religion in England, 1400–1580* (New Haven, CT: Yale
University Press, 1992), p. 381.
20 Marshall's *A Goodly Prymer in Englyshe, Newly Corrected and Printed* (London, 1535), collated
with the 1534 edition, *A Prymer in Englyshe, with certeyn prayers & godly meditations*, was
reprinted in [E. Burton (ed.),] *Three Primers Put Forth in the Reign of Henry VIII* (Oxford University Press, 1848), pp. 1–302; on Marshall and Redman, see Charles C. Butterworth, *The English Primers, 1529–1545* (Philadelphia: University of Pennsylvania Press, 1953), pp. 70–91.

vindicating traditional religion in England. The earlier is *A Dialogue . . . Wherein Be Treated Divers Matters, As of the Veneration and Worship of Images and Relics, Praying to Saints, and Going on Pilgrimage. With Many Other Things Touching the Pestilent Sect of Luther and Tyndale* (1530 – more commonly and colourlessly known as *A Dialogue concerning Heresies*) and *The Confutation of Tyndale's Answer* (1532–3).[21] Fault-lines beyond the control of any authority were opening ever more perceptibly in English religious culture, taking shape in active support of reforms in the church and a heightened role for the laity. As symptomatised in the relaxing of capital penalties on heretics that opened the way for pope-bashing, England's religious climate – while traditionalist overall – contained currents of reform that conjoined and compounded force in the 1530s. Among these, Lollardy, long since driven underground without being extinguished, was a century and a half old; newer currents, less than two decades old, were Erasmian humanism and Lutheranism.[22]

Lollardy was the unique English example of a heresy with learned university roots that had successfully become a popular movement, adhering (though often in crudely polemical reformulations) to the teachings of John Wyclif. In its own time and in the Reformation era, the most revolutionary Lollard tenets were insistence on a literate laity and on open access to the Bible in English as the foundations of a vernacular English literature. Other key tenets included redefinition of the 'saints' as the 'true men and women' recognisable by right belief and upright life; disparagement of celibacy in favour of the married state; denial of papal supremacy and transubstantiation; rejection of pilgrimages, the worship of saints and images, purchased pardons or other papally authorised means of remitting punishment for sin; and a wholesale condemnation of the institution of the church and its clergy as betraying the example of Christ, who had set care for the poor and the preaching of God's truth at the centre of his ministry. The Midlands and London were particular sites of an underground Lollardy. Among all their tenets, unrestricted lay access to the Bible in English would remain a uniquely stymied objective.[23]

21 For the full texts of these two works, see *The Complete Works of St Thomas More*, gen. eds. Louis L. Martz, Richard S. Sylvester and Clarence H. Miller, 15 vols. (London, and New Haven, CT: Yale University Press, 1963–97), vol. 6, Parts 1 and 2; and vol. 8, Parts 1, 2 and 3. On More's qualities and tactics as a controversialist, see Janel Mueller, *The Native Tongue and the Word: Developments in English Prose Style, 1380–1580* (University of Chicago Press, 1984), pp. 201–25.

22 On these convergent currents, see Dickens, *English Reformation*, chs. 2, 4.

23 See Steven Justice, 'Lollardy', in *The Cambridge History of Medieval English Literature*, ed. David Wallace (Cambridge University Press, 1999), pp. 662–89; Margaret Aston, *Faith and Fire: Popular and Unpopular Religion 1350–1600* (London: Hambledon Press, 1993), chs. 2, 3; Anne Hudson, *The Premature Reformation* (Oxford University Press, 1988); John A. F.

Archbishop Thomas Arundel's Oxford Constitutions of 1408–9 aimed to quash the Lollards by prohibiting the possession, reading or reproduction of any excerpt of vernacular Scriptures by any person of any rank, unless a bishop gave express permission. This absolute prohibition had no analogue in Western Christendom. In practice, however, the result was less than complete deprivation, for portions of vernacular Scripture circulated in works of devotion and meditation written for the pious laity, ranging across a spectrum of genres. John Fisher's sermons on the penitential Psalms, which went through several editions, demonstrate the deeply scriptural basis of his spirituality and theology.[24] In this regard Fisher contrasted sharply with his co-religionist More, who opposed Bible-reading by the laity, but on every other issue stood together with Fisher in refusing the Oath of Supremacy, for which both men were beheaded in 1535 as traitors to the Crown. A wealth of scriptural echoes and allusions, typically unidentified by book, chapter or verse, also distinguishes the several publications of Richard Whitford, a Brigittine monk of Syon House – especially his englishing of Thomas à Kempis's *Imitation of Christ* (1530). Finally and most pervasively, after about 1530 the traditional primers – or devotional books compiled for lay use during divine service in Latin – increasingly included portions of vernacular Scripture.[25]

While the Ten Commandments and the Lord's Prayer were staples of this pre-Reformation body of texts, the preponderant English scriptural content consisted of excerpts from the Psalms. Repeated reading and recitation of these highly wrought lyric texts gave practice in the sometimes joyous, often penitential and always God-dependent mode of their imputed, inspired author – thus forming the devout user into a generically devout soul. Modelling the true Christian by tracing the heights and depths of spiritual experience, the first-person utterances of King David gave access to devotional intensity and immediacy that all ranks of the social hierarchy could readily make their own. Excerpts from Psalm 130 ('*De profundis*') in Thomas Godfray's *A Primer in English* (1534–5) will illustrate:

> Lorde / here thou me: Let thy eares be attente unto my depe desyre.
> If thou shuldest loke narowly upon our wyckednesses (o lorde)
>   lorde / who might abyde the?
> But there is mercy with the: and therfore arte thou worshypped.

Thomson, *The Later Lollards, 1414–1520* (London: Oxford University Press, 1965); Brigden, *London and the Reformation*, ch. 2.

24 See Richard Rex, *The Theology of John Fisher* (Cambridge University Press, 1991).

25 See Helen C. White, *Tudor Books of Private Devotion* (Madison: University of Wisconsin Press, 1951); Butterworth, *English Primers*.

I abyde the lorde / my soule abydeth him: and I tarye lokynge up
alwaye for thy promyses.
My soule wayteth for the Lorde: as desyerously as do the watchmen
in the mornynge watche / desyre the daye spring.
Let Israhell wayte for the lorde: for with the lorde is there mercy &
plentuouse redemptyon.[26]

Women as well as men, servants as well as masters, could pattern their spirituality on such a personage: beset by his enemies, tearful and abject for his sins, heartened and even exultant in his perception of divine deliverance and blessing. Thomas Wyatt attests the imaginative as well as spiritual hold exerted by the figure of the Psalmist in some of the earliest verse to bear the stamp of the English Reformation – his metrical versions of the seven penitential Psalms, composed, perhaps, during imprisonment in the Tower of London in 1536, or, somewhat later, in the 1540s. This excerpt, reminiscent of Godfray's text in its monosyllabic diction, compact phrasal units and emotional intensity, comes from Wyatt's prologue to Psalm 143, the last of the set:

> Shew me by tyms thyn Ayde
> For on thy grace I holly / do depend.
> and in thi hand sins all my helth is stayd
> do me to know / what way thou wolt I bend
> For unto the I have reysd up my mynd.[27]

Beyond and above the Psalmic David, however, the figure of the crucified Christ is the ultimate focus of this pre-Reformation body of devotional and meditative works. He is graphically visualised and affectively addressed in his serial sufferings – betrayal by Judas, mockery, scourging, crucifixion, and death from exposure and exhaustion – excerpted or paraphrased from the Gospel narratives. In the vernacular works of pre-Reformation spirituality, the Psalmist is the prototype of the true Christian soul, but divinity itself is disclosed in Christ's Passion, which authenticates the self-sacrificing Redeemer of boundless love, while also warning terribly of his Second Coming in judgement on unrepented and unexpiated human sin.[28] Godfray's *Primer* is typical in offering

---

26 [Thomas Godfray, comp.], *A primer in Englysshe / with dyuers prayers & godly meditations* (London, [*c.* 1535]), unpaginated late section 'Here after foloweth the seuen Psalmes'.
27 Cited from Thomas Wyatt's holograph manuscript of his penitential Psalms, BL, MS. Egerton 2711, by Rivkah Zim, *English Metrical Psalms: Poetry as Praise and Prayer 1535–1601* (Cambridge University Press, 1987), p. 68. In her appendix of printed editions, Kim records as No. 25 (p. 225) the first publication of Wyatt's penitential Psalms by John Harrington (of Stepney) in 1549.
28 See Duffy's magisterial account of the spirituality of the English primers in *Stripping of the Altars*, chs. 6–8.

an alternation of Gospel extracts and commentary to evoke Jesus' agony in the garden of Gethsemane. The urgent rhythms of the passage, again produced by copious monosyllables and brief phrasal units, fix attention on this supreme precedent for any fearful soul's outcries in the presence of God:

> Now began he to be in a greuouse anguysshe . . . / sayeing / full heuy is my mynde euyn into deethe (so wolde he shewe himselfe to be very man / and to be lyke vs his bretherne in all poyntes / . . . nat onely in body / but in mynde / for What is the tormentynge of the body / if the mynde fele it natte?) Whan he was in this paynfull affliction . . . he fled vnto his father / as it was his maner / and is the maner also of all sayntes / . . . and there he fell down flatte vpon therth and prayed / sayeng. Father / if it be possyble / Uere [Veer] ouer this passyon fro me / neuertheles nat my wyl / but thyne be done (for he made rather his complaynte here before his father / than desyred his passyon to be tourned from him) for he came into this houre well wyllynge / but with howe heuy and tremblynge mynde / (for that his deth was now at hande) no man maye expresse.[29]

The sensibility of the great Dutch humanist, Desiderius Erasmus, bore the stamp of much popular, pre-Reformation spirituality. As fiercely as any Lollard, as fiercely as Luther (with whom he came into conflict), Erasmus could denounce papal pretensions to define holiness and dispense salvation through pilgrimages, prayers to images, bulls and externally holy works. Like the Lollards too, he conceived true Christianity in terms of the ministry of Jesus, his preaching, his care for the poor and unfortunate, his moral example, and he wished the Bible to be available to all people – preeminently the Gospels, the source-texts for what he termed '*philosophia Christi*', the normative truths of how to live a godly life. However, Erasmus himself was an elite figure, a scholar of international repute, issuing the first critical edition of the Greek New Testament (1516) together with a translation into the masterly Latin prose for which he and his large corpus of original writings became famed. The direct English influence of Erasmus registered in learned circles – first through friendship with such London intellectuals as More and John Colet, then in somewhat belated appreciation among a younger generation of scholars at Cambridge University, where he had taught Greek from 1513 to 1516.

William Tyndale, an Oxford graduate who may also have studied at Cambridge, made a (now lost) English translation of Erasmus's *Enchiridion Militis Christiani* [Handbook of a Christian Soldier] (1516) and otherwise showed

---

29 [Godfray,] *A primer in Englysshe*, unpaginated second part of 'The passion of our sauyour Christ / deuyded into ten partes', which immediately follows the prayers for 'Laudes'.

responsiveness to Erasmus's Greek-Latin edition of the New Testament, with its preface and annotations that exalted the Gospel narratives as means of vital personal access to the Christ who spoke, healed, died and rose from the dead. In 1524 Tyndale solicited Cuthbert Tunstall, Bishop of London, to sponsor an English translation of the New Testament. Tunstall's firm rejection may have been triggered by a sense of connection between Tyndale's admiration for Erasmus and a broader context of English heresy. Erasmus had urged oral reading and recitation of the Bible to promote lay understanding (already a longstanding Lollard practice in England) and proposed that Psalm texts be set to popular tunes so that ploughmen and weavers might sing them, and women and children might savour God's Word.[30] Tyndale promptly went to Germany; there his English New Testament appeared in 1525. Very soon thereafter, copies were circulating in England.

During his German sojourn, if not before, Tyndale came under the influence of Lutheran theology – especially its tenets of *sola scriptura, sola fides*: that the Bible is the only authority for Christian truth, and that justification by faith alone is its fundamental truth, as expounded by St Paul in Romans and Galatians. Tyndale's New Testament includes English translations of several of Luther's prefaces to Biblical books, and his prose tract, *Parable of the Wicked Mammon* (1527), on justification by faith in the Gospel 'promises' of Christ as Redeemer, draws heavily on Luther's work of the same title. But Luther's influence was by no means exclusively theological: his fierce polemics against such purported religious frauds as the selling of indulgences, the worship of images, the alleged efficacy of pilgrimages, the requirement of clerical celibacy, as well as his exaltation of the godly prince over corrupt papal authority re-echo in Tyndale's *Obedience of a Christian Man*. In this vigorous, encyclopaedic tract Tyndale in effect new-models England after a Lutheran prototype, reinforcing the fabric of social and political hierarchy through his emphasis on secular obedience but shaking traditional institutionalised religion with his far-reaching claims that Scripture as apprehended, believed and internalised by each Christian for himself or herself, is the only means of salvation through Christ (the theme that Luther labelled the 'priesthood of believers'). Nor is Tyndale unique in registering the impact of Lutheranism. This is a feature shared by the first

---

30 The soon-ensuing tide of English metrical Psalm books with musical settings would confirm this proposal. See, further, Donald Dean Smeeton, *Lollard Themes in the Reformation Theology of William Tyndale*, Sixteenth Century Essays & Studies, 6 (Kirksville, MO: Sixteenth Century Journal Publishers, 1986), pp. 249–58, and Zim, *English Metrical Psalms*, especially her appendix listing English Psalm versions printed 1530–1601, pp. 211–59.

Literature and the church

generation of sixteenth-century English reformers and evangelicals: Robert Barnes and George Joye most clearly, but also Thomas Cromwell and Thomas Cranmer in significant if subtler respects.[31]

The sustained incentive to circulate the Bible in English is the single most conspicuous front on which religious conviction and rhetorical suasion outpaced and outmanoeuvred official Crown and Church policy in the era of the English Reformation. Tyndale was consistently branded a heretic, meeting a heretic's death by burning at Vilvorde in the Spanish Netherlands in 1536. His corpus of Biblical translation – the New Testament, the first five books of the Old Testament, and the book of Jonah, all of them the first renderings in English from the original Greek and Hebrew – could never have been authorised to circulate in England if attributed to him by name. When More in his *Dialogue concerning Heresies* and Tunstall in a sermon at Paul's Cross in 1528 denounced as damnable and dangerous error certain key vocabulary choices – 'congregation' rather than 'church', 'love' rather than 'charity', 'favour' rather than 'grace', 'repentance' rather than 'penance' – they accurately pinpointed the reformist orientation of Tyndale's English New Testament. But, by far a greater influence than ideology registered in Tyndale's translations was the sense of direct access and immediate comprehensibility of the Biblical text, produced by his spare, sinewy renderings of the clausal and phrasal parallelisms of his originals. So-called 'sense' parallelisms (saying the same or nearly the same thing in paired phrases) alternating with antitheses (saying unlike things in paired phrases) are a stylistic resource that the Bible shares with other Semitic literatures; these parallelisms and antitheses create poetic compression and poetic rhythms in the medium of prose. Here is Tyndale's version of the episode cited above from Godfray's English primer – Jesus' agony in the garden of Gethsemane (Matthew 26:36–42):

> Then went Iesus with them into a place which is called Gethsamane / and sayde vnto the disciples / syt ye here / whyll I go and praye yonder. And he toke with him Peter and the two sonnes of zebede / and began to wexe sorowfull and to be in an agonye. Then sayd Iesus vnto them: my soule is hevy even vnto the deeth. Tary ye here and watche with me. And he went a lytell aparte / and fell flat on his face / and prayed sayinge: O my father / yf it be possible / let this cuppe passe from me: neverthelesse / not as I wyll / but as thou wylt. And he came vnto

31 See W. A. Clebsch, *England's Earliest Protestants, 1520–35* (New Haven, CT: Yale University Press, 1964); Basil Hall, 'The Early Rise and Gradual Decline of Lutheranism in England (1520–1600)', in *Reform and Reformation England and the Continent c 1500–c 1750*, ed. Derek Baker (Oxford: Basil Blackwell, 1979), pp. 103–31.

the disciples / and founde them a slepe / and sayd to Peter: what / coulde ye not
watch with me one houre: watche and praye / that ye fall not into temptacion.
The spirite is willyng / but the flesshe is weake.[32]

The sense parallelism, 'to wexe sorowfull and to be in an agonye', gradates into
a subsequent pair, 'Tary . . . and watche', 'watche and praye' – both, pivots in
the narrative of how the disciples fail Jesus. The antithesis of willing spirit and
weak flesh crystallises a more profound pathos: Jesus registers their failure as
a doubt he also has about himself.

Whether in narrative or in doctrinal exposition, Tyndale sustains a plain –
both a manifest and an unadorned – colloquialism of phrasing and rhythm, combined with reiteration for emphasis and maximal comprehension. Of Tyndale's
englishings of Scripture, 90 per cent survive intact in authorised English Bibles
through the King James Version of 1611. This commonplace of Reformation
history bears reiterating for the evidence it gives of the power – specifically, the
staying power – of compelling and effective verbal expression. Nor is Tyndale's
stylistic achievement some kind of happy accident or beginner's luck. His
observations on how favourably the capacities of English accommodate those
of the original Biblical languages, Greek and Hebrew, are at once the product of a philologist's intent study and the earliest recorded commendation of
English as a literary medium.[33] Tyndale reflects in his *Obedience* on the bishops
and polemicists who violently oppose the Bible in English and insist not just
on the authority but the superiority of the Latin Vulgate:

> They will say it can not be translated into our tounge, it is so rude. It is not
> so rude as they are false lyers. For the Greeke tounge agreeth more with the
> English then with the Latin. And the properties of the Hebrue tounge agreeth
> a thousand tymes more with the Englishe then with the Latyn. The maner
> of speaking is both one, so that in a thousand places thou needest not but to
> translate it into the English, worde for worde, when thou must seeke a compasse
> in the Latin, and yet shalt haue much worke to translate it welfauouredly.
>
> (*Whole Workes*, p. 102)

32 [William Tyndale,] *The Newe Testament, dylygently corrected and compared with the Greke by
    W. Tindale* (Antwerp, 1534), rendering Matthew 26:36–42, in *The English Hexapla, Exhibiting
    the Six Important English Translations of the New Testament Scriptures* (London: Samuel Bagster
    & Sons, 1841), n. p.
33 On the unprecedentedly early appreciation accorded to English by the Lollards and Tyndale,
    see Mueller, *Native Tongue and the Word*, pp. 111–13, 183–7; for discussion of the general
    humanist slowness to acknowledge the literary potentialities of English, see Richard Foster
    Jones, *The Triumph of the English Language: A Survey of Opinions concerning the Vernacular from
    the Introduction of Printing to the Restoration* (Stanford University Press, 1953), pp. 3–31,
    68–141.

Despite initial successes of five editions in four years – epitomised in Foxe's story of how the merchant Augustine Packington duped Bishop Tunstall to pay enough for confiscated copies of Tyndale's New Testament to finance a new edition[34] – English Bibles ceased to be imported during the period 1530–4. Ranking opponents of the Bible in English spoke out, setting a trend that would steadily define the traditionalist Catholic position. Edmund Bonner, a strong advocate of an English Bible in 1534, would, as Bishop of London and chief prosecutor of heretics under Mary, take the Bibles out of English churches and English hands. John Stokesley and Stephen Gardiner, in their turns, would seek to impede or defeat initiatives for a vernacular Bible. With time, opposition to the circulation of the Bible in English would prove a seriously flawed strategy on the part of the traditionalists, as popular reaction became a more crucial factor in determining religious policy. Archbishop Cranmer took a key step in presenting a divided clergy with a proposal to petition Henry for royal authorisation of an English Bible in December 1534. About this same time Miles Coverdale assembled the first complete version of an English Bible, augmenting Tyndale's incomplete translations with his own made from Latin and German; this he printed in Germany in 1535, with a dedication to Henry VIII.[35]

From this point onward, the cause of legitimating an English Bible for public access advances or recedes in accordance with the zigzag course traced by the official 'formularies' – declarations of fundamental and necessary beliefs – issued by the emergent Church of England. Thus 1536 witnesses Cromwell's injunctions promoting public reading of the Bible in English in every parish church of the realm as well as the issuance of the first of the formularies, the 'Ten Articles'. Their Lutheran orientation has often been emphasised – for example, the reduction of the sacraments from seven to three: baptism, penance and 'the sacrament of the altar', where 'the very selfsame body and blood of Christ is corporally, really, and in very substance exhibited, distributed, and received unto and of all them which receive the said sacrament'.[36] Far more significant, however, for the future institutional identity of the Church of England is the particular logic of reformation perceptible in the Ten Articles – a logic inclusive

34 Foxe, *Acts and Monuments*, ed. Cattley, 4:670.
35 The 'Coverdale Bible' is *Biblia the bible, that is the holy scripture . . . out of Douche and Latyn in to Englishe. M.D.XXXV.* [Cologne or Marburg, 1535]. The contemporary sources on its production are a Paul's Cross sermon by Coverdale, as reported by William Fulke in his *Defence of Translation* (*English Hexapla*, pp. 46–8).
36 [Henry VIII,] *Articles devised by the kynges highnes maiestie, to stablyshe christen quietnes and unitie amonge us, and to avoyde contentious opinions: which articles be also approved by the consent and determination of the hole clergie of this Realme. Anno MDXXXVI* [Thomas Berthelet's edn], in *Formularies of Faith Put Forth By Authority During the Reign of Henry VIII*, ed. Charles Lloyd (Oxford University Press, 1856), p. xxv.

in the practices it permits but no less insistent that these be both explicable and explained, not mystified, in their use. Holy water is 'to put us in remembrance of our baptism and the blood of Christ sprinkled for your redemption', and candles are permissible if they are lit 'in memory of Christ the spiritual light'. Images understood as 'representers of virtue and good example' may remain in the churches, but preachers must warn against 'censing of them, and kneeling and offering unto them, with other like worshippings'. Prayers to saints and the keeping of their holy days are 'laudable' practices only if the people remember that no saint 'is more merciful than Christ' or 'doth serve for one thing more than another, or is patron of the same'.

Similarly, the article on purgatory acknowledges the 'due order of char-ity ... to pray for souls departed ... and to cause others to pray for them', but stresses the need that 'such abuses be clearly put away, which under the name of purgatory hath been advanced to make men believe that through the bishop of Rome's pardon souls might clearly be delivered out of purgatory, and all the pains of it ... The place where they be, the name wherof and kind of pains there, also be to us uncertain by Scripture.' This same, at once inclusive and explanatory, logic extends to the article on justification, defined as 'remission of our sins, and our acceptation or reconciliation into the grace and favour of God, that is to say, our perfect renovation in Christ', before being expounded in a very un-Lutheran fashion as a reciprocal and participatory relation of 'con-trition and faith joined with charity' (Lloyd (ed.), *Formularies*, pp. 12–17).

The inclusive, articulatory logic of reformation traceable in the Ten Articles is, however, repeatedly nullified or displaced by the dynamic of opposition or 'othering' that has already been noted in Fish, More, Tyndale and Latimer. Concurrently with the Ten Articles, Thomas Cromwell, Henry's Vice-gerent for Spirituals, and the clergy of Convocation promulgated an act 'for the abro-gation of certain holydays' intended to rationalise and regulate the accretions of tradition. All feast days in the harvest season from July through September as well as those in the Westminster law terms were abolished, except those of the apostles, the Blessed Virgin, Saint George and the nativity of John the Baptist; Ascension, All Saints' and Candlemas would also be observed. This rupturing of the ritual patterns of religious observance in the parishes of the realm spurred a dangerous but short-lived uprising centred in the north of England – the self-styled 'Pilgrimage of Grace' – whose armed supporters, numbering 40,000 at the peak of the action, marched under banners figuring the five wounds of Christ, an intensely venerated holy image in England, and demanded that the King roll back church reform by rejecting his new men and their new ways.[37]

---

37 On English devotion to the five wounds of Christ, see Duffy, *Stripping of the Altars*, pp. 238–48.

Henry's immediate reaction was to assert royal authority decisively with numerous hangings of the defeated leaders and to advance still further the cause of reform. Quite possibly he thought himself divinely confirmed in doing so, for Queen Jane Seymour bore Henry his only legitimate son, the future Edward VI, in October 1537. Royal injunctions issued in 1536 and 1538 insisted on the clergy's obedience in renouncing the Pope's jurisdiction, in expounding the Ten Articles, in providing Bibles in both Latin and English and encouraging their parishioners to read them, but without disputatiousness. Parents and masters were admonished to catechise every household member in the Apostles' Creed, the Lord's Prayer and the Ten Commandments in English, to which end the so-called *Bishops' Book* (1537) provided a copious set of specimen expositions of these texts and the Ten Articles.

Soon, however, contradictions intrinsic to an era of cultural transformation surged to the fore. On the one hand, in late 1538 Henry VIII authorised the popular use of English Scripture in the form of the so-called 'Great' Bible. On the other hand, in April 1539 he issued a royal proclamation 'for uniformity of religion', deploring the

> great murmur, malice, and malignity . . . risen and sprung amongst divers and sundry of his subjects by diversities of opinions . . . Each of them dispute so earnestly against the other of their opinions as well in churches, alehouses, taverns, and other places . . . that there is begun and sprung among themselves slander and railing each at other as well by word as writing, one part of them calling the other papist, the other part calling the other heretic; whereby is like to follow sedition and tumult and destructions.

Tartly reminding the people that 'the Scripture is permitted to them by the King's goodness in the English tongue', Henry forthwith rescinded its reading aloud in churches or chapels during divine service, allowing only quiet and reverent private access, 'to increase thereby godliness and virtuous reading'.[38]

The 'Great Bible' so momentously licensed by Henry was credited to one 'Thomas Matthew', but was in fact compiled by Miles Coverdale and John Rogers, who added English translations and revisions by Coverdale to complete Tyndale's abortive project.[39] Cromwell and Cranmer secured and then implemented this wholesale reversal of Crown and Church policy in 1538–40,

---

38 Paul L. Hughes and James F. Larkin (eds.), *Tudor Royal Proclamations*, 2 vols. (New Haven, CT: Yale University Press, 1964–9), 1:284–5.

39 The 'Great Bible' is *The byble in Englyshe, that is to saye the content of all the holy scrypture* ([Paris and London], 1539); Thomas Cranmer contributed a prologue to the revised editions beginning a year later, of which the first is *The byble in Englyshe, with a prologe by Thomas archbysshop of Cantorbury* ([London], 1540).

as successive editions of these outsized vernacular tomes printed by Richard Grafton and Edward Whitchurch began to circulate legally to the laity for the first time in 130 years. The title-page of the Great Bible (1539) adapts a 1535 woodcut by Hans Holbein to symbolise Henry's royal supremacy in a graded hierarchy of images: uppermost, the King like Moses on Sinai receiving God's law directly from God's hand; next the King handing 'Verbum Dei' to Cranmer and Cromwell accompanied by bishops and nobles; then across the lowest composite register of vignettes, the circulation of the text to clergy and laity is figured, with the speech banners of the more learned crying 'Vivat Rex', the less learned 'God save the Kynge'. Reminiscent of Erasmus's Latin preface to his New Testament but also of the Lollards' objective of a laity literate in the vernacular, Cranmer's English preface to the Great Bible exhorts those active in their vocations to lay hold of Scripture as the instrument for the working-out of their salvation in their everyday lives:

> Doest thou not marke and consider howe the smyth, mason, or carpenter, or any other handy craftesman, what neade so euer he be in . . . he wyll not see or laye to pledge the toles of hys occupacyon, for then howe shulde he worke his feate or get hys lyuinge therby? Of lyke mynde and affeccyon ought we to be towardes holye scripture, for as mallettes, hammars, sawes, chesylles, axes, and hatchettes be the tooles of theyr occupacyon. So bene the bokes of the prophetes, and apostelles, and all holye wryte inspired by the holy ghost, the instrumentes of our saluacyon. Wherefore, let us not stycke to bye and prouyde vs the Byble, . . . a better Iuell in our house then eyther golde or syluer.[40]

The tonality of this passage confirms the master narrative of a recent authoritative biography that closely tracks Cranmer's course as a committed, activist Reformer.[41] In the Great Bible, however, Cranmer shuns the oppositional rhetoric that predominantly characterises zealots of both the traditionalist and the reformist camps and instead applies the inclusive, articulatory logic of reformation already noted in the Ten Articles. He explains as follows the intermittent insertion of material 'in small letters in the texte':

> So moche as is in the small lettre . . . is more in the common translacyon in Latin, then is founde ether in the Hebrue or in the Greke, whych wordes and sentences we have added, not only to manyfest the same vnto you, but also to satisfye and content those, that here before tyme, hath myssed soche sentences in the Bybles and new Testaments before set forth.   (English Hexapla, p. 58)

---

40 Charles C. Butterworth, *The Literary Lineage of the King James Bible, 1340–1611* (Philadelphia: University of Pennsylvania Press, 1941), pp. 110–19, 129–45; quotation at p. 138.
41 Diarmaid MacCulloch, *Thomas Cranmer: A Life* (New Haven, CT: Yale University Press, 1996).

In effect, Cranmer informs the reader, the words in smaller typeface are English translations of additions made to the Hebrew or Greek in the Vulgate Latin; these have been inserted to 'satisfye and content' those readers who know the Vulgate well enough to 'mysse' them but are marked off by different typography so that they are not mistaken for original wording. In the garden of Gethsemane passage (Matthew 26:36–9) quoted earlier, Cranmer utilises the Vulgate to make local adjustments in Tyndale's translation:

> *Tyndale*: into a place which is called Gethsemane/
> *Cranmer*: vnto a farme place (which is called Gethsemane)
> *Vulgate*: in villam quae dicitur Gethsemani
>
> *Tyndale*: began to wexe sorowfull and to be in an agonye
> *Cranmer*: began to wexe sorowfull and heuye
> *Vulgate*: coepit contristari et maestus esse

Such minute adjustments as these make little difference to the overall sense of the Gospel narrative. The effect is quite otherwise, however, in a passage on faith and works (Romans 3:19–29) that was central to Reformation theology. Now Cranmer's version distinguishes itself from Tyndale's in turns of phrase that preserve resonances of Vulgate vocabulary even as they register and transmit Pauline paradox. The difference shows clearly in the excerpt below, where Tyndale's phrasing sets God's redemptive gift of righteousness over against obedience to God's law. Cranmer rephrases tellingly; the redemptive gift of righteousness is without reference to God's law to the extent that God's law itself allows this. Construing the Vulgate's participial construction (testificata . . .) as having concessive force, Cranmer mediates a paradoxical divide between divine righteousness and divine law:

> *Tyndale*: Now verely is the rigtewesnes that commeth of God declared without
>   the fulfillinge of the lawe / havinge witnes yet of the lawe and of the Prophetes
> *Cranmer*: But now is the ryghtewesnes of God declared without the lawe, for
>   as moch as it is alowed by the testimony of the lawe and the Prophetes
> *Vulgate*: nunc autem sine lege iustitia Dei manifestata est, testificata a lege et
>   prophetis

At a later juncture in the same passage from Romans, Tyndale employs a brief, metaphorical characterisation that conflates the objective and subjective aspects of Christ's role as Saviour ('a seate of mercy') and the believer's saving 'faith in his bloud'. Cranmer, by contrast, marshals the specificity of the Vulgate's prepositional formulations ('per fidem, in sanguine, . . . ad ostensionem') to distinguish the objective role of Christ ('the obtayner of mercy') from the subjective means of apprehension ('thorow fayth'). Cranmer then conjoins Christ and the believer with the phrase 'by the meanes of his bloud', which in the local context applies equally well to both, thus felicitously binding the two together in the act and effect of salvation.

> *Tyndale*: Christ Iesu / whom God hath made a seate of mercy thorow faith in his bloud / to shewe the rightewesnes which before him is of valoure /
> *Cranmer*: Chryst Iesu, whom God hath set forth to be the obtayner of mercy thorow fayth, by the meanes of his bloude, to declare hys ryghteousnes
> *Vulgate*: Christo Iesu, quem proposuit Deus propitiationem per fidem in sanguine ipsius, ad ostensionem iustitiae suae

Although Cranmer's combinatory strategy in the 1539 text of the Great Bible did not prevail in the englishing of God's Word, he would later apply this strategy with success in two other widely circulating works, the Edwardian *Homilies* and the Book of Common Prayer.

The political no less than the religious context in 1539 proved unfavourable to Cranmer's appeal that the Church of England constitute a comprehensive Christian collectivity through the reading and internalising of vernacular Scripture. Factional struggles in court and Council yielded shifting policies on reform, first advancing it, then repressing it. July 1540 saw the fall, trial and execution of Cromwell, the last of Henry's principal ministers. Cromwell was brought down by influential traditionalist adversaries who profited from the King's repudiation of accords that Cromwell had been promoting with German Lutheran princes and divines, but that now seemed only to abet exponents of radical reform in England. (It did not help Cromwell that he had negotiated Henry's ill-fated marriage to Anne of Cleves, whom the King was unable to stomach in person.) Henry's recoil from reform was already detectible in late 1538, when he interrogated and sent to the flames a ranking evangelical, John Lambert, for denying the bodily Real Presence of Christ in the sacrament, and when he recalled Gardiner from three years' absence in France on diplomatic assignment. In May 1539, one month after the royal proclamation limiting Bible-reading, Convocation and Parliament joined to issue the most savage penal act against heresy that had ever been known in England – the Act of Six Articles or, as it was termed in Foxe's *Acts and Monuments*, 'the whip with six strings' (Cattley (ed.), 5:262). By comparison with the Ten Articles, the rhetoric of the Six Articles sustained a premium on expository specificity while firmly precluding any latitude in interpreting its key formulations.

The first article asserted the dogma of transubstantiation – that 'in the most blessed Sacrament of the altar . . . is present really, under the form of bread and wine, the natural body and blood of our Saviour Jesus Christ... and that after the consecration there remaineth no substance of bread or wine, nor any other substance, but the substance of Christ, God and man' – specifying the penalty for denial as death by burning. No longer would a heretic be given the chance to recant or abjure. The second article held it unnecessary for all persons to communicate 'in both kinds', to receive both bread and wine – in effect reinstating the traditional practice of reserving the chalice for the officiating priest. The third and fourth articles held that 'preists... may not marry, by the law of God' and that 'vows of chastity... by man or woman made to God... ought to be observed'. The fifth and sixth articles termed private masses (said on behalf of dead souls, in the absence of living communicants) 'meet and necessary' and 'auricular confession' (recital of one's sins to a priest, to be absolved before receiving communion) 'expedient and necessary'. Although previous injunctions had declared this pair of practices impermissible, in the former case, and purely discretionary, in the latter, both became obligatory again. The Six Articles markedly reduced lay agency and status within the Church of England as institution, while as markedly increasing clerical agency, status and authority.[42]

The impact of the Six Articles on leading English Reformers was immediate: Latimer resigned his bishopric, and John Bale, Thomas Becon, Miles Coverdale, John Hooper and William Turner left England for Antwerp, Strasbourg or Zurich. But the enforcement of the Six Articles through inquests for heresy began only in the summer of 1540 after Henry married his fifth wife, Catherine Howard, in a triumph of the traditionalist faction, and after the beheading of Cromwell and the burnings of Robert Barnes, Thomas Garrett and William Jerome, prominent Lutherans falsely accused of being Anabaptists who denied Christ's incarnation. These conspicuous executions of July 1540 became landmark events in the London popular consciousness by way of the ballad controversy they provoked. Thomas Smith advanced to the fray with his abusive 'Ballad on Thomas Cromwell' ('Thou did not remember, false heretic / One God, one faith, and one King Catholic / For thou has been so long a schismatic. / Sing troll on away, troll on away, &c'). William Gray came to Cromwell's defence with 'A Ballad against Malicious Slanderers' ('The sacrament of the altar, that is most highest / Cromwell believed it to be the very body of Christ / Wherefore in thy writing, on him thou liest'). Most vindictive, however, were the attacks on Barnes, styled 'the vicar of Hell' in 'This lytle treatyse declareth the study and fruits of Barnes burned' (1540), which also gleefully recounts the former friar's last moments with eyewitness specificity:

O how like a Christian man he died
Stiffly holding his hands by his side
Saying, if ever were any saint, that died
I will be one, that must needs to be tried.
Without repentance, the Devil was his guide.
All this was said like a false friar
Yet all could not save him from the fair fire.[43]

In the vacuum of leadership left by Cromwell's death, the later years of Henry VIII's reign registered sharp oscillations as court and Council factions failed to gain an upper hand and yet intensified their animosities as proponents, now, of the old faith and the new learning, respectively. Gardiner and the Duke of Norfolk aimed to restore Catholic orthodoxy with a selective drive to expose the networks of patronage and persuasion linking the Reformist nobility and gentry, leading citizens and common people through pivotal intermediaries – the Reformist writers and printers of London and the most committed Reformist clergy. Religious controversy ran at high tide in the capital through 1540 and 1541 as heresy inquests proceeded, the defenders of reform strategically recanting their voiced convictions so that they might testify to them again when occasion arose. As late 1541 brought to light Queen Catherine Howard's treasonous adulteries, and the disgraced Norfolk could no longer make effective common cause with Gardiner, the prime locus of conservative animosity became the English Bible itself. The Convocation that met with the 1542 Parliament debated whether the Great Bible could be retained 'without scandal, error, and manifest offence to Christ's faithful people'. After Gardiner listed a hundred words that should not be translated from Latin or Greek in order 'to teach the laity their distance', Henry ordered that the universities examine the whole text, thus halting the printing of the Great Bible.[44]

The final significant convergence between the issue of a publicly circulated English Bible and the zigzag course traced by the official 'formularies' of Henry's reign occurs in 1543. This year saw the publication of the highly traditionalist compilation, *A Necessary Doctrine and Erudition of a Christian Man* – known as *The King's Book*, after Henry's direct role in its compilation. Concurrently, Parliament passed an act forbidding the use of Tyndale's translation anywhere in the King's dominions and permitting the use of other, unannotated versions only to chief public officers of the Crown, noblemen, gentlemen, and merchants if they were householders. Disobedient persons of any

---

43 Ballad quotations from Brigden, *London and the Reformation*, pp. 322–4, citing respectively E. W. Dormer, *Gray of Reading* (Reading, 1923), pp. 76–82, and the unique copy of STC 1473.5 preserved in the library of Shrewsbury School.
44 Thomas Fuller, *The Church-History of Britain*, 2:109, cited in *English Hexapla*, p. 68.

other category would incur the pain of a month's imprisonment.[45] But the subsequent exercise of the royal supremacy regarding access to the Scriptures in English took a more straightforward course. When Edward acceded to the throne, his religious orientation was confirmed in an injunction of May 1547 that restored Bible-reading in English without specified limitations and stipulated the Great Bible as the version to be used. Upon her accession, Mary issued injunctions of August 1553 forbidding any reading, teaching or interpretation of English Scripture or point of doctrine 'in churches or other public or private places (except in the schools of the universities)', citing 'her just possession of the imperial crown of this realm and other dominions thereunto belonging' as her warrant for this action (*Tudor Royal Proclamations*, 2:6, 5).

The abrupt and contradictory assertions of both the formularies of faith and the injunctions permitting or forbidding Bible-reading starkly witness the instability that beset the doctrinal core of the Church of England throughout the Reformation era and affected the highest political levels, where control ostensibly resided. Contrary to the national interest in unity and uniformity proclaimed in these texts, their cumulative effect was to foster contentiousness, divisiveness, confusion and anxiety in English society at large. Reformers recognised in the newly issued *King's Book* strong evidence of Gardiner's sway over the royal will in the determination of religious orthodoxy. This formulary equates the necessary points of Christian faith with the traditional contents of the English primers: the Apostles' Creed, the seven sacraments, the Ten Commandments, the Paternoster and the Ave Maria. In its penultimate section, however, where it purports to synthesise free will, justification and good works in pointedly un-Lutheran fashion, the *King's Book* displays the inclusive, articulatory logic observed earlier in the Ten Articles – at once expressed and evoked by the paired correlative constructions (albeit...yet) and the nested subordinate clauses of this capacious single sentence:

> And albeit God is the principal cause and chief worker of this justification in us, without whose grace no man can do no good thing, but following his free will in the state of a sinner, increaseth his own injustice, and multiplieth his sin; yet so it pleaseth the high wisdom of God, that man, prevented by his grace, (which being offered, man may if he will refuse or receive,) shall be also a worker by his free consent and obedience to the same, in the attaining of his own justification, and by God's grace and help shall walk in such works as be requisite to his justification, and so continuing, come to the perfect end thereof by such means and ways as God hath ordained.
>
> (Lloyd (ed.), *Formularies*, pp. 364–5)

45 Burnet, *History of the Reformation*, 1:497, cited in *English Hexapla*, p. 69.

That the primer-like *King's Book* could or should replace the vernacular Bible for the majority of the people was the distinct implication of the oddly named parliamentary 'Act for the Advancement of the True Religion' (May 1543), which, as noted above, reserved to Henry the statutory right to decide who in England might read the Bible and who might not. It asserted that 'the highest and most honest sort of men' benefited from such reading, but the 'lower sort' only fell into error and dispute; therefore 'no women, nor artificers, prentices, journeymen, serving men of the degree of yeomen or under, husbandmen nor labourers' might henceforth read the Bible 'privately or openly'. The measure scored a further victory for Gardiner, who had long feared that open access to the Bible might 'beguile the people into the refusal of obedience'.[46]

In the event, the Act for the Advancement of the True Religion proved a pyrrhic victory for English traditionalists in two ways – first, by saddling them with a deeply counter-intuitive policy (heavily restricted popular access to God's Word); and second, by inciting a wide and prolonged wave of protest, often rising to outrage, in Reformist writings and publications. Henry Brinkelow's mordant *Complaint of Roderick Mors* (1542?) multiplied images of necromancy and bestiality to depict the conduct of Henry's prelates: 'How haue they bewitched the parlamenthouse in making such viperous actes as the beast of Rome neuer made him self?... How shamfully haue they and their membres in many places of England driuen men from reading the bible?' The self-exiled Thomas Becon, writing under the pseudonym 'Theodore Basil', likewise turned an exuberant pen to the defence of Reformation. His tendencious account of his motive for compiling what eventually became more than two dozen prose tracts, mostly consisting of scriptural quotations, uses alliteration ('bloudy boistrous burning') and assonance ('odious... owles') to render opponents of Bible-reading as shameful as if they stood in the pillory:

> In the bloudy boistrous burning time, when the reading of the holy bible, the word of our soules health, was forbidden the pore lay people, I gathered out of the holy scriptures, and caused to be printed for thedifying of the simple and vnlearned Christians: Yet suppressing my name which at the time was odious to those owles that could not abide the glorious light of Gods blessed word, that the boke might haue the better succes, & be the more fre from Antichristes thondreboltes.[47]

---

46 Brigden, *London and the Reformation*, pp. 346–7, citing 34 & 35 Henry VIII c. 1; Lacey Baldwin Smith, *Tudor Prelates and Politics, 1536–1558* (Princeton University Press, 1953), p. 245.

47 Henry Brinkelow, *The complaynt of Roderick Mors... vnto the parlament house of Ingland hys naturall countrey: For the redresse of certeyn wycked lawes, euell custumes & cruell decrees* (Strasbourg? 1542?), sigs. Fviii v, Fv v; Thomas Becon, preface to 'The Gouernance of Vertue', in *The*

These are also the years, from 1543 onward to the end of Henry's reign, when his sixth wife, Queen Katherine Parr, laboured over her *Prayers or Meditations* (1545), a free redaction of excerpts from Richard Whitford's English text of *De imitatione Christi*, and also composed – while postponing the publication of – *The Lamentation of a Sinner*. First published in November 1547, nine months after Henry's death, Parr's *Lamentation* opens with a remarkable passage of self-abasement that could not have reached print while Henry remained on the throne. In fervent first-person locutions, his self-identified wife, a Queen of England, abjects herself for her blind, foolish embrace of worldly wisdom. She then evokes her exaltation in love and gratitude when Scripture – what she calls 'the boke of the crucifix' – opened her eyes and heart to justifying faith in Christ's redemptive death. Parr's is the earliest published instance of the conversion narrative, a genre that would become central in English Nonconformity a century and a half later. Lavishly interspersed with Biblical citations, her *Lamentation* gradates from initial self-castigation through a series of reflections on the sins of the age to culminate in a hortatory vision of England as a harmonious Christian commonwealth of all estates and vocations, bonded in love and concern for one's fellow Christian souls. Parr lodges a prescient reproof to the polemical excesses of the age in urging that Reformation be pursued by looking to oneself, not by faulting others:

> Verely yf all sortes of people would loke to theyr owne vocacion, and ordeyne the same according to Christes doctrine: we should not have so many eyes and eares to other mennes fautes as we have ... God knoweth of what intent and minde I have lamented myne owne sinnes, and fautes, to the worlde. I trust no bodye will judge I have doon it for prayse, or thanke of any creature, since rather I might be ashamed then rejoice, in rehersall therof ... I seeke ... none other wise, then I am taught by Christe to dooe, according to Christen charitie.[48]

Besides her own writing, Queen Katherine attended carefully to the religious and intellectual development of her stepdaughter, Princess Elizabeth, who carried out several pious literary projects in Henry's last years. The precocious twelve-year-old translated *Prayers or Meditations* into Latin, French and Italian as a New Year's gift for her father in 1546. She had already translated Marguerite d'Angoulême's profusely scriptural *Miroir de l'âme pécheresse* from

---

Worckes of Thomas Becon, whiche he hath hyther to made and published, vol. 1 (London, 1564), fol. ccxxvi.

48 Katherine Parr, *The Lamentacion of a Sinner* (London: Edward Whitchurch, 1547), sigs. Gii v, Giii v.

French to English as a New Year's gift for Queen Katherine in 1545, possibly using the 1533 French edition that had been in Anne Boleyn's library. John Bale, in exile in Marburg, saw Elizabeth's translation of the *Miroir* into print as *A Godly Meditation of the Christian Soul* in 1548, the first of its several Continental editions.[49]

In these years, too, at the behest of Gardiner's faction and as part of a plot to incriminate Queen Katherine as a heretic and subversive subject, Anne Askew underwent the heresy investigation that she narrates in her *First Examination* and *Latter Examination* (1546). This spare, gripping text, in unadorned prose, records one woman's steadfast resistance to the cumulative force of ecclesiastical and civil authority. Askew's style is as understated as the proceedings against her are desperate – and illegal, when a member of the King's Council cranks with his own hands the torture rack on which she is bound. Before her high-ranking interrogators cause her to despair of her release and to incriminate herself fatally by denying transubstantiation, her constant and wary response to questioning is 'I believe as the scripture teacheth me' – itself a courageous statement since she belonged to a borderline category of those permitted to read Scripture after 1543. Undeterred by the horrific example of Askew's burning and her own narrow escape from Henry's displeasure, Queen Katherine contrived to write and eventually to publish her *Lamentation of a Sinner*. It is no overstatement to claim that the first instances of female authorship and publication in sixteenth-century England arise in Reformist circles as spirited reflex actions against the reinstated prohibition of the English Bible by the King and the clergy. The women's showing is the more remarkable in view of the meagre literary output of Archbishop Cranmer in this same dangerous and troubled period. Among his dearly held objectives of an English service book and the reform of canon law, only the English *Litany* (1544) found realisation in this period. Quite possibly Henry gave permission for Cranmer's English litany so that his subjects could pray for him as he pursued his increasingly expensive and doomed efforts in 1544 to recapture former English territories in France.

Reformation unleashed: the Edwardian turn of events

An enormous increase in the volume of printed materials in English followed the accession of the nine-year-old Edward VI in February 1547 and the ascendancy of the forces of religious reform that lasted until Edward's death in July

---

49 See [Elizabeth I], *Elizabeth's Glass*, ed. Marc Shell (Lincoln: University of Nebraska Press, 1993).

1553.[50] Factional struggles were incessant at court and in the Council – first between Edward's two uncles, Edward Seymour, Lord Protector, and Thomas Seymour, Lord Admiral, and subsequently between Protector Seymour and John Dudley, Earl of Northumberland, who unseated Seymour and installed himself as Protector. Yet the reign of the godly Boy-King has been hailed as the first significant instance of 'freedom of speech and publication' in England because the Henrician statutes against heresy and treason (including the Act of Six Articles) were repealed, and the reading and expounding of the Bible and related writings were 'auctorised and licensed' once again by the royal injunctions of July 1547. The 'freedom' was extremely lopsided, however. Reformist authors and publishers brought out more than 200 items in 1548 alone, thus swamping the Catholic opposition, who are represented by only 4 surviving pamphlets printed in England during the entire reign.[51]

In confronting this highly selective 'freedom of speech and publication', the key referent is, once again, the royal supremacy, now as exercised in turn by Somerset and Northumberland. Public defence of Catholic doctrine and ritual was outlawed (as tantamount to affirming papal authority), and certain Anabaptist beliefs were disallowed – for example, the holding of property in common, which contravened English rights accorded by the Crown. Edward VI's reign unleashed the evangelical extremities of the oppositional dynamic that infuses much of the cultural energy of the English Reformation era, just as Mary's reign would unleash traditionalist extremities that produced the burnings of nearly 300 men, women and children as heretics and spurred the enthralling narratives of John Foxe's monumental documentary history, the *Acts and Monuments* (first English edition, 1563). In Edward's reign, specifically, a superabundance of textual production and circulation both eroded stability and advocated it as the chief desideratum for church and state alike. The extraliterary period evidence yields telling signs of upheaval and ruptural change. London youth, disproportionately attracted to the cause of Reform, became more assertive, violent and unruly. Iconoclasm – expressed in the damaging of English rood screens, images, altars and stained-glass windows as well as the pilfering of church property and the daily incivilities that inflected parish and local life with sectarian rancour – reached endemic levels across the land. In the opinion of the parishioners of Stanford in the Vale, 'the wicked time of schism' dated

---

50 See Diarmaid MacCulloch, *The Boy King: Edward VI and the Protestant Reformation* (New York: Palgrave, 2001).
51 John N. King, *English Reformation Literature* (Princeton University Press, 1982), pp. 76–113; quotation at p. 86. King remarks: 'The government silenced Richard Smith and Miles Hogarde for writing these works' (p. 89).

not from King Henry's reign but from the beginning of Edward's, when 'all godly ceremonyes and good usys were taken out of the Church'.[52]

Textual counterparts and concomitants of the Edwardian cultural ferment include the earthy satires on Catholicism produced by a range of Reformist writers in both prose and verse. John Bale's widely influential *Image of Both Churches* (1548) develops simultaneously as a polemical construal of the cataclysmic end-time prefigured in the last book of the Bible and as a would-be resolution of the existential and epistemological problem posed by the new learning itself. In dispensing with external authority in the matter of salvation and making the individual's heart and soul the site of justifying faith, Protestantism rendered the search for the true image of the church and oneself a strenuous, perilous process. That outward works could often prove hypocritical or fraudulent merely intensified the peril, which Bale projects in an extended and highly charged personification allegory as the ongoing effort of distinguishing rightly between the Roman church as the crafty, dissimulating whore of Babylon and the reformed church as the pure and single-hearted woman clothed with the sun (Revelation 12:1).[53]

Luke Shepherd's verse satires also turn crucially on the Reformation imperative of discerning the truth amidst misleading appearances. Thus in *John Bon and Mast Person* the plain-spoken ploughman John puts his questions about the mass to his traditionalist priest on the eve of Corpus Christi, the festival instituted to honour the mystery of transubstantiation, which Cranmer disestablished in 1548 (a possible dramatic date for this verse dialogue). Against Mast Person's assertions of clerical authority, John Bon pits his concern with knowledge and proof – he cannot believe in transubstantiation because he does believe his senses:

> Yea but mast parson thynk ye it were ryght
> That if I desired you to make my blake oxe whight
> And you saye it is done, and styl is blacke in syght
> Ye myght me deme a foole for to believe so lyght.

More securely associated with Cranmer's liturgical reforms of 1548 is Shepherd's *The Upcheering of the Mass*, which extends Bale's identification of the Roman church with the whore of Babylon by casting 'Mistress Missa' – Latin for 'mass' – as a harlot hailing from the brothels of Southwark, which lay within

---

52 S. E. Brigden, 'Youth and the English Reformation', *Past and Present* 95 (1982), 37–67; Duffy, *Stripping of the Altars*, chs. 13–14, quotation at p. 532.

53 See McEachern, *Poetics of English Nationhood*, pp. 26–9.

Gardiner's properties as Bishop of Winchester. Missa falls ill and dies, receiving an obscene mock lament and a burlesque dirge: 'A good mestres missa / Shal ye go from us thissa? ... / Because ye muste departe / it greveth many an herte / ... / But what then tushe a farte.'[54]

In at least one significant aspect, the social violence and iconoclasm of the literature of Edward's reign proved newly excessive. This was the tendency to turn the rhetoric of othering – previously directed by Protestants and Catholics against each other – inward against one's own, against the hypocrisy and venality of many professed Protestants. Ferociously negative characterisations of the condition of England abounded in sermons delivered by ranking preachers at court, at St Paul's and other public places as well as in polemical tracts by prominent authors. Their analyses are remarkably consistent: despite the free and open circulation of God's Word, self-love and self-interest, expressed in rampant covetousness for money, goods and land, have deprived the people at large of hospitals and schools and have brought oppression, starvation and vagrancy upon the poor and humble. Hugh Latimer conducted the era's most notorious character assassination in his seventh sermon before Edward (Lent, 1549). Relentlessly multiplying his colloquial, reiterative clausal units, Latimer aimed at reducing to literal nullity the figure of Thomas Seymour, widower of Dowager Queen Katherine Parr, and the younger of the King's uncles, who had been executed on treason charges a month earlier: 'He was a couetous manne, an horrible couetous man. I wolde there were no more in England. He was an ambitious manne, I woulde there were no mo in Englande. He was a sedicious man, a contemnar of commune prayer. I would there were no mo in England. He is gone, I wold he had left none behind him.'[55]

Covetousness is also the ubiquitous trope of Robert Crowley's *Philargyrie of Great Britain* (1551), a verse satire in expressively rough metre and rhyme that tells the fable of a giant of immense strength and insatiable appetite for swallowing gold, who suddenly appears and terrorises the people of England. Philargyrie (Greek for 'love of silver') gets their gold and everything else of value by threatening them with eternal damnation unless they buy indulgences, propitiatory masses and prayers for their souls. Glorying in his success, Philargyrie decides to entrust to Hypocrisy the enforcement of his power over the people. Hypocrisy soon realises that he can effectively challenge Philargyrie

54 Luke Shepherd, *John Bon and Mast Person* (London, [1548]), lines 128–31; *The vpcheringe of the messe* (London, [1548]), lines 347–50, in *An Edition of Luke Shepherd's Satires*, ed. Janice Devereux (Tempe, AZ: Medieval and Renaissance Texts and Studies, 2001), pp. 55, 24.

55 Hugh Latimer, *Seven Sermons before Edward VI on each Friday in Lent 1549*, ed. Edward Arber, English Reprints (Westminster: Archibald Constable, 1895), pp. 197–8.

by practising hospitality – 'as many as wyll / Shall haue theyr fyll / Of meate and
drynck wyth me / Boeth lowe and hye / Shall haue plentie' – and enlisting the
people to defy the giant-extortioner by preaching this doctrine to them:

Open your eies	Your selfe can praye
If you be wyse	As wel alwaye
And se to your owne gayne	As he, and also feede
Let not thys slaue	All such as ye
The ryches haue	Shall knowe to be
That you haue gote with payn	Pore and nedie in deede
You nede not passe	His prayars shall
For his vayne masse	Helpe none at all
Hys diryge and prayars longe	Christis bloude hath paid the price
For well we see	You nede therefore
All those thyngis be	To do no more
But laboure of the tonge	That one price doth suffice.[56]

But the 'Reformer' Hypocrisy utterly fails to foresee the effects of his preaching
upon the people. The independence of Philargyrie which Hypocrisy instils first
makes each man 'loue him selfe' and then, in quick succession, 'this worlds pelfe'
(sig. Dv r). At this point, late in the narrative, Philaute ('Self-Love') successfully
courts the people's allegiance and enthrals them again to Philargyrie and his
exactions. In conclusion, Truth abruptly informs the King of the ruinous state
of his realm and threatens God's wrath if he does not act in vengeance. The
King reads his Bible, then falls prostrate in penitent prayer, which God answers
with a miraculous, but woefully unspecific deliverance of England:

> Then God him sent
> Men that were bent
> Oppression to expell
> ...
> And then all thyngs were well.
>
>   (sig. Dviii v)

Bale, the fiery ex-Carmelite, is one of the most poignant contemporary witnesses to the loss of books and manuscripts that accompanied the dissolution of
the monasteries and changes in Crown policy. His analysis begins predictably
enough by lumping latter-day carnal Reformers with earlier dissolute monks

---

[56] Robert Crowley, *Philargyrie of great Britayne*, in *The Fable of Philargyrie the Great Gigant*,
Reprinted from the only known copy, intro. W. A. Marsden (London: Emery Walker, 1931),
sigs. Cii v–Ciii r, Div r–v.

in an accusation that England has not cared enough for its achievements in learning: 'O cyties of England, whose glory standeth more in bellye chere, than in the serche of wysdome godlye. How cometh it, that neyther you, nor yet the ydell masmongers, have regarded thys most worthy commodyte of your contrey? I meane the conseruacyon of your Antiquytees, and of the worthy labours of your lerned men.' But as Bale's negative assessment proceeds, his vision registers ever more danger from enemies within, allowing, at best, muted hope regarding the legacy of England's learning under a Protestant regime. His chief bogeys are the Anabaptists, a radical sect widely vilified for their belief in communal ownership of property and their record of militant destructiveness on the continent. Bale calls upon all ranks of Englishmen to unite in suppressing such a menace:

> The Anabaptystes in our tyme, an vnquyetouse kynde of men, arrogaunt without measure, capcyose [captious] and vnlerned, do leaue non olde workes vnbrent...I wyshe all naturall noble hartes, and fryndely men to theyr contrey, as wele worldelye occupyers as men of bloude ryall, to consydre...these wycked Anabaptistes, that they myghte so abhorre them, and wyth all endeuour possyble auoyde the lyke.[57]

Thomas Lever, a prominent London preacher, delivered three sermons in 1550 – two at St Paul's, one at court – that found their way promptly into print. His exhortations to obedience, his invectives against covetousness and the decay of learning, sustained by heaping catalogues of nouns and phrases, are altogether typical of the polemics turned inward against fellow Protestants in Edward's reign. In the open-air pulpit at Paul's Cross he presents his credentials as a God-sent, latter-day prophet of the nation's all too manifest evils: 'Heare therefore and...ye shall wel perceyue that I speake...euery thyng according to the commaundement of the Lorde your god, whyche hath sent me vnto you hys people'. God directs Lever to instruct his English hearers regarding their singular unnaturalness to one another – thus confirming the betrayal of the natural and scriptural order that Tyndale's *Obedience* had represented as the certain destiny of a reformed England. Lever's God begins with top-down admonitions: 'Shew the nobility that they haue extorted and famished the commynality by the heightening of fynes and rentes of fermes, and decaying of hospitality and good house kepyng.' But God's most scathing denunciations apply from the bottom up: 'Show the comminalitye that they be both traytoures

57 John Bale, *The Laboryouse Journey & serche of John Leylande, for Englandes Antiquitees...with declaracyons enlarged* (1549), ed. W. A. Copinger (Manchester: Priory Press, 1895), pp. 20, 86, 88.

and rebelles, murmuryng and grudgyng agaynst myne ordinaunces: tel the comminality that ... they ... by and sel, make bargaynes, and do al thynges to the grefe and hynderaunce of manne, contrary to my commaundemente.'[58]

Yet, for all the bite and topicality with which he recounts the many failures of Reformation in the England of his day, Lever makes a sustained attempt to develop a compensatory glimpse of Christian community in his sermon in the Shrouds at St Paul's. Paraphrasing his scriptural source, the apostle Paul addressing the wayward church of Corinth in 1 Corinthians 11 as *'Vnus panis vnum corpus multi sumus'*, Lever begins by adapting the Pauline metaphor to the no less wayward Church of England:

> One bred sayeth he, one body we are that be many: by the whiche he declareth that as of diuers cornes of wheate by the liquor of water knoden into dough is made one loafe of breade: so we being diuerse men, by loue and charitie, ... be made as dyuers members of one misticall body of Christe, where by, I say, as by one example in the stede of many, learne that the more gorgeous you youre selues bee in silkes and veluettes, the more shame is it for you to see other poore and neady, beyng members of the same bodye, in ragges and clothe, yea bare and naked ... But as there be dyuers members in dyuers places, hauynge dyuers duties, so to haue dyuers prouision in feedyng and clothyng.

Lever consistently makes effective use of correlative constructions (as ... so, so ... as, even as) as well as serial intensification with comparative constructions (the more ... the more) to expound and exemplify the diverse yet interdependent human relations that must animate and sustain the church as the body of Christ. In rounding out his unusually positive projection, however, he finally cannot manage to figure acts of charity as being as natural to human behaviour as eating and getting dressed. Lever's last correlative construction overextends itself; the analogy ('even as ye do provide ... for. ... your natural body') trails off under the strain of alleged resemblance: 'And as they be all in one body, so none to be without that feedynge and clothyng, whych for that part of the bodye is meete and necessarye, euen as ye do prouide indifferentlye for euery part of youre naturall bodye'. Lever ends his vision abruptly with a 'So' construction that now expresses intent or result, not correlation, while the imaged community itself is deferred to a heavenly future: 'So let no parte or member of your Christen bodye be vnprouyded for: By reason of the whyche bodye, ye be heyres of the heauenly kyngdome' (Lever, *Sermons*, pp. 46–7).

58 Thomas Lever, 'A Sermon preached at Pauls Crosse', in *Sermons of Thomas Lever 1550*, ed. Edward Arber, English Reprints (Westminster: Archibald Constable, 1870), pp. 140, 141–2.

The preponderantly negative and polemical tonality of English Reformation literature at mid-century coalesces in angry laments over the dissolution of community, in which there is very little positive social vision or portrayal. Notwithstanding Lever's efforts in his Shrouds sermon, almost all is gloom and doom, with threatenings of God's wrath to come upon a wicked and unrepentant England. By this cultural logic, Mary's accession and the restoration of Catholicism could even produce a kind of perverse satisfaction in Reformist quarters. What is more, as will be seen below, the Marian era manifests a surprising amount of rhetorical and affective continuity with the Edwardian – the censure and the threats still abound; only their targets have been exchanged. The paucity of constructive social vision in mid-century Tudor England has been ascribed to the absence of frameworks other than religious and moral ones for posing problems and proposing solutions – specifically, to the absence of developed economic reasoning for improving the lot of the poor and for regulating extortionate practices.[59] This suggestive hypothesis does not, however, displace residual questions regarding religious literature in English at this period. Where, if anywhere, does this literature show the capacity to offer constructive images of community, and what are the attendant resources of expression? These questions will claim critical attention in the following section of this chapter, which locates central interest and merit in Cranmer's homiletic and devotional prose.

Comprehensiveness and community: Cranmer's contributions

Amidst the high tide of oppositional rhetoric that characterises the handling of religious themes in Edward's and Mary's reigns, it is Thomas Cranmer, almost uniquely, who solicits England's wholeness in the four major contributions that he is credited with making to the royally authorised *Certain Sermons or Homilies, Appointed To Be Read in Churches* (1547): 'A Fruitefull exhortation to the readyng of holy scripture', 'Of the saluation of all mankynde', 'Of the true and liuely faithe' and 'Of good workes'. Cranmer begins the homily on the reading of Scripture by analogising between the body's need for food and drink and the soul's need for essential knowledge – both, as represented in his sequential correlative conjunctions (so ... as, as ... so), are indispensable to health and life:

59 See Arthur B. Ferguson, *The Articulate Citizen and the English Renaissance* (Durham, NC: Duke University Press, 1965), pp. 3–41, 133–61.

As drynke is pleasaunte to them, that be drie, and meate to them that be hungery, so is the readyng, hearyng, searchyng, and studiying of holy scripture, to theim that be desirous to knowe God, or themselfes, and to do his will . . . As thei that are sicke of an ague, whatsoeuer thei eate or drynke, (though it bee neuer so pleasaunt) yet it is as bitter to them as wormewoode, . . . euen so is the swete-nesse of Gods worde, bitter, not of it self, but onely unto them that haue their myndes corrupted with long custome of synne, and loue of this world. Ther-fore . . . let us reuerently heare and reade holy scriptures, whiche is the foode of the soule.[60]

The phrasing tactfully reprehends opponents of Bible-reading in moral gener-alities (long custom of sin and love of this world), while figuratively assimilating to Bible-reading the sacramental connotations of eating and drinking which traditionalists attached to the mass, rather than Bible-reading, as the essential means of salvation.

Cranmer, however, quickly demonstrates his greater concern to naturalise Bible-reading, imaging it as a life-giving message taken to heart – that is, into the heart – which assumes properties of a living book in the process: 'For that thyng, which (by perpetuall vse of readyng of holy scripture, and diligent searchynge of the same) is depely printed, and grauen in the harte, at length turneth almoste into nature' (*Certain Sermons*, sig. Bi r). In its final thematic and imagistic turn, the homily inverts and intensifies this process of assimilation: the Bible no longer imprints and engraves the true reader so much as the true reader publishes the Bible. Again drawing on quantitative expressions which he now embeds in shapely parallel clauses, Cranmer figures the true reader not as a merely adept finder of passages or a copious reciter – faddish tactics of the day – but as a living Bible, an inspired source of witnessing legible in the virtuous conduct of daily life. This natural, accessible growth is figured as a process to which every sincere and serious reader of Scripture can aspire and attain:

And in readyng of Gods woorde, he moste proffiteth not alwaies, that is most ready in turnyng of the boke, or in saiyinge of it without the booke, but he that is moste turned into it, that is moste inspired with the holy Ghoste, moste in his hart and life, altered and transformed into that thynge, whiche he readeth: . . . he that daily (forsaking his olde vicious life) encreaseth in vertue, more & more.

(*Certain Sermons*, sig. Bi v)

60 [Thomas Cranmer *et al.*,] *Certain sermons, or homilies, appoynted by the kynges maiestie, to be declared and redde, by all persones, vicars, or curates, euery Sonday in their churches, where thei haue cure* (London, 1547), sigs. Aiii v – Aiiii r.

Incomparably deepening the local synthesis of justification, faith and good works proposed in the *King's Book*, Cranmer's triad of homilies on salvation, faith and good works sustain the foregoing emphasis on integrating heartfelt Bible-reading with one's faith and one's mode of life. Here is his comprehensive formulation near the end of the homily on good works, which makes effective use of major features of his stately style and rhythm – correlative and parallel clauses and phrases in flexible groupings of twos and threes – to evoke norms of spiritual balance and social concord:

> Wherefore, as you haue any zeale to the right & pure honoryng of God: as you haue any regard to your awne soules, and to the life that is to come,...applie yourselfes chiefly aboue all thyng, to reade & to heare Gods worde: marke diligently therin, what his wil is you shal do, & with all your endeuor applie yourselfes to folowe the same. First, you muste haue an assured faithe in God, and geue yourselfes wholy vnto him, loue hym in prosperitie & aduersitie, & dread to offend him euermore. Then, for his sake, loue all men, frendes & fooes, because thei be hys creacion and Image, & redemed by Christ as ye are.
>
> (*Certain Sermons*, sig. Kii r)

The at once assimilating and exacting language of this passage builds through the successive homilies as Cranmer expounds Luther's and Tyndale's *sola fides*, then appeals more broadly to English traditionalists by construing 'only' as referring primarily to 'Christ only' rather than 'faith only', and then insists on the concomitance – indeed, evokes the convergence – of good works with true faith.

In an era when competent preaching was often unavailable, and the *Book of Homilies* was to be utilised where divine service specified a sermon, Cranmer's and other contributions must have had frequent and various airings, although it is impossible to quantify the extent of their spiritual and moral impact. With Cranmer's Book of Common Prayer (1st ed, 1549; 2nd ed, 1552), however, a more extensive familiarity can be assumed because church attendance on Sundays and holidays was a legal obligation that brought fines and other penalties for non-compliance. It is also in the 1549 Prayer Book that the broadly inclusive logic of Cranmer's prose attains its finest literary effects, in both substance and form. Now the impetus to accommodate and comprehend while scrupulously respecting the Scriptures, first registered in the 'small letter' Vulgate additions to the text of the Great Bible, finds a later analogue in the following rubric: 'The Supper of the Lorde and the Holy Communion, commonly called the Masse'; this, however, was supplanted in the more reformed revision of 1552, which reads: 'The Order for the Administracion of the Lordes Supper, or Holy Communion'.[61]

Cranmer's exhortation to the taking of the sacrament emphasises the restoration of neighbourly community, thus giving a particular import to the penitence that is to precede worthy reception of the bread and wine. He recalls the worshippers from their sinfulness to their identity as members of the body of Christ – a movement figured expressively in a series of antithetical reciprocal constructions with the verbs 'offend' and 'forgive', 'do wrong' and 'make restitution', 'be in full mind and purpose' and 'else not come':

> I am commaunded of God, especially to moue and exhorte you to reconcile yourselfes to your neighbors, whom you haue offended, or who hath offended you, . . . and to be in loue and charitie with all the worlde, and to forgeue other, as you woulde that god should forgeue you. And yf any man haue doen wrong to any other, let him make . . . due restitucion of all landes and goodes, . . . before he come to Goddes borde, or at the leaste be in ful minde and purpose so to do, as sone as he is able, or els let him not come to this holy table, thinking to deceyue God, who seeth all mennes hartes.   (*Prayer Books*, p. 217)

Here Cranmer shows himself both typical of the Edwardian Reformation and distinctive within it. If other authors employ the oppositional rhetoric of catalogued enormities, invective and denunciation to turn the energy and focus of 'othering' against professed fellow Protestants whose observed behaviour is that of greedy and exploitative worldlings, Cranmer offers reconciliation, forgiveness and restitution as the means by which parishioners and neighbours may prepare for their sacramental reintegration as a human community.

Succeeding portions of the Holy Communion service deploy body imagery subtly but surely in figuring the relationship between the body of Christ and membership in the Christian community of the church. The minister's prayer of consecration begins by evoking the uniqueness and intactness of the body of Christ on the cross, 'who made there (by his one oblacion once offered) a full, perfect, and sufficient sacrifyce, oblacion, and satysfaccyon, for the sinnes of the whole worlde', and then invokes God's 'holy spirite and worde . . . to blesse and sanctifie these thy gyftes, and creatures of bread and wyne, that they may be unto us the bodye and bloude of thy moste derely beloued sonne Jesus Christe' (*Prayer Books*, p. 222). The sacramental result or purpose here – 'that they may be unto us the bodye and bloude of . . . Jesus Christe' – cannot be transubstantiation. For the text proceeds without a break to evoke again

---

61 [Thomas Cranmer,] *The First and Second Prayer Books of Edward VI*, intro. E. C. S. Gibson, Everyman's Library (London: Dent, 1910, 1964), pp. 212, 377.

the uniqueness and intactness of the living body of Christ, now in the act of breaking the Passover bread and giving the Passover wine to his disciples as narrated by St Paul in 1 Corinthians. Twice over, the words of Christ, figured as physically present with his disciples, conjoin predications of identity ('this is my bodye which is geuen for you', 'this is my bloude of the new Testament, whyche is shed for you and for many, for remission of synnes') with exhortations to specific actions ('Take, eate', 'drynke ye all of this') of an equally specific commemorative type ('do this in remembraunce of me').

Now, still addressing God, Cranmer's prayer articulates a specific understanding of what 'we thy humble seruantes do celebrate, and make here before thy diuine Maiestie, with these thy holy giftes, the memoryall whyche thy sonne hath wylled us to make, hauyng in remembraunce his blessed passion, mightie resurreccyon, and gloryous ascencion'. What 'we', the community of worshippers do together, involves a reformed and collective variation on the venerable Catholic ideal of *imitatio Christi* – enacting, to the extent that we can in spirit and body, Christ's supreme example of offering up his life to God and then confirming this in a shared reception of Holy Communion that unites and integrates us as members of Christ's body:

> And here wee offre and present unto thee (O Lorde) oure selfe, oure soules, and bodies, to be a reasonable, holy and liuely sacrifice unto thee: humbly beseching thee, that whosoeuer shalbee partakers of thys holy Communion, may worthely receiue the most precious body and bloude of thy sonne Jesus Christe: and bee fulfilled with thy grace and heauenly benediccion, and made one bodye with thy sonne Jesus Christe, that he maye dwell in them, and they in hym.
>
> (*Prayer Books*, pp. 222–3)

After the administration of the bread and wine with the reiterated phrases – 'The body (The bloud) of our Lorde Jesus Christe whiche was geuen for thee, preserue thy bodye and soule unto euerlasting life' – Cranmer's concluding prayer of thanksgiving lays strong emphasis on the creating and sustaining of Christian community through partaking in Holy Communion. The use of the English language by native English speakers as the means of 'communicating' sacramentally and verbally is manifestly essential. In the consistently clear and modulated unfolding of their capacious, many-membered shape and meaning, the two sentences of this closing prayer may comprise the finest single instance of Cranmer's rhetorical and conceptual affirmation of the Church of England as at once an earthly reality and yet an ideal.

The pervasive period dynamic of dichotomising and othering would show its force at points in Cranmer's 1552 revision – specifically, in the replacement of the foregoing sentences at the administration of the bread and wine with the more assertively memorialist formulations, 'Take and eate this, in remembraunce that Christ dyed for thee, and feede on him in thy hearte by faythe, with thankesgeuing', 'Drinke this in remembraunce that Christ's bloud was shed for thee, and be thankefull' (*Prayer Books*, p. 389). However, the bulk of the text of the Book of Common Prayer underwent relatively small and infrequent changes, thus preserving the spiritual richness and the stylistic felicity of Cranmer's serial affirmations of Christian community at the heart of the English-language Holy Communion service of the Church of England.

Papal – not royal – supremacy: Marian counter-measures

In August 1553 Queen Mary proclaimed Catholicism in an imposing formulation that climaxes expressively in a correlative construction likening her will for herself with her will for her people: 'Her majesty ... cannot now hide that religion which God and world knoweth she hath ever professed from her infancy hitherto, which as her majesty is minded to observe and maintain for herself by God's grace during her time, so doth her highness much desire and would be glad the same were of all her subjects quietly and charitably embraced' (*Tudor Royal Proclamations*, 2:5). The Latin mass was promptly reinstated, displacing English as the language of public worship. English Bibles gave place to the revived genre of the Primer, or lay folks' book of prayers and instruction, with thirty-five editions of the Sarum (Salisbury Use) version published in Mary's reign, fifteen of these in 1555. It is a revealing indication, however, of changes in popular religious sentiment that John Wayland's officially approved Primer (1555) lacks highly affective traditional prayers on the Passion of Christ, the Virgin Mary, and the Blessed Sacrament; instead, it features godly meditations and prayers for ordinary occasions of daily life, some of these even authored by the Reformer Thomas Becon.[62]

By the end of 1554 the official restoration of Catholicism was sufficiently advanced for Mary to cease all use of the title of Supreme Head, which, however repugnant she found it, was indispensable to her objective of returning the Church of England to papal submission. That December, Parliament reinstituted the heresy statutes and capital penalties that had originally been passed against the Lollards between 1381 and 1415. Anti-Catholic polemic proved unexpectedly tenacious, however. The Oxford disputation of 1554 that pitted the arrested and imprisoned Cranmer, Latimer and Nicholas Ridley against

---

62 Duffy, *Stripping of the Altars*, pp. 526, 539.

the combined theological talent of the universities led by Hugh Weston as pro-locutor marks its high point.[63] The now all too familiar mode of *ad hominem* attacks on such ranking Catholics as Edmund Bonner, Bishop of London, and Stephen Gardiner, Bishop of Winchester, mark the low points of this polemical literature.

In 1555 the elimination of heresy in England became the paramount objective of Gardiner and Bonner, the chief instruments of Mary's religious policy. Between February 1555 and November 1558, the duration of the 'English Inquisition', nearly 300 persons met their deaths by burning at the stake, and many others died in prison. Uncountable others were threatened or imprisoned, and submitted. About 800 English Protestants went into exile on the continent, mainly in Germany or Switzerland. The scope of the heresy inquests focused sharply on the southeast of England, with the four dioceses of London, Canterbury, Chichester and Norwich witnessing 85 per cent of the burnings.[64]

While pressing ahead with these prosecutions, Bonner recognised the necessity of re-educating the laity in the benefits of the church's ceremonies and sacraments if English Catholicism was to be securely restored. Accordingly, in 1555 he issued *A Profitable and Necessary Doctrine, With Certain Homilies Adjoined*. Bonner's formulary reprints the text of the *King's Book* of 1543 with many local rearrangements and some additional material. It will be recalled that the *King's Book* represents the traditional contents of the English primers as the core of Christian faith: the Apostles' Creed, the seven sacraments, the Ten Commandments, the Paternoster and the Ave Maria. Bonner follows suit exactly, innovating substantively only at the end of his volume where he adds a brief exposition of the seven deadly sins, the seven principal virtues, and the eight Beatitudes in list form and ends with a primer-like assemblage of fifteen collects in Latin: three prayers 'for the most holy father the Pope', three 'for the mooste reuerend Lorde Cardynall Poole' (Reginald Pole), three 'for the Kyng, and Quenes maiesties, and theyr counsaylers', three 'for the prosperous voyage, and safe returne of oure most noble kynge Phylippe' and three 'for the byshop of London'.[65]

It will also be recalled that the *King's Book* appeals to an inclusive sense of Christian community by offering to synthesise faith, justification and good

---

63 Foxe provides a lengthy account of the proceedings in *Acts and Monuments* (ed. Cattley), 6:439–536.
64 D. M. Loades, *The Reign of Mary Tudor* (New York: St Martin's Press, 1979), pp. 332–3.
65 [Edmund Bonner,] *A profitable and necessarye doctrine, with certayne homelyes adioned thervnto, set forth by the reuerend father in God, Edmunde Byshop of London, for the instruction and enformation of the people being within his diocese of London, & of his cure and charge* (London, 1555), sig. Bbb ii v – end. The homilies section by John Harpsfield and Henry Pendleton, cited subsequently below as '*Homilies Adjoined*' is bound-in continuously but separately foliated.

works. What was the closing strategy in the *King's Book* becomes the opening gambit in *A Profitable and Necessary Doctrine*, which reproduces the synthesis of faith, hope and charity in the earlier text. The recycled material sustains the earlier effectiveness of its appeal to a broad spectrum of English Christians:

> Fayth ... maye not be alone, but muste nedes haue hope, and charitye, annexed and ioyned vnto it ... to attayne all whatsoeuer God hath promised for Christes sake ... The promyses of god ... are not absolutely and purely made, but vnder this condition ... : that man shoulde beleue in God, and with the grace of God geuen for Chrystes sake, endeuer hym selfe to accomplysshe, and kepe the comaundementes of God.   (*A Profitable and Necessary Doctrine*, sig. Bii)

Here, however, a polemical edge is added to the appeal in the *King's Book* for a broadly understood Christian faith: 'There [in Romans 3]', says Bonner, 'is ment not the late inuented and deuised faith that is to say, onely fayth' (*A Profitable and Necessary Doctrine*, sig. Biii v). Considerable accommodation of the appetite for vernacular Scripture also characterises Bonner's formulary and distinguishes it from the briefer *King's Book*. What swells the scope of *A Profitable and Necessary Doctrine*, for the most part, are the copious quotations from the Vulgate followed by English translations, as well as frequent quotations from the Church Fathers, with English translations, inserted typically at the beginning of each new section of exposition – before each of the clauses of the Creed, each of the sacraments, each of the Ten Commandments. Yet these copious quotations are not purely accommodation; they are also a means of controlling the appetite for vernacular scripture by offering preselected portions as a substitute for direct lay access to the text.

The best gauge of the literary character and tonality of Bonner's formulary is provided by the substantial passages that have no source or analogue in the *King's Book*. The new material consistently documents the infusion of the oppositional and othering tactics of mid-century polemic. These additions are admonitory, coercive, suspicious of popular misapprehensions – and, stylistically, are laden with the pleonastic doublings of lexical primaries (nouns, verbs, adjectives and adverbs) that mark the authoritarian mode in sixteenth-century English prose.[66] By way of illustration, here is the heavy-handed reproach Bonner aims at any reader of *A Profitable and Necessary Doctrine* who might suppose that the Bible is the source of the necessary tenets of Christian faith. Such a supposition is swamped by the heaping phrasal constructions of this passage of new material:

---

66 On this style, see Mueller, *Native Tongue and the Word*, pp. 162–77, 201–25.

Although al thynges as they are nowe pertyculerly vsed in the catholyque Churche here in Earth, are not so distinctly, particulerly, and expreslye in all wordes, fashions, cyrcumstaunces, and poyntes, set forth, taught & expressed in Scrypture, yet the pith, the substaunce, the matter, the foundation & grounde, with the effecte thereof in generall wordes are not onelye comprehended & conteyned in Scrypture, but also by expresse wordes confyrmed by other suffi-cient aucthoritie, And seyng the Catholyke Church hath soo receyued, beleued, allowed, and approued the said thinges, time out of mynde, therefore it shalbe a very great presumption and an vncomely part, any man to control or con-tempne any such thinges so receued, beleued, allowed and approued by the said catholique church, and in so doynge the same is in dede not worthy to be taken or reported for a faythfull membre or obedient chyld of the said Church, but for an arrogante, noughty, and very wycked person.

(A Profitable and Necessary Doctrine, sig. Cii r)

The severity of Bonner's additions to the text of the King's Book renders the prospect of a resonant, positive evocation of Christian community extremely unlikely anywhere in A Profitable and Necessary Doctrine. In fact, the two likeli-est sites – the expositions of the tenth article of the Creed, 'the communion of saints', and of 'The Sacrament of the Altar' – find Bonner in the first instance wholly preoccupied with conformity and, in the second, intent not so much on establishing Christian community as excluding any person who might ques-tion the sacramental practice of distributing bread alone to the laity. Within a single sentence, what begins as solemn warning gravitates into thunderous denunciation: 'If any man should teache ... the lay people ... and so cause them to thyncke, that the hole bodye and bloude of Christ, were not comprehended in that onely forme of bread, as wel as in both the kyndes, thys doctrine ought vtterly to be refused and abiected, as a very pestiferouse and diuelysh doctryne' (A Profitable and Necessary Doctrine, sigs. Yi v–Yii r).

Thirteen English homilies by Bonner's chaplains, John Harpsfield and Henry Pendleton, are appended to Bonner's formulary. Ten of these are ascribed to Harpsfield, two to Pendleton; the last, which is unascribed, seems to be Harpsfield's work. The subjects include the creation and fall of man; the mis-ery of all mankind; the redemption of man; how the redemption in Christ is applicable to us; Christian love and charity; how dangerous a thing the break of charity is; the church – what it is, and the commodity and profit thereof; the 'Supremacy' – alternatively entitled, the 'Supreme Power' – which is an exposition and defence of the papacy in two homilies; the true presence of Christ's body and blood in the Sacrament of the Altar; transubstantiation; and, to conclude, certain answers to some common objections made against the

Sacrament of the Altar. As the listing of subjects suggests, a dynamic similar to that of Bonner's formulary characterises the series of homilies. The collection begins on a positive and inclusive note. Harpsfield's treatment of the creation of man offers a lofty, celebratory evocation of how God dignified our unfallen human capacities. His homily on the misery of man draws to a close with a momentary echo of Cranmer's consecration prayer from the Holy Communion service, cited above.[67] The echo is possibly a contemporary tribute to the effectiveness of Cranmer's text, although Harpsfield applies it for his own particular purposes – an evocation of Christ's death as a supreme priestly self-sacrifice: 'He is that hyghe and euerlastynge preiste, whyche hathe offred him selfe to God, when he instituted the sacrament of the Aultar, and once for all, in a bloudye sacrifyce, done vpon the crosse, with whych oblatyon, he hath made perfecte for euermore, them that are sanctified' (*Homilies Adjoined*, fol. 11r).

However, in the very next homily, on how Christ's redemption is applicable to us, Harpsfield adopts the tone of oppositional polemic and gradates to rhetorical coercion even as he affirms the universality of the means of access to salvation, which, he declares, 'no man is able otherwyse to knowe ... but onely by the catholyke Churche':

> This catholike churche, and no other company, hath the true vnderstandinge of scripture, and the knowledge of all thinges necessary to saluation ... So manye as deuyde them selues from this open knowen Churche of Chryst, and refuse the doctryne thereof, thoughe they be neuer so diligent in reading of scripture, yet shall they neuer truelye vnderstand scrypture, but runne continually farther and farther into erroure and ignoraunce, euen as a man that is once out of his way, the farther, and faster he goeth furthe, the more he laseth his labour.
>
> (*Homilies Adjoined*, fol. 18)

The Catholic Church becomes, in fact, the grand theme of Harpsfield's and Pendleton's *Homilies*, personified at one point as 'our lovynge and tender mother' who desires to rescue us from 'heretycall and scysmaticall congregations' (fols. 31v–32r), but much more regularly asserted as and associated with prescriptive, absolute clerical authority, climaxing in that of the papacy: 'The gouernment Ecclesiasticall, and especially of one to be taken, and reputed as Christes vicar, is the best meane, to let and suppresse heresies ... In dede no one thing can so much suppresse heresye as, if the Authoritie, and gouernment Ecclesiasticall, be accordingly therevnto estemed, and obeyed' (*Homilies Adjoined*, fols. 44, 43). The rhetorical climax of the compounding insistence on

---

67 Duffy notes the echo in *Stripping of the Altars*, p. 536.

the power and authority of the Catholic Church in these homilies arrives at an affirmation of Christian community only through a vehement othering of the image of England as an immemorial, independent *imperium* that had been assembled for Henry VIII in the *Collectanea*:

> If you be desirous to haue example in thys matter, loke but on ... our owne country of England, thys maye be truely spoken, that of al realmes christen there is none that hath (besydes the generall duety) so speciall cause to fauour the see of Rome as Englande hath. For from that see, cam the fayth into this Iland ... And what benefittes we haue in our daies receaued of that see of Rome, all menne doo perceyue, and feale in them selues, & do thanke god therefore, or elles the deuyll hath wonderfullye blynded and seduced them.
>
> (*Homilies Adjoined*, fols. 53–4)

The prose here is Harpsfield's, but the relentlessly dichotomous structures of thought and expression are those endemic to the English religious polemics of this mid-century era. If Bonner's *A Profitable and Necessary Doctrine* could extensively reuse Henry's doctrinal formulations in the *King's Book*, nonetheless, as the ideological and rhetorical precondition of its single evocation of Christian community, the *Homilies Adjoined* must anathematise Henry's royal supremacy and the English Reformation:

> Nowe on the other side, what miseries haue befalen emongest vs synce our disobedience agaynst the sea of Rome, and synce the tyme, that temporall prynces dyd take vpon them, that offyce, which is spirituall, and not belongynge to the regall power, but greatly distant, and dyfferent from the same, I nede not in wordes to declare, forasmuch as you haue felt the smart thereof in dede, and to this day are not quyte of Gods plage for the same. Wherefore to conclude in this matter, this shal be to exhort you, and in Gods name to require you to esteme the primacy, and supremitie of the sea of Rome, as an aucthoritie instituted by Christ, for the quyetnes of the christen people, and for the preseruation of chrystendome, in one catholyke, true fayth, & for the defence of it, agaynst al heresy.
>
> (*Homilies Adjoined*, fols. 53–4)

Postscript: Elizabeth in prospect

Neither the objectives nor the linguistic resources of Cranmer's prose of inclusive affirmation were lost on his goddaughter, Elizabeth, when as Queen and Supreme Governor she sought to establish a Church of England as comprehensive as the political nation. The Elizabethan Prayer Book of 1559 preserves all essentials of the Cranmerian texts discussed above and, as is frequently noted, makes two revelatory changes. The 1559 text deletes the so-called 'black rubric', the petition to be delivered 'from the bishop of Rome and all his enormities', in the text of the Litany.[68] The 1559 text of the Order for Holy Communion splices together from the 1549 and the 1552 texts the two sentences spoken by the priest to the communicant in administering the bread and wine, to yield:

> The body of our Lord Jesus Christ which was geuen for thee, preserue thy body and soule into euerlasting life: and take and eate this, in remembraunce that Christ died for thee, and feede on hym in thy hearte by faythe, with thanksgeuinge.

> The bloud of our Lord Jesus Christ which was shed for thee, preserue thy body and soule into euerlasting life: and drynke this in remembraunce that Christes bloud was shed for thee, and be thankeful.[69]

This splicing of sentences may court contradiction in its reach to accommodate the period's range of beliefs regarding the sacrament variously termed the Lord's Supper, Holy Communion, the Sacrament of the Altar, or the Mass. The tactic accords well, however, with the rhetoric of accommodation that pervades the quatrain composed by Elizabeth in prison, probably in 1554 when Gardiner's implacable hostility and Mary's suspicions about her religious beliefs and her possible political intriguing put her in mortal danger:

> 'Twas Christ the Word that spake it.
> The same took bread and brake it,
> And what he there did make it,
> So I believe and take it.[70]

Princess Elizabeth's rhetoric of accommodation, however, develops as the obverse of the inclusive articulations available to Cranmer in his authoritative position as Archbishop of Canterbury and Primate of All England. Like the imprisoned and deeply suspected Anne Askew, Elizabeth employs her correlative constructions ('Twas... The same, And... So) as envelopes for repeated predications with 'it' – a pronoun that remains unspecific because it refers beyond the range of anything explicitly said.[71]

---

68 *The Book of Common Prayer 1559: The Elizabethan Prayer Book*, ed. John E. Booty (Washington, DC: Folger Shakespeare Library, 1976), pp. 69, 293.

69 [Thomas Cranmer,] *The boke of common praier, and administration of the sacramentes, and other rites and ceremonies in the Churche of Englande* (London, 1559), sig. Ni r. I follow Booty's choice of copy text; the quoted sentences are found on p. 264 of his edition.

70 *Elizabeth I: Collected Works*, ed. Leah S. Marcus, Janel Mueller and Mary Beth Rose (University of Chicago Press, 1999), p. 47.

71 The contrast with the declarative assurance of Edward VI's lyric on the Eucharist is also telling. See Chapter 9 above, p. 250.

As in Cranmer's Holy Communion service, the quatrain reprises the Biblical scene of Christ celebrating Passover with his disciples in the breaking of bread. If Christ's physical presence is affirmed to limit construals of the phrase 'what he there did make it', 'make' nevertheless sustains connotations that are compatible with transubstantiation in this underspecified context. 'Make' recurs at crucial junctures in Cranmer's Holy Communion service: it is first used of 'thine only sonne Jesu Christ... upon the crosse' who 'made there' – wording close to Elizabeth's – '(by his one oblacion once offered) a full, perfect, and sufficient sacrifyce, oblacion, and satysfaccyon, for the sinnes of the whole worlde'; it is next used twice of human action in obedience to Christ's commands: 'we thy humble seruauntes do ... make here before thy diuine Maiestie, with these thy holy giftes, the memoryall whyche they sonne hath wylled us to make'. As for 'take' in Cranmer's Holy Communion service, in the 1549 text it appears only in the quotation from I Corinthians, 'Take, eate', but in the 1552 version it appears there and in the decisively altered sentence at the administration of the bread: 'Take and eate this, in remembraunce that Christ dyed for thee, and feede on him in thy heart by faythe, with thankesgeuing.' Cumulatively, the vocabulary of Elizabeth's quatrain appears most closely aligned with Cranmer's formulations of sacramental meanings, while not articulating those meanings as the two texts of his Holy Communion service do. Together with Tyndale's Biblical translations and the soon-to-appear volumes of Foxe's *Acts and Monuments*, Cranmer's studied rhetoric of inclusive affirmation and Christian community comprises the most enduring literary legacy of the Church of England's first three decades of Reformation.[72]

72 On John Foxe's literary legacy, see John R. Knott, Jr, *Discourses of Martyrdom in English Literature 1563-1694* (Cambridge University Press, 1993).

3

THE ERA OF ELIZABETH AND JAMES VI

Chapter 10

LITERATURE AND NATIONAL
IDENTITY

CLAIRE McEACHERN

To describe Scottish, English, Irish or Welsh national discourses in the latter half of the sixteenth century as discrete intellectual traditions would credit unduly the propaganda of nationhood itself, and grant the claim of national autonomy to a moment when national identities were even more interdependent than they would become. Such interdependence is perhaps especially true for members of the British archipelago (both then and now). It is not that the concept of an independent Scotland or England does not exist in this period. (Ireland and Wales are largely beyond the pale of national self-representations at this time – at least in the English language – though they did indeed have identities within an imperial British state thrust upon them.) But the identities of these British nations are developed in relation to each other, both discursively and politically. Their representations are further interwoven both by virtue of their authors' membership in a common cultural milieu, and especially by virtue of the fact that the two countries define themselves first and foremost as an effect of Protestantism, and in relation to its enemies.[1] When Henry VIII declared in 1533 that 'this realm of England is an empire... without restraint or provocation to any foreign princes or potentates of the world',[2] he struck a rhetorical alliance of Protestantism and resistance to alien domination which would circulate throughout the Tudor century, sometimes in ways uncongenial to monarchy.

In discussing the languages of national identity in this period it is also important to keep in mind the multitude of political models that were available to describe a sovereign community, its institutions, and the relations between them. These identities included classical and scriptural notions of the polity (e.g., Augustan Rome, Hebrew commonwealth); multiple theories of political

---

1 For instance, a *British* genealogy of writings on nationhood in the sixteenth century might well look like Boece/Mair/Vergil/Cranmer/Foxe/Knox/Leslie/Jewel/Camden/ Llywd/Buchanan/Holinshed/Hume/Hooker/Craig.
2 Act in Restraint of Appeals, 1533 (24 Henry VIII c. 12).

origin (e.g., natural law, divine law, conquest or consent); institutional identities such as the primitive church or the Ancient Constitution; and contemporary state formations: papal empire, Genevan theocracy, universal monarchy or the Dutch republic. The new world hovered as both antitype and prototype, as did Britain's own colonial pasts. Theories of cultural origin ranged from the theological to the philological, and could even combine the two (for instance, in the Tower of Babel).[3] National representations in the latter half of the sixteenth century draw upon all of these sources, often quite promiscuously. Their genres are diverse (history, sermon, poem and play), as are their tones (elegiac, comic, apocalyptic). The nation-state is arguably an innovative political form in this period, and its authors sought to describe it with all available resources.

Scottish models of national identity

While the inception of the Reformation in Scotland during the late 1550s marks a new era for the Scottish languages of national identity in this period, they were heavily informed by texts of the previous generation and, as ever, by political and historiographical relations with England. Mid to late sixteenth-century writers who sought to describe a cultural identity and history for Scotland had inherited the contrasting claims of writers Hector Boece and John Mair (Major), each of whom sought to establish an understanding of Scotland's historical autonomy with respect to English claims of imperial British sovereignty. Boece's 1526 *Scotorum historiae* (trans. 1531) followed and extended John of Fordun's *Scotichronicon* (1384) in its claim that Scotland was founded by the marriage of the Greek Gathelus to the Egyptian Scotia in 1500 BC. Their descendants were imagined to have conquered both Ireland and Argyll (via Spain, in flight from the Romans), and ultimately generated the unbroken dynasty of Scottish Kings who first became visible (and countable) with Fergus I in 330 BC. Boece claimed, in other words, that Scotland was the oldest nation in Europe, and, unlike the English, had never suffered Roman conquest.

This narrative of Scotland's origin, modelled on Livy, sought to provide a counter-myth to the English location of a greater British sovereignty in the founding of Brutus (great-grandson of Aeneas), and his subsequent tripartite division of the island amongst his sons Locrine, Albanactus and Camber, who received England, Scotland and Wales, respectively; when Albanactus died

---

3 On this point see Colin Kidd, *British Identities before Nationalism: Ethnicity and Nationhood in the Atlantic World, 1600–1800* (Cambridge University Press, 1999).

without issue, Scotland reverted to the possession of Locrine.[4] This latter British myth was first propagated by Geoffrey of Monmouth in the twelfth century, but is addressed with enthusiasm as well as criticism in the sixteenth. It argued for Scotland's origins as a sub-province of a greater Britain, and supported English claims to the homage of Scottish Kings. Scottish writers throughout the period would take issue with this position; Sir Thomas Craig attacks it in 1605 in his contribution to the union debates which followed James I's accession to the English throne: 'I found my choler begin to rise, and that it happened to me exactly as Holinshed had foretold, for there is nothing, says he, which will vex a Scotsman more.'[5] By contrast, Boece's claims for Scottish autonomy rested fundamentally on the notion of an unbroken line of sovereign, non-British and non-homage-paying Scottish Kings. His work thus sought to elaborate upon the seven centuries left unspecified in Fordun, from Fergus I to Fergus II (330 BC to AD 403). He named forty-five kings and their accomplishments, which included resisting Romans, exterminating Picts, subjecting Britons and repulsing Danes; above all, they persistently refused to recognise any subjection to the English.

Boece's work was the reigning Scottish history of the sixteenth century, until George Buchanan's *Rerum Scoticarum historia* appeared in 1582 (and the latter, despite working in a markedly different scholarly mode, drew heavily upon Boece's line of kings for its genealogy of Scottish resistance to tyranny). Later writers such as John Leslie and Robert Pittiscottie would present their own histories as continuations of Boece, picking up where he had left off, with James I; so too David Chambers, in his *Histoire Abbregée de tous les roys de France, Angleterre, et Ecosse* (Paris, 1579), relied on Boece for his Scottish material. Yet its account of Scottish national origins was not uncontested, even in its own moment. In 1521 John Mair had published his *Historia majoris Britanniae*, which sought to discredit the founding story of Gathelus and Scotia (much as Polydore Vergil would do with respect to the stories of Brutus and Arthur). Mair's work, while equally keen to underscore the notion of a sovereign Scotland, was written with a view to the cessation of Anglo-Scots hostility and to promote an ultimate union of Scotland and England as equal partners (perhaps through the marriage of James IV and Margaret Tudor). His attack on the founding myths of both Gathelus and Brutus was less motivated by humanist evidentiary scruples than by a desire to eliminate potential sources of ideological

4 See Roger A. Mason, 'Scotching the Brut: Politics, History and National Myth in Sixteenth-Century Britain', in *Scotland and England, 1286–1815*, ed. Mason (Edinburgh: J. Donald, 1987), pp. 60–84.
5 *Scotland's Sovereignty Asserted*, trans. George Ridpath (London, 1695), sig. B2 r.

division between the two kingdoms by discrediting their xenophobic founding narratives.[6]

Mair's work was perhaps more remarkable for its critique of magnate power, and of a too-mighty nobility as a threat to political stability. Mair consequently elaborated a division between highland/island and lowland Scots (the former unruly, the latter domesticated), a division which encompassed kin and inheritance structures, language and modes of existence.[7] In this division Mair was signally unlike Boece (or Mair's student Buchanan), who emphasised the integral character of Scots culture, and for whom the highlander ethos and its fierce kin-bonds were a source of cultural pride rather than fear. Mair is noted for his practical thinking about how to restructure forms of tenancy in ways that would free tenants of the kin feuds of their landholders; however, he also emphasised the reciprocal bonds of King and people (a constitutional emphasis reiterated by Buchanan).[8]

If Mair's ideological aim of union was a somewhat eccentric one in the 1520s, in the 1540s it attracted writers advancing the prospect of Anglo-Scots union in the marriage of Edward VI and Mary Stuart. Others were not so respectful of the notion of Scottish sovereignty as Mair or Boece. Tellingly, perhaps the most prominent voice in favour of the union was that of Edward VI's Protector, Lord Somerset, whose *An Epistle or exhortacion to unitie and peace, sent to the inhabitauntes of Scotland* (1548) served as a letter of introduction of English troops to Scotland. Support for Somerset in Scotland was voiced by several Scots, among them his protégé the merchant James Henrisoun (or Harrison). Henrisoun's *Exhortation to the Scottes* (1547) presented the story of Brutus' conquest and division of the kingdom as a precedent for Scots recognition of alliance with England.[9] His corresponding attack on Gathelus was based on chronological scruples, and he went on to celebrate an apocalyptic vision of British – and Christian – union much in the mode of later sixteenth-century English writers. This was in sharp contrast to later Scottish apocalypticists who, unlike their English counterparts, avoided the Constantinian model of

---

6 David Norbrook locates Mair in the tradition of scholastic philosophy rather than humanism. See '*Macbeth* and the Politics of Historiography', in *Politics of Discourse*, ed. Kevin Sharpe and Steven N. Zwicher (Berkeley: University of California Press, 1987), pp. 78–116. Also see Roger A. Mason, 'Kingship, Nobility, and Anglo-Scottish Union: John Mair's *History of Greater Britain* (1521)', *Innes Review*, 41.2 (1990), 182–222.

7 See Arthur Williamson, 'Scots, Indians, and Empire: the Scottish Politics of Civilization 1519–1609', *Past and Present* 150 (Feb. 1996), 46–83; and Norbrook, '*Macbeth* and the Politics of Historiography'.

8 R. A. Mason, 'Kingship', 209.

9 See Marcus Merriman, 'James Henrisoun and "Great Britain": British Union and the Scottish Commonweal', in *Scotland and England, 1216–1815*, ed. Roger A. Mason (Edinburgh: J. Donald, 1987), pp. 85–112, for a discussion of the propaganda of this moment.

British union (i.e. by means of a godly prince) due to its imperialist implications for a subjugated Scotland.[10]

This instance of English aggression is relatively typical in Anglo-Scots history, and Henrisoun's voice a minor one. But the moment is remarkable in demonstrating awareness of the role played by foundation stories in contemporary constructions of nationhood as well as the impact of political circumstance on the construction of national mythologies. For Henrisoun, it was possible to discredit Gathelus and yet retain Brutus in the service of Anglo-Scots union. Such persuasive efforts were in vain; alliance with England would come, but by way of an aversion to France and a common cause in Protestantism. Still, the instance of a nation constructed so blatantly through propaganda would serve to instruct later writers who sought to inscribe Scotland with their own purposes. By the 1540s, it is clear that a Scottish nation is not a naturalised identity, organic or self-evident, but one shaped by and for political purposes.

These pre-Reformation texts served as both sources and scapegoats for later writers. They circulated a collection of interrelated ideas: a model of Scottish sovereignty based alternatively on racial and/or institutional grounds; a historiographical contest over foundation myths and their rival representations of England and Scotland within a British *imperium*; a long history of Anglo-Scots animosity which frequently, if paradoxically, sought a vision of union (or at least alliance); a sense of Scottish culture as comprised of either the division or the unification of highland and lowland societies; a notion of the aristocracy as either protectors or predators of national strength. These elements were deployed variously according to the polemical goals of their authors, and would continue to be refigured in subsequent attempts to describe Scotland's identity.

The result was a peculiarly mobile notion of Scottish nationhood, one not wedded by nature or necessity to any particular instance of authority. This effect is present in the language of the first Scottish Reformers, the Lords of the Congregation, who, in 1559, bolstered by the accession of Elizabeth I to the English throne, described their initial attempts to establish a Protestant kirk in Scotland in terms which explicitly severed the notion of national community from the retention of any specific ruler (e.g. Mary of Guise, acting for the absent Mary, Queen of Scots). As Roger Mason has argued, the Lords' representations of their agenda, while derived from religious notions of both conscience and covenant (the latter indebted to the concept of the 'band' or verbal contract), principally invoked the 'commonweal' as the identity which they sought to defend against the incursions of French rule, their fear exacerbated by the

10 See Arthur Williamson, *Scottish National Consciousness in the Age of James VI* (Edinburgh: J. Donald, 1979).

recent marriage of the young Queen to the French Dauphin, with its prospect of subjection to France. Styling themselves as a custodial nobility (à la Mair), they wrote to Mary of Guise on behalf of 'the preservatioun of our common cuntree, whiche we cannot sonnar betray in the handis of strangeris than that one of us distroy and murther ane uther'.[11] This notion of the realm's independence from a particular locus of political authority was to undergird the actions of the first Reformation Parliament which, two years later, following the death of Mary of Guise, established a Protestant Church of Scotland despite the subsequent and predictable refusal of the absent monarch to ratify it.

The idea of a Scotland whose existence was independent of a given monarch (if not monarchy altogether) was to persist in political writings – most famously in Buchanan's *De iure regni apud Scotos, dialogus* (1579). This idea depended on the notion of a line of Kings (and those who resisted them) and its viability was aided by the circumstances of the mid-century Scottish monarchy. Mary Stuart was first a minor, then an absent Queen, and, upon her return to Scotland as an adult in 1561, a Catholic one – the only legal Catholic in Scotland. Her insistence on alliance with France as a given of Scottish political policy further set her at odds with those committed to a sovereign Scotland. Her abdication in 1568 in favour of her infant son left the realm once again in the administrative hands of often short-lived regents, and the young monarch himself subject to the influence of – and even abduction by – rival factions. The Scottish monarchy was not in this period a particularly strong practical site of national identity (and after 1603, its function was even more theoretical). Its lack of immediate charisma as a focus for national imaginings did not take away from its power as an ideal – indeed, such a lack perhaps only intensified its transcendent character.

Monarchy was, however, the prime organising principle of early modern European political sovereignty. The absence of such a focus in Scotland was exacerbated by the fact that the country's other political institutions were not, primarily, centralising ones. Scottish law at this time was comprised of a 'chaos of different customs';[12] its administration was further hampered by the lack of legal codification and by the mediating influence of what was perhaps Scotland's most trenchant political institution, local kin structures. While the

---

11 See Roger Mason, 'Covenant and Commonweal: the Language of Politics in Reformation Scotland', in *Church Politics, and Society: Scotland 1408–1929*, ed. Norman MacDougall (Edinburgh: J. Donald, 1983), p. 106. Mason argues that the 'commonweal' language, as opposed to the religious terminology, was not only a more judicious choice for a movement in search of Elizabethan sanction, but more persuasive to Scots nobility, for whom the Protestant language was as yet unfamiliar.

12 *The Jacobean Union, Six Tracts of 1604*, ed. Bruce R. Galloway and Brian P. Levack (Edinburgh: Clark Constable, 1985), p. 5.

Scottish nobility could be marshalled on behalf of national defence, its social structures were not centripetal in design; further cultural distinctions (such as language) between highland/island and lowland Scots also made the notion of a homogeneous Scotland difficult to imagine as well as to administer. The Scottish kirk certainly conceptualised a unified and uniform polity, but its lack of political traction until the 1590s meant that its social reforms were largely toothless for most of the sixteenth century, and such effect as they had was confined largely to lowland Scotland.[13] Even so, the presbyterian programme was always respectful of local prerogatives.[14]

All of these features meant that the Scottish nation was an especially imaginary community in this moment; however, writers were hardly stopped from imagining it – on the contrary – and they did so in terms marked by these very circumstances. John Knox was the chief architect of a social vision of a unified Scotland. His *First Blast of the Trumpet Against the Monstrous Regiment of Women* (Geneva, 1558) attacked female rulers (implicitly Mary of Guise and Mary Tudor) for, among other things, rendering their realms vulnerable to foreign domination through marriage. The patriotic rhetorical impulse of the *Blast* was similar to that of the Lords of the Congregation in its desire to preserve the realm from 'the confusion and bondage of strangers' even at the expense of its current monarch.[15] However, Knox's goal was not patriotism or Scottish sovereignty per se, but Protestantism, and he invoked the former to that end.

Knox's major work, his *History of the Reformation of Religion in Scotland*, was an innovation in historiography as well as in its locus for Scottish nationhood. As his colleague John Foxe had done for the English church, Knox sought to provide a history for a Protestant church in Scotland. Foxe, however, in his *Actes and Monuments* (1563 and subsequent editions), inscribes the church in England within a prophetic Constantinian imperial model of a British polity (with Elizabeth as the godly prince and England as the elect nation).[16] Knox's *History* eschewed these models. Scotland's institutions lacked the immemorial reputation and the evidentiary traditions of its southern neighbour (the English King Edward I was reported to have destroyed many of Scotland's

---

13 Alan R. McDonald writes that 'The system of kirk session, presbytery and synod did not penetrate the *Gaidhealtachd* in any significant way during the reign of James VI... few ministers from that part of the kingdom participated in general assemblies, let alone in the ecclesiastical politics of the period': *The Jacobean Kirk, 1567–1625* (Aldershot: Ashgate, 1998), p. 6.

14 See, for example, the *First Book of Discipline*, 'Concerning the Policy of the Church' (ch. xi).

15 John Knox, *First Blast of the Trumpet Against the Monstrous Regiment of Women* (Geneva, 1558), sig. A2 v.

16 See Williamson, *Scottish National Consciousness*, especially ch. 1.

legal records). The imagination of Scotland within a British imperial scheme was bound to compromise its autonomy. Hence while Knox nominally begins his account in 1422, it really gets going in 1527, and the burden of his *History* (Books 2 and 3) lies in a detailed account of the six-year period 1558–64, with particular attention to the conflict with Mary of Guise, who appears in his story as virtually a first cousin to the Whore of Babylon.

As Arthur Williamson has described, Knox's mode is more typological than historical, with Scotland as a version of the Hebrew commonwealth (e.g., 'we are bold to affirm that there is no realm this day upon the face of the earth, that hath [the administration of the sacraments] in greater purity; yea (we must speak the truth whomsoever we offend), there is none (no realm, we mean) that hath them in the like purity').[17] Knox's Scotland is not, however, a peculiarly elect nation – or rather it is only one among the several that made up European Protestantism.[18]

Perhaps the most significant contribution of Knox's *History* to a sense of Scottish nationhood resulted from its methodology. Like Foxe, Knox reproduces letters, speeches and proclamations (partly in an attempt to remedy the Scottish antiquarian crisis). Furthermore, the narrative is an extremely intimate account of events, often from an eyewitness perspective (though Knox figures in the third person). The work is as much political memoir as typology, especially in Book 4, as Knox moves into his relations of the progress of the church under Mary, Queen of Scots. Knox portrays his encounters with the Queen as dramatic set-pieces, in which the suspenseful struggle of truth against falsehood is worked out in dialogue both pithy (Knox) and pert (Mary). The effect is to give the reader a front row seat at the scene of Scottish history, revealing that history as simultaneously a local and universal process. Knox himself appears as a Scottish Protestant Everyman up against a tyrant: 'I shall' he tells Mary, 'be as well content to live under your Grace as Paul was to live under Nero.'[19]

Knox's history narrates more a birth than a past, and thus his attempts to invent rather than remember Scotland must call forth a national image. It is his *Book of Discipline* (1561), not a history but a plan for society, which most explicitly spells out his vision. Written in order to detail what, exactly, a Scottish Protestant kirk would look like, the text projects a Scotland comprised of a

---

17 *John Knox's History of the Reformation in Scotland*, ed. William Croft Dickinson (London: Nelson, 1949), 2:3.

18 As Williamson notes, 'it was only in the political circumstances of the 1590s that there was a consistent effort to link a reformed Scottish church with a specifically Scottish nation': *Scottish National Consciousness*, p. 39.

19 Knox, *History of the Reformation*, 2:15.

set of nationally uniform practices and institutions. Knox describes everything from the administration of church property to the amount that university cooks and gardeners should be paid. He pays particular attention to educational reforms, in the hope of provisioning Scotland with a godly and useful citizenry, 'so that the commonwealth may have some comfort by them'.[20] While the polity envisioned by this document would never reach fruition, it is among the most ambitious, eloquent and specific of the Scotlands imagined in this period.

Knox's work underscored the partisan potentials of Scottish history-writing. His account, particularly its portrait of Mary of Guise, provoked the rival narrative of John Leslie, Bishop of Ross, who had been Mary's chaplain and chief advisor. Four editions of Leslie's defence of Mary appeared between 1569 and 1571[21], and his *History of Scotland from the death of King James I . . . to the year MDLXI* appeared in Rome in 1578 (he finished it in 1570). Leslie presents his work as a patriotic corrective to English accounts, which he had been reading while (like Mary) in exile in England, and 'in the quikis [which] I consider mony and sundry thinges sett forth by their authoris, of the deeds and proceedings betwix Scotland and England, far contrar to our anneals, registeris, and trew proceedings collectict in Scotland'.[22] But the true antagonist of his account is Protestant historiography, and Leslie rewrites the conflicts of 1558–61 by casting Knox's patriotic and dutiful Reformers as both anglicised and seditious: 'the tumult incressed dalie within the realme of Scotland, quill at last the precheours begouth [began] to preche opinly in divers partis . . . sindre Inglis buikis, ballettis and treateis was gevin furth be thame amingis the people, to move thame to seditione'.[23]

Leslie ends his account with the death of Mary of Guise, and even Knox had restrained himself from treating the events that led to the abdication of Mary, Queen of Scots. Those events, however, were too rich a dramatic vein to remain unmined for long. The writer Robert Pittiscottie (1532?–1578?) took the story up to 1575 in *his History and Chronicles of Scotland*.[24] Like Leslie, Pittiscottie

---

20 *Book of Discipline*, in Knox's *History of the Reformation*, 2:297.
21 *A Defence of the Honor of the Right high, right mighty, and noble princesse, Marie Queene of Scotland* (London, 1569).
22 John Leslie, *The History of Scotland* . . . (Edinburgh: Bannatyne Club, 1830), p. 7. The vernacular edition of this work (1568–70), unlike the Latin, does not include the description of Scottish counties and islands.
23 *Ibid.*, p. 269.
24 This work was first printed in 1728, though it is believed to have circulated in manuscript from 1565 to 1575 (Pittiscottie, *History and Chronicles of Scotland*, ed. A. E. J. G. MacKay (Edinburgh and London: William Blackwood and Sons, 1891)). For an account of the representational cult of Mary, Queen of Scots, see Jayne Elizabeth Lewis, *Mary Queen of Scots: Romance and Nation* (London: Routledge, 1998).

begins with James I, and he goes even further than Knox in depicting character
as a motive force; indeed, unconcerned with the sanctifying filter of Biblical
typology (though a staunch Protestant), he writes Scotland's recent past as a
drama of powerful personalities.

The collective effect of these Reformation histories is to make it quite clear
that by the 1570s the identity of 'Scotland' existed in the eye of its individual
beholder, who brought his own political and religious lenses to bear on its
representation. There were several Scotlands: Catholic, Protestant, lowland,
highland. Perhaps it was the desire to integrate these in a single nation that
prompted George Buchanan's *Rerum Scoticarum Historia* (Edinburgh, 1582).
Buchanan turns away from a scriptural paradigm of nation-formation. He also
locates the origins of Scottish kingship in election and tanistry rather than divine sanction or succession; like others before him, he rejects both the Gathelus
and Brutus founding stories.[25] The most unique feature of Buchanan's work,
however, was its vision of Scottish culture as an integral whole whose heart lay
in its Gaelic culture. In this, he turns what many (from Mair to James VI) considered a threat to Scottish unity into its defining characteristic.[26] Instead of
seeing Celtic kin-loyalties as divisive, Buchanan figures these as the wellspring
of a Spartan aristocratic virtue which protects Scotland against both tyranny
and the effeminising effects of (English) luxury. The highlanders and islanders
in this account appear nearly prelapsarian in their freedom from southern contamination (not unlike inhabitants of the Americas): 'Being ignorant of luxury
and Covetousness, they enjoy that Innocency and Tranquility of Mind, which
others take great pains to obtain, from the Precepts and Institutions of Wise
Men.'[27] Populated thus, Buchanan's Scotland contains more than one cultural
temporality, as the northern inhabitants provide a primitive mirror and origin
of southern society.

In a similar conversion of a source of cultural division into a national strength,
Buchanan locates the continuity of Scottish society in the revolutionary resistance of its aristocrats to tyranny – a project common to his dialogue on political
models *De iure regni apud Scotus, dialogus*, and his tragedy *Baptistes* (1577). The
bipartisan appeal of this vision of the Highlands is attested in its adoption by

25 As elsewhere in this chapter, I am wholly indebted to the accounts of Arthur Williamson
    and Roger Mason for this understanding of Buchanan's work.
26 For an account of this double valence, see Colin Kidd, *British Identities before Nationalism*
    ('In early modern Scotland Gaeldom defined the historic essence of nationhood, yet also
    represented an alien otherness' (p. 123)).
27 George Buchanan, *The History of Scotland*, trans. J. Watkins (London, 1722), p. 53. See Roger
    Mason, 'George Buchanan, James VI and the Scottish polity', in *New Perspectives on the
    Politics and Culture of Early Modern Scotland*, ed. John Dwyer, Roger A. Mason and Alexander
    Murdoch (Edinburgh: J. Donald, 1982).

the Catholic apologist David Chambers, in his *Histoire Abbregée de tous les roys de France, Angleterre, et Ecosse.* Like Buchanan, Chambers described kin loyalty as a source of strength rather than division, and also as a unifying factor in highland and lowland cultures.

The most extraordinary feature of Buchanan's work is its methodological approach, for it is philology that more than anything else secures an autonomous and integrated Scotland. Buchanan accounts for Scottish origins by means of an inquiry into the common family of Scots and Welsh Gaelics (known by linguists today as 'P' and 'Q' Celtics), which leads him to locate Scotland's first inhabitants as emigrants (via the Iberian peninsula) from Gaul. Buchanan is thus able to claim Scotland's independence from the English as well as its antiquity and continuous sovereignty (for unlike the Welsh, the Scots Celts avoided Roman conquest), to refute the British myth, and to advance a unitary vision of Scottish society based on kinship structures. Buchanan sets these claims within an antiquarian apparatus describing Scotland's geography and customs, much like those that were becoming fashionable in contemporary English works such as Camden's *Britannia* (1586).[28]

Buchanan's opinions about the respective virtues of tyrants and highlanders alike rendered his work politically suspect; his book was called in by the authorities, ostensibly for corrections, and was not reissued. But the Scottish family was to prove an attractive trope of national history to other writers, and in the 1580s David Hume of Godscroft began compiling his *History of the House of Douglas.* Hume is explicit about the larger function of his local account: 'the matter then first is a particular discourse, onely a simple deduction and historie of a private familie, 3 it which discovereth truly, the famous renomine [renown] of an whole nation'.[29] Like Buchanan, Hume's impulses were classicist, and he disallowed natural law as an origin of political authority. Again, the guardians of national virtue are the families whose land-base provides them with means to resist tyranny and other perversions of the court; correspondingly, a presbyterian church was more likely to resist state corruption.

This view of Scots 'kindnesse' coexisted with its contrary, of course. The preacher Robert Bruce linked familial blood bonds and transubstantiation as equally corrupt forms of consanguinity,[30] and James VI himself wrote

28 Buchanan was in fact writing against the accounts of both Camden and Humphrey Llwyd, whose 1572 *Breviary of Britain* had denounced the account of Boece and denied the existence of a Scottish kingdom prior to the fifth century BC.

29 *David Hume of Godscroft's The History of the House of Douglas*, ed. David Reid, 2 vols., (Edinburgh: Scottish Text Society, 1996) 1:8. See Arthur Williamson, 'A Patriot Nobility? Calvinism, Kin-Ties and Civic Humanism', *Scottish Historical Review* LXXII (1993), 1–21.

30 See Williamson, *Scottish National Consciousness*, p. 69.

damningly in *Basilikon Doron* of Gaelic culture, with its 'barbarous feudes',
and, in the *True Law of Free Monarchies*, located the source of monarchy not in
consent but in conquest, 'directly contrarie . . . to the false affirmation of such
seditious writers, as would perswade us, that the Lawes and statutes of our
countrie were established before the admitting of a King'.[31] For James, loyalty
to country was a political menace rather than a virtue, and he scorned as seditious the notion that 'everie man is borne to carrie such a naturall zeale and
dutie to his common wealth, as to his Mother'.[32]

One of the ironies of the Scottish Reformation is that it accentuates the
division of Gaelic from lowland Scotland precisely on the grounds on which
Buchanan sought to integrate them. Despite Buchanan's focus on linguistic
families as well as the other kind (and Hume went so far as to claim that English
itself was derived from Scots), the fact was that the media of the Reformation
were to a large extent English. No Scots Bible was published during this time,
and Reformers' urgings for a vernacular Scripture meant, in effect, worship
in a tongue quasi-alien in the south and wholly so in the north. Knox's work
was written in English, and Buchanan's in Latin; while writers such as Leslie,
Pittiscottie and Hume wrote in Scots, the last of these recognised the foolhardi-
ness of the choice: 'My tongue and words bewray my Country; the subject of this
discourse, the persones described, the author, and what els, al inioying the
honour and covered with the lustre of a Scottis habit. Nather find I reason to
employ my penne in the envious recherce of any highborne idiome, against the
custome almost of al prudent writers' (Hume, *House of Douglas*, 9). It is perhaps
due to the failure of the kirk to embrace Scots that a popular belletristic tradition
of national imaginings did not fully materialise in Scotland at this time. James I
was the centre of a court group of poets (the 'Castalian Band') that thrived from
the mid 1580s to the mid 1590s, and attempted to launch a movement of Scots
poetry, for 'Poesie now . . . being come to mannis age and perfectioun . . . there
hes neuer ane of thame [poets] written in our language.'[33] But perhaps because
this elite circle had the King at its centre, it did not generate a patriotic poetry,
for Scottish patriotism had long existed in some tension with its monarchy.

The usual places where we look for the writing of nationhood – or rather, the
places that English languages of nationhood have accustomed us to look – did

31 James I, *Basilikon Doron*, in *The Political Works of James I*, ed. Charles McIlwain (Cambridge,
   MA: Harvard University Press, 1918), p. 25; *The True Law of Free Monarchies* (Edinburgh,
   1598), sig. D5 v.
32 *True Law*, sig. D5 v.
33 *Ane Schort Treatise, Contening some Revlis and cautelis to be observit and eschewit in Scottis Poesie*
   (Edinburgh, 1585), repr. in English Reprints, ed. Edward Arber (Westminster: Archibald
   Constable, 1869), p. 54.

not exist in the same way that they did in England. The kirk in Scotland moved to suppress drama by the late sixteenth century, and is also thought to have suppressed one of Scotland's earliest literary anthologies, the Bannatyne MS of 1568, though that was itself a collection of largely medieval poetry. Indeed, medieval poets still served to speak for Scotland in this period. Blind Harry's *Acts and Deeds of Sir W. Wallace* (*c.* 1492) was reissued in 1570, 1594, 1600 and 1611, as was Barbour's *Bruce* (*c.* 1375) in 1571 and 1616. It is thus to the more ephemeral traditions of ballads and broadsides that we must turn for a literary Scotland. The events of Mary's reign, for instance, provided poetic fodder for anonymous rhymers, and the poet Robert Sempill flooded the market in the early 1570s with occasional 'ballats' on subjects like the siege of Edinburgh, 'the Lamentation of Lady Scotland' and 'ane fugitive Scottisman that fled out of Paris at this lait Murther'.[34] One might think that the polemical divisions engendered by the Reformation accorded with the adversarial temper of flyting, a contest of poetical invective. The allegorical *Cherrie and the Slae* (1597) of Alexander Montgomerie, which addressed religious difference, might be considered to be implicitly addressing a distinction important to nationhood. As the historiography of this period suggests, imagining Scotland was always a polemical act, and the most engaging visions of the Scottish nation did not disguise the fact of the divisions that constituted it.

English models of national identity

If the Scottish nation existed in some tension with the institution of monarchy, its English counterpart was shaped by a relative identification between them. Writers figured this identification as an essential, organic and divinely engineered fact, cemented by the providential progress of English Protestantism. This fiction of intimacy between Crown and community helped to breed a brief but powerful patriotic literature whose sentimental force can often mask the cultural contradictions of its moment. Nonetheless, the centripetal vision of an internally unified England singled out by divine providence always coexisted with counter-images of England's internal divisions and of its dependence upon the common European contexts of nation-formation.

It is not, for instance, that mid-century England was lacking in strong criticism of monarchic power; the Marian persecutions of Protestants had

---

34 *The Sempill Ballates* (Edinburgh: T.G. Stevenson, 1872). See also the work of Sir Richard Maitland, e.g., 'Of the Assemblie of the Congregatioun, 1559'; 'On the New 3eir, 1560'; 'Of the Quenis Maryage' (1558); 'Of the Wynning of Calice' (1558).

guaranteed it. Like John Knox, writers such as Christopher Goodman and John Ponet in the late 1550s elaborated a notion of community which could if necessary supersede an ungodly monarch, and which developed the notion of popular responsibility for national identity.[35] Legal forms and traditions also provide for an extra-monarchic understanding of the continuity and inviolability of English customs and institutions. The notions of the Ancient Constitution and the immemorial custom undergirding English common law, and protected in the reiterated performances of Parliament, served to identify a non-monarchic locus of political continuity, community and authority. Written in the mid 1560s, Sir Thomas Smith's *De Republica Anglorum* (London, 1583) sited English communal identity in participatory and consensual practices, describing Parliament as a place 'the most high and absolute power of the Realm of England', where 'everie Englishman is entended to be there present, either in person or by procuration and attornie, of what preheminence, state, dignitie or qualitie soever he bee, from the Prince ... to the lowest person of Englande. And the consent of Parliament is taken to be everie man's consent.'[36] The independence, and interdependence, of royal and parliamentary authorities was focused quite early on in Elizabeth's reign by debate on questions of the succession and Elizabeth's marriage, and it is present in full force in the union debates which followed James I's accession to the English throne in 1603. The play *Gorbuduc* (1565), by Thomas Sackville and Thomas Norton, written for the 1561–2 Christmas festivities at the Inner Temple, considers the disasters that result from a monarch who fails to heed the advice of his counsellors on the question of succession; it was reprinted in 1590, at a time when Elizabeth's age and persistent refusal to name her successor made the question even more acute.

This 'parliamentary' strain of political thought argued for a nation that transcended the authority of any particular ruler; hence, if monarchy was the most long-standing and appropriate form of English rule, it was because the nature of the English people preferred it to any other form. The tone of such thought tends towards the integrative rather than revolutionary: people/Parliament/law and monarch are ideally imagined in a mutually supportive and tolerant relation. The most assiduous literary expression of this national synthesis would appear in Michael Drayton's *Poly-Olbion* (1612), annotated by John Selden. This poem appeared in the wake of parliamentary debates over

35 Christopher Goodman, *How Superior Powers Ought to be Obeyed* (Geneva, 1558); John Ponet, *A Shorte Treatise of Politike Power* (Strasbourg, 1556). Also by Henry VIII's chaplain Thomas Starkey, the *Dialogue Between Reginald Pole and Thomas Lupset*, ed. Kathleen M. Burton (London: Chatto & Windus, 1948), unpublished until the twentieth century.
36 Thomas Smith, *De Republica Anglorum* (London, 1583), ed. Mary Dewar (Cambridge University Press, 1982), pp. 78–9. Also see Chapter 7 above, p. 207.

British union, in which the monarch and Parliament, and British union and English custom, came into fierce rhetorical conflict; it celebrates the tenuous communion of local and national allegiances through a personification of the rivalry and interdependence of geographical features.

Nor was the idea of England's status as *the* – as opposed to *an* – elect nation, without its qualifications.[37] John Aylmer may have notoriously said in 1558 that 'God was English', and Elizabeth's relative reluctance to involve her military resources in the various plights of European Protestants gave a practical resonance to English claims of a religious exclusivity and insularity.[38] But even the most zealous patriots acknowledged the hyperbolic status of such claims to singularity. The sheer fact of Protestant-Catholic antagonism meant that the triumphalist voices of English Protestantism had to be conscious of their own braggadocio, and the need for worthy antagonists against whom to shape a national identity. So too the shaping presence and pressure of the former Genevan exiles in constructing an English church under Elizabeth meant that English Protestantism was always aware of its membership in an international movement, its status as one godly nation among others (often more godly). England's relation to a larger universe was also provided by the activities of trade and exploration; it was the goal of Richard Hakluyt's *Principal Navigations, Voyages, Traffiques, and Discoveries of the English Nation* (1598; enlarged edn, 1598–1600) 'to describe the world and show the English active in it'.[39] Hakluyt's project was one of a number of like efforts designed to bring the New World to the attention of the English, and the English – and their merchants – to the attention of Europe; Sir Humphrey Gilbert's, Sir Walter Ralegh's and Thomas Hariot's works were prominent among them.[40]

Notwithstanding these qualifiers about England's unity and its exclusivity, the language of English community under Elizabeth I was marked by an idealised affiliation between monarch and people, institutionalised – insofar as possible – by the protocols of an official church. Perhaps the most succinct

---

37 For discussion, see William Haller, *Foxe's Book of Martyrs and the Elect Nation* (London: Jonathan Cape, 1963); Katharine R. Firth, *The Apocalyptic Tradition in Reformation Britain, 1530–1645* (Oxford University Press, 1979); and Jesse Lander, 'Foxe's Books of Martyrs: Printing and Popularizing the *Acts and Monuments*', in *Religion and Culture in Renaissance England*, ed. Claire McEachern and Debora Shuger (Cambridge University Press, 1997), pp. 69–92.

38 For an account of England's insular and peculiar identity, see Jeffrey Knapp, *An Empire Nowhere: England, America, and Literature from 'Utopia' to 'The Tempest'* (Berkeley: University of California Press, 1992).

39 Richard Helgerson, *Forms of Nationhood: The Elizabethan Writing of England* (University of Chicago Press, 1992), p. 171.

40 See Mary C. Fuller, *Voyages in Print: English Travel to America, 1576–1624* (Cambridge University Press, 1995).

expression of this community appears in Book 8 of Richard Hooker's *Laws of Ecclesiastical Polity* (1593):

> We hold that... there is not any man of the Church of England, but the same man is also a member of the Commonwealth, nor any man a member of the Commonwealth which is not also of the Church of England, yet as in a figure triangular the base doth differ from the sides thereof, and yet one and the selfsame line, is both a base and also a side.[41]

Hooker's attempt to cement commonwealth to church, and both to the governance of the monarch, certainly had a polemical force; he sought to counter sectarian claims for independence from the official church. Other claims for the intimacy of ruler and people also had an ideal rather than actual force, and were phrased in the organic languages of family, nature and providence.

This intimacy is forged out of various political circumstances and ideological inheritances. The Elizabethan church drew its sense both of cohesion and of uniqueness from earlier Protestant thinkers. From Thomas Cranmer's architecture for an Edwardian Protestantism, resurrected and modified with the accession of Elizabeth I, Elizabeth's subjects received a sense of their national homogeneity constituted through liturgical practices. The Book of Common Prayer proclaimed that 'where heretofore there hath been great diversity in saying and singing in churches within this realm, now the whole realm shall have but one use'.[42] *The Book of Homilies*, on subjects ranging from idolatry to apparel, provided the ill-educated or idiosyncratic preacher with an official text and his parishioners with a nationally uniform message about the organic and divine order of English social life (these were considered so useful a governmental tool that the Marian regime had adopted them as well). From John Bale's *Image of Both Churches* (1545?), Elizabethan writers inherited a language of antithesis between the true church and Antichrist, which would be fuelled punctually throughout the latter sixteenth century by events which helped to keep alive the sense of threat and vulnerability so necessary to the silencing of internal dissension: the papal bull excommunicating Elizabeth (1570), the Admonition Controversy (from 1572), the usurpation intrigues of Mary, Queen of Scots (1580s), the Armada expedition (1588) and the Nine Years' war in Ireland (beginning in 1593). Successive editions of John Foxe's *Acts and Monuments* would have kept alive the memory of the Marian martyrs, as would

---

41 Richard Hooker, *The Laws of Ecclesiastical Polity*, ed. P. G. Stanwood, vol. 3 of *The Folger Library Edition of the Works of Richard Hooker*, gen. ed. W. Speed Hill, 6 vols. (Cambridge, MA: Belknap Press of Harvard University Press, 1977–98), p. 319.
42 *The Book of Common Prayer* (1559), ed. John E. Booty (Washington, DC: Folger Shakespeare Library, 1976), p. 16.

continental religious conflict. Drawing on the methods of both Cranmer and Bale, John Jewel's *Apology of the Church of England* (1564) defines and defends an English church and its practices, in which much of the definition occurs through the process of defence.

The sense of England created through a xenophobic opposition to Catholic excess often permeates literary works. Robert Greene's *Spanish Masquerado* (1589) depicts the defeated Spanish after the Armada; the Pope, for instance, 'sitting Male-contented, scratching of his head, throwing away his keys and his Sworde, in great choller'.[43] The burden of Greene's polemic consists in glosses on his tableaux, which generally rehearse the usual perfidies of Catholic practices and those who embrace them. Shakespeare's history plays *King John* and *Henry VIII: All is True* (the latter co-authored with John Fletcher) are unusually aggressive among his works in their portrayals of a nefarious and meddling Catholic clergy, from medieval papal legates to Wolsey. 'No Italian priest / Shall tithe or toll in our dominions' cries King John, in distinctly Tudor tones, 'I alone, alone do me oppose / Against the Pope and count his friends my foes'.[44] A similar though less religiously explicit animus against foreign perversions ('the art of atheisme, the art of epicurising, the art of whoring, the art of poysoning, the art of sodometrie') drives the journey of Nashe's Jack Wilton in his *Unfortunate Traveller* (1594), though Nashe's text is as much fascinated as repulsed by the excesses it describes.[45]

Spenser's *Faerie Queene* (1590–6) begins with an explicit invocation of the struggle between true and false churches in Book 1, and is concerned throughout with the conduct of its heroes in an alien landscape, their resistances to it and their seductions by it. Like Nashe's Wilton, Spenser's knights are innocents abroad, whose knowledge of their own identity is forged through encounters with foreigners. Much as an English church, in order to remain a visible and recognisable form, had to share in ritual practices common to its antagonists (a fact which rendered it vulnerable to sectarian charges of papistry), so being English required a diffident affiliation with the foreign. This dynamic is also present in self-caricatures of English fashion in this period, in which the inherently fickle nature of an Englishman's dress was compounded by an indiscriminate appropriation of foreign styles, regardless of their national origin (such charges were lodged against English vocabulary as well).

43 Robert Greene, *Spanish Masquerado*, in *The Life and Complete Works*, in *Prose and Verse, of Robert Greene*, ed. A. B. Grosart, 15 vols. (London: Huth Library, 1881–6), 5:242.
44 *King John*, ed. L. A. Beaurline, in *The New Cambridge Shakespeare* (Cambridge University Press, 1990), 3.1.170–1.
45 Thomas Nashe, *The Unfortunate Traveller, and Other Works*, ed. J. B. Steane (Harmondsworth: Penguin, 1972), pp. 342–6.

However, of all the writers who contribute to an English national language and image under Elizabeth, it is perhaps John Foxe who stands out (if alongside Shakespeare). His *Acts and Monuments* first appeared in English in 1563 (and reached seven editions by 1631). Foxe's text combined legal and ecclesiastical history, eyewitness accounts, letters and other official documents; perhaps most important of all for bringing English history alive to his audience, his volumes were illustrated with large and detailed woodcuts. Page upon page of English persons of all ranks (and genders) die for their faith, dignified in the face of papal tyranny; the effect is at once tragic and triumphant.

Significantly, Foxe includes Elizabeth herself among them, in a treatment of a 'tragical matter' that unites her with her people in their suffering. This is her plight under Mary, with which he concludes his narrative (though the portrayal appeared when 'the Lady Elizabeth' had been Queen for twenty-four years):

> we have first to consider in what extreme misery, sickness, fear, and peril her Highness was; into what care, what trouble of mind, and what danger of death she was brought, . . . clapped in the Tower, and again tossed from thence, and from house to house, from prison to prison, from post to pillar, and guarded with a sort of cut-throats which ever gaped for the spoil.[46]

Elizabeth's human (and very feminine) vulnerability renders her as one with – if not of – her eventual subjects, 'left destitute of all that might refresh a doleful heart, fraught with full terror and thraldome'.[47] As with some of Shakespeare's kings, such sufferings include the conventional 'it's lonely at the top' moment, in which Elizabeth 'hearing upon a time out of her garden at Woodstock a milkmaid singing pleasantly, wished herself a milkmaid as she was, saying that her case was better, and life more merrier, than was hers'.[48] Unlike most of her fellow martyrs, of course, Elizabeth is providentially preserved rather than burnt at the stake – 'of a prisoner made a princess'.[49] But the lingering effect of her trials is to collapse the distance between ruler and subject, to imagine the sovereign as a suffering subject in the time prior to her assumption of rule and duty. Elizabeth's trials served to underscore those of her subjects. As Foxe writes, 'such was then the wickedness and rage of the time, wherein what dangers and troubles were among the inferior subjects of this realm of England may be easily gathered, when such a princess of that estate, could not escape without her cross'.[50]

46 John Foxe, *Acts and Monuments*, ed. Stephen Reed Cattley, 8 vols. (London: R. B. Seeley and W. Burnside, 1839 *et seq.*), 8:605.
47 *Ibid.*, p. 619.   48 *Ibid.*, p. 619.   49 *Ibid.*, p. 624.   50 *Ibid.*, p. 604.

This portrait of England's Queen as a damsel in distress resonates in other images of England as well: Spenser's Una, John of Gaunt's (in Shakespeare's *Richard II*) 'dear dear land, / Dear for her reputation throughout the world'.[51] The intended literary effect is to summon the chivalrous indignation of the audience in defence of a tender national honour. Elizabeth's notorious rhetorical identification of her virginity with England's national defence invokes this effect as well. It was a homology made clear by the Ditchley portrait, in which the voluminous farthingale Elizabeth is wearing skirts the edges of a map of England, thus sketching the sense of the nation as a space both capacious and vulnerable.

The personified representation of rule would prove a hallmark of much national discourse in this moment – not least in Elizabeth I's own self-representations. Throughout her career, in both her speeches and public appearances, Elizabeth invoked a language of her own personhood, her common affinity with and for her subjects, and the affective nature of her bond to them. An account of her passage through London on the day before her coronation shows her cultivating a charismatic public persona:

> For in all her passage she did not only show her most gracious love toward the people in general, but also privately. If the baser personages had either offered her grace any flowers or such like as a signification of their good will, or moved to her any suit, she most gently, to the common rejoicing of all the lookers-on and private comfort of the part, stayed her chariot and heard their requests.[52]

Here we see the beginnings of the myth of Elizabeth's common feeling, and the way in which her presence temporarily suspends the hierarchies which configured English society. So too the account imagines the feelings between sovereign and subjects as mutual and reciprocal, an impression which Elizabeth herself frequently encouraged: her love for her subjects is only exceeded by theirs for her, 'more staunch than ever I felt the care in myself for myself to be great. Which alone hath made my heavy burden light and a kingdom's care but easy carriage for me.'[53] This rhetoric is designed to configure the bonds of state as a natural and spontaneous exchange of affections rather than obligations.

Far from attenuating the force of power, such imagery worked to reinforce it. Elizabeth's self-presentation of the monarchy as a feeling person also worked to deflect questions of her marriage (and succession), which were

51 Shakespeare, *Richard II*, ed. Andrew Gurr, in *The New Cambridge Shakespeare* (Cambridge University Press, 1984), 2.1.56–8.
52 *Elizabeth I: Collected Works*, ed. Leah S. Marcus, Janel Mueller and Mary Beth Rose (University of Chicago Press, 2000), p. 53.
53 *Ibid.*, p. 106.

raised by Parliament soon after her accession. 'To conclude', went one of her replies to the Commons, 'I am already bound unto an husband, which is the Kingdom of England . . . And reproach me no more, that I have no children: for every one of you, and as many as are English, are my children and kinsfolks.'[54] Though Elizabeth did not shirk from suggesting the iron fist inside her velvet glove – 'I trust you likewise do not forget that by me you were delivered whilst you were hanging on the bough ready to fall into the mud . . . neither yet the promise which you have here made concerning your duties and obedience' – she was careful to accompany demonstrations of authority with ones of affection: 'though after my death you may have many stepdames, yet shall you never have any a more mother than I meant to be unto you all'.[55] Such figures of queenship rely upon the homological equivalences between natural and cultural orders so frequent in this culture's political discourse, where they worked to secure the hierarchies of civic life by reference to those of the family and nature (themselves divinely ordained). As Elizabeth aspires to be a natural rather than unnatural mother in her care for her subjects, so she insists that they be like dutiful children to her. Such language renders order all the more trenchant for being an effect of feeling.

Elizabeth's language of royal personhood thus serves both to reinforce and yet to render familiar the bonds of state, which, because natural, become all the more binding. Her imagination of herself as a person could include the saucy as well as the sublime:

> though I be a woman, yet I have as good a courage answerable to my place as ever my father had. I am your anointed Queen. I will never be by violence constrained to do anything. I thank God I am indeed endued with such qualities that if I were turned out of the realm in my petticoat, I were able to live in any place of Christendom.[56]

This disingenuous image of Elizabeth defrocked summons a veritable arsenal of rhetorical devices designed to make rule appealing: she is at once resolute, father-identified, divinely ordained, vulnerable, female and flirtatious – both farthingale and petticoat. Moreover, like many of Shakespeare's kings, Elizabeth had frequent recourse to the 'burdens of rule' topos, a rhetorical martyrdom akin to Foxe's own: 'To be a King and wear a crown is a thing more glorious to them that see it than it is pleasant to them that bear it'[57]; 'The cares and troubles of a crown I cannot resemble more fitly than to the confections of a learned physician, perfumed with some aromatical savor, or to bitter pills

---

54 *Ibid.*, p. 59.   55 *Ibid.*, p. 72.   56 *Ibid.*, p. 97.   57 *Ibid.*, p. 339.

gilded over.'[58] While such statements call attention to royalty as a thing apart, they do so by emphasising the element of personal sacrifice required of a ruler, and thus the ultimate commonality between ruler and ruled. This fiction of community was especially resonant in a Christian culture whose central myth related the divinity of a common man.

Charismatic monarchy is thus a powerful component of a language of national fellowship. Admittedly, the intimacy and familiarity so cultivated is not always guaranteed to serve the monarch. Nor was Elizabeth the sole source of such a language. Foxe's representation of the Queen, however gushing, was carefully designed to script a role for Elizabeth as God's own handmaiden, sent to deliver England from papal tyranny into a paradise of Protestantism. Furthermore, the fact remains that Foxe's text honours as martyrs hundreds who defied the combined authority of Crown and church.

Other texts also served to cultivate a double-edged intimacy with the workings of state. From 1559 the stanzaic verses of William Baldwin's compilation, *A Mirror for Magistrates* (in four editions by 1610), presented the rise and – more often – fall of princely personages. Their examples, like the tradition of medieval *de casibus* tragedy, could indeed provide food for thought about the mutable fortunes of worldly glory, but they could also serve as studies of the conduct of rulers, meditations about how not to come to grief, both here and in the hereafter – i.e. what kinds of rule produced what kinds of resistance, and whether such resistance was justified.[59] The chronicles of Holinshed, Grafton, Stowe and Speed made available for review, reflection and perhaps even judgement the conduct of England's past rulers, as not only God's will but also human character became a causal force of political events.[60] Members of the Society of Antiquaries were even more daring in their inquiries into the constructed nature of apparently immemorial institutions. Descriptions, perambulations, surveys and maps of England gave the English a new literacy regarding their political institutions, a sense of their beginnings and mutations in time.

Perhaps most influential of all was the Bible, which made newly visible God's own judgement on a variety of rulers. Despite its official sanction, and exhortations to consensual interpretation, the printed Bible also provided for individual reflection on the moral content of one's own actions as well as others'. The various editions of the Bible (e.g., Geneva, Bishops', Rheims) further made

---

58 *Ibid.*, p. 342.
59 See Andrew Hadfield, *Literature, Politics, and National Identity* (Cambridge University Press, 1994), pp. 81–107.
60 Annabel Patterson has argued that what appears the very shapelessness of this genre indicated a potentially subversive inclusiveness: *Reading Holinshed's Chronicles* (University of Chicago Press, 1994).

evident its own polemical location. Elizabethan England's political culture was indeed built on the axiom of the divine right of Kings and its corollary, passive obedience unto tyrants, but while individual royal excesses and errors in such historical materials are usually recuperated by a providential purposiveness (all roads led to the godly reign of Elizabeth I), the familiarity that they encouraged with England's ruling institutions could not always be guaranteed to serve them as dutifully as might be desired.

A measure of the potentially wayward interest such history could generate can be taken from the literary historiography of the late sixteenth century, both poems and plays. Christopher Marlowe was among the first to realise that, while happy rulers might be all alike, unhappy rulers are miserable in unique and dramatically interesting ways, and his central portrayal in *Edward II* (1594) exploits the conflict between duty and desire to render the vulnerability of royal personhood far more pathetic than Elizabeth herself ever would. Michael Drayton, too, displayed an affinity for the 'human interest' side of England's rulers, and in his long poems *Piers Gaveston* (?1594) and *Mortimeriados* (1596) – later revised as *The Barons' Warres* (1619) – he repeatedly returned to the subject of the King torn between his passions and his kingdom, the mixed motives of his usurper and the plight of his Queen. Drayton had a particular fondness for the private lives of the rich and famous, and his *England's Heroicall Epistles* (1597), modelled on Ovid's *Heroides*, portrayed a series of letters between royal couples (Edward IV and Jane Shore; Rosamond and Henry II; Matilda and King John) conducting themselves as if the chief cares of state are intrusions upon their erotic interests. Again, the effect is to animate power, to render it at once more familiar (in its common pastimes) and more elevated (in the exquisiteness of its sentiments); as in the rhetoric of Elizabeth, the reader is meant to feel both sympathetic to and awed by the sacrifices rule requires. At the same time, there is something rather, well, *familiar* about Drayton's representations of royalty. In a sense, the 'fierce warres' and 'faithfull loves' of Spenser's *Faerie Queene* mine the same sentimentalised image of rule, while the assiduous veil of his allegory suggests that inquiry into political matters is in and of itself a daringly covert activity.

Shakespeare and national identity

The consummate writer of royal character is of course Shakespeare, and his history plays cultivate a volatile vision of the inmost workings of power. Criticism has found evidence for both a subversive and a celebratory Shakespeare, a duality which perhaps testifies to the multiplicity of perspectives required by drama, as well as those inherent to the nature of performance. Monarchy is Shakespeare's recurrent subject, almost to the exclusion of other institutions – law, church or land – no doubt because it is the national abstraction best animated by the body of an actor. From early in his career Shakespeare had fuelled the pace of his literary production with the episodic fortunes of the fifteenth-century civil wars, a subject that Samuel Daniel, in his *Civil Wars* (1595, 1609), had explored as well. What we term the 'first tetralogy' (the three *Henry VI* plays, plus *Richard III, c.* 1589–94) staged the swashbuckling conflicts of civil unrest, which are ultimately harmonised by the providential arrival of Henry Tudor (Elizabeth I's grandfather). Nevertheless, the charismatic villainy of Richard III can threaten to overwhelm the pieties of his downfall, an effect which raises the question why the political (or at least performative) success of God's scourges is so often at odds with a conduct becoming heaven – and so much fun while it lasts.

Shakespeare's second tetralogy, treating the events that provoke the fourteenth-century wars, mounts his most sustained inquiry into the varieties of kingship and the kinds of subjectivity – and subjection – they engender. *Richard II* (*c.* 1595–6) explores the conflict between the sacred kingship of Richard and the political pragmatism of his usurper Henry Bolingbroke in ways that reveal the merits and disadvantages of both styles of rule – as well as the fact that rule, far from being a divinely guaranteed certainty, is often a matter of style. Richard is the most eloquent of Shakespeare's Kings on the personhood of royalty; he trumps both Henry VI (on his molehill) and Henry V (on the eve of Agincourt), not to mention Elizabeth I, on the nearly Christ-like sufferings of the burdens of rule. Henry IV's experience of the civil wars unleashed by his deposition of God's anointed ruler is mainly one in which being King is not what it used to be, and both parts of *Henry IV* confront the discordance of loyalties and values such transitions breed.

However, the loss of former certainties opens up new possibilities for both rebellion and rule, and the plays on the reign of Henry IV are marked by their attention to new sites and styles of political identity. The two *Henry IV* plays (1596–7, 1597) represent this thematic diversity of political identity formally, as a rapid sequencing of court, rebel and tavern scenes which forces an ironic commentary on the respective values of each that works to dissolve the ostensible differences between rule and rebellion. Not just kings but their unruly subjects compete for our attention and affections, including some not found in the chronicle sources, or those who find themselves transformed for the purposes of dramatic effect – for instance, Sir John Falstaff (a Lollard knight become tavern Bacchus) or Henry Percy (a contemporary of Henry IV become a rival of his son). The second part of *Henry IV* echoes the structure and conflicts of the first part, with deliberately exhausting effect, presenting a world aged by the corrosive effects of civil war, in need of moral and political rejuvenation;

the play's focus shifts away from the performance of heroic military action to the desires of old men.

Both parts of *Henry IV* devote substantial space to the youthful career of Henry V, or Prince Hal, who held a shining reputation among England's Kings as a prodigal success whose wayward youth was followed by an improbable military triumph in foreign war. The conversion was positively Biblical, and made for irresistible theatrical and patriotic material; Shakespeare's play was not the only one on this subject (e.g., *The Famous Victories of Henry V* (1594)). Amidst the broils of civil war, the *Henry IV* plays contemplate what goes into the making of a Christian king. Shakespeare credits his profligate prince with a keen theatrical sense of his own reputation and how best to craft it, as if Prince Hal shared with his sixteenth-century audience the knowledge of his own legend. The tension between royalty's private pleasures and public duties is figured by Shakespeare in the tug-of-war terms of morality-play psychomachia (with Falstaff and Hotspur as vice and virtue), but is also self-consciously stage-managed by a prince conscious of his own prodigal myth-in-the-making, and more sophisticated than either of his foils about the rhetorical functions of pleasure and honour alike. However, his rejection of Falstaff at the end of 2 *Henry IV* is no less painful for being known and anticipated, as Shakespeare makes his audience too suffer the sacrifices required of rule.

In *Henry V* the focus shifts from the making of the 'mirror of all Christian kings' (II Chorus) to the making of a political community. Having taken his father's advice to 'busy giddy minds with foreign war', Henry V orchestrates a nation by means of war in France. The shifting scenic perspectives of the Henry IV plays are here complicated by Shakespeare's addition of a Chorus figure whose idealised vision of everything from the valour of English soldiery to the common touch of Henry is repeatedly qualified by the often more equivocal events themselves. The play presents a British nation of sorts, and of all sorts: Welsh, Irish, Scots, English, tavern denizens and nobles unite as a 'band of brothers' to defeat a common enemy. However, the union is temporary and not without frictions, both social and regional. Though the play works towards a truimphalist conclusion, in which the marital union of Henry V to the French Princess Katherine evokes an international harmony and a vision of English strength on a global stage, these are, as the final Chorus atypically admits, highly provisional and even wholly imaginary satisfactions. The play is as much elegy as comedy. It forces us to confront the limits of community as much as it urges their suspension.

The ultimately tragic form of national narratives is a marked feature of the Elizabethan historical imagination, and a striking one, given the ostensible confidence in Elizabethan England's providential place in a divine plan. In Shakespeare's plays especially there is always a sense of the tenuousness of political satisfactions, and *Henry V* is rare in its even sporadic optimism about national coherence. Both *King Lear* and *Macbeth* generate their visions of royal heroism against the backdrop of a nation whose centre cannot hold. So too Spenser's footsore knights, Drayton's heartsore royals and Foxe's suffering bodies all render an England as much melancholy as merry. This mood could result from a number of factors: the formal influence of *de casibus* tragedy, or the dramatic appeal of loss. It may be fostered by Calvinist-inflected English Protestantism, in which the confident election of either nations or persons was always accompanied by the anxious knowledge that the disposition of divine salvation was never entirely clear in this world.

It may equally be a feature of realism – that is, these writers' sense that a community transcending the boundaries of region, status and gender was not only, strictly speaking, illegal but also highly improbable, given the political anxieties in England at this time. For far more threatening to national peace than a foreign invasion by the minions of Antichrist were the sources of internal division. England in the late sixteenth century, the period of its most patriotic literary production, was a small country with no standing army, with astronomical rates of inflation, war with Ireland, sectarian dissension, and preoccupied by the question of who would succeed Elizabeth upon her death. Perhaps the most grating of these threats was religious dissent, not only the Counter-Reformation, but that resulting from Protestantism itself, as those who found the Elizabethan church too tolerant of Catholic practice lodged repeated public grievances. These proponents of further reformation included both those who wished to 'purify' the state church further and those who wished to disassociate themselves from it. By the 1590s, the national church's ability to produce a community both deep and wide had been realised as fully as is possible, but so had its limits – a fact which perhaps accounts more than any other for the plethora and tone of patriotic writing during this decade.

It is curious that Shakespeare's history plays, with few exceptions, do not explicitly address the fact that the English past they represent was a Catholic one. Falstaff is more riotous knight than Lollard, and dies from fever not fire; Henry VIII's Reformation is a marital rather than doctrinal or political event; the clergy throughout are usually scheming and hypocritical, but this is a literary convention which operates from Chaucer to Milton to Molière and beyond. Whether this lack of explicit address is because the Reformation was a less remarkable cultural breach to those who lived in its immediate wake than it is to us, or whether it was so sensitive a political subject that it could only be addressed obliquely, or whether this was a culture which styled the Reformation as a return rather than a revolution, or because, as some have argued, Shakespeare disapproved of it, the fact remains that his plays address the theme of a cultural transition – from a community bound by a transcendent truth to a polyphonic universe of competing claims – through the medium of mortal kingship. In the process, the plays suggest that the sentiment that most mobilises national feeling is pathos – the sense of lost sanctities and certainties all the more precious because they only ever exist in retrospect.

Reinforcing the sectarian assault upon an idealised image of national unity is that posed by the divisions of Britain itself at this time (which were also, of course, religious). While *Henry V* celebrates (?) British union in its congregation of its four captains – a 'weasel Scot', a choleric Irishman, a fawning Welshman and a patronising Englishman – the tensions among them figure among the play's most frank confessions of its own ideality. The notion of an English-British identity which amicably (or even militarily) comprehended the differences of these four regions (cultures? nations?) was among the greatest challenges to what John of Gaunt brazenly described as a 'sceptered isle . . . this little world, / This precious stone set in the silver sea'.[61] This was brought home forcefully with the accession of James VI to the English throne in 1603, and his claim that the island had only '*now* become a little world within itself'.[62] The new King sought initially only to extend the union of crowns to the removal of xenophobic laws and those inhibiting free trade between the two countries, but the questions raised by the ensuing debates about the relations of Kings and laws produced – in addition to a spate of anti-Scots propaganda citing the alien quality of Scots geography and its inhabitants – a parliamentary and juridical defence of English liberty, indigenous custom and cultural integrity whose true linchpin was not an English church but English law.[63]

Studies in contrast: Wales and Ireland

The easiest way for the English to accommodate themselves to the union with Scotland was to invoke the model of the union with – or absorption of – Wales. Henry VIII had annexed Wales to England in 1536, by implementing

---

61 *Richard II*, 2.1.40–8.
62 James I, 1603 Entry Speech, in *A Collection of Scarce and Valuable Tracts* [Somers Tracts], ed. Walter Scott, Esq., 13 vols. 2nd, rev. and enlarged edn (London: T. Cadell *et al.*, 1809–15), 2:62; my italics.
63 For an account of these debates and their literary registers see Claire McEachern, *The Poetics of English Nationhood, 1590–1612* (Cambridge University Press, 1996), pp. 138–91.

the institution of shire boundaries and the English juridical system; the Book of Common Prayer, in English, came into Wales with the 1549 Act of Uniformity. This was a union which, however much still in progress, was finessed at the level of ideology by the identification of the Tudor dynasty with Wales, and imperial myths of the Welshmen Brut and Arthur. Shakespeare's portrait of the Welsh Fluellen as the colonial cosiest with the English King bespeaks England's sense of having mastered the difference of Wales (Fluellen is even permitted, under Gower's supervision, to beat and force-feed the unsavoury Londoner Pistol with his leek on St Davy's Day). Tracts such as Thomas Churchyard's *Worthiness of Wales* (1587) celebrated the admirable ease of Welsh assimilation – 'Kings are obayd, where they were never seene' – although, as in descriptions of other colonial territories, Wales appears somewhat wasted on Welshmen:

> Where if men would, take payne to plye the Plough
> Digge out of drosse, the treasure of the earth,
> And fall to toyle, and labour from their birth,
> They should as soone, to store of wealth attaine
> As other Soyles, whose people takes great paine.[64]

Given, as we have seen, Scotland's own long history with the British myth and its assumptions about the subordinate relation of Scotland to England, the invocation of Wales's status with respect to England was hardly a persuasive model for union.

For if Wales was one model of the relations between England and its fellow occupants of the British isles, Ireland was another; a sense of the relative tractability of the former was conditioned by the difficulties of the latter. In 1565, under the direction of Sir Henry Sidney, Elizabethan policy shifted from the Henrician 'surrender and regrant' model (by which Irish lords would concede allegiance and their lands to the English King, who would then return the lands to the new subjects) to a two-pronged effort to secure Irish soil and allegiance based on both conquest and colonisation. The project was spurred on by the sense of Ireland as a possible port of entry for continental enemies of English territory and ideology (in 1555 the Pope had issued a bull declaring Ireland a kingdom). The first book printed in Ireland was the English Prayer Book, in 1551. Repeated efforts to mount the 'plantation' of Ireland aggravated the existing cultural mixture of 'old English' (in the Dublin pale and towns) and Gaelic Irish (sixty-six feudal chieftains of a largely nomadic culture) by the addition of the 'new English' and Scots settlers, Edmund Spenser among them.

---

64 Thomas Churchyard, *Worthiness of Wales* (London, 1587), sigs. C3 r, F2 v.

However, Elizabeth's reluctance throughout most of her reign to mount decisively the large-scale military conquest considered necessary to secure colonisation meant that Irish settlements were hard put to plant themselves thoroughly.
These settlements were in any case largely a matter of private enterprise rather
than state-supported. By 1593, the increasingly evident failure of these means
to secure an English place in Irish soil and political loyalties resulted in the
Nine Years' war.

Elizabethan writings on Ireland throughout this period portray Irish culture and inhabitants as, in essence, a reprobate horde: lewd, tyrannical, pagan
and dangerous. Where the Welsh, according to Churchyard, were just lazy –
liking 'better ease and rest, meat and mirth, and harmlesse quiet days' – Irish
resistance to the self-styled civilising efforts of the English revealed their barbarian identity (comparable to that of the ancient Scythians), and rationalised
attempts to bring them to subjection and modernity alike.[65] To a culture newly
aware of its own historical identity, characteristics of Irish society appeared as
failures of social progress rather than forms of cultural difference. These included such practices as partible systems of land tenure (tanistry and gavelkind
rather than patrilineal inheritance); the great power of feudal lords (which the
English thought tyrannical); the apparent lack of social hierarchies (the Irish
were believed to consider every man of gentle birth); systems of justice (brehon
law); religion (pagan rather than Christian); dress (the unisex Irish cloak was
thought to facilitate both sex and violence); and a wayward commitment to
herding rather than a rooted husbandry.

The 'old English' writer Richard Stanyhurst begins the Elizabethan tradition with his 1577 *Description of Ireland*, a text which served widely to characterise the country and its inhabitants by its inclusion in editions of Holinshed.
Stanyhurst's Ireland is a potentially bountiful space, Eden without the snakes:
'as nature seemed to have framed this countrie for the storehouse or jewelhouse
of hir chiefest thesaure'. However, like other locations devoid of agrarian culture, it is one wasted on its inhabitants, in whom 'she instilleth a drousie
lithernesse to withdraw them from the insearching of hir hoarded and hidden
jewels'.[66] Stanyhurst is atypical in his ability to endow the Irish with some
virtues; he paints them as a poetic and passionate people, 'religious, franke,

---

65 *Ibid.*, sig. F2 v. The Irish counterpart to Churchyard's *Worthiness of Wales* was his account
    of Irish military experiences in *A Generall Rehearsal of Warres (Churchyard's Choice)* (1597).
66 Richard Stanyhurst, *A Description of Ireland* in *Holinshed's Chronicles of England, Scotland, and
    Ireland*, 6 vols. (London: J. Johnson, 1807–8), 6:41. Other tracts besides those mentioned
    included Sir Philip Sidney, *A Discourse on Irish Affairs* (1577); Sir William Herbert, *Croftus
    sive de Hibernia Liber* (1588); Barnaby Rich, *Allarme to England* (1578), *A Shorte Survey of Ireland*
    (1609), *A New Description of Ireland* (1610); Francis Bacon, *Certain Considerations touching the
    Plantation in Ireland* (1606); Sir John Davies, *A Discovery of the True Causes why Ireland was
    never entirely Subdued* (1612).

amorous, irefull, sufferable of infinit paines, verie glorious, manie sorcerers, excellent horsemen, delighted with words, great almesgivers, passing in hospitalitie . . . Greedie of praise they be, and fearfull of dishonor and to this end they esteeme their poets.'[67] Much as he pictures Irish nature as alluring, Stanyhurst credits the Irish with great powers of cultural seduction over those English insufficiently wary of Irish ways: 'the verie English of birth, conversant with the savage sort of that people become degenerat, and as though they had tasted of Circe's poisoned cup, are quite altered'.[68] As in Brabantio's vision of the alien Othello's power over his gently reared daughter, the Irish here have a sorcerer's power to convert.

Stanyhurst's ability to romanticise the Irish is unusual in this period; or rather, as the trials and tolls of colonial and military efforts mounted, the condescension implicit in his portrait became explicit. For other writers, it was importantly the Irish, not the English, who needed to be converted by intercultural contact, by force if necessary. John Derricke's *The Image of Ireland* (1581) notes the lustful nymphs who populate the landscape, but also its equally unregenerate soldiers, 'with glibbed heddes like Mars hymself, / their malice to expresse: With Irefull hartes and bloudie hands / soone prone to wickednesse'.[69] It is this inflection that governs much of the period's subsequent writing about Ireland. While some writers, such as Richard Becon in the dialogue *Solon His Follie or A politique Discourse Touching the Reformation of Common-Weales conquered, declined or corrupted* (1594), entertained the notion of controlling Ireland through reforming its political culture by instituting common law, other writers such as Edmund Spenser thought such a method pointless in a place with so little regard for the law. For Becon, the Irish are a conquered people, 'still one capable of incorporation into the republic or common weal'; for Spenser, they have yet to achieve the civility which would qualify them for such courtesy.[70] In his *View of the State of Ireland*, also a dialogue, Spenser frankly puts forth the view that possession in Ireland will only be secured through a comprehensive military subjugation. Two divergent views of cultural difference underwrite the discrepancy between these positions: it is either so superficial as to be amenable to a kind of evolution, or so intransigent that it can only be cast off by a people completely broken.[71]

---

67 Stanyhurst, *A Description of Ireland*, p. 67.   68 *Ibid.*, p. 69.
69 *The Image of Ireland, with a Discoverie of Woodkarne* (London, 1581), sig. D1 v.
70 On Becon see Clare Carroll and Vincent Carey (eds.), *Solon His Follie* (Binghamton, NY: Medieval and Renaissance Texts and Studies, 1996), esp. pp. xxvi–xxviii.
71 Though submitted to the Stationers' Company in 1596, Spenser's work was not registered, which some scholars have taken to be a sign that its recommendations were considered extreme even for its own moment. For accounts of its method and subject, see Ciaran Brady, 'Spenser's Irish Crisis: Humanism and Experience in the 1590s', *Past and Present* 111

These images of Ireland are also images of England. The alien quality of Irish culture was, on the one hand, a representation of contemporary English territories remote from the pale of the southeastern counties, and, on the other, a version of England's own past identity, prior to its colonisation and civilisation by Rome. In this sense, the Irish resemble Buchanan's highlanders – although their own obdurate refusal to assimilate to English ways serves as a sign of rebellion rather than a cornerstone of national virtue.

Furthermore, unlike the case of Scotland, no English discourse of Irish nationhood exists in the English language at this moment. The first book printed in Gaelic was the alphabet and catechism, in 1571, and while a translation of the New Testament into Gaelic was underway by 1563 it was not published until 1603. Nicholas Canny notes that while Irish chronicles evince a growing abusiveness towards the English in this period, and Irish warriors often signalled renewed resistance by exchanging English garb for Irish, symbolic warfare in the literary modes of the invading force was not the medium of choice. The works of bardic poets (conscious, like their English counterparts, of their own dependence on patronage) were principally epideictic in nature. Whatever the political choices of the lord in question, few of the *filí* 'sought fit to recommend a coalition of Gaelic chieftains against the common foe. Instead they left political decisions to their betters and praised them in whatever action they undertook whether it was directed against the English or a neighbouring lord.'[72] Ireland would begin to write back, in the Latin of the Counter-Reformation, in 1621.[73] In the sixteenth century, however, the Irish chose to fight their would-be colonisers with real rather than rhetorical weapons.

(1986), 17–49; Julia Reinhard Lupton, 'Mapping Mutability: or, Spenser's Irish plot', in *Representing Ireland: Literature and the origins of conflict, 1534–1660*, ed. Brendan Bradshaw, Andrew Hadfield and Willy Maley (Cambridge University Press, 1993), pp. 93–115; and Debora Shuger, 'Irishmen, Aristocrats, and Other White Barbarians', *Renaissance Quarterly* 50 (1997), 494–525.

72 Nicholas Canny, *The Elizabethan Conquest of Ireland* (Sussex: Harvester Press, 1976), p. 138.

73 With the publication of Philip O'Sullivan Beare's *History of Ireland* (Lisbon) and, in 1634, Geoffrey Keating's *Forus Feasa ar Eirinn*.

Chapter 11

LITERATURE AND THE COURT

―――

CATHERINE BATES

A vast machine – teeming with people and abuzz with opportunity – the royal court in the Elizabethan period was a centre of political happenings, a cultural nexus and a powerhouse of literary activity. Much of that literature came from the top. As the seat of government and as home to the monarch, the court generated a whole promotional literature – public speeches and sermons, official histories and prayers, carefully staged processions and executions, state-sponsored pageants and shows – designed to disseminate power and to maintain civil order by cowing foreign ambassadors and the native populace alike. But the court was also a place where literature came up from below and where writing enabled men to work their way up to what Sir Thomas Wyatt had called 'the slipper top / Of court's estates'.[1] Under the guise of entertaining the court with music, poetry, tournament and dance, upwardly mobile courtiers – and the equally ambitious men in their employ – used literature as a direct way of getting themselves noticed and of advancing their own personal or political cause. Above all else the court was a public space – a place for display and showing off – where all aspects of the drama were cultivated, developed and exploited to the full. But it was also the place where some of the period's most private and intensely introspective poetry was written. The court was an exclusive preserve of aristocratic privilege, a rarified coterie setting in which courtiers amused each other by imitating poetic models then fashionable on the continent and circulating them privately in manuscript among themselves. But it was also an object of popular fascination whose social borders were surprisingly permeable. When in 1557 Richard Tottel published what was to become one of the most popular poetry anthologies of the time – the *Songs and Sonnets*, carefully headed with the name of the Earl of Surrey – he was marketing an idea of courtliness that was immediately seen as saleable, imitable and accessible to a far wider readership. The courtesy book – that unique genre so characteristic

―――

1 'Stand whoso list upon the slipper top / Of court's estates', in *Sir Thomas Wyatt: The Complete Poems*, ed. R. A. Rebholz (Harmondsworth and New York: Penguin, 1978), p. 94. Also see Chapter 8 above, p. 237; and, on *Tottel's Miscellany*, pp. 230–2, 252–6.

of the sixteenth century – also contrived to preserve the mystique of an exclusive courtly class while giving detailed instructions on how to join it. Much of the literature associated with the court was London-based. Yet the court also brought art out into the provinces when, roaming around the country on its annual progresses, it was fêted by the nation's aristocratic houses and by its port, market and university towns. These perennial descents of the court on the regions gave local communities a chance to exercise their own literary and artistic skills. The three-week extravaganza of rustic games, pastoral interludes and costumed masques with which the Earl of Leicester entertained Queen Elizabeth at Kenilworth in 1575 was a remarkable collaboration of sophisticated literary talent brought up from London (including the poet George Gascoigne) and the enthusiastic if more homespun contributions of local folk from the neighbouring Warwickshire villages.

The court was a fount of and focus for every kind of literature from public to private, formal to informal, official to popular, urban to regional. As the centre of intellectual and artistic activity, it exerted a gravitational pull on the literary productivity of the time, even setting a national standard for speech. For George Puttenham, writing in *The Arte of English Poesie* in 1589, the accepted form of English and received pronunciation was to be 'that which is spoken in the kings Court'.[2] As an object of universal aspiration, a site of vicious competition, an inveterate subject of gossip and (more often than not) a source of bitter disappointment, the court provided an occasion and focus for the whole nation's literary output. Indeed, whether it was written by the court, at the court, for the court or about the court – from the most slavish propaganda to the most rancorous anti-court satire – there is scarcely a category of literature (religious writing, perhaps, excepted) that was not in some way influenced or affected by it. So closely were literature and the court identified that, if you were to take the court away, it is no exaggeration to say that nine-tenths of the period's literature, probably more, would go with it.

There were a number of reasons for this. As homes to an aristocratic class which enjoyed the means and the leisure to cultivate the arts, courts had, of course, long been centres of excellence and places of literary and cultural refinement. In the twelfth century, the great lyric and romance traditions of courtly love had evolved and flourished in the seigneurial courts of Languedoc and of northern France. In the fifteenth and sixteenth centuries, however, Europe witnessed a dramatic shift towards the centralisation of political power. The

---

2 George Puttenham, *The Arte of English Poesie*, ed. G. D. Willcock and Alice Walker (Cambridge University Press, 1936), p. 144.

complex and unstable system of baronial courts – cause of so much internecine feuding throughout the Middle Ages – gave way to the gradual emergence of the modern nation-state. Baronial courts that had once been alternative centres of power – internally divided and in competition with each other – were replaced by regimes of strong monarchical and, most frequently, autocratic rule. Once-powerful local potentates were reduced to what Lawrence Stone calls a class of 'fawning courtiers' as kings began to assert their supreme – indeed, divine – right to rule over them.[3] It was in the sixteenth century that kings laid claim to imperial titles and began to be addressed for the first time as 'Your Majesty'. The sixteenth century was the age of *The Courtier* and *The Prince*, Castiglione's and Machiavelli's classic texts being written within a decade of each other (in 1508–18 and 1513 respectively) and setting the tone for the whole of the century to follow. By the sixteenth century the English court came to be spoken of in the singular rather than the plural and it invariably meant the royal court, the centre of the realm and hub of political power. All aspects of court life were enlarged accordingly: its size, its importance, its infrastructure, its organisation, and not least its cultural activity. No longer the leisure pursuit of an aristocratic elite, literature came to be seen as a key form of public relations which could, as Machiavelli observed, be harnessed to serve the encomiastic needs of the prince and so contribute to the smooth running of the state as a whole.

As a burgeoning administrative centre, the court had quickly to develop a well-managed and effectively staffed office system, and in the course of the sixteenth century it became a complex bureaucratic machine. Specific reforms instituted by Thomas Cromwell in the 1530s made for an efficient and streamlined organisation to which our modern system of bureaucratic government stands as the not so distant heir. In the words of one historian, the sixteenth century marked 'the first great age of government by paper', and literary skills were, as a result, in greater demand than ever before.[4] Bureaucracy gave writing a new functionality – and with it a new priority if not prestige – as state service increasingly took the form of literacy rather than military expertise. Abilities which, in the Middle Ages, had largely been confined to the clerical class were now being developed by a newly educated professional and secular class. From keeping records and drafting reports to turning out panegyrics on request, the ability to write became what would these days be called a transferable skill, and men like Edmund Spenser and John Donne, trained at the universities and Inns of Court,

3 Lawrence Stone, *The Crisis of the Aristocracy, 1558–1641* (Oxford: Clarendon Press, 1965), p. 385.
4 J. H. Elliott, *Europe Divided 1559–1598* (London: Collins, 1968), p. 77.

were able to put themselves forward as private secretaries, civil servants and officers of the state. At the most practical level, such posts furnished would-be writers with a livelihood, enabling them to pursue literary careers in tandem with their official duties. It was as a civil servant in Ireland that Spenser wrote *The Faerie Queene* and as secretary to the Lord Keeper, Sir Thomas Egerton, that (at least for the five years before he was ignominiously dismissed for eloping with Egerton's niece) Donne was able to support himself and his Muse.

Although the sixteenth century saw the gradual rise of the professional writer – with dramatists like Shakespeare and authors of popular romances like Thomas Lodge and Robert Greene managing to make a living from their pens – this remained impossible for the majority. For the most part, writers were dependent on a system of patronage, and this was centred firmly on the court. The monarch stood at the top of a pyramidal system in which favoured courtiers could, in their turn, bestow sought-after positions as administrators and tutors on men for whom writing was a direct way of demonstrating their intelligence, learning and intellectual clout. Literature became the unofficial currency of the patronage system – well-turned sonnets, graceful compliments and effusive book-dedications being among the recognised ways by which hopeful candidates would present themselves for the job. Patronage came in all shapes and sizes, from permanent positions to more sporadic offerings, gifts or payments in kind. As tutor to the children of Mary Herbert, Countess of Pembroke, Samuel Daniel enjoyed a comfortable and privileged position in one of the most cultured households of the period, gratefully describing her estate at Wilton as his own 'best Schoole' and his pupil – her son, William Herbert – as 'the fosterer of mee and my Muse'.[5] Donne received £30 from Lucy Russell, Countess of Bedford, to help pay his debts and, as he acknowledged in one of his own favourite poems, the ever-needy Ben Jonson received a whole roebuck from the same lady. Patronage was a two-way system of exchange which gave writers a very concrete reason for putting pen to paper and which sometimes, as in these cases, supported them in their writing. As the focal point for a system that percolated outward and down through a myriad interconnected layers, the court fostered a climate of literary production and contributed both directly and indirectly to making what remains to this day perhaps the richest period in the nation's literary history.

It is impossible to think of literature and the court separately in this period. Indeed, it is a sign of how closely the two were identified that for many years the best and most detailed historical account of the court – its physical

---

5 Samuel Daniel, *Poems and a Defence of Ryme*, ed. Arthur Colby Sprague (University of Chicago Press, 1965), p. 129. On literary patronage, see also Chapter 4 in this volume.

layout and administrative structure – was to be found in the first volume of E. K. Chambers's classic study, *The Elizabethan Stage* (1923).[6] For Chambers the court stood as backdrop to what he saw as the most important feature of the literary landscape of that time – the urban, professional theatre of Marlowe and Shakespeare. That great flowering of Elizabethan drama, unequalled in the country's history, emerged directly from the tradition of spectacle and pageantry for which the court had long been a focus. The Renaissance passion for drama evolved, as he saw it, from a whole array of courtly forms which were not in themselves originally mimetic: state entries and coronation pageants, tournaments and dances, mummeries and triumphs. It was in this context – as the seedbed from which the unparalleled achievements of the Elizabethan dramatists would grow – that Chambers investigated the Revels Office, that key court department which sponsored, commissioned, licensed, regulated, superintended and generally monitored all public events and theatrical shows. To lay the ground for this research he studied the larger body of which the Revels Office formed a part, producing what would remain for at least half a century the most thorough study of that vast conglomeration – at once royal residence, government centre, embassy, stable, hotel and enormous catering operation – which constituted the royal court. The court took its definition first and foremost as a cultural centre, and it says something about Chambers's priorities – and those of so many scholars after him – that understanding how the court worked was a step on the way to understanding the literature of the time and not the other way round.

Not everyone was satisfied with this ordering of priorities, however. In his presidential address to the Royal Historical Society in 1976 the eminent Tudor historian Geoffrey Elton expressed his concern. When he had turned to scrutinise the political, administrative and bureaucratic workings of the court, he said, all he had found were descriptions of gorgeous spectacle and lavish display which, as he saw it, stood as so many enticing veils between the historian and the hard facts he was after. When researching the council and Parliament as political centres he had found a large body of established and well-documented knowledge on which to rely. But in considering the role of the royal court he was bereft of such information and confessed to being 'more baffled than ever'. 'We all know that there was a Court, and we all use the term with frequent ease', he protested,

> but we seem to have taken it so much for granted that we have done almost nothing to investigate it seriously. Lavish descriptions abound of lavish occasions . . . but the sort of study which could really tell us what it was, what part it

6 E. K. Chambers, *The Elizabethan Stage*, 4 vols. (Oxford: Clarendon Press, 1923).

played in affairs, and even how things went there for this or that person, seems
to be confined to a few important articles. At times it has all the appearance of a
fully fledged institution; at other it seems to be no more than a convenient conceptual piece of shorthand, covering certain people, certain behaviour, certain
attitudes.[7]

In Elton's mind 'no one has yet made a proper study of Elizabeth's Court
as a political centre' precisely because it had for so long been seen primarily
as a cultural centre. His attitude was uncompromising. 'We need no more
reveries on accession tilts and symbolism, no more pretty pictures of gallants
and galliards; could we instead have painful studies of Acatery and Pantry, of
vice-chamberlains and ladies of the Privy Chamber?'[8]

The historian's insistence on hard fact and painful study as against what
he clearly regarded as whimsical and self-indulgent accounts of court entertainments is revealing, and since 1976 there have been a number of studies
which have looked into the organisation of the royal household – acatery and
pantry included. David Starkey's work has given us some important insights
into the reorganisation of the Privy Chamber and David Loades has investigated the interdepartmental structures of the court's overall organisation. But
Elton's barely disguised impatience with descriptions of pageantry and costume as obscuring the truth from the historian's penetrating gaze runs counter
to the development of newer historicist approaches to Renaissance literature.
Since the early 1980s these have come to regard cultural manifestations not as
somehow irrelevant or foreign to 'real', painful history, but as the very stuff
of history – and of history-making – itself. In fact in recent years it has been a
question not so much of stripping away the layers of representation in order
to uncover 'the court' lying underneath but rather of seeing the court as itself
a representation – as a dense network of public relationships, a 'work of art
in its own right', as David Loades suggests – and of showing that, quite apart
from anything else, it was in exactly this way that the court was perceived by
the Elizabethans themselves.[9]

In Puttenham's *Arte of English Poesie*, for example, literature and the court are
not presented as two separate if related or even parallel operations. Rather, they
form a continuum. Courting is poetry and poetry courting because composing
oneself and composing a poem essentially come down to the same thing. To
be at court, to play the courtier, to fawn, flatter and ingratiate oneself are

---

7 G. R. Elton, *Studies in Tudor and Stuart Politics and Government*, 3 vols. (Cambridge University
   Press, 1983), 3:38–9.
8 Elton, *Studies in Tudor and Stuart Politics*, 3:53.
9 David M. Loades, *The Tudor Court* (London: Batsford, 1986), p. 7.

specifically seen as forms of self-making – of being on the make – and are therefore forms of *poesis*, the careful cultivation of appearances and of rhetorical artifice. This merging of courting and poetry is nowhere more explicit than in Puttenham's famous allegory of Allegory, the master trope which hides meaning under a cloaking guise and which becomes for him the 'Courtly figure' *par excellence*, 'chiefe ringleader and captaine' of all the other figures which his rhetorical handbook describes.[10] Personified, the figure of *Allegoria* springs to life as the quintessential Elizabethan courtier and we are invited to imagine him, in doublet and hose, alternately creeping, courting and cavorting his way through Puttenham's text. Allegorise Allegory, and when you try to penetrate the surface – to excavate the 'core' meaning lying underneath – you'll find nothing beneath the mask but a masking figure, and nothing beneath that but another, opening up the dizzying prospect of an infinite recess in which any stable meaning or identity is indefinitely postponed. Historians like Elton are cheated of the solid instruction and hard fact they seek as these disappear behind a tantalising veil of rhetorical veils.

For Puttenham the courtier is a creature of pure surface, pure appearance, and his personification of Allegory suggests nothing so much as that the successful Elizabethan courtier might just as well be a rhetorical figure. Sir Thomas Hoby does something rather similar when, in introducing his translation of Castiglione's *Book of the Courtier* in 1561, he too personifies his text as a courtly gentleman who, having 'a long time haunted all the Courtes of Christendom' is at last 'willing to dwell in the Court of England'.[11] If Castiglione's characters had contrived to 'shape in wordes a good Courtier' and Castiglione had, in his turn, shaped these discussions into a book, then Hoby goes one step further by turning the book itself back into a courtier. The book *of* the courtier becomes the book *as* courtier – the refined ambassador of manners to the English court. The Courtier is a book and the book is a courtier, each one as carefully constructed and as tricky to read as the other and both operating under the same masquerade of *beau semblant*, 'the chiefe profession', as Puttenham was to put it, 'of Courting as of poesie'.[12]

This merging of courtship into poetry might encourage us to pause and reflect for a moment on our two terms – literature and the court – and on the relation between them which that small but far from innocent conjunction 'and' implies. To what extent are we justified in seeing literature and the court

---

10 Puttenham, *Arte of English Poesie*, p. 186.
11 Baldassare Castiglione, *The Book of the Courtier*, trans. Sir Thomas Hoby (London: Dent, 1928), p. 2; the following quotation, p. 29.
12 Puttenham, *Arte of English Poesie*, p. 158.

as two distinct if contiguous realms? The matter invites reflection because it leads on to the more extensive question posed by this volume as a whole, and indeed by the larger series to which it belongs, namely, the relation between literature and history. To write about literature 'and' the court is, explicitly or otherwise, to assume a theory of this relation. In the past, critics typically called on the one to account for the other – on the court to explain literature or on literature to explain the court. Scholars of the medieval courtly love lyric, for example, looked to the social mobility and high male-to-female sex ratio of twelfth-century feudal courts to account for the poetic scene of eroticised aspiration there rehearsed. For Johan Huizinga, writing in *The Waning of the Middle Ages* (first edn, 1919), the court of fifteenth-century Burgundy was so imbued with the literary ideals of chivalric romance as to influence not only manners and dress but foreign policy and decisions of state as well – the mindset of an entire age and class so dominated by a poetic fiction that life itself took on the colours of a fairy tale. However different in their trajectory and approach, these accounts each perceive literature and history in the same essentially passive, illustrative relation. Life and letters are seen peaceably to relate, formality being their common theme. A ponderous, elaborate and highly stylised way of life finds itself reflected in the literature and vice versa. Literature mirrors history and history literature, the two solemnly facing each other across a small but unbridgeable gulf, reflecting, symptomising, even embellishing each other yet held apart as firmly, if as delicately, as the two panes of a folding glass.

For Puttenham, by contrast, literature and history exist in an infinitely more dynamic relation. Life and letters are not inert, static categories, reflecting each other across the void. History is not a given, something immanent and already there waiting to be influenced by literature. The court is not the more or less colourful backdrop against which poetry emerges in all its colourful array. On the contrary, the court is relentlessly shown to be a literary construction – actively produced with words – and the outcome of a complex network of propaganda, anecdote, narrative and myth. Indeed, as a structure of power and interlocking relationships, the court does not exist *except* in such representations. 'The court' constitutes the sum total of all such discourses, and *The Arte of English Poesie* – like *The Book of the Courtier* – is nothing less than a detailed programme of their production, laying down exactly how the appearance of courtliness is rhetorically to be constructed and maintained. Courtliness depends, Puttenham shows, on the effectiveness of the representation, on the ability to persuade, to master the art of rhetoric. It depends on the consistency and plausibility of the surface narrative. Poetry is not the natural offshoot of refined and civilised surroundings. It is the collective name for the set of social and political processes by which those surroundings are brought about.

So our theme is less 'literature and the court' than the court *as* literature, courting *as* poesie. As so much new historicist writing has emphasised since the early 1980s, this gives literature a new agency – a power to create worlds and selves. Literature does not just reflect things. It makes things and it makes things happen. Puttenham's self-declared aim in the *Arte* is 'to make of a rude rimer, a learned and Courtly Poet', such making (from the Greek ποιειν) figuring in the book's opening sentence as the very definition of poetry itself.[13] As Sidney noted in the *Apology for Poetry*, the English followed the Greeks in calling the poet 'a maker', adding 'how high and incomparable a title it is'.[14] Making a poem, making a poet, making a personality – they all boil down to the same thing. Like Spenser's hope that *The Faerie Queene* would serve 'to fashion a gentleman' – to civilise and advance him – this ambition belonged to the new humanist doctrine of the Renaissance which saw man as a work of art. It was within the power of every individual to work, mould and shape himself – to make gold out of the brazen, and to sculpt from the raw material of nature a more perfect human being. 'As though the maker and moulder of thyself', wrote Pico della Mirandola in his oration *On the Dignity of Man* (1486), 'thou mayest fashion thyself in whatever shape thou shall prefer'.[15] The manipulation of appearances, the invention of an identity, the construction of a self and presentation of it to the world, the ability to gauge and to calculate effects – all these were rhetorical skills, ones which the new humanistic education saw as its first duty to teach.

As a public sphere where such self-making was practised, honed and (in the whole courtesy-book genre) examined with a self-consciousness never before imagined – and where opportunism, enterprise and initiative could lead in some cases to the most spectacular material rewards – the court has often held a special fascination for new historicist critics. Geoffrey Elton wanted to get behind appearances to the hard facts below, but it is no accident that he remained baffled – that no one had (to his mind) satisfactorily done so before him and that no one has really been moved to do so since. For the question hangs uncertainly: what exactly *was* the court? It wasn't a particular building – the sovereign and the royal retinue moved from palace to palace every five or six weeks, putting up in buildings around London or in the countryside, some of which belonged to the Crown and others to courtiers or high-ranking

---

13 *Ibid.*
14 Sir Philip Sidney, *An Apology for Poetry*, ed. Geoffrey Shepherd (Manchester University Press, 1973), p. 99.
15 Pico della Mirandola, *Oration on the Dignity of Man*, trans. Elizabeth Livermore Forbes, in *The Renaissance Philosophy of Man*, ed. Ernst Cassirer, Paul Oskar Kristeller and John Herman Randall (University of Chicago Press, 1948), p. 225.

officials. Nor was it a particular set of individuals – from residents to those passing through, from the monarch's immediate entourage to the whole army of servants, stableboys, cooks and clerks who were answerable to the Lords Steward and Chamberlain, the court's personnel was in a constant state of flux. Both physically and socially the court was a place of extraordinary mobility. Our ability to think of it as a single entity – as an institution, as what Elton dismissively calls a 'conceptual piece of shorthand', as a centre of power which irresistibly drew to it the nation's centripetal gaze – is entirely a result of well-managed presentation and public relations. 'The court' was a concerted representation, and it is a sign of its success rather than failure as a propaganda exercise that, for all the vagueness about what the court actually consisted of, 'we all know that there was a Court', as Elton exasperatedly puts it, and still 'use the term with frequent ease'.

Literature – defined, at its broadest, as rhetoric, discourse and representation – is the stuff of ideology and no one knew this better than the princes and monarchs who shed their lustre over the period as a whole. Indeed, the Tudors – like those other great dynasties of the sixteenth century, the Stuarts, Valois, Habsburgs, Sforzas and Medici – owed no small part of their success to their masterful grasp of rhetoric and canny handling of public relations. This was an age in which knowing how to use words got you somewhere and was clearly understood as being a first step in the exercise of power. Take, for example, the conduct of the young James VI of Scotland who in 1584, aged only eighteen, published a collection modestly entitled *Essayes of a Prentise* which included, among various poems and translations, a treatise on poetics, *Some Revlis and cautelis to be obseruit and eschewit in Scottis Poesie*. Having escaped from the clutches of the dour, older Protestant lords of the Ruthven Raid, James's aim was to revive the glittering court culture which had first been brought over from France by his cousin Esmé Stuart and had been figureheaded by the great Scottish poet, Alexander Montgomerie. The *Essayes* were a public statement, a clarion call to establish the Scottish court as a brilliant cultural centre and home to a Scottish poetic Renaissance. The *Revlis and cautelis* detailed an ambitious programme for verse. It was specifically a Scottish treatise for Scottish poetry, tapping into a spirit of nationalism which the cult of the vernacular had (from the time of Dante on) mobilised throughout Europe. James's idea was to bring to Scottish culture the great literary achievements of the continent, and he succeeded. The next few years saw the translation into Scots of Guillaume du Bartas's *Judith*, by Thomas Hudson (1584); of Petrarch's *Trionfi*, by William Fowler (1587); and of Ariosto's *Orlando Furioso*, via the French version of Philippe Desportes, by John Stewart of Balynneis (1583–4). James gathered such poets together into the self-styled 'Castalian band' named after Castalia – the fountain on Helicon, mount of the Muses. As leader of the group, James drew attention to his own self-appointed role as Apollo, the god of the sun and of poetry, a role which was to become a central motif in his personal iconography.

There was, however, a more specific point to the publication of the *Revlis and cautelis* in 1584. James was not just presenting himself as the refined and sophisticated monarch of a refined and sophisticated court. He assumed the role of poet for a more specific reason – namely, to show the world that the first thing he had power over was words. It was a Renaissance commonplace that poets had been the first legislators of mankind. As rhetoricians never ceased to reiterate, words had the power to bring men to order, to subdue and to civilise them. Speech makes 'of wilde, sober: of cruel, gentle: of foles, wise: and of beastes, men', as Sir Thomas Wilson wrote in *The Arte of Rhetorique* (1553): 'such force hath the tongue, and such is the power of eloquence and reason, that most men are forced even to yelde in that, whiche most standeth against their will'. Master rhetoric and you were a leader of men. The adept orator could so lead crowds with his golden chain of rhetoric that 'no one man was able to withstand his reason, but everye one was rather driven to do that whiche he woulde, and to will that whiche he did'.[16] James self-consciously styled himself as a poet–King not simply to show himself a cultured, educated prince on the model of other European Renaissance monarchs but more than anything else to act out and live up to this rhetorical ideal, to justify the source of his power. For a King, the very first thing to be seen to rule over – to legislate for – was language, and the *Revlis and cautelis* laid down rules of metrical composition whereby each word was carefully positioned, assigned a fixed and specific place. The authority of Kings was thus projected (and idealised) as being the same as that of authors, the command of a literary subject as being the same as the command of subjects. The point of the *Revlis* was to demonstrate this, as Gabriel Harvey, jotting marginalia in his copy of James's text, immediately understood – 'the excellent'st, & finest Art, that the King could learne, or teach, in his kingdom. The more remarkable, how worthie the pen, & industrie of a king'.[17]

Power did not flow in only one direction, however. James had opened the *Revlis and cautelis* by setting out what he saw as its ideal audience: neither the ignorant (who knew nothing) nor the learned (who knew it all) but rather those who were willing to learn, who were poised to yield to his dictates – the

16 Sir Thomas Wilson, *The Arte of Rhetorique*, ed. Thomas J. Derrick (New York: Garland, 1982), pp. 18–19.
17 Cited in Virginia F. Stern, *Gabriel Harvey: His Life, Marginalia, and Library* (Oxford: Clarendon Press, 1979), p. 173.

already 'docile bairns of knawledge'.[18] For all his command of language, in other words, the rhetorician was nothing without an audience and a submissive one at that. In his sonnet 'Decifring the Perfect Poete', James's list of the ideal poet's attributes – a quick wit, skill, memory, fame and so forth – had similarly culminated in 'others wondering', that is, in the rapt appreciation of a teachable audience as the surest sign of the wordsmith's success.[19] Even a poet–King needed an audience – indeed, his self-styled role as a poet could only bring home to him his unsettling vulnerability to this need. It was not just a matter of asserting power over his subjects. The King too was subjected to language. His manipulation of appearances and power to command had another side – a dependency – for, as the work of Foucault and others has long since accustomed us to recognise, power circulates, existing in a dynamic and dialectical relation between oppressor and oppressed, the two parties locked together in mutual interdependence.

Such circulations are nowhere more evident than in those occasions when Renaissance rulers set themselves before literal audiences, namely those public speeches, pageants and processions of which they were such past masters. 'We princes are set on stages in the sight and view of all the world', Queen Elizabeth told a parliamentary deputation in 1586.[20] In an age when princes could not rely on a standing army, a national police force or any comprehensive system of surveillance with which to enforce their rule, it was a cliché of Renaissance statecraft that the most efficient means to that end was the calculated use of ceremony and show. From their point of view, the most effective events were those like the tilt performed at Westminster before Elizabeth and the Duc de Montmorency in 1572 in which the Queen, lords and ladies were all 'sumptuously apparelled' and lit by torches so that, in the awed words of one spectator, 'those that beheld the Tarrace in this sort furnished, deemed it rather a Theater celestiall, then a pallace of earthly building'. Here was command of the theatrical scene at its best, a moment of perfectly controlled visibility which had the wholly desired effect of dazzling and reducing to speechless wonder 'those that were below looking vpward'.[21]

The performer, however, was also dependent on an audience – indeed, was non-existent without one. The dialectic between player and beholder made for

18 James VI, *The Poems of James VI of Scotland*, ed. James Craigie, 2 vols. (Edinburgh: William Blackwood and Sons, 1955–8), 1:66.
19 *Ibid.* 1:69.
20 Cited by J. E. Neale in *Elizabeth I and her Parliaments*, 2 vols. (London: Jonathan Cape, 1965), 2:119.
21 William Segar, *Honor, military and ciuill* (London, 1602), pp. 195, 196.

a fundamental insecurity in the power game whereby performance was seen as a form of predicament. Not only that, the performer played to an audience of other performers. For it was not only the Prince who acted, of course. The whole court was a scene of role-play and dissimulation from the top down – a collective masquerade from the prince to the courtiers to the whole host of hopeful would-be's clustered along the margins and in the wings. Through the humanistic training in rhetoric (now available, via the grammar schools, to a wider social group than ever before) and through the popular genre of the courtesy book, people were made more aware of how reputations could be produced and appearances maintained. Indeed, practical advice on how to mask at court – how to walk, talk and generally carry it off – was at one and the same time an unmasking, a ruthless exposé of pretension and of the mechanics of making-believe. No age except perhaps our own has been so conscious of power as illusion, a piece of theatre, a shimmering mirage, a fiction which depends for its survival on the ability to pass itself off as truth. The art which concealed art was exposed for all the world to see. The sixteenth century was a time when the state use of public shows in creating an aura of princely magnificence and controlling the population at large was arguably more effective than it had ever been. But it was also a time of political questioning when the mechanics of power and workings of propaganda were more open to debate than ever before. It was an age when texts like Shakespeare's history plays were able to reveal princely power to be the fraud that it was before audiences, the subjects of that very power, who were not only drawn to accept that power but to pay money and applaud.[22]

It is for this reason that in recent years literary historians have found particularly compelling those texts which expose the circulations of power most openly to view. One such text is the account of Queen Elizabeth's coronation procession through the streets of London in January 1559, probably written by Edmund Spenser's schoolmaster, Richard Mulcaster. The pamphlet presents the whole occasion in terms of a theatrical encounter between the prince and her people which strikingly replicates the contractual relation between player and audience. The city is described as 'a stage wherein was shewed the wonderfull spectacle, of a noble hearted princesse toward her most louing people' (sig. A2v).[23] On one side, Elizabeth is received with 'prayers, wishes, welcomminges, cryes, tender woordes' which, as the chronicler goes on to describe,

---

22 See Stephen Greenblatt, *Shakespearean Negotiations: The Circulation of Social Energy in Renaissance England* (Oxford: Clarendon Press, 1988), especially ch. 2. Also see Chapter 10 above, pp. 334–8.

23 *The passage of our most drad Soueraigne Lady Quene Elyzabeth through the citie of London to westminster the daye before her coronacion* (London, 1559).

'argue a wonderfull earnest loue of most obedient subiectes towarde theyr soueraigne'. 'On thother syde', meanwhile, the Queen declares herself with gestures and 'most tender & gentle language'. Gladness, prayer and comfort are thus said to exist 'on eyther syde' (A2r). The city receives her with the most tender obedience and love while she 'lykewise of her side' showed herself to be the 'ymage of a woorthye Ladie and Gouernour' (E2v). Such image-making is explicitly shown to be the result of the mutually dependent relation between beholders and beheld. As she passed on her route through the city, moreover, the Queen twice saw representations of herself. At Gracious Street a tripartite stage represented the figures of Henry VII and Elizabeth of York, Henry VIII and Anne Boleyn, and lastly of Elizabeth herself – an icon that was both visual and discursive since 'all emptie places thereof were furnished with sentences concerning unitie' (B1r). At Cornhill a child represented Elizabeth on her 'seate of worthie gouernance', and again any blank spaces were filled with 'proper sentences' (B3r). Should she have been in any doubt about the matter (which is unlikely) nothing would have reminded Elizabeth more poignantly of the fact that, as Queen, she too was a representation – the product of a whole series of discourses in which many others apart from herself had a part to play.

In the course of the sixteenth century Tudor monarchs and their apologists had revived the old medieval idea of the King's 'two bodies', a legalistic distinction which differentiated between the frail, earthly body of the mortal King and the permanent, official body of the Crown. Individual Kings came and went but the Crown accrued the permanence and stability of an institution which could be passed down with uninterrupted continuity. The representation of such a body, however, remained as dependent on the spin-doctors and image-makers then as it does today. A cult of royalty had to be manufactured and maintained – palaces had to be built, portraits painted, pageants written and designed. Those icons on Elizabeth's procession route had to be devised and constructed – with plaster, costume and carpentry. 'The Queen' meant not only the person of Elizabeth Tudor but also the Queen-as-subject – the subject of and in her subjects' discourse.[24] Producing shows at and for the court thus gave writers an opportunity to reflect on their own powers of representation and on the sway which they themselves might exercise over the power to which they were also at one and the same time subject – often with intriguing results.

Walking down a shady grove in the grounds of the Earl of Leicester's house at Wanstead in May of 1578 or 1579, the Queen suddenly found herself in the

24 See Louis A. Montrose, 'The Elizabethan Subject and the Spenserian Text', in *Literary Theory / Renaissance Texts*, ed. Patricia Parker and David Quint (Baltimore, MD: Johns Hopkins University Press, 1986), pp. 303–40.

midst of a play that had been specially written for the occasion by Leicester's nephew, the young Philip Sidney. The show took the form of a pastoral debate in which (after much to-ing and fro-ing) Elizabeth was invited to arbitrate a dispute between two suitors – a shepherd and a forester – competing for the hand of the Lady of the May, who was unable to decide for herself. On one level it is true to say that Elizabeth did not appear here as a representation. Indeed, one could see it as a brilliant stroke on Sidney's part that, rather than figure her (as in the coronation pageant) frozen in stiff and doll-like rigidity, he chose instead to incorporate the Queen 'herself' into his text – to fold her into the fantasised world of his pastoral disguising. This dramatisation of the royal presence could be read as the supreme compliment, and it was part of a tradition in which, in countless progresses and royal entries, Elizabeth's arrival at a house or town would – as if by magic – cause locked doors to spring open, the blind to see, sleepers to wake, and trees to come back to life as once over-ardent lovers who had been transformed into laurel, oak and holly bushes by malicious spirits. At another level, however, by writing Elizabeth into his play Sidney was also reminding her of her dependence on men like himself – on courtly poets and image-makers whose compliments secured her elevated status but who might also have their own ideas about public policy and matters of state. For the *Lady of May*, as it came to be known, was written in the context of Elizabeth's proposed marriage to a French Catholic prince, the Duc d'Alençon – a subject of profound antipathy to the Protestant faction headed at court by Leicester. Sidney did not write the Queen's lines for her – like any courtly *questione d'amore* the issue between the lovers was left open-ended. But it was Sidney who created the occasion and who actualised in poetic form a choice of suitors which had at that time an immediate topical and political relevance. He may not have scripted her lines but he gave Elizabeth a place and a part to play, and to that extent she could not fail to have been reminded of how much, ultimately, she owed to such courtly makers.

In the end, in fact, compliment and counsel were not entirely reconciled and sat rather awkwardly together. Most critics agree that Elizabeth wilfully failed to choose the forester-figure towards whom Sidney had been steering her, opting instead for the shepherd and so calling the courtier's bluff. But even if he did not succeed in making Elizabeth do what he wanted, Sidney was able to rehearse in this one short text his power as well as powerlessness – his ability to fashion the Queen-as-subject as well as his own subjection to royal whim – thus articulating those circulations of energy which typify so much courtly writing in the period. Subjects had the power to fashion the Queen, who in turn had the power to fashion them. This was not an altogether comfortable arrangement, as Fulke Greville clearly expresses when, in the biography of his famous friend, he describes Sidney's strained and difficult relationship with Elizabeth in a tortuous rhetoric that reeks of dodge and compromise:

> so that although he found a sweet stream of sovereign humours in that well-tempered lady to run against him, yet found he safety in herself, even against that selfness which appeared to threaten him in her; for this happily born and bred princess was not (subject-like) apt to construe things reverently done in the worst sense, but rather – with the spirit of anointed greatness, as created to reign equally over frail and strong – more desirous to find ways to fashion her people than colours or causes to punish them.[25]

A few years after the *Lady of May* Sidney was again involved in a court show, this time a much larger and more public event – a tournament held at Whitehall in May 1581. In scale and scope the tournament was on a par with the Accession Day Tilts, those lavish occasions which from the 1570s had made of the Queen's Accession Day on 17 November an annual national festival. Courtiers in elaborate allegorical costumes would joust against each other in a tiltyard built specially for the purpose, mobilising a whole chivalric fiction of knightly service and reward. The occasion in 1581 belonged to the same tradition and was performed before Elizabeth and a group of French Commissioners who had come over to negotiate the proposed match with Alençon, which even then was still pending. Sidney, along with Fulke Greville, Lord Windsor and the Earl of Arundel entered the tiltyard as the four 'foster children of desire' and proceeded to assault the 'fortress of perfect beauty' – Elizabeth's viewing platform – with rose petals, sugar water and pomades in the manner of the mock sieges which went back to Henrician days and beyond those to Burgundian court extravaganzas. The point of the elaborate charade was that the foster children's ardent 'desire' for the Queen was unacceptable (a clear message to the French Commissioners here), an unacceptability which was acted out in the endless series of courtly 'challengers' who came forward to defend the Queen and to oppose the foster children in knightly combat. Defeated and chastened by such chivalrous opposition, the foster children re-entered the following day in the ash-coloured garments of submission, pledging to sublimate their amorous advances and to serve the Queen as steadfast and loyal subjects. What makes a text like this so intriguing is that it is less the slavish glorification of state power which it might at first seem and more the illustration of a cult in the making. Elizabeth's position as an object of universal devotion depended on

---

25 Fulke Greville, *The Prose Works of Fulke Greville, Lord Brooke*, ed. John Gouws (Oxford: Clarendon Press, 1986), p. 37.

her unattainability. *The Four Foster Children of Desire* shows Elizabeth's courtiers working out for themselves the mechanics of what would gradually become formalised as the cult of the Virgin Queen – while cautioning presumptuous French princes to know their place at the same time.

One of the most important figures in the writing of court drama in this period was John Lyly who, throughout the 1580s and 1590s, wrote a series of elegant comedies which were performed at court by the Children of the Chapel Royal. An ambitious man who had been educated at Oxford, Lyly had his eye on gaining the prestigious and lucrative post of Master of the Revels and he used his graceful entertainments as a means to securing that end. In the epilogue to the early play *Campaspe* (*c*. 1582), he paid Elizabeth the ultimate tribute of suggesting that she – in her act of appreciation – was the very maker of the play. Yet the text is one in which an artist wins out over a prince. The painter Apelles and emperor Alexander are both in love with the same woman, Campaspe. One of them has to yield and (unexpectedly, perhaps) it is Alexander, although Lyly softens the blow by presenting his relinquishing as the heroic act of a leader who is redefining himself as a warrior-prince. All the same, Apelles gets the better of Alexander in love just as, elsewhere in the play, the crusty philosopher Diogenes gets the better of him in argument – signs that Lyly was, in an indirect way, flexing his poetic muscle and making play of the power the artist has over the representation he has made.

In a similar way, Lyly flattered Elizabeth by concluding *Euphues and his England* (1580) – the sequel to his enormously popular prose romance *Euphues* (1578) which had set all the court talking – by describing her and her court as the 'Glasse for Europe', that is, as a model and exemplar for the whole of Europe to follow. By using the image of a mirror Lyly modestly suggests that he is merely reflecting what he could not possibly represent. Elsewhere in the 'looking glass', however, he puts himself forward as a painter of the scene. And, 'though it be not requisite that any should paynt their Prince in England', nonetheless, all modesty aside, Lyly undertakes to 'set downe this Elizabeth, as neere as I can'.[26] Lyly evidently understood all too well the role of the artist in producing the royal image. In the final analysis, however, circulations of power could not be guaranteed to come round full circle. Cycles of reciprocity did not always flow evenly and not every ambitious gambit paid off. Lyly never got the post he wanted and nothing expresses the frustration and despair of the Elizabethan courtly writer so eloquently as the plaintive wail that goes up from Lyly's

---

26 John Lyly, *Euphues and his England*, in *The Complete Works of John Lyly*, ed. R. Warwick Bond 3 vols. (Oxford: Clarendon Press, 1902), 2:204, 205.

second petition to the Queen in 1598: 'thirteen yeares yo': Highnes Servant: Butt; yett nothinge, Twenty ffrindes that though they say, they wilbee sure, I ffinde them, sure to slowe, A thowsand hopes, butt all, noethinge; A hundred promises, butt yett noethinge, Thus Castinge vp an Inventorye of my ffrindes, hopes, promises, and Tymes, the; Summ Total: Amounteth to Just nothinge'.[27]

A similar figure is cut by George Gascoigne. A member, like Lyly, of the newly educated gentry class, Gascoigne came up through the Inns of Court. It was at Gray's Inn that in 1566 he presented two plays – the *Supposes* (based on Ariosto's *I Suppositi*) and *Jocasta* (adapted from Euripides). In the years that followed he tried to get himself noticed at court in the time-honoured fashion – by dedicating works such as his poem 'Woodmanship' to designated courtiers, Lord Grey of Wilton in particular – and he succeeded in bringing himself to the Queen's attention in July 1575 when he was hired by the Earl of Leicester to compose entertainments for Elizabeth's visit to his castle at Kenilworth that summer. Gascoigne made the most of this golden opportunity, writing, devising and personally performing in a two-part show on the subject of Elizabeth's beauty and desirability. Part of the show involved Gascoigne leading her to an enchanted grove of lovers who had been metamorphosed into trees by their cruel mistress 'Zabeta' – including a holly bush ('Deep Desire' on account of his pricks), a laurel ('Due Desert') and an oak ('Constance'), each of which began to shake violently in her presence. There is a touch of homeliness about Gascoigne's efforts, not to mention inadvertent comedy. In the first part of the show he had nearly brained Elizabeth with a club – an 'Oken plant pluct vp by the roots' – which he had over-zealously brandished in his role as a Salvage Man.[28] Elizabeth, however, seems to have taken the gaffe in good humour, and Gascoigne popped up again a few weeks later when, continuing on her progress, the Queen stopped off at Woodstock – the home of her Champion, the inspiration behind the Accession Day Tilts, Sir Henry Lee. Gascoigne composed another show for the occasion – the *Tale of Hemetes the Hermit* – a complicated story of separated lovers who are miraculously reunited in Elizabeth's presence and a blind hermit who is, similarly miraculously, restored to sight (this was Lee).

Either Elizabeth was genuinely delighted with the show or Gascoigne judged that she should have been. In the New Year he followed up his opportunity by presenting her with a lavish manuscript containing the *Tale of Hemetes*

---

27 Lyly, *Works*, 1:70–1.
28 R[obert] L[aneham], *A Letter whearin Part of the Entertainment vntoo the Queenz Maiesty at Killingwoorth Castl iz Signified* (London, 1575), p. 18.

written out in four different languages – English, French, Latin and Italian – an obvious way of demonstrating his own linguistic abilities while at the same time complimenting hers. The handsome volume was fronted by a drawing in Gascoigne's own hand which epitomises the position of the aspiring court writer. The poet is shown kneeling humbly at the Queen's feet and offering up his book to her in clear expectation of acceptance and reward – a visual representation of the plea contained in the dedication that, his truth having hitherto been 'unemployed', this worthy man now presumes 'to knock att the gates of yo' gracyous goodnes hopyng that yo' highnes will sett me on worke though yt were noone and past before I soughte service'.[29] The year 1576 saw furious productivity on Gascoigne's part – no fewer than eight publications – but no such service was forthcoming. He died in 1577. Gascoigne speaks for countless sixteenth-century writers who jostled hopefully for court attention, using their art to sell themselves, but who fell victim to a patronage system which was, at its best, arbitrary and inconsistent, and within which by far the most part were destined to fall bitterly by the wayside.

Such calculations, compromises and (often invidious) cycles of exchange would have been found operating in any court – in any setting where power was centralised and distributed unevenly through a hierarchy of rank. But there was a peculiarity that was special to the court of Elizabeth. Because it was headed by a woman, it was a place where the whole rhetoric of courtly service and reward could readily be transposed into an erotic key. Some male members of that court ostentatiously exploited this for their own political ends, for courtiership could blend seamlessly into courtship when men found themselves fawning to, flattering and suing for, the favour of a female prince. With its large entourage of female attendants the court naturally had a bigger female presence than ever before – 'A fairer crew yet no where could I see, / Then that braue court doth to mine eie present', as Spenser wrote in his dedicatory sonnet 'To all the gratious and beautifull Ladies in the Court'.[30] The femaleness of Elizabeth's court had, incidentally, an important payoff of its own, for it provided an unprecedented opportunity for women to add their voice and make their contribution to the great literary outpouring of that time. In general, it was only aristocratic women who were educated and who had the wealth and leisure to cultivate the arts. Given, through their domestic proximity to Elizabeth, a position so close to the centre of power, courtly

---

29 George Gascoigne, *The Complete Works of George Gascoigne*, ed. J. W. Cunliffe, 2 vols. (Cambridge University Press, 1907–10), 2:476.

30 Edmund Spenser, *The Faerie Queene*, ed. A. C. Hamilton (London and New York: Longman, 1977), p. 743.

women seized the chance to participate in the literary scene, both indirectly as patrons and directly as writers themselves. The last decade of the sixteenth century was an initiating era for great patronesses – Lucy Russell, Countess of Bedford, friend and supporter of John Florio, George Chapman, Sir John Davies, Samuel Daniel, Michael Drayton, Ben Jonson and John Donne; Margaret Clifford, Countess of Cumberland, dedicatee of Aemelia Lanyer's country-house poem, *The Description of Cooke-ham*; and Mary Herbert, Countess of Pembroke, the sister of Sir Philip Sidney and namesake of his *Arcadia*, whom, as Thomas Nashe enthused, 'our Poets extoll as the Patronesse of their inuention'.[31] Elizabeth's court was also an environment in which texts by women were recorded and preserved in a way they might not have been otherwise – where manuscript poems survive by Gentlewomen of the Bedchamber like Anne Vavasour or by ladies-in-waiting like Lady Mary Cheke. Elizabeth wrote herself, and was hailed by George Puttenham as 'the most excellent Poet'.[32] At intervals in her reign she authored sometimes playful, sometimes mournful lyrics. Mary Herbert – most famous for her translation of the Psalms and completion of her brother's unfinished Psalter – also translated Petrarch's *Triumph of Death* and continental closet dramas, as well as composing panegyrics and elegies in her own right.

It was, however, as the home of a sovereign female power – as the setting for Gloriana, Astraea, Belphoebe, Cynthia, Diana or England's Eliza, as she was variously known – that the court of Elizabeth I is seen in the popular imagination as having lent its distinctive colour to the best-known poetry of the period. This was a place where grown men could invent and enter into a fiction of amorous longing and abject devotion with an ardour we can only wonder at. It was a place where a man like Sir Christopher Hatton – who wrote letters to Elizabeth saying things like 'passion overcometh me. I can write no more. Love me, for I love you' – went around as the Queen's pet 'sheep'.[33] It was a place where Sir Walter Ralegh – who wrote letters saying 'my heart was never broken till this day, that I hear the Queen goes away so far off' – went around as her 'silly pug'.[34] Courtiers fought like children

---

31 Thomas Nashe, Preface to *Astrophel and Stella* (1591), in *The Works of Thomas Nashe*, ed. R. B. McKerrow, 5 vols. (London: A. H. Bullen, 1904–10), 3:331. See also Chapter 4 above, pp. 133–6.

32 Puttenham, *Arte of English Poesie*, p. 4.

33 Sir Harris Nicolas (ed.), *Memoirs of the Life and Times of Sir Christopher Hatton* (London: Richard Bentley, 1847), pp. 26–7.

34 Sir Walter Ralegh, *The Life of Sir Walter Ralegh Based on Contemporary Documents... Together with His Letters*, ed. Edward Edwards, 2 vols. (London: Macmillan, 1868), 2:51; 'silly pug' from Elizabeth's poem to Ralegh, in *The Elizabethan Courtier Poets: The Poems and Their Contexts*, ed. Steven May (Columbia: University of Missouri Press, 1991), p. 318.

for her favours and not infrequently came to blows. Lord Mountjoy (then Sir Charles Blount) challenged the envious Earl of Essex to a duel when the latter scornfully disparaged a gift the Queen had made him of a golden chess piece (a queen, naturally) for having 'run very well a Tilt'.[35] 'The Queene stoode up and bade me reache forthe my arme to reste her thereon', noted Sir John Harington happily in his diary, 'Oh, what swete burden to my next songe – Petrarke shall eke out good matter for this businesse'.[36] In a world where the normal gender roles were reversed and where men were forced to sue to a woman for favour, courtiers found in the Petrarchan conventions of courtly love a ready-made language of gesture and ornament with which to declare their devotion and to pledge themselves as the Queen's most faithful servants to command. Elizabeth, it seems, did nothing to stop them. Such effusions made up her queenly cult, even if she didn't find all of them personally appealing. Elizabeth 'allowed herself to be wooed and courted, and even to have love made to her', sighed Sir Francis Bacon, looking back over her reign – admitting, however, that such 'dalliances detracted but little from her fame and nothing at all from her majesty'.[37] It was, of course, through this canny exploitation of her femininity that Elizabeth not only controlled the men at her court but also kept the whole of Europe guessing. Moreover, as a strategy which made an inaccessible female the object of universal inquiry and fascination, it could be argued to lie behind what became one of the most prolific literary vogues of the day: the fashion for the Petrarchan sonnet sequence which flourished throughout the 1580s and 1590s and to which everyone – from Sidney (with *Astrophil and Stella*), to Spenser (with the *Amoretti*), Shakespeare (with his *Sonnets*), Daniel (with *Delia*), Drayton (with *Idea*), Greville (with *Caelica*), Henry Constable (with *Diana*) and a whole host of others – signed up with equal enthusiasm.

For many readers, the sonnet is perhaps *the* definitive product of the Elizabethan age. A diminutive of *suono* ('sound'), the word could be used loosely – as in 'songs and sonnets' – of any short lyric or song-like poem, although by the end of the sixteenth century it had generally come to mean the fourteen-line, decasyllabic poem with a complex rhyme scheme which it designates today. The undisputed father of the sonnet form was Petrarch (1304–74) whose *Canzoniere*, an exhaustive sequence of 366 lyrics, stands as a great paean to his mistress, Laura. Petrarch's sonnets were brought to England early in the

---

35 Robert Naunton, *Fragmenta Regalia or Observations of the Late Queen Elizabeth, Her Times and Favourites* (1641), ed. Edward Arber (Birmingham: English Reprints, 1870), p. 52.

36 Sir John Harington, *Nugae Antiquae*, ed. Thomas Park, 2 vols. (London: Vernor and Hood, 1804; repr., New York: AMS Press, 1966), 2:211.

37 Francis Bacon, *In Felicem Memoriam* (1608), in *The Works of Francis Bacon*, ed. J. Spedding et al., 14 vols. (London: Longman, 1857–74), 6:317.

sixteenth century, translated by Wyatt and Surrey and popularised by *Tottel's Miscellany* (1557). Ostensibly, sonnets were poems of praise for an ethereally remote and supremely idealised mistress, and as such they became a vehicle for the unearthly longings of Neoplatonic aspiration. But, as theorists of epideictic poetry had noted from Aristotle on, the language of praise was also self-reflexive, for the poet's glorious subject shed her lustre over the poet himself, revealing him to be an adept and masterly handler of words.

The sonnet's formal brevity made for a compact and epigrammatic style where intensity was at a premium. Samuel Daniel described the sonnet as an 'Orbe of order and forme'.[38] In praising the woman he loved, the poet would frequently itemise her attributes in a *blason*, her fetishistically worshipped body-parts – lips of coral, eyes of diamond, hair of topaz or gold, skin of alabaster, nipples of porphyry – becoming a staple of the sonneteering tradition for centuries to come. These effusions were compressed into hard, glittering, jewel-like poems, lending adornment less to the female beloved than to her male admirer. If narcissism lay behind the heterosexual relationship which, however infinitely deferred, was supposedly the object of the whole enterprise, for Petrarch's heirs there was also an explicit relation between man and man. Caught in an oedipal rivalry which expressed itself as an anxiety of influence, the aspiring young poet struggled both to emulate and to differentiate himself from his towering poetic forefather – rather as Sidney's Astrophil vainly seeks to reject 'poore *Petrarch's* long deceased woes' while at the same time acknowledging the derivativeness and citationality of all human desire.[39]

As a self-conscious, arch and highly writerly form, the sonnet lent itself as much to the bathos or self-parody of Sir John Davies's *Gullinge Sonnets* (1594) or of the lover described by Jacques who sighs out ballads to his mistress's eyebrow (*As You Like It*, 2.7.149) as it did to rhetorical perfectionism. Meditative and deeply introspective in tone, however, the sonnet vogue also developed what one critic has termed a specifically 'inward' language – an inner sanctuary or chamber of the mind where the poet might retire and, like Donne's lover, 'build in sonnets pretty rooms'.[40] Although in their formal appearance discrete and supremely self-contained, sonnets were also arranged in sequences, and this seriality helped to create an illusion of fictional depth and of narrative and

---

38 Daniel, *A Defence of Ryme* ; p. 138.
39 Sir Philip Sidney, *Astrophil and Stella*, Poem 15, in *The Poems of Sir Philip Sidney*, ed. W. A. Ringler, Jr (Oxford: Clarendon Press, 1962), p. 172.
40 See Anne Ferry, *The 'Inward' Language* (University of Chicago Press, 1983), and John Donne, 'The Canonisation', in *The Complete English Poems of John Donne*, ed. C. A. Patrides (London: Dent, 1985), p. 8.

dramatic continuity which, for some critics, makes them the first articulation of a distinctly modern subjectivity.[41]

One of the reasons why Petrarchism left so indelible a mark on the literature of the period was that it served so many different purposes. On one level, it was the obvious way to flatter the Queen or a female patron, serving as a cover for more private affections as well. On another level, Petrarchism allowed men to rehearse in powerfully charged words their condition of disempowerment. All the introspection and self-searching of the lyric tradition could be brought to bear on their immediate subjective experience while at the same time questioning whether that experience itself were not just another form of play-acting: 'My love lyke the Spectator ydly sits / beholding me that all the pageants play' wrote Spenser in the *Amoretti* .[42] When Sidney wrote *Astrophil and Stella* he was, in career terms, a failure. The conventions of Petrarchism gave him a 'paper stage' (as Nashe put it in his preface to *Astrophil and Stella* (1591)) on which to act out his despair.[43] Not only a route to successful courtship at court – which was rare enough anyway, and no less precarious once attained – Petrarchism also provided a well-versed vocabulary with which to articulate disappointment, rejection and failure. Thrown ignominiously in the Tower in 1592 for having committed the most heinous crime in Elizabeth's emotional book (secretly marrying one of her ladies-in-waiting), Ralegh wrote the strangely fragmented *Ocean to Cynthia*. Its tortuously dense verse not only attempts to make grovelling amends to Elizabeth but also explores the emotional and psychological depths of a most profound state of masculine abjection. Petrarchism gave such men a chance to air their frustration, to rail against their mistress and even to curse her – as Astrophil does in the fifth song of *Astrophil and Stella* – as a devil, tyrant, witch and thief. It was a compensatory poetic in which men, otherwise humiliated and disempowered, could reassert their mastery and – in their fictions if nowhere else – speak for, silence and generally subdue a powerful woman to whom in every other respect they remained subject. By making her the subject of their verse, they brought those circulations of power back within their own control and redirected them towards the rhetorical mastery of perfectly turned sonnets and triumphant monuments of wit.

Such adventitious recuperations of power did not go nearly far enough for some, however. For them the court was a place only of yes-men and hangers-on.

41 See, for example, Joel Fineman, *Shakespeare's Perjured Eye* (Berkeley: University of California Press, 1986).
42 Edmund Spenser, *Amoretti*, Poem 54, in *The Yale Edition of the Shorter Poems of Edmund Spenser*, ed. William Oram *et al.* (New Haven, CT: Yale University Press, 1989), p. 632.
43 Nashe, *Works*, 3:329.

The court and its rituals of courtship were beyond redemption and the only thing to do was to stand well clear of them. The court glowed and shone like rotten wood, in Ralegh's striking image (in 'The Lie'), its thin veneer of sparkle concealing the utmost corruption and decay. It was as a place of smooth talking and unctuous guile that the court came to be caricatured if not characterised in the often savage anti-court satire of the period. 'For there thou needs must learne, to laugh, to lie', wrote Spenser in *Mother Hubberds Tale* (1591), 'To face, to forge, to scoffe, to companie, / To crouche, to please, to be a beetle stock / Of thy great Masters will, to scorne, or mock.'[44] Anti-court satire traditionally involved the speaker gathering himself up and ostentatiously leaving the false and empty world of 'courting vaine' for the rustic simplicity of the pastoral life. Unlike the flapping court insect whom he captures so brilliantly in his fourth satire, Donne's speaker remains true to himself, in quiet retirement 'At home in wholesome solitariness'.[45] In a tradition which went back to Horace and Virgil, the satirist removed himself from the public whirl and, from his elevated position of moral superiority, 'looked down on the stage of the world', as Ben Jonson put it, 'and contemned the play of fortune'.[46]

Yet even here the most vigorous protestations of virtue were not immune from worldly considerations of self-interest and self-advancement. When all was said and done, golden ideals had a way of falling back into the brazen world of the *quid pro quo* where everything had its market value and everyone had his price. The most vituperative criticism was not above calculation, the most aloof stand-off no stranger to compromise. In fact the cult of sincerity and pose of plainness served more often than not to differentiate the speaker from the crowd of beetling minions in order to promote himself as a true and deserving servant to those in power. It was rarely expedient to name and shame individuals. Satire more often took the form of a generalised invective which managed, by attacking the many, to spare the few, making blame not infrequently an inverted form of praise. This explains why the pastoral genre lent itself so well to the deliberate cultivation of ambiguity for, as in Sidney's *Lady of May*, praise and blame had a way of sitting uneasily side by side. Pastoral was anciently perceived as being the vehicle of social comment and political critique, the frenetic world of the court being set critically against its own contemplative country life. In the sixteenth century, however, pastoral was also recognised as being, paradoxically, the definitive genre of duplicity and

44 Spenser, *Yale Edition of Shorter Poems*, p. 352.
45 *Complete Poems of John Donne*, ed. Patrides, p. 236.
46 Ben Jonson, *Timber or Discoveries*, in *Ben Jonson*, ed. Ian Donaldson (Oxford University Press, 1985), p. 551.

dissimulation in which 'much matter [was] vttered somewhat couertly', as William Webbe wrote of Spenser's *Shepheardes Calender*, and where greater matters could be glanced at 'vnder the vaile of homely persons', as Puttenham put it, or 'under the pretty tales of wolves and sheep', as Sidney proposed.[47]

It is in this context that we should consider one of the most important literary texts of the Elizabethan period – Sidney's great pastoral romance, the *Arcadia*. Begun at some point between 1578 and 1580, the *Arcadia* was, appropriately enough, not written at court – the scene of Sidney's difficult relationship with the Queen and frustrated lack of advancement – but rather at his sister's country seat at Wilton. As Sidney wrote in the dedicatory letter to his sister, the book was composed 'in loose sheets of paper, most of it in your presence, the rest by sheets sent unto you as fast as they were done', evoking a relaxed and intimate family setting that was poles apart from the ruses and machinations of Whitehall.[48] Modelled on Jacopo Sannazaro's *Arcadia* (1504) and its imitation, the *Diana* (1559), by Jorge de Montemayor, Sidney's text alternates poetry and prose as pastoral eclogues interrupt at intervals the ongoing narrative romance. This arrangement brings out the inherent contrast between the pseudo-simplicity of the courtly characters who are – for a number of political and amorous reasons – playing at being shepherds, and the genuine rustic community that is playing host to them. Negotiating the delicate balance between castigating and idealising court *mores*, Sidney's text passes comment on courtly standards with an archness that is peculiar to the pastoral genre. The Third Eclogues, for example, celebrate the wedding – between a shepherd Lalus and a shepherdess Kala – which is patently the outcome of a conventional courtship that has been concluded 'with the consent of both parents'. The 'greater persons' of the story, meanwhile – the prince Pyrocles and his beloved, the princess Philoclea – are, as the narrator wryly puts it, 'otherwise occupied', that is to say, in bed together.[49]

In its first, 'old' version, Sidney's *Arcadia* tells the story of a King, Basilius, who disastrously attempts to escape the fate of an oracle by retiring from court and taking himself and his family into pastoral seclusion. The results of this princely dereliction of duty are dire, ranging from gender confusion to jealousy, adultery, rape, abduction, rebellion and the near-death of the King himself who

47 William Webbe, *A Discourse of English Poetrie* (1586), in *Elizabethan Critical Essays*, ed. G. Gregory Smith, 2 vols. (Oxford University Press, 1904), 1:264; Puttenham, *Arte of English Poesie*, p. 38; and Sidney, *Apology for Poetry*, p. 116.
48 Philip Sidney, *The Countess of Pembroke's Arcadia (The Old Arcadia)*, ed. Jean Robertson (Oxford: Clarendon Press, 1973), p. 3.
49 *The Old Arcadia*, pp. 244–5.

is saved only in the nick of time by a comic dénouement. This version of the story was never published – at least, not until 1926 – for after finishing it Sidney embarked on a wholesale rewriting. Although the principal characters and its basic plot outline remain the same, the 'new' *Arcadia* is, in its narrative complexity and overall scope, a quite different creature. Left unfinished at the time of Sidney's death in 1586, it was first published in this truncated form in 1590 and then again – with the end of the *Old Arcadia* tacked on – in 1593. The third-person narrative and narratorial coyness of the *Old Arcadia* give way in the *New* to an altogether darker and more fragmented vision. Moral absolutes become relative as different characters narrate different stories – many of them inset tales of intrigue, cunning, treachery, murder and incest – so that the response to and evaluation of human conduct is angled from individual and subjective points of view.

The critique of those in positions of power takes on a tone that differs from the generally more playful world of the *Old Arcadia*, producing a cynicism which ranges from a glancing spat at the cult of Elizabeth in the description of one character as 'a queen, and therefore beautiful' to a more protracted if ambiguous commentary on the statecraft of the Renaissance prince.[50] Destined to be torn by irresolvable internal conflicts, the troubled hero, Amphialus (who does not appear at all in the *Old Arcadia*), is described as preparing his country for war in typically Machiavellian fashion: 'First he dispatched private letters to all those principal lords and gentlemen of the country ... conforming himself, after their humours: to his friends, friendliness; to the ambitious, great expectations; to the displeased, revenge; to the greedy, spoil – wrapping their hopes with such cunning, as they rather seemed given over unto them, as partakers, than promises sprong of necessity.' Knowing how few there are who can discern 'between shows and substance', Amphialus 'caused a justification of this his action to be written (whereof were sowed abroad many copies) which with some glosses of probability might hide indeed the foulness of his treason'. In a text which is – as these examples show – so acutely conscious of its own status as a rhetorical performance, the ambiguous description of such a character who is 'amplified with arguments and examples, and painted with rhetorical colours' cannot but reflect back upon the author, and Sidney's own command of an art that is openly shown to manipulate and control speaks more subtly than anything else of the invidious circulations of power and of their ultimate inescapability.[51]

50 *The Countess of Pembroke's Arcadia (The New Arcadia)*, ed. Victor Skretkowicz (New York: Oxford University Press, 1987), p. 96.
51 *The New Arcadia*, pp. 324, 325, 326.

No account of literature and the court in this period would be complete without mention of the inimitable mixture of Virgilian epic, Ariostan romance, Arthurian fantasy, medieval dream-vision, topical satire, contemporary humanistic learning and archaic Chaucerian diction which makes up that great monument to the age and the longest poem in the English language – Edmund Spenser's *Faerie Queene*. Educated at the Merchant Taylors' School and at Cambridge, Spenser spent his working life as a government servant – for the most part, as private secretary to Lord Grey of Wilton, the new Lord Deputy of Ireland. He moved to Ireland in 1580 and it was there that *The Faerie Queene* was written, its first three Books being published in 1590 and all six in 1596. Although written at a distance from the court (Ireland frequently appears as a place of pastoral retreat in Spenser's poetry), *The Faerie Queene* was wholly geared around Elizabeth's court in London and takes its entire definition and rationale from that cultural centre and seat of power. Not only the poem's namesake and dedicatee, Queen Elizabeth was also its structuring principle, for the annual feast of the Faery Queene – a clear allusion to Elizabeth's Accession Day festivities – serves as the starting point for the knights whose trials, adventures and quests form the body of the poem. *The Faerie Queene* pivots round the court, and none of the actions of the poem – even actions of knightly disobedience or dereliction – make sense except in relation to it.

'The generall end therefore of all the book', wrote Spenser in his prefatory letter to the 1590 edition, 'is to fashion a gentleman or noble person in vertuous and gentle discipline.'[52] *The Faerie Queene* is an openly didactic poem, yet nothing demonstrates so well the old saw that poetry should both teach and delight. In Saint George (the knight of Holiness), Sir Guyon (the knight of Temperance), Britomart (the female champion of Chastity), Sir Artegall (the defender of Justice), Sir Calidore (the knight of Courtesy) and Arthur (representative of that supreme princely virtue, Magnificence), Spenser creates a cast of characters who personify the virtues and bring the moral struggle to life by battling with all the monsters, dragons, witches, wizards, goblins, dwarves and giants in whom evil had habitually been symbolised by a whole romance tradition.

With its myriad characters, welter of literary analogues and multiple intersecting story-lines, *The Faerie Queene* is designed to confuse. It confronts the reader rather like the 'wood of error' which is the scene of the poem's first adventure and which effectively stands as a gateway into the poem as a whole. Like the Redcrosse Knight and his lady, the reader is drawn into an

---

52 Spenser, *The Faerie Queene*, ed. Hamilton, p. 737.

initially attractive but quickly labyrinthine text, for – as the Italian epic poet Torquato Tasso wrote – poetry is 'like a dark forest, murky and without a ray of light'.[53] As the poem's first protagonists lose their way in the wood and stumble across the monstrously embodied figure of Error – a half-woman, half-snake who vomits up gobbets of flesh, books, papers and eyeless toads – so Spenser unforgettably dramatises the struggle between getting things right and getting them wrong, indicating to the reader at this inaugural moment in the poem, the lures, traps and pitfalls that lie ahead.

The Faerie Queene is an assault course in which readerly skill and expertise are tested to the limit. Complacency invariably comes before a fall. By the end of Book 1, for example, we may feel sufficiently familiarised by that Book's pervasive religious imagery – drawn largely from Genesis, Revelation and the Pauline epistles – to feel ready to tackle Book 2. When, towards the beginning of that Book, we read of a child with bloody hands that cannot be washed clean in a nearby stream, a whole raft of explanatory religious reference seems readily available. Just when we might feel confident about interpreting its symbolism, however, the poem does an about-face, offering not a Christian but a quite alternative classical and pagan field of reference. The unwashable hands allude, in this instance, not to Cain's bloodguilt or Pilate's pusillanimity but rather to some Ovidian tale about a chaste nymph transformed into a pure and unsulliable stream in order to preserve her honour.

The Faerie Queene bristles with doubles, parodies and simulacra. In Book 3, for example, the fair Florimel – a beautiful damsel and classic object of the erotic chase – is indistinguishable from a false Florimel, an animated mannequin fashioned out of snow, wax and golden wire who is made to walk and talk by a witch of evil intent. Archimago, the wicked worker of magic and master of deception, finds his counterpart in Merlin, wonder-worker and magus of the heroic Arthurian tradition. Radegund – the impressively feisty Amazon and champion of women's rights – meets her match in the equally impressive and equally feisty female warrior, Britomart, who yet restores male sovereignty over women in the person of her future husband and partner in justice, Sir Artegall. The Bower of Bliss – a beautiful yet hauntingly sterile place where golden ivy is painted green to tickle the eye – is held up against the Garden of Adonis, the scene of swelling fertility and nature's seedbed of distinctly non-mechanical reproduction.

53 Torquato Tasso, *Discourses on the Heroic Poem* (1594), ed. and trans. Mariella Cavalchini and Irene Samuel (Oxford: Clarendon Press, 1973), p. 21.

Pairing like with unlike, opposite with imago, Spenser invites his readers to compare and contrast, and, in the process, to adapt, adjust and revise their judgements. Reading is a continuous practice of re-evaluation, and it leads less to the enlightenment of some dazzling truth than to an acknowledgement that the world is only darkened by human error and misprision. In what stands (although the poem was left unfinished) as its final Book – the Book of Courtesy – Spenser investigates, as incisively as Castiglione or Puttenham, the peculiar qualities of that virtue which is by no means unproblematically linked to the court from which it appears, etymologically, to derive: 'Of Court it seemes, men Courtesie doe call' (*FQ*, 6.i.1). As the actions of Sir Calidore show, courtesy is more often than not a requirement to compromise, fudge and economise with the truth. Ultimately, *The Faerie Queene* delivers its readers not so much into the floodlights of wisdom as into the murky, flickering, candle-lit world of Bacon's 'Essay on Truth' (1597):

> This same truth is a naked and open day-light, that doth not shew the masks and mummeries and triumphs of the world, half so stately and daintily as candle-lights. Truth may perhaps come to the price of a pearl, that sheweth best by day; but it will not rise to the price of a diamond or carbuncle, that sheweth best in varied lights.[54]

In the course of reading the poem, the reader learns to interpret – to discriminate, to evaluate, to weigh things up, to remember, to compare and contrast, to construe and infer, to consider and make decisions or changes of mind, to read signs more carefully – in short, to become a better reader. By means of carefully laid traps and false trails, Spenser deliberately trips the reader up – a virtuous-seeming hermit turns out to be the arch-villain, Archimago; a beautiful lady his wicked accomplice, Duessa – so that, far from being a passive or recreational experience, reading *The Faerie Queene* is from the very beginning an engaged and active process. The reader has embarked on his or her own quest for enlightenment and self-improvement. As the character Belphoebe remarks, 'Abroad in armes, at home in studious kind / Who seekes with painfull toile, shall honor soonest find' (2.3.40). The painful toil of reading is the same as that of combat, both equivalent ways of fighting the good fight. *The Faerie Queene* achieves this aim by being an allegory – that form which, because it distances sign from referent, surface from meaning, was for George Puttenham the quintessential 'courtly figure'. The reader is invited to penetrate the surface – to

54 Bacon, *Works*, 6:378.

find the core of moral instruction behind the delightful intricacies of the story –
but also to become an expert in the attractions and deceptions of a surface narrative. The reader is asked to be vigilant, to respond intelligently to doubtful
show, and to cultivate all the arts of suspicion – and it is clear that, as far as
Spenser was concerned, no skill could have been more necessary in the dark
and devious courtly world for which he was writing.

In October 1589 Spenser went to London to deliver the first three Books of
The Faerie Queene to Elizabeth in person. She graciously received what would
quickly come to be recognised as a literary masterpiece and national epic, and in
February 1591 awarded Spenser an annual pension of £50. Spenser was (with
the somewhat inexplicable exception of the mediocre poet, Thomas Churchyard) the only writer to be accorded so public a sign of royal favour and recognition. But even a poet of Spenser's standing had to tread carefully. In Book
5 of *The Faerie Queene* Spenser describes the fate of a poet 'whose tongue was
for his trespasse vyle / Nayld to a post', his name 'Bonfont' being scratched
out and replaced by 'Malfont', 'bold title of a Poet bad' (v.ix.25). The incident
graphically conjures the repressiveness of a regime which would – as in the
case of John Stubbes, author of a libellous pamphlet attacking the proposed
French match in 1579 – punish seditious writers with the loss of one hand.
Writers were directly answerable to the state, and Spenser's account of Bonfont's fate strikingly anticipates his own vulnerability to state power. For the
very same canto caused such offence to James VI for appearing (as he saw it) to
defame his mother Mary, Queen of Scots in the person of Duessa, that he immediately demanded of Elizabeth that her poet 'be dewly tryed & punished'.[55]
Elsewhere in *The Faerie Queene*, Spenser hints that his poem has aroused the disapproval of important people, in particular the 'rugged forhead that with graue
foresight / Welds [Wields] kingdomes causes and affaires of state' – generally
taken to be Elizabeth's chief minister, Lord Burghley – who 'My looser rimes
(I wote) doth sharply wite, / For praising loue' (4. Pro.1). The poem indeed ends
by alluding to the same 'mighty Peres displeasure' (6.12.41). The Blatant Beast –
monster of detraction, slander and ill fame which the knight of Courtesy, Sir
Calidore, had struggled in the course of Book 6 to restrain and subdue – in
the closing stanzas of *The Faerie Queene* breaks loose again to roam free and
uncontrolled:

55 From a letter by Robert Bowes, Scottish ambassador to England, to Lord Burghley, dated
12 November 1596, cited in *The Works of Edmund Spenser: A Variorum Edition*, ed. Edwin
Greenlaw et al., 10 vols. (Baltimore, MD: Johns Hopkins University Press, 1932–49),
5:244.

So now he raungeth through the world againe,
And rageth sore in each degree and state;
Ne any is, that may him now restraine,
He growen is so great and strong of late,
Barking and biting all that him doe bate.
(6.12.40)

Not even the poet is spared. Through Spenser's sad if realistic appraisal of his own position as a writer, *The Faerie Queene* shows how the circulations of power between state and subject were worked out in perhaps their most subtle and complex articulation.

Chapter 12

LITERATURE AND THE CHURCH

PATRICK COLLINSON

I

'Religious literature' is a category which cannot be measured with statistical precision. What we in a more secular age call 'religion', a discrete phenomenon, permeated many areas of early modern life and much of its book production. Broadsheet ballads and pamphlets, precursors of both newspapers and novels, may have entertained, even titillated, but they professed to teach moral lessons. Preachers and journalistic hacks, writers of murder pamphlets and the like, invaded each others' generic spaces. Popular songs were instantly 'moralised', with improving lyrics set to the same tunes.[1] Historians and poets disputed which of their disciplines was in the better position to encourage 'virtue'. Sir Philip Sidney thought poetry more 'doctrinable'.[2] 'Truth' was at a premium. The Bible was the ultimate in truth, but chronicles, too, were said to 'carry credit'.[3]

But religious books, by a more exclusive and conventional criterion, will be found to have been the single most important staple of the publishing industry, making up roughly half of its output.[4] This suggests considerable public interest in the subject, although two factors other than piety must be taken into account

---

1 Alexandra Walsham, *Providence in Early Modern England* (Oxford University Press, 1999); Peter Lake, 'Deeds against Nature: Cheap Print, Protestantism and Murder in Early Seventeenth-Century England', in *Culture and Politics in Early Stuart England*, ed. Kevin Sharpe and Peter Lake (Basingstoke: Macmillan, 1994), pp. 257–83; Alexandra Walsham, ' "A Glose of Godlines": Philip Stubbes, 'Elizabethan Grub Street and the invention of Puritanism', in *Belief and Practice in Reformation England*, ed. Susan Wabuda and Caroline Litzenberger (Aldershot: Ashgate, 1998), pp. 177–206; Patrick Collinson, *From Iconoclasm to Iconophobia: the Cultural Impact of the Second English Reformation* (University of Reading, 1986).
2 Sir Philip Sidney, *An Apology for Poetry*, ed. G. Shepherd (Manchester University Press, 1973).
3 Raphael Holinshed, *The Firste Volume of the Chronicles of England, Scotlande, and Irelande* (London, 1577), p. 766.
4 Edith L. Klotz, 'A Subject Analysis of English Imprints for Every Tenth Year from 1480 to 1640', *Huntington Library Quarterly* 1 (1938), 417–19. See also Maureen Bell's statistical analysis of *STC* imprints in John Barnard and D. F. McKenzie (eds.), *A History of the Book in Britain*, vol. 4 (Cambridge University Press, 2002).

in explaining the volume of religious publication. On the one hand there were the commercial motives of printers and booksellers (presumably responsive to demand); on the other, the interest of state and church and of organised bodies of religious opinion, often critical, even dissident. These were factors of 'push' rather than 'pull'. Even supposedly 'popular' literary forms may have been popular only in the sense that they were products intended by their social and intellectual betters for the improvement of the semi-literate, a process of downward cultural mediation.

It is hard to disentangle the strands. At one extreme, religiously committed printers, Catholic and Protestant, put their livelihoods and even their very lives at risk. At the other, the same printing house or balladmonger might publish texts favouring both confessions and none, books and ballads deemed to be 'unchaste' and 'bawdy', and publications which deplored the public taste for such trash. The Lutheran Reformation in Germany was a huge propaganda exercise for an embattled cause, but it revived the flagging fortunes of the printing industry, and virtually created it in Wittenberg, the birthplace of the Reformation, where there was fierce competition among the printers.[5] The story of the printed English Bible in the Reformation began with the personal mission of a highly motivated translator, William Tyndale, then became a lucrative branch of the book trade, and was presently taken over by the official patronage and authority of the English Crown, but never to the exclusion of more private and partisan interests. The book which ranked as almost a second Bible, John Foxe's 'Book of Martyrs', was the personal brainchild of its author and his many collaborators. But it was made possible, practically and financially, by the commercial printing house of John Day and his backers, and it enjoyed a measure of official promotion from a government which had not commissioned its publication, and which bore none of the costs.[6]

A rather extreme case of ideological 'push' is represented by the little books which conveyed to English readers the eclectic doctrines of the Dutch prophet and founder of the reclusive sect (or cult) known as the Family of Love, Hendrik Niclaes, always known by his initials, 'H. N.' A small library of H. N.'s writings in English translation was printed in Cologne in the mid-1570s, and distributed

---

5 John L. Flood, 'The Book in Reformation Germany', in *The Reformation and the Book*, ed. J.-F. Gilmont, trans. Karin Maag (Aldershot: Ashgate, 1998), pp. 21–103.

6 David Daniel, *William Tyndale: A Biography* (New Haven, CT, and London: Yale University Press, 1994); Gerald Hammond, *The Making of the English Bible* (Manchester University Press, 1982); David Loades (ed.), *John Foxe and the English Reformation* (Aldershot: Scolar Press, 1997), and (ed.), *John Foxe: An Historical Perspective* (Aldershot: Ashgate, 1999), esp. Brett Usher, 'Backing Protestantism: The London Godly, the Exchequer and the Foxe Circle', pp. 105–34.

in England by Familist colporteurs, much as *The Watchtower* and kindred publications have been taken door-to-door by Jehovah's Witnesses in the twentieth century.[7] A differently motivated push may lie behind the books in which tiny groups of radical Puritan exiles attacked and anathematised each other. Why did they do this in print? And how were their publications financed?[8]

Print and Protestantism have been regarded as virtually symbiotic. It was Luther himself who called printing 'God's ultimate and greatest gift', through which the whole world would learn true religion, while for Foxe it was 'a divine and miraculous invention'.[9] But there are two important reasons why the history of religious publication in this period is not identical with the advance of the Protestant Reformation. In the first place we should not exaggerate the importance which Protestants attached to the printed word. Faith, according to St Paul, cometh by hearing, and hearing by the word of God (Romans 10:17), a word preached rather than read. The story that Luther told the Strasbourg Reformer Martin Bucer, who had reproached the Wittenbergers for not going out to preach, that they did that with their books, is probably apocryphal, and it is more certain that Luther believed in the primacy of what he called 'living books' – preachers. In Geneva, John Calvin's 2,300 (known) sermons were intended, at least by him, for their hearers, not for publication.[10] In England, the sermons of some of the most celebrated preachers were never put into print, and some nonconformist ministers overcame the inhibiting stigma of print only when they were suspended and no longer able to preach in public, apparently intending their published sermons primarily for their own flocks. There was a complex relationship between the word as uttered and the word as read, and Protestant culture was an oral as well as a scribal and print culture.[11]

Nor should we forget the other media through which the Protestant message was communicated, especially to the illiterate majority of the population. Songs, pictures, plays and street demonstrations were all exploited, although these forms of protest and evangelism were more typical of German Lutheranism than of the Reformed ('Calvinist') tendency which came to prevail in England. This was increasingly iconoclastic, not to say iconophobic,

---

7 Christopher Marsh, *The Family of Love in English Society, 1550–1630* (Cambridge University Press, 1994), pp. 79–85.
8 Peter Milward, 'Schisms among Separatists', in his *Religious Controversies of the Jacobean Age: A Survey of Printed Sources* (London: Scolar Press, 1978), pp. 48–71.
9 Gilmont, *The Reformation and the Book*, pp. 1–2, 266; *Acts and Monuments of John Foxe*, ed. S. R. Cattley, 8 vols. (London, 1837–41), 3:720.
10 Gilmont, *The Reformation and the Book*, pp. 474n, 146, 484.
11 Arnold Hunt, *The Art of Hearing* (Cambridge University Press, forthcoming).

frowning on the visualised representations of sacred things, the mingling of religion with 'mirth'. In the early Elizabethan decades, popular ballads like *A newe northern dittye of the Lady Green Sleves* (1580), which were sung in streets and fairs by those, like Shakespeare's Autolycus, who hawked them, were promptly 'moralised to the Scriptures', parodied in improving texts set to the same tunes. The Clown tells Autolycus in *The Winter's Tale* about the Puritan who 'sings psalms to horn-pipes' (4.3. 44–5). But later the Psalms and those who sang them distanced themselves from the popular musical scene. Both Thomas Nashe and William Shakespeare refer disapprovingly to the practice of singing Psalms to 'Greensleeves'.[12] However, the Scottish case, despite a more pronounced commitment to Calvinism, was rather different. In 1567 John Wedderburn published his *Compendious book of godly Psalms and spiritual Songs*, culturally derivative from Lutheran Germany. The 'spiritual songs' were parodies, 'ballads changed out of profane Songs into godly songs', and sung to tunes like the English *Johne, cum kis me now*. 'Good and godly ballads' retained their popularity well into the seventeenth century.[13]

Our second point, qualifying the Protestant/print symbiosis, is that English Catholics, forced after 1559 into the invidious position of a repressed and sectarian minority, made as much use of the press as Protestants did. The impression that this was not the case derives, in part, from the sense that the Bible was a peculiarly Protestant thing, and – in the Tyndale version which, a few translations on, begat the Authorised Version (or King James Bible) of 1611 – quintessentially English. In Scotland, Sir David Lindsay has 'Dame Veritie' denounce 'the New Test'ment, / In Englisch toung, and printit in England, / Herisie, herisie, fire, fire incontinent'.[14] This is by no means a false perception. Whereas there had been fourteen printed Bibles in High German and four in Low German before Luther was ever heard of, in England the indelible association of vernacular Scripture with heresy meant that no part of the Bible had been printed in English before Tyndale began his Protestant and oppositional enterprise in Cologne and Worms in 1525 and 1526. Thereafter the vernacular Bible held a commanding position in English religious experience, and was disseminated in more copies per capita than anywhere else in Europe. In effect, the English Bible *was* English Protestantism.[15]

12 Collinson, *From Iconoclasm to Iconophobia*; Tessa Watt, *Cheap Print and Popular Piety, 1550–1640* (Cambridge University Press, 1991).
13 Brother Kenneth, 'The Popular Literature of the Scottish Reformation', in *Essays on the Scottish Reformation 1513–1625*, ed. David McRoberts (Glasgow: Burns, 1962), pp. 173–7.
14 *Ibid.*, p. 170.
15 Ian Green, *Print and Protestantism in Early Modern England* (Oxford University Press, 2000).

For historians, the sense that the printing press was God's gift to nascent Protestantism also relates to their knowledge that the Reformation in Germany, and to a much lesser extent in England, began with an explosion of ephemeral pamphlet literature, much of which professed to address the 'simple' and uneducated – a revolution in communication arguably more important than the invention of printing itself. This populist strategy went against the grain with the Catholic authorities, and Catholic publicists were slow to catch up.

But catch up they eventually did. In the spirit of joining their opponents if they could not beat them, English Catholic exiles even produced their own English New Testament at Rheims in 1582, with the Old Testament following from Douai in 1609–10. However, these translations were from the Latin Vulgate rather than from the original Greek and Hebrew, and their use was hedged about with spiritual health warnings to the unwary. The Rheims–Douai Bible was but a small part of a massive exercise in print communication. English Catholics became a people of the book, every bit as much as their Protestant antagonists. Given the circumstances, this was hardly surprising. The evangelical and pastoral enterprise of Catholicism depended heavily upon print in the comparative absence of human resources. Much of this printing was necessarily clandestine, with secret presses in England and books smuggled into the country from abroad. This activity was on a much larger scale than the equivalent enterprise of dissident Protestants, although much less notice has been taken of it: which is to say that the brilliant publications of the Catholic exile Richard Verstegan are not as well known as, say, the Marprelate Tracts. For a time, the Protestant book trade actually lagged behind the Romanist competition. Allison and Rogers's catalogue of Catholic imprints lists 932 items in English and no fewer than 1,619 in other languages. By 1570, 60 of the English titles and 90 of the non-English had already appeared.[16]

II

In undertaking a more detailed survey and analysis of the religious literature of this period, we may distinguish: (1) books intended to indoctrinate and instruct;

16 Gilmont, *The Reformation and the Book*, pp. 487–8; A. F. Allison and D. M. Rogers, *The Contemporary Printed Literature of the English Counter-Reformation between 1558 and 1640*, 2 vols. (Aldershot: Scolar Press, 1989, 1994); Alexandra Walsham, ' "Domme Preachers": Post-Reformation English Catholicism and the Culture of Print', *Past and Present* 168 (August 2000), 72–123. I owe much of my knowledge of Catholic imprints to Dr Walsham and am grateful to her for permission to include material from the chapter we have co-authored with Dr Arnold Hunt in Barnard and McKenzie (eds.), *A History of the Book in Britain*, vol. 4.

(2) religious controversies; (3) works of devotion and piety; and (4) literature in a broader sense – prose and poetry deemed to possess literary merit, which reflected and refracted religious concerns and tastes. This last category includes works of imaginative fiction which were provoked by the political anxieties of an age when politics, too, was charged and overheated with religious issues. Such was the early Elizabethan play *Gorboduc* by Thomas Sackville and Thomas Norton, which used classical, Senecan tragedy to deal obliquely but undisguisedly with the problems of royal marriage and succession;[17] and, twenty years later, Philip Sidney's *Arcadia*, which commented critically through the medium of romantic fiction on a later phase of this long-running crisis, and, more broadly, on the problem of irresponsible monarchy in the Europe of Sidney's day.[18] This last category would also encompass the Spenser of *The Shepeardes Calender* and much that is spiritually profound but opaque in the plays of Shakespeare, but it is a necessary economy to exclude religious literature in that broad sense from the remainder of this chapter.

The publishing sectors which remain for consideration were not hermetically sealed off from each other: (3) merges with (1); (2), in the case of Catholic works, often disguised itself as (3).

Pride of place in the first category must go to the English Bible, which we encounter at every turn in the fourth category. Barbara Lewalski has written of the rich ubiquity of Scripture in seventeenth-century lyric poetry, with its many 'tentacular' tropes and metaphors. John Donne wrote: 'There are not so eloquent books in the world, as the Scriptures.' To single out only one of the scriptural 'books', a considerable portion of the literature of the age was, in effect, a meditative commentary on the Book of Psalms.[19]

As Janel Mueller has demonstrated, scripturalism was a potent force in the creation of English as a literary language long before the second half of the sixteenth century.[20] But the Victorian historian J. R. Green was not wrong when he wrote that the eighty or so years separating the accession of Elizabeth from the Civil War saw the English people become the people of the book, the book being the Bible. The statistics of Bible publication have now been compiled by Professor Ian Green, and they show that by the end of this period

---

17 Greg Walker, *The Politics of Performance in Early Renaissance Drama* (Cambridge University Press, 1998), pp. 196–221.
18 Blair Worden, *The Sound of Virtue: Philip Sidney's 'Arcadia' and Elizabethan Politics* (New Haven, CT, and London: Yale University Press, 1996).
19 Barbara K. Lewalski, *Protestant Poetics and the Seventeenth-Century Religious Lyric* (Princeton University Press, 1979); Lily B. Campbell, *Divine Poetry and Drama in Sixteenth-Century England* (Cambridge University Press, 1959).
20 Janel Mueller, *The Native Tongue and the Word: Developments in English Prose Style, 1380–1580* (University of Chicago Press, 1984).

all those able to make use of the text and to afford it (shall we say the upper third of the population?) possessed a Bible of their own or had ready access to one.[21]

London was also supplying a growing market for Bibles in Scotland. That the Bible was not printed in Scotland, in that radically variant form of the English language which was Lowland Scots, had two consequences. Negatively, it finished Scots as a language of print and erudition, and led to a greater differentiation between the spoken and printed language than obtained in England. More positively, the lack of a Scots Bible contributed to the growth of a common Anglo-Scottish Protestant culture.[22] The Highlands and islands of Scotland, the Scottish Gaidhealtachd, absorbed its Protestantism in a different way. There was as yet no Gaelic Bible, but the evangelism of the kirk successfully appropriated the oral, bardic culture of the region in a process of Protestantisation which never occurred in Irish Gaeldom.[23]

Wales, home to one of the oldest vernacular literatures in Europe, was yet another case. Early in the reign of Elizabeth, critical decisions were taken in high quarters to promote Welsh as the language of religious knowledge and devotion for the Welsh people. The New Testament was printed in Welsh in 1551 and 1567; William Morgan's complete Bible, which had much the same significance for the Welsh language as Tyndale's for English, appeared in 1588. It is a commonplace of Welsh history that this ensured the survival of both language and literary culture. Religion, language and literature were interwoven with a compelling sense of Welsh national identity.[24]

Every version of the English Bible (and there were half a dozen between 1525 and 1611) was, in effect, a revision of William Tyndale – which is to say, of those parts of the Bible which Tyndale lived long enough to translate. In Elizabethan England, the Bishops' Bible, the successor to Henry VIII's 'Great Bible', was set up and read publicly, in churches. But the most popular version for personal and domestic use was the Geneva Bible, first published by English

---

21 Green, *Print and Protestantism in Early Modern England*.
22 Brother Kenneth, 'The Popular Literature of the Scottish Reformation', p. 171; Jane Dawson, 'Anglo-Scottish Protestant Culture and Integration in Sixteenth-century Britain', in *Conquest and Union: Fashioning a British State, 1485–1725*, ed. Steven G. Ellis and Sarah Barber (London: Longman, 1995), pp. 87–114.
23 Jane Dawson, 'Calvinism and the Gaidhealtachd in Scotland', in *Calvinism in Europe, 1540–1620*, ed. Andrew Pettegree, Alastair Duke and Gillian Lewis (Cambridge University Press, 1994), pp. 231–53.
24 Glanmor Williams, 'Religion and Welsh Literature in the Age of the Reformation', *Proceedings of the British Academy* 69 (1983), 371–408; Glanmor Williams, 'Unity of Religion or Unity of Language? Protestants and Catholics and the Welsh Language 1536–1660', in *The Welsh Language before the Industrial Revolution*, ed. Geraint H. Jenkins (Cardiff: University of Wales Press, 1997), pp. 207–33.

Protestant exiles in Geneva in 1560, and printed in England itself in numerous editions from 1576. Later it would take some time for the Authorised Version of 1611 to overtake the Geneva Bible in public esteem. Of 280 editions of the complete Bible published by 1640, only 35 had appeared before 1570, but by the end of Elizabeth's reign there had been almost twice as many again. (The equivalent figures for New Testaments are, respectively, 175, 69 and 50 or so.) In all, there were 18 editions of the Bishops' Bible, 91 of the Geneva Bible (some 70 of them in Elizabeth's reign, an astonishing 66 between 1580 and 1609), and, after 1611, 140 of the Authorised Version. These figures do not take account of the many 'pirated' editions printed overseas, which broke the monopoly legally enjoyed by the English Bible printers.[25]

In this period, Bibles came in three formats, from which different uses can be inferred: folios, for reading aloud in church or in large households; quartos and octavos for individual use. The smaller duodecimos, suitable as presents on the occasion, perhaps, of a christening, were not produced before the seventeenth century. Virtually all New Testaments were quartos or octavos – books for (large) pockets. A Shakespearean scholar has concluded from a study of Biblical references and echoes in the plays that Shakespeare's early knowledge would have been of the Bishops' Bible, heard in church and school, but that, later, Shakespeare may have come to own and make private use of the Geneva Bible.[26] Was that indicative of his passage from the old religion professed by his father to the new?

Bibles are excellent examples of the interplay of government and society which was so characteristic of the English Reformation, and indeed of the political and social culture of early modern England. The Book of Common Prayer, backed up by an Act of Parliament which required its presence and continual use in every parish church in the country, where everyone was supposed to be present, more obviously bore the official imprimatur. More than 9,000 parish churches required the production of the Prayer Book on an industrial scale, as did the more occasional and special liturgies called for at moments of national crisis. If lay people commonly owned their own copies of the Prayer Book, that sector of the book trade would obviously have had to work that much harder. Often, however, we find versions of the Prayer Book and of the Psalter in its metrical 'Geneva' version bound up with the Geneva Bible; this was probably the object which most religious people carried to church.[27]

25 The facts and statistics will be found in Green, *Print and Protestantism in Early Modern England.*
26 Richmond Noble, *Shakespeare's Biblical Knowledge and Use of the Book of Common Prayer* (London: SPCK, 1935).
27 Ian Green, ' "Puritan Prayer Books" and "Geneva Bibles": An Episode in Elizabethan Publishing', *Transactions of the Cambridge Bibliographical Society* 11 (1998), 313–49.

The two books of *Homilies*, sermons to be read in church, especially when the minister was not qualified or licensed to preach sermons, 'for the better understanding of the simple people', were obviously 'official' publications. Queen Elizabeth took an active personal interest in what they had to say, and made so clear her preference for homilies over sermons that her unyielding stance triggered the dismissal/resignation of her second Archbishop of Canterbury, Edmund Grindal.[28] For E. M. W. Tillyard, the speech of Ulysses in *Troilus and Cressida*, extolling the cosmic order of things, was a resonance of the Homily of Obedience which the young Shakespeare would have heard read in church.[29]

But catechisms, from which these generations learned their religion in their youth *en masse*, were a different matter. Available in longer and shorter versions, a more or less official *Catechism*, linked with the Prayer Book, was the work of one of Queen Elizabeth's favourite clerics, Alexander Nowell, Dean of St Paul's. Nevertheless, the entrepreneurial energy that could flourish in the less than tightly regulated society of early modern England is demonstrated by the hundreds of alternative catechisms, the work of private clergymen, which were launched into the free market and often kept in print for sixty or seventy years. Ian Green has counted many hundreds of these enterprising publications, appearing over a period of two centuries. However, the reader who hopes to find an interesting chaos of competing theologies in the catechisms will be disappointed. For the most part, they spoke with one consensual voice. Either there were no significant theological differences in the Church of England, or, more plausibly, it was not thought appropriate to discuss these things in front of the children.[30]

What is often described as the second most important text in the making of Protestant England was another, and singular, case of intertwining private and public interest. *The Acts and Monuments of the Church*, popularly known as 'The Book of Martyrs', first appeared in English from John Day's printing shop in 1563. John Foxe, the principal author (for he had many collaborators), had already published, in continental exile, two modest Latin versions of his martyrology, which were intended to tell a learned, European audience about the history of persecution in England from the time of John Wyclif. The 1563

---

28 *The Two Books of Homilies Appointed to be Read in Churches*, ed. John Griffiths (Oxford University Press, 1859), Preface; Margaret Aston, *England's Iconoclasts*, 2 vols., vol. 1, *Laws Against Images* (Oxford University Press, 1988), pp. 320–4; Patrick Collinson, *Archbishop Grindal, 1519–1583: The Struggle for a Reformed Church* (London: Jonathan Cape, and Berkeley: University of California Press, 1979), ch. 13, 'A Scruple of Conscience'.

29 E. M. W. Tillyard, *The Elizabethan World Picture* (London: Chatto & Windus, 1943), p. 82.

30 Ian Green, *The Christian's ABC: Catechisms and Catechizing in England c. 1534–1740* (Oxford: Clarendon Press, 1996).

edition, a much larger book, celebrated the restored peace of the church, especially in its dedication to Queen Elizabeth, comparing her to the first Christian Emperor, Constantine. In 1570, a not only greatly enlarged but substantially recast book addressed a new set of circumstances, reflecting a sense of renewed unease about the security of the Protestant religion in a country still menaced from within and without by resurgent Catholicism, and by no means safe in the hands of a Queen whose own religious commitment appeared to be lukewarm. The story of persecution and martyrdom in England was now set in a much larger framework, taking the story back to the early history of the church and shaped by the sense of God's purposes in history which Foxe and other 'apocalyptic' writers read into and out of the Book of Revelation (or 'the Apocalypse'). A third edition in 1576 added more material, and in 1583 there was a fourth and greatly expanded version, the last to be published in Foxe's lifetime.[31]

According to a once popular interpretation, Foxe instilled in the English people a sense of their unique status in God's plan as his elect nation. That was not at all the intention of Foxe himself, who saw his subject as the Church Universal, not England and its national and imperial destiny, and who fully expected the imminent end of all things. But authors cannot control the use which readers will make of their books. One of those readers, a friend of Foxe, Sir Francis Drake, took the 1576 edition on board the *Golden Hind*, where it became an object of almost cultic devotion, and was displayed to Drake's Spanish prisoners as proof of the Pope's arrogance and cruelty and the imminent end of popery. So Foxe can be said to have circumnavigated the globe, an event of at least proleptic significance.[32]

Although it was soon matched by Holinshed's *Chronicles*, Foxe's *Acts and Monuments* was in its time the largest book ever published in English, fleshed out as it was with all those 'monuments' – original documents from both official and unofficial sources – and first-hand accounts of the Marian trials and burnings, stunningly illustrated with vivid, action-packed woodcuts. But the sheer scale of the enterprise was self-defeating. Although the book was accorded a kind of canonical status among those who read it regularly and 'throughly', and was notorious among Catholic publicists, who wrote hundreds of pages in its

---

31 Loades (ed.), *John Foxe and the Reformation*, and (ed.), *John Foxe: An Historical Perspective*.
32 William Haller, *Foxe's Book of Martyrs and the Elect Nation* (London: Jonathan Cape, 1963); Katharine R. Firth, *The Apocalyptic Tradition in Reformation Britain 1530–1645* (Oxford University Press, 1979); V. Norskov Olsen, *John Foxe and the Elizabethan Church* (Berkeley and Los Angeles: University of California Press, 1973); Glyn Parry, 'Elect Church or Elect Nation? The Reception of the *Acts and Monuments*', in *John Foxe: An Historical Perspective*, ed. Loades, pp. 167–81.

denunciation, it cannot have been well known to 'the simple flock of Christ, especially the unlearned sort', for whom Foxe, following a familiar convention of writers in the vernacular, purportedly wrote. This was a book which cost most of a year's wages for a workingman. Official steps were taken to install it in cathedral churches and in the various offices of Court, but it is not true that it was set up by order in all parish churches. Nor would this have been feasible, for we know that only 1,350 copies of the 1596 edition were printed, and all the editions printed up to the end of the sixteenth century probably amounted to more than 7,500 copies in all. There was need for an abridgement, but restrictive practices in the book trade created difficulties, and the early abridgements, themselves quite long, failed to become best or steady sellers. Only Clement Cotton's *The mirror of martyrs* (1613), which reduced Foxe, *Reader's-Digest* style, to a collection of improving stories, enjoyed any lasting success.[33]

III

If the Elizabethan Settlement of Religion, the main elements of which were set in place by the first Parliament of the reign in 1559, had settled everything, there would have been no Elizabethan religious controversies. In the event, a religious package often misleadingly described as a compromise failed to satisfy or even contain the two religious extremes in a church which a contemporary called 'a constrained union of Papists and Protestants',[34] either by what it defined or by what it left undefined. The Elizabethan church was not a compromise between Rome and Geneva, in spite of the fact that from time to time it proved convenient to claim for it the Aristotelian virtues of the *via media*, and notwithstanding some deliberate concessions made to old-fashioned religious values in some details of the Settlement. These included Holy Communion administered with words which could (but did not necessarily) imply the Real Presence in the elements, and in the form of traditional wafers rather than ordinary bread; some of the vestments and other 'ornaments' of traditional Catholicism; the fundamental structures of a church which retained a liturgical shape of worship; and government by bishops. The Prayer Book of 1559 was, however, in all other and essential respects Cranmer's unmistakably Protestant

---

33 Leslie M. Oliver, 'The Seventh Edition of John Foxe's "Acts and Monuments" ', *Papers of the Bibliographical Society of America* 37 (1943), 243–60; Damian Nussbaum, 'Whitgift's "Book of Martyrs": Archbishop Whitgift, Timothy Bright and the Elizabethan Struggle over John Foxe's Legacy', in *John Foxe: An Historical Perspective*, ed. Loades, pp. 135–53; Clement Cotton, *The mirror of martyrs* (five editions, 1613–39).

34 Henry Ainsworth, *Counterpoyson. Considerations touching the points in difference between the Church of England and the seduced brethren of the separation* (Amsterdam, 1608), p. 228.

liturgy. The only sermons which the clergy were required by order to preach were denunciations of the Pope, and it became almost a doctrine for the English church, not a radical extravagance, to equate the Pope with Antichrist. Apologists for the church, official and unofficial, assumed that England was not out on its own limb of 'Anglicanism' but aligned not only with the Protestant world but with the so-called Reformed churches of Switzerland and south Germany rather than with the Lutherans.

Whatever her personal religious opinions, and she has recently been called both 'an odd sort of Protestant' and 'an old sort of Protestant', Elizabeth was mostly content to govern a church so defined and constituted.[35] From John Foxe and his friend and fellow Protestant propagandist, John Bale, to later Elizabethan panegyrists, she was not only celebrated but in a sense constructed, we might well say invented, as the godly prince par excellence. The most voluminous of these celebrations was Thomas Bentley's *The Monument of Matrones*, a 1,600-page tome divided into seven 'lamps of virginitie'. This was a kind of 'album' which showcased a catalogue of famous and virtuous women, a biographical concordance of every woman mentioned in the Bible, prayers for women of all kinds, including many ecstatic prayers for the use of the Queen herself, and the Protestant version of a pious French work which Elizabeth had translated in her youth, here called *The Queenes meditation*. Bentley's underlying purpose was prescriptive, providing a model of 'praiers, precepts and examples', not least for the Queen herself; this was a book written by men for the benefit of women. In an invented conversation between Elizabeth and God, she was warned never to forget who had placed her where she was: 'Beware therefore that yee abuse not this authoritie given unto you by me, under certaine lawes and conditions.'[36]

The semi-official *Apologia ecclesiae anglicanae* (1562) composed by John Jewel, Elizabeth's first Bishop of Salisbury, should properly be regarded not as the assertion of a *sui generis* religion called Anglicanism, but as a defence offered *by* the Church of England on behalf of the essential Protestantism which it shared with other Reformed churches. 'We burned them', Jewel could write of two radical heretics – including the Unitarian Michael Servetus – who, truth to tell, were executed far from England.[37] Jewel had already fired the first shots in a literary

35 Patrick Collinson, 'Windows in a Woman's Soul: Questions about the Religion of Queen Elizabeth I', in his *Elizabethan Essays* (London and Rio Grande, OH: Hambledon Press, 1994), p. 114; Susan Doran, 'Elizabeth I's Religion: The Evidence of Her Letters', *Journal of Ecclesiastical History* 51 (2000), 699–720.
36 Collinson, 'Windows in a Woman's Soul', pp. 104–8, 116–17.
37 Patrick Collinson, *Godly People: Essays on English Protestantism and Puritanism* (London: Hambledon Press, 1983), pp. 213–24.

war which has been called 'The Great Controversy'.[38] In a sermon preached at the national pulpit of Paul's Cross on 29 November 1559, and subsequently repeated at court, he challenged Catholics to prove that four principal articles of their belief and practice had been known in the first six Christian centuries: communion in one kind, prayer in a language unknown to the people, the papacy and transubstantiation. If any of these things could be found in the primitive church, Jewel would 'give over'. This preemptive appeal to antiquity was a clever response to the stock Catholic taunt: 'Where was your church before Luther?' The gauntlet was taken up by Thomas Harding, a Catholic in exile who came from Jewel's native Devon and who had been his contemporary and co-religionist in Edwardian Oxford. Harding's *Answere to Maister Iuelles chalenge* (Antwerp, 1564) brought *A replie* from Jewel (1565), which duly provoked Harding's *A reiondre to M. Jewels replie* (1566). By this time, Harding had published his *Confutacion* of Jewel's *Apologie*, to which, of course, Jewel promptly responded. A. C. Southern counted sixty-four titles published in the course of this controversy. Harding denounced Jewel's 'impudencie in lying', 'his continuall scoffing', 'his immoderate bragging'. Jewel's abuse was more urbane: 'If ye shall happen to write hereafter, send us fewer words and more learning.'[39]

These were only the opening rounds of a battle of the books which continued for decades, gaining in sophistication as Catholic controversialists of the stature of Nicholas Sanders, Thomas Stapleton and Robert Persons, not to mention the great Cardinal and Saint Robert Bellarmine, met their match (or not, according to taste) in Protestant divines who made the learned confutation of 'popery' their life's work: John Rainolds in Oxford, William Whitaker in Cambridge. Andrew Willet published a *Synopsis papismi* (1592) which addressed 'three hundreds of popish errors'. These grew to 400 in 1594 and 500 in 1600. And all this preceded James I's founding of Chelsea College to serve as a kind of anti-Catholic research institute. Catholic controversialists in the meantime had made the correction and confutation of Foxe's 'Book of Martyrs' more than a cottage industry. Nicholas Harpsfield, who had been instrumental in the making of Foxe's martyrs in Mary's reign, led the way in attacking 'Joannis Foxi mendacia' with *Dialogi sex contra ... oppugnatores et pseudomartyres* (Antwerp, 1566); Robert Persons followed with his *Treatise of three conuersions of England* (1603–4).[40]

38 A. C. Southern, *Elizabethan Recusant Prose, 1559–1582* (London and Glasgow: Sands, 1950), pp. 61–6. See also Peter Milward, *Religious Controversies of the Elizabethan Age: A Survey of Printed Sources* (London: Scolar Press, 1977), ch. 1, 'Anglican Challenge'.
39 *The Works of John Jewel*, ed. J. Ayre, 4 vols., Parker Society (Cambridge University Press, 1845–50), 4:1092.
40 Glyn Parry, 'John Foxe, "Father of Lyes", and the Papists', in *John Foxe and the English Reformation*, ed. Loades, pp. 195–305; Ceri Sullivan, ' "Oppressed by the Force of Truth":

In Scotland there were some literary confrontations between Protestants and Catholics, but on a much less heroic scale; no one has thought of calling this a 'great controversy'. On the Protestant side, the principal protagonist, was, of course, John Knox, who had used his pen and foreign presses in Geneva and elsewhere to such devastating effect in his pamphlets against the Catholic queens who had briefly dominated the politics of what he called 'the Isle of Great Britanny' in the 1550s: most notably in his (in)famous *The first blast of the trumpet against the monstrous regiment of women* (1558).[41] In 1562 Knox was in Ayrshire, a stronghold of the Reformation, but uncomfortably close to the staunchly Catholic Kennedy clan, one of whom, Quintin Kennedy, Abbot of Crossraguel, challenged him to a disputation on his own turf on the subject of the mass. What ensued 'was too crude and knock-about to be called a disputation'. But Abbot Kennedy struck Knox a shrewd blow when he claimed to have no choice but to put up with Knox's 'babbling and barking' since 'princes' (by implication, Mary, Queen of Scots) were equally on the receiving end.[42]

A more talented opponent was Ninian Winzet, schoolmaster of royal Linlithgow (Mary's birthplace) until, 'expellit and schott out of that my kyndly toun', he went into exile, finishing as abbot of a Scottish–Irish monastery in Ratisbon. After disputing with Knox at Linlithgow, Winzet addressed him in a series of *Tractates* and a cleverly entitled *Last blast of the trumpet*, both printed in Edinburgh, in 1562. There followed, from an Antwerp press, *The buke of four scoir thre questions*. This could have been a great controversy, since the ground on which Winzet chose to fight was the Harding–Jewel ground of Christian antiquity. But it takes two to make a quarrel and Knox failed to respond. Winzet explained that he had put his questions into print because Knox may have had difficulty in reading his handwriting, and that he would gladly translate them into Latin, since the anglophile Knox had apparently forgotten 'our aulde plane Scottis quhilk 30ur mother lernit 30u', while Winzet was 'nocht acquyntit with zour Southeren'. Knox may have thought that he had nothing to gain and much to lose by engaging with Winzet, or he may have feared that his own knowledge of the primitive church was not equal to that of his opponent, who had something of a reputation, hardly deserved, as

Robert Persons Edits John Foxe', in *John Foxe: An Historical Perspective*, ed. Loades, pp. 154–66.

41 *John Knox On Rebellion*, ed. Roger A. Mason (Cambridge University Press, 1994).

42 *Heir followeth the coppie of the ressoning which was betuix the Abbot of Crosraguell and John Knox in Mayboil concerning the Masse* (Edinburgh, 1563), and in *The Works of John Knox*, ed. David Laing, 6 vols. (Edinburgh: Bannatyne Society, 1846–64), vol. 6; Jasper Ridley, *John Knox* (Oxford: Clarendon Press, 1968), pp. 411–14; Michael Lynch, 'John Knox, Minister of Edinburgh and Commissioner of the Kirk', in *John Knox and the British Reformations*, ed. Roger A. Mason (Aldershot: Ashgate, 1998), p. 260.

an authority on the Fathers.[43] Three years later the Scottish Jesuit James Tyrie was more successful in forcing Knox into an engagement on the same issue; but it was only in 1572, in his last published treatise, that Knox was provoked by Tyrie's continued activities into publishing his *Answer to a letter of a Jesuit named Tyrie*. Tyrie replied, but Knox was dead, and this promising controversy petered out.[44]

One other Scottish Catholic controversialist deserves a mention, since he was sufficiently celebrated to have had his *Opera omnia* published in Paris in 1644: Adam Blackwood. Blackwood played a prominent part in the posthumous canonisation of Mary, Queen of Scots in his *Martyre de la royne d'Escosse*, published within months of her execution in 1587. Blackwood, predictably, cast Queen Elizabeth as Jezebel, declared her 'intierement incapable de regner', and called Mary 'vraye et legitime Royne de toute la grand Bretaigne'.[45]

Back in England, while Protestant authors stood shoulder to shoulder against the common enemy, they were at the same time engaged in what one Elizabethan called 'civil wars of the Church of God'. These were also literary wars which had their roots in the moderation of the Elizabethan Settlement, in its deliberate liturgical concessions to conservative opinion and its failure to make a clean sweep of the infrastructure, ministry and discipline of the old church by means of what critics of the Settlement called 'a thorough Reformation'. Addressing the Queen directly, one such critic complained: 'But halflie by your Majesty hath God bene honoured, his Church reformed and established.'[46] Hostilities began over an apparently trivial issue, the requirement that ministers of the church conform to the rubrics of the Prayer Book in the use of traditional vestments, especially the white linen surplice, and other articles of clerical attire, such as the square, cornered cap; and the resistance to these things offered by the first nonconformists and their people, militant lay Protestants, the original 'Puritans'. The year 1566 saw the first printed Puritan manifesto, *A briefe discourse against the outward apparell of the popishe church*, the work of a printer–preacher called Robert Crowley, assisted, it was said, by 'the whole multitude of London ministers'. A reply attributed to none other than

43 Ninian Winzet, *Certain Tractates Together With The Book of Four Score Three Questions*, ed. J. K. Hewison, 2 vols. (Edinburgh and London: William Blackwood, 1888, 1890); David F. Wright, 'John Knox and the Early Church Fathers', in *John Knox and the British Reformations*, ed. Mason, pp. 114–15.
44 Ridley, *John Knox*, pp. 509–11; Maurice Taylor, 'The Conflicting Doctrines of the Scottish Reformation', in *Essays on the Scottish Reformation*, ed. McRoberts, p. 271.
45 Adam Blackwood, *Martyre de la Royne d'Escosse* ('Edinburgh' (*recte* Paris), 1587), sig. Aij, p. 1.
46 Albert Peel (ed.), *The Seconde Parte of a Register*, 2 vols. (Cambridge University Press, 1915), 2:52.

Archbishop Matthew Parker himself was at once answered by the ministers. The Puritan Controversy, which would last intermittently through a century of changing ecclesiastical and political circumstances, had begun.[47]

In 1572, two of the younger London ministers, John Field and Thomas Wilcox, raised the stakes with a militant pamphlet which they called *An admonition to the Parliament*. Claiming that earlier critics of the Elizabethan Settlement had concerned themselves with mere 'shells and chippings', Field and Wilcox launched a fundamental and witty assault on things of real substance – episcopacy and the Prayer Book. The rhetorical decibels were also heightened. Wilcox wrote in measured tones: 'We in England are so fare of, from having a church rightly reformed, according to the prescript of Gods worde, that as yet we are not [subsequently altered to 'scarce'] come to the outwarde face of the same.' In his contribution, Field, who took the credit for 'the bitterness of the style', employed the satirical mode: 'In all their order of service there is no edification . . . but confusion, they tosse the Psalmes in most places like tennice balls. The people some standing, some walking, some talking, some reading, some praying by themselves, attend not the minister. He againe posteth it over, as fast as he can gallop.' Field and Wilcox were marginal figures, repudiated by their seniors, and this could have been a nine days' wonder. But when John Whitgift, the future archbishop, assumed John Jewel's mantle and answered the *Admonition* (soon followed by an anonymous *Second admonition*), and when Whitgift's arch-enemy in Cambridge, Thomas Cartwright, replied to his answer, another battle of the books was under way, known to history as 'The Admonition Controversy'. By 1577 Cartwright, driven out of the university and into continental exile, had got to *The rest of the second replie* to Whitgift, itself a fat little book of hundreds of pages.[48]

There followed two decades of controversial exchanges in print: the Puritans versus the bishops and their conformist defenders. John Field seems to have masterminded much of the propaganda, which the dedicated Robert Waldegrave put into print. This print campaign accompanied much agitation, in Parliament and elsewhere in the public domain, and some direct action, to advance a 'further reformation' on radical, presbyterian lines, and to curb the alleged 'tyranny' of the bishops, who were clamping down on nonconformity. Field, who had helped John Foxe with his martyrology, now compiled his own 'Acts and Monuments' of the sufferings of a new generation of Puritan 'martyrs',

47 Patrick Collinson, *The Elizabethan Puritan Movement* (London: Jonathan Cape, and Berkeley: University of California Press, 1967; Oxford University Press, 1990), pp. 71–97.
48 *Ibid.*, pp. 109–55; Peter Lake, *Anglicans and Puritans? Presbyterianism and English Conformist Thought from Whitgift to Hooker* (London: Unwin Hyman, 1988).

some of it published in *A parte of a register contayning sundrie memorable matters for the reformation of our church*, which appeared from a foreign press in 1593.[49]

With the aid of some of the materials which Field had collected and the assistance of the printer Waldegrave, operating clandestinely out of a series of safe houses, the most remarkable of all Puritan propagandists and satirists burst into print in the Armada autumn of 1588. This was the pseudonymous individual (or syndicate?) called 'Martin Marprelate'. Martin went after the bishops and subjected them to a torrent of fast-talking, scandalous ridicule without precedent in English literature. The weighty conformist tome to which Martin was purportedly responding, was described as 'a very portable booke, a horse may cary it if he be not too weake'. Martin's repertoire included what might now be called 'rap', mimicking the stage performances of Dick Tarleton: 'Ha ha ha', 'Wohohow brother London', 'Py hy hy, I cannot but laugh'. Churchmen have ever provided the best of targets for the satirist. But if we find the Marprelate Tracts entertaining, they were also seditious, and, as a kind of ultimate weapon in these bishops' wars, an admission of failure. Martin was answered 'in his own vein' in a series of anti-Martinist pamphlets, and even on the stage, and the cause of further reformation was discredited.

A long-running debate about the identity of 'Martin', now resolved to the satisfaction of many in favour of the radical Parliamentarian Job Throckmorton, has largely missed the point.[50] Authorship hardly matters. The Tracts are above all evidence of the interaction of print with the popular theatre and the street culture of Elizabethan England, where it was common practice to attack enemies and unpopular figures with handwritten libels or placards; they are evidence, too, of how reality and distorted perceptions and projections of reality, fact and fiction, theatre and life, could interact. The anti-Martinist reaction, as theatrical as Martin himself, seems to have created the stock figure of the stage Puritan, a type with which Shakespeare experimented in *Twelfth Night* and which helped to make a career for Ben Jonson and, further, to create the stereotype of the Puritan himself, who from now on was always presented as seditious, avaricious, randy, but, above all, as an arch-hypocrite.[51]

---

49 Patrick Collinson, 'John Field and Elizabethan Puritanism', in his *Godly People*, pp. 335–70.
50 Leland H. Carlson, *Martin Marprelate, Gentleman: Master Job Throckmorton Laid Open in his Colors* (San Marino: The Huntington Library, 1981).
51 Patrick Collinson, 'Ecclesiastical Vitriol: Religious Satire in the 1590s and the Invention of Puritanism', in *The Reign of Elizabeth I: Court and Culture in the Last Decade*, ed. John Guy (Cambridge University Press, 1995), pp. 150–70; Patrick Collinson, 'Ben Jonson's *Bartholomew Fair*: The Theatre constructs Puritanism', in *The Theatrical City: Culture, Theatre and Politics in London, 1576–1649*, ed. David L. Smith, Richard Strier and David Bevington (Cambridge University Press, 1995), pp. 157–69.

The sequel to the Martinist episode saw a state trial of a select group of lead-ing Puritans, including Cartwright, and a relentless persecution of the radical, separatist wing of Puritanism. It also included the publication of two vicious attacks on the Puritans by Richard Bancroft, a client of Whitgift and a future Archbishop of Canterbury, who for many years had tracked their subversive activities with all the dedication of the priest hunter and pursuivant, Richard Topcliffe, and who had masterminded anti-Martinism. These (anonymous) di-atribes, called *Daungerous positions and proceedings*, and *A suruay of the pretended holy discipline*, lambasted 'their bastardly Discipline, that secretlie and seditious-lie eight or nine yeares since, they have agreed uppon (after their fashion like dogges and cats) in manie of their assemblies . . . But doe I call it a schisme? The worde is too milde.' The same year, 1593, launched the first four portions of a large and more respectable book by a somewhat reclusive divine called Richard Hooker: *Of the lawes of ecclesiasticall politie*. This magisterial work transcended all earlier ecclesiological debates between conformists and nonconformists, especially in its reduction of the issues at stake to their legal-philosophical es-sentials, and, according to some scholars, it did not so much defend Anglicanism as invent it. Much Anglican historiography conveys the impression that, with Hooker in play, it was game, set and match for the Church of England. In any case, public interest in polemical ecclesiology was by now nearly exhausted, so that Hooker was only able to publish his book with the aid of a subvention from two of his former pupils.[52]

The idea, however, that the Puritans had lost the argument or had nothing more to say is mistaken. Their place of dominance in early American soci-ety, and, and, briefly, in a mid-century English Revolution which would temporar-ily eclipse episcopacy and the Prayer Book, was still to come. The passing of Elizabeth I, ever their most relentless enemy, and the accession of James I had reactivated hopes of reform and the redress of grievances. When these things failed to materialise, presses at home and overseas were soon turning out a new wave of Puritan apologetics and polemics, and the inevitable responses from the other side. A bibliographical guide to Jacobean and immediately post-Jacobean controversies lists 160 items in the section called 'Anglican v. Puritan', and a further 73 titles published in a rather more recondite series of exchanges between various kinds of radical Puritans and separatists.[53]

52 A. S. McGrade (ed.), *Richard Hooker and the Construction of Christian Community* (Tempe, AZ: Medieval and Renaissance Texts & Studies, 1997); Lake, *Anglicans and Puritans?*, pp. 145–230; C. J. Sisson, *The Judicious Marriage of Mr Hooker and the Birth of the 'Laws of Ecclesiastical Polity'* (Cambridge University Press, 1940).
53 Milward, *Religious Controversies of the Jacobean Age*, pp. 1–71.

However, to write the literary history of English religion as it entered the seventeenth century in terms of 'Anglican versus Puritan' would be a grave distortion. There was a substantial amount of consensual religious literature, including published sermons, Biblical commentaries, books on the religious and moral issues of the time, such as poverty and the charitable response to poverty, as well as the ceaseless flow of anti-Catholic polemic, which is suggestive of a broad middle ground, wide enough to accommodate both conformists and nonconformists. It is impossible and unnecessary to attach the labels of 'Puritan' or 'Anglican' to one of the most prolific of the religious authors of the age, Bishop Joseph Hall (145 entries in the *Revised Short-Title Catalogue*), or to the Shakespeare of Jacobean preachers, Thomas Adams.[54] English Protestantism was still a coherent structure, and the incipient theological battles between Calvinists and so-called 'Arminians' had yet to register themselves in print.[55]

This section would be incomplete without some reference to a controversial literature aimed at the supposed enemies of all religion, those Satanists in the woodwork of Elizabethan England known to their fearful neighbours as witches.[56] According to the *Daemonologie* published in Edinburgh in 1597 by King James VI (but as James I, he later changed his mind on the matter), it was as requisite to believe in the reality of the Devil and his human instruments as it was to believe in God – a necessary part of a coherent theological world view as well as a prop for kingship.[57]

Total sceptics who doubted that there were such things as witches, and who were accused by the more orthodox of the heresy of 'Sadduceeism' (for the Sadducees had doubted the existence of a spirit world transcending materiality), seem to have been rare, in print at least. One such Sadducee was the Kentish gentleman Reginald Scot, enemy of his local Puritans, author of a famous passage in Holinshed describing the building of Dover Harbour, and of

---

54 Patrick Collinson, *The Religion of Protestants: The Church in English Society, 1559–1625* (Oxford: Clarendon Press, 1982); Patrick Collinson, *The Puritan Character: Polemics and Polarities in Early Seventeenth-Century English Culture* (Los Angeles: Clark Memorial Library, 1989); Sears McGee, 'On Misidentifying Puritans: The Case of Thomas Adams', *Albion* 30.3 (1998), 401–18.

55 Nicholas Tyacke, *Anti-Calvinists: The Rise of English Arminianism c. 1590–1640*, rev. edn (Oxford University Press, 1990); Anthony Milton, *Catholic and Reformed: the Roman and Protestant Churches in English Protestant Thought, 1600–1640* (Cambridge University Press, 1995).

56 From an immense (recent) literature, an account of the intellectual and literary history of witchcraft must single out for reference Stuart Clark, *Thinking With Demons: The Idea of Witchcraft in Early Modern Europe* (Oxford: Clarendon Press, 1997).

57 Stuart Clark, 'King James's *Daemonologie*: Witchcraft and Kingship', in *The Damned Art: Essays in the Literature of Witchcraft*, ed. Sydney Anglo (London: Routledge, 1977), pp. 156–81; Christina Larner, 'James VI and I and Witchcraft', in *The Reign of James VI and I*, ed. A. G. R. Smith (London and Basingstoke: Macmillan, 1973), pp. 74–90.

the standard manual on the husbandry of hops. Scot's *Discouerie of witchcraft* (1584), a work of intellectual distinction carefully researched not only from books but from first-hand observation (Gabriel Harvey wrote that he 'hitteth the nayle on the head with a witnesse'), came very close to concluding that there was nothing to discover, apart from vulgar credulity and official cruelty. For Scot, the true crime of witchcraft was the belief that such a nonsense was possible. The radical premise of his argument was that spirits and demons do not exist, or at least do not intervene in human affairs. The victims were, typically, 'old, lame, bleare-eied, pale, fowle, and full of wrinkles' – and, of course, female. It is very remarkable that sixteenth-century rural Kent should have produced one of the most radically sceptical intellects of the whole Renaissance era, although Scot's scepticism was limited by his Protestant belief in the authority of the Word of God as the only basis on which miracles were to be credited.[58]

Among more orthodox writers on the subject, the great theologian William Perkins (who quoted a Hebrew proverb, 'the more women, the more witches') rejected Scot's opinions. There were witches, and they were persons who wittingly and willingly collaborated with the Devil or devils, who just as certainly existed, in order to work wonders. Their offence was not so much the crime of 'maleficium', doing harm, as the Satanic league or covenant itself, and in his *Discourse of the damned art of witchcraft* (1590s?) Perkins even argued that the 'good witch', or wise man or woman, was actually the 'more horrible and detestable', since whereas wicked witches were objects of natural revulsion, people were tempted to solve their problems by resort to so-called 'good witches'. It was because the witch had renounced God that he or she was justly sentenced, by God, to death: 'He may not live.'[59]

While distancing themselves from Scot's outright scepticism, there was in these clerical writers a significant corrective to what has come to be known as the early modern 'witch craze'. The preacher George Gifford lived and wrote in Essex, a county where the prosecution of witches was threatening to get out of hand. His sensitive ear for what ordinary people said and thought and his sharp eye for what happened to them has won him the accolade of 'Tudor anthropologist'. We encounter this in Gifford's *A discourse of the subtill practises of deuilles* (1587):

58 Sydney Anglo, 'Reginald Scot's *Discoverie of Witchcraft*: Scepticism and Sadduceeism', in *The Damned Art*, ed. Anglo, pp. 106–39; Stuart Clark, *Thinking With Demons*, pp. 211–12, 249, 544–5. Scot's anti-Puritanism is inferred from identifying him with 'R. S.', author of a (manuscript) attack on the Kentish Puritans (*A Seconde Parte of a Register*, 2:230–41).

59 *The Work of William Perkins*, ed. Ian Breward, Courtenay Library of Reformation Classics, 3 (Abingdon: Sutton Courtenay Press, 1970), pp. 587–609.

Some woman doth fal out bitterly with her neighbor: there followeth some great hurt...There is a suspicion conceived. Within fewe years after she is in some iarre with an other. Hee is also plagued...Wel, mother W. doth begin to bee very odious and terrible unto many. Her neighbors dare say nothing but yet in their heartes they wish shee were hanged.

Gifford saw in such rumours a typical ruse of the Devil, whose business was to tempt men to abandon their belief in God, and who distracted attention from their own moral state by persuading them to blame all their misfortunes on witches. So 'witches' could be a red herring. Disease was often due to natural causes. Told that a witch caused the death of cattle, Gifford's interlocutor, 'Daniel', says 'It may be he did: but how know you that?...A witch by the Worde of God ought to die the death, not because she killeth men, for that she cannot,...but because she dealeth with devils.' Gifford's concern was to urge his readers to search their own hearts, to stand on their own moral feet and to put their entire trust in God and his providence. But no one knew better that this strenuous and in some ways stark advice often went down badly with those country people who had more time for 'cunning' folk than for 'scripture men'. It is very striking that, in Gifford's *A dialogue concerning witches and witchcraftes* (1593), all the evidence alleged by the unlearned participants is anecdotal and based on hearsay, whereas 'Daniel' stands firmly on the Word of God.[60]

IV

Both Perkins and Gifford are usually referred to as 'Puritans', although whether that label can account for their views on the subject of witchcraft is open to question. But there was one religious genre which we probably ought to classify as 'Puritan', and which was almost peculiar to the religious culture of Protestant England: so-called 'practical divinity'.[61] This was a system and a literature designed to guide and direct the anxious personal soul through the intricate obstacle race which was the *ordo salutis*: how a man, and very often a woman, might find him or her self, and even know him or her self, to be in a state of elect grace. For assurance of salvation, the assurance of a lively, efficacious faith, was not only something comforting to know. It was actually instrumental. These were potential quicksands, however, for who was to know

---

60 George Gifford, *A discourse of the subtill practises of deuilles by witches and sorcerers* (London, 1587); George Gifford, *A dialogue concerning witches and witchcraftes* (London, 1593); Alan Macfarlane, 'A Tudor Anthropologist: George Gifford's *Discourse and Dialogue*', in *The Damned Art*, ed. Anglo, pp. 140–55.

61 These paragraphs rely on Jason Yiannikkou, 'Protestantism, Puritanism and Practical Divinity in England, c. 1570–c. 1620', unpublished University of Cambridge Ph.D. thesis, 1999.

when faith might prove fraudulent, hypocritical? It was a Calvinist dogma, the very heart of Calvinism, that the elect do not, cannot, fall away. But then it follows that those who do fall away, in their own or others' perception, may never have been elect in the first place.

However, it would be wrong to focus excessively on what has been called the 'practical syllogism' of proving one's election, within the dogmatics of Calvinism. Almost regardless of that issue, those religious professionals who were the divines, in print as well as in face-to-face pastoral contact, were fostering that godly and sanctified style of life which Protestants believed to be the necessary fruits of justification – salvation not so much an event as a process. The intensity of this shared religious experience is well conveyed by a Suffolk preacher: those that 'truly love Christ' were to be 'ever inquiring after him, comforting one another, conferring, meditating, praying, stirring up one another'.[62] One of many treatises turning the process into something of a science bore the subtitle *Physicke for the soule* (John Abernethy, 1615). Perkins, the most widely read of these practitioners, who died in 1602, remained a best-selling commodity for half a century: a dozen editions of the complete *Works*, a total of 200 items up to 1640 listed in the *Revised Short-Title Catalogue*. Perkins was also translated into several foreign languages, including Hungarian.[63]

This is a subject which belongs to the early seventeenth century, the age of what William Haller chose to call *The Rise of Puritanism* (1938). One of the most influential of practical works, *Seven treatises* by the Essex preacher (and diarist) Richard Rogers, was first published in 1603, and had reached its fifth edition by 1629, and there were also six editions of an abridgement of what was a large and scarcely affordable book. *A garden of spirituall flowers*, a collection of practical divinity by Rogers and other preachers, achieved at least twenty editions between 1609 and 1638. Practical divinity has been explained as a line taken by Puritan divines only after the path of further reformation by public authority had been blocked, in order to construct that godly nation and people which was the Puritan aspiration pastorally rather than politically: by penetrating individuals, households, gathered groups.[64]

But the pastoral technique of comforting wounded consciences, which was at the heart of practical divinity, had its roots in earlier years, when John Knox had devoted his professional skills to massaging the religious doubts and fears of his mother-in-law, Elizabeth Bowes, and when the Marian martyr John

---

62 Bartimaeus Andrewes, *Certaine verie worthie, godly and profitable sermons upon the fifth chapiter of the Songe of Solomon* (London, 1583), p. 185.

63 *William Perkins*, ed. Breward, pp. 613–32.

64 Collinson, *The Elizabethan Puritan Movement*, pp. 433–7; Christopher Hill, *Society and Puritanism in Pre-Revolutionary England* (London: Secker and Warburg, 1964), pp. 501–6.

Bradford had exercised a similar ministry through his letters from prison.[65] There was an Elizabethan literature which followed in this train, notably the sermons and letters of the exemplary Puritan divine, Edward Dering (who died in 1576), which were gathered together in 1590 in *Maister Derings workes*, a publishing enterprise in which Knox, John Field, and Dering's widow and Knox's dear friend, Anne Locke, were all in their various ways complicit.[66] Until the end of the sixteenth century, godly letters were the main vehicle for sharing with the religious public at large counsel originally given privately to individuals: for example, *Large letters... for the instruction of such, as are distressed in conscience* (1589), by Field's sometime accomplice, Thomas Wilcox. Thereafter, this personal approach gave way to an increasingly technical casuistry, user-friendly manuals for the troubled soul, or disordered conscience.

In spite of this growing literature expressive of a more or less Puritan spirituality, balanced by more 'Anglican' works such as Bishop Joseph Hall's *Meditations and vowes divine and morall* (many editions from 1605), it could be said that the Reformed Church of England starved its children of spiritual food, and that this was available in greater measure from Roman Catholic sources – specifically from Catholic writers touched by the intensely circumstantial spirituality of the Society of Jesus and of its founder, Ignatius Loyola. Here was instruction in how to pray, how to confess, how to receive the eucharist. Translations were made, not only into English but into Irish and Scots Gaelic, and into Welsh, from modern classics of spirituality, Spanish and Italian, and from older texts such as the prayers of the fourteenth-century mystic Henry Suso. There was also a steady production of the manuals of Catholic devotion and instruction: missals, breviaries, catechisms. English Catholics were part of a pan-European book culture, and contributed significantly to it. A single work by Edmund Campion, *Rationes decem*, first secretly printed at Stonor Park in Oxfordshire in 1581, achieved forty-five editions in the original Latin, and was translated into Czech, Dutch, Flemish, French, German, Hungarian and Polish.[67]

65 Yiannikkou, 'Protestantism, Puritanism and Practical Divinity', pp. 26–40, and Dr Thomas Freeman's forthcoming edition of the *Letters of the Marian Protestants* for the Church of England Record Society; Patrick Collinson, 'John Knox, the Church of England and the Women of England', in *John Knox and the British Reformations*, ed. Mason, pp. 74–96.
66 Collinson, 'Knox, the Church of England and the Women of England', pp. 94–5; Patrick Collinson, 'A Mirror of Elizabethan Puritanism: The Life and Letters of "Godly Master Dering"', in his *Godly People*, pp. 288–324.
67 Allison and Rogers, *Contemporary Printed Literature of the English Counter-Reformation*, 1:24–9; T. A. Birrell, 'English Counter-Reformation Book Culture', *Recusant History* 22 (1994), 113–22.

Much Catholic devotional literature was not quite what it professed to be, and followed a double agenda. There was a hidden polemical intention, not only to nourish the piety of the faithful but to define the distinct existence of the Catholic community. Closet Catholics who in practice were often obliged to conform and compromise were told in print, in such tracts as the Jesuit Robert Persons's *Certayne reasons why Catholiques refuse to goe to church* (1580), that refusal (technically 'recusancy') was the only way to be sure of their salvation, a message intended for the Protestant enemy as much as for the faithful. The literature of persecution and martyrdom, a kind of Catholic *Acts and Monuments*, was no less double-edged, part of the politics of a mission, which, as Persons well knew, could never succeed without a change of regime which would probably require foreign intervention.[68]

But if this was religious war, it was a war which allowed for some spiritual fraternisation. Imitation is the sincerest form of flattery, and the best testimony to the quality of the spiritual sustenance offered by the English Counter-Reformation was its appropriation by Protestants. The most celebrated of Catholic devotional manuals was *The Christian directory guiding men to eternall saluation*, often called *The resolution*, or *The first booke of the Christian exercise*, a text by the Spanish Jesuit Gaspar Loarte, freely adapted by Persons. In 1584, the Yorkshire minister Edmund Bunny, conventionally classified as a moderate Puritan, published a carefully doctored version of Persons's adaptation which, with all references to purgatory and free will excised, still retained 90 per cent of the original text. It is hard to say whether one should be encouraged or discouraged by this evidence of the common Christian ground shared by embattled religious parties who would continue to consign each other to the Devil for generations to come. Bunny's version went through many more impressions than the original. By 1623, the ratio was 24:1. The fact that no fewer than sixteen editions of Bunny/Persons were produced in the single year 1585 is the best evidence we have that the most freely flowing springs of Christian spirituality were still Catholic, even if they were made to pass through a Protestant filter.[69]

68 I owe this point to Dr Alexandra Walsham. See her ' "Domme Preachers"', and also her *Church Papists: Catholicism, Conformity and Confessional Polemic in Early Modern England*, 2nd rev. edn (Woodbridge: Boydell and Brewer, 2000). See also Michael Questier, *Conversion, Politics and Religion in England, 1580–1625* (Cambridge University Press, 1996).

69 Brad S. Gregory, 'The "True and Zealouse Service of God": Robert Parsons, Edmund Bunny, and the *First Booke of the Christian Exercise*', *Journal of Ecclesiastical History* 45 (1994), 238–68; and, for a different interpretation, Victor Houliston, 'Why Robert Persons Would not be Pacified: Edmund Bunny's Theft of the *Book of Resolution*', in *The Reckoned Expense: Edmund Campion and the Early English Jesuits*, ed. Thomas M. McCoog (Woodbridge: Boydell and Brewer, 1996), pp. 159–77.

Another Jesuit work of devotion, Luca Pinelli's *Meditationi brevi del santis-simo sacramento*, received two English translations, one for Catholics, edited by Henry Garnet and published in about 1600, another for Protestants, edited by Christopher Sutton and first published in 1601. The Sutton version omitted references to such beliefs and practices as transubstantiation and penance, but retained most of the original prayers and meditations, especially those concerned with self-examination before receiving communion.[70] It is a fact often overlooked that English Protestants, even Puritans, focused much of their piety on the sacrament of the eucharist.[71] It is also a distressing fact that Garnet was hanged, drawn and quartered for his supposed role in the Gunpowder Treason of 1605. On the other hand, Sutton's *Disce mori. Learne to die*, and his *Disce vivere. Learne to live* were popular with the Anglo-Catholics of the nineteenth century, including John Henry Newman, who went back to Rome and became a cardinal.[72] When, in Kipling's phrase, the tumult and the shouting died, it appears that these were, after all, all Christians.

70 Henry Garnet (ed.), *Briefe meditations of the most holy sacrament and of preparation for receiving the same* (English secret press, *c.* 1600); Christopher Sutton, *Godly Meditations upon the most holy sacrament of the Lordes supper* (London, 1601). I owe these references to Alex Walsham.
71 Arnold Hunt, 'The Lord's Supper in Early Modern England', *Past and Present* 161 (1998), 39–83.
72 *DNB*, s.v. Christopher Sutton.

Chapter 13

LITERATURE AND LONDON

LAWRENCE MANLEY

The literature of early modern England was shaped by the manifold developments that made London, with a population of perhaps 50,000 in 1500 and 250,000 in 1600, the second largest metropolis in Europe by the later seventeenth century. With this growth came an increasing variety of communities and cultures. A well-established citizenry of craftsmen, retailers and wholesale traders enjoyed the traditional freedoms of London by virtue of membership in the guilds or 'livery' companies that organised the City's trades. The expansion of international markets and the establishment of trading outposts around the globe transformed large portions of this citizenry into a wealthy, mobile and literate merchant class. At the same time, the permanent residence of the royal court in Westminster brought increasingly large numbers of the nobility to London, while the legal proceedings of Parliament, the chief courts of the realm and the Inns of Court drew officials, petitioners and litigants from throughout the counties. As the main conduit for the exchange of landed wealth, London became home to the aristocratic marriage market; its social season and developing luxury and leisure industries were attractive to urbanising gentry disposed to conspicuous consumption. The City harboured a large 'youth culture' of apprentices and domestic servants, male and female, recruited from the often distant countryside. Substantial portions of the greater London population were 'strangers' – continental traders, immigrants and communities of Flemish and French religious refugees – and 'foreigners' or non-free English migrants: the artisans, casual labourers, criminals, homeless and unemployed who frequented the rapidly growing suburbs outside the City walls. The ravages of poverty and epidemic disease meant that London's expansion could only be fuelled by patterns of migration: in 1590, one-eighth of the English people became Londoners at some point in their lifetimes.[1] London thus visibly embodied the social possibilities of Britain. The preacher Thomas Adams

---

1 Roger Finlay, *Population and Metropolis: The Demography of London 1580–1650* (Cambridge University Press, 1981), p. 9.

described the City as an anamorphic picture, representing 'to divers beholders, at divers stations, divers forms'.² This diversity of forms helped shape the
discursive possibilities of early modern English literature.

In literature and culture as in other spheres, London exerted its growing
influence through a paradoxical combination of centripetal and centrifugal
effects: its contribution to consolidation and cohesion was linked to forces
that also undermined older traditions and led to greater heterogeneity, mobility, innovation and specialisation in markets, social roles and literary cultures.
The claim that 'Tudor despotism consisted in London's domination over the
rest of England'³ derives in the first instance from the City's decisive role in
promulgating the Reformation and in providing the principal source of Crown
revenues and finance, but it applies to virtually every sphere of life. National
standards in wages, prices, weights and measures were set by the standards of
the London markets; the ordering of time and the movement of heavenly bodies were calculated in almanacs set 'to the meridian of London'. For its carefully
maintained public order during the Reformation, the 'noble and faithful city
of London' was held up as a political example to the 'rude countries' of the
remoter provinces.⁴ The norms proposed for the English language were those
derived from 'the vsuall speech of the Courte and that of London and the shires
lying about London within lx. myles, and not much above'.⁵ The humanist
school texts of the London educators John Colet and William Lily became
the basis for the 'Royal Grammar' promulgated by Henry VIII (1542) and his
successors. Grammar schools, religious benefices, and charities throughout
the countryside were heavily endowed by wealthy London merchants.⁶ The
city's role as an intellectual centre was enhanced by the presence of the Inns of
Court, 'nurses of humanity and liberty' that enabled London to claim 'the name
and stile of an Universitie' and to count itself 'a chief place in the catalogue
of Universities'.⁷ The incorporation of the Company of Stationers in 1557

2 Thomas Adams, 'The City of Peace' (London, 1612), in *Works*, ed. Joseph Angus, 3 vols.
   (Edinburgh: J. Nichol, 1861–2), 3:331.
3 A. F. Pollard, 'Local History', *Times Literary Supplement*, 19 (1920), 161.
4 *A lamentation in which is showed what ruin and destruction cometh of seditious rebellion* (1536), in
   Humanist Scholarship and Public Order, ed. David Berkowitz (Washington: Folger Shakespeare
   Library, 1984), p. 97.
5 John Hart, *A methode . . . to read English* (1570), in *John Hart's Works on English Orthography and
   Pronunciation*, ed. Bror Danielsson, Stockholm Studies in English, 5 (Stockholm: Almqvist,
   1955), p. 234; George Puttenham, *The Arte of English Poesie*, ed. G. D. Willcock and A.Walker
   (Cambridge University Press, 1936), pp. 144–5.
6 Wilbur K. Jordan, *The Charities of London* (London: George Allen and Unwin, 1960),
   pp. 308–18.
7 Sir George Buc, 'A Discourse or Treatise of the third universitie of England', in John Stow,
   Annales (London, 1615), p. 984; Ben Jonson, Dedication to *Every Man Out of His Humour*, in
   The Complete Plays, ed. G. A.Wilkes, 4 vols. (Oxford: Clarendon Press, 1981–2), 1:279.

restricted printing to London (except for presses at Oxford and Cambridge) and placed the ownership and reproduction rights of intellectual 'copy' in the hands of enterprising London publishers. Thanks to London's presses, markets and migration patterns, much of what made its way into literary circulation as a purchasable commodity had first been enacted in the courtrooms and pulpits, on the stages, scaffolds and streets of London. As the source from which intellectual life radiated, London was both 'the Epitome and Breviary of all Britain' and 'the spectacle of the whole realm whereof all other cities and places take example'.[8]

The influence of the metropolis destabilised traditional English society throughout the realm and reconfigured the terms in which it was imagined. During the sixteenth century, the traditional model of the Three Estates of knights, clergy and commons, which accorded the functions of learning and textuality to the clergy, was replaced by a triadic model that divided the realm into Country, Court and City. Based on geographical rather than social 'place', this model took for granted a mobility with regard to geographic space, social status and discursive norms. As the site where Country, Court and City converged, London was the catalyst for both social transformation and a new heterogeneity in expression and ideas. The City contributed to interaction between the expanding classes of landed gentry and urban citizenry, who changed estates 'by a mutual conversion of the one into the other'.[9] With a population that was 'by birth for the most part a mixture of all the countries' of the realm, London functioned as a 'rich and wealthy seedplot' from which newly wealthy social hybrids were in turn 'continuously transplanted' back to the countryside.[10] But London was also the miserable destination of hordes of farmers and villagers, vagabonds, rogues and paupers who, in traditional complaints, were described as casualties of the City's disruption of traditional local economies. Early modern England was thus an urbanising society that had until recently been primarily agrarian and consequently lacked strong traditions of urbanism. This situation presented extraordinary challenges and opportunities for the creators of early modern English literature. In keeping with the burgeoning possibilities for interchange offered by the metropolitan environment, the work of many early modern English writers of literature is marked by

---

8 William Camden, *Britannia*, trans. Philemon Holland (London, 1610), p. 421; Corporation of London Records Office, *Journals of the Common Council*, fo. 65 (1572–3), quoted in Michael Berlin, 'Civic Ceremony in Early Modern London', *Urban History Yearbook* (1986), 23.

9 William Harrison, *The Description of England* (1587), ed. Georges Edelen (Ithaca: Cornell University Press, 1968), p. 115.

10 *Apologie of the Cittie of London*, in John Stow, *The Survey of London*, ed. C. L. Kingsford, 2 vols. (1908; rpt, Oxford: Clarendon Press, 1971), 2:207; Thomas Gainsford, *The Glory of England* (London, 1618), p. 318.

extraordinary ethical and expressive innovation and by a widened sense of the human and social variety that enriches and complicates the experience of living in community.

Ministers and magistrates

The normative background against which literary innovation was defined in Elizabethan London was a holdover from the medieval world of the Three Estates: an alliance between ministry and magistracy, holy word and civic sword. This alliance was both a political arrangement that sustained the oligarchic civic core of London itself – a world of municipal freemen government, guilds, parishes and local vestries – and a conceptual model for acceptable forms of public expression. In London, earlier than elsewhere, the political authority of the magistrate had become a focus of public awareness and expression. In the later Middle Ages, the religious feast of Corpus Christi, which had served to define the body of the local community in religious terms, gave way to the ceremonial preeminence, visible authority and organised structure of the city's guilds and government. At the coming of the Reformation, with the systematic suppression of traditional religious institutions and practices, a revision of the collective memory of the local community brought further prestige to the civic authorities, around whom ritual and public memory were increasingly concentrated.[11]

One prop of civic prestige was a longstanding scribal culture of record-keeping and notarial memory. In the 1580s, London's civic authorities were sequestering and recopying the custumals in which medieval town clerks and chamberlains had inscribed civic precedents and chronicled the city's achievement of its jealously guarded liberties.[12] More crucially, the work of early London chroniclers like Arnold Fitz-Thedmar, William Gregory and Richard Arnold formed a basis for the greater chronicles by Tudor Londoners like Sheriff Robert Fabyan and the City Common Sergeant and prison official Edward Hall. The work of Fabyan and Hall, along with Fabyan's annalistic practice of dating each new year from the mayoral inauguration, made its way into the chronicles of the two great rivals, Richard Grafton, a London Grocer and enterprising publisher, and John Stow, a Merchant Taylor and

---

11 Mervyn James, 'Ritual, Drama, and the Social Body in the Late Medieval English Town', *Past and Present* 98 (1983), 3–29; Robert Tittler, *The Reformation and the Towns in England* (Oxford: Clarendon Press, 1998), pp. 19–20, 270–304.

12 Piers Cain, 'Robert Smith and the Reform of the Archives of the City of London, 1580–1623', *London Journal* 13.1 (1987–8), 3–16.

innovative antiquarian. Thomas Nashe ridiculed the citizen mentality of 'good master Stow' and 'lay chronographers, that write of nothing but of Mayors and Sheriefs, the dear year and the great frost'.[13] Nevertheless, the work of Grafton and Stow was incorporated by the London antiquary Lawrence Fleming into the 1587 edition of Holinshed's *Chronicles*, where the quotidian urban temporality that London annalists had set against the cataclysms of dynastic change became part of a widely influential history of the English nation.

London received its most lavish chronicle and panegyric, however, in Stow's monumental *Survey of London* (1598, 1603), a history of the City's institutions and a ward-by-ward perambulation of its streets and buildings based on meticulous archival research, novel methods of topographical description, and vivid powers of personal observation. The recurring themes of Stow's survey include admiration for the order and 'good amity' of the citizenry, a traditionalist's lament for the loss of the religious ceremonies, institutions and charities that had unified the pre-Reformation community, and an octogenarian's dismay at the overcrowding, impersonality and polarisation of rich and poor that accompanied an ever-accelerating pace of change. Expanded by Anthony Munday in the seventeenth century and by John Strype in the eighteenth, Stow's project continues to this day in the modern *Survey of London*. The pattern of post-Reformation civic writing in London was repeated elsewhere, in descriptions of Great Yarmouth by Henry Manship, Chester by David Rogers, Exeter by John Vowell and Canterbury by William Somner. Together with descriptions of all of England's leading towns included in William Camden's *Britannia* (1586) and John Speed's *Theatre of the Empire of Great Britain* (1611), these works suggest the ways in which, while initially contributing to the decay of provincial towns, London's impressive exemplarity and far-flung influence eventually led to an 'urban Renaissance' throughout the realm.[14] A description of Edinburgh by the Scottish humanist Alexander Alesius appeared alongside a description of London in Sebastian Münster's *Cosmographia* (1550), where the two capitals dominated the section 'de insulis Britannicis'. The reappearance of Alesius's description alongside accounts of London, Norwich, Bristol and other leading British and European cities in Georg Braun's and Franz Hogenberg's massive *Civitates Orbis Terrarum* (1572 *et seq.*) demonstrates the extent to which early modern towns, tied by trade and migration, no matter how distant, were more like each other than like their own more proximate hinterlands.

13 Thomas Nashe, *Works*, ed. R. B. McKerrow (Oxford: Blackwell, 1958), 1:317, 194.
14 Peter Borsay, *The English Urban Renaissance: Culture and Society in the Provincial Town, 1660–1770* (Oxford: Clarendon Press, 1989).

Just as important as scribal culture were the public, performative modes of expression that upheld the authority of magistrates. In London, the coming of the Reformation brought a shift from religious celebrations of commensality to ceremonies that extolled the London magistracy and the wealthiest companies from which leaders were chosen. By the 1540s, the communal ceremonies of the Midsummer Watch, which themselves replaced the earlier pageants of Corpus Christi as the preeminent civic event, were in turn replaced by ceremonies focusing on the inauguration of London's chief magistrate, the Lord Mayor (so styled only from the same period).[15] With processions that displayed the hierarchies of the City government and guilds (and thus defined for spectators the *cursus honorum* of civic officeholding), the inaugural shows began to feature allegorical pageants and spoken verse by the 1560s. Richard Mulcaster composed for the Merchant Taylors in 1568 one of the earliest such texts to survive. By the 1580s, the pageant-scripts, typically commissioned from playwrights by the sponsoring guilds, began regularly to appear in printed form; later pageant writers like Anthony Munday and Thomas Middleton enjoyed official patronage through the newly created post of City Chronographer, a position subsequently occupied by Ben Jonson and Francis Quarles.

In their overt mythologising of London's chief officers and guilds, the inaugural shows formed part of a considerable epideictic literature devoted to the magnanimity, virtue and chivalric aspirations of London's merchant class. William Nelson's celebration of the legendary mayor William Walworth in an inaugural show written for the Fishmongers in 1590 became, along with a related play on the *Life and Death of Jack Straw* (1593), part of a wave of civic mythmaking that included popular civic plays like *The Book of Sir Thomas More* (c. 1593), Dekker's *The Shoemakers' Holiday* (1600) and Heywood's *The Four Prentices of London* (c. 1592), *Edward IV* (1599) and *If you Know Not Me You Know Nobody* (1605). Illustrious merchant-heroes were celebrated in pamphlets like Richard Johnson's *Nine Worthies of London* (1592) and Richard Niccols's *Londons Artillery* (1616), in now-lost plays and ballads on the miraculous youth of Mayor Richard Whittington (1605) and in William Jaggard's woodcut *View of all the Right Honourable Lord Mayors of this Honourable City of London* (1601).[16] Mixing traditional deference with undisguised ambition, and an outmoded chivalric manner with modern mercantile heroics, such civic mythmaking was an improbable and socially threatening hybrid that became a frequent target

15 David M. Bergeron, *English Civic Pageantry, 1558–1642* (London: Edward Arnold, and Columbia: University of South Carolina Press, 1971), chs. 4–9.
16 Laura Caroline Stevenson, *Paradox and Praise: Merchants and Craftsmen in Popular Elizabethan Fiction* (Cambridge University Press, 1984), pp. 108–29.

of ridicule on stage and page, most notably in Beaumont's parody of citizen tastes, *The Knight of the Burning Pestle* (1609).

Civic expression in London was in theory linked to the discursive authority of the clergy; 'the heart of the magistrate... and the loose tongue of the preachers' were supposed to govern the metropolis 'both with the sworde and the worde'.[17] London had always been a great centre of preaching, but in the post-Reformation climate, its pulpits made it 'the very Arke of the presence of God, above all other places in this land'.[18] The City's most important pulpit was the outdoor structure at Paul's Cross in the cathedral churchyard. A site for public proclamations, for sermons inculcating official doctrine and policy, and for dramatic spectacles of public punishment and recantation, Paul's Cross was closely supervised by the authorities. John Aylmer, an Elizabethan Bishop of London, referred to it as 'my chaire'.[19] Sermons in the City churches were supplemented by a number of civic preaching venues: the multi-storeyed pavilion at St Mary Spital, where City officials gathered to hear sermons during Easter week; the London Guildhall, where sermons were preached at election time; and the halls of individual London companies, where sermons were delivered by divinity students whose fellowships were sponsored by the guilds. A precedent for fiery preaching on social themes and public morals had been established by such famous Edwardian sermons as Thomas Lever's *Sermon in the Shrouds* (1550) and Hugh Latimer's *Sermon of the Plough* (1548) at court. This tradition was continued by the many unbeneficed ministers who supplemented preaching by regular parish clergy in lectureships sponsored by the vestries of congregations receptive to Puritanism. John Field and Robert Crowley lectured at Puritan hotbeds like Holy Trinity at the Minories and St Antholin's, Budge Row, while the 'silver-tongued' Henry Smith held forth at St Clement Danes and Thomas Sampson occupied a pulpit at Whittington College.[20] Sermons poured from the presses, and whole London congregations were observed by foreign visitors taking notes during sermons. A country preacher at Paul's Cross in 1571 exclaimed that 'when I come out of the country hither to the city, methink I come into another world, even out of darkness into light, for here the word of God is plentifully preached'.[21]

17 John Northbrooke, *A Treatise of Dicing, Dansing, Plays, and Interludes* (1577), ed. J. P. Collier (London: Shakespeare Society, 1843), p. 84.
18 Thomas Jackson, *The Conuert's Happines* (London, 1609), p. 30.
19 Millar Maclure, *The Paul's Cross Sermons 1534–1642* (University of Toronto Press, 1958), p. 113.
20 Paul Seaver, *The Puritan Lectureships: The Politics of Religious Dissent* (Stanford University Press, 1970).
21 E. B., *A Sermon preached at Pauls crosse on Trinity Sunday, 1571* (London, 1576), n.p.

Sermons on social themes and public morals often took the form of a 'weekly "check-up"',[22] in which preachers offered diagnoses and then called upon the magistrates 'to play both the Phisition and the Surgeon... to launce out all corruption... gathered in the bowels of the city'.[23] Freak occurrences and epidemics were compared to God's wrath on Biblical cities, while the image of Jerusalem fallen and restored was offered as a model for the godly Reformation of London: 'the city of Jerusalem', Henry Smith declared, 'had never so many prophets crying at once in her streets as this city wherein we dwell'.[24] Sermons on social themes ran a gamut, from sexuality and marriage, to domestic and public order, to the proper uses of wealth and law and the obligations of earthly stewardship. Special favourites were the twin evils of prodigality and avarice, one the gentleman's sin, the other the merchant's, linked to each other through financial practices to which preachers gave the blanket term 'usury'. Usury was traditionally associated with prodigal borrowers and avaricious creditors who breached the intimate and informal terms of petty transactions; but by the later sixteenth century 'usury' denoted disturbing transformations in the social order – the changing relationships between land and money, between the aristocratic and business classes, and in the credit relationships of small producers to dealers, the developing relationship between wage earners and employers.[25]

It was supposedly the role of 'the magistrate to punish' and 'the preacher to reprove usury'. But the growth of London as a financial centre, especially after the 1571 repeal of the 1552 statute against usury, sometimes brought preachers into conflict with the merchant and magisterial classes, which had developed their own civic literature and secular outlook. Nicholas Ridley, the Edwardian Bishop of London, boasted that his colleagues Latimer, Lever, Bradford and Knox had so 'ripped' and 'purged' Londoners 'of insatiable covetousness... that these men, of all other, these magistrates could never abide'.[26] The potential for conflict surfaced in the fictional debate between a London merchant and a London minister in Thomas Wilson's *Discourse upon Usury* (1572) and in frequent disputes over benefices, support of the preaching clergy and the sometimes unwelcome content of sermons. The Court of Aldermen, for example, complained that Aylmer's chaplain 'had publicly defamed them to

22 Maclure, *Paul's Cross Sermons*, p. 121.
23 Thomas White, *A Sermon Preached at Paules Crosse... 1577* (London, 1578), sig. F7.
24 Henry Smith, 'The Art of Hearing', *Works*, 2 vols. (Edinburgh: James Nichol, 1866), 1:319.
25 R. H. Tawney, 'Introduction' to Thomas Wilson, *A Discourse upon Usury* (London: G. Bell and Sons, 1925), pp. 16–42.
26 Nicholas Heming, *The Lawful Use of Riches* (London, 1578), cited in Tawney, 'Introduction', pp. 112–13; Nicholas Ridley, *A Pious Lamentation of the Miserable Estate of the Churche* (1566), in *The Works of Nicholas Ridley* (Cambridge: Parker Society, 1843), p. 59.

their faces' in a 1581 Paul's Cross sermon.[27] In 1586, after the Puritan George Closse accused Mayor Wolstan Dixi of fraud and partiality in a Paul's Cross sermon, Closse was summoned back to the pulpit for public chastisement. Dixi's inauguration and the glory of London's magistracy, meanwhile, had just been celebrated in the first of many printed texts of a mayoral show, George Peele's *The Device of the Pageant Borne before Wolstan Dixi* (1585).

In the mid-Elizabethan period, however, increasingly iconoclastic Puritan attitudes sometimes united ministry and magistracy in opposition towards many secular forms of public expression. The opposition of both ministers and magistrates to London's developing theatres was part of a broader antipathy to all of the alternative media developing in the city: 'ballads, books of love, and idle discourses and histories', 'wanton Pamphlets and Promiscuous love-bookes', 'libels, invectives and Satyres', the works of 'Pamphletters and ballad-Writers', of 'poets, pipers, and such peevish cattle'.[28] Critics described the booksellers' stalls in Paul's Churchyard, adjacent to the pulpit Cross, as a 'confused world of trumpery' where 'every stationers shop, stal, & almost every post, gives knowledge of a new toy'.[29] Supported by an extreme scripturalism that condemned as idolatry all words not spoken 'out of the mouth of the Lord' (Jer. 23:16), Protestant resistance to popular and secular urban writing also expressed anxieties about the contaminations (both physical and social) associated with the socially mixed audience of the theatre and the popular press.[30] Extending the logic of a mid-Tudor policy that had classified popular players and ballad-sellers among the species of vagabonds, the authorities stigmatised other forms of expression as the transgressions of men (and women) without a proper vocation for public speech; 'the life and behavior of citizens', they maintained, should be 'subject neither to a Poetes inkhorne, or a players tongue, but the Seate of Justice'.[31] To survey the officially condemned forms of popular and secular expression, and to explore their transgressive novelty, is not just to encounter the burgeoning literary kinds associated with metropolitan life – a plethora of ballads, moral

27 Seaver, 'The Puritan Lectures', p. 122.
28 William Perkins, *A Direction for the Government of the Tongue according to God's Word* (London, 1593), p. 88; Henry Crosse, *Vertues Common-Wealth* (London, 1603), sig. N8; William Vaughan, *The Spirit of Detraction* (London, 1611), sigs. O4, P; Stephen Gosson, *The School of Abuse* (1579) (London: Shakespeare Society, 1841), pp. 14–15.
29 Abraham Holland, *Continued Inquisition against Paper Persecutors*, quoted in Hyder Rollins, 'The Black-Letter Broadside Ballad', *PMLA* 34 (1919), 323; Crosse, *Vertues Common-Wealth*, sig. P.
30 See Sharon Achinstein, 'Plagues and Publication: Ballads and the Representation of Disease in the English Renaissance', *Criticism* 24.1 (1992), 27–49.
31 Stephen Gosson, *Plays confuted in five actions* (1582), in *Markets of Bawdrie: The Dramatic Criticism of Stephen Gosson*, ed. Arthur F. Kinney, Salzburg Studies in English Literature, 4 (Salzburg: Institüt für englischen Sprache und Literatur, 1974), p. 179.

poems, pamphlets, plays and satires – but to discover the depth and richness of London's contribution to early modern English literature.

Minstrels and moralists

Printed on one or both sides of the same single sheet that served for civic proclamations and church edicts, and selling for less than a penny on average, the ballad was a publication novelty that shared a number of oral and performative features with civic expression and preaching. From the 1560s, the outpouring of ballads and ballad-jigs was associated with the popular performances of authors like William Elderton, clowns like Richard Tarlton and William Kemp, and singing ballad-sellers like Stephen Peele and Richard Sheale.[32] The musical settings, choric refrains, rounds, multi-part dialogues and accompanying dances of ballads incorporated the traditional sorts of public communication associated with festive gatherings, mimicry and folk memory. Cheap publishing adapted these oral and performative practices to the wider urban environment, where 'print was everywhere present, posted, exhibited, cried in the streets, and highly visible'.[33] Ballads were were in turn marketed orally by pedlars throughout the countryside and then put 'to independent use and interpretation' by readers who sang them.[34] In *Kind-Hartes Dream* (1592), the London playwright and Stationer Henry Chettle describes how ballads, having 'infected London the eie of England', circulated contagiously throughout the realm at the hands of ballad-mongers, who could 'spred more pamphlets by the State forbidden than all the Booksellers in London'.[35]

The Elizabethan broadside ballad was quickly adapted to communicating information, entertainment, protest, advice and instruction, a range of matters that Thomas Middleton termed 'fashions, fictions, felonies, fooleries'.[36] When reproduced rapidly and in bulk (as many as 1,000 ballads could be produced in a single night), the ballad could swiftly address current events: within five days of the 6 April 1580 earthquake in London, eight tracts and ballads had been entered in the Register of the Stationers' Company. In treating sensational crimes

32 Hyder Rollins, 'William Elderton: Elizabethan Actor and Ballad-Writer', *Studies in Philology* 17 (1920), 199–245; 'The Black-Letter Broadside Ballad', p. 260.
33 Roger Chartier, *The Cultural Uses of Print*, p. 347, cited in Tessa Watt, *Cheap Print and Popular Piety, 1550–1640* (Cambridge University Press, 1991), pp. 5–6.
34 Joy Wiltenberg, *Disorderly Women and Female Power in the Street Literature of Early Modern England and Germany* (Charlottesville: University Press of Virginia, 1992), p. 28.
35 *Kinde-Hartes Dream*, sigs. Cv, C2v, cited in Achinstein, 'Plagues and Publication', pp. 318–19.
36 Thomas Middleton, *The World Tost at Tennis* (1620), in *Works*, ed. A. H. Bullen (rpt; New York: AMS Press, 1964), 7:154.

and murders (the 1594 murder of the London merchant Thomas Merry inspired four ballads and a play by Robert Yarrington), writers turned to scandals and calamities that did not exclude audiences for social or religious reasons.[37] With their potential for sensationalism, ballads could arouse or exploit public emotion in connection with portents, prodigies and political crises (as they did during the Northern Rebellion of 1569–70). Combined with reproducibility, such features as the reuse of popular tunes, the publishing of sequels and the internal use of dialogue, round and refrain also helped to mime, at a quickened tempo, the nature of speech and public debate. Such early ballad wars as the flyting between Thomas Churchyard and Thomas Camell, or the ballad war that ensued from William Fulwood's attack on the 'filthy rimes' of Elderton, helped to bring the immediacy of oral debate into the public realm of print and thus to prepare the way for such later pamphlet wars as the Marprelate debate, the controversy between Thomas Nashe and Gabriel Harvey, and the feminist polemics of the early seventeenth century.

As an ephemeral and down-market form subjected to the 'base...servile' exigencies of the commercial press, the broadside was a medium against which other literary aspirations defined themselves.[38] The amateur productions of courtly poets, meant for the 'priuate recreation...of Ladies and young Gentlemen, or idle Courtiers', were contrasted to 'the uncountable rabble of rhyming ballad-makers', with their 'small & popular Musickes...old romances or historicall rimes, made purposely for the recreation of the common people'.[39] At the same time, religious and moral objections to ballads became the basis for non-courtly poetry devoted to moral and societal reform. John Hall's poetic collection *The Court of Virtue* (1565) was published as a moral alternative to the 'fylthy trade' of 'lecherous Ballades'.[40] Like Robert Crowley's *One and Thyrtye Epigrams* (1550, 1573), Hall's collection carried older traditions of verse complaint into the mid-Tudor period, where they influenced the London satires of Edward Hake in *Newes out of Powles Churchyarde* (1567, 1579), the ballad complaints of Thomas Churchyard, and the attacks on city

---

37 Natascha Würzbach, *The Rise of the English Street Ballad, 1550–1650* (Cambridge University Press, 1990), pp. 17, 25–6, 64–74; Frederick O. Waage, 'Social Themes in the Urban Broadsides of Renaissance England', *Journal of Popular Culture* 11 (1977), 730–42.

38 Sharon Achinstein, 'Audiences and Authors: Ballads and the Making of English Renaissance Literary Culture', *Journal of Medieval and Renaissance Studies* 22 (1992), 311–26.

39 William Webbe, *A Discourse of English Poetrie* (1586), in *Elizabethan Critical Essays*, ed. G. Gregory Smith, 2 vols. (1904; rpt, Oxford University Press, 1971), 1:246; Puttenham, *The Arte of English Poesie*, pp. 83, 158.

40 John Hall, *The Court of Virtue*, ed. Russell A. Fraser (New Brunswick: Rutgers University Press, 1961), p. 16; *Certain Chapters of the Proverbs* (1550), quoted in *The Court of Venus*, ed. Russell A. Fraser (Durham, NC: Duke University Press, 1955), p. 56.

vices in George Gascoigne's *The Steel Glass* (1576) and George Whetstone's *Rock of Regard* (1576).

Hall's collection included the kind of moralising ballads that quickly became a popular staple in the growing broadside trade. Although the genre began with clerical protests like William Birch's *A Warninge to Englande, Let London Begin to Repent* (1565) and the ballad *Against Filthy Writing* (1562) by the London preacher and Sheriff's attorney Thomas Brice, it was quickly adopted by secular moralists and popular professionals. The 'citizein' John Carr composed *A Larum Belle for London* (1573), for example, while William Fulwood, a Merchant Taylor, drew the tune for his *New Ballad Against Unthrifts* (1562) from a love ballad in *The Handful of Pleasant Delights*. John Barker, the author of ballads *Declarying how neybourhed love and trew dealyng is gone* (1562) and lamenting the *Horyble and woful destruccion of Jerusalem* (1569), was among the 'semi-professionals' who turned the evangelising ballad into a profitable medium; his example, subsequently imitated by Elderton and by Thomas Deloney in *Canaan's Calamity* (1597–8), helped to inspire the sensational monitory ballads that were a stock-in-trade for writer–publishers like John Awdeley, William Griffith, Richard Jones and William Pickering.[41]

The homiletic stance imitated in moralising ballads was also adapted to the medium of popular theatre developed in such belated urban morality plays as Robert Wilson's *Three Ladies of London* (1584) and *Three Lords and Three Ladies of London* (1590). In Lodge's and Greene's long-running *Looking-Glass for London and England* (1594), which recounted the story of Jonah's reluctance to prophesy in Nineveh, the dramatists adopted the stance of preachers, attacking London's ineffectual clergy as 'careless guides' who 'presume to force / And tie the power of heaven to their conceits'.[42] The scandal of such writing was not simply that interloping clowns and wits usurped the preacher's function, but that, in turning that function into a profitable enterprise, they revealed a disillusioning presence of market forces in the sphere of religious and moral expression.

The empowering effects of the urban environment on professional writing are exemplified in the work of Isabella Whitney, the first would-be professional woman writer in the English language. A poetic moralist of the generation of Brice, Hake, Griffith and the printer Richard Jones, Whitney came from a landowning Cheshire family. While her eldest brother Geoffrey Whitney achieved success as a lawyer and emblem-writer, Isabella, another brother and

---

41 Watt, *Cheap Print and Popular Piety*, pp. 41, 50–2.
42 *A Looking Glass for London and England*, 3.1.95–103, in *Drama of the English Renaissance. Volume I: The Tudor Period*, ed. Russell A. Fraser and Norman Rabkin (New York: Macmillan, 1976), p. 395.

two sisters were, according to her poems, 'servinge in London' in 1573. The verse epistles of *The Copy of a Letter* (1567) and *A Sweet Nosegay* (1573) refer obliquely to her lucklessness, her unrequited love, and her dismissal from service for what may have been scandal or slander – experiences of a kind probably familiar to many female domestic servants drawn to the metropolis.

As Whitney's work demonstrates, the experience of London varied with differences in gender, which, like those in wealth and status, produced different orientations towards urban space. Recent work suggests that in London, where more than half the population was female, women – especially those of lower status – may actually have been acquainted with a wider spectrum of the city's cultural geography than men. The wives of tradesmen may have moved more widely through London's neighbourhoods in the course of meeting household needs than did their shopkeeping husbands, while the far-flung errands of apprentices and waiting-women may have taken them into a wider orbit than their masters; the greatest mobility may have been experienced by those who were in casual labour, serving on short-term contracts or unemployed.[43] The anonymous *Letter sent by the Maydens of London* (1567) adopts a feminine persona to refute objections to the 'overmuch liberties' of female domestics who were said to 'stray abrode' in the City; it mischievously defends women's mobility by recognising the need of a casually employed serving-woman for 'a candle's ende . . . to light her home in a dark night'.[44]

Whitney's own interrelated ventures into the streets of London and into the realm of professional publication challenge cultural perceptions that typically associated the presence of women in public spaces with wantonness, prostitution and – in caricatures extending from Skelton's Eleanor Rumming and Robert Copland's *Jyl of Brentford* to the hostess of *Mother Bunches Merriments* (1604), Shakespeare's Mistress Quickly and Jonson's Ursula – with the last resort of the female unemployed: ale-brewing and tavern-keeping. The tavern-keeping jest-book heroine *Long Meg of Westminster* (1582) first 'came to London' with a wagonload of Lancashire lasses, 'to get her a service'; and the notoriously mobile and outspoken Moll Frith, daughter of a London shoemaker, was first 'put out to service' but found herself 'too great a Libertine . . . to be enclosed

---

43 See Ilana Krausman Ben-Amos, *Adolescence and Youth in Early Modern England* (New Haven, CT: Yale University Press, 1994), pp. 150–5; Mark Thornton Burnett, *Masters and Servants in English Renaissance Drama and Culture: Obedience and Authority* (New York: St Martin's, 1997), pp. 118–29.

44 Ed. R. J. Fehrenbach, in *Women in the Renaissance: Selections from 'English Literary Renaissance'*, ed. Kirby Farrell, Elizabeth H. Hageman and Arthur F. Kinney (Amherst: University of Massachusetts Press, 1990), pp. 38, 39, 45.

in the limits of a private Domestique Life'.[45] In response to such stereotypes, Whitney conceives her *Sweet Nosegay* – a versified epitome of the Senecan *sententiae* collected in Hugh Plat's *Flowres of Philosophie* (1572) – as a literal *vade mecum* that enables her to circulate publicly in a pestilent world without risk of infection. 'Harvestlesse, / and serviceless also: / and subject unto sicknesse, that/ abrode I could not go', Whitney takes up the professional pen in order to release herself at once from poverty, silence and confinement.[46] From Plat's *sententiae*, and from the ballad-moralising pieties in his accompanying *Pleasures of Poetrie*, Whitney derives a properly public, moral savour, 'which might be my defence / In stynking streets, or lothsome lanes, / which else might mee infect' (sig. A6 v). By assimilating the moral outlook of male writers, she empowers herself to circulate both in London and in print.[47]

In her masterly 'Last Will and Testament' Whitney employs a variety of conventions to turn the unrealised wishes and disappointments of a London serving woman into the tart and witty public speech of a professional urban satirist. 'Loth to leave the Citie', but 'constrained to departe' by poverty (sig. E2), Whitney adopts the fiction of writing a legal testament in order to exploit rules of gender that licensed the moment of a woman's death as one of the few acceptable occasions for the verbal expression of her 'will'.[48] In taking this small freedom, however, she claims greater literary licence, situating herself in a tradition of satiric will-making that extends from *The Wyll of the Devyll and Last Testament* (1548) and *Jyl of Braintfords Testament* (1567) to Robert Greene's *Groatsworth of Wit* (1592).[49] Her will also parodies encomia that celebrated wealthy citizens' grand bequests to the municipality by recording the parting words of an impoverished woman writer to whom London has left nothing to bequeath but her moral education. Whitney's knowing perambulation of the City's streets transforms the public, processional form of civic pageants into the kind of subjective, nightmare *voie* where disenfranchised countrymen are stripped of their possessions and illusions; in this respect her poem adds an

45 *The Whole Life and Death of Long Meg of Westminster* (London, 1582), pp. 2–3; *The Life and Death of Mrs Mary Frith, Alias Moll Cutpurse* (1662), in *Counterfeit Ladies*, ed. Janet Todd and Elizabeth Spearing (London: William Pickering, 1996), p. 11.

46 *A Sweet Nosgay* (London, 1573), sig. A6, in *'The Flowers of Philosophie' (1572) by Hugh Plat and 'A Sweet Nosgay' (1573) and 'The Copy of a Letter' (1567) by Isabella Whitney*, ed. Richard J. Panofsky (Delmar, NY: Scholar's Facsimiles and Reprints, 1983): subsequent references are to this facsimile collection.

47 Ann Rosalind Jones, *The Currency of Eros: Women's Love Lyric in Europe, 1540–1620* (Bloomington: Indiana University Press, 1990), p. 46.

48 Wendy Wall, *The Imprint of Gender: Authorship and Publication in the English Renaissance* (Ithaca, NY: Cornell University Press, 1993), pp. 299–300.

49 Eber C. Perrow, 'The Last Will and Testament as a Form of Literature', *Transactions of the Wisconsin Academy of Sciences, Arts, and Letters* 17 (1911–13), 682–750.

important feminine perspective to a moral tradition extending from Dunbar's *London Lickpenny* and the mid-Tudor *Conscience* (*c*. 1540) to Anthony Munday's 'Woodeman's walke' (1600) and Martin Parker's *Robin Conscience* (1635).

Above all, however, in taking stock of the City's 'Treasury' and honouring its wondrous plenty – a bounty glimpsed but not enjoyed – Whitney's 'wylling minde' takes mental possession of the metropolis, encompassing all that is 'within thee, and without' (sigs. E2v, E7v). By treating London as an unrequiting lover, she uses the anti-Petrarchan conventions of female complaint to underline the City's 'great cruelnes' and lack of 'love and charity' (sigs. E2v-E3). Whitney's impoverished and wandering experience of the city thus paradoxically becomes the basis for moral and discursive power, as she juxtaposes against the City's brave streets, buildings and well-stocked shops a telling inventory of its dispossessed: imprisoned debtors and criminals, the 'blynd and lame' (sig. E7), Bridewell workhouse inmates and Bedlam lunatics 'that out of tune doo talke' (sig. E7). Lacking discursive licence, and writing in an innovative moral vein outside the official channels, Whitney enters the public sphere on the sole authority of her private experience, in a will recorded 'with mine owne hand', and witnessed only by the 'Paper, Pen, and Standish' that 'were / at that same present by' (sig. E8v).

Pamphlets and prose fiction

Developed in the ballad form and in the work of Whitney, literary professionalism reached its culmination in the later Elizabethan age among a generation of remarkable London writers that included Thomas Lodge, Robert Greene, Thomas Nashe and Thomas Dekker. University-educated in every case but the last, but lacking official place or patronage, these writers gravitated towards London and the new economic enterprises of the popular theatre and pamphlet publication.[50] Not so much a genre as a medium, varying in length and format, and costing from twopence to sixpence, the popular pamphlet accommodated a variety of the demands created by increased literacy, from works of piety, pedagogy and self-improvement to current news and polemic.[51] In the hands of the new professionals, who wrote from the literary-social margins of the

---

50 Edwin H. Miller, *The Professional Writer in Elizabethan England* (Cambridge, MA: Harvard University Press, 1959); Phoebe Sheavyn, *The Literary Professional in the Elizabethan Age* (New York: Barnes and Noble, 1967); Jean-Christophe Agnew, *Worlds Apart: The Market and the Theater in Anglo-American Thought, 1550–1750* (Cambridge University Press, 1986).

51 Sandra Clark, *The Elizabethan Pamphleteers: Popular Moralistic Pamphlets, 1580–1640* (Rutherford, NJ: Fairleigh Dickinson University Press, 1985), pp. 17–39.

burgeoning metropolis, the pamphlet became a medium for an innovative style of seriocomic prose that contaminated the humanistic canon of Ciceronian prose with the colloquial idiom of tavern, marketplace and theatre. To the novelties of print and popular circulation the Elizabethan pamphleteers added several further innovations: an urbanised folklore; a colloquial, performative rhetoric; a representational mode of 'realism'; a cult of celebrity; and a satiric vision that contributed to a new secular, urban mentality.

The quick tempo, ready circulation and ad hominem potential of cheap publication made the pamphlet a useful medium for controversy. By focusing on matters of contemporary concern and by encouraging debate and serialisation, pamphleteering brought readers and writers into closer proximity; it transformed readers into participants and their daily experience into the subject of writing.[52] *Jane Anger Her Protection for Women* (1589) exposed readers to the first contemporary, colloquial female voice to intervene in the controversy about women. Whether or not she was the creation of a female author, Jane's persona, tartly answering a now-lost misogynistic pamphlet, made common cause with her readership through witty allusions to the contemporary London scene and by calling on 'all women in generall, and gentle reader whatsoever' to 'aide and assist me in defense'. In the same year, Puritan propagandists invented the carnivalian persona named Martin Marprelate in order to open up the intricacies of anti-episcopal polemic to the needs of popular readership. Responding to Martin Marprelate's discovery that 'the humours of men in these times . . . be given to mirth', the bishops recruited Nashe and other London wits to answer Martin in scurrilous kind. In the ensuing pamphlet war, the traditional grounds of discursive authority – learned theology and academic rhetoric – were supplemented by the authority of common experience and the language of the marketplace. The nature of public debate was transformed by a new criterion of 'representational authority', which adapted controversial issues to the realities of 'the material world and lived experience' of writers and readers.[53]

The ambiguous social status and degraded circumstances of the new urban literary professionals enabled them to claim this new authority, to probe morality 'more searchingly than common soule-Surgions accustome' and, as Nashe put it, 'to build virtue a church on that foundation that the devil built his chapel'.[54] But their literary projects were so intertwined with their reputations

---

52 Lennard J. Davis, *Factual Fictions: The Origins of the English Novel* (Philadelphia: University of Pennsylvania Press, 1997), pp. 58–9.
53 Alexandra Halasz, *The Marketplace of Print: Pamphlets and the Public Sphere in Early Modern England* (Cambridge University Press, 1997), p. 110.
54 *Works*, 2:80, 1:305.

as prodigals and 'prandial libertines'[55] that they also came to exemplify both the dangers of licentiousness and the scandal of literary professionalism. In one round of the Marprelate controversy, the Oxford don Gabriel Harvey upheld the authority of traditional learning by connecting Greene's 'dissolute and licentious living' with his 'impudent pamphletting' and by insisting that Nashe's dissolute life 'daily feedeth his stile; and his stile notoriously bewraieth his life'.[56] By opening the medium of print to the hitherto repressed realms of scurrility and marketplace values, the pamphleteers became what Humphrey King called 'publicans and sinners, (or sinners in publique) in that infortunate Art of Printing'. Writing, in John Danby's terms, 'down' Fortune's Hill to an increasingly popular and socially mixed audience, the pamphleteers parlayed their status as placeless, degraded urbanites into a previously unrecognised form of moral authority. Their ability to read the mobile urban landscape, which was becoming increasingly opaque to official culture, confirms an observation of the twentieth-century urban sociologist Robert Park: 'neither the criminal, the detective, nor the genius has the same opportunity to develop his innate disposition in a small town that he invariably finds in a great city'.[57] The genius of the pamphleteers as urban writers was to have combined, in a novel literary enterprise, the perspectives of the criminal and the policeman, thereby creating new perspectives on urban life.

This double perspective was first developed in the *Mirour for Magestrates of Cyties* (1584) and in *An Alarum Against Usurers* (1584), secular anti-usury pamphlets respectively authored by George Whetstone, the son of a London haberdasher, and Thomas Lodge, the second son of a Lord Mayor who 'went banquerout to the grete slander of the citie' during his tenure in office. Offering their personal experience as moral compensation for their prodigality (the censorious Stephen Gosson labelled Lodge a 'vagrant, looser than libertie, lighter than vanitie'), Lodge and Whetstone addressed the forms of economic deviance that had traditionally been policed by magistrates and ministers but that 'neither honourable may controll ... not divine admonition reclaim'. Their profligacy thus authenticated the very moral compensation for which it also

55 M. Bakhtin, *Rabelais and his World*, trans. H. Iswolsky (1968; rpt, Bloomington: Indiana University Press, 1984), p. 297.
56 Gabriel Harvey, *Foure Letters & Certaine Sonnets*, ed. G. B. Harrison (London: The Bodley Head, 1922), pp. 19–20; *Pierces Supererogation: Or, A New Prayse of the Old Asse* (London, 1593), p. 45.
57 Humphrey King, *An Halfe-Penny-Worth of Wit, in a Penny Worth of Paper* (London, 1613), sig. A4; John Danby, *Poets on Fortune's Hill* (London: Faber and Faber, 1952), p. 16; Robert Park, 'The City: Suggestions for the Investigation of Human Behavior in the Urban Environment', in *Classic Essays on the Culture of Cities*, ed. Richard Sennett (Englewood Cliffs: Prentice-Hall, 1969), p. 126.

created the need; while their ostensible task was to teach moral lessons to young gentlemen, their status as experienced prodigals also enabled them to provide more practical advice on negotiating London's perilous landscape, to 'guide you, as the Clue of the Threede did Theseus, in the Laberinth'.[58]

In the later seriocomic works of Robert Greene and Thomas Nashe, rhetorically mobile styles and personae transformed the pamphlet into a performative medium whose methods were those of 'spoken dialectic' and improvisation.[59] Nashe's powers of ridicule and colloquial expression helped to mobilise and transform traditional prose expression. On the one hand, Nashe wrote in such native and 'traditional' forms as the sermon (*Christes Teares Over Jerusalem*), the complaint or petition (*The Supplication of Pierce Penniless*), the moral interlude (*Summer's Last Will and Testament*), the chronicle (*The Unfortunate Traveller*) and chorography (*Nashe's Lenten Stuffe*). Yet on the other hand he changed the tenor of these forms through the rhetorical immediacy, unconventional perspectives and 'despised and neglected' personae of their outlawed and unlicensed speakers. The prodigal Pierce Pennilesse, addressing his *Supplication* to the devil, thus becomes the 'devil's Orator'; Jack Wilton, a former 'page or appendix' to noblemen, writes his own trickster's version of the history of the sixteenth-century 'Renaissance'; the running colloquial commentary of the motley Will Summers undermines the masque of the seasons in *Summer's Last Will and Testament*; the fugitive author of the *Lenten Stuffe* transforms his exile into a paradoxical praise of the economic and literary marketplace; the despised and persecuted Christ, 'a mean-titled man' who 'kept company with Publicans and sinners, the very out cast of the people', delivers a blistering low-style sermon to Jerusalem-London, castigating its 'chuff-headed Burgomasters' and its inept preachers, who 'fitte us with a cheap religion... being covetous yourselves'. In its combination of homiletic forms and improvisatory comic style, Nashe's work bears out the view that the primary models for early modern prose were the performative routines of the preacher and the clown.[60]

58 Gosson, *Plays confuted*, in *Markets of Bawdrie*, ed. Kinney, p. 141; Thomas Lodge, *An Alarum Against Usurers*, in *The Complete Works*, intro. by Edmund Gosse, 4 vols. (Glasgow: Hunterian Club, 1883), 1:14, 6; George Whetstone, *A Mirour for Magestrates of Cities* (London, 1584), sig. B v.

59 L. C. Knights, 'Elizabethan Prose', in *Drama and Society in the Age of Jonson* (1937; rpt, New York: Norton, 1968), p. 311; cf. Walter Ong, 'Oral Residue in Tudor Prose', in *Rhetoric, Romance, and Technology in the Interaction of Expression and Culture* (Ithaca: Cornell University Press, 1971), pp. 34–5; Neil Rhodes, *The Elizabethan Grotesque* (London: Routledge and Kegan Paul, 1980), pp. 25–6.

60 Marshall McLuhan, *The Gutenberg Galaxy: The Making of Typographic Man* (University of Toronto Press, 1962), p. 136.

Nashe's prolific contemporary Robert Greene used the prose pamphlet to transform his experience of the London demimonde into profitable celebrity. Greene's late work, retracting his earlier Euphuistic romances and playwriting, is a pamphlet-saga of cautionary tales and thinly disguised autobiographies repenting his dissolute and prodigal life. Greene's early repentance pamphlets, *Greenes Mourning Garment* (1590), *Greenes Never Too Late* (1590), *Greene's Farewell to Folly* (1591) and *The Repentance of Robert Greene* (1592), gave way, following the uncertainly authored *Greenes Groats-worth of witte* (1592), to a host of eponymous sequels: *Greenes Vision* (1592), *Greenes News* (1593), *Greenes Funeralls* (1594), *Greene in Conceipt* (1598) and *Greenes Ghost* (1602). Greene exploited his wayward career and the 'stretching Adios' of his repentance tracts in a related project of 1591–2, the half-dozen enormously successful 'cony-catching' pamphlets in which he purported to anatomise criminal techniques discovered through his personal acquaintance with the London underworld. The genre had made earlier appearances in the *Caveat of Common Cursitors* (1566), in which the Kentish gentleman and justice Thomas Harman published his personal examinations of criminal vagabonds, and in John Awdeley's *Fraternity of Vagabonds* (1561), which professed to transcribe the confession of a criminal tramp. Greene's treatment of the genre, however, transformed it into a staple of popular seriocomic prose fiction that was imitated by such contemporaries as Dekker, Middleton, Samuel Rowlands, Richard Johnson and others.

Geared to the instabilities of the marketplace – and to the tempo by which their author was reputed to 'haue yarkt up a Pamphlet in a day & a night' – Greene's cony-catching pamphlets were not only a portrait of London's criminal underworld, but an extended apologia for commercialised fiction-making and its innovative moral functions. One of Greene's major strategies was to transform the expositor's status, replacing the sober magistrate, Thomas Harman, arch-persecutor and taxonomist of rogues, with the persona of a quasi-criminal professional writer. Greene thrives on a rhetorical and theatrical mobility that he shares with his cony-catcher subjects. His pamphlets are in fact themselves literary confidence games modelled on the deceptions of Greene's ostensible subject, the clever criminal who 'counterfets many parts in one . . . and shifts himselfe into so many shapes'. In contrast to the sober dupes – students, merchants, farmers and gentlemen – exploited as both the targets of the criminals and the target audience of the pamphlets themselves (they are the groups typically addressed on the title-pages and in the prefaces), both the professional writer and the cony-catcher share an understanding of their own intense estatelessness, which they parlay into a new form of social competence and versatility. Both cony-catcher and writer profess to read the opaque urban populace, to 'interpret their conceipts, and...decipher their qualities'.[61] As themselves the most avid 'readers' of Greene's pamphlets, his cony-catching criminal adversaries become locked with him in an ever-spiralling pattern of reading and retaliation; the potential for comic escalation – and thus for increased writerly profit – is immense. Always just one small jump ahead of Greene's latest exposé, Greene's criminal subjects – both invisible (Greene does not concern himself with the more visible threats of vagabonds) and protean – are the perfect subject for professional writing: as 'readers' of Greene themselves, they circumvent each published exposé, thereby guaranteeing the need for further sequels.

From its beginnings in Harman, the cony-catching pamphlet was modelled on traditional forms of social inventory, anatomy and taxonomy; just as the law-abiding world was governed by 'ye ordinance of good men', so the underworld was said to be organised by 'a multitude of hateful rules'.[62] For Greene, however, this analogy between the two worlds yielded satiric equation between capital and crime: 'all conditions of men seeke to liue by their wittes, and he is counted wisest, that hath the deepest insight into the getting of gaines' (11:51). Preferring the clever deceptions of cony-catchers to the more vicious hypocrisies of their wealthier and socially superior victims, the criminal pamphlets of Greene and his successors became – within their rhetoric of paranoia – a genre of fearlessness, particularly in their glorification of the urbanity of the man who goes louse-ridden, lame, unregarded and unrewarded: 'The whole kingdome is but his Walke, a whole Cittie is but his parish'.[63] Perhaps only in certain kinds of pastoral – of which the cony-catching pamphlet is a variation – does one find a similar potential to make 'the classes feel part of a larger unity or simply at home with each other'.[64] By 'indeauouring' as Barnabe Rich observed, 'by their pennes to set upp lightes, and to giue the world new eyes to see into deformitie',[65] Greene and his contemporaries defined a new mode of vision. They contributed to the moral technology of

61 A Notable Discovery of Coosnage, in The Life and Complete Works, in Prose and Verse, of Robert Greene, ed. A. B. Grosart, 15 vols. (London: Huth Library, 1881–3), 10:6; subsequent citations of Greene are from this edition.
62 Dekker, The Belman of London, in Non-Dramatic Works, ed. A. B. Grosart, 5 vols. (London, 1881–6), 3:117.
63 Dekker, Non-Dramatic Works, 3:10.
64 William Empson, Some Versions of Pastoral (1935: rpt, New York: New Directions, 1974), p. 199.
65 The Honesty of this Age (1614), ed. Thomas Wright (London: Percy Society, 1843), 11:3–4.

urbanisation by transforming London into a profane and 'intricate laborinth' that could be negotiated by being read.

As a group, the pamphleteers of Elizabethan London derived their vision not so much from *a priori* standards as from the dynamism of the City itself. As playwrights forced to turn to pamphleteering during periods when the theatres were closed by plague, they depended for a living on the exploitation of sensational disasters, economic downturns and disruptive changes in the social order. The unsettling events of urban life enabled them, however, to reflect in new ways on the conditions of early capitalist society. Thomas Dekker's pamphlets are especially notable for turning social catastrophe to advantage, discovering a paradoxically abiding beauty and permanence in the City's turbulent life. Dekker's first pamphlet, *The Wonderfull Yeare. 1603*, was devoted to that year's devastating plague, and nearly all of Dekker's subsequent London pamphlets concerned themselves with disasters – with war, pestilence, famine, crime, social conflict and economic hard times. Despite their often grim, macabre detail and homiletic digressions, they remain essentially seriocomic rhapsodies. Though he shares with his preaching contemporaries a fascination with cities 'rooted up and swept from the face of the earth',[66] Dekker parts with them by finding in the City's ever-shifting possibilities of exchange and transformation both a fundamental consistency and the potential for endurance.

Dekker's pamphlets typically move from disaster towards celebration of the City's dynamic equilibrium; in doing so, they turn from satire to saturnalia, from abstract social anatomy to grotesque realism, from literal report and sober counsel to conscious counterfeiting, picture- and fiction-making. Dekker's detached, pictorial manner transforms the embattled marginality affected by Greene and Nashe into the anonymity of the urban voyeur. Largely free of the professional's shame and the satirist's guilty complicity, Dekker renders the traditional functions of complaint obsolete in his celebration of the unstable and profane rhythms of the urban marketplace. In his fascination with counterfeit and parody – reflected in his mock-sermons, mock-almanacs, mock-handbooks, mock-wills, and in his accounts of the creative uses of counterfeit and print by criminals – Dekker shows a profound scepticism towards the documenting and authorising powers of language. His narrative and descriptive powers transform moral anatomy and urban topography into a landscape from romance: dangers and opportunities alike abound; the vices are those

---

66 *A Rod for Run-awayes* (1625), in *The Plague Pamphlets of Thomas Dekker*, ed. F. P. Wilson (Oxford: Clarendon Press, 1925), pp. 140–1.

of inflexibility and social pretension; the virtues those of adaptability and a tolerance for heterogeneity and change.

Dekker thus created a social vision akin to that elaborated in the popular prose romances of Lodge and Greene and in the staging of historical romance in plays like Greene's *James IV* and Heywood's *Edward IV*. The mixed decorum and socially inclusive vision of such works – their mingling of high and low, nature and nurture, noble blood and noble conduct – helped a diversifying society and urbanising readership to imagine new forms of community in a changing world. The roots of such popular romance in commerce and social mobility are clearly visible as well in the innovative fiction of Thomas Deloney, a weaver and ballad writer who turned to prose narrative after publishing some officially suppressed economic complaints in the mid-1590s. Mingling anecdote, jest, dialogue and song in the manner of popular pamphlets, Deloney's fictions are historically 'revisionist' in nature; their narratives revolve around the mythical careers of aspiring and successful artisan heroes, 'honest men' whose 'memorable lives' were 'omitted by Stow, Hollinshed, Grafton, Hal, . . . and all the rest of those wel deserving writers'.[67] Like the literature and civic pageants that celebrated London's leading merchant worthies, Deloney's fictions use the decorum of chivalric romance to effect a rapprochement between aristocratic tradition and the economic ambition of such entrepreneur-heroes as the provincial clothiers John Winchombe of Newbury and Thomas Cole of Reading and the London shoemaker-magnates Simon Eyre and Richard Casteller. In *Jack of Newbury* (1597), the plucky and patriotic weaver-hero contributes to the making of the Tudor state by preparing to fight against the Scots during the absence of Henry VIII and his nobles; in *Thomas of Reading*, the commerce and solidarity of leading provincial clothiers link countryside manufacturers to the metropolis, creating a socio-economic nation out of a twelfth-century monarchy still torn by primitive dynastic rivalries.

In contrast to much of London's encomiastic literature, in which a neofeudal ethos assimilates commercial and civic values to the aristocratic past and traditional social order, Deloney's works more radically revise the past in order to model a more inclusive social vision and to accommodate a broader popular readership.[68] In his self-proclaimed reign as 'Prince of Ants', the industrious Jack of Newbury fashions an alternative monarchy that protects 'poore and painfull subiects, from the force of the idle Butterflies, their sworn

67 *Kemps Nine Daies Wonder* (1600), ed. Alexander Dyce, Camden Society no. 11 (London: J. B. Nichols and Son, 1840), pp. 20–1.
68 David Margolies, *Novel and Society in Elizabethan England* (London: Croom Helm, 1985), p. 148.

enemies'.[69] His refusal of a knighthood and his career as an MP and organiser of the clothing trades are marked by confident rejection of the pride and privilege of overweening courtiers, interloping foreigners and avaricious financiers, the usual villains in Deloney's tales. 'Infected with Luthers spirit', Jack's reformist opposition to Cardinal Wolsey points the way, in historical retrospect, to a prosperous and Protestant English future (the present in which Deloney writes), where every man 'liues well contented with his state'.[70]

In uniting the mighty and the humble around the virtues of honest labour and the fraternal bonds of 'worthy deeds and great Hospitality', Deloney gestures towards the vision of social harmony popularised in the pastoral romances of Lodge and Greene. Social differences are transcended most completely in the romance disclosures of Deloney's *The Gentle Craft*, where the tales of Crispin and Crispianus combine exiled princes masking as cobblers with the sons of cobblers discovered as princes. Unlike Lodge and Greene, however, Deloney never fully endorses the pastoral fantasy he invokes, a fantasy in which nature and nurture, noble birth and noble conduct converge with the rediscovery of a lost aristocratic identity. The shoemaking exile of the princely St Hugh and his beloved Winifred ends not with nobility restored but with a Platonic love and martyrdom that validate the humble contentment of shoemakers, as the bones of St Hugh become the tools of a merry trade. In the tale of Simon Eyre's rise to the London mayoralty, subsequently dramatised by Dekker, the wonders of a saint's life and Greek romance give way to the mundane realities of economic enterprise, as Winifred's Platonic love for Hugh is replaced by Mistress Eyre's earnest lectures on the virtues of self-confidence and venturing on credit. Eyre's election to the London mayoralty brings to historic fruition the providence of a Protestant God who effects a genuine social transformation when He 'setteth up the humble, and pulleth down the proud, to bring whom he pleaseth to the seat of Honour' (p. 132).

An imagined solidarity between masters and artisans masks the new socio-economic differences implied by Deloney's celebration of busy clothing factories employing weavers by the hundred. Manufacture in quantity yields qualitative change, as prosperous masters blossom into merchant-traders and skilled artisans dwindle into labourers. The older oppressive relationship between London creditors and provincial producers gives way, with the triumph of the latter, to a new oppression, as prosperous producers become the capitalist

---

69 *Jack of Newbury*, in *The Works of Thomas Deloney*, ed. Francis Oscar Mann (Oxford: Clarendon Press, 1912), p. 27; subsequent Deloney references are to this edition.
70 On Deloney's historical hindsight, see Michael McKeon, *The Origins of the English Novel* (Baltimore: Johns Hopkins University Press, 1987), pp. 225–6.

employers of wage-earning workers. Even while relationships between Deloney's heroes and their wives provide a universal model for domestic contentment and familial order, his narratives also enforce the specific structural differences necessary to new forms of economic life. In the last and darkest of Deloney's narratives, *Thomas of Reading* (c. 1598–9), a series of melancholy events – the blinding of Robert, Duke of Normandy, for loving a clothier's servant, the murder of the prosperous clothier Thomas Coles by envious tavern-keepers, and the abandonment of the bankrupt manufacturer Tom Dove by his rebellious employees – undermines the confident equation in the earlier works between contented labour, individual prosperity and social harmony. In its preoccupation with the effects of shifting socio-economic differences, Deloney's fiction exemplifies the ways in which early modern English literature was shaped by its engagement with the multiplying social roles and economic functions of an urbanising world.

Satire and society

At the end of the sixteenth century, the culture of the metropolis provided an important stimulus for experiments in a variety of classically inspired verse forms, which challenged the preeminence of Elizabethan courtly norms and laid the basis for neo-classical poetry in the following two centuries. Marked by a self-conscious sense of genre, these experiments in elegy, epistle, epigram and satire – modelled on Catullus and Ovid, Horace, Martial, Juvenal and Persius – defined a new kind of laureate ambition, which was based on the assertion of classical pedigree, a sharpened critical spirit and an implicit rejection of both courtly and popular literary kinds.[71] The pursuit of distinctive wit and clever judgement in these new forms, linked to the emergence of a fashionable 'Town' culture in the West End of late-Elizabethan London,[72] was both a literary innovation and a novel mode of socialisation; it responded to the complexities of metropolitan life by means of disassociation and the urbane cultivation of literary–social exclusivity.

---

71 On the laureate potential of satire, see Ronald Corthell, 'Beginning as a Satirist: Joseph Hall's *Virgidemiarum Sixe Bookes*', *Studies in English Literature, 1500–1900*, 23 (1983), 47–60.
72 On the development of 'The Town', see Martin Butler, *Theatre and Crisis, 1632–1642* (Cambridge University Press, 1984), p. 141; F. J. Fisher, 'The Development of London as a Centre of Conspicuous Consumption', in *Essays in Economic History*, ed. M. Carus-Wilson, 3 vols. (New York: St Martin's Press), 2:197–207; R. Malcolm Smuts, *Court Culture and the Origins of a Royalist Tradition in Early Stuart England* (Philadelphia: University of Pennsylvania Press, 1987), ch. 3.

The developing 'Town' culture of Elizabethan London was dominated at first by the Inns of Court, which offered professional legal training while serving as fashionable residences and finishing schools for young gentlemen on their way to power.[73] A few practitioners in the new classically inspired forms, including the actor Ben Jonson and Joseph Hall, of Emmanuel Hall, Cambridge, had no close association with the Inns, but most of the late Elizabethan wits had studied or resided there, including such innovative verse satirists as Thomas Lodge, John Donne, John Marston and Everard Guilpin and the epigrammatists Thomas Bastard, John Weever and Sir John Davies. The work of these poets was shaped decisively by the culture of the Inns – by exposure to the contingencies of common law and legal argument, emphasised in such rhetorical handbooks as Abraham Fraunce's *Lawiers Logike* (1588) and John Hoskins's *Directions for Speech and Style* (1599); by classroom moots and mock pleadings that placed an emphasis on improvised wit; and by habits of revelry and dissipation that (according to the Gray's Inn Revels of 1594–5) encouraged residents to 'frequent the Theatre, and such like places of Experience; and resort to the better sort of Ord' naries for Conference, where they may . . . become accomplished with Civil Conversations'.[74] The worldliness and sophistication of life at the Inns contributed to the anti-idealistic critique of courtly Petrarchanism in John Donne's innovative love poems, including both the elegies that (along with Marlowe's daring translation of the *Amores*) cultivate Ovidian erotic wit, and the *Songs and Sonnets*, with their vividly dramatic speakers and situations, pungent colloquialism, striking metaphors and witty quarrels with love and the busy world's demands. The competitive uses of barbed and clever expression at the Inns contributed as well to the curt Senecan style and compressed form of Sir Francis Bacon's *Essays* (1597), to the 'sense, shortnesse, and salt' of the satiric epigram, to the 'accurate and quick description' of the prose character, and to the 'snaphaunce quick distinction' of formal verse satire.[75]

In both satiric epigram and formal verse satire, the pursuit of distinction through classical imitation proceeded in dialogue with both urban popular culture and native literary traditions. Ultimately modelled on the lapidary

73 Philip J. Finkelpearl, *John Marston of the Middle Temple: An Elizabethan Dramatist in his Social Setting* (Cambridge, MA: Harvard University Press, 1969); Wilfred R. Prest, *The Inns of Court under Elizabeth I and the Early Stuarts, 1590–1640* (Totowa, NJ: Rowman and Littlefield, 1972).

74 *Gesta Grayorum*, ed. Desmond Bland (Liverpool University Press, 1968), p. 41.

75 *Paroemiographia* (1659), in *Lexicon Tetraglotton* (London, 1660), unpaginated preface; John Stephens, *Satyricall Essayes, Characters and Others* (London, 1615), title-page; John Marston, *The Scourge of Villanie* (1598), in *The Poems of John Marston*, ed. A. Davenport (Liverpool University Press, 1961), p. 122.

character of inscriptions and epitaphs, the formal features of the epigram – concision, balance, antithesis and point – provided schematic resources for demonstrating cultural competence by encoding commonplace materials in definitive and memorable encapsulations. At the same time, however, the epigram overlapped with such popular, performative and still primarily oral forms as ballads, jests and proverbs. The epigram was a social activity that crystallised in printed form the revelry 'of our tavernes and common tabling houses', where 'many merry heades meete, and scrible with ynke, with chalke, or with a cole such matters as they would every man should know, & descant upon'.[76] It added the stamp of classical authority to the behaviour of the anonymous wits who scrawled facetious epitaphs on the tombs of public figures or circulated libels against their enemies (the young John Davies found himself libelled in epigrams 'set up against him in all the famous places of the City').[77] While the competitive energy and rapid tempo of urban life encouraged aggressive verbal wit, facility and concision, the city's scope, variety and complex life posed a challenge to the epigram's formal precision. Satiric epigrams of the period are animated by tensions between compression and prolixity, individuation and repetition, tightly contained schemes and exfoliating series, sharply etched portraits and sweeping surveys. By the turn of the century, as the genre passed from Inns of Court wits into the hands of popular professionals like Samuel Rowlands and John Taylor the Water Poet, the aspiration to neat formulation increasingly gave way to expansive narratives and catalogues (the longest of Jonson's epigrams was the scatological nightmare, 'On the Famous Voyage'). The art began to be associated with the hitherto loathed trade of balladry and to lead its practitioners into an obsession with their own ephemerality.[78]

In a closely related experiment, writers used the improvised premises and idiosyncratic perspectives of formal verse satire to address and adapt themselves to a changing urban environment. The satirists based their unprecedented claims to moral authority on a highly provisional and performative rhetoric.[79] The apparent moral spontaneity in the satiric spokesman's voice as he surveyed the social scene was rhetorically improvised through a myriad of incidental techniques (such as comparison, parenthesis, digression and catalogue) that

---

76 Puttenham, *The Arte of English Poesie*, p. 54.
77 Benjamin Rudyerd, *The Prince d'Amour* (London, 1660), pp. 78–9.
78 Lawrence Manley, 'Proverbs, Epigrams, and Urbanity in Renaissance London', *English Literary Renaissance* 15 (1985), 247–76.
79 Roma Gill, 'A Purchase of Glory: The Persona of Late Elizabethan Satire', *Studies in Philology* 72 (1975), 408–14.

contributed to the notorious heterogeneity of classical *satura or farrago*. A key to improvisation was the social relationship established in the satirist's *indicatio*, an invective gesture of reference that conjured up a society of distinguishing minds by marking a moral distinction between 'that-over-there' and 'you-and-me-here'.[80] At the heart of this gesture of distinction was a metacommunication implicitly celebrating what Donne called 'a confident and mutuall communicating of those things which we know'.[81] This imaginative creation of a privileged moral community in turn provided satirists like Donne, Hall, Marston and Guilpin with a standpoint from which to survey the follies and vices of anomalous groups and restless individuals who were outrageously exploiting the opportunities available for mischief in an urbanising society.

The unstable relationships between satirist and scene, between like-minded moral community and diversifying society, created a variety of tonal possibilities for verse satire, which ranged between occasional aspirations to a Horatian poise and more frequent recourse to Juvenal's savage *indignatio*. The harshness of the latter was more in keeping with native traditions of complaint and with a false Elizabethan etymology that derived the term 'satire' from the uncouth and hircine savagery of satyrs.[82] The social insecurity of the satirists themselves and the potentially dangerous consequences of writing satire added to these instabilities, but so did the moral ambiguities of the London and Inns of Court environments. Students at the Inns found themselves in an environment that was both morally and intellectually challenging. Study of the common law, based on the empirical complexities of cases and precedents, was a prolonged ordeal lacking in method and tutorial guidance; the occasional lectures were 'long, obscure, and intricate, full of new conceits, like rather to riddles than to lectures'.[83] Moreover, the extramural lives of students, which exposed them to the City's manifold activities, communities and cultures, went largely unsupervised. 'Crept from the cradle of learning to the court of liberty . . . from his tutor to the touchstone of his wits', the typical student was 'his own man now',[84] left to improvise morally where social tradition and religious authority had been slow in adapting to the needs of an increasingly secular society. This moral

80 Walter J. Ong, *Interfaces of the Word: Studies in the Evolution of Consciousness and Culture* (Ithaca: Cornell University Press, 1977), pp. 62–6.

81 Donne, *Letters to Severall Persons of Honour* (1651), quoted in Arthur F. Marotti, *John Donne: Coterie Poet* (Madison: University of Wisconsin Press, 1986), p. 21.

82 Alvin Kernan, *The Cankered Muse: Satire of the English Renaissance* (1959; rpt, Hamden, CT: Archon Books, 1976), ch. 3.

83 Sir Edward Coke, quoted in James Biester, *Lyric Wonder: Rhetoric and Wit in English Renaissance Poetry* (Ithaca: Cornell University Press, 1997), p. 85.

84 Francis Lenton, *The Young Gallants Whirligigg* (1629), quoted in Prest, *The Inns of Court*, p. 141.

predicament was embodied in the dynamics of verse satire, where attempts to imagine moral community led most commonly to expressions of the satirists' own social isolation, rage and moral contamination: 'instead of a norm against which the immediate object of satire stands out', C. S. Lewis observed, 'we have vistas opening on corruption in every direction'.[85] The Horatian poise of Donne's first two satires thus yielded to an anxious search for 'true Religion' in the third and, with the perceptions of bottomless political corruption in the fourth and fifth, to open disillusionment and the guilty realisation that 'to my satyrs there belongs some feare'.[86] Similarly, the philosophic temper of Marston's *Certaine Satires* (1598), borrowed from Persius, gave way entirely in the slightly later *Scourge of Villainie* (1598, revised and enlarged 1599) to the lashing, cynic manner that made Marston (accused by a contemporary of 'lifting up your leg and pissing against the world')[87] the *enfant terrible* of the genre and the model of choice for a fashion of satiric scourging subsequently pursued in works like Middleton's *Microcynicon or ... Snarling Satyres* (1598), the anonymous *Whipping of the Satyre* (1601), Davies of Hereford's *The Scourge of Folly* (1611), George Wither's *Abuses Stript and Whipt* (1613), Richard Brathwait's *Strappado for the Divell* (1615) and John Taylor's *Superbiae Flagellum* (1621).

In the lashing satires of these later popular writers, verse satire was extended and disseminated, like the epigram, to a broader reading public. The urban perspective of the Inns of Court satirists thus survived – in altered popular form – the official attempt to curb the innovative liberty of satire in a ban of 1 June 1599, which called for the satires of Hall, Marston, Middleton, Guilpin and Davies, along with 'all Nashes bookes', to be 'broughte to the Bishop of London to be burnte' and commanded that 'noe Satyres or Epigrams be printed hereafter'.[88] The more enduring heritage of Inns of Court culture, however, was the adaptation of coterie exclusiveness and critical discrimination to the more expansive imitation of classical verse that accompanied the development of a more broadly based elite 'Town' culture in early seventeenth-century London. The social modulations of epistle, epigram, elegy and ode, pioneered by Donne, Jonson, Michael Drayton and others, revealed new 'ways to be more intimate

85 *English Literature in the Sixteenth Century Excluding Drama* (Oxford: Clarendon Press, 1954), p. 470.
86 John Donne, *Selected Prose*, ed. Evelyn Simpson, Helen Gardner and Timothy Healy (Oxford: Clarendon Press, 1967), p. 111.
87 *The Second Part of the Return from Parnassus*, in *The Three Parnassus Plays*, ed. J. B. Leishman (London: Nicholson & Watson, 1949), p. 241.
88 E. Arber (ed.) *A Transcript of the Registers of the Company of Stationers of London*, 5 vols. (London, 1875–94), 3:316.

and informal' in a metropolitan setting of increasing scale and grandeur.[89] Like satire, but in a more composed and intimate vein, these classicising experiments enabled poets to work out a cosmopolitan 'way of life' by means of a selective appeal to the privatised domains of self, friends, distinctive place and occasion. The 'differentiation, refinement, and enrichment' of the person demanded and enabled by the pace and scale of urban life thus contributed not only to new literary kinds and tastes but to their stratification. In early modern English literature, as in early modern London, disassociation paradoxically helped to construct a society by multiplying differences and 'effecting distances'[90] between groups, individuals, tastes and modes of expression.

89 Alastair Fowler, *Kinds of Literature: An Introduction to the Theory of Genres and Kinds* (Cambridge, MA: Harvard University Press, 1982), pp. 195–202.
90 Georg Simmel, 'The Metropolis and Mental Life', in *Classic Essays on the Culture of Cities*, ed. Sennett, p. 53.

Chapter 14

LITERATURE AND THE THEATRE

DAVID BEVINGTON

Although the Reformation is often blamed for suppressing popular drama, and did indeed become a potent oppositional force to be reckoned with in the later sixteenth and early seventeenth centuries, that opposition was by no means evident at first. In Scotland, for example, surviving evidence from the mid sixteenth century shows that theatrical activity, carried out in open-air public venues, could serve the Protestant cause. In 1571 John Knox watched a play that dramatised the current siege of Edinburgh Castle 'according to Mr Knox doctrin'.[1] Although the texts for this and a number of other such plays do not survive, we do have a full text and records of performance of Sir David Lindsay's *Ane Satyre of the Thrie Estaits*, staged first in 1540 before the King and Queen at Linlithgow, then at Cupar, Fife, in 1552, and finally at the public playfield in Edinburgh in 1554 in the presence of Marie de Lorraine, Queen Regent, along with 'ane greit part of the Nobilitie' and 'ane exceding greit nowmer of pepill'.[2] Its avowedly political allegory invites John the Common-Weill to take part in a thoroughgoing redistribution of political responsibility and thereby rescue the King (Rex Humanitas) and his three Parliamentary 'estaits' (Spiritualitie, Temporalitie and Merchand), from those whose loyalties are 'speciallie vnto the Court of Rome' (line 286). The King's tempters are variously named Sensualitie, Flatterie, Falset and Dissait, until, as often happens in such morality drama, they adopt the disguise names of Devotioun, Sapience and Discretioun. This lengthy play of some 4,630 lines was mounted out of doors in the manner of medieval cycle drama and of panoramic entertainments like *The Castle of Perseverance* (c. 1405–25). Its staging calls for various 'scaffolds' or elevated 'seats' reached by ladders and towering above

---

1 R. D. S. Jack (ed.), *The History of Scottish Literature*, vol. 1: *Origins to 1660* (Aberdeen University Press, 1987) p. 204. I am indebted to Janel Mueller for invaluable suggestions here and throughout this chapter.

2 Charteris's preface to *The workis of . . . Schir Dauid Lyndesay of the Mont* (1568), and *The Works of Sir David Lindsay of the Mount*, ed. Douglas Hamer, 4 vols. Scottish Text Society (Edinburgh and London: W. Blackwood & Sons, 1931–6), 4:139–42.

the 'feild' or 'green' (lines 1940–54, 2036), an open playing area that features a body of water along with a pulpit, and stocks and gallows on which the villains are to be hanged. All ends happily when Diligence and others proclaim the 'Nobill Actis of Parliament' (line 3789) forbidding pluralism of benefices, church hierarchy and payments of annates (papal exactions, due yearly) to Rome.[3]

Scottish drama made other faltering attempts to bring a 'Renaissance' in theatre to that northern and Calvinist-ridden country. The anonymous *Philotus*, a late sixteenth-century comedy published in 1603, reveals an interest in the Italianate plot of sexual disguise and mistaken identity. King James VI's determined defiance of the Reformed Church of Scotland achieved a potentially significant victory in 1599 when the King arranged, and forced the church to accept, public performances by a troupe of English actors in Edinburgh.[4] This, however, appears to have been the first and only move towards establishing a commercial public theatre in Scotland. Unlike London, Scotland's capital did not support a regular playhouse. *Philotus* may have been a closet drama never intended for performance. Certainly the tragedies of James VI's courtier Sir William Alexander were conceived as closet dramas. A noted poet and companion of the King, Alexander followed James to London in 1603 and dedicated to him the four *Monarchicke Tragedies: Darius, Croesus, The Alexandrian Tragedy* and *Julius Caesar*. If James had remained in Edinburgh, Scottish drama might have found ways to develop in the new and varied modes of the Renaissance. Once the court had gone, the theatre lost its chief patron, and Scotland lost its cultural and political stimulus.

Even at that, James's interests were more intensely literary than theatrical. He took part in some court masques and court entertainments in Scotland, wrote at least one such work, and devised part of the shows for Prince Henry's baptism. Yet his move to London brought with it little Scottish influence on the English stage. Royal sponsorship of the Stuart masque, that was to bring the genre to heights of visual and verbal extravagance in the last two decades of his reign, was often more at the initiative of Queen Anne and then of Prince Henry than of the King himself; at performances he was sometimes seen to be bored and irritated.[5] James's influence on English theatre was more that of patron: he officially adopted the Lord Chamberlain's Men, whose roster included William Shakespeare and Richard Burbage, as the King's Men in 1603, and often saw

3 David Lindsay, *Ane Satyre of the Thrie Estaits*, ed. James Kinsley (London: Cassell, 1954).
4 Jack (ed.), *History of Scottish Literature*, p. 210.
5 David Bevington and Peter Holbrook (eds.), *The Politics of the Stuart Court Masque* (Cambridge University Press, 1998), pp. 27–37, 121–75.

such plays as *Measure for Measure*, *Othello* and *King Lear* in specially arranged performances at court.

In England, the Reformation church certainly made use of the theatre for what essentially amounted to propaganda purposes.[6] John Skelton, though himself not a supporter of the new humanist learning and too early in any case to write drama for the English Reformation, nonetheless provided a significant model for a polemical theatre that could be turned to advantage by the authorities of the new order once Henry VIII had broken with Rome in 1531–6. Skelton's *Magnificence* (1515–18) anticipates many of the allegorical devices employed by David Lindsay some three or four decades later. A royal figure, Magnificence, is tempted towards ruinous extravagance and corruption by a bevy of insidious counsellors with names like Counterfet Countenaunce, Crafty Conveyaunce and Cloked Colusyon, disguising themselves in the King's presence as Good Demeanance, Sure Surveyance and Sober Sadness. Some of their abuses are priestly; Cloked Colusyon is dressed in an ill-fitting cleric's robe and practises the flattering duplicity of a religious hypocrite. Satire of the church is of the familiar stamp one finds in Chaucer or Langland. Yet the marked resemblance of Magnificence to the young Henry VIII gives a polemical edge to the satire that is distinctly topical, and provides a compelling example of how morality drama could be shaped into an attack on political and religious abuses. The object lesson is unmistakable and is perhaps directed at Henry's dangerous partiality towards Cardinal Thomas Wolsey, his chief councillor: liberality is becoming in a prince, but capricious prodigality is not, and woe betide the monarch who cannot sort out the crucial difference. Skelton's allegiances were to the Dukes of Norfolk, whose ancient high status got no special deference from the new Tudor rulers and who were especially contemptuous of self-serving upstarts like the butcher's son Wolsey. The morality play tradition provided Skelton with a formula for turning conventional topics of satire – extravagance in dress, political scheming, favouritism, clerical worldliness – into weapons of contemporary ridicule.[7]

6 For perspectives on the Reformation and propaganda that have informed this chapter generally, see Rainer Pineas, 'The English Morality Play as a Weapon of Religious Controversy', *Studies in English Literature 1500–1900* 2 (1962), 157–80; Ritchie D. Kendall, *The Drama of Dissent: The Radical Poetics of Nonconformity, 1380–1590* (Chapel Hill: University of North Carolina Press, 1986); Greg Walker, *Plays of Persuasion: Drama and Politics at the Court of Henry VIII* (Cambridge University Press, 1991); and Paul Whitfield White, *Theatre and Reformation: Protestantism, Patronage and Playing in Tudor England* (Cambridge University Press, 1993). I am deeply indebted to Paul White, who has read a version of this chapter with extraordinary care and insight, and whose work has taught me so much.

7 See Walker, *Plays of Persuasion*; Alistair Fox, *Politics and Literature in the Reigns of Henry VII and Henry VIII* (Oxford: Blackwell, 1989); and David Bevington, *Tudor Drama and Politics:*

The Reformation authorities – especially Thomas Cromwell and Thomas Cranmer in the later years of Henry VIII's reign, then the Lord Protector Somerset in the reign of Edward VI, and then Lord Warwick (later Duke of Northumberland) after the Lord Protector's fall in 1550 – seemed to have had no hesitation in abetting the writing and active dissemination of Protestantised religious drama.[8] They did so by commissioning plays and by sponsoring troupes of players who could perform at court, in royal households and on tour. The plays were unmistakably created to fulfil a political and religious mission rather than to serve a disinterested sponsorship of the performing arts, though the Reformers were also avidly interested in education and looked upon the drama as a weapon of educational as well as religious reform. (Earlier humanist plays like John Rastell's *The Nature of the Four Elements, c.* 1517–18, are indicative of this trend.) The Reformers did not speak out against any supposedly inherent evils in drama during this period; their response to the presumed political dangers of a Catholic religious drama was to replace it with theatrical activity of a more friendly persuasion. In some instances, as at Coventry, they also reformed the traditional civic religious drama by bringing it into line with Protestant dogma rather than simply suppressing it.[9]

John Bale, for one, quickly saw the potential, so vividly suggested by Skelton, of a drama that could be polemicised for the English Reformation. Himself a Carmelite friar turned avid Protestant, Bale was the ideal person to 'convert' into Protestant terms the religious plays he had long known as a Catholic. He exploited every genre: saints' lives, as in his play about the Preaching of John the Baptist in the Wilderness (though of course Catholic saints were off limits); Biblical and cyclical plays adapted to anti-Catholic purposes on the subjects of the Temptation in the Wilderness, the Raising of Lazarus, and the Last Supper; open polemics against the Treacheries of the Papists in two parts; a Pater Noster play; another on the Seven Deadly Sins; and morality plays, such as his *Three*

A *Critical Approach to Topical Meaning* (Cambridge, MA: Harvard University Press, 1968), pp. 54–63. See also Arthur Kinney, *John Skelton, Priest as Poet: Seasons of Discovery* (Chapel Hill: University of North Carolina Press, 1987), p. 193.

8 See John N. King, *English Reformation Literature: the Tudor Origins of the Protestant Tradition* (Princeton University Press, 1982), pp. 103–21 and 271–84.

9 Paul White, 'Reforming Mysteries' End: A New Look at Protestant Intervention in English Provincial Drama', *Journal of Medieval and Early Modern Studies* 29.1 (Winter 1999), 121–47, challenges the prevailing view of Protestant confrontation with the drama in order to show how Protestantism engaged positively with the theatre in several provincial communities. White draws on the Records of Early English Drama (REED) series, especially R. W. Ingram (ed.), *Coventry* (University of Toronto Press, 1981). See also Pamela King, 'The York and Coventry Mystery Cycles: A Comparative Model of Civic Response to Growth and Recession', *REED Newsletter* 22 (1975), 25.

Laws of Nature, Moses, and Christ, Corrupted by the Sodomites, Pharisees, and Papists.
Most such plays, including many that are lost, were written in the 1530s and
1540s. Indefatigable, zealous, intemperate, Bale provided scripts that could be
substituted for the older drama in much the way that unreconstructed priests
were being shovelled out of their parishes to make way for men of the new faith.
He obligingly facilitated doubling of parts in order to provide texts that could
be acted by a troupe of five actors, for example (as in the case of *Three Laws*).[10]
Most intriguingly, he showed how historical materials could be adapted to the
new mode of disseminating religious doctrine.

One would like to know what assaults Bale committed on history in his
lost *The Knaveries of Thomas Becket* (*c*. 1536–9), but perhaps the pattern
is clearly enough indicated in his best-known pair of plays about *King Johan*
(A-version, 1538; B-version as late as 1562). The revisionism which the Tudor
rulers unblushingly demanded of their prose historians, in order to refute
Polydore Vergil and other denigrators of King John, takes on dramatic form
in Bale's depiction of the King as martyr to a noble but unrealised cause. John
comes before us as a Protestant centuries ahead of his time, a John the Baptist
to Henry VIII's role as the saviour of the English church. The revisionist historical line is that of William Tyndale and Robert Barnes, who may indeed have
provided Bale a model for attacking the Catholic chroniclers and transforming
John into a dauntless if unsuccessful challenger of Rome.[11] John Foxe was to
take up the cudgels in his *Acts and Monuments*, and thereby transmit to succeeding generations an interpretive view of King John that would leave its mark on
Shakespeare's dramatic version in 1595.[12] Bale's play is a diatribe about the evils
of historical misinterpretation and of religious backsliding. His title figure,
only distantly related to the historical King John, is much more transparently a
Protestant saint: intemperate, offended by profane language, virulently hostile
to 'yowre traysh, yowre ryngyng, syngyng and pypyng' of the papal Antichrist

10 Paul White, *Theatre and Reformation*, pp. 1–41; David Bevington, *From 'Mankind' to Marlowe:
    Growth of Structure in the Popular Drama of Tudor England* (Cambridge, MA: Harvard Univer-
    sity Press, 1962), pp. 129–30; and *The Complete Plays of John Bale*, ed. Peter Happé, 2 vols.
    (Cambridge: D. S. Brewer, 1985–6), 1:22–3, 152–6.
11 Irving Ribner, *The English History Play in the Age of Shakespeare*, rev. edn (New York, 1965),
    p. 35; Honor McCusker, *John Bale, Dramatist and Antiquary* (Bryn Mawr, PA, 1942), pp. 90–
    3; and Janette Dillon, *Language and Stage in Medieval and Renaissance England* (Cambridge
    University Press, 1998), pp. 87–105.
12 Richard Helgerson, *Forms of Nationhood: The Elizabethan Writing of England* (University of
    Chicago Press, 1992), pp. 260–1, notes that Foxe accentuates the aspiration for nationhood
    by organising his *Acts and Monuments* into chapters on the reigns of England's monarchs
    rather than, in Catholic tradition, papal regimes. See also Dillon, *Language and Stage*,
    pp. 107–12, and Huston Diehl, *Staging Reform, Reforming the Stage: Protestantism and Popular
    Theater in Early Modern England* (Ithaca: Cornell University Press, 1997), pp. 22–52.

(line 1392), obsessed with the rightness of his cause, and defiantly ready for martyrdom. [13] John is thus presumably much like Bale himself, and like many other Reformers for whom drama was, potentially at least, an organ for the advancement of truth. The play was designed for doubling by a small acting troupe capable of going on tour, as is evidenced by stage directions telling various actors to exit and dress for another part. Almost certainly these were 'Lord Cromwell's players', specifically commissioned by Thomas Cromwell, with Archbishop Cranmer's active support, to spread propaganda by means of antipapal plays.[14]

The anonymous *Nice Wanton*, played by Paul's Boys before Queen Elizabeth in August of 1560, offers an illustration of how the mixed genre of the quasi-allegorical moral interlude could serve the purposes of the early Elizabethan state. Mary's reign, 1553-8, had seen the performance of pro-Catholic plays, such as *Respublica* (Christmas season, 1553), but designed chiefly for a courtly audience; while the play deplores 'thabuses which hithertoo hath been' and celebrates the recovery of Respublica 'from hir late decay' (line 116),[15] it does so seemingly for a select group of spectators instead of reaching out to the English nation as a whole. Elizabeth and her ministers, the Earl of Leicester notable among them, were not to make Mary's mistake of neglecting the propaganda potential of the drama. *Nice Wanton* is just the kind of play that seems to have been commissioned by the Protestant authorities, returning after years of exile, and burning with zeal to reverse the presumed errors of lost years.

Accordingly, *Nice Wanton* is at pains to castigate backsliding and to warn against the dangers of any such deplorable behaviour in the future. Its Prologue is the pronouncement of a committed Calvinist preacher, quoting Solomon to the effect that to spare the rod is to spoil the child. Humans must be restrained from their 'natural wont evil' (lines 1-11). As his case in point, the dramatist brings on two children spoiled by an indulgent mother, who end in richly deserved misery, in contrast to the virtuous Barnabas, who is wholly aware that 'Man is prone to evil from his youth' (line 27).[16] Ismael, the wicked brother, is ultimately hanged in chains; their sister, Dalila, dies for her crimes as well, though repentant at the last moment. Education is highlighted as of central

---

13 *King Johan*, in *Complete Plays*, ed. Happé, 1:29-99.

14 Bevington, *From 'Mankind' to Marlowe*, p. 268; Dillon, *Language and Stage*, pp. 93 and 234; and Paul White, *Theatre and Reformation*, pp. 12-17.

15 *Respublica*, ed. Leonard A. Magnus, Early English Text Society, extra ser., 94 (London: K. Paul, Trench, Trübner, 1905).

16 *Nice Wanton*, in *The Tudor Interludes: 'Nice Wanton' and 'Impatient Poverty'*, ed. Leonard Tennenhouse (New York: Garland, 1984). See also *Jacob and Esau* (c. 1550-7), acted by an unknown boys' company, analysed by Paul White, *Theatre and Reformation*, pp. 118-23.

concern to the new state, and Calvinist doctrines of election and reprobation are made manifest in the contrasting portraits of two brothers even while the play also holds out to Christian audiences the hope of salvation for those who truly repent. Other plays of Elizabeth's early years offer similar ideological programmes, often written for popular touring companies and provided with doubling charts to facilitate performance by a group of four to six players: *New Custom* (*c*. 1570–3) for four actors, *The Longer Thou Livest the More Fool Thou Art* (*c*. 1559–68) for four, *The Life and Repentance of Mary Magdalene* (*c*. 1550–66) for four, *Like Will to Like* (1562–8) for five, *The Tide Tarrieth No Man* (published 1576) for four, and still others.

The plays for which the English Renaissance is truly memorable begin early in Elizabeth's reign. At first they too cannot have displeased the Calvinist Reformers; they are suffused with moral earnestness and object lessons from history or legend. *Cambises*, for all its comical horseplay among the lower-class characters, offers a sober homily in definition of good government versus its opposite. The Prologue cites Agathon and Seneca in support of the 'honest exercise' of rule by just law and in condemnation of the kind of tyranny that will deservedly inherit 'ignomy and bitter shame'. Because the title figure displays both virtuous and deplorable rule in 'his one good deed of execution, after that many wicked deedes and tirannous murders', *Cambises* is an edifying exemplar of the moral points about good government that the play wishes to inculcate. The author, Thomas Preston (whose zealotry in the Protestant faith is attested elsewhere by his *The Second Book of the Garden of Wisdom* and his later fulminations against the Northern Rebellion of 1569), castigates those who regard themselves as above the law (see line 117), even while he also defends the right of responsible citizens to speak freely in criticism of tyrannous behaviour. An allusion to Bishop Bonner, Queen Mary's hated Bishop of London (line 1141), makes plain the play's alignment on the Protestant side. *Cambises* may well have been written in about 1560–1 for performance at court by Robert Dudley's Men, and was thus sanctioned by Elizabeth's favourite leader of the reforming group in her Privy Council who was soon to become the Earl of Leicester. Significantly, the presentation at court was only part of its performance history: it was designed, like *Nice Wanton* and *New Custom*, for a mobile troupe of players, since it features a 'division of the parts' for eight actors, seemingly six men and two boys. Probably this represents the capacity of Dudley's acting company at that time – a notably larger group than that needed for *Nice Wanton* and other moralities cited above. Surely this acting company was widely employed by Dudley in the service of the new religion. The burlesque comic routines of the Vice Ambidexter and his noisy companions adopt the style of the morality play, presumably as crowd-pleasers, but they also address serious moral and religious issues of public order and the nature of true obedience to the throne.[17]

Gorboduc was the combined effort of two Parliamentary leaders on the side of religious reform. Thomas Norton was a former tutor of Edward Seymour, Earl of Hertford, who in 1560 had secretly married the young woman named as an heir presumptive in Henry VIII's will, Lady Katharine Grey. Norton was also related by marriage to Archbishop Cranmer, and served in Parliament with such energetic advocacy of Protestant succession to the throne and Parliamentary prerogative that he was a continual thorn in Elizabeth's flesh. His interest in the drama did not cease with Gorboduc; he plainly regarded it as a potential weapon for the truth, though he also worried, in An Exhortation, or Rule, set down by one Mr Norton, sometime Remembrancer of London (1574), about 'unnecessary and scarcely honest resorts to plays' in the City of London 'and especially the assemblies to the unchaste, shameless, and unnatural tumbling of the Italian women'.[18] Thomas Sackville, later Baron Buckhurst and then Earl of Dorset, was a more moderate politician who nonetheless joined forces with Norton in an emblematic union of the two Houses of Parliament to set Elizabeth straight on the issue of royal succession: namely, that its line of descent should be clearly stipulated in advance of any need for implementation. The play is significant not only for its adoption of blank verse in tragedy but also for its exploration of presumably authentic British history in support of the Protestant Reformation and its attendant political agenda. Shadowed forth in the play's fiction about a royal family divided against itself is the appalling spectre of civil war in the 1560s – a prospect immeasurably heightened by Elizabeth's nearly fatal bout with smallpox in 1562, the persistent plotting of Catholics on behalf of Mary, Queen of Scots, and then the Northern Rebellion of 1569. A recently noted eyewitness report indicates that the play, under Dudley's sponsorship, commented on issues of royal marriage, favouring Dudley and attacking 'foreign' prospects like that of King Eric of Sweden.[19]

One other example of the moral earnestness of drama in Elizabeth's first years is Richard Edwards's Damon and Pythias, a tragicomedy acted at court by

17 Cambises, by Thomas Preston, in Elizabethan and Stuart Plays, ed. C. R. Baskervill, Virgil B. Heltzel and Arthur H. Nethercot (New York: Holt, Rinehart and Winston, 1934).

18 An Exhortation, or Rule, set down by one Mr Norton, sometime Remembrancer of London, whereby the Lord Mayor of London is to order himself and the city (1574), from a MS of Sir Christopher Hatton, now BL, MS Additional 32379, fo. 36, reprinted in E. K. Chambers, The Elizabethan Stage, 4 vols. (Oxford: Clarendon Press, 1923), 4:273.

19 Norman Jones and Paul Whitfield White, 'Gorboduc and Royal Marriage Politics: An Elizabethan Playgoer's Report of the Premiere Performance', English Literary Renaissance 26 (1996), 3–16.

the Chapel Children, seemingly in 1565. Here we can see how courtly drama for boy actors could address much the same agenda as did the plays for adult actors. Like Cambises, the Dionysius of this play is a legendary tyrant from the ancient world, the despot whom Plato had held up as an example to warn philosophers against the futility of taking an advisory role in government. (Seneca was another such object lesson.) Yet Edwards's serious idealism prompts him to argue that even such a ruler as Dionysius can be swayed to goodness by the disinterested example of virtuous friendship. Despite the Prologue's insistent disclaimer eschewing any political application, Edwards plainly envisages a viable role in Elizabeth's government for himself and like-minded Protestant humanists.[20]

The play abounds in edifyingly contrastive types: Aristippus the worldly philosopher versus Damon and Pythias as unbiased, stoic philosophers, Carisophus the parasite versus Eubulus the pragmatically brave counsellor. Eubulus is also counterposed to Damon and Pythias on the crucial issue of whether philosophers should compromise at all with stern realities, and on this score Edwards is uncompromising: Damon and Pythias's selflessness and serenely detached candour produce the play's almost miraculous conversion of the ruler to virtue, in the face of well-nigh universal cynicism. Although the play does not address directly the issues of Reformation, it does enlist drama – including the courtly drama of the boy actors – on the side of virtuous persuasion. Edwards's Prologue to *Damon and Pythias* is at pains to warn its audience not to expect 'toying Playes' in 'commycall wise' (lines 4–6).[21] Edwards himself seems to have been an ordained minister, who was trained at Oxford and was elected there to be one of the 'theologians' of Christ Church in 1550. Elizabeth's demonstrated approval of Edwards as playwright (she publicly thanked him and rewarded him for his *Palamon and Arcite* at Oxford in 1566) bespeaks her endorsement of the serious moral drama that he wrote for her.[22] Calvinist and Puritan disaffection with the theatre seems a long way off.

What sorts of stages and acting venues were provided for the actors who put on the drama of the early Reformation, and in what ways did those stages provide a vital dimension to the ideological changes that were beginning to

---

20 Bevington, *Tudor Drama and Politics*, pp. 164–7. See also Marie Axton, *The Queen's Two Bodies: Drama and the Elizabethan Succession* (London: Royal Historical Society, 1977), pp. 52–3, on Edwards's commitment to carrying on the work of the Reformation in his plays, including *Palamon and Arcite*.

21 *Richard Edwards' Damon and Pithias: A Critical Old-Spelling Edition*, ed. D. Jerry White (New York: Garland, 1980).

22 *Damon and Pythias*, ed. White, pp. 1–3.

take place in Reformation England? What is the link between theatrical space and Reformist ideology? As we have seen, Sir David Lindsay's *Ane Satyre of the Thrie Estaits*, staged at Cupar in 1552 and at the public playfield in Edinburgh in 1554, fashioned its playing arena in the style of medieval cycle plays in the round, with elevated scaffolds on the periphery of a ground-level plateau. Presumably the spectators were situated around the periphery as well, on the lower slopes of Calton Hill at the Greenside. Some comfort needed to be provided, since royalty and nobility were present and since the performance in 1554 lasted 'fra ix. houris afoir none, till .vi. houris at evin'.[23] More customarily, early moralities and interludes were variously staged in inns and innyards, the great halls of royal and noble households, churches and outdoor spaces such as village greens. The disparateness of acting conditions encouraged richness and diversity in early and mid sixteenth-century drama, and has led to an intriguing debate as to the origins of the great London theatres of the later sixteenth and early seventeenth centuries with which we are, conjecturally at least, more familiar. The development is of crucial importance, since the new theatre spaces created in the later sixteenth century were to house, and give visual expression to, new ideas of social and religious conflict.

Did the Globe Theatre, the Rose and the Swan, along with other theatre buildings, owe more to traditions of an itinerant platform stage or to performance in the great halls of the wealthy? The first view hypothesises a platform stage erected on trestles with a curtain for a backdrop to conceal a place for the actors to change and to provide them with means for entrances and exits. Such a booth stage, easily transported and set up in village greens or at fairs, might well be taken into the yard of an inn and set up against one wall of that enclosed space. In such an arrangement, the 'gate' could be controlled by access to the innyard, often through an arched gateway. The resulting 'theatre' would resemble a later Elizabethan theatre in a number of respects. A rectangular platform, presumably more wide than deep and elevated perhaps five feet above the floor of the innyard, would stand against a back wall; at its rear would be a 'tiring-house' or dressing area improvised by a curtain. Surrounding this platform on all sides, the inn would ordinarily provide galleries looking down into the yard from outside the guests' sleeping quarters.[24]

23 *Works of Lindsay*, ed. Hamer, 4:139–42. Paul White devotes chapter 5 of his *Theatre and Reformation* to playing venues during the early Reformation.
24 See, for example, C. Walter Hodges, *The Globe Restored: A Study of the Elizabethan Theatre* (London: Benn, 1953; 2nd edn, New York: Coward McCann, 1963); Glynne Wickham, *Early English Stages, 1300 to 1660* (London: Routledge and Kegan Paul, 1959–72), and Richard Southern, *The Staging of Plays before Shakespeare* (London: Faber & Faber, 1973).

One advantage of this scenario has to do with financial arrangements. Presumably the guests of the inn would have access to the play as a benefit of their occupancy of rooms; the innkeeper's profit would come in the form of entertaining his guests and thereby attracting customers. The players, meanwhile, could control the 'gate' and require some small payment for entrance to the play from other interested playgoers. In Lewis Wager's *The Life and Repentance of Mary Magdalene* (*c*. 1550–66), for example, the speaker of the Prologue declares to his audience, 'Truly, I say, whether you give halfpence or pence, / Your gain shall be double, before you depart hence'; presumably the acting troupe is following the model of *Mankind* (*c*. 1471). If such an arrangement did occur in England of the mid sixteenth century, it would have anticipated and no doubt set an example for theatres like the Rose, where admission through the gate cost the spectator a basic penny whereas further payment was required for access to the gallery seats; the acting company normally collected the admission price, whereas the owner of the building could count on the revenues from the gallery seats in a range of prices mounting to the most expensive seats in the 'Lord's room'.

A corollary attraction of this booth-stage hypothesis is that it fits well with the idea of a heterogeneous audience composed variously of 'groundlings' standing next to the stage for a small fee and the gentry occupying the seats. Medieval staging often postulates this kind of mixed yet separated audience, as in the reference to 'ane greit nowmer of pepill' at Lindsay's *Ane Satyre* in 1552, or *The Castle of Perseverance*'s distinction between the 'syrys semly' that 'syttyth on syde' and the 'wytes' who are in the 'pleyn place'.[25] *Mankind* addresses 'ye souerns that sytt, & ye brothern that stonde ryghte wppe' (line 29).[26] The later Elizabethan theatre remains solidly in contact with this tradition of a socially diverse assembly.

Yet the platform stage set in an innyard is only one possible model. No less attractive is the great hall of the well-to-do.[27] Skelton's *Magnificence* was probably

25 Robert Weimann, *Shakespeare and the Popular Tradition in the Theater*, ed. Robert Schwartz (Baltimore: Johns Hopkins University Press, 1978); Bevington, *From 'Mankind' to Marlowe*, pp. 48–50.
26 *The Macro Plays: The Castle of Perseverance, Wisdom, Mankind: A Facsimile Edition with Facing Transcriptions*, ed. David Bevington (New York: Johnson Reprint Corp., 1972).
27 See Richard Hosley, 'The Origins of the Shakespearian Playhouse', in *Shakespeare 400*, ed. James G. McManaway (New York: Holt, Rinehart and Winston, 1964), pp. 29–39; Hosley, 'The Playhouses and the Stage', in *A New Companion to Shakespeare Studies*, ed. Kenneth Muir and S. Schoenbaum (Cambridge University Press, 1971), pp. 15–34; Richard Southern, 'The Contribution of the Interludes to Elizabethan Staging', in *Essays on Shakespeare and Elizabethan Drama in Honor of Hardin Craig*, ed. Richard Hosley (Columbia: University of Missouri Press, 1962), pp. 3–14; and David Bevington, 'Popular and Courtly Traditions on

staged in the presence of the Norfolk family, wherever else it may also have been put on. Appearances 'at the door' (line 32), entrances into and exits '*out of the place*' (line 824), abundant changing of costume, and asides to the audience would all be perfectly feasible in a great hall, with the guests of an evening's banquet presumably close at hand, as in Henry Medwall's *Fulgens and Lucrece* (*c.* 1490–1501). The fact that such simple demands could also be met by a more portable booth stage meant that plays of this nature could borrow elements from popular drama and appeal to various audiences in almost any locale that occasion might demand. John Rastell's *The Nature of the Four Elements*, with its undisguised borrowing from popular comic traditions, was probably intended for a stage that Rastell himself designed as a way of bringing humanist issues before select audiences of intellectuals and also a broader public. Many humanist interludes, such as John Heywood's *The Play of the Weather* (1525–33), were conceived for evening gatherings of the elite in a noble or royal banqueting hall. Bale's *Three Laws* and *King John* are uncomplicated in their staging demands in such a way as to render them adaptable to itinerant stages or the great hall; *Three Laws* requires chiefly that its three protagonists be able to sing to the glory of God (line 1922), a common requirement of plays of the period, whereas *King John*'s concern in its many stage directions is with the costuming changes that its characters must anticipate as they exit. As these brief descriptions suggest, staging requirements in the early and mid sixteenth centuries did not importantly differentiate popular from elite drama; on the contrary, the plays that the Reformers found useful to their purposes were so precisely because they were designed for performance in varying sorts of locales.

Visually, the great hall provides the advantage of resemblance to the later Elizabethan theatres in certain ways that booth stages and innyards could not provide. If we imagine the action of a play taking place at the lower end of a great hall, opposite the dais for the host and his chief guests at the upper end, then we can visualise the action in front of a hall screen that grew increasingly elaborate as the Renaissance went on. Two or three doors, often elaborately carved, provided access to a transverse passageway leading to the kitchen and the outside. Those doors, curtained presumably to reduce draughts, bear some resemblance to those of the so-called 'De Witt' drawing of the Swan (*c.* 1596), the earliest and most informative contemporary drawing we have of an Elizabethan theatre interior from a viewpoint facing the stage.[28] More

the Early Tudor Stage', in *Medieval Drama*, ed. Neville Denny, Stratford-upon-Avon Studies, 16 (London: Edward Arnold, 1973), pp. 91–108.
28 Johannes De Witt's drawing is reproduced in *The Complete Works of Shakespeare*, ed. David Bevington, 4th edn updated (New York: Harper Collins, 1997), p. xlvi.

importantly, perhaps, the passageway was surmounted by a gallery that could serve as a music room, so that in appearance the lower end of a great hall featured above the doors a gallery not unlike that shown in the De Witt drawing. In the Cambridge colleges, as Alan Nelson has shown, spectators could be seated behind and above the elaborate stages constructed there for performances, thus providing a seating arrangement 'in the round' not unlike that of the London public theatres.[29]

Yet the staging of plays in great halls cannot be shown conclusively to have taken place at the lower end; some contrary evidence suggests use of the upper end on occasion, and also the centre of the long side of a room around a large fireplace.[30] Guests at a banquet in such a space, seated at rows of tables, could be variously arranged to make any of these options possible. Moreover, the great hall hypothesis does little to anticipate the circular rows of galleries for spectators shown plainly in the De Witt sketch. Conversely, the booth stage hypothesis does not account well for the music room above a tiring-house façade in which elaborate doors are to be found. Perhaps the Elizabethan public theatre building is the product of a number of disparate factors; the best way to resolve the dispute between booth-stage and great-hall hypotheses is to grant a significant measure of plausibility to both, and to conclude that the purpose-built theatre buildings were deliberate hybrids commissioned by actor-entrepreneurs who knew from experience the advantages of both theatrical traditions.

What we know about private theatre spaces in the late sixteenth century, such as Blackfriars, suggests that this venue may indeed have resembled the façade of a great hall in some more detail than did the public theatre façade. Another architectural influence may have been the college halls at the universities, where sophisticated and elaborate, albeit temporary, staging structures were assembled for performance events and then taken down again to be used at a later date.[31] A line of descent from the aristocratic great hall and the college hall to the elite 'private' theatres of late Elizabethan and early Jacobean London would make sense in terms of social alignment. Nevertheless, the overall impression is one of coalescing between aristocratic and more public modes of theatre production in the early and mid sixteenth century. Court dramatists, encouraged by Reformist Privy Councillors like Somerset and Leicester

---

29 Alan H. Nelson, *Early Cambridge Theatres: College, University, and Town Stages, 1464–1720* (Cambridge University Press, 1994).
30 Alan H. Nelson, 'Hall Screens and Elizabethan Playhouses: Counter-Evidence from Cambridge', in *The Development of Shakespeare's Theater*, ed. John H. Astington (New York: AMS, 1992), pp. 57–76.
31 Nelson, *Early Cambridge Theatres*, ch. 7.

to peddle their wares in the public forum, devised plays that could please their noble sponsors and also do the work of the new order in London and in the countryside. Even plays specifically designed for boy actors, like *Nice Wanton* or Edwards's *Damon and Pythias*, adopted a style that incorporated broadly comic elements sure to appeal to popular audiences.

The argument for 'rival traditions' between popular and elite drama, championed by Alfred Harbage,[32] needs to be redefined in the context of early and mid sixteenth-century English drama. Even later, as Ann Jennalie Cook and others have shown, theatre audiences in London were a relatively sophisticated and well-to-do group,[33] so that we must be careful not to overstate the difference. Public and private theatre spaces resembled each other in ways often more significant than the differences; audiences overlapped; and, most importantly, in the earlier years of the century the dramatists and their sponsors were actively intent on courting a wide national audience for drama in order to carry out the programme of the Protestant Reformation.

A thesis of the remainder of this chapter will be that the place to look most of all for 'rival traditions' is in the growing antipathy pitting City moralists, in their attacks on the theatres as places of immoral assembly, against the theatrical community under attack, which understandably grew more edgy and defensive as the vitriol accelerated.[34] The result is an irony: a drama of nascent national and Protestant identity, which had been actively fostered by Reformed courtiers and their London allies, became all too soon an object of intense suspicion when it was regarded as no longer wedded to the concerns of the Reformed community. Later Elizabethan drama was, if you like, a Frankenstein's monster brought to life by Protestant zeal. It turned out to have a mind and agenda of its own.

This chapter will further argue that a sense of 'rival traditions' did in fact then develop between elite and popular to the significant extent that sophisticated drama tended to be perceived by the bourgeois Elect as particularly and

---

32 Alfred Harbage, *Shakespeare and the Rival Traditions* (New York: Macmillan, 1952).
33 Ann Jennalie Cook, *The Privileged Playgoers of Shakespeare's London, 1576–1642* (Princeton University Press, 1981).
34 E. N. S. Thompson, *The Controversy between the Puritans and the Stage*, Yale Studies in English, 20 (New York: H. Holt, 1903); M. M. Knappen, *Tudor Puritanism* (University of Chicago Press, 1939); William Ringler, 'The First Phase of the Elizabethan Attack on the Stage, 1558–1579', *Huntington Library Quarterly* 5 (1942), 391–418; Russell Fraser, *The War against Poetry* (Princeton University Press, 1970); Jonas Barish, *The Antitheatrical Prejudice* (Berkeley: University of California Press, 1981), pp. 82ff.; Jonathan V. Crewe, 'The Theater of the Idols: Theatrical and Anti-theatrical Discourse', in *Staging the Renaissance: Reinterpretations of Elizabethan and Jacobean Drama*, ed. David Scott Kastan and Peter Stallybrass (New York and London: Routledge, 1991), pp. 49–56, rpt from *Theatre Journal* 36 (1984), 321–44.

repellently ungodly. Some of that 'ungodly' drama appeared on public stages, so that the 'rival traditions' did not cleanly separate the private theatres from the public. The commercial and partly ideological war in the late 1590s between the Chamberlain's Men and the Admiral's Men at the Rose was in good part a battle in which the Admiral's Men made an open appeal for the support of London's 'silent majority' of God-fearing, reform-minded citizens. The Admiral's Men succeeded for a time in holding onto Puritan-leaning audiences. Nevertheless, the hostilities were destined to drive a wedge between the London authorities and all forms of drama, obliging acting companies to seek shelter in the private theatres and at court. The English Reformation did much to create, and then to demolish, the drama of the English Renaissance.

Signs of trouble are visible on the horizon even in the 1560s. Richard Edwards's angry denunciation of 'toying Playes' plainly indicates that there are kinds of dramatic entertainment that he, as a practising Reform playwright, refuses to countenance – even the sort that he himself appears to have written in earlier years. Lewis Wager, in his manifesto-like Prologue to *The Life and Repentance of Mary Magdalene*, is similarly aware of a controversy brewing between Reformers like himself, who believe in the use of 'godly mirth' to advance the true faith through popular teaching, and reforming opponents who attack plays as frivolous and immoral.[35]

Popular drama was certainly ready to move in a new romantic direction that would give censorious moralists grounds for loud complaint. *Tom Tyler and His Wife* (1558–63) borrows from morality elements, especially in the play's Vice figure named Desire, but the play is essentially a comic treatment of domestic discord played by boy actors. Tom's wife, bearing the ominous name of Strife, thinks of her husband as a silly creature whom she loves to beat; she is encouraged in her domineering ways by her gossips and drinking companions, Sturdie and Tipple. Their behaviour sends Tom Tyler to Tom Tayler (an 'artificer') for advice on how to tame a shrew, though it all ends in reconciliation.[36] Lost comedies, like *As Plain as Can Be* and *Jack and Jill* (both written for boys in 1567–8), may point to the kinds of plays of which Edwards disapproved. No less unsettlingly, *Clyomon and Clamydes* (c. 1570) initiates a genre of romances that were to become the rage in the 1570s and 1580s, including

35 Lewis Wager, *The Life and Repentaunce of Marie Magdalene*, ed. Frederic Ives Carpenter (University of Chicago Press, 1904). The Prologue is a telling document on the relationship of the Reformed clergy to the popular drama of the early Elizabethan era; see Paul White, *Theatre and Reformation*, pp. 80–7.
36 *Tom Tyler and His Wife*, 2nd impression, 1661, ed. G. C. Moore Smith and W. W. Greg, Malone Society Reprints (1910).

the lost *Cloridon and Radiamanta* and *Theagenes and Chariclea* (both performed at court in 1572–3), *Mamillia* (presented by Leicester's Men at court in 1573), *Herpetulus the Blue Knight and Perobia* (at court, 1574), *The Red Knight* (1576) and still others in increasing numbers. Here we find in abundance the sagas of wandering knights, ladies in distress, fearsome opponents like Bryan Sancefoy (in *Clyomon and Clamydes*), uses of disguise, storms at sea, encounters with dark forests, trials by combat and eventual happy endings that Philip Sidney amiably deplores in *The Defense of Poesie* (*c.* 1581). Sir Philip of course wrote and then rewrote his own 'serious' romance in *Arcadia*, but his religious politics were close to those of Leicester and the Reform party, and it is arguable that his *Arcadia* was intended as an attempt to recuperate, for the purposes of belles lettres, a venerable classical genre that was in imminent danger, on the stage, of becoming vulgarised into trivial entertainment. The burgeoning London theatre was not yet offering offensive satire of London citizens and Puritan ministers, but it was, from many Reformers' point of view, losing its focus on the purposes of the break with Rome.

James Burbage's construction of the Theatre in 1576, immediately outside of London's walls in Shoreditch, to the northeast, can only have accelerated the trend. Burbage enjoyed the patronage of the Earl of Leicester, still immensely influential with the Queen. The location chosen for the site of what may have been London's first permanent theatrical building was in Middlesex, outside the jurisdiction of the city of London. Other locations, both within the city and in its suburbs, had provided more temporary housing for theatrical activity in the 1560s and 1570s; as early as the 1560s, London appears to have had a theatre district of sorts in the vicinity of Gracechurch Street, where the Crosskeys and the Bell were located, and with the Bull in Bishopsgate, Leadenhall and the Merchant Taylors' Hall all nearby. The Red Lion opened in Stepney in 1567, perhaps featuring a large amphitheatre-type venue.[37] Obviously London

---

37 William Ingram, 'The "Evolution" of the Elizabethan Playing Company', in *The Development of Shakespeare's Theater*, ed. John H. Astington (New York: AMS, 1992), pp. 13–28, and *The Business of Playing: The Beginnings of the Adult Professional Theater in Elizabethan London* (Ithaca: Cornell University Press, 1992). On London's theatre district in the 1560s, see Paul White, *Theatre and Reformation*, pp. 132–3; White notes that the Bell Inn was right across the street from St Benet Gracechurch, the parish church of William Wager, author of *Enough Is as Good as a Feast* (*c.* 1559–*c.* 1570) and *The Longer Thou Livest the More Fool Thou Art*. See also Paul White, 'Playing Companies and the Drama of the 1580s: A New Direction for Elizabethan Theatre History?', *Shakespeare Studies* 29 (2000), 265–86. On the Red Lion, see Janet S. Loengard, 'An Elizabethan Lawsuit: John Brayne, His Carpenter, and the Building of the Red Lion Theatre', *Shakespeare Quarterly* 34 (1983), 298–310. On the social matrix for theatre in London, see Lawrence Manley, *Literature and Culture in Early Modern London* (Cambridge University Press, 1995), and Steven Mullaney, *The Place of the Stage* (University of Chicago Press, 1988).

was the place to be, and the touring companies that the reformers had initially encouraged tended to gravitate to that great City.

We can sense the gathering disquiet of the City fathers in an order promulgated by the Common Council of London in December of 1574, well before construction of the Theatre was underway. The order inveighs against 'evil practices of incontinency in great inns' occasioned by the staging of plays. The players are castigated for 'uncomely and unshamefast speeches and doings', for withdrawing the Queen's subjects from divine service on Sundays and holidays, for wasting the money of 'poor and fond persons', for giving opportunity to pickpockets and other vandals, and for creating conditions in which innocent people could be injured by the falling off of scaffolds and the use of weapons and gunpowder during performances. More serious still, perhaps, is the spectre of 'busy and seditious matters' uttered by the players. The conclusions to be drawn from this appalling spectacle are deeply religious: God's wrath is manifest in the plague that has closed down theatrical activity, so that a reopening of the theatres would only be to invite a virulent resumption of the plague. As a consequence, the Common Council orders that no innkeeper, tavernkeeper or other person is to countenance 'any play, interlude, comedy, tragedy, matter or show' which has not been first licensed by the Mayor and Court of Aldermen.[38] Plainly, the city intended to do away with such popular entertainments entirely if it could; it was prevented from doing so by influential support for the players at court and by the availability of the suburbs.

The timing of this confrontation in 1574 can hardly be coincidental. That the building of the Theatre only served to exacerbate an inflamed situation can be seen in the following excerpt from a sermon delivered at Paul's Cross in 1577 by Thomas White:

> Looke but vppon the common playes in London, and see the multitude that flocketh to them and followeth them: beholde the sumptuous Theatre houses, a continuall monument of Londons prodigalitie and folly. But I vnderstande they are nowe forbidden bycause of the plague. I like the pollicye well if it holde still, for a disease is but bodged or patched vp that is not cured in the cause, and the cause of plagues is sinne, if you look to it well: and the cause of sinne are playes: therefore the cause of plagues are playes. (1578)[39]

---

38 Reprinted, for example, in Chambers, *Elizabethan Stage*, 4:273–4, and in *Complete Works of Shakespeare*, ed. Bevington, pp. xliii–xliv.

39 *A Sermon Preached at Paul's Cross . . . in the Time of the Plague* (London, 1578). Reprinted in Chambers, *Elizabethan Stage*, 4:197, and *Works of Shakespeare*, ed. Bevington p. xliv. See also *A Sermon Preached at Paul's Cross* in the same year by John Stockwood, and John Northbrooke's *A Treatise wherein dicing, dancing, vain plays or enterludes, with other idle pastimes, etc., commonly used on the Sabbath day, are reproved by the authority of*

The next unsettling development, from the point of view of city authorities and church alike, was the discovery of the 'liberty' of Blackfriars as a playing venue for companies of boy actors. Although inside London's walls, Blackfriars (originally a monastic house on sloping ground between St Paul's and the Thames) enjoyed its own local government and was thus removed from the immediate jurisdiction of the city. Here, from 1576 to 1584, the Children of the Queen's Chapel made use of a hall to put on plays. Nominally, they were rehearsing for performance before the Queen, and indeed they did appear frequently at court, but the 'rehearsals' soon took on a life of their own. Paul's Boys availed themselves of the same useful fiction, since it gave them all a 'cover' from the wrath of the city fathers. The court position was clear: how could anyone object to rehearsals of performances intended for the Queen's benefit? Into this controversy marched John Lyly, whose *succès de scandale* with *Euphues* in 1578–9 had already made him notorious.

Lyly's meteoric rise to fame as a dramatist can hardly have pleased the more radical of the Reformers. He was soon to be justly suspected of having authored (along with Thomas Nashe) some of the pamphlet attacks on Martin Marprelate – the *nom de plume* of ultra-reforming controversialists whose excesses the established church found disquieting. He was a protégé of and personal secretary to the Earl of Oxford, a known Catholic and a despicable man in family matters. (Oxford married Lord Burghley's daughter and proceeded to make her life unbearable.) Gabriel Harvey no doubt spoke for an influential segment of London opinion when he inveighed against Lyly as, in 1589, 'a professed iester, a Hick-scorner, a scoff-maister, a playmunger, an Interluder: once the foile of Oxford, now the stale of London'.[40]

The scandalous nature of the boys' drama at the 'private' theatres in Blackfriars began with the very fact that boys were acting onstage, aping the mannerisms of their elders, poking fun at respectability, dressing up as women, and inviting irreverent laughter at anything sacred in the realm of politics, religion and morals. (In Lyly's *Galatea*, 1584–8, the two boys playing young women disguise themselves as males and proceed to fall in love with one another under this mistaken impression; at last, a sex change for one of them is

the word of God and ancient writers (London, 1577), in Chambers, *Elizabethan Stage*, 4:198–200.

40 *The Complete Works of John Lyly*, ed. R. Warwick Bond, 3 vols. (Oxford: Clarendon Press, 1902), 1:44. This is not to deny a certain 'popular element' in Lyly's plays, written as they were for well-to-do paying audiences and not simply for the court; see Kent Cartwright, *Theatre and Humanism: English Drama in the Sixteenth Century* (Cambridge University Press, 1999), pp. 167–93, reviewed by White, 'Playing Companies and the Drama of the 1580s', pp. 278–9.

required to make a happy ending possible.) The boys' best idiom, it seemed, was the satirical. Despite influential protection from the Crown and powerful aristocrats, the boys' theatre was in fact shut down during most of the 1590s for the scurrilousness of its attacks. When they were allowed to reopen in 1599, their plays assailed targets of bourgeois respectability with the pent-up fury of an animal too long kept in its cage.

Prior to that, in the 1580s, controversy was their stock in trade. Lyly's *Endymion* (early 1588) looks innocent enough in its fable of a man in love with the moon; but by reversing the emphasis of the received legend (in which the moon falls in love with a mortal) to stress instead the love of Endymion for Queen Cynthia, Lyly clearly points to the Queen of England (commonly identified with Cynthia and Diana) and invites titillating speculation as to who is meant by Endymion. Although the matter remains uncertain, a circumstantial case has been put forward (by this writer) that the portrayal of Endymion points to the Earl of Oxford. Lyly may have left the Earl's employment about the time of writing this play, but his obligations to Oxford and Burghley were still strong. To the extent that Lyly's drama portrays a young man longing for the Queen's affection but compromised by his involvement with another, more worldly woman, the situation depicts Oxford's prolonged and reckless infatuation with Catholicism. Tellus, the woman with whom Endymion is unhappily involved, bears a number of resemblances to Mary, Queen of Scots: she is jealous, a defiant rival of Cynthia, flirtatious, dangerous, conspiratorial. Courtly audiences in early 1588 could hardly have missed the pertinency of current events: with Mary recently executed, Philip II of Spain was mounting a huge invasion of England. Would English Catholics prove loyal to Elizabeth, or would they, as Philip hoped and assumed, come over to his side once the Armada invasion began? This was the burning question of the hour. The loyalty of English Catholics was on the line.

By dramatising the plight of a young man who has imprudently flirted with a seductive siren call, thus necessitating a punitive and corrective rustication in sleep (much as Oxford had suffered times of disfavour and banishment from court), *Endymion* urges reconciliation with those who, like the title character, are essentially good-hearted and loyal even if they have committed sins for which they need the Queen's forgiving kiss. Lyly necessarily adopts a tactful line, and cloaks his argument in the kind of allegory for which he had become famous – and which he used, in earlier plays like *Campaspe* and *Sappho and Phao*, both in 1584, to address similar issues of relationship between Queen Elizabeth and her subjects. Oxford's Boys had performed those earlier plays before the Queen and at Blackfriars. *Endymion* was acted by Paul's Boys in early 1588, but the Oxford connection is still vibrantly alive in that play as well. The close if troubled relationship that Lyly and Oxford enjoyed with Lord Burghley must have accentuated the worries of those who, like Gabriel Harvey, regarded Lyly as 'the minion secretary' to a dangerously influential Catholic right at the heart of Elizabeth's government.[41]

The threat to moral and religious reform represented by Christopher Marlowe is of a different and more unorthodox sort. Whatever the truth of the allegations being brought against Marlowe at the time of his death in 1593, there can be no doubt that he was regarded by many respectable Londoners as an emissary of the devil. His smouldering reputation can have done little to reassure Puritan-leaning Londoners that the theatre might still be of some avail in the building-up of the New Jerusalem, as it had been regarded in the days of mid-century. The so-called 'Baines note', brought in evidence against Marlowe and supposedly representing what Thomas Kyd and other acquaintances reported him to have said, is hearsay that would not meet rules of evidence in a court of law today, and may well have been exaggerated in an atmosphere of heightened emotions, but it is still useful to us as an index of what many Londoners evidently believed was credible. Marlowe is reported to have expressed the opinion that John the Evangelist and Christ were lovers, that Moses led his people on a wild-goose chase of forty years that any sane person could have accomplished in less than one year, that 'all they that love not tobacco and boys were fools', and so on.[42] Marlowe's untimely and violent death in a Deptford rooming house was widely viewed as an edifying illustration of God's punishment upon the wicked.[43] Surely the divine wrath that descended on one of the unregenerate in this compelling instance was promise of more destruction to come for a theatre of profanity.[44]

We do not know if some Londoners shook their heads in wonderment that *Edward II* (1593) seemed far too sympathetic towards royal homosexuality,[45]

---

41 *Endymion*, ed. David Bevington (Manchester University Press, 1996), pp. 27–35, and Bevington, 'Lyly's *Endymion* and *Midas*: The Catholic Question in England', *Comparative Drama* (a special issue on 'Drama and the English Reformation') 32 (1998), 26–46. Also published in *Reformations: Religion, Rulership, & the Sixteenth-Century Stage*, ed. Grace Tiffany (Kalamazoo, MI: Medieval Institute Publications, 1998), pp. 26–46.

42 Quoted, for example, in J. B. Steane, *Marlowe: A Critical Study* (Cambridge University Press, 1965), pp. 363–4.

43 Thomas Beard, *The Theatre of God's Judgements* (London, 1597). On the rooming house where Marlowe died, often referred to as 'a tavern', see Charles Nicholl, *The Reckoning: The Murder of Christopher Marlowe* (University of Chicago Press, 1992), pp. 17–21.

44 David Riggs, 'Marlowe's Quarrel with God', in *Marlowe, History and Sexuality: New Critical Essays on Christopher Marlowe*, ed. Paul Whitfield White (New York: AMS, 1998), pp. 15–37.

45 See Jonathan Goldberg, 'Sodomy and Society: The Case of Christopher Marlowe', in *Staging the Renaissance*, ed. David Kastan and Peter Stallybrass (New York and London: Routledge, 1991), pp. 75–82, rpt from *Southwest Review*, 69 (1984), 371–8. See also Mario DiGangi, *The Homoerotics of Early Modern Drama* (Cambridge University Press, 1997), pp. 107–15;

or if they interpreted *Doctor Faustus* (1588) as dangerously heterodox. As some modern critics have shown, *Faustus* can instead be interpreted as confirmedly orthodox, since its final chorus (in both A and B versions) asks the audience to 'regard his hellish fall, / Whose fiendful fortune may exhort the wise / Only to wonder at unlawful things'.[46] The play can be seen as orthodox even (or especially) from a Calvinist point of view, in that it delineates the downward career of a reprobate sinner to whom God's mercy is justly denied. We do know, however, that what audiences most wanted out of performances of *Faustus* was the frisson of seeing devils and conjuration onstage. The anecdote of a performance in which the actors looked around uneasily to find one more devil in their midst than the company roster could account for [47] is a tale-type, no doubt, but it does speak to audience fascination with the occult and forbidden. Similarly, the huge success of Marlowe's two *Tamburlaine* plays, the first so popular as to require a sequel (1587–8), must have rested on the heady prospects of undreamed-of social and political advancement. Tamburlaine surely struck some viewers as a bad man, ruthless, violent and Machiavellian, but he was also undeniably charismatic, and he did in fact thrive in a world where effete and corrupt monarchies offered such an easy target for unabashed *virtù*. His death, nowhere envisaged at the end of Part I, seems no more than a biological necessity at the end of Part II. The decidedly nonprovidential concept of history that holds together these gigantic and sprawling chronicles gives an unsettling view of historical events as existential and as dominated by certain compelling masters of their own fates. The genie of nonprovidential history, once let out of the bottle, was something that Puritan divines could fulminate against but scarcely restrain.

Staging added to the vibrancy of the newly existential theatre of the late 1580s and 1590s. The ruthless villains of Kyd's *The Spanish Tragedy* (?1588–94) string up Don Horatio for all the audience to behold, and then mangle his corpse: '*They hang him in the arbor . . . They stab him*' (2.4.53–5).[48] The vivid crime is all the more jarring because it follows immediately upon Horatio's torrid wooing of Bel-imperia, the savvy mistress of Horatio's recently deceased best

also, 'Marlowe, Queer Studies, and Renaissance Homoeroticism', in *Marlowe, History and Sexuality*, ed. White, pp. 195–212.

46 *Doctor Faustus: A- and B-Texts (1604, 1616)*, by Christopher Marlowe and His Collaborator and *Revisers*, ed. David Bevington and Eric Rasmussen (Manchester University Press, 1993). For a critique of the orthodox view, see Jonathan Dollimore, *Radical Tragedy: Religion, Ideology and Power in the Drama of Shakespeare and His Contemporaries*, 2nd edn (University of Chicago Press, 1989), pp. 109–19.

47 Printed in Chambers, *Elizabethan Stage*, 3:324–4.

48 Thomas Kyd, *The Spanish Tragedy*, ed. David Bevington (Manchester University Press, 1996).

friend Don Andrea. Their love duet, cast in the familiar Petrarchan metaphor of military combat, climaxes in assassination and abduction. The littering of the stage with corpses at the end of this sensational play does inflict a deserved death on Lorenzo and some lesser villains. At the same time it also claims not only the lives of innocent persons but the political and military welfare of two adjoining states. 'What age hath ever heard such monstrous deeds?' exclaims the grief-stricken Spanish King, who has done his best to seek out wrong. 'My brother, and the whole succeeding hope / That Spain expected after my decease!' (4.4.251–3). Final satisfaction is claimed only by the ghost of Don Andrea, now uncontrollably in the grip of a revengeful fury, and the allegorical figure of Revenge – who has engineered the whole plot, from his entirely pagan perspective, as a way of drawing in, frustrating, antagonising and finally gratifying both Don Andrea and the audience. As a figure of the playwright, satisfying his spectators' desire for sensation and blood, Revenge betokens a new breed of writers for the stage. The immense and continuing success of this play in revival throughout the 1590s ensured its influence on popular taste and styles of playwriting.

Shakespeare's mode of presentation is less brash than that of Kyd and Marlowe, but his use of the theatre is innovative in ways that again exploit a hunger for historical or legendary immediacy largely untrammelled by providential concerns. Siege warfare abounds in the *Henry VI* plays and *Richard III* (c. 1589–94), making vivid use of the whole theatre building. When Lord Talbot attacks the French at Orleans in Act 2 scene 1 of *1 Henry VI*, he and his forces enter onto the main stage '*with scaling-ladders*'. By these means they 'ascend' and 'mount' the walls, that is to say the wall of the tiring-house façade, at three locations, one leader in each 'corner' and one (presumably Talbot) in the centre, thereby clambering into the tiring-house at gallery level and taking the self-indulgent and drunken French by surprise. At this point, '*the French leap o'er the walls in their shirts*' – that is, jump down from the gallery to the main stage and thereby beat an undignified retreat. The Bastard and Orleans, Reignier and the other French leaders, also '*half ready and half unready*', scurry about until one of Talbot's soldiers scares them away, '*leaving their clothes behind*'.[49]

Throughout, the theatre façade represents, with visual plausibility, the walls and gates of the besieged town. Later on, in 3.2, Joan la Pucelle and four French soldiers come onstage, disguised as French peasants '*with sacks on their backs*' and obligingly telling the audience, 'These are the city gates, the gates of Rouen', thereby letting the spectators know what city they are now facing.

49 Citations are from Shakespeare, *Works*, ed. Bevington.

Once Joan has gained access to the town (i.e. entered the tiring-house through a stage door) by means of a ruse, she suddenly appears '*on the top, thrusting out a torch*' to signal her countrymen to storm the gates. Where exactly '*on the top*' signifies in architectural terms is not entirely clear, but unmistakably the whole building is being pressed into service for the duration of the conflict. '*Alarums*' and '*excursions*' call for the sound effects of war. Appearances '*on the walls*' to those standing below, as when Pucelle and her allies mock the Dukes of Bedford and Burgundy standing disconsolately on the main stage outside of the beseiged town (3.2.40.3–4), give spatial plausibility to the vertical separation between the gallery surmounting the tiring-house façade and the stage below it.[50]

Richard II's appearance '*on the walls*' of Flint Castle to negotiate with and then capitulate to the besieging forces of Bolingbroke in *Richard II* (*c*. 1595–6, 3.3.61.1–4) takes similar advantage of spatial and vertical separation to play mordantly on the theme of a Phaethon-like descent (178–82). *King John* (*c*. 1594–5) makes use of similar appearances '*upon the walls*' (2.1.200.1). *Romeo and Juliet* turns these same walls into the façade of Juliet's family's house, with her 'window' (not 'balcony') located in the gallery and the garden where Romeo hides on the stage below (2.1.2).[51] These last-named plays were very probably performed in the Theatre, where Shakespeare wrote plays and acted as a member of the Chamberlain's Men, newly formed in 1594. One cannot be sure where the *Henry VI* plays and *Richard III* were performed, but clearly the walls offered similar staging opportunities.

Although these theatrical gymnastics are not subversive in themselves, one can nevertheless feel the pull away from moral edification and towards the sheer vitality of a mimetic representation. The *Henry VI* plays are replete with moral object lessons in the horrors of civil war, and *Richard III* provides the language needed by any viewer or reader impelled to seek a providential reading of history. Even so, mimesis poses a dangerous threat to moral idealists, as Plato urged long ago in his *Republic*. Poetry and drama tell lies. And, as Stephen Gosson intently argues in his *Plays Confuted in Five Actions* (1582), drama is by far the worse of the two. 'The argument of Tragedies', he wrote, 'is wrath, crueltie, incest, injurie, murther eyther violent by sworde, or voluntary by poyson'; 'The ground work of *Commedies*, is love, cosenedge, flatterie, bawderie, slye conveighance of whoredome' (231). Even plays that 'conteine good matter' and 'may be read with profite' 'cannot be playd, without a manifest breach of Gods

50 See David Bevington, *Action Is Eloquence: Shakespeare's Language of Gesture* (Cambridge, MA: Harvard University Press, 1984), pp. 99–134, esp. 102–3.
51 *Ibid.*, pp. 104–5, 111–12.

commaundement'.[52] The physical act of performing is what is so menacing in its claim of presenting vividly a representation of what purports to be truth. Gosson, himself a lapsed playwright and no friend of Puritanism, knew whereof he spoke. His denunciations are mild compared with those that would follow from William Prynne half a century later, who insists that popular stage plays, 'the very Pompes of the Divell which we renounce in Baptisme', are 'sinfull, heathenish, lewde, ungodly Spectacles, and most pernicious Corruptions'.[53]

In view of the abundant evidence that Puritan opposition to the stage was very specifically fuelled by the building of new theatre structures in the 1570s, 1580s, and 1590s, and by the 'profane' kinds of drama that those locations were generating, we should not be surprised to find, in the 1590s, a battle in the theatre itself for the heart and soul of Londoners. Not all citizens of that great city were zealots of Prynne's stamp, after all. They had come to enjoy the-atre, and they had long enjoyed a theatre tradition that catered specifically to Reformation inclinations. At the same time, the pronouncements of the City Council plainly indicate that Londoners were uneasy, even if fascinated by the new sensationalism, violence and romantic fantasising of the drama now avail-able to them. One acting company that seems to have been intent on capturing this large segment of London's audience was the Admiral's Men at the Rose.

The hands of the Admiral's Men were not spotlessly clean, to be sure. They made a good thing out of *Tamburlaine* and *Doctor Faustus*, with Edward Alleyn in the title role of each. They took over George Peele's *The Battle of Alcazar* by 1594 and Kyd's *The Spanish Tragedy* by 1597. No doubt they launched their successful career in blood and thunder. The titles of many lost plays suggest a search for whatever might prove economically viable. On the other hand, a number of their staple items, such as Henry Porter's *The Two Angry Women of Abingdon*, Part I (*c*. 1585–9), Anthony Munday's *John a Kent and John a Cumber* (*c*. 1587–90), William Houghton's *An Englishman for My Money, or A Woman Will Have Her Will* (1598) and Thomas Dekker's *Old Fortunatus* (1599) classify as family entertainment. Dekker's *The Shoemaker's Holiday* (also in 1599), for all its gentle ribbing of mercantile opportunism and Puritan mannerism, comes across as a wry tribute to the kind of bourgeois temperament that Thomas Deloney, in the source narrative, had treated with unblushing reverence.[54] And when

---

52 Stephen Gosson, *Plays Confuted in Five Actions*, in *Markets of Bawdrie: The Dramatic Criticism of Stephen Gosson*, ed. Arthur F. Kinney, Salzburg Studies in English Literature, 4 (Salzburg, 1974), pp. 160, 177–8. Cited in Barish, *Antitheatrical Prejudice*, pp. 231, 325.
53 William Prynne, *Histriomastix* (London, 1633), title-page.
54 See David Scott Kastan, 'Workshop and/as Playhouse', *Studies in Philology* 84 (1987), 324–37; and essays by Paul S. Seaver and David Bevington on *The Shoemaker's Holiday* in *The Theatrical*

the Admiral's Men went head to head with their chief competitors, the Lord Chamberlain's Men, they were likely to opt for the side of the bourgeois and Puritan-leaning citizenry.

The story of Falstaff–Oldcastle is by now well known and pretty well agreed upon. Shakespeare seems to have written *1 Henry IV* in 1596 with 'Sir John Oldcastle' as the name for Prince Hal's disreputable comic companion, taking the name from the anonymous *Famous Victories of Henry V* (1583–8). To have done so, however, meant taking in vain the name of a revered saint of activist Protestant tradition. The historical Oldcastle had been executed in the time of Henry V for his Lollard extremism, and his death had been fashioned into a martyrdom by John Foxe and other polemicists. The chief living descendant of Oldcastle, Henry Brooke, 8th Lord Cobham, may well have taken umbrage at Shakespeare's irreverent use of the name, or Cobham's many allies may have done so. Shakespeare appears to have changed the name, and to have written 2 *Henry IV* and then *Henry V* using the name, 'Fastolfe' or 'Falstaff', of a cowardly knight who ran away from battle at the siege of Rouen – as portrayed in *1 Henry VI*, 3.2. (The change from quarto 'Brooke' to folio 'Broome' in *The Merry Wives* may have been occasioned by a similar tactful retreat.)[55]

Alleyn and his Admiral's Men did not fail to capitalise on the affront. Their *1 Sir John Oldcastle*, written by Michael Drayton, Richard Hathway, Anthony Munday and Robert Wilson for performance in 1599, assures its viewers in the Prologue that 'no pampered glutton we present, / Nor agèd counselor to youthful sins'. Instead, their Oldcastle will be one 'whose virtues shone above the rest, / A valiant martyr and a virtuous peer' (6–9). In the play itself, Oldcastle is only purportedly on the Wycliffite side championed by Lord Powis. On the crucial issue of the King's prerogative, Oldcastle is anything but a danger to the state. He believes in the exercise of conscience, and he is impatient with the mumbo-jumbo ceremonies of the traditional Roman faith, but he draws the line at seditious talk. The dramatists thus stake out a moderate

---

City: Culture, Theatre and Politics in London, 1576–1649, ed. David L. Smith, Richard Strier and David Bevington (Cambridge University Press, 1995).

55 See Stanley Wells and Gary Taylor (eds.), *William Shakespeare: A Textual Companion* (Oxford: Clarendon Press, 1987), pp. 329–32; Douglas Brooks, *From Playhouse to Printing House: Drama and Authorship in Early Modern England* (Cambridge University Press, 2000); and Peter Corbin and Douglas Sedge (eds.), *The Oldcastle Controversy: Sir John Oldcastle, Part I, and The Famous Victories of Henry V* (Manchester University Press, 1991), pp. 1–28. According to Andrew Cairncross, the name 'Brooke' was also dropped from the folio edition of *3 Henry VI*, along with the expunging in *2 Henry VI* of the passage in 1.4 in which Eleanor Cobham is implicated in a treasonous plot, perhaps also as a result of censorship relating to the Cobham/Oldcastle controversy (Cairncross, ed., *The Second Part* and *The Third Part of King Henry VI*, Arden Shakespeare, 2 (London: Methuen, 1962)).

position, calculated, it would seem, to please a broad spectrum of London spectators. Puritan-leaning reformers, the play suggests, can truly be loyal and should not be accused otherwise. Oldcastle's King (Henry V) certainly takes this view. The dictates of conscience, he urges, are to be respected, but they also demand loyalty to King and country. The correct way to achieve reform is to make grievances known to the King 'And pray amendment, not enforce the same'. He adds, 'Unless their King were tyrant' – which, of course, this King is not (xii, 21–4). Implicitly, Elizabeth deserves no less respect and love from her people.[56]

The Admiral's Men's plays by Henry Chettle and Anthony Munday on *The Downfall of Robert, Earl of Huntingdon* and *The Death of Robert* (etc.), or *1 and 2 Robin Hood*, 1598, address the theme of political exile, as does Shakespeare's *As You Like It*, presented at about the same time by the Chamberlain's Men, but with a perspective that is decidedly more impatient with the world of the court. 'A shame upon this peevish, apish age, / These crouching hypocrite dissembling times!' exclaims Lord Fitzwater (*Downfall*, sc. viii, 1050–1). In the absence of the crusading Richard Lionheart, England is in a perilous state, allowing the iniquitous Justice Warman, Prior of York, to betray Earl Robert (Robin) and lead to his being declared an outlaw. Robin is a particularly useful character for the dramatists because he is both an aristocrat and a believer in human equality. His role is like that of Duke Senior in *As You Like It*, and yet the egalitarian appeal of the Robin Hood story takes the *Huntingdon* plays considerably farther towards a new order of social levelling. 'No man must presume to call our master, / By name of Earle, Lord, Baron, Knight, or Squire, / But simply by the name of Robin Hoode', reads one of the articles of the band of brothers. Members of this society are never to wrong the poor, 'Nor spare a priest, a usurer, or a clarke' (sc. ix, 1329–31, 1355). Justice is unattainable from the incumbent regime, with Warman as the new Sheriff of Nottingham. He is a 'viper of the land', 'lust-defiled, mercilesse', a 'false prior' (sc. xii, 1738, 1743).[57] More seriously, the Earl of Leicester openly defies King John, not for rebellion's sake, but nonetheless through armed resistance in the name of Richard I, prompting John to quake in cowardly fear. Ultimately both this play and its sequel settle for the nostrum that subjects may not mend their plight with violence against the monarch (*Death*, sc. xv, 2315–16), but the martyrdom of Robin has led to popular outcry and armed rebellion against tyranny.

56 Quotations are from the edition by Corbin and Sedge cited in the previous note.
57 Anthony Munday, *The Downfall of Robert Earl of Huntingdon* and *The Death of Robert Earl of Huntingdon*, Malone Society Reprints (Oxford University Press, 1964, 1967, respectively). The latter play is normally attributed to Munday and Henry Chettle.

Look About You (*c*. 1598–1600) brings Robin back to life in a happier world: aided by Robin's 20,000 men, Henry II is crowned in a ceremony that also provides a coronet for Robin.

The less egalitarian thrust of many Chamberlain's Men's plays, especially those of Shakespeare, is not confined to their purportedly cavalier treatment of Oldcastle–Cobham. The presentation of the mob in *Julius Caesar* (1599), as in the earlier 2 *Henry VI*, for example, and in the later *Coriolanus*, is wary of any endorsement of political activism by the citizenry. This is not to argue that Shakespeare was himself a conservative, or that his plays offer a programmed resistance to religious and social reform. It is to argue that Shakespeare and his colleagues seem to have chosen not to endorse the rewriting of social history in order to bestow new prominence on a rising bourgeois class, such as one finds, for example, in *The Four Prentices of London*, acted by the Admiral's Men sometime in the 1590s. Shakespeare's *King John*, *c*. 1594–6, illustrates the point: in its lack of clear endorsement of the extreme Protestant vindication of John espoused by Foxe and other writers, it offers instead a balanced, dual view of a complex monarch as both proto-Protestant victim of Rome's machinations and as a weak, selfishly motivated ruler. *The Book of Sir Thomas More*, acted perhaps by the Chamberlain's Men *c*. 1593–1601 with revisions by Shakespeare, sympathises with London's complaints but not with the May Day uprising itself. Jonson's *Every Man Out of His Humour*, acted by the Chamberlain's Men in 1599, revels in its satirical vein of London City comedy with such acerbity that one could well imagine the play written instead for a boys' company.[58] In this respect it is notably different from Chapman's earlier and more good-natured 'humours' comedies acted by the Admiral's Men, like *The Blind Beggar of Alexandria* (1596) and *An Humorous Day's Mirth* (1597).

Appeals to dreams of social and religious reordering did their work for a time. The great commercial success of the London theatre in the 1590s surely rested on the ability of playwrights and acting companies to avoid alienating the sensitivities of their audiences. The closing of the boys' companies during almost all of this decade must have helped. Yet the satirical thrust of a more court-oriented drama was always there, ready to reassert itself as it did in 1599 and subsequent years. The targets of the reemergent boys' drama were unabashedly urban: foolish cuckolded husbands and shopkeepers, their randy wives and hypocrites of all stripes, especially of a Puritan persuasion. The adult acting companies jumped on this bandwagon too, as they saw London bourgeois audiences turning away from City comedy in distaste. Shakespeare's

58 Bevington, *Tudor Drama and Politics*, pp. 230–59.

company, having hedged its bets by acquiring Blackfriars in 1596, reclaimed the use of that building from the Children of the Chapel (the Children of the Queen's Revels in 1604 and afterwards) for their own use in 1608 and increasingly used it as a winter playhouse for their own productions. No doubt the extremists among the Reformers did their part to goad the acting companies into satirical venom. Wrong belongs to both sides, as is normally the case when extremes make a middle position untenable.

The wonder is not that London citizens abandoned the theatre when they did but that the drama's version of a Great Compromise worked for so long. Indeed, as Martin Butler, Jerzy Limon and Margot Heinemann have argued, 'puritan-oriented' plays persisted on into the 1620s and even 1630s in such works as Middleton and Rowley's A *Game at Chess* (1624).[59] The incredible flourishing of attendance at plays during the 1580s and 1590s, and on briefly into the next century, owed much to the inclusive and generous vision of men like Dekker and Shakespeare. But the Jonsons and Marstons of this competitive world were sure to prevail, unknowingly aided and abetted as they were by the extreme opposition. We can perhaps hear Shakespeare worrying about the social and artistic consequences of unleashed satire in the amiable but edgy debate of Duke Senior and Jaques in *As You Like It*, 2.7, with Duke Senior taking the view that satirists are too likely to be motivated by spleen and Jaques insisting to the contrary that satire must say what it has to say.

One wry view of the impasse with which to end this chapter is to be found in the *Parnassus* plays, acted at St John's College, Cambridge, between 1599 and 1603. The witty, circumstantial satire of these three plays (*The Pilgrimage to Parnassus* and *The Return from Parnassus* in two parts) attests at once to the enormous vitality of the City theatres and to an anxious anticipation of decline. The social conditions deplored in this student-oriented drama are those that concerned Sir Francis Bacon in his essay 'Of Seditions and Troubles': 'the multiplying of nobility and other degrees of quality, in an over-proportion to the common people', 'an overgrown clergy' who 'bring nothing to the stock', and the unemployment of bright young men that results 'when more are bred scholars than preferments can take off'.[60] At the university, in the *Parnassus* plays, the students seem to run into little else than strait-laced Puritanism and

59 Martin Butler, *Theatre and Crisis, 1632–1642* (Cambridge University Press, 1984), pp. 84–99; Jerzy Limon, *Dangerous Matter: English Drama and Politics in 1623/24* (Cambridge University Press, 1986); Margot Heinemann, *Puritanism and Theatre: Thomas Middleton and Opposition Drama under the Early Stuarts* (Cambridge University Press, 1980). See also Martin Butler's chapter in this present volume.
60 Francis Bacon, 'Of Seditions and Troubles', in *Francis Bacon*, ed. Brian Vickers (Oxford University Press, 1996), pp. 366–71, esp. 368.

empty scholasticism. When they come to London in search of opportunities, they encounter ungenerous patrons, vituperative lawyers and quack doctors, obliging them finally to try out for some role in the burgeoning London theatre. Richard Burbage and Will Kemp put them through their paces, commenting the while on the musty academism of much university writing and boasting of 'our fellow *Shakespeare*' who 'puts them all downe' (*Return*, Part II, 4.3).[61] Driven to the expedient of writing satirical plays for the boys' companies, Ingenioso and his fellows find themselves in trouble with the law. Nothing will do, finally, but to beat a hasty retreat, either to the cloistered precincts of the university once more or to a shepherd's life in Kent, where the students can perhaps hope to live out their days in alienated poverty. Drama of the Renaissance, once a bright hope of the Reformers, has become commercialised and satirical to the extent that thoughtful intellectual observers are ready to give it up for lost. So too, increasingly, would London popular audiences. The Reformers, who had done so much to give birth to this great drama in the mid sixteenth century, were now prepared to close its doors. The greatest drama in the history of England would soon give way to the only prolonged period in which the public performance of all drama was officially forbidden.[62]

61 *The Three Parnassus Plays (1598–1601)*, ed. J. B. Leishman (London: Nicholson & Watson, 1949).
62 See the section on 1642–60 in this present volume, especially Chapter 19.

4

THE EARLIER STUART ERA

Chapter 15

LITERATURE AND NATIONAL
IDENTITY

JOHANN P. SOMMERVILLE

In 1603, the Scottish King James VI inherited the throne of England. The following year, he issued a proclamation, changing his title from 'King of England and Scotland' to 'King of Great Britain'.[1] James wanted to unite more than just the crowns of the two kingdoms. His ultimate goal was to create 'a united British nation'.[2] He introduced a new gold coin, called the 'unite' (unit), which featured an inscription declaring 'I will make them one nation.'[3] The English and Scots, he argued, were currently 'two nations', but both inhabited 'one Ile of *Britaine*', and they were 'alreadie ioyned in vnitie of Religion and language'. In time, he hoped, the two nations would become one.[4] The ultimate political allegiance of all his subjects – English, Scots, Welsh and Irish – was to himself.[5] It made sense for countries that were already united by their political and religious loyalties, and by geography and language, to enter into still closer union. Writing in favour of the Union, the Scotsman Robert Pont found it remarkable that his countrymen and the English had so long been mortal enemies. In times past, he argued, God had 'armed these nations with mallice and hatred one against another' in punishment of their popish idolatry. Since the Reformation, however, God had changed his attitude towards the two peoples, and if they refrained from angering him by sinning too seriously, it was now possible for them to live together as 'one commonwealth ... in a lovelie and perpetuall peace'. Peace, he declared,

---

1 James F. Larkin and Paul L. Hughes (eds.), *Stuart Royal Proclamations. Volume I. Royal Proclamations of King James I 1603–1625* (Oxford: Clarendon Press, 1973), pp. 94–8.
2 *The Jacobean Union. Six Tracts of 1604*, ed. Bruce R. Galloway and Brian P. Levack, Scottish History Society, 4th ser., 21 (Edinburgh: C. Constable, 1985), p. ix.
3 Stephen Mitchell and Brian Reeds (eds.), *Standard Catalogue of British Coins. Coins of England and the United Kingdom*, 22nd edn (London: Seaby, 1986), pp. 158, 310. The coin reads 'Faciam eos in gentem unam.' This is a Latin rendition of Ezekiel 37:22, which is translated in the King James or Authorised Version as 'I will make them one nation.'
4 King James VI and I, *Basilicon Doron*, in *Political Writings*, ed. Johann P. Sommerville (Cambridge University Press, 1994), p. 59.
5 James VI and I, Speech to Parliament of 31 March 1607, in *Political Writings*, p. 169.

'under one king, one law, one religion and fayth shal be the true happines of Brittaine'.[6]

Both England and Scotland were Protestant countries. But bishops held much greater power in the English than in the Scottish church. Again, the English had retained a number of religious ceremonies which the Scots had abolished. James made some efforts to bring the Scottish church into line with the English, and his son Charles pursued the same policy with greater vigour. In 1637, the King in company with William Laud, Archbishop of Canterbury, introduced a new Prayer Book in Scotland. James had hoped that the Scots and the English would in time come to see themselves as a single British nation. The hope bore little fruit in his own lifetime, or that of his son. The Scots disliked the Prayer Book partly because they thought it was popish, but also because they believed it had been illegally foisted on them by the English. Rioting broke out in Edinburgh. In 1638 the Scots subscribed to a National Covenant, undertaking to defend 'the true reformed religion' and the 'liberties, and laws of the kingdom'.[7] War between Charles and the Scots resulted, and in 1640 the Scots won. Charles was compelled to call an English Parliament. It soon attacked his recent policies, on the grounds that they had violated the liberties and established religion of England. In 1641, the Irish rose in revolt against Charles, and in the following year the English Parliament went to war with him. In each of the three kingdoms, Charles faced resistance because many felt that he (or his wicked advisers) had transgressed their nation's rights and religion. James wanted a united British nation, in which his subjects' primary political allegiance would be to the King. By 1642, however, many people in each of the three kingdoms were placing their particular country before their King, and before Britain. In each, too, national identity was closely linked to religious self-perceptions.[8] This chapter traces the interplay of these themes – national identity and religious and political allegiances – in the literature of the years between the accession of James I and the outbreak of the English Civil War.

The first section considers Jacobean debates on the Union, and on national identity more generally. The second focuses on notions of allegiance to the Crown, and particularly on the debate over the Oath of Allegiance of 1606 – a debate to which the King himself contributed, as did John Donne, Lancelot

---

6 Robert Pont, 'Of the Union of Britayne', in *The Jacobean Union*, ed. Galloway and Levack, pp. 1–38, at pp. 26–7, 16.

7 Samuel R. Gardiner, *History of England from the Accession of James I to the Outbreak of the Civil War 1603–1642*, 10 vols. (London: Longmans, Green and Co., 1883–4), 8:311 (popish and English), 314–21 (rioting), 331 (National Covenant).

8 For discussion of this intersection during the Civil War period see Chapters 21 and 22 in this volume.

Andrewes and many other divines and gentlemen. James and his son held high-flown views on royal authority, but not all of their subjects shared such attitudes. The third section discusses English writers who rejected the King's opinions on royal power, and argued that English subjects enjoy traditional ancient liberties, which the monarch is bound to respect. The next section treats Scottish works on nationhood, and the equation of Scottishness with anti-popery and limited monarchy. While the English and the Scots identified their nation with Protestantism, in Ireland national feelings commonly fused with Catholicism. The fifth and final section analyses writings on nationhood by the Irish, and by English settlers in Ireland. The present chapter argues chiefly that a strong sense of nationhood was a major theme in the literature of all three of the kingdoms which James and Charles tried to rule. National allegiances were often in tension with allegiance to the Crown, despite the Kings' efforts to identify the nation with themselves. Such claims might not seem contentious to students of literature. The pioneering work of Richard Helgerson has demonstrated the importance of nationhood in English writing under Elizabeth, before the Stuarts succeeded.[9] Scholars in other disciplines, however, are often sceptical that nationhood mattered much in pre-industrial times.

Nationhood and the Union

Sociologists and political scientists often assert that nationalism is a modern phenomenon, dating only to the French and Industrial Revolutions. But Claire McEachern has convincingly argued that the English developed a strong sense of nationhood before the end of the sixteenth century, and Liah Greenfeld has gone as far as to claim that the early modern English were the first nation.[10] It is easy to think of passages in the writings of Shakespeare or others which sound nationalistic, or at least patriotic. Henry V's famous speech before Agincourt springs to mind, as do his words to the troops at Harfleur, ending with the rousing cry "'God for Harry, England, and Saint George'".[11] Of course, this is a call to fight for the *King* as well as the country. Proponents of the idea that

9 Richard Helgerson, *Forms of Nationhood: The Elizabethan Writing of England* (University of Chicago Press, 1992).
10 Claire McEachern, *The Poetics of English Nationhood, 1590–1612* (Cambridge University Press, 1996), esp. pp. 5–6. Liah Greenfeld, *Nationalism: Five Roads to Modernity* (Cambridge, MA: Harvard University Press, 1992). Amongst the works which develop the thesis that nationalism began only in the late eighteenth and nineteenth centuries are Benedict Anderson, *Imagined Communities: Reflections on the Origin and Spread of Nationalism*, rev. edn (New York: Verso, 1991); Ernest Gellner, *Nations and Nationalism* (Oxford: Blackwell, 1983); Gellner, *Nationalism* (New York University Press, 1997); Eric Hobsbawm, *Nations and Nationalism since 1789* (Cambridge University Press, 1991).
11 William Shakespeare, *Henry V*, 4.3.18–67 (Agincourt), 3.1.1–34 (Harfleur).

nationalism is a modern invention argue that before the eighteenth century people conceived of their political loyalties in *dynastic* rather than national terms. They focused their feelings of loyalty on a King, so the argument goes, or on a dynasty, which was often seen as mystically endowed with some sort of divine power. Only when the 'dynastic realm' and 'sacral monarchy' declined in the eighteenth century could nationalism arise.[12]

If the loyalties of James I's subjects had been solely to his person or dynasty, and not in any sense to their nations, it is difficult to see how he could have encountered such serious problems in his attempts to unite England and Scotland. In fact, the English and Scots saw themselves as two separate nations, and many people in both countries came to believe that their nation would not benefit from the Union. The Scot Sir Thomas Craig was at first an enthusiastic advocate of a full union, but like many of his countrymen he feared that it might eventually subordinate his land to its more powerful southern neighbour. In 1605 he wrote a treatise supporting Union but urging that 'each nation be governed in accordance with its own laws and customs'. Earlier, he penned a lengthy rebuttal of the thesis that Scottish kings had in times past acknowledged their subordination to the English monarchy.[13] The Scots had good grounds for suspecting that Union might cost them their independence, for in the English House of Commons much was said of Scotland's poverty and inferiority, and members who rejected other forms of union were willing to countenance the straightforward incorporation of the northern kingdom into England.[14] Sir Francis Bacon insisted that, as the lesser kingdom, Scotland should be subordinated to England if union were to be workable.[15] Arguably, Shakespeare had this sort of incorporative union in mind in *Henry V*, for there the Scots, Welsh and Irish fight for England, not for a Britain in which they are all equal partners.[16] Arguably, too, the play also foreshadowed the difficulties of bringing this kind of union into being.[17]

---

12 Gerald Newman, *The Rise of English Nationalism: A Cultural History 1740–1830* (New York: St Martin's Press, 1987), p. 53. Anderson, *Imagined Communities*, pp. 19, 21, 36.

13 Sir Thomas Craig, *De Unione Regnorum Britanniae Tractatus*, ed. with a translation by C. Sanford Terry, Publications of the Scottish History Society, 60 (Edinburgh: T. & A. Constable, 1909), p. 465. His Latin manuscript treatise *De Hominio* was published in an English translation by George Ridpath as *Scotland's Soveraignty Asserted* (London, 1695).

14 *The Jacobean Union*, ed. Galloway and Levack, pp. xxii, xxv, xxxvi; Brian P. Levack, *The Formation of the British State: England, Scotland, and the Union 1603–1707* (Oxford: Clarendon Press, 1987), pp. 34, 41.

15 Sir Francis Bacon, 'A Brief Discourse, Of the Happy Union of the Kingdomes of England and Scotland', in Bacon, *Resuscitatio* (London, 1671), first pagination, pp. 153–9, at p. 159.

16 Jonathan Dollimore and Alan Sinfield, 'History and Ideology: the Instance of *Henry V*', in *Alternative Shakespeares*, ed. John Drakakis (London: Methuen, 1985), pp. 206–27, at p. 217.

17 McEachern, *The Poetics of English Nationhood*, p. 138.

The English also had things to fear from union with the Scots. Sir Henry Spelman expressed many views typical of English opinion in his manuscript treatise 'Of the Union'. He doubted that economic union would bring his country significant advantages, for 'in trafficque Scotland hath neede of England but not England of Scotlande'. Scotland supplied few commodities that the English needed. Union was, indeed, likely to bring poor Scots south of the border in search of wealth, but England was already 'overladen with multitudes of people'. The English ought to look after their own people before they gave 'entertainment to strangers'. Spelman had no doubt whatsoever that the Scots and the English were two separate nations, and that each should pursue its own goals. The Scots as well as the English ought to oppose the union, for it would tempt Scottish nobles and gentry south of the border, and they would benefit Scotland much more if they stayed at home. Spelman argued that 'what devideth all the nations of the worlde one from another' is 'difference of lawes, manners and language', claiming that the Scots were closer to the French than the English in their laws, and to the Irish in their manners and language. They were different nations and should remain so.[18] Writers who favoured the Union admitted that the Scots and the English were separate nations, but argued that they were close enough in laws, manners and language – and religion, location and climate – for it to make sense to unite them.[19]

Authors gave varying stresses to the components of nationhood, but all accepted its existence, and importance. It was widely agreed that people across the globe normally live in nations. Bacon's *New Atlantis* was a highly influential description of a scientifically advanced utopia in the remote south Pacific. When English sailors first arrive there, they almost at once assume that the inhabitants constitute a nation, though they have seen little of them. Bacon took it for granted that the world was divided up into nations or countries, using the two terms interchangeably.[20] 'All Nations love their owne Countrey best', said Thomas Gainsford, and as an Englishman he wrote at length in

---

18 Sir Henry Spelman, 'Of the Union', in *The Jacobean Union*, ed. Galloway and Levack, pp. 161–84, at p. 162 ('trafficque') p. 174 (multitudes), p. 175 (strangers), p. 179 (Scottish nobles), p. 180 (nations).
19 Sir Henry Savile, 'Historicall Collections', in *The Jacobean Union*, ed. Galloway and Levack, pp. 185–239, at pp. 213–15; Sir John Hayward, *A Treatise of Vnion of the two Realmes of England and Scotland* (London, 1604), p. 31. The Scot John Russell argued in the same way in 'A Treatise of the Happie and Blissed Unioun', in *The Jacobean Union*, ed. Galloway and Levack, pp. 75–142, at p. 78. Bacon, 'A Brief Discourse, Of the Happy Union of the Kingdomes of England and Scotland', in *Resuscitatio*, p. 155, observed that there was not sufficient linguistic diversity, nor large enough mountains or rivers, to keep the two kingdoms divided.
20 Bacon, *New Atlantis*, in *Francis Bacon*, ed. Brian Vickers (Oxford University Press, 1996), pp. 457–89, at pp. 462–3, 466–7.

favour of the notion that 'England commeth neerest the patterne of a happie Countrey, before others.' Gainsford rightly supposed that there would be little controversy about this thesis among his compatriots.[21] English travel writers commonly compared overseas lands with England, to the latter's advantage – though they argued that the English could learn from foreigners, and that there were important ways in which they could improve their institutions. Gainsford himself criticised a number of practices, including the hanging of poor thieves who stole out of necessity.[22] The cleric William Biddulph argued that all 'other nations, both heathen and Christian, go before us . . . in reverencing and providing for clergymen', but nevertheless declared that 'God hath blessed our country above others.'[23] Writing in 1638, the merchant William Bruton described the inhabitants of Bengal as 'Barbarous and Idolatrous people' but praised their love of truth, severity against perjurers, ingenuity and industriousness.[24] Differences in national characteristics were attributed to religion, climate and custom, but rarely to race. If you were pure in religion, it was claimed, God was likely to pour blessings upon you. The fact that the English had the true religion was therefore closely linked to their wider good fortune.

The English, so it was commonly said, were freer than other peoples. William Davies, a barber-surgeon who travelled extensively in America, Africa and Asia, invited the English reader to be thankful to God 'for electing him above all other nations of the earth, to the true and perfect knowledge of his blessed Gospel, but also for preserving him so long from so many miseries and wretched thraldoms whereunto most nations of the earth are subject'.[25] English women, Biddulph typically remarked, enjoyed great freedom, and ought to 'learn to love their husbands, when they shall read in what slavery women live in other countries'.[26] Larger liberties enjoyed by the English, it was said, resulted in greater national prosperity. 'The Husbandmen', declared Gainsford, 'are happier in England then in other nations', since their lords held less power over them than in other countries. Merchants were also well off and 'our *England* is

---

21 Thomas Gainsford, *The Glory of England, or a true description of many excellent prerogatives and remarkeable blessings, whereby she triumpheth over all the nations of the world* (London, 1618), sigs. π 4a, π 8a.

22 Gainsford, 'Observations of State and Millitary Affaires for the most parte collected out of Cornelius Tacitus', Huntington Library, MS Ellesmere 6857, p. 10.

23 William Biddulph, *The travels of certaine Englishmen into Africa, Asia, Troy, Bythinia, Thracia, and to the Blacke Sea* (London, 1609), p. 62, sig. A2a.

24 William Bruton, *Newes from the East-Indies: Or, A Voyage to Bengalla* (London, 1638), pp. 33–4.

25 William Davies, *A true relation of the travailes and captivitie of William Davies, Barber-Surgion of London, under the Duke of Florence* (London, 1614), sig. E4a–b.

26 Biddulph, *Travels*, sig. A2a.

the shop of the world, and *London* the *Magazin* of natures dainties'. As a result of their wealth, the English had proper food to eat. Spaniards might brag of their 'sallets, fruits, and herbs' but Gainsford recalled

> Sr *Roger Williams* answer to an idle *Spanyard*, boasting of his countries citrons, orenges, olives, and such like: I, but (sayd he) in *England* we have dainty veale, and well fed capons to eat with this sawce, and many delicate dishes worthy the name of sustenance indeede. For God made the beasts of the earth to live on the grasse and fruits of the same; but man to live upon them, and command all.[27]

The English, so it was commonly supposed, fed well on roast beef, and wore leather shoes on their feet, while foreigners wore wooden clogs, and dined on bread and vegetables. Such attitudes were sometimes linked to a potent and persuasive political theory connecting English prosperity with limited royal power, and foreign poverty with absolutism. We shall return to this theory in due course.

There was, then, a well-defined sense of English nationhood in the early seventeenth century. James I hoped to create a *British* nation, but was largely – though not wholly – unsuccessful. There were three main contexts in which the idea of Britishness developed. Firstly, in the Ulster Plantation, the Scots and English settlers were sometimes collectively described as 'British', though even there the English tended to regard the Scots as inferiors and to use them as a shield against the Irish.[28] Secondly, the sugar islands of the Caribbean were called the British rather than the English West Indies, and attracted a substantial number of Scottish and Irish as well as English immigrants (and Cromwell sent many Scots and Irish there against their wills). In the later seventeenth century, there was much Irish and Scottish emigration to the middle Atlantic colonies, and there too the settlers were called 'British', though all enjoyed English legal rights.[29] Philip Vincent spoke in 1638 of the 'British Ilanders' who had settled in New England, and detected 'a facultie that God hath given' them 'to beget and bring forth more children, than any other nation of the world'. He had proof of the prowess of the British in this regard from Dutch people, who told him that women in the Netherlands had been having more children ever since 'the English and Scotch frequented their warres and married with

27 Gainsford, *The glory of England*, pp. 251, 304, 233.
28 M. Perceval-Maxwell, *The Outbreak of the Irish Rebellion of 1641* (Montreal: McGill-Queen's University Press, 1994), p. 7. Nicholas Canny, 'The Origins of Empire: An Introduction', in Nicholas Canny and Alaine Low (eds.), *The Oxford History of the British Empire. Volume 1. The Origins of Empire. British Overseas Enterprise to the Close of the Seventeenth Century* (Oxford University Press, 1998), pp. 1–33, at pp. 12–13.
29 Canny, 'The Origins of Empire', pp. 23–4.

them'.[30] Wars abroad were a third context in which a sense of Britishness arose. Many English, Scots and Irish fought alongside each other as volunteers or mercenaries in the Thirty Years' War and other continental conflicts. The author of *Tom Tell Troath* – a scathing attack on royal policies of the early 1620s – argued that the best means by which the King could truly unite the English and Scots was to drop his pacific policies and lead both of these 'two nations' into religious war in Europe. There, 'one victory obtained by the joint valour of English and Scots will more indelibly Christen your Majesties Empire greate Brittaine, then any acte of Parliament or artifice of State'.[31]

The commonest usage of the term 'British' predated James's efforts at union, for the word had long been employed to describe the pre-Roman Celtic inhabitants of the island, and their descendants, especially the Welsh. Wales was divided from England by language, since the vast majority of the Welsh spoke Welsh. But their national awareness did not lead them to take political action to secure their independence. The only talk of a Welsh parliament occurred in anti-Welsh satires like the pseudonymous Morgan Loyd's *Newes from Wales, or the Pritish Parliament* of 1642.[32] In the sixteenth century, the Welsh prided themselves on the Welsh ancestry of the Tudors, whom they saw as reviving an ancient British monarchy.[33] They developed 'an ideology of "British" unity based on loyalty to the monarchy and the Protestant cause'.[34] The thesis that Britain had at first been a united kingdom drew inspiration from the twelfth-century writings of Geoffrey of Monmouth, who recorded that the kingdom of Britain had been founded by Brutus, great-grandson of Aeneas. On Brutus' death, his three sons divided the kingdom, but it was soon reunited, and later kings of Britain included Leir and Arthur. In the 1540s, when the English hoped to take over Scotland by arms and matrimonial diplomacy, the story of Brutus was pressed into ideological service.[35] The proclamation changing James I's title to King of Great Britain spoke of the 'blessed Union, or rather

---

30 Philip Vincent, *A True Relation of the Late Battell fought in New England, between the English, and the Pequet Salvages* (London, 1638), sig. D2a.

31 *Tom Tell-Troath or a free discourse touching the manners of the tyme* (no place or date), p. 28.

32 Philip Jenkins, 'Seventeenth-century Wales: Definition and Identity', in *British Consciousness and Identity. The Making of Britain, 1533–1707*, ed. Brendan Bradshaw and Peter Roberts (Cambridge University Press, 1998), pp. 213–35, at p. 215n7. Another example is *The Welch-mens Prave Resolution: In Defence of Her King, Her Pritish Parliament, and Her Country, against te malignant party* (London, 1642).

33 Brendan Bradshaw, 'The English Reformation and Identity Formation in Wales and Ireland', in *British Consciousness*, ed. Bradshaw and Roberts, pp. 43–111, at p. 74.

34 Jenkins, 'Seventeenth-century Wales', p. 216.

35 Roger A. Mason, 'Scotching the Brut: Politics, History and National Myth in Sixteenth-century Britain', in Roger A. Mason (ed.), *Scotland and England, 1286–1815* (Edinburgh: J. Donald, 1987), pp. 60–84.

Reuniting' of the two kingdoms, and James himself briefly referred to the legend of Brutus in his book of advice for his son, *Basilicon Doron*.[36] However, educated opinion was turning sharply against the story in the sixteenth and early seventeenth centuries. Camden, in his extremely influential *Britannia*, was polite but unconvinced.[37] Sir Philip Sidney and his friend Hubert Languet scoffed at the tale, and Edmund Spenser was sceptical (though in *The Faerie Queene* he exploited it for his own poetic and political purposes).[38] Annotating Michael Drayton's *Poly-Olbion* of 1612, the great scholar John Selden noted that the legend still had a vogue amongst the Welsh, but he himself rejected it.[39] So too did many Scots and Irish, who regarded it as a cloak for English imperialist ambitions.[40]

Between 1603 and 1605, some twenty-eight tracts were written on the Anglo-Scottish Union.[41] A far larger body of literature arose from the pan-European debate over the Oath of Allegiance, enacted by the English Parliament in 1606 as part of new anti-Catholic legislation.[42] The Oath rejected papal claims to be able to depose temporal rulers. People who twice refused to swear it could be imprisoned indefinitely, and forfeit their goods to the Crown. The Pope forbade Catholics to take it, and the eminent Italian Cardinal Bellarmine wrote against it. Soon, James I penned a defence of the Oath. This book came out anonymously early in 1608 under the title *Triplici Nodo, Triplex Cuneus, or an Apologie for the Oath of Allegiance*. It was attacked by a number of English and continental Catholics. James's supporters counterattacked. The debate on the Oath of Allegiance is a good place to begin a discussion of the question of allegiance in general, and of absolutism.

36 Larkin and Hughes (eds.), *Stuart Royal Proclamations*, 1:95. King James VI and I, *Basilicon Doron*, in *Political Writings*, p. 42.
37 William Camden, *Britain, Or a chorographicall description of the most flourishing Kingdomes, England, Scotland, and Ireland*, trans. Philemon Holland (London, 1610), pp. 5–8, 154–5.
38 W. A. Bradley (ed.), *The Correspondence of Philip Sidney and Hubert Languet* (Boston: Merrymount Press, 1912), pp. 36–7. Edmund Spenser, *A View of the State of Ireland*, ed. Andrew Hadfield and Willy Maley (Oxford: Blackwell, 1997), p. 44.
39 Michael Drayton, *Poly-Olbion* (London, 1612), sig. A2a. Welsh uses of the story of Brutus and his descendants are discussed in Peter Roberts, 'Tudor Wales, National Identity and the British Inheritance', in *British Consciousness*, ed. Bradshaw and Roberts, pp. 8–42, at pp. 15–24. The legend is discussed in the context of changing attitudes towards early British history in T. D. Kendrick, *British Antiquity* (London: Methuen, 1950).
40 Colin Kidd, 'Protestantism, Constitutionalism, and British Identity under the Later Stuarts', in *British Consciousness*, ed. Bradshaw and Roberts, pp. 321–42, at p. 322.
41 *The Jacobean Union*, ed. Galloway and Levack, p. xxviii. Their edition prints six of them, and at pp. 241–9 gives bibliographical details of the other twenty-two.
42 Much relevant material is listed in Peter Milward, *Religious Controversies of the Jacobean Age* (London: Scolar Press, 1978), and in James VI and I, *The Political Works of James I*, ed. Charles Howard McIlwain (Cambridge, MA: Harvard University Press, 1918), pp. xcv–cxi.

Allegiance and absolutism

We tend to see the English Catholics around 1600 as a persecuted minority, oppressed by a bigoted and authoritarian government. One highly influential account of John Donne's writings stresses the extent to which he was wracked by feelings of guilt at having betrayed the Catholic faith into which he was born, and suggests that Donne's especial dislike of Jesuits may be related to the emotional hold which these 'stern devoted men' of 'unswerving probity' had over 'his mother's love and allegiance'.[43] However, there is no evidence that Donne saw his departure from the Catholic Church as in any sense a betrayal or apostasy, and he insisted that his decision to abandon his old faith was taken with the greatest deliberation, and only after he had thoroughly examined the questions at issue.[44] On the other hand, there were very good reasons why many people of Donne's generation felt suspicious and fearful of Catholics, and doubted that Jesuits were men of unswerving probity. Robert Parsons, the leader of the English Jesuits on the continent, lobbied for a Spanish invasion of England, to be followed by the rigid suppression of any religion but Catholicism. In 1605, a group of Catholic gentlemen plotted to blow up the King and both Houses of Parliament. The leader of the Jesuits in England, Henry Garnet, knew of the conspiracy, but did nothing to inform the government. He also penned a defence of the practice of equivocation or mental reservation, which looked to many people like lying. It was the discovery of the Gunpowder Plot that led to the enactment of the Oath of Allegiance. In the debate on the Oath, Parsons and like-minded Catholics asserted that the Pope was empowered to discipline all Christian rulers – Protestants as well as Catholics – by means that included deposing them. That is to say, if the Pope judged it appropriate he could deprive a king (or any kind of government) of political authority. If this happened, the king would cease to be a king and become a usurper, who could be removed by anyone.

The Catholic case in favour of the papal deposing power rested on the contentions that God has established two distinct forms of government in the world, one temporal and the other spiritual, and that the spiritual is superior to the temporal. Our immortal souls, they claimed, are more important than our perishable bodies; and the Pope, as custodian of our souls, is therefore superior to secular rulers, whose concern is only with our material welfare here on earth.

43 John Carey, *John Donne. Life, Mind and Art*, new ed. (London: Faber and Faber, 1990), esp. pp. 1–45 (guilt), p. 7 (mother and Jesuits).
44 John Donne, *Pseudo-Martyr*, ed. Anthony Raspa (Montreal and Kingston: McGill-Queen's University Press, 1993), p. 13.

Though the Pope's power is essentially spiritual, he can use temporal means to enforce his commands if he sees fit. Supporters of the papalist position typically argued that temporal power in any state belonged originally to the whole people, or at least to adult male heads of households. For their own convenience, the people might decide to grant authority to a king or other ruler, and when they did this they could impose contractual obligations upon him. If he misruled or failed to fulfil his obligations, the people could call him to account. By contrast, the Pope drew his power from God alone, for Christ had personally authorised him when he said 'Thou art Peter, and upon this rock I will build my church' (Matthew 16:18).[45] Jesuits and other papalists granted the Pope supreme power over the Christian world in temporal as well as spiritual matters. It was therefore not unreasonable for the dramatist Thomas Middleton to allege, in his lively political satire *A Game at Chess*, that the Jesuits aimed at 'universal monarchy', and that their doctrines drew people from their political allegiances.[46]

James and his supporters in the controversy over the Oath of Allegiance answered the Catholic argument by denying that churchmen, including the Pope, have any authority to use temporal punishments. Clerics, they said, could preach and administer the sacraments, and they could discipline sinners by cutting them off from the church through the penalty of excommunication. But no cleric had the right to overrule temporal sovereigns in secular questions, nor to deprive them of authority, nor to incite their subjects to violence against them. Catholics who acknowledged that the Pope did have such rights were nearly traitors, and deserved to be punished. The King's supporters also standardly rejected the claim that rulers derive their power from the people, arguing instead that they draw their authority from God alone. Everyone – Catholics and Protestants – believed that political power came from God, and the Bible seemed to provide incontrovertible evidence of this, for St Paul stated that 'The powers that be are ordained of God' (Romans 13:1). To say that rulers get their power *directly* from God was to deny that it stemmed from the people; it was not at all to suggest that God somehow came down on the clouds in person to present James with a crown. Writers frequently insisted that they did not ground political authority in any supernatural actions by God. Everyone agreed that societies and states arise *naturally*, not supernaturally. God, it was

45 The points made in this and the next few paragraphs are more fully developed in J. P. Sommerville, *Royalists and Patriots. Politics and Ideology in England 1603–1640* (London: Longman, 1999).
46 Thomas Middleton, *A Game at Chess*, 1.150–1, 242–3, 324–5, in *Women beware Women and other plays*, ed. Richard Dutton (Oxford University Press, 1999), pp. 244, 249, 252.

said, designed human nature, humans naturally lived in societies, and societies required governments. In this sense, God was the author of government – as St Paul said. There was nothing very mystical or pre-modern about these views, and they were perfectly compatible with a strong sense of nationhood.

James's supporters admitted that on occasion kings in the past had been elected by their subjects. However, they argued that elective monarchy was not the original form of government, and that typically elections had involved no transfer of power from the people to the king, but only the naming of the person of the ruler, whose title thus came from his subjects, though his power stemmed from God. As Donne's friend and patron Bishop Thomas Morton put it, 'the title unto an authority is not without the meanes of man, but the authority it selfe is immediately from God'.[47] Donne himself remarked that if a company of savages agreed 'to a civill maner of living', 'Magistracie, & Superioritie, would necessarily, and naturally, and Divinely grow out of this consent'. Whatever the form of government, the powers of the governors would be derived directly from God, not from the people: 'And into what maner and forme soever they had digested and concocted this Magistracie, yet the power it-selfe was *Immediately* from God'.[48] Since kings and other rulers got their authority from God alone, it followed that only He could call them to account. The people could not take up arms against their monarch, even if the Pope invited them to do so by deposing the ruler – as Pius V had deposed Elizabeth in 1570. During the 1580s and 1590s, France was ravaged by a civil war, fought against King Henri IV by the Catholic League. Three main principles of the League were that kings get their power from the people, that Catholic subjects can resist a king who tolerates heretics, and that the Pope can depose heretical rulers. A leading purpose of the political writings of Donne, James and their allies was to combat such ideas, and so to prevent a war of religion from breaking out in England.

The Catholic opponents of the Oath of Allegiance said that kings got their powers from the people. James's adherents took issue with this claim on Biblical and historical as well as theoretical grounds. In 1606 the English clergy endorsed canons which were largely aimed at combating Catholic political ideas. They rejected the thesis that power had originally inhered in the people, observing that this conflicted with Biblical evidence. For the Old Testament recorded that in the earliest times Adam and then 'the rest of the patriarchs and chief fathers successively before the flood' held power over their offspring. In those days, the canons concluded, fatherly and royal power had effectively

47 Thomas Morton, *The Encounter against M. Parsons* (London, 1610), p. 246.
48 Donne, *Pseudo-Martyr*, p. 79.

been the same thing.[49] Similarly, Lancelot Andrewes argued that royal power was derived from fatherly power.[50] There was very wide agreement amongst early seventeenth-century writers on social and political theory that fathers have authority over their children by nature, and not by the children's consent. The purpose of comparing or equating royal and paternal power was to suggest that kings do not get their authority from their subjects' consent and cannot be violently resisted by them. The most famous expression of the thesis that political and fatherly power are essentially the same thing was Sir Robert Filmer's *Patriarcha*, probably written by 1632, later revised, and first published in 1680.[51]

Filmer combined his patriarchalist view on the origins of government with an emphasis on the theory of absolute and indivisible sovereignty. Drawing on the work of the French political theorist Jean Bodin, Filmer argued that in every state there must be a single sovereign – whether one person or one assembly – and that this sovereign was not accountable to the people, could never be actively resisted, and had to be obeyed except when his commands conflicted with the laws of God and nature. Donne took much the same line. He claimed that 'God inanimates every State with one power, as every man with one soule'. Subjects could not limit this power any more than parents could alter the souls of their children: 'when therefore people concurre in the desire of such a *King*, they cannot contract, nor limit his power: no more then parents can condition with God, or preclude or withdraw any facultie from that Soule, which God hath infused into the body, which they prepared, and presented to him'.[52] James I, the poet and lawyer Sir John Davies and many leading divines adopted much the same position, which is sometimes called absolutism.[53] Sir Francis Bacon, too, shared the King's basic political stance, but without the theoretical trappings. Though he usually sided with James in disputes over the royal prerogative, he displayed little interest in political theology, preferring the more pragmatic approach to political life taken by Machiavelli, and devoting his philosophical energies to the cause of organised scientific advance, based on experiment and induction – most notably in *The Advancement of Learning* (1605) and the *Novum Organum* (1620).[54]

---

49 *The Convocation Book of MDCVI. Commonly called Bishop Overall's Convocation Book* (Oxford: J. H. Parker, 1844), pp. 2–3.
50 Lancelot Andrewes, *A Sermon preached before his Maiestie, on Sunday the fifth of August last* (London, 1610), p. 13.
51 Sir Robert Filmer, *Patriarcha and Other Writings*, ed. Johann P. Sommerville (Cambridge University Press, 1991), pp. viii, xiv, xxxii–xxxiv.
52 Donne, *Pseudo-Martyr*, p. 133.
53 See the discussion in Sommerville, *Royalists and Patriots*, especially pp. 9–54, 228–50.
54 Bacon praises Machiavelli's practical approach to politics in *The Advancement of Learning*, in *Francis Bacon*, ed. Vickers, pp. 20–299, at p. 254. Bacon's political thought is

In some recent criticism, absolutism is portrayed as a wholly oppressive means of government in which the King's mere will dominated everything, reason was rejected as valueless in political decision-making, no importance was placed on giving the monarch good advice, and participation in political life was strongly discouraged – except for the King and a few courtiers. According to this view, a concern with the public good, with giving the King good counsel, with basing political decisions on reasoned discussion rather than arbitrary decree, and with encouraging wide and active participation in political life were characteristic of subversive, oppositionist and republican thinking, but in no way of absolutism or royalism.[55] The problem with this approach is that James I and his supporters themselves forcefully argued that governments ought to advance the public good – in Scotland, the King issued coins inscribed 'Salus Populi Suprema Lex' ('The safety of the people is the supreme law') – and that rulers should appoint as courtiers and officials only people of the highest intellectual and moral qualities.[56] The King insisted that monarchs ought to abide by the law, and that it was far preferable to live in a state where the law was certain than under arbitrary rule.

Far from affirming that only he himself and some courtiers should be politically active, James insisted that the gentlemen who ran the localities as commissioners of the peace had an obligation to be active in 'the service of the King and countrey', and not like 'idle Slowbellies ... abide alwayes at home, given to a life of ease and delight, liker Ladies then men'.[57] One recent account of republican ideas in seventeenth-century literature suggests that this kind of remark about ladies was characteristic of Machiavellian republicans, while Royalists gave women 'a kind of public sphere' at court: 'The Machiavellian ideal of

discussed in Markku Peltonen, 'Bacon's Political Philosophy', in *The Cambridge Companion to Bacon*, ed. Markku Peltonen (Cambridge University Press, 1996), pp. 283–310; his links with Machiavelli are surveyed at pp. 301–4. The *Novum Organum* first appeared in Bacon, *Instauratio Magna* (London, 1620), pp. 35–360; a modern English translation is Bacon, *The New Organon*, ed. Lisa Jardine and Michael Silverthorne (Cambridge University Press, 2000).

55 The dominance of absolutism is stressed in Jonathan Goldberg, *James I and the Politics of Literature* (Baltimore: Johns Hopkins University Press, 1983). Alternative ideologies, including republicanism, are discussed in David Norbrook, *Writing the English Republic* (Cambridge University Press, 1999); Norbrook, 'The Monarchy of Wit and the Republic of Letters: Donne's Politics', in *Soliciting Interpretation. Literary Theory and Seventeenth-Century English Poetry*, ed. Elizabeth D. Harvey and Katharine Eisaman Maus (University of Chicago Press, 1990), pp. 3–36; Michelle O'Callaghan, '"Talking Politics": Tyranny, Parliament, and Christopher Brooke's *The Ghost of Richard the Third*', *Historical Journal* 41 (1998), 97–120.

56 Peter Seaby and P. Frank Purvey, *Standard Catalogue of British Coins. Volume 2. Coins of Scotland, Ireland & the Islands* (London: Seaby, 1984), pp. xi, 58. James VI and I, *Basilicon Doron*, in *Political Writings*, pp. 35–7.

57 James VI and I, *Political Writings*, pp. 184 (law-abiding), 163 (arbitrary), 221–2 (Slowbellies).

virtù was firmly masculine.' James, however, was no republican. It is sometimes supposed that he mistrusted the public, and that it was only after his reign that a 'public sphere' came into existence in England. Such a sphere has been styled 'a space for the critical discussion of public issues independent of the traditional monopolies of discourse held by the church, the court, and the professions', and dated to various periods from the 1640s onwards.[58] Yet, in 1622 James published a pamphlet explaining to the public at large why he had dissolved the recent Parliament. In order to show that he delighted 'in the goodnesse & benignitie of our government' he offered the people 'the reasons of a resolution of State' which most monarchs would have kept private. No previous ruler had given such a public account of the Crown's disputes with the House of Commons and of the reasons for ending a Parliament. Charles I trod in his father's footsteps by publishing declarations explaining each dissolution of Parliament between his succession and 1640.[59] It is worth emphasising that both Kings recognised that there was a literate, politically aware public beyond the court and beyond Parliament. Both also evidently thought it worthwhile to present the public with a reasoned discussion of their conduct towards Parliament, in the hope of convincing public opinion that the House of Commons and not the King was at fault. The two Kings believed that the actions of members of their Parliaments challenged their sovereignty, and it was for this reason that they grew angry with them. The next section surveys the writings and speeches of those who opposed royal policies in and out of Parliament.

English liberties and the opponents of royal policy

Seventeenth-century English political writing is sometimes discussed in terms of royalism and republicanism.[60] The word 'Royalists' occurs in a book which Sir Edwin Sandys completed in 1599, and which was first published in 1605.[61] Sandys, however, used it exclusively to describe a French political grouping. Randle Cotgrave's French–English dictionary of 1611 defined the French word 'Royaliste' as '*Taking the Kings part, siding with the King*'.[62] By 1627 the word had become English, for in that year the absolutist cleric Robert Sibthorp employed

---

58 Norbrook, *Writing the English Republic*, pp. 20 (masculine), 13 (public sphere).
59 James VI and I, *Political Writings*, p. 250. Sommerville, *Royalists and Patriots*, p. 37.
60 E.g. Norbrook, *Writing the English Republic*.
61 Sir Edwin Sandys, *A Relation of the State of Religion: and with what Hopes and Pollicies it hath beene framed, and is maintained in the severall States of these Westerne parts of the world* (London, 1605), sig. R3b.
62 Randle Cotgrave, *A Dictionarie of the French and English Tongues* (London, 1611), sig. 4A6b.

it, and clearly expected his readers to know that it meant a person who takes a high view of royal power.[63] Not long afterwards, Sir Robert Filmer wrote of the 'new coined distinction of subjects into royalists and patriots'.[64] About 1624 another writer alleged that Catholics were plotting to divide the English into 'regians and Republicans', by persuading the first group to emphasise the people's duty to obey the King's 'absolute will', and the second to argue that 'the lawe of the land' is a more compelling guide to their obligations.[65]

The term 'Royalists' was to acquire a wider vogue than 'regians'. 'Republican' did not catch on much before the 1640s and 1650s, and when used appears to have referred not to a form of government without kings, but to a limited monarchy in which the ruler was under the law.[66] Though the press was censored in early Stuart England, a great deal of scurrilous manuscript material circulated, poking fun at leading courtiers and politicians.[67] Such writings could be outspokenly critical of royal policy and officials, but rarely put forward ideas that can convincingly be described as republican. It has been suggested that people who favoured limited monarchy may in an extended sense be regarded as republicans, since the notion that 'excessive royal power' might threaten the common good 'could easily facilitate a move towards more radically anti-monarchical sentiment in times of crisis'.[68] But, of course, crises could also lead people to acknowledge the quasi-dictatorial powers of a king or military leader, and to recognise that the common good requires emergency measures that might not be strictly legal. Many of those who opposed Charles I's policies were later to endorse the activities of Cromwell and his army, and it was a political crisis that enabled Oliver to establish his military rule. The most thorough modern investigation of republican ideas in pre-Civil-War England convincingly concludes that there was no 'coherent republican tradition' then.[69]

The regimes of James I and his son attracted criticism not because they were monarchies but because they pursued unpopular policies. James, it was widely

63 Robert Sibthorp, *Apostolike Obedience. Shewing the duty of subjects to pay tribute and taxes* (London, 1627), p. 13.
64 Filmer, *Patriarcha and Other Writings*, p. 5.
65 Washington, DC, Folger Shakespeare Library MS V. a. 24, pp. 27–8.
66 Norbrook, *Writing the English Republic*, p. 16.
67 Thomas Cogswell, 'Underground Verse and the Transformation of Early Stuart Political Culture', in *Political Culture and Cultural Politics in Early Modern England*, ed. Susan Amussen and Mark A. Kishlansky (Manchester University Press, 1995), pp. 277–300; Alastair Bellany, ' "Rayling Rymes and Vaunting Verse": Libellous Politics in Early Stuart England, 1603–1628', in *Culture and Politics in Early Stuart England*, ed. Kevin Sharpe and Peter Lake (Stanford University Press, 1993), pp. 285–310.
68 Norbrook, *Writing the English Republic*, pp. 16–17.
69 Markku Peltonen, *Classical Republicanism in English Political Thought 1570–1640* (Cambridge University Press, 1995), p. 12.

felt, was misguided in failing to support the Protestant cause more actively in the opening years of the Thirty Years' War, and especially in negotiating with Spain for a marriage between his son and a Spanish princess. The passivity of the King's foreign policy led people to look back nostalgically on the glorious days of Elizabethan military success, and to suspect that the royal court had fallen prey to popery and corruption – a theme featured in the writings of Drayton, William Browne, Philip Massinger and others.[70] The high cost of Elizabeth's wars against Spain, especially in Ireland, had depleted the Crown's resources, and James's heavy spending did nothing to solve the problem. In 1608 his Treasurer, the Earl of Salisbury, attempted to improve the royal finances by means which included the introduction of extra-Parliamentary impositions on exports and imports. Both James I and Charles I made a great deal of money from this source. In the House of Commons, however, impositions aroused protests on the grounds that they struck at the English tradition that taxation requires the consent of the taxed, represented in Parliament. If the King could tax without consent there would be no need for him to call Parliament. In 1610, the Commons pronounced impositions unconstitutional, but James continued to collect them anyway. There were fears that he had wider ambitions to overthrow English common law, and these were linked to his Scottish origins and his scheme for union.

Suspicions that the King planned to overthrow the established constitution, or the fundamental laws, grew still greater under Charles I, who did not call Parliament for eleven years between 1629 and 1640 – the longest period without a Parliament since the 1200s, when that institution began. Charles took money from his subjects without their consent, using force to compel them to pay in 1626–7, and imprisoning refusers without showing any legal cause for doing so. His Arminian ecclesiastical policies offended the religious sensibilities of Puritans, and of many who considered themselves orthodox, non-Puritan Protestants. When James and Charles abandoned the Spanish match in 1624, the court briefly befriended patriotic Protestants. In his *Game at Chess* Thomas Middleton gave a dramatic treatment of religious and political issues topical at this juncture. His portrayal of Charles as the man responsible for exposing and punishing the wiles of the Spaniards and Jesuits marked the rapprochement of Royalists and patriots.[71] However, Charles's ignominious failure in

70 Thomas Cogswell, *The Blessed Revolution: English Politics and the Coming of War, 1621–1624* (Cambridge University Press, 1989), pp. 25–7. The best discussion of corruption as a theme in political writings is Linda Levy Peck, *Court Patronage and Corruption in Early Stuart England* (London: Unwin Hyman, 1990).
71 Cogswell, 'Thomas Middleton and the Court, 1624: *A Game at Chess* in Context', *Huntington Library Quarterly* 48 (1984), 273–88; Cogswell, *The Blessed Revolution*, pp. 302–7.

the war against Spain, and his suspect religious and financial policies, soon led to renewed criticism.

Under both James and Charles, there were dangers in voicing voluble attacks on royal actions. It was safer to do so in the House of Commons than in most other places, since the Commons enjoyed the privilege of free speech, at least in theory. Parliamentary speeches circulated widely in manuscript. William Hakewill's *The libertie of the subject, against the pretended power of impositions* and James Whitelocke's *A learned and necessary argument to prove that each subject hath a propriety in his goods* were delivered in 1610, but first published only in 1641, after the Long Parliament had met and royal censorship had collapsed. The central argument of both speeches was that by ancient English law, which the King could not break, only Parliament had the authority to legislate and tax. The lawyer Nicholas Fuller ventured into print illicitly in 1607, expressing similar ideas about royal authority. Fuller's pamphlet was also republished in 1641. Some of the law reports of the extremely influential judge and legal writer Sir Edward Coke contained passages which endorsed the same view, and stressed the limits of royal power. James tried to pressure Coke into deleting the objectionable material, but without success, and the judge's recalcitrance was one of the reasons why he was removed from the bench in 1616. Coke became a vocal opponent of royal policies in the Parliaments of the 1620s and along with John Selden was one of the main architects of the Petition of Right of 1628.[72] In his Parliamentary speeches, Selden deployed his formidable learning to defend the subject's liberties against royal encroachment. In his printed works, he was much more cautious. Efforts have been made to discover a theory of mixed monarchy in his writings on English history (and especially in the second edition of *Titles of Honor*, 1631), but these are not fully convincing. In 1616 Selden did, however, edit Sir John Fortescue's *De laudibus legum Angliae* (*In praise of the laws of England*), a fifteenth-century classic of theorising about limited government, and probably the work of English political theory most frequently quoted in early Stuart times.[73]

Other lawyers critical of Crown policy included Richard Martin, John Hoskins and Donne's friend Christopher Brooke, who attacked impositions in the Parliament of 1614. They have been seen – along with Hakewill and Donne himself – as part of a literary circle called the 'Sireniacs'. Brooke wrote a verse denunciation of tyranny entitled *The Ghost of Richard the Third*, which was published in 1614. It has been read as a coded attack on the corruption

---

72 Sommerville, *Royalists and Patriots*, pp. 82, 91–2, 142–3, 221.
73 Paul Christianson, *Discourse on History, Law, and Governance in the Public Career of John Selden, 1610–1635* (University of Toronto Press, 1996).

of James's court, the King's policies and Spanish plotting.[74] Far more open and vigorous assaults on the King's pro-Spanish and unpatriotic foreign policy came from the pen of Thomas Scott in the 1620s. In a series of pamphlets, Scott equated arbitrary government with popery, Spanish guile and corrupt courtiers, while linking Protestantism with English liberties. The connection between English liberties and the Protestant religion was also central to the writings of the young John Lilburne and of the so-called Puritan triumvirate – John Bastwick, Henry Burton and William Prynne – who suffered maiming and imprisonment for their pamphlets of the 1630s. More circumspect critics of the Crown published anonymously. *The Practise of Princes* (1630) argued that the government was now in the hands of a popish and Arminian faction of 'private Agents for Rome, France & the howse of Austria', and predicted that 'who so lives but a few yeares shall see a greater rot of Nobilitie and Prince-like clergie, then ever was seene in this Land'. It approvingly cited Thomas Scott's *Vox Populi*, and the anonymous *Tom Tell Troath*.[75] The latter pamphlet (written around 1624) made many acerbic comments on recent royal policy, lamenting the King's tolerance of popery, and the fact that nothing could now be preached 'but courte divinitie'. It was fortunate, the author claimed, that James ruled over Protestants, for they could be relied on to be loyal even if the King spent his time in his bedchamber, like a Turkish sultan in his seraglio, taking the 'Lords Temporall for his Eunuchs, and whom he will for his Incubus. There he may kisse his minions without shame, and make his Grooms his companions without danger.' The King, said *Tom Tell Troath*, pursued a policy of 'choosing the Minion alternatively out of each nation' in an effort to unite the English and Scots, but this was not turning out to be effective.[76]

After the Long Parliament met in 1640, the need for anonymity rapidly receded. John Pym, Oliver St John and other Members of Parliament denounced royal policy in speeches which printers speedily and openly published for a market keen to learn the latest political news. The key claim of Pym and his allies was that English kings are bound by the law, and that the subject's duty of allegiance is primarily to the nation and its laws and customs rather than to the King – or, what amounted to the same thing, the subject is bound to obey the King only according to the law. The reason why Members of Parliament were able to make such claims with impunity, and why the King had called Parliament, was that the Scots had taken up arms against the King in defence of their own liberties and religion, and had defeated him.

---

74 O'Callaghan, '"Talking Politics"', pp. 102 ('Sireniacs'), 115–20 (Brooke).
75 *The Practise of Princes*. Published by A. Ar. (no place, 1630), pp. 8, 21, 7.
76 *Tom Tell-Troath*, pp. 2–3, 25, 28.

Scottish liberties and nationhood

The standard early modern history of Scotland, and a source of Shakespeare's *Macbeth*, was George Buchanan's *Rerum Scoticarum Historia* (*History of Scottish Affairs*), first published in 1582. Two years later, it was denounced in the Scottish Parliament, and people who owned copies of it were required to hand them in within forty days. Buchanan's *De jure regni apud Scotos* (*The Law of the Kingdom amongst the Scots*, 1579) met the same fate.[77] Both the *De jure* and the *Historia* were trenchantly anti-absolutist works. The first was a short discussion of Scottish government which argued that the monarch drew authority from the people and could be disciplined by them or by inferior magistrates (state officers or nobles) acting on their behalf. Rulers who failed to abide by the conditions upon which they had been appointed could be resisted and even deposed. Buchanan's *Historia* gave detailed evidence to show that the Scots had frequently put these ideas into practice. Protestant resistance theorists like Buchanan firmly rejected the Catholic idea that the church has power to depose secular sovereigns. They argued that the clergy have only spiritual authority. To a king like James VI and I, their doctrines resembled those of the Jesuits. Scottish Presbyterians subjected the King to the church in ecclesiastical matters. If Buchanan's theories were right, a king who failed to heed the church's pronouncements could easily find himself being disciplined by the people. For though clerics could not themselves take temporal action against kings, they could command the people to do so under penalty of spiritual sanctions. Buchanan was James's tutor, and he did not spare the rod in carrying out his pedagogical duties. In later life, James reacted violently against his teachings. He wrote at length against Buchanan's theories in The *Trew Law of Free Monarchies* (1598), and in *Basilicon Doron* (1599) castigated the *Historia* as an infamous libel, advising his son and heir to punish anyone who still had copies of it.[78]

The King's efforts to suppress Buchanan's works and ideas were largely unsuccessful. In the seventeenth century, the *Historia* and the *De jure* were repeatedly published together in Germany, and by the leading Dutch firm of Elzevir. The *Historia* established itself as the standard history of Scotland, and was widely used even by those whose political principles were very different from Buchanan's. Scottish writers whose general political position resembled that of James rather than his tutor include Alexander Irvine, Sir Thomas Craig,

---

77 I. D. McFarlane, *Buchanan* (London: Duckworth, 1981), p. 414.
78 James VI and I, *Trew Law*, in *Political Writings*, pp. 62–84, does not mention Buchanan, but takes issue with doctrines strikingly like his; *Basilicon Doron*, in *Political Writings*, p. 46.

William Drummond of Hawthornden, and John Spottiswoode. Irvine was the author of a political treatise *De jure regni diascepsis* (*An examination of the law of the kingdom*, 1627), the title of which alluded to Buchanan's book, though its contents rejected the claim that kings get their authority from the people and may be resisted by them[79]. Like Irvine, Craig took a high view of royal power. But he found aspects of Buchanan's historical vision congenial, as did many other Scots. According to Buchanan, the kingdom of Scotland was extremely ancient and had never been subject to the English. He endorsed the notion that King Fergus had established the Scottish state at the same time that Alexander the Great was conquering the East. But he poured scorn on the old English myth that Brutus had founded Britain. Craig repeatedly and enthusiastically cited Buchanan's attack on the legend of Brutus.[80]

John Spottiswoode was appointed by James VI and I to the bishopric of Glasgow, and later to the archbishopric of St Andrews. When Charles I went to Scotland for his coronation in 1633, it was Spottiswoode who crowned him. The Archbishop wrote a *History of the Church of Scotland*, which appeared posthumously in 1655, and is one of the two main Scottish ecclesiastical histories to be published in the seventeenth century. The other was David Calderwood's *The True History of the Church of Scotland*, which put forward an account of post-Reformation Scottish history very much in the spirit of Buchanan. Calderwood's views won him James's disfavour, and for a while he lived in exile in the Netherlands. Spottiswoode, on the other hand, was one of the warmest supporters of the King's church policy in Scotland. In his *History*, he sharply criticised Buchanan for 'depressing the Royal authority of Princes, and allowing their controllment by subjects'. But he treated Buchanan as a great authority on early Scottish history, following him on Macbeth and much else. Indeed, he accepted virtually the whole of Buchanan's patriotic but fictitious account of ancient Scotland, with its insistence on the great antiquity of the Scottish state and church, and on Scotland's unsullied record of independence from England. Despite Buchanan's political incorrectness, Spottiswoode declared that 'no man did merit better of his nation for learning, nor thereby did bring to it more glory'. He was, in short, 'a man so well deserving of his countrey, as none more'.[81] William Drummond of Hawthornden penned an

---

79 Alexander Irvine, *De jure regni diascepsis* (Leiden, 1627), pp. 31, 233–4.
80 George Buchanan, *The History of Scotland* (London, 1690), pp. 97, 41–4. Craig, *Scotland's Soveraignty Asserted*, pp. 20, 66, 72.
81 John Spottiswoode, *The History of the Church of Scotland* (London, 1655), pp. 2, 3, 4, 6, 7 and very frequently elsewhere (citations of Buchanan), 28–9 (Macbeth), 325 (Buchanan criticised and praised).

Entertainment for Charles I's arrival in Edinburgh in 1633. It featured a replica of Mount Parnassus, along with Apollo, the Muses and the 'ancient Worthies of Scotland'. The latter included Buchanan, whom Charles's father had so roundly condemned.[82]

Buchanan's patriotic virtues led even Royalists to celebrate his fame. In the later 1630s, the policies of Charles and his advisers seemed to threaten Scottish liberties and religion. Their defenders mined the works of Buchanan for arguments. Sir Archibald Johnston of Wariston made extracts from the writings of Buchanan and John Knox in order to justify the Covenanters' decision to go to war early in 1639. Alexander Henderson, reputedly their best writer, revived resistance theory at the same time to show that the Scots were merely doing their duty in defending 'God's right' and preserving 'the peoples peace against the unjust invasion of the Supream Magistrate'.[83] Henderson's colleague Samuel Rutherford drew heavily on Buchanan to confirm the same claims a few years later.[84]

In England, James I tried to associate opposition to the royal prerogative with popery. But the project for a Spanish Match in the early 1620s persuaded many that popery was really linked to arbitrary or absolute government, and not to ideas of limited kingship. Charles I attempted to show that the Covenanters had adopted the same wicked Jesuitical principles as the Gunpowder Plotters. He cited his father's writings to prove the point. John Corbet's *The Epistle Congratulatorie of Lysimachus Nicanor of the Societie of Jesu, to the Covenanters in Scotland* (1640) levelled the same charge in satirical form. Adopting the persona of a Jesuit, Corbet congratulated the Covenanters on borrowing and implementing Catholic political principles. He argued that Buchanan and others whom the Covenanters treated as authorities maintained positions that were even more radical than those of the Jesuits.[85] Corbet provided a great deal of evidence to support his claim. On the whole, however, this sort of propaganda fell on deaf ears. There *were* Scottish Royalists and even absolutists. But in Scotland as in England patriotic feelings mostly tended to fuse with anti-popery and with ideas of limited government. The Scottish tradition, claimed the historian

---

82 William Drummond of Hawthornden, *The Poetical Works of William Drummond of Hawthornden*, ed. L. E. Kastner, 2 vols. (Manchester University Press, 1913), 2:123.

83 David Stevenson, *The Scottish Revolution 1637–1644. The Triumph of the Covenanters* (Newton Abbot: David & Charles, 1973), p. 133. [Alexander Henderson], *Some Speciall Arguments which warranted the Scottish subiects lawfully to take up armes in defence of their Religion and Liberty* (Amsterdam, 1642), p. 5.

84 Samuel Rutherford, *Lex, Rex: the Law and the Prince* (London, 1644), pp. 448–52.

85 Charles I, *A Large Declaration concerning the late tumults in Scotland* (London, 1639), pp. 3–4. [John Corbet], *The Epistle Congratulatorie of Lysimachus Nicanor of the Societie of Jesu, to the Covenanters in Scotland* (London, 1640), pp. 33–49.

David Hume of Godscroft, was to defend customary rights by taking action against the ruler's evil advisers, and, if necessary, against the monarch too.[86] In Ireland also, national feeling often became linked with opposition to government policy. There, however, the religious colouring which patriotism took on was Catholic, not anti-popish.

Religion, nation and literature in Ireland

In October 1641 a rising began in Ulster, and thousands of British settlers were massacred. The rebellion spread elsewhere, and in 1642 Irish rebels joined with the 'old English' to form the Confederate Catholics, now often referred to as the Confederation of Kilkenny. In earlier times, the 'old English' had viewed themselves as quite distinct from the Irish. They were descendants of Anglo-Normans who had settled in Ireland during the Middle Ages, and they had prided themselves on their origins. However, most 'old English' families remained Catholic after the Reformation, and the distinctions between them and the Irish grew less sharp. Increasingly, too, the English government came to rely on new Protestant settlers – the 'new English'. In the early seventeenth century, the traditional political importance of the 'old English' was being undermined, and this helped to push them towards the native Irish. 'New English' commentators on Irish affairs sometimes optimistically argued that peace had been firmly established when the Nine Years' War ended in English victory in 1603, and that the various inhabitants of the country would eventually coalesce into a single nation. But there was much evidence that pointed in a different direction in the writings of both the Irish and the 'old English'.[87]

Edmund Spenser had hoped that tough action would quash Irish rebelliousness and independence.[88] Under James VI and I, Sir John Davies claimed that Ireland had never before been properly subdued, but that the King had now finally accomplished the task. He praised the policy of colonising Ulster, and

---

86 David Hume of Godscroft, *A generall history of Scotland, together with a particular history of the houses of Douglas and Angus* (Edinburgh, 1648), pp. 418–23.
87 The outbreak of the Irish revolt is discussed in M. Perceval-Maxwell, *The Outbreak of the Irish Rebellion of 1641* (Montreal: McGill-Queen's University Press, 1994). The Catholic Confederation is discussed in Micheál Ó Siochrú, *Confederate Ireland 1642–1649: a Constitutional and Political Analysis* (Portland, Oregon: Four Courts Press, 1999). Aidan Clarke argues that the old English retained and indeed accentuated an identity distinct from that of the Irish in the early seventeenth century: *The Old English in Ireland 1625–42* (Ithaca: Cornell University Press, 1966); 'Colonial Identity in Early Seventeenth-century Ireland', in *Nationality and the Pursuit of National Independence*, ed. T. W. Moody, Historical Studies, 11 (Belfast: Appletree Press, 1978), pp. 57–71. Brendan Bradshaw argues against this position in 'The English Reformation and Identity Formation in Wales and Ireland', p. 55.
88 Spenser, *A View of the State of Ireland*. See also *Faerie Queene*, 5. 12. 26–7.

so creating a 'mixt plantation of Brittish & Irish, that they might grow up togither into one Nation'.[89] Barnabe Rich acknowledged in 1610 that many feared the plantation would fail and the Irish would 'one night . . . lay wast and consume al with fire and sword'. He assured his readers that this would not happen, and that rebellion in Ireland was a thing of the past: 'the Rebel of Ireland shall never more stand out hereafter, as they have done in times past'. It has rightly been noted that there is an 'apparent contradiction' in Spenser's *A View of the State of Ireland*, for the poet at once asserts that Ireland can be reformed, and yet stresses the implacable opposition of the Irish to all things English. The same tension is visible in other writers on Ireland. A Jacobean 'Survey of the present estate of Ireland' observed that the ordinary Irish were well aware of the advantages of the peace which James's reign had brought to the country, but nevertheless warned that it would be unwise for the English to appoint them to positions of trust: 'When an Irishman is made a Sheriffe, there is little better then a legall, and formall Rebell erected'.[90] David Rothe, a leading Catholic churchman, attacked the English regime as oppressive and intolerant in his *Analecta sacra et mira* (1616–19). Responding, Sir Thomas Ryves stressed the peace and prosperity of Ireland and went so far as to claim that the inhabitants lived together in harmony, without any discrimination on national grounds. But he admitted that this was not universally true, and that some of the Irish wanted civil war – as did some of the English. To the charge that the English persecuted Catholics, he replied that they took justified action against disloyalty, and that Rothe's brand of Catholicism was disloyal, for he followed Bellarmine in defending the papal deposing power and condemning the Oath of Allegiance. As long as there were people in Ireland who held such poisonous views, it was incorrect to claim that the island lacked snakes.[91]

It has recently been suggested that English thinking on the Irish changed drastically after the rising and massacres of 1641. Spenser and Davies, so the

89 Sir John Davies, *A Discoverie of the true causes why Ireland was never entirely subdued, nor brought under Obedience of the Crowne of England, untill the beginning of his Maiesties happie raigne* (London, 1612), p. 281.

90 Spenser, *A View of the State of Ireland*, p. xxi. 'A Survey of the present estate of Ireland Anno 1615', San Marino, CA, Huntington Library, MS Ellesmere 1746, fols. 8b–26b, at 23a, 21a. This manuscript is dedicated to James by the author, who signs himself 'E.S.' (fol. 8b).

91 David Rothe, *The Analecta of David Rothe, Bishop of Ossory*, ed. Patrick F. Moran (Dublin: M.H. Gill & Son, 1884); first published in three parts, 1616–19. Sir Thomas Ryves, *Regiminis Anglicani in Hibernia Defensio* (London, 1624), first pagination, pp. 1–2, 67; second pagination, pp. 38–9, 59, 10. Another response to Rothe, in 1,500 lines of verse, is the 'Newes from the Holy Ile' of the English soldier and settler Parr Lane, printed in Alan Ford, 'Parr Lane: "Newes from the Holy Ile"', *Proceedings of the Royal Irish Academy*, Section C, No. 99 (1999), 115–56, at 121–56.

case goes, believed that the people of Ireland could become civilised if their foolish customs on landholding were abolished, and neither author placed much emphasis on the Catholicism of the Irish, seeing them as ignorant rather than popish. Both held that in time the Irish could be educated into becoming English. But after the massacres, the argument proceeds, John Temple published *The Irish Rebellion* (1646), and it established the new orthodoxy about the Irish, claiming that they were racial inferiors and convinced Papists, who were quite irredeemable.[92] In fact, the notion that the Irish were thorough Papists long predates 1641. Thomas Stafford's book on the wars in Ireland and especially Munster around 1600 stressed that the leading Irish rebels portrayed themselves as fighting for the faith against English heresy, persecution and tyranny.[93] Barnabe Rich gave particular weight to the Catholicism of the Irish, claiming that if it could be eradicated there would be no other obstacles to a full union between them and the English. Popery, he declared, underlay the 'sluttishnesse', 'uncleanlinesse', 'rudenesse' and 'inhumane loathsomenes' of the Irish. The Pope told them to rebel against their rulers, for popery was a rebellious religion. The Irish therefore wanted 'to shake off the English government'. Moreover, the fact that they disagreed with the English in religion led them to disagree in everything else too. Turning the maxim 'Love me, and love my Dog' on its head, they rejected anything that the English approved, including 'civility, humanity, or any manner of Decencie'. Rich admitted that the Irish were ignorant and superstitious, but thought these qualities perfectly compatible with popery. His main argument was that once the Irish had been cured of Catholicism they might become quite civilised. At times, however, he acknowledged that popery was not their only problem. The 'Irish by nature are inclined unto cruelty', he affirmed, and observed that they enjoyed being cruel to each other as well as to the English. Still, with time and education they could be improved. One important way in which this might be done would be by undermining their reverence for their hereditary rhymers, to whose 'fabulous fixions' they were 'wonderfully addicted'. These lying bards taught them nothing but theft, murder and rebellion.[94]

Philip O'Sullivan Beare likewise thought that the Irish poets related many things that were untrue. There was not much else on which he agreed with

92 Kathleen M. Noonan, ' "The cruell pressure of an enraged, barbarous people": Irish and English Identity in Seventeenth-century Policy and Propaganda', *Historical Journal* 41 (1998), 151–77, at 154–6, 158, 161–2, 168.
93 Thomas Stafford, *Pacata Hibernia. Ireland Appeased and Reduced or, an Historie of the late Warres of Ireland, especially within the Province of Mounster* (London, 1633), pp. 21, 142, 145–6, 228–9.
94 Barnabe Rich, *A New Description of Ireland* (London, 1610), pp. 16, 17, 21, 41, 39.

Protestant commentators such as Rich. O'Sullivan Beare's family had been deeply involved in resistance to the English during the opening years of the seventeenth century, and he lived in exile in Spain and then Portugal – where his *Historiae Catholicae Iberniae Compendium* (*Compendium of the Catholic History of Ireland*) was published in 1621. Like Rothe, he argued that the English were oppressors of the Irish and persecutors of the faithful. He stressed the unswerving loyalty of the Irish to Catholicism, but argued that from early times the English had been shaky in their religion – and now, of course, they were outright heretics bent on overthrowing religion altogether. English government in Ireland was multiply illegal. The Pope had not, as some supposed, authorised Henry II to rule Ireland. The exclusion from office of all but English settlers – he called them the 'New Irish' – was contrary to the laws of nature and nations. The Irish nobility were not summoned to Parliament as they should have been, and the so-called Parliaments were therefore invalid. The English were a people full of treachery and guile. In past times, Ireland had been famous for its achievements in scholarship, literature and religion. Decline in these fields was not the fault of the Irish but of the Danish and then English invaders, who had brought centuries of destructive war to the country. The reason why God had permitted the English to conquer Ireland was to punish Irish divisions and greed for each other's land. This did not at all mean that God approved of what the English did, and the Pope had been quite right to depose Elizabeth. O'Sullivan Beare dedicated his book to Philip IV of Spain, stressed the supposed Spanish origins of the ancient Irish, and pointed out what an excellent base Ireland would make for attacking the heretics in England, Scotland and the Netherlands.[95]

Attitudes similar to those of O'Sullivan Beare feature in the *Annála Ríoghachta Éireann* (*Annals of the Kingdom of Ireland*), a vast compilation of historical and mythical material drawn from earlier sources by the Franciscan lay brother Mícheál Ó Cléirigh (Michael O'Clery) and others, and completed in 1636. Usually known as *The Annals of the Four Masters* (after its four compilers) this work records how the kingdom of Ireland was established by the Firbolgs, who elected Slainge as their King some 1,934 years before the birth of Christ. From very ancient times, then, there had been a united Irish kingdom. The English were intruders and heretics, against whom the Irish fought nobly in defence

---

95 Philip O'Sullivan Beare, *Historiae Catholicae Iberniae Compendium* (Lisbon, 1621), fols. 37b (lying poets), 37b–38b (Irish loyalty to faith), 67a–68a (English shaky in religion), 58a (English overthrow religion), 59a–63b, 70a (illegal actions and treachery of English), 34b ('Novi Hiberni'), 55a (long war harms culture), 74–5 (God punishes Irish divisions), 70b (Pope right to depose Elizabeth), 2b–3a, 31b–32a (Spanish origins), 10b–11a (good base for attacking heretics).

of their religion and country. The defeat of the Irish at Kinsale in 1601 was a lamentable disaster, 'for the prowess and valour, prosperity and affluence, nobleness and chivalry, dignity and renown, hospitality and generosity, bravery and protection, devotion and pure religion, of the Island, were lost in this engagement'. The book ended by recording the martyrdoms of Catholics recently killed by the English on charges of treason, and the death at Rome in 1616 of the Earl of Tyrone, the leader of the Irish in the Nine Years' War. The English saw him as a traitor and troublemaker, but the *Annals* praised his heroism 'in defending his religion and his patrimony against his enemies'.[96]

O'Sullivan Beare regarded old English families as now effectively Irish.[97] The Catholic priest Geoffrey Keating also assimilated the two groups, asserting that both the 'old foreigners' (the old English) and the Irish, who intermarried with them, were treated unfairly. English commentators, intent on denigrating both, ignored their fine achievements, and gave a distorted and lying account of Ireland. Instead of praising the Irish and old English nobles for founding abbeys and funding scholarship, the 'new foreigners' 'take notice of the ways of inferiors and wretched little hags, ignoring the worthy actions of the gentry'. It was easy to pretend that the Irish were uncivilised if you concentrated on 'the hovels of the poor, and of miserable people'. This proved little, for 'there is no country in the world without a rabble'. In fact, Ireland was a very ancient kingdom that had never been subject to foreign rule until the Norman invasion. Among the new foreigners who told lies about the Irish was Spenser, who perhaps allowed himself licence as a poet to make up 'romances with sweet-sounding words to deceive the reader', and whose account of Irish history (in the *View of the State of Ireland*) was ignorant and erroneous.[98]

Keating used history to vindicate the Irish from the charges levelled against them by the English and other foreigners – for instance denying that they had been cannibals, on the grounds that the only recorded cannibal was Eithne the loathsome, who had been reared 'on the flesh of children, in hope that thereby she would be the sooner marriageable'. Barnabe Rich wanted peace in Ireland and thought that much Irish history was best forgotten: in Ireland, he said, 'there are no histories worthy to be followed, but Tragedies of crueltie, fit to be abhorred'. In Ireland, as in Scotland and England, a sense of nationhood was

---

96 *Annedla Ríoghachta Éireann. Annals of the Kingdom of Ireland, by the Four Masters, from the Earliest Period to the Year 1616*, ed. John O'Donovan, 7 vols. (Dublin: Hodges and Smith, 1848–51), 1:13, 6:2287–9, 2371–5.
97 O'Sullivan Beare, *Historiae Catholicae Iberniae Compendium*, fols. 34b–35a.
98 Geoffrey Keating, *The History of Ireland*, ed. David Comyn and Patrick S. Dineen, Irish Text Society, 4, 8–9, 15, (London: D. Nutt, 1902–14), 1:2–3 (unfairness), 33 (intermarriage), 5 (achievements), 7 (gentry), 53 (rabble), 17 (unconquered before Normans), 31 (Spenser).

closely linked to beliefs about history. Rich hoped that the different groups in Ireland would come to live together in harmony, at least if popery was suppressed. He was fully aware of the reality of national divisions. Commenting on why the Nine Years' War had lasted so long, he argued that the fundamental mistake of the English had been to hire Irish soldiers, who promptly went over to the rebels. 'And it hath', he remarked in terms surely incomprehensible to anyone lacking a strong sense of nationhood, 'ever beene thought a most daungerous thing, to have friendes and enemies both of one Nation'.[99]

99 Keating, *History of Ireland*, 1:9. Rich, *New Description of Ireland*, pp. 4, 113.

Chapter 16

LITERATURE AND THE COURT

LEAH S. MARCUS

In his dedication of the 1616 folio version of *Cynthia's Revels*, Ben Jonson addressed the early Stuart court as 'A bountiful and brave spring' that

> waterest all the noble plants of this island. In thee, the whole kingdom dresseth itself, and is ambitious to use thee as her glass. Beware, then, thou render men's figures truly, and teach them no less to hate their deformities than to love their forms; for, to grace there should come reverence, and no man can call that lovely which is not also venerable.

Thus described, the court is inseparable from the nation at large: not only does it 'water', or offer economic and other sustenance, to the 'noble plants', the aristocracy and gentry, but it also 'mirrors', or provides through its own collective outward 'grace' and loveliness, and its inward sagacity and probity, a set of patterns against which other elements of the kingdom define themselves and each other and determine their relative worth.

It is doubtful whether the Stuart court was as central to all areas of the emerging nation as Jonson claimed it was: in defining it as he did, Jonson, whom James I appointed Poet Laureate and granted an annual pension in that very year of 1616, sought in part to establish the value and significance of his new position. But his definition also points towards an important historical truth: under James, significant elements of court culture were more visible to the nation at large than they had been at any previous time in British history if only because so much of the literature associated with the court was routinely brought into print. Elizabeth I had not published any of her own writings in her own name, and literature produced by (rather than for) the Elizabethan court usually circulated only in manuscript, if at all. James I was the first British monarch who fully understood and exploited the power of print to publicise his own treatises, royal entertainments, proclamations and other materials closely associated with the court.

If the print medium allowed the monarch and his court to receive an unprecedented level of visibility in an emerging 'public sphere', it also created an unprecedented potential for tension between the idealised images of royal policy and of court life typically promulgated by the court itself and other more negative images – hence Jonson's warning that courtiers must offer the nation a 'glass' worthy of emulation. Even more than the theatre, the medium of print had the power to 'make greatness familiar' in both the positive and negative connotations of the phrase, and to make conflicts newly visible to a public at large. Neither the Jacobean nor the Caroline court was by any means an ideological monolith. As recent historians have emphasised, both courts are better understood as heterogeneous groupings of contrasting interests and affiliations. To mention only one salient area where this heterogeneity was visible to contemporaries, both Queen Anne and Queen Henrietta Maria had their own households that functioned in considerable independence from – and sometimes in gleeful opposition to – the policies of their respective husbands. Yet the literature closely associated with the court often portrays it as a monolith, effacing, or at least rendering less visible, the perception of heterogeneity that we receive from other sources. If there was such a thing as early Stuart 'absolutism', that ideology of the power and centrality of the monarch was much more an artifact of literary portrayals than it was an accurate depiction of the ruler, court and nation in interaction. One aim of the present chapter will be to trace some of the ingenious strategies by which literature closely associated with the early Stuart court sought to erase its own highly specific affiliations and present itself as offering broadly accepted truths that belonged to the nation as a whole.

As amply indicated in Catherine Bates's and Patrick Collinson's chapters in this volume (see Chapters 11 and 12), James I was a published author well before he assumed the English throne. His writings as James VI were recognised in England as well as Scotland. By 1601, Gabriel Harvey had referred to the 'King of Scotland' as 'sovereign of the divine art'; before 1603 Harvey owned James's *Essays of a Prentice in the Divine Art of Poesie* (Edinburgh, 1585), which, Harvey claimed, offered 'the excellentest rules and finest art that a king could learn or teach in his kingdom', and *His Majesty's Poetical Exercises at Vacant Hours* (Edinburgh, [1591]), in which Harvey's marginalia particularly commend James's epic 'Lepanto' as 'a gallant and notable poem, both for matter and form'.[1] Although Harvey was an unusually prolific reader and book collector, his interest in the writings of the Scottish monarch was not unusual for the period. During the final decades of the sixteenth century, James sought

---

1 Virginia F. Stern, *Gabriel Harvey: His Life, Marginalia, and Library* (Oxford: Clarendon Press, 1979), pp. 79n., 126 and 223.

through print to become known abroad for his 'Castalian band' of poets, in imitation of the French Pléiade, and for the broad humanist erudition displayed through such literary pursuits.

When James became King of England in 1603, he was deluged with printed tributes, and many of his major works appeared in London editions: *Daemonologie* (which argued for the reality and danger of witchcraft), *The True Law of Free Monarchies* (which expounded and defended the theory of the divine right of kings) and especially his *Basilikon Doron* (James's advice-book on rule for the heir-apparent Prince Henry), which was widely praised as a 'true image' of the mind of the king.[2] *Basilikon Doron* went through eight English editions during 1603 alone. The royal writings offered panegyrists a gold mine of material to admire and imitate, and inspired in English writers the hope that James I would prove more receptive to their offerings than Elizabeth had been. Thomas Greene's 1603 tribute *A Poet's Vision and a Prince's Glory* celebrated James for the 'triple crown' of rule over England, Scotland and Ireland, but also for a 'triple crown' of laurel earned through his accomplishments as a poet. When a poet is also a king, 'He then is equal with a deity.'[3] The most enduringly famous of volumes celebrating James I's accession is surely Ben Jonson's, which combined *His Part of the King's Entertainment in Passing to His Coronation* in 1604 with Jonson's *Althorpe Entertainment*, performed before Queen Anne and Prince Henry in 1603 on their way to England from Scotland, and Jonson's 'Panegyre on the Happy Entrance of James... to His First High Session of Parliament' (1604). This volume echoed James's writings at several turns and revived the classical Roman tradition of address to Roman emperors on important state occasions; in its published form, it included numerous erudite notes that gave it the appearance of a Renaissance edition of a classical author.[4] In the immediate aftermath of James's arrival in England, the English printing scene was further internationalised by the publication of works by James's Scottish courtiers: preeminently William Alexander, later Earl of Stirling, whose volume of verses, *Aurora, Containing the First Fancies of the Author's Youth*, and his *Monarchic Tragedies*, treating Croesus and Darius, appeared in London in 1604; and Sir Robert Aynton, whose Latin verses entitled *Basia* appeared in 1605. William Drummond of Hawthornden was perhaps the most prolific of Scots poets who received a new, English audience for his work as a result of James's

---

2 See James Doelman, ' "A King of Thine Own Heart": The English Reception of King James VI and I's *Basilikon Doron*', *Seventeenth Century* (1994), 1–8; the cited phrase is from James's 1603 preface to the work.

3 Thomas Greene, *A Poet's Vision and a Prince's Glory* (London, 1603), sigs. B4v–C1r.

4 David Riggs, *Ben Jonson: A Life* (Cambridge, MA: Harvard University Press, 1989), pp. 109–12.

accession. Though Drummond continued to publish primarily in Edinburgh rather than London, he wrote in English rather than Scots as an acknowledgement of his newly expanded readership.

The advent of a writer-king gave new meaning to the inexpressibility topos: numerous poets communicated their sense of futility in writing panegyric for a monarch who was his own best poet. But James's enormous largesse towards his new English subjects, combined with his well-publicised interest in literary pursuits, gave poets hope that they would enjoy new prominence and esteem. John Chamberlain cynically observed, 'the very poets, with their idle pamphlets, promise themselves great part in his favour'.[5] In the first years after his accession, there were from three to seven times as many books dedicated to James each year as there had been books dedicated to Elizabeth on average in each of the final years of her reign.[6] The players certainly benefited from the King's show of interest. James I made the drama a royal monopoly by issuing new patents to all of the major London dramatic companies that removed them from the patronage of chief nobles of the realm and attached them instead to members of the royal family, thereby bringing them at least nominally under the wide umbrella of early Stuart court culture. James called for plays at court far more frequently than Queen Elizabeth had, although he appears not to have savoured them as much as she did: for him, they were less important as entertainment than as a display of royal magnificence.

One salient effect of James's published self-presentation as an author was to efface any clear distinction between literary production that belonged to the court and that which only aspired to it. As John Donne was to put the matter in the preface to his *Pseudo-Martyr* (1610), the King had descended 'to a conversation with your subjects by way of your books', encouraging men of letters to ascend to his presence by the same means. This printed 'conversation' constituted what we might call a 'virtual court' much broader than the actual numbers of subjects who had personal access to the monarch. How can we assess the impact of James's writings on this 'virtual court' that existed in the public sphere? Certainly, after James's accession, we find that many of his keynote political and moral themes are echoed repeatedly by other writers. His famed love for a *via media* and 'moderation in all things' as articulated in *Basilikon Doron* was a frequently echoed topos, as was his articulation of the divinity

5 *The Letters of John Chamberlain*, ed. Norman Egbert McClure, 2 vols. (Philadelphia: The American Philosophical Society, 1939), 1:192 (letter of 12 April, 1603). See also Curtis Perry's discussion in *The Making of Jacobean Culture* (Cambridge University Press, 1997), pp. 15–49.
6 Perry, *Jacobean Culture*, p. 24.

of kings in a prefatory sonnet to the same work: 'God gives not kings the style of Gods in vain'. It is often impossible, however, to determine the extent to which a given work was meant to be read as part of the royal 'conversation'.

As an illustration of this point, we might consider James's well-known interest in Roman imperial themes, as applied in particular to his project for the creation of Great Britain through the union of England and Scotland. Already in 1603, poets were beginning to praise the Stuart monarch for the creation, through his own person, of an empire of Britain. Jonson's court masque *Hymenaei*, performed in 1606 for the marriage of the Earl of Essex and Frances Howard, daughter of the Earl of Suffolk, used the occasion of the marriage of two very different families – Essex, a scion of the Puritan nobility and ally of anti-Spanish interests at court, and Howard, daughter of a strongly pro-Spanish and pro-Catholic faction – to celebrate James's project for the Union of the Kingdoms, figured in the masque through a giant 'microcosm or globe' reportedly turned by Ben Jonson himself. Although not ratified until a century later, the project for union was weighed by Parliament, defended in a number of published treatises, and strongly identified with James I in a wide variety of literary forms during the period, including Shakespeare's *Cymbeline*, which is saturated with symbols and prophecies of the 'union' and repeats *Hymenaei*'s allegorical device of a marriage of highly disparate partners to figure James's projected marriage of the kingdoms. How, then, are we to read literature from a similar milieu that appears to rework the same subject, but renders it more equivocally?

A much discussed case in point would be Shakespeare's *King Lear*, which was first performed at court in the same year as *Hymenaei*: 1606. Shakespeare's play begins with a united Britain, a subject dear to James's heart, and displays the disastrous effects of Lear's plan to divide it into three kingdoms corresponding roughly to England, Scotland and Wales (or Cornwall). But depending on the degree to which one wished to press the play's potential analogy between the riven family of Lear and the larger body politic, the play could easily be read as obliterating the possibility for the kind of beneficent, fruitful unity of kingdoms that the King himself was campaigning so hard to achieve. The emptied, exhausted nation at the end of *King Lear* is at the farthest possible remove from the luminous globe that emblematises political union at the end of Jonson's *Hymenaei*, or the re-energised imperial Britain at the end of *Cymbeline*. Moreover, the personality of the British King in *King Lear* – his outbursts of rage, his carelessness about the daily business of running the government, his propensity for endless gallops about the countryside – reflects widely noted defects of James I. The play's obvious participation in James's public 'conversation' about

Britain does not render the dramatic work more legible in terms of the Jacobean policy initiative; rather, that participation makes more troubling and powerful the play's association of divinely ordained kingship with fallibility and disorder. Similarly, *Macbeth* is a play that explores the Scottish underpinnings of James's English rule and forecasts a glorious future for the monarch and his offspring, the line of Banquo; but at the same time, in the person of Macbeth, the play explores darker, destructive elements of the monarch's 'imperial theme'. Macbeth's ruination comes about in part because he takes to heart Jacobean myths about the unassailability of royal prerogative powers.

Alvin Kernan has recently emphasised the undeniable fact that Shakespeare the player, as a member of the King's Men, was a paid, liveried servant of James I. Kernan contends that such a close courtly affiliation precludes readings of plays like *King Lear* or *Macbeth* that interpret them as fundamental assaults on James's high-flown theories of monarchy, at least in terms of their performance and reception at court.[7] Most other critics, however, would resist Kernan's argument as oversimplification of a knotty set of interpretive problems. Indeed, our present critical debate about topical meaning in early modern plays in many ways recapitulates the liveliness and uncertainty expressed about topical meaning during early decades of the seventeenth century. James's 'conversation' with his subjects about some of the most vital principles of his belief and rule may at first have dazzled them with its learning and rhetorical power, as Donne compares the influence of 'your majesty's books' to that of 'the sun which penetrates all corners' (dedication to *Pseudo-Martyr*, 1610). But the very pervasiveness of the royal rhetoric – penetrating, at least, all the literate corners of the kingdom – made it difficult to control in terms of imputed interpretations, and therefore difficult to restrain within the idealising perspective that had so entranced James's subjects on his first arrival in England. Donne himself freely appropriated the sun imagery so closely associated with the monarchy to his own role as poet–lover in poems like 'The Sun Rising', which dismisses James I as otherwise occupied ('tell court huntsmen that the King will ride') and adopts the language of royal absolutism to conjure up a world emptied of all but the poet's own prerogative and his obedient subject(s): 'She is all states, and all princes, I, / Nothing else is.'[8]

Perhaps the best illustration of the pitfalls of literary production under James I derives from the career of Ben Jonson. As noted above, Jonson seemingly

7 Alvin Kernan, *Shakespeare, the King's Playwright: Theatre in the Stuart Court 1603–1613* (New Haven: Yale University Press, 1995), pp. 89–105.
8 *John Donne*, ed. John Carey (Oxford and New York: Oxford University Press, 1991), p. 93.

pulled out all the stops in celebrating James's accession, and continued to praise the King in masques at court and in his *Epigrams*, mostly written by 1612 and first published as a collection in his *Works* of 1616. The *Epigrams* honoured the Stuart monarch as 'best of kings' and 'best of poets' (no. 4) and immortalised the King's project for the union of England and Scotland by depicting it as the marriage of two kingdoms with James as officiating priest and the encircling seas as the ring (no. 5). At the same time, however, Jonson had little but scorn for courtiers considered collectively: the court in the *Epigrams* is comically reduced to a 'Something that Walks Somewhere', a Lord who is only nominally alive, buried in his own 'flesh and blood' (no. 11), a 'Court-Worm' whose garments encircle just such a larva as spun them (no. 15), spiteful 'Courtlings' who ignorantly aspire to be public arbiters despite their utter lack of taste (nos. 52 and 72), or a 'Fine Lady Would-Be' who has aborted her offspring so as not to miss the holiday revelry at court (no. 62). When he praises courtiers by name in the *Epigrams*, Jonson as a rule praises them for personal attributes and fails to note their courtly affiliations. In order to maintain an idealising perspective on the King and principal ministers like Robert Cecil, Earl of Salisbury, Thomas Egerton, Lord Ellesmere, and Thomas Howard, Earl of Suffolk, Jonson separates the monarch and chief ministers from the lesser courtiers and projects many of James's known weaknesses onto the latter group. Anonymous 'courtlings' are excoriated for their officiousness, voluptuousness, arbitrariness of judgement, and intoxication with the latest fashion, while the chief ministers, often in poems provocatively juxtaposed with the more overtly satiric epigrams, are praised by name for truth and virtue.

During the same years, however, Jonson wrote a series of plays that got him into considerable trouble at court. His frequent adoption of Roman imperial themes in his plays from 1603 onward is surely to be interpreted as part of the developing Jacobean 'conversation' about empire, divine right and good rule. But if Jonson hoped for royal approbation through his use of such materials, he was more than once disappointed. After his *Sejanus* was performed at court in the 1603–4 holiday season, Jonson was called before the Privy Council for it and accused of popery and treason by Lord Henry Howard (shortly to become Earl of Northampton).[9] *Sejanus* demonstrates the decline of the Roman Emperor Tiberius after he lapsed into tyranny as a result of overdependence on evil counsellors like Sejanus. It is easy to imagine how such a subject could arouse the paranoia of Privy Councillors who were similarly attempting to influence James I. In taking on such a topic, Jonson may well have placed too much trust

9 Riggs, *Ben Jonson*, p. 105.

in James I's power over his courtiers, and in his humanist love of learning and debate. But it is equally likely that Jonson was venting hostility against some of the very leitmotifs of Jacobean rule that elsewhere he praised.

In 1605 he got in worse trouble for his part in *Eastward Ho*, co-authored with Chapman and Marston, a play that had a seemingly innocent plot but ventured several incidental jabs against James I, his insolent Scottish courtiers and his notorious sale of titles to gain additional revenue. One of the characters, in a marked Scots accent, acknowledges another as 'one of my thirty pound knights'. The play even makes fun of James's project for union by wishing that the Scots who have invaded England could be banished to the New World instead. For his part in *Eastward Ho* Jonson was precipitously thrown into jail. By what schizophrenic logic could he have collaborated in such a production at a time when he was seeking court patronage? The answer lies in a recognition of the fractured allegiances that marked the Jacobean court beneath the public paeans to union and unity. Many English nobles felt enormous resentment at the power and influence wielded by James's Scottish favourites, who had a virtual monopoly on close access to the King. Jonson's patroness for the production of *Eastward Ho* was Queen Anne, who also smarted under exclusion from access to her husband as a result of the dominance of his favourites. The Children of the Chapel Royal, who performed the play at court, were attached to Queen Anne's household. The French ambassador reported at this period that the Queen attended plays for the express purpose of laughing at satiric portrayals of her husband. This was one of the many cases in which Queen Anne's interests as a patron of poets diverged markedly from the King's.[10] Indeed, we can speculate that it may have been in part Queen Anne's influence that got Jonson released from prison and saved him from the threatened punishment of the loss of his ears and nose.

Clearly what Jonson needed in order to bring his savage satiric impulses into line with his equally strong need to idealise the monarch was a literary form that could successfully accommodate both passions. Jonson's greatest triumphs as court poet came from his masques, elaborate entertainments using music, dancing and sudden, spectacular shifts of scenery; these productions typically modulated from strenuous critiques of court vices in the early scenes into wondrous visions of moral transformation and transcendence. In our study of the development of the masque, as in many areas of the study of literature

---

10 For Queen Anne's court see Leeds Barroll, 'The Court of the First Stuart Queen' in *The Mental World of the Jacobean Court*, ed. Linda Levy Peck (Cambridge University Press, 1991), pp. 191–208; and Barbara Lewalski, *Writing Women in Jacobean England* (Cambridge, MA: Harvard University Press, 1993), pp. 15–43.

and the Jacobean court, we have placed too little emphasis on the innovative activities of women. One of Jonson's most important early patrons was Lucy, Countess of Bedford, one of Anne's ladies-in-waiting, and it is perhaps she who recruited him to write *The Masque of Blackness*, performed by the Queen and her ladies on Twelfth Night, 1605, and its sequel *The Masque of Beauty*, performed on Twelfth Night, 1608. The Queen and her inner circle of women devised the subjects of both masques, and may have been at least partially responsible for their engagement with the Jacobean leitmotif of empire. If *Eastward Ho* envisions the beggarly Scots as swarming like a species of vermin over the whole earth, *Blackness* and *Beauty* offer a more positive vision of imperial expansion: the sunlike rays of the King pierce even as far as Africa to 'heal' the blackness of the Queen and her courtiers, imagined as women of Niger. These early masques inaugurate an 'imperial theme' that was to become increasingly prominent in Jonson's later masques and other works such as Shakespeare's *The Tempest* (1611), which both invokes and critiques the masque form as part of a broader set of colonial encounters. Jonson's language of colonial transformation in the Jacobean masque helped courtiers and poets imagine the sweep and power (along with potential dangers) of imperial rule at a time when the British Empire was only embryonic.

Jonson specifically credits Queen Anne with the invention of the antimasque, 'some dance or show that might precede hers and have the place of a foil or false masque' which appeared first in the *Masque of Queens*, performed at court in February 1609.[11] This sumptuous entertainment moved from an antimasque of evil witches to the main masque's idealised procession of queens enacted by Queen Anne and her ladies. Of course the King was free, if he desired, to see Queen Anne and her ladies in the witches rather than in the idealised matriarchs of the main masque: *The Masque of Queens* takes on particular bite if we imagine it as dealing with the 'problem' of women's power and independence at court. Kathryn Schwarz has recently analysed the masque as a systematic dismemberment of the King's 'body politic'.[12] Perhaps not coincidentally, this was the last masque designed by Jonson explicitly at the prompting of Queen Anne and her circle, although they continued to take major roles in the planning and performance of later court entertainments.

From 1616 – the year of Jonson's laureateship – onward, his court masques typically have a bipolar structure in which the antimasques boldly satirise

---

11 Cited from Inigo Jones, *The Theatre of the Stuart Court*, ed. Stephen Orgel and Roy Strong (London: Sotheby Parke Bernet, and Berkeley: University of California Press, 1973), 1:132.
12 See Kathryn Schwarz, *Tough Love: Amazon Encounters in the English Renaissance* (Durham, NC, and London: Duke University Press, 2000), pp. 160–97.

national and courtly vices and the main masques celebrate James's proposed solutions. The increased satiric thrust of his masques from this period may stem in part from the fact that his patron the Earl of Pembroke had been appointed Lord Chamberlain in 1615. Pembroke was as well known for his 'ultra-Protestant' leanings as for his great 'friendship' towards poets, and may have encouraged Jonson's reforming tendencies in the court masque. As part of his 'conversation' with his subjects, James I was prone to issue lengthy, published proclamations that not only announced a policy decision, but explored it in terms of the pragmatic and conceptual problems it was designed to correct. Jonson's and other court masques belonged to the same conversation; they were usually also published within a short interval after their performance, so that both they and the royal policies they celebrated could be aired and debated not just by the courtiers and visiting ambassadors who attended the actual performance, but by the nation at large.

As an example of the daring Jonson was willing to venture in praise and correction of the 'glass' the court offered to the nation, we might consider *Pleasure Reconciled to Virtue*, performed in early 1618 to celebrate James I's landmark visit to Scotland during the previous summer, his efforts there to break the power of the Kirk and impose the governance and liturgy of the Church of England, and his promulgation of an important document that became known as the *Book of Sports* after its publication in 1618. The *Book of Sports* was one of several policy initiatives of the King's designed to reduce the size and dominance of London and to revitalise the countryside, in this case by encouraging traditional communal sports and pastimes – such as church ales, dancing about maypoles, and lavish holiday hospitality on the part of local gentry and aristocrats – all of which customs had 'decayed' in rural parts or been actively suppressed by ecclesiastical reformers and local magistrates concerned with the pastimes' potential for fomenting 'disorders'.

In *Pleasure Reconciled to Virtue*, Jonson brilliantly unites the King's recent ecclesiastical and rural policy initiatives by displaying them as instances of James I's self-characterisation as a mediator, a creator of a fruitful 'middle way' in all things. The masque demonstrates royal power in action through the person of Hercules, who successfully vanquishes excess at both the extremes of Catholic superfluity and Puritan spareness in order to revitalise the countryside and the nation as a re-equilibrated vision of unity. The dances of the main masque show the courtiers' successful assimilation of Hercules' lessons in moderation – a 'mirror' to the nation, of grace and reverence brought into a single whole. The dances end with Prince Charles and the other masquers poised to inherit the role of Hercules for themselves. But the antimasques of *Pleasure Reconciled to Virtue* demonstrate how closely the extremes which James moderates are

associated with the court itself. Comus the belly-god and his drunken retinue are introduced by an erotically charged cupbearer to Hercules who bears
a strong resemblance to the royal favourite George Villiers, later Duke of
Buckingham, and who admits that it is Hercules' own cup that is being dishonoured through the drunken orgies of Comus and his courtiers. The antimasque
points at James's own excess along with that of his courtiers – his excessive
fondness for Buckingham, upon whom he lavished titles, wealth and sexual
favours; his frequent inebriation; and his squandering of court revenues on
over-lavish banqueting and drink.[13] In its original form, *Pleasure Reconciled to
Virtue* was not successful at court; Jonson scrapped the original antimasques for
a less controversial display of loyal Welshmen when it was newly performed
six weeks later in honour of Prince Charles under the title *For the Honour of
Wales*.

Despite the palliative revisions, however, the strong medicine of this entertainment demonstrates just how intellectually and morally challenging court
entertainments could be under the early Stuarts. Despite their brave shows
and huge expense, much resented by many contemporaries, they were not
mere empty spectacles but strenuously dialogic mediations between the ideals
of the court and fallible human behaviour. In 1618, Jonson himself travelled to
Scotland in imitation of James I's celebrated visit of the year before. Jonson's
three weeks' stay with William Drummond of Hawthornden at Drummond's
estate south of Edinburgh resulted in the remarkable *Conversations* collected
by his host. Jonson's table talk reveals much of his ambivalence about his career as court poet, including his wish that he had been a churchman so that,
finding favour with the King, he might preach before James and not flatter
the monarch even if Jonson were staring death in the face. Whatever else it
may have signified, his statement was surely a rueful comment on the adula-
tory stance towards the monarch that was an unavoidable part of being chief
masque writer at court.

After the 1618 onset of the Thirty Years' War in Europe, the Stuart court
masque increasingly took on international subjects and offered a vaster vision of
the transforming power of the King. One of James's mottos was 'blessed are the
peacemakers'. To the despair of English ultra-Protestants, James steadily refused military involvement in the European conflict, even after his own daughter Elizabeth, Queen of Bohemia, was ousted by Catholic forces from the
throne she held along with her husband the Elector Palatine. Prince Henry,
in marked independence from the pacifism of his father, had been strongly

13 Leah S. Marcus, *The Politics of Mirth: Jonson, Herrick, Milton, Marvell, and the Defense of Old
    Holiday Pastimes* (University of Chicago Press, 1986), pp. 106–39.

associated with the ultra-Protestant, interventionist faction in England and with the revival of chivalry at court, but after his death in 1612 that faction lost its chief support within the royal family. After the outbreak of war in 1618, English militants stood by helplessly, fearing that international Protestantism was about to be engulfed and destroyed. Jonson's masque for 1620, *News from the New World Discovered in the Moon*, attempts to bridge the widening gap between the pacifism of the King and the war hunger of many of his subjects by associating royal power with the universal operation of planetary magic.

The antimasques of *News from the New World Discovered* acknowledge the division of the nation over British intervention in the European war by satirising various commercial agents by whom the new war was reported in England, and whom James had attempted to suppress through another of his public proclamations – an ominous instance in which the royal penchant for print was used to silence public debate rather than furthering literary 'conversation' between James and his subjects. Once the antimasques' erratic, illicit 'news' has been silenced, the main masque ascends to a new world that does not change – the mind and ethos of the King, depicted as a universal *primum mobile* constant in 'perfection' and 'pure harmony' and securely controlling the movement of all the planets (that is, the courtiers, the nation at large and even the international community as a whole) despite the huge cataclysm even then being enacted in Europe and the seriously divided opinion it had kindled at home. In the new world of the main masque, what many subjects saw as James's narrow, dangerous isolationism is recast as breadth of vision: Jonson celebrates the monarch as a divinity who controls a universe rather than a mere island kingdom.

Scholars have tended to see masques like *News from the New World*, which link royal power with Neoplatonic planetary magic, as simply communicating James's own grandiose notions of royal absolutism. But we need to recognise how far Jonson's vision of the operation of royal power goes beyond James I's usual assertions of it. It is Jonson, not James, who dramatises through sweeping, cosmic imagery the absolute, universal operation of royal power. Jonson and other masque writers in the 1620s and thereafter were enormously aided by Inigo Jones's innovative uses of perspective in his staging designs for the masque, which increased the audience's visual perception of distance, broadened the imaginable range of royal authority, and thereby extended the dream of empire almost infinitely. Jones's scenic designs also introduced a newly Romanised architecture anchored in the principles of the ancient Roman Vitruvius, and serving visually to imprint a connection between Roman and Jacobean 'empire' upon the minds of viewers and readers of the published version of the masque. The court masque helped James and Charles I and other courtiers to expand their own understanding of the meaning and potential scope of royal power, and that was surely a large part of the fascination this art form held for three decades at court.

One of the most central critical debates of recent decades concerns the degree to which the very pervasiveness and insistence of James's own rhetoric may have created an 'opposition' literature, or at least individual dissenting voices, in writings of the period. The most direct form of 'anti-court' literature was prose and verse libels, sometimes hilariously scurrilous and almost always circulated only anonymously in manuscript. These clandestine but very popular tidbits tended to cluster with particular frequency around lurid episodes in the life of the court, such as the Essex–Howard divorce case (only a few years after the marriage had been celebrated with such pomp in *Hymenaei*). During the widely publicised divorce proceedings, James I sided with the dissolute but putatively virgin Lady Howard against the advice of his own archbishop, since he wanted to free her to marry one of his Scottish favourites, Robert Carr, Lord Rochester. Worse yet, in the ensuing Overbury scandal it was revealed that Frances Howard had gone so far as to murder the courtier Sir Thomas Overbury in order to obliterate evidence that might have blocked her divorce. Elements of the Essex–Howard divorce and Overbury scandal are satirised in plays like Jonson's *The Devil Is an Ass*, but unprinted libels went considerably further in their contempt for the sorry assortment of sorcerers and fashion mavens surrounding Frances Howard. Before his death, Thomas Overbury and his circle, centred on the courtier Cecily Bulstrode, a kinswoman of the Countess of Bedford, had played a manuscript game called 'news' in which they had circulated parodies of prominent courtiers. In the aftermath of the Overbury scandal bits of this 'news' slipped into print as tantalising appendixes of 'Conceited News' provocatively attached to posthumous editions of Overbury's *The Wife*.[14]

The so-called 'Robert Herrick's Commonplace Book'[15] is but one interesting example of a collectively compiled manuscript book that crackles with squibs against the main contenders in the Overbury scandal; against Robert Cecil, Lord Salisbury; and against the Duke of Buckingham, particularly during his and Prince Charles's ill-fated clandestine voyage to Spain to secure the hand of the Spanish Infanta for Charles. The proposed Spanish match was enormously unpopular, satirised as early as Thomas Scott's virulently anti-Spanish *Vox Populi* (printed four times in 1620 alone and eventually suppressed, but

---

14 See *The 'Conceited News' of Sir Thomas Overbury and His Friends*, ed. James E. Savage (Gainesville, FL: Scholars' Facsimiles and Reprints, 1968); and the discussion of manuscript libels in Ann Baynes Coiro, 'Milton and Class Identity: The Publication of *Areopagitica* and the 1645 *Poems*', *Journal of Medieval and Renaissance Studies* 22 (1992), 261–89.

15 Harry Ransom Humanities Research Center, University of Texas, Austin, Pre-1700 MS 79. Most scholars now agree that Herrick's hand is not represented in this manuscript, though it may have been closely tied to his circle at Cambridge.

continuing to circulate widely in manuscript), and as late as Thomas Middleton's hilariously scurrilous play *A Game at Chess* (which enjoyed wild popularity on stage in 1624 until the King acceded to pressure from the Spanish
ambassador and suppressed it). Not content with his proclamations that had
attempted to curb inflammatory debate and news from abroad, James I himself issued a verse reply to 'railing rhymes and vaunting verse' lampooning the
Spanish match.[16]

The royal favourite George Villiers, Duke of Buckingham, was another perennial butt of libels. He had originally been introduced at court by Pembroke and
the anti-Spanish faction, but his precipitous rise to a dukedom, and his enormous and carelessly wielded power as a close intimate of the King's, earned him
many enemies. He accompanied Prince Charles on his ill-fated trip to woo the
Spanish Infanta, and had little better luck in his later anti-Spanish phase, when
he shamed the nation with the disastrously ill-managed Île of Rhé expedition to
relieve continental Protestants. By the time of Buckingham's assassination in
1628, he was called the most hated man in England, and one of the many libels
celebrating his death was written in a style so similar to that of Ben Jonson
that the laureate was for a time accused of its authorship.[17]

Writers willing to acknowledge their own literary offspring had to be more
circumspect. Sir Francis Bacon was very much of the court during most of
the years in which he was writing and expanding his brilliantly terse *Essays*
(published in 1597, 1612 and 1625, with frequent reprints in between); yet he
was insistent on the subject of favourites and evil counsellors: let the King not
divulge his own 'inclination', lest his councillors do nothing but 'sing him a
song of *placebo*'; let kings not purchase friendship 'at the hazard of their own
safety and greatness'; let the King not align himself with a single faction or party,
for when those are 'carried too high and too violently, it is a sign of weakness in
princes'. Bacon's *Essays* circumspectly revise the masque's idealised depiction
of James I: 'Princes are like to heavenly bodies, which cause good or evil times;
and which have much veneration, but no rest.' The King is to remember that
he is a man, and to remember that he is a god, or 'God's lieutenant' – 'the one
bridleth their power, and the other their will'.[18]

16 Kevin Sharpe, 'The King's Writ: Royal Authors and Royal Authority in Early Modern
England', in *Culture and Politics in Early Stuart England*, ed. Sharpe and Peter Lake,
(Basingstoke: Macmillan, 1994), pp. 117–38.
17 See Alastair Bellany, ' "Raylinge Rymes and Vaunting Verse": Libellous Politics in Early
Stuart England, 1603–1628', in *Culture and Politics*, ed. Sharpe and Lake, pp. 285–310.
18 Citations are to *Francis Bacon*, ed. Brian Vickers (Oxford and New York: Oxford Univer-
sity Press, 1996): 'Of Counsel', p. 382; 'Of Friendship', p. 391; 'Of Faction', p. 441; and
'Of Empire', p. 379.

There were other indirect ways of indicating distrust of unbridled 'power'. As David Norbrook has argued, there was a loose coterie of poets sometimes called the 'Spenserians' who harked back to the style, Protestant poetics and apocalypticism of Edmund Spenser and other Elizabethans as a way of communicating their dissatisfaction with the monarch and dominant elements of the Jacobean court. To some degree, these poets were disgruntled by their failure to receive preferment under James. Fulke Greville, Lord Brooke, was one such poet: his *Life of Sidney*, which was not published until 1652, idealised Sidney as 'the last representative of a heroic age of austere Protestant militancy which had now given way to luxury and cowardice'.[19] Samuel Daniel, another poet associated with the 'Spenserian' label, started out with a verse 'Panegyric' to the newly crowned James I and a commission to devise a masque for the first season at court, but was increasingly edged out by Jonson as the poet of choice at court. Daniel's services as poet and masque writer were nevertheless called for by the ultra-Protestant faction. He, not Jonson, created the entertainment for Prince Henry's installation as Prince of Wales: *Tethys' Festival* (1610), danced by Queen Anne, her daughter Elizabeth, and her ladies. Other 'Spenserians' include Michael Drayton, Giles and Phineas Fletcher, William Browne and George Wither, but these figures varied widely in their degree of opposition to the court, their willingness to take on specific issues and their readiness to allow their work to be printed.

The simplest, yet subtlest, way 'Spenserians' indicated their dissatisfaction with the Jacobean court was their refusal to participate in its dominant cultural norms. James prided himself on his 'plain style' as part of his quest (at least in theory) for 'moderation in all things'; the Spenserians tended to prefer the ornate, highly coloured and complex style of Edmund Spenser. Instead of praising James, they harked back to the glory days of Elizabeth. If James I modelled himself upon Augustus Caesar, the 'Spenserians' and their fellow-travellers chose instead to emphasise the virtues of the Roman republic. While James sought to link himself with the epic glories of urban Rome, the 'Spenserians' preferred pastoral, a genre associated from ancient times with the critique of courts. In works like William Browne's *Britannia's Pastorals* (the first part of which was published in 1613) the court is conspicuously absent and the countryside is instead offered as a model for national virtue. Similarly, Michael Drayton's mammoth *Poly-Olbion* (the first part of which was published in 1612) was dedicated to Prince Henry, not James I, and maps the entire nation

19 David Norbrook, *Poetry and Politics in the English Renaissance* (London: Routledge and Kegan Paul, 1984), pp. 195–214; quotation from p. 196.

county by county, placing particular emphasis upon the local notables in each area to the neglect of, and in implicit criticism of, the court.

Lady Mary (Sidney) Wroth's long pastoral romance *Urania* (of which the first part was published in 1621) can be interpreted as belonging to the same anti-Jacobean literary strain, even though its author was very much a fixture at court, unlike most of the 'Spenserians'. At the height of England's 'war fever' and James's pacifism, Wroth's romance constructs an alternative candidate for imperial ruler of the west – the young Amphilanthus, whose internationalism reflects the political stance of Wroth herself, Wroth's lover the Earl of Pembroke, and others who favoured intervention on the continent against the Catholic powers. Wroth's titillating romance aroused outrage on the part of many courtiers who saw themselves personally satirised in its pages; the second half of the manuscript, presently at the Newberry Library in Chicago, never saw print in its own era, although it may well have circulated in manuscript to the special delectation of court ladies who despised both James's political quietism and his well-known contempt for women.[20]

The tendency of early Stuart court literature, however, was to attempt to absorb the opposition. If the Spenserians used pastoral eclogue and romance to suggest simpler, purer alternatives to the values that prevailed at court, the court developed its own forms of pastoral that sought to move a purified court out into the countryside. From 1614 through the 1620s, James I issued a series of proclamations ordering the gentry and aristocracy who swelled the urban population of London, leaving the countryside neglected, to return to their proper spheres of influence and 'keep hospitality' on their rural estates, for the better health of the countryside and of the nation as a whole. Immediately, the masques presented at court began to reflect the policy initiative through their use of pastoral motifs. In *The Golden Age Restored* (1615), for example, Pallas reveals a seductive landscape of the countryside as its culminating vision and admonishes its aristocratic onlookers, 'Behold you here / What Jove hath built to be your sphere; / You hither must retire.'[21] The King even wrote his own Horatian elegy to support the policy initiative, though, uncharacteristically, no printed copy is extant and the poem may have remained in manuscript.

20 Both volumes of the *Urania* are now, for the first time, in print. See *The First Part of the Countess of Montgomery's Urania*, ed. Josephine A. Roberts (Binghamton, NY: Medieval and Renaissance Texts and Studies, 1995); and *The Second Part of the Countess of Montgomery's Urania*, ed. Josephine A. Roberts, Suzanne Gossett and Janel Mueller (Tempe AZ: Medieval and Renaissance Texts and Studies, 1999).

21 Quotation is from *Ben Jonson: The Complete Masques*, ed. Stephen Orgel (New Haven, CT: Yale University Press, 1969), p. 231. See also Marcus, *Politics of Mirth*, pp. 64–105; and, for a more complex reading of the political statement of the masque, Martin Butler, 'Ben Jonson and the Limits of Courtly Panegyric', in *Culture and Politics*, ed. Sharpe and Lake, pp. 91–115.

In one copy, the poem is entitled 'An Elegy Written by the King concerning His Counsel for Ladies and Gentlemen to Depart the City of London according to His Majesty's Proclamation'. Like many Jacobean masques, the poem disparages Whitehall's baubles, plays and 'debauched' manners, and offers more wholesome country arts and increased prosperity as part of his incentive to get the upper classes back to rural life: 'The country is your orb and proper sphere. / There your revenues rise; bestow them there.'[22] James's poem was widely imitated; it may well be that the early Stuart subgenre of the country-house poem arose out of the same policy initiative.

In all likelihood, the first country-house poem was written by a woman, Aemilia Lanyer, wife of the court musician Alfonso Lanyer. Her *Salve Deus Rex Judaeorum*, published in 1611, was dedicated to Queen Anne, Princess Elizabeth and a number of other prominent women. Lanyer's is rare among published volumes in that it gives us a sense of the interests and values a woman author, herself marginally attached to the court, thought likely to appeal to Queen Anne's circle of courtly women. It includes 'The Description of Cooke-ham' honouring the Dowager Countess of Cumberland and her estate, and incorporating many of the themes that were to become staples of the country-house poem: praise of its varied landscape, stately oaks, crystal streams and welcoming flora and fauna. Ben Jonson's 'To Penshurst' is the most famous poem of the subgenre, written about the same time as Lanyer's. It celebrates a seigneurial way of life in which a great family, that of Sir Robert Sidney, Viscount Lisle, lives in symbiotic interaction with the people and products of the surrounding countryside – very much the image of rural retreat celebrated in Stuart court pastoral. But the Stuart country-house poem, unlike Spenserian pastoral, does not elide the monarchy. In 'To Penshurst' one demonstration of the wholesomeness of the estate is the fact that it was able to offer appropriate hospitality to 'our James', even in the absence of its lord and lady.

In the work of Jonson's followers the 'Sons of Ben', however, more and more elements of court life are incorporated into the rural retreat: the subgenre, over time, was 'colonized' by the court, and the owner of the estate increasingly imagined as a surrogate of the monarch. In Thomas Carew's 'To Saxham', for example, which probably dates from the late 1620s, the country estate is cut off from its surrounding fields and villages by winter weather, but, within, the house enjoys a 'spring' of bounty and delicacies that appears to be miraculously supplied from the heavens, much as they might appear in the culminating vision of a masque. Carew's 'To My Friend G. N. from Wrest', probably written

22 *The Poems of James VI of Scotland*, ed. James Craigie, 2 vols., Scottish Text Society (Edinburgh: Blackwood, 1955–8), 2:179.

in 1639, severs the estate even more literally from its surroundings: it offers its courtier visitors a magical self-enclosed space of peace and plenty while the First Bishops' War rages around it. In later examples of the subgenre written during the 'Cavalier winter' of the Civil War and its aftermath, the rural estate becomes not a mere reflection of the court but its only remaining image.[23] Early Stuart pastoral castigates the vices of the court and repudiates it in favour of rural simplicity, as one would expect in a pastoral, but the countryside is infused with purified and rarified simulacra of the values promulgated at court.

If anything, Stuart court pastoral increased in popularity after the death of James I, for his son Charles continued many of his father's major policy initiatives. These included renewal of the earlier proclamations ordering gentry and aristocrats with no specific business in London to return to their country estates; a ceremonial visit to Scotland in 1633 to attempt, yet again, to impose Anglican church government upon the Scottish Kirk; and, as part of the same effort, reissuance of the *Book of Sports* the same year, amidst a new round of controversy over the propriety and lawfulness of traditional customs like church ales and dancing about maypoles. Queen Henrietta Maria made a regular practice of acting in pastorals at court, and even received drama coaching from a member of the King's Men.[24] But a key difference between Charles and his father was that, while James had styled himself a 'bard' unto his people and had kept up a steady, often garrulously intrusive 'conversation' with them via the printed page, Charles prided himself instead upon his silence, informing his first Parliament that it did not 'stand with my nature to spend much time in words' – a statement he often repeated.[25]

Charles did not share his father's relative tolerance for the messy rough and tumble of public debate: his early speeches before Parliament repeatedly if reluctantly broke his preferred silence to interpret differing political opinion as a form of abuse of his authority. After 1629, he silenced Parliament altogether in favour of his own eleven years' 'personal rule' (1629–40), during which he showed little inclination to communicate with his subjects in print. Charles's court, in marked contrast with James's, was generally well run, with much emphasis on order and decorum and (especially after Buckingham's assassination in 1628, which removed the chief impediment to intimacy between Charles and his Queen Henrietta Maria) little tolerance for open displays of drunkenness and sexual depravity. Charles's interests were more visual than literary:

23 Leah S. Marcus, 'Politics and Pastoral: Writing the Court on the Countryside', in *Culture and Politics*, ed. Sharpe and Lake, pp. 139–59.
24 Martin Butler, *Theatre and Crisis, 1632–1642* (Cambridge University Press, 1984), p. 101.
25 Sharpe, 'King's Writ', pp. 131–4.

under his rule, particularly given the relative public silence in which he conducted the business of state, the Stuart court masque achieved even greater sumptuousness and prominence as a vehicle for the communication of royal policy initiatives. Charles also developed his own roster of favoured poets and his own set of royal themes and motifs distinct from his father's – most notably, after the death of Buckingham, the cult of chaste 'Platonic' love he celebrated with Queen Henrietta Maria.

Much has been made of Charles I's 'neglect' of Ben Jonson, who at least nominally retained the title of Laureate until his death in 1637, but was called upon relatively seldom to provide masques and entertainments at the Caroline court. He composed *Love's Triumph through Callipolis*, the King's Twelfth Night masque for 1631, and *Chloridia*, Queen Henrietta Maria's Shrovetide masque performed in February of the same year. Both of these lavish works complemented the ethos of the new court by exquisitely celebrating the pair's highly publicised cult of married chastity and Platonic love. Jonson also composed a handful of congratulatory verses for Charles and two rural entertainments for the King on progress, the *Entertainment at Welbeck* (1631) and *Love's Welcome at Bolsover* (1634), both commissioned by the Earl of Newcastle, Jonson's most significant patron at court after the death of the Earl of Pembroke in 1630. Jonson himself felt slighted by Charles's evident preference for younger poets like Thomas Carew, Aurelian Townshend and William Davenant. In an epilogue added to the printed version of his play *The New Inn* (1628–9; published 1631), which had been intended for court performance but was never staged there because of its utter failure at Blackfriars, Jonson went so far as to suggest that any waning in his own artistry could be attributed to royal neglect: 'And had he lived the care of king and queen, / His art in something more yet had been seen'.[26] But Jonson arguably brought this neglect on himself through his own strategic silence. At the time of Charles I's coronation, the new King had been greeted by the customary verse encomia from many corners of the kingdom, but not one word, so far as we know, from Jonson. His *Underwood*, published only posthumously in 1640, includes several poems addressed to Charles or his consort (numbers 62–7, 72); but these poems, unlike the bulk of the collection, are explicitly dated by Jonson either through their occasion or in their titles, the earliest belonging to 1629. It would appear that only when Buckingham was safely dead was the Poet Laureate actually willing to address panegyric verses to the monarch. At the end of his life, we find Jonson frantically attempting

26 Cited from *Ben Jonson: The New Inn*, ed. Michael Hattaway, The Revels Plays (Manchester and Dover, NH: Manchester University Press, 1984), p. 203 (Epilogue, lines 21–2).

to make amends: he wrote *The Tale of a Tub* (1633) in part to commemorate Charles's reissue of James's *Book of Sports* the same year, and when he died he left unfinished *The Sad Shepherd*, an exquisite piece designed to meet the seemingly inexhaustible demand for pastoral drama at court. But these efforts were too little, too late. Charles never forgave Jonson for his impolitic silence during the first years of the reign.

As Jonson's popularity waned at court, his arch-rival, the engineer and architect Inigo Jones, assumed increasing dominance as a deviser of masques. Jones's first production after he definitively broke with Jonson was *Albion's Triumph* (1632), for which the verses and elements of the 'invention' were supplied by Aurelian Townshend. Through its depiction of the divinely ordained union of the Emperor Albanactus (performed by the Scottish-born Charles I himself) and Alba, goddess of Albion (performed by Queen Henrietta Maria), *Albion's Triumph* combines the imperial themes and celebration of Anglo-Scottish Union familiar from the Jacobean masque with the motif of Platonic love that was a special hallmark of courtly entertainments during the 1630s. In case Charles's performance fails to live up to the masque's high visions of perfection, there is an antimasque character named Platonicus who instructs sceptical viewers that the monarch should be viewed not with mere sight, but through the eyes of intellect as an emperor over all base passions: 'For a supplement to thy lame story, know I have seen this brave Albanactus Caesar, seen him with the eyes of understanding, viewed all his actions, looked into his mind, which I find armed with so many moral virtues that he daily conquers a world of vices.'[27]

It is enormously significant that, unlike his father, Charles I performed as chief masquer in his own masques; indeed, he had been brought up on the art form in the Jacobean court. As a monarch who witnessed his own courtly entertainments, James I had preserved at least a semblance of distance from their assertions of royal divinity and omnipotence, but Charles instead made himself part of the vehicle by which the masque communicated the 'removed mysteries' behind its glorious shows. Indeed, *Albion's Triumph* and other Caroline masques announced themselves, in all their grandiosity and sumptuousness, as revelations of the mind of the King. Did Charles I make the mistake of confusing life and art – actually believe in the highly ritualised 'magic' of his masques to transform the guiding myths of his reign into reality? Many of his sceptical subjects feared that he did, and in the Caroline masque, the issue of the entertainment's credibility, its power to win over its audience, becomes newly prominent.

27 Inigo Jones, *The Theatre of the Stuart Court*, 2:455.

Given the pervasiveness of the Platonic imagery of chaste love in the culture of the Caroline court, a cynical backlash against that particular set of idealisations was perhaps inevitable. Some of the most beautiful love lyrics in the language date from the Caroline era – such as Thomas Carew's 'Song': 'Ask me no more where Jove bestows / When June is past the fading rose'. But the same poet, who as a Gentleman of the Privy Chamber was very much a court insider, also wrote 'A Rapture', with its clever invitation to unchastity: 'Then tell me why / This goblin Honor, which the world adores, / Should make men atheists, and not women whores.' Sir John Suckling, who was later to demonstrate his passionate devotion to the Cavalier cause, was nevertheless a steady debunker of royal platonising, as in his 'Loving and Beloved', which likens lovers to kings on the grounds that both rule through the art of dissembling, or in his 'Against Fruition,' which begins, with wittily scathing reference to the royal dyad as depicted in the masque, 'Fie upon hearts that burn with mutual fire! / I hate two minds that breathe but one desire.' The frequent misogyny of Caroline love lyrics has caused them to lose popularity during recent decades; and, indeed, to read these graceful expressions of male nonchalance alongside women's diaries of the period – which typically record the pain of constant child-bearing and the anguished loss of offspring – is to receive a salutary correction of the Cavaliers' strangely limited, hothouse perspective on women.

To what extent might the fashionable undercurrent of Cavalier literary misogyny reflect an uneasy awareness of the independence of Queen Henrietta Maria? Like Queen Anne before her, Henrietta Maria had her own circle of intimates at court. During the early and mid 1630s, she served as a focal point for the militant anti-Spanish faction: ambassadorial reports record, 'the queen allies herself to the puritans', and she showed special favour for plays and verses that cast Spain in a negative light, such as the revival of *Alphonsus, Emperor of Germany*, an old Elizabethan play about Spain's cruelty towards the Protestants in Germany, which she attended at Blackfriars along with the German Prince Rupert in 1636.[28] During the final years of the decade, by contrast, Henrietta Maria became the centre of a strong Catholic revival, particularly among English noblewomen, many of whom converted to Catholicism. Counter-Reformation devotional literature flowed relatively freely into England under her sponsorship; its effects can be seen, for example, in the highly florid baroque style of Richard Crashaw's book of Latin epigrams (1634), and later poems like his 'Flaming Heart' and hymn to St Theresa. During the 1640s, if not earlier, Crashaw himself converted to Catholicism

28 Butler, *Theatre and Crisis*, p. 33.

under the patronage of the Countess of Denbigh, one of Henrietta Maria's ladies-in-waiting.

The popularity of Catholicism at court was worrisome to many strong Protestants, particularly since, in their view, Charles I's own love for ritual and liturgical forms seemed to be moving the nation dangerously close to 'popery', quite apart from the activities of the Queen. During the mid and late 1630s, a long-brewing controversy over the proper place of liturgical forms became increasingly visible in published writings, in part because of the unprecedented thoroughness with which King Charles and Archbishop Laud sought to impose conformity. What later became known as the 'Laudian' party favoured the retention of ancient pre-Reformation rituals like making the sign of the cross, giving a ring in marriage, and placing the altar against the east wall, at a hieratic distance from communicants in parish churches. What was sometimes disparagingly termed a 'Puritan' current of counter-opinion branded all such practices as unacceptably 'popish' and profane. Increasingly, battles over liturgical forms and the pastimes traditionally bound to religious holidays were fought out in the courts, with the common law venues pitted against the so-called royal prerogative courts, particularly the dreaded High Commission and Star Chamber, where Charles could enforce obedience to royal proclamations over the objections of the lower courts. Particularly after Charles's reissue of the *Book of Sports* in 1633, any literary defence of ritual and ceremony came to be politically coded as pro-Caroline and pro-Laudian. So we find the 'Son of Ben' Robert Herrick, who had court connections and had served earlier as chaplain to the Duke of Buckingham, commending 'May-poles, Hock-carts, Wassails, Wakes', and other forms of holiday mirth as part of a broader agenda to support ritualism per se against its many contemporary enemies. In Herrick, however, as in most of the Cavalier poets, ceremony and seduction are never entirely separable: in 'Corinna's Going a-Maying', for example, he urges Corinna to 'obey' Charles's 'Proclamation made for May' in the *Book of Sports* as part of an effort to seduce her into rural dalliance.

In the masque, Charles sought to legitimise ecclesiastical ritual practices and purge them of such licentious admixtures by tying them to solemn, ancient British usages that predated even the importation of Catholicism from Rome. If religious ritualism was purely British, a mystical intimation of Christian truth *avant la lettre*, then it could scarcely be repudiated as some dangerous foreign import. In *Albion's Triumph* the Emperor Albanactus is also a proto-Christian high priest whose quasi-liturgical rites are innocent precursors of Anglican worship. Perhaps the most sumptuous Caroline masque was Sir Thomas Carew's *Coelum*

Britannicum (performed at court during Shrovetide, 1634), in the thick of the controversy surrounding the *Book of Sports* and Laudian 'innovations' more generally. *Coelum Britannicum* is in many ways a rewriting of Jonson's *Pleasure Reconciled to Virtue* in that it sets a love for traditional communal pastimes within a larger set of ritual structures that redeem it from its excesses. The masque begins with an intriguing vision of the 'ruins of some great city of the ancient Romans or civilized Britons' which Jove vows to restore. The scene changes to a depiction of the night sky, which is gradually darkened through a series of antimasques that one by one extinguish its stars. Several of the antimasques represent grotesque perversions of Charles's actual policies, such as the cultivation of art and connoisseurship, the alleviation of harmful monopolies, the restoration of the countryside, and the reformation of morals at court. Then the scene changes again, revealing a mount holding the 'three kingdoms of England, Scotland, and Ireland' that comprise modern Britain. The divine dyad Carlo-Maria, imagined as a sun or noonday star in the night sky, gradually re-illumines the 'darkened sphere' of the British heavens through a series of highly elaborate ritualised dances.[29] With each dance, some of the stars re-emerge until all are once more visible. The newly furbished, star-studded heavens are depicted as a restoration of ancient pattern, not a novelty, but they also pointedly echo the star-painted ceiling of the court of Star Chamber, which Charles I used during the period of personal rule as a quasi-legal instrument to enforce his visions of political and liturgical order. In Carew's amazing tour de force, ritual is naturalised and linked, through the pointed allusion to Star Chamber, with royal prerogative powers. The dance of ritual, in effect, is identified as the performance of Charles's divinity on earth.

To what extent was the extreme hieraticism of the Caroline masque reflected or reworked in other literary forms of the period? The striking allegorical tableaux of the masque – a Mercury or Peace or Platonic Passion seemingly frozen into an eternal present during their time on centre stage – may well stand behind hyper-real, strongly visualised and highly equivocal images in Caroline lyrics like Andrew Marvell's 'The Unfortunate Lover', possibly written before 1640, his later Mower Poems and 'Upon Appleton House', as well as numerous other poems that post-date the period covered in this chapter. As Martin Butler discusses at greater length below in his chapter on 'Literature and the Theatre to 1660', Caroline drama, both the so-called 'court' drama and the newly genteel public theatres, took up many of the same troubling subjects that were investigated in the masque: the extent and efficacy of royal prerogative

29 Cited from Inigo Jones, *The Theatre of the Stuart Court*, 2:570–80.

powers, the importance of good counsel and the (sometimes unbridgeable) gap between appearance and reality in matters of rule.

In considering the theatrical production of the 1630s, we must take care not to rely on hindsight: the ultimate isolation and shipwreck of the Caroline monarchy should not be read back into cultural productions of a decade earlier; indeed our perception of the artistic integrity and independence of the Caroline drama has suffered greatly from an inability to separate it from the 'decline' of the monarch. Plays written by courtiers for performance before the King are often narrower and more insular than plays written for the public theatre, yet even the court plays echo earlier work by Shakespeare, Jonson and others, in that they explore controversial subjects with considerable freedom. Robert Davenport's *King John and Matilda* (*c.* 1634), which was acted 'often before their majesties', demonstrates through the case of King John how absolutism allied with personal vices can defile church and state; Sir William Davenant's *The Unfortunate Lovers* (1638) shows how a monarch's authority can be perverted through the 'intricate / Though powerful influence of love' and reflects upon Charles I's lack of accountability for his decisions during the period of personal rule; Davenant's *Fair Favourite* from the same year depicts a king who is 'outwardly absolute' but 'inwardly unfree'.[30]

Even John Milton's *Maske at Ludlow* (1634) is of the court in the sense that it was created for an important royal servant, John Egerton, Earl of Bridgewater, on the occasion of his formal installation as President of the Council in the Marches of Wales, one of the courts by which Charles I was attempting to secure and extend his royal prerogative powers. The *Maske* was performed by court musician Henry Lawes and the Earl's own children, who had danced in masques at court, most recently in Carew's *Coelum Britannicum* the same year. But Milton's masque takes place in a wilderness that is far removed from the civilised ethos of the court. Its tempter figure Comus recalls the sinister Comus of Jonson's *Pleasure Reconciled to Virtue*, and attempts to seduce Milton's Lady with deliberate echoes of the very language of Carew's 'rewrite' of Jonson in *Coelum Britannicum*. Through Comus's appeal to the Lady, Milton also echoes and critiques the standard Cavalier invitation to sexual incontinence under the guise of 'harmless mirth'.[31] On the occasion of the performance of Milton's *Maske at Ludlow*, courtiers danced in an entertainment that disassociated the authority of the Earl of Bridgewater from many standard elements of court ideology. During the same decade the public theatres dared to take on issues

30 Butler, *Theatre and Crisis*, pp. 73, 58.
31 Marcus, *Politics of Mirth*, pp. 169–212. Also see Chapter 20, p. 627, below.

like Laudian ritualism, monopolies, the lawfulness of the King's efforts to forbid gentry to reside in London, and un-Parliamentary taxation.

Though some of these productions were suppressed either by the Privy Council or by ecclesiastical officials, the freedom with which the drama treated such sensitive subjects suggests that it, at least, preserved some of the dynamic richness and diversity of the Jacobean 'virtual court', where considerable freedom of debate was frequently tolerated. The plays of James Shirley and Richard Brome, in particular, display and resist the court's tendency to colonise and monopolise the national culture. Brome's *Queen and Concubine* (which Butler suggests may have been acted at court in 1636) offers a scathing portrait of a royal pair – the King of Sicily and his concubine – addicted to the 'top of sovereignty'. The King calls Parliament only to dominate it, despite the objections of his subjects, and ignores the advice of honest courtiers in favour of the toadying Horatio, who consistently holds that 'the king's power warrants his acts'. Similarly, Shirley's *The Lady of Pleasure* (1635) and *The Example* (1634) show how the insistent encroachments of court culture can tyrannise over the lives of those who wish to live separate from it.[32]

By the late 1630s, in the eyes of at least some loyal subjects, the court's profound influence over the rest of the country was identified with the unlawful assertion of prerogative powers by Charles I and his ministers: Jonson's enticing earlier model of the court as a 'spring' or 'glass' to nurture the nation as a whole was reinterpreted as an imposition of cultural tyranny. William Davenant and Inigo Jones's *Salmacida Spolia* (1640), the last masque presented by Charles I and Henrietta Maria at court, offers a final depiction of Charles's idealised nation, a pastoral landscape 'with all such things as might express a country in peace, rich and fruitful'. But the masque also newly acknowledges the frailty and evanescence of the royal vision, showing antimasques of Furies that plunder the rural abundance through political and economic discord, and even acknowledging a stubborn people who fail to value the 'easy blessing' they have received through the King's care. *Salmacida Spolia* ends on an elegiac note: looking upon the royal 'blessings that descend so fast', the Chorus of Beloved People, who have belatedly learned to prize Charles I's blessings upon the nation, grieve that they are 'too great to last'.[33]

32 Butler, *Theatre and Crisis*, pp. 35–42 and 166–74.
33 Inigo Jones, *The Theatre of the Stuart Court*, 2:729–34.

Chapter 17

LITERATURE AND THE CHURCH

DEBORA SHUGER

The early Stuart era begins with the 1604 disputation between the bishops' party and the Puritans at Hampton Court and it ends thirty-seven years later in a civil war between much the same two groups, although over far more complicated issues. Throughout the period one finds religious tensions and conflicts, many with a marked political dimension. Early Stuart controversial divinity centres on issues of authority, jurisdiction, power, obedience, conformity and outward worship. The religious controversies respond to and are inseparably intertwined with the ecclesio-political crises of the age: the Gunpowder Plot of 1605 and the subsequent imposition of the Oath of Allegiance; the outbreak of the Thirty Years' War in 1618; the dissolution of the 1629 Parliament that ushered in Charles's eleven-year Personal Rule; the Bishops' Wars of 1639–40; the English Civil War.

These crises spawned an immense corpus of religious polemic, including a fair amount of hate literature[1] and the anti-Catholic, anti-Laudian conspiratorial fantasies that seem to have been largely responsible for the breakdown of Caroline rule.[2] Yet these polemics also include Donne's witty and searching anti-Jesuit satire, *Ignatius his Conclave* (1611); the providential, almost mystical, nationalism of Lancelot Andrewes's Gunpowder Plot sermons, which, in their fusion of English Protestant triumphalism with radiant evocations of

My deepest thanks to David Loewenstein, Janel Mueller, Anthony Milton and Ramie Targoff for their wonderful comments, criticism and encouragement.

1 For example, *A Discoverie of the most secret and subtile practises of the Iesuites* (London, 1610); John Brereley's semi-pornographic *Luthers Life* (Saint-Omer, 1624), a Jesuit work; and the savagely anti-Laudian *Letany of John Bastwick* (Leiden, 1637).

2 See the articles by Peter Lake, 'Anti-popery: The Structure of a Prejudice', in *Conflict in Early Stuart England*, ed. R. Cust and A. Hughes (London: Longman, 1989), pp. 72–106; Robin Clifton, 'Fear of Popery', in *The Origins of the English Civil War*, ed. Conrad Russell (Basingstoke: Macmillan, 1973), pp. 144–67; Patrick Collinson, *The Birthpangs of Protestant England* (Basingstoke: Macmillan, 1988), p. 148; William M. Lamont, *Marginal Prynne, 1600–1669* (London: Routledge and Kegan Paul, 1963), pp. 1–3, 119–26, 131–7; Anthony Fletcher, *The Outbreak of the English Civil War* (London: Edward Arnold, 1981); Nicholas Tyacke, *Anti-Calvinists: The Rise of English Arminianism c. 1590–1640* (Oxford: Clarendon Press, 1987), pp. 139, 243.

sacral monarchy and a deep abhorrence of religious persecution, gave expression to the ideals at the heart of James's own pacifist and absolutist Christian politics; and William Chillingworth's brilliant *Religion of Protestants* (1638), published only a few months after Descartes's *Discourse on Method* (1637), which radicalised theology via the same epistemic turn that Cartesianism gave to philosophy: a *summa theologiae* that treats not the objects of belief but the act of believing.

The following discussion of Jacobean and Caroline religious literature largely omits this controversial divinity, partly due to space constraints (William Prynne alone wrote over 200 tracts, including a 1,006-page anti-theatrical diatribe), partly because this material has been treated extensively by early Stuart church historians, but primarily because the major religious *literature* of the period does not map, at least not in any straightforward way, onto the ecclesio-political conflicts.[3] This need not have been the case. Edmund Spenser, the one great Elizabethan religious poet, makes eclogues out of the suspension of Archbishop Grindal and epic out of Tudor church history. One can find counterparts to this in the early Stuart period – the attack on the Laudian clergy in Milton's *Lycidas* (1637), Phineas Fletcher's mini-epic on the Gunpowder Plot (*The Locusts* [1627]) – but not often.[4] Yet the early seventeenth century witnesses the flowering of English sacred poetry, a poetry that, although marked by the opposing visions of Christianity that convulsed the English church and nation in 1641, bears little resemblance to the controversial divinity of the age. George Herbert's *The Temple* and John Donne's hymns do not stake out a position in contemporary ecclesio-political debates. Like most early Stuart sacred poetry, these are devotional lyrics, closer to prayer than polemic.

3 The belletristic definition of 'literature' implicit here remains, however controverted and problematic, the operative one; a study of the English Renaissance that focused on the writings of Perkins and Montagu rather than Shakespeare and Donne would not, I think, be considered even now a history of English Renaissance literature. Such a definition does not imply that literature should be studied in isolation from other sorts of texts but precisely the opposite: that one can only study literature's relation to other cultural discourses by first differentiating literature from them; if one calls all colours 'green', it becomes impossible to remark how close green is to aqua and yet how different from lilac.

4 Brief mention should also be made of the religious satirists, in particular, Sir John Harington (1561–1612), whose epigrams ridiculing Puritan hypocrisy, condemning the lay despoliation of church revenues, and defending Lenten abstinence and religious images suggest a more complex cultural genealogy for Laudianism than the standard focus on its clerical lineage allows. Harington, better known for his translation of Ariosto, was a layman, a courtier and a wit. The epigrams were posthumously published, the fullest edition being *The most elegant and witty epigrams of Sir J. Harrington, knight, digested into foure bookes* (London, 1618); see especially 1.13, 20, 88, 90; 2.7, 39, 56, 63, 90; 3.17; 4.30, 36, 38, 83–4, 92. The other important religious satirist of the period, Bishop Corbett, is discussed briefly in Chapter 22 below.

In a letter dated 25 July 1635, James Howell notes that for his 'privat cubicular devotions' he uses 'Hymns, and various prayers of my own penning . . . divers of them written in my own bloud'.[5] The art of poetry flows into the act of worship. 'Soliloquies', which the devotional manuals use for one type of prayer, is also Francis Quarles's title for several lyrics in *Divine Fancies* (1632). 'Pious ejaculations', the subtitle of Herbert's *Temple* (1633), reappears in these manuals as the standard term for another type.[6] This is not mere nomenclature. Herbert repeatedly presents versing as itself worship, as communion: 'that which while I use / I am with thee'.[7] Almost all the devotional manuals of the period include poems. Michael Sparke's demotic and Puritan *Crumms of Comfort* (41 editions between *c.* 1623 and 1652) ends with a beautifully crafted lyric on the brevity of man's life. John Cosin's Laudian *Devotions* (1627) intersperses numerous poems, mostly translations of early Christian hymns but also a variant of Ben Jonson's 'Hymn to God the Father'.[8] William Crashaw's *Manuale Catholicorum* (1611), subtitled 'A Handful: or Rather a Heartfull of holy meditations and Prayers', is mostly poetry – mostly, in fact, although Crashaw was a staunch Protestant, medieval Latin hymns.[9] George Wither's preface to *Haleluiah or, Britans Second Remembrancer* (1641) describes the work as sacred poetry in the tradition of Herbert and Quarles, yet the volume is structured as a devotional manual: daily prayers to be said upon waking, dressing, washing, before meals, at bedtime; followed by prayers for specific occasions like sheep-shearing, house-warming, taking a walk in one's garden.[10]

In general, the sacred poetry of the early Stuart period has deep and myriad affinities with the genres of what Wither calls '*holy-Prose*':[11] sermons,

---

5 James Howell, *Epistolae Ho-Elianae. Familiar Letters Domestic and Forren*, 3rd edn (London, 1655), pp. 274–6.

6 Michael Sparke, *Crumms of Comfort, The Valley of Teares, and the Hill of Joy*, 6th edn (London, 1627), sig. A6r; John Cosin, *A collection of private devotions* (1627), ed. P. G. Stanwood (Oxford: Clarendon Press, 1967), p. 65.

7 George Herbert, 'The Quidditie', in *The Works of George Herbert*, ed. F. E. Hutchinson, 2 vols. (Oxford: Clarendon Press, 1941). Further citations from Herbert are from this edition.

8 Jonson does not publish 'A Hymne' under his own name until the 1641 *Underwood*. Earlier, around 1635, the piece seems to have been used as an anthem in the royal chapel. Thus, more or less the same text functions as private devotion, public worship and poetry. See Stanwood's commentary in Cosin, *Private Devotions*, pp. 122, 340.

9 William Crashaw was also the father of the great Roman Catholic poet, Richard Crashaw, who, ordained an Anglican priest in the 1630s, converted in 1645.

10 The volume provides for occasions sadly neglected by modern hymnals, including 'For Lovers tempted by carnal Desires' (a very chaste rewrite of Jonson's 'Come, my Celia'), 'For a Widower, or a Widow delivered from a troublesome Yoke-fellow' and 'For a Prisoner at the Place of Execution'. On Wither's debt to Tudor devotional manuals, see Stanwood's introduction to Cosin, *Private Devotions*, p. xxvii.

11 George Wither, *Haleluiah or, Britans Second Remembrancer* (1641), The Spenser Society (Manchester: Charles Simms, 1879), p. 479.

meditations, spiritual guides, emblem books, rules for holy living and holy dying, manuals of public and private prayer. It makes sense to treat these together as the religious literature of the age. The same metaphors and motifs thread from one genre to another and across the ecclesio-political spectrum:[12] the flower in spring as an image of spiritual rebirth;[13] faith piercing the 'mask' of God's anger;[14] the angels of Andrewes's 1618 Nativity sermon who 'now, upon His *Birth* . . . disarme' and Milton's 'bright-harnest' ones, who seem unlikely to beat their swords into harp frames any time soon;[15] the sensuous supernatural pictorialism of militantly Calvinist works like Phineas Fletcher's *Locusts* and Lewis Bayly's *Practise of Pietie* (*c.* 1612; 50 editions by 1700), which spends pages describing heaven's 'walls of jasper stone', its gates 'each built of one Pearle . . . and at each gate an Angell', the saints whose bodies 'shine as bright as the sun in the firmament' and 'being made transparent, their soules shall shine throw';[16] the vivid, darting imagery of early seventeenth-century sermons – Andrewes's 'CHRIST, is no wild catt', Thomas Adams's 'Pleasure like an Irishman, wounds with a dart, and is sodainely gone' – that led an earlier generation of scholars to speak of 'metaphysical' preaching.[17]

12 With respect to literature, in contrast to liturgy, there seems to be no correlation between style and churchmanship. Christopher Harvey is clearly a Laudian, but the devotional lyrics of his *Synagogue* (1640) are written in the intimate colloquial plain-style of Herbert's *Temple* and Sibbes's *Bruised Reed*. The richly sensuous ornament, mythological imagery, ceremonious elevation and self-conscious formal brilliance of Milton's early poetry cannot be meaningfully characterised as Puritan.

13 Richard Sibbes, *The Bruised Reed and Smoking Flax* (1630), intro. P. A. Slack (Menston, Yorks.: Scolar Press, 1973), pp. 93, 253; William Prynne, *Mount-Orgueil* (1641), intro. Edmund Miller (Delmar, NY: Scholars' Facsimiles and Reprints, 1984), p. 119; Herbert, 'The Flower'; Lancelot Andrewes, *XCVI Sermons* (London, 1629), p. 514 (Easter 1617).

14 Sibbes, *Bruised Reed*, p. 165; John Donne, 'A Hymne to Christ, at the Authors last going into Germany', lines 5–8, in *The Divine Poems*, ed. Helen Gardner, 2nd edn (Oxford: Clarendon Press, 1978).

15 Andrewes, *XCVI Sermons*, p. 116; John Milton, 'On the Morning of Christs Nativity', line 245, in *English Poems; Comus, 1645* (Menston, Yorks.: Scolar Press, 1968).

16 Lewis Bayly, *The Practise of Pietie*, 13th edn (London, 1621), pp. 122–43. Fletcher wonderfully describes heaven's citizens as 'Full of unmeasur'd blisse, yet still receiving, / Their soules still childing joy, yet still conceiving' (*The Locusts, or Apollyonists*, canto 1, st. 35, reprinted in *Giles and Phineas Fletcher: Poetical Works*, ed. Frederick Boas, 2 vols. (Cambridge University Press, 1908–9), 1:126–38); William Drummond of Hawthornden, *Flowers of Sion or Spirituall Poems* (1623), 'Hymne ii', 'Hymne iii', reprinted in Drummond, *Poems and Prose*, ed. Robert MacDonald (Edinburgh: Scottish Academic Press, 1976).

17 Andrewes, *XCVI Sermons*, p. 144 (Christmas 1622); Thomas Adams, *The Workes of Tho: Adams* (London, 1630), p. 535. On 'metaphysical' preaching, see W. Fraser Mitchell, *English Pulpit Oratory from Andrewes to Tillotson: A Study of its Literary Aspects* (1938; rpt, New York: Russell and Russell, 1962); Horton Davies, *Like Angels from a Cloud: English Metaphysical Preachers 1588–1645* (San Marino: Huntington Library, 1986). For an overview of the scholarship on Tudor–Stuart sermon literature, see Lori Anne Ferrell and Peter McCullough, 'Revising the Study of the English Sermon', in *The English Sermon Revised: Religion, Literature and History 1600–1750*, ed. Ferrell and McCullough (Manchester University Press, 2000), pp. 2–7, 18–19.

Sites of production

To refer to this corpus as 'literature' implicitly homogenises it into a shelf of books. Yet before becoming texts, early seventeenth-century religious compositions often existed as performance, song, pageant, prayer, ritual, wall hanging or even talisman. In their original venues, they seem either more public or more private than what we normally think of as literature. The sermons at Paul's Cross, the Spital (the churchyard of St Mary's hospital) and Whitehall's Preaching Place were huge open-air events drawing up to 5,000 hearers, from cutpurses to Privy Councillors. The audience at Donne's first Paul's Cross sermon (24 March 1617) included the Archbishop of Canterbury, the Lord Keeper, the Lord Privy Seal, the Earl of Arundel, the Earl of Southampton and Sir Ralph Winwood.[18] On Good Friday each year there was a Passion sermon at Paul's Cross – which was also where proclamations and news reports were read out – followed on Easter Monday through Wednesday by Spital sermons on the Resurrection, the series concluding on Sunday with the Rehearsal sermon, which summarised and critiqued the preceding four. For these occasions, writes an Elizabethan chronicler, 'the mayor, with his brethren the aldermen, were accustomed to be present in their violets at Paules on Good Friday, and their scarlets at the Spittle in the holidays, except Wednesday in violet, and the mayor with his brethren on Low Sunday in scarlet, at Paules Cross'.[19] It was at Paul's Cross that the keynote sermons of the English liturgical year – Accession Day, the anniversaries of the Gowrie and Gunpowder conspiracies – were preached, and with similar ceremonious pageantry. The Whitehall Lenten sermons, held on the grounds of the royal palace, were likewise major cultural occasions, the King often listening from the windows of the Council Chamber above the thronged courtyard. London letter writers transcribed the schedule of Lent preachers for their correspondents and reported on the speakers' performances; suitors sent their sermon notes as gifts to prospective court patrons.[20]

On Sundays and holy days, the court entered the chapels royal in solemn hierarchical procession: first gentlemen, barons, earls, knights of the garter, then the Lord Chancellor flanked by two earls bearing the sceptre and the sword of state, and finally the monarch.[21] In these chapels, where Andrewes

---

18 John Chamberlain, *The Letters of John Chamberlain*, ed. N. E. McClure, 2 vols. (Philadelphia: American Philosophical Society, 1939), 2:67.
19 John Stow, *The Survey of London*, cited in Millar Maclure, *The Paul's Cross Sermons 1534–1642* (University of Toronto Press, 1958), p. 9.
20 Peter McCullough, *Sermons at Court: Politics and Religion in Elizabethan and Jacobean Preaching* (Cambridge University Press, 1998), pp. 44–7, 134–5.
21 *Ibid.*, pp. 25–6.

preached most of his great festal homilies, the pulpit faced the enclosed and elevated royal pew, whose latticed window James would often open at the end of the sermon to thank or chastise the minister. At St Paul's, where Donne served as Dean from 1621 until his death ten years later, decorum was more precarious. Services took place in the choir, divided by only a screen from the infamous nave, where London merchants, lawyers, gallants and riff-raff met for *otium* and *negotium* alike. Yet if many of Donne's late sermons were delivered in this atmosphere of 'prevailing irreverence', the Cathedral remained a locus for the old stately rituals of civic piety. Donne's Candlemas sermons would have been preached before the Lord Mayor and Corporation of the City of London, who had processed, their way lit by torchbearers, to St Paul's for the service in honour of the Blessed Virgin.[22]

As preached but also as published text, these sermons exist in public space-time. Editions of early Stuart sermons, even those first printed years after their original delivery, indicate not only when they were preached but where and to whom: *A Sermon Preached to the Honourable Company of the Virginian Plantation. 13 November 1622*; *The First Sermon Preached to King Charles, at Saint James: 3. April. 1625*; *The White Devill or the Hypocrite Vncased: In a Sermon Preached at Pauls Crosse, March the seuenth, 1612*. Howell's hymns 'written in my own bloud', however, were not social performances, nor the religious lyrics that make up the final third of Greville's *Caelica*, most of which probably belong to the period of Greville's tenure as Chancellor of the Exchequer (1614–22). The dates are all conjectural. Like Donne's *Holy Sonnets* and Herbert's *The Temple*, *Caelica*'s lyrics make no reference to times, places, persons, events. They did not circulate in manuscript, and were only published after their author's death.[23] Although Herbert may have composed musical settings for some of his poems, and possibly sung them in 'private Musick-meeting[s]' following Evensong at Salisbury Cathedral, mostly he seems to have shown them to no one: at the time of his death, his closest friends did not know he wrote English verse.[24] Donne's *Devotions upon Emergent Occasions*, by contrast, were published at once, yet they began as meditations jotted down during the course of a serious illness, during days when Donne lay in bed with dead pigeons tied to his feet, during days when he knew he might be dying.

22 George Potter and Evelyn Simpson, 'Introduction' to vol. 4 of John Donne, *The Sermons of John Donne*, ed. Potter and Simpson, 10 vols. (Berkeley: University of California Press, 1959), pp. 1–5.
23 R. A. Rebholz, *The Life of Fulke Greville, First Lord Brooke* (Oxford: Clarendon Press, 1971), pp. 338–9.
24 Amy Charles, *A Life of George Herbert* (Ithaca: Cornell University Press, 1977), pp. 78–9, 166.

In his life of Donne, R. C. Bald describes the *Holy Sonnets* (*c.* 1609–10) as records of 'a spiritual crisis which was in large measure concealed from those closest to him', although years later Donne would allude in his sermons to 'the despair and suffering through which he had passed'.[25] Recent scholarship, whose alertness to the socio-political dimensions of existence comes at a price, has argued for reading the *Holy Sonnets* as coterie verse rather than the poetry of meditation, but without much plausibility. While Donne did show virtually all his writings to a handful of close friends, the divine poems seem not to have circulated more widely; in sharp contrast to the *Satires* and *Elegies*, they leave almost no trace in the verse miscellanies of the period. The late sonnets, including the one on his wife's death, are preserved in a single manuscript.[26]

A good deal of religious verse was, however, written for publication, but not necessarily in book form. Wither's *Hymnes and Songs of the Church* (1623), Quarles's *Divine Fancies* (1632), Milton's *Lycidas* (pub. 1638) appear as or in books, but religious verse printed on a single sheet decorated the walls of many a godly household, a function indicated by titles like 'The Christians jewell [fit] to adorne the hearte and decke the house of every Protestant' (1624). Intended not simply to be read but 'consulted, memorized, recited, meditated upon, pointed to for authority', these texts-for-walls also served an aesthetic function as a Protestant substitute for religious images.[27] Some of the verse is mere doggerel, but the eight-line poem printed below an engraving of an elderly bearded man in the 1607 'The good Hows-holder' is, except for two parentheses of metrical filler, more than competent, and the rhythm of the final lines, where the morality suddenly shifts from prudential to Christian, has unexpected power.

> The good Hows-holder, that his Howse may hold,
>   First builds it on the Rock, not on the Sand,
>   Then, with a warie head and charie hand
>   Prouides (in tyme) for Hunger and for Cold:
> Not daintie Fare and Furniture of Gold,
>   But handsom-holsom (as with Health dooth stand),
>   Not for the Rich that can as much command
>   But the poor Stranger, th'Orfan & the Old.

25 R. C. Bald, *John Donne: A Life* (Oxford: Clarendon Press, 1970), pp. 233–6.
26 Gardner, 'Introduction' to Donne, *Divine Poems*, p. lxxxi.
27 Tessa Watt, *Cheap Print and Popular Piety, 1550–1640* (Cambridge University Press, 1991), pp. 221–7.

In John Taylor's 1630 broadside, 'A Meditation on the Passion', the typographic ornaments outline three crosses; within the crosses are three sets of Biblical verse – the speeches of Christ, the good thief and the bad thief from Luke 23:39–43 – laid out vertically, one letter beneath another. Then, outside the crosses, running horizontally across the page and in a different font, is a poem on the Passion. Since there are three crosses, the verse lines intersect the Bible passages at three points, and, each time, the letter within the cross becomes part of the horizontal as well as the vertical text. The words within the crosses do not need the poem, but the poem needs the letters of Scripture to complete its meaning. The conception is very close to that of Herbert's 'Coloss. 3.3. Our life is hid with Christ in God', and one is tempted to call it a metaphysical pattern-poem; but it is also a devotional object and down-market interior decoration.[28]

The original venue and format of early Stuart religious discourses are not irrelevant to their meaning. Thus, for example, Andrewes's repeated criticism of a sermon-centred piety that neglects the worship of prayer and praise looks like an anti-Puritan swipe until one realises that the King before whom these sermons were preached required that at his entrance into the royal pew the minister immediately switch from the liturgy to his sermon, after which the King would depart.[29] Yet, on the whole, the contexts in which early Stuart religious 'literature' was first produced and performed make surprisingly little difference – surprising, that is, to us, since the private and public discourses of modernity differ radically: the confessional lyrics of Sylvia Plath or John Berryman do not resemble verse found on wall-posters; our languages of inwardness, psychoanalytic and literary, do not resemble public speaking. Early Stuart religious utterance is less venue-specific. After hearing Andrewes's 1609 Nativity sermon, James asked for a copy in order to 'lay yt still under his pillow'.[30] One can also find pillow-talk migrating to the pulpit; thus, for example, the violent sexualised imagery of Donne's 'Batter My Heart' recurs in the sermons, which describe the Holy Ghost falling upon men 'as a Hawk upon a prey, it desires and it will possesse that it falls upon' (*Sermons*, 5:1.511–13) and the 'Commanding love' of God who 'offers those, whom he makes his, his grace; but so, as he sometimes will not be denyed' (9:3.430–3). His *Essayes in Divinity*, written shortly before his ordination in January 1615, strike one as learned and technical experiments in Biblical exegesis, yet they were apparently private devotions, written, as Donne explains in a letter to Goodyer, during the 'few daies' he had 'seposed … for my preparation to the Communion of

---

28 Both broadsides are reproduced in *ibid*. pp. 226, 233.
29 McCullough, *Sermons at Court*, pp. 155–6. 30 *Ibid.*, p. 126, citing Chamberlain's letters.

our B. Saviours body; and in that solitarinesse and arraignment of my self, digested some meditations of mine, and apparelled them (as I use) in the form of a Sermon'.[31] Richard Sibbes's *The Bruised Reed and Smoking Flax* (1630), probably the greatest work of Puritan spirituality prior to 1641, focuses on the dark and painful recesses of inner life – on guilt, weakness, failure, despair; its deep affinities with Herbert's *Temple* have long been noted.[32] Sibbes's book, however, was based on sermons he had preached at Gray's Inn, where he served from 1617 until his death in 1635. The searching and tender spiritual psychology of *The Bruised Reed* is not the sort of material one imagines being preached to a congregation of early Stuart common lawyers.

Sibbes himself revised the sermons into *The Bruised Reed*, shepherding them from performance to literature. Making the necessary qualifications, however, the same could be said of Donne, Herbert, Greville and Andrewes, although the books on which their fame rests were all posthumously printed: Andrewes's sermons in 1629; the poetry of Greville, Donne and Herbert in 1633; Donne's sermons in 1640. They were published – were publishable – because there was a manuscript fair copy, as opposed to a sheaf of sermon notes or verses scribbled on the flyleaf of a prayer book. So, a few months before his death, Herbert entrusted Nicholas Ferrar with a manuscript of *The Temple* to print or burn as he saw fit. So, in 1625, Donne, who preached from notes, wrote out and revised these into continuous prose.[33] That these early Stuart clergymen reconceived their devotions and preaching as literature, as readerly text, is perhaps more remarkable than their anterior embeddedness in the 'thicker' contexts of social and spiritual praxis. Two hundred years earlier, sermons were preached at court and there must have been individuals who composed prayers, poems, meditations – in their hearts if not on paper – which maybe they showed or sang to a few friends; but these occasional, oral and/or private compositions were not such stuff as medieval books are made on. It was not until the early seventeenth century that what the prince heard in his royal chapel might be read by commoners, and a layman's private struggle with despair read by strangers.

---

31 Bald, *Donne*, pp. 298–9.
32 Richard Strier, *Love Known: Theology and Experience in George Herbert's Poetry* (University of Chicago Press, 1983), pp. xv, 84–6, 145, 205.
33 Bald, *Donne*, pp. 407, 479–80. Although the textual history of Donne's poetry is complicated, the first edition (1633) seems to be based on a copy of a manuscript Donne himself compiled in 1614, when he briefly contemplated printing a collection of his poems (Gardner, 'Introduction' to Donne, *Divine Poems*, pp. lxii–lxvi). On Greville's careful revision of his own collected poems, see Geoffrey Bullough's introduction to his *Poems and Dramas of Fulke Greville, First Lord Brooke*, 2 vols. (Edinburgh: Oliver and Boyd, 1939), 1:27–32.

Aesthetics, ethics and inwardness

The great flowering of religious literature, both poetry and prose, in the early seventeenth century was partly a reaction against the polemical flood-tide impelling the fractious currents of ecclesio-political history. The literature focuses on the interior life of the spirit – a matter to which we shall return shortly. One notes, time and again, the turning from 'curious questions and divisions' (Herbert, 'Divinitie') towards the aestheticised spirituality of the Stoic sublime. 'Whatsoeuer is *rare*, and *passionate*, carries the *soule* to the thought of *Eternitie*', Owen Feltham thus writes in 1628: 'When I heare the *rauishing straines* of a *sweet-tuned voyce*, married to the *warbles* of the *Artfull* instrument; I apprehend by this, a higher *Diapason*... And, this makes me beleeue, that con-*templatiue Admiration*, is a large part of the *worship* of the *Deity*.'[34] Feltham is an Anglican Royalist, but Milton says much the same in 'At a solemn Musick', and 'Il Penseroso' ends with an extraordinary evocation of such ravishing worship:

> There let the pealing Organ blow,
> To the full voic'd Quire below,
> In Service high, and Anthems cleer,
> As may with sweetnes, through mine ear,
> Dissolve me into extasies,
> And bring all Heav'n before mine eyes.
>
> (lines 161–6)

Although clearly akin to the Laudian beauty of holiness and the aestheticised Neoplatonism of the Caroline court masques,[35] the aural sublime seems to have had no ideological markers.[36] If Feltham celebrates a poetry (and preaching) that 'giues vp a man to *raptures*' (43), so does William Prynne, who wrote an entire volume of flat-footed devotional lyrics, *Mount-Orgueil* (1641), while confined in a prison of that name. His 'A Christian Paradise' begins:

34 Owen Feltham, *Resolves, A Duple Century*, The English Experience, 734 (Amsterdam: Theatrum Orbis Terrarum, 1975), pp. 42–4. On the Stoic sublime, see Seneca, *Moral Epistles*, 41.

35 Erica Veevers, *Images of Love and Religion: Queen Henrietta Maria and Court Entertainments* (Cambridge University Press, 1989); Peter Lake, 'The Laudian Style: Order, Uniformity and the Pursuit of the Beauty of Holiness in the 1630s', in *The Early Stuart Church, 1603–1642*, ed. Kenneth Fincham (Stanford University Press, 1993), pp. 161–85.

36 James Cannon notes that by the 1620s 'the devotional value of music was becoming increasingly recognized... not only by proto-Laudians, but also by moderates within the Church' ('The Poetry and Polemic of English Church Worship c. 1617–1640', Ph.D. thesis, Cambridge University, 1998, p. 10).

Soare up my *Muse* upon the Eagles Wings,
Above the Clouds, and scrue up all thy strings
Unto their Highest Straines, with Angels Layes
Mens Soules to ravish, and their Hearts to raise
From Earth to Heaven, with those sweetest Notes.

(p. 115)

Moreover, it is the fervently sabbatarian Bishop Bayly who writes

When thou hearest a sweete Consort of *Musicke*; meditate how happy thou shalt
bee when (with the Quire of Heauenly *Angels* and *Saints*) thou shalt sing a part in
that spirituall *Alleluiah* . . . [And] when wee behold the admirable *colours* which
are in *Flowers*, & *Birds*, and the louely *beautie* of *Women*: let vs say, How *faire* is
that God, that made these so faire!   (*Practise of Pietie*, pp. 152, 155)

One had not expected to find this sort of aesthetic spirituality on the Protestant
left, nor a God of flower-like female beauty.

Herbert's 'The Forerunners' is about bringing this 'lovely enchanting language' to church, but it is also about the insignificance *sub specie aeternitatis* of
this project, 'so all within be livelier than before'. The recording of 'all within'
characterises this literature, yet never, I think, for its own sake. Its lyric introspection is always a version of Christian pastoral – the cure of souls, not
sheep. 'By declaring his own spiritual conflicts', Izaak Walton writes, echoing Herbert's dying words, *The Temple* 'hath Comforted and raised many a
dejected and discomposed Soul'.[37] Such deeply private lyrics matter not as
self-portraiture but because, as Richard Baxter writes, 'the transcript of the
heart hath the greatest force on the hearts of others'; so Andrewes puts it,
'none so fit to preach . . . as one that hath been in the *whale's* bellie'.[38] Wither
describes the compositions he refers to interchangeably as '*poësie*', '*Personall
Hymns*' and '*Devotions*' in the same terms: works written 'out of my owne bowels' and 'by searching mine owne heart' to 'stir up mens affections to the love
and practis of holines'.[39] As Herbert explains in *The Country Parson*, the combats
and conquests of a good man, 'being told to another, whether in private conference, or in the Church, are a Sermon . . . for though the temptations may be
diverse in divers Christians, yet the victory is alike in all, being by the self-same
Spirit'.[40]

37 Izaak Walton, *The Lives*, 4th edn (London, 1675), pp. 55, 321.
38 Richard Baxter, *The Autobiography of Richard Baxter, Being the 'Reliquiae Baxterianae' Abridged
     from the Folio (1696)*, ed. J. M. Lloyd Thomas (London: Dent, 1925), p. 95; Andrewes, *XCVI
     Sermons*, p. 516 (Easter 1617).
39 Wither, 'To the Reader', in *Haleluiah*, pp. 21–4.
40 George Herbert, *A Priest to the Temple, or, The Country Parson*, 1:224–90, in *Works*, 1:278–9.

Given the not unjustified tendency to stress what is new and distinctive about the literature of any given era, it is worth noting, however briefly, the persistence throughout the early Stuart period of centuries-old religious topoi, especially the *contemptus mundi* and *memento mori*.[41] Both poetry and prose exhibit a deep otherworldliness, in contrast to which the ending of *Lycidas*, with its double movement past heaven's 'sweet Societies' – first to Lycidas's role as 'Genius of the shore' and then the poet's renewed interest in the woods and pastures of this world – is truly remarkable. So, too, virtually all the religious literature of the period concerns itself, at least in passing, with Christian ethics; the morality is again traditional – surprising only in its sharp and self-conscious divergence from the secular aristocratic code. Modesty, purity, charity, obedience, mildness and humility are religious virtues, not honour, valour and magnanimity. 'As for *Man*', Feltham writes, Christianity 'teaches him to tread on *Cottons*, milds his wilder *temper*: and learnes him in his *patience*, to affect his *enemies*' (*Resolves*, p. 55). Herbert's 'Church Porch' is a rare, and not wholly successful, attempt to reconcile the two codes. The social justice themes of medieval and Tudor preaching likewise continue into the early Stuart period.[42] In Wither's 'A Christmas Caroll' (1622), reminders of the bitter inequities of ordinary time give a disturbing, satiric edge to its celebration of rural festive custom:

> Brisk Nell hath bought a ruff of lawn
> With droppings of the barrel;
> And those that hardly all the year
> Had bread to eat or rags to wear,
> Will have both clothes and dainty fare,
> And all the day be merry.[43]

---

41 Drummond, *Poems* (1616), 'Sonnet iv', 'Song ii' and *Flowres of Sion*, Sonnets i–v, xxv–xxvi (reprinted in *Poems and Prose*); Francis Quarles, *Diuine Fancies: A Critical Edition (1632)*, ed. William Liston (New York: Garland, 1992); Herbert's 'Pearl', 'Mortification', 'The Size', 'The Pilgrimage', 'Dotage'; Bayly, *Practise*, pp. 59–65. For the persistence of such medieval topoi in the ballads and penny-pamphlets of early seventeenth-century popular culture, see Watt, *Cheap Print and Popular Piety*, pp. 86, 104–5, 111, 120–2, 126.

42 Maclure, *Paul's Cross*, p. 122; Helen White, *Social Criticism in Popular Religious Literature of the Sixteenth Century* (New York: Octagon, 1973); Debora Shuger, 'Subversive Fathers and Suffering Subjects: Shakespeare and Christianity', in *Religion, Literature, and Politics in Post-Reformation England, 1540–1688*, ed. Richard Strier and Donna Hamilton (Cambridge University Press, 1995), pp. 46–69. See, for example, Richard Bernard, *The Isle of Man* (London, 1630), whose Calvinist psychological allegory gives way at the end to a medieval diatribe against thrift, economic individualism, profit-motive, all of which Bernard exposes as euphemisms for the sin of covetousness.

43 George Wither, *Fair-virtue, the Mistresse of Philarete* (London, 1622); 'A Christmas Caroll' appears among the miscellaneous verses printed at the end of this volume.

Thomas Adams's 1612 Paul's Cross sermon, *The White Devil*, anatomises the sharp practices of London's piously respectable civic elite with savage circumstantiality:

> [You act] as if you had two gods: one for Sundayes, another for worke daies; one for the *Church*, another for the *Change* . . . It is not seasonable, nor reasonable charity, to vndo whole townes by your vsuries, enclosings, oppressions, impropriations; and for a kind of expiation, to giue three or foure the yeerely pension of twenty marks: an Almeshouse is not so big as a village, nor thy superfluitie wherout thou giuest, like their necessity whereout thou extortest: he is but poorely charitable, that hauing made a hundred beggars, relieues two.
>
> (*The Workes*, p. 48)

The contrastive pairing of 'superfluitie' / 'necessity' calls to mind Shakespeare's *King Lear* of a few years earlier, which invokes the same medieval Christian social ethic informing *The White Devil*:

> Not many rich, not many mighty, not many noble are called . . . [but] a piercing miserie will soften your bowels, and let your soule see through the breaches of her prison, in what need distresse stand[s] of succour. Then you will be charitable or neuer . . . Oh, how vnfit is it among Christians, that some should surfet, whiles other hunger?   (*The Workes*, p. 41)

It is Adams's version of Lear's prayer on the heath for the 'poor, naked wretches' whose suffering his own suffering has let him both see and show compassion for.

Yet, in general, early Stuart religious literature focuses on the soul alone with God. A longing to withdraw 'farre from the clamorous World' to 'converse with that Eternall Love' reverberates through these works.[44] This interior self is the principal subject (in both senses) of Puritan preaching and spiritual guides like Sibbes's *Bruised Reed*. It also provides the subject for the sermons of Andrewes and Donne and for the new style of emblem books first appearing in the mid 1630s, whose 'symbols represent the individual experience of the human soul in its search for sanctity' rather than moral lessons.[45] It is likewise the voice that speaks in the prayers, meditations, soliloquies and ejaculations of the devotional manuals, and, of course, in the sacred lyrics of Herbert, Donne, Greville and their successors.

This is not, on the whole, a particularly decorous voice. These works again and again register doubt, anxiety, frustration, misery, confusion and bleak self-pity. It is easy to misunderstand these rough and transgressive edges of feeling, to

---

44 Drummond, *Flowres of Sion*, Sonnet xxii. See Richard Rambuss, *Closet Devotions* (Durham, NC: Duke University Press, 1998).
45 Rosemary Freeman, *English Emblem Books* (London: Chatto & Windus, 1948), p. 119.

read them as compromising the language of devotion rather than constituting it. God may have higher standards now, but in the seventeenth century He seemed not to mind such unguardedness. So Sibbes urges, 'Art thou bruised? Be of good comfort, he calleth thee; conceale not thy wounds, open all before him' (*The Bruised Reed*, p. 25). The sestet of Donne's 'Holy Sonnet I' borders on a threat:

> Why doth the devill then usurpe in mee?
> Why doth he steale, nay ravish that's thy right?
> Except thou rise and for thine owne worke fight,
> Oh I shall soone despaire.

God had better get busy and do something, or the speaker will join the devil's party. Critics have found these lines (and much else in the *Holy Sonnets*) angry, mixed-up and theologically improper.[46] This does not seem far off the mark, yet a similar threat shows up in Adams's *White Devil*: an anecdote about a man 'that vpon his *Sheeld*, painted God on the one side, and the Deuill on the other: with this *Motto: Si tu me nolis, iste rogitat: if thou, oh God wilt none of mee, heres one will*' (*The Workes*, p.59). Adams never suggests that good Christians ought not to speak to God like this. 'The Christian hart', Joseph Hall writes, 'pours out it selfe to his maker ... All his annoyances, all his wants, all his dislikes, are poured into the bosome of his inuisible friend; who likes vs still so much more, as we aske more, as wee complaine more.'[47]

The language of devotion in early Stuart England can be unhappy, unmannerly and uneasy, yet it also registers, time and again, the wondrous moments when God 'dost turn, and wilt be neare' (Herbert, 'The Search'). Thus in Donne's 'A Hymne to God the Father', the fierce plea for final forgiveness – 'Swear by thy selfe, that at my death thy sonne / Shall shine' – which seems to well up from an abyss of panic, concludes with the astonishing 'as he shines now, and heretofore'.[48] The plea, one suddenly realises, responds to a sense of present grace and benediction; it is an act of trust, of assurance seeking reassurance. Herbert is, of course, the great poet of sacred intimacy, especially in the colloquy poems. The speaker in 'Even-song', bitterly conscious of having wasted the day in vanities, finds that God is not angry, but, like a mother

---

46 Richard Strier, 'John Donne Awry and Squint: the "Holy Sonnets", 1608–1610', *Modern Philology* 86 (1989), 357–84.
47 Joseph Hall, *Heauen vpon Earth: Of true Peace, and Tranquillity of Minde*, 3rd edn (London, 1607), p. 171.
48 This is the reading of the first edition (1633) of Donne's poems; Gardner prints a manuscript reading, which gives 'Sunne' rather than 'sonne' and, in the next line, 'it shines' rather than 'he shines' (*Divine Poems*, p. 51).

putting her child to bed, 'now with darknesse closest wearie eyes', and then the words of comfort: '*It doth suffice: / Henceforth repose; your work is done.*' This is a profoundly happy poem.

'The Christians Life what'

In an undated letter, Donne notes what he considers the key differences between Roman and Reformed Christianity. There are only two: the Roman church 'carries heaven farther from us, by making us pass so many Courts, and Offices of Saints, in this life, in all our petitions', whereas the Protestant stands *coram Deo*, directly before God – a difference that may have something to do with the intimate lyrics, soliloquies and ejaculations of Stuart devotional literature.[49] The second difference is unexpected: 'the *Roman* profession', Donne maintains, 'seems to exhale, and refine our wills from earthly Dregs, and Lees, more then the Reformed, and so seems to bring us nearer heaven'.[50] Protestantism, with its emphasis on faith rather than works, its dark view of fallen nature and its mistrust of asceticism, rejected the whole notion of spiritual superheroes or, in the Catholic sense, saints. As Catholic controversialists regularly note with scorn, Protestantism had no holy virgins, mystics, anchorites, monks or miracle-workers.[51] This is a more significant difference than it might seem. Saints represent the possibility of achieved holiness, of a spiritual grandeur that, by God's grace, men and women could attain in this life. This is what Donne's *Anniversaries* are about: Elizabeth Drury's death marks the loss of heroic sanctity, of those 'to whose person Paradise adhear'd'.[52]

Protestant religious literature can, in turn, be seen as a rethinking of Christian selfhood and Christian virtue. Stuart holy lives register the shift

49 This contrast should not be pressed too hard: the devotional lyrics of the great Elizabethan recusant poets William Alabaster and Robert Southwell are close to those of Donne and Herbert.

50 Letter to Sir Henry Goodyer, in John Donne, *Letters to Severall Persons of Honour (1651)*, ed. M. Thomas Hester (Delmar, NY: Scholars' Facsimiles and Reprints, 1977), p. 102. I have emended the 'Drugs' in the original to 'Dregs'. The letter probably dates from 1610-15.

51 *The Life and Death of Mr Edmund Geninges Priest, Crowned with Martyrdome at London, the 10 day of November, in the year MDXCI* (n.p., 1614), pp. 74, 99; so the Anglican deacon turned Jesuit, Francis Walsingham, contrasts the 'purity and integrity of the practice of holy men and saints' to what he considers Luther's disgusting claim that "Nothing is more sweet or loving uppon earth than is the love of woman, if a man can obtain it... He that resolves to be without a woman, let him lay aside the name of a man, and make himself an angel or a spirit"' (*A Search made into Matters of Religion* (1609; rpt, London, 1843), p. 137; see also pp. 8–9).

52 Donne, 'The Second Anniversarie', line 77, in *The Epithalamions, Anniversaries, and Epicedes*, ed. W. Milgate (Oxford: Clarendon Press, 1978).

with particular clarity. The Roman Catholic *Life and Death of Mr Edmund Geninges* (1614) pictures its subject, a Jesuit priest executed in 1591, as an impersonal site where God works wonders and miracles – he is born with teeth, his thumb falls off; he has no conflicts, no failings, no personality, just hagiographic attributes ('inflamed with burning Charity', 'the very patterne of piety').[53] Protestant lives of holy men differ markedly. George Carleton's *Life of Bernard Gilpin* narrates the Tudor Reformer's slow, hesitant break with Rome, his lingering theological doubts, his frightened silence during the Marian persecution.[54] Walton's life of Donne records his struggles with near-suicidal depression both before and after his ordination (*Lives*, pp. 25–8, 42–3). These are hagiographic narratives, but Protestant ones, shaped by the same vision of sanctity informing Sibbes's observation that what the church treasures about its 'great worthies' is not their 'Heroicall deeds . . . so much, as their falls and bruises' (*The Bruised Reed*, p. 17).[55]

The Protestant model is based on Romans 7 ('For the good that I would I do not: but the evil which I would not, that I do'), which, following Augustine, both Catholics and Protestants read as an account of Christian inwardness.[56] The passage, however, is far more central to Protestant spirituality, where inner conflict and self-division characterise the lives of the elect. 'No sound whole soule' Sibbes avers, 'shall ever enter into heaven' (*The Bruised Reed*, pp. 27–8). As Donne writes in his *Devotions* (1623), the work of God's 'piercing Spirit' is to create in us 'a melting heart, and a troubled heart, and a wounded heart, and a broken heart'.[57] Grace tears the self apart into warring imperatives of flesh and spirit; it produces not heroic sanctity but the imperfect holiness of the brokenhearted.

This Augustinian self is the subject of early Stuart religious literature. Often the soul's inner combat discloses itself as acute sinfulness, as the wracking guilt felt only by the Calvinist elect. A model 'godly Prayer' from Sparke's *Crumms of Comfort* reads, 'I runne after sinne as Swine after filth, I delight in euill . . . I am prone and apt to all badnesse . . . my thoughts wicked, my deeds damnable, my life impious' (n.p.).[58] Greville's finest devotional poems, 'Wrapt up, o Lord,

53 *Geninges*, pp. 32, 42–4.
54 George Carleton, *The life of Bernard Gilpin, a man most holy and renowned among the northerne English* (London, 1629).
55 This understanding of Christian holiness lies behind the great Puritan spiritual autobiographies of the late seventeenth century – above all, John Bunyan's *Grace Abounding*.
56 David Steinmetz, 'Calvin and the Divided Self of Romans 7', in *Augustine, the Harvest, and Theology (1300–1650)*, ed. Kenneth Hagen (Leiden: E.J. Brill, 1990), pp. 300–13.
57 John Donne, *Devotions upon emergent occasions* (1624; rpt Ann Arbor: University of Michigan Press, 1959), p. 74.
58 See also Arthur Dent, *The plaine mans path-way to heauen* (London, 1601), pp. 10–12, 408.

in mans degeneration' and 'Downe in the depth of mine iniquity' record the torment, guilt and terror experienced at the deepest stratum of the self: 'this depth of sinne, this hellish graue', the 'vgly center of infernall spirits'.[59] Yet Herbert's 'Giddinesse' and 'Miserie' are almost as bleak: man is 'A lump of flesh, without a foot or wing / To raise him to a glimpse of blisse', who would not interrupt his nap or dinner 'to purchase the whole pack of starres'; sermons give him a headache. The speaker in these poems is not talking about the heathen or the reprobate but about baptised Christians – about himself. So too Feltham's essay, 'The Christians Life what', defines this life as 'almost nothing but a *vicissitude* of sinne, and sorrow. First, he *sinnes*, and then hee *laments* his folly... Our owne *corruptions* are diseases incurable: while we liue, they will breake out vpon vs, we may *correct* them, we cannot *destroy* them' (*Resolves*, pp. 361–2).

Yet equally often – especially in Herbert, Andrewes, Sibbes and Donne – the anguish of interiority takes the form of longing rather than sin: the longing of what Sibbes calls 'poore distressed man', torn between hope and fear, seeking love with 'restlesse desire' (*The Bruised Reed*, pp. 11–12); the 'holy thirsty dropsy' of Donne's *Holy Sonnets*[60] and of Sparke's 'Soliloquy at midnight': '*humble me, O humble mee, and make me but one of thy number: O come Lord God, come sweet Christ, let mee finde comfort, let mee feele some taste, let me feele some touch, let my heart bee prepared, touch my heart*' (n.p.). The prayer's abject pleading verges on bathos. Yet some of Herbert's lyrics say much the same, albeit 'with more embellishment' ('Forerunners'):

> Bowels of pitie, heare!
> Lord of my soul, love of my minde,
> Bow down thine eare!
> Let not the winde
> Scatter my words, and in the same
> Thy name!
>
> Look on my sorrows round!
> Mark well my furnace! O what flames,
> What heats abound!
> What griefs, what shames!
> Consider, Lord; Lord, bow thine eare,
> And heare!   ('Longing')

---

59 Fulke Greville, *Caelica*, 98–9, in *Certaine Learned and Elegant Works (1633)*, intro. A. D. Cousins (Delmar, NY: Scholars' Facsimiles and Reprints, 1990).
60 'Since she whome I lovd', line 8 (*Divine Poems*, pp. 14–15).

As in Sparke's prayer, the language here, particularly in the second stanza, registers an unconcealed erotic urgency (which the word 'shames' at once insists upon and de-Petrarchanises). In both works one notes the same anguished sense of God's remoteness and the same craving for the intimacies of touch and acknowledgement. This yearning for any contact with God, even painful, forms a steady refrain in Donne's sermons. So, preaching before King Charles, he exclaims, 'let *God* handle me how he will, so hee *cast* mee not out of his hands: I had rather *God* frownd upon mee, then not looke upon me; and I had rather God pursued mee, then left mee to my selfe' (*Sermons*, 7:2. 345–8). There is in these sermons an acute sense of the Protestant remotion of the supernatural. A 1623 Lenten sermon preached from the great outdoor pulpit at Whitehall grapples with why Jesus wept at Lazarus' grave, despite knowing his soul was in heaven. He wept for Lazarus, Donne concludes, '*Quia mortuus*, that he was dead', and when a man 'is gone out of this world he is none of us, he is no longer a man . . . Here, in this world, we who stay, lack those who are gone out of it: we know they shall never come to us; and when we shall go to them, whether we shall know them or no, we dispute . . . Therefore we weep' (*Sermons*, 4:13.279– 322). The dead do not return to us – not as purgatorial spirits, not as *Lycidas*'s desperate fiction of a 'Genius of the shore' – nor perhaps do they recognise each other. One feels here the loss of the medieval ligatures binding the living to their loved dead, binding earth to heaven.[61] Jesus 'wept as man doth weepe' (4:13.136). The self in such works is that of a creature 'tortur'd in the space / Betwixt this world and that of grace', '*Amor amarè flens*, Love running downe the cheekes'.[62]

This Augustinian conception of Christian life as the imperfect holiness of the brokenhearted was challenged by Arminianism.[63] It is not the good Christian, Arminius argued, who is 'affected with a painful sense of sin, is oppressed with its burden, and who sorrows after a godly sort', but rather the 'unregenerate', those whom Scripture calls 'SINNERS . . . POOR and

---

61 See Stephen Greenblatt, *Hamlet in Purgatory* (Princeton University Press, 2001).
62 Herbert, 'Affliction [IV]'; Andrewes, *XCVI Sermons*, p. 534 (Easter 1620).
63 'Arminianism', the anti-predestinarian theology based on the writings of the Dutch minister Jacob Arminius (1560–1609), quickly became a label with which to tar Anglo-Catholic divines (a nineteenth-century phrase, but accurate enough), a misnomer productive of much subsequent confusion. Arminius, at least in his less rebarbative moments, reads like a mix of Calvin and Seneca, and one might usefully think of Arminianism as Protestant neo-Stoicism. See William Bouwsma, 'The Two Faces of Humanism: Stoicism and Augustinianism in Renaissance Thought', in *Itinerarium Italicum: The Profile of the Italian Renaissance in the Mirror of Its European Transformations*, ed. Heiko Oberman with Thomas Brady (Leiden: Brill, 1975), pp. 3–60.

NEEDY...BROKEN-HEARTED'. A regenerate man, conversely, 'has affections that are mortified, and delivered from the dominion and slavery of sin...a will reduced to order, and conformed to the will of God... that is, he actually desists from evil and does good'.[64] Arminius thus holds, against the entire western theological tradition from Augustine on, that Romans 7 does *not* describe Christian inwardness. Rather, the 'contest of the mind or conscience with the inclinations and desires of the flesh and of sin' precedes regeneration. Grace, by contrast, 'conforms the will... restrains and regulates the affections, and directs the external and internal members to obedience to the divine law'.[65] 'Nothing can be imagined more noxious to true morality', he concludes, 'than to assert, that "it is a property of the regenerate *not to do the good which they would, and to do the evil which they would not*" ' (2:519, 539, 659).

In early Stuart England, Arminianism has a complicated afterlife. One detects its accents now and then in the Senecan essayist, Owen Feltham ('Hee that is borne of *God*, sinnes not; and the Spirit of Sanctification will not let him resolue vpon ill' (*Resolves*, p. 339), as well as the Senecan bishop, Joseph Hall. Hall is generally viewed as one of the few firm Calvinists among the Caroline episcopate, and yet he would write in *Heauen vpon Earth*, 'Wherefore serves Religion, but to subdue or gouerne Nature? Wee are so much Christians, as we can rule our selues' (p. 67); the saints are 'Heroicall spirit[s]', not men with a 'wauering heart, that findes continuall combates in it selfe' (pp. 175–7).

One also, however, detects something that sounds a great deal like Arminianism in *most* Puritan writers of the period, because a stringent moralism is inseparable from the whole notion of the 'godly' central to Puritan (and separatist) spirituality. Puritans were, of course, not Arminians, but their violent hostility towards Arminius might be thought to fetishise small differences. According to Bayly, '*Christ Jesus came into the world to saue sinners, &c*. True: But such sinners, who, like *Paul*, are conuerted from their wicked life' (*The Practise of Pietie*, p. 177). Thus Bayly denies that Proverbs 24:16 ('*A just man falleth seuen times in a day*') concerns 'falling into sin, but falling into *trouble*, which his malicious *Enemie* plots against the iust' (p. 177), which is exactly how Arminius reads it (*Works*, 2:481). Hence, Bayly warns, 'Deceiue not thy selfe with the *name* of a *Christian*: whosoeuer liueth in any *customary grosse sin*, hee liueth not in the state of *Grace*' (*The Practise of Pietie*, p. 180). One is either *iustus* or *peccator*,

---

64 Jacobus Arminius, *The Works of James Arminius*, trans. James Nichols and William Nichols, intro. Carl Bangs, 3 vols. (Grand Rapids, MI: Baker Book House, 1986), 2:497–8, 543.

65 Arminius objects to certain Calvinist doctrines – unconditional predestination, final perseverance – precisely because they encourage moral complacency. See *Works*, 2:474, 658–60.

but not, *contra* Luther, both.[66] Prynne at one point seems to make the efficacy of grace contingent on moral self-reform:

> So Rockes and Stones of *Sinne decay*,
> And make Men *fruitelesse till remov'd away*.
> No fruites of Grace will ever grow, or sprout
> Up in them, till these Stones be digged out.
>
> (*Mount-Orgueil*, p. 22)

Similarly in Milton's *Comus*, the Attendant Spirit, on his own admission, cares only about the virtuous:

> Yet som [mortals] there be that by due steps aspire
> To lay their just hands on that Golden Key
> That ope's the Palace of Eternity:
> To such my errand is, and but for such,
> I would not soil these pure Ambrosial weeds,
> With the rank vapours of this Sin-worn mould.
>
> (lines 12–17)[67]

And yet – with the exception of Milton, whose theology is consistently and self-consciously Arminian – the same writers, often in the same works, draw on very different theologies. Hall's neo-Stoic moralism simply abuts, with no attempt to iron out contradictions, the evangel of imputed righteousness and vicarious atonement that characterises Reformation Augustinianism.[68] Bayly's model prayers, which incorporate the harsh self-vilification typical of Puritan devotion, are likewise at odds with his insistence on the godliness of the godly: for example, the daily morning prayer in which one confesses to having 'broken every one of thy Commandments, in thought, word, and deede' (*The Practise of Pietie*, p. 269), a prayer that assumes Christians commit 'grosse sin' on a regular basis.

---

66 In his *Commentary on Galatians*, Luther defines a Christian as '*simul justus et peccator, sanctus, prophanus, inimicus et filius Dei*' (at once righteous and a sinner, holy [and] profane, an enemy and son of God): *D. Martin Luthers Werke: Kritische Gesamtausgabe*, 99 vols. (Weimar: Hermann Böhlau, 1883–1963), 40 (1):368.

67 It is instructive to compare the claim implicit in both passages that moral goodness can, and therefore must, be attained by one's own efforts – before even the first sprouts of grace appear – with the classic Protestantism of the 1547 *Book of Homilies*: 'We are all become vncleane, but we all are not able to clense our selfes, nor to make one another of vs cleane ... We are sheepe that ronne astraie ... but we cannot of our awn power, come agayn to the shepefold, so great is our imperfeccion & weakenes' ('Of the miserie of all mankynd', in *Certayne Sermons, or homelies, appoynted by the kynges Maiestie, to bee declared and redde, by all persones, Vicares, or Curates, euery Sondaye in their churches* (London, 1547), sig. Div).

68 See, for example, Hall's *Heauen vpon Earth*, pp. 40–53.

The question haunting these works, and the whole of Stuart Protestantism – does God save the weak, wavering and sinful? – provides the unresolved theological dialectic of Amelia Lanyer's *Salve Deus Rex Judaeorum* (1611), whose Passion narrative returns time and again to the fate of Christ's tormenters – a high-stakes issue, since all sinners are complicit in the Crucifixion.[69] The poem depicts Christ as dying precisely to save those responsible for his death:

> In midst of bloody sweat and dying breath,
> He had compassion on these tyrants fell:
> And purchast them a place in Heav'n for ever
> When they his Soule and Body sought to sever.[70]

Although the Roman soldiers are 'Vipers' (365) and the Apostles 'Scorpions bred in Adams mud' (381), Christ loves both: loves those 'whose sinnes did stop thy breath', 'Who from thy pretious blood-shed were not free' (388–92). Yet the poem elsewhere condemns Christ's tormenters as 'Hel-hounds' (689) and makes it quite clear they and all the 'wicked' will be 'damn'd in Hell' (729–44). Only those 'Whose life is uncorrupt', 'shall within his Tabernacle dwell' (129–30). As for 'wicked worldlings' (150), however,

> Froward are the ungodly from their birth,
> No sooner borne, but they doe goe astray;
> The Lord will roote them out from off the earth.
>
> (113–15)

The poem fissures along the same theological fault-line running through the Calvinist devotions of Hall and Bayly, reproducing the pervasive tension in early Stuart religious culture over 'how much a little grace will prevaile with GOD for acceptance': whether Christ 'as a mother tendereth most the most diseased, and weakest childe', or whether, 'if we behaue not our selues chastly', God, like 'a iealous husband, whose feruent loue ... [is] abused, will burst foorth into the strongest hatred'.[71]

---

69 'Of the Passion, for good Friday', in the Elizabethan *Homilies*, 1st edn (London, 1563); Herbert, 'Self-condemnation'; G[eorge] W[ither], 'Good Friday', in his *The Hymnes and Songs of the Church* (London, 1623), song 55, st. 16.
70 Aemilia Lanyer, *Salve Deus Rex Judaeorum* (London, 1611), lines 677–80; see also lines 937–52.
71 Sibbes, *Bruised Reed*, pp. 257, 29; John Dod, *A Plaine and Familiar Exposition of the Ten Commandements* (London, 1610), p. 77.

A church divided

These tensions, insofar as they concern the soul's relation to God, seem as much tensions within the culture – and within individuals – as between the subspecies of early Stuart Protestantism. I have said very little about these subspecies thus far, partly to avoid treating poetry and prayer as mystified polemic, partly to avoid a distorting focus on the familiar cluster of divisive issues. Yet with respect to the church and the nature of Christian community, the question of 'how much a little grace will prevail with G O D for acceptance' produced the sharply different answers that divided those whom subsequent usage would call 'Anglicans' and 'Puritans'.[72] It is here that the devotional literature intersects the ecclesio-political struggles of the earlier seventeenth century. At issue was whether ordinary sinful Christian folk belonged among the elect. The classic statement of the Puritan view is Arthur Dent's immensely popular *Plaine mans path-way to heauen* (25 editions between 1601 and 1640). In response to the grilling of the godly minister Theologus, a simple villager named Asunetus ventures,

> As long as I serue God, and say my prayers duly, and truly, morning and euening, and haue a good faith in God, and put my whole trust in him, and do my true intent, and haue a good mind to Godward, and a good meaning: although I am not learned yet I hope it will serue the turn for my soules health.

The minister, unimpressed, replies, 'all your praiers, your fantasticall seruing of God, your good meanings, and your good intents, are to no purpose, but most loathsome, and odious in the sight of God' (p. 28). Still not convinced 200 pages later, Asunetus urges that 'God is mercifull, and therefore I hope he will saue the greatest part for his mercy sake' (p. 292), but Theologus will have none of this: 'tell me', he asks Asunetus, how many sincere 'worshippers of God

72 There are at present no agreed-upon names for the opposing sides in the intra-Protestant conflicts of the period, nor agreement over what the sides were. To describe the conflict as one between 'Anglicans' (a mid seventeenth-century coinage) and 'Puritans' locates the central fault-line from the 1570s onward in the tension between those committed to an inclusive national church, the Book of Common Prayer and the episcopate, and those who insisted upon the 'absolute and unreserved difference and antipathy between godly and ungodly', and viewed the established church as gravely defective both in its worship and 'in its lack of scriptural discipline and order' (Collinson, *Birthpangs*, pp. 143–6; see also Peter Lake, 'Calvinism and the English Church, 1570–1635', *Past and Present* 114 (1987), 32–76). This tension need not have led to catastrophic polarisation; that it did so after 1620 was due to various additional factors (the Thirty Years' War, the ascendancy of Laud), but the faultline remains the same: which is why in 1641 the entire Caroline episcopate – Calvinists and Anglo-Catholics alike – ended up on one side, with Arminians like John Hales and John Milton on the other. Also see Derek Hirst's remarks in Chapter 21, p. 648 below.

wil be found amongst us? I suppose we should not need the art of Arithmetick to number them: for I thinke they would be very fewe in euery Village, Towne, and Citie. I doubt they would walke very thinly in the streets, so as a man might easily tel them as they goe' (p. 287). Nor is it just in England that the redeemed are in short supply: 'heauen is emptie, and hell is full' (p. 294). There is a pastoral purpose to all this – one that succeeds, since Asunetus does finally have a spiritual crisis in which he recognises his total depravity, at which point he can then be assured of mercy. Yet even though Theologus may be preaching the Law as preparation for grace, his fundamental point remains that the simple, unexceptional piety of the ordinary English layman is 'odious in the sight of God'.

One can trace the same view through the Puritan mainstream over the next forty years.[73] Greville's 'A Treatise of Religion' ends with a contrast between 'that litle flocke, Gods owne elect' who obey 'His Lawe' and the unregenerate who merely 'thincke God good, and so his mercie trust: / Yet hold good life impossible to dust'.[74] Prynne, in his own poetic devotions, similarly distinguishes the elect from 'Common Christians, who have no degree, / Of heate or saving grace' (*Mount-Orgueil*, p. 167). 'Common', with its contemptuous side-glance at the Book of Common Prayer, drives home the polemical point.

The ordinary lay piety condemned in these texts should not be confused with vestigial Romanism or, for that matter, popular Pelagianism. It is, however, indistinguishable from the belief that William Crashaw locates at the dead-centre of Christianity:

> our fathers in former times were not of the Romish faith, but of our Religion: excluding, disclayming, & renouncing all their owne merits, and cleauing only to Gods mercy, and the merits of Iesus Christ for their saluation. This was the faith of the ancient Church... Saint *Augustine* saith, Sin is ours, Merit is Gods... And long after euen in the darkest times; deuote *Bernard* saith... *My merit is the mercy of the Lord*.[75]

---

73 See, for example, Bayly, *Practise*, pp. 232–4; Dod, *Ten Commandements*, p. 336; Stephen Marshall, *A Sermon Preached before the Honourable House of Commons... November 17. 1640* (London, 1641), pp. 30–1; for William Bradshaw, see Tyacke, 'Archbishop Laud', in *The Early Stuart Church, 1603–1642*, ed. Fincham, p. 55.

74 Greville, 'A Treatise of Religion', sts. 110–11, in *The Remains: Being Poems of Monarchy and Religion* (London: Oxford University Press, 1965). The poem was first published in 1670, having been excised, probably by Laud, from the 1633 edition of Greville's *Workes*.

75 William Crashaw, *Manuale Catholicorum. A Manuall for True Catholickes* (London, 1611), sigs. A5v–A6v. That the religion of the Church of England, including justification by faith and salvation through Christ's merits alone, was 'no other but what was anciently recieved in the Church, and namely in the ancient Church of Rome' was a standard claim among Anglican writers of the period. See Peter Milward, *Religious Controversies of the Jacobean Age:*

Dent's Asunetus had said almost as much. The same stress on God's mercy towards sinners, on Christ's paying the debt of justice in our stead, shows up in the *Homilies* and Prayer Book; in Andrewes's insistence that Christ's *'bitter teares . . .* [were] *shedd for us*: for us (I say) that should, but are not able to doe the like for our selves: that what is wanting in ours, may be supplied from thence' (*XCVI Sermons*, p. 211); in Adams's epitome of '*the new Couenant*' as 'Not *Doe this and liue*: but *belieue* on him that hath done it for thee, and liue for euer' (*The Workes*, p. 532); and in Herbert's description of Mary Magdalene washing Christ's feet, though 'stain'd her self', because 'Deare soul, she knew who did vouchsafe and deigne / To bear her filth' ('Marie Magdalene'). So too the speaker in 'Judgement', when God calls 'For ev'ry mans peculiar book', resolves

> when thou shalt call for mine,
> That to decline,
> And thrust a Testament into thy hand:
> Let that be scann'd.
> There thou shalt finde my faults are thine.

As William Haller many years ago observed, Puritans had little use for 'the lamb of God sacrificed in vicarious atonement for the sins of man'; what mattered was 'the crucifixion of the new man by the old', 'the active struggle on the part of the individual against his own weakness'.[76] One should die trusting in Christ's mercy, writes Bayly, but 'Liue . . . as though there were no *Gospell* . . . Passe thy life, as though thou wer't vnder the conduct of *Moses*' (*The Practise of Pietie*, p. 209). This emphasis on regeneration, which makes Puritanism the strange bedfellow of Arminius, also grounds its divisive contrast between the profane multitude of 'common Christians' and God's 'chosen crue' (Prynne, *Mount-Orgueil*, p. 152). The political burden of this contrast is visible enough in Greville's dark intimations that the English church has nothing to do with the Church of Christ:

> [God] keepes one course with *Israel*, and us;
> The fleshe still knewe his power, but not his grace:
> All outward Churches ever knowe him thus,
> They beare his name, but never runne his race.
>   ('A Treatise of Religion', st. 62)

A Survey of the Printed Sources (Lincoln: University of Nebraska Press, 1978), pp. 141, 210; Anthony Milton, *Catholic and Reformed: The Roman and Protestant Churches in English Protestant Thought 1600–1640* (Cambridge University Press, 1978), pp. 286–90.
76 William Haller, *The Rise of Puritanism* (New York: Columbia University Press, 1938), pp. 150–1.

It is equally visible in Bayly's insinuation that the English nation – its rulers, its people, its culture – has nothing to do with the Church of Christ: a main obstacle to piety being the fact that 'the *greatest men* in the State, and many chiefe *Gentlemen* in their *Countrey*... be *Swearers, Adulterers, Carowsers, Oppressors*', so that, misled by their betters, men 'suffer themselues to bee carried with the multitude, downe-right to Hell, thinking it impossible that God will suffer so many to be damned' (*The Practise of Pietie*, pp. 200–1).

The Puritan agenda from the beginning sought to purify the worship of the English church. But whereas Elizabethan Puritanism mainly targeted the papist residue contaminating the Prayer Book, the Puritan writings of the early Stuart period tend to oppose true worship not only to the religion of Rome but also to that of 'ordinary professing Christians'.[77] The main function of sabbatarianism, which became a Puritan hallmark around 1600, was, as Bayly implies, to differentiate the godly from the profane multitude: 'God hath *bound* vs to the obedience of *this Commandement*, with more forcible reasons, than to *any* of the rest ... because he did fore-see, that irreligious *men* would either more carelesly *neglect*, or more boldly *breake* this *Commandement*, than any other'. The inference works in both directions: not only do irreligious persons neglect the Sabbath, but someone who neglects the Sabbath will in all probability, Bayly continues, also 'breake any of the other Commandements, so hee may doe it without *discredit* of his reputation, or *danger* of Mans Law' (pp. 401–2). The really serious sins are, like Sabbath-breaking, ones that mere common Christians (and those who govern the English church) do not consider sins at all. Yet, according to Prynne, these

> sunke Rockes of *secret Sinnes that lye*
> *Hid in our Hearts, and worldly jollity,*
> *Mirth, Pastimes, Pleasures, (where we least suspect,*
> *Or feare a danger) most soules still have wrekt.*
> (*Mount-Orgueil*, p. 23)

The discourses of early modern English nationhood, as Richard Helgerson has observed, are largely about inclusion and exclusion.[78] Puritanism is ferociously, triumphantly exclusionary. Although the label of 'Puritan' fits Milton only in a qualified and complicated sense, the movement of his 'On the Morning

77 James McGee, *The Godly Man in Stuart England: Anglicans, Puritans, and the Two Tables, 1620–1670* (New Haven, CT: Yale University Press, 1976), p. 177.
78 Richard Helgerson, *Forms of Nationhood: The Elizabethan Writing of England* (University of Chicago Press, 1992), p. 9.

of Christs Nativity' from peace on earth to down went Dagon – the poem's identification of Christian time, the time between Nativity and Apocalypse, with the expulsion of the idols – brilliantly renders the Puritan vision of profane multitudes trooping, flock upon flock, to 'th' infernal jail'. In Milton, as in most Puritan literature, this is an exultant vision: the glory of God shining forth in his elect, the power of God victorious over his enemies. So Prynne, looking out the window of his Jersey prison, meditates on the rock-strewn shore:

> Rockes most despised and neglected are,
> As worthlesse Creatures: Thus *Gods Saints oft farre*
> *Contem'd, abbor'd of Most, as vile and base,*
> *Though of Mankinde the onely Pearles, Starres, Grace.*
> (*Mount-Orgueil*, p. 23)

In Greville, however, such triumphalism is recast as *Trauerspiel*, the splendours of the elect invisible, obscured by the dark reality of the world's exclusion – the exclusion of the visible church and its congregations – from grace. So in the final poem of *Caelica*, 'Syon lyes waste',

> Mans superstition hath thy truths entomb'd,
> His Atheisme againe her pomps defaceth,
> That sensuall vnsatiable vaste wombe,
> Of thy seene Church, thy vnseene Church disgraceth,
>   There liues no truth with them that seem thine own,
>   Which makes thee liuing Lord, a God vnknowne.

The grave Latinate stateliness of the quatrain's apocalyptic vision of national apostasy gives way in the couplet to a raw and painful confession of alienation: the poet's alienation from the church; the church's alienation from God; but also, since the syntax does not specify to whom God is unknown, the poet's alienation from God.

It is neither modern secularism nor modern sentimentality to treat 'Puritanism' and 'Anglicanism' as differing visions – one exclusive, the other inclusive – of Christian community. The struggle between these two visions goes back to the first major crisis of the western church, the Donatist schism of the late fourth and early fifth centuries.[79] English Protestantism polarises along these ancient lines from the mid-Elizabethan period on – years before

---

79 Puritans get called 'Donatists' from the 1570s on: see the preface to *An Admonition to the Parliament* (1572), reprinted in W. H. Frere and C. E. Douglas (eds.), *Puritan Manifestoes: A Study of the Origin of the Puritan Revolt* (London: SPCK, 1954); Thomas Fuller, *The Holy State and the Profane State* (Cambridge, 1642), pp. 396–405.

Laudianism or, for that matter, Arminianism. One of the most eloquent statements of the Anglican ideal occurs, in fact, in a 1619 *ad clerum* sermon by the
Calvinist vicar of Boothby Pagnall, Robert Sanderson. There is, he argues,

> good need the very *strongest* of us all should ... take heed of despising even the
> very *weakest* ... [The latter] is not only thy *Neighbour* as a *man*; but he is thy
> *Brother* too, as a *Christian* man. He hath imbraced the *Gospell*, he beleeveth in
> the Sonne of God, he is within the pale of the *Church*, as well as thou.[80]

The Laudians Robert Skinner and John Cosin invoke the same ideal. Preaching
before King Charles in 1634, Skinner raises and answers the pivotal question:
'What shall the sinner doe, that is destitute of *holy hands*? What else, but to the
Temple with the Publican? ... For thus it is ever in these sacred meetings; All
for every one, and every one for all, that God may be gracious and have mercy
upon all'.[81] An exquisite passage from Cosin's 1621 Epiphany sermon describes
the joy felt by the outcast and unclean among the Jews

> when they saw Christ keep company with them, and send into the hedges and
> contemned places for the halt and the heathen, then they began to take heart;
> then, saith St Luke, drew near unto Him all the publicans and sinners. So,
> though we were afraid before, yet when we hear God say once, 'As I live, I will
> not the death of a sinner', and Christ, that there is room yet at supper for them
> which sat at the land's end in corners and hedges, that breeds some comfort.

The un-Judaean hedges and the pun on 'land's end' transpose the image of
Christ seeking Israel's lost sheep to England, where Christ, like Herbert's Love,
even now sends for those 'guilty of dust and sin', bidding them to his supper.[82]

Some of the loveliest lyrics of the age play variations on the same theme:
Herbert's 'The Invitation', where carnal, sinful Christians find themselves welcomed to the eucharistic table; 'Redemption', whose Christ dwells among the
profane multitude with its unsanctified, ragged mirth. Herbert's 'Faith' and
Sidney Godolphin's exquisite 'Lord, when the wise men came from far' affirm
the equality *coram Deo* of wise and simple, strong and weak (Dent's Asunetus
and Theologus), since 'A peasant may beleeve as much / As a great Clerk, and

---

80 Robert Sanderson, *Twelve Sermons* (1632), 3rd edn (London, 1637), pp. 10, 35. See also Peter
    Lake, 'Serving God and the Times: The Calvinist Conformity of Robert Sanderson', *Journal
    of British Studies* 27 (1988), 81–116. Although Lake prefers the term 'conformist', this is a
    superb study of early Stuart Anglicanism.
81 Robert Skinner, *A Sermon Preached before the King at White-hall, the third of December* (London,
    1634), pp. 24–5.
82 John Cosin, *The Works of the Right Reverend Father in God, John Cosin, Lord Bishop of Durham*,
    5 vols. (Oxford: John Henry Parker, 1843), 1:14; Herbert, 'Love [III]'.

reach the highest stature' ('Faith'). So in Godolphin's poem, the adoration of the ignorant shepherds is no less acceptable in God's sight than the Magi's 'studied vows':

> Shepheards with humble fearefulnesse
> Walke safely, though their light be lesse:
> Though wisemen better know the way,
> It seems no honest heart can stray. [83]

Wither's communion hymn from his 1623 *Hymnes and Songs of the Church* dedicated to King James invokes the same levelling vision of weak and strong united by the cords of charity into the body of Christ:

> So, if in vnion vnto thee,
> Vnited we remaine,
> The *Faith* of those that stronger be,
> The weaker shall sustaine:
> Our Christian *loue* shall that supply,
> Which we in *knowledge* misse,
> And humble thoughts shall mount vs hie,
> Eu'n to eternall blisse.
> ('For the Communion', st. 6)

The famous meditation on the tolling of the passing bell in Donne's *Devotions*, which celebrates the mystical solidarities binding the community of the parish and, ultimately, of all persons, begins with observing that when the church 'baptizes a child, that action concerns me; for that child is thereby... ingrafted into that body whereof I am a member' (pp. 107–8). Baptism, which virtually every English child received, suffices for membership in the body of Christ; that is, as Cosin writes in his 1627 *Devotions*, the baptised are God's 'elect Children' (p. 117).[84] The conviction that ordinary Christians remained within the pale of salvation implied and was implied by the conviction that the Holy Spirit operated in the ordinary rites of English parish worship, that its liturgy and sacraments were, in Thomas Adams's words, 'conduict-pipes to conuey vnto our soules those graces, from the fountaine of all grace' (Adams, *The Workes*, p. 540). 'On some, lesse', as Lancelot Andrewes puts it, 'on some, more... but

---

83 The lyric is reprinted in *The Oxford Book of Seventeenth Century Verse*, ed. H. J. C. Grierson and G. Bullough (Oxford: Clarendon Press, 1934), pp. 372–3. The poems of Godolphin (1610–43) remained in manuscript until 1931.

84 See also Herbert's two poems on baptism. For the Puritan distinction between common grace bestowed in baptism and saving grace given only to the elect, see McGee, *The Godly Man*, pp. 176–8.

every one, his *Gomer* at least. Some *feathers* of the *Dove*' (*XCVI Sermons*, p. 702 (Whitsunday 1617)).

This inclusive vision of the church underwrites the unexpected generosity characteristic of early seventeenth-century Anglican writers towards what Milton's *Areopagitica* would later term 'moderat varieties and brotherly dissimilitudes'. They do not defend religious toleration in the modern sense, but rather the Erasmian position that charity dare not exclude from salvation any who, in Hall's lovely phrasing, 'professe the blessed name of God, our Redeemer, and looke to be saved by his blood ... *Grecians, Russians, Georgians, Armenians, Iacobites, Abassines*; and many other sects serving the same God ... aspiring to the same Heaven; and like Bees, though flying severall wayes, and working upon severall meadowes, or gardens, yet in the evening, meeting together in the same hive'.[85] Ussher, Sanderson, Chillingworth, Donne and even Laud, for all his insistence on outward conformity and press censorship, make the same proto-Miltonic argument that pieces of the Lord's Temple need not be of one form.[86] The 'universalist and inclusive tones which Laudians adopted in viewing the totality of Christian churches on earth', as a distinguished historian has recently observed, mirrored their refusal 'to privilege the "godly" parishioners over the rest of the congregation'.[87] In contrast to Milton, that is, what mattered to Laudians – and, more generally, to early Stuart Anglicans – were the bonds of charity, not the search for truth.

'These fragments I have shored against my ruins'

The religious politics of the years immediately preceding the English Civil War are marked, on the one side, by the increasingly bitter rhetoric of Prynne, Milton, Henry Burton, John Bastwick and the infamous 1640 Fast Sermons; as, on the other, by the state's increasingly heavy-handed efforts to strangle dissent, climaxing in the fiasco of the Bishops' War. These deepening antagonisms make themselves felt in late Caroline devotional literature: Prynne's *Mount-Orgueil* and Christopher Harvey's *Synagogue* (1640) have a partisan defensiveness absent from the religious poetry of preceding decades. One has the sense of lines being drawn in the sand, of factions hardening. This is, of course, what one would

---

85 Joseph Hall, *Christian Moderation. In two books* (London, 1640), pp. 131–2.
86 W. K. Jordan, *The Development of Religious Toleration in England from the Accession of James I to the Convention of the Long Parliament (1603–1640)* (London: George Allen & Unwin, 1936), pp. 135–7, 147–9; Tyacke, *Anti-Calvinists*, p. 182. William Laud, *The Works*, ed. W. Scott and J. Bliss, 7 vols. (Oxford: John Henry Parker, 1847–60), 2:29, 60, 400–2.
87 Anthony Milton, *Catholic and Reformed*, p. 530.

expect. Yet one also finds what one had not expected: works that, although directly engaging the religio-political crisis, are neither Puritan nor Laudian nor Calvinist nor Arminian, but rather seem to speak from a moment before it became necessary to take sides, a moment when it was still conceivable that the centre might hold. Although their authors ended up on opposite sides of the fence, Thomas Fuller's *Holy State* (1642), Quarles's *The Shepheards Oracles* (written *c.* 1632–41) and Wither's *Hallelujah* (1641) are, all of them, moving reaffirmations of the traditional ideals of Tudor–Stuart conformity.[88]

The Holy State's vision of Christian social order makes no mention of images, altar rails, divine right episcopacy or the other fiercely contested fine points tearing apart the fabric of the Caroline church. What matters to Fuller is the right use of power, unperverse relationships, the practical goodness of ordinary time. His good wife is thus a woman who manages her short-fused husband with tact and patience; his good master one who provides his servants with fair wages, wholesome food and a retirement plan. Although mistrustful of extremism in both its Roman and Genevan forms, Fuller does not write against the barbarians at the gate. He does not, on the whole, write *against*, but rather affirms the quotidian charities – the 'pedestrian obligations and virtues', as Douglas Bush somewhat ungenerously puts it – of a world that had not yet been lost.[89]

Unlike *The Holy State*, *The Shepheards Oracles* directly engage their ecclesio-political moment, the tenth eclogue lamenting the death of Gustavus Adolphus in 1632; the sixth satirising Archbishop Laud.[90] These have been cited as evidence of Quarles's 'Puritan' sympathies, yet this cannot be right. The seventh eclogue denounces the non-conformist clergy for concocting tales of persecution to win sympathy for their faction; the eighth, the arrogance of their claim to be 'That blessed handfull, that selected few / That shall have entrance'. The final eclogue, and almost certainly the last written, responds to the parliamentary attack on the episcopate (the 1640 Root and Branch petition and/or the Bishops' Exclusion Bill of 1641–2). It begins with two good shepherds blaming the bishops' own prelatical ambition for the current crisis, but, rather than endorsing the proposed legislation against them, the eclogue unexpectedly

---

88 These bear witness to John Morrill's revisionist thesis that as late as 1642 most people 'desperately wished to avoid a conflict or, at least, to let it pass them by. The war began despite, yet also because of, the longing for peace. For while the moderates, as always, talked and agonised, extremists seized the initiative' (*Revolt in the Provinces: The People of England and the Tragedies of War 1630–1648*, 2nd edn (London: Longmans, 1999), p. 62).

89 Douglas Bush, *English Literature in the Earlier Seventeenth Century, 1600–1660*, 2nd edn rev. (Oxford and New York: Oxford University Press, 1962), p. 216.

90 Francis Quarles, *The Shepheards Oracles*, 3:199–236, in *The Complete Works in Prose and Verse*, ed. Alexander Grosart, 3 vols. (1880, rpt, New York: AMS, 1967). See also the discussion of Quarles's *Oracles* in Chapter 22 of this volume.

unfolds into a moving defence of episcopacy. The shepherds recall how the bishops

> maintain'd
> Those love-preserving Festivals which chain'd
> Our mutuall hearts in links of love; which clad
> The naked Orphan, and reliev'd the sad
> Afflicted widow, and releas'd the bands
> Of the lean Prisoner grip'd with the hard hands
> Of his too just oppressor.

Although the rest of the eclogue will go on to express a hesitant confidence in Parliament's ability to resist the surging currents of extremism, the shepherds' tribute to the *pastores* of the English church ends on a note of elegiac anxiety: 'this they say / Is to be shortned, if not snatcht away'. When Quarles's wife published *The Shepheards Oracles* in 1646, she tried to define her husband's ecclesiastical politics; he was, she wrote, 'a true sonne of the church of England'.[91]

The same might almost be said for Wither, at least until 1641, although by that date he had cast his lot with the Long Parliament, to which he dedicated his revised version of the 1623 *Hymnes and Songs*, renamed *Haleluiah, or Britans Second Remembrancer*. The changes between the two versions are all in the direction of Puritanism, the 1641 text dropping both the Christmas carol celebrating the festal hospitality enjoined by 'good English custom' and the stanzas defending open communion quoted above. Yet, more significant than the changes is the remarkable similarity between the two volumes. *Haleluiah* retains the 1623 hymns for the Christian year (Advent, Christmas, Pentecost, etc.), the Marian feasts (Purification, Annunciation) and the Anglican saints' days; if it omits the 1623 Christmas carol, it includes two lovely and traditional new ones. Like the contemporaneous works of Fuller and Quarles, Wither's volume refuses to yield the middle ground, to leave it a no-man's-land between polarised antagonists. Like the others, that is, it imagines community on the commons of historical memory – the commons of a faith as well as a nation – in an act of anguished resistance to the imminent but yet inevitable division of a kingdom. The concluding stanzas of Wither's 'Hymn for the Lords Supper' are no less movingly prescient for being more doggerel than poetry:

> For, Love is that strong Cyment, Lord,
> Which us must reunite.
> In bitter speeches, Fire, and Sword;
> It never takes delight.

91 Quarles, *Divine Fancies*, p. xviii.

Meere carnall Instruments, these are;
   And, they are much beguild;
Who dreame that these ordained were,
   Our Breaches to rebuild.

* * *

Confessors, *Martyrs*, Preachers, Lord,
   The *Battails*, fight for thee.
Thy *Holy Spirit*, and thy *Word*,
   Their proper weapons be.

This, if we credit; we shall cease
   The worldlings parts to play,
Or, to beleeve GODS blessed peace,
   Shall come the *Devils* way.
                    (sts. 12–13, 16–17)

Chapter 18

LITERATURE AND LONDON

THOMAS N. CORNS

This chapter aims to describe the complexities which characterise the relation-ship between the literary arts, especially those of an officially sanctioned kind, and political circumstances in the metropolis during the period 1603–40. At one level, this is a narrative of continuities. The principal forms in which the city of London constructed and celebrated its own image remained the same as in the Elizabethan period. Royal processions once more expressed the as-pirations and the loyalism of the City towards the monarchy. Although there are significant silences, such as the cancelled celebration of the coronation of Charles I and the curtailed rites for the funeral of the Duke of Buckingham, the return of Charles I in 1641 from the Scottish crisis was commemorated as emphatically as the coronation entry of James I. The procession to commem-orate the installation each year of a new Lord Mayor, a ritual established in its fullest form towards the end of the Elizabethan period, continued, arguably with increasing pomp, throughout our period. Paul's Cross remained the most public and the most influential preaching platform in the City, and its careful control ensured a continuing loyalism in the majority of sermons preached there, many of which were subsequently printed.

Likewise, outside the arenas of state control, the self-representation of the metropolis appeared remarkably stable. City comedy, apparently holding up a mirror to the lives of London's citizens, continued to be an extremely popular dramatic form, and its assumptions and values changed only a little between the late Elizabethan paradigms, such as *The Shoemakers Holiday* (1599), and early Stuart examples within that tradition. Plague pamphlets and such quasi-satirical forms as coney-catching pamphlets also exhibited remarkable con-tinuity between the Tudor and Stuart eras.

Yet, for all the carefully developed image of London as bastion of civic loy-alism, by the early 1640s its status as a stronghold of support for Parliament against the King was recognised by both sides. How may this radical ideol-ogy be tracked in literary culture and literary representation of London in the 1620s and 1630s? The answer, explored in the second section of this chapter, is twofold. In part, alternative, less loyalist perspectives, especially in matters of religion, found expression in forms that were far less likely to be printed for a reading public, especially in the preaching practices of Puritan London congregations. In part, the discourse of the political establishment at its most brutal was itself subverted by those it aimed to suppress, especially as spectacular punishments mirrored the great ceremonies of state. The public mutilations of John Bastwick, Henry Burton and William Prynne and the flagellation of John Lilburne are ceremonies as tractable to 'reading' as the coronation of James I or the investiture of a Lord Mayor. Here, however, the principal protagonists wrested the message from those agents of repression who seemed best placed to write on their tortured bodies the familiar lessons of order and control.

Such possibilities of inversion remind us that domination of most aspects of the cultural superstructure of the metropolis does not, in episodes of particular crisis, necessarily reflect or influence the political consciousness of the people who live within it. Indeed, as I shall show, huge discrepancies may emerge at such times between the official view of London and the probable experience of most who lived in and near the city. Thus, that in 1640–2 those realities should break through the agreeable fictions of the London establishment and its royal masters is perhaps less paradoxical than at first it may seem.

The most elaborate civic pageants celebrated the coronation of monarchs. James I's entry into the City on 15 March 1604, following a pattern that had been developing since the fourteenth century, took place on the day before his coronation in Westminster.[1] Ben Jonson and Thomas Dekker, the latter in collaboration with Thomas Middleton, were primarily responsible for writing the pageant, which, following earlier examples, was focused on a series of triumphal arches located at traditional sites within the City. Three accounts are extant: Jonson's *B. Jon: His Part of King James his Royall and Magnificent Entertainement through his Honorable Cittie of London, Thursday the 15. of March. 1603* [i.e., 1604] (1604), Dekker's *The Magnificent Entertainment: Given to King James, Queene Anne his wife, and Henry Frederick the Prince, upon the day of his Maiesties Tr[i]umphant passage (from the Tower) through his Honourable Citie (and Chamber) of London, being the 15, of March. 1603* [i.e., 1604] (1604) and *The Arches of Triumph* (1604), an illustrated account of the triumphal arches by their architect and builder, Stephen Harrison. Each account deals primarily with its author's contribution, but collectively they afford a singularly good record of events.

1 Lawrence Manley, *Literature and Culture in Early Modern London* (Cambridge University Press, 1995), p. 216.

It is striking how readily London-generated panegyric picked up on the principal themes of James's political ideology, supplementing them with a neatly inflected celebration of the city's ancient loyalism. Though the pageant scaffolds are explicitly arches of triumph, peace not victory is the recurrent theme. James, self-styled as the most irenic of monarchs, brings an assurance of peace and thus prosperity. At the last arch, at the Temple Bar, Jonson has the Genius Urbis observe,

> This [James] hath brought
> Sweet peace to sit in that bright state shee ought,
> Unbloudie, or untroubled; hath forc'd hence
> All tumults, feares, or other darke portents
> That might invade weake minds; hath made men see
> Once more the face of welcome libertie:
>
> * * *
>
> No more shall rich men (for their little good)
> Suspect to be made guiltie.[2]

This exit from the City repeats a Jacobean refrain introduced at the first arch. As James was to remark in his first speech to his first Parliament, four days later, 'although outward Peace be a great blessing; yet is it as farre inferiour to peace within, as Civill warres are more cruell and unnaturall then warres abroad. And therefore the second great blessing that GOD hath with my Person sent unto you, is Peace within.'[3]

Other political and civic themes recur. Since James as King of England and Scotland is King of a re-founded British state, the role of London as capital of Britain is reiterated in its persistent styling as 'Troynovant', the capital of the legendary Brutus' British kingdom.[4] London is, moreover, from the first arch to the last, repeatedly termed 'Camera regia' (the royal chamber), sometimes with the suggestion that it is, more specifically, the bridal chamber of James and his kingdom. Thus Dekker has the boys of St Paul's Cathedral sing:

> *Troynovant* is now a Bridall Chamber,
>   Whose roofe is gold, floore is of Amber,
> By vertue of that holy light,
> That burnes in *Hymens* hand, more bright.[5]

---

2 *The Works of Ben Jonson*, ed. C. H. Herford, Percy Simpson and Evelyn Simpson, 11 vols. (Oxford: Clarendon Press, 1925–52), 7:102–3.
3 *A Speach, as it was delivered in the Upper House of Parliament... Munday the XIX day of March 1603* [i.e., 1604], in King James VI and I, *Political Writings*, ed. Johann P. Sommerville (Cambridge University Press, 1994), p. 134.
4 For example, Jonson, *Works*, 7:107; *The Dramatic Works of Thomas Dekker*, ed. Fredson Bowers, 4 vols. (Cambridge University Press, 1953–61), 2:257.
5 Dekker, *Dramatic Works*, 2:280.

James's own political rhetoric favoured the notion of the monarchic role in government as a sort of marital consummation: 'What God hath conioyned then, let no man separate. I am the Husband, and the whole Isle is my lawfull Wife; I am the Head, and it is my body'.[6] London functions as the site of that intimate and yet public union.

The 1604 royal entry would seem to have been a success both for the Crown and for the London establishment. Livery companies lined the streets, and the drinking water supply, through the system of conduits, 'ran Claret wine very plenteously',[7] though memories of the previous plague year remained as a poignant contrast to present pleasure.[8] James had other entries of various kinds: in 1605 after the Gunpowder Plot; in 1606 to greet his brother-in-law, Christian IV of Denmark; in 1610 on Henry's installation as Prince of Wales; and in 1613 on the wedding of his daughter Elizabeth.[9]

Charles I was altogether less fortunate in his ceremonial interaction with London. For reasons of fiscal stringency his own installation as Prince of Wales was done privately and without cost.[10] The year 1625 was as grim a plague year as 1603, and a London entry as prelude to the coronation was impossible. The royal wedding to Henrietta Maria was conducted by proxy, precluding the possibilities of public celebration (which may well have been somewhat muted, given her Catholicism). Her later refusal to participate in the coronation unless she were crowned by a Catholic bishop indicates her limited sympathies with playing to the English public. The first attempt at a state occasion during the reign of Charles I was the funeral of the assassinated favourite, the Duke of Buckingham. The funeral procession, by torchlight, had a curtailed and beleaguered aspect, and, though large numbers of Londoners lined the street, the noise they made, according to the Venetian ambassador, sounded 'more like joy than commiseration'. The trained bands were mustered in force, though not as an honour guard but to police the crowds.[11] Perhaps the very fact that Charles could inflict this ceremony on London made it a ritual of power,

6 A Speach . . . delivered in the Upper House of Parliament, in Political Writings, p. 136.
7 Stephen Harrison, The Arches of Triumph, quoted by David M. Bergeron, 'Harrison, Jonson and Dekker: The Magnificent Entertainment for King James', Journal of the Warburg and Courtauld Institutes 31 (1968), 447.
8 See, for example, Jonson's marginal gloss on the speech he gave Electra at the final arch: 'this speech might be understood by Allegorie of the Towne here, that had beene so ruined with sicknesse' (Works, 2:107).
9 R. Malcolm Smuts, 'Public Ceremony and Royal Charisma: The English Royal Entry in London, 1485–1642', in The First Modern Society, ed. A. L. Beier et al. (Cambridge University Press, 1989), pp. 82, 87.
10 Smuts, 'Public Ceremony', p. 89.
11 Roger Lockyer, Buckingham: The Life and Political Career of George Villiers, First Duke of Buckingham 1592–1628 (London and New York: Longman, 1981), pp. 457–8.

though it was scarcely a commemoration of a bereavement shared by King and people.

It has recently been demonstrated that older theories about Charles's inherent hostility to public ceremony and civic pageants are overstated.[12] Yet, though he frequently progressed elsewhere in his kingdoms, including a spectacular visit to Scotland for his coronation in 1633, it was not until 1641 that he made a formal entry into London. The occasion, somewhat unconvincingly, was his triumphant return from the Prayer Book crisis in Scotland, but the loyalism of the London establishment could still ensure a warm response, and he was greeted with shouts of welcome, though a mounted guard was deemed necessary to guarantee his safety.[13] By then, however, as we shall see, a rather different political consciousness was animating Londoners outside the charmed circle of the political elite of the City.

Among the rituals of the civic year, the Lord Mayor's Show had developed by the 1590s into the most important, and its ambitious scope was confirmed and extended in the Jacobean period. Although the pageants characteristically celebrated the ancient foundation of London (and by implication suggest the revered longevity of the rite itself), the show was something of an innovation in metropolitan public life. It emerged probably at the expense of the decline and slide into eventual discontinuation of the revels to celebrate the vigils of St John the Baptist and St Peter (23 and 28 June), the so-called Midsummer Watches. Indeed, John Stow, in his *Survey of London*, omits discussion of the show's origins, perhaps because 'he felt that such recently invented traditions lacked an authentic quality, that they were a poor substitute for the incorporative rituals of the past'.[14] Indeed 'the spotty documentation suggests that the inaugural show was not yet a fully established ceremony at the time that the *Survey* was published'.[15]

The show was staged annually in late October to mark the entrance of the new Lord Mayor into the City of London. Its cost was met by the livery company to which the new mayor belonged, and typical expenditure ran to several hundreds of pounds (at a time when an agricultural day-labourer could be hired for 6d a day); the 1605 show, funded by the Merchant Taylors' Company, cost £710, because it had rained so hard when it was first performed that

---

12 Kevin Sharpe, *The Personal Rule of Charles I* (New Haven, CT, and London: Yale University Press, 1992), p. 630.
13 Sharpe, *The Personal Rule*, p. 631; Smuts, 'Public Ceremony', pp. 91–3.
14 Ian Archer, 'John Stow's *Survey of London*: The Nostalgia of John Stow', in *The Theatrical City: Culture, Theatre and Politics in London, 1576–1649*, ed. David L. Smith, Richard Strier and David Bevington (Cambridge University Press, 1995), p. 24.
15 Lawrence Manley, 'Of Sites and Rites', in *The Theatrical City*, ed. Smith *et al.*, pp. 47–8.

it was felt necessary to repeat it.[16] Costs included the hire of actors, both adults and children, and musicians, the construction of pageant scaffolds and other props, appropriate apparel for participants, the payment of the pageant writer, and frequently the cost of printing accounts of the events. These quarto booklets, rather like printed accounts of individual court masques, served the combined purposes of newsbooks, commemorative programmes and dramatic texts. They are rare before the Jacobean period, though frequent thereafter,[17] and, since their printing was subvented by livery companies, they must reflect a sustained ambition on the part of the sponsors to memorialise their own munificence.

The pageants of Anthony Munday, 'Citizen and Draper of London',[18] the most prolific author of City pageants in the years 1604 to 1623, demonstrate particularly vividly the characteristic thematic and dramatic concerns of the form as they mutate through the Jacobean period. Munday collaborated with Ben Jonson on the first Jacobean show in 1604 (the 1603 pageant had been cancelled because of the plague); thereafter, Munday worked alone. In 1605, his *Triumphes of Re-United Britannia*, rather like the 1604 royal entry, demonstrated how alertly metropolitan ideology aligned itself with the emerging themes of the new regime.

Munday, himself something of an antiquary, and editor of the 1618 edition of Stow's *Survey*, takes as the informing image of his pageant the revival of Britain, founded by Brute as one state, and now re-united under its second Brute, James I. The figure of Neptune speaks thus, seated on a lion:

> Blest be that second *Brute, James* our dread king,
> That set this wreath of Union on her head,
> Whose verie name did heavenlie comfort bring,
> When in despaire our hopes lay droping dead,
> When comfort from most harts was gon and fled,
> Immediatlie the trumpets toong did say,
> God save king *James*: Oh twas a happie daie.[19]

The constitutional unification of England and Scotland was an immediate objective of James I, though one which he never realised. The theme poignantly remained part of the early Stuart political agenda, rehearsed, for example, in

16 *Pageants and Entertainments of Anthony Munday*, ed. David M. Bergeron (New York and London: Garland, 1985), p. 18.
17 Manley, 'Of Sites and Rites', p. 48.
18 As the title-pages of printed pageants usually style him.
19 Munday, *Pageants and Entertainments*, p. 14.

one of the larger panels of Rubens's ceiling paintings for the Banqueting House. It had been a significant motif in the 1604 royal entry.[20]

Munday prefaces the printed version of his pageant with an antiquarian narrative that sets Brute's landing in Britain at '1116 [years] before Christs nativity',[21] though he is at pains to make associations between the City of London in general (and the sponsoring Merchant Taylors' Company in particular) and more recent royal patronage. Voicing the aspiration that James I may extend similar benevolence, and like other Kings before him accept the freedom of the company, 'Epimeleia' (i.e., Diligence) speaks:

> Have our discourses (*Pheme* [i.e., Fame]) let thee know,
> That seaven Kings have borne free brethrens name,
> Of this Societie, and may not time bestow
> An eight, when Heaven shall so appoint the same?[22]

Seven earlier Kings had been associated closely with the guild, which obviously would have liked James I to play a similar role as patron. So Munday, then, affirms the ancient loyalism of the City and the antiquity of its institutions in a self-representation of its ruling elite addressed both to the cadre of liverymen and to the regal establishment. Similar civic themes recur in the pageants that follow *The Triumphes of a Re-United Britannia*. Thus, in *Camp-bell, or The Ironmongers Faire Feild*, for the installation of Sir Thomas Campbell in 1609, Munday has the twin figures of Saint Andrew and Saint George address the new incumbent. Picking up on another favoured motif of James's ideology, the blessings of peace, he has a tableau represent the importance of irenic government:

> In the most eminent place behinde, and back to backe with Soveraigne
> *Majestie*, we seate that ever blessed Companyon of all Royall Kingdomes,
> *Tranquillity*, a Nimphe of gracious and Majesticke presence, attired in
> Carnation, with a rich Tinsell veyle likewise upon her head, a branch of Palme
> in one hand, and a fayre Chaplet or wreath of floures in the other.[23]

The emblem once more recalls a significant detail of the 1604 royal entry.[24]

In *Chruso-thriambos. The Triumphes of Golde*, performed in 1611 for Sir James Pemberton of the Goldsmiths' Company, Munday, drawing on Stow's *Survey*, has the mayor greeted by '*Leofstane* a Gold-Smith, the first Provost that bare authoritie in London', and Nicholas Farringdon, 'Foure times Lord Maior', rises from his tomb and joins Pemberton at his feast.[25] Munday's objectives are twofold. He rehearses another point about the relationship of the City to the

---

20 *Ibid.*, p. 21.   21 *Ibid.*, p. 4.   22 *Ibid.*, p. 13.   23 *Ibid.*, pp. 28–30.
24 *Ibid.*, p. 32.   25 *Ibid.*, pp. 51, 56, 58.

Crown. It is the case that, constitutionally, on the death of the monarch, 'the Lord Mayor of Tudor–Stuart London was . . . the highest ranking officer in the kingdom'.[26] Hence, Faringdon concludes by reminding Pemberton that

> You are Lieutenant to your King,
> And 'tis a very worthy thing,
> To minde Gods blessing, and his grace,
> That brought yee to so high a place.[27]

The second principal objective is to reiterate yet again the myth of London's ancient continuities. The 'traditional' show itself, however, is a relatively recent innovation through which the richest companies maintained an oligarchic control over public celebration as surely as they controlled the instruments of civic government. Moreover, the economy and social structure of the London area were changing rapidly, alarmingly and inexorably. Although the number of inhabitants remained broadly stable within the City, the population of the metropolis was hugely augmented by the growth of the suburbs.[28] Thus, the demography of the region altered discernibly, and with it the regional economy. The volume of trading in the City was overhauled by the manufacturing activities of the suburbs.[29] Munday, by foregrounding continuities, averts the watchers' gaze from the plain evidence of economic transformations in the vital sectors of the region, suggesting that the City carries on much as the City has always carried on – and always will. The conservative message no doubt soothed those that commissioned the pageants, but, as others have observed, 'whether the royal entrances and Lord Mayors' shows made much impact in . . . [the suburbs] seems doubtful'.[30]

Munday's mayoral pageants are extant for 1614, 1615, 1616, 1618 and 1623. His editor observes that, after 1610, he 'makes no extended reference to King James; instead, the national and civic life that he honors centers on the city and guilds and their historical past', which may suggest that Munday shared a general disillusionment with the King by the end of his first decade on the English throne.[31] Possibly so, but Munday remains, though in a less nuanced way, committed to reiterations of the City's ancient loyalty to the throne.

26 Lawrence Manley (ed.), *London in the Age of Shakespeare: An Anthology* (London and Sydney: Croom Helm, 1986), p. 3.
27 Munday, *Pageants and Entertainments*, p. 62.
28 A. L. Beier and Roger Finlay, 'The Significance of the Metropolis', in *London 1500–1700: The Making of the Metropolis*, ed. Beier and Finlay (London and New York: Longman, 1986), p. 8.
29 A. L. Beier, 'Engine of Manufacture: The Trades of London', in *London 1500–1700*, ed. Beier and Finlay, pp. 141–67.
30 Beier and Finlay, 'The Significance of the Metropolis', p. 21.
31 Munday, *Pageants and Entertainments*, p. xv.

In *Metropolis Coronata, The Triumphes of Ancient Drapery* (1615) the figure of Sir Henry Fitz-Alwine, a draper and the first Mayor, again recalls the institution of the office by Richard I,[32] while in *Chrysanaleia: The Gold Fishing: Or, Honour of Fishmongers* (1616), another revived worthy, Sir William Walworth, fishmonger and Mayor, recalls his role (and the role of the City) in the Peasants' Revolt of 1381, when 'in my Soveraigns sight, there I strooke dead / Their cheifest Captaine and commanding head'.[33] But perhaps the boldest of Munday's affirmations of the antiquity of London institutions and their place in the fabric of a Merry England has Robin Hood and his band appear, on the pretext – apparently Munday's invention – that Fitz-Alwine was his father-in-law.[34]

In 1603 and 1625 there were major outbreaks of the plague, which disrupted the rituals of the City, though significantly, in the latter year, as an attempt to suggest continuities among the chaos, the Lord Mayor arranged a public funeral attended by 244 troops for a captain of the trained bands, 'to confute rumours in the country that the city was in total disarray in the face of the plague'.[35] In general, the epidemics devastated London life, and recollection and anxious anticipation of them surely shaped the collective consciousness of the London area. In the Stuart period, plague was endemic at moderate levels for years at a time, raising normal mortality figures sometimes by 10 per cent, sometimes much less. There were massive increases in infection, however, in 1603, 1625, 1636 and 1665; and in two periods between 1606 and 1610 and between 1640 and 1647 (with a slight remission in 1643) plague was responsible for more than 10 per cent of recorded burials every year.[36] The plague was – and to some extent remains – something of a medical mystery, and even the pathogenic organisms primarily responsible have not been identified beyond doubt.[37]

Understandably, a phenomenon that in London accounted for 'at least a fifth of all deaths from 1603 to 1665'[38] deeply marked the literary culture of the metropolis as surely as it deformed its social life. Outbreaks of plague provided both a context for medical counselling and a platform for spiritual meditation (though the latter tended to be something of a paper exercise, since ministers frequently quit the metropolis to avoid infection).[39] In 1603–4, 'twenty-eight books dealing in some way or other with plague were published, of which

32 *Ibid.*, p. 88.   33 *Ibid.*, p. 116.   34 *Ibid.*, pp. 93–6, 99.
35 Paul Slack, *The Impact of Plague in Tudor and Stuart England* (1985; Oxford: Clarendon Press, 1990), p. 297.
36 *Ibid.*, p. 145.
37 Graham Twigg, 'Plague in London: Spatial and Temporal Aspects of Mortality', in *Epidemic Disease in London*, ed. J. A. I. Champion, Centre for Metropolitan History, Working Papers Series, no. 1 (London: Institute of Historical Research, 1993), pp. 1–17.
38 Slack, *Plague*, p. 147.   39 *Ibid.*, p. 287.

fifteen were of a religious character', for the most part associating the aetiology of the disease with a general sinfulness and urging a penitential response; between 1625 and 1627 there were thirty-six plague-related titles, over twenty of them religious. At the same time, it was widely recognised that the safest strategy was to leave plague cities – especially London – with all expedition, avoiding them assiduously during the summer months. As Thomas Lodge, the man of letters turned physician, remarked, 'The first and cheifest remedy, then, is to fly far and return late.'[40] Again, it was understood, as later historians of the disease have confirmed, that mortality rates varied from parish to parish, usually corresponding to levels of prosperity or poverty, and that the suburbs suffered worse than the City. Both facts provide the premise for Ben Jonson's *Alchemist* (1610), in which the householder, Lovewit, has quit London for the duration of the plague; the dénouement has him return and surprise the tricksters, who had thought he would wait till the suburbs were free of plague deaths, not just the City.[41] The extraordinary achievement of *The Alchemist* rests at least in part in its depiction of London's social life in a state of high anxiety about the ravages of a bewildering and devastating disease; it is a comedy acted out on the edge of the precipice where all Londoners too poor or too trapped by their business commitments lived through plague years.

Jonson, whose own family was touched keenly by the ravages of plague,[42] did not gloss over the horrors which form the background of his play. Nevertheless, the most vivid literary engagement occurs in the plague pamphlets of Thomas Dekker, author of the Lord Mayor's Show in 1612, and in 1627-9. Dekker took a rather different approach. He memorialised 1603, a plague year and the year of Elizabeth I's death, in the pamphlet *The Wonderfull Yeare. Wherein is shewed the picture of London, lying sicke of the Plague* (1603). Though he takes some comfort in pondering the late Queen's apotheosis,[43] the initiation of the Stuart dynasty, and the 'solemne wedding day' of James's coronation, which married England and Scotland,[44] yet the 'annus mirabilis' is less persuasively argued for than in Dryden's analogue for 1666. Dekker, with his vigorous fusion of journalistic topicality and moralising morbidity, does not understate the horrors of the London experience:

40 Thomas Lodge, *A Treatise of the Plague: A Rule and Instruction to Preserve such as be in Health from the Infection* (1603), quoted in Manley (ed.), *London in the Age of Shakespeare*, p. 199.
41 Ben Jonson, *The Alchemist*, 4. 7.115-17, in *Works*, vol. 5 (1937), p. 386.
42 David Riggs, *Ben Jonson: A Life* (Cambridge, MA, and London: Harvard University Press, 1989), pp. 96-7.
43 *The Plague Pamphlets of Thomas Dekker*, ed. F. P. Wilson (Oxford: Clarendon Press, 1925), p. 18.
44 *Ibid.*, p. 21.

thou shalt see, and be assured (by tokens sent thee from heaven) that to morrow
thou must be tumbled into a Mucke-pit, and suffer thy body to be bruised
and prest with threescore dead men, lying slovenly upon thee, and thou to be
undermost of all! yea and perhaps halfe of that number were thine enemies!
(and see howe they may be revenged, for the wormes that breed out of their
purifying carcasses, shall crawle in huge swarmes from them, and quite devoure
thee).[45]

However, Dekker insists that flight offers only a poor option. If the one who
flees escapes, the family he leaves behind may perish. Moreover, life outside
London is persistently represented as more dangerous than life at home. The
pamphlet abounds with anecdotes of the sick left uncared-for at the doors of
country inns or plundered and buried in shallow and unconsecrated graves
through the 'turkish and barbarous actions' of 'Hobbinolls'.[46]

Dekker rehearses the same thesis in the plague year of 1625 in *A Rod for
Run-awayes. Gods Tokens, Of his feareful Iudgements, sundry wayes pronounced upon
this City, and on severall persons, both flying from it, and staying in it* (1625), which
again elaborates a moralised fatalism: 'Why should any man, (nay, how dare
any man) presume to escape this Rod of Pestilence, when at his back, before
him, round about him, houses are shut up, Coarses borne forth, and Coffins
brought in?'[47] An essentially secular narration is coloured by penitential and
pious responses to the visitation. Again, Dekker offers anecdotes of Londoners'
maltreatment once they flee, how they are spurned or fleeced by country folk:
'Who then would flye from his owne Nest, which hee may command, to be
lodged amongst Crowes and Ravens, that are ready to picke out our Eyes, if we
offer to come amongst them?', asserting, 'Flocke not therefore to those, who
make more account of Dogges then of Christians.'[48]

At the level of practical advice, Dekker's contention made no sense: of course,
if one could flee, one would flee. But his grim perseverance offers some comfort
to the majority of Londoners unable to take the route of their more affluent
neighbours. Like the civic funeral of the captain of the trained bands, his pamphlets urge and demonstrate a kind of resolute endurance in a civic system that
continued to function despite the huge strains placed upon it. His impractical,
irrational insistence on a kind of solidarity among City dwellers projects an excited ambivalence towards the horror and heroism of living in the early modern
metropolis. These pamphlets perhaps exhibit such sympathy with the disadvantaged because of their author's own condition. A modern editor surmises
that poverty probably kept Dekker in London in 1603 and 1625, citing the

45 *Ibid.*, p. 29.   46 *Ibid.*, p. 59.   47 *Ibid.*, p. 152.   48 *Ibid.*, p. 156.

satirical comments made by some actors[49] on his behaviour in the plague of 1625 that may perhaps hold good for the earlier occasion also: Dekker, they said, would himself have fled from London like them 'if only he could have got hold of a horse'.[50]

Dekker's other London writings, however, show a similar vein of civic pride and stoical resilience. His contributions to the coney-catching genre, richly developed in the Elizabethan period by Robert Greene, attest to a continuity of experience from the sixteenth to the early seventeenth centuries, though in so doing his writing substantially ignores those subtler forces, already maturing in the metropolitan context, that would prove so divisive in the 1640s. For Dekker, the principal threat to Londoners (apart from plague) was the guile and knavery of the City's rogues, but these could in turn be countered by reading his own narratives and absorbing the vicarious experience they offer. The assumptions are ultimately optimistic and normative: learn well, and survive the evils of the City. Thus, he begins *Lanthorne and Candle-light. Or The Bell-mans second Nights walke* (1608), with a dictionary of thieves' argot that would let 'the gentry cove of Romeville spot a thief before he mills his ken, and send him off to cly the jerk'.[51] The same text tells its readers how not to be bamboozled by the equivocating oaths of horse-sellers at Smithfield fairs:

> if an ignorant chapman coming to beat the price say to the horse-courser 'Your nag is very old' or 'Thus many years old' and reckon ten or twelve, he claps his hand presently on the buttock of the beast and prays he may be damned if the horse be not under five – meaning that the horse be not under five years of age, but that he stands under five of his fingers when his hand is clapped upon him.[52]

In Dekker's writings London crime seems manageable; the structures of civic authority remain fundamentally unchallenged, and the cautious, duly warned, enjoy the frisson of successfully encountering those who would take advantage of them.

The Guls Horne-booke (1609), perhaps his most ambitious and successful essay on metropolitan society, is once more premised on confident civic assumptions. In this satirical reflection on the manners, values and folly of City gallants, such

49 In B. V. et al., *The Runaways' Answer* (London, 1625), sigs. B1–B1v.
50 Thomas Dekker, *The Wonderful Year, The Gull's Horn-Book, Penny-Wise, Pound-Foolish, English Villanies Discovered by Lantern and Candlelight and Selected Writings*, ed. E. D. Pendry, The Stratford-upon-Avon Library, no. 4 (London: Edward Arnold, 1967), p. 5.
51 In other words: 'let the gentleman of London identify a thief before he robs his house, and send him to the whipping post'.
52 Dekker, *The Wonderful Year*, in *Selected Writings*, p. 238.

gulls are there for the taking: 'Your hands are ever open, your purses never shut: so that you stand not in the common rank of dry-fisted patrons who give nothing, for you give all. Scholars therefore are as much beholden to you as vintners, players and punks are.'[53] Thus, the gull behaves aggressively in public places, loses money to rogues, drinks to excess, gambles and dissipates the money others have accumulated through their labour. He rises late, behaves churlishly to his family – 'Bid not "Good morrow" so much as to thy father, though he be an emperor. An idle ceremony it is, and can do him little good'[54] – and thereafter his conduct deteriorates. Against the gull stands the implied figure of the honest citizen, rising early, eschewing excess, working hard, and warily anticipating and avoiding the traps of a city that the good man can negotiate successfully. *The Guls Horne-book* offers a sober citizen's perspective on the stereotypical gallant; and thereby it resembles the kinds of social critique developed in City comedy, a genre which owed much in its origins to Dekker's *The Shoemakers Holiday*.

Dekker's play, however, is perhaps atypical of the mature form in celebrating a relatively unprestigious manufacturing guild, rather than depicting the merchants and goldsmiths who more usually people the stage. Most significantly it is a history play, set in the late Middle Ages – and, rather like a Munday pageant, concerned with depicting the origins of City institutions and the ancient loyalism of citizens to the Crown. The plots and characters in City comedies usually conform to a common pattern. Lord Mayors will figure somewhere, either as major participants or as authority figures intervening *ex machina*. The love story will involve the daughter(s) of a prosperous burger and contrasting and competing suitors, some worthy lovers prepared to risk all, others gullish gallants or contriving money-grabbers, only interested in the loved one's financial prospects. Countrymen – usually impecunious gentry-class villains – will figure too, sometimes on the make and looking for rich wives, sometimes as precursors of the stereotypical Cavaliers of the 1640s, debauchees and whoremongers likely to cuckold the citizens and deprave their daughters. Mock funerals, elopements and actions of debt drive the plots, most of which find resolution in good marriages for the worthy lovers (and bad ones for the haughty and appetitive), and a return to prosperity for those who have lived by the bourgeois ethic of hard work.[55] Civic hostility to theatrical enterprises evidently eased in the early Stuart period as London's authorities arrived at an easier relationship with the acting companies and the operation of their theatres.[56] At the same time and

---

53 *Ibid.*, p. 69.   54 *Ibid.*, p. 82.   55 See also Martin Butler, Chapter 19 below, pp. 577–80.
56 Butler, Chapter 19 below, p. 571.

perhaps reciprocally, a dramatic idiom developed that was in closer harmony with the values and assumptions of civic culture.

Yet how is London depicted in these scenes? Jonson's plays are the more disturbing. His London, as we have seen, is plague-haunted. 'Poetic justice' is rarely served – rogues escape punishment in both *The Alchemist* and *Bartholomew Fair* (1614), despite the scenes of apparent retribution with which they conclude. Most significantly, his London is stalked by the new men who will finally destroy the peace of the metropolis, the Puritans Tribulation and Ananias and Zeal-of-the-Land Busy. However good-natured his adaptation of coneycatching elements to dramatic form, Jonson's vision offers a shrewder account of the tensions within the metropolis than the complacent alternatives offered by most of his contemporaries.

More typically, the moral tale of Philip Massinger's *The City-Madam* (?1632) has the haughty, who have aspired to courtly rather than citizen life styles, brought to recognise their errors, and become better people:

> *Sir John [Frugal].* . . . Make you good
> Your promis'd reformation, and instruct
> Our city dames, whom wealth makes proud, to move
> In their own spheres, and willingly to confess
> In their habits, manners, and their highest port,
> A distance 'twixt the city, and the court.[57]

Thus the tone and terminology of the pulpit find their way into the discourse of the theatre. Again, Thomas Middleton's *A Chaste Maid in Cheapside* (?1613) has the good and bad couples neatly paired in its hymeneal resolution:

> *Yellowhammer:* So fortune seldom deals two marriages
> With one hand, and both lucky: the best is,
> One feast will serve them both: marry, for room
> I'll have the dinner kept in Goldsmiths' Hall,
> To which kind gallants, I invite you all.[58]

While the feast is shared, the ethical status of the pair of couples is sharply differentiated. At the conclusion of this kind of drama, no honest trader languishes in prison, no bounder marries a rich heiress; the audience's expectations and aspirations are rarely frustrated.

---

57 Philip Massinger, *The City-Madam*, ed. T. W. Craik (London: Benn, 1964), 5.3.149–55.
58 Thomas Middleton, *A Chaste Maid in Cheapside*, ed. Alan Brissenden (London: Benn, 1968), 5.4.122–6.

Francis Beaumont's *The Knight of the Burning Pestle* (?1607) confidently assumes the formula of City comedy to be so well established that it is ripe for variation and parody of an outrageous kind. The play within the play has a familiar cast: a rich merchant's daughter and her rival suitors, the unloved Humphrey, 'of gentle blood',[59] and the apprentice cashiered from his post, somewhat against the spirit of his indenture, to clear the field for his opponent. Humphrey, of course, loses, and the marriage eventually receives the merchant's blessing. To these familiar components Beaumont adds the disruptive presence of Rafe, an apprentice plucked from the audience at the behest of his master and mistress and thrust into the plot in ways that gently ridicule their chivalric aspirations and bourgeois values.

Yet Beaumont's play engages no more than Massinger's or Middleton's with the immediate crises of London. Its healthy apprentices and its happy bride contrast with the grimmer realities of the mortality rates for young people entering the metropolis. The study of one London parish discloses that in years not marked by visitations of the plague 24 per cent of recorded deaths in the early Stuart period were of people aged 16 to 25, a group which 'includes a large population of immigrant apprentices and servants, plus young wives – two groups particularly at risk'.[60] Adolescents were almost as likely to perish as infants. The likeliest fate of London entrepreneurs differs sharply from the dramatic accounts of virtue rewarded. The career chances of bankruptcy for a businessman were 10 or 15 per cent, and while death was the likeliest conclusion to a business career, bankruptcy was as likely as retirement.[61] Personal financial ruin may well have originated in under-capitalisation, deceit, robbery or the vagaries of trade, rather than profligacy and a failure to adhere to middle-class virtues.

The apparent verisimilitude of City comedy thinly disguises a literary form for the most part carefully disengaged from the society it purports to reflect. That image confirms a version of London as ultimately content with itself. But it does so – with the exception of Jonson's towering achievement – at the price of falsifying the true nature of London's social and economic relationships, though presumably they remained clear enough to any businessman or apprentice who spent the occasional afternoon at the theatre, and who was, no

59 Francis Beaumont, *The Knight of the Burning Pestle*, ed. John Doebler (London: Arnold, 1967), 1.82.
60 Paul S. Seaver, *Wallington's World: A Puritan Artisan in Seventeenth-Century London* (Stanford University Press, 1985), p. 71.
61 Peter Earle, 'The Middling Sort in London', in Jonathan Barry and Christopher Brooks, eds., *The Middling Sort of People: Culture, Society and Politics in England, 1550–1800* (Houndmills and London: Macmillan, 1994), p. 152.

doubt, much less likely than the citizen and his wife of *The Knight of the Burning Pestle* to confuse such art with his own life. Fascinatingly, City comedy, which seems superficially so mimetic, offers a transformation of everyday experience of a fantastic or escapist kind, in which the certainties of art replace the high risk and random nature of metropolitan living.

Jonson's poetry, like his City comedies, draws heavily on the stereotypes of coney-catching literature, though once more he transforms the commonplace into a unique and startling vision of the metropolis. Though the satirical poems among his *Epigrammes* (first published in his *Works* (1616)) are more often concerned with courtiers and courtly aspirants, the rogues, whores and swaggerers of *Bartholomew Fair* or *The Alchemist* people his urban landscape, joined by cashiered and hungry soldiers of a more threatening aspect. In Epigram 133, his boldest depiction of the City, Jonson imagines an improbable journey of two heroes and their ferrymen, by rowing boat, up the Fleet Ditch from its junction with the Thames to Holborn. It becomes a mock-epic descent to the underworld. Cities may be characterised by their sewage systems as well as by their civic rituals, and early modern London's is alarming. The Fleet Ditch functions as a major conduit for human waste. A mud bank of ordure guards its entrance, 'which, when their oares did once stirre, / Belch'd forth an ayre, as hot, as the muster / Of all your night-tubs'.[62] The pie-shops of Fleet Lane discharge their greasy and suspect waste – dead dogs and cats constitute a prominent component of their effluent.[63] The privies open over the waterway, and, since this is the season for peas, 'Laxative lettuce, and such windie meate', 'each privies seate / Is fill'd with buttock'.[64] Jonson is less concerned to show the skull beneath the skin than the jakes in every backyard.

Yet the sense of surrounding horror also informs the most delightful of his urban poems, Epigram 101, 'Inviting a Friend to Supper'. This text develops a distinction between the private sphere of the poet's home and the threatening City outside it. Within, the countryside figures in the form of the bounteous and healthy produce of its farms, fields and foreshores, and literary culture thrives, reserved from the vulgarity of the wider worlds and the pressures of patronage-hunting.[65] Yet this is a temporary respite from the activities of the City, and above all from the malign work of informers:

> and we will have not *Pooly*, or *Parrot* by;
> Nor shall our cups make any guiltie men:
> But, at our parting, we will be, as when

---

62 Epigram 133, lines 62–4, *Works*, 8:85.   63 Lines 142–54, in *ibid.*, 8:88.
64 Lines 166–9, in *ibid.*, 8:88.   65 Epigram 101, lines 9–23, in *ibid.*, 8:64–5.

> We innocently met. No simple word,
> That shall be utter'd at our mirthfull boord,
> Shall make us sad next morning: or affright
> The libertie, that wee'll enjoy to night.[66]

The poem offers a version of the literature of retirement, celebrating the contemplative over the active life. But such peace is unsustainable: the 'libertie' may be enjoyed only tonight. Jonson's epigram, as many have remarked, is profoundly shaped by similar poems by the Roman Imperial poet, Martial. Those resonances pertinently link the London of James I with the Rome of the reign of the tyrannical Domitian – both dangerous, threatening environments in which to establish, however transiently, a fragile place of retreat, even for a writer of genius. Perhaps, in a sense, all metropolises embody a common threat. Just as in *Volpone* Venice supports a City comedy akin to that of London-set plays, so, too, the City around Jonson promotes recollections of another poet in another site of metropolitan crisis.

Thus far this chapter has considered the role of secular literary forms in producing and maintaining an image of early modern London. A more frequent presence in the cultural lives of its citizens than either plays or literary prose, however, were the sermons that made up the dominant discursive experience of Sundays and holidays, and among these the Paul's Cross sermons were the most conspicuous and prestigious. Preached till 1633 in the open air in the churchyard of St Paul's Cathedral – thereafter the venue moved inside – their original setting 'reminds us of the Elizabethan theatre: groundlings and notables, pit and galleries, and, in the midst, the pulpit as stage'.[67] Sermons there clustered around Eastertide and Whitsun week, and the major anniversaries of the royal calendar, such as accession day and commemorations of the Gunpowder Plot and the Gowries' Conspiracy. As its most accomplished historian concludes, 'The Paul's Cross pulpit was nothing less than the popular voice of the Church of England ... And, the unkind might add, nothing more either.'[68] Appointment to preach was carefully regulated and distributed among reliable university men and rectors or curates of City churches. The duty of appointment rested ordinarily with the Bishop of London, who often preached himself.[69]

By these means, a watchful orthodoxy was maintained. In the Jacobean period, rather like the pageants for the Lord Mayor's inauguration, the sermons

---

66 Lines 36–42, in *ibid.*, 8:65.
67 Millar Maclure, *The Paul's Cross Sermons 1534–1642* (University of Toronto Press, 1958), pp. 18, 4.
68 *Ibid.*, p. 167.   69 *Ibid.*, p. 13.

rehearsed a studied loyalism: 'the loyal and sycophantic preachers affirmed that the highest gift of God to England was the King. On him they heaped praise without stint.'[70] In the Caroline period, there was 'a steady chorus of exhortation to obedience in Church and State'.[71] The 'Register of Sermons' for the period 1603–40 eloquently confirms the carefully limited repertoire of the preachers. Take a year for which the record is particularly full, 1613. We find in January a sermon against sin, of a general kind. In February, a sermon against murder, fraud, drunkenness and 'abomination of women's fashions'. In March, a preacher attacks usury and another offers a 'holy panegyric' on the anniversary of the accession. In May, a sermon engages with the tenet of justifying faith. In June, Londoners could hear a general reproof of the sins of the City. In October, a sermon explains how the death of Prince Henry could have been divinely sanctioned and another expatiates on how godliness is more important than earthly gain. In November, there is a Gunpowder Plot sermon.[72] Of course, these are metropolitan sermons for metropolitan audiences, and the status of the City as a commercial centre is as much a presence in this discourse as in civic pageants. Yet the calls to godliness and attacks on excessive materialism are generalised and disengaged, while the prevailing ideology confidently affirms the continuities of interest between the City and Crown. As has been observed, 'Denunciations of deviants from the social model of complaint – usurers, extortioners, rapacious landlords, prodigal gentry, and the varieties of vagabonds – were thus entirely common, while pointed attacks on the structure of society were not.'[73] A high proportion of Paul's Cross sermons from the early Stuart period were subsequently printed since they were showcase presentations for their authors, and their pious orthodoxy ensured that publication carried no risk of legal action whatsoever.

Among mere journeymen-clerics, John Donne appears as a preacher of exceptional style and power. Several London pulpits were open to him in the 1620s. Most significantly, as Dean he preached frequently at St Paul's; and as a beneficiary of royal patronage and an astonishing performer of obvious orthodoxy and loyalty, he preached at Whitehall, often to Charles I. The sermons we know him to have given at Paul's Cross, however, are some of his most politically engaged and and ideologically careful. Consider, for example, the sermon he preached on 15 September 1622, which was his first to be printed; both the order to preach and the order to print came from James. The sermon offers a staunch defence of James's recent decree, 'Directions concerning Preachers',

70 *Ibid.*, p. 97.   71 *Ibid.*, p. 107.   72 *Ibid.*, pp. 234–5.
73 Manley, *Literature and Culture*, p. 310.

which had occasioned some clerical resistance. Donne praises the King 'who as he understands his dutie to God, so doth he his Subjects duties to him'.[74] Donne's thesis develops distinctions between sound and frivolous sermons in terms which acknowledge an anxiety about less authorised voices than his own: 'Those Preachers which must save your soules, are not ignorant, unlearned, extemporall men; but they are not over curious men neither.'[75] In the rejection of the 'curious', the gratuitously and inappropriately inquisitive (*Oxford English Dictionary*, 5. a.), Donne acknowledges the limitations and imperatives of self-censorship for clergy close to the court and dependent on its patronage.

But those other voices in London pulpits, those he characterises as 'ignorant, unlearned, extemporall', were not to be silenced. From the 1620s onwards, the Puritan movement in London had been associated with a number of prominent clergymen, who, 'although they were in a minority among the City clergy, enjoyed great influence and popularity with the citizens'.[76] Preachers like William Gouge, George Hughes, John Davenport and John Goodwin attracted large audiences to sermons and lectures, and the endowment of 'lectureships', primarily preaching appointments, gave unbeneficed Puritan clergy another platform. Puritanism drew the godly into parochial organisations that gave them an experience of the political process that proved highly relevant in the open conflicts of the 1640s.[77] City radicals thus came to those struggles practised in committee work, familiar with collaborating with like-minded people, and interconnected through informal networks.

Perhaps the best insights into the consciousness of such ordinary Londoners come from the extraordinary manuscript meditations and journals of Nehemiah Wallington, so helpfully analysed by Paul Seaver. Wallington was a 'turner', a woodworker, and a petty master and shopkeeper, recognisably a Puritan in the 1620s and 1630s, and an active Presbyterian in the 1640s. Too poor to leave his business and quit the City in times of plague, Wallington articulates a simpler kind of holy terror than Dekker, 'hearing the bells tolling and ringing out continually'. He reflects, 'What if the sickness should come into this house, who would I be willing to spare? Then would I say, the maid. Who next? Myself. But what if God should strike thy wife, or thy father or

74 *The Sermons of John Donne*, ed. George R. Potter and Evelyn M. Simpson, 10 vols. (Berkeley and Los Angeles: University of California Press, 1953–62), 4:207.
75 *Ibid.*, 4:209.
76 Valerie Pearl, *London and the Outbreak of the Puritan Revolution: Civil Government and National Politics, 1625–43* (London: Oxford University Press, 1961), p. 162.
77 Keith Lindley, *Popular Politics and Religion in Civil War London* (Aldershot: Scolar Press, 1997), pp. 407–8.

thy brother John? How would I take it then?'[78] The easy certainties and social hierarchy of Paul's Cross afford no comfort to Wallington; rather, he seeks out sermons by Presbyterians, and by more radical eminences like Goodwin and Hugh Peter.[79] Among these, the more oppositional clergy did not publish significant amounts in the years of Star Chamber control of the press, for obvious reasons, though the sermons they preached and the instructions they gave plainly shaped the religious sensibility of generations of pious Londoners.

A different kind of pageantry shaped Wallington's civic consciousness, especially in the years of crisis from 1637 onwards. Michel Foucault has argued that in the early modern period the condemned man is the 'symmetrical, inverted figure of the king'.[80] London witnessed the negative counterpart to royal entries in grim pageants of inversion, the spectacular mutilations by earcropping of Bastwick, Burton and Prynne and the flagellation and pillorying of Lilburne. Yet such events, witnessed not by the ordered ranks of liverymen carrying out the rituals and instructions of their companies, but by ordinary Londoners, including the Puritan godly, proved to be more impressive ideological structures than entries and shows, though not in the way the state had intended. Neither spectacle produced an immediately contemporary narrative by its participants, though each of them did voice opposition. One manuscript account notes that for Prynne the scaffold became a sort of pulpit, from which he lectured, 'It is for the general good and your liberties that we have engaged our own liberties'; for Burton, it was more of a stage to act out a vivid *imitatio Christi*, calling, as the blood flowed from the artery in his temple, clipped by the executioner's knife, 'be content, it is well, blessed be God'. The crowd, more animated surely than at a royal pageant, gave out 'a mournful shout and a compassionate crying for the chiru[r]geon'.[81]

Those gory processions and tableaux comprised one defiant discourse of opposition in the controlled and repressive days of the late 1630s. The entry of Charles I on his return from Scotland, cheered by a marshalled claque, may have seemed a gratifying public relations coup; but it was eclipsed by the triumphal entry of the heroes of 1637 on their release. Late in 1640 Prynne and Burton led a procession of 'more than ten thousand people on horseback or on foot, with rosemary (for remembrance) or bay (for victory)'.[82] A few days later, to

78 Seaver, *Wallington's World*, p. 79.   79 *Ibid.*, p. 172.
80 Michel Foucault, *Discipline and Punish: The Birth of the Prison*, trans. Alan Sheridan (Harmondsworth: Penguin, 1977), p. 27.
81 Bodleian, Tanner MS 299, fols. 140–6, quoted by Sharpe, *The Personal Rule*, p. 762. On John Lilburne's own spectacular punishment and his brilliant and courageous subversion of it, see his *The Christian Mans Triall*, 2nd edn (London, 1641).
82 Pearl, *London*, pp. 211–12.

greet Bastwick, Wallington himself 'went to Blackheath and did see many coaches and horses and thousands on foot with their rosemary and bays in their hands'.[83] The procession had ceased to function simply as a formal discourse; it had become a proto-revolutionary praxis.

Contemporary observers as diverse as the Earl of Clarendon and Milton remarked on the role of London after the assembling of the Long Parliament as the seedbed and the fortress of opposition to the Crown. Yet for much of the period 1603–40 the image of London life commemorated in its civic functions, nurtured in its prestigious sermons, and reflected in plays and pamphlets was of a loyal society in which hard work was rewarded, authority always reasserted after comic interludes, law and order maintained despite the threats of rogues and vagabonds, and even the visitations of plague endured and survived. But much of the official cultural activity of the period reflected aspirations of the oligarchic groups that controlled the guilds and the governing bodies of London till the early 1640s, and took little account of changes to the economy and the social structure of the metropolitan area posed by the growth of the suburbs. Moreover, the grand occasions of Paul's Cross sermons probably left many ordinary Londoners to find edification in the more frequent – and more stimulating – teachings of a committed minority of Puritan clergy. Popular literary forms offered an image of London as an exhilarating but ultimately moral society in which virtue found its reward, while Dekker's plague pamphlets contended that the City was a better place to die. Nevertheless, a quotidian experience of economic realities and the risks of City living left agreeable fantasies easily recognisable as exactly that, while the sermons of Puritanism and the heroism of its martyrs confuted any notion of the unity of metropolitan opinion and demonstrated the limitations of civic ideology in shaping the consciousness of Londoners.

83 Seaver, *Wallington's World*, pp. 150–1.

Chapter 19

LITERATURE AND THE THEATRE
TO 1660

MARTIN BUTLER

The story of early Stuart theatre is a narrative almost entirely confined to England and Wales. The austere Calvinism of Stuart Scotland did not encourage the development of secular theatre, and the kirk bitterly resented the English travelling companies that occasionally visited Edinburgh while James still resided there. Once the court went south in 1603, leaving the kingdom without a king, Scotland's fragile drama withered away to nothing. The only significant plays written by a Scot during the entire period were Sir William Alexander's *Monarchic Tragedies* (1607) – four closet dramas in intricately Senecan style that were not intended for performance, by a courtier who followed James to London and became completely anglicised.[1] Ireland had a more developed native drama – at Kilkenny, ecclesiastical pageants survived into the 1630s – and English companies occasionally visited Dublin, but the only sustained attempt to establish a professional theatre was the Werburgh Street playhouse, opened by John Ogilby in 1637. These were the years when Lord Deputy Wentworth was living at Dublin in ostentatiously vice-regal style, and Ogilby, his children's tutor, received a new office of Irish Master of the Revels. But since Werburgh Street performed an essentially English repertoire, with actors and a playwright (James Shirley) recruited from London, it inevitably exhibited the tensions of cultural colonialism. Shirley's prologues express an outsider's discomfort with the Dublin audience, and although he wrote one play on Irish history, *St Patrick for Ireland* (c. 1639), it represented the locals as sullen, barbaric and needing acculturation.[2] One Irish dramatist emerged – Henry Burnell, author of *Landgartha* (1639) – but

---

1 Bill Findlay (ed.), *A History of Scottish Theatre* (Edinburgh: Polygon, 1998), pp. 1–79; Anna Jean Mill, *Mediaeval Plays in Scotland* (Edinburgh: W. Blackwood, 1927), pp. 299–306.
2 Alan J. Fletcher, *Drama, Performance and Polity in Pre-Cromwellian Ireland* (Cork University Press, 2000); Patricia Coughlan, ' "Cheap and common animals": The English Anatomy of Ireland in the Seventeenth Century', in *Literature and the English Civil War*, ed. Thomas Healy and Jonathan Sawday (Cambridge University Press, 1990), p. 209.

this theatrical outpost of empire unsurprisingly failed to survive the 1641 rebellion.

In the English countryside and Welsh marches, theatrical companies travelled as they had done in Tudor times, performing in towns, villages and aristocratic households. However, under the Stuarts the volume of performance declined sharply, although the practice of touring survived to the Civil War.[3] Gaps in the records make it difficult to construct a reliable picture of provincial playing. Because of changes in the licensing system, players arriving at a country town no longer automatically registered with the mayor, and visits often went unrecorded. A don's diary mentions that the King's Men visited Oxford in 1635, but the city archives are silent; similarly, we cannot substantiate Ben Jonson's claim, in 1607, that *Volpone* had been seen at both universities.[4] Performances outside the major towns are difficult to track. Only a chance appearance in Quarter Sessions records reveals that an unlicensed troupe led by one Richard Hudson was touring North Yorkshire villages in January and February 1616.[5] Nonetheless, trends in the archives do suggest that after 1610 the numbers of visits were slowly declining. Commonly, towns rid themselves of strollers by paying them to leave without playing, preventing their performances without challenging the authority of their licences. This device has been attributed to the spread of puritanical sentiment, though the inference is questionable. Paying off the players could be due as much to anxiety about their disrupting trade as concern for morality, and some towns with reputations for Puritanism, such as Coventry, were among those still welcoming players in 1640. While the penetration of godly sentiment into local oligarchies made life difficult for the strollers, the underlying direction of change owed as much to economics as to ideology. The focus of the theatrical market was shifting to London.

This change was already underway in the 1570s, with the establishment of purpose-built playhouses in the metropolis, and the emergence of players like the Burbages, who had financial interests in both performance spaces and acting companies. The troupes that in mid-Tudor times regarded touring as their core activity were increasingly using London as their prime base of operations.

3 The pioneering discussion is by Leo Salingar, Gerard Harrison and Bruce Cochrane, 'Les Comédiens et leur public en Angleterre de 1520 à 1640', in *Dramaturgie et société*, ed. J. Jacquot, 2 vols. (Paris: Centre National de la Recherche Scientifique, 1968), 2:525–76. The as yet incomplete picture developing from the REED project is summarised by Peter Greenfield's 'Touring', in *A New History of Early English Drama*, ed. J. D. Cox and D. S. Kastan (New York: Columbia University Press, 1997), pp. 251–68.
4 Andrew Gurr, *The Shakespearean Playing Companies* (Oxford University Press, 1996), pp. 41, 164–5.
5 G. W. Boddy, 'Players of Interludes in North Yorkshire in the Early Seventeenth Century', *North Yorkshire County Record Office Journal* 3 (1976), 112.

But the most decisive factor in undermining provincial playing was the new licensing system imposed after James's accession. During 1603–4, the leading London companies were taken under the patronage of members of the royal family, and the statutory right to support players was withdrawn from the inferior nobility. These developments were critical for provincial drama, since they severely reduced the numbers of companies who were licensed to tour. Thereafter, noble families who wanted drama could promote private theatricals on their estates,[6] but they could no longer maintain their own companies or foster any more dispersed kinds of theatrical activity. Most early Stuart strollers were linked to the London troupes, travelling with licences duplicated from those held by the parent companies.[7] A new perception of theatrical geography arose: the provinces had become the periphery, and London the centre.

How far the new licensing system increased the players' dependence on the court remains a controversial question. Many historians have seen the changes as a turning point in a process by which Crown and theatre contracted an intimacy that lasted until both were overthrown by Parliament in 1642. Certainly Stuart Whitehall was renowned for its cultural patronage, and employed many distinguished poets, musicians, artists and architects. With its ostentatious masques harnessing the power of drama, scenery and music to the praise of monarchy, the court became closely associated with expensive political theatre and needed actors to handle the masques' dialogue. Players also performed regularly at court during the winter season, and Whitehall's support benefited the companies in their dealings with an often hostile City. Shakespeare's company, the King's Men, were the troupe most frequently seen at court, and they capitalised on their favoured status, which helped them achieve preeminence amongst the London companies. Shakespeare's Jacobean plays frequently seem designed to interest their royal patron. It is no accident that he wrote a tragedy on Scottish history, or that *King Lear* and *Cymbeline* draw on the British legendary myths that were germane to James's project for Union of the kingdoms. These plays do not exactly endorse James's policies – their relationship to contemporary affairs is much more oblique – but by addressing such themes, Shakespeare contributed significantly to Jacobean England's developing political culture.[8]

---

6 For example, the Hastings family in Leicestershire (where John Marston's Ashby entertainment was performed, 1607), the Spencers at Harefield (for whom Milton wrote *Arcades*, c. 1634) and the Cliffords at Skipton (who mounted a masque of 'Comus', now lost, in 1637: see Martin Butler, 'A Provincial Masque of "Comus"', *Renaissance Drama* n.s. 17 (1986), 149–73).

7 Gurr, *The Shakespearean Playing Companies*, p. 49.

8 The fullest recent statement of this case is by Alvin Kernan, *Shakespeare, the King's Playwright* (New Haven: Yale University Press, 1995).

Whether royal patrons took a close interest in the daily activities of their companies is another matter. There are few signs that James paid much attention to the affairs of the King's Men. Though not the donnish imbecile of historical myth, his tastes ran to hunting and debate rather than theatre, and his recorded comments on drama are unappreciative – most famously his cry of boredom at Jonson's masque *Pleasure Reconciled to Virtue* (1618), 'What did they make me come here for? Devil take all of you, dance!'[9] The one play for which he expressed enthusiasm was George Ruggle's *Ignoramus* (1615), a Latin academic satire staged at Cambridge University, and an unlikely prospect for any modern revival.[10] By contrast, Queen Anne's court was, in some ways, a rival cultural centre to her husband's, with her own network of friends who were dissociated from the outlook of his servants.[11] She was the great sponsor of the early masques, and in 1604 lent her name to a boys' company, the Children of the Queen's Revels, delegating the licensing of their productions to her poet Samuel Daniel. Whether by coincidence or design, the Queen's Revels at once undertook a series of satires that sailed dangerously close to the political wind. At first Anne seems to have condoned their activities: the French ambassador said James was under attack from pulpit and stage, and his wife 'attends these representations in order to enjoy the laugh against her husband'.[12] The boys' behaviour, however, eventually distanced them from the Queen. Daniel was sacked as licenser, and the troupe downgraded to the Company of the Revels; in 1608 they folded completely. As other players would find in 1624 and 1640, companies caught up in the court's factional struggles put their own survival at risk.

It was the commercial opportunities of the metropolis, not the uncertain rewards of court service, that made London so magnetic. By 1599 the urban marketplace was showing it could sustain a flourishing theatrical industry. Three large amphitheatre playhouses stood on the Bankside in Southwark – the Swan, the Rose and the Globe – and these were shortly joined by two more to the north, the Fortune in Golding Lane (built in 1600) and the Red Bull in Clerkenwell (built 1605). The Rose would shortly close, but the rest were new buildings that proclaimed their companies' prosperity. The Globe was financed by seven of the Lord Chamberlain's Men (the future King's Men), and

9 Inigo Jones, *The Theatre of the Stuart Court*, ed. Stephen Orgel and Roy Strong, 2 vols. (London: Sotheby Parke Bernet, 1973), 1:283.
10 Sir Edmund Kerchever Chambers, *The Elizabethan Stage*, 4 vols. (Oxford: Clarendon Press, 1923), 3:475–6; and see J. Leeds Barroll, 'A New History for Shakespeare and his Time', *Shakespeare Quarterly* 39 (1988), 441–64.
11 Leeds Barroll, 'The Court of the First Stuart Queen', in *The Mental World of the Jacobean Court*, ed. Linda Levy Peck (Cambridge University Press, 1991), pp. 191–208.
12 Chambers, *Elizabethan Stage*, 1:325.

the Fortune was built by the impresario Philip Henslowe for the Admiral's Men (the future Prince's Men). These two theatres, the first built 'for the sole use of a London company whose residence was officially approved',[13] signal a new permanency in the players' affairs. Hereafter the leading companies were identified with their settled playing spaces. Beside these, two smaller roofed theatres accommodated companies of boys, one in the precincts of St Paul's Cathedral (operative 1599–1606), the other in former monastic buildings in the Blackfriars liberty within the city walls (used by the boys 1600–8). These theatres' adventurous repertoires gave them high visibility, but they only performed weekly, and their audience capacity was small (500 at Blackfriars, perhaps only 100 at Paul's). By contrast, the amphitheatres, with their tiered seating arranged economically around a central open space, could accommodate audiences of many hundreds: the Globe's maximum capacity was about 3,000 people.

Only London could provide the numbers of spectators to keep this many theatres in business. In 1600, London held 200,000 souls, and was growing by about 8,000 a year (half the annual population increase for England and Wales). By 1700, London's unique combination of political, economic and social functions had doubled the City's size. As the home of the court, law courts and Parliament, it was the nation's administrative centre; as a major port, it was the heart of commerce; and it was coming to figure as a tourist destination, visited for its own sake or for the emergent realm of fashion. The City drew labourers seeking work, craftsmen looking for citizenship, students residing at the Inns of Court, and gentlemen pursuing business, wives, court office or just the metropolitan round of pleasure and company. Though individual theatres attracted different constituencies, these categories of playgoers all figured in eyewitness accounts of the audiences. Moreover, Jacobean London was compact: the Tower in the east was only a mile from Ludgate in the west, and all the playhouses were within easy walk of Cheapside. Since the City authorities disapproved of the players residing permanently in London, the theatres had to be situated at a distance where they could operate free from mayoral interference. Hence they were built just outside the City limits, in Southwark or the northern suburbs, or in 'liberties' within the walls, zones of special privilege like the Blackfriars, which, for historical reasons, were legally distinct.

It is easy to see why the authorities disliked the theatres. They disturbed trade, drew citizens from their work, unsettled the ideology of thrift, and assembled large crowds, with all the attendant problems of crime, disorder and transmission of plague. There were also religious objections: that play-acting

13　Gurr, *The Shakespearean Playing Companies*, pp. 4–5.

was ungodly, encouraged vice and sexual licence, and undermined the sobriety of a Christian commonwealth. Yet while the City never reconciled itself to the playhouses, they gradually became established as a permanent presence in its cultural and social life. Incessant collisions between the Privy Council and the Mayor over the players' freedom to act around London were highly character-istic of Elizabethan records, but much less in evidence after 1603. In 1601, the usual mayoral complaint against the disorders of players met with the usual conciliar reply that the magistrates were to suppress unauthorised playhouses. This was the last general complaint until 1642, when Parliament closed the playhouses: such protests must have seemed increasingly futile once the royal family had given players their own licence.[14] In the ensuing decades, the City resisted the extension of theatrical activity in Blackfriars precinct, the one place within the walls where a permanent playhouse operated. Proposals for a new theatre at Puddle Wharf were opposed in 1615, and the Blackfriars residents petitioned against traffic congestion caused by the theatre in 1619, 1631 and 1641.[15] In 1609, however, silence greeted the takeover of the Blackfriars by an adult company, perhaps reflecting the fact that the noisy and popular amphithe-atres in the suburbs were the real objects of dislike. The absence of protest was all the more striking because the precinct's legal status had been changed by a financial deal in 1608, in which James returned control of the liberties to the aldermen. The failure to react to the Blackfriars until ten years after the adults had moved in was symptomatic of the lower ideological temperatures aroused by such issues under the Stuarts.

One influential school of modern criticism has seen the theatres' marginality as the key to their drama. Anthropologically minded critics have linked the drama's power to the playhouses' geographical situation, viewing their situa-tion at the edge – their location in ambiguous terrain beyond the reach of civic authority – as the condition of their success. Liminality, in this view, made for aesthetic flexibility: the playhouses 'experiment[ed] with a wide range of avail-able ideological perspectives and . . . realize[d], in dramatic form, the cultural contradictions of the age'.[16] Yet Jacobean London lacked a simple opposition between ordered centre and disorderly periphery; rather, the playhouses were increasingly part of that metropolitan scene to which, superficially, they seem

---

14 Chambers, *Elizabethan Stage*, 4:333–4.
15 Gerald Eades Bentley, *The Jacobean and Caroline Stage*, 7 vols. (Oxford: Clarendon Press, 1941–68), 1:4–5, 31–4, 64; 6:77–86.
16 Stephen Mullaney, *The Place of the Stage: License, Play and Power in Renaissance England* (University of Chicago Press, 1988), pp. ix–x. Compare the critique of these views by Dou-glas Bruster in *Drama and the Market in the Age of Shakespeare* (Cambridge University Press, 1992), pp. 9–10.

opposed. This relationship intensified as the period proceeded. Early Stuart companies were no longer temporary London residents but established economic enterprises, while their drama's preoccupation with the pleasures and perils of City life confirmed the theatres' function as conduits of urban experience. At the same time, the status of plays and playwrights was beginning to attract apologists who intuited the connections between commerce and comedy. If in his *Defence of Poetry* (pub. 1595), Sir Philip Sidney offered only qualified praise for drama, Thomas Heywood's *Apology for Actors* (1612) linked the stage more confidently with a flourishing metropolitan ethos. Far from inhibiting enterprise, said Heywood, the playhouses were 'an ornament to the city, which strangers of all nations repairing hither report of in their countries, beholding them here with some admiration: for what variety of entertainment can there be in any city of Christendom more than in London?'[17] Not everyone agreed. Heywood's arguments were soon attacked in J. G.'s *Refutation of the Apology for Actors* (1615), but they voiced attitudes that were starting to gain ground. When Jonson published his plays in 1616 under the provocative title *Works*, he implied that they were as much the product of serious labour as was any other commodity.[18]

The early Jacobean theatre

The most self-consciously ambitious of the new wave of Jacobean playwrights, Jonson outlined his aspirations in *Poetaster* (1601), performed by the Blackfriars Boys. In this transparent allegory of London rivalries projected onto Augustan Rome, Jonson's ideal writers are an intellectual elite, consorting on equal terms with great aristocratic patrons despite the social disparity. Jonson shadows his own career in Horace, whose work balances in a middle way between Ovid's sensuality and Virgil's sublimity. An independent man of letters, protected by the Emperor Augustus, Horace writes without sullying contact with the market. His enemies are the philistine magistrates and money-grubbers who do not sufficiently value literature, and the incompetent poetasters who envy his skill. These last figures lampoon real-life rivals, John Marston and Thomas Dekker, the former for inflated vocabulary, the latter for hack-writing, and Jonson pointedly distinguishes himself from other dramatists in a scene parodying the overblown acting of the adult troupes 'on the other side of

17 Thomas Heywood, *An Apology for Actors* (London: The Shakespeare Society, 1841), p. 52.
18 The relationship between theatres and markets is explored from a philosophical perspective by Jean-Christophe Agnew, *Worlds Apart: The Market and the Theater in Anglo-American Thought, 1550–1750* (Cambridge University Press, 1986).

the Tiber'.[19] Unfortunately, these jokes backfired, for Dekker's response, *Satiromastix*, reanimated Horace in much less flattering terms, as a servile journeyman-poet sucking up to rich patrons and hammering out rhymes with a distinct lack of inspiration. *Satiromastix* deftly exposed the social agendas that lay just below Jonson's lofty aesthetic discriminations. Far from establishing Jonson's independence of the literary marketplace, *Poetaster* demonstrated how firmly he was embedded within it.[20]

Poetaster and *Satiromastix* exemplify the complex forces that were transforming the situation of the early Stuart dramatists. Late shots in the so-called 'War of the Theatres' – a period of crossfire between rival dramatists working for the boy and adult companies – they testified to a perception that new rewards and opportunities were starting to develop. Few playwrights shared Jonson's expectation of becoming unofficial advisors to Kings, but all were affected by the climate of greater professionalism created by the larger numbers of London playhouses and companies, and by the increased specialisation it entailed. At this time, *Poetaster*'s discrimination between legitimate and illegitimate theatres, true poets and unsophisticated hacks, was still far from obvious. Antagonisms between playwrights and companies did not run on party lines (or 'rival traditions', as Alfred Harbage put it), and were prone to shift unpredictably.[21] *Satiromastix* was staged by both the adults and the boys; and despite his lampooning in *Poetaster*, Marston dedicated *The Malcontent* (1603) to Jonson, and collaborated with him on *Eastward Ho!* (1605).[22] Quarrels between playwrights were as symptomatic of likeness as of difference, indicating the felt necessity to stake out a place in a literary market that had suddenly started to seem congested. Meanwhile, a slowly developing hierarchy of audiences, with diverging tastes served by different repertoires at particular playhouses, brought professional antagonisms and distinctions between playwrights to the surface. Jonson may have misrepresented his situation by linking himself to a classic writer completely distanced from the world of commerce, but this was symptomatic of the new, and frequently contradictory, aspirations aroused by the more established theatrical marketplace.

One trigger for the 'War of the Theatres' was the re-appearance of the boy companies, and the emergence of the indoor houses at St Paul's and the Blackfriars as competitors to the adults. These companies deliberately pitched

19 *The Works of Ben Jonson*, ed. C. H. Herford, Percy Simpson and Evelyn Simpson, 11 vols. (Oxford: Clarendon Press, 1925–52), 4:251.
20 This exchange is discussed by Jonathan Haynes, *The Social Relations of Jonson's Theatre* (Cambridge University Press, 1992), pp. 86–8.
21 Alfred Harbage, *Shakespeare and the Rival Traditions* (New York: Macmillan, 1952).
22 In the dedication to *The Malcontent*, Marston called Jonson his 'candid and heartfelt friend'.

themselves towards select audiences. Since their theatres were small, and admission prices started at sixpence, six times higher than the amphitheatres, their spectators were drawn from a narrower field than those who saw the adult companies. Their playwrights, too, had class. Few were as well connected as William Percy, son to the Earl of Northumberland, who wrote six comedies for Paul's, but Francis Beaumont and John Fletcher, whose names were synonymous with Blackfriars, were sons of, respectively, a bishop and a judge. Others, like Marston and John Webster, had links with the Inns of Court, the lawyers' colleges where a sophisticated tone and *avant garde* interests prevailed.[23] The boys became known for witty and sometimes outrageous drama which relished novelty and innovation and reflected the more unsettling intellectual currents of the time. They could even run ahead of their own audiences, as when Fletcher's *Faithful Shepherdess* (1608) – an Italianate pastoral modelled on Guarini's *Il Pastor Fido* – met with incomprehension and flopped at the Blackfriars. In general, Paul's was more cautious and never so politically or theatrically adventurous as its rival. Yet, both theatres expected their audiences to exhibit critical detachment, enjoy sophisticated alienation effects, and consider themselves 'judging spectators'.[24] These effects were a far cry from the robust festive enthusiasms typical of the amphitheatres.

The boys' drama differed radically in acting style from the adults'. Intensely aware of their own artifice, their plays relished devices that undermined the simple representation of reality. Partly this was the irony of boy actors in adult roles, but there were also hyper-sophisticated metatheatrical effects, such as sudden narrative twists, surprising combinations of naivety and contrivance, and self-conscious allusions to the playwright's hidden hand. Marston's *Antonio and Mellida* (for Paul's Boys, 1600) showcased the style. In Marston's induction, the boys enter in their own persons and discuss their parts with witty detachment, but once the action starts, they shift from stereotyped posturing to passionate emotionalism.[25] The flimsy plot follows the relationship between Antonio, heir to the Duke of Genoa, and Mellida, daughter of his enemy, Piero, Doge of Venice, but what really counts are the fantastic situations and the bitter parody of court manners that interweaves events. Characters teeter on the verge of extreme emotions which are complicated in turn by their language's rhetorical contrivance and by the perception that every persona is a

23 See Philip J. Finkelpearl, *John Marston of the Middle Temple* (Cambridge, MA: Harvard University Press, 1969).
24 Jonson, *Works*, 5:294.
25 The play is discussed by G. K. Hunter, *English Drama 1586–1642* (Oxford: Clarendon Press, 1997), p. 284. See also Jonathon Dollimore, *Radical Tragedy* (Brighton: Harvester Press, 1984), pp. 29–40.

performance. For example, Antonio laments despairingly, thinking he has lost Mellida, but she actually stands next to him in disguise and, when he recognises her, the two characters shift into ecstatic Italian: his plight is made to seem both serious and faintly ridiculous. At such moments, the play oscillates disconcertingly between tragic situations and an ironic preoccupation with its own artifice. Its colliding representational planes leave no stable frame of reference for a coherent action.

   The startling juxtapositions of this deliberately discontinuous dramaturgy left their mark on Jonson, Webster, and Beaumont and Fletcher, but it was Marston who pursued them to the extremes that suited his radically sceptical world view. His plays lurch unpredictably between philosophic idealism and corrosive cynicism, two sides of the same ideological coin: all values are exploded, and all systems of order equally fraudulent. In *Antonio's Revenge* (1601), the sequel to *Antonio and Mellida*, fantastical comedy converts to tragedy, for Piero kills Antonio's father, provoking a hyperbolical vengeance in which all characters seem unhinged by their sufferings. Although Antonio's party does justice on Piero, there is no coherence between their idealistic language and the savagery of his butchery, and Piero's elaborately contrived death seems an empty theatrical ritual. No less disturbing is the dark comedy *The Dutch Courtesan* (1604), in which the naïve moralist Malheureux falls victim to his own lusts, despite his rational Stoicism and the advice of his libertine friend Freevill. Brought to the scaffold by his desires, Malheureux avoids hanging for a crime he never committed but his narrow escape conveys scant reassurance. It is, though, Altofront, the title-character of *The Malcontent* (1605), who most fully expresses Marston's universal scepticism. The rightful but dispossessed Duke of Genoa, he hangs around his old court disguised as Malevole, a discontented nobleman. As two persons in one, he embodies in his uniquely divided perspective the dislocations to which the other plays allude. As Altofront, he is a stoical moralist and defender of providential orthodoxy, but as Malevole he is the cynical libertine, a snarling satirist who sees corruption in every corner. The ending restores him to his dukedom, proving that Providence underwrites the legitimate ruler, but only after the malcontent's demystified view of the world has been fully established. The play's hankering after order issues from a disenchanted perspective; its idealism is rooted in an equally extreme conviction of the worthlessness of things. Little wonder that when the boys ceased playing, Marston turned from the world, entering the church and ending his life as a country parson.

   The other distinction of the boys' drama was its political risk-taking; as one character complained in *Poetaster*, they staged 'nothing but humours, revels and satires, that gird and fart at the time'.[26] Both companies found satire good for business, but Blackfriars farted the most. No sooner was Daniel appointed their governor than he was hauled before the Privy Council to explain his tragedy *Philotas* (1604). Set in the days of Alexander the Great and depicting the fall of an ambitious aristocrat whose popularity drew down his monarch's envy, this was decoded as an allegory of Elizabeth's treatment of her disgraced favourite, Essex. A year later Jonson, Marston and Chapman's *Eastward Ho!* joked undiplomatically about James's Scottish courtiers and newmade knights. Marston fled, and for a time Jonson and Chapman seemed likely to lose their ears. In 1606, the boys were again reprimanded, and some jailed, over John Day's *The Isle of Gulls*, a seemingly naïve Arcadian tale spiced with personal satire on the King, his first minister and Scottish courtiers. Royal patience finally snapped in 1608, when the boys satirised Scottish industry in a lost play, and brought the French court on stage in Chapman's *Conspiracy and Tragedy of Byron*. This time James publicly swore they would 'never play more but should first beg their bread'.[27] Even allowing for the popularity of anti-Scottish sentiment, this level of scandal-mongering was extreme. No other troupe took such risks, and other companies must have worried about damage to their own affairs. Heywood spoke for many when he attacked writers who commit 'their bitterness and liberal invectives against all estates to the mouths of children, supposing their juniority to be a privilege for any railing', and urged the boys 'to curb and limit this presumed liberty' for the sake of the profession.[28]

In the event, Heywood's pragmatism triumphed, for once the boy companies faded, most troupes kept their plays within acceptable limits of conformity. The spectacular altercations of 1603–8 gave way to a better understanding with the Master of the Revels, the court official responsible for administering London's drama, and the climate of the ensuing decade was considerably less fraught.[29] Nonetheless, the expectation persisted that plays should incorporate searching scrutiny of their times, and much Jacobean drama routinely addressed contemporary life and manners. James generally tolerated satire that eschewed scandal, and the playwrights thus avoided serious confrontations with Whitehall. In an

---

26 Jonson, *Works*, 4:251.
27 Chambers, *Elizabethan Stage*, 2:54. For a fuller narrative, see Albert H. Tricomi, *Anti-Court Drama in England 1603–42* (Charlottesville: University Press of Virginia, 1989).
28 Heywood, *An Apology for Actors*, p. 61.
29 The major discussions of censorship are by Janet Clare, '*Art Made Tongue-Tied by Authority': Elizabethan and Jacobean Dramatic Censorship* (Manchester University Press, 1991); Richard Dutton, *Mastering the Revels: The Regulation and Censorship of English Renaissance Drama* (London: Macmillan, 1991); and Nigel Bawcutt, *The Control and Censorship of Caroline Drama* (Oxford University Press, 1996).

age without modern newspapers and media, the theatres took on some functions eventually performed by journalism – retailing information and new ideas,
and consolidating public opinion. Plays like Middleton's *A Yorkshire Tragedy*
(1606) or Heywood and Brome's *The Late Lancashire Witches* (1635) dramatised
newsworthy events for a rapidly developing market eager for gossip. But the
theatre also helped to shape the audiences' mentality in more complex ways,
by dramatising and exploring their assumptions about their own identities and
society. In the busy urban world of Stuart London, drama was a sounding board
for change, managing its spectators' collective experience, their anxieties and
aspirations.

If London was the commercial and administrative focus of Stuart theatre,
it was also its frequent preoccupation, since the metropolitan scene offered
an almost inexhaustible fund of comic material. The late Elizabethan vogue
for comedies satirising 'humorous' characters – eccentrics behaving oddly
because of a physiological imbalance – had already compiled a gallery of stock
urban life. While the courtly locations of George Chapman's humour plays –
Sir Giles Goosecap (1602), *The Gentleman Usher* (1602), *Monsieur D'Olive* (1604) –
bespeak roots in humanistic drama, the trend was towards city settings and familiar characters of the middling sort. Jonson's *Every Man In His Humour* (1598)
depicted citizens and wits in contemporary Florence, but its revised version
(1616) effortlessly translated the Italian topography to London. *Every Man Out
of His Humour* (1599) is even more a mirror, its long central scene set in the public
meeting-place in St Paul's Cathedral, where courtiers, gentlemen and citizens
do business, exchange gossip or just hang out. This was not the first dramatic
pastiche of everyday conversation in a familiar urban setting – that honour
goes to William Haughton's *Englishmen for my Money* (1598) – but it is easily the
most elaborate, and the first to explore the comedy of manners generated by
London life.[30] What Jonson calls a 'humour' is, in fact, a mechanism of social integration. Characters are 'humorous' if their behaviour is aberrant or affected –
in other words, if it offends notions of good manners taken for granted within
the play's world. To Jonson's moral commentators, Asper, Mitis and Cordatus,
norms are fixed, but it is evident from the play's focus on fashion and customs
of speech that they change according to the urban community's shifting social
expectations. Hence although *Every Man Out* is presented as judicial satire,
affirming absolute notions of good and bad, in practice the boundaries it patrols

---

30 See Helen Ostovich, "'To behold the scene full'": Seeing and Judging in *Every Man Out
of His Humour*', in *Re-Presenting Ben Jonson: Text, History, Performance*, ed. Martin Butler
(Basingstoke: Macmillan, 1999), pp. 76–92.

are fluid. Like virtually every other City comedy, it trains attention on the age's most hotly contested category – the problematic but intensely desired label of 'gentleman'.

The range and significance of City comedy can be suggested by comparing plays by Jonson and Middleton. Jonson's three major comedies celebrate the plenitude of urban life but worry about its consequences for systems of social control. Typically, they unsettle the audience's attitudes towards metropolitan enterprise and self-advancement by making criminals their most witty and attractive characters. In *Volpone* (1606), the title-character exploits the self-interest of stereotyped urban figures – lawyer, miser and merchant – who put money into his scams in the false hope of fantastic returns. Volpone's schemes brilliantly expose the shortcomings of what is, in effect, the futures market, but his attempt to rape the merchant's wife, Celia, shows the danger of his own uncontrolled desires. However, the judges who try to restore order have no special insight into the City's activities, but are themselves just as much prey to its illusions, and an unsatisfactory justice is achieved only when Volpone reveals his own criminality. In *The Alchemist* (1610), the concern with governance is more overt. Here the tricksters, who pretend to be making gold from base metal, are selling get-rich-quick schemes, and their dupes are small citizens and would-be gentlemen who think alchemy will bring power and respect. The ensuing commercial competition threatens the City with chaos: each client hopes purchasing power will advance him, and some expect to remake society in their own image. Normality is restored by the gentleman Lovewit, but since he excels only in his ability to beat the rogues at their own game, there is no guarantee of a different future. On the contrary, Lovewit's victory merely reproduces the commercial ethos in a socially acceptable form. In both of these plays, the City is uneasily poised between order and anarchy, its swirling population magnetised by the hope of gain and bent on achieving their private desires. Higher authority is conspicuous by its absence, while ties of friendship and blood dissolve in private self-seeking. In the wonderfully panoramic comedy *Bartholomew Fair* (1614), it is less avarice than sheer idiocy that unites the characters. Two families and a pair of friends visit the Smithfield fair, lured by its reputation for strange sights, and one by one they succumb to the pleasures of food, fighting and sex. Their group ties disintegrate as each sets off after novelty, and the claims to superiority held by authority-figures dissolve: magistrate, preacher and tutor all find themselves punished for disturbing the peace. The witty gentleman, Quarlous, finally comes out on top, but everyone must confront their inability to govern others or themselves. The only figure who can oversee this vigorous but squalid cityscape is the play's principal spectator – the King, addressed in the court prologue as its ultimate judge.[31]

Jonson's comedies are unimaginable without their London setting, but they present the City with profound ambivalence, as a place caught between burgeoning commercialism and the failure of inherited authority. Thomas Middleton's plays celebrate the City less equivocally. His London is full of follies, but the shortcomings of his characters arise environmentally, from their circumstances rather than inherent character flaws. Middleton's more sociologically oriented comedy concerns itself with the injustice of things, the disadvantages that people endure simply because of who they are. His heroes are less than angels – frequently, even, victims of their own prodigality – but they also suffer from the double-dealing condoned in business, or the robbery legitimised by the inheritance system. Consequently, his plays celebrate ingenuity as a means of remedying misfortunes of birth, subterfuge being his heroes' response to the institutionalised inequities which have dispossessed them. A recurrent Middletonian figure is the cunning young gentleman, footloose and indigent, who carves himself a city living by his wits. So too is the independent woman, a character Middleton presents contradictorily as both a victim and a threat. All his plays voice the misogyny of their times and assume that women are 'leaky vessels' incapable of self-control. However, they also present strong women who challenge misogynist assumptions – notably Moll Cutpurse, the transvestite heroine of *The Roaring Girl* (1611; written with Dekker), who beats up the man who takes her for a whore. If Middleton's plays generally reaffirm gender categories, their intermittent concern with women as victims of circumstance unsettles simple gender stereotyping.[32]

Two of Middleton's comedies must suffice for discussion here. *A Trick to Catch the Old One* (1606) is a perfectly plotted action that adapts New Comedy motifs to contemporary urban circumstance. Witgood, the feckless gentleman, has frittered away his estate; to regain it he must deceive his uncle, the usurer Lucre, to whom it is mortgaged. Witgood convinces everyone he is about to wed a rich widow, upon which his credit recovers so miraculously that he reestablishes himself in society and takes revenge on his creditors. The beauty of this plot is its strictly economic analysis of city life as a struggle between haves and have-nots. The grasping citizens want land, the spendthrift gentlemen

---

31 This summary draws on Haynes, *The Social Relations of Jonson's Theatre*, and Peter Womack, *Ben Jonson* (Oxford: Blackwell, 1986).
32 See Gail Kern Paster, *The Body Embarrassed: Drama and the Disciplines of Shame in Early Modern England* (Ithaca, NY: Cornell University Press, 1993), pp. 23–63; Jean Howard, 'Sex and Social Conflict: The Erotics of *The Roaring Girl*', in *Erotic Politics*, ed. Susan Zimmerman (London: Routledge, 1992), pp. 170–90.

need cash: the exact balance and endless circularity of this equation stage the liquidity of money and status. Unlike Jonson, Middleton largely endorses his hero's immorality, for if Witgood does not bite he will be bitten. He is simply playing the system, and his survival depends on manipulating his rivals' social and economic aspirations (to which Witgood is sensitised because of his own status insecurities). In *A Chaste Maid in Cheapside* (1613), the sense of system is even greater, for this play's multiple plots are skilfully bound in interlocking symmetry. A penniless young gentleman, Touchwood, loves a goldsmith's daughter, Moll Yellowhammer, whose parents intend to bestow her on the courtier Sir Walter Whorehound. Unbeknown to the Yellowhammers, however, Sir Walter keeps a mistress and a family of bastards in the household of the complaisant City cuckold Allwit, and his own wealth depends on the infertility of Sir Oliver Kix, to whom his inheritance goes should Kix produce children. All the dominoes collapse when Touchwood's brother secretly impregnates Lady Kix: Sir Walter is disinherited; the Allwits disclaim knowledge of him; and Moll's brother Tim finds himself unwittingly married to one of Walter's castoff whores. The Kixes and Touchwoods go up, Walter and Tim go down, and the Allwits console themselves by investing what remains of their patron's money in fashionable lodgings in the Strand. In this wonderfully engineered plot, every part of the City is intricately tied to every other part, so that business in one quarter impacts on events elsewhere: no one is advantaged without someone else being disadvantaged. This makes Middleton's London seem a place of inexorable economic law, but also an interlinked, knowable community. Unlike the centripetal structure of *The Alchemist*, where the characters are connected only by the accident of being simultaneously in London, *A Chaste Maid* understands the City as a place of neighbourliness as well as double-dealing.[33]

Jonson's and Middleton's comedies do not exhaust the range of representations of urban life on the Jacobean stage, but they help to indicate the variety of responses that the City provoked. By exploring these tensions, Jacobean City comedies helped their audience come to terms with the new urban environment and the processes of economic and social change that it encapsulated. Of course, their picture of the early modern metropolis was far from reliable. Plots derive as much from jest-book and classical comedy as from life, their dim magistrates and enterprising wits not really being representative of the urban

---

33 The social relations of Middleton's comedy are discussed in Margot Heinemann, *Puritanism and Theatre: Thomas Middleton and Opposition Drama* (Cambridge University Press, 1980), and Swapan Chakravorty, *Society and Politics in the Plays of Thomas Middleton* (Oxford University Press, 1995).

scene. But in manipulating such character-types, the dramatists located moral and social polarities that seemed to make sense of London, while expressing both its excitement and its power to alienate.

The so-called 'tragedy of state' performed equivalent functions for the court, managing the depiction of changes in contemporary political life. Since tragedy was expected to deal with the fall of princes, Elizabethan tragic drama always had a political dimension, but it was under the early Stuarts that tragedy became preoccupied with the tensions inherent in the exercise of power. Ambitious and autocratic monarchies were coming to dominate the political geography of early modern Europe. In James's Whitehall, as in other Renaissance courts, power was held by a tiny, aristocratic elite, who lived ostentatious and expensive lives surrounded by burgeoning armies of bureaucrats. In London, Paris, Florence and Madrid, much the same cast of courtiers and favourites, secretaries and counsellors could be found, whose duties expressed the often conflicting needs of the early modern prince. As the court was the fountain of honour, arena of business and source of rewards, it provoked aspiration and envy in equal measure. At the same time, more searching attitudes towards the state as a political mechanism were creating a pragmatic understanding of *realpolitik*. Although the stage representation of living rulers was forbidden, preventing drama from reflecting directly on politics, Jacobean tragedies were deeply conditioned by the anxieties that political change aroused. Often depicting the corridors of power and the toils of intrigue, their version of the tragically hostile universe unfolded in the mysterious and inescapable workings of the state.

One way playwrights could indirectly explore political issues was to dramatise stories from the remote past. The seminal tragedy of Machiavellian duplicity, Jonson's *Sejanus* (1603), staged the rise and fall of a client of the Emperor Tiberius, using material drawn from Tacitus. A Roman precursor of Machiavelli, Tacitus depicted a world ruled by expediency and unaffected by morality; Jonson's deeply unsettling play explores these terms of analysis. In *Sejanus*, men of principle lament the servility of Tiberius' flatterers, but they stand helplessly on the sidelines. The real interest inheres in the emperor's skills of political management and the struggle for supremacy between him and his creature, supposedly his friend but actually a rival. In the event, however, historical distance gave Jonson no protection, for the Privy Council thought the play seditious. Like Daniel's *Philotas*, its story probably seemed too similar to Essex's,[34] though perhaps the real problem was *Sejanus's* cool appreciation of the new statecraft, viewing it with both fascination and fear. As Tiberius

---

34 See Philip Ayres, 'Jonson, Northampton, and the "Treason" in *Sejanus', Modern Philology* 80 (1983), 356–63.

artfully outmanoeuvres Sejanus, striking him down from afar with a masterly stratagem, the play shows a disturbingly sophisticated understanding of the modern technologies of power. Other classical tragedies represented the reason of state in more qualified ways. In Shakespeare's *Antony and Cleopatra* (1606), the future belongs to the astute politician Octavius, but he seems dull beside the rich imaginative life of the lovers. Although Antony is defeated, Cleopatra's suicide testifies to the power of his memory, circumventing Octavius and establishing a counter-history that gives the lovers a pyrrhic victory. In *Coriolanus* (1608), events are again driven by political imperatives, but here the state seems to be perpetually at war with itself. Rome's plebeians and patricians are locked in 'antagonistic dependence', neither being able to trust or to master the other, and Coriolanus is sacrificed to this unresolvable conflict.[35] Each of these plays dramatises a tension between the ambition and the fragility of the hero's warrior ethos. Each hero lives by a code that requires him to be a leader, but the consequences of his self-assertion are inevitably catastrophic. Under threat from politicians with more cunning ways of clinging to power, neither hero can 'hold [his] visible shape'.[36] The state legitimises their warrior status, then destroys them for it.

The situation of these heroes resembles that of contemporary aristocrats like Essex, Buckingham and Strafford, high-profile political casualties who ended their lives under the executioner's axe or assassin's knife. Such careers exemplified the risks and rewards of high place, together with the difficulties faced by the nobility in securing roles within the modern bureaucratised state. The great exponent of such dilemmas was George Chapman, whose *Bussy d'Ambois* (1605) and *Charles, Duke of Byron* (2 parts, 1608), tragedies based on the lives of two sixteenth-century French courtiers, study an aristocracy conscious of being in crisis. These old-style aristocratic heroes are at odds with Machiavellian courts that value functionaries and administrators more dearly than charismatic noblemen. In *Bussy d'Ambois*, Bussy parades arrogantly around the court, seducing the wives of powerful men, fighting duels and speaking dangerous truths about the King's brother. His boasting advances him, for the King protects him, recognising (on the divide-and-rule principle) that the envy Bussy's charisma provokes diverts potential challenges to the Crown. However, the court is destabilised by Bussy's arrogance. The sole survivor of a duel involving six men, he argues that, as king of himself, he is exempt from the punishment that should follow by law, but his rivals' enmity finally overwhelms him. Killed by a pistol shot from off-stage, his death confirms the outdatedness of his ethos: this supremely modern weapon undermines claims to aristocratic

35 Dollimore, *Radical Tragedy*, p. 227.   36 *Antony and Cleopatra*, 4.4.14.

prowess in hand-to-hand combat. Chapman's tragedies thus explore the contradictions triggered by changes in the structure of court life. The court is emptied of divinity, its leaders ruling by expediency rather than innate authority, but Bussy's code of honour, though seen nostalgically, is dangerously individualistic. At such a claustrophobic court there seems to be no modus vivendi for an old-style courtier whose greatness is precisely what makes him problematic.

Chapman's heroic aristocrats at least command admiration for the ambition of their lives. Other Jacobean tragedies deal with court life more disenchantedly, demystifying the aristocratic ethos and refusing to take court ceremony at its own valuation by uncovering a desperate brutality behind the seemingly glamorous exterior. Such effects are typical of the many tragedies set in Italian dukedoms, locations that serve as dramatic shorthand to evoke worlds dominated by policy, that inspire an uneasy mix of fascination and disgust. John Webster was the great specialist in this kind. His *The White Devil* (1612) centres on Vittoria Corrombona, mistress to the Duke of Bracciano, whose relationship with her lover is illicit but thrilling, a passionate entanglement in an otherwise sordid world. For her sake, Bracciano murders his wife, sister to the powerful Duke of Florence; the violence and cunning of Florence's revenge bear out his status as Duke of Machiavelli's city. Webster depicts Italian court life realistically, foregrounding its business and diplomacy, and dwelling on the contradiction between outer opulence and inner bankruptcy. Tilts and ceremony are juxtaposed with the stratagems through which Florence traps Bracciano, his confederacy with assassins and cynical collusion with the great churchman Monticelso. Unlike Chapman's heroes, the sympathetic characters are the small people – Vittoria and her brother Flamineo (Bracciano's henchman) – who get caught up in the power-games of the great. These unlikely heroes, sister and brother, are deeply flawed: she is an adulteress, and he prostitutes her to gain Bracciano's favour. However, their immorality is explained, if not excused, by their reduced circumstances: she is desperate to escape a loveless marriage, and he needs to rebuild an inheritance wasted by his father. Their bloody ends punish their crimes, but the ultimate guilt lies elsewhere, with the powerful men who have thoughtlessly used and discarded them.

The social contrast is even sharper in *The Duchess of Malfi* (1614), which follows the Duchess's attempt to achieve private happiness within the hostile court world. A young widow, she loves a worthy gentleman of low status, but her choices are policed by her two brothers, Duke Ferdinand and the Cardinal, who determine to keep her single. The Duchess marries secretly, and vengeance inevitably follows: her happy domesticity is destroyed by men whose misplaced obsession with the purity of their blood leads to savage sadism. A powerful contrast develops between the worthy but unfortunate lovers and the Duchess's brothers, who, despite their greatness, are shams: 'Glories, like glow-worms, afar off shine bright, / But looked to near, have neither heat nor light'.[37] But the sharpest critique comes from Bosola, the brothers' henchman. A murderer with a conscience, Bosola would be good if the times allowed it. He tries to square faithful service to the brothers with the evil they command him to do, and ends the play killing them for having procured the Duchess's murder, even though he was her assassin. His inconsistencies and confused attempts to rationalise his situation expose a statecraft that demands unquestioning service and offers unpredictable rewards. Yet the play finds no coherent alternative to put in its place.[38]

Moral polarisations are even more acutely drawn in Middleton's Italianate tragedies. In *The Revenger's Tragedy* (*c.* 1606) and *The Lady's Tragedy* (1611) – anonymous plays now generally attributed to him – the courts are frankly stereotyped worlds, whose inhabitants bear allegorical names, or (like the Tyrant and the Lady in *The Lady's Tragedy*) never acquire names at all. They present diametrical oppositions between good and evil, country and court, and elaborate these moral and political contrasts through rhetorical denunciation that taps into a vein of popular satire. Middleton's dukes are godless, his courtiers knee-crooking knaves, his country a rich source of cash bled dry by the centre, and his women either heroically chaste saints or whores who would do anything for advancement. In *The Lady's Tragedy*, the ruler is a usurper whose one desire is to bed the wife of the Duke whose power he has assumed. She commits suicide rather than face rape, but he pays court to her corpse, and is poisoned by her cosmetics. Similar polarities structure *The Revenger's Tragedy*, in which Vindice's attack on the Duke's family is motivated by wrongs done to his father, sister and lover. Disguised as a serviceable knave, Vindice scourges the court's sexual and economic sins, focusing obsessively on its extravagance and luxury, his tirades presenting court life as an endless round of prodigality. Yet for all Vindice's seeming Puritanism, the effect is anything but puritanical, for he seems as much excited as offended by the pursuit of pleasure, participating eagerly in the world he seeks to destroy and reproducing its competitiveness in his own vengeance. At the end, he has destroyed the ducal family but seems

---

37 John Webster (dramatist), *Works of John Webster*, ed. David Charles Gunby, Antony Hammond and Doreen Del Vecchio (Cambridge University Press, 1995–), 1:543.

38 There are suggestive readings of Webster's plays in Frank Whigham, *Seizures of the Will in Early Modern English Drama* (Cambridge University Press, 1996); and Dollimore, *Radical Tragedy*, pp. 231–46.

tainted by his revenge, his violence against the court differing little from the backstabbing that characterises its life. No wonder he is sentenced to death by the nobleman who takes the old Duke's place.

Middleton's and Webster's tragedies are not attacks on the Jacobean Whitehall, for their fantastic or geographically remote settings distance their events, and their plots are framed by the ideologies of their times. They concentrate as much on sexual as political peccadilloes, and their villains are moral grotesques, the harshest satire being reserved for usurpers who lack legitimate status. But the dukes they depict are never unproblematically divine, and the tension and strain that play across their fictional worlds testify to anxieties about the early modern state that could not easily be discharged. Given the playhouses' institutional situation, Jacobean tragedy could never be oppositional in the full modern sense. Nonetheless, the sceptical attitudes that it voiced sat uneasily with orthodox pieties, and promoted a disenchanted understanding of the world of power.

Later Jacobean and Caroline theatre

The extraordinary achievements of early Jacobean drama were produced in a theatre where audiences were still socially mixed, and where considerable cross-fertilisation took place between popular and elite dramatic forms. In the ensuing decades, as individual playhouses began to address distinct playgoing constituencies, tastes gradually began to differentiate. By the 1630s the amphitheatres were playing to a largely citizen clientele, while the more expensive roofed theatres played to fashionable spectators. The volume of indoor playing also increased markedly. In 1609, after the demise of the Revels' Children, the King's Men regained control of the Blackfriars, and began performing there in tandem with the Globe, using the indoor house in the winter and the amphitheatre in summer. As the Blackfriars prospered, other impresarios sought to develop indoor playing spaces for adult troupes. In 1617, Christopher Beeston commissioned Inigo Jones to convert a cockpit in Drury Lane into a playhouse which quickly acquired a reputation similar to Blackfriars. A third indoor theatre, converted from a barn at Salisbury Court (in Whitefriars), opened in 1629. By the 1630s, the number of playhouses had stabilised at six – the three indoor venues, and three amphitheatres, the Globe, the Fortune and the Red Bull – but the indoor houses, with their predominantly genteel audiences and exclusive tone, were the most prestigious venues. This separation was never a simple polarity – the King's Men alternated between their houses down to 1642, and other companies crossed the same theatrical line – nor did it happen overnight. Indeed, when Francis Beaumont satirised popular taste in *The Knight of the Burning Pestle* (1607), in which citizens interrupt a performance of 'The London Merchant' and call for 'The Grocer's Honour' instead, the Blackfriars audience was baffled, not grasping 'the privy mark of irony about it'.[39] But the location of these new venues, towards the west of the City and in the developing fashionable quarter between London and Westminster, did signal a shift in the theatres' social topography. Predominantly attracting aristocrats, gentlemen, lawyers and the wealthier citizenry, the hall theatres came to function as social arenas for an emergent *beau monde*.

The repertoire at the Jacobean and Caroline amphitheatres was increasingly pitched towards citizen audiences whose tastes were nostalgic, patriotic and robust. The Admiral's Men had begun to move this way in the 1590s. In the new reign, renamed the Prince's Men, they presented at the Fortune their so-called 'Elect Nation' plays, Samuel Rowley's *When You See Me You Know Me* (1604) and Thomas Dekker's *The Whore of Babylon* (1606). These plays dramatised the lives of Henry VIII and Queen Elizabeth from a perspective deeply indebted to Foxe's *Acts and Monuments*, representing Tudor history as a sensational struggle between Protestant and Catholic for world dominion, in which servants and citizens sometimes played heroic parts. At the Red Bull, Queen Anne's Men depicted the young Elizabeth's persecution and eventual accession, and London's greetings to its new sovereign, in Heywood's *If You Know Not Me, You Know Nobody* (1604). The 'Elect Nation' plays were among the most frequently revived of the period; they celebrated a civic ideal of a people happily bound in social and religious unity. Other amphitheatre plays foregrounded themes appealing to the religious and class sensitivities of citizens. Day, Rowley and Wilkins's *The Travels of The Three English Brothers* (1607), on the overseas adventures of the real-life Sherleys, was one of many exotic fantasies depicting the triumphs of ordinary Englishmen. Rowley's *A Shoemaker a Gentleman* (1608?) is a lively account of a mythical British past, in which good princes and common men combine to defend Christianity against Roman persecution. Dekker's *If It Be Not a Good Play, The Devil is In It* (1611) mixes comic devils and social satire in a mirror for misruling princes. Heywood's epic series *The Golden Age, The Silver Age, The Brazen Age* and *The Iron Age* (1611–13) staged an anthology of classical myths with all the spectacular resources of the Red Bull. In later years, the amphitheatres became identified with plays featuring action, clowning and fantasy, a performance style that valued spectacle, exaggeration and rant, and a

---

39 *The Dramatic Works in the Beaumont and Fletcher Canon*, gen. ed. Fredson Bowers, 10 vols. (Cambridge University Press, 1966–96), 1:13.

repertoire in which revivals significantly outnumbered new plays. They were still playing *Tamburlaine* and *The Spanish Tragedy* on the eve of the Civil War. This taste must have seemed vulgar by contrast with the refined atmosphere of the halls, though it could simply be called conservative. The amphitheatres remained loyal to the ideological outlook of ordinary craftsmen, citizens and apprentices, and preserved festive and celebratory performance styles from which the indoor playhouses gradually withdrew.

The hall theatres were hospitable to quieter, more intimate styles of drama, gradually acquiring a social tone that reflected the greater exclusiveness of their audiences. In the 1630s the Blackfriars became the favourite meeting ground for London high society, but in the Jacobean period its drama was already serving as a mirror for manners, instructing a genteel elite in codes of dress, language and etiquette. In Jonson's *The Devil is an Ass* (1616), the idiotic gull, Fitzdottrel, is desperate to show off his new cloak at the Blackfriars, and there is a society scene in which the ladies compare fashions and exchange recipes for cosmetics. An even earlier society comedy is Jonson's *Epicoene* (1609), performed by the Revels' Children, which is set entirely among the fashionable rich who lodge in the Strand and kill time with empty chat. Its opening depiction of Clerimont's early morning toilette directly foreshadows the levée scene in Etherege's *Man of Mode* (1676), and its gull, Morose, a gentleman with a morbid allergy to noise, is punished for the crime of unsociability. If Morose hates noise, the moral seems to be, he should not be living in London.[40] The early master of the witty style, however, was John Fletcher, whose comedies were the Blackfriars staple in the later Jacobean period. His most dazzling play, *The Wild Goose Chase* (1621), concerns the courtship games between three Parisian gallants and their women, particularly the stratagems by which the bedhopper Mirabell is finally drawn into marriage. Unlike Middletonian comedy, where the marriage market is powered by the need for money, no inheritance is at issue and no older generation stands in the way. The obstacles to love are internal, the play exploring the mechanisms by which marital partners find one another without forfeiting too much personal autonomy. Fletcher's comedies exhibit less misogyny than many contemporary plays: his women seem to have as much right to (and responsibility for) their own desires as do the men, and the double standard is less in evidence. In *The Wild Goose Chase* society seems happily at play, exploring its own dynamics and untroubled by sexual guilt or status

---

40 See Leo Salingar, *Dramatic Form in Shakespeare and the Jacobeans* (Cambridge University Press, 1986), pp. 175–88.

anxiety, while Mirabell's smart conversation and casual libertinism made him a real culture-hero. 'You have the gift of impudence', says his friend Bellure; no wonder the play was a hit.[41]

Fletcher's other signature form was tragicomedy, which in James's second decade was a Blackfriars speciality. It was taken up by virtually all playwrights, eventually becoming a dominant Stuart mode. Tragicomedy emerged naturally from the early Blackfriars style, for its delightful surprises, teasing juxtapositions and relish for artifice used devices pioneered by the boys. Shakespeare's *Winter's Tale* (1610), *Cymbeline* (1610) and *The Tempest* (1611) – with their amazing epiphanies, self-conscious theatricality, and characters helplessly buffeted by mystifying chance – have sometimes been seen as designed specifically for the new theatre. This exaggerates their novelty, since each had to please Globe audiences too, and their characters never exhibit the dislocated psychologies of Fletcherian tragicomedy. Nonetheless, the general trend led towards sophisticated delight in intractable entanglements in which intense and contradictory emotions were played out. In *Philaster* (1609) and *A King and No King* (1611), both written jointly by Beaumont and Fletcher, the characters are confronted with impossible choices that plunge them into mental torture. The Sicilian Prince Philaster, whose throne has been usurped by the King of Calabria, is forced to watch helplessly while his mistress, the Princess Arethusa, is offered to a Spanish rival, and his sufferings increase when it seems that Arethusa has betrayed him with her page, Bellario. Philaster oscillates between love for Arethusa, anger at her betrayal and regret at his own behaviour, and he performs sensational, self-destructive acts, attempting to kill Arethusa and wounding Bellario in his sleep. He is saved by a rebellion against the King and by the discovery that Bellario is a woman, but the real focus is the exquisite psychological reversals produced by his circumstances. In *A King and No King*, the emotional conflicts are yet more acute, for King Arbaces loves his sister Penthea, and falls into a passion somehow both bestial and idealising. Although the outcome seems destined for tragedy, Arbaces is saved by the belated discovery that he is not Penthea's brother, but was substituted for the Prince at birth. As suggested by the play's quibbling title, Fletcherian tragicomedy orchestrated apparent contradictions into a higher unity, yoking seriousness and levity and plucking surprising resolutions from seeming chaos. To modern tastes these plots can seem contrived, but Stuart audiences found

---

41 Beaumont and Fletcher, *Dramatic Works*, 7:258. Compare Sandra Clark, *The Plays of Beaumont and Fletcher* (Hemel Hempstead: Harvester Wheatsheaf, 1994).

irresistible their mix of intense feeling and sophisticated artfulness. These inhibited but passionate heroes are the first English examples of theatrical baroque.[42]

Fletcherian comedy and tragicomedy set the theatrical trend for the mid-Jacobean years, a decade of relative peace between the Twelve Years' Truce (1609) and the crisis caused when James's son-in-law, the Palatine Prince Frederick, assumed the Bohemian crown (1619). But when Spain and Austria drove Frederick from Bohemia and the Palatinate, the ensuing thirty years of war drew most European nations into battle lines reflecting the religious divide. Many in England were eager for war to recover Frederick's lands, but James saw his interests in friendship with Spain, and declined to fight since he thought peace necessary for stability at home and abroad. England had, indeed, little to gain from a foreign war, but the frustration generated by appeasement of Spain helped to polarise attitudes and erode confidence in the Crown. The 1620s saw the Jacobean consensus shaken by religious and political disagreements, compounded with anxiety about a court that seemed out of step with national aspirations. Such a climate inevitably politicised the drama, which became preoccupied with wartime settings and constitutional themes.

The European war greatly enhanced the market for news, which the drama increasingly helped to satisfy. One important early news-play was *Sir John van Olden Barnavelt* (1619), by Fletcher and Massinger, which dramatised the fall of a leading Dutch politician. Barnavelt's story was highly topical (he had only recently been executed). A leader of the Dutch rebellion against Spanish rule, and an Arminian in religion (Protestantism's liberal wing, at odds with Calvinist orthodoxy), his career raised explosive issues. Although the authors trod this ground diplomatically, it was unusual for plays to represent living statesmen, such as Barnavelt's rival Prince Maurice, or to address theologically controversial topics. The Bishop of London stayed the performance, and the Master of the Revels demanded extensive revisions; print publication was not attempted. Anti-Spanish sentiment colours other dramas, such as Heywood's fantasy of naval adventure, *Dick of Devonshire* (1626). Similar material probably appeared in plays of which only the titles survive – Henry Shirley's *The Spanish Duke of Lerma* (c. 1625?), Richard Gunnell's *The Hungarian Lion* (1623) and *The Spanish Contract* (1624; the King's Men were prosecuted for performing this without a licence). The great topical success, however, was Middleton's *A Game at Chess*

42 The seminal account is Eugene M. Waith's *The Pattern of Tragicomedy in Beaumont and Fletcher* (New Haven, CT: Yale University Press, 1952). See also Arthur C. Kirsch, *Jacobean Dramatic Perspectives* (Charlottesville: University Press of Virginia, 1972), and Gordon McMullan, *The Politics of Unease in the Plays of John Fletcher* (Amherst: University of Massachusetts Press, 1994).

(1624), staged at the Globe for nine days running after the collapse of James's negotiations for a Spanish bride for Prince Charles. This political comedy represented the transactions with Spain as a struggle for European mastery, veiled allegorically as a chess game: the Spanish think they have duped the English but are unexpectedly checkmated at the climax. Recent critics have argued that the King's Men could only have staged such sensitive material with the court's support, and that it echoed the outlook of Charles and Buckingham, who by 1624 wanted more military action than James would allow. However, the play certainly caused a scandal: the Privy Council suspended the company, and Middleton prudently made himself scarce. Discussion of foreign affairs was precluded by royal prerogative, but the play framed European events as an eschatological conflict, thus fanning popular anti-Catholic sentiment.[43] Two years later, Jonson's *The Staple of News* (1626) satirised public interest in affairs, depicting a news 'shop' with correspondents selling far-fetched stories to gullible customers. Arguably, Jonson's exposé testified backhandedly to the vitality of the appetites against which it inveighed.

The climate of crisis affected Middleton and Massinger the most. In his three late tragedies Middleton's sceptical, ironic mode hardened into increasing radicalism and apocalyptic foreboding suggesting considerable disenchantment with the present state of things. The earliest of the three, *The Mayor of Queenborough* (c. 1620), is a pseudo-historical tragedy set during the Saxon invasion of Britain. But its incompetent kings, ambitious favourites and sensationally violent conclusion evoke contemporary anxieties regarding a nation that has lost its ideal purity and earned providential punishment. Better known is *The Changeling* (1622; co-authored with William Rowley), a domestic tragedy politicised by its Spanish setting and its concern with paternal power. The situation of the title-figure, the aristocratic lady Beatrice-Joanna, harks back to the scandal that erupted at the Jacobean court in 1615 when the Countess of Somerset was found to have contrived the death of Sir Thomas Overbury, who opposed her marriage to James's favourite. In order to escape marriage to a man she does not want, Beatrice-Joanna commissions a servant, De Flores, to murder her suitor, but is unable to escape being ensnared by him in a sordid union. Her plight presents a powerful social moral. This great lady assumes

---

43 The interpretation by Margot Heinemann (*Puritanism and Theatre*, pp. 151–71) has been contested by Trevor Howard-Hill, 'Political Interpretations of Middleton's *A Game at Chess*', in *Patronage, Politics and Literary Traditions in England, 1558–1658*, ed. Cedric C. Brown (Detroit: Wayne State University Press, 1993), pp. 268–79, and partially endorsed by Tom Cogswell, 'Thomas Middleton and the Court, 1624: *A Game at Chess* in Context', *Huntington Library Quarterly* 47 (1984), 273–88.

her status protects her autonomy but finds herself overtaken by a retribution that is no respecter of persons, while murder and adultery are shockingly disclosed at the heart of her seemingly urbane world, as if by the eye of God. Middleton's most accomplished tragedy is *Women Beware Women* (1623?), which explores the divide between the worlds of the ordinary citizen and the court. The declassed Venetian gentlewoman Bianca elopes to Florence with a merchant's clerk, Leantio, and marries him for love. Uprooted from her sphere, she is drawn into the Florentine court by the Duke's attentions, where, raped and despoiled of her honour, she becomes his glorious concubine, while Leantio's objections are stifled with cheap court favours. After he gets involved with the great lady, Livia, he is killed by her brother, jealous at the dishonour the liaison does his family. The play's brilliance lies in its absence of sentimentality or cynicism, the almost scientific detachment with which it presents its two worlds. The city is sober but dull, the court glamorous but sinful, and the characters' tragedies arise from social conditioning rather than any inner evil. In Florence, corruption spreads downwards from the Duke, and retribution finally arrives during a masque, as if the gap between the court's image and its reality had finally collapsed. Some critics have seen Middleton as an oppositional playwright, deeply sceptical about the Jacobean court. Certainly his late tragedies show scant ambivalence, and endow their bad characters with little charisma. There is only a severe moral accountancy that pays crime with punishment, at whatever level.[44]

Philip Massinger, a much less puritanical dramatist, eschewed the popular theatrical formulae within which Middleton worked. Massinger's plays are notable for their fluent and correct language (he never once used prose), and for their gravely reflective skills of argument. Nonetheless, their plots frequently evoke current events or address sensitive constitutional topics. Both *The Maid of Honour* (1622?) and *The Bondman* (1623) take up the question of war and the obligations that arise from it. *The Maid of Honour* contrasts the cowardly Sicilian King Roberto with his heroic brother Bertoldo, the one failing to help an ally in time of need, the other enthusiastic for war. However, the antithesis is not clear-cut, for the war is not self-evidently just, while Bertoldo rashly gets captured, then betrays Camiola (the maid of honour), who had supported his soldiering despite the King's disapproval, and resisted seduction by the court favourite. In a surprise ending, Camiola chooses to enter a nunnery rather than

---

44 Heinemann's powerful account of these plays in *Puritanism and Theatre* has been critiqued by Christina Malcolmson, 'As Tame as the Ladies: Politics and Gender in *The Changeling*', *English Literary Renaissance* 20 (1990), 320–39; and Nigel Bawcutt, 'Was Thomas Middleton a Puritan Dramatist?', *Modern Language Review* 94 (1999), 925–39.

ratify the arguments of either party through marriage. *The Bondman* is even more transparently topical. Set in ancient Syracuse, it depicts the unwillingness of the citizens to defend themselves from Carthaginian attack. They are roused to war by the foreign general Timoleon, and shamed into financing it by the heroic lady Cleora. But when the gentlemen go to war, the slaves – led by Marullo, who secretly loves Cleora – revolt against their masters. This turn of events allows a radical re-examination of Syracuse's political and social order, and although the returning soldiers suppress the revolt, Marullo makes a powerful case against tyrannical government, which Cleora endorses by marrying him. Of course, Marullo turns out to be a disguised gentleman, but the play has posed hard questions about social order. It is typical of Massinger's drama to move from circumstantial topicalities to a generalised concern with the liberties and justice by which men live.[45]

After the death of King James, Charles did indeed go to war against Spain and France, but with disastrous consequences. His bungled campaigns were funded by taxes widely seen as unconstitutional, and anxieties on this score persisted into the years after 1629, when Charles ruled without parliamentary finance. Massinger's plays of the later 1620s are preoccupied with tyrannical rulers and dilemmas of obedience. In some, such as *A New Way to Pay Old Debts* (1625) and *The Unnatural Combat* (1626), the issue arises obliquely. A City comedy in a country setting, *A New Way* depicts the attempts of the parvenu Sir Giles Overreach to buy his way into the old aristocracy. Overreach's name, and the schemes by which he garners wealth, allude to Sir Giles Mompesson, a cousin of Charles's favourite, Buckingham, who had been central to a scandal over monopolies. Overreach is a domestic tyrant and monstrous power-seeker, thwarted by aristocrats who are responsible, caring father-figures and serve their country well in the wars. Their attack on Overreach, though socially conservative, implies a dissenting view of the nature of political obligation.[46] Similarly, *The Unnatural Combat* is set amongst idle soldiers and seamen in France, and its lurid violence seems informed by contemporary concern about that nation's leaders. Other plays by Massinger signalled their politics more overtly. *The Roman Actor* (1626) depicts the tyrannical Emperor Domitian and his contempt for the lives and liberties of his citizens. His fall is preceded by portents

45 See the discussion by Margot Heinemann in *Theatre and Government under the Early Stuarts*, ed. J. R. Mulryne and Margaret Shewring (Cambridge University Press, 1993), pp. 237–65.

46 This summarises the account of the play in Martin Butler, '*A New Way to Pay Old Debts*: Massinger's Grim Comedy', in *English Comedy*, ed. Michael Cordner, Peter Holland and John Kerrigan (Cambridge University Press, 1994), pp. 119–36, and 'Insider as Outsider', in *The Theatrical City*, ed. David L. Smith, Richard Strier and David Bevington (Cambridge University Press, 1995), pp. 193–208.

of divine displeasure, and the Stoics who oppose him endure his tortures with saintly indifference. One of several contemporary plays to show the overthrow of Roman despots – such as the anonymous *Nero* (1624?), Thomas May's *Julia Agrippina* (1628) and Nathaniel Richards's *Messallina* (*c.* 1635) – it is difficult not to regard *The Roman Actor* as a disenchanted version of the Stuart imperial ethos, a critique of the system that lay behind Augustan imaginings.[47] Even more clearly oppositional was Massinger's remarkable *Believe As You List* (1631), which stages the sufferings of the sixteenth-century Portuguese pretender, Don Sebastian, at the hands of his Spanish usurpers. Written while Charles was making peace with Spain, the play was refused a licence, and Massinger rewrote it, moving events back to the second century BC; even so, it was never published. Another intriguing but lost Massinger text is *The King and the Subject* (1638), details of which survive only because Charles objected to lines that seemed critical of the unparliamentary tax Ship Money. Ultimately, Massinger was not a rebel, for his plays always upheld responsible paternalism. Nonetheless, his preoccupation with monarchs who fell short of this standard made his plays scarcely less unsettling to Stuart orthodoxy than Middleton's.

The climate of crisis subsided once Charles extricated himself from the conflicts of the 1620s and began a programme of retrenchment. Making peace his first priority, he disentangled himself from expensive warfare and attempted to live on his own resources, avoiding the need to call potentially explosive Parliaments. His income afforded him relative stability down to the Scottish revolt of 1637, although it hobbled his foreign policy and still left the need for controversial money-raising devices at home. The political polarisations of the 1620s also left a legacy. At Whitehall Charles cultivated an ethos of efficient and modernising kingship, but, as events showed, this imagery did not take root in a nation anxious over constitutional issues and disappointed at the neglect of overseas Protestantism. Nonetheless, the calm of these years was reflected in the prospering fortunes of London's theatres. With the three indoor houses established as the premier venues, and with Whitehall keenly interested in drama – a court playhouse was built in 1629, and Henrietta Maria sponsored amateur theatricals among her ladies – the social tone of some theatres became very refined. Caroline drama was not simply 'Cavalier', as is sometimes supposed: the three amphitheatres still played to citizens, while the Drury Lane and Salisbury Court playhouses attracted mixed, if wealthy, audiences. In the 1630s, however, Blackfriars was the meeting ground for a smart set,

---

47 See Martin Butler, 'Romans in Britain: Massinger's *The Roman Actor* and the Early Stuart Classical Play', in *Philip Massinger: A Critical Reassessment*, ed. Douglas Howard (Cambridge University Press, 1985), pp. 139–70.

and the natural home for a new wave of courtly amateur playwrights: William Davenant, John Suckling, the royal huntsman Lodowick Carlell and others. Patterns of production were also changing. Since stocks of tested favourites had accumulated, the frantic output of earlier times was much reduced, and the practice of staging a different play every day began to give way to extended runs for single plays.[48] In the 1630s the market for printed drama ballooned, as did the circulation of plays in manuscript.[49] Library lists attest that playbooks were becoming collectable: in *Histriomastix* (1633) William Prynne complained they were often better printed than Bibles.[50] A critical discourse about drama also crystallised: commendatory poems and marginal annotations marked the arrival of a shared set of aesthetic values, while Sir Richard Baker's riposte to Prynne, *Theatrum Redivivum* (1634), displayed an informed understanding of the arts of performance. Such changes showed how far drama was coming to be understood as literature, as a legitimate topic for study.

James Shirley, John Ford and Richard Brome best exemplify the theatrical climate of the Caroline years. Shirley was house dramatist at Drury Lane, writing twenty plays for the Cockpit during the decade to 1636; in 1640, he became principal dramatist at the Blackfriars. Whitehall admired the fluency and politeness of his work. The Master of the Revels said his tragicomedy *The Young Admiral* (1633), 'being free from oaths, profaneness or obsceneness... may serve as a pattern to other poets', and his masque *The Triumph of Peace* (1634) was a widely noticed public event. Certainly plays like *The Wedding* (c. 1626), *The Witty Fair One* (1628), *Hyde Park* (1632), *The Ball* (1632) and *The Lady of Pleasure* (1635) offered models of language and conduct for a fashionable society establishing itself as a metropolitan elite. Set in the drawing rooms and green spaces of contemporary London, these plays depicted a leisured class evolving norms of behaviour that apparently mirrored those of their audiences. Shirley's dramatic territory is bounded by romance (in *The Wedding*, *The Witty Fair One* and *Hyde Park* characters apparently return from the dead), but his plays frequently interrupt their action with plotless scenes that focus on the polyphonic interplay of voices. The three plots of *Hyde Park* come together in seemingly artless episodes depicting ordinary life in the park, and the finely contrived links between them are made to seem random, as if their interconnections

---

48 See Gurr, *The Shakespearean Playing Companies*, pp. 84–5.

49 See Martin Butler, *Theatre and Crisis, 1632–1642* (Cambridge University Press, 1984), pp. 105–6.

50 James Knowles, 'Jonson's *Entertainment at Britain's Burse*', in *Re-Presenting Ben Jonson*, ed. Butler pp. 124–5; G. W. Prothero, 'A Seventeenth-century Account Book', *English Historical Review* 7 (1892), 88–102; A. C. Baugh, 'A Seventeenth-century Play List', *Modern Language Review* 13 (1918), 401–11.

arose from everyday encounters and casual happenstance. In the levée scene of *The Lady of Pleasure*, the nameless lord dictates a letter to his secretary in one voice (as it were) while carrying on dialogue with friends and servants in another. This tour-de-force conversation exhibits Shirley's densely nuanced verbal texture; his characters move with apparent ease but actual calculation between formality and intimacy, public and private. Their speech brilliantly captures the language of a high society still in the process of inventing itself. It seems courteous and controlled, yet hints at underlying feelings that are strong but can only be tentatively expressed.

Like many Caroline dramatists, Shirley appears ambivalent towards the society he depicts. His plays celebrated their audiences' world, setting the vogue for a series of topical urban comedies, such as Brome's *The Weeding of Covent Garden* (1632), Nabbes's *Tottenham Court* (1633) and Davenant's *The Wits* (1634). These plays, however, stand at a remove from courtly dramas like Davenant's *Love and Honour* (1634) or Suckling's *Aglaura* (1637), which present romantic stories appealing to an overtly aristocratic mentality. In Shirley's characteristic plots, overbearing and self-willed aristocrats are brought to heel, typically by the women they have attempted to seduce – as when Julietta disciplines Lord Bonvile in *Hyde Park*, and Celestina rebukes the lord in *The Lady of Pleasure*. The social thrust of such encounters is carefully limited, for Shirley's plots leave hierarchies of birth unscathed. His aristocrats are less put under control than recalled to a sense of their inherited obligations, while his women, for all their free speech, usually dwindle into a predestined domesticity. But while Shirley respects inherited structures, he represents them as systems of checks and balances that ought to protect all members of society. Even his last plays, *The Cardinal* (1641) and *The Court Secret* (1642), voice anxieties about uncontrolled power that their endings manage only partially to resolve.[51]

In John Ford's plays, an aristocratic ethos is more self-evidently under strain. Ford was a lawyer whose theatrical career began in collaborations with professional writers, and developed in the Caroline period into solo work for Blackfriars and Drury Lane. His plays present intensely ritualised worlds dominated by highly wrought ceremonial and codes of manners, elaborately stylised language and intricately balanced plots. Frequently his characters act (consciously or unconsciously) as players within a play: either they attune their behaviour to the modes of collective conduct that prevail in their societies, or

51 For discussion, see Martin Butler, 'The Condition of the Theatres in 1642', in *The Cambridge History of British Theatre*, ed. Jane Milling and Peter Thomson (Cambridge University Press, 2003).

they assume deliberately theatrical styles, projecting their identities as willed performances. They are obsessed with maintaining personal integrity or stoical self-sufficiency, yet, typically, the roles they want to affirm are either impossibly extreme or incompatible with their environment.[52] So in *'Tis Pity She's a Whore* (1633?), Giovanni acts and speaks like a heroic Petrarchan lover but, disturbingly, the object of his desires is his sister. He would be Romeo to her Juliet were it not that their love is incestuous. In *The Broken Heart* (1631?), Penthea's only wish is to be a devoted wife but she endures a living death in marriage to a husband she did not choose. Her desires are blocked in every direction: it is a kind of adultery to give herself to either husband or lover. Similarly, in *Perkin Warbeck* (1634?), Perkin thinks himself the true English King but cannot make the rest of the world believe him. Since the truth of his identity is never revealed, he appears both a deluded charlatan and a saintly tragic victim. Like Perkin, all Ford's tragic characters seem trapped in the wrong play. The master-plots by which they live are somehow dislocated at the source.

Although Ford's plays never depict contemporary English life, instead taking place in remote or fantasy locations, their focus on the gap between the individual's desires and society's requirements gives them a powerful political dimension. Their societies are always under strain, their characters' subjectivities always at odds with their social roles. In *'Tis Pity*, Giovanni's inner passion is mysterious and overwhelming; it cannot possibly be brought within the structures of his rather ordinary urban community. In the chaotic conclusion, when he brandishes his sister's heart on a dagger before her husband, his shocking and inexplicable act seems to render meaningless the normality of family and state. In *The Broken Heart* – set in an austerely classical Sparta – it is the individual, rather than society, that shatters. Penthea is the play's most inhibited character, but all are blocked one way or another, in love with people they cannot possess, or consumed by envy or frustration. Since the Spartan ethos binds them to silent endurance, their torrential passions are inexpressible. Penthea's brother dies immobilised in a torture chair; his lover, the Princess Calantha, dances with perfect composure while news arrives of his death, but dies in the final scene of a broken heart, her body outwardly intact but overwhelmed by inner suffering. Neither play offers much expectation that the world could be better organised, or that alternatives exist to this endless dialectic of rebellion and conformity. Passions so turbulent need a strong social frame, even if its

52 The case advanced here is elaborated by a number of essays in Michael Neill (ed.), *John Ford: Critical Essays* (Cambridge University Press, 1988). See also the discussion by Ira Clark in *Professional Playwrights: Massinger, Ford, Shirley and Brome* (Lexington: University Press of Kentucky, 1992), pp. 73–111.

order inspires little confidence. The characters are condemned to an aesthetic of suffering, the wondrous self-possession by which they turn their frustrations into psychological art.

By contrast, Richard Brome's plays engage more directly with contemporary events, exploring critical and sometimes controversial perspectives upon them.[53] Brome was a professional dramatist of humble origins – he is first recorded as Ben Jonson's domestic servant – and his output includes plays written for amphitheatre companies as well as for all the indoor playhouses. A friend of the popular playwrights Heywood and Dekker, he specialised almost entirely in comedy, his robust manner contrasting vividly with Ford's and Shirley's refinement. Brome's predominantly satirical and theatrically inventive plays are enlivened with song and dance, pastiche, allegory and burlesque, even his three tragicomedies, rare ventures into courtlier styles, are complicated by self-parody. His most characteristic plays depict contemporary urban life from a detached, ironical perspective, taking nothing at face value and dispensing satire even-handedly on all targets. They are especially critical of pompous authoritarians, always siding with the underdog against sexual, social and political intolerance. In *The Weeding of Covent Garden* (1632), fashionable society is ridiculed equally with Puritan fanaticism: all London seems to be composed of interfering fathers laying down the law for their children, provoking a backlash of disobedience. In *The City Wit* (1630), the unconventional hero, Crazy, is a young citizen getting back at gentlemen who will not pay their debts, and bringing his domineering wife to heel. Crazy's disguises culminate in a mock masque that turns the world upside down: as so often in Brome, moral expectations are dizzyingly inverted, unleashing anarchic possibilities within traditional frameworks. Nor are Brome's gender politics always one-sided, for in *A Mad Couple Well Matched* (1639), even though the philandering gentleman is condoned, the double standard of male freedom and female fidelity is also recognised as problematic.

At Salisbury Court and Drury Lane, Brome's free-wheeling comedies kept alive a tradition of popular and carnivalesque drama at a time when courtly dramatists such as Davenant and Suckling were coming to dominate Blackfriars. His plays were also politically adventurous, their contemporaneity and panoramic scope permitting opportunities for reflection on present-day England. These possibilities were first explored in the loose plot of *The Weeding of Covent Garden*, which mixes a cross-section of London life with topical allusions to Caroline paternalism. The most developed example is the multilevelled

53 These paragraphs summarise my more extended treatment of Brome in *Theatre and Crisis*, supplemented by the thoughtful discussion in Clark, *Professional Playwrights*, pp. 155–96.

comic fantasy of *The Antipodes* (1638), where characters supposedly journey to the other side of the world and find an anti-England that teasingly and ambiguously reverses the order of home. Anti-England collapses customary distinctions between utopia and dystopia, and echoes the sicknesses of 'real' England, currently in the grip of plague: the theatre, Brome seems to imply, is the best cure for society's ills. His politics were much sharper two years later, when *The Court Beggar* (1640) included sharp remarks about Charles's failed military campaign against the Scots, attacked amateur courtly playwrights, and called for the reform of economic monopolies granted to favoured courtiers. Written to coincide with the assembling of the first Parliament for eleven years, the play was performed without licence at the Drury Lane Cockpit. The Master of the Revels stopped it, sacked the playhouse manager and appointed Sir William Davenant to govern the company more reliably. A year later, however, after Davenant was brought down by his part in a failed coup against Parliament, Brome created his last and finest political panorama. In *A Jovial Crew* (1641), a quartet of ladies and gentlemen, bored by home life, decide to sample life among the beggars, but quickly lose their romantic escapism. Vagrancy proves painful and squalid, and they return home with a chastened awareness of their responsibilities, especially once the beggars have admonished them, in a masque, about the dangers of neglecting their social obligations. The play may be nostalgic for a better world where the unprivileged are cared for, but it is coloured with a tough political scepticism and a deeply resonant mood of foreboding.

Drama without a court

A Jovial Crew was the period's last major play, for in September 1642 Parliament issued an order temporarily suspending theatre performances until further notice. The playhouses were not officially allowed to reopen until Charles II returned in 1660, by which time the drama's character had completely altered. This eighteen-year hiatus is usually seen as confirming the enduring hostility between Puritanism and the stage, and the ideological identification of monarchy and theatre. And certainly the drama's suppression was paralleled in other cultural reforms: in 1643 Charles's *Book of Sports* (the proclamation that licensed games on Sundays) was burned, maypoles were banned in 1644, and in 1647 Christmas was abolished.[54] For the ministers and godly magistrates who

54 See Christopher Durston, 'Puritan Rule and the Failure of Cultural Revolution, 1645–1660', in *The Culture of English Puritanism, 1560–1700*, ed. Christopher Durston and Jacqueline Eales (Basingstoke: Macmillan, 1996), pp. 210–34.

wanted to inculcate social and moral discipline, stopping stage-plays was on
step in a programme that embraced curbs on promiscuity, swearing, Sabbath
breaking and drunkenness. Yet the ascendancy of Parliament did not in itse
spell the end for the playhouses. Parliament's first order against plays was
temporary measure suspending performances only for a limited period, an
there were enthusiastic playgoers among the MPs, many of whom sat in th
pre-Civil War audiences or took advantage of London residence in 1640-2 t
enjoy the theatre.[55] Moreover, as the plays of Ford, Shirley, Massinger an
Brome show, there was no simple identity of outlook between theatre an
court, even at this late date. The playhouses were licensed and patronised b
the Crown, but they still attracted a broad clientele and reflected a correspond
ingly diverse body of opinion.[56] This last decade had seen a marked rise in th
drama's political temperature. Besides Brome's *Court Beggar* and Massinger
The King and the Subject (both censored), the amphitheatres had staged play
reflecting on Laudian ceremonial, the Scottish war, economic monopolies an
the church courts. The theatres' robustness demonstrated how beneficial ha
been the commercial stability of the last decade, and how far the drama was fror
lapsing into a 'decadence' that critics used to suppose the closure indicated.

The 1642 restraining order was an emergency measure responding to th
greatest political upheaval experienced by early modern England, and it sus
pended playing 'while these sad causes and set times of humiliation do con
tinue'.[57] Public peace had been under threat since 1637, when Charles faile
to suppress rebellion in the north, despite two military campaigns against th
Scots. In 1640 two successive Parliaments met in an atmosphere of deepenin
crisis; in 1641, the Irish rebelled, and in August 1642 – just two weeks befor
the inhibition – Charles declared war on his own Parliament. In this contex
the statement that plays had to be suspended for the sake of order confirme
that the main issue was not ideological principle but the uncertainty of th
moment: it was at least theoretically possible that, if public quiet returned, th
status quo ante might be restored. As for the audiences, they continued to de
sire plays after 1642. A trickle of surreptitious and underground performance
can be traced throughout the 1640s, from the actors arrested while playin
A King and No King at Salisbury Court in October 1644, to the four companie

---

55 These observations are explored more fully in my *Theatre and Crisis*, pp. 133-5, and 'The
    Condition of the Theatres in 1642'.
56 Unsurprisingly, after the playhouses closed, most players seem to have sided with the Crown,
    but at least two went the other way: Elliard Swanston became a Presbyterian and John Harris
    wrote propaganda for the army.
57 Bentley, *Jacobean and Caroline Stage*, 2:690.

found acting in January 1648, one of which had apparently drawn 120 coaches to the Fortune.[58] Only in the more polarised conditions of the second Civil War (1648) did Parliament take Draconian anti-theatrical action, issuing a new order that condemned playing in clear moral terms and commanded that the playhouses be rendered unusable. The interiors of the Blackfriars, Cockpit, Fortune and Salisbury Court were gutted (the Globe had already been demolished), though the Red Bull remained standing, and reports eventually emerge of performances in private houses and tennis courts. The years 1649–53 saw the ban most strictly enforced, but plays continued to be written and sometimes staged in corners for much of the eighteen-year 'gap'. Printed drama also still attracted a reading public: the collected editions of plays by Beaumont and Fletcher (1647) and the amateur dramatist William Cartwright (1651) issued by the publisher Humphrey Moseley were collectable objects as well as declarations of cultural Royalism.[59]

One immediate legacy of the pre-war theatre is seen in the polemical pamphleteering of the turbulent years down to Charles's execution, which frequently and conveniently fell into semi-dramatic modes.[60] The controversial literature pouring from the presses in the first Civil War meant that dialogue was often the form of choice, allowing competing positions to be debated pro and con. At the same time, short pamphlet-plays, in which public figures were caricatured, shamed or made to 'confess' their crimes, presented news and views to a mass public in a manner patently indebted to the popular stage. Archbishop Laud was mocked by a fool and had his nose put to the grindstone in *Canterbury his Change of Diet* (1641); the King's erstwhile favourite confessed his crimes in *The Earl of Strafford's Ghost* (1644); in *Articles of High Treason* (1641), Cheapside Cross made its will before being pulled down as an idol. It cannot be proved that any of these skits were actually performed, but it is tempting to suppose that some were: they appropriated the resources of jig and farce, and traded on the appeal of plays and 'news' to a common market. The second

58 See Judith Milhous and Robert D. Hume, 'New Light on English Acting Companies in 1646, 1648, and 1660', *Review of English Studies* n.s. 42 (1991), 487–509.
59 See Louis B. Wright, 'The Reading of Plays during the Puritan Revolution', *Huntington Library Bulletin* 6 (1934), 73–108.
60 The seminal discussion of drama between 1642 and 1660 is by Leslie Hotson, *The Commonwealth and Restoration Stage* (Cambridge, MA: Harvard University Press, 1928). The following paragraphs draw on Alfred Harbage, *Cavalier Drama* (Oxford University Press, 1936); Lois Potter, *Secret Rites and Secret Writing* (Cambridge University Press, 1989); Nigel Smith, *Literature and Revolution in England 1640–1660* (New Haven, CT: Yale University Press, 1994); Dale B. J. Randall, *Winter Fruit: English Drama 1642–1660* (Lexington: University Press of Kentucky, 1995); and Susan J. Wiseman, *Drama and Politics in the English Civil War* (Cambridge University Press, 1998).

Civil War gave rise to a new wave of polemical plays that were altogether more elaborate in scope. Depicting events and personalities in plots harking back to Marlowe, Shakespeare and Jonson, they suggest that for contemporaries the structures and motifs of the earlier drama could help frame their response to the traumas of the day. In John Crouch and Marchamont Nedham's *Crafty Cromwell* (2 parts, 1648), the shade of the radical MP John Pym rises like Sulla's ghost in Jonson's *Catiline*, and reveals Cromwell as his puppet, while in scenes reminiscent of Shakespeare's histories, ordinary soldiers guarding the King argue about questions of loyalty. Samuel Sheppard's *The Committee-Man Curried* (1647) satirises one of the Parliamentary officials levying financial penalties on defeated Royalists in an action that imitates the humiliating situations of City comedy. Moreover, the anonymous *Famous Tragedy of King Charles I* (1649) staged the martyrdom of Cavalier heroes at the siege of Colchester, depicting Cromwell as a Marlovian machiavel, and ending with a chorus of lament at Charles's execution. While these plays present Cromwell and the generals as the main villains, it is insufficient simply to label them as 'Royalist', for their attitudes are frequently contradictory and reflect the fragmented ideologies of the moment. Almost certainly some were part-authored by the Leveller pamphleteer Richard Overton, whose polemical writings show a keen appreciation of satirical devices derived from the performed drama.[61]

In the years after the regicide, plays continued to be written by amateurs who had no expectation of performance, but who found in drama a way of giving shape to the chaotic history through which they were living. Many Interregnum plays are lightly veiled allegories, the reader being expected to decode similarities between their action and current events. *The Rebellion of Naples* (by 'T. B.', 1649) parallels Cromwell's career in a tragedy of Italian demagogery; Robert Baron's *Mirza* (1655) uses tyrant and martyr figures from recent Persian history; Christopher Wase pointedly dedicated to Charles's daughter his translation of Sophocles' *Electra* (1649) – that tragedy of a Princess whose father has been murdered. One especially recurrent mode was pastoral tragicomedy, a trend set by Richard Fanshawe's translation of Guarini's *Pastor Fido* (1647), which represents a blighted Arcadia and expresses nostalgia for peace in a manner that invites application to present circumstances. In later examples, such as William Lower's *Enchanted Lovers* (1658) and Cosmo Manuche's *The Banished Shepherdess* (1660), the pastoral world is more emphatically a space of exile, where feelings of deprivation can be vented and plots show lost rulers

---

61 See Heinemann, *Puritanism and Theatre*, pp. 237–57, and Wiseman, *Drama and Politics*, pp. 40–61.

returning and loyal subjects miraculously rewarded. This genre shades into the semi-autobiographical romance, best represented by the plays of Manuche, a former Royalist officer, and the exiled courtier Thomas Killigrew, whose tragicomedies are frankly compensatory fantasies for military failure and social dispossession. By contrast, the anonymous but impressive *Tragedy of that Famous Roman Orator Marcus Tullius Cicero* (1651) stands out for its investment in non-monarchical values. Depicting Antony's bloody murder of Cicero in revenge for his criticisms of Caesar, it underwrites the defender of liberty while representing republican ideals as vulnerable to statecraft and ambition.

Although unperformed and frequently unperformable, such plays prepared the ground for the tragicomic modes of the post-1660 theatre.[62] Indeed, for some amateurs – such as Margaret Cavendish, Duchess of Newcastle, author of numerous plays written in exile at Antwerp, and the most important female dramatist to emerge before Aphra Behn – the impossibility of staging may have been liberating. With their lax plotting, female protagonists and preoccupation with issues of feminine identity, Cavendish's plays were calculated for a theatre of the mind, enabling her to find a dramatic voice at a time when playwriting was not yet a career option for women.[63] But with the creation of Cromwell's Protectorate, circumstances began to develop that allowed some limited state-sanctioned theatre to reestablish itself. The Cockpit Theatre was refitted in 1651; in 1653 a masque, *Cupid and Death*, was staged for the Portuguese ambassador; in 1655 the annual Lord Mayor's shows were resurrected. Much the most substantial development was a proposal for a reformed stage that Cromwell received in 1653 from the former Poet Laureate, William Davenant. Davenant suggested erecting a kind of didactic theatre that would regale spectators with plays on moral themes. Diversified by 'heroical pictures and change of scenes . . . music and wholesome discourses', these shows would encourage civic-spiritedness, educate the people and bring money into London.[64] The eventual outcome was the hybrid drama that Davenant was allowed to mount for paying audiences: *The First Day's Entertainment* and *The Siege of Rhodes* (both 1656) at Rutland House, and *The Cruelty of the Spaniards in Peru* (1658), *The History of Sir Francis Drake* (1659) and *The Siege of Rhodes, Part 2* (1659) at the Cockpit. The first of these was essentially a disputation

62 See Nancy Klein Maguire, *Regicide and Restoration* (Cambridge University Press, 1992).
63 Of course, some single plays had been written by aristocratic women (such as Mary Sidney, Elizabeth Cary and Mary Wroth), but Cavendish was far more prolific a dramatist, and shaped her literary output around the drama.
64 J. R. Jacob and Timothy Raylor, 'Opera and Obedience: Thomas Hobbes and *A Proposition for Advancement of Moralitie* by Sir William Davenant', *Seventeenth Century* 6 (1991), 205–50.

enlivened by music, but the others were conflations of drama and masque that are often regarded as the first English operas. They made themselves acceptable to the Republic by eschewing the overt Royalism of the pre-1642 masques and embracing a mercantile nationalism that echoed the imperialist ambitions of Cromwell's regime. Harking back to an Elizabethan expansionist past from which the intervening Stuart period had been erased, and avoiding hot domestic topics by setting their plots amongst Turks and Spaniards, Davenant's operas suggest how drama might begin to remake itself under conditions of restricted tolerance. Of course, when Charles II returned in 1660, he was followed by a theatre that, with its women actors and changeable scenery, differed radically from that known by his father. Nonetheless, although the break in continuity was acute, the eighteen years that had passed were not simply a gap. Professional drama returned not as an adjunct to the court, but as part of a complex metropolitan culture that, across the period as a whole, it had itself helped to bring into being.

Chapter 20

LITERATURE AND THE
HOUSEHOLD

BARBARA K. LEWALSKI

No doubt authors in every age have written poems and plays, stories and tracts in their studies or bedchambers. But in the late sixteenth and early seventeenth centuries, households of various kinds – from noble estates headed by literary patrons to the private dwellings of the 'middling sort' – emerged as a prominent site of literary production for male as well as female authors, offering an alternative to the court or the church. In these years also, the activities, inhabitants and ideological underpinnings of such households form the subject matter of many kinds of literary and rhetorical texts, addressed to various audiences and serving both private and public purposes.

Ben Jonson's ode 'To Penshurst' was published in his folio of 1616 but written before Prince Henry's death on 6 November 1612.[1] It celebrates the estate of Sir Robert Sidney, Viscount Lisle and later Earl of Leicester, younger brother of the deceased Sir Philip Sidney and of Mary Sidney Herbert, Countess of Pembroke, and himself author of a sonnet sequence, *Rosis and Lysa*.[2] Jonson's poem, in heroic couplets, presents Penshurst as an idealised noble household, a counterweight to the Jacobean court and to more recent 'prodigy' houses like Knole or Longleat, built for ostentatious display and to entertain the court in progress. Penshurst is a *locus amoenus* or delightful place with nature and human society in harmony and with pastoral *otium* happily associated with georgic cultivation. The woods are inhabited by nature gods and family memorials intimating permanence and stability, and on this quasi-Edenic estate fruit is ready to hand, fish leap willingly into nets, and game gladly offers itself to the lord's table. The house is characterised by simplicity and usefulness, with the large extended family – lord, lady, children, servants and retainers – all fulfilling their specific, useful functions and coming together for prayer and

---

1 *The Workes of Benjamin Jonson* (London, 1616). Line 77 refers to King James's visit to Penshurst with Prince Henry.
2 *The Poems of Robert Sidney*, ed. P. J. Croft (Oxford University Press, 1984).

for dinner in the Great Hall. Around it flourishes an agricultural community of interdependent classes linked together in harmony and generosity, with tenants tendering their produce out of love rather than need, and the hall offering ready hospitality to guests of all stations. The poem ends by praising the virtue and fruitfulness of the lady (Barbara Gamage Sidney), which ensure a worthy and religious progeny, and by identifying Robert Sidney as the benevolent and virtuous patriarch who gives order and stability to the entire social community: King James's new nobility have built 'proud, ambitious heaps' but 'thy lord dwells'.[3] The poem's images of profusion and natural abundance disguise, as Raymond Williams observes, the harsh realities of arduous rural labour and landowners' power and greed.[4] They also disguise the realities Robert Sidney's more than 320 letters to his wife reveal: his frequent absences from Penshurst because of court duties, and his mounting financial difficulties. In one letter he complains that he has not money to buy 'necessary clothes for this winter or to pay for man's meate nor horsmeate', and he often underscores the need to retrench Penshurst's hospitality.[5] Jonson's poem, however, is concerned not with fact but with myth, with portraying the Sidneys' estate as a microcosm of an ideal social order founded on patriarchy and older aristocratic values.

Jonson (1572–1637) was not a resident of Penshurst, but he was, he implies, a frequent guest, welcomed as warmly as the King himself: 'As if thou, then, wert mine, or I raign'd here' (line 74). As Jonson's career was taking hold (1602–7) he lived with Esmé Stuart, Lord Aubigny, a cousin of King James. He wrote successful plays for the public theatre and enjoyed the patronage of King James and Queen Anne for his court masques, but he looked especially to the Sidney–Herbert households as patrons and often subjects for his poetry, the literary mode he sought to cultivate especially in his later years. Assimilating models from the classical world, notably Horace, Jonson often constructs an ideal self-image: bluff, scrupulously honest, witty, scornful of flatterers, a lover of wine, capable of self-irony and, above all, a keenly perceptive judge of men and women.

Members of the Sidney–Pembroke household and the Aubigny household loom large as subjects and addressees in his early poetry. His 1616 folio contains

---

3 'To Penshurst', line 102. Jonson's poems are quoted from the standard edition, *The Works of Ben Jonson*, ed. C. H. Herford, Percy Simpson and Evelyn Simpson, 11 vols. (Oxford: Clarendon Press, 1925–52), 8:96.
4 Raymond Williams, *The Country and the City* (Oxford University Press, 1973), pp. 26–34; cf. Don E. Wayne, *Penshurst: The Semiotics of Place and the Poetics of History* (Madison: University of Wisconsin Press, 1984).
5 Kent County Archives Office, Maidstone, Kent, letter of 10 November 1607, Penshurst Papers, U 1475, C 81/158 (cf. letter of 29 September 1609, U 1475, C 81/192).

a book of *Epigrammes*, which he termed 'the ripest of my studies' in a dedicatory preface to William Herbert,[6] Mary Sidney Herbert's elder son, who became Earl of Pembroke in 1601 and Lord Chamberlain in 1615. These 133 epigrams and epitaphs, the finest that had yet appeared in English, present an entire moral and social universe. The several satirical epigrams, indebted especially to Martial, are brief, pithy, witty poems that usually have a surprise turn at the end – a 'sting in the tail'. Under type names (e.g. 'On Gut', 'Sir Cod') they present examples of evils or follies to be shunned. A larger number praise under their own names notable persons who are exemplars of virtue, learning and artistic merit. Along with William Camden, John Donne, Lucy, Countess of Bedford, Sir Henry Saville and Lord Aubigny, are many Sidneys and Herberts: Elizabeth, Countess of Rutland (Philip Sidney's daughter); Lady Mary Wroth and Philip Sidney (Robert Sidney's daughters); William Herbert, Earl of Pembroke; and Susan, Countess of Montgomery (wife of Philip Herbert, William's brother). Especially poignant are two epitaphs on members of Jonson's own family: his first daughter, dead at six months, and his first son, dead at seven years; the latter poem registers profound grief through the very restraint imposed by the spare epitaph form and plain style. The very long Epigram 101, 'Inviting a Friend to Supper', makes a proposed dinner party at Jonson's house a symbol of moral, social and aesthetic values: good taste, good conversation, good books, the gracious civility of host and guest, and a 'liberty' that stands in sharp contrast to the enslaving licentiousness, drunkenness and gluttony characterising the banquets of Imperial Rome or the Jacobean court. The poem's very pure plain style embodies these ideals.

A second book in the 1616 Folio, fifteen poems entitled *The Forest* in allusion to miscellaneous classical collections entitled *Sylva*, is virtually a Sidney volume. It contains, in addition to 'Penshurst', a verse epistle praising Sir Robert Wroth (husband of Lady Mary Wroth) for choosing to escape court and city corruptions at his country estate, Durrants; a comic poem, 'That Women are but Mens Shaddowes', prompted by a jesting debate between William, Earl of Pembroke and his wife on that theme;[7] and a verse epistle to Elizabeth, Countess of Rutland, praising her for qualities of mind and character. Another verse letter praises Katherine, Lady Aubigny, wife of his first patron Esmé Stuart, with similar focus on her 'good minde'. A Pindaric ode to William Sidney

6 Jonson, *Works*, ed. Herford and Simpson, 8:25. The *Epigrammes* were registered in 1612, but not published then.
7 In *Conversations* recorded by Jonson's friend, the poet William Drummond of Hawthornden, Jonson stated that he had sided with Pembroke in this debate and 'my Lady gave a penance to prove it in Verse, hence his Epigrame' (Jonson, *Works*, ed. Herford and Simpson, 11:38).

(Robert Sidney's first son) on his twenty-first birthday is apprentice work for Jonson's later great Pindaric on the friendship of Lucius Cary and Henry Morison, on the occasion of the latter's death in 1629.

Most of the poems in the later collection entitled *Underwood*, as well as many uncollected poems also published in the two-volume posthumous edition of Jonson's *Workes* (1640), have no such family focus. They display Jonson's mastery of many lyric kinds, metres and stanzaic forms: verse satires and verse epistles in pentameter couplets, love elegies sometimes surprisingly 'Donnean' in manner, funeral poems, delicate songs of love or praise (often in complex metrical patterns) and a witty dramatic sequence of ten poems about love, *A Celebration of Charis*, pitting his own against court values. In addition to such poems and works that articulate the principles of his classical poetics – a verse translation of Horace's 'Art of Poetrie' and a prose commonplace book, *Timber, or Discoveries* – that edition also includes his *Conversations* with his friend William Drummond of Hawthornden. During this 'Table Talk', recorded by Drummond and imagined to occur in private, domestic circumstances, Jonson delivers penetrating and sometimes caustic judgements of Donne, Shakespeare and other contemporaries.

While Jonson's 'Penshurst' celebrates an estate and household founded on patriarchy, the other great households that served as sites or stimuli for writing in the period were headed by women. The Countess of Pembroke's Wilton in the 1580s and 1590s offered hospitality for some periods of time to writers who shared her staunch Protestant convictions and literary interests – the poets Nicholas Breton, William Browne, and Samuel Daniel (1562–1619), tutor to her eldest son William Herbert, as well as to the physician–naturalist Thomas Moffett and the cleric Gervase Babington, who were also authors.[8] During his rustication from court in the early 1580s, Sir Philip Sidney wrote his *Countess of Pembroke's Arcadia* at Wilton. Later, John Aubrey termed Wilton 'a little college'.[9] The Countess (1561–1621) completed a verse translation of the Psalms begun by her brother, rendering 107 Psalms in an amazing variety of stanzaic and metrical patterns; she also wrote a powerful elegy for Philip Sidney, a pastoral entertainment for Queen Elizabeth, and translations of Petrarch's *Triumph of Death* and the French Protestant Philippe de Mornay's *Discourse of Life and Death*.[10] While associated with the Countess of Pembroke's circle,

---

8 See Margaret P. Hannay, *Philip's Phoenix: Mary Sidney, Countess of Pembroke* (Oxford University Press, 1990), p. 112.
9 John Aubrey, *Brief Lives*, ed. Oliver Lawson Dick (London: Secker and Warburg, 1949), p. 138.
10 *The Collected Works of Mary Sidney Herbert, Countess of Pembroke*, ed. Margaret Hannay, Noel Kinnamon and Michael G. Brennan (Oxford: Clarendon Press; and New York: Oxford University Press, 1998).

Daniel wrote a sonnet sequence, *Delia*, published with the Ovidian 'Complaint of Rosamond' (1592).[11] He also wrote the first four books of a historical epic called *The Civil Warres betweene the two houses of Lancaster and Yorke* (1594) in *ottava rima*, which earned him the epithet, 'the English Lucan'; the 1609 edition of 7,000 lines in eight books carries a dedication to the Countess of Pembroke.[12] Later Daniel turned to prose history, publishing in 1613 a *History of England* to the reign of King Stephen, expanded in 1618 to the reign of Edward III.[13]

The Countess of Pembroke's Wilton also fostered the development of a line of Senecan tragedies in the French manner; they were not intended for the stage but were a recognised vehicle for exploring dangerous political topics, with their long rhetorical monologues and debates on the wickedness of tyrants, the dangers of absolutism, the modes of and justifications for resistance, the folly of princes, the corruption of royal favourites, the responsibilities of counsellors. While these tragedies do not sanction or encourage rebellion, they often make a strong case for the heroes' resistance to tyranny, and highlight conflicting theories of monarchy, tyranny and rebellion. The Countess of Pembroke's translation of Robert Garnier's *Marc-Antoine* (1592) inaugurated this genre in England.[14] Samuel Daniel followed with *Cleopatra* (1594) – revised in 1607 with Essex's execution, Ralegh's imprisonment and James's absolutism in the background – and with *Philotas*, staged at Blackfriars and published in 1605.[15] The latter work brought Daniel before the Star Chamber.

A still more complex exploration of responses to tyranny from a member of the Sidney–Pembroke coterie was Fulke Greville's *Mustapha*, written in the mid-1590s and heavily revised in two Jacobean versions which highlight a monarch's tyrannical suspicions of his subjects and the danger of rule by favourites.[16] Greville (1554–1628), a close friend of Sir Philip Sidney, was a great landowner in Warwickshire and MP in five Parliaments; his family seat was at Alcester and later he transformed Warwick Castle, granted him by

---

11 Samuel Daniel, *Delia. Contayning certayne Sonnets: With, The Complaint of Rosamond* (London, 1592).
12 Samuel Daniel, *The Civile Warres betweene the two houses of Lancaster and Yorke* (London, 1594); *The Civile Warres . . . Corrected and continued* (London, 1609).
13 Samuel Daniel, *The First Part of the Historie of England* (London, 1613); *The Collection of the History of England* (London, 1618).
14 Mary Sidney Herbert (trans.), *A discourse of life and death by Ph. Mornay; Antonius, a tragedie, written also in French by Ro: Garnier* (London, 1592).
15 Samuel Daniel, *The Tragedie of Cleopatra* (London, 1594; rev. edn, 1607); *Certaine Small Poems lately printed: With the tragedie of Philotas* (London, 1605; rpt, 1607, 1611, 1613).
16 Fulke Greville, *The Tragedy of Mustapha* (London, 1609) contains a truncated version; a manuscript version written 1607–10 was eventually published in *Certaine Learned and Elegant Workes of the Right Honorable Fulke Lord Brooke* (London, 1633). See Ronald A. Rebholz, *The Life of Fulke Greville, First Lord Brooke* (Oxford: Clarendon Press, 1971).

King James, from a decaying ruin into a splendid residence. Though he was a favourite of Queen Elizabeth and served as Chancellor of the Exchequer under James, his writings often incorporate a critique of absolutism and a Calvinist sense of the sinfulness of human nature infecting all human institutions and activities. Greville revised over several years and left in manuscript at Warwick Castle a sonnet sequence *Caelica*, verse treatises on *Monarchy, Human Learning Religion, Fame and Honour* and *Wars*, and another Senecan drama, *Alaham* – al published posthumously in 1633. His is a poetry of dense, often abstract intellectual argument, marked by pervasive irony as well as by thickly clustered images and strained syntax. His highly honorific *Life of the Renowned Sir Philip Sidney* was published in 1652.

Though based in households unconnected with the Sidneys and Pembrokes. Elizabeth Tanfield Cary, Viscountess Falkland (1585–1639), adapted their sort of Senecan drama to explore the analogy between domestic and state tyranny in her *Tragedie of Mariam* (1613).[17] A commendatory poem praising that drama. along with the poetry of the Countesses of Pembroke and Bedford, by Cary's erstwhile tutor, the poet John Davies of Herefordshire, suggests that he may have introduced her to that Senecan genre.[18] The first Englishwoman to write a tragedy, Cary grew up at Burford Priory and Great Tew, the only child and heir of Sir Lawrence Tanfield, a wealthy and successful lawyer, judge and (after 1607) chief Baron of the Exchequer. While the husband she married in 1602, Sir Henry Cary, fought and was imprisoned on the continent (1602–6), Elizabeth lived first at home and then with her mother-in-law who, according to a *Life* written by one of Cary's four daughters, confined her to her chamber and removed her books, at which point she began writing verse.[19] Henry Cary's elevation as Comptroller of the Royal Household, Viscount Falkland in the Scottish peerage and Lord Deputy of Ireland brought Elizabeth to live at court for a time and then in Ireland; the *Life* portrays her as struggling continually to conform her own inclinations and 'strong will' to that of her 'very absolute' husband.[20] She bore eleven children between 1609 and 1624, and nursed them all except for the eldest, Lucius, who was brought up by his grandfather at

17 E. C., *The Tragedie of Mariam, the Faire Queene of Jewry* (London, 1613); Elizabeth Cary, Lady Falkland, *The Tragedy of Mariam the Fair Queen of Jewry*, with *The Lady Falkland her Life, By one of her Daughters*, ed. Barry Weller and Margaret W. Ferguson (Berkeley: University of California Press, 1994).
18 John Davies of Hereford, *The Muses Sacrifice* (London, 1612), sigs. *** 2r–3v. His poem to Cary attributes to her another (apparently lost) tragedy set in Sicily. Davies also wrote *Microcosmos: The discovery of the little world, with government thereof* (London, 1603, 1605, 1611), as well as sonnets and epigrams.
19 *The Lady Falkland her Life*, ed. Weller and Ferguson, p. 189.
20 *Ibid.*, p. 194.

Great Tew. He later inherited that estate and made it the centre of a coterie of rationalist intellectuals, among them the writer William Chillingworth, who had been a tutor in Elizabeth Cary's household.[21] Cary's lifelong attraction to Roman Catholicism culminated in an open profession in 1626, after which she found herself isolated, cast off by husband and family, and in acute financial distress. After her husband's death in 1633 she converted several of her children to Catholicism: four daughters became nuns, and two sons, abducted by her from Great Tew and sent to France, became monks.

Like the other Senecan dramas, *Mariam* intertwines the spheres of public life and private desire, but this work – probably written in either her mother-in-law's or her husband's household – makes issues of love and domestic tyranny central. Prior to the drama's action, Herod the Great had supplanted and executed the hereditary King and High Priest of Israel; divorced his first wife to marry the singularly beautiful Mariam; arranged a drowning accident to remove the new High Priest, Mariam's brother; and twice, when he was called to Rome, left orders that Mariam be killed in the event of his death, out of fierce love and jealousy lest any other man possess her. The play begins with news of Herod's death, bringing a sense of relief, liberation and new beginnings, but these are quashed upon his unexpected return. The good counsellor Sohemus, who had declined to kill Mariam, is executed – accused by Salome, his wife and Herod's sister, of adultery with Mariam. Mariam refused Herod's love and bed as a gesture of protest and an affirmation of personal integrity. Salome engineers a plot to make Mariam seem guilty of attempting to assassinate Herod and then goads him to execute her. After a messenger relates her courageous death, Herod runs mad with grief and remorse, admitting that his tyrannical actions would justify rebellion against him. Mariam is positioned against two principal foils. The chorus, who in this genre do not speak from an authoritative vantage point, claim that a wife owes entire subjection of mind as well as body to her husband. Salome, though thoroughly wicked in flaunting her illicit affairs and arranging the deaths of two husbands, speaks forcefully for a woman's right to divorce and for evenhanded justice for unhappy wives. Mariam admits in soliloquy that she has invited her death by refusing to live by the accepted female triad of virtues: she is chaste but manifestly neither silent nor obedient. But she is unrepentant: she challenges patriarchal control within the institution of marriage, refusing to have her love commanded and claiming a wife's right to her own speech – public and private – as well as to the integrity of her own

---

21 William Chillingworth's best-known work is *The Religion of Protestants a Safe Way to Salvation* (London, 1638). Lucius Cary was celebrated by Jonson in his Pindaric ode on Cary and Morison – see above, p. 606.

emotional life. Such integrity, Cary's tragedy intimates, is the foundation for resistance to tyranny in every sphere. Cary also published a translation (1630) of Cardinal du Perron's *Reply* to King James's argument in support of the Oath of Allegiance, and probably wrote *The History of the Life, Reign, and Death of Edward II*, published much later; if so, she was the first Englishwoman to write a political history.[22]

The author most directly associated with Penshurst and other Sidney–Herbert households was the eldest daughter of Robert Sidney, Mary Wroth (1587?–1651?), whose published work includes the first prose romance and first sonnet sequence by an Englishwoman. The 400,000-word romance, *The Countesse of Mountgomeries Urania* (1621), includes more than 50 poems, and concludes with *Pamphilia to Amphilanthus*, 103 sonnets and songs, many of which circulated earlier in manuscript.[23] Works left unpublished in her lifetime include a few more poems; a 280,000-word, nearly complete continuation of the *Urania*; and a pastoral drama, *Love's Victory*,[24] also a first for an Englishwoman. While the male Sidney authors provided major generic models – Petrarchan sonnet sequences and Philip Sidney's romance, *The Countesse of Pembroke's Arcadia* – Wroth's aunt, Mary Sidney Herbert, the Countess of Pembroke, offered a precedent for female authorship and perhaps some contact with the literary and intellectual coterie associated with Wilton. Married in 1604 to Sir Robert Wroth, the King's riding forester charged with facilitating the royal hunt, Mary Wroth divided her time between the court, the various Sidney–Pembroke family residences, and Wroth's estates – Durrants at Enfield and

---

22 *The Reply of the Most Illustrious Cardinal of Perron, to the Answeare of the Most Excellent King of Great Britaine* (Douay, 1630). E.[lizabeth] F.[alkland?], *The History of the Life, Reign, and Death of Edward II, King of England, and Lord of Ireland. With the Rise and Fall of his Great Favourites, Gaveston and the Spencers* (London, 1680), written around 1627. On the authorship issue, see Barbara K. Lewalski, *Writing Women in Jacobean England* (Cambridge, MA: Harvard University Press, 1993), Appendix A, pp. 317–20. An epitaph on Buckingham is attributed to her in the manuscript, BL, MS Egerton 2725, fol. 60. The daughter's *Life* mentions several unpublished works.

23 *The Countesse of Mountgomeries Urania, Written by the right honorable the Lady Mary Wroath, Daughter to the right Noble Robert Earle of Leicester. And Neece to the ever famous and renowned Sr Philip Sidney, knight. And to the most excellent Lady Mary Countesse of Pembroke late deceased* (London, 1621). Josephine A. Roberts has edited *The First Part of the Countess of Montgomery's Urania* (Binghamton, NY: Medieval and Renaissance Texts and Studies, 1995), and *The Poems of Lady Mary Wroth* (Baton Rouge and London: Louisiana State University Press, 1982).

24 The unpublished *Urania* exists uniquely as a holograph manuscript (Newberry Library, Case MS fY 1565. W95). *The Second Part of the Countess of Montgomery's Urania*, ed. Josephine Roberts, completed by Suzanne Gossett and Janel Mueller (Tempe, AZ: Medieval and Renaissance Texts and Studies and Arizona Center for Medieval and Renaissance Studies, 1999). *Love's Victory* exists in an almost complete manuscript at Penshurst, and in a truncated manuscript at the Huntington Library (HM 600); *Lady Mary Wroth's Love's Victory: The Penshurst Manuscript*, ed. Michael J. Brennan (London: Roxburghe Club, 1988).

Loughton Hall in Essex. After Wroth's death in 1614 a love affair between Mary Wroth and her married first cousin, William Herbert, Earl of Pembroke, produced two illegitimate children. Apparently she also exchanged poems with Pembroke, who was not only a powerful courtier but also a major patron of theatre, music, literature and art. Wroth alludes to their relationship in the two principal characters of her romance, who are also the title personages of her sonnet sequence, Pamphilia ('all loving') and Amphilanthus ('lover of both').

Pamphilia to Amphilanthus claims the Petrarchan tradition for an English woman poet and gives voice and subjectivity to a sonnet lady, normally the silent object of the sonneteer's desire. In taking up the *passé* genre of the sonnet sequence, Wroth was not simply imitating, belatedly, her uncle's *Astrophil to Stella*, but rather adapting to a female lover-speaker the genre that had long been used to analyse a male lover's desire, passions, frustrations and fantasies, while also reflecting cultural and sometimes career anxieties. Petrarchan in form, Wroth's sonnets are interspersed with elegant songs in a variety of metres; the collection also includes a carefully executed 'Corona' of fourteen interlinked sonnets. She retained several conventional Petrarchan motifs: wounding eyes, fiery darts, absence, night, flowing tears, time, puns on the beloved's name 'Will'. But Wroth does not simply reverse the usual sonnet roles. Pamphilia addresses very few sonnets to Amphilanthus: there are no praises of his overpowering physical beauty or charms, no narratives of kisses or other favours received or denied, no blazons scattering his parts as a gesture of aggrandisement or control, no promises to eternise him through the poet's songs, no palinodes or renunciations of love. Nor does she often assume the Petrarchan lover's position of abject servant begging pity from a cold and cruel beloved. Instead, Pamphilia portrays herself as subject to Cupid, God of Love, usually identified here, through introspection and self-analysis, with the force of her own desire. She deals with a beloved flawed by inconstancy by making the love experience itself – not the beloved – the locus of value and the stimulus to poetry, tracing through the sequence the woman lover's movement from the bondage of chaotic passion to the freedom of self-chosen constancy. While this ending point may seem compliant with contemporary patriarchal ideology, it is not: Wroth's female speaker affirms constancy not chastity, to a lover not a husband, as a matter of choice not cultural imposition, and as a means to personal and artistic growth.

Wroth's massive romance, *Urania*, claims the Sidney mantle ostentatiously by its title and by structural, thematic and verbal allusions to Philip Sidney's *Countesse of Pembrokes Arcadia*. There are the expected generic markers: a multitude of characters; numerous interwoven and interpolated tales; knights fighting giants, pirates, monsters and usurping kings; Spenserian symbolic places, e.g., the Palace of Love and the Temple of Love. Wroth, however, again revises the generic topoi from a Jacobean woman author's perspective. She breaks the romance convention of a plot centred on courtship, portraying instead married heroines and their love relationships, both inside and outside of marriage.[25] At the level of fantasy all the characters are, or are discovered to be, kings, queens, emperors and their heirs, with the power and comparative freedom incident to those positions. But the landscape is not Arcadia or Fairyland; it is war-torn Europe and Asia, a world rife with rape, incest, tortured women, endangered children, forced marriages, murderous jealousies, court treacheries. This world produces intense psychological pressures because of the tyranny of love (which no one escapes) and the ubiquity of male inconstancy in heroes who are otherwise courageous fighters and attractive lovers. The higher heroism belongs to a few women and involves the preservation of personal integrity and agency amid such pressures and constraints. The work is in part a *roman à clef*, with allusions to some notorious scandals in Jacobean England, one of which, concerning Lord Edward Denny and his daughter, provoked a firestorm of protest from that Lord and a probably disingenuous offer by Wroth to recall the book. The romance, however, more consistently alludes to members of the Sidney households: Wroth herself; Pembroke; Robert Sidney; Sir Philip Sidney; Mary Sidney Herbert, Countess of Pembroke; Robert Sidney's daughter and her death in childbirth. Many of the interpolated stories reprise Wroth's own situation – unhappy arranged marriage, unfaithful courtier-lover, psychic suffering, arbitrary censure, disgrace, writing – offering it as the story of (almost) Everywoman, at least in the higher social ranks. A major means of self-definition and agency for Wroth's heroines is literary composition – the telling of tales about themselves and others, and the making of poems. Of the fifty-five poems in many genres and verse forms in the published *Urania*, twice as many are assigned to female speakers as to men, and Pamphilia, Wroth's surrogate as poet and storyteller, is singled out as a poet by vocation.

Wroth's unpublished tragicomedy, *Love's Victory*, stands in the tradition of Tasso's *Aminta*, Guarini's *Pastor Fido*, Samuel Daniel's *Queenes Arcadia* and John Fletcher's *Faithfull Shepheardesse*,[26] but it is even more clearly a family affair. Its characters allude to members of the Sidney–Herbert–Wroth households and

25 Paul Salzman, *English Prose Fiction, 1558–1700: A Critical History* (Oxford: Clarendon Press, 1985), p. 141. See Naomi J. Miller, *Changing the Subject: Mary Wroth and Figurations of Gender in Early Modern England* (Lexington: University Press of Kentucky, 1996).

26 Torquato Tasso, *Aminta* (Cremona, 1580); Battista Guarini, *Il Pastor Fido* (Venice, 1590), trans. [anon.] as *The Faithfull Shepheard* (London, 1602); Samuel Daniel, *The Queenes Arcadia* (London, 1606); John Fletcher, *The Faithfull Shepheardesse* (London, [1610?]).

it was probably performed at Durrants or Penshurst, with musical settings for the all-pervasive and various songs. Here Wroth reworked another genre which traditionally served as a vehicle for male desire, nostalgia and political commentary to develop a female pastoral fantasy whose elements are a nonhierarchical community, close female and cross-gender friendships, female authorship and female agency. Even more than in the *Urania*, it is the women who solve the love problems that almost destroy their pastoral society, and who nurture its values of love, leisure, wit, artful play and harmonious community.

Another noble household that nurtured literary production was that of Margaret Russell Clifford, Countess of Cumberland (1560–1616), whose husband, the dashing sea adventurer George Clifford, was often absent from England, and then estranged from his wife for several years before his death in 1605. These circumstances evidently made a space within which the Countess could develop an important role as patron of poets and Reformist clergymen. Among those who expressed gratitude for her patronage were Spenser, Henry Lok, Robert Greene, William Perkins and Samuel Hieron.[27] Some of them may have been guests at one or another of the Clifford castles and estates in Cumberland, Yorkshire or Westmorland, or at Cookham, the royal estate leased to her brother, William Russell of Thornhaugh, and occupied by her on occasion both before and probably shortly after George Clifford's death.[28] The writers most closely associated with her household were her own daughter, Anne Clifford (1589–1676), the poet Samuel Daniel who became Anne's tutor in the later 1590s (Anne later attributed her good education to her mother and 'that religious and honest poet' Daniel)[29] and the poet Aemilia Lanyer (1569–1645).

Anne Clifford's writings – diaries, family history, autobiography and biography, all unpublished until this century[30] – were prompted in part by family pride but especially by her long struggle and continual litigations, at first in conjunction with her mother, to maintain Anne's legal claim, as her father's

27 Literary works acknowledging her patronage include Spenser, *Fowre Hymnes* (London, 1596); Henry Lok, *Ecclesiastes* [with] *Sundrie sonets of Christian passions* (London, 1597); and Robert Greene, *Penelope's Web* (London, 1587). Theological works include William Perkins, *Salve for a Sicke Man* (London, 1611) and *Workes* (London, 1600); and Samuel Hieron, *Certain Meditations* (London, 1615) and *Sermons* (London, 1620).
28 During the period September–November 1604, Margaret Clifford dated five letters from 'Cookham in Berkshire' (Longleat, Portland Papers, vol. 23, fols. 24–8); Anne Clifford's *Diary* records one visit to Cookham in 1603, but its record then skips to 1616.
29 Anne Clifford, *Lives of Lady Anne Clifford and of Her Parents*, ed. J. P. Gilson (London: Roxburghe Club, 1916), p. 28.
30 *The Diary of Anne Clifford, 1616–1619*, ed. Katherine O. Acheson (New York and London: Garland, 1995); *Diaries*, ed. D. J. H. Clifford (Wolfeboro Falls, NH: Sutton, 1991); *The Diary of Lady Anne Clifford*, ed. Vita Sackville-West (London: Heinemann, 1923); *Lives*, ed. Gilson.

only child, to a large inheritance in properties and offices in Westmorland and Yorkshire. George Clifford's will, ignoring an ancient entail to legitimate Clifford heirs regardless of sex, had willed these properties to his brother who automatically inherited the Cumberland earldom. Anne and her mother compiled massive tomes of records and family papers called 'The Chronicles', by analogy with the chronicle histories of princes; later she collected and organised records and eyewitness accounts pertaining to her father's sea voyages.[31] In 1609, by marriage to Richard Sackville, she became Countess of Dorset, and her remarkable *Diary* records the day-by-day activities of her marital and legal struggles in the years 1616–17 and 1619.[32] The focus is her resistance to her husband's continual pressure – by exiling her to his great country estate Knole in Kent, cutting off her allowance and taking away her beloved child – to give over her suits in exchange for a monetary award, which he needed desperately to keep up his flamboyant life style at court. She also records, as a series of understated dramatic encounters, her resistance to an awesome assemblage of powerful men engaged on Dorset's side: the King, the Chief Justice, several peers, lawyers and the Cliffords. Beyond that, her *Diary* affords an insight into her lonely daily life at Knole: the small milestones in her daughter's life, the books she read or had read to her, card games with the servants. It offers, as most diaries in this period do not, some expression of personal emotion and judgements of people and events. In 1630, by a second marriage to Philip Herbert, Anne Clifford became Countess of Pembroke and Montgomery and mistress of Wilton. But she kept up her suits and petitions for her property, at last obtaining it in 1643 upon the death of her uncle and his male heirs. In 1653 she wrote retrospective memoirs of her father and mother in the vein of Plutarch's moralised *Lives*, as well as a lively and sometimes reflective autobiography, *A true memorial of the life of me the Lady Anne Clifford*.[33]

While living in the Clifford household Daniel published *Poeticall Essayes* along with a remarkable verse colloquy on the purpose of writing poetry, *Musophilus* (1599), dedicated to Sir Philip Sidney's friend Fulke Greville.[34] He also wrote several fine verse epistles to patrons or would-be patrons, among them Margaret

---

31 'Great Books of the Records of Skipton Castle', 3 vols., Kendal, Cumbria Record Office, WD/Hoth/Great Books. 'A brief Relation of the Severall Voyages undertaken and performed by the Right Honourable George, Earle of Cumberland', Cumbria Record Office, WD/Hoth/Additional Records, 70.

32 There is extant also a retrospective summary of the year 1603, describing, from the perspective of the teenager she then was, the momentous events of the change of reigns.

33 An eighteenth-century copy of these works (from the third volume of the 'Great Books') is in BL, MS Harleian 6177; it is the basis of *Lives*, ed. Gilson.

34 Samuel Daniel, *Poeticall Essayes* [with] *Musophilus* (London, 1599).

and Anne Clifford, and a prose *Defence of Rhyme* addressed to his erstwhile pupil William Herbert (Pembroke), which defends English accentual verse forms against Thomas Campion's classicising brief for quantitative metres. In 1603 he published a long poem entitled *A Panegyrike Congratulatory* to James I, appending these works to it; that volume paved the way for his appointment to various offices in the court of Queen Anne, for whom he also wrote masques.[35] All these poems are marked by clarity, restraint, moral earnestness and quiet eloquence; his verse epistles to patrons and even *A Panegyrike* to James contain as much grave and thoughtful advice as praise.

The work most directly associated with the Clifford household is Aemilia Lanyer's *Salve Deus Rex Judaeorum* (1611), the first substantial volume of original poems published by a woman.[36] Daughter to an Italian-Jewish family of court musicians, Lanyer (1569–1645) was educated in the aristocratic household of Susan Bertie, Countess of Kent, before becoming the mistress of Queen Elizabeth's Lord Chamberlain, Henry Carey, Lord Hunsdon, after which she married into another family of musicians, the Lanyers. For some period of time she resided with Margaret Clifford and her young daughter Anne at Cookham, and her several tributes to Margaret Clifford associate that place with her religious conversion and with the confirmation of her role as poet. Lanyer may also have received some support from Margaret Clifford in the unusual venture of offering her poetry for publication. Her volume has a feminist thrust. Nine dedicatory poems to former and hoped-for patrons, in a variety of stanzaic forms, praise them as a community of contemporary good women: these include a poem to Queen Anne; a long verse epistle to Anne Clifford as Countess of Dorset, seeking a renewal of association with her; and a dream-vision poem asking the Countess of Pembroke to recognise Lanyer as her successor in a female poetic line. A prose address to Margaret Clifford identifies her as the volume's primary patron and audience, while another, 'To the Virtuous Reader', offers a spirited defence of women's moral and spiritual equality or superiority to men in both Old and New Testament stories. The long title poem, a baroque meditation on Christ's Passion,[37] locates the Passion Week narrative within an extended frame (about one-third of the whole) focused on Margaret Clifford as chief meditator on, and participant in, Christ's sufferings.

---

35 Samuel Daniel, *A Panegyrike Congratulatory delivered to the Kings most excellent majesty at Burleigh Harrington in Rutlandshire. Also certaine epistles. With a defence of ryme* (London, 1603).
36 Aemilia Lanyer, *Salve Deus Rex Judaeorum* (London, 1611); *The Poems of Aemilia Lanyer: Salve Deus Rex Judaeorum*, ed. Susanne Woods (Oxford University Press, 1993).
37 See Susanne Woods, *Lanyer: A Renaissance Woman Poet* (New York and Oxford: Oxford University Press, 1999).

The poem continually contrasts the good women who figure in the Passion story with the weak or evil men who tormented or betrayed Jesus, and also incorporates a spirited defence of Eve and all women against the imposition of male dominance.

The final poem, 'The Description of Cooke-ham', in 210 iambic pentameter lines, celebrates that estate in elegiac mode, as a valediction to an ideal female social order. This poem may or may not have been written before Jonson's 'To Penshurst', commonly assumed to have inaugurated the country-house genre in English literature, but it was published first. Its myth contrasts sharply with that developed in 'To Penshurst'. No lord dwells here, only three ladies who are about to leave forever – Margaret to go to her widow's dower house, Anne to her conflict-ridden marriage to Dorset, Lanyer to social decline. The estate is described in evocative pastoral imagery as a *locus amoenus*; it enacts the pathetic fallacy continually as it responds joyously to Margaret's arrival and takes on the appearance of a ravaged Eden when she departs. Moreover, there is no larger society at Cookham as at Penshurst: no extended family, no servants, no villagers, no visitors, no men at all. Cookham is conceived as a lost female paradise, an ageless, classless society in which the three women lived without mates but found contentment and delight in nature, God and their own companionship.[38]

Literary activity also flourished in the household of Lucy (Harington) Russell, Countess of Bedford (1581–1627), the favourite of Queen Anne, a power-broker at court and the most important literary patroness of the Jacobean era. Her husband Edward, the third Earl, remained mostly in the country after his part in Essex's rebellion, and the Countess was left to make her own way and follow her own interests. When not at court, Lucy Bedford resided at her estate, Twickenham, just outside London, making it into a salon of sorts for female and male friends, most of whom were also courtiers and occasional poets. Among them were her kinswomen Cecilia Bulstrode and Bridget, Lady Markham, Sir Henry Goodyer and the diplomats Sir Thomas Roe and Sir Henry Wotton. Writers associated with her included Michael Drayton, John Florio, John Davies of Hereford, George Chapman, Samuel Daniel and Ben Jonson, whose masques she helped to promote at the new court.[39] Jonson wrote three

38 See Lewalski, *Writing Women*, pp. 234–41.
39 She is addressed as patron by Michael Drayton in *Endimion and Phoebe* (London, [1595]); John Florio in *A World of Wordes, or Most copious, and exact Dictionaries in Italian and English* (London, 1598), sig. A 3v, and *The Essays or Morall, Politike, and Militarie Discourses of Lo. Michell de Montaigne* (London, 1603), sigs. A2–A4; George Chapman in *Homer Prince of Poets*, sig. Ec 2; and John Davies of Hereford in *The Muses Sacrifice*, sigs. ✳✳✳ 2–2v. Samuel Daniel dedicated his Christmas masque of 1604, *The Vision of the 12 Goddesses* (London, 1604), to her and wrote one of his verse epistles about her (*Panegyrike*, sig. E3).

epigrams praising her mind and character in a tone of great judiciousness, one of which accompanied his presentation of Donne's *Satyres* to her. But she fell out with Jonson over a vitriolic epigram he wrote on Cecilia Bulstrode, 'On the Court Pucell', and his strained epitaph for Bulstrode's death in 1609, praising her improbably as a virgin, did not repair the breach. The collegiate ladies in Jonson's stage comedy *Epicoene* (also 1609) seem to satirise her circle at Twickenham and their 'President', Lady Haughty. John Donne (1572–1631), introduced into Lucy Bedford's circle by Sir Henry Goodyer around 1607, became for the next five years virtually her laureate.

Donne's imprudent clandestine marriage in 1601 to the daughter of Sir George More ended the much-desired career in public service he had begun as Secretary to the Lord Keeper, Sir Thomas Egerton (More's kinsman), forcing Donne to accept such employment as he could find, and the largesse of friends, to support his rapidly expanding family. After residing for a time in the household of Francis Wolley in Surrey, and after some travel on the continent as companion to Sir Walter Chute, he reconciled with Anne's father in 1606, receiving a small stipend from him that enabled the Donnes to move to a cottage at Mitcham, near London.[40] From that retirement Donne continued to write letters in prose and verse to Goodyer, Wotton and other friends, reporting on his difficult domestic arrangements and frustrated ambition,[41] commenting on their successes and sometimes offering moral advice. Around 1607–8, as a way of coping with anxieties and melancholy, he also wrote a long, scholarly disquisition on suicide, *Biathanatos*, suspending judgement as to circumstances and motives that might justify it. A few years later he wrote and published in both Latin and English two polemics against papal authority and the Jesuits, *Pseudo-Martyr* (1610) and *Ignatius his Conclave* (1611), to reintroduce himself as a fit candidate for public service.[42]

Though most of Donne's poems cannot be dated with certainty, he evidently wrote several of his *Songs and Sonnets* at Mitcham. His elegies and satires and some of the wittily salacious love poems probably belong to his life as a young man about town at the Inns of Court, while some poems dealing with the discovery and growth of mutual love and its dangers and problems – e.g. 'The Sunne Rising', 'Loves Growth', 'A Lecture upon the Shadow', 'The Anniversarie' – may have been courtship poems to Ann More.[43] Among those which almost

---

40 R. C. Bald, *John Donne: A Life* (Oxford University Press, 1970), pp. 140–54.
41 See John Carey, *John Donne: Life, Mind, and Art* (New York: Oxford University Press, 1981), pp. 60–130.
42 *Biathanatos* (London, 1646) was published posthumously by Donne's son; *Pseudo-Martyr* (London, 1610); *Conclave Ignatii* [London,1611]; *Ignatius his Conclave* (London, 1611).
43 Arthur F. Marotti, *John Donne: Coterie Poet* (Madison: University of Wisconsin Press, 1986), pp. 44–178.

certainly belong to the difficult early years of his marriage are 'The Sunne Rising' and 'The Canonization', which locate the speaker away from London and court life; they seem to address a male audience and argue – perhaps too vociferously – that the world is well lost for love. Certain of the valedictions – 'Of the Book', 'Of Weeping' and especially 'A Valediction: forbidding Mourning' – may have been addressed to Ann on an occasion of parting, either in 1605 or 1611, offering assurances, answering fears and insisting that love will conquer absence. Most of Donne's love poems, whether witty or serious, whether they play off Ovid (as in 'The Indifferent'), or overturn Petrarch (as in 'The Funerall' and 'The Relique') or revise Neoplatonic love theory to exalt sexual union as essential to the union of souls (as in 'The Extasie'), are marked by distinguishing stylistic features that define a new path for the English love lyric. These include complex, witty argument, a dramatised speaker and scene, learned and often abstruse imagery, colloquial and sometimes unmelodic verse, and surprising conceits that often (as in 'The Canonization') conflate or transpose the spheres of human love and religion into one another. Several of Donne's 'Holy Sonnets', also written in the Mitcham years, make comparable transpositions.

While living at Mitcham, Donne was a frequent guest at Twickenham. He depended on the Countess of Bedford as a patron but he also exchanged verses with her as a member of her coterie, on one occasion complimenting her poems as excellent exercises on an 'ill' subject.[44] Donne's 'Twick'nam Garden' – an exaggerated Petrarchan lament in which the sighing speaker bemoans his mistress's cruelty in the 'paradise' of the Countess's garden – probably belongs to some such game of poetic exchanges on conventional love themes. 'Aire and Angels', 'The Feaver' and 'The Funerall' may also have been written for such occasions.[45] The title of 'A Nocturnall upon S. Lucies Day', in which the speaker imagines his reduction to the 'quintessence of nothingness', suggests that it was written for Lucy Bedford. Donne also addressed six verse letters to the Countess and wrote funeral elegies for her friends Lady Markham and Cecilia Bulstrode and for her brother John Harington. His first elegy for Bulstrode recants the defiance of his 'Death be not Proud' sonnet, but almost elides Bulstrode herself in portraying the whole world as a universe of death. The Countess wrote an elegy in response and implicit reproof (her single surviving poem), arguing that the death of the just, like Bulstrode, is a summons from God, not from Death. Donne's second elegy for Bulstrode appears to correct the first in the light

---

44 *The Life and Letters of John Donne*, ed. Edmund Gosse, 2 vols. (London: Heinemann, 1899) 1:217–18. The letter probably dates from 1609 but her poems are not extant.
45 See Marotti, *John Donne: Coterie Poet*, p. 211.

of that poem, focusing now on her friends' sorrow and Bulstrode's worth.[46]
Donne's many verse letters and funeral elegies, and chiefly those for the Countess, transformed the poem of praise from conventional hyperbolic compliment
or quasi-Petrarchan adulation into audaciously witty, outrageously hyperbolic,
logically contorted, but also serious, metaphysical inquiry. These poems display the strains of courtiership as Donne strives to assert his own worth before
the Countess and other powerful women patrons, even as he offers to meditate
on them as images of God and as fit subjects through which to explore some
general proposition about virtue, or religion, or death or sorrow.[47]

The *Anniversaries*, Donne's most elaborate poems in this vein and virtually
his only poems published in his lifetime, were produced in tribute to the young
daughter of Sir Robert Drury, who died in December 1610, just before her fifteenth birthday. Donne evidently presented his 'Funerall Elegie' to Sir Robert
shortly after Elizabeth's death, and by it gained Drury's settled patronage and
an invitation to accompany him for a period of travel and residence in Europe
in 1611–12. The *First Anniversarie: An Anatomy of the World* (1611) was written
and published before they left; the *Second Anniversarie: Of the Progres of the Soule*
was written in Amiens, France, and the three poems were published together in
1612. The subtitle of the *Anatomy* designates the 'Untimely Death' of the young
and innocent Elizabeth as an 'Occasion' to explore 'the Frailty and the Decay
of this whole World'.[48] Its speaker assumes the role of an anatomist displaying
all the corruptions in man the microcosm and in the entire cosmos that began
with the Fall and have steadily worsened. In the *Progres of the Soule* the speaker
offers to meditate on what he now terms the girl's 'Religious Death', to explore
a new theme, the comparative state of the regenerate soul in this world and in
the next.[49] The extravagant hyperbole praising the young girl as counter to all
the world's corruption serves as patronage verse and also as a vehicle for some
stunning poetic passages, among them a description of the impact of the new
philosophy and science as evidence of the approaching dissolution into chaos
of both the physical world and society: ''Tis all in pieces, all cohaerence gone'.[50]
Another portrays the soul's trajectory through the heavens, joyfully escaping
all the physical and social incommodities of earthly life.[51] Upon his return from

46 Donne's elegies for Bulstrode are in *John Donne, The Epithalamions, Anniversaries, and Epicedes*,
    ed. W. Milgate (Oxford: Clarendon Press, 1978), pp. 59–63; the Countess's elegy is also in
    that volume, Appendix B, pp. 236–7.
47 See Barbara K. Lewalski, *Donne's Anniversaries and the Poetry of Praise: The Creation of a
    Symbolic Mode* (Princeton University Press, 1973), pp. 42–70.
48 *The Epithalamions, Anniversaries*, ed. Milgate, p. 20.
49 *Ibid.*, p. 39.   50 *Anatomy of the World*, line 213, in *ibid.*, p. 28.
51 *Progres of the Soule*, lines 179–218, in *The Epithalamions, Anniversaries*, ed. Milgate.

France, Donne moved with his family to a house belonging to Sir Robert in Drury Lane, where he lived until he became Dean of St Paul's in 1621.

Households of the lesser gentry or the bourgeoisie also provided sites for and stimuli to literary production. Several marriage manuals or advice books, mostly by Puritan clerics, undertook to define the institution of marriage; the hierarchical relationship between the sexes; the specific spheres and duties of husband, wife, children and servants within the family; and the analogy of household and commonwealth, with the *paterfamilias* standing in the place of the King in the state and God in the universe. The often-reprinted *Godlie Forme of Householde Government* (1598) by Robert Cleaver, revised in 1612 by John Dod, details the duties of all household members, emphasising the parallel between family and state and describing the household as 'a little common-wealth' where the father 'is not only a ruler, but a King, and Lord of all'.[52] William Whateley's *Bride-Bush* (1616) underscores the separate spheres of men and women: 'He without doores, she within, he abroad, she at home.'[53] William Gouge in *Of Domesticall Duties* (1622) goes farther than some in insisting that women owe total obedience even to evil husbands, though he also emphasises women's intelligence and other merits, and the husbands' duty to win their compliance through gentle treatment.[54] More pragmatically, Gervase Markham in *The English Hus-wife* (1615) focuses on the duties of women in the middle and lower ranks to take an active part in cookery, the growing of herbs and the preparation of medicines for their families.[55] Thomas Fosset details the duties of householder and servants, emphasising that the former must take responsibility for the religious and moral education of their servants, and that servants must give unstinting obedience to both master and mistress unless commanded to something sinful.[56] In a treatise on the Ten Commandments (1604) John Dod emphasises the reciprocal duties of parents and children: parents should correct children physically in order to break their wills which are infected by original sin; mothers ought to breast-feed their own children (an uncommon practice among the middle and upper classes); and children owe both parents absolute obedience.[57]

Women also wrote books of domestic advice. *The Countess of Lincolnes Nurserie* (1622) was written to urge women to breast-feed, as a thing ordained by God

52 R.[obert] C.[leaver and John Dod], *A Godlie Forme of Householde Government: for the Ordering of Private Families, According to the Direction of Gods Word* (London, 1612), pp. 13–15.

53 William Whateley, *A Bride-Bush: or, A direction for married persons* (London, 1619), p. 84.

54 William Gouge, *Of Domesticall Duties: Eight Treatises* (London, 1622), p. 318.

55 Gervase Markham, *The English Hus-Wife, Contayning, the Inward and Outward Vertues which ought to be in a compleat Woman* (London, 1615).

56 Thomas Fosset, *The Servants Dutie. Or the Calling and Condition of Servants* (London, 1613).

57 John Dod, *A Plaine and Familiar Exposition of the Ten Commandements* (London, 1604).

and proper to their nature and biological function. She explains the urgency of her campaign as an effort to make up for the fact that she did not suckle her eighteen children, having been 'overruled by anothers authority' – presumably her husband's.[58] But most mothers' manuals were written by women of less exalted status, as deathbed advice to their own children. That often true circumstance served to counter the social strictures on female authorship by appealing to a mother's unquestioned right and authority to teach and testify in such circumstances. Elizabeth Grymston (c. 1563–1603) introduces herself as a dying Roman Catholic mother who also fears that her husband may not live long, and whose *Miscelanea, Meditations, Memoratives* (1604) is meant to teach her only son, Bernye, how to live a virtuous and religious life.[59] That book is a mixture of paraphrase and quotation (sometimes altered) from the Bible, the church fathers, and classical and contemporary poets, all assimilated to Grymston's persona as a dying mother and arranged according to the doctrine of each chapter; its popularity led to four editions before 1618. Elizabeth Jocelin (1595–1622), prophetically fearing death in childbirth, addressed her book, *The Mother's Legacie to her unborne Childe* (1624), to the child in her womb, claiming authority to write, despite her female defects, based on her 'motherly zeale' and right to teach that child.[60] The work, however, also reaches out to a larger audience: her suggestions concerning the child's education – clearly conflicted in the case of a daughter – are addressed to her husband, and a prefatory Approbation by Thomas Goad affirms the value of her book to others by stressing Jocelin's excellent education in the classics, history and literature. Much the most popular of these manuals, a brief, pocket-sized volume entitled *The Mother's Blessing* (1616) by an otherwise unknown Puritan, Dorothy Leigh, went through at least fifteen editions before 1640. The full title identifies it as a legacy of instruction from a now-dead mother to her three sons, written in part to fulfil the charge of their dead father to see to their education.[61] But in providing advice on a variety of topics, from children's names, to their education, to female chastity, to the loving partnership that should define her sons' relationship with their wives, she continually moves beyond her immediate audience, to address at times all women, at other times all the faithful. She thereby extends the role of mother-teacher in the household into the public sphere.

58 Elizabeth Clinton, Countess of Lincoln, *The Countess of Lincolnes Nurserie* (London, 1622), p. 16.
59 Elizabeth Grymston, *Miscelanea, Meditations, Memoratives* (London, 1604).
60 Elizabeth Jocelin, *The Mothers Legacie to her unborn Childe* (London, 1624), sig. B.
61 Dorothy Leigh, *The Mothers Blessing; or, the godly Counsaile of a Gentlewoman, not long since deceased, left behind her for her children. Containing many good exhortations and good admonitions profitable for all Parents, to leave as a Legacy for their Children* (London, 1616).

Several households provided sites for self-reflective writing. Owen Feltham (1602?–1668), who spent much of his adult life as Steward of the household of the Earl of Thomond at Great Billing, Northamptonshire, published in several editions a highly popular and often expanded collection of moral essays, entitled *Resolves, Divine, Morall, Politicall* (1623?).[62] Felltham claims to have written his essays, on such topics as 'Of Puritans', 'Of Preaching', 'Of Women', 'Of Idleness', 'Of Poets and Poetry', more for himself than for others, but he offers them also 'to the middle sort of people... to give the world some account of how he spent his vacant hours', and 'to show myself to the world'.[63] Whereas Bacon adopts an objective stance and an often aphoristic style for his essays, Felltham presents himself more discursively, as a likeable, tolerant, witty gentleman offering a picture of his mind in tones of genial reflection and conversational intimacy.

The Puritan emphasis on self-examination was a stimulus to the *Diary* produced by Lady Margaret Hoby (1571–1633), covering the years 1599–1606.[64] This wealthy Puritan gentlewoman, who owned a manor house and large estates near Hackness in North Yorkshire, was married first to William Devereux, brother of the Earl of Essex, then to Thomas Sidney, younger son of Robert Sidney of Penshurst, and finally (in 1596) to Sir Thomas Posthumous Hoby. Her *Diary* records the quotidian activities of the mistress of such a household: supervising house and gardens, paying bills, caring for the sick and injured, taking walks, writing letters, enduring illnesses, offering hospitality to neighbours. It also affords a picture of the religious practice in such a household: private prayers, attendance at church, reading of Scripture and other books, annotations of sermons, meditation and daily examination of conscience, readings by and discussions with the chaplain.

The young Puritan Rachel Speght (1597–16??), daughter of a London clergyman who evidently arranged for her good education and allowed her to write and publish, produced a remarkable 300-line autobiographical poem, 'The Dream', in the mode of medieval dream visions, which seems to rework the *Romance of the Rose*. Described by Speght as 'imaginarie in manner; reall in matter', 'The Dream' prefaces a longer though less interesting meditative poem, *Mortalities Memorandum* (1621), produced and published on the occasion of her

---

62 The first edition, *Resolves, Divine, Morall, Politicall* [London, 1623?] contained 100 short essays; the second and third, *Resolves, A Duple Century* (London, 1628) added a second century of poems. The eighth edition (1661), thoroughly revised, was dedicated to the Dowager Countess of Thomond.

63 *Resolves*, 1628, sigs. A 4r–v.

64 *The Private Life of an Elizabethan Lady: The Diary of Lady Margaret Hoby, 1599–1605*, ed. Joanna Moody (Stroud, Gloucestershire: Sutton, 1998).

mother's death and dedicated to her godmother, Mary Moundford.[65] In 'The Dream' Speght fictionalises the obstacles she encountered and the rapturous delight she experienced in her pursuit of learning. A series of allegorical personifications – e.g. Ignorance, Thought, Age, Experience, Dissuasion – represent the psychological and societal forces that hinder or assist her entry into the Garden of Erudition; and she puts into the mouth of Truth a strong defence of women's education. In this book she also reasserts her authorship of an earlier polemic tract defending women, *A Mouzell for Melastomus* (1617), her response to a rambling, boisterous, tonally confused but lively attack on women by Joseph Swetnam (1615).[66] This is the only contribution to the controversy touched off by Swetnam that appears under the author's own name and that is certainly by a woman. At the end of 'The Dream' Rachel laments that her education was terminated by some 'occurrence' (line 234) – perhaps her mother's illness, perhaps arrangements for her marriage in 1621, which apparently ended her writing career.

The Memorandum of Martha Moulsworth, Widow is an autobiographical poem by a gentlewoman whose sensibilities are clearly not Puritan. Carefully dated on her birthday, 10 November 1632, it presents in a wryly judicious tone a retrospective on her life (fifty-five couplets for her fifty-five years).[67] With attitudes sometimes reminiscent of Chaucer's Wife of Bath, Moulsworth (1577–16??) describes her enjoyment of a good social standing and satisfying sexual life with her three husbands, and especially the large amount of control over the household accorded her by the last one. Yet she also testifies to her delight in and intention to retain the new freedom she enjoys as a widow. But these satisfactions are tempered by an awareness of loss: because of disuse she has forgotten all the Latin she learned from her clergyman father, all her children have died, and she still grieves for her last husband. At one point she undertakes to speak for all women, urging that they receive a university education. This is a thoroughly radical proposal for the period, rendered more so by her claim that women would then outstrip men in intellectual achievements.

65 *Mortalities Memorandum, with A Dreame Prefixed, imaginarie in manner; reall in matter* (London, 1621); *The Polemics and Poems of Rachel Speght*, ed. Barbara K. Lewalski (New York: Oxford University Press, 1996), pp. 43–60.

66 [Joseph Swetnam] Tom Tel-troth, *The Araignment of Lewde, idle, froward and unconstant women: Or the vanitie of them, choose you whether* (London, 1615); Rachel Speght, *A Mouzell for Melastomus, the Cynicall Bayter of, and foule mouthed Barker against Evah's Sex* (London, 1617).

67 The manuscript is in the Beinecke Library, Yale, MS Osborn fol. 150; *'My Name Was Martha'*: *A Renaissance Woman's Autobiographical Poem*, ed. Robert C. Evans and Barbara Wiedemann (West Cornwall, CT: Locust Hill Press, 1993).

John Milton wrote some Latin poetry and prose orations (*Prolusiones*) while studying for his Baccalaureate and Master of Arts degrees at Christ's College, Cambridge (1625 to 1632), but many of his finest early poems were written at home, and at first in London where his father, a scrivener and amateur musician, kept a shop and apartments in Bread Street.[68] 'Elegy I', a Latin verse letter to his dearest friend Charles Diodati, protests a little too vigorously that he is greatly enjoying his temporary 'rustication' from Cambridge (probably in March 1626) as a result of some altercation with his tutor. In London, he reports, he enjoys girl-watching and leisure for poetry. He probably wrote his Ovidian Latin 'Elegy VII' the next spring: it reports an amorous springtime adventure in London, perhaps real, perhaps wholly literary, in which the speaker is smitten with the beauty of a young woman who vanishes before he approaches her, leaving him to savour his delightful misery. In January 1628, he wrote his first original English poem, a funeral ode for his sister's child, 'On the Death of a Fair Infant Dying of a Cough'.[69] It melds Chaucerian rime royal with the Spenserian stanza, apostrophising the infant as a maiden unwittingly destroyed by the bumbling caresses of Winter, who (rather like Donne's Elizabeth Drury) is made to embody the power of innocence to slake God's wrath for sin and drive off 'black perdition' and 'slaughtering pestilence' (lines 67–8). In December 1629, he addressed another Latin verse letter to Diodati from London, in which he associates styles of life and kinds of poetry. In urbane and playful tones, Milton associates Diodati's enjoyment of Christmastide festivities in the country with the light elegy, and his own abstemious life with epic or sacred subjects, such as the ode 'On the Morning of Christ's Nativity' which he was then writing.

That ode, Milton's first major poem, already displays elements that remain constants in his poetry: allusiveness, revision and mixture of genres, stunning originality, cosmic scope, a complex interplay of classical and Christian stories, prophetic voice and Reformist politics. The poem looks back to classical and Christian odes and literary hymns, and incorporates many Spenserian elements: allegorical personifications, the masque-like descent of the 'meek-eyd Peace' (line 46) and onomatopoeia, including a striking evocation of the music of the

---

68 For Milton's life, see William R. Parker, *Milton: A Biography*, 2 vols. (Oxford: Clarendon Press, 1968; rev. edn, ed. Gordon Campbell, 1996); Barbara K. Lewalski, *The Life of John Milton: A Critical Biography* (Oxford: Blackwell, 2000). Except where otherwise noted, Milton's early poems discussed here are quoted from *Poems of Mr John Milton, Both English and Latin* (London, 1645).

69 The poem was first published in and is quoted from Milton, *Poems, &c. Upon Several Occasions* (London, 1673); it is there dated by Milton to his seventeenth year (two years earlier), but the subject is almost certainly his two-year-old niece, buried on 22 January 1628.

spheres. As a pastoral it revises Virgil's 'Fourth Eclogue', celebrating the birth of the Messiah rather than the Roman consul Pollio's son as the herald of the true Golden Age. Its theme is the Incarnation and its meaning to nature, humankind and the entire cosmos, and it centres on the uneasy encounter of the natural order with this supernatural event, which leads both nature and the poet to imagine that the Millennial Golden Age is imminent. But then he is abruptly recalled to the nativity moment and to history. The final third of the poem is a long catalogue of the pagan gods expelled from their shrines, registering Puritan anxiety in 1629 about the 'papist idolatry' fostered by soon-to-be Archbishop Laud, and suggesting, by a kind of formal mimesis, the long and difficult process that must precede Christ's Second Coming: ridding humankind of all its idols, lovely as well as hideous.

When the University was closed by plague in the spring of 1630, Milton evidently lived and wrote in the London suburb of Hammersmith, to which his father had recently retired. That rural retreat may well have prompted a return to topics of springtime and love: a lighthearted English aubade with affinities to Elizabethan lyricists, 'On May Morning'; an English sonnet, 'O Nightingale', which recalls medieval debates between the nightingale as harbinger of love and the cuckoo as emblem of infidelity; and a Petrarchan mini-sonnet sequence in Italian. He affixed the date 1630 to his first published poem, the sixteen-line 'Epitaph on the admirable Dramatick Poet, W. Shakespeare', for the Second Folio of Shakespeare's plays (1632); the invitation to contribute probably came about through his father's associations in musical and theatrical circles. The poem reworks the conventional conceit that a poet's best monument is his works, making Shakespeare's readers his true 'live-long Monument' (line 8), turned to marble in wonder at his genius. Milton also claims the Bard as a model for himself, terming him 'my Shakespeare' and his poetry 'Delphic' (lines 1, 12).

Milton stated that he spent the summer of 1631 in a delightful village that greatly stimulated his intellectual and poetic growth – probably Hammersmith – and among its poetic fruits were probably the brilliantly inventive companion poems *L'Allegro* and *Il Penseroso*.[70] These poems explore the ideal pleasures appropriate to contrasting life styles – 'heart-easing Mirth' and 'divinest Melancholy'[71] – that a poet might choose, or might choose at different times, or in sequence. Milton is now so skilful with metrics that he can use the same verse form – a ten-line prelude with alternating lines of six and ten

70 He made the statement in *Prolusion VII*, his academic oration the following spring; *Complete Prose Works of John Milton*, ed. Don M. Wolfe *et al.*, 8 vols. (New Haven, CT: Yale University Press, 1953–82), 1:289.
71 *L'Allegro*, line 13; *Il Penseroso*, line 12.

syllables, followed by octosyllabic couplets – to produce wholly different tonal effects. In *L'Allegro* the quick short vowels, the monosyllables, the liquid consonants and the frequent trochaic rhythms trip over the tongue in a mimesis of youthful frolic. In *Il Penseroso* polysyllables, clusters of consonants and a liberal use of near-spondaic feet produce a deliberate and sombre tone. *L'Allegro* is a poem of youthful mirth, innocent joy, lighthearted pleasure and freedom from care, rendered through the activities and values of the pastoral mode. *Il Penseroso* celebrates Melancholy as the saturnine temperament that seeks solitude, the scholarly life and religious contemplation, evoking the topics and atmosphere of medieval romance. The title personages of both poems are ideal but exaggerated types, yet a progression is implied by the eight-line coda to *Il Penseroso* that disrupts the poems' parallelism. While *L'Allegro* portrays the life of youth as a cyclical round, *Il Penseroso* opens to the future, offering to lead, after 'long experience', to ecstatic vision, all-embracing scientific learning and prophetic poetry – 'something like Prophetic strain' (lines 173–4).

When Milton graduated as Master of Arts in 1632 he went to live with his parents at Hammersmith, undertaking for nearly six years a course of private study and writing. On or shortly before his twenty-fourth birthday he wrote an anxious sonnet that begins 'How soon hath Time the suttle theef of youth / Stoln on his wing my three and twentieth yeer', voicing profound psychological and spiritual anxiety about his belatedness in choosing a vocation. With the Laudian takeover of the church his earlier plans to become a minister seemed less and less viable, and no seventeenth-century gentleman could imagine making a career, much less a living, as a poet, unless he found settled patronage. About this time Milton also wrote three short odes on religious themes in complex metrical patterns, of which the finest is 'At a solemn Musick', an ecstatic praise of sacred vocal music and poetry.

Perhaps to attract patronage as tutor or secretary in a noble, soundly Protestant, household, Milton accepted a commission in 1632 to write an 'Entertainment' for the birthday of the Countess of Derby, erstwhile patron of Spenser and a long line of Protestant writers.[72] In that work, *Arcades*, Milton began to develop a stance towards art and recreation that repudiates the court aesthetics and rural sports fostered by King Charles and Queen Henrietta Maria, but also the wholesale denunciations of court masques, dramas, mixed dance and rural festivals by the rabid Puritan William Prynne.[73] Milton's entertainment

---

72 The commission probably came through the musician Henry Lawes, music master to the Countess's Egerton grandchildren and likely known to Milton through his father.

73 See Charles I, *The King's Majesty's declaration to his subjects concerning lawful sports to be used* (London, 1633); William Prynne, *Histrio-mastix* (London, 1633).

proposes to reclaim pastoral from the court, intimating the superiority of this noble Protestant lady and her household at Harewood over the Roman Catholic Queen. Here, visitors (the Countess's grandchildren and others) come in pastoral guise from the 'Arcadian' court to pay homage to a far superior rural queen of a better Arcadia, directed by Genius, who embodies the curative and harmony-producing powers of music and poetry.

Two years later (1634) Milton wrote *A Maske Presented at Ludlow Castle*, popularly known as *Comus*, for another soundly Protestant household, that of Sir John Egerton, Earl of Bridgewater, and son-in-law of the Countess of Derby, to celebrate his appointment as Lord Lieutenant of Wales and the border counties. The work builds brilliantly on the family occasion. The hinge of the plot is a journey by the Earl's fifteen-year-old daughter, Alice, and her two younger brothers to their father's house for a celebration, aided by an Attendant Spirit who is Lady Alice's music master, Henry Lawes. That journey, however, comes to figure the journey of life to a divine Father's house, as the young people become lost in the dark woods and the Lady is tempted and held captive by Comus – not the traditional belly god of drunkenness and gluttony but a suave seducer with the power and attractiveness of natural sensuality and of a contemporary cultural ideal. He presents these young aristocrats with the refined, dissolute, licentious Cavalier life style they must learn to resist,[74] as the Lady does through chastity and a vigorous defence of the right uses of natural goods.

Both in its acting version and in the longer published versions in 1637 and 1645,[75] Milton's masque undertakes to reform that genre, delivering a trenchant critique of the Caroline ethos mystified in such court masques as Thomas Carew's *Coelum Britannicum* (also 1634).[76] With his bestial rout Comus is made to figure on one level Cavalier licentiousness, Laudian ritual, the depravities of court masques and feasts, as well as the unruly holiday pastimes denounced by Prynne. In form, theme and spirit Milton's *Maske* projects Reformist religious and political values. The ideal masque world is Ludlow Castle, not the Stuart court, and it is attained through pilgrimage: it does not simply appear and dispel all discord, as is usual in court masques. Nor are monarchs the agents of cure and renewal. That role belongs to the nymph Sabrina who is, at one level, an instrument of divine grace from the Welsh countryside; her power is necessary

---

74 See Cedric C. Brown, *Milton's Aristocratic Entertainments* (Cambridge University Press, 1985), pp. 57–77.

75 For the various texts see *John Milton: A Maske. The Earlier Versions*, ed. S. E. Sprott (University of Toronto Press, 1973).

76 Thomas Carew, *Coelum Britannicum*, in *Poems* (London, 1640). Also see Chapter 16, p. 510 above.

to release the Lady, who, as a fallen human, cannot attain the father's house by her own efforts. Evil is conceived in Protestant, not courtly Platonic terms: at the end of the masque the dark wood is still dangerous to pass through and Comus is neither conquered, nor transformed nor reconciled. Comus himself is a court masquer who casts 'dazzling Spells' that 'cheate the eye with bleare illusion' (154–5), and the court scene that appears after the dark wood is Comus's own residence, not the locus of virtue and grace that a masque audience would expect. Comus exhibits the seductive power of false rhetoric, against which is posed the better art displayed in the songs and poetry of the Lady, the Attendant Spirit and Sabrina, and especially in the masque dances at Ludlow Castle. That better art, nurtured in the virtuous households of the sound Protestant aristocracy, helps define Milton's principle of chastity – not ascetic denial but the principle that orders sensuality, pleasure and love, holding nature, human nature and art to their right uses.

Sometime in 1636 the Milton family moved to Horton, a peaceful Berkshire village, where Milton continued his studies, prepared *Comus* for publication and wrote his great funeral elegy, *Lycidas*, to commemorate his college associate Edward King, drowned in a shipwreck en route to Ireland. *Lycidas* was published in a Cambridge memorial volume early in 1638.[77] Though King was not a close friend, the sudden death of this young man, three years Milton's junior and likewise committed to serving the church and writing poetry, forced Milton to confront his deepest anxieties about unfulfilled vocation, early death, belatedness and the worth of poetry. Also, the death of Milton's own mother in 1637 and the arrival of the plague in Horton that year surely intensified his sense of vulnerability even in his own rural household. Accordingly, *Lycidas* contains intense feeling fused with its consummate art. Virtually every line alludes to some other classical or Renaissance pastoral funeral elegy, yet no other funeral poem has the scope, dimension, poignancy and power of this one. The verse form – chiefly iambic pentameter with occasional short lines and a very irrgular rhyme scheme – builds tension, denies surface smoothness and prevents facile resolutions. Milton calls upon the rich symbolic resources of pastoral to associate his shepherd speaker with several roles: poet, minister or pastor of a flock, and Biblical prophet called to that role from tending sheep. As he develops some familiar topics of pastoral elegy, the Miltonic 'uncouth swain' again and again evokes the pastoral vision of the harmony of nature and humankind, then dramatises its collapse as it proves unable to supply satisfactory answers to hard questions about poetic fame, or the loss of good men

---

77 *Lycidas*, in *Justa Edouardo King naufrago* (Cambridge, 1638).

from the ministry that badly needs them, or the terror of the drowned body weltering in the monstrous deep. The death of Lycidas/King seems to demonstrate the futility of exceptional talent, lofty ambition and noble ideals, and to show human life and nature alike given over to meaningless chaos. In Saint Peter's fierce tirade the poem also sounds some leitmotifs of Milton's Reformist politics: the dangers posed by a corrupt clergy and church, the menace of Rome, and the adumbrations of apocalypse. At length the swain catches up the various signs of resurrection in nature and in myth into a vision of Lycidas enjoying the perfected pastoral of heaven, and after that vision he is able take up his own pastoral roles in this world – 'warbling his Doric lay' and donning the prophet's 'mantle blue' (lines 189, 192).[78]

At about this time, probably, Milton also wrote *Ad Patrem*, a sophisticated Latin verse epistle that is in part a praise of his father for fostering his education and self-education, in part a defence of poetry against his father's supposed disparagement of it, and in part an implicit persuasion to that father to accept and continue to support him in his now openly declared vocation as poet. Milton's insistence that he owes his development as a poet to natural abilities, a divine call, the educational opportunities and support afforded by his father, and his own self-directed study, points away from more public institutions – court, church, noble patrons, great estates – to the private household as the seed-bed for poetry. Milton's later works also register the increasing importance and centrality to the social order of the nuclear family and household. After he left his father's house Milton sent forth from his own private households his polemic advice to Parliaments and statesmen on the great issues of church and state. In *Areopagitica* he imagines reformation being best advanced by scholars reading and writing independently in their own studies and publishing freely; and in his divorce tracts he insists that no reformation in church or state can succeed unless liberty is first restored to the household by allowing miserable, incompatible spouses to divorce. Two decades later he will cast as protagonists of England's greatest epic a domestic couple tending their garden.

78 Joseph A. Wittreich, Jr, *Visionary Poetics: Milton's Tradition and his Legacy* (San Marino: Huntington Library, 1979), pp. 142–3.

5

THE CIVIL WAR AND COMMONWEALTH ERA

Chapter 21

LITERATURE AND NATIONAL
IDENTITY

DEREK HIRST

In the later 1630s, as he was writing *Religio Medici*, Sir Thomas Browne proclaimed England's transcendent nature: 'All places, all ayres make unto me one
Country; I am in *England*, every where, and under any meridian.' Such relaxed
confidence in what England stood for, and its ability to overcome local distractions and inconveniences, may seem characteristic of the Caroline peace; it
surely became untenable by the time Browne's book was published, in 1643.[1]
By then, everything England stood for – its past, its present, its future, not to
mention the geopolitical implications of its location among the islands at the
edge of the European land-mass – was a matter of war. If Browne and his England were somehow immanent, transcending the world, it was not long before
John Milton sharply raised the stakes, only to seem to throw over the game altogether shortly thereafter. To Milton at the start of England's troubles, the nation
as nation had deep apocalyptic purpose. In *Of Reformation* (1641), he prophesied
that Christ would 'judge the severall Kingdomes of the World, . . . distributing
Nationall Honours and *Rewards* to Religious and just *Common-wealths*'. Further,
he proclaimed the next year in *The Reason of Church-Government*, the nation was
also the divinely ordained agent of cultural regeneration, for 'all the kinds of
Lyrick poesy, . . . the inspired guift of God rarely bestow'd . . . , [are instituted]
in every Nation: and are of power beside the office of a pulpit to imbreed and
cherish in a great people the seeds of vertu, and publick civility'.[2] Yet in just
over a decade, in his *Second Defence of the English People* (1654), Milton reduced
England to a few against a largely hostile world,[3] and soon after – if we accept

---

1 Sir Thomas Browne, *Religio Medici* (1643), in *The Major Works*, ed. C. A. Patrides (London:
  Penguin Books, 1977), p. 133. Notwithstanding Browne's determined eirenicism, his was not
  an unpolemical claim even in the later 1630s, when some disaffected Puritans were looking
  to North America and others were in contact with the Scots.
2 John Milton, *Complete Prose Works* [hereafter *CPW*], gen. ed. Don M. Wolfe, 8 vols. (New
  Haven, CT: Yale University Press, 1953–82),1:616, 816.
3 The isolation of the cause of virtue was as great within England as without. In Europe, Milton
  found Queen Christina of Sweden to celebrate, and paid warm tribute to his reception years

that he began work on his great epic sometime in the later 1650s – came to the conviction that the real drama lay within the human heart.[4] Browne in the later 1630s thought himself somehow the emblem and repository of England; Milton's only apparently similar words of 1666 – 'One's *patria* is wherever it is well with him'[5] – are a measure of the distance travelled. As in so much else, Milton's writings signalled major innovations in the way the nation's identity was imagined and written out across a revolution.

The upheavals of the years between 1640 and 1660 occasioned intense debate over the direction of the nation and the meaning of its experience. These were decades of wars, of civil wars, of revolutions, which sorely tested political allegiances; they were also decades in which questions of identity were central to every writer, and every genre. The omnipresence of such concerns provides impressive testimony of the depth and extent of cultural and intellectual crisis. Yet how could it have been otherwise? By their very nature, civil wars and revolutions are struggles for control over collective identity. But England's were something more: to borrow from the opening words of Lucan, the poet-historian of the Roman republic's civil wars – whose newly translated work inspired many in mid seventeenth-century England – these were 'wars more than civil'.[6] Perspectives on the matter of identity therefore shifted. Questions about the meaning of community were inevitable when Englishmen were killing one another, dismantling the monarchy that had figured centrally in almost a millennium of England's history, and fragmenting the national church. Questions of a different kind arose, however, when English partisans looked for aid not just to France, to Spain, to the Netherlands, to Germany, to Sweden, but also to the other British kingdoms, Scotland and Ireland. Those questions became more urgent, and more bitter, when English soil and bodies were trampled upon by Scots and Irish forces. Then when England's sword was in turn wielded, increasingly successfully, against Ireland and Scotland, and then against the Dutch and the Spanish, and in the Mediterranean, the Caribbean, the Baltic, still other questions came to the fore. Partisanship, religious intolerance, xenophobia, empire, and indeed the beginnings of a reaction against all these, inflected a discourse of nationhood that was fast spawning

ago in Florence; in England, he saw a dwindling band of heroes, and the possibility that there might survive only the memory of the lone prophet, John Milton. *CPW*, 4:556–7, 604–6, 609, 615–17, 636–9, 671–86.
4 John Aubrey reported that Milton commenced writing *Paradise Lost* '2 yeares before the King came-in', in other words, sometime in 1658. John Aubrey, *Brief Lives* (London: Penguin Books, 1960), p. 274.
5 Letter to Peter Heimbach, *CPW* 8:4 (I am grateful to David Loewenstein for this reference). Note that Milton did not say 'England is...'
6 *Lucan's Pharsalia*, trans. Thomas May, 2nd edn, rev. (London, 1631), sig. A1.

new terms. One of the most potent of these was generated by developments far from the battlefield. The fast-expanding transoceanic trade routes, around which the Navigation Acts of 1650–1 attempted to build a quasi-imperial framework, were beginning to bring in their first material returns. To a nation that treasured memories of Sir Francis Drake, empire was a familiar – and, to most, an attractive – category; but in these years, poets like Denham and Waller found a more surprising theme in commerce, and the plenty it brought.[7] Milton's attacks on luxury in *Paradise Lost* suggest less his rediscovery of the Seven Deadly Sins from some medieval morality play than his acute sensitivity to the possibilities, and the dangers, of a dawning commercial age.[8]

If the ways people wrote about the nation and its identity shifted in this time of upheaval, there was one constant. Partisanship, whether crude or sophisticated, was everywhere. Both sides sought to exclude their enemies from the national community through calumny and invective; the invective did not die down with the fighting, though it lessened in intensity as many defeated Royalists withdrew into introspective pursuits. Much of that polemical energy was expended on defining and controlling England's religious identity, and consigning the foe to the outer darkness, or worse. The period used to be called 'the Puritan Revolution', and, while that term has gone out of scholarly fashion, it did serve to register the force that brought Charles I to the scaffold on 30 January 1649. The conviction of so many godly men and women that England was a second Israel found expression not only in Milton's antiepiscopal tracts of 1641–2 but in many works that had greater influence on contemporary readers. The most important of these was undoubtedly Stephen Marshall's sermon *Meroz Cursed* (1641), which he preached first to Parliament, and then to steadily widening audiences, to remind them of the sufferings God had inflicted on those who withheld their hands from the shedding of blood for his purposes.[9] If we are to look for writings that drove great events we must look here, to the familiar story of England as Israel, with its swelling crescendo in the 1640s and diminuendo in the following decade.[10] But that story was not

7 For evidence of Drake's currency, see Sir William Davenant's musical entertainments of 1658–9, *The History of Sir Francis Drake* and *The Cruelty of the Spaniards in Peru*. For the new economic possibilities in the 1650s, see Derek Hirst, 'Locating the 1650s in England's Seventeenth Century', *History* 81 (1996), 359–83.

8 See, for example, Satan's enrapturement with what seemed 'Odours from the spicie shoar / Of *Arabie* the blest.../ So entertained those odorous sweets the Fiend.' *Paradise Lost*, 4, lines 162–3, 166, in *The Complete Poetry of John Milton*, ed. John T. Shawcross, rev edn (New York: Anchor Books, 1977), p. 321.

9 Stephen Marshall, *Meroz Cursed* ([London], 1641).

10 Christopher Hill has addressed these issues at length; see in particular his *Antichrist in Seventeenth-Century England* (Oxford University Press, 1971).

written in a wholly partisan language. As we shall see, Royalists did not cede Israel to zealous Parliamentarians, nor was Israel the only model for England offered, even by Parliamentarians.

There were other stories of place. Rome provided the second great national history and source of exemplars, and though in the later seventeenth century interest in the Roman model grew in almost inverse relationship to a declining taste for Israelite examples,[11] the mid-century traffic between the two, Israel and Rome, was more complex, and often more contestatory. Perhaps the most striking address to the two models for a polity is Andrew Marvell's *The First Anniversary of Government under the Lord Protector* (1655), a poem that seems almost programmatically to survey classical and apocalyptic frames for England, and finds them all wanting. Others were readier to build forthwith, and Thomas Hobbes spent many pages of *Leviathan* (1651) denying the applicability of both visions of a nation to a commonwealth whose agonies he sought to resolve by building out from an irreducible core, the fear-ridden individual absent all prior allegiances.

The other geography of the imagination, no less complex or contested, was a modern one. It involved matters of territory and allegiance: Was the nation which so many texts sought to express the old political and administrative unit of England, or was England part of a larger polity? Peter Heylyn, a dispossessed churchman trying to earn his bread by gratifying the burgeoning demand for travel books and compendia, suggested lightheartedly in his encyclopaedic *Cosmographie* (1652) that no talk about 'Great Britaine' was needed, since it was his readers' home and they therefore knew it well enough already.[12] Taking our cue from such confidence, we might think that Milton and all those others who addressed the meaning of nationhood repeatedly through the period and expressed such profound ambivalence about its geographic extent – whether England or Britain – had an interest in exploiting the ancient ambiguity as circumstances suggested.

Polemical exploitation certainly cannot be discounted, yet there were deeper issues. The ancestral migrations of the various peoples of the islands – the outlines of which were familiar to many seventeenth-century writers – meant that apparent confusion might not be mere disingenuousness. When and what

---

11 Steven Zwicker, 'England, Israel and the Triumph of Roman Virtue', in *Millenarianism and Messianism in English Literature and Thought, 1650–1800*, ed. Richard H. Popkin (Leiden: Brill, 1988), pp. 37–64.
12 He did not take his own advice; no better founded was his confidence that the English and the Scots, though old enemies, were now 'one onely Nation'. Peter Heylyn, *Cosmographie in four bookes* (London, 1652), pp. 257, 299.

was Britain? When and what was England? These were legitimate questions. Some writers sought answers by almost unthinkingly associating the land with its present occupants, using possession of the land to shape identification of a people. Although Sir Robert Filmer's *Patriarcha* was written before the Civil Wars, and was not published until 1680, it is worth quoting for its suggestive, and surely unintended, slippage into the first person plural: 'When Julius Caesar landed [in Britannia] he found four kings in Kent..., and the British names of Danmonii, Durotriges... and the rest are plentiful testimonies of the several kingdoms of the Britons when the Romans became our lords. As soon as ever the Romans left us, the Saxons divided us into seven kingdoms.'[13] Milton showed the same capacity for retrospective identification with the land and its people, however ancient, and in his *Observations upon the Articles of Peace* (1649) condemned the conduct of the Scots in Ulster, to which they had been 'neighbourly admitted... not as the *Saxons*, by merit of thir warfare against our [i.e. the ancient Britons'] enemies'. Pre-modern analysts were as capable as we of recognising such slippage. John Hare, the author of *Saint Edward's Ghost, or Anti-Normanisme*, a radical tract of 1647, noted that his Saxon heroes' claims to England rested on their conceit that 'they had their Originall and Spring (like the Gyants, Myrmidons, Cadmus his new men, and other warlick breeds) from the soyle and earth under them, as which was never known otherwise then appropriate to their name and possession'.[14] So easily were myths made.

Such myths had consequences. In the radicals' canon in particular, the English and the British represented different values. Thanks to the *Germania* of the great Roman historian Tacitus, the Germanic peoples were a byword for sturdy independence, incorruptibility, valour. The English, undoubtedly Germanic as they were, could be celebrated for their stirring past by those minded to praise them for their struggles against tyranny in the 1640s. Yet when they converted to Christianity the ancient English had admitted agents of the Pope into their land, whereas the ancient Britons – whom the English pushed northwards and westwards – had maintained a non-papalist Christianity despite their military weakness. The British therefore provided precedents and exemplars in pure churchmanship. Milton was not alone in ambivalence towards progenitors whose heroism took such different forms. The varying degrees of respect for the English shown in, for example, the *History of Britain* and the *First Defence of the English People* can be matched in the writings of the republican lawyer

13 Sir Robert Filmer, *Patriarcha and Other Writings*, ed. J. Sommerville (Cambridge University Press, 1991), p. 53.
14 *CPW*, 3:333; John Hare, *Saint Edward's Ghost, or Anti-Normanisme* (London, 1647), p. 4.

and Parliament man Nathaniel Bacon when his concerns similarly swung from religious to political liberty.[15]

All of the stories told about a national community reflect at least tension, more usually contestation. The Civil Wars were fought by forces each claiming to represent or to embody England, and those claims were of course liable to polemical appropriation, and to challenge. The vulnerability of Parliament's representational claims, when the large majority of the nation could not vote, was all too apparent. The claim to embody, to include the whole nation in one body politic, underwent a more interesting transformation. Powerfully deployed – but by no means possessed[16] – by the King up to and through his trial, it brought not just the brutal retort of regicide but also the visceral response of John Milton's *Eikonoklastes* (1649). From the shock of dismemberment, the ideal of the body politic that had long sustained and expressed the English polity never fully recovered. The sundering of that body elicited Hobbes's polity, so carefully defined and structured in *Leviathan*, with its mathematical reduction of collectivity to the individual who transfers his will to the sovereign. Though few accepted Hobbes's bleak judgement that true political community was no more, there were many whom the pains of war and revolution drove to a not dissimilar conclusion: that the public drama was not an individual's concern. So while in 1640 the ideal of the inclusive body politic dominated most discourse, by 1660 there was a growing readiness to imagine a denatured public world, outside of which the individual found private consolations.

Travails of a kingdom

The period opened with a fierce challenge to the nation's geopolitical frame: the Scottish National Covenant of 1638, which precipitated the Bishops' Wars of 1639–40, and thus England's crisis. The literary record of the 1640s opened at court with a dramatic assertion of a supra-national identity centring in the King. Sir William Davenant's masque, *Salmacida Spolia*, was performed in January 1640. The court masques of the Stuarts had always ventured far from conventional English rhetorics of nationhood.[17] Such early masques of the

---

15 See the discussion of Bacon's *Historical and Political Discourse of the Laws and Government of England* (1647) in Colin Kidd, *British Identities before Nationalism* (Cambridge University Press, 1999), pp. 87–8, 103–4.

16 Perhaps the most graphic deployment of the body politic argument as a whole came in Thomas Edwards's *Gangraena* (London, 1646).

17 See Richard Helgerson, *Forms of Nationhood* (University of Chicago Press, 1992), for a powerful account of the construction of a national myth in the years around the turn of the century.

Scoto-English James VI and I as *The Irish Masque* swiftly proclaimed the British dimension of the new dynasty's rule;[18] the accession of the thoroughly anglicised Charles I made little difference, and the court was soon asked to admire idealisations of British virtue and imperial potency in masques like *Coelum Britannicum* and *Britannia Triumphans*.[19] Davenant's 1640 masque was therefore following a distinguished tradition in suggesting the extent and complexities of the King's rule.[20] Although it extenuated the discomforts of a present in which political challenge was building north of the Scottish border, the masque offered little indulgence to English solipsism. Willing subjects could be found among the better sort of all three kingdoms, but – and here Davenant offered one more episode in a story as old as Herodotus, of challenge to the arable heartland from the regions beyond – Charles's lands were troubled by wild tribesmen from the mountains. Masquers held out ideals to the spectators' view, but Davenant's anti-masquers also enacted a disturbing image of England's place in an unstable British world.

Many critics of recent royal policies needed little invitation to set their experiences and hopes in a wider context. It had been the King who turned his back on involvement in Europe's wars of religion in the 1630s, whose poets had celebrated England's 'halcyon days' of peace, and whose churchmen had insisted on a reverend English self-sufficiency. Despite the determined patriotism of John Foxe's *Acts and Monuments*, the so-called 'Book of Martyrs', the godly sense of the Christian community had never been confined to national churches. Even the most inveterate Scottish Presbyterian nourished hopes of exporting the true kirk, while in England the tradition of extolling the pattern of the 'best reformed churches' in Scotland and across the Channel was well established.[21] Had Charles chosen to recast his policies and his commitments in 1640, late though that was in the Thirty Years' War, many Englishmen

18 Martin Butler, 'The Invention of Britain and the Early Stuart Masque', in *The Stuart Court and Europe*, ed. R. M. Smuts (Cambridge University Press, 1996), pp. 65–85; and see the arguments of Leah Marcus in Chapter 16, above.
19 There is a significant contrast here with the vision of an English church held forth so insistently by Charles and Archbishop Laud. Such ambiguities in the Crown's claims before the onset of trouble indicate how much the developments in the 1640s represented not so much new departures as the elaboration of lines of thought that were already in place. For Charles's and Laud's ecclesiastical vision, see Julian Davies, *The Caroline Captivity of the Church* (Oxford: Clarendon Press, 1992), and Peter Lake, 'The Laudian Style', in *The Early Stuart Church, 1603–1642*, ed. Kenneth Fincham (Stanford University Press, 1993), pp. 161–86.
20 Whatever the English application of its performance: see Martin Butler, 'Politics and the Masque: *Salmacida Spolia*', in *Literature and the English Civil War*, ed. Thomas Healy and Jonathan Sawday (Cambridge University Press, 1990), pp. 59–74.
21 See the essays in John Morrill (ed.), *The Scottish National Covenant in its British Context* (University of Edinburgh Press, 1990).

would have eagerly supported a British king who sought to project and protect a forward Protestantism in Europe. One barometer was provided by the very popular poet and future Parliamentarian, George Wither, who addressed his *Haleluiah, or Britans [sic] Second Remembrancer* (1641), 'To the thrice Honorable, the high Courts of Parliament, now assembled, in the Triple-Empire of the British-Isles'.[22] Britishness was not a label to be discounted, and it was no accident that the leading Parliamentarian newsbook during the first English Civil War was entitled *Mercurius Britanicus*.

John Milton provides a measure of the complexities of identity in the world in which Davenant's masque was imagined and performed, and also of how changing political realities could change a writer's sense of who he was and was not. In his anti-episcopal tracts the young poet and pamphleteer poured encomia on England, 'the first Restorer of buried Truth', and 'a right pious, right honest, and right hardy nation'.[23] Although he showed himself in his 1648–9 writings, *Observations upon the Articles of Peace* and *The Tenure of Kings and Magistrates*, capable of deep contempt for intolerant Scots Presbyterians, in 1641 Milton saw such closeness between 'ENGLAND and SCOTLAND dearest Brothers both in Nature, and in CHRIST', that all the wiles of the popish enemy would be needed to dissolve it.[24] 'Go on both hand in hand O NATIONS never to be disunited, be the *Praise* and the *Heroick Song* of all POSTERITY': the fervour of Milton's prayer in *Of Reformation* is striking, in view of what was to come.[25] But Milton was not about to cede equality, though he claimed fraternity and liberty. Instead, he practised the comfortable elision of England and Britain that inhabitants of England from Shakespeare's John of Gaunt forward have managed so regularly, and that has so often infuriated England's British neighbours. In *Of Reformation's* closing pages he celebrated God's English dispensations, that 'didst build up this *Britannick Empire* to a glorious and enviable heighth with all her Daughter Ilands about her'; similarly, in *Areopagitica* (1644), he juxtaposed too neatly praise for the English as 'a Nation not slow', with proud acknowledgement of the Roman governor Agricola's preference for 'the naturall wits of Britain' over the French.[26] Yet though he repeatedly declared himself 'John Milton Englishman', he was no simple little-Englander. In 1643, in

---

22 Sig. A2. Wither's text calls for religious solidarity with the Scots in the greater cause.
23 It was in fact to 'this Iland' that Milton gave credit for finding buried truth, but he had just made clear he was talking of England: *CPW*, 1:525–6, 797.
24 *CPW*, 1:596. For further discussion of Milton's views of Ireland, see Willy Maley, 'Milton and the "complication of interests" in Early Modern Ireland', in *Milton and the Imperial Vision*, ed. Balachandra Rajan and Elizabeth Sauer (Pittsburgh: Duquesne University Press, 1999), pp. 155–68.
25 *CPW*, 1:597.   26 *CPW*, 1:614, 2:552.

The Doctrine and Discipline of Divorce, he showed a salutary awareness – rare among his contemporaries – that England was entitled to 'scarce...a third part of the Brittish name'.[27]

The British identifications that came so naturally to Milton were also part of the booksellers' stock-in-trade. Along with Bibles and catechisms, almanacs were the most widely distributed printed works of the seventeenth century. They proliferated through every decade, and they ran into millions of copies. Almanacs' staples may have been seasonal advice and astrological predictions, but along with the stars they increasingly carried texts of nationhood: chronologies, regnal lists and a constant chorus of the nation's dimensions and rhythms – catalogues of the distances on the roads to London, evocative lists of all the May fairs throughout England and Wales, all the Midsummer fairs and so on. Ordinary consumers might perhaps be able to admire one of the quality maps of England pulled from Speed or Saxton if they had occasion to do business in a fashionable inn. Even the illiterate, gazing with their literate neighbours on the almanacs – those compendia, those troves of essential information and advice – could form a basic idea of the dimensions of England, of Scotland too, and at least of Ireland's location. The geography – indeed, the political geography – of the nation was there to see. And the almanacs schooled readers in a British frame, since, from at least the time of the 1607 debates on Anglo-Scottish Union, almanacs had emphatically declared their Britishness. Title pages in increasing numbers claimed the relevance of predictions to 'all' or 'the most part of Great Britaine', while tide-tables ranged from Aberdeen and Dunbar to Great Yarmouth and Plymouth. What had been a steady current in 1640 became a torrent. Readers of almanacs could have little doubt that climatically, chronologically, astrologically at least, they were part of the British Isles.[28]

The broader printed record helps fill in the outline presented in the almanacs. As partisanship intensified between 1640 and 1643, title-page appeals to English ways roughly doubled.[29] Rising authorial and political passions seem to

<hr />

27 *CPW*, 2:231. That rare recognition of cartographic realities did not, of course, prevent Milton joining almost all his English compatriots in steadfastly assuming – whether in 1641, 1643 or 1648 – England's proprietary right in Ireland.

28 But not necessarily politically: see, for example, Thomas White, *Almanacke and Prognostication* (London, 1642). For fuller discussion of almanacs, see Bernard S. Capp, *English Almanacs, 1500–1800. Astrology and the Popular Press* (London: Faber, 1979).

29 The 'WorldCat' catalogue of the OCLC data-base – by no means a perfect index, but broadranging, compendious and fairly easily manipulated – lists some 8,000 entries for works (including multiple editions) published in English between 1640 and 1643. In 1640, 7% of entries displayed the word 'England' somewhere on their title pages, 11% in 1641 and 12% in 1642; by 1643 the proportion had increased to 15%.

have found a response at the bookstalls, where money and attention were clearly being invested in explicitly national matters, though the marketplace was a very competitive one, in which the number of publications of all kinds was soaring. To judge once again by the title pages, 'Britain' or 'British' issues seem to have held much less appeal; but in fact almost half of all the title-page salutes to England in 1640–3 coupled England with Scotland and/or Ireland, or with New England. In these years, the many tracts that touted Scottish sufferings in, or Irish practices against, a common cause were joined by a significant number urging England to model itself on some transatlantic city on a hill. In other words, gestures towards England alone were nearly matched by recognition of England's membership of a larger whole, whether geopolitical or spiritual. The court poets who had invoked a British identity in the 1630s could now hear oddly distorted echoes from the other side of a fast-emerging partisan divide.

They also heard angry assertions of an English virtue centred in English liberty. The challenges of 1640–1 to the King's government and practices of the 1630s were mounted in the press as well as in Parliament, and the cases of Ship Money, and of the decade's assorted martyrs, were soon the stuff of broadside and pamphlet.[30] The claim advanced in the famous *Second Part* of Sir Edward Coke's *Institutes of the Laws of England* (1642) had already been declared to a wider audience on many fronts, perhaps above all in the outpourings surrounding the 1641 trial of the Earl of Strafford: England was defined by the fabric of its laws.[31] That story of fortunate exceptionalism had long been a-writing, but it gained an urgent polemical edge as Parliament men and their publicist allies strove to protect common law and subjects' rights against prerogative and popery. At an increasing rate, printed parliamentary speeches, genuine and fictive, wove together a disjointed but powerful narrative of those rights and institutions that had denominated England in history.[32]

If there was to be a debate over the meaning of the nation, Charles's natural supporters were slow to develop a new script. In some quarters the halcyon 1630s lingered for a while. Neither Thomas Carew's *Poems* (1640) nor Francis Quarles's *Threnodes* (1641) showed much anxiety over England, its condition

---

30 See, for example, Henry Parker, *The Case of Shipmony Briefly Discoursed* (London, 1640); *An Humble Remonstrance to His Majesty, against the Tax of Ship-Money* (London, 1641); *Several Humble Petitions of...Bastwicke...Burton...Prynne* (London, 1641); William Prynne, *Lord Bishops: None of the Lords Bishops* ([Amsterdam], 1640). A full listing would run well into the hundreds.

31 See, for example, *The Declaration of John Pym Esquire, upon the Whole Matter of the Charge of High Treason* (London, 1641); *An Answer to the Lord Digbies Speech in the House of Commons to the Bill of Attainder* (London, 1641); *The Petition of the Citizens of London to both Houses of Parliament, 1641* (London, 1641); *The Earle of Strafford Characterized* (London, 1641).

32 See Ernest Sirluck's introduction to *CPW*, 2:1–52; A. D. T. Cromartie, 'The Printing of Parliamentary Speeches, November 1640 – July 1642', *Historical Journal* 33 (1990), 23–44.

or its identity; the identity such authors asserted was cultural and social rather than national. While the last new play before the closure of the London theatres, Richard Brome's *A Jovial Crew* (performed 1641, published 1652) did interrogate social relations, its merry beggars on the open road seemed in the end merely to affirm commonplaces of harmony and inclusiveness that must to many in 1641 have seemed at best irrelevant or desperately hopeful. This was not the script with which to counter the opposition's writing of England as the chosen nation or the law-inscribed nation.

The ambivalence of so many of the King's critics, their tendency to look to Geneva, to Edinburgh, to New England, even while they wrote of England, provided the King's friends their opening. Despite the long-practised British posture of Charles and his father,[33] there was now much to gain polemically, and even more emotionally, by claiming a purely English identity. Accordingly, 1641 saw the construction, mainly in printed Parliamentary speeches, of competing, and enduring, visions of the nation. On the one hand, John Pym's allies among the King's critics stressed England's defining inheritance of the common law, and an anti-Catholic imperative binding magnate and miller alike. That case was to find its finest expression in Milton's vision in *Areopagitica* (1644), of Englishmen banded together in their great workshop of war and ideas, hammering out a stirring future, 'a Nation not slow and dull, but of a quick, ingenious, and piercing spirit', rousing itself like Samson from its sleep to do great deeds.[34] On the other hand, Parliamentary rhetoricians like the poet–MP Edmund Waller wove a very different fabric of order, nobility, property and English self-sufficiency in church and state alike. That attractive case laid the groundwork for what was later to become known as moderate or 'constitutional' Royalism.[35]

The new Royalist account of England found its most imaginative version in Sir John Denham's topographical poem *Coopers Hill*, written in late 1641 and first published the following year.[36] Taking a particularly hallowed tract

33 This posture was not quickly abandoned: when the King returned in late 1641 from visiting Edinburgh to a lavish reception in the city of London, an account of the civic festivities was published as *Great Britaines time of triumph* (London, 1641).

34 *CPW*, 2:551, 553–4.

35 For example, *Mr Waller's Speech in Parliament at a conference of both Houses* (London, 1641), and *The third speech of the Lord George Digby to the House of Commons concerning bishops and the citie petition* (London, 1640/1); more generally, see David L. Smith, *Constitutional Royalism and the Search for Settlement, c. 1640–1649* (Cambridge University Press, 1994).

36 For a collation of the various versions of Denham's poem, see Brendan O Hehir, *Expans'd Hieroglyphics* (Berkeley and Los Angeles: University of California Press, 1969). The new editions with substantial revisions – in 1655 more clearly 'Royalist', in 1668 more emphatically commercial – indicate the centrality of Denham's work to the Stuart camp. For additional discussion of Denham, see Chapter 25 below.

of English soil as the emblem of the nation and its history, and tying this to the King, Denham gave the powerful topos of place to a royal cause in danger of floundering. The argument of identity seems as clear as the Virgilian assurance of the writing, for the bounteous landscape of the Thames Valley sets the scene for a claim of continuity between the English liberties secured at Runnymede, the gentle hill, and the royal castle at Windsor and its occupants: 'no threatning heights / Accesse deny, no horrid steepe affrights' (lines 57–8). There is partisan work to be sure, as Denham celebrates in a scene of a stag hunt the magnanimity of the Crown and its supporters, while advertising the violence and rapacity of the (Parliamentary) hunting-dogs. But it is not only the partisanship of others that threatens the pastoral world he opens by celebrating. London is part of the poem's imagined landscape, and its commerce and greed offer a disturbing lesson in self-consumption to labouring humanity who, 'increasing with their store, / Their vast desires, but make their wants the more' (lines 31–2). The boldness of Denham's poem lies in the way he tranquillises these disruptive forces of commerce by folding them into an imperial vision: a well-regulated river, like a proper economic order, 'makes both Indies ours', and London 'the worlds Exchange' (lines 216, 218). The fruits of empire, with their promise of power and abundance, are brought up a river that is in a very real sense tributary to the Crown. Denham came close to imagining a new, royal, political stability resting on commerce and empire, even while celebrating an essential English balance rooted in an idealised yet localised past. For a moment, the anxiety that characterises so many evocations of England in these years seemed held at bay.

In the crisis of 1641 Denham approached that defence of monarchy which Dryden was to make characteristically his own.[37] Far more important at the time to those who were not yet persuaded that England stood on the edge of the apocalypse was the King's *Answer* to Parliament's *Nineteen Propositions* of 1642.[38] The royal advisors who crafted this powerful document turned the figure of the river – up which Denham's tribute goods wafted – into what was to become a central Royalist metaphor. It promised more than fertility and renewal; as a figure for history, or the people, it also threatened inundation once its banks were breached.[39] Not only did the *Answer* conjure the general catastrophe that must follow any violent disruption of the current of

---

37 The *locus classicus* for Dryden's account is *Annus Mirabilis* (London, 1667).

38 For the text of the *Answer*, see Joyce Lee Malcolm, (ed.), *The Struggle for Sovereignty: Seventeenth-Century English Political Tracts*, 2 vols. (Indianapolis: Liberty Fund, 1999), 1:154–78, esp. pp. 167–71; for its centrality to English history, see Betty Kemp, *King and Commons, 1660–1832* (London: Macmillan, 1957).

39 The destructive capacity of the river figured as the people is the argument of the 1655 edition of Denham's *Coopers Hill*.

English history. It also asserted ringingly that descent and succession alone gave England its identity: without them, 'this splendid and excellently distinguished form of Government, [would] end in a dark equall *Chaos* of Confusion, and the long Line of Our many noble Ancestors in a *Jack Cade*, or a *Wat Tyler*'.[40]

However powerful the *Answer's* claim to royal custody over England's past, present and future, there was no mistaking its social exclusiveness. Hymns to noble virtue as the essence of England soon became deeply partisan as Royalists inscribed a social definition of the nation. Parliamentarian woodcuts contested Royalist attempts to appropriate aristocratic honour, and flaunted a succession of their own mounted commanders, from the Earl of Essex to Colonel Poyntz. John Vicars's *England's Worthies* (1647) contested the matter more systematically in his catalogue of Parliament's stalwarts of honour. By giving pride of place (or at least of space) to London's darlings, Generals Edward Massey and Sir William Waller, Vicars challenged the association of heroic virtue with ancient acres and royal service, and advanced instead the integrity and valour of the citizen. The Royalists won this encounter, at least rhetorically. Not only did the noble commanders around the King outface the smaller number of titled nobility and their companions whom Vicars and his like celebrated; they also had a polemical advantage in their press agent, Sir John Berkenhead, editor of the main Royalist news-sheet. Berkenhead's *Mercurius Aulicus* kept up a vivid refrain of panegyric salute on the one hand, and satire and calumny on the other, as it strove to marginalise the enemy as tub-thumpers, fanatics, un-English in their rebelliousness and ingratitude.

The social contours of Englishness emerged most elegantly in what promised to be the supreme literary contribution to the King's cause, Abraham Cowley's *The Civil War*.[41] That unfinished epic, aborted in late 1643, opened with protestations of dismay at a growing calamity – 'What rage does *England* from it selfe divide?' – and with nostalgia for the glories the nation had won under Elizabeth and her forebears: 'To her great *Neptune* homag'd all his Streames, / And all the wide strecht Ocean was her *Thames*' (Bk 1, lines 1, 63–4). As it tracked the descent into civil war, the poem oscillated between vilification of vulgar Parliamentarians and salute to the Royalist nobles who had been victors in the early months of the war. But when the victories began to dry up, Cowley's conviction of noble, and Royalist, virtue gave place to a bitter lament for nation

40 Malcolm (ed.), *Struggle for Sovereignty*, p. 171. Cade and Tyler had led popular revolts in 1450 and 1381 respectively.
41 See Abraham Cowley, *The Civil War*, ed. Allan Pritchard (University of Toronto Press, 1973).

and hierarchy alike. The Puritan artisans who died in the sack of Birmingham formed a fitting pyre for the fallen Royalist Earl of Denbigh, while the Welsh foot soldiers who built Denbigh's pyre could be included in the panegyric host, because they had been 'high-borne' and doughty in their deeds against the plebeian foe. The poem closes abruptly, condemning the 'Wretches' who killed Viscount Falkland at the Battle of Newbury, with the bathetic 'Our Sinnes are great, but Falkland too is slaine' (II, 77; III, 623, 648). True nobility, custody of the national tradition, and of course partisan allegiance thus constituted the vital distinction that Royalists drew against the enemy as they strove vainly to define the nation around themselves.

Defeat soon made history more appropriate than epic as a vehicle for the development of the Royalist case. As he began to write his *History of the Rebellion* in 1646, Edward Hyde redirected his acute intelligence and eloquence from the pursuit of royal victory to the pursuit of understanding, or so he claimed: he would observe 'the faults and infirmities of both sides'; and indeed, he did not spare even Charles himself.[42] But Hyde was as convinced as Cowley that the Royalists had embodied true aristocratic virtue and Englishness alike, while the disorderly crowds and preachers who swelled the Parliamentarians' ranks, as well as their Scottish allies, disqualified that cause from the patriotism it so often claimed. The social complaint, and scorn, that Hyde directed against enemies who drew their strength disproportionately from London and the cloth-making areas is deservedly famous.[43] Yet Hyde's was emphatically a national history, and its urbane political commentary and its brilliant character sketches of leading friends and foes are interspersed with reflections on nation as well as history. His avowed purpose as a historian was to study individual choices, to praise the worth of some and to blame the vice of others. Hyde's was thus the voice of the moralist, and through the *History* can be heard echoes of the royal Psalmist, King David, who had also reflected on his countrymen's desertions and their consequent sufferings. Hyde denies at the outset that there was any 'universal apostacy in the whole nation', but he quickly concedes that 'the immediate finger and wrath of God must be acknowledg'd in these perplexities and distractions', and that the nation had been brought, through complacency and luxury, to the 'signal mortification, and castigation

---

42 Edward Hyde, Earl of Clarendon, *History of the Rebellion*, ed.W. D. Macray, 6 vols. (Oxford: Clarendon Press, 1888), 1:1–2.

43 Hyde's comments provide essential evidence for neo-Marxist arguments about the English Revolution: see, for example, Brian Manning, *The English People and the English Revolution*, 2nd edn. (London and Chicago: Bookmarks, 1991).

of Heaven'.[44] Catastrophe and exile made the model of the Psalms compelling, and Hyde occupied much of his European wanderings of the 1650s with meditations on, and translation of, King David's book. If, as a commoner, he could not speak for his people as could David, he could still draw out the national meaning of the Psalms.[45]

The identification of England and Israel was never a Puritan, still less a Parliamentarian, monopoly. Recognising the importance of the Parliamentarians' claim to a divine mandate, Hyde and many others did all they could to reappropriate Scripture, the vital source of legitimacy and power. Hyde's adoption of the Psalmist's voice was one way to comprehend the meaning of loss in a nation that remained for him, as for his enemies, elect; Bishop Henry King's 1651 verse translation of *The Psalmes of David* gave an even more pointedly Royalist application of Scripture to nationhood and prophetic identity. It is easy to assume that the defeated turned to the Psalms for simple consolation, and to overlook the argument that underlay the solace. As befitted a royal successor to David, Charles made that argument clear with a singular act of prostration. To every chapter of historical reflections in the brilliantly successful *Eikon Basilike* (1649) was appended a set of meditations that powerfully cast Charles as suffering servant of his people, a Christic King sacrificed for and by a successor nation to Israel: 'O let not My bloud be upon them and their Children, whom the fraud and faction of some, not the malice of all, have excited to crucifie Me.'[46] As with Biblical Israel, moreover, nation as well as King would be redeemed. The argument of redemption was comforting, but also polemical – 'Nor will he suffer those men long to prosper in their *Babel*, who build it with the bones and cement it with the bloud of their Kings.'[47] *Eikon Basilike* enabled its countless purchasers to practise private devotions even as they privately asserted, against the usurping republic, a national identity rooted in monarchy and liturgical devotion alike.

In the throes of a republic

The works with black-edged pages that flooded from the presses in 1649, the elegies that lamented the death of all civility, even society itself, with the King on the scaffold, contended more or less crudely that monarchy gave England its

---

44 Clarendon, *History of the Rebellion*, esp. 1:1–2.
45 Hyde's translation of the Psalms was published in *A collection of several tracts of the Right Honourable Edward, Earl of Clarendon* (London, 1727).
46 *Eikon Basilike* (London, 1649), Meditations at the close of ch. 26, 'Upon the Armies surprisall of the King at Holmeby'.
47 *Ibid.*, 'Meditations upon Death', appended to ch. 27, 'To the Prince of Wales'.

identity. But many on the late King's side were eager to appropriate the liturgical, rather than the monarchical, gestures of his book. Although much of their work was either unpublished or unfinished at the Restoration, churchmen in the 1650s crafted a number of histories as a means of asserting England's episcopal heritage and preserving what we know as the Anglican Church. Thomas Fuller's *Church-History* (1655), Peter Heylyn's *Cyprianus Anglicanus* (1668), John Hacket's work on his *Scrinia Reserata* (1693), Bishop Morley with his patronage of John Spottiswoode's *History of the Church of Scotland* (1655), Sir William Dugdale with his *Monasticon Anglicanum* that began to appear in 1655, all sought to recapture England's past and appropriate its future for the church as embodiment of the nation. The disestablishment of the episcopal church in 1645 had thus provoked an argumentative counter. Political and military defeat effectively confined this to the pages of learned tomes, so the efforts of Izaak Walton to memorialise individual churchmen as models of humane and sympathetic learning – including a life of Sir Henry Wotton, Provost of Eton College, published in 1651, and an expanded 1658 version of his earlier (1640) life of John Donne – probably did more to advance the argument that the nation's values were best embodied in a particular style of churchmanship. Not for nothing was the term 'Anglican' now coming into use.[48]

Churchmen were not the only ones to attempt an archaeology of nationhood. Just as the dismantling of the episcopal church drove its devotees to a programme of recovery and vindication, so the fracturing of the nation's culture in war, symbolised most vividly by the closing of the theatres by Parliament, prompted similar efforts of retrieval and reassertion. The flurry of republished dramatic works in the 1640s and 1650s, especially those of Beaumont and Fletcher, suggest a broad attempt to locate in the cultural record a national identity that was not the spiritually exclusive preserve of the godly.[49] The huge array of prefatory tributes to William Cartwright's *Comedies, Tragi-Comedies, with Other Poems* (1651) marked it as one of the publishing events of the decade, a Royalist attempt to offer the native theatrical tradition as a prime constituent of cultural continuity and national community.

Claims to continuity with the old ways also found more fleeting expressions. The Cavalier lyric, which flourished in many collections in the 1640s and 1650s,

---

48 The *Oxford English Dictionary* attributes the first use of the term to James Howell, *Familiar Letters* (London, 1650), 2:23. The *OED* also notes that Howell himself attributed it to 1635; but since he is notorious for retrospective inventions, 1650 seems the safer date.

49 For the history of the stage in these years, see Dale B. Randall, *Winter Fruit: English Drama 1642–1660* (Lexington: University of Kentucky Press, 1995). Also see Chapter 19, pp. 597–602 above.

spoke of style, carelessness, friendship and loyalty, of enjoyment, abandonment and loss, a certain aristocratic abandon.[50] Those lyrics have become a byword for celebrations of drunkenness and debauchery, though the most celebrated collection, Richard Lovelace's *Lucasta* (1649), might warn us against travesty with its moving expression of suffering and captivity. The milkmaids, nymphs and shepherds who cross paths with Chloris, Sylvia and the raised glass in the collection in fact suggest the positive core of the Cavalier ethos. However ribald, their gestures towards the nation as festive community draw on the old and powerful organic vision of the nation, and seek to reconstitute a body politic distressed and decapitated. The nation as festive and ritual community is the claim above all of Walton's *Compleat Angler* (1653), along with *Eikon Basilike* the great publishing success of these years. Piscator's wanderings and musings along the Hertfordshire river-bank challenge Puritan sourness with values that are polemically inclusive: friendship, fellowship and a concord both social and natural. The milkmaid who entertains the meandering fishermen with 'that smooth Song which was made by *Kit Marlow*, now at least fifty years ago', and is answered by her mother with one 'which was made by Sir *Walter Raleigh* in his yonger dayes', projects harmonies of more than one kind.[51] When Alexander Brome greeted the second edition of 1655 by saluting the work's contribution to the Royalist cause he surely had in mind the way it conjured within an emphatically Anglican religious vision a unitary culture that embraced the classical lore of fishing, banter with the milkmaids, Ralegh's poems, recipes for cooking fish, and the natural history of 'little living creatures with which the Sun and Summer adorn and beautifie the river banks and meadows'. Of course, such assertions of what readers were urged to think true English values could scarcely be misty-eyed, since they emerged from the depths of defeat. Robert Herrick's 'The Hock-Cart', composed around 1647, recognises the inevitability of pain even as it enfolds labourers and lord alike in a community that is not merely festive in its address to 'Rurall Younglings' and 'frollicke boyes' (line 43), but also deeply Christian:

> And, you must know, your Lords word's true,
> Feed him ye must whose food fils you,
> And that this pleasure is like raine,
> Not sent ye for to drowne your paine,
> But to make it spring againe.   (lines 51–5)[52]

---

50 It was the particular product of the printing-house of Humphrey Moseley, who made an
    industry out of high-level literary nostalgia. See also Chapter 25 in this volume.
51 Izaak Walton, *The Compleat Angler* (London, 1653), pp. 63–4.
52 *Ibid.*, p. 98; *Works of Robert Herrick*, ed. Alfred Pollard, 2 vols. (London, 1891), 1:125–6.

The England imagined on the other side of the partisan divide proved harder to describe. Royalists looked firmly back to an idealised and harmonious England; their enemies, as befitted the victors, could not rest in such simple verities. Yet perhaps only George Wither managed to combine consistent support for England's new republican rulers with the outlines of a social vision; his attacks on privilege, and praise for Parliament as the people's representative, suggest the potent Cromwellian alliance of lesser gentlemen and urban and professional middling sorts. Wither's 1648 call for a remodelling of Parliament gives poetic expression to what may seem the true spirit of the revolution, though it yielded verse that was often somewhat strained:

> The *Fathers* of your *being*, in this *Nation*,
> Were an unsound, corrupted *Generation*;
> And, did begin a *Representative*,
> As like themselves, as ever, man alive
> Begot a child: with *members*, crooked, lame,
> Blind, deaf, and dumb, into the world you came.[53]

In a godly republic that prized freedom of the spirit, Wither was far from alone in blending castigation with ostentatious gestures of encouragement and support. For all his polite gestures to the Lord Megaletor – a thinly disguised Oliver Cromwell – the classical republic that James Harrington elaborately configured in *Oceana* (1656) was a not-so-veiled criticism of the Protectorate. Harrington viewed social competition and change with equanimity, and outlined how it was that the 'balance' of property in England had devolved upon a virtuous citizenry in arms. Few others could imagine England, still largely arable, populated by citizens. Although his England was even more bound to the soil and rooted in suffering than was Herrick's, the strange tragicomedy of universal love and sibling rivalry told by Gerrard Winstanley the Digger, notably in his *Fire in the Bush* (1649) – 'these two powers are Jacob and Esau, flesh and spirit, struggling within the womb of the living earth, who shall rule first' – somehow promised an egalitarian transcendence for nation and individual alike.[54] Indeed, his regimented communitarian utopia, *The Law of Freedome* (1652), with its vision of a nation and people made whole by communion with the earth they dug, gave a

---

53 George Wither, *Prosopopoeia Britannica* (London, 1648), p. 66.Wither declared his enthusiastic support for the revolution in *The British Appeals* (London, 1651), p. 29: 'we, with *open face*; / *By Publick Justice*; in a *Publick place*; /... / *Try'd, Judg'd* and *Executed*, without fear; / The greatest *Tyrant*, ever reigning here'. For fuller discussion of Wither, see David Norbrook, *Writing the English Republic* (Cambridge University Press, 1999).
54 Winstanley, *The Law of Freedom and Other Writings*, ed. Christopher Hill (Harmondsworth: Penguin Books, 1973), pp. 213–72, esp. 253.

radical twist to assumptions of the unity of nation and land. Whether Diggers or early Quakers, most who wrote of the plight of the countryman in the post-war depression and dearth could manage only a lament that fast became an apocalyptic indictment. Exceptions were Walter Blith's *English Improver* (1649) and *English Improver Improved* (1653), which urged agricultural improvement as the means to a just commonwealth. On such dreams, of improvement and of agrarian equality, Marvell reflects quizzically in *Upon Appleton House* (1651).[55] The house opens reassuringly onto 'a stately frontispiece of poor', but the woman gleaning after the harvest speaks disruptively out of the body of the poem, while the varied landscapes, of improvement and of Levellers alike, seem only to disorient (lines 65–6, 405–8, 449–50).

Marvell's England was no easier to locate in time than in a social universe. The poet who could offer a wistful salute, in language redolent of Genesis as well as Shakespeare's John of Gaunt, to what might have been, 'that dear and happy Isle / The Garden of the World ere while, / Thou Paradise of four Seas' (*Upon Appleton House*, lines 321–3), seems for a moment close to those Royalists who pine for their 'halcyon days'. Yet Marvell watches time nervously as he tries to gloss the meaning of destiny for a patron, Lord Fairfax, who has just decided to resign his army command at the crisis of the young and embattled republic. Questioning the dynastic and the public future, the poet's instinct is to freeze the moment, and the young Maria (Fairfax's daughter and the poet's tutee), in a crystalline present; watching day's end creep across the river, that universal metaphor for time, the narrator, the tutor and the tutee in the poem head for the safety of the house. Marvell's evocation of temporal suspension was not limited to his great topographical poem, for he was famously preoccupied by time's hold on the nation, its rulers and its writers. Here was a poet who could imagine the ideologically unnerving juxtaposition of 'ancient rights' and mere physical strength more explicitly than most writers dared (*An Horatian Ode*, lines 37–40). Yet he could no more fix the nation in time than he could Lord Fairfax's estate at Nun Appleton. *An Horatian Ode* (1650) reveals him palpably – and ironically – unsure whether Cromwell had brought England to the moment of new foundation, and *The First Anniversary* (1655) baulks at the full implications of elect nationhood. Even as he slapped at those saints who proclaimed the imminent supersession of all earthly authorities and national distinctions, Marvell for a moment held out to England, and

55 For the date of this poem, see Derek Hirst and Steven Zwicker, 'High Summer at Nun Appleton, 1651: Andrew Marvell and Lord Fairfax's Occasions', *Historical Journal* 36 (1993), 247–69. Quotations from Marvell's poetry are from *The Poems and Letters of Andrew Marvell*, ed. H. M. Margoliouth, 3rd edn rev. Pierre Legouis with E. E. Duncan-Jones (Oxford: Clarendon Press, 1971).

to Cromwell, a vision of a prophetic future. Yet though he castigated his countrymen for standing woefully 'unprepared', the poet was himself prepared to ask whether Cromwell might be the shaper of a classical rather than a godly republic, and to allow that England might move in a regular temporal succession after all (*The First Anniversary*, lines 150, 293–320, 401–2). The elegiac mood of his *Poem upon the Death of O.C.* (1659), with its lament for the dead hero, a merely mighty human being, provided its own answer.

To Milton such questions once seemed plain. The prophetic and patriotic voice of the anti-episcopal tracts at the start of the 1640s still resounded confidently as war followed. In *Areopagitica* (1644) the nation was indubitably elect, and God revealed himself 'as his manner is, first to his English-men'.[56] But even as Milton's own voice strengthened, his sense of England's prophetic mission waned. In the disillusioning months after the end of the fighting, the majority of his countrymen swung against the heroic freedom of which he dreamed, and in his *History of Britain* he meditates gloomily on their status and capacity.[57] Although he discerns an admirable yearning for freedom in the natives' resistance to empire, he is left lamenting the inability of these northerners, whether the British or the English who displaced them, to absorb or equal the civility of the Roman conquerors: the Britons were 'at first greedy of change, and to be thought the leading Nation to freedom from the Empire', though they soon relapsed into licence and servitude; 'the *Saxons* were now full as wicked as the *Britans* were at their arrival, brok'n with luxury and sloth, either secular or superstitious'. Whatever the dating of the angry 'Digression' on the backsliding Long Parliament, it is clear that Milton at this period resented the Anglo-Saxon settlers for their failure to seize on the republican, and the spiritual, possibilities offered by the collapse of empire, and their willingness to turn to a new Romish thraldom.[58] Such failure, his historical analysis and present political experience led him to fear, was characteristic of the English. There was a regicidal moment in 1648–9 of renewed political hope, expressed in *The Tenure of Kings and Magistrates* (1649); but the strange passion his countrymen immediately showed for the 'King's Book', *Eikon Basilike* (1649), led him to conclude in *Eikonoklastes* (1649) that they were almost irremediably

56 *CPW*, 2:553. Here too, however, Milton had recognised decadence, especially in the vulgar: 'What more Nationall corruption, for which England hears ill abroad, then houshold gluttony; who shall be the rectors of our daily rioting?' (*ibid.*, pp. 525–6.)

57 The date of this work is sharply contested. Much was surely written in the later 1640s, and the 'Digression' on the history of the Long Parliament was probably partly written in 1647 and revised in 1655. See Nicholas von Maltzahn, *Milton's 'History of Britain': Republican Historiography in the English Revolution* (Oxford: Clarendon Press, 1991).

58 *CPW*, 5:130–1, 259.

corrupt. Something smacked of class analysis in his condemnation: it was the 'mad multitude', 'the ignorant and wretched people', who were eagerly fooled by the *Eikon*, and he confessed he could not 'willingly' attribute such 'low dejection and abasement of mind ... to the natural disposition of an Englishman'.[59] From then on, Milton increasingly spoke past the backsliding English to the international – and republican – republic of letters, and to a distant posterity. A story of nationhood remained, but that story was no longer one of election. The celebration of England's 'glorious and immortal actions' in *The Reason of Church Government* (1642), the vision of Samson in *Areopagitica* and of a people marked out for action, the tributes to British valour and nobility in the *History*, all herald the argument Milton was to advance so strenuously in his *First Defence* (1651) and *Second Defence of the English People* (1654). English nationhood was itself an epic, its high point the public trial and execution of Charles I. Of this nation and epic, as the concluding peroration to the *Second Defence* made breathtakingly clear, John Milton was poet as well as historian and prophet.[60]

The widespread irresolution in face of the competing attractions of Jerusalem and Rome is a measure of the perplexity generated by the experience of revolution in a tradition-bound society. In *Vox Pacifica* (1645), George Wither imagined himself steering to a political Antipodes by 'some Utopian-Map' (pp. 123–4). Marvell too, at the end of *Upon Appleton House*, yearned for a map as his mind turned towards the Antipodes (lines 761–8, 771). The sense that England stood at some great turn into the unknown, perhaps into greatness, helps account for the vogue for Longinus' aesthetics of precipitousness, translated into English by John Hall as *On the Sublime* (1652). It is thus no anomaly that James Harrington's *Oceana* (1656), the greatest work of political theory after Hobbes's *Leviathan* and famous now for its sweeping historical analysis, is among other things a Utopian romance, in which Queen Elizabeth bids fair for readers' admiration; or that one of the more controversial republican works of 1659, a time of creative ferment, was boldly entitled *Chaos*.[61]

The most accessible guide for those who sought to comprehend the trauma of revolution was Scripture, which told an unmistakable story of the destruction of earthly power. At times of particular crisis, as in 1653–4 and again in 1659, the presses abounded in works proclaiming Dagon's imminent downfall, and calling on the saving remnant to implement God's purpose for England and

59 *Ibid.*, 3:345, 367, 344.   60 *Ibid.*, 4:684–6.
61 For discussion of the romance theme, see Nigel Smith, *Literature and Revolution in England 1640–1660* (New Haven, CT: Yale University Press, 1994), pp. 246–9. For discussion of *Chaos*, see Nigel Smith's Chapter 23 below.

the world. That road, with its promise of triumph over all earthly distinctions, and even over time, was taken by numerous prophets both male and female – notoriously by such Fifth-Monarchy men as Feake and Simpson whom Marvell excoriates in *The First Anniversary* (line 305). But the availability of another powerful account of the fall of kings, and one that did not end in the apocalypse, allowed others to imagine their situation within time, rather than think themselves under the most urgent pressure to transform and transcend it. In *An Horatian Ode* Marvell famously balances forces that hint of the apocalypse against the pattern of the Roman republic; in *The First Anniversary* (where he had polemical reasons for claiming, and containing, the realm of prophecy for Cromwell) the classical acts explicitly as a brake on the apocalyptic.[62] Even Harrington's *Oceana*, for all its classical republicanism, was the site of some tension over time.[63]

Amidst a revolution, however, Rome could not be merely a means to hold the apocalypse at bay. For some, it presented a model almost as powerful as others found Jerusalem. England, a new republic formed through the expulsion of its ruling dynasty, could find its very type on the banks of the Tiber, where for a time conquest and glory had inhabited republican forms. As the republic established itself with the 1650 campaign into Scotland, the journalist and polemicist Marchamont Nedham hammered the point home. In a series of brilliant and witty editorials in *Mercurius Politicus*, Nedham exhorted England on from acts of foundation to a republican empire, while his scathing attacks on 'the young Tarquin' (the younger Charles Stuart) coupled monarchy with rape.[64] The application of that Roman model in Harrington's *Oceana* generated a still more confident elaboration of the English republic's expansionist destiny. More ponderous exercises in classicising, such as John Streater's newsbook editorials against the newly installed Lord Protector as hungry Caesar in 1654, sought to take the stern republican case out to plebeian readers.[65] As Milton looked back from 1660 on such aspirations, he could only lament in *The Readie and Easie Way* the wasting of an opportunity to build 'another Rome in the West'.[66]

---

62 For this argument, see Derek Hirst, '"That Sober Liberty": Marvell's Cromwell in 1654', in *The Golden and the Brazen World*, ed. John M. Wallace (Berkeley and Los Angeles: University of California Press, 1985), pp. 17–53.

63 See especially Harrington's reference to 'this empire...the kingdom of Christ', in *The Political Works of James Harrington*, ed. J. G. A. Pocock (Cambridge University Press, 1977), p. 332.

64 See the opening editorial pages of *Mercurius Politicus* between September 1650 and 1652, republished in *The Excellencie of a Free State* (London, 1656).

65 *Perfect and Impartial Intelligence*, 23 May–2 June 1654. Nigel Smith discusses Streater further in Chapter 23 below.

66 *CPW*, 7:357.

For many, however, Rome wrote the language not primarily of political forms and the confident projection of power, but of virtue and elevation above the vicissitudes of power. Its history abounded in examples of duty and self-sacrifice, often in face of imperial corruption, and these proved attractive for a state that justified itself insistently in terms of 'the public interest' against the selfishness of kings.[67] But duty and the public interest did not suffice to outline a national identity. The example of selfless heroes like Henry Ireton inspired little beyond elegiac tributes, while the gallery of public-spirited English worthies in Milton's Latin *Second Defence* was aimed at a European rather than an English audience. Lucan, the epic celebrant of the Roman republic, certainly had his eager followers – not least, his translator, Thomas May, whose impressive *History of the Long Parliament* (1647) and its continuation in the *Breviary* (1650) rested on an extended parallel between England's civil wars and Rome's. But Lucan's Rome could be at best a compromised pattern for England, since his *Pharsalia* celebrated virtuous republicans in the moment of their destruction; May's untimely death in 1650 spared him from having to continue this story.[68] Yet very different constructions of Roman virtue still held their appeal, to which John Ogilby's splendid illustrated edition of Virgil (1654) testified.[69] The broad political range of the subscribers to its lavish dedicative plates suggests that this was not altogether a partisan venture. Every European state looked to Virgil, the poet of empire and glory, for patterns and parallels, and England was no different. The reigns of the early Stuarts had abounded in Augustan gestures, and when, from the chaos of revolution, again a great man rose to power, celebrations of Lord Protector Cromwell as a new Augustus were quickly heard.[70] Denham and Harrington made more serious, albeit still partisan, attempts to recast Virgil's narrative of the Trojan Wars, which provided one of the primal stories of politics, in terms suitable to a kingless England.[71] The Royalist Denham's aim was undoubtedly partly

---

67 This was the dominant motif of Marchamont Nedham's semi-official defence of the Protectorate, *The True State of the Case of the Commonwealth* (London, 1654).

68 On May as a historian, see Nigel Smith, *Literature and Revolution*, pp. 205, 342–4, and J. G. A. Pocock, 'Thomas May and the Narrative of Civil War', in *Writing and Political Engagement in Seventeenth-Century England*, ed. Derek Hirst and Richard Strier (Cambridge University Press, 2000), pp. 112–44. For the influence of Lucan throughout the period, see Norbrook, *Writing the English Republic*.

69 John Ogilby, *The Works of Publius Virgilius Maro, translated, adorn'd with sculpture, and illustrated with annotations* (London, 1654).The first edition of 1650 had lacked plates.

70 David Armitage, 'The Cromwellian Protectorate and the Languages of Empire', *Historical Journal* 35 (1992), 531–55.

71 Sir John Denham, *The Destruction of Troy* (London, 1655), and James Harrington, *Aeneid* (London, 1658).

consolation, and the republican Harrington's was affirmation; but both efforts converged in proclaiming the English to themselves as a stirring and exalted people.

Such powerful Virgilian echoes comment ironically on one dimension of the literature of national identity during the English republic. Title pages at the end of the 1640s and through the following decade less frequently summoned the reader with appeals to 'England' or 'English' – indeed, the decline in such appeals was steeper than the overall reduction in publications.[72] Although a powerful discourse of England continued even as the Parliamentarian cause fragmented, paeans to English nationhood, as we shall see, tended to come from those who looked askance at the regime.

Royalists were to take some time to arrive again at the unalloyed espousal of Englishness that Denham had achieved in 1641. The Stuart claim to pan-British loyalties regained momentum in the war as Charles turned to Wales to recruit his regiments, and to professionals like the Scottish Earl of Forth to command his forces. Cowley's tribute in *The Civil War* to the valiant Welshmen was part of a larger British polemic, in which he attributed to witchcraft the Parliamentarians' success in subduing 'Great *Brittaines* aged *Genius*' and seducing their countrymen to battle (II, lines 1–20). Still more suggestive of the partisan identifications drawn in the war were the series of elegies composed in 1645 by Edward Walsingham of Warwickshire for fallen Royalist commanders: *Alter Britanniae Heros* (Sir Henry Gage); *Britannicae virtutis imago* (Major-General Smith); *Hector Britannicus* (Sir John Digley). But as the Royalists confronted an increasingly imperial republic and pondered the Scots' hand-over of Charles I to Parliament in early 1647, their stance changed. They soon produced a series of constructions of a nostalgic and idealised Englishness. The nascent literary canon, elaborated with the tributes in Walton's *Compleat Angler* to Ralegh and Marlowe, the republication of Beaumont and Fletcher and of Donne, certainly speaks of a commercial interest and popular taste; but the new edition of Denham's *Coopers Hill* (1655) and the partisan gestures in the materials appended to Cartwright's *Comedies, Tragedies*, declared a political meaning and purpose as well. Although the Royalists had once again discovered England, their arguments of identity were always susceptible to political recalculation.

The road on the other side was no more straightforward, except where it led through the radical camp. The Leveller John Lilburne directed his repeated

---

72 This claim is based on a rough analysis of title-page data gleaned from the 'WorldCat' data-base.

claims to be a 'freeborn Englishman' against intolerant Scots and persecuting noblemen alike.[73] As Lilburne well knew, the rhetoric of sturdy Englishness served as a critique of all forms of privilege, whether aristocratic (as in Hare's *St Edwards Ghost, or Anti-Normanisme* of 1647) or army grandee (as in the Levellers' *England's New Chains Discovered* of 1649). It serves the same polemical purpose in the radical Thomas Lord Grey of Groby's *Old English Blood Boyling in Leicestershire-men* (1648), his call to the people to take arms against Scottish invaders and their intolerant allies; and in Milton's *First* and *Second Defence of the English People*.[74] Much less clear-cut is the verse of Wither, which oscillates between a British and an English pole according to topical need. The titles of Wither's works are suggestive: *Haleluiah, or Britans Second Remembrancer* (1641), *Opobalsamum Anglicanum* (1646), *Amygdala Britannica* (1647), *Prosopopoeia Britannica* (1648), *The British Appeals* (1651), *Fides-Anglicana* (1660). It was not that those who came into power had ceased to see themselves as custodians of England's weal. Indeed, Cromwell probably thought himself the quintessential sturdy Englishman. Nothing better suggests the dilemmas of a republic whose history could be proudly recounted in 1654 as *Britannia Triumphalis* than the decision of one of its greatest servants, the ex-Royalist Roger Boyle, Lord Broghill (later Earl of Orrery), to write out his trials and tribulations as an Anglo-Irish politician in *Parthenissa* (1651–69), an extravagant romance of love and honour.[75]

After the conquest of Scotland in 1652 the republic announced itself as, if not a British commonwealth, then at least a composite commonwealth – the commonwealths of England, Scotland and Ireland. It thereby found itself, ironically, close to the plight of the King in 1640, appealing to claims and loyalties that were not quite there. Indeed, the republic's predicament was more acute, since the early Stuart monarchy had left the political institutions of Scotland and Ireland more or less intact, while the republic endeavoured to bring all into a single political frame built in England. It thus gave ample encouragement to the venerable English tendency to confuse little England with greater Britain. In this at least, Wither was close to the mainstream when he addressed

73 See Keith Thomas, 'The Levellers and the Franchise', in *The Interregnum*, ed. G. E. Aylmer (London: Macmillan, 1972), p. 74, for oddities in Lilburne's signature claim. Equally polemical use of the claim to nationhood is made in John Vicars's parade of *England's Worthies*, directed as this was against the wartime Royalist array of noble 'British' heroes.

74 The occurrence of 'English People' in the title of the *First Defence* presumably explains Lilburne's praise of Milton in his *As You Were* (London, 1652). I am indebted to David Loewenstein for this point.

75 For the location of this text in a British frame, see John Kerrigan, 'Orrery's Ireland and the British Problem', 1641–1679, in David Baker and Willy Maley, eds. *British Identities and English Renaissance Literature* (Cambridge University Press, 2002), pp. 197–255.

his revealingly titled *The British Appeals* (1651), 'To the Soveraigne MAIESTY of the Parliament of the English Republike...Keepers of the Liberties of England'.

Ambiguities and uncertainties abounded in the state England was building from the islands of the Atlantic archipelago. The assemblage of communities that the new state claimed to embody was not easily imagined, while the wars and material demands entailed were all too easily resented. Furthermore, animosities intensified as interactions with neighbours multiplied, often bringing with them not the conviction of common interest and destiny of which apologists, and a few idealists, dreamed but a sharper and more exclusive sense of identity.[76] At the very moment of the republic's expansion, Marvell, writing *An Horatian Ode*, hovered between dreams of freeing England's neighbours – presumably those on the European continent – from tyranny, and grimmer thoughts of hunting and conquering Scots and Irish. If this seems a typically English double standard, it would be one of the many ironies to be found in the *Horatian Ode*. Writing *Leviathan* (1651) as an emergent scientist of politics and of human behaviour, Hobbes had less interest in irony; his adaptation of the standard Royalist sneer at Scottish 'Judases' – for 'selling' the King to Parliament in the negotiations of 1646–7 – therefore suggests the more strongly how increased familiarity could breed contempt or worse.[77] Indeed, Scotland was generally cast as the site of villainy, oppression and hypocrisy, from Henry Parker's diatribe of 1650, *The False Brother*, through to Samuel Butler's scorn for Sir John Presbyter in the defining early Restoration satire, *Hudibras* (1664). Ireland – predictably enough, in view of the 1641 revolt – fared worse, most substantially in Sir John Temple's signal contribution to the literature of vengeance, his *History of the Irish Rebellion* (1646). Unlike Scotland, however, Ireland was also central to England's growing literature of empire. Gerald Boate's *Irelands Naturall History* (1652), the most substantial non-polemical work, imagines physical and even climatic improvement of Ireland completing the work of anglicisation that the sword had not yet effected. In its imposition of the intellectual categories and economic priorities of the conqueror, Boate's constitutes a classic imperial text. Yet it is the work whose title seems to promise coordination, perhaps even cooperation, for the territories

---

76 Thus, after recognising that the English were the ancient enemies of the Scots, Heylyn in his *Cosmographie*, p. 299, intoned the hope, 'One onely Nation now are we, / And let us so forever be.'

77 In ch. 3 of *Leviathan*, Hobbes ingenuously considers the worth of a Roman penny – the measure of the price set on Christ's head and, by extension, on Charles I's when the Scots handed him over.

of the archipelago, James Harrington's *Oceana* (1656), that demonstrates best the subordinated status of the non-English commonwealths. If a wider Britain has any part to play in Harrington's republic beyond providing an occasion for writing, it is as a source of manpower (Scotland) and revenues (Ireland) for a purely English expansionism understood and justified in terms of the Roman virtue of benevolence: 'If the empire of a commonwealth be patronage, to ask whether it be lawful for a commonwealth to aspire unto the empire of the world is to ask whether it be lawful for her to do her duty, or to put the world into a better condition than it was before.'[78] That classically shaped understanding of empire as a benevolent, improving force explains how Milton in his *Observations upon the Articles of Peace* could excoriate the Irish for their ingratitude to English conquerors, for showing a disposition 'not onely sottish but indocible and averse from all Civility and amendment... rejecting the ingenuity of all other Nations to improve and waxe more civill by a civilizing Conquest'.[79]

Abroad and at home

Expansion seems the one distinctive imaginative claim advanced by pro-government writings in the 1650s. In its romance with Elizabeth as well as in its dreams of empire, if not in its republican critique, Harrington's *Oceana* draws surprisingly close to the rhetoric of the establishment. Cromwell's declaration justifying the dispatch of the Western Design into the Caribbean appeals self-consciously to Elizabethan tropes and Elizabethan history: it was 'the Spaniards perpetual Jealousies of the English, in respect of his Treasure' in the Americas, as well as their subservience to the Pope, that caused the war with Elizabeth and the attempt in 1588 at 'a total Conquest of this Nation, which must needs ly close by English mens hearts'.[80] In awkward but officially licensed dramatic works, *The Cruelty of the Spaniards in Peru* (1658) and *Sir Francis Drake* (1659), Davenant developed these themes to construct what later centuries would understand as a jingoistic campaign masquerading as art. The harnessing of commercial wealth and empire evoked in Denham's *Coopers Hill* was fast becoming a reality in the aftermath of the First Dutch War; and Waller saw both its polemical and its expressive potential. Although his *Panegyric to my Lord Protector* (1655) opens by saluting England as the arbiter of the Atlantic archipelago, 'the seat of Empire, where the Irish come, / And

78 Harrington, *Political Works*, ed. Pocock, p. 328.   79 *CPW*, 3:304.
80 *A Declaration of His Highness... Setting forth, On the Behalf of this Commonwealth, the Justice of their Cause against Spain* (London, 1655), p. 119 (unconventional pagination).

the unwilling Scotch, to fetch their doom' (lines 15–16), it moves swiftly into
a celebration of oceanic glory and gain:

> The taste of hot Arabia's spice we know,
> Free from the scorching sun that makes it grow:
> Without the worm, in Persian silks we shine;
> And, without planting, drink of every vine.
>
> (lines 57–60)[81]

Waller uses the nation's steady acquisition of prosperity, strength and glory as a
platform on which to raise a crown for the Protector – if only of bays and olive.[82]

   Expansion into blue waters appealed to many, not just among the lesser
London merchants who might seem its and perhaps the republic's natural
constituency: certainly to many even among the conquered Scots, surely to
Harrington and to other former Royalists too. Cowley lamented lost maritime glory in *The Civil War*, and *Coopers Hill* was republished in 1655. Waller's
panegyric thus suggested how projections into a world abroad could serve
to consolidate identifications at home. Hobbes's pupil Sir William Davenant
had made the calculus explicit in the separately published *Preface* (1650)
to *Gondibert*, when he warned against imagining England a second Israel:
'narrow Dominion breeds evil, peevish, and vexatious mindes, and a National
self-opinion, like simple Jewish arrogance; and the Jews were extraordinary
proud in a very little Country'.[83] Yet empire could not be a panacea, for it
generated new tensions and divisions. A patrician distaste for merchants' work
and ways lurks in *Coopers Hill*; similar ambivalence characterises the work of
another conforming ex-Royalist, Sir Richard Fanshawe, whose translation of
the Portuguese maritime epic, Camoens's *Lusiads*, appeared in 1655. With its
delight in chivalric exploits, hierarchy and glory –

> I only, with my Tenants, and with this
> (And at that word he pull'd out half his Blade)
> Will save from force, and all that shameful is,
> This land, which hitherto hath liv'd a Maid

---

81 Milton surely had these lines in mind when he wrote of Satan's olfactory delights in *Paradise
   Lost*, 4: lines 160–6.
82 The promise of a crown is too neatly qualified – the 'bays and olive' are confined to a
   separate stanza: see Waller, *A Panegyric to my Lord Protector*, lines 184–5, in *Poems of Edmund
   Waller*, ed. G. Thorn Drury (London: Routledge, and New York: E. P. Dutton, 1904), 2:11.
   The second (1655) edition of this work contains the more explicit development of the theme
   of empire.
83 The *preface to Gondibert, an heroick poem, written by Sir William D'Avenant; with an answer to
   the preface by Mr Hobbes* (Paris, 1650), p. 4.

– and its unease about merchant profits and pelf, Fanshawe's *Lusiad* seems the emblematic text of an aristocratic order experiencing the formation of commercial empire.[84] Such unease straddled the spectrum, for an equivalent disdain for empire and profit is evident among radical republicans. Lucy Hutchinson, famous for the fiercely republican *Memoirs* she wrote of her husband Colonel John Hutchinson, promptly answered Waller's verse with a manuscript anti-panegyric, denouncing the corruptions of commerce and empire, and any prospect of a Cromwellian monarchy, in the name of a sterner English virtue.[85] For his post, John Milton began to write his anti-imperial epic in the later 1650s, certainly by 1658.[86]

A new traffic between the external and the domestic became paradoxically the most striking characteristic of a period that began as partisan competition for the soul of England. On the one hand, the victors' attempts in the 1650s to articulate their own vision of the nation made little progress: Cromwell's occasional calls for days of humiliation, casting England still as a beleaguered Israel, soon became a party shibboleth, and perhaps not even that, for many of the godly had begun to look within themselves.[87] On the other side, the great Royalist party-piece, Cartwright's *Tragedies, Comedies* of 1651, looks far more played-out than its gallery of dedicatory materials would suggest. Many Royalists and Parliamentarians alike found greater satisfaction in a more privatised imagination that pulled them away from the travails of a body politic that had been sundered in 1649. In that privatising process the literature of friendship, self-conscious as it clearly was, played a central part: particularly through the efforts of Katherine Philips, the 'matchless Orinda', and her circle, but also James Howell's *Dodona's Grove* (1644 and multiple editions), and such guides to the epistolary craft as that of Thomas Blount.[88] Working to the same effect was the growing fashion for polite local histories, represented in the Midlands by the circle of Sir William Dugdale (whose *Antiquities of Warwickshire* appeared in

84 *The Lusiad, or, Portugals Historicall Poem...Now Newly put into English by Richard Fanshaw* (London, 1655), p. 78.
85 David Norbrook, 'Lucy Hutchinson versus Edmund Waller: An Unpublished Reply to Waller's *A Panegyrick to my Lord Protector*', *The Seventeenth Century* 11 (1996), 61–86.
86 See David Armitage, 'John Milton: Poet against Empire', in *Milton and Republicanism*, ed. David Armitage, Armand Himy and Quentin Skinner (Cambridge University Press, 1995), pp. 206–25; see also the essays in Balachandra Rajan and Elizabeth Sauer (eds.), *Milton and the Imperial Vision*.
87 The rise of the Quakers, and Milton's turn within, are symptomatic. For Cromwell's calls to humiliation as a shibboleth, see Derek Hirst, 'The Fracturing of the Cromwellian Alliance', *English Historical Review* 108 (1993), 883–4.
88 Thomas Blount, *The Academie of Eloquence* (London, 1654). For further discussion of these themes, see Chapter 25 in this volume.

1656), or in Yorkshire by Roger Dodsworth (who collaborated with Dugdale on *Monasticon Anglicanum*) and the Fairfaxes, and the Marvell of *Upon Appleton House* too. All these represented a turn away from the national drama towards local and even familial concerns. More striking, however, are new currents in the romance. Partly under the influence of French fashions, perhaps under pressure too of an expanding and mixed readership, romances modelled on or deriving from Sir Philip Sidney's *Arcadia* were giving place to works that seem much less organic and socially embedded. Escapism may figure in Davenant's huge but unfinished *Gondibert* (1651), since its author did indeed try to find an escape in America from the Royalist débâcle; in a time of perplexity, his text celebrates not public loyalties but noble heroism, private obligations and sacrifice – extravagances of deed and passion. Yet the new style had its politics. In his contribution to the *Preface* to *Gondibert*, Hobbes instructed his protégé Davenant that the function of imaginative literature was to entertain and to distract; Davenant replied by declaring an absolutist politics, and – in the poem proper – by placing his great spirits in courts and camps. Davenant's literary rival, Lord Broghill, responded to the difficulties of maintaining a politician's footing in the morass that lay between London and Dublin by turning instead to extremes of love and honour in his unfinished blockbuster, *Parthenissa* (1651–69). It was as though the old national body politic had dissolved, to be replaced by two emerging polarities. One, a newly articulated private world, was expressed in the growing taste for the romance and in the cult of friendship; the other was a public sphere both more distant and more daunting. Hobbes recognised that dynamic when he prefaced *Leviathan* with a salute to the lost world of his friend Francis Godolphin, the complete gentleman.

The great emblem from these years that saw the nation re-imagined is not therefore their most famous artifact, the frontispiece to *Leviathan* representing the state as the sum of its human and material parts. It is surely the juxtaposition of Hobbes's elegiac preface with that blunt engraving; and indeed, it is the juxtaposition of both of these with Hobbes's contemporaneous preface to Davenant's *Gondibert*. These years were not only ones of an all-consuming drive for partisan commitment; they also saw the birth of Leviathan, the creation of the modern state. The responses to that unattractive coupling register variously, from the vogue for impossible heroics as well as the romance, to the pastoral perplexity of Herrick and Marvell, as well as to Walton's meanderings, and the writings of private friendship. The sundering of the body politic found expression not only in the elegies for the dead King but also in a literature of retreat. Yet the private world that emerged from the explorations of these years was not only that of Walton and Phillips, or of Milton in the great epic that he had already begun to write. Another emblem might be taken from William Faithorne's impressive 1658 map of London, which emphasised the shipping, with all the new commercial – and private – wealth it brought into the capital: 'her Commerce and Trafick dilatinge it selfe to the utmost ends of the Earth'.[89] Commerce, power and an increasingly fully articulated realm of the private – these were the novel contributions of the writings of the 1650s to the imagining of England.

89 The 1658 map of London by William Faithorne and Richard Newcourt was published in *London Topographical Society: Publications* 18 (1905).

Chapter 22

LITERATURE AND RELIGION

DAVID LOEWENSTEIN AND JOHN MORRILL

The context

There was a war of words and images as well as a war of swords and muskets in mid seventeenth-century Britain, and it was a war fought with the same venom and the same determination. It was, to an even greater extent than the clash of arms, a war of religion or a series of wars of religion: the established Church of England was dismantled and the unity of the godly disintegrated.[1] On the battlefield, the fighting followed existing good military practice, and the codes of honour were adhered to.[2] There was no such restraint on the printed page: innovation, inventiveness, a spoliating invective was everywhere to be found. The heady cause of religious liberty was advanced with a freedom of form, syntax and vocabulary that startled, troubled and disturbed.[3] This war of religion was waged across the period in a bewildering diversity of polemical strategies and forms in both prose and poetry.

On all sides, but perhaps especially on the Puritan side of the polemical exchanges, the religious writing in the period 1640–60 is a literary equivalent of the mid nineteenth-century opening up of the American West. It was frequently characterised by an exhilarating freedom, a high dependence on contingency, a rugged individualism, extraordinary improvisation and a central authority trying and largely failing to impose rules and inappropriate order. The most exhilarating (for us) and alarming (for many contemporaries) feature of this was the freedom that men and (more dramatically) women had to think

---

1 For the case that the Civil Wars were the last of the European 'Wars of Religion', see John Morrill, 'The Religious Context of the English Civil War', *Transactions of the Royal Historical Society* 5th ser. 34 (1984), 155–78 (rpt in John Morrill, *The Nature of the English Revolution* (Harlow: Longman, 1993), pp. 45–68)); and for a critical assessment, see Glenn Burgess, 'Was the English Civil War a War of Religion?: The Evidence of Political Propaganda', *Huntington Library Quarterly* 61.2 (2000 for 1998), 173–201.
2 Barbara Donagan, 'Codes and Conduct in the English Civil War', *Past and Present* 118 (1988), 65–95.
3 The most exciting exploration of this literary dynamic is Nigel Smith, *Literature and Revolution in England 1640–1660* (London and New Haven, CT: Yale University Press, 1994).

unthinkable thoughts, to challenge those beliefs about the way the world was that previous generations had been incapable of thinking of questioning.[4] As men and women saw institutions vanish which had seemed as fixed and permanent as the peak of a mountain or the course of a river – monarchy, House of Lords, the established church – so the social and cultural constructions which had seemed just as adamantine came under challenge. The Diggers called for an end to private property,[5] the Levellers called for an end to primogeniture, and they and other radical groups sought to put an end to professional lawyers and the universities.[6] In no area, however, was the freedom to think more courageously taken up than in religion. Not only was the authority of churchmen challenged; so was the authority of the creeds, of the Fathers, of Scripture itself.[7] No one better represents this freeing of the human mind to think unthinkable thoughts than John Milton. His attacks on the existing church in 1641-2 were more far-reaching than anyone else's; his plea for a radical rethinking of the law of marriage and divorce was as fundamental a humanist challenge to received wisdom as anything written in the 1640s; his *De Doctrina Christiana* is so remarkable an assault on patristic learning and on the pillars of received Christian wisdom that even the imprudent Milton thought twice about publishing it.[8] He was as uncompromising in criticising the Puritan establishment as he was towards its predecessor; he had a visceral distrust of all authority, historical or present. He is an epitome of what became possible during the English Revolution.

Teeming liberty had as much shape as a lava flow. But some channels are clear amidst the smoke and the glow. Not even in the first great era of Reformation was there such a relentless testimony to the immanence and imminence of God. Hundreds of occasional sermons and pamphlets testified to the intense personal involvement of God in the present events, and in his personal call to each and every individual to participate in personal and national reformation. The rhetoric is more restrained on the Royalist side of the arguments, but it

---

4 The classic statement of this is Christopher Hill, *The World Turned Upside Down: Radical Ideas During the English Revolution*, 2nd edn (Harmondsworth: Penguin, 1975).

5 For contrasting views on this, see Christopher Hill, *Gerrard Winstanley: The Law of Freedom and Other Writings* (Harmondsworth: Penguin, 1973), esp. pp. 20-31, and J. C. Davis, *Utopia and the Ideal State: A Study of English Utopian Writings 1516-1700* (Cambridge University Press, 1981), pp. 169-204.

6 For the best introduction to the social ideas of the Levellers, see Margaret James, *Social Problems and Policy during the Puritan Revolution 1640-1660*, 2nd edn (London: Routledge, 1966). For a brief summary, see John Morrill, 'The Impact on Society', in *Revolution and Restoration: England in the 1650s*, ed. Morrill (London: Collins and Brown, 1992), pp. 91-111.

7 See below, pp. 698-713.

8 For a robust analysis of Milton's radical religious thought, see Christopher Hill, *Milton and the English Revolution* (London: Faber, 1977), chs. 18-26.

was omnipresent. The immanence of God was reinforced with an immensely powerful providentialism;[9] and the Old Testament was ransacked for parallels with the present of God's invitation to his chosen people, his rewarding of them when they obeyed his call and his terrible punishment on them when they failed to heed it. The imminence of God was reinforced with overwhelming testimony that the Second Coming was nigh; and the Pauline epistles were ransacked by many and the books of Daniel and Revelation ransacked by some for the language of an eschatalogical destiny for the revolutionary impulse.[10] There were plenty of Englishmen immune to this language. It was, however, politically incorrect to challenge it, at least until Royalist satirists, with nothing to lose, began to cudgel the godly in the 1650s.

All this fuelled the wars of words that were to define the great literary responses to the religious and institutional struggles of the period. Sir Thomas Browne, who eschewed Puritan zeal and iconoclasm, was unusual in this fiercely contentious age: regarding 'discourse in matters of Religion', he found himself 'neither violently defending one, nor with that common ardour and contention opposing another'.[11]

Wars of words sometimes sought to make sense of events as they unfolded, and sometimes they helped to define and shape crisis. It was a war of words that helped to determine what became the Royalist party in the Civil Wars and the Parliamentarian party of the 1640s. This verbal conflict focused on the reform or replacement of the hybrid religious settlement of 1559 – specifically on the nature of the Royal Supremacy in matters ecclesiastical, on the future of episcopacy and of episcopal oversight of the church, and on the retention in any form of the Book of Common Prayer.[12] This print war was at its height in the period from the spring of 1641 to the summer of 1642. It thus ran strictly parallel to the Parliamentary skirmishing launched by the presentation of the roots-and-branches[13] petition for 'reforming the reformation' of

9 For which see Alexandra Walsham, *Providence in Early Modern England* (Oxford University Press, 1999).
10 This can be seen in any or all of the Fast Sermons preached before the Long Parliament, most of which were published. For a list, see J. F. Wilson, *Pulpit in Parliament: Puritanism during the English Civil Wars 1640–1648* (Princeton University Press, 1969), pp. 255–75.
11 Sir Thomas Browne, *Religio Medici* (1643) in *Religio Medici and Other Works*, ed. L. C. Martin (Oxford: Clarendon Press, 1964), p. 3.
12 Anthony Fletcher, *The Outbreak of the English Civil War* (London: Edward Arnold, 1981); John Morrill, 'The Attack on the Church of England in the Long Parliament', in Morrill, *The Nature of the English Revolution*, pp. 69–90.
13 Usually known as 'root and branch'. But that is incorrect. The original petition clearly uses the plural form: see Richard Strier, 'The Root and Branch Petition and the Grand Remonstrance: from Diagnosis to Operation', in *The Theatrical City: Culture, Theatre and Politics in London, 1576–1649*, ed. David L. Smith, Richard Strier and David Bevington (Cambridge University Press, 1995), pp. 225–7.

1547–59.[14] In the course of this skirmish more than half the bishops were impeached, and proposals laid out for the suspension of the rest pending a full review by an assembly of divines. The war of words was to rumble on for the next eighteen years.

This war of words over religion between Royalists and Parliamentarians was soon strictly subsidiary to the verbal skirmishes within the Parliamentarian movement. All hope that the Elizabethan Church Settlement could be replaced by a system rooted in the application of Biblical (specifically Pauline) ecclesiology and the witness of Protestant churches elsewhere quickly faded. Paul's pronouncements were found to be Delphic; and the evidence of incompatible models – those of the Scottish church and of the New England churches specifically – was just too great.[15] Between June 1643 and late 1646, the Westminster Assembly of Divines wrestled with these issues.[16] It was made up of two representative 'godly' ministers from each county, two from each university and four from London (nominated by the MPs from each area) with ten Lords chosen by the upper house and twenty members chosen by the Lower House. To these 120 Englishmen, a small but relentless group of Scottish delegates was added as a consequence of the Solemn League and Covenant. This was the treaty by which the two kingdoms undertook to bring about a uniformity of faith and practice in England, Scotland and Ireland. The Assembly was successful in agreeing to a new model of worship and new doctrinal statements acceptable to most Calvinistic groups and churches; but there was no agreement on church government. The 'Presbyterians' stressed the need for a strong uniformity of belief, worship and discipline policed by a bottom-up series of assemblies and jurisdictions (at the equivalent of deanery, county and national levels). The later 'Independents' or non-separating Congregationalists made each local church community responsible for its own forms and practices, but with regional and national advisory bodies to which – it was argued – individual churches would want to show all due respect and regard. This was a debate about the appropriate form of the national church in a confessional state. It was not a debate about the cause of religious toleration or pluralism.

Cutting across and complicating both these debates was another, increasingly strident debate about the authority of the clergy – to define religious

---

14 The phrase comes from a Fast Sermon by Edmund Calamy, *England's Looking Glass*, preached on 22 November 1641. This and other sermons to the Long Parliament were consulted in the facsimile edition: R. Jeffs (ed.), *Fast Sermons to the Parliament, November 1640 – April 1653*, 34 vols. (London: Cornmarket Press, 1970–1).

15 Tom Webster, *Godly Clergy in Early Stuart England: The Caroline Puritan Movement c. 1620–1643* (Cambridge University Press, 1997), ch. 17.

16 The fullest modern account is Robert Paul, *The Assembly of the Lord: Politics and Religion in the Westminster Assembly and the Grand Debate* (Edinburgh: T. and T. Clark, 1985).

truth, to monopolise the right to proclaim it from the pulpit, and to exercise ecclesiastical jurisdiction – and the challenge to those clerical claims.[17] It had been a key element in the Laudian strategy of the 1630s to remove the shackles that the Reformation had placed on churchmen. The Royal Supremacy was to be exercised through the bishops and Convocation; the church courts were to be freed from the supervision and intervention of the common law courts; and much of the wealth and jurisdiction stripped from the church in the mid seventeenth century was to be restored. Much of the opposition to Laudianism was opposition to clerisy. There was, however, a high *iure divino* Presbyterianism as well as a high *iure divino* episcopalianism and very much the same men who had written against the latter came to fulminate against the former – John Milton and Henry Parker are only the first two who spring to mind. Virtually no one argued the case for Laudianism in the 1640s (although some, like Herrick in *His Noble Numbers*, memorialised it); the Royalists pinned their faith in an episcopalianism shorn of coercive power and firmly under lay control ('Erastianism'). There was, however, a vigorous debate within Presbyterianism and Presbyterianism's enemies were not shy about commenting on that debate. That debate, moreover, became intertwined with the debate between English and Scottish churchmen.[18] The latter maintained that their participation in the English Civil War after 1643 had, as its principal purpose, the establishment of a strong theocratic polity of the kind established in Scotland in the years 1639–43. There the General Assembly paralleled the Parliament in authority, and there the power of excommunication (and therefore the power to exclude from public office) lay with the clerical estate. At least eighty pamphlets addressed by Scottish ministers to an English audience or by English clergy and laymen in response were published in the thirty months following the signing of the Solemn League and Covenant between the two nations in the autumn of 1643.[19]

In the following years, Parliament – acting on advice from the Westminster Assembly of Divines – set out to dismantle the old church. Episcopacy was formally abolished in 1646, and bishops' and cathedral lands were sold off to tenant farmers, to local landowners and to London business-men. The cathedrals themselves were recycled for a variety of purposes – prisons, barracks,

---

17 William Lamont, *Godly Rule: Politics and Religion 1603–1660* (Basingstoke: Macmillan, 1969).
18 Joong-Lak Kim, 'The Debate on the Relations Between the Churches of Scotland and England During the British Revolution (1633–1647)', unpublished Ph.D. thesis, University of Cambridge, 1997; John Coffey, *Politics, Religion and the British Revolutions: The Mind of Samuel Rutherford* (Cambridge University Press, 1997), ch. 6.
19 Kim, 'Debate on the Relations between the Churches', ch. 7.

shopping precincts as well as local preaching centres. Use of the Prayer Book was proscribed in 1644 but the ban was ineffectual, and the book was used – normally shorn of its rubrics – for the sacraments and other rites of passage in many churches throughout the period, and probably in a majority of churches by and from the mid 1650s.[20] Meanwhile a bitterly divided Assembly propounded an alternative authoritarian structure of church government, discipline and practice that would be binding on all inhabitants of Britain and Ireland.[21] Parliament diluted its provisions, however, and put it firmly under lay control locally and at the centre. This 'lame erastian presbytery' as Robert Baillie termed it,[22] was half-established in just under half of England. Bishops and church courts had been swept away, but alternative policing structures withered on the vine. The Commonwealth inherited the rights to present to livings (and the tithes, the payments of one tenth of one's income to the church as decreed by Holy Scripture) for all Crown livings, all episcopal and dean and chapter livings, and all those previously held by those convicted of active Royalism (the 'malignants' and the 'delinquents'). The Commonwealth secured and retained perhaps 40 per cent of the patronage. The remainder lay with the laymen who had controlled this since the Reformation or even before. There thus remained a 'state church' in the sense of a parish system with a publicly approved ministry supported by tithes which everyone was required to pay (a principle seriously challenged by a Quaker campaign throughout the 1650s). But the laws requiring church attendance, and the laws prescribing forms of worship had been repealed. Even the parochial registration of baptisms, marriages and deaths was abolished in 1653 in favour of civil registration. Celebration of Prayer Book services in or outside parish churches, and Catholic rites of all kinds were proscribed, but the proscription was enforced only occasionally and laxly.[23]

In effect, from 1647 on, the case for the confessional state had collapsed. Too many separatist assemblies had established themselves, too many prophets gathered believers around them, too many mainstream Congregationalists had opted out of the system, even before the one true mass movement of the Revolution – the Quakers – emerged in the mid 1650s.[24] It is probably true that the remarkable debate in print on the nature and extent of religious liberty exaggerates the scale of the dis-integration of religious unity in the 1650s. On

20 Morrill, *The Nature of the English Revolution*, pp. 148–76.
21 Elliot Vernon, 'The Sion College Conclave and London Presbyterianism in the English Revolution', unpublished Ph.D. thesis, University of Cambridge, 2000.
22 *The Letters and Journals of Robert Baillie*, ed. David Laing, 3 vols. (Edinburgh: Bannatyne Club, 1841–2), 2.90.
23 Morrill, *The Nature of the English Revolution*, pp. 163–70.
24 For a discussion of their writings, see below, pp. 703–6.

no Sunday in that decade is it likely that more than 5 per cent of the population were attending religious services outside their parish churches (with a great concentration in London).[25] Nonetheless, religious liberty was the issue dominating the print culture of the decade. Oliver Cromwell was famously to tell Parliament in January 1655 that 'religio[us liberty] was not the thing at the first contested for, but God brought it to that issue at last and gave it to us by way of redundancy'.[26] Yet only five months earlier he could complain to that same Parliament about 'the carnal divisions and contentions among Christians', and at the end of his life, in an outburst of exhausted ferocity, he could bewail how every sect 'strove to be uppermost'[27] and that

> we have an appetite to variety, to be not only making wounds, but as if we should see one making wounds in a man's side and would desire nothing more than to be groping and grovelling with his fingers in those wounds. This is that men will be at; this is the spirit of those that would trample on men's liberties in spiritual respects. They will be making wounds, and rending and tearing, and making them wider than they are.[28]

Cromwell's problem as head of state was to differentiate those who sought liberty as a way of seeking God from those who sought liberty as a justification for moral licentiousness or as a means of imposing their own visions on others. There were those who demanded liberty for themselves, but saw no reason to extend it to others; there were those who demanded liberty for everyone as the only way of ensuring liberty for themselves; and there were those who wished to confer liberty on others, with or without restriction. Most obviously the issues at the heart of these debates concerned the right of religious assembly, the right freely to preach and to publish religious opinion, and the containment of the moral chaos that was alleged to have ensued from the collapse of the confessional state.[29]

The period witnessed the production of many thousands of polemical tracts of all sizes, from 8 to 300 pages in length; hundreds of sermons on contemporary events; hundreds of declarations, orders and other propaganda statements put out in the name of political authority in forms which gave them a quasi-legal status. Then there were the dozens of Socratic dialogues with increasingly mordant satirical content; dozens of poems on the state of the church and the public

25 J. F. McGregor and Barry Reay (eds.), *Radical Religion in the English Revolution* (Oxford University Press, 1984), pp. 9–11.
26 *Speeches of Oliver Cromwell*, ed. Ivan Roots (London: Dent, 1989), p. 67.
27 *Ibid.*, p. 33.   28 *Ibid.*, p. 180.
29 John Coffey, *Persecution and Toleration in Protestant England 1558–1689* (Harlow: Longman, 2000), ch. 6.

and private sins of churchmen couched more in scatological than in eschatological doggerel;[30] and foolscap broadsheets, replete with evocative woodcuts or
engravings for display on the walls of the taverns and alehouses of England and
Wales.[31] Passionate pleading and savage mockery were in incongruous partnership, as explicitly religious publication averaged between twenty and fifty
titles a month on the shelves of George Thomason's bookshop over the 220
months that spanned the calling of the Long Parliament in November 1640 to
the demise of the restored Rump in February 1660.

One simple way of measuring the impact of particular religious debates is to
look at the presence of key words in the titles of publications: thus the word
'bishop' appears in 363 titles between 1603 and 1659, and 207 of those (almost
60%) occur in the years 1640–3.[32] There is a similar percentage in relation to
the smaller number of publications containing the word 'episcopacy' and the
words 'prelate' and 'prelacy' (neither of which are visible in the publications
of the years 1620–39). By contrast only 6% of the 401 occurrences of the word
'presbyterian' in all titles published 1640–59 appeared in 1640–2, compared
with 60% in the years 1643–8 (a similar proportion for each period to that for
works whose titles included the word 'Independent' as a religious denomina-
tor). A study of the word 'liberty' in titles tells a slightly different story. The
word appears at a steady rate across the period, but whereas less than a quarter
of the uses in 1640–1 are religious (more typical are such uses as 'The Liberty
of the Manor of Stepney', and ' . . . against the subject's liberty'), by 1646 the
proportion had risen to two thirds, and by 1654 to three quarters.[33]

Literature and church government

The war of words was a war that fragmented debate. It was a war of literary
grapeshot. Within the anarchy of themes and enthusiasms, however, in which
so many taboos were challenged, and so many unthinkable thoughts given an
airing, some core arguments held steady. Two prominent ones that will be used
as organising principles within this chapter are, first, the running argument

30 Probably the best way of gaining a sense of this pattern remains the chronologically arranged
    G. K. Fortescue, *Catalogue of the Pamphlets, Books, Newspapers, and Manuscripts . . . Collected
    by George Thomason*, 2 vols. (London: William Claudes and Sons, 1908).
31 Tessa Watt, *Cheap Print and Popular Piety, 1550–1640* (Cambridge University Press, 1991).
    A great many of the broadsheets published between 1640 and 1660 were collected together
    by George Thomason, and are catalogued by the British Library as the 669 series. They
    are gathered together in the microfilm edition of the Thomason Tracts (Ann Arbor, MI:
    University Microfilms International, 1977–81), 256 reels with index.
32 This and similar calculations are derived by key-word searches on *EEBO (Early English Books
    Online)*.
33 Based on searches made of the title pages as printed in *EEBO*.

about church government between the advocates of a confessional state and the champions of religious pluralism, and second, the literature of the Holy Spirit.

Much of the first debate was stimulated by 'official publication', the commissioned polemic licensed by the parties to the political conflict, the making public and the formal endorsement of that which had hitherto been private and privileged. Thus from 5 April 1641 the two Houses of Parliament – but fairly soon the Commons alone – appropriated to itself the right to place its imprimatur on what became a vast publicity enterprise. About 1,300 of the 8,000 or so items published in the years 1641–5 were authorised by one or both of the Houses and bore their official commendation.[34] In the spring of 1643 Edward Husbands (publisher to the Parliament) could publish *An exact collection of all remonstrances, declarations, orders ... betweene the Kings most excellent Majesty and his high court of Parliament*, a collection of not fewer than 410 items. Parliament was confident enough to republish most of Charles's formal statements. The Houses were convinced that his own words, as glossed by theirs, would reveal a conspiracy by wicked counsellors to befuddle and confuse the King so as to induce him to deliver the country up to popery and to an arbitrary government in which he was a puppet and the papists the puppet-masters. The King in his publication alleged that a sinister and malignant minority were seeking personal power and were allying with dissolute sectaries in an unholy alliance that could lead only to anarchy. In a known world where religious wars had led to the dissolution of governments, the language of anarchy was more terrifying than the language of tyranny, and fear of social and moral inversion read into religious separatism was equally powerful. Many of the documents reproduced in Husbands's *Exact collection* were originally printed on folio sheets and both sides in the disputes gave them the familiar form of royal proclamations. They were pinned to many church doors, on inn walls and in market squares. A rhetoric of mutual respect masked tense, terse language in which each side claimed to be protecting true religion and English liberties from imminent catastrophic assault.

This was a message reinforced by the semi-official publication of the speeches of some forty-five MPs – many fabricated by or published with the collusion of their purported authors.[35] For example, thirty-three speeches were published as by John Pym; no more than eighteen of these were ever delivered

34 Sheila Lambert, 'Printing for Parliament 1641–1700', *List and Index Society*, spec. ser. 20 (1981); Sheila Lambert, 'The Beginning of Printing for the House of Commons, 1640–1642', *The Library* 6th ser. 3 (1981), 43–61.
35 Alan Cromartie, 'The Printing of Parliamentary Speeches, November 1640–July 1642', *Historical Journal* 33. 1 (1990), 23–42.

in Parliament, and there was significant adaptation of the content in many of those eighteen.[36] An average of ten supposed Parliamentary speeches were published in each month of the first session of the Long Parliament (November 1640–August 1641) and then a more fluctuating number (peaking at twenty-seven in January 1642) before MPs receded back into public silence from the spring.[37]

By far the commonest subject matter of these speeches was church government: on the need for reform and on the need for fundamental reform ('roots and branches' were the watchwords) or for a return to 'the pure religion of Queen Elizabeth and King James' (or 'the pure true Protestant religion by law established without any connivance of popery or innovation' – that is, the Elizabethan Settlement shorn of Laudian adornments) as the future Royalists put it.[38] In addition, with the active collusion of the King's ministers and of Parliamentary leaders, many of the petitions presented from a majority of English counties for and against roots-and-branches reform of the church were printed.[39] Finally, from the summer of 1641 Parliament routinely ordered the publication of the sermons preached – always in pairs – on the monthly Fast Days.[40] These sermons were uncompromising in identifying the incompleteness of England's sixteenth-century Reformation, the subsequent falling back into popery and the certainty and imminence of God's wrath if there was not a rapid, thorough and universal national reformation. The preachers made clear what they would not have rather than what they would have, but there was a providentialist imperative in their rhetoric. The pattern was repetitive but powerful. The preacher took a story from the Old Testament in which God had given freedom of choice to the people of Israel: they could obey and be rewarded or disobey and be punished – typically by being enslaved (in, for example, Egypt or Babylon). The preacher then looked at the condition of England at that moment and showed in great detail the parallels with the Biblical situation and the necessity of a dynamic response (personal and national reformation).

36 John Morrill, 'The Unweariableness of Mr Pym: Influence and Eloquence in the Puritan Revolution', in Susan Amussen and Mark A. Kishlansky (eds.), *Political Culture and Cultural Politics in Early Modern England* (Manchester University Press, 1995), pp. 36–43.

37 Cromartie, 'Printing', p. 27.

38 *Bibliotheca Lindesiana: A Bibliography of Royal Proclamations of Tudor and Stuart Sovereigns*, ed. R. R. Steele, 2 vols. (Oxford University Press, 1910), 1:295. For a general discussion of this point, see Morrill, *The Nature of the English Revolution*, pp. 69–90.

39 Judith Maltby, *Prayer Book and People in Elizabethan and Early Stuart England* (Cambridge University Press, 1998), chs. 4 and 5. For the texts of most of the petition, see Sir Thomas Aston, *A collection of sundry petitions presented unto the Kings Most Excellent Majesty* (London, 1642).

40 For a complete list of all these Fast Sermons, see Wilson, *Pulpit in Parliament*, pp. 255–74.

The titles of the sermons are evocative of those choices: Stephen Marshall (who preached more than anyone else to the Long Parliament) in February 1642 published his sermon *Meroz Cursed* on the text from Judges 5:23: 'Curse ye Meroz (said the Angell of the Lord) curse we bitterly the inhabitants thereof, because they came not to the helpe of the Lord, to the help of the Lord against the mighty';[41] two months later Thomas Goodwin published his plea for the completion of a reformation left unfinished for eighty years just as Solomon's Temple had been left unfinished after his death for eighty years during which it had become polluted with the pagan rites of the Samaritans, as now the English church had been by those of the Laudians: *Zerubbabel's Encouragement to finish the Temple* (text from Zechariah 4:6–9).[42] There was no Royalist equivalent.

In deepest Suffolk, a yeoman farmer took out a subscription to the published sermons, and month by month he read and annotated them. In due course it was the cumulative message of the sermons about God's punishment of idolaters that led him to volunteer to remove all 'monuments of idolatry and superstition' from the churches of East Anglia. His name was William Dowsing and he got the job.[43] Across England, this proliferation of official and semi-official publications amazed, startled, challenged men and women at all social levels, whether they sat at home and read them to themselves and their households, or heard them read out in churches on Sundays or in town squares on market days. It is a vital context for the flood of publications aimed at literate, politically active and independent folk eager to purchase, to pass around, to discuss the future shape of the religious institutions, forms of worship, codes of discipline that would shape their lives. The great literary debate on church government and liturgy followed on not so much from parliamentary action as the publication of materials relating to parliamentary debate.

The first great series of polemical exchanges was generated by the publication of Bishop Joseph Hall's *Humble Remonstrance to the High Court of Parliament* (London, 1641). Hall had been pressed into service as a veteran Jacobean bishop,[44] relatively uncontaminated by links with, or dependency on, the hated Archbishop Laud (the target by name of thirty-seven pamphlets in

41 Stephen Marshall, *Meroz Cursed* (London, 1641). Marshall took this sermon on tour, repeating it in up to twenty major towns. It was reprinted in 1645, and its reprinting provoked a flurry of replies.
42 T. Goodwin, *Zerubbabel's Encouragement to finish the Temple* (London, 1642).
43 John Morrill, 'William Dowsing and the Administration of Iconoclasm in the English Revolution', in *The Journal of William Dowsing: Iconoclasm in East Anglia in the English Civil War*, ed. Trevor Cooper (London: The Ecclesiological Society, 2001), pp. 6–10.
44 Hall deserves and requires a major modern study. In the meantime, F. L. Huntley, *Bishop Joseph Hall 1574–1656: A Biographical and Critical Study* (Cambridge: D. S. Brewer, 1979), established the context for his important writings of the 1640s.

1641 and 1642).[45] Hall's assignment was to challenge the Scottish Parliament's abolition of episcopacy and specifically the Bishop of Orkney's renunciation of the indelible mark of his episcopal consecration. *Episcopacy by Divine Right Asserted* is an uneasy, self-conscious document (perhaps because Hall felt the Primate's hot breath on his neck as he wrote it) with unstable pronominalisation and an accompanying unwillingness to move from the apostolic and patristic ages into the present. *The Humble Remonstrance* is altogether stronger intellectually and stylistically. The earlier tract begins with 'an expostulatorie entrance': 'Good God! What is this, that I have lived to heare? That a Bishop in a Christian Assembly, should renounce his Episcopall function, and cry mercy for his now-abandoned calling? Brother that was (who ever you be) I must have leave a while to contest seriously with you; the act was yours, the concernment the whole Churches.'[46] There is an instability in the audience, the pitch and focus here. *The Humble Remonstrance* is one tenth the length but more coherent in its defence of Biblical imperative and of tradition, and in its evocation of the hazards to social cohesion if ecclesiastical hierarchy is replaced by ecclesiastical egalitarianism.[47] It was an argument fully developed by Sir Thomas Aston in his *Remonstrance against Presbytery*:

> let us then ere we imbrace the thoughts of such a totall subversion of the fabrick of a Church and State examine whether such Reformers aime at our liberty or theire own advancement... is it not really to pull downe 26 bishops or set up 9324 potentiall popes... [they would] Sampson-like in their full strength... lay hold of those pillars of our state that prop up the regulated fabrick of this glorious monarchy, and by cracking them, wilfully burie themselves and us in the rubbish of chaos.[48]

Despite the unease of this conceit (Samson was, after all, God's chosen instrument, and however much he had betrayed his calling, his self-sacrificial massacre of the Philistines was redemptive in Old Testament terms), the essentially anarchistic consequences of Puritan institutional iconoclasm are powerfully expressed.

The first serious response to Hall's *Remonstrance* came in a pamphlet put together by five Puritan ministers, all of whom had gritted their teeth and kissed the Laudian rod in the 1630s, preferring to compromise with the dictates of conscience so as to protect their flocks from worse, rather than opt

---

45 Calculated from *Early English Books Online*.
46 Joseph Hall, *Episcopacie by Divine Right. Asserted* (London, 1640), pp. 1–2.
47 Joseph Hall, *An Humble Remonstrance* (London, 1640), pp. 3–4.
48 Sir Thomas Aston, *A Remonstrance against Presbytery* (London, 1642), sig. A13.

out of prudent minimalist conformity into the bracing freedom of the 'howling wilderness' of New England.[49] All five had received and still received the discreet patronage of Puritan peers, and their initials made up the mnemonic SMECTYMNUUS[50]: the pamphlet's title was *An Answer to a booke entituled, An Humble Remonstrance*. It suffers from collective authorship, with a rather relentless earnestness and repetitiveness, its prose drained of individual flights of fancy. It launched a rapid succession of exchanges of twenty-three separate publications, and it drew John Milton into the fray, in defence (as he claimed) and perhaps at the behest of one of the Smectymnuans, his old schoolmaster Thomas Young. In a succession of five tracts – notably *Of Reformation* and *Of Prelatical Episcopacy*[51] – published in 1641 and 1642, Milton compared the purity of gospel ordinance and the liberty within the primitive church with 'the chaffe of overdated Ceremonies, ... [the] stumble forward another way into the new-vomited Paganisme of sensual Idolatry', a catastrophe he laid firmly at the door of a haughty clergy.[52] Milton's writings are indeed a harbinger of the extraordinary usurpation performed by a generation of Biblically immersed and theologically informed laymen on the near-monopoly of the clergy not only in the pulpit but in religious print. Later, Henry Lawrence – Oliver Cromwell's landlord in the 1630s and President of his Council of State in the 1650s – was publishing, with Milton's help, a definitive 210-page tract on angelology, as close to a holy of holies of clerical writing as can be imagined.[53] And Milton's fierce anti-clericalism – soon to be directed against Puritan ministers as much as against Laudian ceremonialists – was equally precocious and anticipatory of one of the major discourses of the whole period. His contempt for the conformist clergy reaches its apogee at the fiery end of *Of Reformation*. There he calls for worldly punishment of them for their pride and arrogance. But he also predicts that hereafter the bishops will 'be throwne downe eternally into the darkest and deepest Gulfe of HELL, where under the despightfull controule, the trample and spurne of all

49 A phrase used by the Lord Protector in addressing Parliament on 22 January 1655: *Speeches of Oliver Cromwell*, ed. Roots, p. 67.

50 An acrostic made up the initials of Stephen Marshall, Edmund Calamy, Thomas Young, Matthew Newcomen, UUilliam Spurstowe.

51 But also *Animadversions upon the Remonstrants Defence, The Reason of Church-governement urg'd against episcopacy* and *An Apology against a pamphlet call'd a modest confutation of the animadversions upon the Remonstrant against Smectymnuus.*

52 *Of Reformation*, in *Complete Prose Works of John Milton*, gen. ed. Don M. Wolfe *et al.*, 8 vols. (New Haven, CT: Yale University Press, 1953–82), 1:519–20; subsequent quotations ave cited parenthetically in our text with the abbreviation *CPW*.

53 Henry Lawrence, *Of our communion, and warre with angels* (London, 1646). Milton's assistance is noted in *STC*.

the other Damned ... they shall remaine in that plight for ever, the basest, the lowermost, the most dejected, most underfoot and the downe-trodden Vassals of Perdition'.[54]

One of Milton's stock devices in his early zealous prose was coarse abuse, burlesque as much as satire, a device he boldly defended at length in the preface to the *Animadversions*: 'such a grim laughter ... hath oft-times a strong and sinewy force in teaching and confuting'.[55] By contrast, Royalists' stock device was haughty hyperbole. It also has to be said that the vigour and spontaneity began to disappear on both sides of the debate in the summer of 1642. Although Charles I claimed to be fighting for the church as well as the Crown, Anglican polemic reached a low point in the years 1643–6. It consisted of the tracts of a handful of Scottish bishops, especially the unyielding John Maxwell (author of *Sacro-Sancta Regum Majestatis: or, the sacred and royall prerogative of Christian kings* (1644)) and of a handful of Irish bishops, especially John Bramhall (as in *A fair warning* (1649)). The English bishops, however, hid themselves away or went into exile and did little by word or deed to sustain their cause. Even their spokesmen fell silent. Peter Heylyn, Laud's sharp-tongued speechwriter in the 1630s, and the most strident voice of second-generation Laudianism in the 1660s and 1670s, was mute between his *Rebel's Catechism* (1643) and the eve of the Restoration.[56] It was left to a younger generation of royal chaplains and a sprinkling of pious laymen to keep the case for the Elizabethan Church alive. More than sixty pamphlets printed between 1646 and 1659 contained the word 'episcopacy' in the title, with peaks in 1648, 1654 and 1656, and a trough in the years 1650–3 (between one and three titles per annum). Although this younger generation mounted a series of oblique defences of non-Laudian Anglicanism (Henry Hammond's *Considerations for present use* (1644) and *Of the power of the keyes* (1647) and Jeremy Taylor's *Treatise of Episcopacy* (1648) are representative), what anchored the case for the disestablished Anglican Church was the publication in 1649 of *The Papers which passed at Newcastle Betwixt his sacred Majesty and Mr Al: Henderson concerning the Change of Church Government*. This, together with the immensely popular *Eikon Basilike*, with its Christic apotheosis of the executed King Charles, provided the manifesto for the Church-and-Crown alliance of the second half of the century. One should not underestimate the quiet and moderate witness of this young generation

---

54 Milton, *CPW*, 1:616–17. 55 *Ibid.*, 1:663–4.
56 Heylyn had, for example, written Laud's published judgement against Burton, Bastwicke and Prynne in 1638 and was later to publish the principal apologias for Laud, *Cyprianus Anglicus* (London, 1668) and *Ecclesia Restaurata* (London, 1670).

in keeping before a shell-shocked gentry the image of a clergy theologically prudent, socially deferential and liturgically restrained. They were to inherit the kingdom in 1662.

That said, the episcopalians left the field to the Puritans to engage in spectacular public disagreements amongst themselves. With Laudians mute, and the defenders of episcopacy spending half their space disclaiming Laud's 'English popery' before defending the office and the men Charles nominated to replace the disgraced Laudians, the advocates of reformation fired on all cylinders and united their natural constituency while alienating much moderate, thoughtful opinion.

What united them was pent-up fury at Laudian clerisy and the liturgical aesthetic which Laud himself had christened the 'beauty of holiness'.[57] The snag, however, was that reform made for an untidy alliance. There was a profound anti-clericalism at the heart of the anti-episcopal campaign, and that soon came to be redirected towards all those Puritans who wanted to replace *iure divino* bishops by *iure divino* presbyters. Milton was not alone in finding that 'New Presbyter is but Old Priest writ large' (see pp. 683–4, 688 below). Henry Parker wrote some of the most powerful critiques of episcopal claims in 1641–2;[58] but he was no less relentless in his criticisms of *iure divino* Presbyterianism in the following years.[59] William Prynne, having had the tips of his ears sliced off in 1633 for libelling the Queen and the stumps sliced off in 1637 for libelling the bishops, spent much of the early 1640s in a relentless attack on the latter (*A catalogue of such testimonies in all ages as plainly evidence Bishops and Presbyters to be both one* (London, 1641); *Lord Bishops: None of the Lord's Bishops* (London, 1640); *A New Discovery of the Prelates Tyranny* (London, 1641)) and in managing and publicising the trial of Laud (*Canterburies Doome*) and publishing – with inflammatory annotations – Laud's diary.[60] But he also untiringly assaulted the proposals for a Presbyterian church settlement (as in *Diotrephes catechised: or sixteen important questions... challenged by a divine right by some over-rigid Presbyterians and Independents* (London, 1646)) as he did the claims of anyone to toleration outside the state church. He was extreme in his Erastianism, and his prolix lambasting of those he disapproved of was relentless, but his visceral

57 Early Stuart usage is examined and exemplified in *The Stuart Constitution: Documents and Commentary*, ed. J. P. Kenyon, 2nd edn (Cambridge University Press, 1986), pp. 148–9.
58 E.g. Henry Parker, *The Question Concerning the Divine Right of Episcopacie Truly Stated* (London, 1641) and *The True Grounds of Ecclesiastical Regiment* (London, 1641).
59 E.g. Parker, *Ius Regum* (London, 1645) and *The Trojan Horse of Presbyteriall Government Unbowelled* (London, 1646).
60 William Prynne, *A breviate of the life of William Laud, Arch-bishop of Canterbury* (London, 1644).

anti-clericalism found a large constituency. Prynne did set the tone for the 'Erastian controversy' of 1644–6, hard won by the anti-clericalists, but at the heavy cost of schism.[61] His mission statement, laid out in *Independency Examined, Unmasked, and Refuted* (September 1644), asked

> whether a Parliament...assisted with the advice and judgement of an Assembly of the most orthodox, pious conscientious learned Ministers in our church...be not more fit to form and fashion the government of the churches of Christ, and...determine...what church government is agreeable to the Word of God and fittest for every parish church throughout this land, for the advancement of the God's glory, the people's salvation, the general peace and tranquillity of church and state than any one or two Independent ministers.[62]

Two months later, however, Milton, now the implacable enemy of Presbyterianism, would dismiss false prophets who 'prognosticate a year of sects and schisms'.[63]

The contribution of the Scots to the debates on church government in England was important (if often counter-productive) throughout the 1640s. Perhaps the most important single contribution was Samuel Rutherford's *Lex Rex* (1643) which combined a message that all Parliamentarians wanted to hear – the right of lesser magistrates to call the people to self-defence against a tyrant – with a message that they were more uneasy about, concerning the relationship of church and state.[64] It is suggestive that, as early as 1641, the Scots commissioners asked Robert Baillie to focus on the case for Presbyterian government against episcopacy, George Gillespie to focus on plain style in worship against ceremonialism, and Robert Blair to focus on the case for Presbyterianism against the New England way (Congregationalism). The high earnestness, the humourless word-plays and self-righteous bluster make most of these works unappealing, although Alexander Henderson's *Government and Order of the Church of Scotland* (1642) has a calm authority and clarity, and George Gillespie's *Aaron's Rod Blossoming. Or The Divine Ordinance of Church Government Vindicated* (1646) has a tense passion that stimulated lively responses.

The case against replacing one authoritarian, rigid church structure (episcopalianism) with another (Presbyterianism) was never effectively made because what was called, at the time and since, 'Presbyterianism' consisted of a loose

---

61 For an introduction, see G. Yule, *Puritans in Politics: The Religious Legislation of the Long Parliament* (Sutton Courtney: The Sutton Courtney Press, 1981), pp. 149–208.
62 William Prynne, *Independency Examined, Unmasked, Refuted* (London, 1644), title-page.
63 Milton, *Areopagitica*, in *CPW*, 2:588.
64 John Coffey, *Politics, Religion and the British Revolutions: The Mind of Samuel Rutherford* (Cambridge University Press, 1997), ch. 6.

congeries of overlapping positions on church government in great tension with one another. 'Presbyterians' could agree on the shape and the form of worship, on moral theology and Calvinist soteriology, on the need for strong discipline rooted in an alliance of godly minister and magistrate, but there was no agreement on government. Thus there was a large audience for the *Large Catechism* and for the *Small Catechism* produced by the Westminster Assembly, and for its *Confession of Faith*, all of which retained and retain a hold in evangelical Protestant traditions in the English-speaking world in the centuries that followed. Their literary qualities, as in the case of the King James Bible and Cranmer's service books, are an important part of their longevity. The parts of the *Confession* dealing with the sacraments (chapters 27–9) were never bettered in Protestant apologetic. 'Presbyterians' could also agree that while *primary* discipline should be exercised within each parish, there needed to be a hierarchy of courts, consisting of representatives from the next layer down, to ensure consistency of judgement and the maintenance of uniformity. How much authority should be held at each level, how much reserved to the clergy and how much shared with godly laymen, and whether or not there should be constant moderators of local regions who could bear the title 'bishop' were all deeply disputed. Too much ink was spent on defending the minutiae of these differences to allow a coherent 'Presbyterianism' to emerge. When Parliament took the recommendations from the Assembly and Erastianised them, incoherence compounded itself.[65]

There was an understanding amongst the clerical protagonists of 'reforming the reformation' that they would not anticipate the outcome of the Westminster Assembly by promoting particular schemes. This was partly prudence and partly a recognition that reconciling the advocates of the Genevan-Scottish model and of the Massachusetts model would need imagination and generosity on both sides. Perhaps it was really also a hope that 120 or so godly men praying sincerely together and reading the Scriptures under the guidance of the Holy Spirit would recover a model of church government answerable to the precepts of Christ and the needs of the times. It was the minority of men returned from semi-voluntary exile who broke the self-imposed bar on public disputation. As the arrival of Scots observers in the wake of the Solemn League and Covenant strengthened the prospect of a scheme based on Genevan principles, five 'Congregationalist' ministers published *An Apologetical Narration, Humbly Submitted*

---

65 The fullest account remains Paul, *The Assembly of the Lord*. Chad von Dixhoorn is re-editing the minutes of the Assembly and transforming our understanding of them.

to the Honourable Houses of Parliament (1643), thus launching a campaign for the right to opt out of what seemed likely to be proposed by the Assembly for all those who could not in conscience accept the Presbyterian principle. This brought the haughty vituperation of the Scots and others on their heads, but it also brought out passionate defences of their position, much of the best of it from Congregationalist ministers testifying from across the Atlantic: John Cotton's *The Keyes of the Kingdom of Heaven* (1644) and *The Way of the Churches of Christ in New England* (1645) represent the most lucid of the defences, with Thomas Shepard's *New England's Lamentation for Old England's present errours and divisions* (1645) close behind. The 'Presbyterians' as usual were more effective in challenging what they could not stomach rather than in promoting what they could, with Thomas Edwards to the fore in his *Antapologia* (1644). In all, the *Apologeticall Narration* generated an ongoing debate lasting for seven or eight months as well as comment in dozens of published sermons. In the event, legislative action destroyed episcopacy; legislative inaction destroyed the case for an effective Presbyterianism. There was a fresh series of exchanges in the high summer of 1647, this time less densely theological and more satirical and scatological (three of the sequence of a dozen titles are *The lamentation of the ruling lay-Elders, sadly bemoaning the death of their late foster-father Sir John Presbyter*; *The Last Will and Testament of Sir James Independent*; and *The infamous history of Sir Simon Synod and his son Sir John Presbyter. Describing the Acts* [*of*] *their youth, Autumne and Old Age* (all in August 1647)). At last Presbyterians and Independents were able to laugh at one another (though certainly not with one another).

By 1649, a loosely confederated, Erastian national church closer to Congregationalism than to anything else, existed by default. Except for spasmodic campaigns by London Presbyterian ministers organising themselves in and around Sion College, the principal debates in print ceased to be how best to structure the national church. The key issue now became how far to permit freedom of religious assembly, practice and testimony outside that church: the case for religious freedom.

First in the field was Henry Burton (one of those whose ears had been cropped in 1637 for libelling the bishops). Inflamed by the language of the Protestation Oath of May 1641 (aimed to bind all Protestants together against Catholics and their fellow-travellers by swearing to uphold 'the true reformed Protestant religion expressed in the doctrine of the Church of England'), Burton published *The Protestation Protested*, a passionate defence of the proposition that a true church 'consists of none, but such as visible living members of Christ the head, and visible Saints under him' (sig. A3). This brought powerful rebuttals by John Geree[66] and Thomas Edwards,[67] and defences of Burton's position from the radical Robert Lord Brooke and from the most articulate of the female Baptists, Katherine Chidley[68] (considered later in this chapter). The publication in this area which did most, however, to stimulate literary debate was undoubtedly Roger Williams's *Bloudy Tenent of Persecution, for cause of Conscience* (1644). Williams, who had fled from persecution in England only to be driven out of Massachusetts for his heterodox ideas, wrote from the tiny gathered community in Providence, Rhode Island, to plead that 'the blood of so many hundred thousand souls of Protestants and Papists, spilt in the Wars of present and former Ages, for their respective Conscience, is not required nor accepted by Jesus Christ, the Prince of Peace'.[69] Yet even Williams was not a lover of those Christians who did not share his anxious chiliasm. Toleration was necessary to prevent the wheat from falling amongst tares. Freeing Catholics to worship openly would merely be the efficient means of an idolatrous and sacrilegious descent into hell. A more charitable defence of religious liberty as a natural right as articulated by a wide range of authors can be found in the writings of Richard Overton and other Levellers.[70]

Yet it remained the case that most of those demanding unfettered liberty were in need of it. Those in authority who favoured liberty for others saw it as the duty of magistrates to set prudential limits to prevent public scandal and blasphemy. If liberty ran to licence then God would show his displeasure. This was the clear position of Oliver Cromwell, whose published speeches make some of the most passionate pleas against prescription in matters of religious faith, but who still believed that there should be a state church to teach and regulate a great majority of the people (with a public ministry regulated by the state and paid by a universal financial levy) and that there should be a limit to what could be done in the name of religion.[71] He believed passionately that men and women should be able to worship God in their own way:

---

66 John Geree, *Judah's Joy at the Oath* (London, 1641).
67 Thomas Edwards, *Reasons against the independent government of particular congregations* (London, 1641).
68 Katherine Chidley, *A Justification of the Independent Churches of Christ* (London, 1641).
69 Roger Williams, *The Bloudy Tenent of Persecution, for cause of Conscience, discussed, in a conference between Truth and Peace* (London, 1644), sig. A2.
70 See below, p. 700.
71 The biography by Robert Paul, *The Lord Protector* (Grand Rapids, MI: Eerdmans, 1955), is the most thorough study. But see now J. C. Davis, 'Oliver Cromwell's Religion', in *Oliver Cromwell and the English Revolution*, ed. John Morrill (Harlow: Longman, 1990), pp. 181–208.

And what would God do? To what end? That he might plant in the wilderness the cedar and the shittah tree, and the myrtle and the palm tree together. To what end? That they might know and consider, and understand together that the hand of the Lord hath done this; and that the Lord hath created it, that he wrought all salvation and deliverance which he hath wrought, for the good of the whole flock. Therefore . . . have a care of the whole flock. Love all the sheep, love the lambs, love all, tender all, and cherish all, and countenance all in all things that are good.[72]

Cromwell also recognised that the state had the duty to restrain licentious behaviour masquerading as religious practice and to prevent members of one denomination from abusing people in another. The Commonwealth and Protectorate did see a greater degree of religious freedom – freedom of expression, freedom of religious assembly, freedom for those who opted out of state religion to participate in public life – than Britain was to see again until the end of the nineteenth century, but it was prudential state-regulated liberty, not the unfettered liberty pleaded for by the Levellers William Walwyn and Richard Overton.

The main debate concerned the liberty of individuals to live out their lives in covenanted communities without state interference. It was a case to be made by Baptists and in due course by a multitude of small sects, often gathering around a charismatic leader or a specific apocalyptic moment. And it led not only to rational debate about the desirability of pluralistic religious practice in a commonwealth of sinful men and women, but also to a nightmare literature, in which the neuroses of the godly were given angry expression. Foremost amongst such heresiographies was Thomas Edwards's *Gangraena: Or a Catalogue and Discovery of Many of the Errours, Blasphemies, Heresies and Pernicious Practices of the Sectaries of this time*, published in three editions. In the first edition (February 1646) he enumerated 16 sorts of sects, 180 errors or heresies and 28 forms of malpractice. Anxious godly from across England bombarded Edwards with fresh horror stories – the second edition added a further 34 errors and the third edition called itself *A new and higher discovery*. Milton's divorce writings constituted error 154 in the first part, and Milton memorialised Edwards in his satirical sonnet on the politics of religious persecution, 'On the New Forcers of Conscience under the Long Parliament':

---

72 Spoken by Cromwell to the Nominated Assembly on 4 July 1653: *Speeches of Oliver Cromwell*, ed. Roots, p. 22.

Men whose life, learning, faith and pure intent
Would have been held in high esteem by Paul
Must now be named and printed heretics
By shallow Edwards.[73]

As the Army (whose officers were much chastised by *Gangraena* and accused
of tolerating much blasphemous behaviour, such as the baptising of horses as
well as promoting the error of lay preaching) took political power in London in
1647, the capital became too hot for Edwards, who withdrew to Holland where
he promptly caught an infection and died. The work of naming and shaming
heretics passed to Ephraim Pagitt, whose *Heresiography: or, A description of the
Heretickes and Sectaries of these latter times* went through many editions and
expansions, without gaining the shapelessness and shrillness of *Gangraena*. It
was still being reprinted in 1662.

There was, then, a great debate on the nature and extent of rights of
conscience conceived as the liberty of individuals to live out their lives in
covenanted communities without state interference. There was also, however,
a subsidiary debate in which men of personal or intellectual substance pleaded
for a much more personal liberty to think unthinkable thoughts and to express
them. Back in 1641 this was the case made by Robert Lord Brooke (the adopted
son of Fulke Greville) in *The Nature of Truth, its union and unity with the soule*,
and both he and William Fiennes, Viscount Saye and Sele, published shorter,
more polemical (bitterly anticlerical) works in 1642.[74] The latter demanded
that men (and women) of wisdom, discernment and means should be exempt
from religious prescription of all kinds:

> I am not satisfied that a certaine number of men should usurpe an authority
> unto themselves to frame certaine prayers and formes of Divine service and,
> when that is done, under the name of the Church to injoyne them upon all
> persons . . . If because some men had need to make use of crutches, all men
> should be prohibited the use of their legges and injoyned to take up such
> crutches as have been prepared for those who had no legs. This I confesse I am
> not satisfied in.[75]

---

73 John Milton, *Complete Shorter Poems*, ed. John Carey, 2nd edn (London: Longman, 1997),
pp. 298–9.

74 *A discourse opening the nature of episcopacie which is exercised in England . . . by the Right Honourable
Robert, Lord Brooke* (London, 1641); and for Saye, see below, n. 75.

75 *A speech of the Right Honourable William, Lord Viscount Saye and Sele in answer to the Lord Archbishop of Canterburies Last Speech and concerning the Liturgie of the Church of England* (London,
1641). See also his companion piece: *A speech of the Right Honourable William, Lord Viscount
Saye and Seale, Upon the Bill against Bishops power in civill affaires and Courts of Iudicature*
(London, 1641).

The most powerful and – both at the time and ever since – influential such plea, however, was that of Milton's *Areopagitica*, which vigorously defends the freedom of the sects and gathered churches (but not of Catholics).

Poetry and religious conflict

The war of words over religion was likewise expressed in the diverse religious poetry written or published during the mid seventeenth century as poets responded – often polemically – to the assault on the Church of England and its rituals mounted by the godly and to the threatening forces of sectarianism. Godly regimes imposed cultural values upon the English nation, augmenting the tension between traditional religious practices and Puritan reform. The vitality of popular church rituals and older religious forms during these years of national turmoil and godly reform also found lively and defiant expression in religious poetry.[76] This section thus examines how poets responded to the period's acute religious tensions and divisions.

The religious conflicts of the 1640s and 1650s prompted satirical responses from pro-Royalist poets who registered anxiety about a breakdown of ecclesiastical control that was unleashing new religious freedom, zeal and lower-class radical preaching. Alexander Brome satirised the voice of iconoclastic Puritan saints who hypocritically encouraged their soldiers to fight for 'true Religion' and 'the Kingdomes good, / By robbing Churches, plundring men, / And shedding guiltlesse blood', and who wished to advance godly religion by encouraging 'mechanic preachers', artisans (like Bunyan) and uneducated laymen who had found the liberty to preach during the revolutionary decades:

> We must preserve Mecannicks now,
> To Lecturize and pray;
> By them the Gospel is advanc'd,
> The clean contrary way.[77]

John Taylor, the 'King's Water-poet' (referring to his trade as a waterman), likewise engaged himself in religious polemic on the side of the old church by publishing popular (and often clumsy if energetic) satirical verses and emblems expressing his anxieties about the madness of 'these Distracted times' as he defended ceremony in worship, attacked popery and ridiculed the emergence

---

76 On widespread attachment to Church of England rituals, see Morrill, *The Nature of the English Revolution*, ch. 7.

77 'The Saints Encouragement' (1643), in *Alexander Brome: Poems*, ed. Roman R. Dubinski, 2 vols. (University of Toronto Press, 1982).

of 'peevish Sects, / Full of foule errors, poore, and bare of sence'.[78] Meanwhile, John Cleveland and Abraham Cowley produced high-spirited verse satires in the 1640s: these included the former's 'A Dialogue between Two Zealots' (mocking the zany apocalyptic interpretations of Puritan clergymen), 'Smectymnuus, or the Club-Divines' (ridiculing, with contemptuous wit and linguistic ingenuity, the monstrosity of the five Puritans whose initials made up the acronym 'Smectymnuus'), 'The Mixt Assembly' (a scathing satire on the Presbyterian Westminster Assembly and the reformation of the English Church) and a polemical, hyperbolic elegy 'On the Archbishop of Canterbury' and on the destruction of the country ('The state in *Strafford* fell, the Church in *Laud*').[79] Cowley's anti-Puritan verses included *The Puritans Lecture* (1642; first printed as *A Satyre Against Separatists*) and *The Puritan and the Papist* (1643); these aggressive partisan satires of London Puritan lecturers and contemporary religious extremes (e.g. the Puritan left and the papist right) assault the English church and state, and resemble scurrilous anti-Puritan prose and poetic satires of the early 1640s (e.g. John Taylor's *A Swarme of Sectaries* (1641); *A Tale in a Tub or, A Tub Lecture* (1641); *A Cluster of Coxcombes* (1642)). They likewise complement Cowley's seething satirical depiction in *The Civil War* (1643) of multitudes of 'base Mechanicks', loathsome heresies and monstrous sects spawned by 'the Furies' in London.[80]

Moreover, though Parliament abolished episcopacy in 1646, its poetic defenders were by no means silenced. A 'Profest Royalist' engaged in 'His Quarrel with the Times', Francis Quarles included in his posthumously published *The Shepheards Oracles* (1646) a pastoral debate between Anarchus and Canonicus in which the former speaker condemns set forms, the Book of Common Prayer ('a meer Relique of the Romane Whore') and popish church rituals, while the latter sharply counters: 'What Apostle taught your tongue / To gibe at Bishops? Or to vex and wrong / Your Mother Church?'[81] Richard Corbet, Bishop of Oxford

---

78 *Mad Fashions, Od Fashions, All out of Fashions* (London, 1642); *A Swarme of Sectaries, and Schismatiques* ([London], 1641), p. 2. See also Bernard Capp, *The World of John Taylor the Water-Poet, 1578–1653* (Oxford: Clarendon Press, 1994).

79 See *The Poems of John Cleveland*, ed. Brian Morris and Eleanor Withington (Oxford: Clarendon Press, 1967).

80 See, for the first two anti-Puritan satires and *The Civil War*, *The Collected Works of Abraham Cowley*, vol. 1, ed. Thomas O. Calhoun, Laurence Heyworth and Allan Pritchard (London and Toronto: Associated University Presses, 1989). Cowley's attack on sectarianism occurs in Book 3 of *The Civil War*. For other anti-Puritan satires, see *Rump: Or An Exact Collection of the Choycest Poems and Songs...By the most Eminent Wits, from Anno 1639 to Anno 1661* (London, 1662). See also Nigel Smith, *Literature and Revolution in England*, ch. 9.

81 *The Shepheards Oracles* (London, 1646), Eclogue 8, esp. pp. 90–2; elsewhere Quarles condemned separatist anarchy and root-and-branch reform – see Eclogue 11 (printed separately in 1644): *The Complete Works in Prose and Verse of Francis Quarles*, ed. A. B. Grosart, 3 vols.

and Norwich during the 1630s, died in 1635, at the height of Archbishop Laud's power; his miscellaneous poems, published posthumously in 1648, mocked as a kind of madness Puritan expressions of zeal, apocalyptic rhetoric and martyrdom inspired by Foxe: 'Boldly I preach, hate a Crosse, hate a Surplice, / Miters, Copes, and Rotchets [i.e. vestments worn by bishops]'.[82] Even Milton's nephew John Phillips would publish verses in rhyming couplets and coarse, scurrilous language mocking Puritan fast-day sermons, church services, pious parishioners, zealous Biblical language, and mechanics moved by the Spirit to preach; though Milton himself was fiercely anti-clerical and would attack London Presbyterian preachers in coarse satirical prose, it is hard to believe that he would have completely endorsed such anti-Puritan verses written in the mode of Royalist satire.[83]

In the midst of the religious conflicts intensified by civil war, Milton published his 1645 *Poems* in which he self-consciously presented himself as poetic *vates* or seer. While displaying the extraordinary variety and precocious achievements of his early generic experiments (some of which reveal his mastery of Cavalier poetic modes), the volume also highlights his Reformist Protestant outlook, his fierce antagonism towards the Laudian church and his emerging radical apocalyptic voice. He placed first among his English poems his ambitious Nativity Ode, a militantly Protestant poem envisioning the expulsion of pagan idolatry and refusing to represent Christmas as a festival.[84] Milton's prophetic poem already had polemical significance when it was composed in 1629, the year Charles I began his Personal Rule (the eleven-year period when he ruled without Parliament) and the year after Laud became Bishop of London. It now took on fresh apocalyptic resonance in 1645, the year Laud was executed; the abolition of episcopacy would soon follow. While the Ode suggests that England is not yet ready for the millennium – 'But wisest Fate says no, / This must not yet be so' (lines 149–50) – the conditions for its coming would have seemed more promising with the destruction of Laudian 'popish' idolatry. Other poems in the volume also had telling political and religious

---

(Edinburgh: T. & A. Constable, 1880–1), 3:233–6. *The Profest Royalist: His Quarrel with the Times* (Oxford, 1645) is the title of his volume of three tracts defending the King's ecclesiastical and political positions. See also the discussion of Quarles in Chapter 17 above.

82 'The Distracted Puritane', in *Poetica Stromata or A Collection of Sundry Pieces* (1648); see *The Poems of Richard Corbett*, ed. J. A. W. Bennett and H. R. Trevor-Roper (Oxford: Clarendon Press, 1955).

83 [John Phillips], *A Satyr Against Hypocrites* (London, 1655); *Sportive Wit* (London, 1656); Barbara K. Lewalski, *The Life of John Milton* (Oxford: Blackwell, 2000), pp. 333–4, 336.

84 Cf. the minor poet Thomas Philipott who, in 1646, likewise envisioned in verses on the nativity the silencing of pagan oracles, though without the detail and polemical force of Milton's Ode: *Poems* (London, 1646), pp. 45–6.

resonance: early paraphrases of Psalms 114 and 136 emphasised the hard struggle for liberty, God's protective power and the Lord's power to quell 'wrathfull
tyrants'; *A Maske Presented at Ludlow Castle*, a bold revision of the Caroline court
masque, emphasised the 'hard assays' required to test the virtue of England's
young aristocrats (represented by the Earl of Bridgewater's three children)
if they are to withstand the dangers of Cavalier licentiousness and Laudian
ritual (represented by Comus and his rout); and 'In quintum Novembris' – a
mini-epic inspired by the Gunpowder Plot (1605) – expressed Milton's militant national Protestantism by linking Satan with diabolical papist powers.
Moreover, Milton now added a headnote to *Lycidas* (1637) announcing that
his apocalyptic pastoral elegy 'by occasion foretels the ruine of our corrupted
Clergy then in their height': retrospectively he presents his poem – with its
furious jeremiad by Saint Peter and its ominous warning of the 'two-handed
engine' standing ready 'at the door' 'to smite once, and smite no more' – as
a fiery prophecy anticipating the English Revolution and the destruction of
a ceremonial clergy whose 'lean and flashy songs' had left their flocks hungry
and 'swoln with wind' (lines 113–30).[85]

Although Milton produced little new religious or prophetic poetry during
the 1640s, the few sonnets he produced put that form to fresh satirical uses
as he savagely attacked the Presbyterian clergy and pamphleteers who had
slandered him as a heretic because of his divorce tracts. In 1646, as Parliament
strengthened Presbyterian church government nationwide and worked to curb
blasphemies and heresies, Milton produced his confrontational 'On the New
Forcers of Conscience'. There he warned Parliament, in a stinging epigrammatic coda, of a new Pharisaical hypocrisy – equal to that of the Laudian clergy –
that would force 'Consciences that Christ set free': 'New *Presbyter* is but Old
Priest writ large'.[86]

Though the son of a Puritan preacher and polemicist, Richard Crashaw nevertheless found himself attracted to the world of elaborate church ritual and sacra-
mentalism which godly reformers considered ecclesiastical 'innovations'. His
Counter-Reformation aesthetics articulate an extreme form of high-church devotional expression, aligned at first with the world of Caroline ceremonialism,
in this age of religious conflict. He became a Fellow of Peterhouse, Cambridge,
in 1635 and until the early 1640s sought refuge there from escalating religious
and political tensions. The College's elaborately decorated chapel exemplified
Laud's concern with the 'beauty of holiness' and external ceremony; the fierce

---

85 Quotations are from *Poems of Mr John Milton, Both English and Latin* (London, 1645).
86 Milton, *Complete Shorter Poems*, pp. 298–300.

Puritan polemicist William Prynne condemned Peterhouse's chapel as a place of 'Popish Ceremonies' and 'Anti-Christian Innovations' encouraged by the College's Laudian Master John Cosin.[87] But for Crashaw, who yearned for a religion that put on 'A majestie that [might] beseem [God's] throne',[88] the chapel offered stained-glass windows, a marble altar, gilded candlesticks, representations of angels, a large crucifix, a wooden statue of Peter and the crossed keys, as well as other ceremonial ornaments. During the Civil War, however, this cloistered Laudian sanctuary would suffer at the hands of iconoclastic Puritans eager to demolish 'Monuments of Idolatry and Superstition' in order to 'accomplish the blessed Reformation so happily begun'; Crashaw was ejected from his Fellowship in April 1644, causing, as he poignantly writes in his sole surviving letter, nothing less than 'a dislocation of [his] whole condition'.[89] Fleeing to the continent, he converted to Catholicism about 1645–no doubt yearning for the protectiveness and ceremonial religion the shattered Church of England could no longer provide – and Henrietta Maria, Charles's Catholic wife (then in exile), wrote to the Pope, recommending Crashaw's services to the Catholic Church. His sacred poems, *Steps to the Temple*, first appeared in 1646 (the second, enlarged edition appeared in 1648), a striking poetic monument to the Counter-Reformation sensibility which, in Laudian form, had exacerbated religious and political tensions during the 1630s and 1640s and which drove Crashaw, in the mid 1640s, to turn to the baroque culture of continental Catholicism.

Crashaw's poems are not characterised by spiritual doubt, anguished introspection and inward struggle as the religious poems of Donne and Herbert often are; rather, his Counter-Reformation and baroque poetic imagination focuses on saints, sacraments, the cult of tears, and the Holy Name of Jesus. Yet his sacred verses express his own extreme intensity of emotion as he writes sensually about Mary Magdalene's nourishing stream of tears which rise up to heaven (as in 'The Weeper' where a cherub feeds upon her tears 'Whose sacred influence / Adds sweetness to his sweetest Lips'),[90] or when he writes about the suffering martyrdom, spiritual ecstasy and burning piety of Saint Teresa

87 *The Stuart Constitution*, ed. Kenyon, pp. 148–9 (for Laud); William Prynne, *Canterburies Doome* (London, 1646), pp. 73–5. On Crashaw and Laudian contexts, see also Thomas F. Healy, *Richard Crashaw* (Leiden: E. J. Brill, 1986).
88 'On a Treatise of Charity', in *The Poems, English, Latin and Greek, of Richard Crashaw*, ed. L. C. Martin, 2nd edn (Oxford: Clarendon Press, 1957); subsequent quotations are from this edition.
89 'An Ordinance for the further demolishing of Monuments of Idolatry and Superstition' (May 1644) in *Acts and Ordinances of the Interregnum, 1642–1660*, ed. C. H. Firth and R. Rait, 3 vols. (London: Wyman & Sons, 1911), 1:425–6; *Poems*, pp. xxv, xxx–xxxii, 419–20.
90 We quote from the revised (1648) version of 'The Weeper': *Poems*, p. 309.

of Avila, the sixteenth-century Spanish mystic and key figure of the Catholic Counter-Reformation. Crashaw's poetics of excessive emotion and extravagant adoration reach a climax in his veneration of Saint Teresa's mystical and sensuous death: 'O how oft shalt thou complaine / Of a sweet and subtile paine?' he asks as he imagines her 'delicious wounds that weep / Balsome' ('In memory of... Lady Madre Teresa', lines 97–8, 108–9). Recognising that such Counter-Reformation verses would likely be read with hostility by English Protestant readers, Crashaw wrote a poem defending his verses to Saint Teresa against anti-Catholic, anti-Spanish sentiments: 'O 'tis not Spanish, but 'tis heaven she speakes' ('An Apologie', line 23), he proclaims, suggesting that such intense religious devotion, and the creative sensibility it inspires, transcend national boundaries. Crashaw died in exile in August 1649, serving as a subcanon in Loreto and never returning to revolutionary England; his poetry and aesthetics articulated a distinctive, even *sui generis* form of high-church devotional expression – one that moved from Caroline ceremonialism to the baroque culture of the Catholic Counter-Reformation – in an age of diverse and clashing religious beliefs.

The conflict between two competing cultures – Puritan reformism and a native traditionalism with its tolerance of festivals, drinking and popular recreations – is also apparent in the poetry of Robert Herrick, as well as the posthumously published *Poems* (1640, 1643, 1652) of Thomas Randolph who celebrated the old summer games, rural festivity and 'harmelesse May-poles' which 'are rail'd upon / As if they were the towers of *Babylon*'.[91] A poet of sensuous lyrics and epigrams about 'Times trans-shifting' ('The Argument of his Book', *Hesperides*), Herrick found religious ceremonialism and ritual, including old festive customs, especially appealing. Parson of Dean Prior in Devon from 1629 to 1647, when he was ejected from his ecclesiastical living, Herrick published his *Hesperides* in 1648 (dedicated to Charles, Prince of Wales), followed in the same volume by his sacred poems, *Noble Numbers* (1647). Herrick's poetry of pagan festivity and the English ritual year warmly portrays harvest celebrations, as well as Christmas ceremonies, New Year's gifts, mumming and decking with greenery. His poems illustrate the vitality of popular rituals, as

---

91 Thomas Randolph, *Poems*, 3rd edn (London, 1643), p. 105; the 4th edition appeared in 1652. For the Puritan attack on traditional festive culture, see David Underdown, *Revel, Riot and Rebellion: Popular Politics and Culture in England, 1603–1660* (Oxford: Clarendon Press, 1985); Ronald Hutton, *The Rise and Fall of Merry England: The Ritual Year, 1400–1700* (Oxford University Press, 1996), chs. 5–6. See also Leah S. Marcus, *The Politics of Mirth: Jonson, Herrick, Milton, Marvell, and the Defense of Old Holiday Pastimes* (University of Chicago Press, 1986).

well as a nostalgia for a ceremonial pre-war church, in the midst of 'TIMES most bad' caused by 'our wasting Warre';[92] they can thus be regarded as a defiant expression of Royalist opposition and the old festive culture. The king's *Book of Sports*, reissued in 1633, sanctioned 'lawful recreations' on Sundays and holy days, thereby enraging sabbatarian reformers committed to godly devotion and offended by idolatrous ecclesiastical policies; during the Civil War an ordinance for 'the better observation of the Lords-Day' (April 1644) ordered local magistrates to burn the declaration and banned Sunday games, dancing, wakes and other festive pastimes, including the erecting of maypoles, 'a Heathenish vanity'.[93] Yet in the argument to his book Herrick proclaims: 'I sing of *Maypoles, Hock-carts, Wassails, Wakes*'. Poems such as 'The Hock-Cart, or Harvest home' and 'The Wake' deliberately valorise traditional rituals and recreations in order to affirm social and religious order. 'Corinna's Going a Maying', with its fusion of pagan and Christian devotion and festive licence, explicitly evokes the *Book of Sports* – 'that sinful book of liberty', the Puritan Nehemiah Wallington called it – which had fuelled cultural and religious tensions:[94]

> Come, we'll abroad; and let's obay
> The Proclamation made for May:
> And sin no more, as we have done, by staying;
> But my *Corinna*, come, let's goe a Maying.
>
> (lines 39–42)

Herrick's poetic celebrations of Christmas festivities (e.g. his 'Ceremonies for Christmas') likewise defiantly spurned Parliament's ordinance against Christmas (December 1644) as a feast 'giving liberty to carnall and sensuall delights', as well as Parliament's new Directory for Public Worship (1645) which declared that 'Festival dayes' have 'no Warrant in the Word of God'.[95]

Other poems, including 'Mattens, or morning Prayer' and 'Evensong', express Herrick's commitment to the Church of England's liturgy. Even his 'secular' lyrics, including those addressed to Julia, are rich in ceremonial details

---

92 'Upon the troublesome times', in *Poetical Works of Robert Herrick*, ed. L. C. Martin (Oxford: Clarendon Press, 1956), p. 211. See also Chapter 25 below for Herrick's convivial poetry in relation to political disorder.

93 *The Constitutional Documents of the Puritan Revolution, 1625–1660*, ed. S. R. Gardiner (1906; rpt, Oxford: Clarendon Press, 1979), pp. 99–103; *Acts and Ordinances*, ed. Firth and Rait, 1:420–2; Hutton, *Merry England*, pp. 200–1, 203–8.

94 Paul S. Seaver, *Wallington's World: A Puritan Artisan in Seventeenth-Century London* (Stanford University Press, 1985), p. 51.

95 *Acts and Ordinances*, ed. Firth and Rait 1:580, 607. See also the ordinance of June 1647 'for Abolishing of Festivals', including Christmas, Easter and Whitsuntide: 1:954.

and church 'rites' – offering incense and sacrifices, wearing clerical vestments, kneeling at altars, erecting images, praying to his patron saint (Ben Jonson) for 'old *Religions* sake' and giving him candles – that would have surely been provocative in the context of godly reform and its assault on ritualised religion and 'Monuments of Idolatry'.[96] Meanwhile, Herrick's satiric epigram on the zealous Puritan whose ears had been cropped evokes the religious conflicts of the 1630s: 'Is *Zelot* pure? he is: ye see he weares / The signe of *Circumcision* in his eares'.[97]

Herrick's Laudian sensibility is also notable in *His Noble Numbers*, consisting of 272 'PIOUS PIECES' in which he sings 'the Birth of his Christ and sighes for his *Saviours* suffering on the *Crosse*'; in these poems, moreover, he eschews the grim Calvinist emphasis on predestination to damnation and hell, emphasising instead a happier doctrine of predestination to salvation and heaven: 'PREDESTINATION is the Cause alone / Of many standing, but of fall to none'. Human agency too can stimulate God's response and contribute to salvation: 'If thou canst change thy life, God then will please / To change, or call back, His past *Sentences*'. The poet's Laudianism, with its emphasis on ceremonial worship, sacerdotal rites and the sanctity of the altar, is apparent when he addresses God ('With golden Censers, and with Incense, here, / Before Thy Virgin-Altar I appeare'), when he writes of the circumcision ('Then, like a perfum'd Altar, see / That all things sweet, and clean may be') or when in priestly fashion he asserts the subordination of the laity.[98] Herrick's Easter poems concluding *His Noble Numbers* depict the suffering Christ as tragic actor (not unlike the Christic Charles of *Eikon Basilike*), scorned by the rude, inconstant multitude: such verses become a defiant means of responding to the tragedy of defeated Royalism in 1648.

Henry Vaughan's religious poetry likewise responds to the assault on the Church of England by zealous reformers; finding consolation in the poetry of Herbert – that poet-pastor of the church – he seeks to retreat from the darkness of civil war and human sinfulness into a world of inner, spiritual life and illumination.[99] His collection of sacred poems, *Silex Scintillans* (1650, 1655), also engages with contemporary religious politics, expressing his acute sense of loss

---

96 See Achsah Guibbory, *Ceremony and Community from Herbert to Milton: Literature, Religion and Cultural Conflict in Seventeenth-Century England* (Cambridge University Press, 1998), ch. 4; for 'His Prayer to Ben. Jonson', see *Poetical Works*, pp. 212–13.

97 'Upon Zelot', in *Poetical Works*, p. 232.

98 *Poetical Works*, pp. 337, 389, 368, 366; see also Thomas N. Corns, *Uncloistered Virtue: English Political Literature, 1640–1660* (Oxford: Clarendon Press, 1992), pp. 120–2.

99 See Chapter 25 below on Vaughan's poetry of retirement.

over the destruction of the traditional ecclesiastical order.[100] A Royalist poet educated in Oxford and London, Vaughan returned to his native Wales at the outbreak of the war. However, the Act for the Better Propagation and Preaching of the Gospel in Wales (February 1649/50) reinforced a godly ecclesiastical and political presence in his homeland; it resulted in the ejection of his twin brother, Thomas, from his Breconshire parish and, alarmingly, in the presence of itinerant radical preachers, including Vavasor Powell, William Erbery and Morgan Llwyd (also the author of much millenarian verse).[101] Vaughan thus found himself writing 'out of a land of darknesse', as he put it in one devotional work, 'where destruction passeth for propagation'.[102] In another devotional work, *The Mount of Olives* (1652), he appealed to those who dare to '*look* upon and *commiserate* distressed Religion' and noted (as he paid homage to Herbert) the 'many blessed Patterns of holy life in the *British Church*, though now trodden under foot, and branded with the title of *Antichristian*'.[103] In his poem 'The Brittish Church', Vaughan laments the devastation suffered by the old church and the persecution caused by revolutionary Puritans. England has become a wasteland as a result of the church's destruction, and the poem's desolated speaker – the Bride of Christ with her 'ravish'd looks / Slain flock, and pillag'd fleeces' – poignantly implores Christ's swift return (since the British church's 'glorious head' is 'fled'). In 'Religion' Vaughan laments the poisoning of the once-pure spring of religion – now 'a tainted sink' – and prays for its purification, while in 'The Search' he yearns for 'those calme, golden Evenings' of ancient Biblical times.[104] Moreover, in the second part of the 1655 *Silex*, a defiant Vaughan opens with poems affirming the liturgical calendar of the Church of England ('Ascension-day' and 'Ascension-Hymn' followed soon after by 'Trinity-Sunday' and 'Palm-Sunday'). In response to contemporary religio-political tensions, Vaughan also produced much anti-Puritan satire in both prose and verse.[105] His less known Welsh contemporary, Rowland Watkyns, was likewise a religious poet bitter about the Puritan regime and loyal to the

100 During the Interregnum Thomas Washbourne likewise published *Divine Poems* (1654) lamenting the state of the church and its threatened traditions.
101 *Acts and Ordinances*, ed. Firth and Rait, 2:342–8; F. E. Hutchinson, *Henry Vaughan: A Life and Interpretation* (Oxford: Clarendon Press, 1947), ch. 9; Stephen Roberts, 'Religion, Politics and Welshness', in *'Into Another Mould': Aspects of the Interregnum*, ed. Ivan Roots, 2nd edn (University of Exeter Press, 1998), pp. 30–46; Robert Wilcher, *The Writing of Royalism, 1628–1660* (Cambridge University Press, 2001), pp. 323–7.
102 *Flores Solitudinis* (preface dated April 1652), in *Works of Henry Vaughan*, ed. Leonard C. Martin, 2nd edn (Oxford: Clarendon Press, 1957), p. 217.
103 *Works*, pp. 138, 186.   104 *Ibid.*, pp. 410, 404–7.
105 See James D. Simmonds, *Masques of God: Form and Theme in the Poetry of Henry Vaughan* (University of Pittsburgh Press, 1972), pp. 85–116.

church; he wrote verses against lower-class preachers and schismatics (mad fanatics setting 'on fire/The peaceful Kingdom'), while writing on Christ's nativity and Easter (feasts abolished by Parliament), justifying predestination ('Who's sav'd, or damn'd, none knows') and depicting the dead King Charles I as a holy martyr.[106]

The shock of the English church violently assaulted was conveyed not only by numerous sermons and pamphlets canonising the executed Charles I as 'Britaines Josiah' and audaciously comparing him to Christ,[107] but in an out-pouring of extravagant poetic laments, elegies and epitaphs produced as a re-sult of the 'horrid sin' of the regicide.[108] As in the immensely popular 'King's Book', *Eikon Basilike*, the Christic, sacerdotal King who had suffered afflictions at the hands of newfangled reformers was depicted as 'The most Constant of Martyrs', as well as the 'best of Divines' and 'the Churches Cittadell'. Verse elegies lamenting the dead King conveyed a sense of incredulity ('Such a Fall / Great Christendome ne're Pattern'd'); because of his violent death and the 'Convulsions' shaking the land, 'Religion put's on Black'.[109] The persecuted King was a saint: as patient as Job, as mild as Moses, as wise as Solomon and as valiant as David.[110] Yet in Bishop Henry King's eyes, searching Scripture for such comparisons only confirmed 'That Charls exceeds Judea's Parallels'.[111] Meanwhile, radical religion had justified 'the Savages' or 'Bloudy *Rebells*' whose butchery and treachery was comparable to that of 'the guilty *Cain*' or evoked the Biblical parallels of Judas Iscariot and 'Pilate Bradshaw with his pack of Jews',

---

106 Rowland Watkyns, *Flamma Sine Fumo* [1662], ed. Paul C. Davies (Cardiff: University of Wales, 1968), pp. 3, 4–5, 12, 43–4, 101, 109; a clergyman ejected from his living, Watkyns seems to have written many if not all of his poems during the Interregnum. On Vaughan and Watkyns, see Alan Rudrum, 'Resistance, Collaboration, and Silence: Henry Vaughan and Breconshire Royalism', in *The English Civil Wars in the Literary Imagination*, ed. Claude J. Summers and Ted-Larry Pebworth (Columbia, MO, and London: University of Missouri Press, 1999), pp. 102–18.

107 See, e.g., [William Juxon], *The Subjects Sorrow: or, Lamentations upon the Death of Britaines Josiah, King Charles* (London, 1649); Anon., *The Tears of Sion upon the Death of Josiah* ([London], 1649); Henry Leslie, *The Martyrdom of King Charles, or His Conformity with Christ in His Sufferings* (The Hague, 1649); Anon., *The Life and Death of King Charles the Martyr, Parallel'd with our Saviour in all his Sufferings* (London, 1649).

108 See 'An ELEGY in Memory of His late MAJESTY', in *Two Elegies. The One on His late Majestie* ([London], 1649), p. 5.

109 *Monumentum Regale or A TOMBE, Erected for that incomparable and Glorious Monarch, CHARLES THE FIRST* (n.p., 1649), pp. 4, 46, 38, 2–3. See also *An Epitaph on the KING, Who was beheaded at White-Hall* (n.p., 1649), bound with an edition of *Eikon Basilike*; and the elegies in *Vaticinium Votivum* (1649). On verses lamenting the King, see Wilcher, *The Writing of Royalism*, ch. 11.

110 *The Monument of Charles the First, King of England* ([London, 1649]).

111 'An Elegy upon the most Incomparable King Charls the First', in *The Poems of Henry King*, ed. Margaret Crum (Oxford: Clarendon Press, 1965), pp. 117–32 (lines 17–52).

a biting reference to the republican lawyer, John Bradshaw, who presided at the King's trial.[112] The savage rebel was 'a Tiger without faith' who, King wrote after Charles's funeral, had 'mangled' the church: 'Her Massacre is on thy Block display'd'.[113] Another elegist bemoaned that his reason is now 'cast away in this *Red floud*, / Which ne'r o'reflowes us all' and, extending the Biblical allusion, lamented that Britain, 'O'recast with *darknesse*, and with bloud o'rerun', was suffering two of the plagues inflicted by God on Egypt.[114] Despite the traumatic events culminating in the regicide, the King's martyrdom and his book would nevertheless vindicate the desecrated Church of England: 'His *Book*, his *Life*, his *Death*, will henceforth be / The *Church of England's* best *Apologie*'.[115]

In the midst of the religious tensions of the Interregnum, An Collins published 'Theological employments' – devotional verses composed to help her rise above the mental and physical anguish caused by her chronic illness.[116] While her 'homely' poetic 'offspring',[117] as she calls her *Divine Songs and Meditacions* (1653), become the occasion for thoughtful meditations on key Protestant themes (e.g. the need for saving grace, the role of Scripture in the life of the godly, her belief in the Trinity, justification by faith), her poems, in contrast to Elizabeth Major's,[118] are not silent about contemporary religious controversies and the need for moderation and order in church and state. Dismissing religious 'Novelties', Collins depicts radical sectaries as introducing 'New . . . Glosses' on 'old Heresies' ('The Preface'). Yet writing 'Betimes in Truths defence' involves a complex perspective that more than simply repudiates the novelties of religious radicalism; Collins is not easily aligned with one particular religious group. In 'A Song composed in time of the Civill Warr', she expresses her concern about 'false Worships', 'Errors', 'Carnall Liberty' and 'Disorders' encouraged by radical sectaries; however, she also criticises Parliamentary oaths (e.g. the Commonwealth's loyalty or Engagement Oath of

---

112 *Monumentum Regale*, p. 6; Henry King, 'An Elegy upon . . . King Charls', lines 368, 445. See also King's elegy 'A Deepe Groane, fetch at the Funerall of . . . Charles the First', in *Poems*, pp. 110–17, for the sin of Cain (lines 23–4).
113 *Monumentum Regale*, p. 7; Henry King, 'A Deepe Groane', lines 25–6.
114 *Jeremias Redivivus: or, An Elegiacall Lamentation on the Death of our ENGLISH JOSIAS, CHARLES the First* (n.p., 1649), pp. 1, 2; also in *Monumentum Regale*, p. 40.
115 *Monumentum Regale*, p. 23.
116 On Collins from the perspective of the godly household, see Chapter 24 below.
117 An Collins, *Divine Songs and Meditacions*, ed. Sidney Gottlieb (Tempe, AZ: Medieval and Renaissance Texts and Studies, 1996), p. 5.
118 See *Honey on the Rod; or a comfortable Contemplative for one in Affliction; with sundry Poems on several Occasions* (London, 1656), concluding with poems about her physical and spiritual afflictions.

1650) and imprisonment used to restrain religious and political freedom and promote Protestant unity:

> And to bind Soul and Body both
> To Sathans service sure
> Therto they many ty by Oath,
> Or Cause them to endure
> The Losse of lightsom Liberty.[119]

Furthermore, Collins can express apocalyptic fervour (as at the end of this poem), and elsewhere she writes that, while she rejoices in God's appearance 'in Gospel-voyce' (i.e. through Scripture), she takes no offence at the 'greater Light' ('The Preface'), the inner light illuminating sectarians, including Quakers, during the Interregnum. Yet she also takes a stand against the dangerous heresy of mortalism or 'soul-sleeping', a 'falacy' held by religious radicals (including Milton and the Leveller Richard Overton) which maintained that 'the Soul doth with the Body dy' but is resurrected at the last day.[120]

Religious controversy likewise emerges as a key issue in John Collop's *Poesis Rediviva* (1655), the product of retirement during the Interregnum.[121] As the author of *Medici Catholicon* (1655), a tract whose title recalls the tolerant and sceptical writing of Sir Thomas Browne, Collop denied allegiance to any faction; he wrote verses (e.g. 'The Church') commending Christian charity as 'Religions light', while deriding religious factions manifested by rapacious Romanists ('Romish Wolves'), radical sectarians ('schismatick Foxes'), as well as polemical Presbyterians.[122] Drawing frequently upon that moderate and learned defender of the Church of England, Henry Hammond ('bright Evangelist'), Collop's verses ridicule the pretentious inspiration of the enthusiast ('Who doing ill, sayes th' Spirit acts within') and depict sectaries as volatile with their perverse imaginations and glosses: 'All these adulterers of Sacred Writ, / Each doth a Concubine to his fancy fit'. In an age disturbed by the rash zeal and bitter contention of religious fanaticism, the satiric and melancholy Collop favoured 'orderly zeal', presenting himself as a voice of moderation.[123]

Poetry, moreover, expressed the conflict between radical religious agitation and moderate godly reform, as strident sectarianism increasingly threatened

---

119 *Divine Songs*, pp. 60–3.   120 *Ibid.*, pp. 5, 86–7.
121 On the collection's literary qualities, see Chapter 25 below; Nigel Smith, *Literature and Revolution in England*, pp. 315–17.
122 *The Poems of John Collop*, ed. Conrad Hilberry (Madison: University of Wisconsin Press, 1962), pp. 47–50, 61.
123 *Poems*, pp. 61–3, 54–5.

Protestant unity and reformation during the Interregnum. Anna Trapnel the Fifth Monarchist visionary (discussed below) issued fiery millenarian verses criticising the conservative Protectorate (established in December 1653) for betraying the revolution, and Cromwell for attempting to supplant King Jesus, while the finest poem defending the godly Protector, Andrew Marvell's *First Anniversary of the Government* (1655), satirised a 'frantique Army' (line 299) of sectaries who were fuelling religious tensions. Committed to reformation but frustrated by contentious sectaries opposed to an established clergy, Cromwell complained to the Protectorate Parliament about the deplorable state of 'spiritual things', divisions among the godly created by 'prodigious blasphemies' as well as 'contempt of God and Christ... and of the Scriptures'.[124] Marvell's satirical catalogue of swarming sectarians evokes, in a compressed fashion, a wide range of popular fears and exaggerated representations:

> Accursed Locusts, whom your King does spit
> Out of the Center of th'unbottom'd Pit;
> Wand'rers, Adult'rers, Lyers, *Munser's* rest,
> Sorcerers, Atheists, Jesuites, Possest.
>
> (311–14)[125]

Anti-sectarians were equating the multiplying sects with the terrifying locusts emerging from the bottomless pit in Revelation 9, a new onslaught from the forces of destruction spreading over the nation. The 'frantick Zeale' of inflamed millenarians recalled the religious fervour of the original Münster Anabaptists which (in 1534–5) had resulted in religious and social anarchy: they seemed to breathe 'nothing but fire and sword' as they looked 'upon their countrymen with such an eye as the *Anabaptists* cast upon *Munster*'.[126] Marvell's own response reminds us that Cromwell's priority during the 1650s, despite his own Puritan zeal, was unity among the godly (within a national church) rather than religious diversity and flourishing radical sectarianism. As we shall see in the next section, the sectarian fragmentation of Protestantism also distressed the prominent Puritan writer Richard Baxter, yet generated an outpouring of rich radical religious writing.

---

124 *Speeches of Oliver Cromwell*, p. 31 (4 September 1654); Austin Woolrych, *Commonwealth to Protectorate* (Oxford: Clarendon Press, 1982).
125 *The Poems and Letters of Andrew Marvell*, ed. H. M. Margoliouth, 3rd edn rev. Pierre Legouis with E. E. Duncan-Jones (Oxford: Clarendon Press, 1971).
126 Ephraim Pagitt, *Heresiography, Or a Description of the Heretickes and Sectaries Sprang up in these latter times*, 5th edn (London, 1654), p. 117; William Aspinwall, *The Legislative Power in Christ's Peculiar Prerogative* (London, 1656), p. 37.

The literature of the Holy Spirit
and radical religion

The fall of Laud and the established church was followed by an outburst of sectarian activity which bewildered and frustrated orthodox Puritans. During these turbulent years of civil war and revolution, the disintegration of Puritan unity and the emergence of religious movements and beliefs in conflict with established religion stimulated a remarkable flourishing of radical religious literature and preaching characterised by bold uses of language and unorthodox theological doctrines. Emphasising the immediate guidance and inspiration of the Spirit or the inner light, radical religious writers clashed with institutionalised religion and the state church, often producing texts of unusual verbal and visionary power.

The splintering of Protestantism and the rise of separatism and sects, however, worried the moderate Puritan divine, Richard Baxter of Kidderminster, one of the most prolific religious authors of his age: in his pastoral zeal he wrote, by his own count, 'about 128 books', nearly 40 produced by 1660.[127] Although he served for a short period as a chaplain in the parliamentary Army and had no interest in external forms of worship, Baxter deplored religious enthusiasm and the unbridled language of sectarian discourse; indeed, his service as chaplain during the mid 1640s confirmed his distaste for radical preachers and hot-headed sectaries, so that the perils of antinomianism became the subject of his first published book, *Aphorisms of Justification* (1649). His first large meditative work, the hugely popular *The Saints Everlasting Rest* (1650), was written out of a sense of personal and religious urgency: begun in 1647, as he was languishing in poor health, Baxter anxiously deplores an age 'when almost all the Land is in a flame of contention, and so many, that we thought godly, are busily demolishing the Church'.[128] This text of disillusion, weariness and intense spiritual longing for rest from affliction expresses the anguish of suffering and destruction as a result of civil war: 'we have had a long and perilous War', Baxter writes, in which we have seen 'Families ruined; Congregations ruined ... Cities ruined; Country ruined; Court ruined; Kingdoms ruined; Who weeps not when all these bleed?' Baxter thus urges his readers to 'Beware of extreames in the controverted points of Religion' and to pursue 'The middle way'.[129] For Baxter the greatest danger to reformation was 'Division and Separation' among the godly – he considered such religious strife 'utterly intolerable'.[130] Distressed by fruitless theological

---

127 N. H. Keeble, *Richard Baxter: Puritan Man of Letters* (Oxford: Clarendon Press, 1982), pp. 2, 157–69.
128 *The Saints Everlasting Rest* (London, 1650), sig. A3r.
129 *Ibid.*, pp. 92, 122; sig. A4v.   130 *Ibid.*, sig. (a)r.

speculation, religious contentiousness, and rhetorical ingenuity and wit, Baxter cultivated an unaffected, direct style of preaching and writing.

In his posthumous *Reliquiae Baxterianae* (1696) – a folio volume of 800 pages – Baxter left a rich, disjointed narrative of his 'Life and Times', including his spiritual evolution, the workings of God's providence, and the religious controversies of his age; the text's 'sudden transitions and juxtapositions' register both its heterogeneity and 'the confusions of the times'.[131] In this supreme defence of the Puritans, Baxter also expresses alarm at the spread of heretical beliefs, sects and anti-clerical sentiment during the 1640s and 1650s. Thus in the Parliamentary army Baxter found that among soldiers with sectarian and antinomian leanings 'their most frequent and vehement Disputes were for Liberty of Conscience' and that 'every Man might not only *hold*, but *preach* and *do* in Matters of Religion what he pleased';[132] radical books by Richard Overton and John Lilburne, as well as such popular radical chaplains as John Saltmarsh and William Dell, further encouraged radical religious ferment. Yet despite his antipathy to sectarian enthusiasm and his promotion of unity among the godly, Baxter came to associate the apprehension of God with the indwelling Spirit: 'though the Folly of Fanaticks tempted me long to over-look the Strength of this Testimony of the Spirit, while they placed it in a certain *internal Assertion*, or enthusiastick Inspiration; yet now I see that the Holy Ghost in another manner is the Witness of Christ and his Agent in the World'.[133]

Dell and Saltmarsh, as well as other radical preachers, including Hugh Peter, William Erbery and John Everard, contributed to the spread of radical religious beliefs and lay preaching, and strengthened the reaction against university-trained clergy and formalism in religion.[134] Like the Milton of *Areopagitica* (but unlike Baxter), Saltmarsh could proclaim that 'Divisions ought to be no prejudice to the Truth',[135] and he attacked both the prelates and Presbyterians for fuelling religious factions. As he put in his major work, *Sparkles of Glory* (1647), the Spirit could not be confined 'to one outward form or fellowship of men' ('The Epistle Dedicatory'). A defender of sectarianism, free grace and a free press, the antinomian Saltmarsh argued for religious toleration in a series of works sold through the radical bookseller Giles Calvert (later the publisher of many writings by Gerrard Winstanley and the Quakers): *Free-Grace* (1645), *Groanes for Liberty* (1646), *The Smoke in the Temple* (1646) and *Reasons for Unitie*,

---

131 Keeble, *Richard Baxter*, p. 148.
132 *Reliquiae Baxterianae*, ed. Matthew Sylvester (London, 1696), Part I, p. 53.
133 *Ibid.*, Part I, p. 127.
134 Parliament had issued an ordinance in 1645 prohibiting any person from preaching who was not ordained a minister: *Acts and Ordinances*, ed. Firth and Rait, 1:677.
135 *Groanes for Liberty* (London, 1646), p. 1.

Peace, and Love (1646), among other works. *Free-Grace* boldly asserted his openly antinomian position regarding 'A Beleevers glorious Freedom': 'The Spirit of Christ sets a believer as free from Hell, the Law, and bondage here on Earth, as if he were in Heaven.'[136] In *The Doctrine of Baptisms* (1648), *The Way of True Peace and Unity among the Faithful* (1649) and *The Tryal of Spirits* (1653), Dell likewise rejected the institutional clergy, the visible church (set up by Antichrist) and outward forms of worship, while emphasising the role of the Spirit, the equality of all saints ('having *Christ* and the *Spirit, equally* present with them and in them'),[137] and the true church as an invisible spiritual society. Once persecuted by Laud for heretical beliefs, Everard, a preacher with a large following, was important for encouraging Hermeticism and continental (especially German) mystical theology in radical religious writing and thought. His many translations included works by Nicholas of Cusa, Sebastian Franck, Hans Denck, and the anonymous *Theologia Germanica*, and these texts had an impact on his sermons, published posthumously in 1653 *(Some Gospel-Treasures Opened)*.[138]

During the late 1640s the Levellers were also associated with radical religion and London separatism: among their leaders, John Lilburne, a member of a Particular Baptist church in the early 1640s, was a highly popular separatist regarded by Thomas Edwards the heresy-hunter as 'the great darling of the Sectaries'; Richard Overton was a General (or non-Calvinist) Baptist and mortalist; and William Walwyn, depicted by his enemies as dangerous and antinomian, was a political Independent and a staunch defender of freedom for the sects.[139] The Levellers were as hostile to the professional clergy as they were to professional lawyers or politicians, and they favoured the complete disestablishment of religion and the abandonment of all prescription in forms of worship or patterns of belief. They thus made religious liberty a crucial part of their polemical campaign, which included pungent attacks on Cromwell and the senior army officers for their dissembled godliness, a treacherous cloak for new political despotism and brutal ambition in the Commonwealth: 'did ever men pretend an higher degree of Holinesse, Religion, and Zeal to God and Country than these?'[140]

136 *Free-Grace: or The Flowings of Christs Blood freely to Sinners* (London, 1645), p. 140.
137 *The Way of True Peace and Unity among the Faithful* (London, 1649), p. 13.
138 On Everard, see Nigel Smith, *Perfection Proclaimed: Language and Literature in English Radical Religion, 1640–1660* (Oxford: Clarendon Press, 1989), pp. 110–27, 131–8.
139 Thomas Edwards, *Gangraena* (London, 1646), Part III, p. 153; *The Writings of William Walwyn*, ed. Jack R. McMichael and Barbara Taft (Athens: University of Georgia Press, 1989), pp. 15–16, 23, 56–61, 99–124, 127–30, 138–9, 163–4, 168; Brian Manning, 'The Levellers and Religion', in *Radical Religion in the English Revolution*, ed. McGregor and Reay, ch. 3.
140 *The Hunting of the Foxes* (1649), in *The Levellers in the English Revolution*, ed. G. E. Aylmer (Ithaca, NY: Cornell University Press, 1975), p. 149.

Originating during this period of acute religious and political crisis – stimulated by the overthrow of the monarchy, the defeat of the Levellers (in May 1649) and economic hardship after the Civil War – one group of radical writers, whom contemporaries called 'Ranters', fiercely challenged the strict Calvinist predestinarianism and sexual mores of orthodox Puritans. These extreme antinomians, including Abiezer Coppe, Laurence Clarkson, Joseph Salmon and Jacob Bauthumley, repudiated religious orthodoxy by claiming that 'sin hath its conception only in the imagination', as Clarkson put it in *A Single Eye* (1649).[141] Suddenly emerging into prominence in 1649 – and perceived as a religious and social threat by the cautious Rump Parliament of the Republic – they were never an organised movement; nonetheless, they were feared by the orthodox godly and were the subject of hostile polemics by other religious radicals, including Quakers, Baptists and Diggers. Their proto-Blakean assertions – the 'Devil is God, Hell is Heaven, Sin Holiness, Damnation Salvation'[142] – turned the world of orthodox religion upside down. In *The Light and Dark Sides of God* (1650), Jacob Bauthumley stressed (as did Winstanley) that the carnal Protestant religion encourages men to 'fancy a high place for [God] above the Stars', keeping them 'in bondage to sin, law, [and] an accusing Conscience which is Hell' (pp. 236, 248). Especially shocking to the orthodox godly was the Ranter tendency to dispute the primary authority of the letter of the Scripture – 'for I have a surer word within', Bauthumley proclaims, 'to which I take heed' since the 'Bible without' is 'but a shadow of that Bible which is within' (pp. 253, 260). Moreover, the Ranters provocatively claimed that 'no man could be free'd from sin, till he had acted that so called sin', as Laurence Clarkson asserted in *The Lost Sheep Found*, his vivid account of his spiritual 'Journey through many Religious Countreys' (pp. 180, 176). Because Ranter rebelliousness was often expressed in acts of libertinism, swearing, drinking and blasphemy – acts Ranters considered as holy as praying and preaching – their excesses were excoriated (and their threat to church and state exaggerated) in contemporary newsbooks and heresiographies.

The most notorious Ranter prophet, the itinerant preacher Abiezer Coppe, was imprisoned and censored by Parliament for his two *Fiery Flying Rolls* (1649), which likewise prompted the Rump's Blasphemy Act (August 1650) aimed at cracking down on extreme antinomian behaviour and its alarming writings, and part of a wider government campaign for moral reformation.[143] Coppe's

---

141 *A Collection of Ranter Writings from the 17th Century*, ed. Nigel Smith (London: Junction Books, 1983), p. 169; subsequent quotations are from this edition.
142 Clarkson, in *ibid.*, p. 173.
143 See Christopher Durston, 'Puritan Rule and the Failure of Cultural Revolution, 1645–1660', in *The Culture of English Puritanism, 1560–1700*, ed. Durston and Jacqueline Eales (Basingstoke: Macmillan, 1996), pp. 217–19.

flamboyant visionary tracts mount some of the fiercest attacks in the age on Puritan orthodoxy, religious formalism and conformity. Coppe assaults 'all the Great ones of the Earth' as his fiery prophetic voice merges in his *Fiery Flying Rolls* with that of the dreadful voice of the mighty Lord who levels and over-turns like the God of Ezekiel 21:27 ('I overturn, overturn, overturn') and Isaiah 2:17–21 ('he ariseth to shake terribly the earth'). His prophetic self-fashioning and transgressions, moreover, involve exaggerated, 'strange postures' (inspired by the prophet Ezekiel's ecstatic utterances and pranks) as he preaches in the streets of London and shocks the 'great ones' with 'a huge loud voice proclaim-ing the day of the Lord', while paying homage to the oppressed and suffering poor; he thus makes himself 'a Sign and a Wonder in fleshly *Israel*' (pp. 104–5, 74–5), anticipating the Quakers' use of extravagant symbolic gestures a few years later (e.g. their 'going naked for a sign'). By choosing 'base things, to con-found things that are' (p. 107), Coppe paradoxically aimed to destroy outward hypocritical holiness. His outrageous behaviour, ferocious rhetoric and verbal flamboyance produced some of the sharpest challenges to the Interregnum's Puritan establishment and clerical elite – and some of the most potent radical religious prose of early modern England.

Fervently anti-clerical, Winstanley the Digger was also among the most gifted radical religious visionaries to write during the revolution of 1648–9 and its ambiguous aftermath in a Commonwealth that did little to advance religious, social or legal reform. His pamphlets fused radical theology and com-munism as he attempted to realise a paradisal state through communal activity. Leader of the short-lived agrarian movement to make the earth a 'common treasury' for all (established in April 1649 in Surrey), he reinterprets central myths of the Bible (e.g. Cain versus Abel, Jacob versus Esau, Michael versus the Dragon) to express his vision of class conflict, the exploitation of the poor, and the menacing proliferation of clerical and kingly powers in the Republic. Moved by the Spirit, which he considers above the letter of the Bible, Winstanley freely allegorises its texts, since 'whether there was any such outward things or no, it matters not much, if thou seest all within'.[144] Moreover, acutely sensitive to alienating uses of theological language and concepts by the professional clergy, Winstanley provocatively chooses the word 'Reason' to mean God or the Spirit: as he observes regarding the name God and its oppressive uses, 'I have been held under darknesse by that word, as I see many people are' (p. 105). Addressed to churches with university-educated clergy, his most original religious work,

---

144 *The Works of Gerrard Winstanley*, ed. George H. Sabine (Ithaca, NY: Cornell University Press, 1941), p. 462; further quotations are from this edition.

Fire in the Bush (March 1650), rewrites the Book of Daniel's vision (in chapter 7) of the four beasts or world powers rising out of the chaos of the great sea – a favourite passage for millenarian interpretation in this revolutionary age – as Winstanley gives it new poetic expression and apocalyptic urgency. Winstanley's allegorical version depicts the fantastic beasts as frightening human creations rising 'up out of the deceived heart of mankinde' (p. 464); kingly power, the institutional church, the law and private property are visible manifestations of the Serpent or Dragon within humankind. The fourth beast – representing the oppressive power of the clergy – is, however, more dreadful than the rest. The clergy use verbal and hermeneutic skills to exploit the common people, to bewitch them to conform, and to keep them in darkness: they distort the plainness of the Scriptures 'with their darke interpretation, and glosses, as if it were too hard for ordinary men now to understand them; and thereby they deceive the simple, and makes a prey of the poore, and cosens them of the Earth' (pp. 474–5). Although his Digger experiment had failed by the spring of 1650, Winstanley produced, within a few years of concentrated publication, some of the most moving expressions of class conflict and exploitation in the English language; his visionary, often poetic writing distinctively revealed the interconnections between the institutions of religious orthodoxy, state power and social injustice.

Of all the missionary sects to appear during the Interregnum, the Quakers seemed especially alarming to the orthodox godly, though as a young preacher convinced of sin, damnation and predestination, the anti-authoritarian Bunyan also clashed furiously with them in his early polemical writings.[145] The Quakers' charismatic, itinerant prophets and leaders – George Fox, James Nayler, Edward Burrough, William Dewsbury, Richard Hubberthorne, among others – poured out contentious tracts that proclaimed the supremacy of the inner light, expressed a state of sinless perfection, assaulted ministers and magistrates, repudiated religious formality, promoted the ideology of the Lamb's War (from Rev. 17:14) and spread their heretical ideology well beyond Britain itself. To hostile and bewildered contemporaries the terrifying Quakers seemed extravagant and subversive as they rejected the gestures and language of social deference, disrupted traditional church services, engaged in physical quaking and trembling (as did Old Testament prophets) and responded to the impromptu leadings of the Spirit. Starting in 1652 as Fox and other itinerant preachers

---

145 These include *Some Gospel-Truths Opened* (1656) and *A Vindication of the Book Called, Some Gospel-Truths Opened* (1657); see also Christopher Hill, *A Tinker and a Poorman: John Bunyan and His Church, 1628–1688* (New York: Knopf, 1989), ch. 8.

moved through the rural areas of northern England, this movement of religious protest against the theology and organisation of orthodox Puritanism was having a significant impact by 1654 and 1655, and may have reached 50,000 members by the Restoration, making the Quakers the largest sect of the period.[146] Indeed, those who converted to Quakerism, as Thomas Ellwood and Mary Penington vividly recorded in spiritual autobiographies, often endured great hostility from relations, neighbours and even servants.[147] The early Quakers circulated countless letters (as a crucial means of organising their movement) and, brilliantly exploiting the press to voice their controversial religious views, produced a startling number of printed tracts written in sharp, plain language: 64 titles were published in 1654, 101 in 1655, and 95 in 1656 – powerful evidence that, as Edward Burrough announced in 1654, the Lord was speaking to the nation 'by the mouth of his Servants in word and writing'.[148] Their pugnacious apocalyptic texts included provocative and threatening title-pages announcing the mighty day of the Lord or the vials of God's wrath. Post-Restoration Quakers would alter their polemical strategies in order to weather the storm of religious persecution; the Quakers of the 1650s, however, were by no means pacificists, nor can their apocalyptic militancy easily be reconciled with the image of their later respectability.

The arresting combination of sublime and concrete language (often evoking the conditions of Quaker suffering) and their bold scriptural mythmaking can, at moments, give Fox's apocalyptic writings of the Interregnum an unusual potency. In one of his most notable early tracts, *Newes Coming up out of the North, Sounding towards the South* (1654), Fox draws upon the myth of the Lamb's War, having placed himself in the visionary line of Isaiah, Jeremiah, Ezekiel and Micah; fusing his prophetic voice with that of the 'Lord God of powers', he utters his thundering words against teachers of the world now in England:

146 Barry Reay, 'Quakerism and Society', in *Radical Religion in the English Revolution*, ed. McGregor and Reay, ch. 6; Adrian Davies, *The Quakers in English Society, 1655–1725* (Oxford: Clarendon Press, 2000).

147 Thomas Ellwood, *The History of the Life of Thomas Ellwood* (London, 1714); Mary Penington, *Experiences in the Life of Mary Penington (written by herself)* (1911; London: Friends Historical Society, 1992).

148 Kate Peters, 'Patterns of Quaker Authorship, 1652–1656', in *The Emergence of Quaker Writing: Dissenting Literature in Seventeenth-Century England*, ed. Thomas N. Corns and David Loewenstein (London: Frank Cass, 1995), pp. 17, 21 n. 11; Thomas P. O'Malley, 'The Press and Quakerism, 1653–1659', *Journal of the Friends' Historical Society* 54 (1979), 169–84; Barry Reay, *The Quakers and the English Revolution* (London: Temple Smith, 1985), notes that about 500 titles appeared between 1658 and 1660 (p. 11). For Burrough, see *The Memorable Works of a Son of Thunder and Consolation: Namely, That True Prophet, and Faithful Servant of God* (London, 1672), p. 12.

be valiant for the Lord, bow not to the deceit: tremble all Nations before the Lord, and before his Army, his Host. Sound the Trumpet, sound an Alarm, call up to the battell, gather together for the destruction, draw the sword ... hew down all the powers of the earth ... a day of slaughter is coming to you who have made war against the Lamb.[149]

The sublime Quaker visionary blends the language of Revelation with the militant language of the prophet Joel ('Blow ye the trumpet in Zion, and sound an alarm in my holy mountain', Joel 2:1) and the language of Psalm 114:7, while also evoking a prophetic day of slaughter (as in Jeremiah 12:3). Another of his most forceful apocalyptic texts, *The Lambs Officer*, appeared at a moment of radical exhilaration and intense Quaker pamphleteering fuelled partly by the collapse of the Cromwellian regime in April 1659 and the restoration of the Rump in early May (both a result of revolutionary pressure from the Army). Fox punctuates his flood of rhetorical questions and apocalyptic themes with a constant refrain of 'Guilty, or not guilty?' – a provocative question he poses to priests, magistrates, earthly kings, as well as other antichristian powers, as he imagines them being brought not before the courts of the nation but before the 'Judgement Bar' of the Lamb itself and compelled to drink 'the cup of the indignation of the Almighty' (see Rev. 14:10). Fox's visionary writing is saturated in the language and metaphors of the Book of Revelation, interspersed with concrete details evoking Quaker persecution. He reviles the hireling priests for persecuting the saints in stocks, prisons and houses of correction ('doth not the blood of many lye upon you, as in *York*- Gaol, *Lancaster*- Gaol, *Glouster*') and for knocking them down in 'Steeplehouses', the Quaker deflationary term for churches; the Lamb's officer thus commands the ministers and kings of the earth to face the judgement of the Lamb – 'Come, answer me before the Lambs Power, Throne, and Dominion'.[150]

Moreover, in an age when millenarianism and prophecy were linked with political radicalism, Quaker women, including Elizabeth Hooton, Dorothy Waugh, Anne Audland, Hester Biddle, Mary Howgill, Martha Simmonds, Margaret Fell and Dorothy White, were notable for preaching, writing and printing polemical tracts, thereby boldly challenging conventions of acceptable feminine behaviour and subverting the Pauline injunction that 'women keep silence in the churches: for it is not permitted unto them to speak' (1 Cor. 14:34; see also 1 Tim. 2:11–12).[151] With their vigorous defiance of

---

149 *Newes Coming up out of the North* (London, 1654), p. 31; cf. p. 37.
150 *The Lambs Officer* (London, 1659), pp. 15, 9, 19, 7–8.
151 See Phyllis Mack, *Visionary Women: Ecstatic Prophecy in Seventeenth-Century England* (Berkeley and Los Angeles: University of California Press), chs. 4, 7; Stevie Davies,

traditional gender politics, they often assumed an identity as 'mothers in Israel' and as aggressive public prophets moved by the Lord against ungodly practices. The collectively written *Saints Testimony Finishing through Sufferings* (1655), challenging the persecution of Quakers at Banbury, offered a forceful justification of women preachers 'guided by the Spirit of the Lord' by citing such Biblical prophetesses as Deborah, Miriam and Huldah.[152] In the same year the Quakers Priscilla Cotton and Mary Cole published *To the Priests and People of England;* written while the authors were prisoners in Exeter gaol, this combative visionary polemic, dense with scripturally based arguments, warned of a grim 'persecuting Cainish generation' now in England – hypocritical priests who hate 'the just and pure seed of God' (i.e. the Quakers) – and defended (against Paul's interdictions) the authority of women as spiritual equals of men, to preach and prophesy, for 'Christ appeared to the women first, and sent them to preach the resurrection to the apostles' (Matt. 28:9–10, John 20:14–18).[153] Having converted to Quakerism in 1652 (after hearing Fox preach), Margaret Fell was especially active as a controversialist and could write with great prophetic fervour: she warned the orthodox clergy, reproved the city of London, gave voice to the persecuted Quakers, organised petitions, wrote letters to Cromwell reminding him of his promise of 'liberty of conscience' and highlighted the urgent need to protect that liberty during the 'evil days' (to use Milton's phrase) of the Restoration.[154]

Women thus became increasingly involved in radical religious causes, and the 1640s and 1650s saw the visible emergence of over 300 female visionaries (about 220 were Quakers), a number of whom contributed to the flourishing of radical religious writing.[155] Because these women could not sit in the Parliament or

Unbridled Spirits: Women of the English Revolution, 1640–1660 (London: The Women's Press, 1998); Hilary Hinds, *God's Englishwomen: Seventeenth-Century Radical Sectarian Writing and Feminist Criticism* (Manchester University Press, 1996); Elaine Hobby, 'Handmaids of the Lord and Mothers in Israel: Early Vindications of Quaker Women's Prophecy', in *The Emergence of Quaker Writing*, ed. Corns and Loewenstein, pp. 88–98. Patricia Crawford suggests that writings of Quaker women amounted 'to about 20 per cent of women's output for the whole century': 'Women's Published Writings, 1600–1700', in *Women in English Society, 1500–1800*, ed. Mary Prior (1985; rpt London and New York: Routledge, 1991), p. 213.

152 *The Saints Testimony Finishing through Sufferings* (London, 1655), pp. 15–16; Anne Audland was one of the authors.

153 Hinds prints and annotates the pamphlet in *God's Englishwomen*, Appendix C (pp. 222–6, 238–40); she considers the intersection of discourses of gender and spirituality in ch. 7.

154 Fell's early writings include *False Prophets, Antichrists, Deceivers, which are in the World* (London, 1655), *A Loving Salutation* (London, 1656), *This is to the Clergy* (London, 1660), *The Citie of London Reproved for its Abominations* (London, 1660), *A Declaration and an Information* (London, 1660). See also Bonnelyn Young Kunze, *Margaret Fell and the Rise of Quakerism* (Stanford University Press, 1994).

155 Phyllis Mack, 'Women as Prophets During the English Civil War', *Feminist Studies* 8.1 (1982), 19–45, esp. p. 19. Many of these female visionaries did not publish.

stand in the pulpit, they turned to prophecy and claimed to be vessels of the Lord, engaged in radical actions and words in the public sphere; indeed, they were inspired by the divine promise that in the 'last days' before the second coming of Christ 'your sons and your daughters shall prophesy' (Acts 2:17). The prolific and outspoken gentlewoman Lady Eleanor Douglas (or Davies), who suffered several terms of imprisonment for her prophecies, specialised in predicting events. Between 1625 and 1652, relying often on the Books of Daniel and Revelation for inspiration and apocalyptic interpretation, she produced more than 60 tracts varying in length from a broadsheet to 100 pages; written in the third person, these often omit subjects or verbs, mix the Biblical with the historical and the personal, and abound with anagrams, puns, astrological references and complex images. Her tracts could seem Delphic as they pronounced against the actions of King, bishops and Parliament. Lady Eleanor foretold the downfall of Charles I whom she depicted as Belshazzar ruling over Babylon, and when his execution in 1649 fulfilled her prophecy, her reputation was revived and her energies renewed.[156]

In many cases women prophets were associated with the flourishing sects and gathered churches (by 1646 London had thirty-six separatist congregations); and in some cases, they were able to operate at the highest political levels. Associated with the Baptist congregation of William Kiffin, Elizabeth Poole illustrates how the Spirit could inspire diverse kinds of prophecies. During the critical period of 1648–9 she addressed controversial prophecies to the Council of Officers and 'their High Court of Justice', chastising these mighty authorities for intending to execute Charles whom she likened to the nation's 'Father and husband' who had betrayed the people's trust and had been justly overthrown; developing the analogy of the King as husband with power over his wife's body, she asserted: 'You never heard that a wife might put away her husband, as he is the head of her body, but for the Lords sake suffereth his terror to her flesh, though she be free in the spirit to the Lord.'[157] The outspoken Poole was subsequently disowned by her Baptist congregation.

156 *Prophetic Writings of Lady Eleanor Douglas*, ed. Esther S. Cope (Oxford University Press, 1995); Cope, *Handmaid of the Holy Spirit: Dame Eleanor Davies, Never Soe Mad a Ladie* (Ann Arbor: University of Michigan Press, 1992).
157 *A Vision: Wherein is manifested the disease and cure of the Kingdome* (London, 1648[9]), pp. 4–5; *An Alarum of War, given to the Army* (London, 1649); Manfred Brod, 'Politics and Prophecy in Seventeenth-Century England: The Case of Elizabeth Poole', *Albion* 31.3 (1999), 395–412. Other women writers, including Mary Pope and the Presbyterian Elizabeth Warren (the latter of whom employed sharp prophetic language in her *Warning-Peece from Heaven* [1649]), also argued boldly for the King's exemption from punishment.

Other sectarian women preachers never committed themselves to print and we know about them primarily through hostile observers. Robert Baillie, a Scottish Presbyterian minister and heresy-hunter, considered the enthusiastic and millenarian Mrs Attaway 'the Mistresse of all the She-preachers in *Colemanstreet*' (referring to the parish of the Independent minister and radical Arminian John Goodwin in Coleman Street) and denounced her radical views against infant baptism, while Thomas Edwards denounced her mortalism and alleged interest in Milton's doctrine of divorce.[158] Not all women dissatisfied with the Presbyterian concern for strict uniformity of beliefs and a compulsory national church, however, readily found a spiritual home in the separatist congregations that flourished during the unsettled years of the 1640s and 1650s; in *A Wise Virgins Lamp Burning*, Anne Venn, the daughter of the regicide and Parliamentary radical John Venn, poignantly describes in more than 300 pages her spiritual anguish and her often lonely search for a holy congregation after her disillusionment with the bitter Presbyterians.[159]

Meanwhile, by taking an active part in ecclesiastical controversy, women also gave voice to the Independent congregations slandered by their new religious persecutors. A separatist and later a petitioner on behalf of the Levellers, Katherine Chidley repudiated the antichristian Church of England and was the first woman openly to defend the Independent churches in print, while challenging the Presbyterian minister Edwards in *The Justification of the Independent Churches of Christ* (1641), *Good Counsell, to the Petitioners for Presbyterian Government* (1645) and *A New Year's Gift, or Brief Exhortation to Mr Thomas Edwards* (1645). In her first text urging toleration for separatists (though not for schism or heresy) and defending liberty of conscience, she fearlessly questioned Edwards's calling and compared him to the priest Amaziah who bid the prophet Amos to flee away into the land of Judah (Amos 7:12–13); and she buttressed her authority by citing, on her title page, the story of Jael who slew the Canaanite commander Sisera, the oppressor of Israel (Judg. 4:21). Like Milton, whose *Areopagitica* defended the sects against false (Presbyterian) prophets, Chidley developed plenty of venom for London's Presbyterian ministers as the breeders of religious division, and in *Good Counsell*, where she scorned their reorganisation of the national church, she mounted a short, vigorous defence of 'separated Assemblies' against slanderers. There she entreated 'the truly godly' 'to arise

---

158 Robert Baillie, *Anabaptism the True Fountaine of Independency* (London, 1647), p. 53; Edwards, *Gangraena*, Part II, p. 9; Part III, pp. 26–7.
159 Anne Venn, *A Wise Virgins Lamp* (London, 1658).

and be doing', words exemplifying her own polemical works and bold exertions in the area of religious disputation.

Mary Cary and Anna Trapnel were the most notable visionary women writers to emerge from the Fifth Monarchists, the radical millenarian movement of the 1650s led by such fiery London preachers as Christopher Feake, John Simpson and John Rogers, and committed to the destruction of the antichristian Fourth Monarchy prophesied in the Book of Daniel (chapter 7) and the immediate establishment of Christ's Kingdom on earth. The more intellectual of the two women writers, Cary made thorough studies of mathematics, world history and especially the Bible to support her prophecies justifying regicide. In her prophetic works – *A Word in Season* (1647), *The Resurrection of the Witnesses* (1648, 1653), *The Little Horns Doom and Downfall* (1651), *Twelve Humble Proposals* (1653) – she displayed great ingenuity in scriptural hermeneutics. Appearing under the patronage of wives of Parliamentary leaders and army grandees (notably Cromwell's wife Elizabeth Cromwell and daughter Bridget Ireton), Cary's *The Little Horns Doom* analysed in remarkable detail prophecies from the Books of Daniel and Revelation to explain the upheavals of the English Revolution, including the destruction of Charles I (identified with the little horn of the Beast of Daniel 7:8) who had made war against the saints. A member of John Simpson's congregation, Trapnel was a more flamboyant public figure and her works – *Anna Trapnel's Report and Plea*, *The Cry of a Stone*, *A Legacy for Saints* and *Strange and Wonderful news* (all 1654) – recount her controversial preaching in the west of England and in London, as well as her imprisonments. Exceptional among these texts is *The Cry of a Stone*, prophecies issued in a torrent of popular verse, as well as prose, and delivered during a twelve-day trance at Whitehall during January 1654. Here, at the very centre of power, God's handmaid dared to criticise openly Cromwell's quasi-regal Protectorate – comparing the apostate Protector unfavourably to Gideon who had refused to become king – and, in a tone of fiery millenarian exultation, imagined the Lord in these last days of the world 'gone forth mightily' and casting 'out / The fourth great monarchy' to make way for God's kingdom on earth.[160] Trapnel's sensational political prophecies attracted large inquisitive and enthusiastic audiences ('very many persons of all sorts and degrees'), including members of the aristocracy and members of the recently dissolved 'Barebones'

---

160 *The Cry of a Stone*, ed. Hilary Hinds (Tempe, AZ: Medieval and Renaissance Texts and Studies, 2000), p. 75. On millennial hopes in the period, see Bernard Capp, 'The Fifth Monarchists and Popular Millenarianism', in *Radical Religion in the English Revolution*, ed. McGregor and Reay, pp. 165–89.

Parliament – an indication of ongoing and widespread interest in popular millenarian visions.[161]

The prominent Parliamentarian radical, Sir Henry Vane, the subject of a powerful sonnet by Milton on the urgency of protecting religious liberty, was among the most fervent millenarian writers of the Interregnum – believing with Trapnel that Cromwell had deserted the cause of Christ and his saints – and he remained so right up until his execution in 1662. In his major religious work, the sometimes abstruse *The Retired Mans Meditations* (1655), Vane envisioned the glorious Second Coming of Christ and the rule of the saints;[162] there he also keenly perceived the religious and political upheavals of revolutionary England as evidence of the continuing war between the forces of Christ and Antichrist, whose subtle workings and forms Vane aimed to unmask. By means of scriptural interpretation, Vane sought to open 'mystical and dark prophesies' and to reveal their 'spiritual meaning', as well as their 'literal and historical sense', thereby showing 'how well both' the 'mystical' and 'historical' senses 'may stand together'.[163]

During these years of religious ferment, the radical Protestant Milton himself affirmed that 'each believer, according to his personal talents, should have a chance . . . to prophesy, teach, or exhort';[164] he nevertheless did not include women preachers who, we have seen, refused to keep silent. Although he never joined a separate congregation or sect (despite sharing religious beliefs with General Baptists and Quakers), he made notable contributions to the literature of radical religion during the later Interregnum when he produced radically religious polemics and was preparing a large heretical theological treatise, his 'dearest and best possession' containing views frequently 'at odds with certain conventional opinions' (*CPW*, 6:121). Despite recent questions raised about the authorship of *De Doctrina Christiana* (1658?–1674; the manuscript, in its much-corrected and revised state, was discovered in 1823), most scholars still agree that this treatise of theological and Biblical exegesis, crammed with over 8,000 proof texts, is by Milton (his earliest biographers confirm that he was writing a heterodox 'Body of Divinity') and that its doctrinal positions are indeed his, including anti-Trinitarianism, anti-Sabbatarianism, mortalism, adult baptism of believers, monism and creation *ex deo*, and a radical form of Arminianism (i.e. allowing humans the freedom to accept or reject grace), as well as other heterodoxies.[165] Its emphasis on the 'pre-eminent and

161 *The Cry of a Stone*, pp. 4–5.
162 *The Retired Mans Meditations* (London, 1655), esp. ch. 26.
163 *Ibid.*, 'To the Reader', sigs. a4r – v.   164 *De Doctrina Christiana*, in *CPW*, 6:608.
165 *The Early Lives of John Milton*, ed. Helen Darbishire (London: Constable, 1932), p. 31; also pp. 9–10, 46–7, 192. The scholarly debate includes William B. Hunter, 'The Provenance

supreme authority' (*CPW*, 6:587) of the inward Spirit, even over the letter of the Scripture, aligns Milton with the unorthodox, antinomian spiritual beliefs of Quakers and other religious radicals. Nevertheless, Milton asserts his hermeneutic independence with regard to his radical religious contemporaries as he reexamines theological doctrines in the *Christian Doctrine:* as he engages strenuously with the Holy Scriptures, he insists that he follows 'no other heresy or sect' and works out 'his beliefs for himself' (as he urged every believer to do for himself; *CPW*, 6:123, 118) rather than depending upon human authorities, including radical ones.

At the end of the Interregnum Milton published companion texts highlighting his radical spiritual convictions and rejecting any form of institutionalised religion and theology: *A Treatise of Civil Power in Ecclesiastical Causes*, addressed to Richard Cromwell's newly convened conservative Parliament, and *The Likeliest Means to Remove Hirelings out of the Church*, published in August 1659 when fears of sectarianism (notably anti-Quaker feeling) stirred a pro-Royalist Presbyterian rising led by Sir George Booth. Milton's texts also appeared in the same year that the Puritan minister Baxter, worried about the threat to Protestantism from radical zealots as well as popery, produced *A Holy Commonwealth*, his principal work envisioning England as a 'holy commonwealth' defined by clerical discipline and the magistrate's power in spiritual matters; for this commonwealth Cromwell's son seemed an ideal godly magistrate.[166] Whereas Baxter insisted that it was 'trayterous and intolerable' to affirm that 'Magistrates have nothing to do with matters of Religion, but are to leave all men to their consciences',[167] Milton repudiated Puritan orthodoxy by vigorously challenging the authority of ecclesiastical and political powers when it came to spiritual matters and inward religion. Spiritual inwardness has become Milton's touchstone of integrity, and his polemical strategy involves his own 'free and conscientious examination' (*Civil Power*, *CPW*, 7:258) of divisive religious terms which had aggravated tensions during the revolutionary decades. Thus he defuses (as he does in *Areopagitica*) the invidious terms *'heresie* and *heretic'* – 'another Greek apparition' – by defining a heretic freshly: one who maintains the

of the *Christian Doctrine*', *Studies in English Literature, 1500–1900* 33 (1992), 129–42, with responses by Barbara Lewalski and John Shawcross, 143–66; Hunter, *Visitation Unimplor'd: Milton and the Authorship of De Doctrina* (Pittsburgh: Duquesne University Press, 1998); Gordon Campbell, Thomas N. Corns, John K. Hale, David Holmes and Fiona Tweedie, 'The Provenance of *De Doctrina Christiana*', *Milton Quarterly* 31 (1997), 67–117; Stephen Dobranski and John Rumrich (eds.), *Milton and Heresy* (Cambridge University Press, 1998); Barbara Lewalski, 'Milton and *De Doctrina Christiana*: Evidences of Authorship', *Milton Studies* 36 (1999), 203–28.

166 See Richard Baxter, *A Holy Commonwealth*, ed. William Lamont (Cambridge University Press, 1994); the treatise is unfinished.

167 *Ibid.*, p. 171.

traditions of men or opinions not supported by Scripture; heresy therefore means professing a belief contrary to one's conscientious understanding of and strenuous engagement with Scripture (*CPW*, 7:247–9, 252).[168] Moreover, Milton's emphasis on the guidance of the 'inward perswasive motions' of the Spirit (*CPW*, 7:261), rather than on human laws and commandments, registers his close affinity to religious radicals – the Quakers among them – while anticipating the radical spiritualism of his great poems (expressed, e.g., in the 'strong motion' by which Jesus is led into the wilderness in *Paradise Regained* 1.290); or the 'rousing motions' (line 1382) Samson begins to feel before he destroys, with apocalyptic force, the idolatrous temple of Dagon in *Samson Agonistes*). *Civil Power* is characterised by its emphasis on internal illumination, by Milton's concise uses of scriptural proof texts to emphasise our freedom from ceremonies and the servile laws of men, and by the plainness of its style which conveys Milton's polemical rejection of the learned ministry: for 'doubtless in matters of religion he is learnedest who is planest' (*CPW*, 7:272).

In *The Likeliest Means*, Milton's biting attack on the hireling clergy as wolves and 'greedy dogs' (*CPW*, 7:296; echoing Isa. 56:11) and his hostility to tithes resemble the language and contempt of radical sectarians who reviled the orthodox, university-trained clergy as hirelings for making a trade of their preaching. Tithes remained among the most contentious religious issues of the revolution; religious radicals, including Milton (*CPW*, 7:281–90), argued that they had lost their divine sanction when the ceremonial Law was superseded by the gospel and the Levitical priesthood by an apostolic ministry. Most provocatively Milton commends itinerant, inwardly inspired preachers who preach in informal settings ('we may be well assur'd that he who disdaind not to be laid in a manger, disdains not to be preachd in a barn … such meetings as these being, indeed, most apostolical and primitive') and who model themselves after the apostles (as early Quaker preachers did), for they, though few in number, 'preachd to the poore as well as to the rich, looking for no recompense but in heaven' (*CPW*, 7:303–5).

In his last publication of the Interregnum, Milton showed a reckless disregard for his own safety as he spoke the language of the Commonwealth's 'good Old Cause' and reminded his contemporaries of the divine light which had illuminated a generation of radical Puritans who had sought to act according to it: 'after all this light among us' how could the English allow themselves 'to returne back to *Egypt*', putting their 'necks again under kingship' and

---

168 See also *Of True Religion*, in *CPW*, 8:421, 423; Janel Mueller, 'Milton on Heresy', in *Milton and Heresy*, ed. Dobranski and Rumrich, pp. 21–38.

submitting to the servile worship of an 'idol queen' *(The Readie and Easie Way* [second edition, April 1660], *CPW,* 7:462)? The restoration of the English monarchy and the Church of England, inaugurating a spiritually impoverished age when the 'greater part' of his countrymen would 'deem in outward Rites and specious forms / Religion satisfi'd' *(Paradise Lost,* 12.533–5), would not, however, stifle Milton's radical religious convictions. Baxter, we recall, had lamented a land consumed 'in a flame of contention' fuelling religious divisions during the upheavals of the 1640s and 1650s. In Restoration England, a period marked by ongoing religious tensions and instability, the war of words and contention could still be heard in Milton's poetry as both religious radicals and orthodox Puritans suffered heavy persecution. During the 1660s and the 1670s, the blind visionary poet, illuminated by the 'Celestial Light', would find the courage to write and publish the most enduring poetic tributes to the struggles of dissenters and the religion of the Spirit within: *Paradise Lost, Paradise Regained* and *Samson Agonistes.*[169]

169 These poems are considered in their Restoration context in Chapter 26 below; for their radical religious politics, see David Loewenstein, *Representing Revolution in Milton and his Contemporaries: Religion, Politics, and Polemics in Radical Puritanism* (Cambridge University Press, 2001), chs. 7–9.

Chapter 23

LITERATURE AND LONDON

NIGEL SMITH

London twas thou that didst thy Prince betray
And could thy sable vent no other way.
Fragment of anonymous elegy on Charles I,
Cardiff Central Library, MS 1.482, fo. 33v

Contexts and conditions

As Chapter 21 in this volume demonstrates, the civil crisis of the mid-century was one that embraced three kingdoms and a principality. It drew England into several armed conflicts with other west European states: most significantly, that other maritime and Protestant power, the United Provinces.[1] Additionally, the literary consequences of the war of the three kingdoms, and the First Dutch War (1652–4), were felt in the English language used in the provinces, in Scotland, Ireland and Wales, in the Celtic language cultures of these places, and in Dutch literature.[2]

London, however, was at the heart of the Civil War, and understanding its unique role is one of the keys to understanding the nature of the English Revolution and the literary innovations of these years. London was important not merely because it was the capital city of the nation, the major centre of population and of commerce. It was also near the places where government occurred and where the theatre of state played itself out. London's peculiar urban culture gave the capital a life of its own. We might more accurately say, a set of lives, since in the twenty years of Civil War, revolution and experimentation with non-monarchical forms of government, various forces would emerge from London culture and have a decisive effect on the turn of events in the nation at

---

1 See, e.g., Brendan Bradshaw and John Morrill (eds.), *The British Problem, c.* 1534–1707: *State Formation in the Atlantic Archipelago* (Basingstoke: Macmillan, 1996); Jane H. Ohlmeyer, *Civil War and Restoration in the Three Stuart Kingdoms: The Career of Randal MacDonnell, Marquis of Antrim*, 1609–1683 (Cambridge University Press, 1993).

2 Peter Davidson (ed.), *Poetry and Revolution: An Anthology of British Verse*, 1625–60 (Oxford: Clarendon Press 1998).

large.[3] Each of these forces was associated with, or even defined by, a specific kind of literary activity.

Several major factors should be borne in mind with respect to London and literature during the 1640s. First, London pinned its colours to Parliament in this decade. There was by no means universal consent for this, but as a corporation, the City backed the Long Parliament, and indeed bankrolled it. This was the first of a series of moves that would have a long-term impact on the City. By fleeing Westminster in January 1642, by raising his standard in Nottingham, and by making his headquarters in Oxford, the King was putting himself at a considerable disadvantage. Although no decisive battles took place near London, the King realised that he would have to recapture the City if he was to prevail. The Royalist army advanced as far as Turnham Green, thereby occasioning the mustering of the trained bands of London and the serious fear (expressed in a famous Milton sonnet, 'When the assault was intended to the city') that the City would be invaded.

After the regicide, London's civic identity was closely linked with the Republic and the Protectorate, the two modes of government established between the abolition of the monarchy in January 1649 and its restoration in April 1660. Indeed, the Rump Parliament adopted the arms of London in 1649: the most obvious and visible projection of the English Republic's image, present at the top of every printed document, was the shield of London.[4]

Secondly, the City's lending of support to the Parliament occurred at the same time as a dispute within the corporation itself. This was a power struggle between a generation of older, richer merchants, who had been the beneficiaries of royal monopolies, and a younger generation of less-established merchants who favoured the adoption of free trade.[5] The older generation supported the King, but the younger generation contained some of the more extreme Parliamentarians: men like Henry Robinson who would figure as major

---

3 Valerie Pearl, *London and the Outbreak of the Puritan Revolution: City Government and National Politics, 1625–43* (Oxford University Press, 1961); R. C. Richardson (ed.), *The English Civil Wars: Local Aspects* (Stroud, Gloucestershire: Sutton, 1997); Keith Lindley, *Popular Politics and Religion in Civil War London* (Aldershot: Scolar Press, 1997); Sean Kelsey, *Inventing a Republic: The Political Culture of the English Commonwealth, 1649–1653* (Manchester University Press, 1997); Derek Hirst, ' "That Sober Liberty": Marvell's Cromwell in 1654', in *The Golden and the Brazen World: Papers in Literature and History 1650–1800*, ed. John M. Wallace (Berkeley, Los Angeles and London: University of California Press, 1985), pp. 17–53. For a broader view, see also Valerie Pearl, 'Change and Stability in Seventeenth-Century London', *London Journal* 5 (1979), 3–34; Paul Griffiths and Mark S. R. Jenner, eds., *Londinopolis: Essays in the Cultural and Social History of Early Modern London* (Manchester University Press, 2000).
4 See Kelsey, *Inventing a Republic*, ch. 3.
5 See Robert Brenner, *Merchants and Revolution: Commercial Change, Political Conflict, and London's Overseas Traders, 1550–1653* (Princeton University Press, 1993).

propagandists for both economic liberalism and religious toleration. Visible committed republicans before 1649 were few, but among those who were, like Henry Marten, links with the City radicals were common and important. London was the city of the radicals. However, those in favour of reform had their greatest impact in the summer of 1643. Thereafter, the balance of power shifted to the moderates and conservatives. Indeed, these interests, when allied with the Presbyterian divines, nearly led to a reinstatement of the King in the City. In these circumstances, London might be seen as the fulcrum of a nearly successful counter-revolution, to which several radical writers, including John Goodwin, William Dell and John Milton himself, would respond.[6]

The third significant factor in London's literary life in the mid seventeenth century was its religious life. Its dense urban communities, and, in religious terms, parishes, reflected in an exaggerated way the tensions and divisions at the centre of national religious culture. In other words, in most of the City parishes, the confessional conflicts that were still playing out the Reformation were present in a ferociously inflamed way.[7] A parish vicar might have, on the one hand, evidence of sustained recusancy in his parish, and, more worryingly for him, Roman Catholic proselytes, perhaps in the form of Jesuits. On the other hand, he might well have Puritans of some kind, perhaps even extreme ones, who had thrown aside the idea of a national church, not only because it was insufficiently reformed, but because it was, perforce, tainted. Heaven forbid, the two extremes might even talk to one another, circumventing the centre ground of the national church. Beside the preached word, much of this tension would be expressed by the circulation of written or printed materials, each with their own distinctive literary forms.

The fourth factor is at least as important as all the others. London was, and had always been, the centre of the printing trade in England. However much manuscript circulation accounted for the initial life of literary texts and sustained their circulation in many contexts, notably courtly literature, and however many works began their lives in provincial contexts, such as country houses, the vast majority of all printing was in London.[8] London was especially

---

6 See Valerie Pearl, 'London's Counter-Revolution', in *The Interregnum: The Quest for Settlement, 1646–1660*, ed. G. E. Aylmer (London: Macmillan, 1972), pp. 29–56.
7 David R. Como, 'Puritans and Heretics: The Emergence of an Antinomian Underground in Early Stuart England', unpublished Ph.D. thesis, Princeton University, 1999; Jeremy Boulton, *Neighbourhood and Society: A London Suburb in the Seventeenth Century* (Cambridge University Press, 1987); Peter Lake with Michael Questier (eds.) *The Antichrist's Lewd Hat: Protestants, Papists and Players in Post-Reformation England* (New Haven, CT, and London: Yale University Press, 2002).
8 On manuscript circulation and the relation of printing to literary culture, see also Chapters 2 and 3 in this volume.

well suited to handle a rapid politicisation of letters, once the conflict between King and Parliament got underway. This was precisely what happened: an explosion of printed materials.[9] King Charles was able to make use of the university printing presses in Oxford, and a remarkable amount of Royalist material was published in the first half of the 1640s.[10] But this was because the London presses, often in indirect or covert ways, began to print Royalist books. One of the functions of conventionally defined 'high' literature (play-texts, poems, prose romances) at this time was to speak the 'secret language' of Royalism in the midst of the enemy's camp. It is in no little part because of the power of London publishing activity that the history of the Civil War has been written until very recently in such centralist terms. The greatest single body of printed evidence for the period is the tract collection of a London publisher, George Thomason, who between 1640 and 1661 amassed a collection of more than 22,000 publications out of what he was able to purchase from the shops and stalls of London publishers.[11] The Thomason Tracts constitute by no means all of the total works published in the period, but they do represent a very large proportion. The civic life of London during the period is visible throughout this collection, in every kind of publication. There was a good deal of self-reflection here: *The City Law* (July 1647) was a 68-page account of the constitution and other laws of the capital, 'ENGLISHED, *Out of an ancient French Manuscript*'. One of its publishers was Livewell Chapman, who would be a prominent Fifth Monarchist and republican publisher in the following decade.

The Thomason Tracts provide vivid and various evidence of two crucial changes in London literary life that occurred early in the 1640s and had a profound impact on English history. First, in the summer of 1642, largely as a means of exerting social control, Parliament closed the theatres.[12] They were not to open again in any continuing way until after the restoration of the

---

9 There is no satisfactory study of censorship in the period, but see Annabel Patterson, *Censorship and Interpretation: The Conditions of Writing and Reading in Early Modern England* (Madison: University of Wisconsin Press, 1984), and the forthcoming Cambridge University Press *History of the Book in Britain, 1558–1685*, ed. D. F. Mackenzie, John Barnard and Maureen Bell.
10 See Lois Potter, *Secret Rites and Secret Writing: Royalist Literature, 1641–1660* (Cambridge University Press, 1989).
11 See G. K. Fortescue, *Catalogue of the Pamphlets, Books, Newspapers, and Manuscripts relating to the Civil War, the Commonwealth, and the Restoration, Collected by George Thomason, 1640–1661* (London, 1908). This can be supplemented by Donald Wing's *Short-Title Catalogue of Books Printed in England, Scotland, Ireland, Wales, and British America, and of English books Printed in Other Countries, 1641–1700*, 2nd edn. (New York: Modern Language Association, 1982–98), and the Early English Books Online website (http://www.lib.umi.com/eeebonew/).
12 Leslie Hotson, *The Commonwealth and Restoration Stage* (Cambridge, MA: Harvard University Press, 1928); Susan Wiseman, *Drama and Politics in the English Civil War* (Cambridge University Press, 1998); see also Chapter 19 in this volume, pp. 597–602.

monarchy. Plays were surreptitiously performed (perhaps more away from the capital than within it), and, in the 1640s, theatricality became associated with Royalism. There were some experiments with different kinds of theatre during the 1650s, such as the imperialist quasi-operas of Sir William Davenant; and several prominent republicans called for the opening of suitably reformed theatres. There were also pageants and occasional entertainments for visiting ambassadors. In the main, though, plays were not regularly performed. The most visible presence of the stage was actually in the publishing of plays. During the Civil War and Interregnum periods, largely through the efforts of the publisher Humphrey Moseley, the canons of several pre-war dramatists (e.g. Beaumont and Fletcher, Middleton, Massinger, Ford, Davenant, Brome, Shirley) were established through printed editions.[13] This in itself would have a profound impact upon the development of the drama and drama criticism, once the theatres were again opened after the Restoration.

While the theatres were officially closed, the printed book flourished. The most significant development was the emergence of the printed serial newsbook, among myriad other kinds of shorter publication, such as the published speech, dialogues, accounts of battles and mock sermons.[14] Before 1641, foreign news was sometimes sporadically offered in printed form (the publishing of domestic news was illegal). Handwritten news digests were prepared and sent from London and Westminster to the ruling elite in the provinces. In late November 1641, however, the Long Parliament began to publish an account of its proceedings, as a means of justifying the course it was taking with the King. Soon the King would establish his own newsbook in Oxford. Thus began two decades of polemically directed journalism, in which the parameters of that art were discovered: writing humorously in order to attract readers, exploiting rumours, being economical with the truth or concealing it – in short, lying. Among the more remarkable early practitioners of journalism was Marchamont Nedham, famous for changing sides, and also for developing a theory of the republic in a form that could be readily digested by the lower echelons of the 'middling sort'.[15] Here, for instance, is the beginning of an editorial:

13 Paulina Kewes, ' "Give Me the Sociable Pocket-Books . . . ": Humphrey Moseley's Serial Publication of Octavo Play Collections', *Publishing History* 38 (1995), 5–21.
14 Joad Raymond, *The Invention of the Newspaper: English Newsbooks, 1641–1649* (Oxford: Clarendon Press, 1996); Jason McElligott, 'Edward Crouch (c. 1622–1676): A Poor Printer in Seventeenth-century London', *Journal of the Print History Society* n.s. 1 (2000), 49–73.
15 Blair Worden, ' "Wit in a Roundhead": The Dilemma of Marchamont Nedham', in *Political Culture and Cultural Politics in Early Modern England: Essays Presented to David Underdown*, ed. Susan D. Amussen and Mark A. Kishlansky (Manchester University Press, 1995),

In the last, you had a Touch of some Reasons, justifying the form of a *Free-State* (or a *Government of the People*) to be much more excellent than the *Grandee*, or the *Kingly Power*. By the *People*, we mean such as shal be duely chosen to represent the People *successively* in their *Supream Assemblies*; And that the People thus qualified or constituted, are the best *Keepers of their own Liberties*.[16]

Nedham is often remembered for his jocoserious style, his rendering of news humorously, since he believed that this was the way to sustain and influence a readership. In this passage, however, he reveals his knowledge of classical republican history and literature, and a design to draw the reader carefully into appreciating the essentials of republican political theory (see also below, pp. 724–5, 730–1).

There were also ways in which London was bound together by common ways of writing: in part, due to the hold of traditions and common perceptions that remained despite faction and religious division. Not surprisingly, these concern particular material features of the City, or events in its history. One in particular is fire, often rendered in apocalyptic tones. The Book of Revelation made most Londoners think about the possibility of an imminent fiery consumption in the City. Furthermore, the very flammability of much of the City's fabric, and the nearness in cultural memory of the fiery martyrdoms of early Protestants, meant that London was experienced in reality, and on the written or printed page, as a tinderbox.[17] Metaphor and reality lived side by side: London was politically inflammable, and nowhere was this more apparent than on the printed page. Thus, William Finch, millenarian and follower of the self-proclaimed King of the Jews, Thomas Tany, attracted notice when he set fire to parts of London in 1655 in order to induce divine fiery retribution. Finch himself distributed tracts rich in apocalyptic imagery that explained the action.[18]

Contested space; competing visions

London may have given its support to Parliament, but there were plenty of Royalists within the City. Most supporters of the Long Parliament initially thought that they were rescuing the King from evil advisers. Accordingly,

pp. 301–37; Carolyn Nelson and Matthew Seccombe, *British Newspapers and Periodicals, 1641–1700: A Short-title Catalogue of Serials Printed in England, Scotland, Ireland, and British America* (New York: Modern Language Association of America, 1987).
16 *Mercurius Politicus* 78 (27 Nov. – 4 Dec. 1651), p. 1237.
17 See Nigel Smith, '"Making Fire": Conflagration and Religious Controversy in Seventeenth-Century London', in *Imagining Early Modern London*, ed. J. F. Merritt (Cambridge University Press, 2001), pp. 273–93.
18 [William Finch], *A third great and terrible Fire, Fire, Fire* (1 June 1655), p. 4.

a tradition of associating the City's history with monarchy was used in the Royalist cause. On 7th March 1648, after the King had been captured and handed over to Parliament, and after London had been occupied by the New Model Army, Thomason acquired a poem printed in a quarto pamphlet entitled *London, King Charles His Augusta, or, City Royal*. It claimed to be an English translation by an author who wished to preserve his anonymity, and was found in the study of Sir William Davenant then in exile in Paris, but soon to be captured and imprisoned on a charge of treason for complicity with Royalist plots. Using the works of the great antiquarian scholars of the age in marginal annotations, the poem presented the British Troy as a true expression of the nation's multifarious roots and components, Celtic and Roman, complete with a prophecy from the goddess Diana, as opposed to the London-as-Jerusalem comparison preferred by the Puritans. *London, King Charles his Augusta* is a counterpart to the kind of embattled episcopal defence against Puritan attack, such as *Persecutio Undecima* (November 1648), that appeared at this time.

The poem associated with Davenant was in its way a lament for an urban world that had, from a Royalist viewpoint in 1648, disappeared. Davenant was, effectively, Charles I's laureate and he was now in danger of execution. By 1640 the pleasures of urban refinement and leisure had made London synonymous with Cavalier culture.[19] The experience of aesthetic pleasure in the City was such that those without means could in fact forget that they relied upon the patronage of the great – hence the Tribe of Ben, the group of young poets who gathered around the elderly Ben Jonson in the Mermaid Tavern, and the other drinking, singing and declaiming clubs of the 1630s.[20] These developments stemmed from the growth of the West End, the space between the City and Westminster, with its concomitant new property and financial arrangements, and its new forms of communication. A fashion and residential centre had been created on the edge of the capital, one which drew the country elite to the City in increasing numbers. From 1646, restrictions were imposed on the movements of known Royalists, and some were banished from the capital. What the privileged had experienced as a highly literary and theatrical public culture was now only accessible in the pages of Royalist publications. These were a way of sustaining what had been achieved in a monarchical metropolitan vision for a future age, across a period of disruption. Moseley's publishing activities were part of the bedrock of this activity; other works contained a history of

---

19 See Lawrence Manley, *Literature and Culture in Early Modern London* (Cambridge University Press, 1995), ch. 9.
20 See Timothy Raylor, *Cavaliers, Clubs, and Literary Culture: Sir John Mennes, James Smith, and the Order of the Fancy* (Cranbury, NJ, and London: Associated University Presses, 1994).

the 'Halcyon days' before the war, such as Edmund Gayton's *Pleasant Notes upon Don Quixot* (1654). Anthologies were another way in which this culture was transmitted in the mid-century, and particularly the 1650s: a new phenomenon consisting sometimes of very lengthy collections of various brief, usually light, poems, concerned with city matters, such as *Musarum Deliciae* (1655). Furthermore, where Royalist literature had involved the development of a moral enquiry, as in the plays of Ben Jonson and his followers, the moral dimensions of that literature became an articulating force – hence, the prevalence of Jonsonian and Websterian imitation in the Royalist play-pamphlets of the later 1640s.

A similar but much more extensive work was James Howell's *Londinopolis* (1657), a history of London and Westminster, prefaced by a poem in Latin and English on London Bridge, in which Neptune is impressed because the bridge outdoes the Rialto at Venice. Howell had published some famous Royalist literature in the 1640s, but, in debt and in need of coming to terms with the Commonwealth government, he chose to write a history that played up London's classical heritage, as well as its mercantile prowess. Howell borrowed freely from extant histories and other materials concerned with the City, especially Stow's history, but claimed that he also added his own insights. In *Londinopolis*, Howell's Royalism has vanished, except in odd corners where he seems to have incorporated older materials that were obviously monarchical in orientation: 'And though there be some, who hold such Corporations, and little *Body politiques*, of this kind, to be prejudicial to *Monarchy*; yet they may be said to be one of the *Glories* of *London*, and wherein she surpasseth all other Cities' (p. 46). Moreover, he does not cease to call the country a kingdom (e.g. p. 407). Howell was rewarded in 1660 with the title of Historiographer Royal. His careful hedging of London's identity in 1657 accords perfectly with the political situation at that point. The Republic was finished, and Protectorate circles debated whether Oliver Cromwell would take the crown and thereby help to secure the future of a new dynasty and state.

Meanwhile, across town, Puritan congregations of all kinds were meeting. If the City enabled Anglicans and Catholics to celebrate their communions in secret, the variety of forms of worship and devotion within the Puritan diaspora must have made the City feel like a Tower of Babel. Royalists felt that London radicalism spelt the end of civilisation. By the later 1650s, different Puritan sermon styles were well recognisable, and easily lent themselves to imitation. An important feature of these years was the ecumenical meeting of various kinds of Puritans, to debate matters of faith. The General Baptists in particular encouraged this kind of open-ended speculative meeting.[21] The meeting itself was probably more unpredictable in nature than the prophesyings of the Independent and Baptist churches. Prophesyings began life in the late sixteenth century as meetings of clergy and laity to discuss the meaning of scriptural passages, but later became known for the trance-like deliveries of women like Anna Trapnel, who dared to challenge Cromwell's Protectorate.[22] While worship in most Puritan congregations, as in the established church, banished all singing except for metrical Psalms, which were of course Biblically based, the need for occasional celebrations of more contemporary events (such as victories in battle) resulted in the composition of hymns, especially among some Independent and Baptist congregations. The London gathered churches were in any case highly distinctive literary units, with the Independent congregations most willing to expose publicly in print vast quantities of confessions of experience – the brief spiritual autobiographies that believers had to give before the church in order to join it. Being a Puritan often meant being an author, and nowhere was this truer than in London.[23]

The most astonishing aspect of prophetic culture in the aftermath of the regicide was the emergence of a number of prophets, whose colourful writings were accompanied by highly theatrical 'performances' that inverted the social order in the name of social and economic equality. The Ranters were and are notorious for their alleged practice of free love, but contemporaries were as much amazed by the prophet (in this instance, Abiezer Coppe) who stopped the coaches of the wealthy and who groped gypsies, a holy fool who thought he voiced God and warned that a fiery apocalypse would soon consume everyone's money:

> Wherefore waving my charging so many Coaches, so many hundreds of men and women of the greater rank, in the open streets, with my hand stretched out, my hat cock't up, staring on them as if I would look thorough them, gnashing with my teeth at some of them, and day and night with a huge loud voice proclaiming the day of the Lord throughout London and Southwark, and leaving divers other exploits... falling down flat upon the ground before rogues, beggars, cripples, halt, maimed; blind, &c. kissing the feet of many, rising up againe and giving them money.[24]

21 Nigel Smith, *Perfection Proclaimed: Language and Literature in English Radical Religion, 1640–1660* (Oxford: Clarendon Press, 1989), ch. 1.

22 Anna Trapnel, *The Cry of a Stone* (1654), ed. Hilary Hinds (Tempe, AZ: Medieval and Renaissance Texts and Studies, 2000).

23 Nigel Smith, *Perfection Proclaimed*, chs. 1 and 2.

24 Abiezer Coppe, *A Second Fiery Flying Roule* (1649), in *A Collection of Ranter Writings from the Seventeenth Century*, ed. N. Smith (London: Junction Books, 1983), p. 105.

Fortunately, Coppe's vision of wealthy ladies burning alive in punishment for their fine apparel and cosmetics, filling the streets of London with the stench and smoke of burning flesh, remained in his imagination.[25]

In a way, Puritanism's sway in London was in tune with the old forms of urban regulation: sumptuary laws, sober dress and respect for hierarchy, even if the authorities were not bishops and kings. But equally, as in the instance of the financially successful godly merchants, Puritanism probably helped status differences disappear. Furthermore, if the republicans of the 1650s began by believing in virtue, by the late 1650s most of them understood that it was trade that made a nation strong. In the late 1640s and 1650s an ideology of a kingless state merged with the sense of possessing a burgeoning, prosperous metropolis. Restoration London was a fusion of Commonwealth commercial optimism (which assumed that trade should be backed by military strength) and a literary culture which began by welcoming Royalism, but soon admitted various kinds of Puritan and republican dissent back into its ranks. In the 1640s, the contending forces were pitted against each other in publishing wars that obsessed and horrified the capital's readers. The possibilities and limitations of this London literary world were explored in Milton's famous plea against pre-publication licensing, *Areopagitica* (November 1644).

John Milton and the 'City of refuge'

Milton was a Londoner through and through, the son of a nouveau riche burgher, a son who had been treated to the most privileged of educations. In the summer of 1639 he had returned to reside in the capital after a fourteen-month tour of Europe.[26] His voice in the cause of religious reform equalled in quality the very best of the Puritan Long Parliament sermons. His sense of the poet's role as national prophet was evident in his writings. Furthermore, in 1643, he came out in his true colours as an advocate of divorce for incompatible partners, and became immediately and notoriously identified with the extreme Puritan ferment that was beginning to worry the more conservative wing of the Puritans, the Presbyterians.[27]

Areopagitica appeared towards the end of the next year, in response to Parliament's 1643 Licensing Act, which reintroduced a form of censorship: not

---

25 See [Coppe], *Divine Fireworks* (London, 1657), single sheet.
26 William Riley Parker, *Milton: A Biographical Commentary*, 2 vols., 2nd edn, revised, ed. Gordon Campbell (Oxford: Clarendon Press, and New York: Oxford University Press, 1996), ch. 7.
27 See Thomas N. Corns, 'Milton's Quest for Respectability', *Modern Language Review* 77 (1982), 769–79.

as absolute as the system that had prevailed before 1640, but pre-publication interference in an author's views nonetheless. At the heart of Milton's tract is his first formulation of his free-will theology, central to his great poem *Paradise Lost* (1667, revised 1674), but equally conspicuous is the image of London as a besieged city populated by vigorously inventive writers:

> Behold now this vast City; a City of refuge, the mansion house of liberty, encompast and surrounded with his protection; the shop of warre hath not there more anvils and hammers waking, to fashion out the plates and instruments of armed Justice in defence of beleaguer'd Truth, then there be pens and heads there, sitting by their studious lamps, musing, searching, revolving new notions and idea's wherewith to present, as with their homage, and their fealty the approaching Reformation.[28]

Milton draws his imagery from Numbers 35:6–15 where God commands the Children of Israel to give cities to the Levites 'as a refuge'. The nimble imagery does the work of crossing the boundary between learning and fighting, even though we never see the London trained bands mustered literally before us. Milton had been running a school for his nephews in the City, and he was engaged in the debate for a universal reform of knowledge, at the centre of which was the Hungarian exile then resident in London, Samuel Hartlib. Through this circle, *Areopagitica* was read in England and in Europe, although its ambitious style put its comprehension beyond all but the most serious intellectuals.[29]

Milton's vision of intellectual freedom is intensely urban: he compares the freedom of which London is capable with the intellectually limited world of contemporary Italy. Italian books, subject to Counter-Reformation censorship, have title pages like Italian piazzas, with friars bobbing their heads to give permission: a visual personification of an imprimatur. Behind London and Italy are the city states of the ancient world. The tract takes its title from the Areopagus, the council in ancient Athens that ruled when the assembly of the people did not meet. The Areopagus in fact had the power of censorship, and by likening the English Parliament to the Areopagus, and arguing that there should be no pre-publication censorship, Milton was reversing the usual understanding of the ancient world. On the title-page of *Areopagitica*, Milton quoted translated lines from Euripides' play *The Suppliant Women*. In these lines, Theseus defends the rights of Athenians to participation in government and to free speech, even though Milton inserted the qualifying phrase 'who can',

28 From *Complete Prose Works of John Milton*, gen. ed. Don M. Wolfe, 8 vols. (New Haven, CT: Yale University Press, 1953–82), 2:553. Further references to Milton's prose will be to this edition, abbreviated *CPW*.
29 David Norbrook, *Writing the English Republic: Poetry, Rhetoric and Politics, 1627–1660* (Cambridge University Press, 1999), pp. 124–5.

to suggest that it is those who are either gifted enough, or sufficiently well-educated, to speak publicly who may do so. The quotation says much about Milton's conception of London as a replication of an ancient democracy, its personal and civic values held together by the frequent performance of such anti-tyrannical dramas – if only the theatres had not been closed at the time. The bold thinking and speaking, founded in the proper and uncompelled exercise of reason, that is the foundation of Greek and Roman civic humanism, is thus at the heart of *Areopagitica*, with its theology of free will. Athens and Rome are the foremost of the ancient cities where freedom and learning are tied together, as opposed to 'surly' Sparta, where such freedoms were outlawed. Milton in fact implies a rather unconvincing parallel between Athens and Sparta, and London and Oxford, where Charles I had his headquarters and court during the first Civil War. Certainly, Charles and his court were in a sense 'camping' in Oxford, just as the Spartan males in compulsory military service lived in tents within a defensive citadel rather than in buildings. But Oxford had the chief library of the kingdom, and was a major seat of European learning and religion, and therefore hardly the centre of an invincible warrior culture.

The Parliament at Westminster is offered a rousing speech in which the orator, imitating Isocrates (who always delivered his speeches to the Areopagus in writing rather than in person), speaks from lively London to tell MPs that the nation is not 'beyond the manhood of a Roman recovery' (*CPW*, 2:487). In this capital, books are 'precious lifeblood': they are the 'essence' of human resource and must thus be left to circulate unhindered, so that public debate can establish their relative merit and their eventual contribution to the people's well-being. Constitutional republicanism is not recommended by Milton in the tract, but the sustained alignment of classical and classical-republican sources and frameworks of understanding means that Milton constructs London as a republic of virtue, in which liberty is nourished by free, right-choosing citizen authors.[30] Utopias, the literary tradition extending from Plato to More, are blueprints for ideal societies, in Milton's view. As such, they should be spurned because they are not rooted in a conception of virtuous action (*CPW*, 2:219). Indeed, *Areopagitica* is rightly seen as a crucial point in the emergence of Milton's republican thought.[31] Milton would later think in more detail about the best

---

30 Nigel Smith, '*Areopagitica*: Voicing Contexts, 1643–5', in *Politics, Poetics, and Hermeneutics in Milton's Prose*, ed. David Loewenstein and James Grantham Turner (Cambridge University Press, 1990), pp. 103–22.

31 *Ibid.*; Norbrook, *Writing the English Republic*, pp. 118–39; Martin Dzelzainis, 'Milton's Classical Republicanism', in *Milton and Republicanism*, ed. David Armitage, Armand Himy and Quentin Skinner (Cambridge University Press, 1995), pp. 3–24; Quentin Skinner, *Liberty before Liberalism* (Cambridge University Press, 1998).

form of constitution for a free state, but this was when the Commonwealth was on the verge of becoming a monarchy again. His proposals in *The Readie and Easie Way to Establish a Free Commonwealth* (1660) recommend one: election to a senate with a fixed membership. No doubt Milton was desperate at this stage to imagine a polity that would not slide towards monarchy. But in doing so, he was fatally compromising the exciting vision of urban virtue and literary productiveness first expounded in *Areopagitica*.

Throughout its course, the tract gives a splendidly evocative account of the sense of excitement that surrounded the print market of the early 1640s. This is best perceived in a passage arguing for the sheer impossibility of regulating the presses. Such measures are simply against the politics and economics of early modern London, as well as the nature of composition. After a licence has been granted, an author might have second thoughts, and this creates difficulties for the law-abiding printer who:

> dares not go beyond his licenc't copy; so often then must the author trudge to his leav-giver, that those his new insertions may be viewed; and many jaunts will be made, ere that licenser, for it must be the same man, can either be found, or found at leisure; mean while either the Presse must stand still, which is no small damage, or the author loose his accuratest thoughts, & send the book forth wors then he had made it, which to a diligent writer is the greatest melancholy and vexation that can befall. (*CPW*, 2:532)

Books from foreign presses, even Roman Catholic ones, will be smuggled into the country. Knowledge, like sin, should be thought of as a huge heap 'increasing under the very act of diminishing' (*CPW*, 2:527). The City is thus no place for any kind of covetousness, as the free-trade terms that govern the description of a series of City merchant characters suggest. And because his argument remains so open to the presence of contingency, Milton is quite happy to oppose pre-publication licensing but also to affirm that books that are truly blasphemous, or Roman Catholic, should be summarily burned. His imagery is just as inconsistent: books are men, but eating is the dominant metaphor for the reading of books – cannibalism is at the heart of the tract. In this respect, *Areopagitica* is much more than a defence of press freedom. Its attentiveness to urban experience and tradition make it argue for a profoundly exciting method of enquiry, choosing freely, inevitably within certain limits, but always with the sense that contradiction and reversal are at the heart of all we can know. The urban imagery suggests that Milton understood this paradoxical truth to be intimately associated with the city, and the City of London at that.

London's liberty in chains: Leveller writing and the city

John Lilburne was the best-known of the Levellers, and one of their prominent leaders. Of the three key figures, Lilburne, Walwyn and Overton, Lilburne was the only one to be both an urban activist and a member of the Army. He personified seventeenth-century agitprop. The Levellers themselves are of particular interest because, until the emergence of the Quakers in the 1650s, they capitalised most upon the print opportunities of the 1640s, and, in large part, they defined the heart of the popular politics of Civil War London.[32] The individuals who made up the Leveller party when it emerged as an organised political force in 1646, calling for franchise reform and greater religious toleration, were mostly radical Puritans. In the early 1640s, several of them had made an impact in a series of publications calling for greater religious toleration, against the restrictions urged by the Presbyterians. These works and the meetings of London radicals that accompanied them contributed to the calls for franchise reform in the later seventeenth century.

London's Liberty in Chains Discovered, written when Lilburne was a prisoner in the Tower of London, ties the politics of London's corporation to the radical agendas in the City and in the New Model Army. Lilburne voices his support for London free-trade writings (p. 22), and prints a free-trade petition from two London merchants (pp. 43–5), as well as confessing that he had been robbed by the 'monopolizing merchant-adventurers' (p. 32). Other free-trade writings by London merchants harmonise with Lilburne's methods and outlook.[33] Lilburne calls for an extension of the franchise beyond the Common Council so that every freeman in the City would have the right to vote, rather than the aldermen only. The tract is typical of Lilburne's writing in its length – a good reason to use the printing press – and in its gathering together of different kinds of legal authority. A modern reader, who may think of Lilburne as a proto-democrat, might be surprised by the reference to medieval charters that established the constitution of the capital. This inevitably meant an appeal to a king – King John, who granted a Charter to London, so Lilburne claims, in 1227. Another source of authority involves comparison between

32 Nigel Smith, *Literature and Revolution In England 1640–1660* (New Haven, CT: Yale University Press, 1994), pp. 130–48; Lindley, *Popular Politics*; David Loewenstein, *Representing Revolution in Milton and his Contemporaries: Religion, Politics, and Polemics in Radical Puritanism* (Cambridge University Press, 2001), ch. 1; Smith, 'Naked Space', in *The Public Sphere in Early Modern England*, ed. Peter Lake and Steven Pincus (Manchester University Press, forthcoming).

33 See, e.g., Thomas Johnson, *A Discourse Consisting of Motives for The Enlargement and Freedome of Trade* ([23 April] 1645).

London's free men and virtuous ancient Romans. The denial of the vote to the 'people' is, says Lilburne, an act of tyranny as barbaric as anything in ancient Rome. Moderation in government is achieved by annual election, 'as the *Annuall Consul in Rome*' (p. 2); for 'did Rome ever so flourish, as when, not any thing was done but by the Senate and People there?' (p. 7). In the time of King Alfred, it had been established in London that all government should be elective, the electors being all the freemen (then called 'barons'). It is no surprise then, that in other Leveller tracts those citizens who guard and promote the electoral process are regarded as heroes; in this way, the Leveller pamphleteers eulogistically explained popular political agency and representation.

Since an attempt to silence them was usually the immediate cause of their publications, Leveller books constituted themselves as the act of freedom for which they spoke. Pamphlets were worn in hatbands, especially at Leveller demonstrations and mutinies: the book became the sacrament of the movement. The Levellers exploited the petition – the traditional means by which those outside the political nation presented their grievances to those within it – but once the petition had ceased to function effectively for them, they transformed it, using the pamphlet and incorporating the petition within it, as a means of recruiting public support and generating a unified movement. Although conventional petitioning, such as that offered by women on behalf of imprisoned Leveller leaders in 1649, continued to work effectively, Parliament's refusal to accept Lilburne's petitions was instrumental in a change.[34] The result was a recourse to the kinds of pamphleteering format that Lilburne had developed while taking on the London establishment in the mid-1640s, but this time applied to the national predicament at large. By 1649, the Levellers had exploited a series of polemical techniques: newsbooks with carnivalesque, theatrical and dramatic language; the use of (secret) presses both in London and in the army; engraved title pages (e.g., Lilburne behind bars, Lilburne pleading his case with a common law text in his hands); and a series of stated demands (the *Agreements of the People*) in which franchise extension and regular Parliaments were enshrined. The Protestant martyrological tradition had thus been turned into a modern, popular political movement.[35] There is evidence that the urban Levellers in particular believed that they would be able to persuade people entirely through political meetings and the power of print, and hence overcome the power of the New Model Army commanders who stood in their

34 See David Zaret, *Origins of Democratic Culture: Printing, Petitions and the Public Sphere in Early Modern England* (Princeton University Press, 2000), ch. 8.
35 John R. Knott, *Discourses of Martyrdom in English Literature 1563–1694* (Cambridge University Press, 1993).

way. The fact is that their victory could only have been achieved by a resort to armed force. Their failure in this respect showed the limitations of the power of their books.

Leveller books, pamphlets and broadsides are notable for their exposure of mercantile and artisanal life in the period, and for their incorporation of social relations at large into Leveller propaganda.[36] Of this aspect, there is no greater example than Richard Overton's account of the invasion of his house by New Model Army troopers, on the pretext that he was an adulterous, sexual libertine. The urban and oral vigour of this writing makes the reader experience with the author the violation of the freeborn Englishman's private space. The writing is humorous (Overton was a feared satirist), as it confuses books and people in a sexual farce. This is Overton's mode of responding to the way in which the authorities tried to incriminate radicals on charges of sexual impropriety:

> And we three were together in a Chamber discoursing, he and I intending about our businesse immediately to go abroad, and hearing them knock, I said, Yonder are they come for me. Whereupon, some books that lay upon the table in the room, were thrown into the beds betwixt the sheets (and the books were all the persons he found there in the beds, except that he took us for printed papers, and then there were many) ... the Lieutenant Colonel began to abuse me with scandalous Language, and asked me, if the Gentlewoman who then sate suckling her childe, were not one of my wives, and averred that she and I lay together that night. Then the Gentleman hearing his wife called Whore, and abused so shamefully, got from the souldiers, and ran up stairs; and coming into the room where we were, he taxed the Lieutenant Colonel for abusing of his wife and me, and told him that he and I lay together that night: But the Lieutenant Colonel, out of that little discretion he had about him, took the Gentleman by the hand, saying 'How dost thou, brother Cuckold?'[37]

In this way, the godly householders of 1640s London learned of the new tyranny that was around them, just as they would read how it put unjust pressure on that most urban godly household at the centre of which was the marriage of John and Elizabeth Lilburne.[38]

As we have seen, Lilburne's knowledge of Rome helped him think about London. His deepest engagement with Roman and Machiavellian thought came

36 Alan Houston, 'A Way of Settlement: The Levellers, Monopolies and the Public Interest', *History of Political Thought* 9 (1993), 381–419.
37 Richard Overton, *The Picture of the Counsel of State* (1649) in *Freedom in Arms: A Selection of Leveller Writings*, ed. A. L. Morton (London: Lawrence and Wishart, 1975), pp. 200–1; see, further, Nigel Smith, *Literature and Revolution*, pp. 297–304.
38 See Ann Hughes, 'Gender and Politics in Leveller Literature', in *Political Culture and Cultural Politics in Early Modern England*, ed. Amussen and Kishlansky, ch. 7.

after the defeat of the Levellers, when he was exiled in Amsterdam. But others at home were busy producing a form of popular republicanism, consistent with the Leveller appeal to the common law, and exploiting the possibilities of the printing press. No discussion of popular print and politics in London should ignore in this respect John Streater. Between the dissolving of the Rump Parliament and his enforced silence just over a year later, Streater published a series of mostly newsbook-style writings that challenged the rule of Cromwell's Protectorate. Especially relevant was Streater's newsbook *Observations*. Foreign news was printed at the front, followed by some serious lessons in the formation of popular republics in the form of an extended, paragraph-by-paragraph commentary on Aristotle's *Politics*. Streater's strict view of electoral accountability and his plans for movement of the working population around the country according to need suggest an austere republic, but it was one in which, through a fusion of private and public spheres, and widespread education, all male citizens also become rulers in a commonwealth for increase.[39] Streater's pages document conversations on the London street between republican citizens, even encounters there with powerful Protectorate figures who were charged to silence him, but who could personally see the virtue of his position: they were trying to turn a blind eye.

London and Interregnum writing

Leveller writing was the most significant political thought in the period to have been bequeathed by London to posterity, even if it was not properly recognised for hundreds of years. Just as visible in the early days of the republic were the writing and activity of Gerrard Winstanley the Digger, and the associated writing that recommended the cultivation of common land and the abolition of private property. In calling themselves True Levellers, the Diggers signified that they thought of themselves as a further development of the Levellers, although Lilburne was one Leveller who pointedly dissociated his views from those of the Diggers.[40] The Diggers may have cultivated common land outside London in Surrey and Buckinghamshire, but Winstanley was a failed London merchant. His writings are addressed in part to a city constituency, as if the Digger experiment was a converse but inextricably linked appendage to popular city politics. *A Watch-Word to the City of London* (26 August 1649) is an

---

39 See Nigel Smith, 'Popular Republicanism in the 1650s: John Streater's "heroick Mechanicks"', in *Milton and Republicanism*, ed. Armitage *et al.*, pp. 137–55; Adrian Johns, *The Nature of the Book: Print and Knowledge in the Making* (University of Chicago Press, 1998), ch. 4.
40 See Lilburne, *Legall Fundamentall Liberties* (London, 1649), p. 75.

explanation of digging, a record of attacks on the St George's Hill commune and a warning that London is about to lose its hard-won freedom. The mystical and occult ideas that have such a significant presence in Winstanley's text are also the products of the London book market.[41]

The other great works of political theory from this period, however, have little or nothing to do with London. Hobbes's *Leviathan* was written in exile by an author who had been out of the country for most of the war decade. Before then he had mostly lived in country houses. James Harrington's *Oceana*, the most significant work of republican theory in the period, is an agrarian vision, although he approved of towns, unlike Hobbes, who regarded them as worms in the body politic.[42] Its Platonic categories distance it even further from the immediacy of an urban environment, although executive decisions and representation take place in a capital, 'Emporium'. It was in fact in the later 1650s, when the reception of *Oceana* occurred within the context of the unwinding of the Protectorate, that Harrington's works were broadly discussed in the political circles of London – the early world of the coffee houses. In 1659, on the eve of the Restoration, some attempted a resolution of Leveller and Harringtonian ideas, and Harrington himself convened the decidedly urban Rota Club, a collection of virtuosi who met to debate republican political theory.[43] This writing, and the pamphlets that accompanied it, exchange the almost playful obfuscation and learned allusiveness of early Harrington for writing in a plain, gritty style. This was the republican public sphere at its latest stage of evolution: a brief but intense period of impressive, popular political writing that would never recur again.

The presence of London as a touchstone for Commonwealth literary judgement extended to literature more closely associated with the Protectorate government. Milton's practice of embodying in his tracts, notably *Areopagitica* (1644), quotations from contemporary topical works circulating in the City exemplify the reader/writer's free choice in operation. This practice is taken to a further degree of sophistication by his associate Andrew Marvell, especially in his panegyric of Oliver Cromwell. Marvell had customarily constructed his complicated political verse by ironically quoting or echoing phrases from

---

41 For Winstanley and London, see further David Loewenstein, 'Digger Writing and Rural Dissent in the English Revolution: Representing England as a Common Treasury', in *The Country and the City Revisited: England and the Politics of Culture, 1550–1850*, ed. D. Landry and G. MacLean (Cambridge University Press, 1999), pp. 74–88.

42 *The Political Works of James Harrington*, ed. J. G. A. Pocock (Cambridge University Press, 1977); Anna Strumia, *L'immaginazione repubblicana: Sparta e Israele nel dibattito filosofico-politico dell'età di Cromwell* (Florence: Le Lettere, 1991).

43 Nigel Smith, 'Naked Space'; see also Norbrook, *Writing the English Republic*, pp. 398–400.

political pamphlet literature inside his couplets. The *First Anniversary* praises Cromwell by gathering bits and pieces of polemical publication that appeared during Cromwell's largely successful first year as Lord Protector. The poem does this under the governing image of Cromwell at home in his capital London. Indeed, Marvell reworks some of Milton's more remarkable images of active civic life in *Areopagitica*, and, like that work, the poem demonstrates its author's knowledge of the London publishing scene. Even more than Milton's tract, Marvell's poem lets the City stand for the nation, doing this first in terms of classical myth: Amphion played the city of Thebes into being with his lyre, Cromwell tunes his 'ruling instrument' in order to play the city/nation into being.

Like Milton, Marvell was probably aiming at a sophisticated readership: certainly members of the political nation, those involved in the Protectorate government; recently disappointed supporters of the now-defunct republic; and the Fifth Monarchists, millenarian Puritans, whose power base was in the London congregations. They had originally given the Protectorate their support, but now doubted that Cromwell would deliver the kind of state that would encourage the Second Coming of Christ. Indeed, Marvell's poem ignores most of the problems faced by Cromwell, and his opposition, in order to focus on the millennial theme. Oliver Cromwell, not the Fifth Monarchists, the poem argues, will provide the pathway for King Jesus to return to his Holy City. London becomes the central image for a series of qualities – from imperial might to Old Testament magistracy – by which the Protector's prowess is known. The inflammatory London preaching of the Fifth Monarchists Christopher Feake and John Simpson is explicitly named in the poem (line 305), as Marvell confuses, for the sake of inciting alarm, the urban phenomena of Fifth Monarchists, Quakers and alleged Adamites (lines 293–320). Significantly, Marvell omits the most visible Fifth Monarchist, the prophet Anna Trapnel, who occupied rooms in Whitehall in early 1654 in order to prophesy against the Protectorate. While Trapnel met with serious resistance in Cornwall, where she was tried as a witch, she was popular with many in the Commonwealth establishment in London. Her writings construct London, the geography and buildings of which she records in great detail, as a Holy City to be possessed by the saints. She is its Deborah, or, indeed, its Cassandra, if Cromwell prevails.[44] It may well have been unwise for Marvell to invoke Trapnel by name in his panegyric because she was too popular a figurehead.

---

44 See Trapnel, *The Cry of a Stone* (1654), ed. Hinds, pp. 9, 54.

The place of London in the poem becomes evident when we realise the debt of *The First Anniversary* to Waller's 'Upon his Majesty's Repairing of Paul's' (?1635), as full-blown a celebration of Charles I as one could hope to find. In particular, Marvell compares Cromwell to Amphion as Waller had compared Charles I:

> He, like Amphion, makes those quarries leap
> Into fair figures from a confused heap;
> For in his art of regiment is found
> A power like that of harmony in sound.
> (lines 11–14)[45]

Marvell appropriates an image hitherto associated with royalty and attaches it to the princely Protector, thus making Cromwell more regal. In this instance, royal associations with the capital are used to enhance Cromwell's image. The allusion, which would have been immediately apparent to contemporary *literati*, is designed to amplify the sense of Cromwell as the leader who outstrips all monarchs. Charles's renovation of St Paul's Cathedral was a project begun by his father, while Cromwell, who renovates not merely one church but an entire state, starts from the beginning. (The poem's use of Waller may catch a further irony, since St Paul's was threatened with demolition throughout the 1650s, and during 1654 the south wall partially collapsed.) In Waller's poem, Charles is the recipient of heavenly benevolence, but Cromwell, as prophet and magistrate, is associated with divine agency. Charles is given good weather for his building, but he cannot bring rain (lines 47–50), whereas Cromwell brings the storm that purges the land (lines 233–8); Charles is illuminated by the sun (lines 51–3), whereas Cromwell *is* the sun (lines 342–4); Charles breeds admiration in foreign princes (lines 61–4), whereas Cromwell breeds fear in them (lines 377–8). Amphion was a more politically appropriate musician than King David, who remained a strong component in Royalist iconography. But kings belong in courts, whereas Oliver belongs in his capital, and the capital is the nation. By contrast, Waller's *A Panegyric to my Lord Protector* (1655) focuses almost exclusively on imperial rather than civic imagery.

Yet if Cromwell is the 'protecting weight' on the roof of the lively, but unruly city-state, at the centre of Marvell's poem is the coaching accident that occurred – if not in London then close to it – in Hyde Park on the edge of the new West End. Cromwell's avoidance of disaster is adduced to show the power

45 *Poems of Edmund Waller*, ed, G. Thorn Drury, 2 vols. (1904; rpt, New York: Greenwood Press, 1968).

of Providence that guides both him and his governance of England. While the City of London functions protectively as a presence that prevents the Protector from blatantly appearing as a monarch, the margins of the City are a dangerous place, and the City itself is potentially a turbulent and turbaned anarchy that must be mastered. For all that, the poem draws on the image of citizen Cromwell, sober in his dark clothes and white collar, the godly Londoner and family man. It was, after all, London to which the Protector appealed for support early in his rule, and the City which accepted him after his famously angry Parliamentary speech of 12 September 1654.

Chaos: revived republic and Restoration

On 28 June 1659, Thomason purchased from a London bookstall an eight-page quarto pamphlet called *Chaos*, published by Livewell Chapman, a Fifth Monarchist supporter who had also published Harrington's *Oceana*. Typical of the myriad publications in the capital that followed the recall of the Rump Parliament and the brief restoration of a republic after the failure of Richard Cromwell's Protectorate, *Chaos* is rich with poetic language and reference (Ovid's *Metamorphoses* is quoted in the first sentence), as well as political theory. The nation has returned to its first chaos, much like the contemporary public discussion and debate, so that strong leadership is needed to maintain laws and liberties. The tract urges the elevation of a single common interest for the nation, and makes specific recommendations for the administrating of law, political elections, taxation, trade, agriculture and education. The allegorical description of chaos emphasises the importance of timely reform: 'if . . . we flout and abuse this coy Mistress TIME, and improve not the advantage and opportunity thereof, she will be gone, and then repentance may come too late' (p. 3). At the same time, chaos can only fashion a state out of the materials that prevail there: 'but out of her own store, *Chaos*-like, is her furniture, onely the deck and dress may seem to be sometimes borrowed from one, sometimes from another. Yet unless she be new built, so as to suit with the temper of her own climate, she will be unserviceable, and her fruit abortive' (p. 5). This discussion is typical of the almost frantic operation of London's public sphere in the year before the Restoration, as Commonwealth supporters debated the best form of government for the country. For instance, in *The Readie and Easie Way to Establish a Free Commonwealth* (February and April 1660), Milton was at pains to argue that trade – the life-blood of London – was not incompatible with republican government.

The sense of debate and excited difference prevailed during the Protectorate, despite its harsher terms of governance. But the hopeful urban vision of *Areopagitica*, which was aided by the arrival of the coffee house and attested by the proliferation of the newsbooks, disappeared at the Restoration.[46] Or rather, it disappeared as a dominant presence in printed literature. The second edition of *Chaos* (18 July 1659) contained a new preface that blamed London, Westminster and the suburbs for sucking wealth and population away from other parts of the country. Many republicans, Harrington among them, thought that a kingless state was only possible if there was a workable balance between capital and provinces. Fittingly, in Sir John Ogilby's description of the pageant decorations for Charles II's procession through London, Division and Dissent, and, by implication, Debate, were figured as monsters over which the King stood in triumph. On this occasion, the livery companies of the City stumped up £11,000 to cover the costs, and wine flowed through the Great Conduit in Cheapside. No doubt, this was an image of the good times to come, but it was also chillingly redolent of the blood that had been spilt, and the spilling that would come.

In these circumstances, political and religious dissent would take on very different expressive characteristics from those of the previous two decades. On the other hand, warnings of fiery conflagrations of the City, as a divine punishment for corruption and tyranny, in particular from Quakers, were a feature that straddled the Restoration divide.[47] As things turned out, the warnings were not wrong. The capital would not be ready for its role as commercial and imperial centre, with all of the cultural richness that that entailed, for some time to come. In fact, many of the literary and cultural forms associated with the Restoration (boisterous, lewd short satirical poems and drolleries; poems and plays on colonial and imperial themes, or on the leisure spaces of London; calls for a reborn theatre[48]; new science and proposals for agricultural improvement; grand folio translations of the classics) were already a feature of 1650s literary London. When, on 19 April 1656, the stationer Nathaniel Brooks was reported by Stephen Bowtell for selling *Sportive Wit*, regarded as 'scandalous, if not prejudiciall to the Commonwealth', and was sought by the authorities, alongside the radical publisher Giles Calvert, who had, yet again, been issuing Quaker millenarian writings, the situation resembles the pervasive censorship operated by Roger L'Estrange during the Restoration.[49]

46 See also, below, Chapter 26.

47 See, e.g., George Fox, *A Warning to . . . this Proud City* (London, 1655); Margaret Fell, *The citie of London reproved* (May 1660).

48 See, e.g., Thomas Jordan, *The Walks of Islington and Hogsdon* (London, 1657); anon., *Lady Alimony; or, the Alimony Lady* (London, 1659).

49 John Thurloe, *A Collection of the State Papers of John Thurloe*, 7 vols. (London, 1742), 4:717–18. For a parallel in another city, see Phil Withington, 'Views from the Bridge: Revolution and Restoration in Seventeenth-Century York', *Past and Present* 170 (February 2001), 121–51.

The appearance of Dryden's first royal panegyric at the start of the new decade and regime (*Astrea Redux* (1660)) has been taken as a clear signal of the beginning of a new literary age. But with continuing resistance to the restored monarchy and Church of England in the form of plots, and with the new regime's inability to conduct successful campaigns against the Dutch, the temporal turning-point for London is best seen as the Great Fire of 1666, and the *annus horribilis* that followed, culminating in defeat in the Second Dutch War (1665–7). The City would be constructed after the fire, while dissent and Parliamentary opposition began to find the voices that would eventually lead to Whiggery. The poem that appeared towards the end of 1667 was the first edition of Milton's *Paradise Lost*, which was seen almost immediately by intelligent observers as in large part a covert commentary on the tumult of the previous thirty years. Marvell's allegorical figure of Excise in his *Last Instructions to a Painter* (1667) borrowed from Milton's allegory of Sin and Death in Book 2 of *Paradise Lost*: Marvell's allegory represents a civic and governmental capital grown weak with division and decadence, prone to invasion by less-than-heroic Dutchmen. A surviving early manuscript fragment of this long poem suggests that pictures of corrupt courtiers drawn from it were spread through the court and the City.[50] While a thousand Neros played, Rome burned.

50 See, e.g., BL, MS Additional 18220, fol. 23.

Chapter 24

LITERATURE AND THE
HOUSEHOLD

HELEN WILCOX

The middle decades of the seventeenth century in England were momentous in political, religious and material terms – with the country in the throes of political crises, religious sectarianism, and civil as well as foreign warfare – but they also represent a significant turning point in the history of English literary activity. The structures of patronage which had sustained and framed the literary output of previous generations (as discussed by Graham Parry in Chapter 4) were by now severely weakened and in some cases totally demolished. The court, the focal point of national culture (for good or ill) in the days of Elizabeth I and James I, had become the polarising, unfixed and shadowy entourage of Charles I at war, and after 1649 it moved into exile abroad. The English Church, instigator and inspiration of so much literary production since the Reformation, was divided, fragmented and ultimately disestablished until 1660. The public theatres, the material and financial context for a substantial amount of early modern writing, were closed between 1642 and 1660. Although some of the kinds of writing previously fostered by these three major institutions (for example, the lyric) continued to be produced, and although some of the issues that they had formerly expressed – love, religious devotion, power – continued to drive the texts of the mid-century, these new writings began to reveal the environment from which they predominantly came: the household.

The assumption upon which this chapter is based is that, in mid seventeenth-century England, writing came home (so to speak), driven towards the private sphere by the instability of public social and cultural structures.[1] This apparent shift does not mean that public issues ceased to feature in literary texts – far from it – and it does not indicate a lessening of the quality or even the scale of writing. It does, however, represent a significant change of perspective as a

---

1 I gratefully acknowledge the stimulating discussions of this idea with colleagues at Groningen University, Liverpool John Moores University and Chester College, and I thank the editors of this volume for their range of knowledge and creative view of literary history.

result of which, to put it in sweeping terms, plays became closet dramas and the courtly romance became the narrative of the sociable letter written in the living room. Literature, domesticated through circumstance, was increasingly feminised at this time, not only by the influx of women writers amid the radical uncertainties of the mid-century but also by the elevation of genres associated with the household and female experience, such as domestic religious devotion, autobiography and, ultimately, the novel. A glimpse of the fundamental development from medieval to modern literature may thus be caught here, in miniature, by examining literature in the household sphere. This chapter will approach the topic in two parts: an exploration of the multiple significances of the term 'house' in texts from this period and context will be followed by a survey of the kinds of writing produced in and for the household in mid seventeenth-century England.

Literary images of the household

What does it mean to speak of literature and the 'household'? What definitions of the term 'house' may be found, implicit or explicit, in a range of English literary texts from the middle of the seventeenth century? At the very beginning of the period, the *Poems* of Thomas Carew (1640) include a celebration of Saxham, the home of the Crofts family, written in the tradition of the country-house poem inherited from Lanyer and Jonson.[2] The poem suggests an ideal of a house in its own grounds – the household as estate – handsome, hospitable and welcoming:

> Though frost, and snow, lockt from mine eyes,
> That beautie which without dore lyes;
> Thy gardens, orchards, walkes, that so
> I might not all thy pleasures know;
> Yet (*Saxham*) thou within thy gate,
> Art of thy selfe so delicate;
> So full of native sweets, that blesse
> Thy roofe with inward happinesse;
> As neither from, nor to, thy store
> Winter takes ought, or Spring addes more.[3]

The house is an emblem of domestic virtue and the epitome of apparently permanent values; it stands firm, unchanging despite the changes of nature,

---

2 See Barbara Lewalski's discussion of Aemilia Lanyer's 'The Description of Cooke-ham' and Ben Jonson's 'To Penshurst' in Chapter 20 of this volume.
3 Thomas Carew, 'To Saxham', *Poems* (London, 1640), p. 45.

offering its own intrinsic pleasures and self-sufficient blessings ('native sweets', 'inward happinesse'). In post-Reformation England, it fulfils the social function once carried out by the monasteries with their hospices, as is suggested by the metaphors of pilgrimage employed later in the poem. The 'chearfull beames' from Saxham's lamps and fireplaces

> send forth their light,
> To all that wander in the night,
> And seeme to beckon from aloofe,
> The weary Pilgrim to thy roofe;
> Where if, refresht, he will away,
> Hee's fairly welcome, or if stay
> Farre more, which he shall hearty find,
> Both from the Master, and the Hinde.[4]

Saxham is depicted both physically and symbolically as a beacon in the darkness; it is a place of safety and enlightenment as well as refreshment. Unusually, the longer a guest stays, the heartier is the welcome, and it does not appear to matter whether the 'pilgrim' is rich or poor:

> Thou hast no Porter at the doore
> T'examine, or keep back the poore;
> Nor locks, nor bolts; thy gates have bin
> Made onely to let strangers in.[5]

Unlike the old establishments from which they grew, Carew's idealised country houses are not bolted fortresses but places whose gates stand open in welcome.

It is all too well known that ideals are articulated when felt to be under pressure, and Carew's depiction of the perfect household came at a time when many English homes were about to be cast into completely different roles. The 'locks' and 'bolts' of Lady Brilliana Harley's house (Brampton Bryan) were used a mere three years later to keep out a besieging Royalist army which 'threatened every day' to 'beset' the household, as she wrote to her son in January 1643.[6] Lucy Hutchinson found herself forced to adopt a new home in the same year, also on account of the Civil War; she and her husband, Colonel John Hutchinson, settled uneasily into Nottingham Castle when he became its governor on behalf of the parliamentary cause. They left behind 'a house and a considerable estate to the mercy of the enemie' because, as she wrote in the biography of her husband, he wished rather to 'advance the cause than secure

4 *Ibid.*, p. 46.   5 *Ibid.*, p. 47.
6 *The Letters of Lady Brilliana Harley*, ed. Thomas Taylor Lewis (London: Camden Society, 1854), p. 187.

his owne stake'.⁷ Lucy Hutchinson records poignant scenes from the 1640s
in which the refuge of the ordinary English house was breached, showing the
startlingly mingled worlds of war and domesticity. Typical of this juxtaposition
is the following account of bullets in a bedroom:

> a Cannon shott that came through a house which was deserted of all its inhab-
> itants but only a girle that rockt a little child in a cradle. The girle was struck
> dead and kill'd with the wind of the bullett, which past by and went thorough
> the wall and a bed's-head in the next house, and did some execution there,
> while the child in the cradle remain'd unhurt.⁸

Meanwhile, writing from the other side of the political divide, Margaret
Cavendish, wife of the Royalist Duke of Newcastle, recalled her mother's experience of widowhood and civil war explicitly in terms of the family home:

> She made her house her cloister, enclosing herself, as it were, therein; for she
> seldom went abroad, unless to church. But these unhappy wars forced her out,
> by reason she and her children were loyal to the king. For which they plundered
> her and my brothers of all their goods, plate, jewels, money, corn, cattle and the
> like; cut down their woods, pulled down their houses, and sequestered them
> from their land and livings.⁹

From being a place of calm retreat ('cloister' here recalling Carew's religious
metaphors for Saxham), Cavendish's mother's house has become an emblem
of vulnerability and division. Like the nation in which it found itself in the
1640s, an English house could no longer be guaranteed a continuous or consistent ownership, and was by no means secure. Without a house, however, as
Cavendish's list of plundered items suggests, a family not only lacked a home
but also its 'land and livings'. An early modern household was more than a building and its occupants; it consisted of material goods, from 'jewels' to 'cattle',
and provided the means of subsistence for several families. When, as the poet
An Collins wrote, many were 'of their homes depriv'd' during the Civil Wars,
the 'beuty of the Land' was 'abollisht' but the people of the land, too, were
almost destroyed by the absence of daily 'necessaries' from which they were
thus 'parted by constraint'.¹⁰

7 Lucy Hutchinson, *Memoirs of the Life of Colonel Hutchinson*, ed. James Sutherland (Oxford
   University Press, 1973), p. 87.
8 *Ibid.*, p. 96.
9 Margaret Cavendish, *A True Relation of my Birth, Breeding and Life*, from *Natures Pictures*
   (1656), in *Her Own Life: Autobiographical Writings by Seventeenth-Century Englishwomen*, ed.
   Elspeth Graham *et al.* (London: Routledge, 1989), p. 91.
10 An Collins, 'Another Song [composed in time of the Civill Warr]', in *Divine Songs and
   Meditacions* (1653), ed. Sidney Gottlieb (Tempe, AZ: Medieval and Renaissance Texts and
   Studies, 1996), p. 65.

Like most communities, the mid seventeenth-century household (when not, in Collins's words, 'quite demollisht'[11]) was bound together by rituals, particularly those associated with the beginning and ending of life.[12] The domestic devotions of Elizabeth Egerton, for example, poignantly demonstrate how the processes of birth and death were experienced in the life of her household and reveal that they were all too frequently linked together in the loss of infants. Her prayers (written between her marriage in 1642 and her death in 1663) alternate with sorrowful regularity between devotions written 'when I was with Child' or 'in time of Labour' and those such as 'When I lost my Deare Girle Kate' or on the loss of 'my boy Henry'.[13] It was not only the physical events of birth and death that took place in the home but also, increasingly, the religious ceremonies associated with them. Alice Thornton, for example, records the following bleak entry in her *Book of Remembrances*: 'My sister Danby died at Thorpe, September, 1645, of her sixteenth child, being a son named Francis, whom I baptized.'[14] This brief, matter-of-fact note bears witness to the practical religion of the home as well as to the plight of women during their childbearing years. At the other end of life, too, the wisdom and piety of those who survived to advanced years formed a crucial element in the cycle of the early modern household with its extended family community. Thornton's *Remembrances* also include an account of her mother's last days in 1659:

> In this condition of weakness was my dear mother almost quite without food, rest, ease or sleep for about a week, in which time, as in all her sickness, she expressed extraordinary great patience... She was an example and pattern of piety, faith and patience in her greatest torment, still with godly instructions, gentle rebukes for sin, a continual praying of psalms, speaking to God in his own phrase and word, saying that we could not speak to him from ourselves in such an acceptable manner, as by that which was dictated by his own most holy spirit.[15]

In addition to its devotional function in the tradition of 'holy dying',[16] this passage vividly depicts the elderly woman at the spiritual centre of the

---

11 *Ibid.*, p. 65.
12 See David Cressy, *Birth, Marriage and Death: Ritual, Religion, and the Life-Cycle in Tudor and Stuart England* (Oxford University Press, 1997).
13 Elizabeth Egerton, 'True Coppies of certaine Loose Papers left by the Right honorable Elizabeth Countesse of Bridgewater' (1663), BL, MS Egerton 607, fols. 22v, 28r, 119v, 114v. Elizabeth was the daughter of William Cavendish, Duke of Newcastle, stepdaughter of Margaret Cavendish, and sister of Jane Cavendish with whom she wrote *The Concealed Fancies* (see below). She is sometimes known as Elizabeth Brackley because her husband, John Egerton, was Viscount Brackley at the time of their marriage.
14 Alice Thornton, *Book of Remembrances*, in *Her Own Life*, ed. Graham *et al.*, p. 152.
15 *Ibid.* (1659 entry), p. 155.
16 As implied by Jeremy Taylor in the title of his conduct book, *Holy Dying* (London, 1651).

home, dispensing 'godly instructions' and even 'rebukes' to those around her deathbed. The traditional function of the church, issuing blessings and corrections to the community, is here subsumed into the home.

Thornton's household, like many others, was thus a setting for the cycles of life and death and, thereby, a place of spiritual learning in the context of the family. The responsibility of parents in this matter was particularly emphasised by Jeremy Taylor, who asserted in *Holy Living* (1650) that

> *Parents must shew piety at home*, that is, they must give good example and reverent deportment, in the face of their children; and all those instances of charity, which usualy endear each other; sweetnesse of conversation, affability, frequent admonition, all significations of love and tendernesse, care and watchfulnesse must be expressed towards Children, that they may look upon their parents as their friends and patrons, their defence and sanctuary, their treasure and their Guide.[17]

In Taylor's ideal, the household is where piety and reverence are found, and where, as in the well-known saying, charity begins. The metaphors chosen to fill out the image of the parents – 'defence', 'sanctuary', 'treasure', 'Guide' – are notable for their closeness to the imagery used for the house itself by, for example, Carew and Cavendish; houses and occupants merge as emblems of security.

There was, of course, a less positive side to this idea of the enclosing household, summed up in the telling phrase 'shut up in a Countrey Grange' used by the poet Hester Pulter to describe herself as she lamented being 'tide to one Habitation'.[18] Elizabeth Delaval's *Meditations* offer further insight into the experience of being 'shut up' in a house, with their honest and occasionally disgruntled account of her education under the supervision of her grandmother. She recalls how she would be set 'a tasque . . . ether as to the reading of so many chaptier's in the French Bible and so many in the English one, or that I was to learn so many chapters of the holy scripture by heart, before my play felow's might come to me' but adds that one Mistress Carter would often 'earnestly plead for my liberty before my tasque was done'.[19] The metaphor of begging for the young pupil's freedom reminds us that the house which is a fortress against danger can also be a prison for those living within its walls.

17 Jeremy Taylor, 'The Duty of Parents to their Children', in *Holy Living and Holy Dying* (1650, 1651), ed. P. G. Stanwood, 2 vols. (Oxford: Clarendon Press, 1989), 1:153. The italics are Taylor's.
18 Leeds University Library Brotherton MS Lt q 32, fol. 79r.
19 *The Meditations of Lady Elizabeth Delaval*, ed. Douglas G. Greene, Surtees Society, 190 (Gateshead: Northumberland Press, 1978), p. 29.

The jailor, as it were, in Delaval's house was a loving but dominant grandmother. In most early modern English homes, the educational 'Guide' for the children and the rest of the household was indeed a woman. Milton expressed a commonly held view in *Paradise Lost* when he allowed Adam to comment, addressing Eve, that 'nothing lovelier can be found / In woman, than to study household good'.[20] Such concern for the moral, spiritual and practical 'good' of the miniature society that is found in the home was often specifically the task of the mother of the house. This is attested in texts such as Elizabeth Richardson's *A Ladies Legacie to her Daughters* (1645), in which she transcribes her prayers for special occasions and for each day of the week, to be used by her children as well as the others 'under my care', as she describes the household.[21] Richardson's contemporary, Lady Anne Harcourt, clearly fulfilled a similar function as the teacher of those on her estate, Stanton Harcourt. She was commended after her death as a devout mistress who, after the Sunday sermon, would

> call before her her maid-servants, and such boyes as served in the House, to give account what they had heard; helping their memories wherein they failed, clearing up the sense of what was delivered, wherein it might seem obscure unto them, exhorting and pressing them to be doers of the Word, and not hearers only, concluding *all* in Prayer with them.[22]

The larger household, we are carefully shown here, could extend beyond the family to include servants of both sexes in its concern for spiritual education. To that group one might also add a tutor (such as the poet Andrew Marvell in the Fairfax household) and, if funds and religious practice permitted, a minister. As Edmund Calamy observed in the same funeral sermon on Anne Harcourt:

> Upon the Close of the Late unhappy Wars, so soon as she had a Liberty to return to her Estate and place of Abode near *Oxford*, and when her Estate (through the Calamity of those times) was at a Low ebbe, the first thing she did, was ... to provide and maintain at her own cost (in effect) a preaching Minister there.[23]

The household could thus, by means of formal employment or in unofficial ways (as with the domestic baptism and deathbed teaching in Alice Thornton's home), take on the tasks and the trappings of an entire community of home, school and church.

20 John Milton, *Paradise Lost* (1667, 1674), ed. Alastair Fowler (London: Longman, 1971), 9.232–3.
21 Elizabeth Richardson, *A Ladies Legacie to her Daughters* (London, 1645), p. 48.
22 Edmund Calamy, *The Happinesse Of those who Sleep in Jesus* (London, 1662), p. 28. By the time of her death, Anne Harcourt had been widowed (her husband dying in the Civil War) and had subsequently married again, becoming Lady Anne Waller.
23 *Ibid.*, p. 29.

The early modern household is beginning to be defined by these texts written under its influence, and may already be seen as a place of many symbolic as well as practical functions. It was, at its most basic, a physical house, varying from the modest dimensions of an ordinary home to the grandeur of a castle, but the term 'household' also refers to the community living (and dying) within its walls, from the extended family to the servants of all levels who formed part of a rich estate. However large or small, the household was, in principle at least, a place of learning, particularly spiritual instruction, in which women played a significant role. In fact, women and the house were explicitly identified with one another, as when Lucy Hutchinson reported that her husband's soldiers left the battle in order to find out what was become of 'their wives and houses'.[24] The English household, loaded with traditions and ideals in personal, moral and political dimensions, nevertheless proved deeply vulnerable to physical attack in the revolutionary years (as is demonstrated, for example, by the distressed letters of Brilliana Harley) and remained subject to change and uncertainty throughout the seventeenth century.

As a material reality under pressure and an ideal in transition, the English household was a mirror of the national situation in the middle years of the century. Margaret Cavendish echoed many traditionalists when she wrote in her *Sociable Letters* (1664) that the household is a microcosm, a little kingdom and body politic, and thus that 'when a Master is from Home, his family is like a Body without a Head, like as a King should travel into Foreign Countries'.[25] When the King was at home in his own country, as Robert Filmer asserted in *Patriarcha*, it was customary for him to function in almost every detail like the head of a household: 'As the Father over one family, so the King, as Father over many families, extends his care to preserve, feed, clothe, instruct and defend the whole commonwealth.'[26] The connection between the running of a household and the running of the state was not only made by Royalist writers and philosophers. Gerrard Winstanley, radical Digger and author of *The True Levellers Standard Advanced* (1649), regarded the family as a commonwealth in miniature. In his visionary blueprint for a new political system, *The Law of Freedom* (1652), he replaces the trope of the head of the home as a king with the theory that a father is an 'officer' of the Commonwealth. Such a father, he asserts, would govern the household not as a tyrant but as one 'chosen by a joint consent', through 'the necessity of the young

24 Hutchinson, *Memoirs*, p. 97.
25 Margaret Cavendish, *CCXI Sociable Letters* (London, 1664), p. 127.
26 Sir Robert Filmer, *Patriarcha*, in *Patriarcha and Other Political Works*, ed. Peter Laslett, (Oxford: Clarendon Press, 1949), p. 63.

children' who, implicitly, cry out: 'Father, do thou teach us how to plant the earth, that we may live, and we will obey.'[27] Milton, too, saw the parallel between household and state since both are versions of 'a human society' but, like Winstanley, he challenged the traditional models of both.[28] In *The Doctrine and Discipline of Divorce* (1644) Milton argues that marriage is a covenant which, like that between the ruler and the ruled, 'may be call'd the covnant of God'. But, he asks rhetorically, when there is an 'apparent unfitnes' between man and wife, 'where can be the peace and love which must invite God to such a house?' In such situations, marriage itself must not be made a 'tyrannesse', and divorce is preferable in Milton's view. If the ill-suited couple are made to remain together, he argues, God may instead find himself 'divorced' from the household.[29]

Thomas Fuller's family conduct book, *The Holy State* (1642), was in the meantime attempting to hold together the traditional political as well as matrimonial overtones of the term 'state'. The engraved title page highlights the interconnectedness of monarch, church and state, while the work itself presents the characters of good wife, husband, parent, child, master and servant as well as advocate, minister, soldier and statesman. In his preface, Fuller laments the unfortunate timing of his publication amidst 'the distractions of this age' (at the very start of the Civil Wars) but explains, in a revealing metaphor, that he was overtaken by events: 'when I left my home, it was fair weather, and my journey was half past, before I discovered the tempest'.[30] 'Home', we are once again reminded, represents familiarity and safety, the refuge from bad (political) weather. Interestingly, his account of the household gives a certain prominence to the feminine: the good wife precedes the good husband in the sequence of chapters, and the house is seen as 'the womans centre'.[31] The patriarchal order, however, is never in doubt and is restored when the mistress of the house submits to the 'good Master' who is 'the heart in the midst of his household'.[32] As the work proceeds, it becomes clear that Fuller is under no illusions about the glories of domesticity. In his description of the 'constant Virgin', he notes that 'Housekeepers cannot so exactly mark all their family-affairs, but that

---

27 Gerrard Winstanley, *The Law of Freedom and Other Writings*, ed. Christopher Hill (Harmondsworth: Penguin, 1973), p. 317.
28 'The ninth reason', in *The Doctrine and Discipline of Divorce* (1643, revised 1644), in John Milton, *Complete Prose Works of John Milton*, gen. ed. Don M. Wolfe *et al.*, 8 vols. (New Haven, CT: Yale University Press, 1953–82), 2:275.
29 Milton, *Divorce*, pp. 276–7.
30 Thomas Fuller, 'To the Reader', in *The Holy State and the Profane State* (Cambridge, 1642), sig. A2r.
31 *Ibid.*, p. 2.   32 *Ibid.*, p. 17.

sometimes their ranks will be broken', and he goes on to demonstrate in some detail the 'encumbrances' from which the virgin is freed:

> No lording Husband shall at the same time command her presence and distance...so that providing his break-fast hazards her soul to fast a meal of morning prayer: No crying Children shall drown her singing of psalmes, and put her devotion out of tune: No unfaithfull Servants shall force her to divide her eyes betwixt lifting them up to God and casting them down to oversee their work; but making her Closet her Chappell, she freely enjoyeth God and good thoughts at what time she pleaseth.[33]

The association of the house with holiness – the closet as a chapel – is here shown to be, potentially, in tension with the practical demands of running a household. Family life was not always marked by what Taylor had termed 'sweetnesse of conversation';[34] the state, both civil and marital, was often troubled.

In addition to being the physical, metaphorical and ideological entity that we have so far encountered, the early modern house fulfilled an important financial function which should not be overlooked. It often represented a source of livelihood for one or more families, as Margaret Cavendish bitterly observed after her mother's 'land and livings' had been confiscated,[35] but it further signified the status and inheritance of its owner. This point is teasingly made by Dorothy Osborne as she reports, in a letter written to William Temple in January 1653, the method of her triumphant rejection of an unwanted suitor:

> As my last refuge, I gott my Brother to goe downe with him to see his house, whoe when he cam back made the relation I wisht. He sayed the seate was as ill, as so good a country would permitt, and the house so ruined for want of living int, as it would ask a good proportion of time, and mony, to make it fitt for a woman to confine her self to, this (though it were not much) I was willing to take hold of, and make it considerable enough to break the agreement.[36]

In such circumstances, the house was the man: the unattractiveness of the house's position and state enabled Osborne to refuse him in refusing it, and thereby to avoid confining herself (to borrow her own powerful expression) to either its proportions or his affections. Bearing in mind how the house belonged to the male line and the woman was absorbed into it by marriage (like a tributary into a river, as one commentator put it),[37] it is all the more

---

33 *Ibid.*, p. 35.   34 Taylor, *Holy Living*, p. 153 (see above, p. 742).
35 Margaret Cavendish, 'True Relation', p. 91 (see above, p. 740).
36 Dorothy Osborne, *Letters to Sir William Temple*, ed. Kenneth Parker (London: Penguin, 1987), p. 42.
37 See T. E., *The Lawes Resolutions of Womens Rights* (London, 1632), pp. 124–5.

striking that the seventeenth-century diarist Lady Anne Clifford appropriated the male perspective in fighting to inherit her father's lands and castles. After a long struggle and with a massive sense of relief, she came into her inheritance and, leaving her own husband's home, moved north to the Clifford estates. In 1651 she recorded in her diary the satisfaction of living there:

And in this settled aboad of mine in theis three ancient Houses of mine Inheritance, Apleby Castle and Brougham Castle in Westmerland, and Skipton castle or House in Craven, I doe more and more fall in love with the contentments and innocent pleasures of a Country Life. Which humour of mine I do [wish] with all my hearrt (if it bee the Will of Almightie God) may be conferred on my Posteritie that are to succeed mee in these places, for a Wife and Lady oneself, to make their owne houses the place of Selfe fruition and bee comfortably parte of this Life.[38]

In this revealing passage, the house is multi-faceted, symbolising the wealth of the family both in the past ('ancient Houses of mine Inheritance') and in the future ('my Posteritie that are to succeed mee in these places'). We are reminded that a house is not only a material building but also a genealogy, the 'house of Clifford' as it were. In this 'settled aboad', both physical and psychological, Clifford discovers a stable identity. A sign of her contentment is that, as she flourishes, she wishes upon her successors the same opportunity to make 'their owne houses the place of Selfe fruition'.

A house, then, is more than an expression of family and community, inheritance and loyalty; it can come to be identified with the individual who owns or occupies it and who may well experience 'Selfe fruition' by means of it. This is clearly to be seen from the perspective of the individual concerned, as in the personal bond with her homes recorded in Anne Clifford's diary, but it may also be seen from without by those who visit the house or observe the householder. In the opening stanzas of 'Upon Appleton House', for example, Marvell identifies the modest and balanced dimensions of this 'sober' building with the 'Humility' of the Fairfax family who inhabit it.[39] A little later in the century, the diarist John Evelyn noted that Sir Thomas Browne was the possessor of many curiosities for the visitor to admire but concluded that Browne's 'whole house & Garden [is] a Paradise and Cabinet of rarities'.[40] The fascinations of the man who lived there were to be discerned

38 *The Diaries of Lady Anne Clifford*, ed. D. J. H. Clifford (Stroud, Gloucestershire: Alan Sutton, 1990), p. 112.
39 Andrew Marvell, 'Upon Appleton House', in *The Poems and Letters of Andrew Marvell*, ed. H. M. Margoliouth, 2 vols., 2nd edn (Oxford: Clarendon Press, 1963), 1:59–60.
40 John Evelyn, *Diary*, ed. E. S. de Beer, 6 vols. (London and New York: Oxford University Press, 1959), 3:62–3 (entry for 17 October 1671).

in his entire estate – and, as Coleridge later pointed out, the greatest rarity of all on display in the 'cabinet' of his house was Browne himself.[41] A house is the frame, whether 'sober' or rare, within which an individual identity can find expression.

Browne's 'Cabinet of rarities' brings us to a further important function of the seventeenth-century household, since, as Evelyn went on to observe in his diary, such cabinets contained 'Medails, books, Plants, naturall things' including even 'a collection of the Eggs of all the foule & birds he could procure'.[42] In the midst of the eggs, feathers, animal skins, coins and other curiosities,[43] it is easy to overlook the 'books' which also feature in Evelyn's list. However, as a seventeenth-century painting of *A Collector's Cabinet* also demonstrates,[44] documents, manuscript notebooks and printed books formed an important part of these collections which were brought to and put on display within the household. Many texts of the time indeed attest that possessing books, reading, displaying and exchanging them, as well as writing and discussing them, were significant activities in the literate early modern household. Dorothy Osborne, for instance, concludes a letter to William Temple in May 1653 with the following practical comments on reading and writing:

> In the mean time I have sent you the first Tome of Cyrus to read, when you have don with it leave it at Mr Hollingsworths and i'le send you another.
> I have my Ladys with me all this Afternoon that are for London to morrow, and now have I as many letters to write as my Lord Generall's Secretary, forgive mee that this paper is no longer, for I am   Yours . . . [45]

Osborne's letter, like many other autobiographical writings from the period, records sociable reading and writing, demonstrating the use of language and literature as a means of social exchange. This was such a commonplace of mid seventeenth-century household life that the appearance of being engaged in letter-writing was mocked by Margaret Cavendish, ironically in one of her

---

41 See Roberta F. Brinkley (ed.), *Coleridge on the Seventeenth Century* (Durham, NC: Duke University Press, 1955), pp. 438–62.
42 Evelyn, *Diary*, 3:595.
43 For a vivid fictional reconstruction of the mid seventeenth-century Tradescant collection of rarities which formed the basis for the Ashmolean collection in Oxford, see Philippa Gregory, *Virgin Earth* (London: Harper Collins, 1999).
44 Frans Francken II, *A Collector's Cabinet* (1617), probably acquired by Algernon Percy, 10th Earl of Northumberland, for Petworth House and recorded in an inventory for 1671 at Petworth. See Terence Rodrigues and Jane Blood (eds.), *Treasures of the North* (London: Christies, 2000), item 25.
45 Osborne, *Letters*, p. 79.

own *CCXI Sociable Letters*, as a frequently dishonest excuse for getting rid of visitors who outstay their welcome. In the past, she comments, the custom was for hosts to 'look in their Watches, or to Gape, or Yawn', but now the trick is 'to have alwayes, or for the most part, Pen, Ink, and Paper lying upon the Table in their Chamber, for an excuse they are writing Letters; as for the first, it is Rude, and the last for the most part is False'.[46] Whether false or not, this practice, as brought to life in Cavendish's vivid observation, conveys a sense of the household as a context in which 'Pen, Ink, and Paper' were very much at home.

The poems of An Collins, while confirming this association of the household with writing, give a quieter picture of the house as a place of literary activity. In 'The Preface' to her *Divine Songs and Meditacions* (1653) she feels the need to justify her poetic 'exercise':

> Being through weakness to the house confin'd,
> My mentall powers seeming long to sleep,
> Were summond up, by want of wakeing mind
> Their wonted course of exercise to keep,
> And not to waste themselves in slumber deep;
> Though no work can bee so from error kept
> But some against it boldly will except:
>
> Yet sith it was my morning exercise
> The fruit of intellectuals to vent,
> In Songs or counterfets of Poesies,
> And having therein found no small content,
> To keep that course my thoughts are therfore bent.[47]

Knowing that some readers would undoubtedly take exception to her literary presumption, Collins meticulously explains that her poetry is precisely the kind of mental activity appropriate to one who is 'to the house confin'd'. The domestic context, though restricting, can enable the harvesting of intellectual 'fruit' and prove a source of 'content'. Collins, it seems, was house-bound through chronic illness (what she termed her 'weakness') and she mentions no other household company than God. This female state of household 'confinement' – the term regularly associated with childbirth and used in Dorothy Osborne's letter and Hester Pulter's poem to indicate a woman's restriction within the home – resulted, in Collins's case, not in the birth of children but in what she called 'the offspring of my mind':

46 Margaret Cavendish, *CCXI Sociable Letters*, p. 90.   47 Collins, *Divine Songs*, p. 3.

Now touching that I hasten to expresse
Concerning these, the offspring of my mind,
Who though they here appear in homely dresse
And as they are my works, I do not find
But ranked with others, they may go behind,
Yet for theyr matter, I suppose they bee
Not worthlesse quite, whilst they with Truth agree.[48]

The descendants of Collins's house, her poetic 'offspring', are clothed in 'homely dresse', immediately associating the household literary context with stylistic simplicity though also thereby claiming the plainness which goes hand-in-hand with 'Truth'. Collins was indeed aware that, though her poetry might suffer if 'ranked with others' on grounds of artistry, its 'matter' is sound and springs (as she put it in 'The Discourse') from 'true intent of mind'.[49] Both house and garden – together forming the estate of a household – are metaphoric, indeed mental, locations for Collins, who describes herself in 'Another Song' as a 'garden ... enclosed', a phrase borrowed from the Song of Songs.[50] While this image was normally interpreted as a reference to chastity, and therefore read allegorically as the safely enclosed fertility of the virgin Mary, Collins uses it to refer not to her womb but to her 'mind', which can produce a 'fruit most rare': her writing.[51]

House, garden, family and household estate thus offered vital contexts, both rhetorical and literal, for the production of early modern writing. But there is one final sense in which the idea of the house could be defined, and that is not as a physical, ancestral or practical institution, but, rather, as a place of religion. Though the spiritual realm is generally described as a state – the kingdom of heaven – the specific metaphor of a house is also present in the Bible, as in Christ's saying, 'In my Father's house are many mansions'.[52] We have already observed how the household could fulfil some of the functions of the church in mid seventeenth-century England: in the case of the infant baptism administered by Alice Thornton, for instance, or the daily prayers and almost catechismal training devised by Anne Harcourt for her household's well-being. We have also seen how the (secular) house could function symbolically as a place of retreat, even a 'cloister',[53] and was associated with private devotion, domestic virtue and the plain truth. In 'Upon Appleton House', Marvell plays wittily on the intersection of religion and houses, recalling the fact that Nun Appleton (as its full name implies) had previously been a convent, while asserting in true post-Reformation manner that

---

48 *Ibid.*, p. 5.   49 Collins, 'The Discourse', in *Divine Songs*, p. 8.   50 Song of Songs 4:12.
51 Collins, 'Another Song' ('The winter of my infancy'), in *Divine Songs*, p. 55.
52 John 14:2.   53 Margaret Cavendish, 'A True Relation', p. 91.

Though many a *Nun* there made her Vow,
'Twas no *Religious House* till now.[54]

While, strictly speaking, no 'religious houses' (in the traditional sense of monasteries and convents) remained in England, yet, Marvell suggests, every devout (Protestant) household could live up to the name and indeed might deserve it more than the pre-Reformation establishments. At the very time when Marvell was making this assertion, however, there were English religious houses in existence on the continent – and these, too, were sites of literary production. One such house belonged to the 'holy Order of S. Benet and English Congregation of our Ladies of Comfort in Cambray' as it was announced on the title-page of *The Spiritual Exercises of the Most Vertuous and Religious D. Gertrude More* (1658). Like An Collins's *Divine Songs and Meditacions*, More's poems were produced in confinement – in More's case, voluntary enclosure – within a house. In her 'Apology' More explains that, although she is 'living in Religion' and, indeed, 'in a Religious community', her heart has 'grown . . . as hard as stone', and 'for this reason by al the meanes I could imagin, I have endeavoured to strengthen my self by writing, gathering, and thus (as in some parts of my papers it wil appeare) addressing my speech to our Lord'.[55] More's explanation not only confirms the house, once again, as a place of writing, but suggests that the household community can include another implied member to whom speech can be addressed: 'our Lord'. A house contains and protects an earthly group of family, guests and, in many instances, servants; it also entertains a spiritual company of ancestors, future descendants (as in Anne Clifford's diary) and, above all, Christ. In one of her household prayers, Elizabeth Egerton asked, with a fine turn of phrase, that God might be 'ever President, and resident with me'.[56] The early modern household may have had a resident woman as its centre and a man as its implied head, but its 'President' was undoubtedly God himself.

Genres of domestic literature

What kinds of literature, then, were produced in English households of the mid seventeenth-century? As will already have become apparent in the process of defining the idea of the 'house' and 'household', the variety of texts associated with the home was considerable; they included lyrics, letters, biography, memoirs, devotions, conduct books, meditations, commemorative sermons,

54 Marvell, 'Upon Appleton House', in *Poems and Letters*, 1:67.
55 Dame Gertrude More, *The Spiritual Exercises* (Paris, 1658), pp. 13–14.
56 Egerton, *True Coppies*, 27r.

prose polemics, diaries and poems of praise. Margaret Cavendish summed up the range as follows: 'Some Devotions, or Romances, or Receits of Medicines, for Cookery or Confectioners, or Complemental Letters, or a Copy or two of Verses'.[57] Her list is succinct, in effect reducing the genres to religious, secular, practical, social and poetic, and I shall follow those categories in my remaining discussion of household writings. However, it is first important to point out that the items in Cavendish's list are specifically identified as the types of writing which women ('our Sex') tended to produce. The parallels between writing from the house and writing by women in this period are striking. It is not clear whether the increase in women's writing was a symptom or a cause of the domestication of literature – indeed, it was probably both – but the two processes converge to change the face of English literature after the mid seventeenth century.

Cavendish's first category of writing, 'Some Devotions', may be typified by the devotional work of Lady Anne Harcourt as described by Edmund Calamy in the sermon preached at her funeral: 'She hath a large Book in Folio written in her own hand, wherein under several Heads of Divinity, she hath registred the Observations of her reading both out of the Scriptures (which were her delight) and out of the Writings of our best Divines, and out of her own experiences.'[58] The nature of household devotional writing is made very clear in this 'large Book' which combines Bible study, commonplace book and spiritual autobiography. The fundamental interaction of reading and writing in devotional life is confirmed here, as is the mixture of Biblical authority, expert knowledge ('our best Divines') and ordinary daily life ('her own experiences'). The fact that the book was in folio format suggests that it was not intended for private use but would have been made accessible to the whole family. Household devotional writing is characterised by a sense of shared practicality, as is also suggested in the preface to Elizabeth Richardson's collection of 'devotions or prayers', *A Ladies Legacie to her Daughters*, in which she asks her readers to 'esteem so well of it, as often to peruse, ponder, practice, and make use of this Booke according to my intention, though of it self unworthy'.[59] If her instruction to her daughters to 'practice, and make use of' the devotional text was followed, then they, and other members of their households, would have interlaced their days with her prayers, from 'first sight of the morning light' until 'in bed before sleep'.[60] The experience of Elizabeth Avery, as recorded in John Rogers's collection of Fifth Monarchist spiritual experiences, *Ohel or Beth-Shemesh* (1653), suggests that the private devotional life continued even between sleep and first light:

57 Margaret Cavendish, *CCXI Sociable Letters*, p. 226.　　58 Calamy, *Happinesse*, p. 28.
59 Richardson, *Ladies Legacie*, p. 2.　　60 *Ibid.*, pp. 19, 26.

I sighed and prayed, and sighed and prayed, went to bed with my heart full, and head full, and eyes full, and all afflicted; at length, I slept and dreamed, That unless Christ were in me, I were damned, a reprobate, undone, and lost for ever. When I awaked, my heart aked, ready to break, I rose up, and wept sore, and with sighs and tears I took the Bible, and looked out for Christ there.[61]

In addition to spelling out the terror which lay behind many a religious act, however, this passage from the life of an extreme Protestant points up the limits of household devotion; Avery's distressed state can only be resolved by going out of the house to attend a public sermon, 'By all which, I was much raised up, and went home with joy, and was sure that I had found Christ now.'[62]

The association of intense devotional life, as well as the household, with women – who, like Avery, 'went home', or remained at home, with a spiritual 'joy' – resulted in a relatively large output of religious writing by women in mid seventeenth-century England. From the convent of Cambray to the private chambers of many an English house, women felt moved and enabled to write when this seemed permitted, or even required, by God. The anonymous author of *Eliza's Babes, or the Virgins-Offering* (1652) explains that, despite being an 'ignorant woman', she has published her devotions because it is God's merciful way to declare his goodness 'by weak and contemptible means'.[63] Elizabeth Major, in *Sin and Mercy Briefly Discovered* (1656), justifies naming sins which should normally not be mentioned by her 'blushing Sex' by referring to the 'holy confidence' that enables her 'not to blush' while writing.[64] The empowering nature of devotion for women writers is further evident in Elizabeth Richardson's preface to *A Ladies Legacie to her Daughters*, where she excuses herself for publishing her own work on the ground that 'the matter is but devotions or prayers, which surely concernes and belongs to women, as well as to the best learned men'.[65] The experience of the early modern household would seem to suggest that this 'matter' belonged even more to women than to 'learned men', as in the case of Elizabeth Egerton whose collection of prayers in manuscript traces the concerns of a mother through expectancy, anxiety, danger, delivery and, frequently, the loss of children. Cumulatively the texts build up an image of maternal prayer as the devotional centre of the household.

---

61 Elizabeth Avery's testimonial as recorded in John Rogers, *Ohel or Beth-Shemesh* (London, 1653), p. 407.
62 *Ibid.*, p. 408.
63 *Eliza's Babes, or the Virgins-Offering* (London, 1652), p. 75. A critical edition of *Eliza's Babes*, ed. L. E. Semler, is forthcoming from Fairleigh Dickinson University Press.
64 Elizabeth Major, *Sin and Mercy Briefly Discovered* (London, 1656), being the second part of *Honey on the Rod*, sig. h3r.
65 Richardson, *Ladies Legacie*, p. 3.

In Egerton's prayer for 'my poore sick Child', her 'Girle Franck',[66] for instance, the frame of reference is consciously gendered: 'O sweet Jesus, say unto me, as thou didst to the woman of Canaan, o woman great is thy Faith, and be it unto thee even as thou wilt, & immediately the Child was made whole from that houre; Lord there is nothing impossible with thee.'[67] The maternal perspective, Scriptural knowledge, personal faith and echoes of the Book of Common Prayer are blended here in a moving testimony to women's devotional life within the household.

Cavendish's categories of writing inevitably overlap, and a number of texts which could be classed as devotional may also appropriately be included under the last of her five headings, 'a Copy or two of Verses', as in the case of An Collins's *Divine Songs and Meditacions*, Elizabeth Major's *Honey on the Rod* (1656) or the anonymous collection of lyrics and meditations entitled *Eliza's Babes: or the Virgins-Offering*. There is a considerable overlap, too, between sacred and secular works, since almost any seventeenth-century mood or event could be seen to have religious significance, as is shown in an extract from Anne Harcourt's summary of God's benefits to her: 'The estate, which I found in all respects very unsettled, is now, through God's goodness to me, very much setled. My hous, soe unlike to proove a comfortable place to inhabite in, is now made very pleasing.'[68]

While the settling of an estate or the improvement of a house could be seen, from Harcourt's perspective, to bring sacred and profane together in a providential way, not all writers gave such matters a religious colouring. The second of Cavendish's list of genres, 'Romances', takes us into the more secular realms of drama and fiction, such as Anna Weamys's 1651 pastoral narrative, *A Continuation of Sir Philip Sidney's 'Arcadia'*, which responds to the invitation at the end of Sidney's *Arcadia* for 'some other spirit to exercise his [*sic*] pen in that wherewith mine is already dulled'.[69] The most striking corpus of purely secular texts produced in or for the household in this period, however, must surely come from the Cavendish family. The two daughters of William Cavendish, Duke of Newcastle – Jane Cavendish and the devotional writer Elizabeth Egerton – collaborated in the early 1640s to create *The Concealed Fancies*, a secular play of imprisonment and honour. The context in which the play was written provides an extreme example of mid seventeenth-century household

---

66 Egerton, *True Coppies*, 18v.　　67 *Ibid.*, 20r.
68 Anne Harcourt, from 'An inumeration of the many mercyes I have receaved', in *The Harcourt Papers*, ed. E. W. Harcourt, 14 vols. (Oxford: Parker, 1880–1905), 1:170.
69 Anna Weamys, *A Continuation of Sir Philip Sidney's 'Arcadia'*, ed. Patrick Colborn Cullen (New York: Oxford University Press, 1994), p. 1.

experience. The family home, Welbeck Abbey, was besieged by Parliamentary forces. The man of the house, the widowed Duke, was away with the Royalist entourage, while his two daughters were left behind in an intensely domestic and sisterly environment within which one of their major pleasures was the reading and writing of literature. In addition to writing prayers, poems and letters, they also created this secular drama for performance on a private stage largely without men (in a notable reversal of the situation in the public theatres before they were closed in 1642). The play's title, *The Concealed Fancies*, highlights its extensive use of the conceit of concealment: two sisters are hidden in a nunnery, their real identities disguised and their emotional desires contained, while the two sisters who wrote the play were imprisoned in their own home and their text remained unpublished until the twentieth century. Femininity, war, love, women's domestic writing – not forgetting drama itself – all involve concealment of one sort or another. There is, perhaps not surprisingly, a claustrophobic mood to the play, despite its happy ending in the rescue of the women by their reformed lovers. As Tattiney, one of the sisters, expresses in verse just before the women's release,

> My grief doth make me for to look
> As if life I had quietly forsook;
> Then for my fine delitive tomb,
> Is my seeled chamber and my dark parlour room.
> Then when my spirit in the gallery doth walk,
> It will not speak, for sin it is to talk.[70]

The image of the tomb as a 'dark parlour room' disconcertingly transforms the idea of the house, and the silent ghost hints at the many early modern household voices, particularly female, which, until recently, remained unheard.

Margaret Cavendish, the stepmother of the Cavendish sisters who is briefly parodied in *The Concealed Fancies* in the character of Lady Tranquility, was the most prolific secular woman writer of the mid seventeenth century and a pioneer in many literary genres (as well the provider of the framework for this discussion of household genres). She was the author of plays, poems, memoirs, scientific and philosophical essays, biography, fiction and letters, and, ironically, she defies categorisation in any one of her own list of literary modes. Indeed, when she puts forward the categories in her *Sociable Letters*, she comments that women writers tend to produce 'Briefs' rather than

70 Jane Cavendish and Elizabeth Egerton, *The Concealed Fancies*, 5.2.19–24, in *Renaissance Drama by Women: Texts and Documents*, ed. S. P. Cerasano and Marion Wynne-Davies (London: Routledge, 1996), p. 150.

'Volumes', expressing 'our Brief Wit in our Short Works' – at which point she cheekily adds, 'to Express my self according to the Wit of our Sex, I will end this Letter'.[71] In most other contexts, however, brevity is not a prominent feature of Cavendish's work, which, on the contrary, swirls with creative imagination and outspoken opinion over many a 'Volume'. Notable among her contributions to English literary activity in the mid-century is her autobiographical memoir, 'A True Relation of my Birth, Breeding and Life', which appeared in *Natures Pictures* in 1656 and is the first secular autobiography known to have been published by an Englishwoman. The 'True Relation' is remarkable for its complete lack of reference to religion as a framework for female self-knowledge. Instead its author balances precariously between claims to bashfulness and a desire for personal recognition. She is happy to 'enclose' herself in the home with her husband, but nevertheless wishes to 'appear at the best advantage...in the view of the public world', not being afraid to climb 'fame's tower, which is to live by remembrance in after-ages'.[72] This almost contradictory (yet readily understandable) position typifies Cavendish's reaction to time, circumstance and literature. Torn between truth and imagination, she was perpetually self-promoting and yet rampantly curious, as the title-page of *Natures Pictures* encapsulates:

> Natures Pictures, Drawn by Fancies Pencil to the Life. Written by the thrice Noble, Illustrious, and Excellent Princess, the Lady Marchioness of Newcastle. In this volume there are several feigned Stories of Natural Descriptions, as Comical, Tragical, and Tragi-Comical, Poetical, Romancical, Philosophical, and Historical, both in Prose and Verse, some all Verse, some all Prose, some mixt,...Also there are some Morals and some Dialogues...and a true story at the latter end, wherein there is no feigning.[73]

A great deal of 'feigning', however, was invested in her 1666 work, *The Blazing World*, a 'Romance' (to use her own generic term) which boldly looks forward to science fiction and fantasy writing.[74] Her 'fantastical' female thoughts, which, as she wrote in 'A True Relation', tended to 'work of themselves, like silkworms that spins out of their own bowels',[75] left their cocoonery to create a 'new' world.

Of all the literature produced in and for the early modern household, the writings which perhaps most readily spring to mind in this connection are those

71 Margaret Cavendish, *Sociable Letters*, p. 226.
72 Margaret Cavendish, 'A True Relation', pp. 98, 97.
73 Margaret Cavendish, *Natures Pictures* (London: 1656), title page.
74 Margaret Cavendish, *The Blazing World and Other Writings*, ed. Kate Lilley (London: Penguin, 1994).
75 Margaret Cavendish, *Poems and Fancies* (London, 1653), sig. A3r, and 'A True Relation', p. 95.

in the third category, the practical texts which record (to borrow Cavendish's phrase) 'Receits of Medicines, for Cookery or Confectioners'. These handbooks, particularly the commonplace books from the period, mingle herbal remedies, culinary recipes, Biblical quotations and scraps of poetry in an inscribed, though often unpublished, epitome of the daily juxtapositions of household life. The middle years of the seventeenth century also witnessed the first publication of what might be termed household manuals. Prominent among these is *A Choice Manual of Rare and Select Secrets in Physick and Chyrurgery Collected and Practised by the Right Honourable, the Countesse of Kent, late deceased*, published together with *A True Gentlewomans Delight Wherein is contained all manner of Cookery* in the early 1650s.[76] This extended title forms a fascinating statement on the skills of housekeeping. They are assumed to be feminine and delightful, and thus convey a sense of secrecy and discovery (the '*Rare . . . Secrets*' echoing the ideas of 'confinement' and 'concealment' encountered in previous texts). In addition, they are recognised as grounded in experience (these tips have not just been '*Collected*' but '*Practised*') and are attributed to Elizabeth Grey, Countess of Kent, a leading hostess of her day. A dedicatory epistle describes the book's contents as 'a rich Cabinet of knowledge', recalling the image of a house as itself a cabinet of rarities; the alphabeticised Table of Contents for the first part of the book indeed indicates the cornucopia of items on offer, from 'Aqua mirabilis, and the vertues thereof' to (as the final entry, under 'W') 'For to cause a young Child to make Water'.[77] The second part moves on to the details of such recipes as 'Quince Cream' and 'Lark Pie', and instruction in the processes of 'Preserving, Conserving, Drying and Candying, Very necessary for all Ladies and Gentlewomen'.[78] Other practical skills appropriate to 'Ladies and Gentlewomen' are indirectly recorded in household writing, as when Elizabeth Egerton, who prayed never to be 'sluggish' or 'linger out' her time, wrote a meditation 'Upon occasion of the unwinding of a skean of Silke'. This homely necessity is transformed into an extended metaphor of spirituality as she prays that Christ will 'unravell the skeane of my transgressions' so that she may start to 'spin the Thread of purity'.[79]

As Cavendish's category, 'Complemental Letters', reminds us, much of the writing associated with the household was social by nature. The most famous

---

76 Elizabeth Grey, Countess of Kent, *A Choice Manual of Rare and Select Secrets*, together with *A True Gentlewomans Delight*, 2nd edn (London, 1653). This is the earliest edition preserved in the British Library collection. *A Choice Manual* predates by more than ten years the better-known *Cook's Guide* published by Hannah Wolley in 1664.

77 Grey, *Choice Manual*, sigs. A2r, A3r, A4v.

78 Grey, *True Gentlewomans Delight*, pp. 3, 91 and title-page.

79 Egerton, *True Coppies*, sigs. 108v, 109v.

letters extant from this period are those written by Dorothy Osborne to
William Temple during their courtship, a correspondence much praised and
enjoyed by generations of readers, and characterised by a sprightly combination
of the homely, the literary and the worldly, rounded out with wit and affectionate self-mockery. A slightly less than affectionate tone, however, is adopted in
her mockery of Margaret Cavendish, 'my Lady New Castle',[80] who, as we have
seen, published a collection of fictional *Sociable Letters* containing, ironically, a
range of wit and comment comparable to that found in Osborne's actual correspondence. As Cavendish wrote in her preface, the letters are 'rather Scenes' in
which are expressed 'the Humors of Mankind and the Actions of Man's Life',
and the opening letter lists among the possible contents of their correspondence 'the several Accidents, and several Imployments of our home-affairs,
and what visits we receive, or entertainments we make . . . and what reports we
hear of publick affairs, and of particular Persons, and the like'.[81] The letters
convey a sense of the self-sufficiency of home life 'free from the Intanglements,
confused Clamours, and rumbling Noise of the World'. Who needs playhouses
and courts when thoughts can 'entertain my Mind with such Pleasures' and
enact plays 'on the Stage of Imagination, where my Mind sits as a Spectator'?[82]

   Two other social kinds of writing practised in the mid seventeenth-century
household served a similar cohesive purpose to that of correspondence: recording the lives of family members in biography, and keeping journals of individual or communal experiences. We have already encountered Lucy Hutchinson
as the writer of the biography of her husband, and Margaret Cavendish also
published a biography of her husband, the Duke of Newcastle, in 1667. An
important addition to this group of texts is the *Life* of Elizabeth Cary, Lady
Falkland (author of *The Tragedie of Mariam*, 1613), written by one or more of
her daughters. All four of them were members of the same convent as Gertrude
More, and the biography, written in the early 1640s, justifies their mother's
conversion to Catholicism as well as recounting her dilemmas as a wife and
writer.[83] The process of remembering – as families, as co-religionists, as households – was also facilitated by journals, for instance in Alice Thornton's *Book of
Remembrances*, where the births and deaths of relatives and friends are recorded
together with confessions and meditations of a more spiritual nature. Here the
borders between devotional, social and autobiographical modes are blurred,

80 Osborne, *Letters*, p. 75.   81 Margaret Cavendish, *CCXI Sociable Letters*, sig. c2r, p. 1.
82 *Ibid.*, pp. 56, 57.
83 Anne (?) Cary, *The Lady Falkland: Her Life*, in Elizabeth Cary, *The Tragedie of Mariam with The
   Lady Falkland: her Life*, ed. Barry Waller and Margaret W. Ferguson (Berkeley: University of
   California Press, 1994), pp. 183–275.

just as in actual household communities. Elizabeth Delaval's *Meditations* provide a further example of this mingling of modes of writing: personal and spiritual narratives converge and at one point become subsumed in a collection of letters from her grandmother.[84] Lucy Hutchinson's *Memoirs of the Life of Colonel Hutchinson*, too, stray on occasion into autobiography despite the deliberately third-person references to the writer herself: when she recounts John Hutchinson's first encounter with the 'unknowne gentlewoman' who will later become his wife, she describes herself in providential terms as 'her that was destin'd to make his future joy'.[85] The personal and the historical, as well as the spiritual and social, intersect in these texts and in the households from which they came.

Margaret Cavendish's final category, 'a Copy or two of Verses', runs like a rich seam through household writing in the middle decades of the seventeenth century. In addition to the many devotional poets considered in the preceding chapters (for whom the household context was both exile and inspiration), those who printed or circulated domestic poems in this era include Carew (1640), the as yet unidentified author of *Eliza's Babes*, Margaret Cavendish (1653), An Collins, Elizabeth Major (*Honey on the Rod*), Katherine Philips (*Poems*, 1664), Hester Pulter, Lucy Hutchinson and Andrew Marvell.[86] Two examples from this list must suffice to illustrate the strong links between poetry and the household in this period. First, 'Eliza' represents the early modern women who wrote simultaneously from a position of concealment (in this instance, anonymity) and freedom, released into creativity by religious experience. She declares herself on the title page to be 'a LADY, who onely desires to advance the glory of GOD, and not her own' and, like Collins and Major, regards her poems as her 'Babes', here specifically identified as the fruit of a 'strict union' with the 'Prince of eternall glory'.[87] Her prefatory epistle continues the metaphor, taking on a maternal tone when she addresses the poems as children leaving the family home: 'Goe you must, to praise him, that gave you me. And more Ile say for you, which few Mothers can, you were obtained by vertue, borne with ease and pleasure, and will live to my content and felicity. And so Adieu.'[88] One of the intriguing elements of the ensuing lyric sequence is the manner in which the poet, who is 'affianced' to God and thinks of heaven as her 'Mansion',[89] deals with the reality of marriage and an

---

84 Delaval, *Meditations*, pp. 70–4.   85 Hutchinson, *Memoirs*, p. 30.
86 Hester Pulter, Lucy Hutchinson and Andrew Marvell wrote their poems during this period but because they remained in manuscript or were posthumously published, they are difficult to date precisely.
87 *Eliza's Babes*, sig. A2r. See also Collins, *Divine Songs*, p. 5 (discussed above) and Major, *Sin and Mercy*, sig. h3v.
88 *Eliza's Babes*, sig. A3v.   89 *Ibid.*, sig. A2r, p. 51.

earthly home. At first she resents the threat of a human husband, experiencing marriage as a betrayal of her heavenly love and seeing that most other married couples 'live in strife'.[90] Ultimately, however, she comes to terms with life in her married home, admitting that God has persuaded her to 'see / We happy in that life may be'. As she approaches death she calmly contemplates her earthly life and relationships in her poem 'To my Husband':

> When from the world, I shall be tane,
> And from earths necessary paine,
> Then let no blacks be worne for me,
> Not in a Ring my dear by thee.
> But this bright Diamond, let it be
> Worn in rememberance of me.
> And when it sparkles in your eye,
> Think 'tis my shadow passeth by.
> For why, more bright you shall me see,
> Then that or any Gem can bee.
> Dress not the house with sable weed,
> As if there were some dismall deed
> Acted to be when I am gone.
>
> * * *
>
> It was my glory I did spring
> From heavens eternall powerfull King:
> To his bright Palace heir am I . . .[91]

As the poem confirms, the material 'house' need not be draped in mourning cloths after her death as 'Eliza' will be sparkling in heaven's 'bright Palace'. Instead of repeating her claim to marriage with Christ, she changes her metaphor to the (equally Bible-sanctioned) terminology of household inheritance: she is a confident 'heir' to the house of God.

My second brief example of household poetry from mid seventeenth-century England is from the work of Andrew Marvell that was produced while he was in residence at the Fairfax family home, Appleton House in Yorkshire, in 1650–1. Ironically, Marvell's domestic setting replicates the rural retreat which he urges the 'forward youth' to 'forsake' at the opening of the 'Horatian Ode' (also written during the Appleton years), where he sings 'in the Shadows . . . / His Numbers languishing'.[92] Ultimately, the 'Shadows' of the peaceful hall and gardens prove just the place for a contemplation of 'Wars and Fortunes' – as well as time, innocence and loss – sharply perceived 'from some shade'.[93] This

---

90 *Ibid.*, 'The change', p. 44.   91 *Ibid.*, pp. 46–7.   92 Marvell, *Poems and Letters*, 1:87.
93 Marvell, 'An Horatian Ode', line 113, 'The Picture of little T. C.', line 24, *Poems and Letters*, 190, 38.

is most profoundly to be seen in 'Upon Appleton House', in which public political dilemmas are framed within the household environment, in a reversal rather than a rejection of the familiar relationship of private to public. The poet commits himself to the house and its principles, even to the extent of mirroring the 'short but admirable Lines' of its humble architecture in his own modest poetic lines. While the opening praises the dedicatee, the 'Master great', the poem as a whole centres upon Fairfax's daughter Mary, in keeping with the feminine associations which we have seen in conduct books, household practice and the literature of this era. The 'easie Philosopher', feminised through his separation from the 'Men' who symbolically 'Massacre the Grass', considers the world's hopes to be epitomised in this aptly named Maria, who 'with Graces more divine / Supplies beyond her Sex the Line'. In her 'Line' a redemptive future is confirmed, parallel to that which Eve promises through the line of descent to Mary at the end of *Paradise Lost*.[94] The link with Eden is deliberate, as the poem's penultimate stanza specifies:

> 'Tis not, what once it was, the World;
> But a rude heap together hurl'd;
> All negligently overthrown,
> Gulfes, Deserts, Precipices, Stone.
> Your lesser World contains the same.
> But in more decent Order tame;
> You Heaven's Center, Nature's Lap.
> And Paradice's only Map.[95]

The 'lesser World' of Appleton House is seen to be of a 'more decent Order' than the larger world – once again, reversing the normal hierarchies – and it offers a blueprint for heavenly perfection. That which is 'lesser' – a word with overtones not only of the small and homely but also of the feminine – in fact turns out to be the image or representation ('Map') of a restored Eden. This recalls Evelyn's description of Thomas Browne's house and garden as 'a Paradise', and Marvell's reference to Appleton slightly earlier in the poem as a 'Domestick Heaven'.[96] The household could not be honoured with any higher regard than this.

This chapter has, I trust, made clear not only the wealth of literary material generated by, for and about the English household in the middle decades of the seventeenth century, but also the ways in which the house itself functioned

---

94 See Milton, *Paradise Lost*, 12.621–3.
95 Marvell, 'Upon Appleton House', stanza lxxxxvi, *Poems and Letters*, 1:82. Earlier quotations from the poem are from stanzas vi, vii, lxxi, xlviii, l, lxxxxiii.
96 Evelyn, *Diary*, 3:594 (see above) and Marvell, 'Upon Appleton House' stanza lxxxxi, *Poems and Letters*, 1:81.

as an emblem and microcosm of human experience. Within its walls it encompassed birth and death, peace and war, tradition and transition, family and individual, earth and heaven. The range of writing emerging from the household is matched by the variety of people and experiences featured in them, from Margaret Cavendish's colourful self to the 'Kitchin-maid' who, she reports in her *CCXI Sociable Letters*, was born to 'Dripping or Basting' but through marriage became 'a gay Lady'.[97] The early modern household configured the public world in terms of its own holy 'state' and the spiritual realm in the dimensions of its earthly 'mansion'. Its prominence in the historical realities of mid seventeenth-century England had a profound impact on this and future generations of writers, and the central place of women, both in the physical household and in the literary genres produced under its influence, was of enormous significance for the development of literary history after the Restoration.

97 Margaret Cavendish, *CCXI Sociable Letters*, pp. 87–8.

Chapter 25

ALTERNATIVE SITES FOR
LITERATURE

JOSHUA SCODEL

This chapter examines a spectrum of civil war and Interregnum venues – literal and textual – in which authors either imagined alternatives to engagement or pursued intellectual projects at some remove from the era's political, religious and military conflicts. Drawing on longstanding generic practices, foreign and native, as well as various philosophical and religious traditions, numerous writers, mainly Royalist, celebrated country life and rural retirement in order to evade or address Britain's crisis.[1] Royalist authors also expressed defiant insouciance, shared values and mutual support-in-adversity with innovative contributions to traditional genres, such as the drinking poem, and newer sorts of publications, such as the anthology of verse 'drollery'. With differing degrees of involvement in current events, like-minded intellectuals, such as Samuel Hartlib's circle, the Oxford scientific club and the Cambridge Platonists articulated new intellectual visions. Others, such as Thomas Browne and Thomas Urquhart, pursued more solitary intellectual and literary paths for a personal purchase on both their age and eternity, or participated in contemporaries' group endeavours with self-conscious distinctiveness – as did John Milton, the Puritan convivial poet and Hartlib's classicising colleague in educational reform.

One of the greatest celebrants of country life and retired contentment, Robert Herrick mixes lyric grace and epigrammatic point in his 1648 volume consisting of the predominantly secular *Hesperides* and religious *Noble Numbers*. *Hesperides* documents '*Times trans-shifting*' ('The Argument of his Book', line 9) – not only seasonal changes, ageing and death, but also English sociopolitical disruption. Yet the polysemous title *Hesperides* evokes England as

---

1 See Maren-Sofie Røstvig, *The Happy Man: Studies in the Metamorphoses of a Classical Ideal, 1600–1700*, 2 vols. (Oslo: Akademisk Forlag, 1954–8), vol 1; and James G. Turner, *The Politics of Landscape* (Cambridge, MA: Harvard University Press, 1979).

a paradisal garden island.[2] Herrick idealises, nostalgically and defiantly, a joyful community centred around the country pastimes promoted by the Stuart court, decried by Puritans as pagan and superstitious, and outlawed by Parliament when *Hesperides* was published.[3] Blending native English custom with classical poetic and mythological allusions, Herrick evokes time-hallowed, nature-sanctioned festivity. His masterpiece in this mode, 'Corinna's going a Maying', adapts the classical *carpe diem* seduction poem to the 'harmlesse follie' (line 58) of Mayday rites. Acknowledging but deflecting critiques associating country pastimes with illicit sexuality, the speaker encourages the virgin Corinna – an innocent, homey English 'sweet-Slug-a-bed' (line 5) though named after Ovid's mistress – with tales of sexual frolics in the woods that eventuate in marriage. The opening characteristically hails the beautiful morning in terms of luminous Greek divinities (Apollo, Aurora) and the responsive Church of England 'Mattens' and 'Hymnes' (lines 10–11) of the creatures.[4]

Herrick thematises his poetic relationship to political disorder. A lament that the poet cannot sing during '*untuneable Times*' makes poetry out of its supposed impossibility. The poet becomes, at times, self-sufficient in adversity: the three-couplet 'Purposes', rendering the opening of Horace's *Ode* 3.3, praises the steadfast Stoic, pursuing his 'purposes' unfazed by 'threats of Tyrants' (lines 2–3); the three-couplet 'His desire', loosely indebted to the same ode, lauds the poet who can 'clearely sing' (line 3) amidst cataclysm. Herrick also escapes into his book, which he declares a 'Dominion' that will 'endure' even 'When Monarchies trans-shifted are' ('On himselfe', lines 3–4); the final, iconically shaped 'The pillar of Fame', asserts its own immortality 'Tho Kindoms fal' (line 10).[5]

Splendid poems, indebted to Herrick's master Ben Jonson and his classical models, treat the gentleman's estate as the centre of a harmonious community. Shorter compositions (including distichs and verses with one- or two-foot lines) more distinctively respond to the times by encapsulating how 'little' – a favourite term of Herrick's – contents the retired countryman. As the modest and ultimately ejected parson of Dean Prior, Devonshire, Herrick instances himself: the poem 'His Grange, or private wealth' details his 'little' (line 8) domain – a maid, farm animals, pets – in couplets whose alternating one-foot

---

2 See Ann Baynes Coiro, *Robert Herrick's 'Hesperides' and the Epigram Book Tradition* (Baltimore and London: Johns Hopkins University Press, 1988), pp. 3–29.
3 See Leah S. Marcus, *The Politics of Mirth: Jonson, Herrick, Milton, Marvell, and the Defense of Old Holiday Pastimes* (University of Chicago Press, 1986), pp. 140–68.
4 Robert Herrick, *The Complete Poetry*, ed. J. Max Patrick (1963; rpt, New York: Norton, 1968), pp. 11, 98–100.
5 *Ibid.*, pp. 118–19, 285, 419, 280, 443.

lines convey delight in 'slight things' (line 32). In poems on his own death, Herrick even imagines, with a world-renouncing diminution, his grave as 'Chamber fit' ('On himselfe', line 7). In 'His content in the Country', Herrick declares satisfaction with the 'poore Tenement' where he lives (line 8); in 'The Bed-man, or Grave-maker', he asks but for 'one Tenement' in which to be laid (line 4).[6]

With the Puritan disenfranchisement of the established church and the Interregnum loosening of religious dogmas, retirement poets increasingly sought God in a personal approach to nature. Herrick addressed poems to Mildmay Fane, Earl of Westmorland, who submitted to Parliament in 1644 and retired from public life after imprisonment. Alongside devotional poems in George Herbert's vein, Fane's *Otia Sacra* (1648) contains translations of Latin retirement poems and a Horatian-style rural epistle. The setting of 'To Retiredness' offers both an escape from worldly cares and an opportunity to admire God's 'works of wonder' (line 22). Fane topically lauds a peaceful landscape where only rustics argue and birds 'contest' (line 57) in song. While his verse can be crabbed or pleonastic, Fane's epigrammatic brevity here conveys mental concentration: 'For so my Thoughts by this retreat / Grow stronger, like contracted heat' (lines 69–70).[7]

The Christian Horatian poetry of the Polish Jesuit, Mathias Casimir Sarbiewski, was translated and imitated during this period; his sacred parody of Horace's *Epode* 2 influentially described the happy countryman worshipping the Creator. Henry Vaughan's Cavalier *Poems* (1646) and *Olor Iscanus* (1647) contain retirement poems and translations; the latter opens with celebrations of Vaughan's local Welsh river – as birthplace, poetic inspiration and solace in troubled times – and includes a translation of Casimir's epode. While extensively echoing his declared model, Herbert, Vaughan in *Silex Scintillans* (1650, 1655) deviates from Herbert's carefully structured lyrics with poems often memorable for great passages rather than as wholes.[8] Replacing Herbert's Calvinism with hermetic philosophy to celebrate a nature alive with divine spirit, Vaughan joyfully describes the innocent creatures' instinctual longing

---

6 *Ibid.*, pp. 324–5, 168, 266, 364. See Joshua Scodel, *The English Poetic Epitaph: Conflict and Commemoration from Jonson to Wordsworth* (Ithaca, NY: Cornell University Press, 1991), pp. 166–93.

7 Mildmay Fane, *Otia Sacra* (1648), intro. Donald M. Friedman (Delmar, NY: Scholars' Facsimiles, 1975), pp. 172–4.

8 See Joan Bennett, *Five Metaphysical Poets* (Cambridge University Press, 1964), pp. 71–89; but for a more positive assessment of the poetic structure of Vaughan's Herbert-inspired verse, see Jonathan F. S. Post, *Henry Vaughan: The Unfolding Vision* (Princeton University Press, 1982), pp. 81–97.

for God, articulates the Paracelsian belief that *all* creatures (not only the 'elect') will be made 'new' on the Last Day ('The Book', line 27) and recalls a childhood innocence when he perceived within nature the 'shadows of eternity' ('The Retreat', line 14).[9] With descriptive precision and mystical fervour, Vaughan worships light. Longing to pierce the 'clouds' of human sinfulness separating him from God, Vaughan celebrates sunrise as nature's awakening to God ('Dawning', 'The Morning Watch') and rapturous Platonic illumination – as in the dazzling opening of 'The World': 'I saw Eternity the other night / Like a great *Ring* of pure and endless light'. He contemplates the night sky's 'ordered lights' as a rebuke to rebellious, war-torn Britain ('The Constellation', line 1) and contrasts the luminous state of the dead with his own isolation in a twilight world: 'They are all gone into the world of light! / And I alone sit ling'ring here' begins a great poem that movingly compares the poet's memory of the dead to evening's lingering 'faint beams' (line 7).[10]

John Hall's 'To his Tutor, Master Pawson' in his *Poems* (1646) beckons the poet's Puritan teacher on a contemplative pilgrimage through and beyond the natural world – first to peruse God's 'book' of 'Nature', which, in Hall's clever but not facile distinction, 'to aread is easy, to understand divine' (lines 3, 11–12); then to contemplate the world with its ruins of former 'kingdoms' (line 42); and finally to ascend to heaven. Hall elsewhere sanitises Cavalier forms: his 'A Rapture' recalls Carew's libertine 'Rapture', as other poems recall *carpe diem* seductions, but Hall demands 'Platonic' rather than sensual fulfilment. Hall's impatient exhortations to Pawson – 'Come, let us run / And give the world a girdle with the sun' ('To his Tutor', lines 13–14), 'Let us tear / A passage through / That fleeting vault above' (lines 50–2) – turn erotic intensity to contemplative otherworldliness, as phraseology shared with Andrew Marvell's 'To his Coy Mistress' suggests ('Let us . . . / . . . tear our Pleasures with rough strife, / Thorough the Iron gates of Life. / Thus, though we cannot make our Sun / Stand still, yet we will make him run', lines 37, 43–6).[11]

---

9 Henry Vaughan, *The Complete Poems*, ed. Alan Rudrum (New Haven, CT, and London: Yale University Press, 1981), pp. 310, 173. On Vaughan's anti-Calvinism, see Alan Rudrum, 'Henry Vaughan, The Liberation of the Creatures, and Seventeenth-Century English Calvinism', *The Seventeenth Century* 4 (1989), 33–54. On the child figure in seventeenth-century poetry, see Leah S. Marcus, *Childhood and Cultural Despair: A Theme and Variations in Seventeenth-Century Literature* (University of Pittsburgh Press, 1978).
10 Vaughan, *Complete Poems*, pp. 227, 230, 246.
11 *Minor Poets of the Caroline Period*, ed. George Saintsbury, 3 vols. (Oxford: Clarendon Press, 1905–21), 2:208–9, 199–200; Andrew Marvell, *The Poems and Letters of Andrew Marvell*, ed. H. M. Margoliouth, rev. Pierre Legouis and E. E. Duncan-Jones, 2 vols., 3rd edn (Oxford: Clarendon Press, 1971), 1:28.

In John Denham's *Coopers Hill*, published in 1642 and updated in 1655, sociopolitical lessons emerge from retired contemplation of nature. The original version urges both King and Parliament to avoid political chaos through moderation. Virgil's *Georgics* is Denham's major model, often understood during the period as an episodic didactic poem, with digressions, on order and disorder in nature and nation.[12] Denham purports to contemplate with wise detachment a landscape that emblematises England's past and present state. Looking down (literally and metaphorically) from Coopers Hill in Surrey upon the 'cloud / Of businesse' in London, where crowds 'Toyle' and 'study plots' in their insatiable 'desires' for wealth and power, 'affraid to be secure', Denham lauds his own rural tranquility: 'O happinesse of sweet retir'd content! / To be at once secure, and innocent' (lines 27–48). Denham's stance is Epicurean, derived from both alternatives in a famous *Georgics* set-piece where Virgil wishes to be either an Epicurean philosopher who fearlessly observes nature or a contented country-dweller (*Georgics*, 2.475–94). Denham also echoes Virgil's own major model, Lucretius, who describes how the Epicurean sage calmly 'looks down from the height' on those who seek riches and political power with vain 'toil' (*labore*) (*De rerum natura*, 2.7–13). Denham politicises such contemplative Epicureanism by suggesting that self-restraint defines kings' and subjects' reciprocal rights and duties. Lucretius claims men are consumed by labour, cares and war because they do not adhere to the proper 'limit' (*finis*) of desire (*De rerum natura*, 5.1423–35). Giving an Epicurean grounding to a recurrent conception of constitutional monarchy in the 1640s, Denham exhorts subject and monarch to 'limit . . . desire' rather than disastrously 'seeking to have more' (lines 330, 349).[13]

While calling for self-restraint to preserve harmony, Denham espouses a contradictory vision of expansionary commerce in 'treasures' (line 212) as the source of England's (and the world's) prosperity. Denham 'discovers' models for both in nature: the Thames's keeping within its banks exemplifies political restraint, while its ceaseless flow around the 'whole Globe' (line 215) exemplifies – indeed activates – English commerce. The 1655 *Coopers Hill* condemns

---

12 See *Expans'd Hieroglyphicks: A Critical Edition of Sir John Denham's 'Coopers Hill'*, ed. Brendan O Hehir (Berkeley and Los Angeles: University of California Press, 1969), pp. 9–13. On georgic as a central seventeenth-century genre, see Alastair Fowler, 'Georgic and Pastoral: Laws of Genre in the Seventeenth Century', in *Culture and Cultivation in Early Modern England: Writing and the Land*, ed. Michael Leslie and Timothy Raylor (Leicester University Press, 1992), pp. 81–8; Anthony Low, *The Georgic Revolution* (Princeton University Press, 1985); and Joshua Scodel, *Excess and the Mean in Early Modern English Literature* (Princeton University Press, 2002), chs. 3–4.

13 *Expans'd Hieroglyphicks*, pp. 111–13, 132, 134.

recent history with a final Virgilian comparison of civil conflict to a destructive, overflowing river. Yet it also praises the Thames in a couplet subsequently celebrated, imitated and parodied by English neoclassical poets as exemplifying the heroic couplet's formal possibilities of antithetical balance: 'Though deep, yet clear, though gentle, yet not dull, / Strong without rage, without ore-flowing full' (lines 191–2).[14] Denham locates beauty in the balancing of divergent impulses.

While Denham sought to give counsel, later Cavalier writers turned to pastoral traditions for consolatory retreat. Richard Lovelace's *Lucasta* (1649), which includes several Royalist lyrics on love, war and their relationship, concludes with 'Aramantha. A Pastoral'. This lengthy poem modifies the Renaissance topos of an enamoured hero's sojourn in a pastoral landscape that he must eventually leave to perform his public duties, as in Book 6 of Spenser's *Faerie Queene*. Lovelace's heroic lover embraces pastoral forever: finding his beloved Lucasta in the woods, Alexis abandons heroic 'arms' to live and die with her in her 'peacefull cave'. Lucasta's bower mythopoetically recreates the (Stuart) court destroyed by civil war's 'fire and blood': Lucasta is 'Queen' of a paradisal garden.[15]

Isaak Walton's *Complete Angler* (1653), which went through five editions before the century's end, is a generic hybrid: part sports manual, part pastoral protest – voiced in terms of Christian quietism – against the Civil War's sociopolitical and religious disruption. Combining the classical triad of divergent ways of life, Walton's fisherman has it all: wholesome pleasure, contemplation of nature and relaxed, 'harmless' (i.e., non-disruptive) action. Echoing the Bible and the then-banned Book of Common Prayer, the work idealises fishermen as uncontentious Christians, while 'Angling' evokes the disestablished 'Ecclesia Anglicana' to which Walton's humble fisherman clings. From the second, 1655 edition onward, Walton's concluding epigraph is 1 Thessalonians 4:11, 'Study to be quiet', while his lucid, unassuming style throughout recalls 'lowly, humble' New Testament epistles written, as he notes, by fishermen.

Walton also wards off his period's conflicts by engaging longstanding literary conventions and values. Citations of Elizabethan and Jacobean lyrics conjure an England of rural harmony and piety.[16] In the friendly debate of the author's mouthpiece, Piscator, with partisans of rival sports, Walton recalls classical and

---

14 *Ibid.*, pp. 124, 151.
15 Richard Lovelace, *Poems of Richard Lovelace*, ed. C. H. Wilkinson (Oxford: Clarendon Press, 1930), pp. 107–18.
16 See Steven N. Zwicker, *Lines of Authority: Politics and English Literary Culture, 1649–1689* (Ithaca, NY: Cornell University Press, 1993), pp. 60–75.

Renaissance works deploying and celebrating civilised dialogue, here implicitly contrasted with contemporary polemic and violence. Pastoral is Walton's main source. Piscatory eclogues had substituted fishermen for shepherds; Walton's angler-as-Christian derives from pastoral's Christian shepherd. Various Renaissance pastorals represent highborn exiles from court appreciating shepherds' humble lives (as in Shakespeare's *As You Like It*); Walton's angler and his fellow sportsmen, bereft of a court, find happy entertainment among simple countryfolk. Walton 'pastoralises' rustics, adapting the genre's singing contest in which rivalry promotes delight and both sides may be deemed winners: a milkmaid and her mother recite Christopher Marlowe's pastoral invitation and Walter Ralegh's response; Piscator and a ploughman with the pastoral sobriquet 'Coridon' praise their respective ways of life in a verse 'match' promoting 'contentment' rather than 'contention' (an expressive verbal juxtaposition).[17]

Formal and thematic affinities with his 'Horatian Ode' (1650) and 'Upon Appleton House' (1651) suggest that Andrew Marvell composed his diverse pastorals around the same time. Self-conscious about generic traditions and possibilities, Marvell's pastorals explore the relationship between lowly subjects and profound themes.[18] His Mower poems, several of which are ostensibly love laments by a humble speaker, treat the human fall from harmony with nature. 'The Mower to the Glo-Worms' evokes 'higher' political themes by denying them:

> Ye Country Comets, that portend
> No War, nor Princes funeral,
> Shining unto no higher end
> Then to presage the Grasses fall.
>
> (lines 5–8)

Introducing the loftiest theme as if it were lowly – 'the grass's fall' is also *the* Fall ('All flesh is grass', Isaiah 40:6) – Marvell analogises the Mower's loss of pastoral harmony with the repudiated, seemingly higher themes of war and royal death, both instances of fallen life. His 'Horatian Ode' rejects pastoral poetry by declaring that in political crisis one can no longer 'in the Shadows sing' (line 3): song-in-the-shade is a Virgilian synecdoche for pastoral's bower, far from political strife (cf. *Eclogue* 1.5). In 'The Nymph complaining for the death

17 Isaak Walton, *The Complete Angler, 1653–1676*, ed. Jonquil Bevan (Oxford: Clarendon Press, 1983), pp. 69, 371, 75, 90–1, 94.
18 On Marvell's generic experimentation, see Rosalie Colie, '*My Ecchoing Song*': *Andrew Marvell's Poetry of Criticism* (Princeton University Press, 1970); and Geoffrey Hartman, '"The Nymph Complaining for the Death of Her Faun": A Brief Allegory', in *Beyond Formalism: Literary Essays 1958–1970* (New Haven, CT, and London: Yale University Press, 1970), pp. 173–92.

of her Fawn', by contrast, Marvell registers war's cost to innocent bystanders: 'wanton Troopers' (line 1) have killed the nymph's fawn and thereby destroyed her innocent, sensual paradise (England?).[19]

'The Garden' has recently been dated to the 1660s on the basis of alleged echoes of Restoration publications.[20] It nevertheless responds to the 'Horatian Ode' by celebrating the 'inglorious Arts of Peace' and 'private Gardens' rejected by Cromwell and his panegyric poet (lines 10, 29), while its thematics and stanzaic form more closely resemble 'Upon Appleton House' than Marvell's major Restoration works. Whatever its date, the poem's playful seriousness reflects upon Interregnum retirement poetry in general. The distinctive wit of 'The Garden' celebrates the sensual, intellectual and spiritual pleasures of retirement as an ascending scale. The superabundant fruits that overwhelm the speaker and make him 'fall on Grass' (line 40) with happy innocence implicitly contrast with the Fall; intellectual pleasures draw the outside world within the mind's reaches, producing, in a gloriously enigmatic phrase, 'a green Thought in a green Shade' (line 48); and the soul delights in its own beauty while preparing for a heavenward 'longer flight' (line 55). For such pleasures Marvell will exchange both public life and erotic desire. Wittily claiming that the ambitious seek the laurels and bays of public honour, and that the pagan gods, too, pursued the plants into which nubile nymphs metamorphosed to escape, Marvell playfully proposes his garden with its 'Garlands of repose' (line 8) as the most comprehensive object of desire. This *reductio ad absurdum* reveals Marvell's sense that wholeheartedly embracing a way of life involves trivialising its alternatives.[21]

'Upon Appleton House', written while Marvell was tutor to Lord Thomas Fairfax's daughter at Nun Appleton House, Yorkshire, concludes otherwise, by spurning the simplifications it considers.[22] The poem, begun as a Jonsonian country-house poem, becomes a multifaceted georgic reflection upon retirement in relation to English history. Playing with multiple, even reversible perspectives, Marvell both honours and questions Fairfax's retirement. While Fairfax's cultivation of his garden evokes his cultivation of conscience

19 Marvell, *Poems and Letters*, 1:47, 91, 23.
20 Alan Pritchard, 'Marvell's "The Garden": A Restoration Poem?' *Studies in English Literature* 23 (1983), 371–88.
21 Marvell, *Poems and Letters*, 1:91–2, 51–2.
22 On 'Appleton House', see Derek Hirst and Steven Zwicker, 'High Summer at Nun Appleton, 1651: Andrew Marvell and Lord Fairfax's Occasions', *Historical Journal* 36 (1993), 247–69 (a contextual reading); and M. J. K. O'Loughlin, 'This Sober Frame: A Reading of "Upon Appleton House"', in *Andrew Marvell: A Collection of Critical Essays*, ed. George deForest Lord (Englewood Cliffs, NJ: Prentice-Hall, 1968), pp. 120–42 (a new critical analysis).

(lines 353–4), comparisons of Fairfax's gardening to his abandoned military life and wistful claims that Fairfax – 'had it pleased him and *God*' (line 346) – might have cultivated all Britain (the former 'Garden of the World', line 322) hint at Marvell's ambivalence even while aligning Fairfax's decision with the course of Providence.[23] Both the virtue and potential taint of Fairfax's garden retirement emerge from framing it with other, corrupt forms of retirement: first, the lubricious lesbian sportiveness of the nuns, who once inhabited Appleton House, is destroyed by mock-heroic valour when Fairfax's ancestor turned the nunnery into a Protestant household; then, the poet's own retirement, which becomes more solipsistic as he walks from Appleton's meadows to its woods.

These ambulations suggest the inescapability, both tactically and morally, of the national crisis. The poet's encounter with Fairfax's mowers in the meadows reaches its wittiest, most telling moment when a 'bloody' labourer saucily responds to the poet's comparison of the mowers to '*Israalites*' (line 389) – and thus implicitly to England's Puritan revolutionaries – by killing rails in place of Biblical quails (lines 406–9). By turning the retired contemplator into an overheard participant, Marvell dissolves the ideal of detachment and literary-political stances like Denham's in *Coopers Hill*, supposedly above and apart from the fray. The effects of the poet's 'retiring' to the woods from the meadow's 'Flood' (line 481) – a frequent metaphor for civil war – undercuts Virgil's and Denham's georgic associations of retirement with contemplative wisdom and calm contentment. While the poet happily reads '*Natures mystick Book*' (line 584) and 'securely play[s]' (line 607) in the woods, this '*easie Philosopher*' (line 561) seems less sage and serene than irresponsible, 'car[e]less' (line 529) in the sense of 'negligent' as well as 'free from care'. He describes himself 'languishing with ease', 'lazy' and 'trifling' (lines 593, 643, 652). He cannot, furthermore, actually escape from crisis by retreating 'within' (lines 504, 505) the wood ('within' is a resonant word in the poem). Observing a woodpecker's felling of an oak tree, which evokes the execution of Charles I (the royal oak), the poet notes that the tree had 'a *Traitor-worm*, within it bred' like 'our *Flesh* corrupt within' (lines 554–5). The self is tainted as much by sin 'within' as is the public domain without. The final section of the poem, which apotheosises Maria Fairfax as the presiding deity of the natural landscape, qualifies celebrations of pastoral retreat like Lovelace's 'Amarantha' by joyfully predicting that Maria will leave the estate to marry for 'some universal good' (line 741). Marvell thus reveals his dissatisfaction with retirement, but also his uncertainty about what can and

23　Contrast Andrew Shifflett, *Stoicism, Politics, and Literature in the Age of Milton* (Cambridge University Press, 1998), pp. 45–52.

should now be done – by Maria, by himself, above all by Lord Fairfax – for the nation.[24]

With a less subtle voice, John Collop's *Poesia Rediviva* (1656) engages the times by echoing (but not always reviving) the past: metrically rough compression and conceits recall Donne, while epigrammatic Stoicism evokes both Donne's and Jonson's epistles. 'On Retirement' celebrates endurance in adversity with the Donnean conceit of the retired man as his 'own *Umbrella*' and 'sun' (line 29), borrowed from Donne's prose letters, published in 1651. Echoing Jonson's 'To Penshurst' but shifting focus from the estate's ideal economy to the exemplary gentleman, 'A Character of a Compleat Gentleman' locates besieged gentry values in the virtuous individual. Other poems condemn Puritans and associate the 'free' Stoic, untroubled by mob or fate, with Charles I's 'Royal' martyrdom.[25]

The writing process itself could provide Royalist solace. The first Englishwoman to publish extensively, Margaret Cavendish, Duchess of Newcastle, declares she wrote her first book, *Poems and Fancies* (1653), to '*divert*' her from sadness, for which she had much cause: Charles I's defeat; the exile of her husband, a Royalist general; and ensuing financial difficulties. She speculates about nature's atoms-in-motion, psychology and morality. She also laments recent English history. While her pentameter couplets remain pedestrian at best, her speculative forays cumulatively engage. Restlessness is Cavendish's most interesting theme, both in *Poems* and in her subsequent Interregnum verse and prose miscellanies – *Worlds Olio* (1655), *Philosophical and Physical Opinions* (1655) and *Natures Pictures* (1656). While restlessness destroys the monarchy (allegorised in the felling of an oak and hunting of a stag) and an island of prosperity and peace (Britain), Cavendish finds pleasurable outlets for her (self-styled) 'restless' mind in fanciful vagaries.[26] Cavendish's dialogue poems between personifications of mental states and passions portray poetic fancy in diverse guises, such as Melancholy, dwelling in a 'lowly *Cell*', whose '*Imagination* severall pleasures gives'; Joy, which lets loose '*Thoughts* in multitude'; and 'Wit', which creates '*new*, and *strange*' '*Ideas*'. Cavendish suggests that fairies inspire poetic '*fancy*'; her fairy kingdom frolics are nostalgic, escapist Royalist evocations of courtly bustle but also allegories and instances of the skittish poetic imagination.[27]

---

24 Marvell, *Poems and Letters*, 1:62–86.
25 John Collop, *Poems*, ed. Conrad Hilberry (Madison: University of Wisconsin Press, 1962), pp. 65–6, 71–2, 88.
26 Margaret Cavendish, *Poems and Fancies* (London, 1653), sig. A7r, pp. 66–70, 113–20; *Natures Pictures Drawn by Fancies Pencil to the Life* (London, 1656), sig. C1r.
27 Cavendish, *Poems and Fancies*, pp. 78, 81–2, 162.

Writing many of her poems during the 1650s when she was the wife of a Parliamentarian but herself a member of a circle with Royalist sympathisers, the other major woman writer of the period, Katherine Philips, celebrates withdrawal from society's troubles: 'When all the stormy World doth roar / How unconcern'd am I?' she asks, rhetorically, in 'A Country-life' (lines 41–2). Philips is at her most innovative and influential in praising (to quote from one poem's title) '*retir'd Friendship*' between women as the source of deep emotional gratification and as a glorious alternative to the 'angry world' ('Friendship's Mystery, To my dearest Lucasia', line 4). Protesting the supposed male monopoly on virtuous friendship, her poem 'A Friend' declares

> ... for Men t'exclude
> Women from Friendship's vast capacity,
> Is a Design injurious or rude,
> Only maintain'd by partial tyranny.
> (lines 19–22)

Paralleling Jonson and his 'Sons', Philips in 'To . . . Ann Owen' hails a woman's '*Adoption*' into her '*Society*'. In her view, same-sex intimacy is purer than marriage, which too often is based upon 'Lust' or material 'Design' ('Friendship', line 31). By adapting the male erotic poet's adoration and censure of his female beloved, however, Philips also infuses female friendship with erotic intensity. Castigating a female companion for inconstancy, for example, she laments that her 'Passion' has met with disdain ('Injuria Amicitiae', line 45).[28]

Philips exploits Donne's treatment of heterosexual love as a religious mystery that mixes souls for the edification of the 'profane': 'There's a Religion in our Love', she declares ('Friendship's Mystery . . . ', line 5), for 'twin-Souls in one shall grow, / And teach the World new Love' ('To Mrs M. A. at parting', lines 49–50). Recalling Donne's metaphysical flights, though little of his playfulness, Philips philosophises, sometimes ponderously, sometimes with epigrammatic force. Loving friends constitute one another's selves: 'We are our selves but by rebound' ('Friendship's Mystery . . . ', line 23). Against Calvinist notions of natural depravity, she argues that friendship's 'united good' arises from a 'Grace' that 'refines' rather than 'destroys' natural goodness ('L'Accord du Bien', lines 57, 41); submerging contemporaneous Calvinist-Arminian

28 Katherine Philips, *Poems* (1667), intro. Travis Dupriest (Delmar, NY: Scholars' Facsimiles, 1992), pp. 89, 28, 21, 95, 32, 79, 54. On Philips' eroticisation of female friendship, see Elaine Hobby, *Virtue of Necessity: English Women's Writing, 1649–1688* (London: Virago Press, 1988), pp. 135–40; and Elizabeth Susan Wahl, *Invisible Relations: Representations of Female Intimacy in the Age of Enlightenment* (Stanford University Press, 1999), pp. 130–70.

debates on salvation in friendship's 'mystery', she pronounces friendship predestined yet freely willed ('Friendship's Mystery...', lines 6–10). 'To my
Lucasia, in defence of declared Friendship' replaces the tetrameter quatrains
of Donne's 'The Ecstasy' with pentameters, and adapts Donne's argument
for heterosexual love's fulfilment in sexual consummation by contending that
the poet's and addressee's mutual 'Love' (line 1) must be nourished by bodily
'Converse' (line 74) – 'transactions' (line 32) of eye and ear.[29]

Philips reworks various Donnean tropes for her gynocentric focus. The twin
compasses in 'A Valediction, Forbidding Mourning' now signify the bond between separated women as Philips replaces Donne's conventionally feminine,
stay-at-home foot that 'leans, and hearkens after' (line 31) the active male with
her own image of responsive equality: 'Each follows where the other leans'
('Friendship in Embleme...', line 27). In 'The Sun Rising', Donne had man-
fully commanded the sun to shine exclusively on himself and his beloved: 'Shine
here to us, and thou art everywhere' (line 29). In 'An Answer to another per-
swading a Lady to Marriage', Philips critiques both the suitor addressed in her
poem and the masculine pride of Donnean verse by contemptuously comparing her addressee's desire to confine a woman in marriage with an attempt to
monopolise the sun:

> First make the Sun in private shine,
> And bid the World adieu,
> That so he may his beams confine
> In complement to you.
>   (lines 9–12)[30]

One of the richest, yet comparatively underappreciated genres in which mid-
century literary expression fashioned alternative domains to public life was
that of poems and songs whose setting is a drinking party often modelled
upon the classical symposium. In symposiastic poems and songs, Cavalier poets celebrated a largely homosocial pleasure – convivial drinking. The Greek
poet Anacreon and the 'Anacreontics' ascribed to him at this period advocated drunken contentment as an escape from anxiety about social standing,
ageing and death. The Roman poet Horace places Anacreontic themes in a
larger context by calling for either moderate drinking or brief but intense indulgence as decorous responses in specified contexts. Together, Anacreontic
and Horatian symposiastic poetry appealed to Royalists deprived of political
power who were eager to license means of pleasurable escape and to mock

29 Philips, *Poems*, pp. 21, 76, 22, 100, 21, 82–5.
30 *Ibid.*, pp. 38, 155; John Donne, *The Complete English Poems*, ed. A. J. Smith (Harmondsworth:
     Penguin, 1971), pp. 85, 81.

Puritan sentiments and Interregnum legislation against drunkenness and alehouses.[31]

Herrick's drinking poetry escapes a harsh present by imaginatively recreating antique festivity. Alone or with fellow revellers, a tipsy Herrick communes with Anacreon, Horace and other ancient poets in 'A Lyrick to Mirth', 'To live merrily, and to trust to Good Verses' and 'An Ode to Sir Clipsbie Crew'. Imitating the *Anacreontea* in 'On himselfe' Herrick declares himself unafraid of 'Earthly Powers', wanting only 'crowns of flowers' and to be with 'Wine and Oile besmear'd' (lines 1–2, 4). 'Wine and Oile' sacralises a Horatian formula for symposiastic luxury ('vina et unguenta', *Ode* 2.3.13) by also evoking a Biblical synecdoche for God's blessings (Deuteronomy 7:13, Psalm 104:15). The rose crown betokens the Royalist Herrick's wish to be a king himself – of his own symposiastic realm. Ordering up a rose crown and an expensive Roman wine reserved for special occasions in Horace (*Ode* 1.20.9, *Epode* 9.1), Herrick's 'A Frolick' exchanges the realities of an English tavern for an imagined world of luxury where he reigns with drunken abandon:

> Bring me my Rose-buds, Drawer come;
> So, while I sit thus crown'd;
> Ile drink the aged *Cecubum*,
> Until the roofe turne round.[32]

Like Jonson and many Cavalier poets, Herrick sometimes distinguishes his own elite wine-drinking, associated with classical culture and poetic inspiration, from the commoners' (sometimes grotesque and comic) consumption of beer and ale. 'The Hock-Cart', Herrick's most famous poem on country festivities, opens with the summons, 'Come Sons of Summer, by whose toile, / We are the Lords of Wine and Oile' – thus grounding the elite's symposiastic (and scriptural) luxury in labourers' seasonal toil. Inviting Mildmay Fane's labourers to celebrate the harvest home, Herrick notes they have no 'Wine' but bids them 'freely drink' 'stout Beere' (lines 36–8) with healths to their lord and their tools – that is, to their servitude. Herrick qualifies his claim that beer 'drowns all care' (line 37) with a reminder that the festival's brief pleasures are 'like raine, / Not sent ye for to drowne your paine, / But for to make it spring againe' (lines 53–5). Social difference, embodied in distinctive regimes of pleasure (and pain or its absence), is naturalised as being akin to weather.[33]

31 For more extensive discussion of Royalist drinking poetry, see Scodel, *Excess and the Mean*, chapters 7–8; see also Lois Potter, *Secret Rites and Secret Writing: Royalist Literature, 1641–1660* (Cambridge University Press, 1989), pp. 140–2, 147–8.

32 Herrick, *Poetry*, pp. 55–6, 113–15, 264, 95, 277.   33 *Ibid.*, pp. 140–2.

While some Royalist poets associated beer and ale with low-class Parliamentarians (and mocked Cromwell as a besotted brewer's son), Herrick provides a more sympathetic portrait of lower-class drinking by associating it with
Anacreontic contentment. Sometimes he does so as a patronising outsider, as
when he apostrophises countryfolk 'Drencht in Ale, or drown'd in Beere' as
'Happy Rusticks, best content / With the cheapest Merriment' ('The Wake',
lines 20-2); but he also ventriloquises the alehouse's drunken contentment in
'The Coblers Catch', 'A Hymne to Bacchus' and 'The Tinkers Song'. The latter's
dimeter lines underscore an admirable contentment with 'little cost' (line 14)
that resembles Herrick's own cult of the 'little', especially since Herrick himself can claim contentment with humble 'North-downe Ale' ('A Hymne, to the
Lares', line 10).[34]

Lovelace's drinking poetry in Lucasta is more topically located within Royalist subcommunities. He celebrates heavy drinking as solace first for Charles I's
soldiers smarting over the ignominious peace with the Scots in 1639 ('Sonnet.
To Generall Goring, after the pacification at Berwicke'), then for Royalist prisoners ('The Vintage to the Dungeon', 'To ALTHEA, From Prison') and finally
for defeated Royalist companions ('The Grasse-hopper. To my Noble Friend,
Mr CHARLES COTTON'). 'To ALTHEA', which hymns the 'Libertie' (line 16)
of inebriation, modifies Horatian symposiastic tropes to praise heavy drinking:
echoing Horace's call for garlands and wine to dispel cares (Ode 2.11), Lovelace
rejects Horace's call for the tempering of wine with water (lines 18-20) by
celebrating 'flowing Cups' without 'allaying Thames' (lines 9-10).[35]

Lovelace's masterpiece, 'The Grasse-hopper', treats drunkenness more com-
plexly as an appropriate response to bleak times.[36] Lovelace draws on an
Anacreontic poem addressing a cicada or grasshopper as lord of the earth and
happy as a king. The Anacreontic poet celebrates this creature, satisfied on
dew, for effortlessly embodying the carefree life that the symposiast must seek
through drunkenness. By contrast, Lovelace's first five stanzas simultaneously
celebrate the 'Drunke' (line 3) grasshopper for its victory over melancholy and
mourn and mock him as a 'verdant foole' unaware that he would turn to 'green
Ice' (line 17). Though Lovelace is too loyal and tactful to criticise his King directly, the Anacreontic subtext permits the English grasshopper to emblematise

34 Ibid., pp. 337, 291, 342, 422, 310.
35 Lovelace, Poems, pp. 81-2, 46, 78-9, 38-40.
36 Ibid., pp. 38-40. See Julia Martindale, 'The Best Master of Virtue and Wisdom: The Horace
   of Ben Jonson and his Heirs', in Horace Made New: Horatian Influences on British Writing
   from the Renaissance to the Twentieth Century, ed. Charles Martindale and David Hopkins
   (Cambridge University Press, 1993), pp. 73-5; and Earl Miner, The Cavalier Mode from
   Jonson to Cotton (Princeton University Press, 1971), pp. 286-95.

monarchy – the deposed Charles I and perhaps, more generally, the defeated Royalists, who enjoyed Charles's reign without realising its vulnerability. Lovelace's claim that he and his symposiastic companion Charles Cotton (the elder) should 'lay in' and 'poize' an 'o'reflowing glasse' against the 'Winter' and 'Raine' (lines 19–20) evokes the Aesopian fable of the improvident cicada and prudent ant. Unlike the grasshopper-king's heedless drinking, Lovelace implies, the poet and his symposiastic companion's heavy carousing is a prudent, considered reaction to wintry times, i.e., a harsh political climate.

Lovelace's retreat to wine, fire and friendship recalls the symposiastic Horace's decorous response to the seasons, particularly *Ode* 1.9. But Lovelace moves farther inward. The 'Genuine Summer in each others breast' (line 22) and the two friends' 'sacred harthes' (hearths/hearts) (line 25) replace Horace's literal fire. The English poet is more hyperbolic and solipsistic regarding his power over external circumstances: the friends will 'whip' and 'strip' darkness to create 'everlasting' day (lines 33–6). Lovelace's hyperboles are partially offset, however, by the sense that they arise from fragile bravado. Against the 'usurping' of December's 'Raigne' (line 30), an allusion to the Parliamentary suppression of traditional Christmas celebrations and to the defeat of the Caroline monarch, the two friends pit 'showers' of wine. December's cry 'he hath his Crowne againe!' (line 32) relies upon an implicit pun. To 'crown' a glass is 'to fill to overflowing' (*OED* definition 8). December has his 'Crowne' again – but only among the drinkers' 'o'erflowing' glasses. (Compare Alexander Brome's drinking song of 1648, 'The New-Courtier': 'Since we have no King let the goblet be crown'd: / Our Monarchy thus we'l recover' (lines 4–5).[37]) Lovelace's monarchic triumphalism is knowingly fictive.

After such drunken bravura, the final stanza rehearses sober Stoic commonplaces that the two friends are 'richer than untempted Kings' in their self-sufficiency while the 'Lord of all what Seas embrace' who 'wants himselfe, is poore indeed' (lines 37–40). The self-sufficient, prudent friends contrast with the foolish grasshopper-king Charles I, monarch of sea-girt Britain who failed to realise that the true kingdom is within. The stanza's opening 'Thus' (line 37) presents the final stanza's Stoic wisdom as arising from Lovelace's vision of future drunken revels. The tonal shift to Stoic moralising suggests that the poet need only imagine the high of intoxication to secure his present sober contentment. While the grasshopper lived in a drunken present without

37 Alexander Brome, *Poems*, ed. Roman R. Dubinski, 2 vols. (University of Toronto Press, 1982), 1:128.

regard for his future, the prudent poet contemplates (and manipulates) past, present and future to create his own equanimity.

Such poise is unusual, however. Drinking poetry becomes both more escapist and more equivocal as Royalist poets lose a sense of ethically viable options. Thomas Stanley, whose original poems are elegant variations on Cavalier conventions, was an accomplished verse translator of both classical authors and early modern continental poets. He also wrote a history of philosophy indebted to Diogenes Laertius. During the late 1640s, Stanley's London home became a centre for Royalist authors, including the playwright–poet James Shirley, the minor poets William Hammond and Edward Sherburne, and possibly Herrick and Lovelace; this seems to have been a Royalist secret society with intellectual ambitions. Perhaps Stanley's greatest translation, his *Anacreontea* (1651) is polished and generally faithful; its major change is to turn homosexual into heterosexual love while reviving a simpler past of erotic and symposiastic joy. Stanley's notes hint at Interregnum connotations by glossing the grasshopper ode with a passage from Philostratus in which a persecuted philosopher contrasts the 'happinesse' of the freely singing insects with the 'misery' of those like himself who cannot even 'whisper' their 'thoughts'. The grasshopper becomes a synecdoche for the Anacreontic world, imagined as a poetic heterocosm without the oppression to which Stanley himself was subject. Yet the ambivalent Stanley can criticise Anacreontic 'Luxury' and drunkenness.[38]

Abraham Cowley's more freely paraphrased, erotic and symposiastic 'Anacreontiques' (1656), prepared for publication while the poet was under arrest as a Royalist spy, both heighten and critique the escapist excess of the genre. Notoriously submitting to the military victors in the preface to this volume, Cowley begins his Anacreontics with a farewell to 'mighty' (and controversial) poetry on '*Heroes*' and '*Kings*'. His version of the grasshopper ode praises the insect for escaping from all cares in a drunken revelry unbroken until death. Unlike the Anacreontic grasshopper, who drinks plain dew and dies peacefully without suffering old age, Cowley's (recalling Lovelace's) drinks the dew's '*Wine*' and dies '*Sated*'. While the Anacreontic grasshopper only sings like a king, Cowley's drunken creature (with a glance at Charles I's fate) is 'Happier then the happiest King!' The poem celebrates never having to wake to sober reality. Yet the final, original elegy on Anacreon provides a palinode: Cowley's mouthpiece Cupid praises Anacreon for spurning 'Bus'iness, Honor, Title, State' for love but condemns Bacchus for the poet's death. Cowley thus defends the erotic escapism but distances himself from the drunken excess of his Anacreontic imitations. He further 'frames' such escapism in the 1656

---

38 Thomas Stanley, *Anacreon, Bion, Moschus* (London, 1651), pp. 107, 85, 87.

volume by placing his Anacreontics before his *Pindaric Odes* and *Davideis*, which are public, heroic works with oblique but insistent topicality.[39]

In other symposiastic poetry of the period a deliberate coarseness intrudes, expressing mounting despair among Royalists that they could do more than survive, however ignobly. Lovelace's 'A loose Saraband', published posthumously in 1659–60, rejects 'Honour' (line 42) for drinking and lovemaking; claiming that 'all the World ... staggers, / More ugly drunk then we', the speaker declares himself only slightly superior to the 'ugly' drunken world drowned in its own 'blood' (lines 25–6, 28). Lovelace's final 'Leave me but Love and Sherry' (line 48) reduces the proud Stoicism that concluded 'The Grasshopper' to bargain-basement Anacreontism.[40]

Brome and Charles Cotton exemplify the coarser mode. In poems spanning the crisis years of the 1640s and 1650s, Brome sometimes treats drinking as defiant loyalty to the Royalist cause, but his most interesting compositions oppose safe inebriation to foolhardy opposition. '*Mirth*. Out of Anacreon' adds to its ancient models an attack upon devisers of 'plots' (line 3) and upon the 'valiant' (line 11) as reckless fools. In 'The Safety' (circa 1648) Brome claims not to care who wins the war; professing contentment with 'little', Brome desires only that 'Canary be cheaper' (lines 26–8). Yet Brome also exposes such contentment's ignobility by claiming 'he that creeps low, lives safe' (line 17). While proclaiming that wine fits men for 'action' (line 8), Cotton's 'Ode', published in a song book of 1659, similarly concludes by settling for raffish hedonism: 'Let me have sack, tobacco store, / A drunken friend, a little wh – re, / Provided, I will ask no more' (lines 40–2). The request for a 'little whore' followed by (and rhymed with) 'no more' brazenly proposes a petite prostitute as an example of virtuous contentment with 'little'. In the posthumous version of 1689, which probably reflects Cotton's original (but, before the Restoration, dangerous-to-publish) wit, 'Provided' reads '*Protector*': asking Cromwell to sanction his modest desires, Cotton juxtaposes and rhymes within an enjambed phrase the words 'wh–re' / 'Protector' to besmirch Cromwell with the poet's own wenching. Effrontery substitutes for 'action'.[41]

Brome and Cotton go beyond their classical models in associating drunkenness not simply with the soothing of worrisome thoughts but with the rejection of thought as such: both contrast (and rhyme) 'drinking' with 'thinking'.[42]

39 Abraham Cowley, *Poems*, ed. A. R. Waller (Cambridge University Press, 1905), pp. 50, 57, 60.
40 Lovelace, *Poems*, pp. 139–41.
41 Brome, *Poems*, 1:138, 129–30; John Gamble, *Ayres and Dialogues ... The Second Book* (London, 1659), p. 47; Charles Cotton, *Poems*, ed. John Beresford (London: Richard Cobden-Sanderson, 1923), pp. 358–9.
42 Brome, *Poems*, 1:110, 125; Cotton, *Poems*, pp. 354, 355.

Cotton's 'Ode' condemns the very poetry he writes: 'Come, let us drink away the time, / A pox upon this pelting rhyme! / . . . / Odes, Sonnets, and such little toys' (lines 1–2, 5).[43] Brome's and Cotton's willed oblivion may be read against their contemporaneous elegies on Charles I and those they idealised as Royalist martyrs, which express the guilt of non-heroic survivors.[44]

Diverse publications sought to keep up gentry spirits in hard times, partly by reaffirming connections to a courtly past. Prefaced with commendatory Cavalier poems, such posthumous publications as Beaumont and Fletcher's *Comedies and Tragedies* (1647) and William Cartwright's *Poems* (1651) commemorated and reaffirmed earlier Stuart literary culture. Song books like John Hilton's *Catch that Catch Can* (1650) and John Playford's *Select Musicall Ayres* (1652) provided recreation with songs, old and new, of conviviality, love and drink. Interregnum verse anthologies implied a contestatory stance by including 'wit' or 'drollery' in their titles. *Witts Recreations*, first published in 1640 and expanded during the Interregnum, collects much early seventeenth-century comic verse, such as humorous epitaphs upon the (increasingly threatening) lower orders (whom the anthology put back in their place).[45] *Choyce Drollery: Songs & Sonnets* (1656), banned by Parliament, and *Parnassus Biceps* (1656), a selection from university 'Wits' which protested Puritan interference with the universities, also recycled early Stuart verse along with some explicitly topical poems like the defiant song of an imprisoned Royalist.[46] Such volumes as *Sportive Wit* (1656), presented as the product of 'a Club of sparkling Wits', as well as *Musarum Deliciae* (1655) and the provocatively titled *Wit Restor'd* (1658), both edited by John Mennes and James Smith (and containing much of their own verse), twitted the Protectorate regime's Puritan highmindedness with insouciant mockery and unabashed frankness about the body's needs and appetites. These anthologies included cynical drinking songs (Brome's were a favourite), bawdy erotic poetry and scatological humour; Stuart courtly verse forms and conventions mingled with popular ballad rhythms and diction. Mennes and Smith specialised in verse epistles on friendship that distantly recalled Jonson but expressed the Royalist predicament with comic bravado in jaunty, metrically careless couplets.[47]

---

43 Cotton, *Poems*, p. 358.
44 See Brome, *Poems* 1:294–9; Cotton, *Poems*, pp. 240–1, 281–3.
45 See Scodel, *English Epitaph*, pp. 160–2.
46 *Choyce Drollery: Songs & Sonnets* (1656), ed. J. Woodfall Ebsworth (Boston, Lincolnshire, 1876); Ab[raham] White (ed.), *Parnassus Biceps or Several Choice Pieces of Poetry* (1656), ed. G. Thorn Drury (London: Etchells and Macdonald, 1927), pp. 107–10.
47 See John Mennes and James Smith (eds.), *Musarum Deliciae* (1655) and *Wit Restor'd* (1658), rpt with intro. Tim Raylor (Delmar, NY: Scholars' Facsimiles & Reprints, 1985); and Timothy

On a self-consciously more dignified plane, in two sonnets of the mid-1650s, 'Lawrence of virtuous father...' and 'Cyriack, whose grandsire...', John Milton captures a distinctively Horatian note in portraying companionable festivity as a restorative rather than a rejection of social responsibilities.[48] Milton contests the Cavaliers' appropriation of convivial poetry by presenting a version of pleasure that can complement rather than affront religious and political reformation. Foregrounding Horatian motifs largely ignored by Cavalier contemporaries, Milton sets ideal recreational moments within a larger order of providential history by combining scriptural echoes with a Horatian-style address to his young invitees in terms of their ancestry, the public-spirited lineage whose values they must uphold. Milton's justification for winter relaxation in 'Lawrence' – the spring will reclothe 'lily and rose, that neither sowed nor spun' (line 8) – presents convivial pleasure as both Horatian deference to the season and, recalling Matthew 6:26–30, trust in Providence. The 'Cyriack' sonnet's final reproach to him who 'with superfluous burden loads the day, / And when God sends a cheerful hour, refrains' (lines 13–14) defends pleasure not only by invoking Christian liberty (recalling Matthew 11:30) but also by echoing Horace's advice to accept 'the gifts of the present hour' (*Ode* 3.8.27), counsel oft forgotten in Cavalier celebrations of endless drinking. Milton's claim that 'For other things mild heaven a time ordains' (line 11) similarly recalls and Christianises Horace's call to enjoy the present moment by entrusting 'other things' (*cetera*) to the gods (*Ode* 1.9.9).

Yet Milton also distances himself from Horatian motifs congenial to Cavalier contemporaries. While Horace and the Cavaliers celebrated wine-drinking parties, Milton implicitly alludes to early modern distinctions between temperate mealtime drinking and intemperate imbibing at other times by inviting Lawrence to drink wine alongside a 'neat repast, light and choice' (line 9). While Milton's early verse portrayed Horace as 'drenched' (*madens*) in wine (*Elegia Sexta*, line 27)[49] and Herrick celebrates rustics 'Drenched in Ale', Milton bids Cyriack 'deep thoughts ... drench / In [innocent] mirth' (lines 5–6); the enjambment elicits, only to reject, the prospect of Horatian–Cavalier inebriation. The 'Lawrence' sonnet ends with a gnomic distillation of Milton's moderate – and anti-Horatian – ethos: 'He who of those delights can judge, and spare /

Raylor, *Cavaliers, Clubs, and Literary Culture: Sir John Mennes, James Smith, and the Order of the Fancy* (Cranbury, NJ, and London: Associated University Presses, 1994).

48 John Milton, *Complete Shorter Poems*, ed. John Carey, 2nd edn (London and New York: Longman, 1997), pp. 344–6. See John H. Finley, 'Milton and Horace: A Study of Milton's Sonnets', *Harvard Studies in Classical Philology* 48 (1937), 63–7; and Niall Rudd, 'Milton, Sonnet xx. An Avoidable Controversy', *Hermathena* 158 (1995), 109–16.

49 Milton, *Shorter Poems*, p. 118.

To interpose them oft, is not unwise'. Critics have disagreed about whether 'spare' means 'refrain' or 'afford (time)', but the former is more syntactically and contextually plausible. Milton imagines 'sometimes' (line 3) enjoying a refined meal, but praises a 'he' who displays his temperance by refraining from such enjoyment 'oft', a self-restraint all the more laudable when one knows how enjoyable such a convivium truly is. Milton thus not only captures the moderating spirit of the aphorism he echoes from the grammar-school compendium, the *Disticha Catonis* – 'Interpose *from time to time* [*interdum*] joys among your cares' – but also rejects Horatian partying 'often' (*Odes* 2.7.6, 3.21.12). Milton's call to 'spare' inverts a fundamental symposiastic value, the reveller's abandon: Horace bids revellers not 'spare' (*parce[re]*) (*Odes* 2.7.20; 3.19.21-2), and numerous Cavalier drinking poems exhort carousers (like this 1656 song) 'Drinke and doe not spare'.[50] Rejecting the Horatian–Cavalier notion that unrestraint has its place in the full life, Milton's final emphasis on moral wisdom contrasts with the conclusion of a Horatian ode that encourages a friend to temper wisdom with 'brief' symposiastic 'folly' since 'it is sweet to be unwise [*desipere*] in season' (*Ode* 4.12.27-8). Such pleasurable unwisdom, the Horatian 'harmlesse follie of the time' of Herrick's 'Corinna's going a Maying' (line 58), was for Milton an aberration of the times.

While Cavaliers formed clubs of wit and conviviality, the universities came into their own during this period as centres for more serious intellectual gatherings. The Cambridge Platonists – principally Benjamin Whichcote, Henry More, John Smith, Ralph Cudworth – were associated (except for More) with Emmanuel College. They sought philosophical, primarily Neoplatonic, foundations for Christian faith. Promoting an ecumenical, eirenic church based on fundamentals, they, like the Puritans, opposed Laudian ritualism. They rejected Calvinist predestinarianism, however, and proclaimed the human capacity for divinisation through right reason, the image of God.[51] Overriding the sense of separate private and public domains articulated in so much retirement and symposiastic poetry, the Cambridge Platonists blur the distinction between the contemplative and active life. In discourses published posthumously in 1660, Smith celebrates the true Christian as the highest version of 'Contemplative man'. Yet the Platonists insist that man's union with God expresses itself in pious action. Smith contrasts the Christian, who imitates divine goodness and is 'full of activity', with the Stoic, 'confined' within his 'private ... cell'. In a

---

50 *Choyce Drollery*, p. 42.
51 See H. R. McAdoo, *The Spirit of Anglicanism: A Survey of Anglican Theological Method in the Seventeenth Century* (London: Black, 1965), pp. 81-155.

1647 sermon to the House of Commons, Cudworth cites Plotinus on divine goodness to define the Christian as one who knows Christ by keeping His commandments.[52]

During the Civil War period More, the most prolific of the group, published didactic verse – *Psychodia Platonica* (1642), *Democritus Platonissans* (1646), *Philosophical Poems* (1647) – before turning to argumentative prose (*An Antidote against Atheism* (1653), *Conjectura Cabbalistica* (1653), *Enthusiasmus Triumphatus* (1656), *The Immortality of the Soul* (1659)). More's lengthy poem *Psychozoia* (1642, revised 1647) expounds the soul's relation to God in largely Plotinian terms, but includes along the way some lively satiric portraits of Calvinists and Laudians. Seeking an authoritative public voice as a poet, More follows Spenser in his archaic diction, verse form and allegory. Professing concern above all for matter, however, More exchanges Spenserian euphony for metrical roughness and technical philosophical coinages (e.g., the currently voguish 'Alterity'). *Cupid's Conflict* deploys pastoral dialogue to contrast sensual with heavenly love; both embrace nature, but the former 'glut[s]' the soul with 'sense' until the soul 'retire[s]' into itself (lines 37, 41) – a theme more playfully taken up in Marvell's 'Garden' – while the latter 'hug[s]' in 'close embrace' the 'works of God', the 'vast Universe' (lines 135, 139–40). More's generic experiments bespeak his didactic anxieties; much of *Cupid's Conflict* worries, revealingly, whether the spiritual song of a 'solitarie' will find a receptive audience (line 421).[53] In his more intimate but characteristically high-minded correspondence with the learned, philosophically inclined Anne, Viscountess Conway, More applies philosophical and religious remedies for their bodily and mental pains (she was an invalid; both were melancholic). The celibate More, who declares himself 'but an *Aggregate* of my friends', finds passionate friendship (as Philips does) outside conventional homosocial parameters; though ever respectful of Conway's rank, he declares her his greatest friend, their virtuous friendship his highest joy.[54]

During the 1640s and 1650s another intellectual coterie centred around the tireless Samuel Hartlib, whose inner circle regarded itself as an intellectual

---

52 *The Cambridge Platonists*, ed. C. A. Patrides (London: Edward Arnold, 1969), pp. 143, 195, 177–8, 98.

53 Henry More, *Philosophical Poems*, ed. Geoffrey Bullough (Manchester University Press, 1931), pp. 11, 110, 113, 123.

54 *The Conway Letters: The Correspondence of Anne, Viscountess Conway, Henry More, and their Friends, 1642–1684*, ed. Marjorie Hope Nicolson, rev. Sarah Hutton (Oxford: Clarendon Press, 1992), p. 165.

and spiritual brotherhood dedicated to public service.[55] This group promoted
Baconian knowledge as useful for improving man's material conditions, and
educational reform as central to any Puritan–Parliamentary 'reformation' of
the nation. Education, primarily for elite males but with some attention to
females and the lower orders, should centre on practical science and Scripture-
based piety. In 1642 Hartlib translated the Moravian educational theorist Jan
Amos Comenius (Komensky). Around 1650, Hartlib's close associate John Dury
detailed a curriculum for forming pious men 'fitt... for any employment' in
church and state. Subordinating women to men and the domestic to the public sphere, Dury provided briefer guidelines for producing godly and sensi-
ble 'housewives'. While stressing, in Baconian fashion, 'things' over 'words',
the Hartlib circle expressed their dedication to the public with scriptural–
Protestant flourishes. Attacking the universities' 'retired and unsociable' learning, Dury called for 'true Israelites' (Englishmen) unwilling to 'burie their
Talents' to combat the universities' 'Monkish disposition'. Like Bacon, who
drew upon mercantilist values to figure knowledge's advancement as intellectual commerce, Hartlib and Dury proposed schemes, such as an 'Office of
Address' modelled on a mercantile exchange, for the public 'Trade' of practical
and spiritual knowledge.[56]

Addressed to Hartlib and sharing the Hartlib circle's sense of the centrality
of education to national reformation, Milton's *Of Education* (1644) posits piety
and Baconian knowledge of 'solid things' rather than mere 'words' as goals.
Milton's curriculum, however, is more humanist than Baconian; it relies heavily on classical texts, which also inform Milton's sometimes grand rhetoric. His
early announcement, for example, that he will conduct his reader to the 'hill
side' of true education, 'laborious... at the first ascent' but 'smooth' and 'full of
goodly prospect' at the summit, closely echoes the *Table of Cebes*, a Greek moral
text which Milton later recommends for inspiring young students with 'love
of virtue and true labor'. In 1649, as Parliament considered proposals for educational reform, John Hall, a friend of Hartlib and Milton as well as Royalists
like Lovelace and Stanley (whom he praised and sought to involve in Hartlib's
schemes), wrote a grandiloquent call to Parliament for university reform as
the culmination of the republican reformation and its 'Heroick designes'.

---

55 See Charles Webster, *The Great Instauration: Science, Medicine and Reform, 1626–1660*
(New York: Holmes & Meier, 1975); and Mark Greengrass, Michael Leslie and Timothy
Raylor, eds., *Samuel Hartlib and Universal Reformation: Studies in Intellectual Communication*
(Cambridge University Press, 1994).
56 John Dury, *Reformed School*, pp. 57, 18, and *Reformed Library Keeper*, pp. 10, 28–31,
in *The Reformed School and The Reformed Library Keeper* (1651; rpt, Menston: Scolar,
1972).

Rhetorically indebted to Milton's high style in prose (particularly *Areopagit-ica* (1644)), Hall proposed an educational overhaul along Baconian lines.[57]

Hall engages public issues in other Bacon-inspired prose. His first publication, his 1646 essays, indebted in vision and style to Bacon's essays on court life, only hint at contemporary crisis by anatomising the horrors of civil war in general terms; in 1650 he adapts Baconian strictures against superstitious reverence for antiquity and premature generalisations to argue the republican case against monarchy. Hall's translations of Longinus (1652), who associated rhetorical sublimity with heroic magnanimity and republican freedom, and of Hierocles (1657), a Neoplatonist esteemed by the Cambridge Platonists who grounded virtuous behaviour in self-respect, reveal his politically inflected promotion of human dignity.

A separate group of scientists and mathematicians who intersected with the Hartlib circle centred around John Wallis and John Wilkins. It began meeting about 1645 in London, and around 1649 became a self-designated Oxford 'club', multiplying in numbers and influence. By 1660 the group had gravitated back to London, where it became formally organised as the Royal Society.[58] This association aimed to build a core intellectual solidarity that would benefit society at large. More religiously and politically diverse than Hartlib's circle, members – who included Robert Boyle and William Petty (friends and correspondents of Hartlib), Seth Ward, Robert Hooke and Christopher Wren – took divergent positions on the Interregnum regimes but found commonality in public-spirited scientific pursuits. Written by Ward, with a preface by Wilkins, *Vindiciae Academiarum* (1654) reveals both men's social conservatism and distaste for radical educational reform of Hartlib's sort: defending the universities, the work argued that both Aristotelian deduction and Baconian induction had their proper curricular roles and that intensive focus upon practical sciences was incompatible with the universities' 'comprehensive' mission and their specific task of shaping the elite into 'Rationall and Graceful speakers'. 'Rationall and Graceful' encapsulates a stylistic ideal of this group, whose pursuit of an urbane, persuasive perspicuity – implicitly or explicitly contrasted with polemical excess – helped forge late seventeenth- and eighteenth-century scientific and polite expository prose. A leading Latitudinarian divine (friendly

---

57 John Milton, *Complete Prose Works, vol. 2: 1643–1648*, ed. Ernest Sirluck (New Haven, CT: Yale University Press, 1959), pp. 369, 376; John Hall, *An Humble Motion ... Concerning the Advancement of Learning and Reformation of the Universities* (London, 1649), p. 6. On Hall and Milton, see David Norbrook, *Writing the English Republic: Poetry, Rhetoric and Politics, 1627–1660* (Cambridge University Press, 1998), pp. 212–21.

58 See Webster, *Great Instauration*, pp. 51–7, 153–78; and B. J. Shapiro, *John Wilkins, 1614–1672: An Intellectual Biography* (Berkeley: University of California Press, 1969), pp. 81–147.

with the ecumenical Platonists) as well as a scientist, Wilkins advocated '*plain*' but graceful preaching in his influential, oft-reprinted *Ecclesiastes* (1646), and sober prayer devoid of both 'affectation' and the radical sects' supposed rhetorical 'negligence' in *Discourse concerning . . . Prayer* (1653).[59]

Seeking certainties as well as persuasiveness, members of both Hartlib's circle and the Oxford group additionally sought to construct a universal writing and language with clear references to real 'things' that would advance scientific knowledge and end the verbal disputes that Bacon had condemned. This goal appeared all the more pressing in light of the period's violent disputes over (diversely defined) political and religious terms.[60] Hartlib's associate, the merchant Francis Lodowyck, propounded his schemes in 1647 and 1652. Wilkins examined secret codes and discussed the feasibility of constructing a universal language in *Mercury* (1641); his friend Ward briefly expounded a system in *Vindiciae Academiarum*, which Wilkins in turn expanded in his *Essay toward a Real Character* (1668).

As a member of an intellectual circle of Royalist exiles in Paris that included Cowley and Hobbes, William Davenant adumbrates the ideal of a Baconian philosophical community dedicated to public service while dissociating it from the Puritan–Parliamentary cause. Despite a cumbersome romance plot (set in medieval Lombardy), a quatrain form that impedes narrative momentum and a tendency to syntactic obscurity, Davenant's incomplete epic romance *Gondibert* (1651) vigorously explores the public issues of the 1650s, often with trenchant, epigrammatic wit. In his preface, Davenant attacks both excessive ambition for leading to political faction, and retired 'contentedness' for excluding the virtuous from power. Yet with topical relevance for defeated Royalists, the poem depicts retirement's attractions by exploiting, like Lovelace, the motif of the courtier-soldier's amorous pastoral sojourn. Falling in love with the polymath Astragon's daughter and consequently scorning the crown he could attain by marriage, the eponymous hero Gondibert prefers his beloved's pastoral 'shade' to 'shining Thrones' and condemns the 'lust of Pow'r' that corrupts even 'wisest Senates' (such as England's Parliament!) (Book 2, canto 8, stanzas 31, 46). Davenant undermines the distinction between retirement and public service,

59 [Seth Ward,] *Vindiciae Academiarum* (1654), p. 50, rpt in *Science and Education in the Seventeenth Century: The Webster–Ward Debate*, ed. Allen Debus (London: Macdonald; New York: American Elsevier, 1970), p. 244; John Wilkins, *Ecclesiastes, or A Discourse concerning the Gift of Prayer* (London, 1646), p. 105, and *Discourse concerning . . . Prayer* (London, 1653), p. 48.
60 See Vivian Salmon, *The Study of Language in Seventeenth-Century England*, rev. edn (Amsterdam: Benjamins, 1988), pp. 129–90; and M. M. Slaughter, *Universal Languages and Scientific Taxonomy in the Seventeenth Century* (Cambridge University Press, 1982), pp. 97–140.

however, by depicting Astragon as presiding over an intellectual institute committed to mastering both the natural and the sociopolitical worlds. His library contains ethicopolitical manuals, teaching how 'Law' must suppress the common people's 'lusts' (Book 2, canto 5, stanza 45). Davenant's completed epic presumably would have shown Gondibert reconciling amorous retirement and political duty, partly encouraged by the public-spiritedness of the 'retired' Astragon.[61]

The Royalist physician Thomas Browne also mixes retired and Baconian values. Inspired by Bacon's call for a catalogue of intellectual errors to advance learning, Browne's encyclopedic *Pseudodoxia Epidemica* (1650) marshals 'reason', 'experience' and a cautious approach to authorities to contend with the credulities and misjudgements that have beset fallen humankind. Addressing the reasonable few, Browne ascribes 'common errors' mainly to ignorant common folks but also to the elite who succumb to 'vulgaritie'.[62] In this most impersonal of his major works, Browne casts himself as part of a collective enterprise, willing that his text be superseded. Yet the work exemplifies his humanist belief that men of special talents like himself must make distinctive public contributions because 'a man should be... individuall'.[63]

Published together, Browne's *Hydriotaphia, or Urne-Buriall* and *The Garden of Cyrus* (1658) combine learned treatise, personal essay and meditation. *Hydriotaphia* proceeds from an antiquarian examination of recently discovered burial urns (which Browne plausibly but wrongly identifies as Roman) and disquisition on the variety of funerary practices to a religio-philosophical meditation upon humanity's vain attempts to escape mortality. As antiquarian, Browne resembles such Royalist contemporaries as William Dugdale, author of *The Antiquities of Warwickshire* (1656) and *The History of St Paul's* (1658), and Thomas Fuller, author of the *Church History of Britain* (1655), who withdrew from the present and rebuked its zealotry through respectful recovery of the British past.[64] Yet Browne redirects his focus from retrospect to a prospect on endtime, praising 'pious spirits' who recognise the vainglory of earthly monuments because they expect the Second Coming. Revealing his distaste for the Interregnum public realm, Browne associates Christian piety with retired

61 William Davenant, *Gondibert*, ed. David F. Gladish (Oxford: Clarendon Press, 1971), pp. 13, 183, 185, 156.
62 Thomas Browne, *Pseudodoxia Epidemica*, ed. Robin Robins, 2 vols. (Oxford: Clarendon Press, 1981), 1:21.
63 *Ibid.*, 1:4, 31.
64 See Graham Parry, *The Trophies of Time: English Antiquarians of the Seventeenth Century* (Oxford University Press, 1995), pp. 249–60.

obscurity: 'To be namelesse in worthy deeds exceeds an infamous history'; 'Happy are they whom privacy makes innocent'.[65] With lengthy learned 'excursions' outside its ostensible subject, *The Garden of Cyrus* celebrates gardens shaped in a 'quincunx' pattern associated with number mysticism. *The Garden* responds to its companion by focusing on life rather than death and Resurrection and by celebrating a more joyous, playful retirement of 'Garden delights' and the speculative 'Problemes' that Browne 'delight[s]' to pose to his reader and himself.[66]

While remaining assured of the essentials for happiness and salvation, Browne luxuriates in speculation for its own sake – he favours 'probably', 'perhaps' and unanswerable questions (sometimes advanced with coy *praeteritio*, the rhetorical figure of passing over a subject while calling attention to it). His protean style combines lengthy sentences loosely connected by parataxis, evoking his mental explorations, and aphorisms (such as those on virtuous obscurity) declaring his certainties. Presenting himself as both a cosmopolitan heir of classical culture and a patriotic lover of his native tongue, Browne powerfully juxtaposes grandiloquent Latinate terms with plain English monosyllables, as when *Hydriotaphia* describes the Christian looking forward to 'annihilation, extasis, exolution, liquefaction, transformation, and kisse of the Spouse'.[67]

A more ebullient mingling of the learned and popular enlivens the works of the Scotsman Thomas Urquhart, whose Englishing of Rabelais (1653) is the period's most successful translation of fiction. Urquhart deftly renders Rabelais's linguistic play – extravagant panegyric and invective; imaginary languages; lists of nouns, verbs or adjectives conveying the richness of life and of learning; high-spirited mixtures of arcane coinages and the demotic, sometimes obscene. Urquhart can even outdo Rabelais with longer lists of derogatory or commendatory epithets. Urquhart suffered imprisonment and financial ruin for siding with the King and against Scottish Presbyterianism. Energised by his likemindedness with his original, he expertly conveys the Frenchman's exuberant vision of pleasure based on Christian freedom and on drinking as a festive rite as well as his attacks on religious hypocrisy, which chimed with Urquhart's detestation of Presbyterian rigour.

Urquhart's original composition, *Ekskubalauron, The Discovery of a Most Exquisite Jewel* (1652), also sports Rabelaisian linguistic inventiveness (its titular

65 Thomas Browne, *Works* ed. Geoffrey Keynes, 4 vols. (University of Chicago Press, 1964), 1:170, 167.
66 *Ibid.*, 1:176, 224.
67 *Ibid.*, 1:170. On Browne's style, see Jonathan F. S. Post, *Sir Thomas Browne* (Boston: Twayne, 1987), pp. 57–68.

coinage, meaning 'gold out of dung', is characteristic). Urquhart relieves a high style – periodic sentences with numerous adjectives and adverbial phrases, aureate doublets and bizarrely learned coinages – with slang, especially in invective, attacking his critics as 'pristinary lobcocks' and 'archaeomanetick coxcombs'. Urquhart petitions Parliament to free him and to return his property as recompense for his universal language scheme. His scheme differs from that of more sober contemporaries in focusing not upon the precise rendering of 'things' but rather upon the language's 'copiousness' and generative capacity, superior to the 'witty compositions' which Urquhart himself produces in his macaronic English.[68]

Ekskubalauron also extensively celebrates Scottish achievements in arms and arts (Urquhart's own points of pride); its centrepiece is the panegyric upon the 'ever-renowned' James Crichton (1560–82), a superlative swordsman, sportsman (the occasion for a Rabelaisian list of sports), debater, mime of all professions (the opportunity for another bravura inventory) and lover. This setpiece celebrates and seeks the comic sublime: Crichton's swordplay arouses spectators' 'ravishment' and his wordplay produces auditors' 'transported, disparpled, and sublimated fancies'. Urquhart's own copious catalogue of Crichton's 'jeers, squibs, flouts, buls, quips, taunts, whims, jests, clinches, gybes, mokes, jerks' similarly seeks to mesmerise. In an uproarious display of textual sexuality, Urquhart uses outlandish coinages and double entendres to describe Crichton's lovemaking: the 'intermutual unlimitedness' of the lovers' arousing 'visuriency' and 'tacturiency' culminate in Crichton's 'luxuriousness to erect a gnomon on her horizontal dyal' and his mistress's 'hirquitaliency at the elevation of the pole of his microcosme'.[69] Obliquity skirts vulgarity, but the linguistic strain also comically conveys lovers' non-linguistic, bodily communication. Urquhart's fanciful genius stands as a final, salutary reminder that authors of the 1640s and 1650s often escape general trends of the period – as many of those discussed here earnestly sought to do.

68 Thomas Urquhart, *The Jewel*, ed. R. D. S. Jack and R. J. Lyall (Edinburgh: Scottish Academic Press, 1983), pp. 71–2, 61, 67.
69 *Ibid.*, pp. 125, 106, 114, 124.

Chapter 26

FROM REVOLUTION TO RESTORATION IN ENGLISH LITERARY CULTURE

JAMES GRANTHAM TURNER

Among Charles II's first political initiatives was an Act of Indemnity and Oblivion, but most recent scholars of the early Restoration have tried to undo both the 'Oblivion' and the 'Uniformity' mandated by the new regime. Literary history no longer separates Milton and Marvell from their context, nor does it confidently proclaim a new 'Age of Dryden' starting in 1660. Sympathetic historians stress the persistence of 'revolutionary' or 'nonconformist' culture under persecution and the continuities in those poets' writing careers; revisionists stress the relative stability of social attitudes before and after the regicide. In this final chapter my task is to bring out connections and continuities with the literary-historical themes and institutions that have shaped the entire volume. Rather than minimising the effect of 1660 or replicating its polarised propaganda, however, I suggest that the epochal changes of the Restoration incorporated and preserved the defeated 'English Revolution' in its memory. My paradigm derives from the Vanity Fair episode in Bunyan's *Pilgrim's Progress*, both a general allegory of the World, the Flesh and the Devil and a precise portrait of the drunken, jeering, conformist culture of the early Restoration, which taunts the austere and disdainful pilgrim for his black clothing and godly dialect, tries to force him into consumerism, and then installs him in a cage at the very centre of the Fairground. That cage preserves the marginalised 'Puritan' at the very centre of the victors' culture, and guarantees some receptiveness, however hostile, to his resurgence. As Dryden reveals during a later crisis, English Royalists were ever ready to see 'the Good Old Cause revived'.

1660: the world turned right side up?

The habit of beginning a new epoch with that ultra-Royalist date 1660 – deeply engrained in modern institutions that teach and publish 'English

Literature' – runs counter to the etymology and ideology of 'Restoration'. Most movements that we would call innovative or revolutionary (like the Protestant urge to regain 'primitive' Christianity or the Baconian 'Instauration' of science) were depicted as a movement backward to a better time. The word 'restoration' itself retained a strong radical connotation right up to the moment that a restored Parliament, from which ex-Royalists were still excluded, voted to invite the return of Charles Stuart, King of Scots (making him in theory an elected monarch, like the King of Poland or the Holy Roman Emperor). Most Britons agreed that the new-old regime of Charles II involved returning to an ancient state, though radicals like Milton identified it as Egyptian bondage rather than British liberty, with power happily shared by King, church and Parliament under the rule of law. Despite all the Royalist propaganda, the old radicalism flared up in incidents like the armed insurrection of Fifth Monarchists under Thomas Venner in 1661 and the 'Bawdy House Riots' of 1668. As we learn from Samuel Pepys's diary – the most vivid and concrete account of the 1660s – fresh revolutions were expected throughout the decade, belying the image created by Royalist poets such as Charles Cotton, who present Restoration England as a unified culture held together by 'One Harmony, one Mirth, one Voice'.[1]

Many aspects of 'Restoration' England, including the repression of religious radicals, had in fact begun by the 1650s. In the middle years of that decade, England had settled down under a quasi-monarchic Protector, who ruled with powers almost as great as those of Charles I in the 1630s (once both leaders dissolved their Parliaments) and with a much more effective army and navy. Cromwell refused the crown but made awkward attempts to revive regal trappings: robes; oil paintings; an appointed Upper House and Privy Council; residence in Whitehall; masques and dynastic wedding ceremonies with verses by Marvell, Waller and Davenant; a full orchestra and 'mixt dancing (a thing heretofore accounted profane)'. Even if these efforts did not convince foreign ambassadors, Cromwell received literary adulation on an epic scale, including Latin verses and the Latin prose *Second Defence* by Milton; English tributes included a collective volume by the 'Oxford Muses' (in which the young John Locke praises the beneficial effect of the Protectorate on merchant shipping) and panegyrics not only by the future opposition MP Andrew Marvell but by

---

1 Pepys, *Diary*, ed. Robert Latham and William Matthews (Berkeley: University of California Press, 1970–83), entries for 7–11 Jan., 1 Dec. 1661; 22 Jan., 25 May, 15 Aug., 26 Oct.–6 Nov. 1662; 1–2 June, 9 Nov. 1663; 5 Aug., 1 Sept. 1665; 19 Oct., 19 Dec. 1666; 14 June 1667; 24–5 Mar. 1668; and notes; Cotton, Epode 'To Alexander Brome', in *Poems*, ed. John Beresford (London: Cobden-Sanderson, 1923), p. 365.

the soon-to-be-fawning Royalists John Dryden and Edmund Waller, a source of embarrassment (and a mine of poetic ideas) for the rest of their lives. The Lord Protector's funeral procession, in which Milton, Marvell and Dryden marched side by side, looked as stately as that of any Grand Duke or Cardinal, and his *crowned* funeral effigy provoked the bitterest criticisms from radicals who had earlier supported him for being 'so zealous to overthrow Images, Pictures, and Idols'.[2]

In the rapid sequence of events between 1642 and 1660 all the institutions that have provided the framework for this *Cambridge History* had been 'turned upside down' or at least subjected to question: court, church and theatre most obviously, but also nation and household. Cromwell's military campaigns strengthened the English nation at the expense of Scotland and Ireland, and after his death even radicals accused the army of making 'England, Scotland, Ireland a chaos, without form and void'. Godly rule changed the concept of the 'nation' as well as its power structure, as we gather from John Eachard's revealing remark about the Restoration: when Charles II heard long speeches full of Biblical allusions to Adam and the Garden of Eden, he must have 'wondered to what *Nation* he was restored' – as if the public display of religiosity had suddenly become un-English. The unrepentant Milton, who had proudly blazoned his Englishness in the Latin defences of the Commonwealth, now feels like an exile, murmuring that 'one's *Patria* is wherever it is well with him'.[3]

Even though many male radicals seemed incapable of applying their levelling ideas to the domestic sphere, enemies of innovation constantly *presented* it as an eruption of disorder in the household and promiscuity in private life. Reacting to the sudden activism of subordinates – 'mechanic' preachers from the servile classes, women preaching and raising petitions – political controversies and demonstrations often imitated rituals of humiliation normally used for domineering wives, cuckolded husbands and lecherous adulterers. But after this ferment or 'chaos' did the world simply turn right side up again? What was 'restored' in 1660, and what had changed utterly? Lords, bishops and church courts certainly came back, along with Gentlemen of the Bedchamber and

2 Contemporaries cited in James A. Winn, 'Theatrical Culture 2: Theatre and Music', in *The Cambridge Companion to English Literature, 1650–1740*, ed. Steven N. Zwicker (Cambridge University Press, 1998), p. 104; David Norbrook, *Writing the English Republic: Poetry, Rhetoric and Politics, 1627–1660* (Cambridge University Press, 1999), p. 380 (381 shows the effigy); Winn, *John Dryden and His World* (New Haven, CT, and London: Yale University Press 1987), p. 80. Locke's poem appears in *Musarum Oxoniensis Elaioforia* (Oxford, 1654), p. 95.

3 Norbrook, *Republic*, p. 408; Eachard, *Some Observations upon the Answer to an Enquiry into the Grounds and Occasions of the Contempt of the Clergy and Religion* (1685), p. 71; Milton, *Complete Prose Works of John Milton*, ed. Don M. Wolfe *et al.*, 8 vols. (New Haven, CT: Yale University Press, 1953–82), 8:4.

Masters of the Revels, Law French, organs and bells, theatres, long hair, Maypoles and Christmas pies; by contrast, nobody tried to revive Star Chamber, Ship Money, feudal tenures or monopolies. The monarchy had been revealed as contingent rather than natural, and it could never be exactly the same again; the royal head, once removed and sewn back, always revealed what Marvell called a 'purple thread' of scar tissue (p. 818 below).

For a brief moment in 1660, former Cromwellians and Puritans might have been forgiven for thinking that a more tolerant era had arrived. Even before Charles II returned (arriving in London on his birthday, 29 May) he proclaimed his support for 'liberty to tender consciences' (Declaration at Breda). Damping down religious conflict was his prime concern, and he even made conciliatory gestures to broaden the national church, offering bishoprics to Presbyterians like Richard Baxter and Edmund Calamy (the 'ec' in Milton's 'Smectymnuus'). The reconciling effect of Charles's Act of Indemnity and Oblivion meant that some of Cromwell's keenest civil servants thrived after the Restoration (like Pepys, who confessed in his diary to having rejoiced at Charles I's execution). One wit remarked that the Act meant Indemnity for his former enemies and Oblivion for his most loyal friends, alluding to Charles's notorious failure to pay out the financial rewards he promised for all favours except sexual ones. Some acts of ferocious judicial revenge took place nevertheless, since named individuals directly responsible for his father's trial and execution were 'exempted': though some (like Edmund Ludlow) escaped to Europe and compiled memoirs of the persecution, and some (like Henry Marten) got away with life imprisonment, many activists were tried and executed for high treason, their blackened heads stuck up on Westminster Hall or London Bridge. The dismembered included Oliver Cromwell himself, whose corpse was unearthed for the ceremony, and several unpopular republicans were also exhumed from Westminster Abbey (among them Thomas May, translator of Lucan's *Pharsalia* and historian of Parliament). Milton, briefly jailed and constantly attacked for his pro-regicide views, could well have been named in this exemption and put to death like his friend Sir Henry Vane; though his prose tracts were burned by the public hangman, Milton's literary friends released him from jail and shielded him from the death penalty. According to the anti-Restoration pamphlet *Mirabilis Annus Secundus, or the Second Part of the Second Years Prodigies* (1662), these executions inspired a gruesome triumphalist humour that further provoked God's wrath against the backsliding nation: 'rejoycing' at the disembowelment of Sir John Barkstead, the Draconian ruler of London under Cromwell, two Royalist revellers actually salvaged his liver from the fire and ate it broiled in a tavern – where divine vengeance struck them with mortal sickness (p. 36).

Restoration legislation also regulated discourse, directly influencing literary culture. Though it lifted the anti-theatrical laws imposed in 1642 – by 'those good people who could more easily dispossess their lawful Sovereign than endure a wanton jest', as Dryden put it – and permitted women actors (to raise the moral tone), the Crown still licensed only two playhouses, closing down the disorderly fringe theatres that had sprung up despite the Commonwealth.[4] Censorship returned with a vengeance (though its effects have been greatly exaggerated), trying to stamp out the clandestine presses that still produced seditious newsbooks like *Mirabilis Annus* and prophecies like Anna Trapnel's immense poem *Voice for the King of Saints*.[5] Manuscript production flourished, for works too heretical, too personal or too licentious to publish in print, the most famous being Milton's *De Doctrina Christiana* (which English secret agents confiscated from the press in Holland) and the burlesque drama *Sodom*. Many important texts of the 1660s and 1670s remained in manuscript for decades or even centuries: the notes of John Aubrey later published as *Brief Lives*; the incomparable diaries of Pepys and Evelyn; the poems of Rochester (and hundreds of other politically or sexually risqué verses); the memoirs of defeated Commonwealthsmen like Ludlow, Baxter and Whitelock and Royalist wives like Anne Halkett and Ann Fanshawe; Clarendon's *Life* and *History of the Great Rebellion*. Lucy Hutchinson left all her works in manuscript – not only her famous memoir of her parliamentary husband, but the first full English translation of Lucretius and an epic-scale Biblical meditation in verse that makes her a true contemporary of Milton and Trapnel.

The new laws extended even to speech acts and vocabulary choice. Under the Act of Oblivion it was actually *illegal* to use 'any name or names, or other words of reproach tending to revive the memory of the late differences or the occasions thereof', though a newly drafted Treason Act equally forbade 'all, writing, printing, or malicious and advised speaking' that envisages 'restraint of the Sovereign' or tends to 'deprive him of his style'. Throughout Charles's reign, government spies picked up obscene slanders from the oral culture of dissent, railing at the King as a whoremonger and a bastard, continuing the

---

4 John Dryden, 'Of Heroick Plays', in *Works*, gen. ed. Edward Niles Hooker, H. T. Swedenberg, Jr, *et al.*, 20 vols. (Berkeley, Los Angeles, London: University of California Press, 1961–2001), 11:9; Jessica Munns, 'Theatrical Culture 1: Politics and Theatre', in *Companion*, ed. Zwicker, p. 83.

5 Surviving only in one mutilated copy without forematter (Bodleian Library, Oxford, shelf-mark S 1.42 Th), the second edition of Trapnel's Fifth Monarchist *Voice* is a folio of almost 1,000 pages (whereas the 1658 version contains some 90 pages in a much smaller format); I therefore propose a post-Restoration date for it, and infer clandestine publication.

Civil War hostility to Henrietta Maria as 'Jezebel' or the 'Whore or Babylon'.[6] Between those who sought to impose some restraint on Charles's more alarming inclinations (to fornication, absolutism and extravagance), those who criticised some aspect of his 'style', and those who pointedly reminded the 'Fanatics' and 'Puritans' of their defeat, virtually the entire population must have broken the law.

1660: panegyrics for the new regime

Propagandists of the Stuart Restoration faced the problem of harnessing the more 'conformable' literary modes to the new aristocratic–loyalist culture. Many of the poets who rushed to build a heroic image of Charles II had performed the same service for Cromwell, and the Protector had already monopolised most of the available heroic tropes (comparison to Augustus, favour of the gods, stern marmoreal grandeur, flourishing Commonwealth at home and military victories abroad). Providential language had likewise been taken over by the godly, and even the most loyal monarchists, who dutifully declared the Restoration God's handiwork, found Charles himself a shallow and unheroic figure. The new King's 'style', however protected by the new Treason Act, never quite matched the office. Clarendon observed that he lacked 'reverence or esteem for antiquity, and did in truth... contemn old orders, forms and institutions'. The age as well as its leader seemed incorrigibly anti-heroic to Clarendon: his often-quoted account of the disastrous effects of the Great Rebellion – when all traditional hierarchy and deference vanished between parents and children, men and women, masters and servants – actually refers to the 1660s, when the King's party dissolved into drunken bickering and Charles indulged his youthful follies instead of uniting the country. As Samuel Butler remarked with his usual perspicuity, 'No Age abounded more with Heroical Poetry' than the Restoration, 'and yet there was never any wherein fewer Heroicall Actions were performed.'[7] Butler's Law posits an inverse relation between celebration and achievement.

6 Legislation cited in Norbrook, *Republic*, p. 1, and Michael Seidel, 'Satire, Lampoon, Libel, Slander', in *Companion*, ed. Zwicker, p. 44. For seditious sexual gossip see Richard L. Greaves, *Deliver Us from Evil: The Radical Underground in Britain, 1660–1663* (Oxford University Press, 1986), e.g. pp. 22–3 (Charles II conceived in adultery with Henry Jermyn, Earl of St Albans), 111.

7 Edward Hyde, Earl of Clarendon, *Selections from The History of the Rebellion and The Life by Himself*, ed. G. Huehns (Oxford, New York, Melbourne: Oxford University Press, 1978), pp. 374–82, 425–6; Butler, *Prose Observations*, ed. Hugh de Quehen (Oxford: Clarendon Press, 1979), p. 175.

Panegyrics and funeral poems on Cromwell constituted both a resource and an embarrassment for the 'forward' young intellectuals evoked in Marvell's 'Horatian Ode', who had indeed 'left their shades' and joined the Protector's service, and who needed to save their necks at the Restoration. A typical contribution to the quasi-monarchic obsequies of Cromwell contains Dryden's *Heroique Stanzas* alongside poems by Thomas Sprat, who became the official historian of the Royal Society, and Edmund Waller, successive panegyrist to Charles I and the Lord Protector. When Charles II asked Waller why he wrote a better panegyric for Cromwell, the answer allegedly came that 'we poets never succeed so well in writing truth as in fiction' – an evasion as dangerous as it was witty, since it could so easily be applied to the new regime. After easing himself back into royal favour Waller revived the topographical genre that he had used to praise Charles I and Inigo Jones, and introduced new kinds of 'Heroical Poetry' like the 'Instructions to a Painter'; Waller's palpably fictive efforts opened a rich vein of satire, culminating in Marvell's splendidly anti-heroic *Last Instructions to a Painter*. Marvell's more passionate 'Poem upon the Death of O. C.' had been dropped from the Cromwell commemorative volume, and significantly Marvell is one of the few poets not to submit a lavish eulogy to Charles. (Two other hold-outs were Milton, who maintained a contemptuous silence on the Stuart Restoration, and George Wither, who addressed the King in an unrepentant prophetic and critical mode, accepting his return as a *de facto* act of conquest that God had mysteriously permitted, but refusing to praise him and warning that the apocalypse would still arrive in 1666, the Year of the Great Beast.) Those who did submit found it easier to turn their coats because they had evolved a panegyric mode – grave, classical, measured, 'Augustan' rather than godly and 'enthusiastic' – that with a little gilding could serve for Charles as well as Oliver. Waller praised his kinsman Cromwell for the kind of non-controversial achievements that even Clarendon could recognise – his greatness, his stabilising effect, his secular power, his imperialist successes in the West Indies and Flanders. Though his reputation as a 'Protector-Poet' put him in some danger, Waller could rapidly whip up an adulation of Charles's absolute power in May 1660, urging him *not* to forgive his 'obnoxious' people too hastily, and recycling many of his Cromwellian tropes – comparisons to ancient empire-builders like Aeneas and Alexander, pathetic fallacies that turn natural features like wheatfields, wind and sea into awestruck, adoring subjects.[8]

---

8 Wither, *Speculum Speculativum* (London, 1660); Waller, *To the King, upon His Majesties Happy Return* (London, 1660), and cf. Norbrook, *Republic*, pp. 426–8.

Dryden presents his 'Heroique' Cromwell as monumental and self-sufficient, his 'Grandeur' derived from Heaven alone. In calm and lofty Gondibert stanzas, the dead dictator is figured as a perfect circle, a sun, an eagle, laureate Caesar, Machiavellian Prince, Alexander, civiliser of Ireland and Scotland (who bless their conqueror), reconciler of warring factions, balancer of power in Europe, leader in the arts of peace as well as war, blender of Love and Majesty. By trimming a few references to the youthful follies of 'rash Monarchs' and the 'sullen' Commons who fade like feeble stars before the Protector's 'Heroique Vertue', Dryden can recycle much of this praise into the open-ended couplets of *Astraea Redux*. The storm at Cromwell's death becomes the sighs of Britain's 'Protecting Genius', and the ensuing calm a sign of divine blessing; a few months later, the same weather can serve as a sinister 'horrid Stillness' betokening God's anger or indifference. The generic shift from state funeral to state triumph requires a May Day drapery of vernal rapture over what is fundamentally the same monument. Charles is naturally the spring thaw, the sun reflected in the water, the bridegroom for whom the entire nation 'groans' with desire. Dryden's sober, controlled verse contrasts with the eclectic profusion of his imagery, which compares Charles to so many legitimising figures that they begin to cancel each other out. As the poem moves on to end with the actual May celebrations, this contradiction of form and content is subsumed into pure emotion. To prepare for a final evocation of the imperial splendour Britain will now enjoy, Dryden recreates the excitement of the spectators as they crowd to gaze on Charles, locating the centre of English Royalism where it still remains, in celebrity hysteria.[9]

If Cowley's 'Ode upon His Majesties Restoration and Return' sounds even lusher than Dryden's *Astraea Redux*, this is because his 'Pindarique' mode reinforces the dithyrambic fervour. Cowley needed extra fireworks to mask his earlier acceptance of Cromwell's *de facto* power and his advice to the Royalists to lay down their pens as well as their swords (a passage that his enemies constantly cited), but his personation of a Restoration 'Priest' and prophet tends to recreate that moment of surrender. Cowley demonises the revolution as the Fall from Eden, melodramatically naming Cromwell and Bradshaw as if he were raising the Great Serpent, thus inadvertently witnessing to their frightening power. The religious interpretation grows more delirious and blasphemous with each new strophe, unwittingly confirming anti-Royalist scepticism. Not content with making Charles I a martyr (soon to be the official Anglican line) and then Christ himself, combining 'suffering Humanity' with 'Power Divine',

9 *Works*, 1:11–16, 22–31.

Cowley turns the young royals into Moses' chosen people crossing the Red Sea and General Monck into Jehovah, bringing light to Chaos. Charles II is equally identified with Christ. Even the ending, when Cowley cheers on the Queen Mother, Monck and Parliament like the spectator of a series of carnival floats, manages to restore some of the 'dread' that has supposedly vanished and to raise new fears of absolutism: the 'Worthies' of the Commons are advised to have durable statues made of themselves, so that they really will be 'the *Long*, the *Endless Parliament*' – a self-memorialisation particularly apt because 'a firmly setled *Peace* / May shortly make your publick labours cease'.[10]

Culture as anarchy: Restoration triumphalism and the 'Sons of Belial'

Though Charles II was clearly ready to show toleration and to defuse the ideological conflicts that had embroiled his country and killed his father, the restored Parliament wanted no such reconciliation. Far from abolishing themselves as Cowley recommended, Parliament soon passed Draconian laws against sects and separatists, the so-called Clarendon Code (after the Chancellor Edward Hyde, Earl of Clarendon, though he did not necessarily support this revenge-driven 'panic legislation'). They made all worship outside the Anglican Church illegal (an act famously enforced in the case of John Bunyan, who chose repeated jail sentences rather than cease preaching), barred members of any other denomination from public office, and lumped together as 'Dissenting' the entire spectrum from dour, disciplined Presbyterians to wild-eyed Quakers, tarring them all with the brush of sedition and regicide. Like loyalists in the 1640s, tainted ministers and university officials were silenced and ejected (the Cambridge Platonist Benjamin Whichcote lost the Vice-Chancellorship of that university, for example). Bishops regained the lands that had been expropriated and profitably sold off. Compulsory church attendance had already been restored by the Protector (in 1657), but now the Episcopalian system was enforced by law, and religious expression forced into a pre-established form of words; the much-hated Book of Common Prayer, now including a liturgy for 'King Charles Martyr' and his 'miraculously' preserved son, had to be accepted

---

10 Cowley, *Poems*, ed. A. R. Waller (Cambridge University Press, 1905), pp. 420–32 (for Cowley's defeatist preface to the 1656 *Davideis*, see p. 820 below). For the star that announced Charles's birth (with parallels to Bethlehem), in panegyrics and in the medal that commemorated the Restoration, see Dryden,*Works*, 1.232–3, and Nicholas Jose, *Ideas of the Restoration in English Literature 1660–71* (Cambridge, MA: Harvard University Press, 1984), p. 39.

in every detail – a compulsion more thorough than anything ordered before 1640. Preaching, still by far the most effective public address system, could only be performed by licensed servants of the state ordained by a bishop, and had to include whatever homiletic propaganda the Crown ordered.

As Chapter 22 shows, conflicts among non-Episcopalians had been furious in the 1640s and 1650s; English radicalism was a coalition of widely differing doctrines and styles, including the sober dialect of the 'Puritan' (a pastiche of the Protestant Bible), the proto-Blakean raptures of the Ranters, and the witty, agnostic republicanism of Henry Marten and Thomas Challoner (vividly brought to life in Aubrey's *Brief Lives*). Restoration repression helped them forget their differences and make common cause for liberty of conscience and the right to resist state coercion in matters of belief, blaming schism on the falsity of enforced unanimity just as Milton had done in the 1640s. In 1672, however, the limits of that liberty and tolerance were rapidly revealed. When Charles unilaterally lifted the restrictions against dissenters in a 'Declaration of Indulgence', the Parliament, the Anglican establishment *and* the oppressed dissenters poured out a stream of denunciation, on the grounds that the measure might benefit that other marginal, demonised figure, the Roman Catholic plotting to overthrow true English liberty. Baxter had rehearsed the same argument in 1660, endorsing the persecution of his own beliefs on the grounds that toleration would 'secure the Liberty of the Papists'.[11] Hatred of Catholicism drove virtually every political agitation and every discussion of toleration, including Milton's last prose work, *Of True Religion* (1673). It is hardly surprising that the elite, in their private opinions, turned away from organised religion entirely and regarded it all as 'priestcraft' and superstition.

The dissenting voice persists in British culture, and may even have been strengthened by temporal, political defeat, but later generations often describe it as purely inward and 'spiritual'. In the 1660s, however, this tradition of pacific containment was not at all self-evident: Venner's rebellion in 1661 revived the spectacle of anti-monarchist violence; regicides were hung, drawn and quartered for a number of years as the secret police rounded them up;

11 Quoted in N. H. Keeble, *The Literary Culture of Nonconformity in Later Seventeenth-Century England* (Leicester University Press, 1987), p. 27, from whom my account of Restoration religion is largely taken; apart from Papists, the one group not accepted into the 'dissenting' fold was Fifth Monarchy, on account of Venner's armed rebellion. The situation in the other kingdoms differed somewhat: the reimposition of episcopacy and Prayer Book was much more deeply resented in Presbyterian Scotland; in Ireland, where no Parliament sat at all during the 'Interregnum' and Cromwellianism never took hold, Restoration laws tried to heal the memory of the 1645 Rebellion by pardoning 'innocent' Catholics (thousands of Certificates of Innocence were dispensed under the relatively moderate rule of Lord Ormonde).

demonstrations like the apprentices' and Bawdy House Riots (with their 'literary' accompaniment of satirical mock-petitions and lampoons) struck terror into the authorities and called out all the forces of military and legal repression. Catastrophic events like the plague of 1665 and the fire that destroyed much of London in 1666 awakened fears of social collapse or insurrection, paranoid blame of foreign and domestic enemies, and primitive supernatural explanations: God was surely punishing his Englishmen for voting back a lewd and profane tyrant like Charles II.

The term 'Restoration culture' generally conjures up something very different from the godliness of Milton and Bunyan, Anna Trapnel and Lucy Hutchinson. Euphoric Royalists (and those who wished to pass as such) conceived the King's return as Carnival defeating the Puritan Lent, the revival of Merry England, the licentious, Dionysian, irreverent reaction against a humourless and vicious theocracy. Historians of the earlier seventeenth century pay increasing attention to popular 'revels' and 'riots' as an expression of political culture, showing that they often constituted a protest against oppression or a rebuke to deviance rather than the innocent 'Sports' that James I and Charles I encouraged as an antidote to Puritanism. The Restoration certainly staged itself as a resurgence of these popular festivities, but even in the pious 1650s government and opposition had exploited them: the punishment of James Nayler for blasphemy in 1656, for example, resembled the charivari or 'rough music' that punished inadequate husbands (the Quaker was seated backwards on a nag to run the gauntlet of derision). In the power vacuum that followed the death of Cromwell, John Tatham's topical farce *The Rump* juxtaposes the Committee of Safety with the female circle of Lady Lambert (a self-proclaimed 'Free Woman'), clamouring to settle new honours and repeal the laws against fornication. Tatham revives the lewd 'Parliament of Ladies' (a favourite theme of the republican Henry Neville) in order to associate activist women with 'unofficial kinds of government, inappropriate kinds of influence, and illusionary forms of power'.[12]

The Restoration depended on outbursts of Royalist sentiment in the popular culture, simultaneously expressed in action and discourse. The first concerted attack on the post-Cromwellian army was launched by an apprentice mob, and the same youth group (traditionally licensed to riot on Shrove Tuesday and to attack unpopular leaders) enforced the new regime through mass assaults

---

12 Tatham, *The Rump* (London, 1661), pp. 24–8, 43; Paula R. Backscheider, *Spectacular Politics: Theatrical Power and Mass Culture in Early Modern England* (Baltimore, MD: Johns Hopkins University Press, 1993), pp. 25, 28.

on Puritans and through publications like *The Out-Cry of the London Prentices for Justice* (1660, a vicious personal attack on the blind Milton). This unleashing of popular festivity could easily shift its meaning or backfire, however. The apprentices' 1660 rising in support of the soldiers' mutiny led to mass arrests, and their 1664 riot against the pillorying of two of their number mobilised the trained bands throughout London. Among the events that led to Clarendon's banishment in 1667, his ostentatious London mansion was 'forced by the women [and] his windows broken'. Women's riots revived a panic fear of their militancy, expressed in direct attacks and in 'porno-political' satire; Fifth Monarchism was particularly associated with insubordinate female libido. Displays of public nudity could represent a Quaker 'sign' of revolutionary protest or an aristocratic 'frolic', like the notorious episode when the poets Sir Charles Sedley and Lord Buckhurst (future Earl of Dorset and Lord Chamberlain of England) stripped naked on the balcony of the Cock Tavern, in Pepys's words 'acting all the postures of lust and buggery that could be imagined'.[13]

This upper-class expropriation of popular 'riot' (in all senses of the word) rapidly passed into fashionable literature, adding an element of raw violence to the Cavalier 'symposiast' pose (see Chapter 25 above). Drunken assaults on prostitutes and constables, or smashing of windows – previously associated with apprentice risings and vigilante protests – acquired an aura of genteel amusement, best exemplified by Sir Frederick Frolick in Sir George Etherege's *The Comical Revenge, or Love in a Tub* (1664). The word 'ranting', applied in the 1650s to those antinomians who declared themselves above the law, now signified the 'frolicks' of a gentleman, expressing ebullient sexual energy rather than religious zeal or class hatred.

When Milton characterised the libertine opponents of his divorce tracts in the 1640s, he used 'the brood of Belial' to mean the very dregs of society 'to whom no liberty is pleasing but unbridled and vagabond lust without pale or partition'. By the time of *Paradise Lost*, however, Milton locates the Sons of Belial among the upper classes, and especially in the newly restored royal entourage. (In contrast, the new Book of Common Prayer calls the 'murderers' of Charles I 'sons of Belial'.) When he describes Belial and his riotous Sons in the epic catalogue of fallen angels Milton slips from the narrative past into the present tense, and transfers the social setting from the lower depths ('vagabond lust') to the highest echelons: 'In Courts and Palaces he also Reigns / And in

13 Pepys, *Diary*, entries for 3 and 12 Feb. 1660, 1 July 1663, 26 Mar. and 26 July 1664 (Quaker nudism); William Riley Parker, *Milton: A Biography* (Oxford: Clarendon Press, 1968), p. 569; Ludlow, cited in Steven C. A. Pincus, *Protestantism and Patriotism: Ideologies and the Making of English Foreign Policy, 1650–1668* (Cambridge University Press, 1996), p. 426.

luxurious Cities' that closely resemble Restoration London.[14] This shift in
the placing of 'Belial' – common throughout the anti-Royalist underground –
identifies social disorder with the oxymoronic conjunction of criminal 'riot'
and courtly arrogance. The rioters of Easter 1668 wondered why they merely
attacked 'the little bawdy-houses and did not go and pull down the great bawdy-
house at White hall' (Pepys, *Diary*, 25 March 1668).

This critique of courtly 'Riot' centres the blame squarely on Charles II
himself. Though James I had been denounced (by Puritans like Lucy
Hutchinson) for encouraging 'bawds' and 'catamites', corrupting the entire
country by 'conformity with the court example', not since Henry VIII had a
monarch openly acknowledged his mistresses and pardoned the 'injury and
outrage' of his courtiers.[15] The promiscuity of the newly restored King (and
his brother James, Duke of York) threw public morality into deep confusion; in
particular, the category of Royal Mistress, lavishly endowed with public funds
and titles, obstructed the attempt to confine illicit sexuality to a nether zone. As
Margaret Cavendish, Duchess of Newcastle, observed of the new generation
of aristocrats, 'the Practise of their Lives' was 'not answerable to the Degree of
their Dignities'; in modern terms 'the Restoration court projected a collective
image of living in ironic and even defiant incompatibility with its inherited
forms of public representation . . . The Court was *both* classical and grotesque,
both regal and foolish, high and low.'[16] The age that invented the 'noble Savage'
– the famous epithet that Dryden coined for his untamed hero Almanzor – also
produced the savage noble.

Alongside the 'Heroic' genres of Royalist panegyric, two kinds of unofficial
literature emanate from this culture of carnivalesque excess. The most characteristic writings of the early Restoration can be classified in two mutually
mirroring categories, which we might call the Voice for the King of Saints
and the Voice for the Sons of Belial. On one side are the 'Puritan' memorials of tribulation, Milton's major poems, Bunyan's spiritual autobiography
Grace Abounding to the Chief of Sinners, Marvell's satires, even Pepys's ebulliently
Royalist and sensual diary, which still records horror at upper-class excess,

---

14 *Complete Prose Works*, 2.225; *Paradise Lost (PL)*, 1.497–505, 4.765–7, 7.26–7, 32 (on the
   'barbarous dissonance' of drunken revellers, a phrase earlier used in *A Mask*, line 550).
   Quotations from Milton's poetry are taken from *John Milton: Complete Poems and Major Prose*,
   ed. Merritt Y. Hughes (New York: Odyssey Press, 1957).
15 Lucy Hutchinson, *Memoirs of the Life of Colonel Hutchinson, with a Fragment of Autobiography*,
   ed. N. H. Keeble (London: Dent, 1995), pp. 63, 67.
16 Margaret Cavendish, *CCXI Sociable Letters* (London, 1664), p. 106; Peter Stallybrass and
   Allon White, *The Poetics and Politics of Transgression* (Ithaca, NY: Cornell University Press
   1986), pp. 101–2.

pain at the mockery of the Puritans, shock at the bawdy talk of wits and actresses, fear of popular dissatisfaction and nostalgia for the solid achievements of Oliver Cromwell. On the other side we can place the inversionary or disorderly genres: the pornographic pamphlet, the mock-petition, the picaresque novel of roguery and the lampoon, obscene personal satire in boisterous verse and wittily ingenious rhyme.

Pornography erupts in the liminal period, after the collapse of 'Puritan' power in a rush of festivity, but before the new state had been fully defined and confirmed. Triumph over the old regime colours salacious gossip-sheets and whore biographies, which compare the brothel to 'our late Commonwealth'. When the courtesan commits herself to 'Nature's Good Old Cause', the phrase links unlimited copulation with anti-Royalism and the political activism of women, as if that were the only 'Cause' natural to them. On the other hand, her partners are not the hypocritical Puritans but the 'lewd Quality', the newly confident Cavaliers and courtiers who 'never yet made conscience to dispense and indulge with their codpiece'; their libertine sexuality lets them ignore the current debate over liberty of conscience and declarations of indulgence, but the sexual metaphor plunges the reader back into these issues. Mock-petitions from the 'poor whores' to the King's Catholic, absolutist mistress sprang up during the 'Bawdy House' insurrection of 1668, infuriating the authorities because the radical underground had dropped its apocalyptic language and adopted the witty, parodic mode of festive culture.[17]

Verse lampoons had been an integral part of festive–aggressive culture for generations – dozens of them mocked the corruptions of James I and the first Duke of Buckingham – but in the Restoration they became altogether more fashionable, sleeker in form and more assuredly outrageous in content. As in the mock-petitions, court ladies are paraded as whores and Lady Castlemaine becomes 'That prerogative Queane', a dense phrase which combines the old pun on quean/queen with a new sense of the complicated relation between political and sexual 'prerogative'. This cultivated disrespect extends to religion too; flippant lampoonists actually do what Marvell feared *Paradise Lost* would do, 'ruin the sacred Truths' of the Bible itself. Butler's *Hudibras* reduces the imaginative search for Paradise to a set of self-evidently absurd questions that only a crack-brained zealot would consider: 'What *Adam* dreamt of when his Bride / Came from the Closet in his side' crunches into two jog-trot lines one of the

17 *The Practical Part of Love* (London, 1660), pp. 43, 44, 73; *The Poor-Whores Petition to the most Splendid, Illustrious, Serene and Eminent Lady of Pleasure the Countess of Castlemayne* (London, 1668); Bodleian Library, Oxford, MS Don. b. 8, fol. 193; Tim Harris, 'The Bawdy House Riots of 1668', *Historical Journal* 29 (1986), 537–56.

most beautiful episodes in Milton's epic, when Adam does indeed recount this dream to Raphael.[18] Butler's mock-epic *Hudibras* (Part I, 1663, Part II, 1664) is the quintessential expression of the festive–aggressive culture. Butler so mastered the comic four-beat couplet that it acquired the name 'Hudibrastic'. The entire poem is a kind of mega-lampoon pinned up over the defeated Puritans, all of whose sins (and more) are summed up in the ridiculous protagonists Sir Hudibras, Ralpho and Sir Sidrophel. The helter-skelter prosody, the crazily improvised imagery and rhyme, the sardonic refusal to take any hierarchy seriously, are all supposed to match the chaos of the revolution, which Butler wants to brand as neither good, nor old, nor even a cause. The very first lines – 'When civil Fury first grew high / And men fell out they knew not why' – establish the theme of causeless blundering. *Hudibras* is weakened by this chaotic–episodic structure and by the bewildering profusion of satiric targets: its wandering hero has to represent the fanaticism of the Good Old Cause, the delusions of a latter-day Don Quixote, the mania for occult and cabbalistic interpretation, even the pedantry of the antiquarian; his squire Ralpho embodies both mystic dreams of personal revelation and plebeian concreteness. These incompatible themes crowd and jostle in exhilarating confusion. *Hudibras* is, as we say, a riot.

There is something parasitic about the mock-heroic, feeding off the energies it ostensibly belittles. One typical festive–violent episode in *Hudibras* shows this clearly. Hudibras and Ralpho stumble across a charivari, the riotous, pan-banging, egg-throwing procession that humiliates a submissive husband. Hudibras interprets this spectacle as a wonderful survival of the ancient Roman triumph, an idolatrous cult of the Whore of Babylon astride her Horned Beast, and an unjust attack on women; since his goal is to gain a rich widow by performing deeds of knight-errantry, he indignantly attacks this anti-feminist slur. Rather than trotting out the usual list of female worthies, however, he defends (and thereby conflates) two specific kinds of active women – 'scolds' and militant supporters of the Good Old Cause. Suddenly the impassioned Hudibras ceases to be the spectator of the charivari and becomes its target-object. The rotten egg that interrupts his eulogy, revealing the text as a kind of pillory, serves to release Butler from the spell of an oration that threatens to compromise the poem's belittling purpose – an unintentionally impressive catalogue of women's political achievement during the revolutionary decades.

18 'A Ballad', Bodleian Library, MS Don. b. 8, fol. 185; Samuel Butler, *Hudibras*, ed. John Wilders (Oxford: Clarendon Press, 1967), 1.i. 175–8 (cf. *PL*, 8.470–7).

Bunyan and Milton in the Restoration context

Milton, Bunyan and Butler inhabit unrelated social worlds and utterly different ideological positions, but they share a radical suspicion of ornamental style
and self-proclaimed heroism. An acute awareness that contemporary 'Actions'
reduce 'Heroique Poetry' to an empty shell cuts across ideological divides, impelling both Butler's carnivalesque cynicism and Milton's abandonment of the
national epic he planned in the 1640s. Set in this context, the great dissenting writers seem less isolated. They find grandeur in the colossal iniquities of
'State' – Marvell's painterly *Last Instructions*, Milton's glittering portrayal of
Satan's empire – and in the solitary 'tender conscience' struggling against it. In
the case of Milton, as we shall see, this struggle forced him to confront not only
the dominant Restoration culture but the accumulated weight and splendour
of literary history.

Milton and Bunyan were not alone in maintaining the alternative voice despite the 'evil days' of the Restoration. Braving the new inquisition, women
like Elizabeth Calvert played a leading part in printing and distributing oppositional literature, while Quaker women continued to claim the right to speak
in religious meetings, using arguments codified in Margaret Fell Fox's *Womens
Speaking Justified* (1666), and to seek out writable sufferings. Roman Catholics
like Hugh Serenus Cressy wrote and imported their own equally dangerous
polemics against intolerance. Like Bunyan, the Welsh Fifth Monarchist Vavasor
Powell defiantly wrote from prison (*The Bird in the Cage, Chirping*, 1661) and
distilled his struggles into the form now called 'spiritual autobiography', a standardised progression from Sin (dramatically exaggerated by a kind of inverse
egotism) through 'conviction' and Satanic counter-temptation to a radiant
sense of salvation. Milton's *Samson Agonistes* can be understood as an educated
man's version of that progress, condensed in the prism of the neo-Aristotelian
unities rather than spread out through the daily events of a humdrum life.

Other nonconformists expressed themselves in 'literary' modes, too. The
epic-length *Order and Disorder, or The World Made and Undone*, a retelling of
Genesis in heroic couplets, is very probably the work of Lucy Hutchinson;
another epic about Adam and Eve – *Mundorum Explicatio* (1661), apparently
by Samuel Pordage and his father John, an associate of Abiezer Coppe and
Jane Lead – keeps alive the mystic, Boehmean side of 1650s religion, and explicitly attacks the idea of 'hyperbolizing' the acts of princes and kings. The
amazing George Wither, whose outspoken poetry earned him imprisonment
under James I and Charles II (and a fine from the parliamentary Army), continued to publish what he endearingly called 'A Personal Contribution to the

National Humiliation', intensifying his prophetic voice as he approached the *annus mirabilis* 1666 (announced by numerous portents including the Great Plague and a comet). Reading Wither's advice to 'us' former revolutionaries in his book-length poem on the Restoration – by laying down the sword, to 'overcome / By being vanquished, and prevail much more / By *loosing* than by *winning* heretofore' – brings into sharper focus Adam's definition of Christian heroism at the end of *Paradise Lost*: under 'heavie persecution' the godly can prevail 'with good / Still overcoming evil, and by small / Accomplishing great things, by things deemd weak / Subverting worldly strong'.[19]

Bunyan's *Grace Abounding to the Chief of Sinners*, first published in that year of miracles 1666, perfectly exemplifies the subversive ascendancy of the weak. Bunyan creates a monument of direct, experiential subjectivity in which the subject seems almost completely passive in his own story. His 'tender' conscience renders every pang of guilt so vividly that at times we seem to be reading the diary of a schizophrenic ('the very stones in the street and tiles upon the houses did bend themselves against me'), but he makes no effort to overcome the guilt – an extreme version of the paradox inherent in Calvinism, that the believer can do nothing to earn God's grace. To dramatise the metaphor of being born again, Bunyan creates a childlike persona: God and Satan 'work upon' him as he squirms helplessly, 'kicking' and 'screaming' like a baby stolen by gipsies or fallen into a millpond. Satan sneaks up behind him and pulls his clothes. Even reading the Bible has an infantile quality, as individual phrases 'drop', 'visit' or 'bolt in upon' him, meaning something entirely different according to the emotion that Bunyan casts upon them at that moment. Cognition depends on sense-impression ('it was fresh upon my Soul, and I believed it'). Bunyan's detachment from his own mental processes borders on scientific curiosity when, trying to reconcile two contradictory lines that imply his salvation or damnation, he speculates 'if both these Scriptures would meet in my heart at once, I wonder which of them would get the better of me'; unlike Boyle, however, he sets up no experiment but simply desires and waits until 'they boulted both upon me at a time'. He must eventually assign himself more agency in his own affairs, as he becomes a public figure; the closing sections relate how he began preaching, confronted the Lord Chief Justice and staved off despair in prison. (He is particularly concerned that he might panic on the scaffold and give 'the enemy' a chance to laugh at the people of God.)

19 Wither, *Sighs for the Pitchers* (London, 1666), title page, and *Speculum Speculativum*, p. 56; *PL*, 12.531, 565–8. The fullest account of 'Puritan' survival is Keeble, *Literary Culture of Nonconformity*.

Even here, however, the principal experience of 'grace abounding' consists of what we might call passive hermeneutics, as Biblical fragments are manifested unto him and interpretation submits to the subjective rapture of the mechanic preacher: 'them Scriptures that I saw nothing in before, are made in this place and state to shine on me.'[20]

In later editions, 'unfolding my secret things' even more fully, Bunyan augments his narrative to emphasise the continuity of 'Puritan' radicalism and Restoration nonconformity. The more distant the dread year 1660, the more Bunyan retrieves and inserts episodes explicitly set in the revolutionary decades – a miraculous escape from a musket bullet when fighting for the parliamentary Army, debates with the Ranters (including a close friend much given to 'whoring') – and amplifies the details of his youthful depravity, which even included dancing and bell-ringing: this wickedness is cured by terrifying thoughts of the bell, and the entire steeple, falling and crushing him to death. We learn more about the hostility of the ungodly, who imagine the unrepentant Puritan 'a witch, a Jesuit, a highwayman' and a sexual libertine. Two years after the appearance of *Samson Agonistes*, Bunyan adds a passage identifying himself with Samson; when Satan daunts him by pointing out that he himself is guilty of the sin his sermon condemns, Bunyan counters 'let me die with the Philistines' – quoting precisely the suicidal line that Milton takes pains to avoid in his drama.[21]

Samson was dangerous material, unstable in its signification. Bunyan's confused citation identifies the Philistines with his own congregation, sinners like himself, and the crashing building with the 'conviction of sin' that his sermon will induce. Marvell, to express his fear that *Paradise Lost* might 'ruin the sacred Truths', imagined his friend overwhelming the world 'to revenge his sight' just as Samson 'groaped the Temples Posts in spight'. Though Milton's achievement removes those fears and replaces them with sublime feelings of 'delight and horrour', Marvell's sceptical interpretation of Samson still stands – 'ruining' the Old Testament hero by making him a barbarian full of vengeance and 'spite'.[22]

Whatever else it signifies about Milton's relation to his contemporaries, realising his old plan to write a tragedy in *Samson Agonistes* allows him to retain his youthful infatuation with complex prosody and rhyme, angrily rejected as

20 *Grace Abounding*, ed. Roger Sharrock (Oxford: Clarendon Press, 1962), paras. numbered 187, 102, 198, 107, 338, 215, 90, 261, 190, 212–13, 22, 334, 321; where Bunyan has later augmented or corrected the text, I use the 1st edn (London, 1666), pp. 49, 58, 87.

21 *Ibid.*, paras. 174, 309, 295.

22 Marvell, 'On Mr Milton's Paradise lost', lines 7–10, 35, in *The Poems and Letters of Andrew Marvell*, ed. H. M. Margoliouth, rev. Pierre Logouis and E. E. Duncan-Jones, 2 vols., 3rd edn (Oxford: Clarendon Press, 1971).

a sign of 'bondage' in the prefatory note to *Paradise Lost* but appropriate in a drama whose theme is bondage. Samson is chained first literally and then metaphorically, in the prison of his own self-pity and anger against God; drama allows raw and vivid expressions of the fury that seethes beneath the surface of the divorce tracts and the agony of blindness, not permitted *in propria persona*. But the dialogue frequently confronts the bondage of the entire nation, the elect Israelites who failed to seize the opportunities provided by Samson's individual acts of terrorism. This makes *Samson* a topical play, an oblique mirror of contemporary England if not a direct allegory. Samson's agony comes first from blaming God (for making the eyeball too vulnerable, for making him strong but stupid) and then from blaming himself so virulently that, as his father Manoah acutely observes, it seems like a kind of egotism (lines 514–15). The drama shows Samson working through the various stages of despair in order to regain the healing rhetoric of self-justification and denunciation.

Milton's Chief of Sinners differs from Bunyan's in one important respect; he is a man of vast passions, boiling with sexuality and anger. Like other Restoration stage-heroes he is torn apart by the conflicts of Love and Honour. Furious denunciations of his own 'foul effeminacy' attack the Dalila within; Samson even pretends to think that his voluptuous married life was worse than his present state of blindness and slave labour (lines 410, 416–18). Milton's theoretical preface defines his goal as the Aristotelian catharsis or purgation of the emotions, and the last words of the play – 'calm of mind, all passion spent' – suggest that the cast as well as the reader should experience this; but many of Samson's passions are not in fact 'tempered and reduced'. Transference of blame to God is clearly condemned, and Samson gains some quiet dignity when he ritually 'acknowledges and confesses' his responsibility (lines 448, 376). Transference of blame to evil women and backsliding compatriots is another matter, however. Samson's forgiveness of Dalila expresses not 'calm of mind' but sexual fury, combining the white-hot resentment of the divorce tracts with contemporary misogynist hatred of the royal mistresses. Likewise, Samson's equally emotional attacks on his countrymen are allowed to stand unchallenged and unpurged: 'Nations grown corrupt' enslave themselves, 'despise, or envy, or suspect' the heroic individual Deliverer, and in short 'love Bondage more than Liberty, / Bondage with ease than strenuous liberty' (lines 240, 268–74, and compare 1213–16). The people thus serve a multiple signification: they are 'my country', 'Israel's sons' whom Samson is proud to acknowledge when he finally stands up to the Philistine bully (lines 1177, 1208);

they are the oppressed godly remnant of Restoration England, their corpses exposed 'To dogs and fowls a prey, or else captived,' abandoned by God 'to the unjust tribunals, under change of times, / And condemnation of the ingrateful multitude' (lines 694–6); and they *are* that contemptible multitude.

Samson Agonistes resonates with the issues of the Restoration, yet cannot be reduced to them; like the 'Samson Hubristes' projected in Milton's earlier Trinity College Manuscript, the protagonist must be considered a Greek tragic hero – noble but flawed, cursed and blessed by a primitive deity. This 'dramatic poem' can even be read as a critique of traditional heroism, especially since in printed sequence it follows the great epic *Paradise Lost* (1667) and the minor epic *Paradise Regained* (published with *Samson* in 1671), both of which explicitly reject his kind of physical valour. Milton has more in common with his contemporary Butler than appears on the surface, since large portions of *Paradise Lost* are best understood as mock-heroic: the Odyssean heroism of the solitary traveller Satan (the hero of his own *Sataniad* or *Annus Mirabilis*, where indomitable Will battles with implacable Fate) ends in grotesque pantomime, of course, but the Iliadic heroism of the warring angels is equally futile, showing that war can achieve nothing even in a good cause. Once he reaches the tragic climax of the Fall, in the invocation to Book 9, Milton makes his contra-heroism explicit, attacking (in suitably sumptuous language) both the ancient focus on martial prowess and contemporary epic's obsession with knightly grandeur and chivalry; on the contrary, it is 'the better fortitude / Of Patience and Heroic Martyrdom' that 'justly gives Heroic name / To Person or to Poem' (9.31–41).

The anti-heroic stance of *Paradise Lost* differs from Hudibrastic mockery, of course. Milton still pours all his poetic gifts into effects that must ultimately be renounced as hollow: the noble music of the fallen angels that 'suspended Hell'; the gilded baroque splendour of Pandemonium and Satan's military parades; the rhetorical splendour of his public speeches encouraging the fallen angels, which nineteenth-century neo-Puritans took out of context and applied to more admirable examples of 'the unconquerable Will'. Like a true tragedian Milton invests in the doomed – a category that comprises not only the sublime depravity of the *Sataniad* but the beauty of the paradisal books, the rolling landscape of Eden (which generations of English landowners will try to recreate in their own 'happy rural seat of various view') or the lyrical eroticism of Adam and Eve, drenched in nostalgia for Elizabethan stateliness as well as for Eden itself. All these must yield to the briefer, tougher, more Protestant style that faces the future rather than the past, exemplified in Eve's contrite confession in Book 10 and in the seminar on future history that Michael gives Adam in Books 11 and 12.[23]

Throughout the poem, in fact, thorny reminders of future history stick out from the texture of the verse, forcing the Restoration reader to make painful applications. As in Bunyan and Trapnel, these pointers convey a general lesson about sin, corruption and redemption, appropriate in a poem that purports to show the origins of the entire human condition. But they are also highly specific, blocking the tendency to separate the contemporary from the 'universal'. When the poet evokes his own blindness and the 'evil times' in which he suffers, he unmistakably presents the historic John Milton in the concrete circumstances of Restoration defeat. We have already seen how sharply he links the Sons of Belial to Restoration decadence. When placed alongside explicitly political works like Wither's *Speculum Speculativum* or Marvell's *Last Instructions*, passages like the allegory of Sin and Death or the praise of 'subverting' weakness seem equally applicable to the abuses of the 1660s. At the level of phrase and image rather than action, *Paradise Lost* can sound as topical as *Samson*. Satan's appearance as an eclipsed sun, a 'disastrous twilight' that 'with fear of change / Perplexes Monarchs', recalls the threatening comets of the *annus mirabilis* 1666, and reportedly aroused the suspicion of Charles II's censor (1.597–9). When Satan reaches Eden and leaps over the wall into Paradise, Milton adds to his epic similes (a wolf raiding the sheepcote, a burglar coming in over the roof) the provocative aside 'So since into his Church lewd Hirelings climbe' (4.193); rather than evoking 'universal' depravity, Milton explicitly recalls the language of the Good Old Cause and his own particular campaign within it, using his own favourite word for salaried priests, blazoned in the title of his revolutionary prose *Likeliest Means to Remove Hirelings* (1659) and in his sonnet advising Cromwell to remove 'hireling wolves'. He cites his own anti-Restoration campaign again in Book 12, where the Israelites cross the desert 'not the readiest way', avoiding 'rash' confrontations with the Philistines that might send them defeated 'back to Egypt' (216–19).

Modern equivalents of the Philistines appear whenever Milton wants to define the purity and beauty of Paradise by contrast: Edenic sexuality is compared to the Balls and 'bought Smiles' of court amours, and the naked simplicity of

---

23 The 1667 version was divided into only ten books, though I refer for convenience to the 12-book division of 1674 (which split the War in Heaven and Michael's history lesson to throw the Abdiel and Nimrod episodes into greater prominence). As well as the well-known pro-Satan assertions of Blake and Shelley, cf. C. H. Firth's preface to his edition of Edmund Ludlow's *Memoirs*, 3 vols. (Oxford: Clarendon Press, 1894), which applies the 'unconquerable Will' passage (*PL*, 1. 105–6) to Ludlow himself (1.xlii).

Adam meeting Raphael to the 'tedious pomp that waits / On Princes' – despised not just for its tacky ornament ('besmeared with Gold') but for its 'dazzling' and stupefying effect on the people (5.354–7). The long discussion of Nimrod and the Tower of Babel in Book 12 is even more critical of monarchic 'tyrants', an arrogant crew who overthrow the original 'fair equalitie, fraternal state', impose an unwarrantable 'Sovereignty' over their fellow men (women are not even mentioned in this discussion) and then dare accuse the egalitarian resistance of 'Rebellion' even though they themselves are the true rebels against God; in a counter-semantic move, Milton even uses the hot Royalist word 'Usurper' to indict royalty itself. Contemporary readers got the message. The ex-radical horticulturalist John Beale wishes the authorities had cracked down on this Nimrod passage, which for him proves that Milton 'holds to his old Principle' – even though Michael (like Samson) actually teaches acceptance of political tyranny, God's punishment for a backsliding people.[24]

Almost as much ink has been spilled on the analogies between Satan and seventeenth-century politics as on the relation between Milton's Eve and twentieth-century feminism, and the range of answers to both questions suggests the inexhaustible polysemy of the poem. Satan, the arch-rebel against divine right, adopts the republican rhetoric of liberation and equality when he seduces his fellow angels (who hail him as 'Deliverer from new Lords') and later when he urges Eve to throw off false restraints on her human potential, so he would certainly be equated with the English Revolution by Royalist readers. The entire action of the poem (narrated by Raphael) begins when the Son is established as King, and even though that kingship is awarded for merit, and will be set aside for a higher cause, the sentimental monarchist could well identify with Milton's opulent evocation of royal splendour; like the Fifth Monarchists, he worships divine kingship as ardently as he despises it on earth. Satan's titanic individualism, self-promotion, charismatic rather than hereditary authority, and manipulation of a Council of State suggests Cromwell to some readers, though his chosen 'style' is distinctly monarchal and his 'God-like imitated State' associates him with the baroque absolutist. Especially in the opening of Book 2 ('High on a Throne of Royal State'), Satan becomes a kitschy agglomerate of every monarch; like his theatrical cousins in the Restoration 'heroic play', he adopts a stagey, bejewelled splendour that Milton associates with the 'barbaric' monarchies of India and the Gulf (though his swarming troops are compared to the northern Goths and Vandals). Satan's palace-cum-temple

---

24 PL 12.26–96; Beale to Evelyn (a correspondence earlier brought to light by Nicholas von Maltzahn), cited in Norbrook, *Republic*, p. 467.

Pandemonium deliriously fuses elements of Babylon, Cairo, St Peter's and Versailles, lit throughout with glowing minerals that Satan's prospectors have dug from the 'wounded' soil; its closest analogue comes in Margaret Cavendish's *Blazing World*, where the absolutist Empress awes her subjects into adoring submission with spectacular displays of luminous stones that her scientists have discovered and mined. Satan's coercive leadership matches his phantasmagoric taste, dazzling his followers into idolatrous worship of himself, reifying his honours and titles, oppressing the faithful by ordering them to worship in ways that break their fealty to God – exactly what the nonconformists denounced in the new Anglican order.

Nimrod-style tyranny clearly shows through the republican rhetoric the moment it is tested by the sole voice of dissent in his tribe, Abdiel. Here the loaded language of Restoration politics comes into the sharpest focus. Expelled from Satan's camp, this 'Servant of God' is repeatedly praised for his 'zeale', his single-handed fight to 'maintain / Against revolted multitudes the Cause / Of Truth' while suffering 'Universal reproach' (6.30–7). When he reappears in the opening scene of the War in Heaven, he tauntingly reminds Satan of his seeming 'dissent'; pointing to the vast army behind him, he boasts 'My Sect thou seest' (6.146–7) – the fighting word reminding us that Milton treated the 'sects' sympathetically even though he joined none. Just as Nimrod 'from Rebellion shall derive his name, / Though of Rebellion others he accuse' (12.36–7), so Satan responds with the loftiest scorn for this 'seditious Angel' (6.152). Abdiel is the new heroic type, foreshadowing the 'one just man', the 'Pilgrim' in Vanity Fair, and ultimately Milton himself, 'in word mightier than they in Armes'. The 'Cause', prominent at the line-break, has been recast not as a mass movement but as the timely utterance of a zealot 'alone / Encompass'd round with foes' (5.875–6), holding fast to the faith when all the weaklings around him are stampeding into bondage and apostasy. This is very much Milton's revolution, as seen through the narrowing lens of the Restoration.

Paradise Lost is the quintessential 1660s text because it looks both ways, summing up the 'early modern' and forging new forms through parody and critique. To echo the last words that Milton wrote, added for the final revision in the year of his death, the poem is poised 'Betwixt the world destroyed and world restored'. Its complex relation to poetic innovation can be grasped in a single line from the invocation, when he prays for divine help in attaining 'Things unattempted yet in Prose or Rhyme'. Certainly this is neither prose nor rhyme but something distinctive between the two, emulating God's own design of the universe by neoclassical symmetry and 'stretching out his Line so far' that it creates new spatial configurations. But how can the subject be *unattempted*, when Milton retells the oldest story in the book and echoes every known epic from Homer to Tasso and Spenser (including the relatively neglected republican civil war poem, Lucan's *Pharsalia*)? Indeed, this line itself is translated from the quintessential chivalric epic, Ariosto's *Orlando Furioso*. The poet's desire for the not-yet-expressed has already been expressed. Milton's solution is to simulate and outperform antique epic, romance and chivalry while defining a new heroic subject – the lonely thinker resisting mass hysteria, the naked couple making serious mistakes but still walking 'hand in hand' into the world of work and pain.[25] Milton's incorporation of psychological nuance and domestic conflict into the unfallen state makes *Paradise Lost* the first novel as well as the last epic.

Paradise Lost's opening prophecy of a single great man who will 'Restore us' prompts Milton's only unequivocally post-1660 poem, *Paradise Regained*, an austere 'brief epic' in four books narrating Christ's temptation in the wilderness but modelled on the story of Job. As in *Samson Agonistes*, Milton takes the classic 'Puritan' strategy of *Grace Abounding* – recreating the Temptation of Christ in terms scaled to the writer's own life – and transmutes it into the high-cultural mode. First Satan, then the narrator, customises the standard temptations to make them appeal to a young, radical Christ uncannily like the young, radical poet–prophet Milton. In council Belial proposes a typical Restoration solution to the problem of how to corrupt the new leader, sending 'women' to 'Enerve, and with voluptuous hope dissolve', just as Louis XIV managed Charles II. But this approach is contemptuously rejected by Satan, who recognises that he is dealing with the anti-sexual zealot of the divorce tracts rather than the Magdalen-loving Christ of the gospels. Even Satan's first temptation is angled to appeal to a young radical (turn stones into bread to ease the 'misery and hardship' of the local people), and before leaving on the first day he slips in another temptation closely related to Milton's poetic vocation: since God permits 'the Hypocrite or Atheous Priest' into his ministry (a glaring reference to the Restoration church as seen through dissenting eyes), surely Jesus can allow the devil to frequent his company and enjoy the aesthetic beauty of his discourse, 'pleasing to the ear, / And tuneable as Silvan Pipe or Song'. Is it Satan or Milton who echoes the Shakespearean sweetness of *A Midsummer Night's Dream* ('more tunable than lark to shepherd's ear')?[26] The most temptingly 'tuneable' passages occur, in fact, not in the speeches of

---

25 *PL*, 12.3, 1.16, 8.102 (cf. Norbrook, *Republic*, p. 473), 12:648.
26 *Paradise Regained* (*PR*), 1.154–68, 338–45, 487, 479–80 (and cf. *PL*, 9.24, 5.149–52); *A Midsummer Night's Dream*, 1.i.184.

Satan (where they would fall directly on Christ's ear, like the blandishments of
Comus or Dalila) but in the narrator's own voice. The languorous alliterations of
the banquet scene (2.358–62), for example, awaken nostalgia for the chivalric,
Spenserian poetic world where Milton himself began his poetic career.

Throughout this Restoration epic of styles, Satan crafts his temptations to
appeal to the kinds of zeal most relevant to contemporary England: sensuous consumption of forbidden foods and equally luscious verse; antinomian
rejection of the Law; a dazzling New Model Army to crush the pagan and
establish God's reign on earth; Machiavellian wisdom that could turn high politics into an instrument of righteousness; counter-counterrevolutionary moral
fervour that could overthrow a 'lascivious', decadent monarch (for Tiberius
read Charles II) and reestablish 'A victor people free from servile yoke'; and finally, the calm retreat of literature and philosophy. Milton's Christ beats away
all these, sometimes in tough, wiry, compressed lines that perfectly embody
the plain style, sometimes by parodies of Satan's own lush verse. This must be
the only Jesus in world literature who can recite the names of expensive wines
in rolling pentameters, just as he is probably the only one to denounce the
people as 'vile and base, / Deservedly made vassal', 'effeminate', 'degenerate,
by themselves enslaved', 'a herd confus'd, / A miscellaneous rabble, who extol /
Things vulgar'.[27] If Royalist culture needed to preserve the Puritan on display,
Milton never ceases to pillory the backsliding nation and the Sons of Belial –
even in the character of the Prince of Peace.

'Augustan' London and the shift in literary modes

Outside the dissenting enclave, how did the changes of the 1660s alter the
landscape of literature? Did the new anti-Puritan culture, and the new emphasis on metropolitan life, affect the sites of literary production and the relation
between the regional varieties of English discourse? Did the Restoration privilege different genres of prose and verse – as we have already seen in the case
of lampoon and burlesque – and did other genres sink from view? And what
became of the 'Heroique' impulse after the first flush of 1660? The comparison
of Dryden's *Annus Mirabilis* and Marvell's *Last Instructions*, later in this section,
suggests that the Restoration's true progeny is satire.

Prose narrative had not yet formed a recognisable 'English novel', prose non-
fiction remained highly miscellaneous, and theatrical writing was still to reach
the streamlined form that we understand by 'Restoration comedy' (a term that

27 *PR*, 2.340–53 (non-kosher food included in the banquet), 3.50–2, 4.91–144.

describes only a few works of 1675–1700 now considered canonical). Fiction was still dominated by the French novels of Honoré d'Urfé and Madeleine de Scudéry, and by Sidney's *Arcadia* (recently extended by Anne Weamys). The fullest contribution to the romance genre was *Parthenissa*, by the Irish aristocrat Roger Boyle, Earl of Orrery (brother of the equally prolific scientist), who also pioneered the rhymed 'heroic play' that took over the themes of French fiction: vast chivalric actions, close analysis of conflicting emotions, idealistic devotion to the beloved.

The great majority of non-fictional prose was still religious, ranging from high-Anglican sermons to spiritual autobiographies like Bunyan's *Grace Abounding* and subversive accounts of God's providence. In the secular realm, publishers catered to a desire for texts that mirrored the newly restored nation or shaped its civil society. Witty conversational gambits, apposite poetic quotations and semifictional correspondence were gathered into how-to anthologies like *The New Academy of Compliments* (1671), whose title-page claims to distil the wit of Sir William Davenant, Sir Charles Sedley and Lord Buckhurst (the two leaders of fashionable society who displayed their scatological humour in the tavern-balcony riot). Antiquarians and biographers, patiently accumulating anecdotes and documents, appealed to the sense that nationality depends on local history; Thomas Fuller's posthumous *Worthies of England* – a county-by-county gazetter with a separate section on Wales that includes proverbs in the original language – records a plethora of local sayings, precious minerals, famous inhabitants and notable buildings. On a much more serious level, Clarendon's autobiography and *History of the Great Rebellion* (written during his two periods of exile, after the Civil Wars and after his ouster from power in 1667) embody the same compilatory urge, building his magisterial account of the 'natural causes' of history around a gallery of character portraits.

To distance themselves from the old 'Puritan' tone both prose and verse aimed to appear *urbane*, metropolitan or 'Augustan', and in many cases this stylistic gesture was reinforced by literally concentrating on the fashionable world of London: the site depicted merges with the site of production. Topographical poetry, for example, continued to appear in the decade after *Coopers Hill*, but it focused much more narrowly upon London, and 1660s drama set virtually no scenes in rural England or in the other British nations.[28] In a parallel

<hr>

28 Robert Arnold Aubin, *Topographical Poetry in XVIII-Century England* (New York: Modern Language Association, 1936) provides a post-1660 listing, supplemented by J. G. Turner, 'The Matter of Britain: Topographical Poetry in English 1600–1660', *Notes and Queries* 223 (1978), 514–24.

development, publication in the regions, and in the other native languages of Britain and her dependencies, shrank after the Restoration reimposed central control (New England is the exception, due to the single-handed work of John Eliot in the Massachuset language). Only 10 Welsh titles appeared in the 1660s, as opposed to over 100 pre-1660 and 47 in the 1680s; the other Celtic languages fared even worse than Welsh, and though the first bilingual work in Irish and English appeared in 1667 it came from a Catholic press in Louvain.[29] Even in Glasgow and Edinburgh, which could still publish legally, the vast majority of titles appear in standard English and some, like Sir George Mackenzie's *Moral Gallantry* (Edinburgh, 1667), explicitly engage the new ethics of urbanity and *politesse*.

We should not make Restoration discourse too homogenous, however. Witty flippancy flourished already in the 1650s, and 'Puritan' earnestness surfaces even in supporters of the new regime – even though satirists and dramatists did their best to exorcise the godly 'enthusiastic' tone through parody. When we read in a spiritual journal 'there befel me a most infinit Desire of a Book from Heaven... this Thirst hung upon me a long time... me thought a New Light Darted in into all the Psalms' we think of Bunyan, but in fact this is the Reverend Thomas Traherne, BD (Oxon), rector of Credenhill and chaplain to the Lord Keeper of the Great Seal (though like Bunyan a poor man's son). If Traherne's rapturous visions of childhood, when 'the Corn was Orient and Immortal Wheat' and 'the Skies were mine, and so were the Sun and Moon and Stars', sound like William Blake, his *Thanksgivings* sound like Abiezer Coppe, celebrating his radiant certainty of salvation in lineated Biblical prose. Nothing could be further from the boisterous rhyming and cheeky cynicism of the Restoration lampoon:

> The Weighty Affairs
> Of Plackets and Players
> Now busy the Heads of our Great Ones.

---

29 Geraint H. Jenkins, *Literature, Religion and Society in Wales, 1660–1730* (Cardiff: University of Wales Press, 1978), pp. 34–5; the first English–Irish printed book is supposedly Richard Arch(e)dekin, *A Treatise of Miracles* (Louvain, 1667); Eliot's work in the 1660s includes his Bible translation, several language primers and *Christiane Oonowae Sampoowaonk* (Cambridge, MA: n.d., reissued 1670). (Outside print culture some genres did flourish, for example the Welsh *halsingod* or manuscript devotional poems and Irish oral tales like 'Cromwell and the Friar', which presumably date from this period.) Oddly, at least four minority-language areas (Cornwall, Jersey, Isle of Man, Orkney) had been treated in English topographical poems before 1660.

But this too is Traherne, simulating the flippant tone of the age in order to critique its frivolity.[30]

The ambiguous, jocoserious attitude of the 'Great Ones' created problems for those who sincerely wanted to put their poetic gift at the disposal of the authorities. As Butler observes, 'Heroical Poetry' fulminated in a void, since 'Heroical Actions' were conspicuously lacking. The best secular poets of the 1660s gravitated towards satire, Marvell being the decisive example. Only Dryden attempted high seriousness, in his bid for the joint posts of Poet Laureate and Historiographer Royal.

After the loss of John Ogilby's twelve-book *Caroleis* in the fire of London, Dryden's *Annus Mirabilis: The Year of Wonders, 1666* must serve as the sole exemplar of the Stuart heroic or 'Historical Poem' – as Dryden himself calls it, even though the events it describes (the naval war with Holland and the Great Fire) took place less than two years earlier. Since Dryden had retired to the country during the Great Plague of 1665–6 he works from official court news releases rather than first-hand witness, and this allows his sense of the 'Epick' free play. A Virgilian epigraph links the fire to the fall of Troy, and quotations in the footnotes identify the classical passages that Dryden emulates and updates. Dryden's vision of the new post-fire capital thus incorporates the enthusiasm of *Areopagitica* into the neoclassicism that gives the name 'Augustan' to this period: 'Me-thinks already, from this Chymick flame, / I see a City of more precious mold, . . . More great than humane, now, and more *August*' – here a note explains that the ancient name of London was Augusta.[31] The goal could hardly be further from Milton's, of course: Dryden must redefine the Year of Wonders as a triumph for the royal family, when many of their subjects regarded them as monsters of incompetence or iniquity, justly struck down by plague and fire in the *mirabilis annus* predicated by George Wither and the Book of Revelation. Confronted by age-old signs of apocalypse such as war, comets, pestilence and fire, which a wide sector of the population still interpreted as portents, Dryden wavers between modern scientific rationalism and ancient superstition. The two comets that terrified the nation are quietly defused, first by domestic imagery ('Tapers') and then by fanciful materialist explanations (stanzas 16–17). Supernatural causation abounds in *Annus Mirabilis* – on behalf

---

30 Thomas Traherne, *Centuries, Poems, and Thanksgivings*, ed. H. M. Margoliouth (Oxford: Clarendon Press, 1958), vol. 1, *The Third Century*, meditations 3, 27, 62; Traherne, *Commentaries of Heaven: The Poems*, ed. D. D. C. Chambers (Salzburg: Institüt für Anglistik und Amerikanistik, Universität Salzburg, 1989), p. 30.

31 Stanza 293; the poem is quoted from Dryden, *Works*, 1:59–105 (with prose forematter, 48–59).

of the Stuarts, at least – but it reads as poetic convention, epic machinery, acknowledged fiction.

Particularly in his dramatisation of the Great Fire, heroic imagery lets Dryden evoke the causes he refuses to credit literally, and at the same time defuse the criticisms of the apocalyptic opposition. Without actually saying that the fanatics caused it (countering the paranoid blame of French/Dutch/Papist arson with a conspiracy theory of his own), he compares it in a lengthy epic simile to 'some dire Usurper' and continues to metaphorise it as an outburst of class hatred moving from the mean streets towards the 'Palaces and Temples' of the great, albeit urged on by a *Belgian* wind' (stanzas 213–15, 230). Though he emphasises the natural, accidental causes of the disaster he still asserts that God burns St Paul's because it has been profaned by the Puritans (who had deconsecrated this supreme 'steeple-house' and used it as a stable). In a dazzling display of the art of concession, Dryden invents a moving episode where, in the midst of his heroic fire-fighting efforts, Charles prays for the wrath of God to fall on him alone – for the unspecified sins of his 'heedless Youth' – rather than on his beloved people. The future Laureate thus finesses the most serious complaint against the King, that his sins were bringing plagues upon England, into a Royalist tear-jerker. Meanwhile Dryden continues to snipe at what he would later call 'the Good Old Cause revived': the desiccated heads of the Fifth Monarchist rebels descend from London Bridge and become 'bold Fanatick Spectres', dancing about the bonfire and singing their Puritan psalms with 'feeble voice'.[32]

Ghosts could perform for either side, however. At the unforgettable climax of *Last Instructions to a Painter*, Marvell imagines a series of cautionary visions appearing to King Charles in the middle of the night. The stripped, gagged and bound figure of Britannia moves him to lust rather than remorse, assuming she is just another mistress delivered to his bed. But then his grandfather Henri IV appears, pointing to the assassin's wound, followed by his own beheaded father: 'ghastly Charles, turning his Collar low, / The purple thread about his Neck does show' (lines 885–922). There could be no more vivid image of the troubled transition 'from Revolution to Restoration'. In the 'Horatian Ode', Marvell had proposed a new significance for an old foundation myth, the portent of a bloody head on the site of the Capitol which frightens those 'architects' unable to interpret it positively; this ghostly scene in *Last Instructions* reminds the King that Restoration England shares the same foundation.

32 *Annus Mirabilis*, stanzas 265, 223; *Absalom and Achitophel*, line 82.

If Dryden's *Annus Mirabilis* fails brilliantly at the impossible task of turning the Restoration into a heroic poem, Marvell's oppositional *Last Instructions* launches the most important literary genre of the Augustan age, the mock-heroic as serious satire. Marvell abandons the burlesque mode of *Hudibras*, though both poems contain an emblematic charivari scene, establishing their affinity with the popular culture of mockery and (as Marvell explains) teaching important lessons by 'Spectacle Innocent' and 'quick Effigy' (lines 389–91). Instead, he adopts a lofty heroic-couplet style in keeping with the epic scale of wrongdoing – the corruption, self-serving and scapegoating of the parliamentary clique around Clarendon, whose mismanagement of the Dutch War caused the worst disaster in English naval history when the fleet was burned in its own harbour, the River Medway. In a passage shimmering with painterly beauty as well as political sarcasm, the Dutch admiral becomes a courtier gliding in Rubensian triumph to woo the English water nymphs. A series of dazzling insider portraits of courtiers, mistresses and MPs builds up the theme of corruption in the body politic, subsuming the pornographic personal lampoon into the Augustan structure. The gross Earl of St. Albans, for example – 'The new *Court's* pattern, Stallion of the old' (line 30) – literally embodies the continuity of the Caroline and Restoration eras (he was reputedly the real father of Charles II). The fornications of Anne Hyde (Clarendon's daughter, who married James, Duke of York, in advanced pregancy) prefigure the corruption that gives us 'a new Whore of State' in the Excise (lines 49–62, 150).

When he moves on from court to Parliament, instead of the Homeric parade of heroes Marvell surveys the serried ranks of procurers and cuckolds entering the House, with Sir John Denham as their leader (line 174). Against this background of lust, frivolity and bungling, one solitary figure stands out. Pointedly, Marvell's sole example of true heroism is not English at all: an intensely erotic portrait of the 'loyal Scot' – undoing Cleveland's vicious Civil War satire against the 'Rebel Scot' – celebrates a boyish naval officer who chose to stand on the burning deck when all around him fled. Unlike Charles I in the 'Horatian Ode', another 'comely Head' who meets his public and theatrical death as if it were a bedroom scene, this figure seems driven by a powerfully active desire, embracing the 'Sheets' of flame 'Like a glad Lover' on his wedding night (lines 677–8). The contrast between this patriotic, poetic death scene and the King's chilly, haunted, conscience-stricken bedroom could hardly be stronger. Despite the ostensible loyalism of its ending, Marvell's great anti-panegyric raises serious questions about British identity and the national interest, dramatised in the troubled relation of 'the Country' to 'the King' (line 974).

Poetic careers and 'conformable' forms

A surprising number of authors produced significant work before and after 1660, whether or not they altered their style or climbed on the Stuart bandwagon. Many of the writers discussed in Chapter 25 renewed their careers in this decade. Abraham Cowley, the boy wonder of Caroline lyric and for Samuel Johnson the epitome of the far-fetched 'Metaphysical' mode, burst out in 1660 with panegyric and comedy (*The Cutter of Coleman Street*, rewritten from his own *Guardian* of 1641), and continued to pour out proposals for a new science college, a botanical epic in Latin, urbane prose essays on country life, and spectacular odes in imitation of Pindar. (In the 1650s he started two incomplete epics in English rhyming couplets; *The Civil War* stayed in manuscript, rendered obsolete by the King's defeat, but Cowley published the fragmentary *Davideis* in 1656, with learned annotations as if it were already a classic, and a preface that got him into trouble four years later, urging Royalists to accept Cromwell and 'lay down our Pens as well as Arms'.) Continuity might have been easier for regional than for metropolitan poets. The Derbyshire gentleman-poet Charles Cotton became increasingly productive after 1660: apart from lyrics, Pindarics and elegies, his poetry includes local-descriptive pieces like *The Wonders of the Peake*, a galloping *Voyage to Ireland in Burlesque*, and the 1664 *Scarronides*, which travesties the *Aeneid* in Hudibrastic metre, turning princesses and heroes into gossiping midwives and village idiots; in prose he continued Walton's *Compleat Angler* (adding new poems) and translated the essays of Montaigne. For poets closer to the court, however, the Caroline 'Cavalier' mode was hard to maintain: the new 'Sons of Belial' (Sedley, Dorset, Etherege, Rochester) accentuated its cynicism and pursued extremer forms of hedonism, so that 'Love and Sherry' were no longer enough to denote wild abandon. It gave no thrill any more to play with the 'Crowne' on a glass of wine or to imagine the late King as a fragile but joyous grasshopper, as Lovelace did (see Chapter 25 above), since the present monarch outperformed that insect.

On the other hand, some poets 'shrunk their streams' or changed course after 1660, whether due to the change of times or to the notion that writing verse belongs only to youth. The Welsh wizard Henry Vaughan lived until 1695, and added some new poems to the 1678 reissue of his work optimistically called *Thalia Rediviva* (*Thalia Renewed*), but mostly busied himself with medicine and Hermeticism. Marvell lived until 1681, but after beginning his Parliamentary career in 1658 he shifted his writing mode dramatically, from lyric and panegyric to satire and prose controversy (though losing none of his surreal inventiveness). Some poets clearly suffered from the change of ethos:

Sir John Denham survived until 1669, and even added a few lines to *Coopers Hill* in praise of global consumerism ('Commerce makes everything grow everywhere'), but the father of Augustan poetics now found himself a ridiculous court cuckold, mocked for his marriage to an eighteen-year-old who had quite openly become mistress to the Duke of York.[33] Herrick, a poet who seems to have sprouted verse as easily as a tree sprouts leaves, left not a scrap of writing after 1648; even though he was restored to his rural parish and lived until 1674, his imaginary 'green world' had vanished completely.

Katherine Philips, in contrast, lived only four years after 1660 and spent most of her time in Wales and Ireland, but went on from strength to strength. Her translation of Corneille's *Pompey* (with added songs) ran successfully in Dublin and later in London, while her own poetry branched out: the ode to retirement becomes more 'Pindarique', the elegies more passionate, the *vers de société* more flirtatiously sophisticated as Philips spends more time with the Irish aristocracy (addressing numerous poems to the ubiquitous Boyle family). The well-crafted, late-Metaphysical lyrics of friendship and retirement develop into raw, direct expressions of baffling love for another woman: the prospect of Lucasia's marriage inspires an Adieu to the 'dear object of my Love's excess' that is closer to Ovid's *Heroides* than to the 'Platonic' model of the 1650s. Philips's early death prevented her from seeing the success of the poems she had evidently prepared for publication, including examples of the new, public, pentameter-couplet voice that she produced for royal occasions; again, the Restoration brought out an extrovert political mode, in contrast to the quiet, nostalgic Royalism that cemented her coterie verse in the 1650s.[34]

Posthumous publication made Philips one of the most celebrated poets of either sex. Everybody from militant feminists like 'Philo-Philippa' to established male literati vied to supply commendatory poems. Cowley devoted two of his elaborate Pindarics to Philips, encrusted with heavily gendered compliments on the 'Tyrannies' of her Wit and Beauty, the fruitfulness of her 'unexhausted and unfathomed Womb', the androgyny of her verse ('than Man

---

33 *Expans'd Hieroglyphicks: A Study of Sir John Denham's 'Coopers Hill' with a Critical Edition of the Poem*, ed. Brendan O Hehir (Berkeley and Los Angeles: University of California Press, 1969), p. 150; Marvell, *Last Instructions*, line 174; 'The Conyborough of Coopers Hill', in Bodleian MS Don. b. 8, fol. 287. Denham also completed Katherine Philips's translation of Corneille's *Horace*, which was apparently staged with burlesque dances between the acts (Pepys, *Diary*, 19 Jan. 1669).

34 *The Collected Works of Katherine Philips, The Matchless Orinda*, vol. 1, *The Poems*, ed. Patrick Thomas (Stump Cross, Essex: Stump Cross Books, 1990), pp. 211–13; for examples of verses datable post-1660, see pp. 109–11, 177–8, 193–5 (as well as the public poems actually addressed to (mostly female) members of the royal family, the Lord Lieutenant of Ireland and the Archbishop of Canterbury).

more strong, and more than Woman sweet'), her purity in contrast to Sappho's 'shame' and her revival of the Welsh 'Race'. Henry Vaughan's eulogy adopts the facetious Hudibrastic mode to complain about the degeneracy of the age; 'noble numbers' are despised and 'great witts have left the Stage' to frivolous 'Drollers', proving that poets 'thrive best in adversity'. Astonishingly, the old Royalist links Cromwellian terror to artistic achievement: 'since the thunder left our air / Their Laurels look not half so fair'. With the divine exception of Philips herself, Vaughan declares the Restoration a disaster for literature because its writers are insufficiently 'oppressed'.[35]

But did these shifts in literary genre and ethos have any impact on the form of verse itself? The acrimonious debate over rhyme – in Milton's prefatory note to *Paradise Lost* as well as in Dryden's criticism – reminds us that such questions cannot be answered in a vacuum: the form of expression *placed* the voice socially and politically. Plain style denoted modernity and a refusal to adhere to the jargons that divided an earlier generation. Poised 'wit' and clean, stylish prose advertised gentlemanly status, membership in the polite classes. Rhyme signalled loyalty rather than dissidence; in the debate over Milton's blank verse, we shall see, rhyme is associated with 'bondage' and blank verse is condemned as 'nonconformable'.

We have already seen in the case of 'Hudibrastics' that specific verse forms become welded to particular attitudes. The four-beat couplet – beautifully used in Milton's *Il Penseroso* and Marvell's lyrics – now signifies facetious banter and anti-Puritan satire. Conversely, certain stanza forms invariably indicated serious nonconformist devotion. Anne Bradstreet for example, whose public poetry maintains a stately, old-fashioned prosody reminiscent of Shakespeare's sonnets, cleaves in her private verso to the old Protestant psalm measure of Sternhold and Hopkins, essentially an Elizabethan fourteener couplet broken into alternating lines of four and three stresses.[36] This is the metre that sustains the million words of Anna Trapnel's *Voice for the King of Saints* and (with additional internal rhymes) the most popular poem in 1660s New England, Michael Wigglesworth's book-length *Day of Doom*. Meanwhile, certain verse forms vanish almost completely. Nobody followed Milton's example by writing sonnets; with the gigantic exception of Milton's *Paradise Lost* nobody tried blank verse for narrative, and even the drama was increasingly written in couplets to

35 Cowley, *Poems*, pp. 404–6, 441–3 ('On the Death of Mrs Katherine Philips'), responding to pro-Welsh and pro-Boadicea sympathies in Philips, *Poems*, pp. 202–3 (in one MS called 'On the Brittish Language'); *The Works of Henry Vaughan*, ed. L. C. Martin, 2nd edn (Oxford: Clarendon Press, 1957), p. 641.
36 Anne Bradstreet, *Works*, ed. Jeannine Hensley (Cambridge, MA: Harvard University Press, 1967), pp. 247–70.

emulate the French model that Charles II favoured. Very few long narratives were written in stanzas, with the exception of the Gondibert stanza (a pentameter quatrain rhyming *abab*, used by Davenant for his failed epic of that name), which expresses the ebb and flow of narration and reflection in Dryden's *Heroique Stanzas* on Cromwell and in his *Annus Mirabilis*. Dryden revives this measure to make his peace with the 1650s and advertise his bid to continue Davenant's Laureate project, but it would soon be wickedly parodied in Rochester's 'Disabled Debauchee'.

Shorter lyric forms, in contrast, proliferated at the metropolitan centre of social change. Lampooning and electioneering generated an impressive variety of stanzas, including one uncannily like that of Tennyson's *In Memoriam*.[37] Higher literary aspirations produced two contrasting modes, the tight lyrics in excruciatingly polite language (or its deliberate opposite) favoured by the 'Mob of Gentlemen' – Dorset, Sedley and Rochester – and the 'Pindarique' form popularised by Cowley, frenetically changing rhyme, metre and line length according to the fluctuations of mood and subject. (The problem with these experiments in prosodic freedom and sublime free association is that unlike the Greek original they are fettered by rhyme, as are parts of *Samson Agonistes*.) The 'Pindarique' form would soon reach its apotheosis with Dryden's funeral ode for the poet Anne Killigrew and his 'Alexander's Feast' for musical setting.

Once the octosyllabic couplet had been Butlerised, the universal default mode for discursive poetry became the so-called heroic couplet, pentameters sharply end-stopped and pivoting around an internal caesura. This flexible measure could be strung together into an endless chain or isolated as an autonomous unit in which metrics coalesced with meaning: as in the famous 'Thames couplets' of Denham's *Coopers Hill*, the see-sawing antithesis defined a pair of intersecting factors with the precision of the new mathematics, which could express a complex variation or motion as a graph plotted by x and y coordinates (like pressure and volume in Boyle's Law, p. 825 below). Dryden rapidly developed ways to vary the potential monotony by adding triplets, the third rhyming line often swelling into six or more feet when the subject inspired metrical mimesis: in *Astraea Redux*, the poem that welcomes the King (and blows a smoke screen over his earlier praise of Cromwell), Dryden compares the deafening and blinding gun salute to 'sudden Extasies', and suddenly adds an extra line (line 228). The orderly couplet – further polished by removing archaisms, hard conceits, pleonasms, clanging rhetorical effects like alliteration, thick sound-clusters, indeed any unlawful assembly of vowels and consonants – stood for everything

37 *Englands Vote for a Free Election of a Free Parliament* (1660), cited in Norbrook, *Republic*, pp. 418–19.

modern, fashionable, spruce and loyalist, as Marvell brilliantly demonstrates when he praises the blank verse of *Paradise Lost* in conspicuously rhymed couplets: 'I too transported by the Mode offend', as if the superficial ornament that 'we for fashion wear', the 'tinkling' rhyme that he both exemplifies and parodies, had 'transported' him like a felon away from his Good Old Cause.³⁸

The most significant moment in the history of the Restoration couplet may therefore be Milton's rejection of it in the growling prose preface he dictated for an early reissue of *Paradise Lost*, and the snappy reply he made when Dryden asked permission to turn his epic into a rhyming musical, 'giving him leave to tag his verses'.³⁹ Despite his odic virtuosity in *Samson Agonistes*, Milton declares rhyme 'the Invention of a barbarous Age, to set off wretched matter and lame Meter', already rejected by 'our best English Tragedies' and quite unnecessary for the combination of formality and fluency that sustains 'the sense variously drawn out from one Verse into another'. Publishing a blank verse epic is 'an example set, the first in English, of ancient liberty recovered to Heroic Poem from the troublesom and modern bondage of Rimeing'. Rising above the 'vulgar' new taste for 'the jingling sound of like endings', Milton stages a one-man Restoration – in the sense of an innovative and politically charged return to ancient splendour. The stage was set for an acrimonious battle over the true nature of 'Heroic Verse', which inevitably involved deeper questions of loyalty and dissidence as well as 'jingling' matters of verse form. Marvell's mockery of rhyming, 'tagging of points' and the heroic play in *The Rehearsal Transpros'd* (1672) brought on a counter-attack – apparently by Samuel Butler himself – that links Marvell's 'transprosing' with his friend Milton's blank verse. Milton is both 'authentick' and seditious, 'Schismatick' and 'nonconformable in point of Rhyme'.⁴⁰

Science, religion and the plain style

In philosophy, both natural and political, eminent figures from the 1650s managed to thrive after the Restoration. Hobbes survived to write *Behemoth* (his controversial analysis of the revolution), numerous philosophical papers

38 'On Mr Milton's Paradise lost', lines 46–51.
39 John Aubrey, *Brief Lives, edited from the original Manuscripts*, ed. Oliver Lawson Dick (London: Secker and Warburg, 1949).
40 Marvell, *The Rehearsal Transpros'd*, ed. D. I. B. Smith (Oxford: Clarendon Press, 1971), esp. p. 78; [Richard Leigh or Samuel Butler?], *The Transproser Rehears'd* (Oxford, 1673), in *Milton: The Critical Heritage*, ed. John T. Shawcross (London: Routledge, 1970), p. 78. Milton's proud claim to be 'the first' epic writer in blank verse is not quite true, if the English version of Payne Fisher's *Marston Moor* (cited from MS in Norbrook, *Republic*, p. 449) predates it.

for the Royal Society, and love poetry in which he identifies himself as 'past ninety';[41] frequenting the court, he became a kind of theory guru for rebellious young wits who supposedly cited him in support of atheism and materialism. On a more ethereal plane, Henry More and Lady Anne Conway continued to correspond on an astonishing variety of subjects (Irish ghosts, cabbala, Quakerism, infinity, Scottish witchcraft, stroking cures), and though he abandoned old-fashioned genres like the neo-Spenserian allegorical poem and the cabbalistic rewriting of Scripture More continued to produce voluminous prose treatises arguing for the reality of the invisible world. Another intellectual force of the Caroline era, the humanist scholar and royal tutor Bathsua Makin, revived her project for women's education – not, now, at court but in Tottenham, where she founded a private school to refute the 'debauched' opinion 'that Women are not endued with such Reason as Men, nor capable of improvement by Education as they are'.[42]

Meanwhile, despite the deep association between the Baconian 'Great Instauration' and the Puritan revolution, most of the male scientists and inventors in the Hartlib circle and the Oxford 'invisible college' continued their research and flourished in the newly constituted Royal Society. Though the King himself approached their work in a frivolous spirit, their membership included the greatest names in physics, anatomy, architecture and 'political arithmetic' (Boyle, Hooke, Wren, Petty) as well as technically minded literati, divines and memoirists such as Dryden, Evelyn, Pepys and Wilkins (who continued his speculations on the international language or 'real character' after his promotion to a bishopric). The Irish peer Robert Boyle's publications alone would make the 1660s illustrious in the history of science, and include *New Experiments Physico-Mechanicall Touching the Spring of the Air*, where he lays out the principle that still bears the name Boyle's Law, an elegant quantitative demonstration that pressure and volume relate inversely at constant temperature. His *Sceptical Chymist*, a dialogue in which representatives of different methodologies debate in a polite, temperate tone, provided the theoretical and stylistic model for other intellectual prose works, such as Dryden's *Essay of Dramatick Poesie* (p. 832 below).

This continuity in 'philosophic' writing was helped by hiding old revolutionary allegiances, by transferring the dangerous-sounding rhetoric of innovation to the natural world, and by emphasising the (supposedly) non-controversial basis of scientific truth. Some Royal Society publications of the 1660s covered

---

41 Aubrey, *Brief Lives* p. 158.
42 *An Essay to Revive the Ancient Education of Gentlewomen* (London, 1673), p. 3.

up traces of the millenarian zeal that had fuelled similar projects in the godly decade: Evelyn's treatise on restoring the nation's forests, *Sylva*, fails to mention the almost identical proposals made ten years earlier by the fiery Puritan reformer Ralph Austen. Nevertheless, 1660s eulogies of the new science could sound like the old revolutionary polemic; Cowley's Pindaric ode 'To the Royal Society', for example, celebrates Philosophy's willingness to fight for his 'long-oppressed Right' (though the corrupt old Authorities call it 'Rebellion'), his smashing of old idols and throwing the Garden of Knowledge 'open and free'.[43] Furthermore, the 'scientific revolution' proceeded in part because a common interest in concrete evidence, independent thinking and unadorned style underlay the warring ideological camps. Boyle constantly urges the scientist to test everything against one's 'own particular knowledge' (or at least check that the fellow-relator speaks from direct 'experience'); Bunyan recalls in *Grace Abounding* being advised 'that we took not up any truth upon trust, as from this or that or another man or men, but to cry mightily to God that he would convince us of the reality thereof'. The verification procedures are obviously quite different, but the need for 'conviction' and the rejection of tainted, second-hand authority are similar.

Both the Puritan and the scientist claim to propagate their discoveries in the plainest language: Bunyan renounces the ornate style when narrating God's interventions ('I may not play in my relating of them, but be plain and simple, and lay down the thing as it was'), while the members of the Royal Society (according to the ex-Cromwellian Thomas Sprat) reject metaphor and 'return back to the primitive purity and shortness, when men delivered so many *things* almost in an equal number of words'. Sprat's campaign for 'Mathematical plainness', like Wilkins's efforts to create a 'real' language that conveys things unmediated by words, takes us back both to paradise ('primitive purity', 'a close, naked, natural way of speaking') and to the true character of England ('sincerity' and 'sound simplicity').[44] Cowley's Ode endorses this revolutionary-sounding move from distracting, ornamental Words (mere 'wanton Wit', idle Images, 'the pleasant Labyrinths of ever-fresh Discourse') to satisfyingly concrete Things – in a dazzlingly complex poetry bursting with images, needless to say.

43 Cowley, *Poems*, pp. 448–53, and compare Christopher Hill, *The World Turned Upside Down: Radical Ideas during the English Revolution* (1972; London: Penguin, 1991), p. 363.
44 Boyle, *The Sceptical Chymist* (London, 1661), cited in Steven Shapin and Simon Schaffer, *Leviathan and the Air-Pump: Hobbes, Boyle, and the Experimental Life* (Princeton University Press, 1985), p. 58; Bunyan, *Grace Abounding*, pp. 3–4 ('The Preface'), para. 117; Sprat, *The History of the Royal-Society* (London, 1667), pp. 111–14 (Cowley's ode appears at the front of Sprat's *History*).

A common commitment to 'experimental' lucidity and 'plain style' rhetoric thus united certain factions that were otherwise totally opposed. Bunyan and the Royal Society each insist on first-hand experience rendered in anti-frivolous, stripped-down language – though in fact Cowley and Sprat celebrate their linguistic revolution in ornate metaphors and Bunyan's humble, earthy style is dense with cryptic religious symbols and fantastically adorned with phrases taken from the Tyndale and King James Bibles. *Hudibras* attacks the Independent Ralpho as much for his obscurantist dialect as for his preposterous claims to personal inspiration; just as his faith is 'a dark-Lanthorn of the Spirit' that nobody else can see by, so the divine afflatus, weirdly sounding through his nose 'like Bag-pipe-drone', produces 'Such language as no mortal ear' can hear (1.i.499–514). Davenant praised the powerful Scots General Monck for the 'gracefull plainnesse' of his style, which 'makes our Nation and our Language free'. Edmund Ludlow, the most feared of the exiled militants, espouses the same 'clearness and perspicuity' in his memoirs that the Latitudinarian bishops used to promote Anglican conformity. *Plain English* was the title of a republican tract (refuted by the official censor Sir Roger L'Estrange), but it also served as the basis for the establishment's new approach to religious controversy and Biblical exegesis. The future Archbishop of Canterbury John Tillotson, as an eager young divine working to shake off his Puritan training, consistently emphasises the simple rationality of non-controversial Christianity and its compatibility with worldly interests: his sermon on Psalm 119:96 ('thy Commandment is exceeding broad') sets aside anything difficult and 'Poetical' in the text and declares its 'main Scope and Design very plain and obvious'; a correspondingly plain doctrine emerges from this interpretive decision, as Tillotson assures his elite audience that 'true Religion' guarantees 'the Happiness of Body and Soul ... both in this World and the next', providing the surest way 'to understand our true Interest' and 'secure the main Chance'.[45]

Margaret Cavendish related only obliquely to this scientific and stylistic revolution, though her ambitious literary and philosophical writings continued to proliferate after 1660. She was alienated from the Royal Society by her sex and by her extreme individualism, preferring to reign as 'Margaret the First' over her own imaginary universe than to share power with unworthy and egotistic contemporaries (as she explains in her utopian space novel *The Description of a New World, Called the Blazing World*). Cavendish's sublime confidence in

---

45 Norbrook, *Republic*, pp. 417, 422–3; Ludlow, *Memoirs*, ed. Firth, 2:357; Tillotson, 'The Wisdom of Religion' (delivered 1664), in *Works*, ed. Ralph Barker, 2nd edn (London, 1717), 1:289–93. Even Milton moved to a plainer prose style in the late 1650s.

unaided reason rather than empirical observation also cut her off from the experimenters. In her two-part treatise *Observations upon Experimental Philosophy* (1666) – combining her theories of physics with the fictional *Blazing World*, where the same scientific problems are debated by half-animal humanoids on another planet – Cavendish explores all the questions that occupied Boyle and the Royal Society, but in the end values only the kind of applied science that improves social harmony; she particularly denounces the microscope and the telescope as 'deluding-Glasses' that sow dissension and futile debate, undermining the hierarchy of reason and sense. Cavendish's theory of self-moving matter may anticipate modern biology and atomic physics, but she had no means of persuading anyone else of its truth; instead she relies on increasingly fantastic fiction, where the scientific theme is mingled with Restoration-era social criticism, sexual transgression and theatrical glamour.[46]

Towards 'Restoration' drama

Margaret Cavendish wrote abundantly before and after the Restoration, in a variety of literary modes including drama and epistolary fiction, but her publishing habits changed to match the new decade. Though she was just as much an outsider as Milton, considered mad because she refused to follow conventional fashions of dress and behaviour, she turned away from poetry almost completely and offered her socially oriented, theatre-going, gossip-loving contemporaries a folio collection of *Sociable Letters*, the utopian-satirical fiction of *Blazing World*, a biography of her husband the Civil War leader and two volumes of plays. Over twenty airy and often amusing closet dramas explore gender-bending themes that have attracted recent critical attention. *The Bridals* explores cross-dressing in the lower stratum, in a greasy kitchen-scene reminiscent of Jonson's *Bartholomew Fair*. On a grander level, in *Bell in Campo* (based on an actual episode in the French civil war known as the Fronde) Lady Victoria raises an intractable siege, rides in triumph into the capital and legislates new freedoms for women; in *Youth's Glory and Death's Banquet* one Gentleman declares 'I wish I were a Woman' after realising the natural abilities of the philosopher Lady Sanspareille (who dies inexplicably, however, as if the modern world could not contain such a marvel). *The Female Academy* satirises male efforts to eroticise women's higher education, as does *The Convent of Pleasure*, a cross-dressing romance that proves Cavendish as heteroclite in her gendering of characters as in her self-proclaimed indifference to grammatical gender: 'A great

---

46 *Observations upon Experimental Philosophy*, 2nd edn (London, 1668), fols. a3v, b2v–3, pp. 7–12, 157; *The Blazing World and Other Writings*, ed. Kate Lilley (London: Penguin, 1994), esp. pp. 124, 140–5, 183, 215, 224.

Foreign Princess...of a Masculine Presence' joins the convent 'to be one of Nature's Devotes'; until the conventional *Epicoene*-style ending reveals her true sex (male), 'she' wreaks havoc with the category of Nature fearfully evoked by Lady Happy when she falls in love with this irresistibly amphibious stranger.[47]

The Puritans had moved rapidly to close the theatres in 1642, but they did not extirpate drama entirely (as Martin Butler shows in Chapter 19 above). Political exiles like Margaret Cavendish and Thomas Killigrew wrote their rambling play-scripts during the Commonwealth period, and a few stage performances were commissioned or tolerated under Cromwell: masques to welcome the Portuguese ambassador, drolls at the Red Bull, operas staged with painted scenery in a private theatre set up by Davenant. But the reestablishment of theatre under royal patronage changed the mode of literary *production*, even if dramatic *writing* did not change completely in the 1660s (when the majority of plays were revivals or adaptations of Jacobean originals). The prospect of live performance by glamorous actresses to a fashionable audience drew the energies of writers who might otherwise have attempted novel or epic, even when (like Dryden) they deprecate their effort as mere popular entertainment. Playwrights earned the box-office profits of the third night (if any), could sell their manuscript to a publisher, and hoped for a donation from whoever agreed to accept the dedication in print. Though triumphal arches and allegorical speeches greeted state occasions like his coronation, Charles II never truly revived the panoply of ceremonial, masque and procession that the earlier Stuarts (not to mention contemporary European Kings and Grand Dukes) depended on for the illusion of magnificence and power. Instead, the court might attend the first night or commission a performance in its own Whitehall theatre (which was more like a commercial, ticket-selling playhouse than the structures put up for Inigo Jones's pre-Civil War masques). Aristocratic patronage returned after the Restoration, but it was never the principal source of an author's income; the 'favours' of a patron like Lady Castlemaine (as Wycherley ambiguously puts it) mainly conferred celebrity value on the commodity, boosting sales of tickets and books. From 1670 Aphra Behn lived largely on the proceeds of drama (her first career in espionage having failed because the Crown never delivered its payments), and even Dryden, Poet Laureate after Davenant's death in 1668, needed to write several plays a year.

London theatre began the decade firmly in the hands of survivors from the old regime. One of only two royal patents was held by Thomas Killigrew, whose

---

47 All the plays cited appear in *Playes* (London, 1662), except for *The Convent of Pleasure, a Comedy*, in *Plays, Never Before Printed* (London, 1668); Cavendish attaches no dates to her closet dramas, but does refer to a passion for home theatricals during her exile in Antwerp in the late 1650s.

revival of his own 1641 *Parson's Wedding* with an all-female cast helped to set the taste for bawdy titillation that peaked in the 1670s. The more innovative Duke's Company was run by Sir William Davenant, who literally embodied historical continuity since he enjoyed the reputation of being Shakespeare's bastard son. Davenant had dominated literary culture during the later years of Charles I with lyrics, stage plays, an epic on the magnificent success of the British in Madagascar, and court masques, including the very last one to be performed before the Civil War, *Salmacida Spolia*. In the 1650s he busied himself with the catastrophic epic *Gondibert*, famous for its prefatory critical essays by himself and Hobbes, and almost single-handedly kept theatre alive by staging his own operatic entertainments at Rutland House and The Cockpit, works that did not quite fall into the categories banned by the anti-theatrical laws; performances like *The Siege of Rhodes* (1656) introduced painted scenery and women actors to the public stage years before the Restoration. In 1660 Davenant was well placed to obtain the other patent that Charles II held out for aspiring theatre managers, even though the restored but powerless Master of the Revels tried to accuse him of having performed that office for 'Oliver the Tyrant'. For eight years Davenant (now Poet Laureate) filled the stage with his own revived compositions – in one case embedded in a surreal, metatheatrical framing device, *The Playhouse to Be Let* – and with highly popular musicals based on Shakespeare, tidied up according to neoclassical criteria and embellished with all the 'Finery' he could muster. *Macbeth* received 'new Cloaths, new Scenes, Machines, as flyings for the Witches, Singing and Dancing'; *The Tempest* (co-adapted with Dryden) adds extra *ingénues* and the kind of anti-Puritan satire that was virtually obligatory in this decade. Building on his Cromwell-era experiments, Davenant established the physical as well as the literary form of the Restoration theatre – a luxurious and flexible auditorium with a range of galleries and boxes for all classes from valets to duchesses, a benched 'pit' for the trendiest critics and the loosest women, and a stage that combined the projecting apron and permanent entry-doors of the Caroline theatre with an inner 'scene' for changeable painted sets; the old 'wooden O' (*Henry V*, Prologue, line 13) and its stinking groundlings had gone for ever. After this triumph the new/old Laureate was laid to rest in Westminster Abbey, in the grave from which Tom May had been exhumed.[48]

As Roger Boyle's stage adaptations of romance material suggest, new writers for the stage largely worked with older materials and squeezed their plays into

---

48 *Dictionary of National Biography*; *Macbeth* playbill cited in George Henry Nettleton, *English Drama of the Restoration and Eighteenth Century (1642–1780)* (New York: Macmillan, 1914), pp. 5–6.

a repertoire dominated by revivals. (Pepys saw Jonson's *Bartholomew Fair* seven times, even though it pained him to see the Puritans mocked, and when Dryden needed to illustrate a perfect English play in the *Essay of Dramatick Poesie* he chose Jonson's *Epicoene*, in which the last surviving boy actor had made a dazzling impact in 1661.) Nevertheless, many younger writers including Dryden were drawn in to the London theatre, either as playwrights or collaborators. Even Margaret Cavendish's old Cavalier husband ventured onto the stage; his *Sir Martin Mar-all* (1667), a farce about a bumbling aristocrat co-written with Dryden with borrowings from Molière, was the smash hit of the decade, perhaps providing comic catharsis for the real-life catastrophes of the Royalist war machine, past and present. At least three women had scripted plays by 1670 (Philips's translated *Pompey* and *Horace*, Frances Boothby's *Marcelia*, Aphra Behn's *The Forced Marriage*), and the theatre also gave brief fame to writers from the outer nations of Britain: the Irish peer Roger Boyle (whose work ranged from the heroic *Henry V* to the picaresque *Guzman* anticipated the later triumph of his countrymen Congreve, Sheridan and Goldsmith; a generation before George Farquhar, the Scots humorist and translator Thomas Sydserff (or Saint Serfe as he became in fashionable London) enjoyed a hit with *Tarugo's Wiles* (1667), a typical mix of Spanish intrigue and knockabout humour in the new setting of a 'Coffee House'.[49]

Compared to sleek performances like *The Country-Wife*, *The Man of Mode*, *All for Love* or *The Way of the World* – canonical 'Restoration' dramas discussed in the next volume of the *Cambridge History* – the theatre of the 1660s looks quite heterogeneous. It mixes serious and comic modes, Spanish and English settings, prose, blank verse and brassy heroic couplets, chivalric Love-and-Honour plots and low topical humour, while rare attempts at uniformly serious tragedy, like Sir Robert Howard's *The Duke of Lerma*, seem to have failed at the box office. Etherege's *Comical Revenge* captures the ethos of the 'Sons of Belial' in the riotous Sir Frederick Frolick, but Etherege also packs in a witty courtship plot (rewarding Sir Frederick with his love object), an anti-French farce involving a cure for syphilis, a lofty sword-and-cape romance in couplets, and a low trickery plot in which an old Cromwellian is married to a whore. City comedy was easily updated into triumphalist anti-Puritan satire, following Tatham's *Rump* and Cowley's *Cutter of Coleman Street* (whose plot is driven by resentment at the plundering of the defeated Royalists); Edward Howard's

---

49 For plot summaries of virtually all the plays of Restoration London, by genre and decade, see Robert D. Hume, *The Development of English Drama in the Late Seventeenth Century* (Oxford: Clarendon Press, 1976).

1664 *The Usurper* thinly disguises the revolutionary leaders in Italian melo-drama, while his brother Robert's *The Committee* (1662) opens the wound of Cromwell-era confiscations and, for good measure, creates a 'lovable' stage Irishman with the ethnic nickname 'Teague'. Etherege's *She Would If She Could* (1668) introduces comic Puritans alongside more typically 'Restoration' mo-tifs (sexual voracity of upper-class ladies, stylishly lewd songs, brilliant repartee between liberated young couples), a good example of the need to display the caged enemy at the heart of Vanity Fair.

The best drama of the decade, ironically, may not be a play at all but a critical dialogue. Dryden's *Essay of Dramatick Poesie* (1668) expands upon the pref-aces and defences that he was starting to attach to his plays, raising their intellectual and commercial value at once. Set disquisitions – on false and true wit, Nature and Imitation, plausibility and poetic licence, ancients and moderns, mixed plots and unity of action, French and English drama, Jonson and Shakespeare – are distributed among a quartet of speakers, emulating the 'Sceptical' and 'modest' discourses of the Royal Society where the issues are 'determined by the Readers'.[50] Dryden's four characters encapsulate the new literary establishment, the two brothers working to dominate the London stage (Sir Robert Howard and Dryden himself, who gets the last and largest speeches), and the two court wits (Sedley and Buckhurst/Dorset) in whom converge the highest and the lowest echelons of Restoration culture, the drunken riot and the hegemonic 'conversation of the gentleman' – increasingly the criterion by which Dryden will judge literary quality. As in contemporary comedy, these interactions are embedded in a topical context. The recent past and the present are vividly brought in as the wits parallel bad poets to 'Levellers' and 'seditious Preachers' and assess the cultural damage done by the revolution; since 'we have been so long together bad Englishmen that we had not leisure to be good Poets', the crucial question then becomes whether Restoration drama can com-pete with the achievement of the Jacobeans. The dialogue takes place during the Anglo-Dutch naval war that Dryden had just raised to epic status in *Annus Mirabilis*: the foursome take a boat down the Thames to catch the sound of gun-fire, prompting their speculations on Englishness in the theatre, on cultural nationalism versus 'submission' to a foreign power – the prescriptive neoclas-sical 'Rules' of French theory, in particular the 'three unities' of time, action and place. Returning to Westminster, they 'stood a while looking back on the

---

50 As Dryden claims in the 'Defence' of the *Essay* prefacing the second edition of *The Indian Emperour* (1668), in *Works*, 9:15; the *Essay* itself is cited from *Works*, 17:3–81, esp. pp. 9–11, 33, 63, 80.

water, upon which the Moon-beams played, and made it appear like floating quick-silver; at last they went up through a crowd of French people who were merrily dancing in the open air', as if oblivious to the imperial might of English culture.

Like Sidney's *Apology for Poetry*, Dryden's *Essay* theorises its chosen genre before it coalesced into canonical form. As in *Annus Mirabilis*, Dryden conjures up a future vision while pretending to celebrate the existing achievements of Royalism: 'with the restoration of our happiness, we see revived poesie lifting up its head, and already shaking off the rubbish' of Civil War barbarism. Yet even this extreme assertion of 'Restoration' discontinuity recalls the most striking moment in 'Revolutionary' discourse – Milton's vision in *Areopagitica* of England rousing herself from her Royalist sleep, shaking her mighty locks.

Chronological outline of historical events and texts in Britain, 1528–1674, with list of selected manuscripts

REBECCA LEMON

Historical events 1528–1558

Monarchs of England: Henry VIII (1509–47); Edward VI (1547–53); Mary I (1553–8).
Archbishops of Canterbury: William Warham (1504–32); Thomas Cranmer (1533–53); Reginald Pole (1554–8).
Monarchs of Scotland: James V (1513–42); Mary Stuart, Queen of Scots (1542–68).

1529 'Reformation' Parliament; fall of Cardinal Thomas Wolsey, succeeded as Lord Chancellor by Thomas More.

1530 Hugh Latimer begins to preach reformation in the west of England.

1533 Thomas Cranmer made Archbishop of Canterbury. Henry VIII divorces Catherine of Aragon and marries Anne Boleyn; birth of Elizabeth. Act in Restraint of Appeals (English subjects prohibited from appealing to Rome for legal judgement in certain types of cases: in effect, termination of papal supremacy in England).

1534 Parliamentary Act of Supremacy designating Henry VIII 'Supreme Head' of Church of England; abjuration of papal supremacy by the clergy. Ignatius Loyola founds the Society of Jesus.

1535 Execution of Sir Thomas More and Bishop John Fisher for refusing to take the Oath of Supremacy.

1536 Ten Articles of Religion; Act for dissolution of smaller monasteries. Henry VIII divorces and beheads Anne Boleyn on charges of adultery and incest. Henry marries Jane Seymour; birth of Edward.

1536–7 Pilgrimage of Grace (armed uprising against Henry's and Thomas Cromwell's religious and political innovations by traditionalists in north of England); Acts of Union of England and Wales.

1536–8 First and second Royal Injunctions of Henry VIII, authorising preparation and publication of an English Bible.

1538 James V of Scotland marries Marie de Guise.

1539 Six Articles of Religion; Act for dissolution of greater monasteries; 'Great Bible' set up in parish churches.

1540 Henry VIII marries Anne of Cleves, marriage annulled; then marries Catherine Howard. Fall and execution of Thomas Cromwell, Henry's chief

[834]

minister. Robert Barnes, Thomas Garrett and William Jerome burned for heresy.

1541 John Calvin founds the 'City of God' in Geneva.

1542 Catherine Howard beheaded. Battle of Solway Moss: Henry VIII defeats James V.

1543 Royal injunctions restricting Bible reading in English. Henry VIII marries Katherine Parr.

1545 Council of Trent convenes, with the aim of reforming the Catholic Church.

1546 Anne Askew burned for heresy.

1547 Execution of Thomas Howard, Earl of Surrey, on imputation of treason. John Knox begins preaching.

1548 Infant Mary, Queen of Scots, betrothed to the Dauphin, the future Francis II of France.

1549 Act of Uniformity of Church of England; first Book of Common Prayer. Hugh Latimer preaches Lenten sermons before Edward. Kett's Rebellion (violent social and political protests in Norfolk and Suffolk that seriously threatened the regime of Lord Protector Edward Seymour).

1552 Revised Book of Common Prayer; execution of Lord Protector Seymour, Duke of Somerset. John Dudley, Duke of Northumberland, becomes Lord Protector.

1553 Forty-Two Articles (set of fundamental religious doctrines of the reformed Church of England under Edward VI). Lady Jane Grey becomes 'Nine Days' Queen'; Mary's claim to the throne vindicated.

1554 Parliamentary Act repealing Royal Supremacy; reinstatement of Latin Mass; revival of heresy Acts. Marriage of Mary to Philip II of Spain. Execution of Lady Jane Grey for treason. Wyatt's rebellion (uprising on behalf of religious reform).

1555 Burnings of Latimer and Nicholas Ridley, deposed Bishop of London. Bull of Pope Paul IV declaring Ireland a kingdom; Mary of Guise Regent in Scotland.

1557 Stationers' Company incorporated in London. First swearing of the Covenant in Scotland by barons who supported the first preachers of reform and bound themselves together for mutual support.

1558 Loss of Calais to France.

Literature of Europe 1528–1558

1528 BALDASSARE CASTIGLIONE, *Il Libro del Cortegiano (Book of the Courtier)*

1529 ANTONIO DE GUEVARA, *Dial of Princes*

1532 FRANÇOIS RABELAIS, *Pantagruel*; *Gargantua* (1534)

1535 *Biblia. The Bible, that is, the Holy Scripture*, the first complete English Bible, compiled by Miles Coverdale (printed in Germany)

1536 JEAN CALVIN, *Institutes of the Christian Religion* (French version; Latin, 1539)

1541 GIAMBATTISTA GIRALDI CINTHIO, *Orbecche*
1543 NICOLAS COPERNICUS, *De Revolutionibus* (exposition of heliocentric theory)
1549 JOACHIM DU BELLAY, *Défense et illustration de la langue française*
1554 ANON., *Lazarillo de Tormes*
1555 LOUISE LABÉ, *Oeuvres*

Literature of Britain 1528–1558

ENGLAND

THOMAS MORE (1477/8–1535). Member of Parliament (1504); Master of Requests
and Privy Councillor (1517); Speaker of the Commons (1523); Lord Chancellor
(1529–32); executed for treason (1535).

1516 *Utopia* (in Latin; English translation, 1551, by RALPH ROBYNSON)
1529 *Dialogue concerning Heresies; The Supplication of Souls*
1532–3 *Confutation of Tyndale's Answer*
1533 *Apology of Sir Thomas More, Knight*
1534 *A Dialogue of Comfort Against Tribulation*

THOMAS CRANMER (1489–1556). Cambridge University (BA 1512; MA 1515).
Attracts Henry VIII's attention with the proposal that he obtain a divorce
(1530). First Archbishop of Canterbury in an autonomous Church of England
(1533–53). Godfather at Princess Elizabeth's baptism (1533). Arrested for
treason under Queen Mary (1553); imprisoned at Oxford with Hugh Latimer
and Nicholas Ridley (1554). Recants his reformed beliefs under threat of
burning for heresy (February–March 1556); reaffirms his reformed beliefs and
dies at the stake (20 March 1556).

1530 with EDWARD FOX, *Collectanea satis copiosa* (*A Sufficiently Plentiful
Compilation*), historical sources on ancient autonomy of English monarchy
1544 compiler of royally authorised English *Litany*
1547 principal contributor to royally authorised *Book of Homilies*
1549 compiler of royally authorised English Book of Common Prayer
1550 *A Defence of the True and Catholic Doctrine of the Sacrament; Answer
unto . . . Stephen Gardiner* (who had sharply attacked the *Defence* in print)
1552 Book of Common Prayer revised

WILLIAM TYNDALE (c. 1494–1536). Magdalen College, Oxford (BA 1513; MA
1515). Unsuccessfully petitions Cuthbert Tunstall, Bishop of London, to
sponsor his proposed English translation of the Bible (1523); leaves England for
Hamburg (1524). Relocates in Antwerp in community of English merchants
(1532); arrested and imprisoned in Vilvorde Castle, a state prison in the Spanish
Netherlands (1535); burned at the stake there for heresy (1536).

1525 *The New Testament*, English translation from Erasmus's Greek–Latin edition.
1527 *Parable of the Wicked Mammon*

1528 *Obedience of a Christian Man*
1530 *Practice of Prelates*
1531 *Answer to Sir Thomas More's Dialogue*
1534 *The New Testament, diligently corrected and compared with the Greek* (pub. Antwerp)

1529 LEONARD COX, *Art or Craft of Rhetoric*
1529 SIMON FISH, *Supplication for the Beggars*
1530 ROBERT COPLAND, *Hye Way to the Spytall House*
1530 THOMAS MOULTON, *The Mirror or Glass of Health*
1530 Debate on Henry VIII's divorce, including 'The Glasse of the Truth';
    WILLIAM MARSHALL, trans. MARSILIUS OF PADUA, *Defensor Pacis*;
    JOHN FISHER, *De causa matrimonii serenissime Regis Angliae*
1531 THOMAS ELYOT, *The Boke Named the Governour*
1531 CHRISTOPHER SAINT GERMAN, *A dyalogue in Engliyshe betwyxt a doctoure of dyvynyte and a student in the lawes*
1532 JOHN SKELTON, *Garland of Laurel* published
1533 *The Court of Venus*
1533 JOHN HEYWOOD, Interludes: *The Play of the Weather; A Play of Love* (1534)
1534 WILLIAM MARSHALL, *A Primer in English*; revised as *A Goodly Primer in English* (1535)
1534-5 THOMAS GODFRAY, *A Primer in English*
1535 STEPHEN GARDINER, *De vera obedientia*
1536 HENRY PARKER, *Tryumphes of Fraunces Petrarcke*
1537 *The Bible, which is all the Holy Scripture*, English compilation by Miles Coverdale and John Rogers ('Thomas Mathew' Bible)
1538 JOHN BALE, *Three Laws of Nature, Moses, and Christ* (pub. 1548); *King John*, Parts 1 and 2; *God's Promises*
1538 THOMAS ELYOT, *Latin–English Dictionary Castel of Helth*; *The Banquet of Sapience* (1539)
1539 *The Bible in English* ('Great Bible') (Paris); *The Bible . . . with a Prologue by Thomas, Archbishop of Canterbury* ('Cranmer's Bible') (London, 1540)
1539 RICHARD MORISON, *An Invective against Treason: An Exhortation to Stir all Englishmen to the Defence of their Country*
1540 JOHN PALSGRAVE, *Acolastus*
c. 1540 THOMAS ELYOT, *The Image of Governance*
1542 ANDREW BORDE, *The fyrst boke of the Introduction of Knowledge* (pub. 1548)
?1542 HENRY BRINKELOW, *The Complaint of Roderick Mors*
1542 JOHN GOUGH, *The Copy of the Submission of O'Neill*
1542 EDWARD HALL, *The Union of the two noble and illustrious families of Lancaster and York* (full text pub. 1548)
1543 *A Necessary Doctrine and Erudition of a Christian Man (The King's Book)*

1544 ELIZABETH TUDOR, *A Godly Medytacyon of the Christen Sowle*, Eng. trans. of
    MARGUERITE DE NAVARRE, *Le Miroir de l'âme pécheresse* (pub. John Bale,
    Marburg, 1548)
1545 THOMAS ELYOT, *The Defence of Good Women*
1545 JOHN HEYWOOD, *The Four P. P.*
1545 KATHERINE PARR, *Prayers or Meditations*
1545 EDWARD WALSHE, *The Office and Duty in Fighting for Our Country*
1546 ANNE ASKEW, *First* and *Latter Examinations*
1546 JOHN HEYWOOD, *Proverbs*
1547 THOMAS BECON, *A New Dialog betwene thangell of God, & the Shepherdes in the
    Felde*
1547 KATHERINE PARR, *Lamentation of a Sinner*
1547 LUKE SHEPHERD, *John Bon and Mast Person; Upcheering of the Mass* (1548)
1548 WILLIAM BALDWIN, *A Treatise of Moral Philosophy*
1548 JOHN BALE, *Image of Both Churches*
1548 HUGH LATIMER, *Sermon of the Plow*
1548 THOMAS STERNHOLD and JOHN HOPKINS, *Certain Psalms; Psalms of David*
    (1549); *Whole Book of Psalms* (1562)
1548–54 ROBERT PARKYN, *Life of Christ*
1549 JOHN BALE, *The Laboryouse journey and serche of Johan Leylande for England's
    antiquities*
1549 JOHN CHEKE, *The Hurte of Sedition*
c. 1549 THOMAS SMITH, *Discourse of the Commonweal of England* (pub. 1581)

THOMAS WYATT (1503–42). Marshal of Calais (1528–30); Commissioner of the
    Peace in Essex (1532). Knighted (1535); imprisoned in the Tower (1536, 1541).
    Ambassador to Spain (1537–9).
    c. 1530s–40s Devonshire Manuscript of verse (BL, MS Additional 17492)
    1540s Seven prologues and seven penitential Psalms in verse (modeled on
    PIETRO ARETINO's prose version of the *Psalms* (Venice, 1534))
    c. 1540–1600 Arundel Harington Manuscript, including verse by Wyatt
    c. 1542–9 Egerton Manuscript of verse (BL, MS Egerton 2711)
    1557 *Tottel's Miscellany* published by Richard Tottel; includes sonnets by Wyatt

HENRY HOWARD, EARL OF SURREY (1517?–47). Travels to France with Henry
    VIII (1532). Imprisoned at Windsor Castle (1537). Knight of the Garter (1541).
    Arrested (1542); imprisoned (1543). Soldier in France (1545–6). Executed for
    treason (1547).
    c. 1540–1600 Arundel Harington Manuscript, including verse by Surrey
    1554; 1557 VERGIL, *Aeneid*, selections; Eng. blank verse trans. published
    1557 *Tottel's Miscellany* published by Richard Tottel; includes sonnets by Surrey

1549 ROBERT CROWLEY, *Voice of the Last Trumpet; The Way to Wealth* (1550);
      Philargyrie of Great Britain (1551)
1550 THOMAS LEVER, *Sermons*
1550 LEWIS WAGER, *Life and Repentance of Mary Magdalene*
1551 RALPH ROBINSON, Eng. trans. of THOMAS MORE's *Utopia* published
1552 NICHOLAS UDALL, *Ralph Roister Doister*
1553 JOHN BALE, *Vocation to the Bishopric of Ossorie in Ireland*
1553 WILLIAM BALDWIN, *Beware the Cat*
c. 1553 W. STEVENSON (?), *Gammer Gurton's Needle*
1553 THOMAS WILSON, *Arte of Rhetorique*
1554 JOHN CHRISTOPHERSON, *Exhortation to all menne to take hede and beware of rebellion*
1554 MILES HOGARDE, *The Assault of the Sacrament of the Altar*
c. 1554 NICHOLAS UDALL (?), *Jacob and Esau*
1555 EDMUND BONNER, *A Profitable and Necessary Doctrine, with Certain Homilies Adjoined* (by JOHN HARPSFIELD and HENRY PENDLETON)
1555 JOHN HEYWOOD, *Two Hundred Epigrams*
1555 JOHN PERKINS, *A Profitable booke treating of the lawes of England*
c. 1555 WILLIAM ROPER, *The Lyfe of Sir Thomas More, knyghte* (pub. as *The Mirrour of Vertue in Worldly Greatnes*, Paris, 1626)
1555 RICHARD SHERRY, *Treatise of Schemes and Tropes*
1555 JOHN WAYLAND, *An Uniform and Catholic Primer*
1556 NICHOLAS HARPSFIELD, *Life and Death of Sir Thomas More*
1556 JOHN HEYWOOD, *The Spider and the Fly*
1556 MILES HOGARDE, *The Displaying of the Protestants*
1556 JOHN PONET, *A Shorte Treatise of Politike Power*
1557 WILLIAM STANFORD, *Les plees del coron*
1557 RICHARD TOTTEL, *Songs and Sonnets, written by the . . . late Earl of Surrey and others* ('Tottel's Miscellany')

SCOTLAND

1537 DAVID LINDSAY, *Deploration of the Death of Quene Magdalene; The Complaynt and Testament of a popinjay* (1538)
1540 HECTOR BOECE, *The historie and croniklis of Scotland* (Scots trans. of Latin original, 1527)
1540 DAVID LINDSAY, *Ane Satyre of the Thrie Estaits* (pub. Edinburgh, 1602); *Tragedie of the late moste reverende father David [Cardinall Beaton]* (1547)
1550 ALEXANDER ALANE, *Edinburgi regiae Scotorum urbis descriptio*, in SEBASTIAN MÜNSTER, *Cosmographia* (Basle)
1550 ROBERT WEDDERBURN, *The Complaynt of Scotland*
1553 GAVIN DOUGLAS, *Virgil's Aeneid Translated into Scottish Verse*

1554 JOHN KNOX, *A godly letter sent to the fayethfull in London, Newcastell, Barwyke, and to all other within the realme of Englande, that loue the comminge of oure Lorde Iesus* (Rome [for London])

1554 DAVID LINDSAY, *Ane Dialog betuix Experience and ane Courteour*

1555 PATRICK COCKBURN, *In dominicam orationem pia meditatio* (St Andrews)

1556 WILLIAM LAUDER, *Ane compendious and breue tractate concerning the office and dewtie of Kingis, spirituall Pastoris and temporall jugis* (St Andrews); *Ane godlie tractate or mirrour* [on doctrine of the elect] (Edinburgh, 1569); *Ane prettie mirrour or conference, betuix the faithfull Protestant and the dissemblit false hypocreit* (Edinburgh, 1570)

WALES

1547 WILLIAM SALESBURY, *A Dictionary in Englyshe and Welshe* (London)

1551 SALESBURY, *Lliver gweddi gyffredin* (Welsh trans. of Book of Common Prayer) (pub. London)

1554 *A Newe Ballade of the Marigolde*

IRELAND

c. 1541 Annals of Ulster

1542 'The copye of the submissyon of Oneyll'

1551 Book of Common Prayer printed at Dublin

1553 JOHN BALE, *God's Promises* performed in Kilkenny

Historical Events 1558–1603

Monarchs of England: Elizabeth I (1558–1603).

Archbishops of Canterbury: Matthew Parker (1559–75); Edmund Grindal (1576–83); John Whitgift (1583–1603).

Monarchs of Scotland: Mary, Queen of Scots (1542–68); James VI (1568–1625).

1559 Queen Elizabeth 'Supreme Governor' of the Church of England (Act of Uniformity); Elizabethan Book of Common Prayer.

1560 Treaty of Edinburgh (Mary agrees to cease styling herself 'Queen of England'). John Knox returns to Scotland. Scottish Parliament abolishes papal jurisdiction; Calvinism adopted.

1562 John Hawkins and Francis Drake initiate slave trade with America.

1562–98 French wars of religion.

1563 Thirty-Nine Articles (doctrinal formulary of the Church of England promulgated during the Elizabethan Settlement of Religion). Act for the Translation of the Bible and the Divine Service into the Welsh Tongue. Severe outbreak of plague in London. Council of Trent adjourned.

1566 James VI of Scotland born. Thomas Gresham founds Royal Exchange in London.

1567–98 Revolt of the Netherlands against Spanish rule.

1568 Battle of Langside, 13 May: Mary, Queen of Scots, flees to England, after defeat by self-appointed custodians of her infant son, James Stuart. English Catholics found college at Douai, France.

1569 Northern Rebellion (armed uprising to place Thomas Howard, Duke of Norfolk, and Mary, Queen of Scots, on the English throne).

1570 Pope Pius V excommunicates Elizabeth and releases her Catholic subjects from loyalty to her.

1571 Subscription Act (oath subscribing to the Thirty-Nine Articles, required of all English clergy).

1571 Act for incorporation of Universities of Oxford and Cambridge. Don John of Austria defeats Ottoman fleet at Lepanto.

1572 Duke of Norfolk executed for treason. Archbishop Mathew Parker founds Society of Antiquaries in London. St Bartholomew's Day massacre: 8,000 Protestants die in Paris and outlying areas.

1574 Leicester's company of actors formed.

1576 The Theatre built in London.

1577 Opening of the Curtain Theatre. Elizabeth suspends Archbishop Edmund Grindal for refusing to suppress Puritan 'prophesyings'.

1577–80 Francis Drake starts his voyage around the world.

1579 Pope Gregory XIII establishes English Jesuit college in Rome.

1581 Scottish National Covenant, or First Covenant (James VI signs a bond, drawn up by Protestant ministers, detailing a Reformed confession of faith and the superstitions and errors to be combated; it is subsequently signed by the courtiers and the people).

1582 Ruthven Raid: William Ruthven, 1st Earl of Gowrie, and other Protestants seize James VI, who escapes (1583); Gowrie executed (1584).

1584 Scottish parliamentary 'Black Acts', establishing royal power over Church of Scotland. Cambridge University Press founded. Sir Walter Ralegh founds first English colony in North America, on Roanoke Island. Oaths (Bonds) of Association for preservation of Elizabeth's life and crown, against plots to replace her with Mary, Queen of Scots.

1586 Robert Sidney appointed Governor of Flushing. James VI signs Treaty of Berwick with Elizabeth I. Trial of Mary, Queen of Scots, for conspiracy against Elizabeth's life. Mary executed (early 1587).

1588 Defeat of the Spanish Armada; Elizabeth's speech at Tilbury. Death of Robert Dudley, Earl of Leicester, Elizabeth's most enduring favourite.

1589 Assassination of Henry III of France.

1591 Ralegh imprisoned and released. Trinity College founded in Dublin.

1592 Rose Theatre opened. Outbreak of plague in London. Galileo invents the thermometer.

1594–6 Swan Theatre built.

1595 Ralegh's voyage to Guiana. English Jesuit priest and author, Robert Southwell, executed for treason.

1596 Blackfriars Theatre opened. Cadiz expedition led by Robert Devereux, Earl of Essex, Elizabeth's last major favourite.
1597 English campaign to aid Protestants in Spanish Netherlands.
1598 Elizabethan Poor Law (also 1601). Death of William Cecil, Lord Burghley, Elizabeth's principal minister.
1598–1603 Rebellion of Hugh O'Neill, Earl of Tyrone; unsuccessfully opposed by Essex; suppressed by Charles Blount, Lord Mountjoy.
1599 Globe Theatre built. Episcopal ban on publication of satires.
1600 Gowrie Conspiracy: John Ruthven, 3rd Earl of Gowrie, attempts to seize James VI (5 August). Fortune Theatre built. East India Company founded in London.
1601 Essex and conspirators unsuccessfully attempt rebellion against Elizabeth; Essex is tried and executed for treason.
1602 Bodleian Library founded.

Literature of Europe 1558–1603

1554–73 MATTEO BANDELLO, *Novelle*, Vols. 1–4
1558 MARGUERITE DE NAVARRE, *Heptameron*
c. 1559 JORGE DE MONTEMAYOR, *Diana*
1561 JULIUS CAESAR SCALIGER, *Poetices libri septem*
1565 GIAMBATTISTA GIRALDI CINTHIO, *Gli Hecatommithi*
1573 TORQUATO TASSO, *Aminta*
1574 GUILLAUME DE SALUSTE DU BARTAS, *Judith*
1575 VERONICA FRANCO, *Terze rime*
1575 PIERRE DE RONSARD, *Sonnets pour Hélène*
1578 GUILLAUME DE SALUSTE DU BARTAS, *La Sepmaine*
1580 MICHEL EYQUEM DE MONTAIGNE, *Essais*, Books 1–2
1580–1 TASSO, *Gerusalemme Liberata*
1582 *The New Testament of our Lord and Saviour Jesus Christ . . . translated out of the Latin Vulgate* (Rheims)
1584 CLAUDIO MONTEVERDI, *Canzonette a tre voci, libro primo* (first book of madrigals)
1585 GIORDANO BRUNO, *Eroici Furori*
1591 TASSO, *Aminta* printed in London.
1594 TASSO, *Discorsi del Poema Eroica*
1595 MONTAIGNE, *Essais*, Books 1–3 (posthumous edition)

Literature of Britain 1558–1603

ENGLAND

1558 CHRISTOPHER GOODMAN, *How Superior Powers Oght to be Obeid* (Geneva)
1559 JOHN AYLMER, *An Harborowe for faithfull and trewe subjects*
1559 WILLIAM BALDWIN, *A Mirror for Magistrates*

c. 1559 JOHN PHILIP, *Patient and Meek Grissel*

1560 *The Bible and holy scriptures . . . with moste profitable annotations* ('Geneva Bible')

1560 ANON., *Nice Wanton*

1560 ANNE LOK DERING PROWSE, Eng. trans. of CALVIN, *Sermons*

c. 1560 W. WAGER, *Enough is as Good as a Feast*

1561 THOMAS HOBY, Eng. trans. of CASTIGLIONE, *Book of the Courtier*

c. 1561 THOMAS PRESTON (?), *Cambyses, King of Persia*

1561 THOMAS SACKVILLE and THOMAS NORTON, *Gorboduc, or Ferrex and Porrex*

1562 JOHN JEWEL, *An Apology of the Church of England*

1563 JOHN FOXE, *Ecclesiastical History*, first Eng. text of *Acts and Monuments* ('Book of Martyrs'); the 1559 Latin version, *Historia ecclesiastica*, is further expanded in subsequent Eng. edns (1570, 1576, 1583)

1563 BARNABY GOOGE, *Eclogues, Epitaphs, and Sonnets*

1563 THOMAS SACKVILLE, Induction to *Mirror for Magistrates*

1564–6 ROGER ASCHAM, *The Scolemaster* (pub. 1570)

1565 WILLIAM BIRCH, *A Warning to Englande; Let London Begin to Repent*

1565 RICHARD EDWARDS, *Damon and Pythias*

1565 JOHN HALL, *The Court of Virtue*

1565 THOMAS SMITH, *De Republica Anglorum* (pub. 1584)

1566 GEORGE GASCOIGNE, *Supposes; Jocasta*

1566 WILLIAM PAINTER, *The Palace of Pleasure*

1567 ANON., *Clyomon and Clamydes*

1567 THOMAS DRANT, *Horace's Art of Poetry, Epistles, and Satires Englished*

1567 ARTHUR GOLDING, Eng. trans. of Ovid's *Metamorphoses*

1567 EDWARD HAKE, *Newes out of Powles Churchyarde*

1567 WILLIAM STANFORD, *An exposition of the kinges prerogative*

1567 GEORGE TURBERVILLE, *Epitaphes, Epigrams, Songs and Sonnets*

1567 ISABELLA WHITNEY, *A Copy of a Letter*

1567–8 'Rogue Tracts', including THOMAS HARMAN, *Caveat or Warning for Common Cursetors*; WILLIAM COPLAND, *Dialogue between Two Beggars*

1568 *The holi bible, conteyning the olde testament and the newe* ('Bishops' Bible')

1572 THOMAS WILCOX and JOHN FIELD, *Admonition to the Parliament*

1572 THOMAS WILSON, *Discourse upon Usury*

1573 GEORGE GASCOIGNE, *Adventures of Master F. J.; A Hundreth Sundrie Flowers*

1573 ISABELLA WHITNEY, *A Sweet Nosegay*

1574 THOMAS CARTWRIGHT, *Second Admonition to the Parliament*

1575 GEORGE GASCOIGNE, *The Glass of Government; Posies; Certain Notes of Instruction; Princely Pleasures of . . . Kenilworth* (1576); *The Steel Glass* (1576)

1576 GEORGE PETTIE, *A Petite Palace of Pettie his Pleasure*

c. 1577 THOMAS LUPTON, *All for Money*

1577 HENRY PEACHAM, *The Garden of Eloquence*

1577–8 RAPHAEL HOLINSHED, *Chronicles of England, Scotland and Ireland*; rev. edn
       (1586–7) incorporates WILLIAM HARRISON, *A Description of England*, and
       RICHARD STANYHURST, *A Description of Ireland*
1579 STEPHEN GOSSON, *The School of Abuse*
1579 THOMAS NORTH, *Lives of the Noble Grecians and Romans*; Eng. trans. of
     JACQUES AMYOT's French trans. of PLUTARCH's Greek.

JOHN LYLY (*c.* 1554–1606). Oxford University (BA 1573; MA 1575). Seeks position
     at court. Receives patronage of Edward de Vere, Earl of Oxford, who helps him
     organise a company of boy players to perform at Blackfriars Theatre. Writes for
     the boys' acting companies of the Chapel Royal and St Paul's Cathedral;
     appointed 'vice master' of St Paul's company. Elected MP three times, starting
     in 1589.
     1578 *Euphues: The Anatomy of Wit*
     1580 *Euphues and His England*
     c. 1582 *Campaspe*
     1584 *Sappho and Phao*
     1585 *Gallathea* (pub. 1592)
     1588 *Endimion, or Man in the Moon* (pub. 1591)
     1589 *Midas*; *Mother Bombie*; *Pappe with an Hatchet*
     c. 1590 *Love's Metamorphosis*

EDMUND SPENSER (*c.* 1552–99). Secretary to John Young, Bishop of Rochester
     (1578). Secretary to Lord Grey of Wilton (1580). Undertaker for settlement of
     Munster (*c.* 1588). Settles at Kilcolman Castle, County Cork. Flees Kilcolman
     during rebellion in Ireland (1598). Dies in London.
     1569 'Visions' and sonnets modelled on Petrarch and Du Bellay, published in *A
           Theatre for Worldings*, Eng. trans. of JAN VAN DEN NOOT's Dutch original
     1579 *The Shepheardes Calender*
     1586 *Astrophel*, pastoral elegy on the death of Philip Sidney
     1587 *Colin Clouts Come Home Again* (pub. 1595)
     1590 *The Faerie Queene*, Books 1–3 (composed after 1580)
     1590–1 *Muiopotmos, or the Fate of the Butterflie*
     1591 *Ruines of Time*; *Complaints, Containing sundrie small Poemes of the Worlds
           Vanity*; *Daphnaida*
     1595 *Amoretti*; *Epithalamion*
     1596 *The Faerie Queene*, Books 4–6; *Fowre Hymns*; *Mutabilitie Cantos*
     1596 *A View of the Present State of Ireland* (attributed)

1580 JOHN STOW, *Chronicles of England*
c. 1581 GEORGE PEELE, *The Arraignment of Paris*
c. 1581 ROBERT WILSON, *The Three Ladies of London*
1582 THOMAS BENTLEY, ed., *Monument of Matrons*

1582 SETPHEN GOSSON, *Plays Confuted in Five Actions*
1582 RICHARD HAKLUYT, *Divers Voyages Touching the Discovery of America*
1583–92 WALTER RALEGH, poems written and circulated at court
1583 WILLIAM CECIL, LORD BURGHLEY, *The Execution of Justice in England*
1583 PHILIP STUBBES, *The Anatomie of Abuses*
1584 CARDINAL WILLIAM ALLEN, *A True, Sincere, and Modest Defense of English Catholics*
1584 ANTHONY MUNDAY, *Fedele and Fortunio*
1584 REGINALD SCOT, *The Discoverie of Witchcraft*
1585 GEORGE PEELE, *The Device of the Pageant Borne before Wolstan Dixi*
c. 1585–9 HENRY PORTER, *The Two Angry Women of Abingdon*, Part 1
1586 ANON., *Arden of Feversham* (pub. 1592)
1586 ANON., *The Famous Victories of Henry V*
1586 WILLIAM CAMDEN, *Britannia*
1586 WILLIAM WEBBE, *Discourse of English Poetrie*
1587 ANGEL DAY, *Daphnis and Chloe*; Eng. trans. of JACQUES AMYOT's French trans. of LONGUS's Greek original
1587 GEORGE GIFFORD, *A Discourse of the subtill practises of devilles; A Dialogue concerning witches and witchcraftes* (1593)
c. 1587 THOMAS KYD, *The Spanish Tragedy*; rev. edn (1592)

SIR PHILIP SIDNEY (1554–86). Witnesses massacre of St Bartholomew's Day (1572). Makes acquaintance of Penelope Devereux, daughter of first Earl of Essex and wife of Sir Robert Rich (1576). Knighted (1582). Marries Lady Frances Walsingham (1583). Appointed Governor of Flushing (1585). Dies at Zutphen, from musket shot wound received in battle.
1577 *Discourse of Irish Affairs*
1578 *The Lady of May*
c. 1580 *The Countess of Pembroke's Arcadia (Old Arcadia)* and *Astrophel and Stella* composed
c. 1581 *Defence of Poesy [Apologie for Poetrie]* written
1582 *Four Foster Children of Desire*
1587 *Of the Trueness of the Christian Religion*; Eng. trans., with ARTHUR GOLDING, of DU PLESSIS MORNAY's French original
1590 *The Countess of Pembroke's Arcadia (New Arcadia)*, Books 1–3, published; five-book, composite, posthumous edn, 1593
1591 *Astrophel and Stella* published
1595 *Defence of Poesy* published

CHRISTOPHER MARLOWE (1564–93). Cambridge University (BA 1584; MA 1587, following the Privy Council's intervention on Marlowe's behalf). Visits Rheims (c. 1585–6). Shares a writing-chamber with Thomas Kyd (c. 1591). Deported from the Netherlands for attempting to circulate forged gold coins

(1592). Killed in a rooming house in Deptford, allegedly in a quarrel over paying the bill.

c. 1585 *All Ovid's Elegies: Three Books* translated (pub. after 1602)

c. 1585–91 *The Tragedie of Dido, Queene of Carthage* (pub. 1594)

c. 1587–8 *Tamburlaine the Great*, Parts 1–2 (pub. 1590)

c. 1588 *Dr Faustus* (pub. 1604)

c. 1589–90 *The Jew of Malta* (pub. 1633)

c. 1593 *Edward II* (pub. imperfect text, 1593; pub. 1598)

    Hero and Leander composed (pub. 1598)

    The Massacre at Paris (pub. 1600)

1588 WILLIAM BYRD, *Psalms, Sonnets and Songs*

1588 ABRAHAM FRAUNCE, *The Arcadian Rhetoricke*

1588 ROBERT WILSON, *The Three Lords and Three Ladies of London*

1588–9 'Martin Marprelate' tracts: attacks on English bishops by Puritan author, JOB THROCKMORTON; answers by JOHN LYLY and THOMAS NASHE

1589 JANE ANGER, *Protection for Women*

1589 ANON., *A Warning for Fair Women*

1589 RICHARD HAKLUYT, *Principal Navigations, Voyages, and Discoveries of the English Nation*; enlarged edn, 1598–1600

c. 1589 ANTHONY MUNDAY, *John a Kent and John a Cumber*

1589 THOMAS NASHE, *The Anatomy of Absurdity*

1589 GEORGE PEELE, *The Battle of Alcazar*

1589 GEORGE PUTTENHAM, *Arte of English Poesie*

ROBERT GREENE (1558–92). Attends Cambridge University (BA 1578; MA 1583). Travels in Spain, France, Italy, Germany, Poland and Denmark (*c.* 1579–82). Marries daughter of a Norwich gentleman (*c.* 1579). Settles in London, abandoning his wife and son (1585). Receives honorary MA from Oxford (1588). Dies, according to legend, of a surfeit of Rhenish wine and pickled herrings.

c. 1587 *Alphonsus, King of Aragon; Euphues His Censure to Philautus*

1588 *Pandosto; Perimedes the Blacke-Smith*

1589 *Menaphon*

1589–92 *Friar Bacon and Friar Bungay* (pub. 1594)

c. 1590 *James IV; George a Greene*

c. 1590 *A Looking Glass for London and England*, with THOMAS LODGE

1591 *A Notable Discovery of Couzenage; Orlando Furioso* (play based on ARIOSTO's epic)

1592–3 *A Disputation between a He Coney-Catcher and a She Coney-Catcher; A Quip for an Upstart Courtier; A Groats-worth of Wit*

WILLIAM SHAKESPEARE (1564–1616). Attends Stratford-upon-Avon grammar school. Marries Anne Hathaway (1582). Leaves wife and three children in

Stratford; moves to London. Member of Lord Chamberlain's Men (1594) and King's Men (1603). Son Hamnet dies (1596). Purchases New Place in Stratford (1597). Shareholder of the Globe Theatre (1599).

1589–94 *Henry VI* Parts 1–3; *Comedy of Errors*; *Titus Andronicus*; *Two Gentlemen of Verona*; *Richard III*; *Taming of the Shrew*; *Love's Labour's Lost*

c. 1590–8 *Sonnets* (pub. 1609)

1593 *Venus and Adonis* published

1594 *The Rape of Lucrece* published

1595–8 *Richard II*; *Romeo and Juliet*; *A Midsummer Night's Dream*; *King John*; *Merchant of Venice*; *Henry IV*, Parts 1–2; *Merry Wives of Windsor*

1599–1602 *Much Ado about Nothing*; *Henry V*; *Julius Caesar*; *As You Like It*; *Hamlet*; *Twelfth Night*; *Troilus and Cressida*

1601 *The Phoenix and the Turtle* published

SONNETEERS

c. 1580–90? FULKE GREVILLE, LORD BROOKE, *Caelica* (pub. 1633)

1582 THOMAS WATSON, *Hekatompathia*

c. 1582–4 PHILIP SIDNEY, *Certain Sonnets*; *Astrophil and Stella*

1590s–1603 WILLIAM SHAKESPEARE, *Sonnets* (pub. 1609)

1592 SAMUEL DANIEL, *Delia, with The Complaint of Rosamond*; rev. text (pub. 1594)

1592 GABRIEL HARVEY, *Certain Sonnets*

c. 1593–4 MICHAEL DRAYTON, *Idea the Shepheards Garland*; rev. as *Ideas Mirrour* (1594); further rev. as *Idea* (1619)

1594 RICHARD BARNFIELD, *Cynthia*; with *Certain Sonnets* (1595)

1595 BARNABE BARNES, *A Divine Century of Spiritual Sonnets*

c. 1595 ROBERT SIDNEY, sonnets composed and circulated

1595 EDMUND SPENSER, *Amoretti*

1597 JOHN DAVIES, *Gulling Sonnets*

c. 1590–1614 JOHN DONNE, *Songs and Sonnets* composed

c. 1590 ANON., *King Leir*

c. 1590 ANON., *Mucedorus*

1590 ROBERT PAYNE, *A Brief Description of Ireland*

1590 GEORGE PEELE, *Polyhymnia*

1590 MARY SIDNEY, COUNTESS OF PEMBROKE, *Tragedie of Antonie*; Eng. trans. of ROBERT GARNIER's French (pub. 1592)

c. 1590 ROBERT WILSON, *The Cobbler's Prophecy*

c. 1591 ANON., *The True Tragedy of Richard III*

1591 ABRAHAM FRAUNCE, *The Countess of Pembroke's Ivychurch, containing the Life and Death of Phillis and Amyntas*; Eng. adaptation from TASSO's Italian

1591 JOHN HARINGTON, *Orlando Furioso in English heroical verse*; trans. of LUDOVICO ARIOSTO's Italian epic

c. 1591 GEORGE PEELE, *Edward I*
1592 HENRY CHETTLE, *A Kind-Harts Dreame*
1592 GABRIEL HARVEY, *Four Letters*
c. 1592 THOMAS HEYWOOD, *Four Prentices of London* (pub. 1615)
1592 RICHARD JOHNSON, *Nine Worthies of London*
c. 1592 THOMAS NASHE, *Summer's Last Will and Testament; Piers Penniless*

SAMUEL DANIEL (1563–1619). Enters Magdalen Hall, Oxford (1579), but leaves
     without taking a degree. Visits Italy, and meets Giambattista Guarini (*c.* 1586).
     Tutor to William Herbert, third Earl of Pembroke, and to Lady Anne Clifford.
     Licenser for Children of the Queen's Revels (1604–5).
     1592 *Delia, with the Complaint of Rosamond*
     1594 *Cleopatra*
     1595 *The Civil Wars between the two houses of Lancaster and York*, Books 1–5
     1599 *Musophilus; Poetical Essays*
     1601 *The Works . . . newly augmented*
     c. 1602 *Defense of Rime*

MICHAEL DRAYTON (1563–1631). Born at Hartshill in Warwickshire. Enters
     service of Sir Henry Goodere of Polesworth, whose daughter Anne may be the
     woman he addresses as 'Idea'. Buried in Westminster Abbey.
     1591 *The Harmonie of the Church*
     1593 *Idea the Shepheards Garland*
     c. 1593 *Piers Gaveston*
     1594 *Ideas Mirrour; Matilda*
     1595 *Endimion and Phoebe*
     1596 *Mortimeriados; Robert, Duke of Normandy*
     1597 *England's Heroical Epistles*

1593 THOMAS NASHE, *Christ's Tears over Jerusalem*
c. 1593 GEORGE PEELE, *Old Wives' Tale; David and Bethsabe*
1594 RICHARD HOOKER, *Of the Laws of Ecclesiastical Polity*, Books 1–4
1594 THOMAS KYD, *Cornelia*
1594 LODGE and GREENE, *A Looking-Glass for London and England*
1594 THOMAS NASHE, *The Unfortunate Traveler*
1595 GEORGE CHAPMAN, *Ovid's Banquet of Sense; The Blind Beggar of Alexandria*
     (1596); *An Humorous Day's Mirth* (1597)
1595 MARY SIDNEY, COUNTESS OF PEMBROKE, *Psalms* (with PHILIP SIDNEY)
c. 1596 FULKE GREVILLE, *Mustapha*
1596 JOHN HARINGTON, *Metamorphosis of Ajax*
1596 WALTER RALEGH, *Discovery of Guiana*
1596 WILLIAM WARNER, *Albion's England*, Books 1–12

1597 FRANCIS BACON, *Essays*; rev. and enlarged edns (1612, 1625)
1597 THOMAS DELONEY, *Jack of Newbury*
1597 RICHARD HOOKER, *Of the Laws of Ecclesiastical Polity*, Book 5

BEN JONSON (1572/3-1637). Soldier with English troops in Netherlands (1594). Employed by Philip Henslowe's companies as a player and playwright (1597). Imprisoned for (now-lost) dramatic satire, *The Isle of Dogs* (1597). Kills fellow actor in a duel (1598). Converts to Catholicism (1598).
1598 *Every Man in His Humour* (pub. 1601)
1599 *Every Man Out of His Humour* (pub. 1600)
1600 *Cynthia's Revels* (pub. 1601)
1601 *Poetaster* (pub. 1602)

1598 GEORGE CHAPMAN, *Seven Books of the Iliades*; Eng. trans. of Books 1-2, 7-11 of HOMER's Greek; twelve-book translation (*c.* 1608); complete translation, *The Iliads of Homer* (1614)
1598 ROBERT CLEAVER, *A Godly Form of Household Government*; enlarged edn, with JOHN DOD (1610)
1598 JOHN FLORIO, *A World of Wordes, or Most Copious and Exact Dictionaries in Italian and English*
1598 FRANCIS MERES, *Palladis Tamia*
c. 1598 HENRY PORTER, *The Two Angry Women of Abingdon*
1598 JOHN STOW, *A Survey of London and Westminster*; rev. edn (1603)
1598 BARTHOLOMEW YONGE, *Diana*; Eng. trans. of JORGE DE MONTEMAYOR's Portuguese
c. 1598-9 THOMAS DELONEY, *Thomas of Reading*
1598-9 JOHN MARSTON, *The Scourge of Villainy*; *Passionate Pilgrim*; *Antonio and Mellida*
1598-1606 ANON., *The Pilgrimage to Parnassus*, Part 1; *The Return from Parnassus* (1602); Part 3 (1606)
1599 ANON., *Club Law*; *A Larum for London*
c. 1599 THOMAS DEKKER, *The Shoemakers' Holiday*; *Old Fortunatus*
1599 MICHAEL DRAYTON, RICHARD HATHAWAY and ROBERT WILSON, *Sir John Oldcastle*, Part 1
1599 JOHN HAYWARD, *The Life and Reigne of Henry IV*
1599 JOHN MARSTON (?), *Histrio-Mastix*
1599 THOMAS NASHE, *Nashes Lenten Stuffe*
c. 1599-1605 MARGARET HOBY, *Diary* composed
c. 1600 ANON., *Thomas Lord Cromwell*
1600 HENRY CHETTLE, DEKKER and WILLIAM HAUGHTON, *Patient Grissel*
1600 CHETTLE and HAUGHTON, *The Blind Beggar of Bethnal Green*, Part 1

1600 JOHN DAY, DEKKER and HAUGHTON, *The Spanish Moor's Tragedy*

1600 WILLIAM HAUGHTON, *The Devil and His Dame*

1600 JOHN MARSTON, *Antonio's Revenge*

1600 *England's Helicon*

c. 1601 THOMAS CAMPION, *A Booke of Ayres*

1601 GEORGE CHAPMAN, *All Fools*

1601 THOMAS DEKKER, *Satiromastix*

1601 ARTHUR DENT, *The Plaine Mans Path-way to Heaven*

1601 JOHN DONNE, *The Progresse of the Soule* (fragmentary epic) composed

1601 JOHN MARSTON, *What You Will*

1601 MARY SIDNEY, *Dialogue between Two Shepherds, Thenot and Astraea*

1602 ANON., *The Fair Maid of the Exchange*

1602 THOMAS CAMPION, *Observations on the Art of English Poesy*

1602 RICHARD CAREW, *Survey of Cornwall*

c. 1602 GEORGE CHAPMAN, *The Gentleman Usher*; *May Day*; *Sir Giles Goosecap*

1602 HENRY CHETTLE, *Hoffman*

1602 FRANCIS DAVISON and WALTER DAVISON, *A Poetical Rhapsody*

c. 1602 THOMAS HEYWOOD, *The Fair Maid of the West, Part 1*; *The Royal King and the Loyal Subject*; *How a Man May Choose a Good Wife from a Bad* (?)

1602 HENRY PERCY, *A Country Tragedy*

SCOTLAND

1558 JOHN KNOX, *Appellation*; *The First Blast of the Trumpet against the monstrous Regiment of Women* (Geneva)

1561 *The confessioun of faith profesit and belevit be the protestantes within the realme of Scotland*

1562 *The Form of Prayers and Ministrations of the Sacraments* (Reformed Church of Scotland's 'Book of Common Order', service-book for public worship in churches)

1562 NINIAN WINZET, *Certain Tractates for Reformation of Doctrine and Manners of... the afflicted Catholics in Scotland*; *Last Blast of the Trumpet of God's Word against the Usurped Authority of John Knox and His Calvinian Brethren, Intruded Preachers* (not printed); *The Book of Fourscore and Three Questions... to the Preachers of the Protestants in Scotland* (Antwerp, 1563)

1564-5 GEORGE BUCHANAN, *Psalmorum Davidis paraphrasis poetica* (Paris; 2nd edn, Paris, 1566; 3rd edn, Strasbourg, 1568)

c. 1565 ROBERT LINDSAY OF PITSCOTTIE, *The Historie and Croniclis of Scotland*

1567 JOHN CARSWELL, trans. of the 'Book of Common Order' into classical Gaelic

1567-8 JOHN WEDDERBURN, *Ane compendious bulk of godlie psalmes and spirituall songis* (Edinburgh)

1568 JOHN LESLIE, *Defense of the Honor of Mary Queen of Scotland and Dowager of France*

1568 DAVID LINDSAY (d. 1555), *Works*; 1st collected edn

c. 1569 WILLIAM LAUDER, *A Godly Tractate or Mirrour; a pretty mirror or conference, betwixt the faithful Protestant and the dissembling false hypocrite*

1570 GEORGE BUCHANAN, *A detection of the Doings of Mary, Queen of Scots; The Chameleon: or the crafty statesman* (not printed); *An Admonition direct to the true Lordes* (1571)

1571 JOHN LESLIE, *Treatise concerning the Right of Mary of Scotland* (Liège)

1572 *The Lamentatioun of Lady Scotland*

1573 JAMES TYRIE, *Refutation of an Answer made by John Knox* (Paris)

1575 JOHN ROLLAND OF DALKEITH, *A Treatise Called The Court of Venus; The Seven Sages* (1578)

1578 GEORGE BUCHANAN, *Baptistes; De Jure Regni apud Scotos* (1579)

1580 JOHN HAY, *Certain Demands concerning the Christian Religion and Discipline . . . of the New Pretended Kirk of Scotland* (Paris)

1580 JAMES MELVILLE, minister of Kilkenny, *Morning Vision: or Poem for the Practice of Piety, Faith and Repentance*

c. 1580s JOHN LESLIE, *History of Scotland from the Death of King James I, in the year 1436, to the year 1561*; Eng. trans. by JAMES DALRYMPLE from Leslie's Latin

1582 GEORGE BUCHANAN, *Rerum Scoticarum Historia*

1584 THOMAS HUDSON, *The Historie of Judith*; Scots trans. of DU BARTAS'S French

1584 KING JAMES VI, *Reulis and Cautelis to be observit and eschewit in Scottis Poesie*, in *The Essayes of a Prentice in the Divine Art of Poesie*; 2nd edn. 1585

1586 JOHN KNOX, *The History of the Reformation of Religion within the Realm of Scotland*

1587 WILLIAM FOWLER, Scots trans. of PETRARCH, *Trionfi*

c. 1590s JOHN COLVILLE, *The Historie and Life of King James the Sext*

c. 1590s ALEXANDER MONTGOMERIE, *The Cherrie and the Slae*; 2nd edn, Edinburgh (1597)

1591 KING JAMES VI, *His Majesty's Poetical Exercises at Vacant Hours*

1594 ALEXANDER HUME, *Ane Treatise of Conscience; A Treatise of the Felicity of the Life to Come*

1594 ANDREW MELVILLE, *Principis scoto-britannorum natalia*

1594 GEORGE THOMSON, *De Antiquitate Christiane e Religionis apud Scotos* (Rome and Douai)

1597 JAMES VI, *Demonologie*; 2nd edn (London, 1603)

1598 [JAMES VI], *Trew Law of Free Monarchies*; 2nd edn (London, 1603)

1599 ALEXANDER HUME, *Hymns or Sacred Songs, wherein the Right Use of Poesie May Be Espied*

1599 JAMES VI, *Basilicon Doron* first printed for private distribution

1601 JOHN COLVILLE, *Paraenesis* (Paris); Eng. trans., *Paraenese or Admonition* (Paris, 1602)

WALES

1573 HUMPHREY LLWYD, *The Breviary of Britayne*, Eng. trans. by THOMAS
      TURYNE from Llwyd's Latin, *Commentarioli Brittanicae descriptionis fragmentum*
      (Cologne, 1572)
1587 THOMAS CHURCHYARD, *The Worthiness of Wales*
1588 WILLIAM MORGAN, *Y Beibl cyssegr-lan*; first Welsh trans. of the Bible (rev.
      edns, 1620, 1630)
1589 WILLIAM MORGAN, revision of WILLIAM SALESBURY's Welsh trans. of the
      Book of Common Prayer

IRELAND

1571 JOHN KEARNEY, *Aibdil Gaoidhilge & Caiticiosma* (Gaelic alphabet and
      catechism), first book published in Gaelic in Ireland
1584 RICHARD STANYHURST, *De Rebus in Hibernia Gestis*; Eng. trans., *A Description
      of Ireland*, pub. in HOLINSHED, *Chronicles of England, Scotland and Ireland*
      (1586–7 edn)

Historical Events 1603–1641

Monarchs of England: James VI and I (1603–25); Charles I (1625–49).
Archbishops of Canterbury: Richard Bancroft (1604–11); George Abbot (1611–33);
      William Laud (1633–40).
Monarchs of Scotland: James VI (1568–1625); Charles I (1625–49).

1603 Theatre companies under royal patronage. Outbreak of plague in London.
1604 Hampton Court Conference (James fails to secure religious conformity of 300
      Puritan clergy and ejects them from their livings).
1605 Gunpowder Plot (Robert Catesby, Guy Fawkes and other English Catholics
      conspire to blow up Houses of Parliament while in session and attended by
      James).
1607 John Smith founds colony of Virginia at Jamestown.
1610 Assassination of Henry IV of France. Reports of Galileo's discoveries with
      telescope.
1612 Death of Prince Henry, King James's eldest son.
1613 Princess Elizabeth marries Frederick, Elector Palatine. Globe Theatre
      destroyed by fire.
1614 'Addled Parliament' (James's term for a Parliament that demanded tax reforms
      and restoration of ejected Puritan clergy instead of voting the expected
      subsidy).
1616 William Harvey lectures in London on circulation of the blood.
1618 Sir Walter Ralegh executed after unsuccessful New World expedition in
      search of gold. Synod of Dort (Netherlands): Calvinists and Arminians debate
      grace, free will and predestination.

1618–48 Thirty Years' War in Europe, begins in Germany.

1619 Death of Queen Anne of Denmark, James I's consort.

1620 Pilgrims (nonconforming Puritans) sail from England in the *Mayflower*, settle at Plymouth, Massachusetts.

1623 Prince Charles and the Duke of Buckingham in Madrid negotiate unsuccessfully for Charles's marriage with the Spanish Infanta.

1624 War declared on Spain.

1625 Death of James I. Charles I succeeds to throne; marries Henrietta Maria of France. Parliament grants Charles tonnage and poundage for one year.

1626–9 War with France; failed English naval expedition to Ile of Rhé to aid Huguenots.

1628 Duke of Buckingham, Charles's favourite, assassinated. 'Petition of Right' (Declaration of the 'rights and liberties of the subject', conceived by Edward Coke in response to the conflict between Charles I and Parliament over the extent of the royal prerogative; it stated parliamentary grievances and forbade levying of taxes without parliamentary consent, arbitrary imprisonment, forced billeting of soldiers by citizenry, and martial law).

1629 Charles dissolves Parliament, beginning twelve years of 'Personal Rule'. Whitefriars Theatre built.

1630 Massachusetts Bay Colony founded.

1632 Anthony van Dyke, Flemish painter, settles in England.

1633 Galileo interrogated by the Inquisition in Rome.

1634 William Prynne imprisoned. Charles I demands payment of 'ship money' (a special tax) without consent of Parliament.

1636–7 Book of Common Prayer and Ecclesiastical Canons imposed on a resistant (Calvinist) Church of Scotland.

1638–9 'Bishops' War' (armed resistance to King Charles's and Archbishop William Laud's imposition of Book of Common Prayer in Scotland); Second Covenant (revival of 1581 First Covenant) sworn to uphold Calvinist Church of Scotland.

1639 'Black Oath' requires Ulster Scots to swear loyalty to Charles.

1640 Long Parliament convenes (to 1653). 'Root-and-Branch' petition, to end episcopacy in the Church of England. Impeachment and execution of Laud. Censorship breaks down.

1641 Rebellion breaks out in Ireland. Execution of the Earl of Strafford. Parliament presents Charles with 'Grand Remonstrance'.

Literature of Europe 1603–1641

1605–15 MIGUEL DE CERVANTES SAAVEDRA, *Don Quixote*

1610 GALILEO, *Siderus Nuncius*

1612 CERVANTES, *Novelas Exemplares*

1613 GIOVAMBATTISTA ANDREINI, *L'Adamo*

1634 Académie Française founded under Louis XIII

1636 PIERRE CORNEILLE, *Le Cid*
1637 RENÉ DESCARTES, *Discours de la méthode*
1639 CORNEILLE, *Cinna*; *Polyeucte* (1640)

Literature of Britain 1603–1641

ENGLAND

BEN JONSON (1572/3–1637). Imprisoned for topicality in *Eastward Ho* (1605).
Reconverts to Church of England (1610). Tutor to Ralegh's son (1612).
Granted pension by King James I (1616). Collaborates with Inigo Jones, set
designer and architect, on a series of court masques.

1603 *Entertainment at Althorpe*
1604 *His Part of the King's Entertainment in Passing to His Coronation*
c. 1612 Epigrams composed
1614 *The Sad Shepherd* (pub. 1641)
1616 *Works*, folio 1st edn, including *Epigrams* and *The Forest*
1616–40 Songs composed
1619 *Conversations with Drummond of Hawthornden*
1640–1 *Underwood*; *Works*, 2nd edn, in 2 vols.; *Timber, or Discoveries*

PLAYS
1603 *Sejanus His Fall* (pub. 1605)
1605 *Eastward Ho*, with CHAPMAN and MARSTON
1606 *Volpone, or The Fox* (pub. 1610)
1609 *Epicoene, or The Silent Woman* (pub. 1610)
1610 *The Alchemist* (pub. 1612)
1611 *Catiline*
1614 *Bartholomew Fair* (pub. 1631)
1616 *The Devil is an Ass*
1626 *The Staple of News*
1629 *The New Inn*
1632 *The Magnetic Lady*
1633 *A Tale of a Tub*

MASQUES
1605 *The Masque of Blackness* (pub. 1608)
1606 *Hymenaei*
1608 *The Masque of Beauty*
1609 *The Masque of Queens*
1611 *Oberon* (pub. 1616)
1612 *Love Restored* (pub. 1616)
1615 *The Golden Age Restor'd*
1616 *Mercury Vindicated from Alchemists at Court*
1618 *Pleasure Reconciled to Virtue* (pub. 1640)

1620 *News from the New World Discovered in the Moon*
1623 *Time Vindicated*
1624 *Neptune's Triumph for the Return of Albion*
1625 *The Fortunate Isles*
1631 *Chloridia*; *Love's Triumph through Callipolis*
1634 *Love's Welcome at Bolsover*

WILLIAM SHAKESPEARE (1564–1616). Purchases 127 acres of land in Stratford
(1602). Daughter Susanna marries (1607); daughter Judith marries (1616).
1603–7 *All's Well that Ends Well*; *Othello*; *Measure for Measure*; *King Lear*; *Macbeth*;
Antony and Cleopatra
1608–11 *Timon of Athens*; *Coriolanus*; *Pericles*; *Cymbeline*; *The Winter's Tale*; *The
Tempest*
1612–13 *Two Noble Kinsmen*, with JOHN FLETCHER; *Henry VIII*
1623 *Works* ('First Folio'), collected by JOHN HEMINGES and HENRY
CONDELL
1632 *Works* ('Second Folio')

THOMAS DEKKER (*c.* 1570–1632). Imprisoned for debt (1597–8; 1612–18).
Engaged as a playwright by Philip Henslowe (1595). Twice arrested as a
recusant, for not attending church. Wife dies while he is in prison (1616).
1603 *The Wonderful Year*
1604 *Westward Hoe*, with JOHN WEBSTER (pub. 1607); *The Honest Whore*, Part 1,
with THOMAS MIDDLETON; *The London Prodigal* (?)
1605 *Northward Ho*, with WEBSTER (pub. 1607); *The Seven Deadly Sins of London*;
Honest Whore, Part 2 (1608; pub. 1630)
1606 *The Double PP*; *The Whore of Babylon*
1608 *The Bellman of London*; *Lanthorne and Candle-light*
1609 *Gull's Horn-Book*
1611 *The Roaring Girl*, with MIDDLETON
c. 1611 *Match Me in London*; *If It Be Not Good, the Devil Is in It*
1620 *The Virgin Martyr*; *Dekker his Dreame*
1621 *The Witch of Edmonton*, with JOHN FORD and WILLIAM ROWLEY
(pub. 1658); *A Rod for Runaways*
1622 *The Noble Spanish Soldier*
1623 *The Spanish Gypsy*, with FORD
c. 1623 *The Welsh Ambassador*

1603 ANON., *Philotus*; *Narcissus*
1603 MICHAEL DRAYTON, *The Barons' Wars*
1603 JOHN FLORIO, *Essayes or morall, politike and millitarie discourses*; Eng. trans. of
MONTAIGNE's French original
1603 THOMAS GREENE, *A Poet's Vision and a Prince's Glory*
1603 THOMAS HEYWOOD, *A Woman Killed with Kindness* (pub. 1607)

1603 JOHN MARSTON, *The Malcontent*

c. 1603 THOMAS MIDDLETON, *The Family of Love*; *The Phoenix* (*c.* 1604)

1603 WILLIAM PERCY, *The Fairy Pastoral*

1603 RICHARD ROGERS, *Seven Treatises, containing such direction as is gathered out of Holy Scriptures*

1604 WILLIAM ALEXANDER, *Croesus*

c. 1604 ELIZABETH TANSFIELD CARY, LADY FALKLAND, *The Tragedy of Mariam, Fair Queen of Jewry* composed

1604 ROBERT CAWDREY, *A Table Alphabeticall*

1604 GEORGE CHAPMAN, *Bussy d'Ambois* (pub. 1607); *Monsieur d'Olive* (pub. 1606); *All Fools* (pub. 1605)

c. 1604 SAMUEL DANIEL, *Philotas*

1604 JOHN DAY, *Law Tricks*

1604 ELIZABETH GRYMSTON, *Miscelanea, Meditations, Memoratives*

1604 JOHN HAYWARD, *A Treatise of Union of the two Realmes of England and Scotland*

1604 THOMAS HEYWOOD, *If You Know Not Me, You Know Nobody*, Part 1; *The Wise Woman of Hogsdon*

1604 JAMES VI AND I, *A Counterblast to Tobacco*

1604 JOHN MARSTON, *The Dutch Courtesan*; *Poetaster or The Fawn*

1604 Revised Book of Common Prayer (England)

1605 JOHN DAY, *The Isle of Gulls* (pub. 1606)

1605 MICHAEL DRAYTON, *Poems*; *Eclogues* (pub. 1606)

1605 THOMAS HEYWOOD, *If You Know Not Me, You Know Nobody*, Part 2

c. 1605 THOMAS MIDDLETON, *Michaelmas Term* (pub. 1607); *A Trick to Catch the Old One* (pub. 1608); *A Yorkshire Tragedy* (with co-author?)

1605 ANTHONY MUNDAY, *Triumphs of Re-United Britannia*

FRANCIS BACON, BARON VERULAM, VISCOUNT ST ALBANS (1561–1626). Elected to Parliament (1584). Associate of Earl of Essex (1590s). Solicitor-General (1607); Attorney General (1613); Lord Keeper (1617); Lord Chancellor (1618). Impeached and convicted on bribery charges (1621).

    1605 *Two Books of the Advancement of Learning*; enlarged Latin version, *De Augmentis Scientiarum* (1623)

    1609 *De Sapientia Veterum*; Eng. trans. (1619)

    1612 *Essays*, 2nd edn, enlarged

    1620 *Novum Organum*, as a part of *Instauratio Magna*

    1622 *History of the Reign of King Henry VII*

    1625 *Essays*, 3rd edn, enlarged

    1627 *New Atlantis* and *Sylva Sylvarum* published

c. 1606 ANON. [THOMAS MIDDLETON, THOMAS DEKKER, CYRIL TOURNEUR?], *The Revenger's Tragedy*

1606 MICHAEL DRAYTON, *Eclogues*

1606 THOMAS MIDDLETON, *A Mad World, My Masters* (pub. 1608); *The Puritan*

c. 1607 FRANCIS BEAUMONT, *The Knight of the Burning Pestle* (pub. 1613)

1607 THOMAS CAMPION, *Lord Hay's Masque*

c. 1607 THOMAS HEYWOOD, *The Rape of Lucrece*

c. 1607 LEWIS MACHIN (?), *Every Woman in Her Humour*

1607 THOMAS MIDDLETON, *Your Five Gallants*

1608 FRANCIS BEAUMONT and JOHN FLETCHER, *Cupid's Revenge*; *Philaster* (1609); *The Coxcomb* (1609)

c. 1608 GEORGE CHAPMAN, *Byron's Conspiracy*; *Byron's Tragedy*

c. 1608 JOHN DAY, *Humour out of Breath*

c. 1608 JOHN FLETCHER, *The Faithful Shepherdess* (pub. 1610)

1608 JOSEPH HALL, *Characters of Vertues and Vices*

c. 1608 WILLIAM ROWLEY, *A Shoemaker, A Gentleman* (pub. 1638)

1609 WILLIAM BIDDULPH, *The travels of certaine Englishmen ... to the Blacke Sea*

1609 SAMUEL DANIEL, *Civil Wars*, Books 6–8

c. 1609 NATHAN FIELD, *A Woman is a Weathercock*

1609 HEYWOOD and WILLIAM ROWLEY, *Fortune by Land and Sea*

c. 1609 MIDDLETON and ROWLEY, *Wit at Several Weapons*

1610 FRANCIS BEAUMONT and JOHN FLETCHER, *The Maid's Tragedy* (pub. 1619); *A King and No King* (pub. 1618)

1610 WILLIAM CAMDEN, *Britain, or a chorographicall description of England, Scotland, and Ireland*, a revised, enlarged version of his Latin *Britannia* (1588); Eng. trans. by PHILEMON HOLLAND

1610 GEORGE CHAPMAN, *The Revenge of Bussy D'Ambois*

1610 SAMUEL DANIEL, *Tethys' Festival*

1610 GILES FLETCHER, *Christ's Victory and Triumph*

1610 THOMAS HEYWOOD, *The Golden Age*

1610 THOMAS MORTON, *The Encounter against M. [Robert] Parsons*

1610 BARNABE RICH, *A New Description of Ireland*

1611 *The Holy Bible, Containing the Old and New Testaments, Translated from the Original Tongues* ('Authorised' or 'King James' Version)

1611 WILLIAM CRASHAW, *Manuale Catholicorum*

c. 1611 JOHN FLETCHER, *Monsieur Thomas*; *The Night Walker*; *The Woman's Prize*; *The Captain* (*c.* 1612); *Bonduca* (*c.* 1613)

1611 FULKE GREVILLE, LORD BROOKE, *Life of Sir Philip Sidney* (pub. 1652)

c. 1611 THOMAS HEYWOOD, *The Brazen Age*; *The Silver Age*

1611 AEMILIA LANYER, *Salve Deus Rex Judaeorum*

1611 THOMAS MIDDLETON, *The Second Maiden's Tragedy*

1611 JOHN SPEED, *Theatre of the Empire of Great Britain*

1611 CYRIL TOURNEUR (?), *The Atheist's Tragedy*

JOHN DONNE (1572–1631). Born into Catholic family descended from Thomas More on mother's side. Attends Hart Hall, Oxford, without taking a degree.

Studies law at Inns of Court (1591–5?). Sails with English expeditions against Cadiz and the Azores (1596–7). Appointed secretary to Thomas Egerton, Lord Keeper (1597). Elopes with Ann More, daughter of Egerton's brother-in-law, and is dismissed by Egerton (1601). MP for Brackley (1601). Accompanies Sir Thomas Drury on European trip (1609–10). Takes holy orders in Church of England; receives DD from Cambridge University at James's behest (1615). Becomes Reader in Divinity, Lincoln's Inn (1615). Wife dies in childbirth (1617). Dean of St Paul's (1621–31).

    c. 1590–1614 Satires, Elegies, Songs and Sonnets composed and circulated in manuscript

    1606–7 *Biathanatos* (pub. 1646)

    c. 1609–17 'La Corona' and Holy Sonnets composed

    1610 *Pseudo-Martyr*

    1611 *Ignatius His Conclave*; concurrent Latin version, *Conclavi Ignatii*

    1611–12 *First* and *Second Anniversaries* composed and published

    1614 *Essays in Divinity* (pub. 1615)

    1622 *Two Sermons*; *Four Sermons* (1624)

    1624 *Devotions upon Emergent Occasions*

    1625 *Sermon before King Charles*

    1632 *Deaths Duell* published

    1633 *Poems* published posthumously

c. 1612 LEWIS BAYLY, *The Practice of Pietie*

1612 MICHAEL DRAYTON, *Poly-Olbion* begun (completed 1622)

1612 THOMAS HEYWOOD, *Apology for Actors*

1612 JOHN WEBSTER, *The White Devil*

1612 THOMAS WILSON, *A Christian Dictionarie*

1613 WILLIAM BROWNE, *Britannia's Pastorals*

c. 1613 THOMAS CAMPION, *Two Bookes of Ayres*

1613 GEORGE CHAPMAN, *The Memorable Masque*

1613 CLEMENT COTTON, *The Mirror of Martyrs*

1613 SAMUEL DANIEL, *History of England* (enlarged edn, 1618)

1613 JOHN HAYWARD, *The Lives of the Three Normans, Kings of England*

1613 THOMAS MIDDLETON, *A Chaste Maid in Cheapside* (pub. 1630); *No Wit, No Help Like a Woman's*; *More Dissemblers Besides Women*; *The Witch* (*c.* 1615); *The Widow* (*c.* 1616); *Hengist, King of Kent* (*c.* 1618)

1613 JOHN STEPHENS, *Cynthia's Revenge*

1613 GEORGE WITHER, *Abuses Stript and Whipt*

c. 1613 MARY WROTH, lyric sequence, 'Pamphilia to Amphilanthus', composed; pub. in *First Part of the Countess of Montgomery's Arcadia* (1621)

1614 CHRISTOPHER BROOKE, *The Ghost of Richard the Third*

1614 GEORGE CHAPMAN, *Homer's Odysses*; Eng. trans. of Greek original

1614 SAMUEL DANIEL, *Hymen's Triumph*

1614 WILLIAM DAVIES, *A true relation of the travailes and captivitie of William Davies, Barber-Surgion of London*

1614 JOHN FLETCHER, *Valentinian; Wit Without Money*

1614 THOMAS OVERBURY, *Characters*, appended to *A Wife, Now a Widow*

1614 WALTER RALEGH, *History of the World* (incomplete)

1615 THOMAS BRIGHTMAN, *A Revelation of the Revelation*

1615 WILLIAM CAMDEN, *Annales rerum Anglicarum, et Hibernicarum, regnante Elizabetha*, Book 1–3; Books 4 (1627); Eng. trans. by R. NORTON (1630)

1615 SAMUEL HIERON, *Certain Meditations*

1615 J. G., *A Refutation of the Apology for Actors*

1615 GERVASE MARKHAM, *The English Hus-wife*

1615 JOSEPH SWETNAM, *The Arraignment of Lewd, Idle, Froward and Unconstant Women*

1615 GEORGE WITHER, *The Shepherd's Hunting*

1616 JOHN BULLOKAR, *An English Expositor*

1616 GEORGE CHAPMAN, trans., *The Whole Works of Homer*

1616 DOROTHY LEIGH, *The Mother's Blessing*

1616 THOMAS MIDDLETON, *Inner Temple Masque* (pub. 1619)

1616 MIDDLETON and WILLIAM ROWLEY, *A Fair Quarrel; The Old Law* (*c.* 1618); *The World Tossed at Tennis* (*c.* 1619)

1616 WILLIAM WHATELY, *A Bride Bush: or, A direction for married persons*

1617 RICHARD BRATHWAIT, *The Smoking Age*

1617 JAMES VI AND I, *Works* (folio vol. dated 1616 on title-page)

1617 ESTER SOWERNAM, *Ester hath hang'd Haman*

1617 RACHEL SPEGHT, *A Muzzle for Melastomus*

1617 JOHN WEBSTER, *Devil's Law-Case* (pub. 1623)

1618 THOMAS GAINSFORD, *The Glory of England*

1618 JAMES VI AND I, *The King's Majesty's Declaration concerning Lawful Sports* (24 May): 'Book of Sports', first issue

1619 JOHN FLETCHER, *The Humorous Lieutenant*

1619 FLETCHER and PHILIP MASSINGER, *The Little French Lawyer; Sir John van Olden Barnavelt; The Custom of the Country; The Double Marriage; The False One* (*c.* 1620)

c. 1619 JOHN FORD, *The Laws of Candy*

1619 JOHN MAYER, *A Pattern for Women*

1619–22 INIGO JONES, designs for the royal Banqueting House in Whitehall

1620 ANON., *Swetnam the Woman Hater, Arraigned by Women*

1620 *Haec-Vir* and *Hic-Mulier*, satires on cross-dressing women and effeminate men

1620 *The Honor of Virtue*, sermon tribute to Elizabeth Crashaw, who died in childbirth

1620 THOMAS MAY, *The Heir*

c. 1620 MIDDLETON, *Mayor of Queenborough*

1621 JOHN BARCLAY, *Argenis*, Eng. trans. (1625)

1621 ROBERT BURTON, *Anatomy of Melancholy*

1621 JOHN DAVIES, *Antiquae linguae Britannicae*

1621 JOHN FLETCHER, *The Wild Goose Chase; The Island Princess; The Pilgrim*

c. 1621 FORD AND DEKKER, *The Witch of Edmonton* (pub. 1658)

1621 PHILIP MASSINGER, *The Maid of Honour*

1621 THOMAS MIDDLETON, *Women Beware Women*

c. 1621 MIDDLETON and WEBSTER, *Anything for a Quiet Life*

1621 THOMAS SCOTT, *Vox Populi*

1621 RACHEL SPEGHT, *Mortality's Memorandum, With A Dream Prefixed*

1621 MARY WROTH, *The Countess of Montgomerie's Urania*, Part 1

1622 ELIZABETH CLINTON, *The Countess of Lincoln's Nursery*

1622 WILLIAM GOUGE, *Of Domestical Duties*

1622 MIDDLETON AND WILLIAM ROWLEY, *The Changeling* (pub. 1653)

1622 HENRY PEACHAM, *Compleat Gentleman*

1622 GEORGE WITHER, *Fair Virtue, The Mistress of Phil' Arete*

1623 HENRY COCKERAM, *The English Dictionarie*

1623 SAMUEL DANIEL, *Whole Works*

c. 1623 OWEN FELTHAM, *Resolves, Divine, Morall, Politicall*

1623 JOHN FLETCHER, *The Wandering Lovers; Rule a Wife and Have a Wife; A Wife for a Month* (1624)

1623 FLETCHER and ROWLEY, *The Maid in the Mill*

c. 1623 MICHAEL SPARKE, *Crumms of Comfort*

1623 GEORGE WITHER, *Hymnes and Songs of the Church*

1624 JOHN FORD, *Perkin Warbeck* (pub. 1634)

1624 THOMAS HEYWOOD, *Gunaikeion: or Nine Books of Various History concerning Women; The Captives*

1624 ELIZABETH JOCELIN, *The Mother's Legacie to her unborne Childe*

1624 PHILIP MASSINGER, *The Bondman, The Parliament of Love; The Renegado; The Unnatural Combat* (*c.* 1624); *A New Way to Pay Old Debts* (1625; pub. 1633)

1624 THOMAS MIDDLETON, *A Game at Chess* (pub. 1625)

c. 1624 JOHN WEBSTER, *Appius and Virginia*

c. 1625 JOHN DAVENPORT, *A New Trick to Catch the Devil*

1625 THOMAS DEKKER, *A Rod for Run-Awayes*

c. 1625 THOMAS HEYWOOD, *The English Traveller; The Escapes of Jupiter*

1625 JAMES SHIRLEY, *The School of Compliment; The Maid's Revenge* (1626); *The Wedding* (1626)

1626 LADY ELEANOR DOUGLAS, *A Warning to the Dragon*

1626 PHILIP MASSINGER, *Roman Actor* (pub. 1629); *The Great Duke of Florence* (1627)

1626 THOMAS MAY, *Cleopatra, Queen of Egypt; Antigone, the Theban Princess* (*c.* 1627); *Julia Agrippina, Empress of Rome* (1628)

1627 JOHN COSIN, *A Collection of Private Devotions*

1627 THOMAS MAY, trans., *Lucan's Pharsalia. The Whole Ten Books* (2nd edn, 1631)

1627 JOSEPH MEDE, *Clavis Apocalyptica* (trans. 1643)
1627 JAMES SHIRLEY, *The Witty Fair One; The Grateful Servant* (1629)
1628 EDWARD COKE, *The First Part of the Institutes of the Laws of England*, a
commentary on THOMAS LITTLETON's *Tenures*
1628 JOHN EARLE, *Microcosmographie*
c. 1628 JOHN FORD, *The Lover's Melancholy; The Queen; The Broken Heart* (1629)

JOHN MILTON (1608–74). Born in London to a prosperous scrivener and musician.
Attends St Paul's School. Studies at Christ's College, Cambridge (BA 1629; MA
1632). Studious retirement at Hammersmith and Horton (1632–5). Deaths of
mother and of classmate, Edward King (1637). Travels in France and Italy
(1638–9). Tutor to nephews John and Edward Phillips (1640).
1629 *On the Morning of Christ's Nativity*
1631 *Arcades*
c. 1631–2 *L'Allegro* and *Il Penseroso*
1634 first performance of *A Maske at Ludlow Castle* ('Comus') (rev., pub. 1637)
1637 *Lycidas* written (pub. 1638)
1641 *Of Reformation; Of Prelatical Episcopacy; Animadversions upon the Remonstrants
Defence; Apology for Smectymnuus*

1630 RICHARD BROME, *The City Wit*
1630 THOMAS HEYWOOD, *The Fair Maid of the West*, Part 2
1630 DIANA PRIMROSE, *A Chaine of Pearle*
1630 THOMAS RANDOLPH, *Amyntas; The Muses' Looking Glass*
1630 RICHARD SIBBES, *The Bruised Reed and Smoking Flax*
1630 JOHN TAYLOR, *Works*
1630–1 RICHARD BRATHWAIT, *Complete Gentleman; Complete Gentlewoman*
1631 THOMAS DEKKER, *The Wonder of a Kingdom*
1631 PHILIP MASSINGER, *Believe as You List; The Emperor of the East*
1631 JOHN SELDEN, *Titles of Honor*
c. 1631 JAMES SHIRLEY, *The Contention for Honour and Riches; The Humorous Courtier;
Love's Cruelty; The Traitor*
1631 ARTHUR WILSON, *The Swisser*
1631 GEORGE WITHER, *Psalms of David*
c. 1632 RICHARD BROME, *The Novella; The Weeding of Covent Garden*
c. 1632 ROBERT FILMER, *Patriarcha* written
c. 1632 JOHN FORD, *'Tis Pity She's a Whore; Love's Sacrifice*
1632 INIGO JONES and AURELIAN TOWNSHEND, *Albion's Triumph*
1632 DONALD LUPTON, *London and the Country, Carbonadoed and Quartered into
Several Characters*
1632 PHILIP MASSINGER, *The City Madam; The Guardian* (1633)
1632 FRANCIS QUARLES, *Divine Fancies; The Shepheards Oracles* (c. 1632–40)
1632 JAMES SHIRLEY, *The Ball; The Young Admiral* (1633); *Hyde Park* (pub. 1637)

c. 1637 JASPER MAYNE, *The City Match*

1638 WILLIAM BRUNTON, *Newes from the East-Indies*

1638 LODOWICK CARLELL, *The Passionate Lovers*, Parts 1 and 2

1638 WILLIAM CHILLINGWORTH, *The Religion of Protestants A Safe Way to Salvation*

1638 WILLIAM DAVENANT, *The Fair Favorite*; *The Unfortunate Lovers*; *The Spanish Lovers* (1639)

1638 JOHN LILBURNE, *The Christian Mans Triall* (2nd edn, 1641); *A Worke of the Beast*

1638 THOMAS RANDOLPH, *Poems*

c. 1638 LEWIS SHARPE, *The Noble Stranger*

1638 JOHN SUCKLING, *Aglaura*

1638 PHILIP VINCENT, *A True Relation of the Late Battell fought in New England*

c. 1639 JAMES SHIRLEY, *The Gentleman of Venice*; *The Politician*; *St Patrick for Ireland*, Part 1

1639 JOHN TAYLOR, *A Juniper Lecture*

1640 ROBERT, LORD BROOKE, *The Nature of Truth*

1640 THOMAS CAREW, *Poems*

1640 JANE CAVENDISH and ELIZABETH EGERTON, *The Concealed Fancies*

c. 1640 WILLIAM CAVENDISH, DUKE OF NEWCASTLE, and JAMES SHIRLEY, *The Country Captain*

1640 WILLIAM DAVENANT and INIGO JONES, *Salmacida Spolia*

1640 JAMES HOWELL, *Dodona's Grove*

1640 FRANCIS QUARLES, *Enchiridion*

1640 MARY TATTLEWELL AND JOAN HIT-HIM-HOME, *The Women's Sharp Revenge*

1640 George Thomason, London printer and bookseller, begins his collection of tracts

1640 ISAAC WALTON, *Life of Donne*

1640 *Witts Recreations*

c. 1641 WILLIAM CAVENDISH, *The Variety*

1641 KATHERINE CHIDLEY, *The Justification of the Independent Churches of Christ*

c. 1641 JOHN DENHAM, *The Sophy*

1641 THOMAS JORDAN, *The Walks of Islington and Hogsdon*

c. 1641 THOMAS KILLIGREW, *The Parson's Wedding*

1641 HENRY PEACHAM, *The Worth of a Penny, or a Caution to Keep Money*

1641 WILLIAM PRYNNE, *Mount-Orgueil*

1641 JAMES SHIRLEY, *The Cardinal*

c. 1641 JOHN TATHAM, *The Distracted State*

1641 JOHN TAYLOR, *A Tale in a Tub or, A Tub Lecture*; *A Swarme of Sectaries*; *A Cluster of Coxcombes* (1642)

1641 JOHN WILKINS, *Mercury*

1641 GEORGE WITHER, *Haleluiah*, rev. and enlarged edn of *Hymnes and Songs of the Church*

SCOTLAND

1603 ROBERT KIRK, Scots Gaelic trans. of New Testament

1604 WILLIAM ALEXANDER, EARL OF STIRLING, *Aurora; Monarchic Tragedies* (London)

1605 SIR ROBERT AYTON (or AYTOUN), *Basia* (London)

1605 THOMAS CRAIG, *Scotland's Sovereignty Asserted*

1607 WILLIAM ALEXANDER, *Monarchic Tragedies* (Edinburgh)

1611 DAVID MURRAY OF GORTHIE, *Caelia; The Tragical Death of Sophonisba*

1613 WILLIAM BARCLAY, *Nepenthes: or the Virtues of Tobacco*

WILLIAM DRUMMOND OF HAWTHORNDEN (1585–1649). Travels in Europe and amasses large library (*c.* 1607–10). His betrothed dies (1614). Visited by Ben Jonson (1618–19). Marries (1623).

1613 *Tears on the Death of Meliades*

1616 *Poems: Amorous, Funeral, Divine, Pastoral*

1617 *Forth Feasting*

1623 *Flowers of Sion; A Cypresse Grove*

1633 *Entertainment of the high and mighty monarch, Charles, King of Great Britain*

1615 WILLIAM BARCLAY, *Callirhoe, the Nymph of Aberdeen* (pub. 1670)

1618 WILLIAM LITHGOW, *The Pilgrim's Farewell to his Native Country of Scotland*

c. 1620 JOHN FORBES, *Disputationes theologicae*

1621 SIR PATRICK HUME and ALEXANDER MONTGOMERIE, *The Flyting of Montgomerie and Polwart*

1625 WILLIAM LITHGOW, *Scotland's Tears*

1627 ALEXANDER IRVINE, *De jure regni diascepsis* (Examination of the laws of the kingdom)

1629 HELEN LIVINGSTON, COUNTESS OF LINLITHGOW, *Confession and Conversion*

1633 DAVID HUME of Godscroft, *The Origin and Descent of the Most Noble and Illustrious Family and Name of Douglas*

1633 WILLIAM LITHGOW, *Scotland's Welcome to her Native Son and Sovereign Lord King Charles*

1633 ANDREW RAMSAY, *Poemata sacra et miscellanea et epigrammata sacra*

1637 *Delitiae poetarum Scotorum huius aevi illustrium*, ed. ARTHUR JOHNSTON (Amsterdam)

1637 ANDREW MELVILLE, *Poemata*

1641 THOMAS URQUHART, *Epigrams Divine and Moral*

WALES

1615 R. A. GENT., *The Valiant Welshman, or The True Chronicle History of Caradoc the Great*

IRELAND

1603 WILLIAM O'DONNELL, Irish Gaelic trans. of New Testament
1634 GEOFFREY KEATING, *Foras Feasa ar Eirinn* (Basis of Knowledge about Ireland)
1636 MICHEAL O'CLEIRIGH, *Annals of the Four Masters*
1640 HENRY BURNELL, *Landgartha*

Historical Events 1642–1674

Rulers of England: Charles I (1625–49); Lord Protector Oliver Cromwell (1653–8); Major-Generals (1655–7); Lord Protector Richard Cromwell (1658–9); King Charles II (1660–85).
The Commonwealth of England (1649–60).
Archbishops of Canterbury: William Laud (1633–40); William Juxon (1660–3); Gilbert Sheldon (1663–77).
Monarchs of Scotland: Charles I (1625–49), Charles II (1649 [proclaimed King] – 1685).

1642 Civil War erupts; Battle of Edgehill (first major engagement between Parliamentarians under Earl of Essex and Royalists under Charles I and Prince Rupert). Closing of the public theatres. Bishops excluded from House of Lords.
1643 Westminster Assembly of Divines constituted. Solemn League and Covenant, originating in Scotland, sworn by sympathisers in England. Pre-publication censorship reintroduced.
1644 Battle of Marston Moor (major Royalist defeat near York). Globe Theatre razed.
1645 New Model Army established; Thomas Fairfax named Lord General. Battle of Naseby (first major victory of New Model Army of Fairfax and Oliver Cromwell, over Royalists led by Charles I and Prince Rupert). Prayer Book abolished. Laud executed.
1646 Episcopacy abolished. First Civil War ends.
1647 Charles I delivered to Parliament by Scots. Putney debates (New Model Army spokesmen deliberate the extension of voting rights in England). King escapes. Declaration of the Army.
1648 Thirty Years' War ends. Second Civil War. Pride's Purge (exclusion of 140 MPs from their seats in House of Commons). Whitehall debates (Army spokesmen deliberate future provisions for toleration of varieties of public worship in England).
1649 Trial and execution of Charles I. Monarchy and House of Lords abolished; Commonwealth declared. Oliver Cromwell's military campaign to reconquer Ireland. Diggers' colonies established.
1650 Battle of Dunbar (Cromwell defeats Scots under Lieut. Gen. David Leslie). Cromwell succeeds Fairfax as Lord General. Blasphemy Act.

1651 Charles II crowned at Scone (last monarch crowned in Scotland).

1652–4 First Dutch War. Settlement of Ireland Act.

1653 Rump Parliament (remnant of Long Parliament after Pride's Purge) dissolved. 'Barebones', or Nominated, Parliament (of 140 'godly men' chosen as MPs by Cromwell and Council of Army officers); after its dissolution, Oliver Cromwell is proclaimed First Lord Protector under the Instrument of Government.

1654–5 Protectorate Parliament.

1655 Rule of the Major-Generals. War with Spain begins (to 1659). Jews readmitted to England. Royalist insurrection at Salisbury fails (Col. John Penruddock's rising).

1656 Second Protectorate Parliament.

1657 Humble Petition and Advice presented by Parliament; Cromwell refuses offer of crown but accepts right to name his successor.

1658 Oliver Cromwell dies; his son, Richard Cromwell, named Lord Protector.

1659 Protectorate abolished; Rump Parliament restored.

1660 Charles II issues the Declaration of Breda (a series of conciliatory assurances to English subjects who had acted against the crown); monarchy restored. Act of Indemnity and Oblivion. Theatres reopen. Bishops and House of Lords restored. Royal Society founded. Sir Isaac Newton discovers the composition of light.

1661 James Venner's rebellion: radical millenarians (Fifth Monarchists and Quakers) are suppressed in London. Cavalier Parliament meets. Clarendon Code (series of Parliamentary measures to reestablish Church of England) enacted (to 1665).

1662 Charles II marries Catherine of Braganza. Introduction of revised Prayer Book. Act of Uniformity (revised Prayer Book mandatory for public worship). Royal Society receives its charter.

1664 Conventicles Act, prohibiting public worship not conducted according to revised Prayer Book. English forces occupy New York (Nieuw Amsterdam).

1665 Great Plague: 70,000 Londoners, 15 per cent of city's population, die. Second Dutch War.

1666 Great Fire of London.

1667 Dutch sail up the Medway. Fall of Edward Hyde, Earl of Clarendon.

1668 John Dryden made Poet Laureate.

1670 Treaty of Dover (Charles II secretly promises to return Britain to papal jurisdiction). Second Conventicles Act (heavier penalties for religious nonconformity, including prison and deportation for repeated offences).

1673 James II marries Mary of Modena. Test Act (all civil and military officials to swear Oaths of Royal Allegiance and Royal Supremacy, also to profess adherence to Church of England, thus excluding Catholics from public office).

1674 Third Anglo-Dutch War ends (Treaty of Westminster).

Literature of Europe 1642–1674

1644 RENÉ DESCARTES, *Principia philosophiae*
1656 BLAISE PASCAL, *Lettres provinciales*
1658 GERTRUDE MORE, *Confessio amoris* (Douai)
1659 JEAN-BAPTISTE POQUELIN (MOLIÈRE), *Les Précieuses ridicules*
1662 MOLIÈRE, *L'Ecole des maris; L'Ecole des femmes*
1666 MOLIÈRE, *Le Misanthrope*
1667 MOLIÈRE, *Tartuffe*
1667 JEAN RACINE, *Andromaque*
1668 JEAN DE LA FONTAINE, *Fables*
1669 PASCAL, *Pensées*
1669 RACINE, *Britannicus*

Literature of Britain 1642–1674

ENGLAND

1642 THOMAS BROWNE, *Religio Medici*
1642 SIR EDWARD COKE, *Second Part of the Institutes of the Laws of England*
1642 ABRAHAM COWLEY, *The Guardian*, rev. and pub. as *The Cutter of Coleman Street* (1663)
1642 JOHN DENHAM, *Coopers Hill* (rev. edns, 1650, 1655)
1642 THOMAS FULLER, *The Holy State*
1642 JOHN GOODWIN, *Anti-Cavalierisme*
1642 THOMAS HOBBES, *De Cive* (Paris)
1642 STEPHEN MARSHALL, *Meroz Cursed, or, A Sermon* (title page dated 1641)
1642 HENRY MORE, *Psychodia Platonica; Psychozoia* composed (rev. 1647)
1642 HENRY PARKER, *Observations upon Some of His Majesties Late Answers and Expresses*
1642 HENRY PEACHAM, *The Art of Living in London*
1642 JAMES SHIRLEY, *The Court Secret* (pub. 1653); *The Sisters* (pub. 1652)

JOHN MILTON (1608–74). Marries Mary Powell, daughter of royalist parents (1642), who separates from him (1643–5), then returns and bears him three daughters and a son, who dies in infancy. Appointed Secretary for Foreign Tongues to Cromwell's Council of State (1649). Total blindness; death of wife Mary (1652). Marries Katherine Woodcock (1656); she dies (1658). Arrested and briefly imprisoned in immediate aftermath of Restoration (1660). Marries Elizabeth Minshull (1662).

1642 *Reason of Church Government; An Apology against a Pamphlet*
1643 *Doctrine and Discipline of Divorce* (rev. edn, 1644)
1644 *Of Education; Aeropagitica*
1645 *Tetrachordon; Colasterion; Poems of Mr John Milton* (pub. 2 January 1646)

1649 *Tenure of Kings and Magistrates; Observations upon the Articles of Peace; Eikonoklastes*
1651 *Defensio Pro Populo Anglicano*
1654 *Defensio Secunda*
1655 *Pro Se Defensio*
1659 *A Treatise of Civil Power in Ecclesiastical Causes; Considerations Touching the Likeliest Means to Remove Hirelings out of the Church*
1660 *The Ready and Easy Way to Establish a Free Commonwealth*
1667 *Paradise Lost, A Poem in Ten Books*
1670 *The History of Britain*
1671 *Paradise Regained; Samson Agonistes*
1673 *Of True Religion, Heresy, Schism, and Toleration; Poems . . . upon Several Occasions*
1674 *Paradise Lost, A Poem in Twelve Books*

ANDREW MARVELL (1621–78). Attends Hull Grammar School and Trinity College, Cambridge. Travels on the continent (1643–7). Tutor to Mary Fairfax, daughter of Thomas Fairfax (1650–2). Tutor to Cromwell's ward, William Dutton (1653). Latin secretary to the Council of State (1657). MP for Hull (1659–78).
1649 Poems to Richard Lovelace, and on the death of Lord Hastings
1650 'An Horatian Ode upon Cromwell's Return from Ireland'
1650–1 'Upon Appleton House' (pub. 1651)
1653 'The Bermudas'
1655 *The First Anniversary of the Government under Oliver Cromwell*
1658 'A Poem Upon the Death of His Late Highness the Lord Protector'
1667 *Last Instructions to a Painter*
c. 1668 'The Garden'; the Mower poems
1672 *The Rehearsal Transpros'd*
1673 *The Rehearsal Transpros'd*, The Second Part
1681 *Miscellaneous Poems*

1643 RICHARD BAKER, *A Chronicle of the Kings of England*
1643 THOMAS BROWNE, *A True and Full Copy of . . . Religio Medici*
1643 ABRAHAM COWLEY, *The Civil War*, fragmentary epic modelled on Lucan (pub. 1679)
1643 GEORGE WITHER, *Campo-Musae, or The Field-Musings*
1643–9 *The Lady Falkland: Her Life, By One of Her Daughters* (biography of Elizabeth Tanfield Cary)
1644 JACOB BOEHME, *The Tree of Christian Faith; Two Theosophical Epistles* (1645), first Eng. trans. of his works
1644 JOHN COTTON, *The Keyes of the Kingdom of Heaven; The Way of the Churches of Christ in New England* (1645)

1644 HENRY PARKER, *Jus Populi*

1644 HENRY ROBINSON, *Liberty of Conscience*

1644 ROGER WILLIAMS, *The Bloody Tenent of Persecution*

1645 KATHERINE CHIDLEY, *A New Year's Gift, or Brief Exhortation to Mr Thomas Edwards; Good Counsel, to the Petitioners for Presbyterian Government*

1645 THOMAS FULLER, *Good Thoughts in Bad Times*

1645 JAMES HOWELL, *Epistolae Ho-Elianae* (2nd edn, 1650; 3rd edn, 1655; 6th edn, 1688)

1645 JOHN LILBURNE, *England's Birthright Justified*

1645 EPHRAIM PAGITT, *Heresiography* (6th edn, 1662)

1645 ELIZABETH RICHARDSON, *A Ladies Legacie to Her Daughters*

1645 THOMAS SHEPARD, *New England's Lamentation for Old England's Present Errours and Divisions*

1645 EDMUND WALLER, *Poems* (6th edn, 1694)

1645 WILLIAM WALWYN, *Englands Lamentable Slaverie*

1645–62 ALICE THORNTON, *Autobiography* composed

1646 ROBERT BAILLIE, *Anabaptism the True Fountaine of Independency*

1646 THOMAS BROWNE, *Pseudodoxia Epidemica*

1646 RICHARD CRASHAW, *Steps to the Temple* (2nd edn, 1648)

1646 THOMAS EDWARDS, *Gangraena* (3rd edn, 1646)

1646 JOHN HALL, *Poems*

1646 JOHN LILBURNE, *Londons Liberty in Chains Discovered; The Charters of London; Plain Truth without Fear of Flattery* (1647)

1646 HENRY MORE, *Democritus Platonissans*

1646 RICHARD OVERTON, *Remonstrance of Many Thousand Citizens; An Appeal from the Degenerate Representative Body* (1647)

1646 JOHN SALTMARSH, *Groanes for Liberty; The Smoke in the Temple; Reasons for Unitie, Peace, and Love*

1646 JAMES SHIRLEY, *Poems*

1646 JOHN SUCKLING, *Fragmenta Aurea* (3rd edn, 1648)

1646 JOHN TEMPLE, *The Irish Rebellion* (4th edn, 1698)

1646 JOHN WILKINS, *Ecclesiastes, or, A Discourse concerning the Gift of Preaching* (7th edn, 1693)

1647 *An Agreement of the People* (1648, 1649), Leveller social contract

1647 FRANCIS BEAUMONT and JOHN FLETCHER, *Comedies and Tragedies*, fol. edn

1647 MARY CARY, *A Word in Season; The Resurrection of the Witnesses* (pub. 1648, 1653); *The Little Horn's Doom and Downfall* (pub. 1651); *Twelve Humble Proposals* (pub. 1653)

1647 ABRAHAM COWLEY, *The Mistress*

1647 RICHARD FANSHAWE, trans. of GUARINI'S *Il Pastor Fido* (unpublished)

1647 THOMAS MAY, *The History of the Parliament of England*

1647 HENRY MORE, *Philosophical Poems*

1647 JOHN SALTMARSH, *Sparkles of Glory*
1647 JOSHUA SPRIGGE, *Anglia Rediviva: Englands Recovery*
1647 THOMAS STANLEY, *Poems and Translations*
1647 JEREMY TAYLOR, *Theologia Eklektiké: A Discourse of the Liberty of Prophesying*
1647 HENRY VAUGHAN, *Olor Iscanus: A Collection of Some Select Poems*
1648 RICHARD CORBETT, *Poetica Stromata or A Collection of Sundry Pieces*
      (posthumous pub.)
1648 MILDMAY FANE, EARL OF WESTMORLAND, *Otia Sacra*
1648 ROBERT HERRICK, *Hesperides; His Noble Numbers* (1647)
1648 RICHARD HOOKER, *Of the Laws of Ecclesiastical Polity: The Sixth and Eighth
      Books* (posthumous pub.)
1648 ELIZABETH POOLE, *A Vision: The Disease and Cure of the Kingdom*
1648 GEORGE WITHER, *Prosopopoeia Britannica*
1648 WILLIAM WALWYN, *The Bloody Project*
c. 1648–63 ELIZABETH EGERTON, *Book of Occasional Meditations and Prayers*
      composed
1649 *A Watch-Word to the City of London*
1649 ANTHONY ASCHAM, *Of the Confusions and Revolutions of Governments*
1649 LAURENCE CLARKSON, *A Single Eye All Light, No Darkness*
1649 ABIEZER COPPE, *Fiery Flying Roll; A Second Fiery Flying Roule*
1649 WILLIAM DELL, *The Way of True Peace and Unity among the Faithful*
1649 JOHN GAUDEN / CHARLES I, *Eikon Basilike* (35 edns in 1649; 39 edns by
      1660)
1649 JOHN HALL, *An Humble Motion to the Parliament . . . Concerning the Advancement
      of Learning*
1649 EDWARD, LORD HERBERT OF CHERBURY, *The Life and Reign of King Henry
      VIII*
1649 JOHN LILBURNE, *England's New Chains Discovered*
1649 RICHARD LOVELACE, *Lucasta: Epodes*
1649 RICHARD OVERTON, *The Baiting of the Great Bull of Bashan Unfolded; A New
      Bull-Baiting; Overton's Defiance of the Act of Pardon*
1649 JOSEPH SALMON, *A Rout, A Rout*
1649 WILLIAM WALWYN, *Walwyn's Just Defence*
1649 GERARD WINSTANLEY, *The True Leveller's Standard Advanced*
1650 JACOB BAUTHUMLEY, *The Light and Dark Sides of God*
1650 RICHARD BAXTER, *The Saints Everlasting Rest; Unreasonableness of Infidelity*
      (1655)
1650 ANNE BRADSTREET, *The Tenth Muse Lately Sprung Up in America*
      (unauthorised pub.)
1650 THOMAS BROWNE, *Pseudoxia Epidemica* (2nd edn)
1650 JOHN HILTON, ed., *Catch that Catch Can*
1650 THOMAS HOBBES, *De Corpore Politico; Humane Nature*

1650 MARCHAMONT NEDHAM, *The Case of the Commonwealth of England Stated*; *The True State of the Case of the Commonwealth* (1654)

1650 JEREMY TAYLOR, *Holy Living*; *Holy Dying* (1651)

1650 GERRARD WINSTANLEY, *New-yeers gift for the Parliament and armie*; *Fire in the Bush*

1651 WILLIAM CARTWRIGHT, *Comedies, Tragicomedies, With Other Poems*

1651 MARY CARY, *The Little Horns Doom and Downfall*

1651 JOHN CLEVELAND, *Poems* (19th edn, 1669)

1651 ROBERT COTTON, *Cottoni posthuma*

1651 NICHOLAS CULPEPER, *Directory for Midwives*, Part 1; Part 2 (1662) (11th edn, 1700)

1651 WILLIAM DAVENANT, *Gondibert*

1651 THOMAS HOBBES, *Leviathan*

1651 WILLIAM LILLY, *Monarchy or No Monarchy in England*

1651 MARCHAMONT NEDHAM begins the newsletter, *Mercurius Politicus*

1651 JOSEPH SALMON, *Height in Depths*

1651 THOMAS STANLEY, *Poems, including 'Anacreontea'*

1651 ANNA WEAMYS, *A Continuation of Sir Philip Sidney's 'Arcadia'*

1651 JOHN WILKINS, *Discourse concerning the Gift of Prayer*

1651 GEORGE WITHER, *The British Appeals*

1652 *Eliza's Babes: or the Virgin's-Offering*

1652 RICHARD CRASHAW, *Carmen Deo Nostro: Sacred Poems*

1652 PAYNE FISHER, *Irenodia Gratulatoria*; *Veni: Vidi: Vici*

1652 GEORGE HERBERT, *A Priest to the Temple* (3rd edn, 1675)

1652 JOHN PLAYFORD, *Select Musicall Ayres*

1652 GERRARD WINSTANLEY, *The Law of Freedom in a Platform*

1653 ELIZABETH AVERY, *Spiritual Autobiography* written

1653 AN COLLINS, *Divine Songs and Meditacions*

1653 JOHN EVERARD, *Some Gospel-Treasures Opened*

1653 JOHN LILBURNE, *Just Defense of John Lilburne*

1653 JAMES NAYLER, *A Discovery of the First Wisdom from beneath, and the Second Wisdom from Above* composed

1653 JOHN ROGERS, *Ohel or Beth-shemesh: A Tabernacle for the Sun*

1653 IZAAK WALTON, *The Compleat Angler* (5th edn, 1676)

MARGARET CAVENDISH, DUCHESS OF NEWCASTLE (1623–73). Serves as maid of honour to Queen Henrietta Maria (1645). Marries William Cavendish, Duke of Newcastle (1645). Lives in exile during the English Civil War (1645–60).

1653 *Poems and Fancies*; *Philosophical Fancies*

1655 *Philosophical and Physical Opinions*; *World's Olio*

1656 *Nature's Pictures Drawn by Fancy's Pencil to the Life*

1662 *Plays*

1664 *Philosophical Letters; CCXI Sociable Letters*
1666 *Description of the New Blazing World; Observations upon Experimental Philosophy*
      (2nd edn, 1668)
1667 *Life of Sir William Cavendish*

1654 THOMAS BLOUNT, *The Academie of Eloquence* (5th edn, 1683)
1654 GEORGE FOX, *Newes Coming up out of the North*
1654 EDMUND GAYTON, *Pleasant Notes upon Don Quixot*
1654 R. C., ed., *The Harmony of the Muses*
1654 ANNA TRAPNEL, *Report and Plea; The Cry of a Stone; A Legacy for Saints;*
      Strange and Wonderful News
1654 SETH WARD, *Vindiciae Academiarum*
1654 THOMAS WASHBOURNE, *Divine Poems*
1655 *The Saints' Testimony Finishing through Sufferings*
1655 ANNE AUDLAND, *A True Declaration of the Suffering of the Innocent*
1655 PRISCILLA COTTON and MARY COLE, *To the Priests and People of England, We*
      Discharge Our Consciences
1655 NICHOLAS CULPEPER, *Culpeper's Astrological Judgment of Diseases from the*
      Decumbiture of the Sick
1655 JOHN DENHAM, *The Destruction of Troy* composed
1655 RICHARD FANSHAWE, Eng. trans. of CAMOENS's *Lusiads* in progress
1655 THOMAS FULLER, *The Church History of Britain*
1655 VINCENT GOODKIN, *The Great Case of Transplantation of Ireland Discussed*
1655 RICHARD LAWRENCE, *England's Great Interest in the Well-Planting of Ireland*
1655 WILLIAM SALES, *Theophania: or Several Modern Histories*
1655 MARTHA SIMMONDS, *A Lamentation for the Lost Sheep*
1655 THOMAS TANY, *Theauraujohn His Aurora in Tranlagorum in Salem Gloria*
1655 JEREMY TAYLOR, *The Golden Grove* (20th edn, 1700)
1655 HENRY VANE, *The Retired Mans Meditations* (3rd edn, 1698)
1655 EDMUND WALLER, *A Panegyric to my Lord Protector*
1656 Satirical verse collections, including *Choyce Drollery: Songs and Sonnets*, banned
      by Parliament; *Parnassus Biceps*, anti-Puritan pieces by University 'Wits'; and
      JOHN MENNES and JAMES SMITH, eds., *Sportive Wit* and *Musarum Deliciae*
1656 JOHN BUNYAN, *Some Gospel-Truths Opened*
1656 JOHN COLLOP, *Poesis Rediviva; Medici Catholicon*
1656 ABRAHAM COWLEY, *Poems* including 'Anacreontiques'; *Davideis* composed
1656 WILLIAM DAVENANT, *The Siege of Rhodes* (pub. 1656)
1656 WILLIAM DUGDALE, *The Antiquities of Warwickshire*
1656 JOHN GAMBLE, *Ayres and Dialogues*, Book 1; Book 2 (1659)
1656 JAMES HARRINGTON, *Commonwealth of Oceana*
1656 ELIZABETH MAJOR, *Honey on the Rod*
1656 HENRY VANE, *A Healing Question Propounded*
1657 JOHN BUNYAN, *A Vindication of the Book Called, Some Gospel-Truths Opened*

1657 JAMES HOWELL, *Londonopolis*
1657 HENRY KING, *Poems, Elegies, Paradoxes and Sonnets*
1657 JAMES NAYLER, *A True Narrative of the Examination, Tryall, and Sufferings of James Nayler* composed
1658 THOMAS BROWNE, *Hydriotaphia, or Urne-Buriall; Garden of Cyrus*
1658 NICOLAS CULPEPPER, *School of Physick*
1658 WILLIAM DUGDALE, *The History of St Paul's Cathedral*
1658 JAMES HARRINGTON, Eng. trans. of VIRGIL'S *Aeneid* in progress
1658 SARAH JINNER, *An Almanack or Prognostication for Women*
1658 JOHN MENNES and JAMES SMITH, eds., *Wit Restor'd*
1658 ANNA TRAPNEL, *Voice for the King of Saints and Nations*
1659 RICHARD BAXTER, *A Holy Commonwealth*
1659 JOHN BUNYAN, *The Doctrine of the Law and Grace Unfolded*
1659 GEORGE FOX, *The Lambs Officer Is Gone Forth*
1659 RICHARD LOVELACE, *Lucasta: Posthume Poems*
1659 JOHN SUCKLING, *Last Remains*
1659 GEORGE WITHER, *Salt Upon Salt*

JOHN DRYDEN (1631–1700). Attends Westminster School and Trinity College, Cambridge (BA 1654). Lives in London (*c.* 1657). Figures in literary quarrels with George Villiers, Duke of Buckingham (1671); Elkanah Settle (1673); and John Wilmot, Earl of Rochester (1679). Appointed Poet Laureate and Historiographer Royal (1670). Receives Customs post (1683). Converts to Catholicism (1685). Deprived of Laureateship and Customs post for not swearing Oaths of Supremacy and Allegiance (1688).
1658 'Heroic Stanzas'
1660 'Astraea Redux'
1663 *The Wild Gallant* (pub. 1669)
1665 *The Indian Queen*
1666 *Annus Mirabilis*
1667 *The Indian Emperor; Sir Martin Mar-all,* with WILLIAM CAVENDISH
1668 *Essay of Dramatic Poesy*
1672 *Marriage à la Mode; Conquest of Granada,* Part 1
c. 1674 *The State of Innocence* (stage adaptation of *Paradise Lost*) (pub. 1677)

1660 *The Out-Cry of the London Prentices for Justice*
1660 HESTER BIDDLE, *Oh! Woe, woe from the Lord*
1660 ROBERT BOYLE, *New Experiments Physico-Mechanicall Touching the Spring of the Air*
1660 ALEXANDER BROME, *The Rump, or, A Collection of Songs*
1660 LAWRENCE CLARKSON, *The Lost Sheep Found*
1660 MARGARET FELL, *The Citie of London reprov'd; A Declaration and an Information from Us; This is to the Clergy*

1660 GEORGE WITHER, *Speculum Speculativum*

c. 1660–9 SAMUEL PEPYS, *Diary* written

c. 1660s LUCY HUTCHINSON, *Order and Disorder, or The World Made and Undone* composed

1661 ROBERT BOYLE, *The Sceptical Chymist*

1661 JOHN BUNYAN, *Profitable Meditations*

1661 JOSEPH GLANVILL, *The Vanity of Dogmatising*

1661 JOHN PERROT, *A Sea of the Seed's Sufferings*

1661 HANNAH WOLLEY, *The Ladies' Directory*

1662 *Mirabilis Annus Secundus, or the Second Years Prodigies*, Parts 1 and 2

1662 ALEXANDER BROME, *Rump: or An Exact Collection of the Choicest Poems and Songs*

1662 JOHN BUNYAN, *I Will Pray with the Spirit* (4th edn, 1692)

1662 EDMUND CALAMY, *The Happinesse of Those Who Sleep in Jesus*

1662 THOMAS FULLER, *The History of the Worthies of England*

1662 ROBERT HOWARD, *The Committee*

1662 MICHAEL WIGGLESWORTH, *Day of Doom*

1662–71 ELIZABETH DELAVAL, *Meditations* composed

1663 SAMUEL BUTLER, *Hudibras*, Part 1 (Part 2, 1664; Part 3, 1678) (34 edns total by 1700)

1664 CHARLES COTTON, *Scarronides: or Virgile travestie*

1664 GEORGE ETHEREGE, *The Comical Revenge, or Love in a Tub* (pub. 1664)

1664 JOHN EVELYN, *Sylva: or A Discourse of Forest Trees* (3rd edn, 1679)

1664 EDWARD HOWARD, *The Usurper*

1664–71 LUCY HUTCHINSON *Memoirs of the Life of Colonel Hutchinson* composed (pub. 1806)

1664 KATHERINE PHILIPS, *Poems* (2nd edn, 1667; 3rd edn, 1669; 4th edn, 1678)

1664–5 ALGERNON SIDNEY, *Court Maxims* composed

1665 JOHN BUNYAN, *One Thing is Needful*

1665 ROBERT HOOKE, *Micrographia*

1665 ISAAC NEWTON at work on calculus

1666 JOHN BUNYAN, *Grace Abounding to the Chief of Sinners* (7th edn, 1695)

1666 MARGARET FELL, *Womens Speaking Justified*

1666 GEORGE WITHER, *Sigh for the Pitchers*

1667 JAMES SHIRLEY, *The Constant Maid* (pub. 1667)

1667 THOMAS SPRAT, *The History of the Royal Society*

1668 ABRAHAM COWLEY, *Works*

1668 WILLIAM DAVENANT, *The Rivals* (pub. 1668)

1668 JOHN DENHAM, *Poems and Translations*

1668 GEORGE ETHEREGE, *She Wou'd If She Cou'd* (pub. 1668; 3rd edn, 1693)

1668 THOMAS HOBBES, *Behemoth, or the Long Parliament* (pub. 1679)

1668 ROBERT HOWARD, *The Great Favorite or, The Duke of Lerma*

1668 HENRY MORE, *Divine Dialogues*

1669 *The New Academy of Compliments* (5th edn, 1698)

1670 APHRA BEHN, *The Forced Marriage* (pub. 1670; 3rd edn, 1690)

1670 FRANCES BOOTHBY, *Marcelia*

1671 APHRA BEHN, *The Amorous Prince*

1671 JANE SHARP, *The Midwives Book*

c. 1671-4 EDWARD HYDE, EARL OF CLARENDON, *History of the Rebellion* (begun 1646; pub. 1702-4)

1672 APHRA BEHN, *The Dutch Lover* (pub. 1673)

1672 WILLIAM WYCHERLEY, *Love in a Wood* (pub. 1672); *The Gentleman Dancing-Master* (pub. 1673)

1673 BATHSUA MAKIN, *An Essay to Revive the Ancient Education of Gentlewomen*

SCOTLAND

1642 [ALEXANDER HENDERSON], *Some Speciall Arguments... to take up armes*

1644 DAVID HUME of Godscroft, *The History of the Houses of Douglas and Angus... From the Year 767, to the Reign of Our Late Sovereign, James the Sixth* (Edinburgh; London edn, 1648); *A General History of Scotland* (pub. 1648-57)

1644 JOHN MAXWELL, *Sacro-Sancta Regum Majestatis: or, The Sacred and Royall Prerogative of Christian Kings* (Oxford)

1646 ROBERT JOHNSTON, *The History of Scotland during the Minority of James VI*, trans. by THOMAS MIDDLETON from Johnston's Latin (2nd edn, 1648)

1652 THOMAS URQUHART, *Ekskubalauron: or, The Discovery of a Most Exquisite Jewel*

1653 THOMAS URQUHART *et al.*, *Whole Works of F. Rabelais, MD, done out of French*, 2 vols. (pub. 1708)

1656 JOHN SPOTTISWOODE, ARCHBISHOP OF ST ANDREWS (d. 1639), *The History of the Church of Scotland*

1667 GEORGE MACKENZIE, *Moral Gallantry*

1667 THOMAS SYDSERFF, *Tarugo's Wiles*

WALES

c. 1640s-50s MORGAN LLWYD, poems composed, including 'The Desolation, Lamentation and Resolution of the Welsh Saints, in the Late Wars' (1643)

1661 VAVASOR POWELL, *The Bird in the Cage, Chirping* (London)

1663 ROWLAND WATKYNS, *Flamma Sine Fumo: or Poems without Fictions* (London)

HENRY VAUGHAN (*c.* 1621-95). Attends Jesus College, Oxford (1638-40). Leaves Oxford to study law in London (1640). Returns home to Brecknocshire, Wales, at outbreak of Civil War and fights on Royalist side. Practices medicine in Newton, on the river Usk.

1646 *Poems*

1650 *Silex Scintillans: or, Sacred Poems* (London) (2nd edn, 1655)

1651 *Olor Iscanus: A Collection of Some Select Poems* (London)

1652 *The Mount of Olives: or, Solitary Devotions* (London)
1678 *Thalia Rediviva* (London)

IRELAND

1649 JOHN BRAMHALL, BISHOP OF DUBLIN (Church of England), *A Fair Warning To Take Heed*
1651, 1655–9 ROGER BOYLE, EARL OF ORRERY, *Parthenissa* (separate issues of Parts 1–6, 1655–69; 11 edns total by 1669)
1665 BOYLE, *Tragedy of Mustapha* (pub. 1668)
1667 RICHARD ARCH(E)DEKIN, *A Treatise of Miracles* (Louvain)

SELECTED MANUSCRIPTS[1]

c. 1501–4 London, British Library (BL), MS Additional 5465. Early Tudor songbook compiled by Robert Fayrfax.

c. 1513–35 BL, MS Additional 31922. Contains many early Tudor songs. Printed by John Stevens, *Music and Poetry in the Early Tudor Court* (Lincoln: University of Nebraska Press, 1961).

c. 1530s; 1542–9 BL, MS Egerton 2711. Manuscript of Thomas Wyatt's poems, with authorial revisions in Wyatt's hand. Other hands annotated and revised poems. MS later in possession of the family of John Harington of Stepney, whose members added other (non-poetic) material. Nineteen Elizabethan poems were added as late as 1600.

c. 1532–*c.* 1539 BL, MS Additional 17492 (Devonshire MS). Late Henrician courtly anthology circulated among several women at court and their lovers or friends. Includes one poem *c.* 1562.

c. 1540–1600 Arundel, Arundel Castle, Arundel-Harington MS. A family commonplace book / verse anthology kept by Sir John Harington of Stepney and his son, Sir John Harington of Kelston. Contains – even after many pages were removed in the eighteenth century – one of the largest collections of Tudor poetry, from the Henrician through the Elizabethan periods. Ruth Hughey (ed.), *The Arundel Harington Manuscript of Tudor Poetry*, 2 vols. (Columbus: Ohio State University Press, 1960).

c. 1555 BL, MS Harley 6254. Biography of Thomas More by William Roper (his son-in-law).

1568 Edinburgh, National Library of Scotland, Advocates Library MS 1.1.6. A collection of Scottish court poetry including works by Robert Henryson, Gavin Douglas, William Dunbar, David Lindsay and Alexander Scott.

c. 1580s BL, MS Harley 7392. An anthology of 153 Elizabethan poems, including more of Edward Dyer's, for example, than any other MS.

---

1 Steven May and Arthur Marotti provided invaluable assistance in compiling this manuscript portion of the chronology. Thanks are also due to Janel Mueller and David Loewenstein for assisting with the final revision of the whole chronology.

1581–1613 Cambridge University Library, MS Dd.5.75. Henry Stanford's anthology of late Elizabethan poetry, much of it private and occasional. Steven May (ed.), *Henry Stanford's Anthology* (New York: Garland, 1988).

c. 1585–1600 Oxford, Bodleian Library, MS Rawl. Poet. 85. A large Elizabethan poetry collection assembled at Cambridge and at court, including poetry by Walter Ralegh, Nicholas Breton, Philip Sidney, Edward Dyer, Arthur Gorges and Edmund Spenser, as well as occasional pieces by members of the University community. Laurence Cummings (ed.), 'John Finet's Miscellany', unpublished Ph.D. thesis, Washington University, 1960.

c. 1585–1600 Arundel Castle, Duke of Norfolk's MSS (Special Case) 'Harrington MS Temp. Eliz'. Includes verse by Thomas Wyatt, the Earl of Surrey, John Harington, Sidney, Ralegh, Fulke Greville and Spenser.

c. 1585–1615 Dublin, Marsh's Library, MS Z. 3.5.21. Includes texts by Henry Constable, Sidney, Ralegh and Edward de Vere, Earl of Oxford.

late 1580s–1590 BL, MS Additional 15232 (Bright MS). A commonplace book kept by the Sidney family; see William A. Ringler, Jr (ed.), *The Poems of Sir Philip Sidney* (Oxford: Clarendon Press, 1962), pp. 538–9.

c. 1592–1602 Bodleian Library, MS Rawl. Poet. 148 (Liber Lilliati). A collection of late Elizabethan verse, much of it by amateurs writing for social occasions. Edward Doughtie (ed.), *Liber Lilliati: Elizabethan Verse and Song* (Newark: University of Delaware Press; London: Asociated University Presses, 1985).

c. 1595–1630 Washington, DC, Folger Shakespeare Library, MS V.a.89 (Cornwallis MS). A two-part collection of verse: the first, poems by John Bentley;

& *c.* 1630–60 the second, such Elizabethan poets as Sidney, Dyer, Oxford and Ralegh, in addition to nine anonymous, apparently unique lyrics.

c. 1596 BL, MS Additional 34064 (Cosens MS). Owned by Anthony Babington of Warrington.

c. 1596–1601 BL, MS Harley 6910. An anthology with poems copied from contemporary printed books, including substantive texts by Sidney, Dyer, Oxford, Ralegh and others.

c. 1600–25 Philadelphia, Rosenbach Museum and Library, MS 1083/15. An Inns of Court manuscript of poetry, containing much verse of Sir John Davies. James Lee Sanderson (ed.), *An Edition of an Early Seventeenth-Century Manuscript Collection of Poems (Rosenbach MS. 186)*, Ph.D. thesis, University of Pennsylvania, 1960.

c. 1604–20 London, Inner Temple, MS Petyt 538.43. Includes selections from the Countess of Pembroke's Psalms, Nashe's 'Choice of Valentines' and verse by Harington, Dr Richard Edes and others.

c. 1605–30 Manchester, Chetham's Library, MS Mun. A.4.15. An Inns of Court miscellany of verse and prose, including poetry by Davies, Donne, Ralegh, Sidney and Oxford. *The Dr Farmer Chetham MS, being a commonplace-book...Temp. Elizabeth, James I. and Charles I*, ed. Alexander B. Grosart, Publications of the Chetham Society, Vol. 89 (Manchester, 1873).

c. 1610–40 London, Victoria and Albert Museum, Dyce MS 44 (Todd MS). A collection of satires, epigrams, verse epitaphs and love poems by Henry Constable, King James, Davies, Harington and others.

c. 1620–40 San Marino, CA, Huntington Library, MS HM 198. Part 1 is a large folio verse miscellany (*c.* 1630s), including 52 poems by Donne. Part 2 includes verse by Donne, Jonson, Harington and Edward, Lord Herbert of Cherbury.

c. 1620–40 Cambridge, MA, Harvard University, Houghton Library MS Eng. 686. An anthology of pre-Civil-War-era texts, including writing by Donne, Corbet, Harington, Ralegh, Henry Wotton and others.

c. 1625–30s London, Westminster Abbey, MS 41. A collection of 118 poems connected with Christ Church, Oxford, owned by George Morley, who became Bishop of Winchester.

c. 1628–60 Bodleian, MS Ashmole 38. A large Caroline anthology of verse, the first 165 pages of which were transcribed before 1638, and the rest between 1640 and 1660, according to Brian Morris and Eleanor Withington (eds.), *The Poems of John Cleveland* (Oxford: Clarendon Press, 1967). Includes Donne, Henry King, Thomas Carew, Robert Herrick, Ben Jonson, William Strode, Richard Corbett, Thomas Randolph, Ralegh, Francis Beaumont, Wotton and James Shirley, as well as many lesser-known and anonymous writers.

c. 1631–3 BL, MS Additional 30982. A verse miscellany compiled by Daniel Leare, a distant cousin of William Strode; it contains one of the largest collections of Richard Corbet's poems.

c. 1630s BL, MS Sloane 1446. An anthology compiled at Christ Church, Oxford, containing works by many poets of the first half of the seventeenth century.

c. 1630s–50s BL, MS Harley 6717–18 (Calfe MS). Two large collections of mostly Jacobean and Caroline verse assembled by Peter Calfe and his son of the same name. The first part has 33 poems by Thomas Carew. There are copies of 30 poems from the book of Thomas Manne, amanuensis of Henry King, and the anthology contains other poems related to the King family.

c. 1650 BL, MS Additional 25707 (Skipwith MS). A poetry collection owned by the Skipwith family, containing verse by Donne, Jonson, Wotton, Beaumont, Carew and others, including Henry and William Skipwith. This is a Jacobean and Caroline anthology; the latest poem is about Charles I's death.

mid seventeenth century BL, MS Additional 53723 (Henry Lawes MS). A large folio collection of over 300 songs and musical dialogues compiled by Henry Lawes (1596–1662) in his own hand. See Peter Beal, *Index of English Literary Manuscripts*, Vol. 2: *1625–1700* (London: Mansell, 1987), p. 532.

Select bibliography

Primary sources

References have been verified against the bibliographical compilations listed below. In them, readers will find more detailed information (for example, about almanacs, Bibles, the Book of Common Prayer, Parliamentary Acts, and royal injunctions and proclamations).

The New Cambridge Bibliography of English Literature, gen, ed. George Watson; Vol. 1: *600–1660*, ed. William A. Ringler, Jr, Cambridge University Press, 1974.

A Short-Title Catalogue of Books Printed in England, Scotland, & Ireland, and of English Books Printed Abroad, 1475–1640, comp. A. W. Pollard and G. R. Redgrave; 2nd edn, rev. and enlarged, W. A. Jackson, F. S. Ferguson and Katharine F. Pantzer, 3 vols., London: The Bibliographical Society, 1986.

A Short-Title Catalogue of Books Printed in England, Scotland, Ireland, Wales, and British America, and of English Books Printed in Other Countries, 1641–1700, comp. Donald Wing; 2nd edn, rev and enlarged, 3 vols., New York: Modern Language Association of America, 1982–98.

A., R., Gent., *The valiant Welshman, or the true chronicle history of Caradoc the great*, [London:] G. Purslowe for R. Lownes, 1615. Mod. rpt, New York: AMS Press, 1970.

Acts of the Privy Council of England, ed. John Roche Dasent, new ser., 32 vols., London: Eyre and Spottiswoode for HMSO, 1890–1907.

Adams, Thomas, *The Workes of Tho: Adams*, London: T. Harper [and A. Matthews] for J. Grismand, 1629 [reissue, 1630].

Alabaster, William, *Sonnets*, ed. G. M. Story and Helen Gardner, London: Oxford University Press, 1959.

Andrewes, Lancelot, *A Sermon preached before his Maiestie, on Sunday the fifth of August last*, London: R. Barker, 1610.

XCVI Sermons, London: G. Miller for R. Badger, 1629.

Sermons, sel. and ed. G. M. Story, Oxford: Clarendon Press, 1967.

Annála Rioghachta Eireann. Annals of the Kingdom of Ireland, by the Four Masters, from the Earliest Period to the Year 1616, ed. John O'Donovan, 7 vols., Dublin: Hodges and Smith, 1848–51.

Argyll, Archibald Campbell, Marquis and 8th Earl, *Instructions to a Son*, Edinburgh and London: for D. Trench, 1661. 3rd edn, 1689.

Arminius, Jacobus, *The Works of James Arminius*, trans. James Nichols and William Nichols, 3 vols., London: Longman, Hurst *et al.*, 1825–75. Rpt, Grand Rapids, MI: Baker Book House, 1986.

The Arundel Harington Manuscript of Tudor Poetry, ed. Ruth Hughey, 2 vols., Columbus: Ohio State University Press, 1960.

Ascham, R[oger], *The Scholemaster*, London: John Daye, 1570. 8th edn, 1589. Mod. edn, *The Schoolmaster (1570)*, ed. Lawrence V. Ryan, Charlottesville, VA: The University Press of Virginia for Folger Shakespeare Library, 1967.

Ashhurst, William, *Reasons against Agreement with a late Printed Paper, intituled, Foundations of Freedome*, [London:] for Thomas Underhill, 1648.

Askew, Anne, *The Examinations of Anne Askew*, ed. Elaine V. Beilin, New York and Oxford: Oxford University Press, 1996.

  The First Examination of Anne Askewe Lately Martyred in Smithfelde by the Romysh Popes Upholders, with the Elucydacyon of Johan Bale, Marburg [Wesel: D. van der Straten,] 1546. 6th edn, 1560.

  The lattre examinacyon of Anne Askewe, with the elucydacyon of J. Bale, Marburg [Wesel: D. van der Straten,] 1547. 6th edn, 1560.

Aston, Sir Thomas, *A collection of sundry petitions presented unto the Kings Most Excellent Majesty*, London: for W. Sheares, 1642.

  A Remonstrance against Presbytery, London: for J. Aston, 1642.

Aubrey, John, *'Brief Lives', chiefly of contemporaries, set down by John Aubrey, between the years 1669 & 1696, edited from the author's MSS*, ed. Andrew Clark, Oxford: Clarendon Press, 1898.

  Brief Lives, edited from the original manuscripts, ed. Oliver Lawson Dick, London: Secker and Warburg, 1949. Rpt Ann Arbor: University of Michigan Press, 1962.

[Audland, Anne, *et al*.,] *The Saints Testimony Finishing through Sufferings*, London: G. Calvert, 1655.

Austen, Ralph, *A Treatise of Fruit-Trees*, Oxford: [L. Lichfield] for T. Robinson, 1653. 3rd edn, 1665.

Aylmer, John, *An Harborowe for faithfull and trewe subjectes*, London: J. Daye, 1559.

Bacon, Francis, *The Advancement of Learning*, ed. Michael Kiernan, The Oxford Francis Bacon, 4, Oxford: Clarendon Press, 2000.

  The Advancement of Learning, in *Francis Bacon*, ed. Vickers, pp. 20–299.

  'A Brief Discourse, Of the Happy Union of the Kingdomes of England and Scotland', in *Resuscitatio*, London: by S. Griffin for W. Lee, 1657. 3rd edn, 1671.

  Francis Bacon, ed. Brian Vickers, Oxford and New York: Oxford University Press, 1996.

  Francisci de Verulamio, . . . Instauratio Magna . . . Novum Organum, London: J. Bill, 1620.

  New Atlantis, in *Francis Bacon*, ed. Vickers, pp. 457–89.

  The New Organon, ed. Lisa Jardine and Michael Silverthorne, Cambridge University Press, 2000.

  'Of Seditions and Troubles', in *Francis Bacon*, ed. Vickers, pp. 366–70.

  The Works of Francis Bacon, ed. James Spedding, Robert Leslie Ellis and Douglas Demon Heath, 14 vols., London: Longmans, 1857–74.

Bacon, Nathaniel, *An Historical and Political Discourse of the Laws and Government of England*, London: for J. Starkey, 1689.

Baillie, Robert, *Anabaptism the True Fountaine of Independency*, London: S. Gellibrand, 1647.

  A Dissuasive from the Errours of the Time, London: S. Gellibrand, 1645.

  The Letters and Journals of Robert Baillie, ed. David Laing, 3 vols., Edinburgh, Bannatyne Club, 1841–2.

Baker, George, *The composition or making of the oil called oleum magistrale*, London: J. Alde, 1574.

Baldwin, William, *The Canticles or Balades of Salomon, Phraselyke Declared in English Metres*, London: W. Baldwin, 1549.

A Marvelous Hystory Intitulede, Beware the Cat, London: W. Gryffith, 1570. 2nd edn, 1584. Mod. edn, *Beware the Cat: The First English Novel*, ed. William Ringler and Michael Flachmann, San Marino, CA: Huntington Library, 1988.

A Myrroure for Magistrates, London: T. Marsh, 1559. 7th edn, 1578. Mod. edn, *A Mirror for Magistrates, Edited from Original Texts in the Huntington Library*, ed. Lily B. Campbell, Cambridge University Press, 1938; rpt New York: Barnes & Noble, 1960.

A Treatise of Morall Phylosophie, Contayning the Sayinges of the Wise, London: E. Whitchurche, 1547. 24th edn, 1639. Facs. of 1620 edn enlarged by Thomas Palfreyman, intro. Robert Hood Bowers, Gainsville, FL: Scholars' Facsimiles & Reprints, 1967.

Bale, John, *A brefe comedy or enterlude concernynge the temptacyon of our lorde*, [Wesel: D. van der Straten, 1547?].

A comedy concernynge thre lawes, of nature, Moses, & Christ. Compyled MDXXXVIII, [Wesel: D. van der Straten, 1548?].

Complete Plays, ed. Peter Happé, 2 vols., Cambridge, Woodbridge, Suffolk: D. S. Brewer, 1985–6.

Illustrium maioris Britanniae scriptorum, summarium, [Wesel: D. van der Straten,] 1548.

The image of both churches, after the revelacion of saynt Johan the evangelyst, [Antwerp: S. Mierdman? 1545?]. 5th edn, 1570. Mod. edn in *Select Works of John Bale*, ed. Revd Henry Christmas, Parker Society, vol. 1, Cambridge University Press, 1849.

King Johan, ed. Barry B. Adams, San Marino, CA: Huntington Library, 1969.

A tragedye or enterlude manyfestyng the chefe promyses of God unto man, [Wesel: D. van der Straten, 1547?].

Vocacyon of Johan Bale to the Bishoprick of Ossorie in Irelande, [Wesel: J. Lambrecht? for H. Singleton,] 1553.

Bale, John [and John Leland], *The Laboryouse Journey & serche of John Leylande, for Englandes antiquitees, geven of hym as a newe yeares gyfte to Kynge Henry the viij . . . with declaracyons enlarged by J. Bale*, London: [S. Mierdman for] J. Bale, 1549. Mod. edn, ed. W. A. Copinger, Manchester: Priory Press, 1895.

Banister, John, *The Historie of Man, sucked from the sappe of the most approved Anathomistes*, London: J. Daye, 1578.

Barclay, Alexander, *Here begynneth the Egloges of Alexander Barclay prest wher of the fyrst thre conteyneth the myserys of courters & courtes*, [Southwark: P. Treveris, c. 1530]. 3rd edn, c. 1560. Mod. edn, *The Eclogues*, ed. Beatrice White, Early English Text Society, orig. ser. 175, London: H. Milford, 1928; rpt, 1960.

Barnes, Barnabe, *Parthenophil and Parthenophe: Sonnettes, madrigals, elegies and odes*, London: [J. Wolfe, 1593]. Mod. edn, ed. Victor A. Doyno, Carbondale: Southern Illinois University Press, 1971.

Barnfield, Richard, *Complete Poems*, ed. George Klawitter, Selinsgrove, PA: Susquehanna University Press, 1990.

Batchiler, John, *The Virgins Pattern*, London: S. Dover, 1661.

Baxter, Richard, *The Autobiography of Richard Baxter*, ed. N. H. Keeble, London: Dent, 1974.

A Holy Commonwealth, London: for T. Underhill and F. Tyton, 1659; 2nd edn, 1659. Mod. edn, ed. William Lamont, Cambridge University Press, 1994.

Reliquiae Baxterianae, or Mr Richard Baxters narrative of the most memorable passages of his life and times, faithfully publish'd from his own original manuscript by Matthew Sylvester, London: for T. Parkhurst, J. Robinson, J. Lawrence and J. Dunton, 1696.

The Saints Everlasting Rest; or, A treatise of the blessed state of the saints in their enjoyment of God in glory, London: T. Underhill and F. Tyton, 1650. 14th edn, 1688. Mod. edn, 2 vols., London: Griffith, Farran, Okeden & Welsh, 1887.

Bayly, Lewis, *The practise of pietie: directing a christian how to walke that he may please God*, London: for J. Hodgetts, 1612. 36th edn, *c.* 1685.

Beard, Thomas, *The Theater of God's Judgments; Or, A Collection of Histories*, London: A. Islip, 1597. 3rd enlarged edn, 1631.

Beaumont, Francis and Fletcher, John, *Comedies and Tragedies*, London: for H. Robinson and for H. Moseley, 1647.

The Dramatic Works in the Beaumont and Fletcher Canon, gen. ed. Fredson Bowers, 10 vols., Cambridge University Press, 1966–96.

Fifty Comedies and Tragedies written by Francis Beaumont and John Fletcher, Gentlemen; all in one volume, published by the authors original copies, the songs to each play being added, London: for J. Martyn, H. Herringman, R. Marriot, 1679.

A King and No King, London: for T. Walkley, 1619.

The Knight of the Burning Pestle, London: for W. Burre, 1613. 3rd edn, 1635. Mod. edn, ed. John Doebler, London: Arnold, 1967.

The Maides Tragedy, London: for F. Constable, 1619. 4th edn, 1638.

Philaster; Or, Love Lyes a Bleeding, London: for T. Walkely, 1620. 5th edn, 1639.

Becon, Richard, *Solon His Follie, or A politique Discourse Touching the Reformation of Common-Weales conquered, declined or corrupted*, 1594, ed. Clare Carroll and Vincent Carey, Binghamton, NY: Medieval and Renaissance Texts and Studies, 1996.

Becon, Thomas, *The Worckes of Thomas Becon, whiche he hath hyther to made and published*, Vol. 1, London: John Daye, 1564. Mod. edn, *The Early Works of Thomas Becon*, ed. J. Ayre, Parker Society, vol. 2, Cambridge University Press, 1843.

Bentley, Thomas, *The monument of matrones: contening seven severall lamps of virginitie, or distinct treatises: whereof the first five concerne praier and meditation: the other two last, preceptes and examples*, London: H. Denham, 1582.

Bibles

Biblia the bible, that is the holy scripture... out of Douche and Latyn in to Englishe. M.D.XXXV, [Cologne or Marburg, 1535]. The 'Coverdale Bible'.

The byble in Englyshe, that is to saye the content of all the holy scrypture, [Paris: François Regnault, and London:] R. Grafton and E. Whitchurch, 1539. The 'Great Bible'.

The byble in Englyshe, with a prologe by Thomas archbysshop of Cantorbury, [London:] E. Whitchurch or R. Grafton, 1540. The 'Great Bible' with Cranmer's prologue and textual alterations.

The bible and holy scriptures conteyned in the olde and newe testament... With most profitable annotations, Geneva: R. Hall, 1560. The 'Geneva Bible'.

The. holie. bible. conteynyng the olde testament and the newe, London: R. Jugge, 1568. The 'Bishops' Bible'.

The new testament of Jesus Christ, faithfully translated into English, out of the authentical Latin . . . In the English college of Rhemes, Rheims: J. Fogny, 1582. Douai-Rheims version (English Vulgate).

The holie bible faithfully translated into English, out of the authentical Latin, Douai: L. Kellam, 1609/10. Old Testament in Douai-Rheims version (English Vulgate).

The holy bible, conteyning the old testament, and the new, newly translated out of the originall tongues: & . . . revised, by his maiesties speciall commandement. Appointed to be read in churches, London: R. Barker, 1611. The 'Authorised' or 'King James' Bible.

The Holy Bible (facsimile edition of the Authorised Version of 1611), Oxford and New York: Oxford University Press, 1911.

Biddulph, William, *The travels of certaine Englishmen into Africa, Asia, Troy, Bythinia, Thracia, and to the Blacke Sea,* London: for W. Aspley, 1609.

Blount, Thomas, *Glossographia: or a dictionary interpreting all such hard words of whatsoever language, now used in our refined English tongue,* London: T. Newcomb, 1656. 5th edn, 1681.

Boate, Arnold, *The Character of a Trulie Vertuous Woman . . . Mistris Margaret Dungan, Wife to Dr Arnold Boate,* Paris: for the author, 1651.

Boece (or Boethius), Hector, *Heir beginnis the hystory and croniklis of Scotland,* trans. John Bellenden, Edinburgh: T. Davidson, 1540. Mod. edn, *The Chronicles of Scotland, compiled by Hector Boece, translated into Scots by John Bellenden, 1531,* ed. Walter Seton, R. W. Chambers and Edith Batho, Publications of the Scottish Text Society, 3rd ser., 10, 15, Edinburgh and London: W. Blackwood & Sons, 1938–41.
Scotorum historiae a prima gentis origine, . . . libri XIX (compiled Paris, 1526), Paris, 1575.

[Bonner, Edmund,] *A profitable and necessarye doctrine, with certayne homelyes adjoined thervnto, set forth by the reuerend father in God, Edmunde Byshop of London, for the instruction and enformation of the people being within his diocesse of London, & of his cure and charge,* London: J. Cawode, 1555.

The Book of Common Prayer

The booke of the common prayer and administracion of the sacramentes, and other rites and ceremonies of the Churche of Englande, London: E. Whitchurch, 1549. First Edwardian Book of Common Prayer. Mod. edn, *The First and Second Prayer Books of Edward VI,* intro. E. C. S. Gibson, Everyman's Library, London: Dent, and New York: Dutton, 1910. Rpt, 1964.

The boke of common prayer, and administracion of the sacramentes, and other rites and ceremonies in the Churche of Englande, London: E. Whitchurch, 1552. Second Edwardian Book of Common Prayer. Mod. edn, *The First and Second Prayer Books of Edward VI,* intro. Gibson.

The boke of common praier, and administration of the sacramentes, and other rites and ceremonies in the Churche of Englande, London: R. Grafton, 1559. Mod. edn, *The Book of Common Prayer 1559: The Elizabethan Prayer Book,* ed. John E. Booty, Washington, DC: Folger Shakespeare Library, 1976.

The Book of Common Prayer, London: By His Majesties printers, 1662. The Restoration Book of Common Prayer.

[Book of Common Prayer in Welsh] *Llyfr gweddi gyffredin*. [London: by S. Dover for Edward Fowks and Peter Bodwel,] 1664. 2nd edn, 1678.

Borde, Andrew, *The breuiary of helthe, for all maner of sycknesses and diseases*, London: W. Myddelton, 1547. 5th edn, 1598.

The fyrst boke of the Introduction of knowledge, London: W. Copland, [1542].

Boyle, Robert, *The Sceptical Chymist*, London: J. Cadwell for J. Crooke, 1661.

Bradford, John, *The copye of a letter, . . . declaring the nature of spaniardes, and discovering treasons, againste Englande*, [Wesel?: J. Lambrecht?, 1556?].

Bradstreet, Anne, *Works*, ed. Jeannine Hensley, Cambridge, MA: Harvard University Press, 1967.

Bramhall, John, *A Fair Warning to Take Heed of Scottish Discipline*, London, 1649. 4th edn, 1674.

The Serpent Salve, or, a Remedy for the Biting of an Aspe, Oxford, 1643.

Brathwait, Richard, *The English Gentleman: containing sundry excellent rules how to accommodate himselfe in the manage of publike or private affaires*, London: J. Haviland, 1630. 2nd enlarged edn, 1633.

The English Gentlewoman, drawne out to the full body: expressing, what habilliments doe best attire her, London: for M. Sparke, 1631.

Whimzies: or, A New Cast of Characters, London: F. K[ingston], 1631.

Breton, Nicholas, *Complete Works and Verse*, ed. Alexander B. Grosart, 2 vols., Edinburgh: T. & A. Constable, 1875-9.

Bridgewater, Elizabeth Egerton, Countess of, 'True Coppies of certaine Loose Papers left by the Right honorable Elizabeth Countesse of Bridgewater', British Library, MS Egerton 607, 1663.

Brinkelow, Henry, *The complaynt of Roderick Mors . . . vnto the parlament house of Ingland hys naturall countrey: For the redresse of certeyn wycked lawes, euell custumes & cruell decrees*, Savoy per Franciscum de Turona [Strasbourg?: W. Köpfel, 1542?]. 4th edn, 1560?

Brinsley, John, *Ludus Literarius; or, the grammar schoole. Intended for the helping of the younger sort of teachers, and of all schollars*, London: H. Lownes for T. Man, 1612. 10th edn, 1639.

Brome, Alexander, *Poems*, ed. Roman R. Dubinski, 2 vols., Toronto and Buffalo, NY: University of Toronto Press, 1982.

[Brome, Alexander,] *Rump: Or An Exact Collection of the Choycest Poems and Songs . . . By the most Eminent Wits, from Anno 1639 to Anno 1661*, London: for H. Brome and H. Marsh, 1662.

Brome, Richard, *Dramatic Works*, ed. J. Pearson, 3 vols., London: J. Pearson, 1873. Rpt New York: AMS Press, 1966.

Five New Playes, London: for H. Moseley, R. Marriot and T. Dring, 1653.

A Joviall Crew: or, The Merry Beggars, presented in a comedie at the Cock-pit in Drury-Lane, in the year 1641, London: J. Y. for E. D. and N. E., 1652.

Brooke, Robert Greville, Baron, *A discourse opening the nature of episcopacie which is exercised in England*, London: R. C. for S. Cartwright, 1641. 3rd edn, 1681.

Browne, Thomas, *The Major Works*, ed. C. A. Patrides, London: Penguin Books, 1977.

Pseudodoxia Epidemica, London: for E. Dod, 1646. 7th enlarged edn, 1672. Mod. edn, 2 vols., ed. Robin Robins, Oxford: Clarendon Press, 1981.

Religio Medici, London: for A. Crooke, 1643. 10th edn, 1682.

Religio Medici and Other Works, ed. L. C. Martin, Oxford: Clarendon Press, 1964.

Works of Sir Thomas Browne, ed. Geoffrey Keynes, 4 vols., new edn, London: Faber & Faber; University of Chicago Press, 1964.

Browne, William, of Tavistock, *Poems*, ed. Gordon Goodwin, intro. A. H. Bullen, 2 vols., London: G. Routledge, and New York: E. P. Dutton, 1905.

Bruton, William, *Newes from the East-Indies: Or, A Voyage to Bengalla*, London: J. Okes, sold by H. Blunden, 1638.

Buchanan, George, *Baptistes, sive columnia, tragoedia*, London: T. Vautroller, 1577. 2nd edn, 1578.

De iure regni apud Scotos, dialogus, Edinburgh: J. Ross for H. Charter, 1579. 5th edn, 1689.

Rerum Scoticarum historia, Edinburgh: A. Arbuthnot, 1582. 4th edn, 1643. Trans. as *The History of Scotland*, London: A. Churchill, 1690. Mod. edn, *The History of Scotland from the Earliest Period to the Regency of the Earl of Moray*, ed. and trans. J. Aikman, 6 vols., Glasgow: Blackie, Fullarton & Co., 1827.

Bullinger, Heinrich (Henry), *The christen state of matrimonie: the orygenall of holy wedlok*, trans. M. Coverdale, [Antwerp: M. Crom, 1541].

Bullokar, John, *An English expositor: teaching the interpretation of the hardest words used in our language*, London: J. Legatt, 1616.

Bunyan, John, *A Few Sighs from Hell, or, The Groans of A Damned Soul*, London: R. Wood for M. Wright, 1658. 10th edn, 1700.

Grace Abounding to the Chief of Sinners, London: George Larkin, 1666. Mod. edn, ed. Roger Sharrock, Oxford: Clarendon Press, 1962.

The Miscellaneous Works of John Bunyan, gen, ed. Roger Sharrock, 13 vols., Oxford: Clarendon Press, 1976–94.

The Pilgrim's Progress, London: for Nathaniel Ponder, 1678. 22nd edn, 1696.

Burton, Robert, *The Anatomy of Melancholy*, ed. Thomas C. Faulkner, Nicolas K. Kiessling and Rhonda L. Blair, 6 vols., Oxford: Clarendon Press, 1989–2000.

Butler, Samuel, *Hudibras*, ed. John Wilders, Oxford: Clarendon Press, 1967.

Prose Observations, ed. Hugh de Quehen, Oxford: Clarendon Press, 1979.

Satires and Miscellaneous Poetry and Prose, ed. René Lamar, Cambridge University Press, 1928.

C., E., [Falkland, Elizabeth Cary, Viscountess,] (trans.) [Cardinal Jacques Davy du Perron,] *The History of the Life, Reign, and Death of Edward II, King of England, and Lord of Ireland. With the Rise and Fall of His Great Favourites, Gaveston and the Spencers*, London: J. C. for C. Harper, 1680.

The Reply of the Most Illustrious Cardinal of Perron, to the Answeare of the Most Excellent King of Great Britaine. The First Tome, Douay: M. Bogart, 1630.

The Tragedie of Mariam, the Faire Queene of Jewry, London: T. Creede for R. Hawkins, 1613. Mod. edn, *The Tragedy of Mariam the Fair Queen of Jewry, with The Lady Falkland her Life, By one of her Daughters*, ed. Barry Weller and Margaret W. Ferguson, Berkeley: University of California Press, 1994.

Cabala, Mysteries of State, London: for G. Bedell and T. Collins, 1654. 3rd edn, 1691.

The Cambridge Platonists, ed. C. A. Patrides, London: Edward Arnold, 1969.

Camden, William, *Annales rerum Anglicarum, et Hibernicarum, regnante Elizabetha, ad annum MDLXXXIX*, Books 1–3, London: G. Stansby, 1615. Book 4: *Tomus alter annalium rerum Anglicarum, et Hibernicarum, sive pars quarta*, London: G. Stansby, 1629. Trans. as *The historie of the most renowned and victorious princess Elizabeth*, trans. R. Norton, London: for B. Fisher, 1630. 5th edn, 1688.

Britannia sive florentissimorum regnorum, Angliae, Scotiae, Hiberniae chorographica descriptio, London: R. Newbery, 1586. 6th edn, 1607. Trans. as *Britain, Or a chorographicall description of the most flourishing Kingdomes, England, Scotland, and Ireland*, trans. Philemon Holland, London: G. Bishop and J. Norton, 1610.

Remaines of a greater worke, concerning Britain, London: for S. Waterson, 1605. 7th edn, 1674. Mod. edn, *Remains Concerning Britain*, ed. R. D. Dunn, University of Toronto Press, 1984.

Campion, Thomas, *Works of Thomas Campion*, ed. Walter R. Davis, New York: Doubleday, 1967.

Carew, Thomas, *The Poems*, ed. Rhodes Dunlap, Oxford: Clarendon Press, 1949.

Carleton, George, *The life of Bernard Gilpin, a man most holy and renowned among the northerne English*, London: W. Jones, 1629.

Cartwright, William, *Comedies, Tragi-Comedies, with Other Poems*, London: for H. Moseley, 1651.

Plays and Poems, ed. G. Blakemore Evans, Madison, WI: University of Wisconsin Press, 1951.

Cary, Mary, *The Little Horns Doom and Downfall*, London: for the author, 1651.

Cavalier and Puritan: Ballads and Broadsides Illustrating the Period of the Great Rebellion, 1640–1660, ed. Hyder E. Rollins, New York University Press, 1923.

Cavendish, George, *The Life and death of Thomas Woolsey, Cardinal, once Arch Bishop of York and Lord Chancellour of England . . . written by one of his own servants, being his gentleman usher*, London: for D. Newman, 1667. Mod. edn, *The Life and Death of Cardinal Wolsey*, ed. Richard S. Sylvester, Early English Text Society, orig. ser., 243, Oxford University Press, 1959.

Metrical Visions, ed. A. S. G. Edwards, Columbia: University of South Carolina Press, 1980.

The Worlds Olio, London: for J. Martin and J. Allestrye, 1655. 2nd edn, 1671.

Cawdrey, Robert, *A Table Alphabeticall, conteyning and teaching the understanding of hard usuall English wordes, borrowed from the Hebrew, Greeke, Latin, or French, &c.*, London: J. R[oberts] for E. Weaver, 1604. 4th edn, 1617.

Caxton, William, *The Prologues and Epilogues of William Caxton*, ed. W. J. B. Crotch, Early English Text Society, orig. ser., 176, London: H. Milford/Oxford University Press for EETS, 1928.

Chalmers, David, *Histoire abrégée de tous les roys de France, Angleterre, et Escosse . . . contenant aussi en brief discours de l'ancienne aliance et mutuel secours entre la France et l'Escosse*, Paris, 1579.

Chaloner, Thomas, *De republica Anglorum instauranda, libri decem* [in verse], London: T. Vautroller, 1579.

Chandos, John (ed.), *In God's Name: Examples of Preaching in England from the Act of Supremacy to the Act of Uniformity, 1534–1662*, London: Bobbs-Merrill, 1971.

Chapman, George, *Al fooles, a Comedy, presented at the Black Fryers*, London: for T. Thorpe, 1605.

Bussy d'Ambois: a Tragedie: as it hath been often presented, London: for W. Aspley, 1607.

Eastward hoe. As it was playd in the Black-friers. Made by G. Chapman. B. Jonson. J. Marston, London: for W. Aspley, 1605. 3rd edn, 1605.

Hero and Leander. Begun by C. Marloe; and finished by G. Chapman, London: for P. Linley, 1598. 9th edn, 1637.

Ovids banquet of sence, London: for R. Smith, 1595. 2nd edn, 1598.

Plays, vol. 1, The Comedies, ed. Allan Holaday, Urbana: University of Illinois Press, 1970.

Plays, vol. 2, The Tragedies, ed. Allan Holaday *et al.* Cambridge: D. S. Brewer, 1987.

The Poems, ed. Phyllis Brooks Bartlett, Oxford University Press, 1941.

[Charles I,] *The Kings Cabinet opened: Or, Certain Packets of Secret Letters & Papers, Written with the Kings own Hand, and taken in his Cabinet at Nasby-Field, June 14. 1645*, London: for R. Bostock, 1645.

A Large Declaration concerning the late tumults in Scotland . . . By the King, London: R. Young, 1639.

Chaucer, Geoffrey, *The workes of our antient and lerned English poet, G. Chaucer, newly printed*, ed. Thomas Speght, London: [A. Islip,] 1598; 1602.

The workes . . . with divers addicions, ed. John Stowe, London: [for J. Wight,] 1561.

The Works of our ancient and learned English poet, newly printed, ed. W. Thynne, London: T. Godfray, 1532.

Cheke, John, *The hurte of sedition, howe greveous it is to a commune welth*, London: J. Daye and W. Seres, 1549. 4th edn, 1576.

Chettle, Henry, *Kind-Harts Dreame. Conteining five apparitions, with their invectives against abuses raigning*, London: for W. Wright, [1592]. Mod. edn, ed. G. B. Harrison, London, 1923; rpt, New York: Barnes and Noble, 1966.

C[hidley], K[atherine], *Good Counsell, to the Petitioners for Presbyterian Government*, [London, 1645].

A Justification of the Independent Churches of Christ, London: W. Larnar, 1641.

Chief Pre-Shakespearean Dramas, ed. John Quincy Adams, Cambridge University Press, 1924.

Choyce Drollery: Songs & Sonnets. Being a collection of divers excellent pieces of poetry, of several eminent authors, London: for R. Pollard and J. Sweeting, 1656. Mod. edn, ed. J. Woodfall Ebsworth, Boston, Lincs.: R. Roberts, 1876.

Christopherson, John, *An exhortation to all menne to take hede and beware of rebellion*, London: J. Cawood, 1554.

The Chronicle of the Grey Friars of London, ed. John Gough Nichols, Publications of the Camden Society, 1st ser., 53, London: Camden Society, 1852.

The Chronicle of King Henry VIII of England. Being a Contemporary Record of Some of the Principal Events of the Reigns of Henry VIII and Edward VI. Written in Spanish by an Unknown Hand, trans. and ed. Martin A. Sharp Hume, London: G. Bell & Sons, 1889.

The Chronicle of Queen Jane, and of Two Years of Queen Mary, and Especially of the Rebellion of Sir Thomas Wyatt, ed. John Gough Nichols, Publications of the Camden Society, 1st ser., 48, London: Camden Society, 1850.

Churchyard, Thomas, *The first parte of Churchyards chippes, containing twelve severall labours*, London: T. Marshe, 1575.

The worthines of Wales, wherein are more then a thousand severall things rehearsed. A poem, London: G. Robinson for T. Cadman, 1587. Rpt, London: for T. Evans, 1776. Facs. edn by the Spenser Society, Manchester, 1876.

Clarendon, Edward Hyde, Earl of, *The History of the Rebellion and Civil Wars in England Begun in the Year 1641 by Edward, Earl of Clarendon; Re-edited from a Fresh Collation of the Original*

Manuscript in the Bodleian Library, ed. W. Dunn Macray, 6 vols., Oxford: Clarendon Press, 1888.

Selections from The History of the Rebellion and The Life by Himself, ed. G. Huehns, Oxford University Press, 1978.

Clarke, Samuel, of St Bennet Fink, *The Lives of Sundry Eminent Persons*, London: for T. Simmons, 1683.

C[leaver], R[obert], *A Godlie Forme of Householde Government, for the Ordering of Private Families, According to the Direction of Gods Word*, London: T. Creede for T. Man, 1598. 4th enlarged edn, subtitled *First, gathered by R. C. And now newly perused, amended, and augmented, by J. Dod, and R. Clever*, London: for T. Man and G. Norton, 1610. 8th edn, 1630.

[Cleveland, John,] *Monumentum Regale, or A Tombe, Erected for . . . Charles the First, Printed 1649*, [London,] 1649.

Cleveland, John, *The Poems of John Cleveland*, ed. Brian Morris and Eleanor Withington, Oxford: Clarendon Press, 1967.

Clifford, Anne, *Diaries*, ed. D. J. H. Clifford, Stroud, Gloucestershire: Alan Sutton, 1990; and Wolfeboro Falls, NH: Sutton, 1991.

The Diary of Anne Clifford, 1616–1619. A Critical Edition, ed. Katherine O. Acheson, New York: Garland, 1995.

The Diary of Lady Anne Clifford, ed. Vita Sackville-West, New York: G. H. Doran, 1923.

Cockburn, Patrick, *In dominicam orationem pia meditatio*, St Andrews: J. Scot, 1555.

Cockeram, Henry, *The English Dictionarie: or, an interpreter of hard English words*, London: Eliot's Court Press for N. Butter, 1623.

Colet, John, *Rudimenta grammatices et docendi methodus*, [Southwark:] P. Treveris, 1529; 10th edn, 1539?

Collins, An, *Divine Songs and Meditacions*, London: R. Bishop, 1653. Mod. edn, ed. Sidney Gottlieb, Tempe, AZ: Medieval and Renaissance Texts and Studies, 1996.

Collop, John, *The Poems of John Collop*, ed. Conrad Hilberry, Madison: University of Wisconsin Press, 1962.

Comenius [Komensky], Jan [Johann] Amos, *A Reformation of Schooles*, trans. Samuel Hartlib, London: for Michael Sparke, 1642; facs. edn, Menston, Yorks.: Scolar Press, 1969.

The complaynt of Scotland, vyth ane exortatione to the three Estaitis, to be vigilante on the diffens of their public veil, Paris, 1549; mod. edn, ed. J. A. H. Murray, Early English Text Society, ext. ser., 17, London: Kegan Paul, Trench, Trübner, 1872. Rpts, 1891, 1906.

The confession of faith, and the larger and shorter catechism, Amsterdam: for A. Wilson, [1649]. 29 London and Edinburgh edns, 1647–1700.

The confessioun of faith profesit and belevit be the protestantes within the realme of Scotland, Edinburgh: J. Scot, 1561.

Constable, Henry, *Poems*, ed. Joan Grundy, Liverpool University Press, 1960.

The Conway Letters: The Correspondence of Anne, Viscountess Conway, Henry More, and their Friends, 1642–1684, ed. Marjorie Hope Nicolson, rev. Sarah Hutton, Oxford: Clarendon Press, 1992.

Coppe, Abiezer, *A Fiery Flying Roll*, London, 1649.

A Second Fiery Flying Roule, London, 1649. Mod. edn of both in *A Collection of Ranter Writings from the Seventeenth Century*, ed. Nigel Smith, London: Junction Books, 1983.

Selected Writings, ed. A. Hopton, London: Aporia Press, 1987.

Coppin, Richard, *Divine Teachings*, preface by Abiezer Coppe, London: G. Calvert, 1649. 2nd edn, 1653.

Corbet, John, *The Epistle Congratulatorie of Lysimachus Nicanor, of the Societie of Jesu, to the Covenanters in Scotland. Wherein is paralleled our sweet harmony and correspondency in divers materiall points of doctrine and practice*, Dublin: Society of Stationers, 1640. 4th edn, London: R. Young and R. Badger, 1640; 5th edn, London, 1684.

Corbet, Richard, *Certain elegant poems*, London: for A. Crooke, 1647.

The Poems of Richard Corbett, ed. J. A. W. Bennett and H. R. Trevor-Roper, Oxford: Clarendon Press, 1955.

Corbin, Peter and Sedge, Douglas (eds.), *The Oldcastle Controversy: 'Sir John Oldcastle, Part I', and 'The Famous Victories of Henry V'*, Manchester University Press, 1991.

Three Jacobean Witchcraft Plays, Manchester University Press, 1986.

Cosin, John, *A collection of private devotions: in the practise of the ancient church, called the houres of prayer*, London: R. Young, 1627. 10th edn, 1719; mod. edn, ed. Paul G. Stanwood, Oxford: Clarendon Press, 1967.

The Works of the Right Reverend Father in God, John Cosin, Lord Bishop of Durham, 5 vols., Oxford: John Henry Parker, 1843.

Cotgrave, Randle, *A Dictionarie of the French and English Tongues*, London: A. Islip, 1611. 10th edn, 1650.

Cotterell, Charles (trans.), [Gualtier de Coste, seigneur de La Calprenède,] *Cassandra. A Romance*, London: for H. Moseley, 1652. 7th edn, 1676.

Cotton, Charles, *The compleat angler, Part II*, London: for R. Marriott and H. Brome, 1676.

Poems, ed. John Beresford, London: Richard Cobden-Sanderson, 1923; ed. John Buxton, London: Routledge, 1958.

Scarronides, or Le Vergile travestie: a mock-poem, being the first book of Virgils Aeneis in English, burlesque, London: for H. Brome, 1664. *Fourth book* added, 1665. 11th edn, 1700. Mod. edn, ed. A. I. Dust, New York: Garland, 1992.

Cotton, Clement, *The mirror of martyrs . . . Expressing the force of their faith* [selections from John Foxe's *Acts and Monuments*], London: for J. Budge, 1613. 5th enlarged edn, 1639.

Cotton, John, *The bloudy tenent, washed and made white in the bloud of the Lambe*, London: for H. Allen, 1647.

Cowley, Abraham, *The Collected Works of Abraham Cowley*, ed. Thomas O. Calhoun, Laurence Heyworth and Allan Pritchard, Newark: University of Delaware Press, 1989– (in progress).

Essays, Plays and Sundry Verses, ed. A. R. Waller, Cambridge University Press, 1906.

A Poem on the Late Civil War, [London,] 1679. Mod. edn, *The Civil War*, ed. Allan Pritchard, University of Toronto Press, 1973.

Poems, London: for Humphrey Mosely, 1656. 2nd edn, Oxford, 1668. Mod. edn, ed. A. R. Waller, Cambridge University Press, 1905.

Craig, Thomas, *Scotland's sovereignty asserted: being a dispute concerning homage, against those who maintain that Scotland is a feu, or fee-liege of England, and that therefore the king of Scots owes homage to the king of England, translated from the Latin manuscript*, trans. George Ridpath, London: for A. Bell, 1695.

De Unione Regnorum Britanniae Tractatus, edited from the manuscript in the Advocates' Library, with a translation and notes, trans. C. Sanford Terry, Publications of the Scottish History Society, 60, Edinburgh: T. & A. Constable, 1909.

[Cranmer, Thomas,] *The booke of the common prayer and administracion of the sacramentes, and other rites and ceremonies of the Churche of Englande*, London: E. Whitchurch, 1549; another edn, R. Grafton, 1549, 1552. See the Book of Common Prayer.

The First and Second Prayer Books of Edward VI, intro. E. C. S. Gibson, Everyman's Library (London: Dev, 1910, 1964).

Miscellaneous Writings and Letters of Thomas Cranmer, ed. John Edmund Cox, Parker Society 16, Cambridge University Press, 1846.

[Cranmer, Thomas, *et al.*,] *Certain sermons, or homilies, appoynted by the kynges maiestie, to be declared and redde, by all persones, vicars, or curates, euery Sonday in their churches, where thei haue cure*, London: R. Grafton, 1547. First Book of Homilies.

Crashaw, Richard, *Carmen Deo nostro, . . . sacred poems*, Paris: P. Targa, 1652.

Poemata et epigrammata, Cambridge: J. Hays, 1670. 2nd edn, 1674.

The Poems, English, Latin and Greek, of Richard Crashaw, ed. L. C. Martin, Oxford: Clarendon Press, 1957.

Steps to the temple: sacred poems, London: for H. Moseley, 1646. 5th edn, 1680.

Crashaw, William, *Manuale Catholicorum. A Manuall for True Catholickes*, London: [N. Okes] for L. Becket, 1611.

Critical Essays of the Seventeenth Century, ed. J. E. Spingarn, 3 vols., Oxford: Clarendon Press, 1908.

Cromwell, Oliver, *Speeches of Oliver Cromwell*, ed. Ivan Roots, London: Dent, 1989.

Writings and Speeches of Oliver Cromwell, ed. Wilbur C. Abbott, 4 vols., Cambridge, MA: Harvard University Press, 1937–47.

Crowley, Robert, *One and thyrtye epigrammes, wherein are bryefly touched so many abuses, that ought to be put away*, London: [R. Grafton for] R. Crowley, 1550. 3rd edn, 1573.

Philargyrie of great Britayne, in *The Fable of Philargyrie the Great Gigant, Reprinted from the only known copy*, intro. W. A. Marsden, London: Emery Walker, 1931. Mod. edn, ed. John N. King, *English Literary Renaissance* 10 (1980), 46–75.

Select Works, ed. J. M. Cowper, London: Early English Text Society, ext. ser., 15, London: N. Trübner, 1872.

Culpeper, Nicholas, *Culpeper's Astrologicall judgment of diseases from the decumbiture of the sick*, London: for N. Brookes, 1655.

Culpeper's directory for midwives: or a guide for women, the second part, London: P. Cole, 1662. 3rd edn, 1681.

Culpeper's school of physick, London: for N. Brook, 1659. 5th edn, 1696.

A directory for midwives, London: P. Cole, 1651. 11th edn, 1700.

The English physician, London, 1652. *The English physician, enlarged*, London: P. Cole, 1653. 17th edn, 1698.

Daniel, Samuel, *The first fowre bookes of the civile Warres betweene the two houses of Lancaster and Yorke*, London: for S. Waterson, 1595.

The Civile Warres betweene the howeses of Lancaster and Yorke corrected and continued, Books 1–8, London: S. Waterson, 1609. Mod. edn, ed. Lawrence Michel, New Haven, CT: Yale University Press, 1958.

A defence of ryme in A panegyrike congratulatory delivered to the Kings most excellent majesty . . . Also certaine epistles. With a defence of ryme, London: for E. Blount, 1603.

Mod. edns, in *Elizabethan Critical Essays*, ed. Smith, 2:356–84; *Poems and a Defence of Ryme*, ed. Arthur Colby Sprague, University of Chicago Press, 1965.

Delia. Contayning certayne sonnets: with, The complaint of Rosamond, London: for S. Waterson, 1592. Mod. edns, in *The Complete Works of Samuel Daniel in Verse and Prose*, ed. Alexander B. Grosart, 5 vols., London: Russell & Russell, 1885, vol. 1; *Poems and a Defence of Ryme*, ed. Sprague.

Poeticall Essayes . . . Newly corrected and augmented (includes 'Musophilus'), London: for S. Waterson, 1599.

Davenant, William, *Dramatic Works*, ed. J. Maidment and W. H. Logan, 5 vols., London: 1872–4. Rpt, New York: Russell and Russell, 1964.

Gondibert, London: for John Holden, 1651. Mod. edn, ed. David F. Gladish, Oxford: Clarendon Press, 1971.

London, King Charles, his Augusta, London: for W. Leybourn, 1648.

The platonick lovers. A tragaecomedy, London: for R. Meighem, 1636.

The preface to Gondibert an heroick poem, written by Sir William D'Avenant; with answer to the preface by Mr Hobbes, Paris: M. Guillemot, 1650.

Salmacida spolia. A masque presented at White-hall, London: for T. Walkely, 1639.

The Shorter Poems and Songs from the Plays and Masques, ed. A. M. Gibbs, Oxford: Clarendon Press, 1972.

The siege of Rhodes, London: for H. Herringman, 1656. 4th edn, 1670.

Davidson, Peter (ed.), *Poetry and Revolution: An Anthology of British Verse, 1625–60*, Oxford: Clarendon Press, 1998.

Davies, John, of Hereford, *The Muses Sacrifice*, London: for G. Norton, 1612.

Davies, Sir John, *A Discoverie of the true causes why Ireland was never entirely subdued, nor brought under Obedience of the Crowne of England, untill the beginning of his Maiesties happie raigne*, London: for J. Jaggard, 1612.

The Poems, ed. Robert Krueger, Oxford: Clarendon Press, 1975.

Davies, William, *A true relation of the travailes and captivitie of William Davies, Barber-Surgion of London, under the Duke of Florence*, London: N. Bourne, 1614.

Day, Angel, *The English secretorie. Wherein is contayned, a perfect method, for the inditing of all manner of epistles*, London: R. Waldegrave, 1586. 9th edn, 1635.

Debus, Allen (ed.), *Science and Education in the Seventeenth Century: The Webster–Ward Debate*, London: Macdonald, and New York: American Elsevier, 1970.

Dekker, Thomas, *The belman of London: bringing to light the most notorious villanies now practised in the kingdome*, London: for N. Butter, 1608. 10th enlarged edn, 1620.

The Dramatic Works of Thomas Dekker, ed. Fredson Bowers, 4 vols., Cambridge University Press, 1953–61.

The guls horne-booke, London: [N. Okes] for R. S[ergier?], 1609.

The honest whore, London: for J. Hodgets, 1604. 6th edn, 1635.

Non-Dramatic Works, ed. A. B. Grosart, 5 vols., London, 1886.

The Plague Pamphlets of Thomas Dekker, ed. F. P. Wilson, Oxford: Clarendon Press, 1925.

The second part of the honest whore, London: for N. Butter, 1630.

Selected Writings [*The Wonderful Year, The Gull's Horn-Book, Penny-Wise, Pound-Foolish, English Villanies Discovered by Lantern and Candlelight*], ed. E. D. Pendry, Stratford-upon-Avon Library, 4, London: Edward Arnold, 1967.

The shomakers holiday. Or the gentle craft. With the life of Simon Eyre, shoomaker, and lord maior of London, London: V. Sims, 1600. 5th edn, 1631.

The wonderfull yeare. Wherein is shewed the picture of London, lying sicke of the plague, London: T. Creede, 1603.

Delaval, Elizabeth, *The Meditations of Lady Elizabeth Delaval Written Between 1662 and 1671*, ed. Douglas G. Greene, Publications of the Surtees Society, 190, Gateshead, Northumbria: Northumberland Press, 1978.

Dell, William, *The Tryal of Spirits*, London: G. Calvert, 1653. 3rd edn, 1699.

The Way of True Peace and Unity among the Faithful, London: G. Calvert, 1649. 2nd edn, 1651.

Deloney, Thomas, *The gentle craft. A discourse containing many matters of delight* [*c*. 1597], London: for E. Brewster, 1627; 3 more edns by 1640.

The pleasant history of John Winchcomb, in his younger yeares called Jack of Newberie [*c*. 1597], *Now the eight time imprinted, corrected and inlarged*, London: H. Lownes, 1619. 11th edn, 1630.

The second part of the gentle craft, London: [E. Allde, *c*. 1600].

Thomas of Reading. Or, the sixe worthy yeomen of the West [*c*. 1602]. *Now the fourth time corrected and enlarged*, London: for T. P[avier], 1612.

The Works of Thomas Deloney, ed. Francis Oscar Mann, Oxford: Clarendon Press, 1912. Rpt, 1967.

Denham, John, *Expans'd Hieroglyphicks: A Study of Sir John Denham's 'Coopers Hill' with a Critical Edition of the Poem*, ed. Brendan O Hehir, Berkeley and Los Angeles: University of California Press, 1969.

Dent, Arthur, *The plaine mans path-way to heaven, Wherein every man may clearly see, whether he shall be saved or damned. Set forth dialogue wise*, London: for R. Dexter, 1601. 25th edn, 1640.

Llwybr hyffordd yn cyfarwyddo yr anghyfarwydd i'r nefoed. Welsh trans. by R. Lloyd, London: N. Okes & G. Lathum, 1630.

The plaine-mans path-way to heaven. The second part, Set foorth dialogue-wise, London: for B. Sutton and W. Barrenger, 1609. 2nd edn, 1612.

Derricke, John, *The image of Irelande, with a discoverie of woodkarne* [*wild kerns*], ... *their aptnesse, celeritie, and proneness to rebellion* (in verse), London: J. Daye, 1581. Mod. edn, ed. John Small, Edinburgh: A. & C. Black, 1883. Facs. of Small's edn, Delmar, NY: Scholars' Facsimiles & Reprints, 1998.

Digby, Kenelm, *Observations Upon Religio Medici*, London: for L. Chapman and D. Frere, 1643. 4th edn, 1659.

Dod, John, *A Plaine and Familiar Exposition of the Ten Commandements, with a Methodicall Short Catechisme*, London: T. C[reede] for T. Man, 1604. 19th edn, 1635.

Donne, John, *The Complete English Poems of John Donne*, ed. A. J. Smith, Harmondsworth: Penguin, 1971; ed. C. A. Patrides, London: Dent, 1985.

Deaths duell, or, a consolation to the soule, against the dying life, and living death of the body. In a sermon, London: for R. Redmer and B. Fisher, 1632. 3rd edn, 1633.

Devotions upon emergent occasions, and severall steps in my sickness, London: for T. Jones, 1624. Mod edn, ed. John Sparrow, Cambridge University Press, 1923. Another edn, with *Death's Duell*, Ann Arbor: University of Michigan Press, 1959.

The Divine Poems, ed. Helen Gardner, Oxford: Clarendon Press, 1952. Rpt, 1978.

Elegies and the Songs and Sonnets, ed. Helen Gardner, Oxford: Clarendon Press, 1965.

The Epithalamions, Anniversaries, and Epicedes, ed. Wesley Milgate, Oxford: Clarendon Press, 1978.

Letters to Severall Persons of Honour, London: for R. Marriot, 1651. Facs. edn intro. M. Thomas Hester, Delmar, NY: Scholars' Facsimiles & Reprints, 1977.

Poems, with elegies on the authors death, London: for J. Marriot, 1633. 7th edn, 1669.

Pseudo-Martyr. Wherein... this conclusion is evicted. That those of the Romane religion ought to take the oath of allegiance, London: for W. Burre, 1610. Mod. edn, ed. Anthony Raspa, Montreal and Kingston: McGill-Queen's University Press, 1993.

Satires, Epigrams and Verse Letters, ed. Wesley Milgate, Oxford: Clarendon Press, 1967.

Sermons of John Donne, ed. George R. Potter and Evelyn M. Simpson, 10 vols., Berkeley and Los Angeles: University of California Press, 1953–62.

Douglas, Gawin, *The palis of honoure*, Edinburgh: T. Davidson, [*c*. 1535]. 3rd edn, 1579. Mod. edn, ed. David Parkinson, Kalamazoo, MI: TEAMS / Medieval Institute Publications of Western Michigan University, 1992.

Poetical Works, ed. John Small, 4 vols., Edinburgh: W. Paterson, 1874.

The .xii. bukes of Eneados... in Scottish metir, bi G. Douglas, London: [W. Copland,] 1553. Mod edn, *Virgil's Aeneid Translated into Scottish Verse (1553)*, ed. David F. C. Coldwell, Edinburgh: William Blackwood, 1957.

Drayton, Michael, *The barons warres in the raigne of Edward the second*, London: for N. Ling, 1619. Extensively revises his *Mortimeriados. The Lamentable civell warres of Edward the second and the barrons*, London: for M. Lownes, 1596.

Englands heroicall epistles, London: for N. Ling, 1597. 6th edn, 1630.

Peirs Gaveston earle of Cornwall. His life, death, and fortune, London: for N. L[ing] and J. Busby, [1594?].

Poems, ed. John Buxton, Cambridge, MA: Harvard University Press, 1953.

Poly-Olbion, London: for M. Lownes *et al.*, [1612]. *Second part, or a continuance of Poly-Olbion*, London: for J. Marriott *et al.*, 1622.

Works, ed. J. William Hebel, 5 vols., Oxford: Blackwell for the Shakespeare Head Press, 1931–41. Rpt, 1961.

Drummond, William, of Hawthornden, *Poems and Prose*, ed. Robert H. MacDonald, Edinburgh: Scottish Academic Press, 1976.

Poetical Works of William Drummond of Hawthornden, with 'A Cypresse Grove', ed. Leon Emil Kastner, 2 vols., Manchester University Press, 1913.

Dryden, John, *Absalom and Achitophel. A poem*, London: for J. T., 1681. 8th edn, 1682.

Annus Mirabilis: the year 1666, London: for H. Herringman, 1667. 3rd edn, 1688.

Aureng-Zebe: a tragedy, London: for H. Herringman, 1676. 6th edn, 1699.

The conquest of Granada, London: for H. Herringman, 1672. 5th edn, 1695.

The Indian emperour, London: for H. Herringman, 1667. 10th edn, 1700.

Marriage a-la-mode, London: for H. Herringman, 1673. 4th edn, 1698.

Miscellany poems, London: for J. Tonson, 1684. In two parts, 1692.

Of dramatick poesie, an essay, London: for H. Herringman, 1668. 3rd edn, 1693.

Works, 4 vols., London: for J. Tonson, 1691–5.

Works, gen. ed. Edward Niles Hooker, H. T. Swedenberg, Jr, *et al.*, 20 vols., Berkeley, Los Angeles, London: University of California Press, 1961–2001.

Dugdale, William, *The Antiquities of Warwickshire*, London: T. Warren, 1656.

Dury, John, *The Reformed Librarie-Keeper*, London: William Dugard, 1650.
The Reformed School, London: for R. Wodnothe, [1649?]. Facs. edns of both tracts in 1 vol., Menston, Yorks.: Scolar Press, 1972.

E., T., *The Lawes Resolutions of Womens Rights, or the Lawes Provision for Woemen*, London: [M. Flesher for] the assigns of J. More, 1632.

Early English Books Online Website (http://www.lib.umi.com/eeebonew/).

Edward VI, *The Chronicle and Political Papers of King Edward VI*, ed. Wilbur K. Jordan, London: Allen & Unwin, and Ithaca, NY: Cornell University Press, 1966.
Literary Remains of King Edward the Sixth, ed. John Gough Nichols, 2 vols., Roxburghe Club, London: J. B. Nichols & Sons, 1857.

Edwards, Richard, *The excellent comedie of two the most faithfullest freendes, Damon and Pithias*, London: for R. Johns, 1571. Mod. edn, *Richard Edwards' Damon and Pithias*, ed. D. Jerry White, New York: Garland, 1980.
Works of Richard Edwards, ed. Ros King, Manchester University Press, and New York: Palgrave, 2001.

Edwards, Thomas, *Antapologia: or A full answer to the apologeticall narration of Mr Goodwin*, London: T. R. and E. M. for R. Smith, 1644.
Gangraena: Or a Catalogue and Discovery of Many of the Errours Heresies, Blasphemies, and Pernicious Practices of the Sectaries of this Time, London: for R. Smith, 1646. 3rd edn, 1646.
Reasons against the independent government of particular congregations, London: for J. Bellamie and R. Smith, 1641.
The Second Part of Gangraena, London: for R. Smith, 1646. 3rd edn, 1646.
The Third Part of Gangraena, London: for R. Smith, 1646.

Eikon Basilike: The Portraiture of His Sacred Majesty in His Solitudes and Sufferings, ed. Philip Knachel, Ithaca, NY: Cornell University Press for the Folger Shakespeare Library, 1966.

[Elizabeth I,] *Elizabeth I: Collected Works*, ed. Leah S. Marcus, Janel Mueller and Mary Beth Rose, University of Chicago Press, 2000.
Elizabeth's Glass, ed. Marc Shell, Lincoln, NE: University of Nebraska Press, 1993.

Elizabethan and Stuart Plays, ed. Charles R. Baskervill, Virgil B. Heltzel and Arthur H. Nethercot, New York: Holt, Rinehart and Winston, 1934.

The Elizabethan Courtier Poets: The Poems and Their Contexts, ed. Steven May, Columbia: University of Missouri Press, 1991.

Elizabethan Critical Essays, ed. G. Gregory Smith, 2 vols., Oxford: Clarendon Press, 1904. Rpt, 1937.

Elizabethan Ireland: A Selection of Writings by Elizabethan Writers on Ireland, ed. James P. Myers, Jr, Hamden, CT: Archon Books, 1983.

Eliza's Babes or the Virgins Offering, London: by M. S. for L. Blaiklock, 1652. Ed. L. E. Semler, Rutherford, NJ: Fairleigh Dickinson University Press, 2000.

Ellis, Henry (ed.), *Original letters illustrative of English history, including numerous royal letters, from autographs in the British Museum, and one or two other collections*, 11 vols. in 3 series. London: Harding, Triphook & Lepard, 1824, 1827, 1846.

Ellwood, Thomas, *The History of the Life of Thomas Ellwood*, London: J. Sowle, 1714. Mod. edn, ed. S. Graveson, London: Headley Brothers, 1906.

Elyot, Sir Thomas, *The boke named the Gouernour*, London: T. Berthelet, 1531. 8th edn, 1580. Mod. edn, *The Book of the Governor: Edited from the First Edition of 1531*, ed. H. H. S. Croft, 2 vols., London: K. Paul, Trench, 1887. Rpt, New York: Burt Franklin, 1967.

The Castel of Helthe, gathered oute of the chyefe authors of phisyke, London: [T. Berthelet, 1537?]. 17th edn, 1610. Facs. of 1541 edn, intro. Samuel A. Tannenbaum, New York: Scholars' Facsimiles & Reprints, 1937.

Four Political Treatises: The Doctrinal of Princes (1533); Pasquil the Playne (1533); The Banquette of Sapience (1534); and the Image of Governance (1541). Facs. edns, intro. Lillian Gottesman, Gainsville, FL: Scholars' Facsimiles & Reprints, 1967.

The English Hexapla, Exhibiting the Six Important English Translations of the New Testament Scriptures: Wiclif (1380); Tyndale (1524); Cranmer (1539); Genevan (1557); Anglo-Rhemish (1582); Authorised (1611); with the original Greek, London: Samuel Bagster & Sons, 1841.

The English Levellers, ed. Andrew Sharp, Cambridge University Press, 1998.

Erasmus, Desiderius, *(Adagia) Proverbes or adagies . . . gathered out of the Chiliades of Erasmus by R[ichard] Taverner*, London: R. Bankes, 1539. 6th enlarged edn, 1622.

Apophthegmes, that is to saie, prompte, quicke, wittie saiynges. First gathered by Erasmus. And now englished by N. Udall, London: R. Grafton, 1542.

De civilitate morum puerilium . . . A lytell booke of good maners for chyldren, with interpretacion in to the englysshe tonge, by R. Whytyngton, London: W. de Worde, 1532. 8th edn, 1560.

Collected Works of Erasmus, gen. eds. Peter G. Bietenholz et al., 100+ vols., University of Toronto Press, 1974– (in progress).

De copia verborum ac rerum, commentarii duo, London: W. de Worde, 1528. 4th edn, 1573.

The first tome or volume of the paraphrase of Erasmus upon the newe testament, ed. Nicholas Udall, London: E. Whitchurch, 1548. 4th edn, 1548.

Opus epistolarum, ed. P. S. Allen and H. M. Allen, 12 vols., Oxford University Press, 1906–58.

The second tome or volume of the paraphrase of Erasmus upon the newe testament, ed. Miles Coverdale, London: E. Whitchurch, 1549. 2nd edn, 1549.

Etherege, Sir George, *The Man of Mode*, London: for H. Herringman, 1676. 3rd edn, 1693.

Plays of Sir George Etherege, ed. Michael Cordner, Cambridge University Press, 1982.

Poems, ed. James Thorpe, Princeton University Press, 1963.

Evans, Rhys, *An Eccho to The voice from heaven. Or a narration of the life, and manner of the special calling, and visions of Arise Evans*, London: for the author, 1652.

Evelyn, John, *Diary*, ed. E. S. de Beer, 6 vols., London and New York: Oxford University Press, 1959. Ed. Guy de la Bédoyère, Woodbridge, Suffolk, and Rochester, NY: Boydell Press, 1995.

Kalendarium hortense: or the gardners almanac, 2nd edn, London: J. Martyn and J. Allestrye, 1666. 12th edn, 1699.

Sylva, or a Discourse of Forest-Trees, London: J. Martyn and J. Allestrye, 1664. 3rd edn, 1679.

Everard, John, *Some Gospel-Treasures Opened*, London: R. W. for R. Harford, 1653.

Fairfax, Thomas Fairfax, Baron, *The Poems of Thomas, Third Lord Fairfax, from MS Fairfax 40 in the Bodleian Library*, ed. Edward Bliss Read, Transactions of the Connecticut Academy of Arts and Sciences, 14, New Haven, CT: Auspices of Yale University, 1909.

The Faith, Doctrine and Religion, Professed, and Protected in the Realm of England . . . Expressed in Thirty-Nine Articles, 1562 and 1604, London: J. Field, 1661.

Fanshawe, Richard (trans.), [Luiz de Camoens,] *The Lusiad, or, Portugals Historicall Poem, . . . Now Newly put into English by Richard Fanshaw*, London: for H. Moseley, 1655.

Poems and Translations, ed. Peter Davidson, 2 vols., Oxford: Clarendon Press, 1997–9.

Fast Sermons to Parliament, ed. Robin Jeffs, 34 vols., London: Cornmarket Press, 1970–1.

Fell Fox, Margaret, *The citie of London reproved*, London: for R. Wilson, [1660].
A loving salutation to the seed of Abraham, London: T. Simmons, 1656.
This is to the Clergy, London: for R. Wilson, 1660.
Womens speaking justified, [London,] 1666. 2nd edn, 1667.
Feltham, Owen, *Resolves, Divine, Morall, Politicall*, London: [G. Purslowe] for H. Seile, 1623. 11th edn, 1696.
    Resolves, A Duple Century, one new, an other of a second edition, London: [G. Purslowe] for H. Seile, 1628. Facs. rpt, The English Experience, 734, Amsterdam: Theatrum Orbis Terrarum, 1975.
Feuillerat, Albert (ed.), *Documents Relating to the Revels at Court in the Time of Edward VI and Queen Mary*, Louvain University Press, 1914.
Field, John and Wilcox, Thomas, *An Admonition to the Parliament*, [Hemel Hempstead?: J. Stroud?] 1572. 3rd edn, 1617. Mod. edn, in *Puritan Manifestoes*, ed. W. H. Frere and C. E. Douglas, London: SPCK, and New York: E. S. Gorham, 1907, 1954.
Filmer, Robert, *Patriarcha: or, the natural power of kings*, London: W. Davis, 1680. 3rd edn, 1685.
    Patriarcha and Other Political Works, ed. Pater Laslett, Oxford: Blackwell, 1949. Rpt, New York: Garland, 1984.
    Patriarcha and Other Writings, ed. Johann P. Sommerville, Cambridge University Press, 1991.
Firth, C. H. and Rait, R. S. (eds.), *Acts and Ordinances of the Interregnum, 1642–1660*. 3 vols., London: Wyman & Sons for HM Stationers' Office, 1911.
Fish, Simon, *A supplicacyon for the beggers*, [Antwerp?: J. Grapheus? 1529?]. Mod. edn, ed. Frederick J. Furnivall, Early English Text Society, extra. ser., 13, London: Trübner, 1871.
Fisher, Payne, *Irenodia Gratulatoria*, London: T. Newcomb for J. Holden, 1652; trans. [Thomas Manley,] *Veni: Vidi: Vici: The Triumphs of . . . Oliver Cromwell*, London: for J. Tey, 1652.
Fletcher, Giles, *Christs victorie, and triumph in heaven, and earth, over, and after death*, Cambridge: C. Legge, 1610. 4th edn, 1640.
Fletcher, Phineas, *Giles and Phineas Fletcher: Poetical Works*, ed. Frederick S. Boas, 2 vols., Cambridge University Press, 1908–9.
    The purple island, or the isle of man, Cambridge: [T. Buck and R. Daniel,] 1633.
    Locustae, vel pietas jesuitica, [Cambridge:] T. & J. Buck, 1627.
Ford, John, *The broken heart. A tragedy*, London: for H. Beeston, 1633.
    The chronicle historie of Perkin Warbeck, London: for H. Beeston, 1634.
    John Ford's Dramatic Works Reprinted from the Original Quartos, ed. Henry de Vocht, 2 vols., Materialen zur Kunde des älteren englischen Dramas, Louvain: A. Uystpruyst, 1927.
    Selected Plays of John Ford, ed. Colin Gibson, Cambridge University Press, 1986.
    'Tis pitty shee's a whore, London: N. Okes for R. Collins, 1633.
Forrest, William, *The History of Grisild the second: a narrative, in verse, of the divorce of Queen Katherine of Arragon*, ed. William Dunn Macray, Roxburghe Club, London: Whittingham and Wilkins, 1875.
Fortescue, Sir John, *De politica administratione et legibus civilibus Angliae commentarius*, London: E. Whitchurch & H. Smyth, [1543?].

The Governance of England: otherwise called The difference between an absolute and a limited monarchy, by John Fortescue, trans. and ed. Charles Plummer, Oxford: Clarendon Press, 1885. Rpt, 1926.

On the Laws and Governance of England: Sir John Fortescue, ed. Shelley Lockwood, Cambridge University Press, 1997.

Fosset, Thomas, *The Servants Dutie. Or the Calling and Condition of Servants*, London: G. Eld, 1613.

Fox, George, *A Journal, or historical account of the life, travels, sufferings, Christian experiences, and labour of love, in the work of the ministry, of . . . George Fox*, London: for T. Northcott, 1694. Mod. edns, *Journal of George Fox*, ed. John L. Nickalls, rev. edn, London: Religious Society of Friends, 1975; *The Journal: George Fox*, ed. Nigel Smith, London: Penguin, 1998.

Newes Coming up out of the North, London: for G. Calvert, 1654.

The Lambs Officer Is Gone Forth, London: for T. Simmons, 1659.

A Warning to All in this Proud City, Called London, [London, 1655].

Foxe, John, *Actes and monuments of these latter and perillous dayes, touching matters of the church* (The 'Book of Martyrs'), London: J. Day, 1563.

The first (second) volume of the ecclesiasticall history contaynyng the Actes and monumentes . . . Newly recognised and inlarged, 2 vols., London: J. Daye, 1570.

The first (second) volume of the ecclesiasticall history contaynyng the Actes and monumentes . . . Newly recognised and inlarged, 2 vols., London: J. Daye, 1576.

Actes and monuments of matters most speciall in the church. Newly reuised and recognised, partly also augmented, and now the fourth time published, 2 vols., London, J. Daye, 1583. Published by Oxford University Press on CD Rom 1999.

The ecclesiasticall historie: conteynyng the Actes and monumentes . . . Newly recognised and inlarged, 2 vols., London: P. Short, 1597.

Acts and monuments of matters most speciall and memorable happening in the church . . . : wherein is set forth at large the whole race and course of the Church . . . with the bloody times, horrible troubles, and great persecutions against the martyrs of Christ sought and wrought as well by heathen emperors, as now lately practised by Romish prelates, especially in this realme of England and Scotland: whereunto are annexed certain additions, 3 vols., London: for the Company of Stationers, 1641.

Acts and Monuments of John Foxe, ed. Stephen Reed Cattley, 8 vols., London: R. B. Seeley and W. Burnside, 1837–41.

Acts and Monuments of John Foxe, ed. Cattley, pref. Revd. George Townsend, 8 vols.; London: Seeley, Burnside, and Seeley, 1843–9. Rpt, New York: AMS Press, 1965.

Fraunce, Abraham, *The Third Part of the Countess of Pembrokes Ivychurch, Entituled, Amintas dale*, London: for T. Woodcocke, 1592. Mod. edn, ed. Gerald Snare, Northridge: California State University Press, 1975.

Frere, W. H. and Kennedy, W. P. M. (eds.), *Visitation Articles and Injunctions of the Period of the Reformation*, 3 vols., London: Longmans, Green and Co., 1910.

Frith, John, *A boke made by John Frith . . . answering unto M. Mores letter*, Munster: C. Willems, [Antwerp: H. Peetersen van Middelburch?] 1533. 4th edn, 1548. Rpt in *The Whole Workes of William Tyndall, Iohn Frith, and Docter Barnes*, London: J. Daye, 1573.

Froissart, Jean, *The Chronicle of Froissart, translated out of French by Sir John Bourchier, Lord Berners, Annis 1523-25*, intro. William Paton Ker, 6 vols., London: D. Nutt, 1901-3. Rpt, New York: AMS Press, 1967.

Fuller, Thomas, *The Church-History of Britain*, London: for J. Williams, 1655.

Good Thoughts in Bad Times, Exeter: for T. Hunt, 1645. 9th edn, 1669.

Good Thoughts in Worse Times, London: for J. Williams, 1647. 7th edn, 1680.

The History of the Holy Warre, Cambridge: T. Buck, 1639. 4th edn, 1651.

The History of the Worthies of England, London: J. G., W. L. and W. G., 1662.

The Holy State and the Profane State, Cambridge: for J. Williams, 1642. 4th edn, 1663.

Mixt Contemplations in Better Times, London: for J. Williams, 1660.

Thoughts and Contemplations, ed. James O. Wood, London: SPCK, 1964.

Gainsford, Thomas, *The glory of England, or a true description of many excellent prerogatives and remarkable blessings, whereby she triumpheth over all the nations of the world*, London: for T. Norton, 1618.

'Observations of State and Millitary Affaires for the most parte collected out of Cornelius Tacitus', San Marino, CA, Huntington Library, Ellesmere MS 6857.

Gale, Thomas (comp.), *Certaine Workes of chirurgerie, newly compiled*, London: T. East, 1563; Part 2, 1567. 2nd edn, 1586.

Gamble, John, *Ayres and Dialogues*, London: W. Godbid for the author, 1656. 2nd edn, 1657. 3rd edn, 1658.

Ayres and Dialogues for one. Second book, London: W. Godbid for N. Elkin, 1659.

A garden of spirituall flowers. Planted by Ri. Ro[gers.] Will. Per[kins.] Ri. Gree[nhame.] M. M[osse?] and Geo. Web[be], London, T. Snodham for T. Pavier, 1609. 3rd enlarged edn, 1609. 16th edn, 1631.

A garden of spirituall flowers, 2. Part, London: T. Snodham for T. Pavier, 1612. 10th edn, 1630. 4th edn of Parts 1 and 2, 1638.

Gardiner, Samuel R. (ed.), *The Constitutional Documents of the Puritan Revolution, 1625-1660*, Oxford: Clarendon Press, 1889. 3rd edn, rev., 1906. Rpts, 1951, 1979.

Gardiner, Stephen, *The Letters of Stephen Gardiner*, ed. James Arthur Muller, Cambridge University Press, 1933. Rpt, Westport, CT: Greenwood Press, 1970.

De vera obedientia oratio, London: T. Berthelet, 1535.

De vera obediencia an oration . . . Nowe translated into english [by John Bale], Rouen: M. Wood [London? J. Day], 1553. Rpt, 'The Oration of True Obedience', in *Obedience in Church and State: Three Political Tracts by Stephen Gardiner*, ed. Pierre Janelle, Cambridge University Press, 1930.

Garman, Mary, Applegate, Judith, Benefiel, Margaret, and Meredith, Dortha, (eds.), *Hidden in Plain Sight: Quaker Women's Writings, 1650-1700*, Wallingford, PA: Pendle Hill, 1995.

Gascoigne, George, *The Complete Works of George Gascoigne*, ed. J. W. Cunliffe, 2 vols., Cambridge University Press, 1907-10.

Gau, John (trans.), Christiern Pedersen, *The richt vay to the Kingdome of hevine is techit heir*, Malmö: J. Hochstraten, 1533. Mod. edn, ed. A. F. Mitchell, Scottish Text Society, 12, Edinburgh and London: W. Blackwood and Sons, 1888.

Gee, Henry and Hardy, William John (eds.), *Documents Illustrative of English Church History*, London: Macmillan, 1896.

Gee, John, *The foot out of the snare: with a detection of sundry late practices and impostures of the priests and jesuits in England. Whereunto is added a catalogue of such bookes as in this authors knowledge have been vented within two yeeres last past in London, by the priests and their agents* ... *[and] the names of such as disperse, print, bind or sell popish bookes*, London: H. L[ownes] for R. Milbourne, 1624. Mod. edn, ed. T. H. B. Harmsen, Nijmegen: Cicero Press, 1992.

Geninges, John, *The Life and Death of Mr Edmund Geninges Priest, Crowned with Martyrdome at London, the 10 day of November, in the year MDXCI*, Saint-Omer: C. Boscard, 1614.

Gesner, Conrad, *The newe jewell of health* ..., *Faithfully corrected and published in Englishe*, trans. G[eorge] Baker, London: H. Denham, 1576.

Gifford, George, *A dialogue concerning witches and witchcraftes*, London: J. Windet for T. Cooke and M. Hart, 1593.

A discourse of the subtill practises of deuilles by witches and sorcerers, London: [T. Orwin] for T. Cooke, 1587.

Gill, Alexander, *Logonomia Anglica. Qua gentis sermo facilius addiscitur*, London: J. Beale, 1619. *Logonomia Anglica (1619)*, trans. Robin C. Alston, ed. Bror Danielsson and Arvid Gabrielson, Stockholm Studies in English, 26 and 27, Stockholm: Almqvist & Wiksell, 1972.

Gillespie, George, *A late dialogue betwixt a civilian and a divine*, London: for R. Bostock, 1644.

Wholesome severity reconciled with Christian liberty, London: for C. Meredith, 1645.

A glasse of the truthe (A dialogue between a lawyer and a divine concerning Henry VIII's proposed divorce), London: T. Berthelet, 1532.

[Godfray, Thomas, comp.,] *A primer in Englysshe / with dyuers prayers & godly meditations*, London: T. Godfray, [*c*. 1535].

Godolphin, Sidney, *The Poems*, ed. William Dighton, Oxford: Clarendon Press, 1931.

Golding, Arthur (trans.), *The fyrst fower bookes of P. Ovidius Nasos worke intitled Metamorphosis*, London: W. Seres, 1565.

The .xv. bookes of P. Ovidius Naso, entytuled Metamorphosis, London: W. Seres, 1567.

Goodman, Christopher, *How superior powers oght to be obeyd of their subjects: and wherin they may lawfully be disobeyed*, Geneva: J. Crispin, 1558.

Goodwin, Thomas, Nye, Philip, Simpson, Sydrach, Burroughs, Jeremiah and Bridge, William, *An Apologeticall Narration*, London: for R. Dawlman, 1643.

Googe, Barnabe, *Eglogs epytaphes, and sonettes. newly written*, London: for R. Newbery, 1563. Mod. edn, *Eclogues, Epitaphs, and Sonnets*, ed. Judith Kennedy, University of Toronto Press, 1989.

Gorges, Arthur, *The Collected Poems of Sir Arthur Gorges*, ed. Helen Sandison, Oxford: Clarendon Press, 1953.

Gosson, Stephen, *Playes confuted in five actions, proving that they are not to be suffred in a christian common weale*, London: for T. Gosson, [1582]. Mod. edn in *Markets of Bawdrie: The Dramatic Criticism of Stephen Gosson*, ed. Arthur F. Kinney, Salzburg Studies in English Literature, 4, Salzburg: Institüt für englischen Sprache und Literatur, 1974.

The s[c]hoole of abuse, conteining a plesaunt invective against poets, pipers, plaiers, jesters, and such like caterpillers of a commonwealth, London: T. Woodcocke, 1579, 3rd edn, 1587.

Gouge, William, *Of Domesticall Duties: Eight Treatises*, London: J. Haviland for W. Bladen, 1622. 3rd edn, 1626.

Grafton, Richard, *An abridgement of the Chronicles of England*, London: R. Tottel, 1563. 3rd enlarged edn, 1572.

A Chronicle at large, and meere history of the affayres of Englande from the creation of the worlde,
unto the first yere of queene Elizabeth, 2 vols., London: H. Denham for R. Tottel and H.
Toye, 1569.

Grafton's Chronicle; or, History of England, 2 vols., London: J. Johnson, 1809.

Great Britain. *Statutes of the Realm, From Original Records and Authentic Manuscripts*, 10 vols.,
London: G. Ayre and E. Strahan, 1810–28.

Graham, Elspeth *et al.* (eds.). *Her Own Life: Autobiographical Writings by Seventeenth-Century
Englishwomen*, London: Routledge, 1989.

Greene, Robert, *The Life and Complete Works, in Prose and Verse, of Robert Greene*, ed.
Alexander B. Grosart, 15 vols., London: Huth Library, 1881–6.

A notable discovery of coosenage, London: [J. Wolfe for T. Nelson, 1591]. 4th edn, 1592. Part
2, as *The second part of conny-catching*, London: J. Wolfe for W. Wright, 1591. 2nd
enlarged edn, 1592. Part 3, as *The third and last part of conny-catching*, London: T. Scarlet
for C. Burbie, 1592. 2nd edn, 1592. Mod. edns of all three tracts, ed. G. B. Harrison,
London: John Lane, The Bodley Head Ltd, 1923. Rpt, New York: Barnes and Noble,
1966.

Plays and Poems of Robert Greene, ed. J. Churton Collins, 2 vols., Oxford: Clarendon Press,
1905.

*A quip for an upstart courtier: or, a quaint dispute. Wherein is plainely set downe the disorders in
all estates and trades*, London: J. Wolfe, 1592. 11th edn, 1635.

The Spanish masquerado. Wherein . . . is discovered the pride and insolencie of the Spanish estate,
London: R. Ward for T. Cadman, 1589.

Greville, Fulke, Baron Brooke, *Certaine Learned and Elegant Workes of the Right Honorable
Fulke Lord Brooke*, London: E. P[urslowe] for H Seyle, 1633. Facs. edn, intro. A. D.
Cousins, Delmar, NY: Scholars' Facsimiles & Reprints, 1990.

Poems and Dramas of Fulke Greville, First Lord Brooke, ed. Geoffrey Bullough, 2 vols.,
Edinburgh: Oliver and Boyd, 1939.

The Prose Works of Fulke Greville, Lord Brooke, ed. John Gouws, Oxford: Clarendon Press,
1986.

The Remains of Sir Fulke Greville, Lord Brooke, Being Poems of Monarchy and Religion, London:
T. N. for H. Herringman, 1670. Mod. edn, ed. G. A. Wilkes, London: Oxford University
Press, 1965.

Grymston, Elizabeth, *Miscelanea, Meditations, Memoratives*, London: M. Bradwood for
F. Norton, 1604.

Guevara, Antonio de, *The Golden Boke of Marcus Aurelius*, trans. John Bourchier, Lord
Berners, London: T. Berthelet, 1535.

Guilpin, Edward, *Skialetheia: or a Shadowe of Truth, in Certaine Epigrams and Satyres*, London:
J. R[oberts] for N. Ling, 1598. Mod. edn, ed. D. Allen Carroll, Chapel Hill: University
of North Carolina Press, 1974.

Haec-vir; or the womanish-man, being an answere to Hic-mulier, In a briefe dialogue, London: for
J. Trundle, 1620.

Hakluyt, Richard, *The Principall Navigations, Voiages, Traffiques, and Discoveries of the English
Nation*, London: G. Bishop and R. Newberie, 1589. 2nd enlarged edn, 1598–1600. Mod.
rpt of 2nd edn, 12 vols., Hakluyt Society, ext. ser., Glasgow: J. Maclehose and Son,
1903–5; mod. rpt, 8 vols., Everyman's Library, London: J. Dent, and New York: E. P.
Dutton, 1907.

Hall, Edward, *Henry VIII by Edward Hall: The Triumphant Reigne of Kyng Henry the VIII*, ed. Charles Whibley, London: T. C. & E. C. Jack, 1904.

The Union of the two noble and illustrate famelies of Lancastre and York, London: R. Grafton, 1548. 3rd edn, 1550.

Hall, John, *The Court of Virtue*, London: T. Marshe, 1565. Mod. edn, ed. Russell A. Fraser, New Brunswick: Rutgers University Press, 1961.

Hall, John, poet, *The Grounds and Reasons of Monarchy Considered, corrected and reprinted according to the Edinburgh copy*, 1650. 3rd edn, 1651.

Horae Vacivae, or Essays, London: E. G. for J. Rothwell, 1646.

An Humble Motion . . . Concerning the Advancement of Learning and Reformation of the Universities, London: for J. Walker, 1649.

Poems, Cambridge: R. Daniel, 1646. Mod. rpt, in *Minor Poets of the Caroline Period*, ed. George Saintsbury, 3 vols., Oxford: Clarendon Press, 1905–21, 2:180–211.

Hall, Joseph, *Christian Moderation. In two books*, London: M. Flesher [and R. Oulton?], 1640.

Collected Poems, ed. Arnold Davenport, Liverpool University Press, 1949.

Episcopacie by divine right. Asserted, London: R. B[adger] for N. Butter, 1640.

Heauen upon earth: or, of true peace, and tranquillitie of minde, London: J. Windet for J. Porter, 1606. 3rd edn, 1607.

An humble remonstrance to the high court of Parliament, London: M. F[lesher] for N. Butter, 1640.

Virgidemiarum; sixe bookes. First three bookes, of toothlesse satyrs, London: T. Creede for R. Dexter, 1597. 3rd edn, 1602.

Virgidemiarum. The three last Bookes. Of byting satyres, London: R. Bradocke for R. Dexter, 1598. 2nd edn, 1599.

Works of Joseph Hall, Bishop of Norwich, London: for T. Pavier, M. Flesher and J. Haviland, 1625. 10th edn, 1648. Mod. edn in 12 vols., Oxford: D. A. Talboys, 1837–9.

Haller, William (ed.), *Tracts on Liberty in the Puritan Revolution, 1638–1647*. 3 vols., New York: Columbia University Press, 1934.

Hammond, Henry, *Five Propositions to the Kings Majesty and the Army concerning church-government*, Cambridge: for N. Smith, 1647.

Harcourt, Edward William (ed.), *The Harcourt Papers*, 14 vols., Oxford: Parker, 1880–1905.

Harington, John, *Letters and Epigrams*, ed. Norman E. McClure, Philadelphia: University of Pennsylvania Press, and London: Oxford University Press, 1930.

The most elegant and witty epigrams of Sir J. Harrington, knight, digested into foure bookes, London: G. P[urslowe] for John Budge, 1618. 3rd edn, 1633.

Nugae Antiquae, being a miscellaneous collection of original papers, in prose and verse . . . by Sir John Harington, ed. Thomas Park, 2 vols., London: Vernor and Hood, 1804. Rpt, 3 vols., Hildesheim: Georg Olms, 1968.

Harington, John (trans.) Ludovico Ariosto, *Orlando Furioso in English heroical verse by John Harington*, London: R. Field, 1591. 3rd edn, 1633. Mod. edn, ed. Robert McNulty, Oxford: Clarendon Press, 1972.

Harley, Lady Brilliana, *Letters*, ed. Thomas Taylor Lewis, Camden Society Publications, 58, London: Camden Society, 1854.

Harpsfield, John and Pendleton, Henry, *Homilies adjoined, in [Bonner, Edmund,] A profitable and necessarye doctrine, with certayne homelyes adioned*, London: J. Cawode, 1555.

Harrington, James, *The common-wealth of Oceana*, London: J. Streater for Livewell Chapman, 1656. Mod. edn, *The Commonwealth of Oceana and A System of Politics*, ed. J. G. A. Pocock, Cambridge University Press, 1992.

The Political Works of James Harington, ed. J. G. A. Pocock, Cambridge University Press, 1977.

Harrison (or Henrisoun), James, *An exhortacion to the Scottes, to conforme to the vnion, betwene Englande and Scotlande*, London: R. Grafton, 1547.

Hartlib, Samuel, *Samuel Hartlib and the Advancement of Learning*, ed. Charles Webster, Cambridge University Press, 1970.

Harvey, Gabriel, *Gabriel Harvey's Marginalia*, ed. George Charles Moore-Smith, Stratford-upon-Avon: Shakespeare Head Press, 1913.

Works, ed. Alexander B. Grosart, 3 vols., London: Huth Library, 1884–5.

H[ayward], J[ohn], *A Treatise of Vnion of the two Realmes of England and Scotland*, London: F. Kingston for C. Burby, 1604.

[Head, Richard,] *The English Rogue Described, in the Life of Meriton Latroon*, London: for H. Marsh, 1665. 6th edn, 1680.

[Henderson, Alexander], *Some Speciall Arguments which warranted the Scottish subiects lawfully to take up armes in defence of their Religion and Liberty*, Amsterdam: Richt Right Press, 1642.

[Henry VIII,] *Articles devised by the kynges highnes maiestie, to stablyshe christen quietnes and unitie amonge us, and to avoyde contentious opinions: which articles be also approved by the consent and determination of the hole clergie of this Realme. Anno MDXXXVI* ('Ten Articles'), London: T. Berthelet, 1536. Mod. rpt in *Formularies of Faith Put Forth By Authority During the Reign of Henry VIII*, ed. Charles Lloyd, Oxford University Press, 1856.

A Necessary Doctrine and Erudition for Any Christian Man, Set Forth by the Kinges Majesty of England (The 'King's Book'), London: T. Berthelet, 1543. Mod. rpt in *Formularies of Faith*, ed. Lloyd.

Herbert, Edward, Lord, of Cherbury, *The Life and Raigne of King Henry the Eighth*, London: E. G. for T. Whitaker, 1649. 9th edn, 1693.

Herbert, George, *The temple. Sacred poems and private ejaculations*, Cambridge: T. Buck and R. Daniel, 1633.

The Works of George Herbert, ed. F. E. Hutchinson, 2 vols., Oxford: Clarendon Press, 1941.

Herrick, Robert, *The Complete Poetry*, ed. J. Max Patrick, New York: Norton, 1968.

Hesperides, London: J. Williams and F. Eglesfield, 1648.

The Poetical Works of Robert Herrick, ed. L. C. Martin, Oxford: Clarendon Press, 1956.

Heylyn, Peter, *Cosmographie*, London: for H. Seile, 1652. 4th edn, 1666.

Heywood, John, *Dramatic Writings*, ed. John S. Farmer, New York: Barnes and Noble, 1966.

Plays, ed. Richard Axton and Peter Happé, Cambridge: D. S. Brewer, 1991.

Proverbs, Epigrams, and Miscellanies, ed. John S. Farmer, New York: Barnes and Noble, 1966.

Works and Miscellaneous Short Poems, ed. Burton A. Milligan, Urbana: University of Illinois Press, 1956. Rpt, Westport, CT; Greenwood Press, 1980.

Heywood, Oliver, *The Rev. Oliver Heywood, BA, 1630–1702: His Autobiography, Diaries, Anecdote and Event Books*, ed. J. Horsfall Turner, 4 vols., Brighouse: A. B. Bayes, 1882–5.

Heywood, Thomas, *An Apology for Actors*, London: N. Okes, 1611. Mod. edn, The Shakespeare Society, 1841.

Dramatic Works, 6 vols., London: J. Pearson, 1874.

Gunaikeion: or Nine Bookes of Various History concerninge Women, London: A. Islip, 1624.

Pageants, ed. David M. Bergeron, New York: Garland, 1986.

Hic mulier: or, the man-woman: being a medicine to cure the staggers in the masculine-feminines of our times, London: for J. T[rundle], 1620.

Hierocles upon the Golden Verses of Pythagoras, trans. J. Hall, London: J. Streater for F. Eaglesfield, 1657.

Hilton, John, *Catch that Catch Can*, London: for J. Benson and J. Playford, 1652. 5th edn, 1685.

Hobbes, Thomas, *Behemoth, or the Long Parliament, Printed 1679*, Mod. edn, ed. Ferdinand Tonnies, intro. Stephen Holmes, University of Chicago Press, 1990.

The English Works of Thomas Hobbes of Malmesbury, ed. Sir William Molesworth, 11 vols., London: John Bohn, 1839–45.

Leviathan, London: for Andrew Crooke, 1651. 5th edn, 1681. Mod. edns, ed. C. B. Macpherson, Harmondsworth: Penguin, 1968; ed. Richard Tuck, Cambridge University Press, 1991.

Hobbes, Thomas (trans.) *Eight bookes of the Peloponnesian Warre written by Thucydides. Interpreted immediately out of the Greeke by T. Hobbes*, London: for H. Seile, 1629.

Hoby, Margaret, *The Private Life of an Elizabethan Lady: The Diary of Lady Margaret Hoby, 1599–1605*, ed. Joanna Moody, Stroud, Glos.: Sutton, 1998.

Hoby, Sir Thomas (trans.), *The courtyer of count Baldessar Castilio*, London: [S. Mierdman for R. Jugge], 1561. Mod. edn [Baldassare Castiglione], *The Book of the Courtier*, trans. Sir Thomas Hoby, Everyman's Library, London and Toronto: Dent, 1928.

[Hogarde (or Huggard), Miles,] *The displaying of the protestantes, with a description of diuers their abuses*, [London:] R. Caly, 1556.

Hogarde (or Huggard), Miles, *A trestise declaring howe Christ by peruerse preachyng was banished out of this realme*, [London:] R. Caly, 1554.

Holinshed, Raphael, *The First Volume of the Chronicles of England, Scotlande, and Irelande*, 2 vols., London: [H. Bynneman] for J. Harrison, 1577.

The First and Second Volumes of Chronicles. Newlie augmented and continued, 3 vols., London: [H. Denham,] 1587. Mod. edn, *Chronicles*, ed. J. Johnson and Henry Ellis, 6 vols., London: J. Johnson, 1807–8.

Hooker, Richard, *Of the lawes of ecclesiasticall politie. Eyght* [i.e., four] *bookes*, London: J. Windet, 1593.

The fift booke, London: J. Windet, 1597.

Of the lawes of ecclesiasticall politie; the sixth and eighth books, London: R. Bishop, 1648.

The Folger Library Edition of the Works of Richard Hooker, gen. ed. W. Speed Hill, 7 vols., Cambridge, MA: Belknap Press of Harvard University Press, 1977–98.

Hoole, Charles, *A New Discovery of the Olde Arte of Teaching School*, London: J. T. for A. Crook, 1660.

Howard, Henry, Earl of Surrey, *Certain bokes of Virgiles Aeneais turned into English meter by Henry earle of Surrey*, London: R. Tottel, 1557. Mod. edn, *The Aeneid of Henry Howard, Earl of Surrey*, ed. Florence Ridley, Berkeley: University of California Press, 1963.

Epigrames &c by the Earle of Surrey, London, 1574.

Poems, ed. Emrys Jones, Oxford University Press, 1964.

Poems of Henry Howard Earl of Surrey, ed. Frederick Morgan Padelford, Seattle: University of Washington Press, 1920.

Songes and sonettes, written by Henry Haward late earle of Surrey, and other, London: R. Tottel, 1557. 9th edn, 1587.

The Works of Henry Howard, Earl of Surrey and of Sir Thomas Wyatt the Elder, ed. George Frederick Nott, 2 vols., London: Longman, Hurst, Rees, Orme and Brown, 1815-16. Rpt, New York: AMS Press, 1965.

Howell, James, *Epistolae Ho-Elianae. Familiar Letters Domestic and Forren*, London: for H. Moseley, 1645. 6th edn, 1688.

Londinopolis; an historical discourse, London: for H. Twiford, G. Sawbridge, T. Dring and J. Place, 1657.

Hume, David, of Godscroft, *David Hume of Godscroft's The History of the House of Douglas*, ed. David Reid, 2 vols., Edinburgh: Scottish Text Society, 1996.

A generall history of Scotland, together with a particular history of the houses of Douglas and Angus, Edinburgh: Evan Tyler, 1648.

Hutchinson, Lucy, *Memoirs of the Life of Colonel Hutchinson*, ed. James Sutherland, Oxford University Press, 1973.

Memoirs of the Life of Colonel Hutchinson, with a Fragment of Autobiography, ed. N. H. Keeble, London: Dent, 1995.

Order and Disorder, or The World Made and Undone, ed. David Norbrook, Oxford: Blackwell, 2001.

An Introduction of Algorisme: to learn to reckon wyth the Pen or wyth the Counters, London: J. Awdeley, 1574.

Irvine, Alexander, *De jure regni diascepsis*, Leiden: Elzevir, 1627.

The Jacobean Union. Six Tracts of 1604, ed. Bruce R. Galloway and Brian P. Levack, Scottish History Society, 4th ser., 21, Edinburgh: C. Constable, 1985.

James VI and I, *Ane Schort Treatise, Conteining some Revlis and cautelis to be obseruit and eschewit in Scottis Poesie* (Edinburgh, 1584). Rpt, English Reprints, ed. Edward Arber, Westminster: Archibald Constable, 1869.

Basilikon Doron, or, his Majesties instructions to his dearest sonne, Henry the Prince, London: F. Kyngston for J. Norton 'according to the copie printed [in 1599] at Edenburgh', 1603.

His Maiesties Poeticall Exercises at vacant houres, Edinburgh: R. Waldegrave, 1591.

The kings majesties speech, . . . in parliament, 19 March 1603, London: R. Barker, 1604. Rpt in vol. 2 (1809) of *A Collection of Scarce and Valuable Tracts . . . Chiefly Such as Relate to the History and Constitution of these Kingdoms* ('Somers Tracts'), 2nd rev. and enlarged edn, ed. Walter Scott, 13 vols., London: T. Cadell and W. Davies, 1809-15.

The Poems of James VI of Scotland, ed. James Craigie, 2 vols., Scottish Text Society, Edinburgh: William Blackwood, 1955-8.

The Political Works of James I, ed. Charles Howard McIlwain, Cambridge, MA: Harvard University Press, 1918.

Political Writings, ed. Johann P. Sommerville, Cambridge University Press, 1994.

Trew Law of Free Monarchies, Edinburgh: R. Waldegrave, 1598.

Jewel, John, *Apologia ecclesiae anglicanae*, London: R. Wolfe, 1562. 9th edn, 1639.

An apologie or answere in defence of the Church of Englande, trans. Lady Ann Bacon, London: R. Wolfe, 1564. 3rd edn, 1635. Mod. rpt, *An Apology of the Church of England*, ed. J. E. Booty, Ithaca, NY: Cornell University Press for the Folger Shakespeare Library, 1963.

Deffynniad ffydd eglwys loegr (Welsh trans. of *Apologie* by M. Kyffin), London: R. Field, 1595.

Works of John Jewel, Bishop of Salisbury, ed. Richard William Jelf, 8 vols., Oxford University Press, 1848.

Works of the very learned J. Jewell, London, J. Norton, 1609. 3rd edn, 1611.

Jocelin, Elizabeth, *The Mothers Legacie to her unborn Childe*, London: J. Haviland for W. Barret, 1624.

Johnson, Samuel, 'Milton', *Lives of the English Poets*, ed. George Birkbeck Hill, Oxford: Clarendon Press, 1905, 1:84–200.

Jones, Inigo, *The Theatre of the Stuart Court: including the complete designs for productions at court, . . . together with their texts and historical documentation*, ed. Stephen Orgel and Roy Strong, 2 vols., London: Sotheby Parke Bernet, and Berkeley: University of California Press, 1973.

Jonson, Ben, *Ben Jonson*, ed. Ian Donaldson, Oxford University Press, 1985.

Ben Jonson: The Complete Masques, ed. Stephen Orgel, New Haven, CT: Yale University Press, 1969.

The Complete Plays, ed. G. A. Wilkes, 4 vols., Oxford: Clarendon Press, 1981–2.

The Complete Poems, ed. George Parfitt, New Haven, CT: Yale University Press, 1975.

The Workes of Benjamin Jonson, London: W. Stansby, 1616. *The second [and third] volume*, London: for R. Meighen [and T. Walkley], 1640.

The Works of Ben Jonson, ed. C. H. Herford, Percy Simpson and Evelyn Simpson, 11 vols., Oxford: Clarendon Press, 1925–52. Rpt, 1988.

Jordan, Thomas, *The Walks of Islington and Hogsdon*, London: T. Wilson, 1657.

Keating, Geoffrey, *The History of Ireland*, trans. and ed. David Comyn and Patrick S. Dinneen, 4 vols., Irish Text Society, London: D. Nutt, 1902–14.

Kent, Elizabeth Grey, Countess of, *A Choice Manual of Rare and Select Secrets in Physick and Chyrurgery*, London: G. D., 1653. 19th edn, 1687.

Killigrew, Thomas, *Comedies and Tragedies*, London: for H. Herringman, 1664.

King, Henry, *Poems, elegies, paradoxes, and sonnets*, London: by J. G. for R. Marriot and H. Herringman, 1657.

The Poems of Henry King, ed. Margaret Crum, Oxford: Clarendon Press, 1965.

Knox, John, *Book of Discipline*, in *John Knox's History of the Reformation in Scotland*, ed. William Croft Dickinson, 2 vols., London and New York: Thomas Nelson, 1949.

The First Blast of the trumpet against the monstruous regiment of women, [Geneva: J. Poullain and A. Rebul,] 1558.

The first (second-thirde) book of the history of the reformation of religion within the realm of Scotland, London: T. Vautroller, 1587 (pp. 17–560; said to have been seized by Archbishop Whitgift's order before completion of printing). Mod. edn, ed. William Croft Dickinson, 2 vols.

John Knox on Rebellion, ed. Roger Mason, Cambridge University Press, 1994.

The Works of John Knox, ed. David Laing, 6 vols., Edinburgh: Bannatyne Society, 1846–64.

Kyd, Thomas, *The Spanish Tragedy*, ed. David Bevington, New York: Manchester University Press, 1996.

Lane, Parr, 'Newes from the Holy Ile', in Alan Ford, 'Parr Lane: "Newes from the Holy Ile"', *Proceedings of the Royal Irish Academy* 99C (1999), 115–56.

L[aneham], R[obert], *A Letter: whearin Part of the Entertainment vntoo the Queenz Maiesty at Killingwoorth Castl iz Signified*, [London, 1575].

Lanyer, Aemilia, *Salve Deus Rex Judaeorum*, London: V. Simmes for R. Bonian, 1611. Mod. edn, *The Poems of Aemilia Lanyer: Salve Deus Rex Judaeorum*, ed. Susanne Woods, Oxford University Press, 1993.

Larkin, James F. and Hughes, Paul L. (eds.), *Stuart Royal Proclamations. Volume I. Royal Proclamations of King James I 1603–1625*, Oxford: Clarendon Press, 1973.

Latimer, Hugh, *Selected Sermons of Hugh Latimer*, ed. Allan G. Chester, Charlottesville: University of Virginia Press, 1968.

Sermons, ed. J. Watkins, 2 vols., Oxford University Press, 1824.

Seven Sermons before Edward VI on Each Friday in Lent, 1549, ed. Edward Arber, English Reprints, Westminster: Archibald Constable, 1895.

Laud, William, *The Works*, ed. W. Scott and J. Bliss, 7 vols., Oxford: J. H. Parker, 1847–60.

Lawrence, Henry, *Of our communion, and warre with angels*, London: for G. Calvert, 1646.

Leigh, Dorothy, *The Mothers Blessing; or, the godly Counsaile of a Gentlewoman, not long since deceased, left behind her for her children*, London: for J. Budge, 1616. 4th edn, [S. Stafford] for J. Budge, 1618. 15th edn, for R. Allot, 1630.

Leland, John, *De rebus Britannicis Collectanea*, ed. Thomas Hearn, 4 vols., London: W. and J. Richardson, 1770.

Leslie, John, *A Defence of the Honor of the Right high, right mighty, and noble princesse, Marie Queene of Scotland*, London: E Dicaeophile, [Rheims: J Foigny,] 1569. 2nd enlarged edn, entitled *A Treatise Concerning the Defence of the Honour of Marie of Scotland*, [Louvain: J. Fowler,] 1571.

The Historie of Scotland wrytten first in Latin by . . . Jhone Leslie, bishop of Rosse, and translated in Scottish by Father James Dalrymple, 1596, ed. E. G. Cody, O. S. B. and William Murison, 2 vols., Scottish Text Society, Edinburgh and London: W. Blackwood & Sons, 1889–95.

Letters of Royal and Illustrious Ladies of Great Britain, ed. Mary Anne Everett Green Wood, 3 vols., London: H. Colburn, 1846.

The Leveller Tracts, 1647–1653, ed. William Haller and Godfrey Davies, New York: Columbia University Press, 1944.

The Levellers in the English Revolution, ed. G. E. Aylmer, Ithaca, NY: Cornell University Press, 1975.

Lever, Thomas, 'A Sermon preached at Pauls Crosse', in *Sermons of Thomas Lever 1550*, ed. Edward Arber, English Reprints, Westminster: Archibald Constable, 1870.

Lilburne, John, *The charters of London*, printed at London. 'Decemb. 18.' 1646.

The Christian Mans Triall. 2nd edn, London: for W. Larnar, 1641.

Londons Liberty in Chains Discovered, [London, 1646].

Lily, William, *An introduction of the eyght partes of speche* ('Lily's Accidence'), London: T. Berthelet, 1542. Later entitled *A shorte introduction of grammar*, London: R. Wolfe, 1548. Many edns.

Libellus de constructione octo partium orationis ('Lily's Grammar'), London: R. Pynson, 1513. Later entitled *Brevissima institutio*, London: R. Wolfe, 1549. Many edns. Facs. rpt, *A Shorte Introduction of Grammar, by William Lily*, intro. Vincent J. Flynn, New York: Scholars' Facsimiles & Reprints, 1945.

Lincoln, Elizabeth Clinton, Countess of, *The Countess of Lincolnes Nurserie*, ed. T. Lodge, Oxford: J. Lichfield and J. Short, 1622.

Lindsay, David, *Ane Satyre of the Thrie Estaits*, ed. James Kinsley, London: Cassell, 1954.

The Thrie Estaitis, ed. R. Lyall, Edinburgh: Canongate Publishers, 1989.

The Works of Sir David Lindsay of the Mount, 1490–1555, ed. Douglas Hamer, 4 vols., Scottish Text Society, Edinburgh and London: W. Blackwood & Sons, 1931–6.

Works, ed. John Small and J. A. H. Murray, 5 vols., Early English Text Society, London: N. Trübner, 1865–1971, Rpt, New York: Greenwood Press, 1969.

The Lisle Letters, ed. Muriel St Clare Byrne, 6 vols., University of Chicago Press, 1981.

Lloyd, Charles (ed.), *Formularies of Faith Put Forth By Authority During the Reign of Henry VIII*, Oxford University Press, 1856.

Llwyd, Humphrey, *The breviary of Britayne, Englished by T. Twyne, 1573*, [London: R. Johnes, 1573].

Llwyd, Morgan, *Gweithiau Morgan Llwyd*, ed. T. E. Ellis and J. H. Davies, 2 vols., Bangor: Jarvis & Foster, 1899, 1908.

Lodge, Thomas, *The Complete Works of Thomas Lodge*, intro. Edmund Gosse, 4 vols., Glasgow: Hunterian Club, 1883. Rpt, New York: Russell & Russell, 1963.

Protogenes can know Apelles (A defence of poetry, music and stage plays, in answer to Stephen Gosson's *School of Abuse*), London: [H. Singleton? 1579].

Lodowyck, Francis, *A Common Writing*, [London:] for the author, 1647. Rpt, Menston, Yorks. Scolar Press, 1969.

The Ground-Work . . . of a New Perfect Language, [London:] 1652. Rpt, Menston, Yorks. Scolar Press, 1968.

Longinus, *Peri Hypsous, or, Dionysius Longinus on the Height of Eloquence*, trans. John Hall, [London:] by R. Daniel for F. Eaglesfield, 1652.

Lord, George deF., *et al.* (eds.), *Poems on Affairs of State: Augustan Satirical Verse, 1660–1714*, London and New Haven, CT: Yale University Press, 1963–75.

Loveday, Robert (trans.), [Gualtier de Coste, seigneur de La Calprenède,] *Hymen's praeludia or Loves Masterpiece, Being the first part of Cleopatra*, London: for G. Thompson, 1652. 17th edn, 1663, enlarging successively through Parts 2–12. Parts 1–12, 1665; 5th edn, 1677.

Lovelace, Richard, *Poems of Richard Lovelace*, ed. C. H. Wilkinson, Oxford: Clarendon Press, 1930.

Ludlow, Edmund, *Memoirs of Edmund Ludlow*, ed. C. H. Firth, 3 vols., Oxford: Clarendon Press, 1894.

Lumley, Jane Lumley, Baroness, *Iphigenia at Aulis, translated by Lady Lumley*, The Malone Society, London: C. Whittingham, 1909.

Luther, Martin, *Luther's Works*, gen. eds. Jaroslav Pelikan and Helmut T. Lehmann, 55 vols., St Louis: Concordia Publishing House, and Philadelphia: Fortress Press, 1958–86.

Lyly, John, *The Complete Works of John Lyly*, ed. R. Warwick Bond, 3 vols., Oxford: Clarendon Press, 1902.

Endymion, ed. David Bevington, Manchester University Press, 1996.

Machyn, Henry, *Diary of Henry Machyn, Citizen and Merchant Taylor of London, from 1550 to 1563*, ed. John Gough Nichols, Camden Society, 42, London: J. B. Nichols, 1848.

The Macro Plays: The Castle of Perseverance, Wisdom, Mankind, A Facsimile Edition with Facing Transcriptions, ed. David Bevington, Folger Facsimiles, Manuscript Series, 1, New York: Johnson Reprint Corp., 1972.

Major, Elizabeth, *Honey on the Rod*, London: T. Maxey, 1656.

Major, John, *Historia majoris Britanniae, tam Angliae quam Scotae*, Paris, 1521; trans. as *A History of Britain, as well England as Scotland*, trans. and ed. A. Constable, Scottish History Society, 10, Edinburgh University Press, 1892.

[Makin, Bathsua,] *An Essay to Revive the Ancient Education of Gentlewomen*, London: J. D., 1673.

Malcolm, Joyce Lee (ed.), *The Struggle for Sovereignty: Seventeenth-Century English Political Tracts*, 2 vols., Indianapolis: Liberty Fund, 1999.

Markham, Gervase, *Countrey contentments . . . The English Hus-wife, Contayning, the Inward and Outward Vertues which ought to be in a compleat Woman*, London: J. B[eale] for R. Jackson, 1615. 2nd edn, 1623. 5th edn, 1633. 5th time augmented, 1637.

Marlowe, Christopher, *Complete Works*, ed. Roma Gill *et al.*, 5 vols., Oxford: Clarendon Press, 1987-98.

Doctor Faustus: A- and B-Texts (1604, 1616), by Christopher Marlowe and His Collaborator and Revisers, ed. David Bevington and Eric Rasmussen, Manchester University Press, and New York: St Martin's, 1993.

The troublesome raigne and lamentable death of Edward the second, [London: R. Robinson] for W. Jones, 1594.

['Marprelate, Martin',] *The Marprelate Tracts, 1588, 1589*, ed. William Pierce, London: J. Clarke, 1911. Facs. edn, *The Marprelate Tracts (1588-1589)*, Menston, Yorks.: Scolar Press, 1967.

Marshall, Stephen, *Meroz Cursed, or A Sermon*, London: R. Badger for S. Gellibrand, 1641.

[Marshall, William,] *A Goodly Prymer in Englyshe, Newly Corrected and Printed*, London: J. Byddell for W. Marshall, 1535.

A Prymer in Englyshe, with certeyn prayers and godly meditations, London: W. Marshall, 1534.

Marston, John, *Works of John Marston*, ed. H. Harvey-Wood, 3 vols., Edinburgh: Oliver and Boyd, 1934-9.

Marvell, Andrew, *Complete Poems of Andrew Marvell*, ed. Nigel Smith, Harlow: Longman, 2003.

The Poems and Letters of Andrew Marvell, ed. H. M. Margoliouth, rev. Pierre Legouis and E. E. Duncan-Jones, 2 vols., 3rd edn, Oxford: Clarendon Press, 1971.

The Rehearsal Transpros'd, ed. D. I. B. Smith, Oxford: Clarendon Press, 1971.

Massinger, Philip, *The City-Madam*, ed. T. W. Craik, London: Benn, 1964.

Plays and Poems of Philip Massinger, ed. Philip Edwards and Colin Gibson, 5 vols., Oxford: Clarendon Press, 1976.

Maxwell, John, *Sacro-sancta regum maiestatis: or, the sacred and royal prerogative of Christian Kings*, Oxford: for H. Hall, 1644.

May, Thomas, *The History of the Parliament of England*, London: M. Bell for G. Thomason, 1647.

May, Thomas (trans.), *Lucan's Pharsalia . . . The whole ten bookes. Englished, by T. May*, London: [A. Mathewes] for T. Jones and J. Marriott, 1627; 2nd edn, 1631; 3rd end, 1633.

M[ennes], J[ohn] and S[mith], J[ames], *Wits Recreations*, London: for Humphry Blunden, 1641. Rev. edn, *Recreation for ingenious head-peeces*, London: M. Simmons, 1650. Rpt, of 1641 edn, with intro. Colin Gibson, Aldershot, Harts.: Scolar Press, 1990.

(eds.), *Musarum Deliciae (1656) and Wit Restor'd (1658)*. Facs. edn, intro. Tim Raylor, Delmar, NY: Scholars' Facsimiles & Reprints, 1985.

Middleton, Thomas, *A Chaste Maid in Cheapside*, ed. Alan Brissenden, London: Benn, 1968.

Women Beware Women and Other Plays, ed. Richard Dutton, Oxford University Press, 1999.

Works of Thomas Middleton, ed. A. H. Bullen, 8 vols., London: J. C. Nimmo, 1885–6. Rpt, New York: AMS Press, 1964.

Milton, John, *An Apology against a pamphlet (Apology for Smectymnuus)*, London: J. Rothwell, 1642.

Areopagitica . . . Printed 1644, [London: 1644].

A Complete Collection of the Historical, Political, and Miscellaneous Works in English and Latin of John Milton, ed. John Toland, 2 vols., Amsterdam, 1698.

Complete Prose Works of John Milton, ed. Don M. Wolfe *et al.*, 8 vols., New Haven, CT: Yale University Press, 1953–82.

Complete Shorter Poems, ed. John Carey, 2nd edn, London and New York: Longman, 1997.

English Poems; Comus, 1645, Menston, Yorks.: Scolar Press, 1968. (Facs. edn omitting the Latin poems of the 1st edn.)

John Milton: Complete Poems and Major Prose, ed. Merritt Y. Hughes, Indianapolis: Bobbs-Merrill, and New York: Odyssey Press, 1957.

Lycidas in *Justa Edouardo King naufrago*, Cambridge: T. Buck and R. Daniel, 1638.

A Maske Presented at Ludlow Castle, 1634, London: [A. Mathewes] for H. Robinson, 1637.

A Maske: The Earlier Versions, ed. S. E. Sprott, Toronto and Buffalo, NY: University of Toronto Press, 1973.

Of Education, [London: T. Underhill, 1644].

Paradise Lost, ed. Alastair Fowler, 2nd edn, London and New York: Longman, 1998.

Paradise Lost. A Poem in Twelve Books, London: S. Simmons, 1674.

Poems, & c. Upon Several Occasions, London: for T. Dring, 1673.

Poems of Mr John Milton, Both English and Latin, London: R. Raworth for H. Moseley, 1645.

Works of John Milton, gen. ed., Frank A. Patterson, 18 vols., New York: Columbia University Press, 1931–8.

The Mirror for Magistrates, ed. Lily B. Campbell, Cambridge University Press, 1938. Rpt, New York: Barnes and Noble, 1960.

Montgomerie, Alexander, *The Cherrie and the Slae*, Edinburgh: R. Waldegrave, 1597.

Poems, ed. David J. Parkinson, Edinburgh: Scottish Text Society, 2000.

More, Dame Gertrude, *The Spiritual Exercises*, Paris: L. de la Fosse, 1658.

More, Henry, *An Explanation of the Grand Mystery of Godliness*, Cambridge: J. Flesher for W. Morden, 1660.

A Modest Enquiry into the Mystery of Iniquity, Cambridge: J. Flesher for W. Morden, 1664.

Philosophicall Poems, Cambridge: R. Daniel, 1647.

Philosophical Poems of Henry More, ed. Geoffrey Bullough, Manchester University Press, 1931.

A Platonick Song of the Soul, ed. Alexander Jacob, Lewisburg, PA: Bucknell University Press, and London: Associated University Presses, 1998.

More, Thomas, *The Complete Works of St Thomas More*, gen. eds. Louis L. Martz, Richard S. Sylvester and Clarence H. Miller, 15 vols., London and New Haven, CT: Yale University Press, 1963–97.

Dialogue of Comfort Against Tribulation, ed. Louis L. Martz and Frank Manley, *Complete Works*, vol. 12 (1976).

The History of King Richard III, ed. Richard S. Sylvester, *Complete Works*, vol. 3 (1963).

The Supplication of Souls, ed. Frank Manley, Germain Marc'hadour, Richard Marius and Clarence H. Miller, *Complete Works*, vol. 7 (1990).

Utopia, ed. Edward Surtz, SJ, and J. H. Hexter, *Complete Works*, vol. 4 (1964).

Morison, Richard, *An exhortation to styrre all Englyshe men to the defence of theyr contreye*, [London: T. Berthelet, 1539].

A lamentation in which is shewed what ruyne and destruction cometh of seditious rebellyon, [London: T. Berthelet,] 1536.

A remedy for sedition, [London: T. Berthelet,] 1536.

Morton, Thomas, Bishop of Gloucester, *The Encounter against M. Parsons*, London: for J. Bill, 1610.

Moulsworth, Martha, *'My Name Was Martha': A Renaissance Woman's Autobiographical Poem*, ed. Robert C. Evans and Barbara Wiedemann, West Cornwall, CT: Locust Hill Press, 1993.

Moulton, Thomas, *This is the myrour or glasse of helth*, [London: R. Wyer, before 1531]. 121-chapter edn, 1536. 133-chapter edn, 1540 *et seq.*

Moxon, Joseph, *Mechanick Exercises on the Whole Art of Printing, 1683–4*, ed. Herbert Davis and Harry Carter, 2nd edn, Oxford University Press, 1962.

Muir, Kenneth, 'Unpublished Poems in the Devonshire Manuscript', *Proceedings of the Leeds Philosophical and Literary Society* 6.4 (1947), 253–82.

[Mulcaster, Richard], *The passage of our most drad Soueraigne Lady Quene Elyzabeth through the citie of London to westminster the daye before her coronacion, 1558*, London: R. Tottel, 1559.

Munday, Anthony [and Henry Chettle?], *The Death of Robert Earl of Huntingdon, 1601*, Malone Society Reprints, Oxford University Press, 1967.

The Downfall of Robert Earl of Huntingdon, 1601, Malone Society Reprints, Oxford University Press, 1964.

Pageants and Entertainments of Anthony Munday: A Critical Edition, ed. David M. Bergeron, New York and London: Garland, 1985.

Myers, James P., Jr (ed.), *Elizabethan Ireland: A Selection of Writings by Elizabethan Writers on Ireland*, Hamden, CT: Archon Books, 1983.

Nashe, Thomas, *The vnfortunate traueller, Or, the Life of Iacke Wilton*, London: T. Scarlet for C. Burby, 1594.

Works of Thomas Nashe, ed. R. B. McKerrow, 5 vols., London: A. H. Bullen *et al.*, 1904–10.

Naunton, Robert, *Fragmenta Regalia or Observations on the Late Queen Elizabeth, Her Times and Favourites*, ed. John S. Cerovski, Washington: Folger Shakespeare Library, and London: Associated University Presses, 1985.

[Nedham, Marchamont,] *The case of the common-wealth of England, stated*, London: for E. Blackmore and R. Lowndes, [1650].

The case of the kingdom stated, printed 1647.

Mercurius Politicus 1650–9, Newsbooks 5, ed. P. W. Thomas, London: Cornmarket Press, 1971–2.

A True State of the Case of the Commonwealth, London: T. Newcome, 1653.

Neville, Henry, *The Isle of Pines, or, a late discovery*, London: S. G. for A. Banks and C. Harper, 1668.

The Ladies Parliament, or Divers Remarkable Passages of Ladies in Spring-Garden, in Parliament Assembled, [London, 1647].

A New Enterlude of Godly Queene Hester, ed. W. W. Greg, Materialen zur Kunde der älteren englischen Dramas 5, Louvain: A. Uystpruyst, 1904.

Newcastle, Margaret Cavendish, Duchess of, *CCXI Sociable Letters*, London: W. Wilson, 1664.

The Convent of Pleasure and Other Plays, ed. Anne Shaver, Baltimore, MD, and London: Johns Hopkins University Press, 1999.

The description of a new world, called the blazing world, London: A. Maxwell, 1666. 2nd edn, 1668. Mod. edn, *The Blazing World and Other Writings*, ed. Kate Lilley, London: Penguin, 1994.

Natures Pictures Drawn by Fancies Pencil to the Life, London: for J. Martin and J. Allestrye, 1656. 2nd edn, 1671.

Paper Bodies: A Margaret Cavendish Reader, ed. Sylvia Bowerbank and Sara Mendelson, Peterborough, Ont., and Letchworth: Broadview Press, 2000.

Philosophical and Physical Opinions, London: for J. Martin and J. Allestrye, 1655. 2nd edn, 1663.

Playes, London: A. Warren for J. Martyn, J. Allestry and T. Dicas, 1662.

Plays, Never Before Printed, London: A. Maxwell, 1668.

Poems and Fancies, London: T. R. for J. Martin and J. Allestrye, 1653. 3rd edn, 1668.

A newe ballade of the marigolde, London: R. Lant, 1554.

Northbrooke, John, *A Treatise wherein dicing, dauncing, vaine plays or enterluds, with other idle pastimes, etc., commonly used on the Sabbath day, are reproved by the authority of the word of God and ancient writers*, London: H. Bynneman for G. Byshop, 1577.

Norton, Thomas, *The tragedie of Gorbuduc, whereof three actes were wrytten by T. Nortone, and the two laste by T. Sackvile. Sett forthe as the same was shewed before the quenes most excellent majestie. 1561*, London: W. Griffith, 1565.

Ogilby, John, *The Entertainment of His Most Excellent Majestie Charles II, in His Passage through the City of London to His Coronation*, London: T. Roycroft, 1662.

Orrery, Roger Boyle, Earl of, *Dramatic Works*, ed. William Smith Clark, Cambridge, MA: Harvard University Press, 1937.

Parthenissa, Parts 1–6, London: H. Herringman and H. Moseley, 1651–69.

Osborne, Dorothy, *Letters to Sir William Temple*, ed. Kenneth Parker, London and New York: Penguin Books, 1987.

O'Sullivan Beare, Philip, *Historiae Catholicae Iberniae Compendium*, Lisbon: P. Crasbeeck, 1621.

Overall, John, *Bishop Overall's Convocation Book, MDCVI [1606], concerning the government of God's catholic church and the kingdoms of the whole world*, London: for W. Kettiby, 1690. Mod. edn, *The Convocation Book, MDCVI*, Oxford: J. H. Parker, 1844.

Overbury, Thomas, *The 'Conceited News' of Sir Thomas Overbury and His Friends: A Facsimile Reproduction of the Ninth Impression of 1616 of Sir Thomas Overbury His Wife*, with commentary and textual notes by James E. Savage, Gainesville, FL: Scholars' Facsimiles & Reprints, 1968.

The Overburian Characters, ed. W. J. Paylor, Oxford: Blackwell, 1936.

A wife now the widow... Whereunto are added many witty Characters, London: E. Griffin for L. Lisle, 1614. 3rd edn, enlarged, 1614. 4th edn, enlarged, 1614.

Overton, Richard, *The Picture of the Counsel of State*, 1649, in *Freedom in Arms: A Selection of Leveller Writings*, ed. A. L. Morton, London: Lawrence and Wishart, 1975.

Oxford, Edward de Vere, Earl of, 'The Poems of Edward de Vere, Seventeenth Earl of Oxford, and of Robert Devereux, Second Earl of Oxford', ed. Steven May, *Studies in Philology* 77 (1980), 5–132.

Pace, Richard, *De fructu qui ex doctrina percipitur: The Benefit of a Liberal Education*, ed. and trans. Frank Manley and Richard S. Sylvester, Renaissance Text Series 2, New York: Renaissance Society of America, 1967.

Pagitt, Ephraim, *Heresiography: or, A description of the Heretickes and Sectaries of these latter times*, London: M. Okes, 1645. 6th edn, London: W. Lee, 1661.

Parker, Henry, *Jus Regum, or, A Vindication*, London: for R. Bostock, 1645.

The Question Concerning the Divine Right of Episcopacie Truly Stated, London: for R. Bostock, 1641.

The Trojan Horse of Presbyteriall Government Unbowelled, [London]. 'Printed in the yeer, 1646'.

The True Grounds of Ecclesiastical Regiment, London: for R. Bostock, 1641.

Parr, Katherine, Queen, *Collected Works and Correspondence of Queen Katherine Parr*, ed. Janel Mueller, in preparation.

The Lamentacion of a Sinner, London: Edward Whitchurch, 1547.

Prayers or Medytacions . . . Collected out of holy woorkes by the most vertuous and graciouse Princess Katherine quene of Englande, Fraunce, and Ireland. Anno domini 1545, London: T. Berthelet, 1545.

Patten, William, *The expedition into Scotland of the most worthy fortunate Prince Edward, Duke of Somerset*, London: R. Grafton, 1547. Rpt in *Tudor Tracts, 1532–1588*, intro. A. F. Pollard, Westminster: A. Constable, 1903.

Paulet, William, Marquis of Winchester, *The Lorde Marques Idlenes: conteining manifold matters of acceptable deuise*, [London:] A. Hatfield, 1586.

Peele, George, *Works of George Peele*, ed. A. H. Bullen, 2 vols, London: John C. Nimmo, 1888. Rpt Port Washington, NY: Kennikat Press, 1966.

Pembroke, Mary Sidney Herbert, Countess of, *The Collected Works of Mary Sidney Herbert*, ed. Margaret P. Hannay, Noel J. Kinnamon and Michael G. Brennan, Oxford: Clarendon Press, and New York: Oxford University Press, 1998.

Pembroke, Mary Sidney Herbert, Countess of (trans.), *A Discourse of life and death by Ph[ilippe de] Mornay. Antonius, a tragedie, written also in French by Ro [bert] Garnier. Both doone in English by the countesse of Pembroke*, London: P. S[hort] for W. Ponsonby, 1592.

The Psalms of Sir Philip Sidney and the Countess of Pembroke, ed. J. C. A. Rathmell, Garden City, NY: Doubleday, 1963.

The triumph of death, and other unpublished and uncollected poems, ed. Gary F. Waller, Salzburg: Institüt für englischen Sprache und Literatur, 1977.

Penington, Mary, *Experiences in the Life of Mary Penington (written by herself)*, London: Headley Bros., and Philadelphia: Briddle Press, 1911. Rpt, London: Friends Historical Society, 1992.

Pepys, Samuel, *Diary: A New and Complete Transcription*, ed. Robert Latham and William Matthews, 11 vols., Berkeley and Los Angeles: University of California Press, 1970–83.

Perkins, John, *Here beginneth a verie profitable booke . . . treating of the lawes of this Realme*, London: R. Tottel, 1555.

Perkins, William, *Christian Oeconomie: or, a short survey of the right manner of ordering a familie according to the Scriptures. Written in Latine and now set forth in the vulgar tongue by T. Pickering*, London: F. Kyngston, 1609.

The Work of William Perkins, ed. Ian Breward, The Courtenay Library of Reformation Classics, 3, Abingdon, Berks.: Sutton Courtenay Press, 1970.

Phaer, Thomas (trans.), *A new booke entyteled the regiment of lyfe*, London: [1543?], 9th edn, 1596.

Philips, Katherine, *Collected Works of Katherine Philips, The Matchless Orinda*, ed. Patrick Thomas, Stump Cross, Essex: Stump Cross Books, 1990–3.

Poems (1667), intro. Travis DuPriest, Delmar, NY: Scholars' Fascimiles, 1992.

Poems: ... to which is added Monsieur Corneille's Pompey and Horace, London: J. G. for Richard Marriott, 1664. 2nd edn, London: J. M. for H. Herringman, 1667.

Phillips, John, *A Satyr Against Hypocrites*, London: N. B., 1655.

Pico della Mirandola, *Oration on the Dignity of Man*, trans. Elizabeth Livermore Forbes, in *The Renaissance Philosophy of Man*, ed. Ernst Cassirer, Paul Oskar Kristeller and John Herman Randall, University of Chicago Press, 1948.

Pollard, A. F. (ed.), *Records of the English Bible*, London: Oxford University Press, 1911.

Ponet (or Poynet), John, Bishop of Rochester and Winchester, *A shorte treatise of politike power, and of the true obedience*, [Strasbourg: heirs of W. Köpfel,] 1556.

Pont, Robert, 'Of the Union of Britayne', in *The Jacobean Union. Six Tracts of 1604*, ed. Galloway and Levack, Scottish History Society, pp. 1–38.

Poole, Elizabeth, *An Alarum of War, given to the Army*, London, 1649.

A Vision: Wherein is manifested the disease and cure of the Kingdome, London, 1648[9].

[Pordage, Samuel,] *Mundorum explicatio, or the explanation*, London: T. R. for Lodowick Lloyd, 1661.

The Practical Part of Love, Extracted out of the Extravagant and Lascivious Life of a Fair but Subtle Female, London, 1660.

Proctor, John, *The historie of Wyates rebellion*, London: [R. Caly,] 1554. Mod. edn, *Tudor Tracts, 1532–1588*, ed. A. F. Pollard, Westminster: A. Constable, 1903.

Prynne, William, *A breviate of the life of William Laud, Arch-bishop of Canterbury*, London: F. L. for M. Sparke, 1644.

Canterburies Doome, London: by J. Macock for M. Sparke, 1646.

Histrio-mastix. The players scourge, London: E. A[llde, A. Mathewes, T. Cotes] and W. J[ones] for M. Sparke, 1633.

Lord Bishops: None of the Lords Bishops, [Amsterdam: Cloppenburg Press,] 1640.

Mount-Orgueil (1641), intro. Edmund Miller, Delmar, NY: Scholars' Facsimiles & Reprints, 1984.

New Discovery of the Prelates Tyranny, London: for M. S[parke], 1641.

New Presbyterian Light springing out of Independent Darkness, London, 1647.

Puttenham, George, *The Arte of English Poesie*, ed. Gladys Doidge Willcock and Alice Walker, Cambridge University Press, 1936. Rpt, 1970.

Quarles, Francis, *The Complete Works in Prose and Verse of Francis Quarles*, ed. Alexander B. Grosart, 3 vols., Edinburgh: T. & A. Constable, 1880. Rpt, New York: AMS Press, 1967.

Diuine Fancies: digested into epigrammes, meditations, observations, London: for J. Marriot, 1632. Mod. edn, ed. William Liston, New York: Garland, 1992.

Rabelais, François, *Gargantua and Pantagruel*, trans. Thomas Urquhart, intro. Charles Whibley, 2 vols., 1900. Rpt, New York: AMS Press, 1967.

Ralegh, Sir Walter, *The Life of Sir Walter Ralegh, Based on Contemporary Documents ... Together with His Letters*, ed. Edward Edwards, 2 vols., London: Macmillan, 1868.

The Poems, ed. Agnes M. C. Latham, Cambridge, MA: Harvard University Press, 1951.

Works of Sir Walter Ralegh, 8 vols., Oxford University Press, 1829. Rpt, New York: Burt Franklin, 1965.

Randolph, Thomas, *Poems*, Oxford: L. Lichfield, 1638. 3rd edn, [London,] printed 1643. 4th edn, 1652. 5th edn, 1664.

Reformation Biblical Drama in England [*The Life and Repentaunce of Mary Magdalene, The History of Iacob and Esau*], ed. Paul Whitfield White, New York: AMS Press, 1992.

Renaissance Drama by Women: Texts and Documents, ed. Susan E. Cerasano and Marion Wynne-Davies, London: Routledge, 1996.

Respublica, AD 1553: A Play on the Social Condition of England, ed. Leonard A. Magnus, Early English Text Society, extra, ser., 94, London: K. Paul, Trench, Trübner, 1905.

Rich, Barnabe, *A New Description of Ireland: wherein is described the disposition of the Irish*, London: [W. Jaggard for] T. Adams, 1610.

Richardson, Elizabeth, *A Ladies Legacie to her Daughters*, [London:] T. Harper, 1645.

Rogers, John, *Ohel or Beth-Shemesh. A Tabernacle for the Sun*, London: for R. I[bbitson] and G. and H. Eversden, 1653.

Rogers, Richard, *Seven treatises, containing such direction as is gathered out of the holie scriptures, leading and guiding to true happines*, London: F. Kyngston for T. Man and R. Dexter, 1603, 2nd enlarged edn, 1604. 3rd enlarged edn, 1610. 4th edn, 1616. 5th edn, 1630.

Rothe, David, *The Analecta of David Rothe, Bishop of Ossory*, ed. Patrick F. Moran, Dublin: M. H. Gill & Son, 1884.

Rowlands, Samuel, *Complete Works*, ed. Edmund Gosse and S. J. H. Herrtage, 3 vols., Glasgow: Huntlerian Club, 1880.

Russell, John, 'A Treatise of the Happie and Blissed Unioun', in *The Jacobean Union. Six Tracts of 1604*, ed. Galloway and Levack, pp. 75–142.

Rutherford, Samuel, *Lex, Rex: the Law and the Prince*, London: for J. Field, 1644.

Ryves, Sir Thomas, *Regiminis Anglicani in Hibernia Defensio, adversus Analecten*, London: [H. Lownes, J. Dawson and J. Haviland] for J. Bartlet, 1624.

Sackville, Thomas, *The tragedie of Gorbuduc, whereof three actes were wrytten by T. Nortone, and the two laste by T. Sackvile. Sett forthe as the same was shewed before the quenes most excellent majestie. 1561*, London: W. Griffith, 1565.

Sadler, John, *The sicke womans private looking-glasse*, London: A. Griffin for P. Stephens and C. Meridith, 1636.

Saint German, Christopher, *An answere to a letter*, London: [T. Godfray, 1535].

A dyalogue in Englyshe betwyxt a doctour of dyvynyte and a student in the lawes, London: [R. Wyer, 1531].

A treatise concernynge the division betwene the spiritualitie and the temporalitie, London: [R. Redman, 1532].

Saintsbury, George (ed.), *Minor Poets of the Caroline Period*, 3 vols., Oxford: Clarendon Press, 1905–21.

Salesbury, William, *A Briefe and A Playne Introduction, Teachynge How to Pronounce the Letters in the British Tong*, London: [R. Grafton for] R. Crowley, 1550.

A Dictionary in Englyshe and Welshe, London: [N. Hill for] J. Waley, 1547.

Saltmarsh, John, *Free Grace: or The Flowings of Christs Blood freely to Sinners*, London: for G. Calvert, 1645.

Groanes for Liberty, London: for G. Calvert, 1646.

Sparkles of Glory, London: for G. Calvert, 1647.

Sampson, Richard, *Oratio qua docet, anglos, regiae dignitati ut obediant . . .* , London: T. Berthelet, 1535.

Sanderson, Robert, *Ten Sermons*, London: R. Y[oung] for R. Dawlman, 1627. 2nd edn, *Twelve Sermons*, 1632. 3rd edn, *Twelve Sermons, . . . Whereunto are added two sermons more*, 1637.

Sandys, Sir Edwin, *A Relation of the State of Religion: and with what Hopes and Pollicies it hath beene framed, and is maintained in the severall States of these Westerne parts of the world*, London: [G. and A. Snowdon for] S. Waterson, 1605.

Savile, Sir Henry, 'Historicall Collections,' in *The Jacobean Union. Six Tracts of 1604*, ed. Galloway and Levack, pp. 185–239.

Saye and Sele, William Fiennes, Viscount, *A speech of the Right Honourable William Lord Viscount Saye and Sele, in answer to the Lord Archbishop of Canterburies Last Speech and concerning the Liturgie of the Church of England*, [London:] 'anno Domini, 1641.'
   A speech of the Right Honourable William, Lord Viscount Saye and Seale, Vpon the Bill against Bishops power in civill affaires and Courts of Iudicature, London: for T. Underhill, 1641.

Scot, Reginald, *The discoverie of witchcraft*, London: [H. Denham for] W. Brome, 1584.

Scott, Alexander, *Poems*, ed. James Cranstoun, Scottish Text Society, Edinburgh: W. Blackwood & Sons, 1896.

Scudéry, Madeleine de, *Artemenes, or the Grand Cyrus*, trans. F. G., London: for H. Moseley and T. Dring, 1653–5. 2nd edn, 1691.

Segar, William, *Honor, military and ciuill*, London: R. Barker, 1602.

Sempill, Robert, *The Sempill Ballates: A Series of Historical. Political, and Satirical Scottish Poems, Ascribed to Robert Sempill, 1567–1583*, Edinburgh: T. G. Stevenson, 1872.

Seymour, Edward, Duke of Somerset, *An epistle or exhortacion to unitie and peace, sent to the inhabitauntes of Scotlande*, London: R. Grafton, 1548.

Shakespeare, William, *The Complete Works of Shakespeare*, ed. David Bevington, 4th edn, New York: Harper, Collins, 1992.
   Mr William Shakespeares comedies, histories, & tragedies. Published according to the true originall copies, comp. Edward Heminges and John Condell, London: printed by I. Jaggard and E. Blount, 1623.
   The New Cambridge Shakespeare, gen, ed. Brian Gibbons, assoc. gen, ed. A. R. Braunmuller, Cambridge University Press, 1984– (in progress).
   The Riverside Shakespeare, ed. G. Blakemore Evans, 2nd edn, Boston: Houghton Mifflin, 1997.

Sharp, Jane, *The Midwives' Book*, London: for Simon Miller, 1671. Mod. edn, ed. Elaine Hobby, Oxford University Press, 1999.

Shepherd, Luke, *John Bon and Mast Person*, London: J. Daye and W. Seres, [1548?].
   Luke Shepherd's Satires, ed. Janice Devereux, Tempe, AZ: Renaissance English Text Society and Arizona Center for Medieval and Renaissance Studies, 2001.
   The vpcheringe of the messe, London: J. Daye and W. Seres, [1548].

Shirley, James, *Dramatic Works and Poems*, ed. Revd Alexander Dyce, 6 vols., London: Murray, 1833.

Sibbes, Richard, *The Bruised Reed, and Smoking Flax. Some Sermons*, London: [M. Flesher] for R. Dawlman, 1630. Facs. edn, intro. P. A. Slack, Menston, Yorks.: Scolar Press, 1973.
   Complete Works of Richard Sibbes, ed. Alexander B. Grosart, 7 vols., Edinburgh: J. Nichol, 1862–4. Rpt, Carlisle, PA: Banner of Truth Trust, 1978–83.

Sibthorp, Robert, *Apostolike Obedience. Shewing the duty of subjects to pay tribute and taxes. A Sermon*, London: M. Flesher for R. M[ynne], 1627.

Sidney, Philip, *An Apologie for Poetrie*, London: [J. Roberts] for H. Olney, 1595. Mod. edn, ed. Geoffey Shepherd, Manchester University Press, 1973.

The Correspondence of Philip Sidney and Hubert Languet, ed. William Aspenwall Bradley, Boston: Merrymount Press, 1912.

The Countess of Pembrokes Arcadia, London: J. Windet for W. Ponsonbie, 1590. Mod. edn, *The Countess of Pembroke's Arcadia (The Old Arcadia)*, ed. Jean Robertson, Oxford: Clarendon Press, 1973.

The Countess of Pembrokes Arcadia. Now since the first edition augmented and ended, London: [J. Windet] for W. Ponsonbie, 1593. Mod. edn, *The Countess of Pembroke's Arcadia (The New Arcadia)*, ed. Victor Skretkowicz, Oxford: Clarendon Press, and New York: Oxford University Press, 1987.

The Poems of Sir Philip Sidney, ed. W. A. Ringler, Jr, Oxford: Clarendon Press, 1962.

Prose Works, ed. Albert Feuillerat, 4 vols., Cambridge University Press, 1962.

Sidney, Robert, *The Poems of Robert Sidney*, ed. P. J. Croft, Oxford and New York: Oxford University Press, 1984.

Skelton, John, *The Complete English Poems*, ed. John Scattergood, London and New Haven, CT: Yale University Press, 1983.

Magnyfycence, a goodly enterlude and a mery, London: [Southwark, P. Treveris for J. Rastell, 1530].

Skinner, Robert, *A Sermon Preached before the King at White-hall, the third of December*, London: J. L[egat] for A. Hebb, 1634.

Smectymnuus [Stephen Marshall, Edmund Calamy, Thomas Young, Matthew Newcomen, William Spurstow], *An Answer to a book entituled, An Humble Remonstrance*, London: for J. Rothwell, 1641.

Smith, Nigel (ed.), *A Collection of Ranter Writings from the 17th Century*, London: Junction Books, 1983.

Smith, Thomas, *De Republica Anglorum. The maner of governement of England*, London: H. Middleton for G. Seton, 1583. Mod. edn, *De Republica Anglorum*, ed. Mary Dewar, Cambridge University Press, 1982.

Smith, William, *Chloris, or the complaint of the passionate despised shepheard*, London: E. Bollifant, 1596.

Poems, ed. Lawrence A. Sasek, Baton Rouge: Louisiana State University Press, 1970.

Southwell, Robert, *Poems*, ed. James H. McDonald and Nancy P. Brown, Oxford: Clarendon Press, 1967.

Saint Peters complaint, with other poems, London: for J. Wolfe, 1595. 8th edn, 1602. Enlarged as *S. Peters Complaint. And Saint Mary Magdalens funeral teares, With sundry other selected, and devout poems*, [Saint-Omer: English College Press,] 1616. 6th edn, 1634.

Sparke, Michael, *Crumms of Comfort, The Valley of Teares, and the Hill of Joy*, 6th edn, London: [I. Jaggard] for M. Sparke, 1627. 20th edn, 1635.

Speght, Rachel, *Mortalities Memorandum, with A Dreame Prefixed, imaginarie in manner; reall in matter*, London: E. Griffin for J. Bloom, 1621.

A Mouzell for Melastomus, the Cynicall Bayter of, and foule mouthed Barker against Evah's Sex, London: N. Okes for T. Archer, 1617.

The Polemics and Poems of Rachel Speght, ed. Barbara K. Lewalski, Oxford University Press, 1996.

Spelman, Sir Henry, 'Of the Union', in *The Jacobean Union. Six Tracts of 1604*, ed. Galloway and Levack, pp. 161–84.

Spencer, Christopher (ed.), *Five Restoration Adaptations of Shakespeare*, Urbana: University of Illinois Press, 1965.

Spenser, Edmund, *The Faerie Queene. Disposed into twelve books, fashioning XII. morall vertues* [Bks 1–3], London: [J. Wolfe] for W. Ponsonbie, 1590.

The Second Part of the Faerie Queene, London: [R. Field] for W. Ponsonbie, 1596. Mod. edn, *The Faerie Queene*, ed. A. C. Hamilton, Shohachi Fukuda, Hiroshi Yamashita, Toshiyuki Suzuki, London and New York: Longman, 2001.

The Works of Edmund Spenser: A Variorum Edition, ed. Edwin Greenlaw, Charles G. Osgood and Frederick M. Padelford, 10 vols., Baltimore, MD: Johns Hopkins University Press, 1932–57.

The Yale Edition of the Shorter Poems of Edmund Spenser, ed. William Oram *et al.*, New Haven, CT: Yale University Press, 1989.

[Spenser, Edmund] (attrib.) *A View of the State of Ireland*, in James Ware, *Two Histories of Ireland, the one written by E. Campion, the other by M. Hanmer*, Dublin: Society of Stationers, and London: T. Harper, 1633. Mod. edn, *A View of the State of Ireland*, ed. Andrew Hadfield and Willy Maley, Oxford: Blackwell, 1997.

Spottiswoode, John, Archbishop of St Andrews, *The History of the Church of Scotland*, London: J. Flesher for R. Royston, 1655. 4th edn, 1677.

Sprat, Thomas, *The History of the Royal-Society*, London: T. R. for J. Martyn and J. Allestry, 1667.

Stafford, Thomas, *Pacata Hibernia. Ireland Appeased and Reduced, or, an Historie of the late Warres of Ireland, especially within the Province of Mounster*, London: A. Mathewes for R. Milbourne, 1633.

Stafford, William, *A compendious or briefe examination of certayne ordinary complaints* [written in 1549], London: T. Marshe, 1581. The authorship of this treatise has been contested by its modern editors. See the attribution to either John Hales or Thomas Smith in *A discourse of the common weal of the realme of England, first printed in 1581 and commonly attributed to W. S., edited from the MSS by Elizabeth Lamond*, completed by William Cunningham; Cambridge University Press, 1893. Rpt, 1929. See, further, *A Discourse of the Commonweal of This Realm of England. Attributed to Sir Thomas Smith*, ed. Mary Dewar, Charlottesville: University Press of Virginia for Folger Shakespeare Library, 1969.

Stanford, William, *An exposition of the kinges prerogative collected out of the great abridgement of justice Fizherbert and other olde writers of the lawes of Englande*, London: R. Tottel, 1567. *Les plees del coron: divisees in plusiours titles*, London: R. Tottel, 1557.

Stanley, Thomas, *The History of Philosophy*, London: for H. Moseley and T. Dring, 1655. Vol. 2, 1656. Vol. 3, 1660. 2nd edn, 1687. *Poems and Translations*, [London:] for the author and his friends, 1647. Mod. edn, ed. Galbraith Miller Crump, Oxford: Clarendon Press, 1962.

Stanyhurst, Richard, *A Description of Ireland*, in Raphael Holinshed, *The First Volume of the Chronicles of England, Scotlande, and Irelande*, 2 vols., London: [H. Bynneman] for J. Harrison, 1577.

Starkey, Thomas, *Dialogue between Reginald Pole and Thomas Lupset*, ed. T. F. Mayer, Publications of the Camden Society, 4th ser., 37, London: Royal Historical Society, 1989.

An exhortation to the people, instructynge them to unitie and obedience, London: T. Berthelet, [?1540].

Stirling, William Alexander, Earl of, *Poetical Works*, ed. L. E. Kaster and H. B. Charlton, Edinburgh: W. Blackwood, 1921–9.

Stow, John, *The Chronicles of England, from Brute unto this present yeare 1580*, London: R. Newberie, at the assignment of H. Bynneman, 1580. 2nd and subsequent edns, *The Annales of England*, 1592, 1600, 1601, 1605, 1615, 1631.

A Summarie of English Chronicles, London: T. Marsh, 1565. 2nd and subsequent edns, 1566, 1570, 1573, 1574, 1575, 1590. Superseded by *Chronicles and Annales*.

A Survey of London, London: [J. Windet for] J. Wolfe, 1598. 2nd and subsequent edns, 1599, 1603, 1618, 1633. Mod. edn, *A Survey of London*, ed. C. L. Kingsford, 2 vols., 1908. Rpt, Oxford: Clarendon Press, 1971.

Strype, John, *Annals of the Reformation and Establishment of Religion, and Other Various Occurrences in the Church of England, during Queen Elizabeth's Happy Reign*, London: for J. Wyat, 1709. Mod. edn, 4 vols., Oxford: Clarendon Press, 1824.

Ecclesiastical Memorials, Relating Chiefly to Religion, and the Reformation of It, and the Emergencies of the Church of England, under King Henry VIII, King Edward VI, and Queen Mary I, 3 vols., London: for J. Wyat, 1721. Mod. edn, 3 vols., Oxford: Clarendon Press, 1822.

The Life of the Learned Sir John Cheke, Kt, London: for John Wyat, 1705. Mod. edn, Oxford: Clarendon Press, 1881.

The Stuart Constitution: Documents and Commentary, ed. John Kenyon, 2nd edn, Cambridge University Press, 1986.

Suckling, John, *The Works of Sir John Suckling: The Non-Dramatic Works*, ed. Thomas Clayton, Oxford: Clarendon Press, 1971.

A supplycacyon to the Queenes Maiestie, London: J. Cawoode, 1550. Strasbourg, W. Rihel, 1555.

Surtz, Edward and Murphy, Virginia (eds.), *The Divorce Tracts of Henry VIII*, Angers: Moreana, 1988.

'A Survey of the present estate of Ireland Anno 1615', San Marino, CA: Huntington Library, Ellesmere MS 1746, fols. 8b–26b.

Tanner, J. R. (ed.), *Tudor Constitutional Documents AD 1485–1603: With an Historical Commentary*, Cambridge University Press, 1922. Rpt, 1951.

[Tany, Thomas,] *A third great and terrible Fire, Fire, Fire*, [London, 1655].

Tasso, Torquato, *Discourses on the Heroic Poem*, trans. and ed. Mariella Cavalchini and Irene Samuel, Oxford: Clarendon Press, 1973.

Tatham, John, *The Rump*, London: W. Godbid for R. Bloome, 1661.

Taylor, Jeremy, *The rule and exercises of holy dying*, London: for R. Royston, 1651. 18th edn, 1700.

The rule and exercises of holy living, London: for R. Royston, 1650. 18th edn, 1700.

Holy Living and Holy Dying, ed. Paul G. Stanwood, 2 vols., Oxford: Clarendon Press, 1989.

Treatises of 1. The liberty of prophesying 2. Prayer Extempore 3. Episcopacie, London: for R. Royston, 1648.

Taylor, John, *Mad Fashions, Od Fashions, All out of Fashions*, London: J. Hammond, 1642.

A Swarme of Sectaries, and Schismatiques, [London:] 1641.

Temple, Sir John, *The Irish Rebellion*, London: R. White for S. Gellibrand, 1646.

The Three Parnassus Plays (1598–1601), ed. J. B. Leishman, London: Nicholson & Watson, 1949.

Three Primers Put Forth in the Reign of Henry VIII, [ed. E. Burton], Oxford University Press, 1848.

Tom Tell-Trath, or a free discourse touching the manners of the tyme. Directed to His Majestie by waye of humble advertisement. Supposed to be printed in the year 1622.

Tom Tyler and His Wife, 2nd impression, London, 1661. Mod. edn, ed. G. C. Moore Smith and W. W. Greg, Malone Society Reprints, 1910.

Tottel, Richard, *Tottel's Miscellany (1557–1587)*, ed. Hyder Edward Rollins, 2 vols., Cambridge, MA: Harvard University Press, 1928–9. Rev. edn, 1965.

Traherne, Thomas, *Centuries, Poems, and Thanksgivings*, ed. H. M. Margoliouth, Oxford: Clarendon Press, 1958.

Commentaries of Heaven: The Poems, ed. D. D. C. Chambers, Salzburg: Institüt für Anglistik und Amerikanistik, Universität Salzburg, 1989.

Trapnel, Anna, *The Cry of a Stone*, [London:] 1654. Mod. edn, ed. Hilary Hinds, Tempe, AZ: Medieval and Renaissance Texts and Studies, 2000.

A Legacy for Saints, London: T. Brewster, 1654.

A Voice for the King of Saints and Nations, or A Testimony Poured Forth by the Spirit through Anna Trapnell, [London:] 1658. Enlarged text, University of Oxford, Bodleian Library, MS. S 1.42 Th., sig. B1ff.

Tryon, Thomas, *Some Memoirs of the Life of Mr Tho: Tryon, late of London, merchant: written by himself*, London: T. Sowle, 1705.

Tudor Interludes, ed. Peter Happé, Harmondsworth: Penguin, 1972.

The Tudor Interludes: 'Nice Wanton' and 'Impatient Poverty', ed. Leonard Tennenhouse, New York: Garland, 1984.

Tudor Royal Proclamations, ed. Paul L. Hughes and James. F. Larkin, 2 vols., London and New Haven, CT: Yale University Press, 1964–9.

Tudor Tracts, 1532–1588, intro. A. F. Pollard, Westminster: A. Constable & Co., 1903. Rpt, New York: Cooper Square Publishers, 1964.

Turberville, George, *Epitaphes, epigrams, songs and sonets, Newly corrected with additions*, London: H. Denham, 1567. Facs. edn, also incorporating *Epitaphes and sonnettes (1576)*, intro. Richard J. Panofsky, Delmar, NY: Scholars' Facsimiles & Reprints, 1977.

Turner, William, *A new herball*, London: S. Mierdman, 1551.

The seconde parte of William Turners herball, Cologne: A. Birckman, 1562.

The first and seconde partes . . . lately oversene, corrected and enlarged with the thirde parte, Cologne: A Birckman, 1568.

Turpyn, Richard, *The Chronicle of Calais in the Reigns of Henry VII and Henry VIII to the Year 1540*, ed. John Gough Nichols, Publications of the Camden Society, 1st ser., 35, London: J. B. Nichols, 1846.

The Two Books of Homilies Appointed to be Read in Churches, ed. John Griffiths, Oxford University Press, 1859.

Two Tudor Interludes: The Interlude of Youth, Hick Scorner, ed. Ian Lancashire, University of Manchester Press, and Baltimore, MD: Johns Hopkins University Press, 1980.

T[yler,] M[argaret] (trans.), [Diego Ortuñez de Calahorra,] *The Mirrour of Princely Deedes and Knighthood*, London: T. East, [1578].

Tyndale, William, *An answere unto sir Thomas Mores dialoge*, [Antwerp: S. Cock, 1531]. Mod. edn, ed. Henry Walter, Parker Society, 45, Cambridge University Press, 1850.

The Newe Testament, dylygently corrected and compared with the Greke by W. Tindale, Antwerp: M. Emperowr, 1534. Rpt, in *The English Hexapla*, London, 1841.

Obedience of a Christen man, and how Christen rulers ought to governe, Marlborow in the lande of Hesse, H. Luft [Antwerp: J. Hoochstraten,] 1528. Mod. edn, ed. Henry Walter, *Doctrinal Treatises and Introductions to Different Portions of the Holy Scriptures*, Parker Society, 44, Cambridge University Press, 1848. Rpt, New York: Johnson Reprint Corp., 1968.

The practyse of Prelates: Whether the Kinges grace maye be separated from hys quene / because she was his brothers wyfe, Marburg, [Antwerp: J. Hoochstraten], 1530.

The whole workes of W. Tyndall, Iohn Frith, and Doct. Barnes, ed. John Foxe, London: J. Daye, 1573.

Tyrone, Con Bacach O'Neill, 1st Earl of, *The copye of the submissyon of Oneyll, which he made the .xxiiii. daye of September, in the .xxxiiii. yere of his maiesties raygne*, London: for J. Gough, 1542.

[Udall, Nicholas,] *'Respublica': An Interlude for Christmas 1553*, ed. W. W. Greg, Early English Text Society, orig. ser., 226, London: Oxford University Press, 1952.

Urfé, Honoré d', *Astrea. A Romance*, trans. J. Davies, London: W. W. for H. Moseley, T. Dring and H. Herringman, 1657.

Urquhart, Thomas, *The Jewel*, ed. R. D. S. Jack and R. J. Lyall, Edinburgh: Scottish Academic Press, 1983.

Urquhart, Thomas (trans.) [François Rabelais,] *The works of the famous Mr Francis Rabelais, doctor in physick: treating of the lives, heroick deeds, and sayings of Gargantua and his son Pantagruel: . . . written originally in French, and translated into English by Sir Thomas Urchard*, London: J. R., 1664. Mod edns, *Rabelais, Gargantua and Pantagruel, translated by Thomas Urquhart*, intro. Charles Whibley, 2 vols., London, 1900. Rpt, New York: AMS Press, 1967.

The Urquhart–Le Motteux Translation of The Works of Francis Rabelais, ed. Albert Jay Nock and Catherine Rose Wilson, 2 vols., New York: Harcourt, Brace, 1931.

Works of Sir Thomas Urquhart, Glasgow: Maitland Club, 1834, rpt, New York: AMS Press, 1971.

V., B., *The run-awayes answer, to a booke called, A rodde for runne-awayes*, London: [A. Mathewes], 1625.

Vane, Henry, *The Retired Mans Meditations*, London: R. W., 1655.

Vaughan, Henry, *The Complete Poems*, ed. Alan Rudrum, London and New Haven, CT: Yale University Press, 1981.

Works of Henry Vaughan, ed. Leonard C. Martin, 2nd edn, Oxford: Clarendon Press, 1957.

Venn, Anne, *A Wise Virgins Lamp Burning*, London: E. Cole, 1658.

Vergil, Polydore, *The Anglica Historia, AD 1485–1537*, ed. and trans. Denys Hay, Camden Society, 3rd ser., 74, London: Royal Historical Society, 1950.

Verstegan, Richard, *Letters and Despatches of Richard Verstegan (c. 1550–1640)*, ed. Anthony G. Petti, Publications of the Catholic Record Society, 52, London: Catholic Record Society, 1959.

Vicars, John, *England's Worthies*, London: for J. Rothwell, 1647.
Former ages never heard of, and after ages will admire. Or a brief review of the most materiall Parliamentary transactions, London: M. S. for T. Jenner, 1654. 2nd edn, 1656. 3rd edn, 1660.

Vincent, Philip, *A True Relation of the Late Battell fought in New England, between the English, and the Pequet Salvages*, London: N. Butter and J. Bellamie, 1638.

Wager, Lewis, *A newe enterlude, never before this tyme imprinted, of the life and repentaunce of Marie Magdalene*, London: J. Charleswood, 1566. Mod. edn, *The Life and Repentaunce of Marie Magdalene*, ed. Frederic Ives Carpenter, University of Chicago Press, 1904.

Walker, Anthony, *The holy life of Mrs Elizabeth Walker . . . with some useful papers and letters written by her on several occasions*, London: J. Leake, 1690. 2nd edn, *The vertuous wife: or the holy life of Mrs Elizabeth Walker*, London: for N. R., 1694.

Walker, Clement, *Anarchia Anglicana: or the history of Independency*, London: printed 1648. *Second Part*, London, printed in the year 1649. 8 more edns in 1649. Another edn in 1661.
Compleat History of Independency, London: for R. Royston and R. Lownds, 1661. 3 more edns in 1661.

Waller, Edmund, *Poems, &c., written upon several occasions, and to several persons*, London: T. W. for H. Mosely, 1645. 7 edns by 1694. Mod. edn, *Poems of Edmund Waller*, ed. G. Thorn Drury, 2 vols., London: Routledge, and New York: E. P. Dutton, 1904. Rpt, New York: Greenwood Press, 1968.

Walshe, Edward, *The office and duety in fightyng for our countrey*, London: J. Herfort, 1545.

Walton, Isaak, *The compleat angler*, London: T. Maxey for R. Marriot, 1653. 5 edns by 1676. Mod. edn, *The Complete Angler, 1653–1676*, ed. Jonquil Bevan, Oxford: Clarendon Press, 1983.
The lives of Dr John Donne, Sir Henry Wotton, Mr Richard Hooker, Mr George Herbert, London: T. Newcomb for R. Marriott, 1670. 4th edn, 1675. Mod. edn, intro. George Saintsbury, London: Oxford University Press, 1936.

Walwyn, William, *The Writings of William Walwyn*, ed. Jack R. McMichael and Barbara Taft, Athens: University of Georgia Press, 1989.

Ward, Seth, *Vindiciae Academiarum, containing some brief animadversions upon Mr Websters book stiled, The examination of academies*, Oxford: by L. Lichfield for T. Robinson, 1654. Mod. rpt in *Science and Education in the Seventeenth Century: The Webster–Ward Debate*, ed. Allen Debus, London: Macdonald; New York: American Elsevier, 1970.

A warninge for Englande, London [Strasbourg]: heirs of W. Kopfel, 1555.

Warren, Elizabeth, *A Warning-Peece from Heaven, against the Sins of the Times*, London: R. Constable for H. Shepherd, 1649.

Warwick, Mary Rich, Countess of, *The Autobiography of Mary, Countess of Warwick*, ed. T. Crofton Croker, London: printed for the Percy Society by Richards, 1848.

W[atkyns], R[owland], *Flamma sine fumo, or poems without fictions*, London: for W. Leake, 1662. Mod edn, ed. Paul C. Davies, Cardiff: University of Wales Press, 1968.

Watson, Thomas, *The Hekatompathia or passionate centurie of love*, London: for G. Cawood, [1582]. Facs. rpt, intro. S. K. Heninger, Gainesville, FL: Scholars' Facsimiles & Reprints, 1964.

Webbe, William, *A Discourse of English Poetrie*, London: J. Charlewood for R. Walley, 1586. Mod. edn in *Elizabethan Critical Essays*, ed. G. Gregory Smith.

Webster, John, chaplain, *Academiarum examen, or the examination of academies*, London: for
   G. Calvert, 1654. Mod. rpt in *Science and Education in the Seventeenth Century: The
   Webster–Ward Debate*, ed. Debus.
Webster, John, dramatist, *The tragedy of the dutchesse of Malfy*, London: N. Okes for
   J. Waterson, 1623.
The white divel, . . . with the life and death of Vittoria Corombona, London: N. O[kes] for
   T. Archer, 1612.
Works of John Webster, ed. David Charles Gunby, Antony Hammond and Doreen Del
   Vecchio, Cambridge University Press, 1995– (in progress).
*The Welch-mens Prave Resolution: In Defence of Her King, Her Pritish Parliament, and Her Country,
   against te Malignant party*, London: J. Harrison, 1642.
Westmorland, Mildmay Fane, 2nd Earl of, *Otia sacra optima fides*, London: by R. Cotes, 1648.
   Facs. edn, intro. Donald M. Friedman, Delmar, NY: Scholars' Facsimiles, 1975.
The Poetry of Mildmay Fane, Second Earl of Westmorland, ed. Tom Cain, Manchester
   University Press, 2001.
Whateley, William, *A Bride-Bush: or, A direction for married persons*, London: F. Kyngston for
   T. Man, 1619.
Whitney, Geoffrey, *A Choice of emblemes and other devises*, Leiden: C. Plantyn, 1586. Facs. edn,
   ed. Henry Green and intro. Frank Fieler, London: Lowell Reeve and Co., 1886; New
   York: AMS Press, 1967.
W[hitney], Is[abella], *The copy of a letter, lately written in meeter, by a yonge gentilwoman: to her
   unconstant lover*, London: R. Jhones, [1567].
A sweet nosgay, or pleasant posye: contayning a hundred and ten phylosophicall flowers, London:
   [R. Jones, 1573].
A sweet nosgay; and the copy of a letter, ed. Richard J. Panofsky, Delmar, NY: Scholars'
   Facsimiles and Reprints, 1982.
[Wigglesworth, Michael,] *The Day of Doom*, London: J. G. for P. C., 1666. 6th edn, 1715. Mod.
   edn, *The Day of Doom . . . With Other Poems*, New York: American News Company, 1867.
Wilkins, John, *A Discourse Concernng the Gift of Prayer*, London: T. R. and E. M. for
   S. Gellibrand, 1651. 9th edn, 1695.
Ecclesiastes, or A Discourse concerning the Gift of Preaching, London: M. F. for S. Gellibrand,
   1646. 7th edn, 1693.
An Essay Towards a Real Character, and a Philosophical Language, London: for S. Gellibrand
   and J. Martyn, 1668.
Mercury, or, The Secret and Swift Messenger, London: I. Norton for I. Maynard and
   T. Wilkins, 1641.
Williams, Roger, *The Bloudy Tenent of Persecution, for cause of Conscience, discussed, in a
   conference between Truth and Peace*, London, 1644.
Wilson, John, *Select Musicall Ayres*, [London:] for John Playford, 1652; 2nd edn., 1653.
Wilson, Thomas, *The arte of rhetorique, for the vse of all suche as are studious of eloquence*,
   London: R. Grafton, 1553. 8th edn, 1585. Mod. edn, *The Arte of Rhetorique*, ed. Thomas
   J. Derrick, New York: Garland, 1982.
A discourse vppon vsurye, by waye of dialogue, London: R. Tottel, 1572. Mod. edn, *A Discourse
   upon Usury*, ed. R. H. Tawney, London: G. Bell and Sons, 1925.

Winstanley, Gerrard, *The law of freedom in a platform*, London: for the author, to be sold by G. Calvert, 1652. Mod. edn, *The Law of Freedom and Other Writings*, ed. Christopher Hill, Harmondsworth: Penguin Books, 1973.

The saints paradice, London: G. Calvert, 1648.

Several pieces gathered into one volume, London: G. Calvert, 1649.

A watch-word to the City of London, London: for G. Calvert, 1649. Mod. edn in *The Law of Freedom and Other Writings*, ed. Hill.

Works of Gerrard Winstanley, with an Appendix of Documents relating to the Digger Movement, ed. George H. Sabine, Ithaca, NY: Cornell University Press, 1941.

Winzet, Ninian, *Certain Tractates Together With The Book of Four Score Three Questions*, ed. J. K. Hewison, 2 vols., Scottish Text Society, Edinburgh and London: William Blackwood, 1888, 1890.

Wit and Drollery, Joviall Poems, London: for N. Brook, 1661.

Wither, George, *The British Appeals*, London: for the author, to be sold by N. Brook, 1651.

Campo-Musae, or the field-musings of Captain George Wither, London: R. Austin and A. Coe, 1643.

Fair-virtue, the Mistresse of Philarete, London: [A. Mathewes] for J. Grismand, 1622.

Fides-Anglicana, London, 1660.

Haleluiah, or Britans Second Remembrancer, London: I. L. for A. Hebb, 1641. Facs. edn printed for the Spenser Society, Manchester: C. E. Simms, 1879.

The Hymnes and Songs of the Church, London: [J. Bill] for G. W[ither], 1623. 9th edn, 1623.

Miscellaneous Works, 6 vols., printed for the Spenser Society, Manchester: C. E. Simms, 1872-8.

Prosopopoeia Britannica: Britans genius, London: R. Austin, 1648.

Vox Pacifica, London: R. Austin, 1645.

Woodhouse, A. S. P. (ed.), *Puritanism and Liberty: Being the Army Debates (1647-9) from the Clarke Manuscripts*, 3rd edn, London: Dent, 1986.

Woolley, H[annah], *The Gentlewomans Companion*, London: A. Maxwell for D. Newman, 1673. 2nd edn, 1675. 3rd edn, 1682.

Woudhuysen, H. R. (ed.), *The Penguin Book of Renaissance Verse*, sel. and intro. David Norbrook, Harmondsworth: Penguin, 1993.

[Wright, Abraham], *Parnassus Biceps or Several Choice Pieces of Poetry*, London: for George Eversden, 1656. Mod edn, ed. G. Thorn Drury, London: Etchells & Macdonald, 1927.

Wriothesley, Charles, *A Chronicle of England During the Reign of the Tudors, from AD 1485-1559*, ed. William Douglas Hamilton, 2 vols., new ser. 11, London: Camden Society, 1875.

Wroth, Mary, *The Countesse of Mountgomeries Urania* (The First Part), London: for J. Marriot and J. Grismand, 1621. Mod. edn, *The First Part of the Countess of Montgomery's Urania*, ed. Josephine A. Roberts, Binghamton, NY: Medieval and Renaissance Texts and Studies, 1995.

'Love's Victory', Penshurst MS. Mod. edn, *Lady Mary Wroth's Love's Victory: The Penshurst Manuscript*, ed. Michael J. Brennan, London: Roxburghe Club, 1988.

The Poems of Lady Mary Wroth, ed. Josephine A. Roberts, Baton Rouge: Louisiana State University Press, 1982.

The Second Part of the Countess of Montgomery's Urania (Newberry Library, Case MS f Y 1565.
    W95), ed. Josephine A. Roberts, completed by Suzanne Gossett and Janel Mueller,
    Tempe, AZ: RETS and Arizona Center for Medieval and Renaissance Studies, 1999.
Wyatt, Sir Thomas, *The Complete Poems of Sir Thomas Wyatt*, ed. R. A. Rebholz, London and
    New Haven, CT: Yale University Press, 1975. Rpt, Harmondsworth and New York:
    Penguin, 1978.
    The Poetry of Sir Thomas Wyatt, ed. Kenneth Muir and Patricia Thomson, University of
    Liverpool Press, 1969.
Wycherley, William, *Love in a Wood, or St James's Park*, London: for H. Herringman, 1672.
Xenophon, *Xenophons treatise of house holde*, trans. G. Heruet, London: Thomas Berthelet,
    1532.

Secondary sources

Achinstein, Sharon, 'Audiences and Authors: Ballads and the Making of English Renaissance
    Literary Culture', *Journal of Medieval and Renaissance Studies*, 22 (1992), 311–26.
    Milton and the Revolutionary Reader, Princeton University Press, 1994.
    'Plagues and Publication: Ballads and the Representation of Disease in the English
    Renaissance', *Criticism*, 24.1 (1992), 27–49.
Aitken, Adam, McDiarmid, Matthew and Thomason, Derick (eds.), *Bards and Makars: Scottish
    Language and Literature: Medieval and Renaissance*, University of Glasgow Press, 1977.
Agnew, Jean-Christophe, *Worlds Apart: The Market and the Theater in Anglo-American Thought,
    1550–1750*, Cambridge University Press, 1986.
Allen, C. G., 'The Sources of Lily's Grammar: A Review of the Facts and Some Further
    Suggestions', *The Library*, 5th ser., 9 (1954), 85–100.
Allison, A. F. and Rogers, D. M., *The Contemporary Printed Literature of the English
    Counter-Reformation between 1558 and 1640*, 2 vols.: Vol. 1, *Works in Languages Other than
    English*. Aldershot: Scolar Press, 1989; Vol. 2, *Works in English, with Addenda and
    Corrigenda to Volume I*, Aldershot: Scolar Press, 1994.
Amos, Flora Ross, *Early Theories of Translation*, New York: Columbia University Press, 1920.
Amussen, Susan D., *An Ordered Society: Gender and Class in Early Modern England*, Oxford
    University Press, 1988.
Amussen, Susan D. and Kishlansky, Mark A. (eds.), *Political Culture and Cultural Politics in Early
    Modern England: Essays Presented to David Underdown*, Manchester University Press, 1995.
Anderson, Benedict, *Imagined Communities: Reflections on the Origin and Spread of Nationalism*,
    rev. edn, New York: Verso, 1991.
Anderson, D. K. (ed.), *'Concord in Discord': The Plays of John Ford, 1586–1986*, New York:
    AMS Press, 1986.
Andrews, K. R., Canny, N. P. and Hair, P. E. H., *The Westward Enterprise: English Activities in
    Ireland, the Atlantic and America, 1480–1650*, Liverpool University Press, 1978.
Anglo, Sydney, *Images of Tudor Kingship*, London: Seaby, 1992.
    Spectacle, Pageantry, and Early Tudor Policy, Oxford University Press, 1969.
Anglo, Sydney (ed.), *The Damned Art: Essays in the Literature of Witchcraft*, London: Routledge,
    1977.

Arber, Edward (ed.), *A Transcript of the Registers of the Company of Stationers of London, 1554–1640 AD*, 5 vols., London and Birmingham: privately printed, 1875–94. Rpt, New York: Peter Smith, 1950.

Archer, Ian, 'John Stow's *Survey of London*: The Nostalgia of John Stow', in Smith, Strier and Bevington (eds.), *The Theatrical City: Culture, Theatre and Politics in London, 1576–1649*, pp. 17–34.

Armitage, David, 'The Cromwellian Protectorate and the Languages of Empire', *Historical Journal*, 35 (1992), 531–55.

'John Milton: Poet Against Empire', in Armitage, Himy and Skinner, (eds.), *Milton and Republicanism*, pp. 206–25.

Armitage, David, Himy, Armond and Skinner, Quentin (eds.), *Milton and Republicanism*, Cambridge University Press, 1995.

Armstrong, Elizabeth, *Before Copyright: The French Book-Privilege System, 1498–1526*, Cambridge University Press, 1990.

'English Purchases of Printed Books from the Continent 1465–1526', *English Historical Review*, 94 (1979), 268–90.

Aston, Margaret, *England's Iconoclasts, Vol. 1, Laws Against Images*, Oxford University Press, 1988.

Faith and Fire: Popular and Unpopular Religion 1350–1600, London: Hambledon Press, 1993.

Lollards and Reformers: Images and Literacy in Late Medieval Religion, London: Hambledon Press, 1984.

Attridge, Derek, *Well-weighed Syllables: Elizabethan Verse in Classical Metres*, Cambridge University Press, 1974.

Axton, Marie, *The Queen's Two Bodies: Drama and the Elizabethan Succession*, London: Royal Historical Society, 1977.

Aylmer, G. E., *Rebellion or Revolution? England, 1640–1660*, Oxford University Press, 1986.

Bailey, Richard W., 'The Conquests of English', in Sidney Greenbaum (ed.), *The English Language Today*, New York: Pergamon, 1985, pp. 9–19.

Baker, David J., *Between Nations: Shakespeare, Spenser, Marvell and the Question of Britain*, Stanford University Press, 1997.

Baker, David J. and Maley, Willy (eds.), *British Identities and English Renaissance Literature*, Cambridge University Press, 2002.

Bald, R. C., *John Donne: A Life*, Oxford University Press, 1970.

Baldi, Sergio, 'The Secretary of the Duke of Norfolk and the First Italian Grammar in England', in Siegfried Korninger (ed.), *Studies in English Language and Literature Presented to Dr Karl Brunner on the Occasion of his Seventieth Birthday*, Vienna: W. Braunmüller, 1957, pp. 1–27.

Barash, Carol, *English Women's Poetry, 1649–1714: Politics, Community, and Linguistic Authority*, Oxford: Clarendon Press, 1996.

Barish, Jonas, *The Antitheatrical Prejudice*, Berkeley: University of California Press, 1981.

Barroll, Leeds, 'A New History for Shakespeare and his Time', *Shakespeare Quarterly*, 39 (1988), 441–64.

Barry, Jonathan and Brooks, Christopher (eds.), *The Middling Sort of People: Culture, Society and Politics in England, 1550–1800*, Houndmills and London: Macmillan, 1994.

Barton, Anne, *Ben Jonson, Dramatist*, Cambridge University Press, 1984.

Bates, Catherine, *The Rhetoric of Courtship in Elizabethan Language and Literature*, Cambridge University Press, 1992.

Baugh, Albert C. and Cable, Thomas, *A History of the English Language*, 4th edn, London: Routledge, 1993.

Bawcutt, Nigel, *The Control and Censorship of Caroline Drama*, Oxford University Press, 1996.

Beal, Peter, *In Praise of Scribes: Manuscripts and Their Makers in Seventeenth-Century England*, Oxford: Clarendon Press, 1998.

  Index of English Literary Manuscripts, Vol. 1: 1450–1625 (2 parts); *Vol. 2 [Part 1]: 1625–1700*, London: Mansell and New York: Bowker, 1980–93.

Beddard, R. A., 'A Traitor's Gift: Hugh Peter's Donation to the Bodleian Library', *Bodleian Library Record*, 16 (April 1999), 374–91.

Bedouelle, Guy, and Le Gal, Patrick (eds.), *Le 'Divorce' du Roi Henry VIII; études et documents*, Travaux d'Humanisme et Renaissance, 221, Geneva: Droz, 1987.

Beer, B. L., *Northumberland: The Political Career of John Dudley, Earl of Warwick and Duke of Northumberland*, Kent State University Press, 1973.

  'Engine of Manufacture: The Trades of London', in Beier and Finlay (eds.), *London 1500–1700*, pp. 141–67.

Beier, A. L. and Finlay, Roger, 'The Significance of the Metropolis', in Beier and Finlay (eds.), *London 1500–1700*, pp. 1–33.

Beier, A. L. and Finlay, Roger (eds.), *London 1500–1700: The Making of the Metropolis*, London and New York: Longman, 1986.

Beier, A. L., *et al.* (eds.), *The First Modern Society*, Cambridge University Press, 1989.

Beilin, Elaine, *Redeeming Eve: Women Writers of the English Renaissance*, Princeton University Press, 1997.

Bell, Michael and Barnard, J., 'Provisional Count of STC Titles 1475–1640', *Publishing History*, 31 (1992), 48–64.

  'Provisional Count of Wing Titles 1641–1700', *Publishing History*, 55 (1998), 89–97.

Bellany, Alastair, ' "Rayling Rymes and Vaunting Verse": Libellous Politics in Early Stuart England, 1603–1628', in Sharpe and Lake (eds.), *Culture and Politics in Early Stuart England*, pp. 285–310.

Belsey, Catherine, *The Subject of Tragedy: Identity and Difference in Renaissance Drama*, London: Routledge, 1985.

Bennett, H. S., *English Books and Readers 1475–1557*, 2nd ed, Cambridge University Press, 1969.

  English Books and Readers 1558–1603, Cambridge University Press, 1965.

  English Books and Readers 1603–1640, Cambridge University Press, 1970.

Bennett, Joan, *Five Metaphysical Poets*, rev. edn, Cambridge University Press, 1964.

Bentley, Gerald E., *The Jacobean and Caroline Stage*, 7 vols., Oxford: Clarendon Press, 1941–68.

  The Profession of Dramatist in Shakespeare's Time, Princeton University Press, 1971.

  The Profession of Player in Shakespeare's Time, Princeton University Press, 1984.

Bercovitch, Sacvan and Patell, Cyrus R. K. (eds.), *The Cambridge History of American Literature: Volume 1 (1590–1820)*, Cambridge University Press, 1994.

Berdan, John M., *Early Tudor Poetry 1485–1574*, New York: Macmillan, 1920.

Berger, Jr, Harry, *Second World and Green World: Studies in Renaissance Fiction-Making*, Berkeley: University of California Press, 1988.

Bergeron, David M., *English Civic Pageantry, 1558–1642*, London: Edward Arnold, 1971.

'Harrison, Jonson and Dekker: The Magnificent Entertainment for King James', *Journal of the Warburg and Courtauld Institutes*, 31 (1968), 445–8.

Berlin, Michael, 'Civic Ceremony in Early Modern London', *Urban History Yearbook* (1986), 15–27.

Berry, Philippa, *Of Chastity and Power: Elizabethan Literature and the Unmarried Queen*, London: Routledge, 1989.

Bevington, David, *Action is Eloquence: Shakespeare's Language of Gesture*, Cambridge, MA: Harvard University Press, 1984.

From 'Mankind' to Marlowe: Growth of Structure in the Popular Drama of Tudor England, Cambridge, MA: Harvard University Press, 1962.

'Lyly's *Endymion* and *Midas*: The Catholic Question in England', *Comparative Drama*, 32 (1998), 26–46.

'Popular and Courtly Traditions on the Early Tudor Stage', in Neville Denny (ed.), *Medieval Drama*, Stratford-upon-Avon Studies, 16, London: Edward Arnold, 1973, pp. 91–107.

Tudor Drama and Politics: A Critical Approach to Topical Meaning, Cambridge, MA: Harvard University Press, 1968.

Bevington, David and Holbrook, Peter, *The Politics of the Stuart Court Masque*, Cambridge University Press, 1998.

Biester, James, *Lyric Wonder: Rhetoric and Wit in English Renaissance Poetry*, Ithaca, NY: Cornell University Press, 1997.

Binns, J. W., *Intellectual Culture in Elizabethan and Jacobean England: The Latin Writings of the Age*, Leeds: Francis Cairns, 1990.

Birrell, T. A., *English Monarchs and Their Books: From Henry II to Charles II*, The Panizzi Lectures, 1986, London: The British Library, 1987.

Blagden, Cyprian, *The Stationers' Company: A History, 1403–1959*, London: Allen & Unwin, 1960.

Blake, N. F., 'Lord Berners: A Survey', *Medievalia et Humanistica*, n.s., 2 (1971), 118–30.

'Wynken de Worde: The Early Years', *Gutenberg Jahrbuch*, 46 (1971), 62–6.

'Wynken de Worde: The Later Years', *Gutenberg Jahrbuch*, 47 (1972), 128–38.

Bland, Mark, 'The London Book-Trade in 1600', in David Scott Kastan (ed.), *A Companion to Shakespeare*, Oxford: Blackwell, 1999, pp. 450–63.

Blank, Paula, *Broken English: Dialects and the Politics of Language in Renaissance Writings*, London: Routledge, 1996.

Blayney, Peter W. M., 'The Publication of Playbooks', in John D. Cox and David Scott Kastan (eds.), *A New History of Early English Drama*, New York: Columbia University Press, 1997, pp. 383–422.

Bolgar, R. R., *The Classical Heritage and its Beneficiaries*, Cambridge University Press, 1954.

Bolgar, R. R. (ed.), *Classical Influences on European Culture AD 1500–1700*, Cambridge University Press, 1976.

Boulton, Jeremy, *Neighbourhood and Society: A London Suburb in the Seventeenth Century*, Cambridge University Press, 1987.

Bouwsma, William J., *The Waning of the Renaissance, 1550–1640*, New Haven, CT: Yale University Press, 2000.

Bowden, Caroline, ' "For the Glory of God": A Study of the Education of English Catholic Women in Convents in Flanders and France in the First Half of the Seventeenth Century', *Paedagogica Historica*, Supplementary Series, 5, University of Ghent: Centre for the Study of Historical Pedagogy, 1999.

Bradbrook, Muriel C., *English Dramatic Form: A History of its Development*, Oxford University Press, 1965.

John Webster: Citizen and Dramatist, London: Weidenfeld and Nicolson, 1980.

The Living Monument: Shakespeare and the Theatre of his Time, Cambridge University Press, 1976.

Braden, Gordon, *The Classics and English Renaissance Poetry*, New Haven, CT, and London: Yale University Press, 1978.

Bradshaw, Brendan, *The Irish Constitutional Revolution of the Sixteenth Century*, Cambridge University Press, 1979.

Bradshaw, Brendan and Morrill, John (eds.), *The British Problem, c. 1534–1707*, Basingstoke: Macmillan, 1996.

Bradshaw, Brendan and Roberts, Peter (eds.), *British Consciousness and Identity. The Making of Britain, 1534–1707*, Cambridge University Press, 1998.

Brady, Ciaran, 'Spenser's Irish Crisis: Humanism and Experience in the 1590s', *Past and Present*, 111 (1986), 17–49.

Braunmuller, A. R. and Hattaway, Michael (eds.), *The Cambridge Companion to Renaissance Drama*, Cambridge University Press, 1990.

Brennan, Michael, *Literary Patronage in the English Renaissance: The Pembroke Family*, London: Routledge, 1988.

Brenner, Robert, *Merchants and Revolution: Commercial Change, Political Conflict, and London's Overseas Traders, 1550–1653*, Princeton University Press, 1993.

Brigden, S. E., 'Youth and the English Reformation', *Past & Present*, 95 (1982), 37–67.

Brigden, Susan, 'Henry Howard, Earl of Surrey, and the "Conjured League" ', *Historical Journal*, 37.3 (1994), 507–37.

London and the Reformation, Oxford: Clarendon Press, 1989.

New Worlds, Lost Worlds: The Rule of the Tudors, New York: Viking, 2001.

' "The Shadow That You Know": Sir Thomas Wyatt and Sir Francis Bryan at Court and in Embassy', *Historical Journal*, 39.1 (1996), 1–31.

Briggs, Katherine, *A Dictionary of English Folk Tales*, 2 vols., London: Routledge, 1970–1.

Brooks, Douglas A., *From Playhouse to Printing House: Drama and Authorship in Early Modern England*, Cambridge University Press, 2000.

Brown, Cedric C., *Milton's Aristocratic Entertainments*, Cambridge University Press, 1985.

Brown, Cedric C. (ed.), *Patronage, Politics and Literary Traditions in England, 1558–1658*, Detroit: Wayne State University Press, 1993.

Brown, Nancy Pollard, 'Paperchase: The Dissemination of Catholic Texts in Elizabethan England', in Peter Beal and Jeremy Griffiths (eds.), *English Manuscript Studies 1100–1700*, Vol. 1. Oxford: Blackwell, 1989, pp. 120–43.

Bruster, Douglas, *Drama and the Market in the Age of Shakespeare*, Cambridge University
  Press, 1992.

Bryant, James C., *Tudor Drama and Religious Controversy*, Macon, GA: Mercer University
  Press, 1984.

Burckhardt, Jacob, *The Civilization of the Renaissance in Italy*, trans. S. G. C. Middlemore,
  Harmondsworth: Penguin, 1990.

Burgess, Glenn, 'Was the English Civil War a War of Religion?: The Evidence of Political
  Propaganda', *Huntington Library Quarterly*, 61.2 (2000), 173–201.

Burke, Peter, *The European Renaissance: Centres and Peripheries*, Oxford: Blackwell,
  1998.

Burnett, Mark Thornton, *Masters and Servants in English Renaissance Drama and Culture:
  Authority and Obedience*, Basingstoke: Macmillan, 1997.

Bush, Douglas, *English Literature in the Earlier Seventeenth Century, 1600–1660*, 2nd edn,
  Oxford and New York: Oxford University Press, 1962.

Bush, M. L., *The Government Policy of Protector Somerset*, London: Edward Arnold, 1975.
  The Pilgrimage of Grace, Manchester University Press, 1996.

Bushnell, Rebecca W., *Tragedies of Tyrants: Political Thought and Theater in the English
  Renaissance*, Ithaca, NY: Cornell University Press, 1990.

Butler, Martin, 'The Invention of Britain and the Early Stuart Masque', in R. M. Smuts (ed.),
  The Stuart Court and Europe: Essays in Politics and Political Culture, Cambridge University
  Press, 1996, pp. 65–85.
  Theatre and Crisis, 1632–1642, Cambridge University Press, 1984.

Butler, Martin (ed.), *Re-Presenting Ben Jonson: Text, History, Performance*, Basingstoke:
  Macmillan, 1999.

Butterworth, Charles C., *The English Primers, 1529–1545*, Philadelphia: University of
  Pennsylvania Press, 1953.
  The Literary Lineage of the King James Bible, 1340–1611, Philadelphia: University of
  Pennsylvania Press, 1941.

Buxton, John, *Sir Philip Sidney and the English Renaissance*, London: Macmillan, 1954.

Cain, Piers, 'Robert Smith and the Reform of the Archives of the City of London,
  1580–1623', *London Journal*, 13.1 (1987–8), 3–16.

Callaghan, Dympna, *Women and Gender in Renaissance Tragedy*, Hemel Hempstead:
  Harvester, 1989.

Camille, Michael, *Image on the Edge: The Margins of Medieval Art*, Cambridge, MA: Harvard
  University Press, 1992.

Campbell, Lorne, *Renaissance Portraits: European Portrait-Painting in the 14th, 15th, and 16th
  Centuries*, London and New Haven, CT: Yale University Press, 1990.

Cannon, James P. D., 'The Poetry and Polemic of English Church Worship c. 1617–1640',
  unpublished Ph. D. thesis, University of Cambridge, 1998.

Canny, Nicholas, *The Elizabethan Conquest of Ireland: A Pattern Established, 1565–76*, Sussex:
  Harvester Press, 1976.
  'The Origins of Empire: An Introduction', in Canny and Low (eds.), *The Oxford History of
  the British Empire. Volume 1. The Origins of Empire*, pp. 1–33.
  'Rowland White's "Discors touching Ireland"', c. 1569', *Irish Historical Studies*, 20
  (1976–7), 439–63.

'Rowland White's "The disorders of the Irisshrey"', 1571', *Studia Hibernica*, 19 (1979), 147–60.

Canny, Nicholas, and Low, Alaine (eds.), *The Oxford History of the British Empire. Volume 1. The Origins of Empire. British Overseas Enterprise to the Close of the Seventeenth Century*, Oxford University Press, 1998.

Capp, Bernard, *English Almanacs, 1500–1800: Astrology and the Popular Press*, London: Faber, 1979.

Capp, B. S., *The Fifth Monarchy Men: A Study in Seventeenth-Century English Millenarianism*, London: Faber and Faber, 1972.

Carey, John, *John Donne: Life, Mind and Art*, new edn, London: Faber and Faber, 1990.

Carlson, David R., *English Humanist Books: Writers and Patrons, Manuscript and Print, 1475–1525*, University of Toronto Press, 1993.

Carlson, Leland H., *Martin Marprelate, Gentleman: Master Job Throkmorton Laid Open in his Colors*, San Marino, CA: The Huntington Library, 1981.

Cave, Terence, *The Cornucopian Text: Problems of Writing in the French Renaissance*, Oxford: Clarendon Press, 1979.

Chakravorty, Swapan, *Society and Politics in the Plays of Thomas Middleton*, Oxford University Press, 1995.

Chambers, E. K., *The Elizabethan Stage*, 4 vols., Oxford: Clarendon Press, 1923.

Charlton, Kenneth, *Education in Renaissance England*, London: Routledge and Kegan Paul, 1965.

' "False Fonde Bookes, Ballades and Rimes": An Aspect of Informal Education in Early Modern England', *History of Education Quarterly*, 27 (1987), 449–71.

Women, Religion and Education in Early Modern England, London: Routledge, 1999.

Chartier, Roger, *The Order of Books*, trans. Lydia G. Cochrane, Stanford University Press, 1992.

Chernaik, Warren L., *The Poet's Time: Politics and Religion in the Work of Andrew Marvell*, Cambridge University Press, 1983.

Chernaik, Warren and Dzelzainis, Martin (eds.), *Marvell and Liberty*, London: Macmillan, 1999.

Chester, Allan G., *Hugh Latimer: Apostle to the English*, Philadelphia: University of Pennsylvania Press, 1954.

'The "New Learning": A Semantic Note', *Studies in the Renaissance*, 2 (1955), 139–47.

Christianson, Paul, *Discourse on History, Law, and Governance in the Public Career of John Selden, 1610–1635*, University of Toronto Press, 1996.

Reformers and Babylon: Apocalyptic Visions in England from the Reformation to the Outbreak of the Civil War, University of Toronto Press, 1978.

Clair, Colin, *A History of Printing in Britain*, New York: Oxford University Press, 1966.

Clancy, Thomas H., *Papist Pamphleteers: The Allen–Parsons Party and the Political Thought of the Counter-Reformation in England, 1572–1615*, University of Chicago Press, 1974. 2nd ed, 1996.

Clare, Janet, *'Art Made Tongue-Tied by Authority': Elizabethan and Jacobean Dramatic Censorship*, Manchester University Press, 1991.

Clark, Ira, *Professional Playwrights: Massinger, Ford, Shirley and Brome*, Lexington: University Press of Kentucky, 1992.

Clark, Sandra, *The Elizabethan Pamphleteers: Popular Moralistic Pamphlets, 1580–1640*, Rutherford, NJ: Fairleigh Dickinson University Press, 1985.

The Plays of Beaumont and Fletcher, Hemel Hempstead: Harvester Wheatsheaf, 1994.

Clark, Stuart, *Thinking With Demons: The Idea of Witchcraft in Early Modern Europe*, Oxford: Clarendon Press, 1997.

Clarke, Aidan, 'Colonial Identity in Early Seventeenth-century Ireland', in T. W. Moody (ed.), *Nationality and the Pursuit of National Independence*, Belfast: Appletree Press, 1978; Vol. 11 of *Historical Studies. Papers Read Before the Irish Conference of Historians*, pp. 57–71.

The Old English in Ireland 1625–42, Ithaca, NY: Cornell University Press, 1966.

Clarke, M. L., *Classical Education in Great Britain 1500–1900*, Cambridge University Press, 1959.

Clarke, P., 'The Ownership of Books in England 1540–1640. The Example of Some Kentish Townsfolk', in Lawrence Stone (ed.), *Schooling and Society. Studies in the History of Education*, Baltimore MD: Johns Hopkins University Press, 1976, pp. 95–111.

Clebsch, W. A., *England's Earliest Protestants, 1520–35*, New Haven, CT: Yale University Press, 1964.

Clegg, Cyndia Susan, *Press Censorship in Elizabethan England*, Cambridge University Press, 1997.

Clement, Wolfgang, *English Tragedy Before Shakespeare: The Development of Dramatic Speech*, trans. T. S. Dorsch, New York: Barnes and Noble, 1961.

Coffey, John, *Persecution and Toleration in Protestant England, 1558–1689*, Harlow: Longman, 2000.

Politics, Religion and the British Revolutions: The Mind of Samuel Rutherford, Cambridge University Press, 1997.

Cogswell, Thomas, *The Blessed Revolution: English Politics and the Coming of War, 1621–1624*, Cambridge University Press, 1989.

'Thomas Middleton and the Court, 1624: *A Game at Chess* in Context', *Huntington Library Quarterly*, 47 (1984), 273–88.

'Underground Verse and the Transformation of Early Stuart Political Culture', in Amussen and Kishlansky (eds.), *Political Culture and Cultural Politics in Early Modern England*, pp. 277–300.

Cohen, Walter, *Drama of a Nation: Public Theatre in Renaissance England and Spain*, Ithaca, NY: Cornell University Press, 1985.

Cohn, Norman, *The Pursuit of the Millennium*, 1957, rev. edn, New York: Oxford University Press, 1970.

Coiro, Ann Baynes, *Robert Herrick's 'Hesperides' and the Epigram Book Tradition*, Baltimore, MD, and London: Johns Hopkins University Press, 1988.

Coleman, D. C., *The British Paper Industry, 1495–1860: A Study in Industrial Growth*, Oxford University Press, 1958.

Colie, Rosalie, *'My Ecchoing Song': Andrew Marvell's Poetry of Criticism*, Princeton University Press, 1970.

Colley, Linda, *Britons: Forging the Nation, 1707–1837*, New Haven, CT: Yale University Press, 1992.

Collinson, Patrick, *Archbishop Grindal, 1519–1583: The Struggle for a Reformed Church*, Berkeley: University of California Press, 1979.

The Birthpangs of Protestant England: Religious and Cultural Change in the Sixteenth and Seventeenth Centuries, Basingstoke: Macmillan, and New York: St Martin's, 1988.

'Ecclesiastical Vitriol: Religious Satire in the 1590s and the Invention of Puritanism', in Guy (ed.), *The Reign of Elizabeth I*, pp. 150–70.

The Elizabethan Puritan Movement, London: Jonathan Cape, and Berkeley: University of California Press, 1967; Oxford University Press, 1990.

From Iconoclasm to Iconophobia: The Cultural Impact of the Second English Reformation, University of Reading, 1986.

Godly People: Essays on English Protestantism and Puritanism, London: Hambledon Press, 1983.

The Religion of Protestants: The Church in English Society, 1559–1625, Oxford: Clarendon Press, 1982.

Collinson, Patrick, Hunt, Arnold and Walsham, Alexandra, 'Religious Publishing in England 1557–1640', ch. 2 in John Barnard and D. F. McKenzie (eds.), *The History of the Book in Britain*, Vol. 4, Cambridge University Press, 2002.

Colvin, Howard M. (ed.), *The History of the King's Works, 1485–1660*, 3 vols., London: HM Stationery Office, 1975.

Como, David R., 'Puritans and Heretics: The Emergence of an Antinomian Underground in Early Stuart England', unpublished Ph.D. thesis, Princeton University, 1999.

Condren, Conal and Cousins, A. D. (eds.), *The Political Identity of Andrew Marvell*, Aldershot: Scolar Press, 1990.

Cook, Ann Jennalie, *The Privileged Playgoers of Shakespeare's London*, 1576–1642, Princeton University Press, 1981.

Cope, Esther S., *Handmaid of the Holy Spirit: Dame Eleanor Davies, Never Soe Mad a Ladie*, Ann Arbor: University of Michigan Press, 1992.

Corns, Thomas N., *Milton's Language*, Oxford and Cambridge, MA: Basil Blackwell, 1990.

Regaining 'Paradise Lost', London and New York: Longman, 1994.

Uncloistered Virtue: English Political Literature, 1640–1660, Oxford: Clarendon Press, 1992.

Corns, Thomas N., (ed.), *The Royal Image: Representations of Charles I*, Cambridge University Press, 1999.

Corns, Thomas N. and Loewenstein, David (eds.), *The Emergence of Quaker Writing: Dissenting Literature in Seventeenth-Century England*, London: Frank Cass, 1995.

Corthell, Ronald, 'Beginning as a Satirist: Joseph Hall's *Virgidemiarum Sixe Bookes*', *Studies in English Literature, 1500–1900*, 23 (1983), 47–60.

Cox, John D. and Kastan, David S. (eds.), *A New History of Early English Drama*, New York: Columbia University Press, 1997.

Crane, D., 'English Translations of the *Imitatio Christi* in the Sixteenth and Seventeenth Centuries', *Recusant History*, 13 (1975), 79–100.

Crawford, Patricia, *Women and Religion in England, 1500–1720*, London and New York: Routledge, 1993.

Cressy, David, *Birth, Marriage and Death: Ritual, Religion, and the Life-Cycle in Tudor and Stuart England*, Oxford University Press, 1997.

'Educational Opportunity in Tudor and Stuart England', *History of Education Quarterly*, 16 (1976), 301–20.

Literacy and the Social Order: Reading and Writing in Tudor and Stuart England, Cambridge University Press, 1980.

Crewe, Jonathan V., *Trials of Authorship: Anterior Forms and Poetic Reconstruction from Wyatt to Shakespeare*, Berkeley: University of California Press, 1990.

Croft, Pauline, 'The Reputation of Robert Cecil: Libels, Political Opinion and Popular Awareness in the Early Seventeenth Century', *Transactions of the Royal Historical Society*, 6th ser., 1 (1991), 43–69.

Cross, Claire, 'The Church in England, 1646–1660', in G. E. Aylmer (ed.), *The Interregnum: The Quest for Settlement, 1646–1660*, London, Macmillan, 1972, pp. 99–120.

Cummings, R. M., *Spenser: The Critical Heritage*, New York: Barnes and Noble, 1971.

Cust, Richard and Hughes, Ann (eds.), *Conflict in Early Stuart England: Studies in Religion and Politics, 1603–1642*, London: Longman, 1989.

Daiches, David, *Literature and Gentility in Scotland*, Edinburgh University Press, 1982.

Daniellson, B., *John Hart's Works on English Orthography and Pronunciation*, Stockholm Studies in English, 5, Stockholm: Almqvist, 1955.

Davies, Horton, *Worship and Theology in England, Vol. II: From Andrewes to Baxter and Fox, 1603–1690*, Princeton University Press, 1975.

Davies, Julian, *The Caroline Captivity of the Church*, Oxford: Clarendon Press, 1992.

Davies, Stevie, *Unbridled Spirits: Women of the English Revolution, 1640–1660*, London: The Women's Press, 1998.

Davis, J. C., *Fear, Myth and History: The Ranters and the Historians*, Cambridge University Press, 1986.

'Oliver Cromwell's Religion', in John Morrill (ed.), *Oliver Cromwell and the English Revolution*, Harlow: Longman, 1990, pp. 181–208.

'Religion and the Struggle for Freedom in the English Revolution', *Historical Journal*, 35 (1992), 507–30.

Utopia and the Ideal State: A Study of English Utopian Writings 1516–1700, Cambridge University Press, 1981.

Davis, Lennard J., *Factual Fictions: The Origins of the English Novel*, Philadelphia: University of Pennsylvania Press, 1997.

Dawson, Jane, 'Anglo-Scottish Protestant Culture and Integration in Sixteenth-Century Britain', in Steven G. Ellis and Sarah Barber (eds.), *Conquest and Union: Fashioning a British State, 1485–1725*, London: Longman, 1995, pp. 87–114.

Dickens, A. G., *The English Reformation*, New York: Schocken Books, 1964.

Late Monasticism and the Reformation, London: Hambledon Press, 1994.

Dickins, B., 'Henry Gostling's Library: A Young Don's Books in 1674', *Transactions of Cambridge Bibliographical Society*, 3 (1961), 216–24.

Diehl, Huston, *Staging Reform, Reforming the Stage: Protestantism and Popular Theater in Early Modern England*, Ithaca, NY: Cornell University Press, 1997.

DiGangi, Mario, *The Homoerotics of Early Modern Drama*, Cambridge University Press, 1997.

Dillon, Janette, *Language and Stage in Medieval and Renaissance England*, Cambridge University Press, 1998.

Theatre, Court and City, 1595–1610: Drama and Social Space in London, Cambridge University Press, 2000.

Dobranski, Stephen B., *Milton, Authorship, and the Book Trade*, Cambridge University Press, 1999.

Dobranski, Stephen B. and Rumrich, John (eds.), *Milton and Heresy*, Cambridge University Press, 1998.

Dolan, Frances, *Dangerous Familiars: Representations of Domestic Crime in England, 1550–1700*, Ithaca, NY: Cornell University Press, 1994.

Dollimore, Jonathan, *Radical Tragedy: Religion, Ideology and Power in the Drama of Shakespeare and His Contemporaries*, Brighton: Harvester Press, 1984. 2nd edn, University of Chicago Press, 1989.

Dollimore, Jonathan and Sinfield, Alan, 'History and Ideology: The Instance of *Henry V* ', in John Drakakis (ed.), *Alternative Shakespeares*, London: Methuen, 1985, pp. 206–27.

Donaldson, Ian, *Jonson's Magic Houses*, Oxford: Clarendon Press, 1997.

Doody, Margaret Anne, *The Daring Muse: Augustan Poetry Reconsidered*, Cambridge University Press, 1985.

Dorian, Nancy C., *Language Death: The Life Cycle of a Scottish Gaelic Dialect*, University of Pennsylvania Press, 1984.

Dowling, Maria, *Humanism in the Age of Henry VIII*, London: Croom Helm Ltd, 1986.

Dubrow, Heather, *A Happier Eden: The Politics of Marriage in the Stuart Epithalamium*, Ithaca, NY: Cornell University Press, 1990.

Dubrow, Heather and Strier, Richard (eds.), *The Historical Renaissance: New Essays on Tudor and Stuart Literature and Culture*, University of Chicago Press, 1988.

Duff, E. Gordon, *A Century of the English Book Trade*, London: The Bibliographical Society, 1905.

Duffy, Eamon, 'The Godly and the Multitude in Stuart England', *The Seventeenth Century*, 1 (1986), 31–55.

    The Stripping of the Altars: Traditional Religion in England, 1400–1580, New Haven, CT, and London: Yale University Press, 1992.

Durston, Christopher, and Eales, Jacqueline (eds.), *The Culture of English Puritanism, 1560–1700*, Basingstoke: Macmillan, 1996.

Dutton, Richard, *Mastering the Revels: The Regulation and Censorship of English Renaissance Drama*, London: Macmillan 1991.

Dutton, Richard and Wilson, Richard (eds.), *New Historicism and Renaissance Drama*, Harlow: Longman, 1992.

Earle, Peter, 'The Middling Sort in London', in Barry and Brooks (eds.), *The Middling Sort of People*, Houndmills and London: Macmillan, 1994, pp. 141–58.

Easthope, Anthony, 'Problematizing the Pentametre', *New Literary History*, 12.3 (Spring 1981), 481–5.

Ebling, Gerhard, *Luther*, trans. R. A. Wilson, Philadelphia: Fortress Press, 1970.

Eddington, Carol, *Court and Culture in Renaissance Scotland: Sir David Lindsay of the Mount*, Amherst: University of Massachusetts Press, 1994.

Edmond, Mary, *Rare Sir William Davenant*, Manchester University Press, 1987.

Eisenstein, Elizabeth L., *The Printing Press as an Agent of Change: Communications and Cultural Transformations in Early Modern Europe*, 2 vols., Cambridge University Press, 1979.

Ellis, Steven G., *Tudor Ireland: Crown, Community and the Conflict of Cultures, 1470–1603*, London: Longman, 1985.

Elton, G. R., *England Under the Tudors*, London: Methuen, 1955.

Policy and Police: The Enforcement of the Reformation in the Age of Thomas Cromwell, Cambridge University Press, 1959, 1972.

Reform and Reformation: England 1509–1558, Cambridge, MA: Harvard University Press, 1977.

Reform and Renewal: Thomas Cromwell and the Commonweal, Cambridge University Press, 1973.

Studies in Tudor and Stuart Politics: Papers and Reviews, 1946–1972, 3 vols., Cambridge University Press, 1974.

The Tudor Constitution, 2nd edn, Cambridge University Press, 1982.

Empson, William, *Some Versions of Pastoral*, London: Chatto & Windus, 1935.

Erickson, Amy Louise, *Women and Property in Early Modern England*, London and New York: Routledge, 1993.

Evans, Albert Owen, *A Memorandum on the Legality of the Welsh Bible and the Welsh Version of the Book of Common Prayer*, Cardiff: William Lewis, 1925.

Evans, Maurice, *English Poetry in the Sixteenth Century*, New York: Hutchinson and Co., 1967.

Evans, Robert C., *Ben Jonson and the Politics of Patronage*, Lewisburg, PA: Bucknell University Press, 1988.

Habits of Mind: Evidence and Effects of Ben Jonson's Reading, Lewisburg, PA: Bucknell University Press, 1995.

Ezell, Margaret J. M., *The Patriarch's Wife: Literary Evidence and the History of the Family*, Chapel Hill: University of North Carolina Press, 1987.

Falco, Raphael, *Conceived Presences: Literary Genealogy in Renaissance England*, Amherst: University of Massachusetts Press, 1994.

Farrell, Kirby, Hageman, Elizabeth and Kinney, Arthur F. (eds.), *Women in the Renaissance: Selections from 'English Literary Renaissance'*, Amherst: University of Massachusetts Press, 1990.

Feather, John, *A History of British Publishing*, London and New York: Routledge, 1988.

Feingold, M., 'Jordan Revisited: Patterns of Charitable Giving in Sixteenth- and Seventeenth-Century England', *History of Education*, 8 (1979), 257–73.

The Mathematicians' Apprenticeship: Science, Universities and Society in England, 1560–1640, Cambridge University Press, 1984.

Ferguson, Arthur B., *The Articulate Citizen and the English Renaissance*, Durham, NC: Duke University Press, 1965.

Ferrell, Lori Anne and McCullough, Peter (eds.), *The English Sermon Revised: Religion, Literature and History 1600–1750*, Manchester University Press, 2000.

Findlay, Alison, *A Feminist Perspective on Renaissance Drama*, Oxford: Blackwell, 1999.

Findlay, Bill (ed.), *A History of Scottish Theatre*, Edinburgh: Polygon, 1998.

Finkelpearl, Philip J., *Court and Country Politics in the Plays of Beaumont and Fletcher*, Princeton University Press, 1990.

John Marston of the Middle Temple: An Elizabethan Dramatist in His Social Setting, Cambridge, MA: Harvard University Press, 1969.

Finlay, Roger, *Population and Metropolis: The Demography of London 1580-1650*, Cambridge University Press, 1981.

Finley, John H., 'Milton and Horace: A Study of Milton's Sonnets', *Harvard Studies in Classical Philology*, 48 (1937), 29-74.

Firth, Katharine R., *The Apocalyptic Tradition in Reformation Britain, 1530-1645*, Oxford University Press, 1979.

Fletcher, A. J., *Drama, Performance and Polity in Pre-Cromwellian Ireland*, Cork University Press, 2000.

Fletcher, Anthony, *The Outbreak of the English Civil War*, London: Edward Arnold, 1981.

Fletcher, Anthony and Roberts, Peter (eds.), *Religion, Culture and Society in Early Modern Britain*, Cambridge University Press, 1994.

Flynn, V. J., 'The Grammatical Writings of William Lily, 1468-?1523', *Papers of the Bibliographical Society of America*, 37 (1943), 85-113.

Fortescue, G. K., *Catalogue of the Pamphlets, Books, Newspapers, and Manuscripts Relating to the Civil War, the Commonwealth, and the Restoration, Collected by George Thomason, 1640-1661*, 2 vols., London: William Clowes and Sons, 1908.

Foucault, Michel, *Discipline and Punish: The Birth of the Prison*, trans. Alan Sheridan, Harmondsworth: Penguin, 1977.

Fowler, Alastair, *The Country-House Poem*, Edinburgh University Press, 1994.

'Georgic and Pastoral: Laws of Genre in the Seventeenth Century', in Michael Leslie and Timothy Raylor (eds.), *Culture and Cultivation in Early Modern England: Writing and the Land*, Leicester University Press, 1992, pp. 81-8.

Kinds of Literature: An Introduction to the Theory of Genres and Kinds, Cambridge, MA: Harvard University Press, 1982.

Fox, Adam, 'Ballads, Libels and Popular Ridicule in Jacobean England', *Past and Present*, 145 (1994), 47-83.

'Custom, Memory and the Authority of Writing', in Paul Griffiths, Adam Fox and Steve Hindle (eds.), *The Experience of Authority in Early Modern England*, Basingstoke: Macmillan, 1996, pp. 89-116.

Oral and Literate Culture in England, 1500-1700, Oxford: Clarendon Press, 2000.

Fox, Alistair, *Politics and Literature in the Reigns of Henry VII and Henry VIII*, Oxford: Blackwell, 1989.

Fox, Alistair and Guy, John, *Reassessing the Henrician Age: Humanism, Politics, and Reform, 1500-1550*, Oxford: Blackwell, 1986.

Foxwell, A. K., *A Study of Sir Thomas Wyatt's Poetry*, University of London Press, 1911.

Frank, Joseph, *The Beginnings of the English Newspaper, 1620-1660*, Cambridge, MA: Harvard University Press, 1961.

Fraser, Russell A., *The War Against Poetry*, Princeton University Press, 1970.

Frearson, Michael, 'The English Corantos of the 1620s', unpublished Ph. D. thesis, University of Cambridge, 1993.

Freeman, Rosemary, *English Emblem Books*, London: Chatto and Windus, 1948.

Freeman, Thomas, 'Fate, Faction and Fiction in Foxe's *Book of Martyrs*', *Historical Journal*, 43 (2000), 601-23.

Fuller, Mary C., *Voyages in Print: English Travel to America, 1576-1624*, Cambridge University Press, 1995.

Gardiner, S. R., *The History of the Commonwealth and Protectorate, 1649–1660*, 4 vols., 1903; New York: AMS Press, 1965.

History of England from the Accession of James I to the Outbreak of the Civil War, 1603–1642, 10 vols., London: Longmans, Green and Co., 1883–4.

History of the Great Civil War, 4 vols., London: Longmans, Green and Co., 1910.

Gascoigne, John, *Science, Politics and Universities in Europe, 1600–1800*, Aldershot: Ashgate, 1999.

Gaskell, Philip, *A New Introduction to Bibliography*, rev. edn, Oxford University Press, 1974.

Gellner, Ernest, *Nationalism*, New York University Press, 1997.

Nations and Nationalism, Oxford: Blackwell, 1983.

Giamatti, A. Bartlett, 'Hippolytus Among the Exiles: The Romance of Early Humanism', in Maynard Mack and George deForest Lord (eds.), *Poetic Traditions of the English Renaissance*, New Haven, CT, and London: Yale University Press, 1982, pp. 1–23.

Gibbons, Brian, *Jacobean City Comedy*, 2nd edn, London: Methuen, 1980.

Gill, Roma, 'A Purchase of Glory: The Persona of Late Elizabethan Satire', *Studies in Philology*, 72 (1975), 408–14.

Gilmont, J.-F. (ed.), *The Reformation and the Book*, trans. Karin Maag, Aldershot: Ashgate, 1998.

Ginzburg, Carlo, *The Cheese and the Worms: The Cosmos of a Sixteenth-Century Miller*, trans. John Tedeschi and Anne Tedeschi, Baltimore, MD: Johns Hopkins University Press, 1980.

Goldberg, Jonathan, *James I and the Politics of Literature*, Baltimore, MD: Johns Hopkins University Press, 1983.

Gordon, D. J., *The Renaissance Imagination: Essays and Lectures*, ed. Stephen Orgel, Berkeley: University of California Press, 1975.

Gordon, D. J. and Robertson, J. (eds.), *A Calendar of Dramatic Revels in the Books of the Livery Companies of London, 1485–1640*, Malone Society Collections, 3, Oxford University Press, 1954.

Gorlach, Manfred, *Introduction to Early Modern English*, Cambridge University Press, 1981.

Grabes, Herbert, *Das englische Pamphlet: Politische und religiose Polemik am Beginn der Neuzeit (1521–1640)*, Tübingen: Max Niemeyer Verlag, 1990.

Grafton, Anthony, 'The Importance of Being Printed', *Journal of Interdisciplinary History*, 11 (1980), 265–86.

From Humanism to the Humanities, Cambridge, MA: Harvard University Press, 1986.

Joseph Scaliger: A Study in the History of Classical Scholarship, 2 vols., Oxford University Press, 1983.

Grafton, Anthony and Jardine, Lisa, 'Teacher, Text, and Pupil in the Renaissance Classroom', *History of Universities*, 1 (1981), 37–70.

' "Studied for Action": How Gabriel Harvey Read his Livy', *Past and Present*, 129 (1990), 3–50.

Graham, Michael F., *The Uses of Reform; 'Godly Discipline' and Popular Behaviour in Scotland and Beyond, 1560–1610*, Leiden: Brill, 1996.

Greaves, Richard L., *Deliver Us from Evil: The Radical Underground in Britain, 1660–1663*, Oxford University Press, 1986.

Greaves, Richard L. (ed.), *Triumph over Silence: Women in Protestant History*, Westport, CT: Greenwood, 1985.

Greaves, Richard L. and Zaller, Robert (eds.), *A Biographical Dictionary of British Radicals in the Seventeenth Century*, Brighton: Harvester, 1982–4.

Green, Ian, *The Christian's ABC: Catechisms and Catechizing in England c. 1530–1740*, Oxford: Clarendon Press, 1996.

Print and Protestantism in Early Modern England, Oxford University Press, 2000.

Greenblatt, Stephen, 'Psychoanalysis and Renaissance Culture', in Patricia Parker and David Quint (eds.), *Literary Theory/Renaissance Texts*, Baltimore, MD: Johns Hopkins University Press, 1986, pp. 210–24.

Renaissance Self-Fashioning: From More to Shakespeare, University of Chicago Press, 1980.

Shakespearean Negotiations: The Circulation of Social Energy in Renaissance England, Berkeley: University of California Press, 1988.

Greenblatt, Stephen (ed.), *Representing the English Renaissance*, Berkeley: University of California Press, 1988.

Greene, Thomas M., *The Light in Troy: Imitation and Discovery in Renaissance Poetry*, New Haven, CT, and London: Yale University Press, 1982.

Greenfeld, Liah, *Nationalism: Five Roads to Modernity*, Cambridge, MA: Harvard University Press, 1992.

Greengrass, Mark, Leslie, Michael and Raylor, Timothy (eds.), *Samuel Hartlib and Universal Reformation: Studies in Intellectual Communication*, Cambridge University Press, 1994.

Greg, W. W., *A Bibliography of the English Printed Drama to the Restoration*, 4 vols., London: Bibliographical Society, 1951–62.

A Companion to Arber, being a Calender of Documents in Edward Arber's 'A Transcript of the Registers of the Company of Stationers of London, 1554–1640', Oxford University Press, 1967.

Some Aspects and Problems of London Publishing between 1550 and 1650, Oxford University Press, 1956.

Greg, W. W. and Boswell, E., *Records of the Court of the Stationers' Company, 1576–1602*, London: The Bibliographical Society, 1930.

Gregory, Brad S., 'The "True and Zealouse Service of God": Robert Parsons, Edmund Bunny, and the First Booke of the Christian Exercise', *Journal of Ecclesiastical History*, 45 (1994), 238–68.

Griffin, Dustin, *Literary Patronage in England, 1650–1800*, Cambridge University Press, 1996.

Griffiths, Paul and Jenner, Mark S. R. (eds.), *Londinopolis: Essays in the Cultural and Social History of Early Modern London*, Manchester University Press, 2000.

Griffiths, R. A. and Thomas, R. S. (eds.), *The Making of the Tudor Dynasty*, Gloucester: Alan Sutton, 1985.

Guibbory, Achsah, *Ceremony and Community from Herbert to Milton: Literature, Religion and Cultural Conflict in Seventeenth-Century England*, Cambridge University Press, 1998.

Gunn, S. J., *Early Tudor Government 1485–1558*, New York: St Martin's, 1995.

Gurr, Andrew, *Playgoing in Shakespeare's London*, 2nd edn, Cambridge University Press, 1996.

The Shakespearean Playing Companies, Oxford University Press, 1996.

The Shakespearean Stage, 3rd edn, Cambridge University Press, 1992.

Gurr, Andrew with Orrell, John, *Rebuilding Shakespeare's Globe*, London: Weidenfeld and Nicolson, 1989.

Guy, John A., 'The Rhetoric of Counsel in Early Modern England', in Dale Hoak (ed.), *Tudor Political Culture*, Cambridge University Press, 1995, pp. 292–310.

Tudor England, Oxford University Press, 1988.

Guy, John A. (ed.), *The Reign of Elizabeth I: Court and Culture in the Last Decade*, Cambridge University Press, 1995.

Hackel, Heidi Brayman, ' "Boasting of Silence": Women Readers and the Patriarchal State', in Kevin Sharpe and Steven N. Zwicker (eds.), *Reading, Politics, and Society in Early Modern England*, Cambridge University Press, 2003.

' "The Great Variety of Readers" and Early Modern Reading Practices', in David Scott Kastan (ed.), *A Companion to Shakespeare*, Oxford: Blackwell, 1999, pp. 139–57.

' "Rowme of Its Own": Printed Drama in Early Libraries', in Cox and Kastan (eds.), *A New History of Early English Drama*, pp. 113–30.

Hackett, Helen, *Virgin Mother, Maiden Queen: Elizabeth I and the Cult of the Virgin Mary*, Basingstoke: Macmillan, 1994.

Hadfield, Andrew, *Literature, Politics, and National Identity*, Cambridge University Press, 1994.

Haigh, Christopher, *English Reformations: Religion, Politics, and Society Under the Tudors*, Oxford University Press, 1993.

Haigh, Christopher (ed.), *The English Reformation Revisited*, Cambridge University Press, 1987.

Halasz, Alexandra, *The Marketplace of Print: Pamphlets and the Public Sphere in Early Modern England*, Cambridge University Press, 1997.

Hale, John K., *Milton's Language: The Impact of Multilingualism on Style*, Cambridge University Press, 1997.

Hall, Basil, 'The Early Rise and Gradual Decline of Lutheranism in England (1520–1600)', in Derek Baker (ed.), *Reform and Reformation: England and the Continent c. 1500 – c. 1750*, Oxford: Basil Blackwell, 1979, pp. 103–31.

Hall, Kim F., *Things of Darkness: Economies of Race and Gender in Early Modern England*, Ithaca, NY: Cornell University Press, 1995.

Hall, Vernon, *Renaissance Literary Criticism: A Study of its Social Content*, Gloucester, MA: Peter Smith, 1959.

Haller, William, *Foxe's Book of Martyrs and the Elect Nation*, London: Jonathan Cape, 1963.

Liberty and Reformation in the Puritan Revolution, New York: Columbia University Press, 1955.

The Rise of Puritanism, New York: Columbia University Press, 1934, 1938.

Halpern, Martin, 'On the Two Chief Metrical Modes in English', *PMLA*, 77.3 (June 1962), 177–86.

Hamilton, Donna B. and Strier, Richard (eds.), *Religion, Literature and Politics in Post-Reformation England, 1540–1688*, Cambridge University Press, 1996.

Hammond, Gerald, *The Making of the English Bible*, Manchester University Press, 1982.

Hannay, Margaret, *Philip's Phoenix: Mary Sidney, Countess of Pembroke*, Oxford University Press, 1990.

Hannay, Margaret (ed.), *Silent But For The Word: Tudor Women as Patrons, Translators, and Writers of Religious Works*, Kent State University Press, 1985.

Harbage, Alfred, *Cavalier Drama*, Oxford University Press, 1936.

Shakespeare and the Rival Traditions, New York: Macmillan, 1952.

Hardison, O. B., *Prosody and Purpose in the English Renaissance*, Baltimore, MD, and London: Johns Hopkins University Press, 1989.

Harrier, Richard, *The Canon of Sir Thomas Wyatt's Poetry*, Cambridge MA: Harvard University Press, 1975.

Harris, Jesse W., *John Bale: A Study in the Minor Literature of the Reformation*, Urbana: University of Illinois Press, 1940.

Harris, Tim, *London Crowds in the Reign of Charles II: Propaganda and Politics from the Restoration until the Exclusion Crisis*, Cambridge University Press, 1987.

Hartman, Geoffrey H., ' "The Nymph Complaining for the Death of Her Faun": A Brief Allegory', in *Beyond Formalism: Literary Essays 1958–1970*, New Haven, CT, and London: Yale University Press, 1970, pp. 173–92.

Harvey, Elizabeth D. and Maus, Katharine Eisaman (eds.), *Soliciting Interpretation. Literary Theory and Seventeenth-Century English Poetry*, University of Chicago Press, 1990.

Hattaway, Michael (ed.), *A Companion to English Renaissance Literature and Culture*, Oxford: Blackwell, 2000.

Haugaard, W. J., 'Katherine Parr: The Religious Convictions of a Renaissance Queen', *Renaissance Quarterly*, 22 (1969), 346–59.

Haynes, Jonathan, *The Social Relations of Jonson's Theatre*, Cambridge University Press, 1992.

Heale, Elizabeth, 'Women and the Courtly Love Lyric: The Devonshire MS (BL Additional 17492)', *Modern Language Review*, 90. 2 (April 1995), 296–313.

Wyatt, Surrey and Early Tudor Court Poetry, London and New York: Longman, 1998.

Healy, Thomas F., *Richard Crashaw*, Leiden: E. J. Brill, 1986.

Healy, Thomas and Sawday, Jonathan (eds.), *Literature and the English Civil War*, Cambridge University Press, 1990.

Heinemann, Margot, *Puritanism and Theatre: Thomas Middleton and Opposition Drama under the Early Stuarts*, Cambridge University Press, 1980.

Helgerson, Richard, *Forms of Nationhood: The Elizabethan Writing of England*, University of Chicago Press, 1992.

Self-Crowned Laureates: Spenser, Jonson, Milton and the Literary System, Berkeley: University of California Press, 1983.

Hellinga, Lotte and Trapp, J. B. (eds.), *The Cambridge History of the Book in Britain, Volume 3, 1400–1557*, Cambridge University Press, 1999.

Herman, Peter C. (ed.), *Rethinking the Henrician Era: Essays on Early Tudor Texts and Contexts*, Chicago and Urbana: University of Illinois Press, 1994.

Hill, Christopher, *Antichrist in Seventeenth-Century England*, 1971; rev. edn, London and New York: Verso, 1990.

The Collected Essays of Christopher Hill, vol. II: Religion and Politics in 17th-Century England, Brighton: Harvester, 1986.

The English Bible and the Seventeenth-Century Revolution, Harmondsworth: Penguin, 1993.

The Experience of Defeat: Milton and Some Contemporaries, London: Faber, 1984.

Milton and the English Revolution, 1977, New York: Viking, 1979.

A Nation of Change and Novelty: Radical Politics, Religion and Literature in 17th-Century England, London: Routledge, 1990.

Puritanism and Revolution, New York: Schocken Books, 1964.

Some Intellectual Consequences of the English Revolution, Madison: University of Wisconsin Press, 1980.

A Turbulent, Seditious and Factious People: John Bunyan and his Church, Oxford: Clarendon Press, 1988.

The World Turned Upside Down: Radical Ideas During the English Revolution, 2nd edn, Harmondsworth: Penguin, 1975.

Hills, Richard L., *Papermaking in Britain, 1488–1988: A Short History*, London: Athlone, 1988.

Hinds, Hilary, *God's Englishwomen: Seventeenth-Century Radical Sectarian Writing and Feminist Criticism*, Manchester University Press, 1996.

Hirst, Derek, *England in Conflict, 1603–1660: Kingdom, Community, Commonwealth*, London: Arnold, 1999.

'The English Republic and the Meaning of Britain', in Brendan Bradshaw and John Morrill (ed.), *The British Problem, c. 1535–1707*, Basingstoke: Macmillan, 1996, pp. 192–219.

' "That Sober Liberty": Marvell's Cromwell in 1654', in John M. Wallace (ed.), *The Golden and the Brazen World: Papers in Literature and History 1650–1800*, Berkeley: University of California Press, 1985, pp. 17–53.

Hirst, Derek and Strier, Richard (eds.), *Writing and Political Engagement in Seventeenth-Century England*, Cambridge University Press, 2000.

Hirst, Derek and Zwicker, Steven, 'High Summer at Nun Appleton, 1651: Andrew Marvell and Lord Fairfax's Occasions', *Historical Journal*, 36 (1993), 247–69.

Hobbs, Mary, *Early Seventeenth-Century Verse Miscellany Manuscripts*, Aldershot: Scolar Press, 1992.

Hobby, Elaine, *Virtue of Necessity: English Women's Writing, 1649–88*, London: Virago Press, 1988. Ann Arbor: University of Michigan Press, 1989.

Hobsbawm, Eric, *Nations and Nationalism since 1789*, Cambridge University Press, 1991.

Hodges, C. Walter, *The Globe Restored: A Study of the Elizabethan Theatre*, London: E. Benn, 1953. New York: W. W. Norton, 1973.

Holstun, James (ed.), *Pamphlet Wars: Prose in the English Revolution*, London: Frank Cass, 1992.

Hosley, Richard, 'The Playhouses and the Stage', in Kenneth Muir and S. Schoenbaum (eds.), *A New Companion to Shakespeare Studies*, Cambridge University Press, 1971, pp. 15–34.

Hotson, Leslie, *The Commonwealth and Restoration Stage*, Cambridge, MA: Harvard University Press, 1928.

Houston, R. A., 'The Development of Literacy: Northern England, 1640–1750', *Economic History Review*, 35. 2 (1982), 199–216.

Scottish Literacy and the Scottish Identity: Illiteracy and Society in Scotland and Northern England, 1600–1800, Cambridge University Press, 1985.

Howard, Douglas (ed.), *Philip Massinger: A Critical Reassessment*, Cambridge University Press, 1985.

Howard, Jean, *The Stage and Social Struggle in Early Modern England*, London: Routledge, 1994.

Hudson, Anne, *The Premature Reformation*, Oxford University Press, 1988.

Hudson, E. K., 'English Protestants and the *Imitatio Christi* 1580–1620', *Sixteenth Century Journal*, 19 (1988), 541–58.

Hudson, Winthrop S., *John Ponet: Advocate of Limited Monarchy*, University of Chicago Press, 1940.

Hughes, Ann, *The Causes of the English Civil War*, 2nd edn, Basingstoke: Macmillan, 1998.

Hull, Suzanne W., *Chaste, Silent & Obedient: English Books for Women, 1475–1640*, San Marino, CA: Huntington Library, 1982.

Hume, Robert D., *The Development of English Drama in the Late Seventeenth Century*, Oxford: Clarendon Press, 1976.

Hunter, G. K., *English Drama 1586–1642: The Age of Shakespeare*, Oxford: Clarendon Press, 1997.

John Lyly: The Humanist as Courtier, London: Routledge and Kegan Paul, 1962.

Hunter, Michael and Gregory, Annabel (eds.), *An Astrological Diary of the Seventeenth Century: Samuel Jeake of Rye, 1652–1699*, Oxford University Press, 1988.

Hutton, Ronald, *Charles the Second, King of England, Scotland, and Ireland*, Oxford: Clarendon Press, 1989.

The Restoration: A Political and Religious History of England and Wales, 1658–1667, Oxford: Clarendon Press, 1985.

The Rise and Fall of Merry England: The Ritual Year, 1400–1700, Oxford University Press, 1996.

Ingram, Randall, 'Robert Herrick and the Making of *Hesperides*', *Studies in English Literature*, 38.1 (Winter 1998), 127–49.

Ingram, William, *The Business of Playing: The Beginnings of the Adult Professional Theater in Elizabethan London*, Ithaca, NY: Cornell University Press, 1992.

'The "Evolution" of the Elizabethan Playing Company', in John H. Astington (ed.), *The Development of Shakespeare's Theater*, New York: AMS, 1992, pp. 13–28.

Ives, E. W., 'Stress, Faction and Ideology in Early Tudor England', *Historical Journal*, 34 (1991), 193–202.

Jack, R. D. S. (ed.), *Medieval and Renaissance*, vol. 1 of *The History of Scottish Literature*, gen. ed. Cairns Graig, 4 vols., Aberdeen University Press, 1987–8.

Jackson, William A., *Records of the Court of the Stationers' Company, 1576–1602*, London: The Bibliographical Society, 1930.

Jacob, J. R. and Raylor, T., 'Opera and Obedience: Thomas Hobbes and *A Proposition for Advancement of Moralitie* by Sir William Davenant', *The Seventeenth Century*, 6 (1991), 205–50.

James, M. E., *English Politics and the Concept of Honour, 1485–1640, Past and Present* Supplement, 3 (1978).

James, Margaret, *Social Problems and Policy during the Puritan Revolution 1640–1660*, 2nd edn, London: Routledge, 1966.

James, Mervyn, *English Politics and Culture: Studies in Early Modern England*, Cambridge University Press, 1986.

'Ritual, Drama, and the Social Body in the Late Medieval English Town', *Past and Present*, 98 (1983), 3–29.

Jardine, Lisa, 'Humanism and Dialectic in Sixteenth-Century Cambridge: A Preliminary Investigation', in R. R. Bolgar (ed.), *Classical Influences on European Culture AD 1500–1700*, Cambridge University Press, 1976, pp. 141–54.

'The Place of Dialectic Teaching in Sixteenth-Century Cambridge', *Studies in the Renaissance*, 21 (1974), 31–62.

Worldly Goods: A New History of the Renaissance, London: Macmillan, 1996.

Jardine, Lisa and Sherman, William, 'Pragmatic Readers: Knowledge Transactions and Scholarly Services in Late Elizabethan England', in Fletcher and Roberts (eds.), *Religion, Culture, and Society in Early Modern Britain*, pp. 102–24.

Javitch, Daniel, *Poetry and Courtliness in Renaissance England*, Princeton University Press, 1978.

Jenkins, Hugh, *Feigned Commonwealths: The Country-House and the Fashioning of the Ideal Community*, Pittsburgh, PA: Duquesne University Press, 1998.

Jenkins, Philip, 'Seventeenth-Century Wales: Definition and Identity', in Bradshaw and Roberts (eds.), *British Consciousness and Identity. The Making of Britain, 1533–1707*, pp. 213–35.

Jentoft, Clyde W., *Sir Thomas Wyatt and Henry Howard, Earl of Surrey: A Reference Guide*, Boston: G. K. Hall, 1980.

Jewell, Helen M., *Education in Early Modern England*, Basingstoke: Macmillan, 1998.

Johns, Adrian, *The Nature of the Book: Print and Knowledge in the Making*, University of Chicago Press, 1998.

Johnson, Francis R., 'Latin vs. English: The Sixteenth-Century Debate over Scientific Terminology', *Studies in Philology*, 41 (1944), 109–35.

Johnson, Gerald D., 'The Stationers Versus the Drapers: Control of the Press in the Late Sixteenth Century', *The Library*, 6th ser., 10 (1988), 1–17.

Jones, Ann Rosalind, *The Currency of Eros: Women's Love Lyric in Europe, 1540–1620*, Bloomington: Indiana University Press, 1990.

Jones, Emrys, *The Origins of Shakespeare*, Oxford: Clarendon Press, 1977.

Jones, Norman and White, Paul Whitfield, '*Gorboduc* and Royal Marriage Politics: An Elizabethan Playgoer's Report of the Premiere Performance', *English Literary Renaissance*, 26 (1996), 3–16.

Jones, R. Brinley, *The Old British Tongue: The Vernacular in Wales, 1540–1640*, Cardiff: Avalon Books, 1970.

Jones, Richard Foster, 'Science and Language in England in the Mid-Seventeenth Century', *Journal of English and Germanic Philology*, 31 (1932), 315–31.

The Triumph of the English Language: A Survey of Opinions concerning the Vernacular from the Introduction of Printing to the Restoration, Stanford University Press, 1953.

Jordan, Wilbur Kitchener, *The Development of Religious Toleration in England from the Accession of James 1 to the Convention of the Long Parliament (1603–1640)*, London: George Allen & Unwin, 1936.

Edward VI, 2 vols., Cambridge, MA: Harvard University Press, 1968–70.

Philanthropy in England 1480–1660, London: Allen and Unwin, 1959.

Jose, Nicholas, *Ideas of the Restoration in English Literature 1660–71*, Cambridge, MA: Harvard University Press, 1984.

Kaplan, M. Lindsay, *The Culture of Slander in Early Modern England*, Cambridge University Press, 1997.

Kastan, David, ' "Holy Wurdes" and "Slypper Wit": John Bale's *King Johan* and the Poetics of Propaganda', in Herman (ed.), *Rethinking the Henrician Era*, pp. 267–82.

' "The Noise of the New Bible": Reform and Reaction in Henrician England', in Claire McEachern and Debora Shuger (eds.), *Religion and Culture in Renaissance England*, Cambridge University Press, 1997, pp. 46–68.

'Opening Gates and Stopping Hedges: Grafton, Stow, and the Politics of Elizabethan History Writing', in Elizabeth Fowler and Roland Greene (eds.), *The Project of Prose in Early Modern Europe and the New World*, Cambridge University Press, 1997, pp. 66–79.

Shakespeare and the Book, Cambridge University Press, 2001.

'Workshop and/as Playhouse', *Studies in Philology*, 84 (1987), 324–37.

Kastan, David Scott and Stallybrass, Peter (eds.), *Staging the Renaissance: Reinterpretations of Elizabethan and Jacobean Drama*, London: Routledge, 1991.

Kay, M. M., *The History of Rivington and Blackrod Grammar School*, Manchester University Press, 1931.

Kay, W. David, *Ben Jonson: A Literary Life*, Basingstoke: Macmillan, 1995.

Keeble, N. H. *The Literary Culture of Nonconformity in Later Seventeenth-Century England*, Leicester University Press, 1987.

' "Take away preaching, and take away salvation"; Hugh Latimer, Protestantism, and Prose Style', in Neil Rhodes (ed.), *English Renaissance Prose: History, Language, and Politics*, Tempe, AZ: Renaissance English Text Society and Arizona Center for Medieval and Renaissance Studies, 1997, pp. 57–74.

Richard Baxter: Puritan Man of Letters, Oxford: Clarendon Press, 1982.

Keeble, N. H. (ed.), *The Cambridge Companion to Writing of the English Revolution*, Cambridge University Press, 2001.

Kelley, D. R. and Sacks, D. H. (eds.)., *The Historical Imagination in Early Modern Britain: History, Rhetoric and Fiction, 1500–1800*, Cambridge University Press, 1997.

Kelliher, Hilton, *Andrew Marvell, Poet and Politician, 1621–78: An Exhibition to Commemorate the Tercentenary of His Death*, London: British Museum Publications, 1978.

Kelsey, Sean, *Inventing a Republic: The Political Culture of the English Commonwealth, 1649–1653*, Manchester University Press, 1997.

Kendall, R. T., *Calvin and English Calvinism to 1649*, Oxford University Press, 1979.

Kendall, Ritchie D., *The Drama of Dissent: The Radical Poetics of Nonconformity, 1380–1590*, Chapel Hill: University of North Carolina Press, 1986.

Kendrick, T. D., *British Antiquity*, London: Methuen, 1950.

Kenneth, Brother, 'The Popular Literature of the Scottish Reformation', in David McRoberts (ed.), *Essays on the Scottish Reformation 1513–1625*, Glasgow: Burns, 1962.

Kerby-Fulton, Kathryn and Despres, Denise L., *Iconography and the Professional Reader: The Politics of Book Production in the Douce 'Piers Plowman'*, Minneapolis: University of Minnesota Press, 1999.

Kerling, Nelly J. M., 'Caxton and the Trade in Printed Books', *Book Collector*, 4 (1955), 190–99.

Kernan, Alvin, *The Cankered Muse: Satire of the English Renaissance*, 1959. Rpt, Hamden, CT: Archon Books, 1976.

Shakespeare, the King's Playwright: Theatre in the Stuart Court 1603–1613, New Haven, CT: Yale University Press, 1995.

Kerrigan, John, 'Orrery's Ireland and the British Problem, 1641–1679', in Baker and Maley (eds.), *British Identities and English Renaissance Literature*, 2002, pp. 197–225.

Kerrigan, William and Braden, Gordon, *The Idea of the Renaissance*, Baltimore, MD, and London: The Johns Hopkins University Press, 1989.

Key, Elizabeth, 'Register of Schools and Schoolmasters in the Diocese of Ely, 1560–1700', *Proceedings of the Cambridge Antiquarian Society*, 70 (1980), 127–89.

Kidd, Colin, *British Identities before Nationalism: Ethnicity and Nationhood in the Atlantic World, 1600–1800*, Cambridge University Press, 1999.

'Protestantism, Constitutionalism, and British Identity under the Later Stuarts', in Bradshaw and Roberts (eds.), *British Consciousness and Identity: The Making of Britain, 1533–1707*, pp. 321–42.

King, Bruce, *Seventeenth-Century English Literature*, New York: Schocken Books, 1982.

King, John N., *English Reformation Literature: The Tudor Origins of the Protestant Tradition*, Princeton University Press, 1982.

'Patronage and Piety: The Influence of Catherine Parr', in Hannay (ed.), *Silent but for the Word*, pp. 43–50.

Tudor Royal Iconography: Literature and Art in an Age of Religious Crisis, Princeton University Press, 1982.

Kinney, Arthur, *John Skelton, Priest as Poet: Seasons of Discovery*, Chapel Hill: University of North Carolina Press, 1987.

Kipling, Gordon, *The Triumph of Honour: Burgundian Origins of the Elizabethan Renaissance*, The Hague: Leiden University Press, 1977.

Kirk, James, 'The Religion of Early Scottish Protestants', in J. Kirk (ed.), *Humanism and Reform: The Church in Europe, England and Scotland; Essays in Honour of James K. Cameron*, Oxford: Blackwell, 1991.

Kirsch, Arthur C., *Jacobean Dramatic Perspectives*, Charlottesville: University Press of Virginia, 1972.

Klotz, Edith L., 'A Subject Analysis of English Imprints for Every Tenth Year from 1480 to 1640', *Huntington Library Quarterly*, 1 (1938), 417–19.

Knafla, L. A., 'The Matriculation Revolution and Education at the Inns of Court in Renaissance England', in A. J. Slavin (ed.), *Tudor Men and Institutions. Studies in English Law and Government*, Baton Rouge: Louisiana State University Press, 1972, pp. 232–64.

Knapp, Jeffrey, *An Empire Nowhere: England, America, and Literature from Utopia to The Tempest*, Berkeley: University of California Press, 1992.

Knappen, M. M., *Tudor Puritanism*, University of Chicago Press, 1939.

Knights, L. C., *Drama and Society in the Age of Jonson*, 1937. Rpt, New York: Norton, 1968.

Knoppers, Laura Lunger, *Constructing Cromwell: Ceremony, Portrait, and Print, 1645–1661*, Cambridge University Press, 2000.

Historicizing Milton: Spectacle, Power, and Poetry in Restoration England, Athens: University of Georgia Press, 1994.

Knott, John R., *Discourses of Martyrdom in English Literature 1563–1694*, Cambridge University Press, 1993.

The Sword and the Spirit: Puritan Responses to the Bible, University of Chicago Press, 1980.

LaCapra, Dominick, *Rethinking Intellectual History: Texts, Contexts, Language*, Ithaca, NY: Cornell University Press, 1983.

Lake, Peter, 'Calvinism and the English Church, 1570–1635', *Past and Present*, 114 (1987), 32–76.

'Feminine Piety and Personal Potency: The Emancipation of Mrs Jane Ratcliffe', *The Seventeenth Century*, 2 (1987), 143–65.

'The Laudian Style: Order, Uniformity and the Pursuit of the Beauty of Holiness in the 1630s', in Kenneth Fincham (ed.), *The Early Stuart Church, 1603–1642*, Basingstoke: Macmillan, 1993, pp. 161–85.

'Serving God and the Times: The Calvinist Conformity of Robert Sanderson', *Journal of British Studies*, 27 (1988), 81–116.

Lake, Peter with Questier, Michael, *The Antichrist's Lewd Hat: Protestants, Papists and Players in Post-Reformation England*, New Haven, CT, and London: Yale University Press, 2002.

Lamont, William M., *Godly Rule: Politics and Religion, 1603–1660*, London: Macmillan, 1969.

Marginal Prynne, 1600–1669, London: Routledge and Kegan Paul, 1963.

Puritanism and Historical Controversy, London: University College London Press, 1996.

Lander, Jesse, 'Foxe's Books of Martyrs: Printing and Popularizing the *Acts and Monuments*', in Claire McEachern and Debora Shuger (eds.), *Religion and Culture in Renaissance England*, Cambridge University Press, 1997, pp. 69–92.

Latham, Robert and Matthews, William (eds.), *The Diary of Samuel Pepys*, 11 vols., London: Bell & Hyman, 1970.

Lathrop, H. B., 'The Sonnet Forms of Wyatt and Surrey', *Modern Philology*, 2 (1905), 463–70.

Translations From the Classics into English from Caxton to Chapman, 1477–1620, Madison: University of Wisconsin Studies in Language and Literature, 35, 1933.

Leech, Clifford and Craik, T. W., *The Revels History of English Drama*, vol. 3, 1576–1613, London: Methuen, 1975.

Leggatt, Alexander, *English Drama: Shakespeare to the Restoration 1590–1660*, Harlow: Longman, 1988.

Lehrer, Seth, *Courtly Letters in the Age of Henry VIII: Literary Culture and the Arts of Deceit*, Cambridge University Press, 1997.

Leinwand, Theodore B., *The City Staged: Jacobean Comedy 1603–1613*, Madison: University of Wisconsin Press, 1986.

Theatre, Finance and Society in Early Modern England, Cambridge University Press, 1999.

Letters and Papers, Foreign and Domestic, of the Reign of Henry VIII, comp. and arr. James Gairdner, vol. 9, London: Her Majesty's Stationers' Office, 1886.

Levack, Brian P., *The Formation of the British State: England, Scotland, and the Union 1603–1707*, Oxford: Clarendon Press, 1987.

Lever, J. W., *The Tragedy of State*, London: Methuen, 1971.

Lewalski, Barbara K., *The Life of John Milton*, Oxford: Blackwell, 2000.

Protestant Poetics and the Seventeenth-Century Religious Lyric, Princeton University Press, 1979.

Writing Women in Jacobean England, Cambridge, MA: Harvard University Press, 1993.

Lewis, C. S., *English Literature in the Sixteenth Century Excluding Drama*, Oxford: Clarendon Press, 1954. Rpt, 1962.

Lewis, Jayne Elizabeth, *Mary Queen of Scots: Romance and Nation*, London, New York: Routledge, 1998.

Limon, Jerzy, *Dangerous Matter: English Drama and Politics 1623–24*, Cambridge University Press, 1986.

The Masque of Stuart Culture, Newark: University of Delaware Press, and London: Associated University Presses, 1991.

Lindenbaum, Peter, 'Milton's Contract', in Martha Woodmansee and Peter Jaszi (eds.), *The Construction of Authorship: Textual Appropriation in Law and Literature*, Durham, NC: Duke University Press, 1994, pp. 175–90.

Lindley, Keith, *Popular Politics and Religion in Civil War London*, Aldershot: Scolar Press, 1997.

Loach, Jennifer, *Edward VI*, ed. George Bernard and Penry Williams, New Haven, CT: Yale University Press, 1999.

Loades, David M., *John Dudley, Duke of Northumberland 1504–1553*, Oxford: Clarendon Press, 1996.

Mary Tudor: A Life, Oxford: Basil Blackwell, 1989, 1991.

The Oxford Martyrs, New York: Stein and Day, 1970.

Politics, Censorship and the English Reformation, London and New York: Pinter, 1991.

The Reign of Mary Tudor: Politics, Government, and Religion in England, 1553–1558, New York: St Martin's Press, 1979; London: Longmans, 1991.

Loades, David M. (ed.), *John Foxe: An Historical Perspective*, Aldershot: Ashgate, 1999.

(ed.), *John Foxe and the English Reformation*, Aldershot: Scolar Press, 1997.

Lockyer, Roger, *Buckingham: The Life and Political Career of George Villiers, First Duke of Buckingham 1592–1628*, London and New York: Longman, 1981.

Loewenstein, David, *Representing Revolution in Milton and his Contemporaries: Religion, Politics, and Polemics in Radical Puritanism*, Cambridge University Press, 2001.

'Treason against God and State: Blasphemy in Milton's Culture and *Paradise Lost*', in Dobranski and Rumrich (eds.), *Milton and Heresy*, pp. 176–98.

Loewenstein, David and Turner, James Grantham (eds.), *Politics, Poetics, and Hermeneutics in Milton's Prose*, Cambridge University Press, 1990.

Loomba, Ania, *Gender, Race and Renaissance Drama*, Manchester University Press, 1989.

Looney, J., 'Undergraduate Education in Early Stuart Cambridge', *History of Education*, 10 (1981), 9–19.

Love, Harold, *Scribal Publication in Seventeenth-Century England*, Oxford: Clarendon Press, 1993.

Low, Anthony, *The Georgic Revolution*, Princeton University Press, 1985.

Loxley, James, *Royalism and Poetry in the English Civil Wars: The Drawn Sword*, Basingstoke: Macmillan, 1997.

Luke, Mary, *The Nine Days' Queen: A Portrait of Lady Jane Grey*, New York: W. Morrow, 1986.

Lupton, J. H., *A Life of Dean Colet DD*, London: Bell, 1887.

Lupton, Julia Reinhard, 'Mapping Mutability: Or, Spenser's Irish plot', in Brendan Bradshaw, Andrew Hadfield and Willy Maley (eds.), *Representing Ireland: Literature and the Origins of Conflict, 1534–1660*, Cambridge University Press, 1993, pp. 93–115.

Lytle, Guy Fitch and Orgel, Stephen (eds.), *Patronage in the Renaissance*, Princeton University Press, 1981.

MacCaffrey, Wallace, *The Shaping of the Elizabethan Regime: Elizabethan Politics, 1558–1572*, Princeton University Press, 1969.

Maclure, Millar, *The Paul's Cross Sermons 1534–1642*, University of Toronto Press, 1958.

MacCulloch, Diarmaid, *The Reign of Henry VIII: Politics, Policy, and Piety*, New York: St Martin's Press, 1995.

Thomas Cranmer: A Life, New Haven, CT, and London: Yale University Press, 1996.

Tudor Church Militant: Edward VI and the Protestant Reformation, London: Allen Lane, 1999.

Mack, Phyllis, *Visionary Women: Ecstatic Prophecy in Seventeenth-Century England*, Berkeley: University of California Press, 1992.

Mackisack, May, *Medieval History in the Tudor Age*, Oxford: Clarendon Press, 1971.

MacLean, Gerald M. *Time's Witness: Historical Representation in English Poetry, 1603–1660*, University of Wisconsin Press, 1990.

MacLean, Gerald M. (ed.), *Culture and Society in the Stuart Restoration: Literature, Drama, History*, Cambridge University Press, 1995.

Madan, Francis F., *A New Bibliography of the Eikon Basilike of King Charles I*, Oxford University Press, 1950.

Maguire, Nancy Klein, *Regicide and Restoration*, Cambridge University Press, 1992.

Maguire, Nancy Klein (ed.), *Renaissance Tragicomedy: Explorations in Genre and Politics*, New York: AMS Press, 1987.

Maltby, Judith, *Prayer Book and People in Elizabethan and Early Stuart England*, Cambridge University Press, 1998.

Manley, Lawrence, *Literature and Culture in Early Modern London*, Cambridge University Press, 1995.

'Of Sites and Rites', in Smith, Strier and Bevington (eds.), *The Theatrical City: Culture, Theatre, and Politics in London, 1576–1649*, ch. 2.

'Proverbs, Epigrams, and Urbanity in Renaissance London', *English Literary Renaissance*, 15 (1985), 247–76.

Manley, Lawrence (ed.), *London in the Age of Shakespeare: An Anthology*, London and Sydney: Croom Helm, 1986.

Manning, Brian, *The English People and the English Revolution*, 2nd edn, London and Chicago: Bookmarks, 1991.

Manning, Brian (ed.), *Politics, Religion and the English Civil War*, London: Arnold, 1973.

Marcus, Leah S., *Childhood and Cultural Despair: A Theme and Variations in Seventeenth-Century Literature*, University of Pittsburgh Press, 1978.

The Politics of Mirth: Jonson, Herrick, Milton, Marvell, and the Defense of Old Holiday Pastimes, University of Chicago Press, 1986.

Margolies, David, *Novel and Society in Elizabethan England*, London: Croom Helm, 1985.

Marius, Richard, *Thomas More: A Biography*, New York: Alfred Knopf, 1984.

Marotti, Arthur, *John Donne: Coterie Poet*, Madison: University of Wisconsin Press, 1986.

Manuscript, Print and the English Renaissance Lyric, Ithaca, NY, and London: Cornell University Press, 1995.

Martindale, Julia, 'The Best Master of Virtue and Wisdom: The Horace of Ben Jonson and his Heirs', in Charles Martindale and David Hopkins (eds.), *Horace Made New: Horatian Influences on British Writing from the Renaissance to the Twentieth Century*, Cambridge University Press, 1993, pp. 50–85.

Martz, Louis, *The Poetry of Meditation*, rev. edn, New Haven, CT: Yale University Press, 1962.

Mason, H. A., *Humanism and Poetry in the Early Tudor Period*, London: Routledge & Kegan Paul, 1959.

Sir Thomas Wyatt: A Literary Portrait, Bristol Classical Press, 1986.

Mason, Roger A., 'Covenant and Commonweal: The Language of Politics in Reformation Scotland' in Norman MacDougall (ed.), *Church, Politics, and Society: Scotland 1408–1929*, Edinburgh: J. Donald, 1983, pp. 97–126.

'Kingship, Nobility, and Anglo-Scottish Union: John Mair's History of Greater Britain (1521)', *Innes Review*, 41.2 (1990), 182–222.

'Scotching the Brut: Politics, History and National Myth in Sixteenth-Century Britain', in Mason (ed.), *Scotland and England, 1286–1815*, pp. 60–84.

Mason, Roger A. (ed.), *John Knox and the British Reformations*, Aldershot: Ashgate, 1998.

Scotland and England, 1286–1815, Edinburgh: J. Donald, 1987.

Masten, Jeffrey, *Textual Intercourse: Collaboration, Authorship and Sexualities in Renaissance Drama*, Cambridge University Press, 1997.

Mathews, William, 'Language in *Love's Labour's Lost*', *Essays and Studies* (1964), 1–11.

Matthews, A. G., *Calamy Revised*, Oxford: Clarendon Press, 1934.

Maus, Katherine Eisaman, *Inwardness and Theater in the English Renaissance*, University of Chicago Press, 1995.

May, Steven W., 'Tudor Aristocrats and the Mythical "Stigma of Print"', *Renaissance Papers* (1980), 11–18.

McAdoo, H. R., *The Spirit of Anglicanism: A Survey of Anglican Theological Method in the Seventeenth Century*, London: Black, 1965.

McClure, J. Derrick, *Scots and Its Literature*, Philadelphia: Johns Benjamins, 1995.

McConica, James K., *English Humanists and Reformation Politics under Henry VIII and Edward VI*, Oxford University Press, 1965.

McConica, James K. (ed.), *The Collegiate University*, Oxford: Clarendon Press, 1986.

McCoy, Richard C., *The Rites of Knighthood: The Literature and Politics of Elizabethan Chivalry*, Berkeley: University of California Press, 1989.

McCullough, Peter, *Sermons at Court: Politics and Religion in Elizabethan and Jacobean Preaching*, Cambridge University Press, 1998.

McDonald, Alan R., *The Jacobean Kirk, 1567–1625: Sovereignty, Polity, and Liturgy*, Aldershot: Ashgate, 1998.

McEachern, Claire, *The Poetics of English Nationhood, 1590–1612*, Cambridge University Press, 1996.

McElderry, Bruce Robert, Jr, 'Archaism and Innovation in Spenser's Poetic Diction', *PMLA*, 47.1 (1932), 144–70.

McFarlane, Ian D., *Buchanan*, London: Duckworth, 1981.

McGavin, John J., 'The Dramatic Prosody of Sir David Lindsay', in R. D. S. Jack and K. McGinley (eds.), *Of Lion and Unicorn: Essays on Anglo-Scottish Literary Relations in Honour of Professor John MacQueen*, Edinburgh: Quadriga, 1993, pp. 39–66.

McGee, James, *The Godly Man in Stuart England: Anglicans, Puritans, and the Two Tables, 1620–1670*, New Haven, CT: Yale University Press, 1976.

McGrade, Arthur S. (ed.), *Richard Hooker and the Construction of Christian Community*, Tempe, AZ: Medieval and Renaissance Texts and Studies, 1997.

McGregor, J. F. and Reay, B. (eds.), *Radical Religion in the English Revolution*, Oxford University Press, 1984.

McKenna, J. W., 'How God became an Englishman', in J. W. McKenna and J. DeLloyd Guth (eds.), *Tudor Rule and Revolution: Essays for G. R. Elton from his American Friends*, Cambridge University Press, 1982, pp. 24–44.

McKenzie, D. F., *The Cambridge University Press 1696–1712: A Bibliographic Study*, 2 vols., Cambridge University Press, 1966.

'Printers of the Mind: Some Notes on Bibliographical Theories and Printing-House Practices', *Studies in Bibliography*, 22 (1969), 1–75.

McKeon, Michael, *The Origins of the English Novel*, Baltimore, MD: Johns Hopkins University Press, 1987.

Politics and Poetry in Restoration England: The Case of Dryden's Annus Mirabilis, Cambridge, MA: Harvard University Press, 1975.

McKitterick, David, *A History of Cambridge University Press*, 2 vols., Cambridge University Press, 1992–8.

McLuskie, Kathleen, *Renaissance Dramatists*, Hemel Hempstead: Harvester Wheatsheaf, 1989.

McMullan, Gordon, *The Politics of Unease in the Plays of John Fletcher*, Amherst: University of Massachusetts Press, 1994.

McMullan, Gordon and Hope, J. (eds.), *The Politics of Tragicomedy: Shakespeare and After*, London: Routledge, 1992.

McRae, Andrew, *God Speed the Plough: The Representation of Agrarian England, 1500–1600*, Cambridge University Press, 1996.

Mendle, Michael, 'News and the Pamphlet Culture of Mid-Seventeenth-Century England', in Brendan Dooley and Sabrina A. Baron (eds.), *The Politics of Information in Early Modern Europe*, London and New York: Routledge, 2001, ch. 3.

Mendleson, Sara and Crawford, Patricia, *Women in Early Modern England*, Oxford: Clarendon Press, 1998.

Merriman, Marcus, 'James Henrisoun and "Great Britain": British Union and the Scottish Commonweal', in Mason (ed.), *Scotland and England, 1216–1815*, pp. 85–112.

Merritt, Julia (ed.), *Imagining Early Modern London*, Cambridge University Press, 2001.

Michael, Ian, *The Teaching of English from the Sixteenth Century to 1870*, Cambridge University Press, 1987.

Milhous, Judith and Hume, Robert, 'New Light on English Acting Companies in 1646, 1648, and 1660', *Review of English Studies*, n.s., 42 (1991), 487–509.

Miller, Edwin Haviland, *The Professional Writer in Elizabethan England*, Cambridge, MA: Harvard University Press, 1959.

Miller, Helen, *Henry VIII and the English Nobility*, Oxford: Basil Blackwell, 1986.

Miller, Naomi, *Changing the Subject: Mary Wroth and Figurations of Gender in Early Modern England*, Lexington: University Press of Kentucky, 1996.

Milton, Anthony, *Catholic and Reformed: The Roman and Protestant Churches in English Protestant Thought 1600–1640*, Cambridge University Press, 1978.

Milward, Peter, *Religious Controversies of the Elizabethan Age: A Survey of Printed Sources*, London: Scolar Press, 1977, and Lincoln: University of Nebraska Press, 1977.

Religious Controversies of the Jacobean Age: A Survey of Printed Sources, London: Scolar Press, 1978.

Miner, Earl, *The Cavalier Mode from Jonson to Cotton*, Princeton University Press, 1971.

Montrose, Louis, *The Purpose of Playing: Shakespeare and the Cultural Politics of the Elizabethan Theater*, University of Chicago Press, 1996.

Moody, T. W., Martin, F. X. and Byrne, F. J. (eds.), *A New History of Ireland*, 9 vols., Oxford: Clarendon Press, 1976.

Morgan, John, *Godly Learning: Puritan Attitudes towards Reason, Learning and Education, 1560–1640*, Cambridge University Press, 1986.

Morgan, P., 'Frances Wolfreston and "Hor Bouks", A Seventeenth-Century Woman Book-Collector', *The Library*, 6th ser., 11 (1989), 197–219.

Morrill, John, *The Nature of the English Revolution*, London: Longman, 1993.

'William Dowsing and the Administration of Iconoclasm in the English Revolution', in Trevor Cooper (ed.), *The Journal of William Dowsing: Iconoclasm in East Anglia in the English Civil War*, London: Ecclesiological Society, 2001, pp. 1–28.

Morrill, John (ed.), *Revolution and Restoration: England in the 1650s*, London: Collins and Brown, 1992.

(ed.), *The Scottish National Covenant in its British Context*, University of Edinburgh Press, 1990.

Morrison, Paul G., *Index of Printers, Publishers and Booksellers in Donald Wing's Short Title Catalogue*, Charlottesville: University Press of Virginia, 1995.

Morton, A. L., *The World of the Ranters: Religious Radicalism in the English Revolution*, 1970. Rpt, London: Lawrence and Wishart, 1979.

Mozley, J. F., *John Foxe and his Book*, New York: Macmillan, 1940.

Mueller, Janel, *The Native Tongue and the Word: Developments in English Prose Style, 1380–1580*, University of Chicago Press, 1984.

Muir, Kenneth, *Life and Letters of Sir Thomas Wyatt*, University of Liverpool Press, 1963.

Mullaney, Steven, *The Place of the Stage: License, Play and Power in Renaissance England*, University of Chicago Press, 1988.

Mulryne, J. R. and Shewring, M. (eds.), *Shakespeare's Globe Rebuilt*, Cambridge University Press, 1997.

Theatre and Government under the Early Stuarts, Cambridge University Press, 1993.

Neill, M. (ed.), *John Ford: Critical Essays*, Cambridge University Press, 1988.

Nelson, Alan H., *Early Cambridge Theatres: College, University, and Town Stages, 1464–1720*, Cambridge University Press, 1994.

'Hall Screens and Elizabethan Playhouses: Counter-Evidence from Cambridge', in John H. Astington (ed.), *The Development of Shakespeare's Theater*, New York: AMS Press, 1992, pp. 57–76.

Nelson, Carolyn and Seccombe, Matthew, *British Newspapers and Periodicals, 1641–1700: A Short-Title Catalogue of Serials Printed in England, Scotland, Ireland, and British America*, New York: Modern Language Association of America, 1987.

Newman, Karen, *Fashioning Femininity and English Renaissance Drama*, University of Chicago Press, 1991.

Nicholls, Mark, *A History of the Modern British Isles, 1529–1603*, Oxford: Blackwell, 1999.

Nicolas, Harris (ed.), *Memoirs of the Life and Times of Sir Christopher Hatton*, London: R. Bentley, 1847.

Noonan, Kathleen M., ' "The cruell pressure of an enraged, barbarous people": Irish and English Identity in Seventeenth-Century Policy and Propaganda', *Historical Journal*, 41 (1998), 151–77.

Norbrook, David, 'Lucy Hutchinson versus Edmund Waller: An Unpublished Reply to Waller's *A Panegyrick to my Lord Protector*', *The Seventeenth Century*, 11 (1996), 61–86.

'*Macbeth* and the Politics of Historiography', in Sharpe and Zwicker (eds.), *Politics of Discourse*, Berkeley: University of California Press, 1987, pp. 78–116.

'The Monarchy of Wit and the Republic of Letters: Donne's Politics', in Harvey and Maus (eds.), *Soliciting Interpretation. Literary Theory and Seventeenth-Century English Poetry*, pp. 3–36.

Poetry and Politics in the English Renaissance, London: Routledge and Kegan Paul, 1984.

Writing the English Republic: Poetry, Rhetoric and Politics, 1627–1660, Cambridge University Press, 1998.

Nuttall, Geoffrey, *The Holy Spirit in Puritan Faith and Experience*, 3rd edn, University of Chicago Press, 1992.

Visible Saints: The Congregational Way, 1640–1660, Oxford: Basil Blackwell, 1957.

O' Cuiv, Brian, 'The Irish Language in the Early Modern Period', in W. Moody, F. X. Martin and F. J. Byrne (eds.), *A New History of Ireland*, vol. 3, Oxford: Clarendon Press, 1976, pp. 509–45.

O'Day, R., *Education and Society 1500–1800*, London: Longman, 1982.

O'Loughlin, M. J. K., 'This Sober Frame: A Reading of "Upon Appleton House" ', in George deF. Lord (ed.), *Andrew Marvell: A Collection of Critical Essays*, Englewood Cliffs, NJ: Prentice-Hall, 1968, pp. 120–42.

Olsen, V. Norskov, *John Foxe and the Elizabethan Church*, Berkeley: University of California Press, 1973.

Ong, Walter J., *Interfaces of the Word: Studies in the Evolution of Consciousness and Culture*, Ithaca, NY: Cornell University Press, 1977.

'Oral Residue in Tudor Prose', in *Rhetoric, Romance, and Technology in the Interaction of Expression and Culture*, Ithaca, NY: Cornell University Press, 1971, pp. 23–47.

Oras, Ants, 'Surrey's Technique of Verbal Echoes: A Method and its Background', *Journal of English and Germanic Philology*, 50 (1951), 289–308.

Orgel, Stephen, *The Illusion of Power: Political Theater in the English Renaissance*, Berkeley: University of California Press, 1975.

'The Renaissance Artist as Plagiarist', *ELH*, 48 (1981), 476–95.

Orlin, Lena Cowen (ed.), *Material London, ca. 1600*, Philadelphia: University of Pennsylvania Press, 2000.

Palmer, Henrietta R., *List of English Editions and Translations of Greek and Latin Classics Printed Before 1641*, London: Blades, East & Blades, 1911.

Palmer, Patricia, *Language and Conquest in Early Modern Ireland: English Renaissance Literature and Elizabethan Imperial Expansion*, Cambridge University Press, 2001.

Parker, William Riley, *Milton: A Biography*, 2 vols., Oxford: Clarendon Press, 1968. Rev. edn, ed. Gordon Campbell, 1996.

Parry, Graham, *The Golden Age Restor'd: The Culture of the Stuart Court*, Manchester University Press, 1981.

'The Great Picture of Lady Anne Clifford', in *Art and Patronage in the Caroline Courts*, ed. David Howarth, Cambridge University Press, 1993, pp. 202–19.

The Trophies of Time: English Antiquarians of the Seventeenth Century, Oxford University Press, 1995.

Paster, Gail K., *The Body Embarrassed: Drama and the Disciplines of Shame in Early Modern England*, Ithaca, NY: Cornell University Press, 1993.

The Idea of the City in the Age of Shakespeare, Athens: University of Georgia Press, 1985.

Patrides, C. A. and Waddington, Raymond (eds.), *The Age of Milton: Backgrounds to Seventeenth-Century Literature*, Manchester University Press, 1980.

Patterson, Annabel, *Censorship and Interpretation: The Conditions of Writing and Reading in Early Modern England*, Madison: University of Wisconsin Press, 1984.

Reading Holinshed's Chronicles, University of Chicago Press, 1994.

Patterson, Bruce, *Music and Poetry of the English Renaissance*, London: Methuen, 1948.

Patterson, Lyman Ray, *Copyright in Historical Perspective*, Nashville, TN: Vanderbilt University Press, 1968.

Paul, Robert, *The Assembly of the Lord: Politics and Religion in the Westminster Assembly and the Grand Debate*, Edinburgh: T. and T. Clark, 1985.

Pearl, Valerie, *London and the Outbreak of the Puritan Revolution: City Government and National Politics, 1625–43*, London: Oxford University Press, 1961.

Peck, Linda Levy, *Court Patronage and Corruption in Early Stuart England*, London: Unwin Hyman, 1990.

Northampton: Patronage and Policy at the Court of James I, London: Allen & Unwin, 1982.

Peck, Linda Levy (ed.), *The Mental World of the Jacobean Court*, Cambridge University Press, 1991.

Peel, Albert (ed.), *The Seconde Parte of a Register: Being a Calendar of Manuscripts under the title intended for publication by the Puritans about 1593, and now in Dr Williams's Library, London*, 2 vols., Cambridge University Press, 1915.

Peltonen, Markku, 'Bacon's Political Philosophy', in Peltonen (ed.), *The Cambridge Companion to Bacon*, pp. 283–310.

Classical Republicanism in English Political Thought 1570–1640, Cambridge University Press, 1995.

Peltonen, Markku (ed.), *The Cambridge Companion to Bacon*, Cambridge University Press, 1996.

Pennington, D. H. and Thomas, Keith (eds.), *Puritans and Revolutionaries*, Oxford: Clarendon Press, 1978.

Perceval-Maxwell, M., *The Outbreak of the Irish Rebellion of 1641*, Montreal: McGill-Queen's University Press, 1994.

Perry, Curtis, *The Making of Jacobean Culture*, Cambridge University Press, 1997.

Philips, I. G. and Morgan, P., 'Libraries, Books and Printing', in *History of the University of Oxford*, gen. ed. T. H. Aston, Vol. 4, *Seventeenth-Century Oxford*, ed. N. Tyacke, Oxford: Clarendon Press, 1997, pp. 659–85.

Pincus, Steven C. A., *Protestantism and Patriotism: Ideologies and the Making of English Foreign Policy, 1650–1668*, Cambridge University Press, 1996.

Pineas, Rainer, 'The English Morality Play as a Weapon of Religious Controversy', *Studies in English Literature 1500–1900*, 2 (1962), 157–80.

Plant, Marjorie, *The English Book Trade*, 2nd edn, London: Allen and Unwin, 1965.

Plomer, Henry, *Wynken de Worde and his Contemporaries from the Death of Caxton to 1535*, London: Grafton, 1925.

Pollard, Graham, 'The Company of Stationers before 1557', *The Library*, 4th ser., 18 (1937–8), 1–37.

Popkin, Richard H. (ed.), *Millenarianism and Messianism in English Literature and Thought, 1650–1800*, Leiden: Brill, 1988.

Post, Jonathan F. S., *Henry Vaughan: The Unfolding Vision*, Princeton University Press, 1982.

Sir Thomas Browne, Boston: Twayne, 1987.

Potter, Lois, *Secret Rites and Secret Writing: Royalist Literature, 1641–1660*, Cambridge University Press, 1989.

Potter, Lois (gen. ed.), *The Revels History of English Drama*, vol. 4, *1613–1660*, London: Methuen, 1981.

Potter, R., *The English Morality Play*. London: Routledge and Kegan Paul, 1975.

Prest, Wilfred R., *The Inns of Court under Elizabeth I and the Early Stuarts, 1590–1640*, London: Longman, 1972.

'Legal Education and the Gentry at the Inns of Court', *Past and Present*, 38 (1967), 20–39.

Price, Glanrille (ed.), *The Celtic Connection*, Gerrard's Cross: Colin Smythe, 1992.

Prior, Mary (ed.), *Women in English Society, 1500–1800*, London and New York: Methuen, 1985.

Pritchard, Allan, 'Marvell's "The Garden": A Restoration Poem?', *Studies in English Literature*, 23 (1983), 371–88.

Questier, Michael, *Conversion, Politics and Religion in England, 1580–1625*, Cambridge University Press, 1996.

Quint, David, *Epic and Empire: Politics and Generic Form from Virgil to Milton*, Princeton University Press, 1993.

Randall, Dale B. J., *Winter Fruit: English Drama 1642–1660*, Lexington: University Press of Kentucky, 1995.

Raylor, Timothy, *Cavaliers, Clubs, and Literary Culture: Sir John Mennes, James Smith, and the Order of the Fancy*, Cranbury, NJ, and London: Associated University Presses, 1994.

Raymond, Joad, *The Invention of the Newspaper: English Newsbooks, 1641–1649*, Oxford: Clarendon Press, 1996.

Reay, Barry, 'Orality, Literacy and Print', in Reay (ed.), *Popular Cultures in England, 1550–1750*, London: Longman, 1998, pp. 36–70.

The Quakers and the English Revolution, London: Temple Smith, 1985.

Rebhorn, Wayne A., *Courtly Performances: Masking and Festivity in Castiglione's 'Book of the Courtier'*, Detroit: Wayne State University Press, 1978.

Records of Early English Drama series, Turnhout, Belgium: Brepols Publishers, and University of Toronto Press, 1976– (in preparation).

Redworth, Glyn, *In Defence of the Catholic Church: The Life of Stephen Gardiner*, Oxford: Basil Blackwell, 1990.

Reed, Arthur W., *Early Tudor Drama: Medwall, the Rastells, Heywood, and the More Circle*, London: Methuen, 1926.

'The Regulation of the Book Trade Before the Proclamation of 1538', *Transactions of the Bibliographical Society*, 15 (1919), 155–86.

Rees, Joan, *Samuel Daniel: A Critical and Biographical Study*, Liverpool University Press, 1964.

Revard, Stella P., *Milton and the Tangles of Neaera's Hair: The Making of the 1645 Poems*, Columbia: University of Missouri Press, 1997.

Rex, Richard, *The Theology of John Fisher*, Cambridge University Press, 1991.

Reynolds, L. D. and Wilson, N. G., *Scribes and Scholars: A Guide to the Transmission of Greek and Latin Literature*, 3rd edn, Oxford University Press, 1991.

Rhodes, Neil, *The Elizabethan Grotesque*, London: Routledge and Kegan Paul, 1980.

Ribner, Irving, *The English History Play in the Age of Shakespeare*, rev. edn, New York: Barnes and Noble, and London: Methuen, 1965.

Richardson, R. C. and Ridden, G. M. (eds.), *Freedom and the English Revolution*, Manchester University Press, 1986.

Riddell, James A. and Stewart, Stanley, *Jonson's Spenser: Evidence and Historical Criticism*, Pittsburgh: Duquesne University Press, 1995.

Riggs, David, *Ben Jonson: A Life*, Cambridge, MA: Harvard University Press, 1989.

Ringler, William, 'The First Phase of the Elizabethan Attack on the Stage, 1558–1579', *Huntington Library Quarterly*, 5 (1942), 391–418.

Roberts, Peter, 'Tudor Wales, National Identity and the British Inheritance', in Bradshaw and Roberts (eds.), *British Consciousness and Identity: The Making of Britain, 1533–1707*, pp. 8–42.

Roberts, Stephen, 'Religion, Politics and Welshness, 1649–1660', in Ivan Roots (ed.), *'Into Another Mould': Aspects of the Interregnum*, University of Exeter Press, 1998, pp. 30–46.

Rogers, John, *The Matter of Revolution: Science, Poetry, and Politics in the Age of Milton*, Ithaca, NY: Cornell University Press, 1996.

Rollins, Hyder E., 'The Black-Letter Broadside Ballad', *PMLA*, 34 (1919), 259–339.
'William Elderton: Elizabethan Actor and Ballad-Writer', *Studies in Philology*, 17 (1920), 199–245.

Ronberg, Gert, *A Way With Words: The Language of Renaissance English Literature*, London: Edward Arnold, 1992.

Rose, Mark, *Authors and Owners: The Invention of Copyright*, Cambridge, MA: Harvard University Press, 1993.

Rose, Mary Beth (ed.), *Renaissance Drama as Cultural History*, Evanston, IL: Northwestern University Press, 1990.

Rosenberg, Eleanor, *Leicester: Patron of Letters*, New York: Columbia University Press, 1955.

Rosenblatt, Jason P. and Schleiner, Winfried, 'John Selden's Letter to Ben Jonson on Cross-Dressing and Bisexual Gods', *English Literary Renaissance*, 29 (Winter 1999), 44–74.

Rosenthal, Bernard M., *The Rosenthal Collection of Printed Books with Manuscript Annotations: A Catalogue of 242 Editions Mostly Before 1600 Annotated by Contemporary or Near-Contemporary Readers*, New Haven, CT: Yale University Press, 1997.

Rostenberg, Leona, *The Minority Press and the English Crown 1558–1625: A Study in Repression*, Nieuwkoop: B. De Graaf, 1971.

Røstvig, Maren-Sofie, *The Happy Man: Studies in the Metamorphoses of a Classical Ideal*, 1600–1700, 2 vols., 2nd edn, Oslo: Norwegian Universities Press, 1962–71.

Rubel, Vere, *Poetic Diction in the English Renaissance: From Skelton to Spenser*, New York: Modern Language Association of America, 1941.

Rudrum, Alan, 'Henry Vaughan, The Liberation of the Creatures, and Seventeenth-Century English Calvinism', *The Seventeenth Century*, 4 (1989), 33–54.

Salingar, Leo G., *Dramatic Form in Shakespeare and the Jacobeans*, Cambridge University Press, 1986.

Salingar, Leo G., Harrison, G. and Cochrane, B., 'Les Comédiens et leur public en Angleterre de 1520 à 1640', in J. Jacquot (ed.), *Dramaturgie et société*, 2 vols., Paris: Centre National de la Recherche Scientifique, 1968, 2: 525–76.

Salmon, Vivian, *The Study of Language in Seventeenth-Century England*, 1979. Rev. edn, Amsterdam: Benjamins, 1988.

Sanders, Eve, *Gender and Literacy on Stage in Early Modern England*, Cambridge University Press, 1998.

Saunders, J. W., 'From Manuscript to Print: A Note on the Circulation of Poetic MSS in the Sixteenth Century', *Proceedings of the Leeds Philosophical and Literary Society*, 6.8 (1951), 502–28.

'The Stigma of Print: A Note on the Social Bases of Tudor Poetry', *Essays in Criticism*, 1 (1951), 139–64.

Scarisbrick, J. J., *Henry VIII*, Berkeley: University of California Press, 1968.

The Reformation and the English People, Oxford: Basil Blackwell, 1984.

Schlauch, Margaret, *Antecedents of the English Novel, 1400–1600*, Warsaw: PWN–Polish Scientific Publishers, 1963.

Schoenfeldt, Michael C., *Prayer and Power: George Herbert and Renaissance Courtship*, University of Chicago Press, 1991.

Schofield, Roger, 'The Measurement of Literacy in Pre-Industrial England', in Jack Goody (ed.), *Literacy in Traditional Societies*, Cambridge University Press, 1968.

Schwarz, Kathryn, *Tough Love: Amazon Encounters in the English Renaissance*, Durham and London: Duke University Press, 2000.

Scodel, Joshua, *The English Poetic Epitaph: Conflict and Commemoration from Jonson to Wordsworth*, Ithaca, NY: Cornell University Press, 1991.

Excess and the Mean in Early Modern English Literature, Princeton University Press, 2002.

Seaver, Paul, *The Puritan Lectureships: The Politics of Religious Dissent*, Stanford University Press, 1970.

Wallington's World: A Puritan Artisan in Seventeenth-Century London, Stanford University Press, 1985.

Sessions, William A., 'The Earl of Surrey and Catherine Parr: A Letter and Two Portraits', *ANQ: A Quarterly of Short Articles, Notes, and Reviews*, n.s. 5. 2–3 (April–July 1992), 128–30.

' "Enough Survives": The Earl of Surrey and European Court Culture', *History Today*, 41 (June 1991), 48–54.

Henry Howard, Earl of Surrey, Boston: G. K. Hall and Co., 1986.

Henry Howard, Earl of Surrey: A Life, Oxford University Press, 1999.

'Surrey's Psalms in the Tower', in Helen Wilcox, Richard Todd and Alasdair MacDonald (eds.), *Sacred and Profane: Secular and Devotional Interplay in Early Modern British Literature*, Amsterdam: VU University Press, 1995, 142–50.

'Surrey's Wyatt: Autumn 1542 and the New Poet', in Herman (ed.), *Rethinking the Henrician Era*, pp. 168–92.

Shapin, Steven and Schaffer, Simon, *Leviathan and the Air-Pump: Hobbes, Boyle, and the Experimental Life*, Princeton University Press, 1985.

Shapiro, B. J., *John Wilkins, 1614–1672: An Intellectual Biography*, Berkeley: University of California Press, 1969.

Sharpe, Kevin, *Criticism and Compliment: The Politics of Literature in the England of Charles I*, Cambridge University Press, 1987.

The Personal Rule of Charles I, New Haven, CT: Yale University Press, 1992.

Reading Revolutions: The Politics of Reading in Early Modern England, New Haven, CT: Yale University Press, 2000.

Remapping Early Modern England: The Culture of Seventeenth-Century Politics, Cambridge University Press, 2000.

Sharpe, Kevin and Lake, Peter (eds.), *Culture and Politics in Early Stuart England*, Basingstoke: Macmillan, 1994.

Sharpe, Kevin and Zwicker, Steven N. (eds.), *Politics of Discourse: The Literature and History of Seventeenth-Century England*, Berkeley: University of California Press, 1987.

Shaw, W. A., *A History of the English Church during the Civil Wars and under the Commonwealth*, 2 vols., 1900; New York: B. Franklin, 1974.

Sheavyn, Phoebe, *The Literary Profession in the Elizabethan Age*, 2nd edn, rev. J. W. Saunders, Manchester University Press, 1967.

Shell, Alison, *Catholicism, Controversy and the English Literary Imagination, 1558–1660*, Cambridge University Press, 1999.

Shepherd, Simon, *Amazons and Warrior Women: Varieties of Feminism in Seventeenth-Century Drama*, Brighton: Harvester, 1981.

Sherman, William H., *John Dee: The Politics of Reading and Writing in the English Renaissance*, Amherst: University of Massachusetts Press, 1995.

Shifflett, Andrew, *Stoicism, Politics, and Literature in the Age of Milton*, Cambridge University Press, 1998.

Shire, Helena Mennie, *Song, Dance, and Poetry of the Court of Scotland under King James VI*, Cambridge University Press, 1969.

Shuger, Debora, *Habits of Thought in the English Renaissance: Religion, Politics, and the Dominant Culture*, Berkeley: University of California Press, 1990.

'Irishmen, Aristocrats, and Other White Barbarians', *Renaissance Quarterly*, 50 (1997), 494–525.

The Renaissance Bible: Scholarship, Sacrifice, and Subjectivity, Berkeley: University of California Press, 1994.

Siebert, Fredrick Seaton, *Freedom of the Press in England, 1476–1776*, Urbana: University of Illinois Press, 1952.

Simon, Joan, *Education and Society in Tudor England*, Cambridge University Press, 1966.

Simpson, Percy, *Proof-reading in the Sixteenth, Seventeenth, and Eighteenth Centuries*, London: Oxford University Press, 1935.

Sinfield, Alan, *Literature in Protestant England, 1560–1660*, London: Croom Helm, 1983.

Sisson, C. J., *The Judicious Marriage of Mr Hooker and the Birth of the 'Laws of Ecclesiastical Polity'*, Cambridge University Press, 1940.

Skinner, Quentin, *The Foundations of Modern Political Thought*, 2 vols., Cambridge University Press, 1978.

Liberty before Liberalism, Cambridge University Press, 1998.

Slack, Paul, *The Impact of Plague in Tudor and Stuart England*, 1985. Oxford: Clarendon Press, 1990.

Slaughter, M. M., *Universal Languages and Scientific Taxonomy in the Seventeenth Century*, Cambridge University Press, 1982.

Smith, David L., *A History of the Modern British Isles, 1603–1707: The Double Crown*, Oxford: Blackwell, 1998.

Smith, David L., Strier, Richard and Bevington, David (eds.), *The Theatrical City: Culture, Theatre and Politics in London, 1576–1649*, Cambridge University Press, 1995.

Smith, Lacey Baldwin, *Henry VIII: The Mask of Royalty*, London: Jonathan Cape, 1971.

Tudor Prelates and Politics, 1536–1558, Princeton University Press, 1953.

Smith, Margaret M., *The Title-Page: Its Early Development, 1460–1510*, London: British Library, 2000.

Smith, Nigel, *Literature and Revolution in England 1640–1660*, New Haven, CT: Yale University Press, 1994.

Perfection Proclaimed: Language and Literature in English Radical Religion, 1640–1660, Oxford: Clarendon Press, 1989.

Smuts, R. Malcolm, *Court Culture and the Origins of a Royalist Tradition in Early Stuart England*, Philadelphia: University of Pennsylvania Press, 1987.

Culture and Power in England, New York: St Martin's, 1999.

'Public Ceremony and Royal Charisma: The English Royal Entry in London, 1485–1642', in Beier *et al.* (eds.), *The First Modern Society*, pp. 65–93.

The Stuart Court and Europe: Essays in Politics and Political Culture, Cambridge University Press, 1996.

Sommerville, J. P., *Royalists and Patriots. Politics and Ideology in England 1603–1640*, London: Longman, 1999.

Southall, Raymond, *The Courtly Maker: An Essay on the Poetry of Wyatt and his Contemporaries*, Oxford: Basil Blackwell, 1964.

'The Devonshire Manuscript Collection of Early Tudor Poetry, 1532–1541', *Review of English Studies*, 15 (1964), 142–50.

Southern, A. C., *Elizabethan Recusant Prose, 1559–1582*, London: Sands, 1950.

Southern, Richard, 'The Contribution of the Interludes to Elizabethan Staging', in Richard Hosley (ed.), *Essays on Shakespeare and Elizabethan Drama in Honor of Hardin Craig*, Columbia: University of Missouri Press, 1962, pp. 3–14.

The Staging of Plays Before Shakespeare, London: Faber & Faber, 1973.

Spearing, A. C., *Medieval to Renaissance in English Poetry*, Cambridge University Press, 1985.

Sprunger, Keith, *Trumpets from the Tower: English Puritan Printing in the Netherlands, 1600–1640*, Leiden: E. J. Brill, 1994.

Spufford, Margaret, *Contrasting Communities*, Cambridge University Press, 1974.

'First Steps in Literacy: The Reading and Writing Experiences of the Humblest Seventeenth-Century Spiritual Autobiographers', *Social History*, 4 (1979), 407–35.

'Literacy, Trade and Religion in the Commercial Centres of Europe', in Karel Davids and Jan Lucassen (eds.), *A Miracle Mirrored: The Dutch Republic in European Perspective*, Cambridge University Press, 1995, pp. 229–83.

Small Books and Pleasant Histories: Popular Fiction and its Readership in Seventeenth-Century England, London: Methuen, and Athens: University of Georgia Press, 1981.

'Women Teaching Reading to Poor Children in the Sixteenth and Seventeenth Centuries', in Mary Hilton, Morag Styles and Victor Watson (eds.), *Opening the Nursery Door: Reading, Writing and Childhood, 1600–1900*, London: Routledge, 1997, pp. 47–62.

Spufford, Margaret, (ed.), *The World of Rural Dissenters, 1520–1725*, Cambridge University Press, 1995.

Spurr, John, *The Restoration Church of England, 1646–1689*, New Haven, CT: Yale University Press, 1991.

Stachniewski, John, *The Persecutory Imagination: English Puritanism and the Literature of Religious Despair*, Oxford: Clarendon Press, 1991.

Stallybrass, Peter and White, Allon, *The Politics and Poetics of Transgression*, Ithaca, NY: Cornell University Press, 1986.

Starkey, David, 'Court and Government', in Christopher Coleman and David Starkey (eds.), *Revolution Reassessed: Revisions in the History of the Tudor Government and Administrations*, Oxford: Clarendon Press, 1986, pp. 29–58.

'The Court: Castiglione's Ideal and Tudor Reality', *Journal of the Warburg and Courtauld Institutes*, 45 (1982), 232–9.

Elizabeth: The Struggle for the Throne, New York: Harper Collins, 2000.

'Preface' and 'Intimacy and Innovation: The Rise of the Privy Chamber, 1485–1547', in Starkey (ed.), *The English Court*, pp. 71–118.

The Reign of Henry VIII: Personalities and Politics, London: George Philip, 1985.

'Rivals in Power, The Tudors and the Nobility', in Starkey (ed.), *Rivals in Power: Lives and Letters of the Great Tudor Dynasties*, London: Macmillan, 1990, pp. 8–25.

Starkey, David, (ed.), *The English Court: From the Wars of the Roses to the Civil War*, London: Longman, 1987.

Henry VIII: A European Court in England, London: Collins & Brown, 1991.

Steen, Sara Jayne, 'Recent Studies in Women Writers of the Seventeenth Century', *English Literary Renaissance*, 24 (1994), 243–74.

Henry VIII: A European Court in England, London: Collins & Brown, 1991.

Stern, Virginia F., *Gabriel Harvey: His Life, Marginalia, and Library*, Oxford: Clarendon Press, 1979.

Stevens, John, *Music and Poetry in the Early Tudor Court*, London: Methuen, and Lincoln: University of Nebraska Press, 1961.

Stevenson, David, *The Scottish Revolution 1637–1644: The Triumph of the Covenanters*, Newton Abbot: David & Charles, 1973.

Stevenson, Laura Caroline, *Paradox and Praise: Merchants and Craftsmen in Popular Elizabethan Fiction*, Cambridge University Press, 1984.

Stoddard, Roger E., *Marks in Books, Illustrated, and Explained*, Cambridge, MA: Harvard University Press, 1985.

Stone, Lawrence, *The Crisis of the Aristocracy, 1558–1641*, Oxford: Clarendon Press, 1965.

The Family, Sex and Marriage in England, 1500–1700, London: Weidenfeld and Nicholson, 1977.

'The Educational Revolution in England, 1560–1640', *Past and Present*, 28 (1964), 41–80.

Strier, Richard, 'John Donne Awry and Squint: The "Holy Sonnets", 1608–1610', *Modern Philology*, 86 (1989), 357–84.

Love Known: Theology and Experience in George Herbert's Poetry, University of Chicago Press, 1983.

Strong, Roy, *The Cult of Elizabeth: Elizabethan Portraiture and Pageantry*, London: Thames and Hudson, 1977.

'Edward VI and the Pope', *Journal of the Warburg and Courtauld Institutes*, 23 (1960), 311–13.

The English Icon: Elizabethan and Jacobean Portraiture, New York: Pantheon Books, 1969.

The English Renaissance Miniature, London: Thames and Hudson, 1984.

Holbein and Henry VIII, London: Routledge and Kegan Paul, 1967.

Tudor and Jacobean Portraits, 2 vols., London: HM Stationery Office, 1969.

Summers, Claude J. and Pebworth, Ted-Larry (eds.), *The English Civil Wars in the Literary Imagination*, Columbia: University of Missouri Press, 1999.

Targoff, Ramie, *Common Prayer: The Language of Public Devotion in Early Modern England*, University of Chicago Press, 2001.

Tavard, Georges Henri, *Holy Writ or Holy Church: The Crisis of the Protestant Reformation*, New York: Burns & Oates, 1959.

Thomas, Keith, 'The Meaning of Literacy in Early Modern England', in Gerd Baumann (ed.), *The Written Word: Literacy in Transition*, Oxford: Clarendon Press, 1986, pp. 97–131.

Religion and the Decline of Magic, London: Weidenfeld and Nicholson, 1971.

'Women and the Civil War Sects', *Past and Present*, 13 (1958), 42–62.

Thompson, E. N. S., *The Controversy Between the Puritans and the Stage*, Yale Studies in English, 20, New York: H. Holt, 1903.

Thompson, Roger, *Unfit for Modest Ears: A Study of Pornographic, Obscene and Bawdy Works Written or Published in England in the Second Half of the Seventeenth Centuries*, London: Macmillan, 1979.

Thomson, John A. F., *The Later Lollards, 1414–1520*, London: Oxford University Press, 1965.

Thomson, Patricia, 'Wyatt and Surrey', in Christopher Ricks (ed.), *English Poetry and Prose, 1540 to 1674*, London: Barrie & Jenkins, 1970, pp. 19–40.

Tittler, R., *The Reformation and the Towns in England: Politics and Political Culture, c. 1540–1640*, Oxford: Clarendon Press, 1998.

Todd, Margot (ed.), *Reformation to Revolution: Politics and Religion in Early Modern England*, London: Routledge, 1995.

Trevor-Roper, H. R., *Archbishop Laud, 1573–1645*, 2nd edn, London: Macmillan, 1962.

Catholics, Anglicans and Puritans: Seventeenth Century Essays, University of Chicago Press, 1988.

Tricomi, Albert H., *Anti-Court Drama in England 1603–42*, Charlottesville: University Press of Virginia, 1989.

Trombly, Frederic B., 'Surrey's Fidelity to Wyatt in "Wyatt Resteth Here"', *Studies in Philology*, 77 (Fall 1980), 376–87.

Trotter, David, *The Poetry of Abraham Cowley*, Basingstoke: Macmillan, 1979.

Tudor-Craig, Pamela, 'Henry VIII and King David', in Daniel Williams (ed.), *Early Tudor England: Proceedings of the 1987 Harlaxton Symposium*, Woodbridge: Boydell Press, 1989, pp. 183–205.

Turner, James Grantham, *Libertines and Radicals in Early Modern London: Sexuality, Politics and Literary Culture, 1630–1685*, Cambridge University Press, 2002.

One Flesh: Paradisal Marriage and Sexual Relations in the Age of Milton, Oxford: Clarendon Press, 1987.

The Politics of Landscape, Cambridge, MA: Harvard University Press, 1979.

Twigg, Graham, 'Plague in London: Spatial and Temporal Aspects of Mortality', in J. A. I. Champion (ed.), *Epidemic Disease in London*, Centre for Metropolitan History, Working Papers Series, 1, London: Institute of Historical Research, 1993, pp. 1–17.

Tyacke, Nicholas, *Anti-Calvinists: The Rise of English Arminianism c. 1590–1640*, Oxford: Clarendon Press, 1987.

Tyacke, Nicholas (ed.), *Seventeenth-Century Oxford*, Oxford: Clarendon Press, 1997.

Underdown, David, *Pride's Purge: Politics in the Puritan Revolution*, Oxford: Clarendon Press, 1971.

Revel, Riot and Rebellion: Popular Politics and Culture in England, 1603–1660, Oxford: Clarendon Press, 1985.

Veevers, Erica, *Images of Love and Religion: Queen Henrietta Maria and Court Entertainments*, Cambridge University Press, 1989.

Von Maltzahn, Nicholas, 'The First Reception of *Paradise Lost* (1667)', *Review of English Studies*, 47 (November 1996), 479–99.

Milton's History of Britain: Republican Historiography in the English Revolution, Oxford: Clarendon Press, 1991.

Waage, Frederick O., 'Social Themes in the Urban Broadsides of Renaissance England', *Journal of Popular Culture*, 11 (1977), 730–42.

Waith, E. M., *The Pattern of Tragicomedy in Beaumont and Fletcher*, New Haven, CT: Yale University Press, 1952.

Walker, Greg, *John Skelton and the Politics of the 1520s*, Cambridge University Press, 1988.

Persuasive Fictions: Faction, Literature and Political Culture in the Reign of Henry VIII, Aldershot, Hants.: Scolar Press, 1996.

Plays of Persuasion: Drama and Politics, Cambridge University Press, 1991.

'Sir David Lindsay's *Ane Satyre of the Thrie Estaitis* and the Politics of Reformation', *Scottish Library Journal*, 16 (1989), 5–17.

Wall, Wendy, *The Imprint of Gender: Authorship and Publication in the English Renaissance*, Ithaca, NY: Cornell University Press, 1993.

Wallace, David (ed.), *The Cambridge History of Medieval English Literature*, Cambridge University Press, 1999.

Waller, Gary, *English Poetry of the Sixteenth Century*, London: Longman, 1986.

Walsham, Alexandra, *Church Papists: Catholicism, Conformity and Confessional Polemic in Early Modern England*, 2nd rev. edn, Woodbridge: Boydell and Brewer, 2000.

' "Domme Preachers": Post-Reformation English Catholicism and the Culture of Print', *Past and Present*, 168 (August 2000), 72–123.

Providence in Early Modern England, Oxford University Press, 1999.

Ward, A. W. and Waller, A. R. (eds.), *The Cambridge History of English Literature*, 15 vols., Cambridge University Press, 1907–27.

Watkins, Owen C., *The Puritan Experience: Studies in Spiritual Autobiography*, London: Routledge and Kegan Paul, 1972.

Watson, Foster, *The English Grammar Schools to 1660*, Cambridge University Press, 1908.

Watt, Tessa, *Cheap Print and Popular Piety, 1550–1640*, Cambridge University Press, 1991.

Wayne, Don E., *Penshurst: The Semiotics of Place and the Poetics of History*, Madison: University of Wisconsin Press, 1984.

Webber, Joan, *The Eloquent 'I': Style and Self in Seventeenth-Century Prose*, Madison: University of Wisconsin Press, 1968.

Webster, Charles, *The Great Instauration: Science, Medicine and Reform, 1626–1660*, New York: Holmes & Meier, 1975.

Webster, Charles (ed.), *Health, Medicine, and Mortality in the Sixteenth Century*, Cambridge University Press, 1979.

Webster, Tom, *Godly Clergy in Early Stuart England: The Caroline Puritan Movement c. 1620–1643*, Cambridge University Press, 1997.

Weimann, Robert, *Authority and Representation in Early Modern Discourse*, ed. David Hillman, Baltimore, MD: Johns Hopkins University Press, 1996.
  Shakespeare and the Popular Tradition in the Theater, ed. Robert Schwartz, Baltimore, MD: Johns Hopkins University Press, 1978.

Westfall, Suzanne R., *Patrons and Performance: Early Tudor Household Revels*, Oxford: Clarendon Press, 1990.

Wheale, Nigel, *Writing and Society: Literacy, Print and Politics in Britain, 1590–1660*, London and New York: Routledge, 1998.

Whigham, Frank, *Seizures of the Will in Early Modern English Drama*, Cambridge University Press, 1996.

White, Helen C., *Tudor Books of Private Devotion*, Madison: University of Wisconsin Press, 1951.

White, Martin, *Renaissance Drama in Action*, London: Routledge, 1998.

White, Paul Whitfield, 'Reforming Mysteries' End: A New Look at Protestant Intervention in English Provincial Drama', *Journal of Medieval and Early Modern Studies*, 29.1 (Winter 1999), 121–47.
  Theatre and Reformation: Protestantism, Patronage, and Playing in Tudor England, Cambridge University Press, 1993.

White, Paul Whitfield (ed.), *Marlowe, History and Sexuality: New Critical Essays on Christopher Marlowe*, New York: AMS Press, 1998.

Wickham, Glynne, *Early English Stages, 1300 to 1600*, London: Routledge and Kegan Paul, 1959–72.

Wilcher, Robert, *The Writing of Royalism, 1628–1660*, Cambridge University Press, 2001.

Wilcox, Helen (ed.), *Women and Literature in Britain, 1500–1700*, Cambridge University Press, 1996.

Wilding, Michael, *Dragons Teeth: Literature in the English Revolution*, Oxford: Clarendon Press, 1987.

Willen, Diane, 'Women and Religion in Early Modern England', in Sherrin Marshall (ed.), *Women in Reformation and Counter-Reformation Europe: Public and Private Worlds*, Bloomington: University of Indiana Press, 1989, pp. 140–65.

Williams, Franklin B., *Index of Dedications and Commendatory Verses in English Books before 1641*, London: Bibliographical Society, 1962.

Williams, Glanmor, 'Religion and Welsh Literature in the Age of the Reformation', *Proceedings of the British Academy*, 69 (1983), 371–408.

Wales and the Reformation, Cardiff: University of Wales Press, 1997.

Williams, Glanmor and Jones, Robert Owen (eds.), *The Celts and the Renaissance: Tradition and Innovation*, Cardiff: University of Wales Press, 1990.

Williams, Neville, *All The Queen's Men: Elizabeth I and Her Courtiers*, London: Weidenfeld and Nicolson, 1972.

Williams, Penry, *The Later Tudors: England, 1547–1603*, Oxford: Clarendon Press, 1995.

Williams, Raymond, *The Country and the City*, Oxford University Press, 1973.

Keywords: A Vocabulary of Culture and Society, rev. edn, New York: Oxford University Press, 1985.

Williamson, Arthur, 'A Patriot Nobility? Calvinism, Kin-Ties and Civic Humanism', *Scottish Historical Review* LXXII, 1. 193 (1993), 1–21.

'Scots, Indians, and Empire: The Scottish Politics of Civilization 1519–1609', *Past and Present*, 150 (Feb. 1996), 46–83.

Scottish National Consciousness in the Age of James VI, Edinburgh: J. Donald, 1979.

Wilson, Jean, *The Archaeology of Shakespeare: The Material Legacy of Shakespeare's Theatre*, Stroud: Alan Sutton, 1995.

Wilson, John F., *Pulpit in Parliament: Puritanism during the English Civil Wars, 1640–1648*, Princeton University Press, 1969.

Wiltenberg, Joy, *Disorderly Women and Female Power in the Street Literature of Early Modern England and Germany*, Charlottesville: University Press of Virginia, 1992.

Wing, Donald G., *Short Title Catalogue of Books Printed in England, Scotland, Ireland, Wales, and British America, and of English Books Printed in Other Countries, 1641–1700*, 3 vols., 2nd edn, New York: Modern Language Association, 1982–98.

Winn, James Anderson, *John Dryden and His World*, New Haven, CT: Yale University Press, 1987.

Wiseman, Susan, ' "Adam, the Father of All Flesh," Porno-Political Rhetoric and Political Theory in and after the English Civil War', in Holstun (ed.), *Pamphlet Wars*, pp. 134–57.

Drama and Politics in the English Civil War, Cambridge University Press, 1998.

Wittreich, Joseph A., Jr, *Visionary Poetics: Milton's Tradition and His Legacy*, San Marino, CA: Huntington Library, 1979.

Womack, Peter, *Ben Jonson*, Blackwell: Oxford, 1986.

Woodbridge, Linda, *Women and the English Renaissance: Literature and the Nature of Womenkind, 1540–1620*, Urbana: University of Illinois Press, 1984.

Woods, Susanne, *Lanyer: A Renaissance Woman Poet*, Oxford University Press, 1999.

Natural Emphasis: English Versification from Chaucer to Dryden, San Marino, CA: Huntington Library, 1985.

Woolrych, Austin, *Commonwealth to Protectorate*, Oxford: Clarendon Press, 1982.

Worden, A. B., *The Rump Parliament, 1648–1653*, Cambridge University Press, 1974.

Worden, Blair, 'Providence and Politics in Cromwellian England', *Past and Present*, 109 (1985), 55–99.

The Sound of Virtue: Philip Sidney's Arcadia and Elizabethan Politics, New Haven, CT: Yale University Press, 1996.

Wormald, Jenny, 'Bloodfeud, Kindred and Government in Early Modern Scotland', *Past and Present*, 87 (1980), 54–97.

Court, Kirk and Community, 1470–1625, London: Edward Arnold, 1981.

Woudhuysen, H. R., *Sir Philip Sidney and the Circulation of Manuscripts 1558–1640*, Oxford: Clarendon Press, 1996.

Wright, George, 'Wyatt's Decasyllabic Line', *Studies in Philology*, 82.2 (Spring 1985), 129–59.

Wright, Louis B., *Middle-Class Culture in Elizabethan England*, Chapel Hill: University of North Carolina Press, 1935.

'The Reading of Plays during the Puritan Revolution', *Huntington Library Bulletin*, 6 (1934), 73–108.

Wrightson, Keith, *English Society, 1580–1680*, London: Unwin Hyman, 1982.

Würzbach, Natascha, *The Rise of the English Street Ballad, 1550–1650*, Cambridge University Press, 1990.

Yates, Frances A., *Astraea: The Imperial Theme in the Sixteenth Century*, London: Routledge and Kegan Paul, 1975.

Young, Alan, *Tudor and Jacobean Tournaments*, London: George Philip & Son, 1987.

Zagorin, Perez, 'Sir Thomas Wyatt and the Court of Henry VIII: The Courtier's Ambivalence', *Journal of Medieval and Renaissance Studies*, 23 (1993), 113–41.

Zim, Rivka, *English Metrical Psalms: Poetry as Praise and Prayer 1535–1601*, Cambridge University Press, 1987.

Zimmerman, Susan (ed.), *Erotic Politics: Desire on the Renaissance Stage*, London: Routledge, 1992.

Zwicker, Steven N., 'England, Israel and the Triumph of Roman Virtue', in Popkin (ed.), *Millenarianism and Messianism in English Literature and Thought, 1650–1800*, pp. 37–64.

'Irony, Modernity, and Miscellany: Politics and Aesthetics in the Stuart Restoration', in Howard Nenner (ed.), *Politics and the Political Imagination in Later Stuart Britain: Essays Presented to Lois Green Schwoerer*, University of Rochester Press, 1997, 181–95.

Lines of Authority: Politics and English Literary Culture, 1649–1689, Ithaca, NY: Cornell University Press, 1993.

Zwicker, Steven N. (ed.), *The Cambridge Companion to English Literature, 1650–1740*, Cambridge University Press, 1998.

Index

Abbot, George 129
Abbot, Robert 132
Abernethy, John 395
abridgements 32, 37, 96
absolutism 465, 468–73, 478, 479, 480, 488
    see also under Charles I; James VI of Scotland
    and I of England
Accession Day celebrations 358, 360, 369, 560
accounting 17, 18–22, 61
acrostics, libels in form of 76
actors
    companies 126, 137, 434–5
        travelling 429, 432, 433, 434, 565, 566–7
        (see also Admiral's Men; Lord
        Chamberlain's Men); women 602, 794,
        829, 830
    BOYS' COMPANIES 441, 442, 445–6, 572–5
    banned in 1590s 446, 454, 572
    Blackfriars Boys (Revels Boys) 445–6, 569,
        571, 573, 575, 584, 586
    last surviving 831
    satire 446, 454, 568, 574–5
    see also Children of the Chapel Royal; Paul's
        Boys
Actors, Peter (stationer to the king) 85–6
adages 95, 184, 187
Adamites 732
Adams, Thomas 392, 399–400, 515, 535, 539
    The White Devil (sermon) 517, 524, 525
addresses to reader 173–5, 185, 190
Admiral's Men 126, 451–4
    and citizen audiences 442, 451–4, 585
    as Prince's Men 569, 585
    war against Lord Chamberlain's Men 182,
        442, 451–4, 572
admiration 178, 182–9, 191
Admonition Controversy 328, 389
Agreements of the People, Levellers' 728
Agricola, Rudolph 48
agriculture 392–3, 735
Alabaster, William 526n49
Alençon, François Hercule de Valois, Duc d'
    357, 358, 359, 372

Alesius, Alexander 403
Alexander, William, Earl of Stirling 65, 161,
    429, 489, 565
allegory 10, 371–2
    Bale 292
    Montgomerie 325
    in performance 242, 245–6, 404, 509,
        600
    Puttenham and 349
    Restoration 194
    Spenser 371–2, 783
    Winstanley's, of Bible 702, 703
Allestree, Richard 32
Alleyn, Edward 451, 452
alliteration 249, 266, 288
Allott, Robert 33
almanacs 18, 36–7, 105, 641
alphabet and catechism, Gaelic 342
alphabetical organisation and the
    commonplace book 187n64
Alphonsus, Emperor of Germany (drama) 507
alteration of texts in manuscripts 57, 59
alternative sites of literature, Civil War and
    Commonwealth era 763–89
    anthologies of 'drollery' 763, 780
    Browne 763, 787–8
    convivial poetry 763, 774–82
    intellectual circles 763, 782–7
    literature of retirement 763–74, 786–8
    Urquhart 763, 788–9
Amadis de Gaul 41, 42
amanuenses 56, 58n13
America *see* Atlantic colonies; New England
Amsterdam 190, 729–30
Anabaptists 285, 291, 295, 697
Anacreontic verse 774–9
anaphora 249, 268
anarchy, culture of 791, 798–804
Andrewes, Lancelot, Bishop of Winchester 46,
    129, 519, 539–40
    and Oath of Allegiance debate 460–1, 471
    sermons 512–13, 515, 520, 522, 524, 528,
        535